THE MILLITARY BALANCE 2020

published by

for

The International Institute for Strategic Studies
ARUNDEL HOUSE | 6 TEMPLE PLACE | LONDON | WC2R 2PG | UK

THE **MILITARY BALANCE** 2020

The International Institute for Strategic Studies
ARUNDEL HOUSE | 6 TEMPLE PLACE | LONDON | WC2R 2PG | UK

DIRECTOR-GENERAL AND CHIEF EXECUTIVE **Dr John Chipman**
DIRECTOR FOR DEFENCE AND MILITARY ANALYSIS **Dr Bastian Giegerich**
EDITOR **James Hackett**
ASSOCIATE EDITOR **Nicholas Payne**

MILITARY AEROSPACE **Douglas Barrie** MRAeS
LAND WARFARE **Brigadier (Retd) Benjamin Barry**
MILITARY FORCES AND EQUIPMENT **Henry Boyd**
NAVAL FORCES AND MARITIME SECURITY **Nick Childs**
DEFENCE ECONOMICS **Dr Lucie Béraud-Sudreau**
RESEARCH AND ANALYSIS **Joseph Dempsey, Yvonni-Stefania Efstathiou, Haena Jo, Amanda Lapo, Yohann Michel, Robert Mitchell, Meia Nouwens, Michael Tong, Tom Waldwyn**

EDITORIAL **Vivien Antwi, Kevin Jewell, Jill Lally, Jack May, Michael Marsden, Bao-Chau Pham**
DESIGN, PRODUCTION, INFORMATION GRAPHICS **John Buck, Carolina Vargas, Kelly Verity**
CARTOGRAPHY **John Buck, Carolina Vargas, Kelly Verity**
RESEARCH SUPPORT **Holly Graham, Katrina Marina, Erica Pepe**

This publication has been prepared by the Director-General and Chief Executive of the Institute and his Staff, who accept full responsibility for its contents. The views expressed herein do not, and indeed cannot, represent a consensus of views among the worldwide membership of the Institute as a whole.

FIRST PUBLISHED February 2020

© The International Institute for Strategic Studies 2020
All rights reserved. No part of this publication may be reproduced, stored, transmitted, or disseminated, in any form, or by any means, without prior written permission from Taylor & Francis, to whom all requests to reproduce copyright material should be directed, in writing.

ISBN 978-0-367-46639-8
ISSN 0459-7222

Cover images: FRONT: DF-17 system at the PRC's 70th anniversary parade (Sheng Jiapeng/China News Service/VCG via Getty); Turkish and Russian military vehicles in northeastern Syria (Delil Souleiman/AFP via Getty); Russian S-70 *Okhotnik* UAV and Su-57 combat aircraft (TASS via Getty); Russian Navy's *Admiral Gorshkov* destroyer arriving in Vladivostok (Yuri Smityuk/TASS via Getty). BACK: Japan Ground Self-Defense Force's AAV-7 amphibious-assault vehicle (Asahi Shimbun via Getty); Russian Mi-26 transport helicopter at *Tsentr*-2019 military exercise (Gavriil Grigorov/TASS via Getty); French *Operation Barkhane* soldier at a Malian armed forces base (Daphne Benoit/AFP via Getty).

The Military Balance (ISSN 0459-7222) is published annually by Routledge Journals, an imprint of Taylor & Francis, 4 Park Square, Milton Park, Abingdon, Oxfordshire OX14 4RN, UK.

A subscription to the institution print edition, ISSN 0459-7222, includes free access for any number of concurrent users across a local area network to the online edition, ISSN 1479-9022.

All subscriptions are payable in advance and all rates include postage. Journals are sent by air to the USA, Canada, Mexico, India, Japan and Australasia. Subscriptions are entered on an annual basis, i.e. January to December. Payment may be made by sterling cheque, dollar cheque, international money order, National Giro, or credit card (Amex, Visa, Mastercard).

Please send subscription orders to: USA/Canada: Taylor & Francis Inc., Journals Department, 530 Walnut Street, Suite 850, Philadelphia, PA 19106, USA. UK/Europe/Rest of World: Routledge Journals, T&F Customer Services, T&F Informa UK Ltd., Sheepen Place, Colchester, Essex, CO3 3LP, UK. Email: subscriptions@tandf.co.uk

Contents

Indexes of Tables, Figures and Maps 4
Editor's Introduction 5

Part One Capabilities, Trends and Economics
Domain trends 7

- **Chapter 1 Defence and military analysis** 9
  China's armed forces: 'informatisation' and 'intelligentisation' 9; Military use of the electromagnetic spectrum: the renewed focus on electronic warfare 13; The space domain: towards a regular realm of conflict? 17

- **Chapter 2 Comparative defence statistics** 21
  Defence budgets and expenditure 21; High-speed helicopters: pushing the rotary limits 23; France's *Scorpion* armoured-vehicle-replacement programme 24; China, Russia and the United States: surface-launched anti-ship missiles 25; Key defence statistics 26

- **Chapter 3 North America** 28
  Regional trends in 2019 28;
  United States: defence policy and economics 30;
  Canada: defence policy 42;
  Armed forces data section 43;
  Arms procurements and deliveries 61

- **Chapter 4 Europe** 64
  Regional trends in 2019 64;
  Regional defence policy and economics 66;
  Germany: defence policy 75;
  Poland: defence policy 77;
  Turkey: defence policy 81;
  United Kingdom: defence policy 82;
  Armed forces data section 86;
  Arms procurements and deliveries 163

- **Chapter 5 Russia and Eurasia** 166
  Regional trends in 2019 166;
  Russia: defence policy and economics 168;
  Armed forces data section 183;
  Arms procurements and deliveries 217

- **Chapter 6 Asia** 220
  Regional trends in 2019 220;
  Regional defence policy and economics 222;
  Australia's modernising armed forces 229;
  China: defence policy and economics 231;
  Japan: defence policy 239;
  North Korea: missile testing in 2019 242;
  South Korea: defence policy 243;
  Singapore: defence policy and economics 246;
  Armed forces data section 250;
  Arms procurements and deliveries 321

- **Chapter 7 Middle East and North Africa** 324
  Regional trends in 2019 324;
  Regional defence policy and economics 326;
  Morocco: defence policy and economics 336;
  Armed forces data section 340;
  Arms procurements and deliveries 385

- **Chapter 8 Latin America and the Caribbean** 388
  Regional trends in 2019 388;
  Regional defence policy and economics 390;
  Armed forces data section 398;
  Arms procurements and deliveries 442

- **Chapter 9 Sub-Saharan Africa** 444
  Regional trends in 2019 444;
  Regional defence policy and economics 446;
  Nigeria: defence policy and economics 453;
  Armed forces data section 460;
  Arms procurements and deliveries 513

- **Chapter 10 Military cyber capabilities** 515

Part Two Reference

Explanatory notes 519
  Principal land definitions 523; Principal naval definitions 524; Principal aviation definitions 525
List of abbreviations for data sections 527
International comparisons of defence expenditure and military personnel 529
Index of country/territory abbreviations 535
Index of countries and territories 536

Index of **TABLES**

1. Selected Russian EW systems reported deployed to the Ukraine and Syrian theatres 15
2. US National Defense Budget Function and other selected budgets, 2000, 2010–2020 40
3. US fixed-wing fighter-aircraft exports, 2010–Oct 2019 62
4. US: new-build armoured-vehicle programmes (in production) 62
5. Littoral Combat Ship programme: planned and achieved IOC dates 63
6. European aerospace industry: participation in combat-aircraft programmes, 2019 74
7. European countries operating LR-SAM systems introduced in the 1980s or earlier 164
8. European LR-SAM programmes with production contracts 164
9. *Boxer* new-build production contracts 165
10. Countries that have selected *Boxer* 165
11. Russian defence expenditure as % of GDP 179
12. Russia's defence industry: annual percentage change of industrial output 181
13. Kazakhstan: aerospace and air-defence procurement, 2010–19 218
14. Turkmenistan: aerospace and air-defence procurement, 2010–19 218
15. Russian Navy: selected ongoing surface-combatant programmes 219
16. North Korea: missile testing as of October 2019 243
17. Royal Malaysian Navy: '15 To 5' transformation programme 322
18. T-50/FA-50 production contracts 323
19. Italy–Israel: defence-equipment procurement agreement 386
20. Oman: defence-equipment procurement, 2010–19 386
21. Egypt: naval procurement, 2008–19 387
22. *Super Tucano* production contracts 443
23. South Africa: real-terms defence spending, 2015–19 453
24. France: naval exports to sub-Saharan African states, 2011–Nov 2019 514
25. Military cyber capabilities: a potential collection plan 516
26. List of abbreviations for data sections 527
27. International comparisons of defence expenditure and military personnel 529
28. Index of country/territory abbreviations 535
29. Index of countries and territories 536

Index of **FIGURES**

North America
1. M1 *Abrams* main battle tank: upgrade timeline, 1979–2019 34
2. US defence expenditure as % of GDP 39
3. US Navy Littoral Combat Ship programme 63

Europe
4. European Union: defence-planning process, 2019–25 69
5. Europe: real-terms defence spending, year-on-year change, 2008–19 70
6. Europe regional defence expenditure as % of GDP 72
7. Europe defence spending by country and sub-region, 2019 72
8. UK future combat-aircraft concept 83
9. Europe: long-range surface-to-air missile (LR-SAM) system modernisation 164
10. ARTEC *Boxer* modular wheeled armoured vehicle 165

Russia and Eurasia
11. Russia: estimated total military expenditure as % of GDP 180
12. Russian Navy: surface-combatant acquisition 219

Asia
13. Asia defence spending by country and sub-region, 2019 225
14. Asia: sub-regional real-terms defence-spending growth, 2018–19 (US$bn, constant 2015) 227
15. Indonesia and Malaysia: real-terms defence spending, 2015–19 (US$bn) 228
16. Asia regional defence expenditure as % of GDP 228
17. China and selected states: domestically built naval vessels launched between 2007–18 235
18. PLAN Type-055 *Renhai*-class cruiser 236
19. Type-16 Mobile Combat Vehicle 241
20. Republic of Korea: FA-50 *Fighting Eagle*/T-50 *Golden Eagle* 323

Middle East and North Africa
21. Saudi Arabia defence expenditure as % of GDP 334
22. North Africa defence expenditure 2019: sub-regional breakdown 335

Latin America and the Caribbean
23. Latin America and the Caribbean defence spending by country and sub-region, 2019 395
24. Latin America and the Caribbean regional defence expenditure as % of GDP 395
25. Embraer: EMB-314 (A-29) *Super Tucano* light-attack/training aircraft 443

Sub-Saharan Africa
26. Sub-Saharan Africa defence spending by country and sub-region, 2019 450
27. Sub-Saharan Africa regional defence expenditure as % of GDP 452
28. Sub-Saharan Africa: total defence spending, 2008–19 452
29. Sub-Saharan Africa: total defence spending by sub-region, 2015–19 (US$bn, constant 2015) 453
30. Denel Group: sales by destination, 2018 453
31. Nigeria: defence budget 2019, breakdown by service 459
32. France: naval exports to sub-Saharan African states 514

Index of **MAPS**

1. Europe regional defence spending 71
2. Poland: selected military facilities 79
3. UK defence companies: European presence, 2019 84
4. Russia: military bases abroad and in disputed territories 170
5. Russia's guided-weapons sector: major manufacturers and products 174
6. Selected maritime capabilities in the Caspian Sea 175
7. Russia and Eurasia regional defence spending 180
8. Asia regional defence spending 226
9. Japan: southern military formations, 2019 240
10. US Central Command (CENTCOM) area of responsibility: force dispositions, 2019 327
11. Middle East and North Africa regional defence spending 334
12. Morocco: principal military bases 338
13. Latin America and the Caribbean regional defence spending 396
14. Sahel region: selected deployed foreign forces, 2019 449
15. Sub-Saharan Africa regional defence spending 451

Editor's Introduction

As the 2020 edition of *The Military Balance* is published, defence debates remain dominated by an unstable international security environment. Some previously held assumptions about the direction of national defence policies and decision-making priorities are being questioned. This is producing further uncertainty and may cause states to hedge their defence relations and procurement priorities. At the same time, advanced military capabilities, augmented by potentially disruptive new technologies, continue to spread.

Globally, key elements of the rules-based international order that characterised the post-Second World War period are being challenged. The demise of the Intermediate-Range Nuclear Forces (INF) Treaty exemplifies this most clearly, with its collapse precipitated by Russian breaches as well as the Trump administration's determination – with an eye to China's military modernisation – that the bilateral accord had outlived its usefulness. Nonetheless, Russia showed United States' inspectors its new *Avangard* hypersonic glide vehicle in late November 2019 as part of its obligations under the New START treaty. Indeed, it is noteworthy that in the current climate, observers are looking nervously not just towards Moscow, but also anxiously in the direction of Washington for signs of interest in maintaining this remaining element of the strategic arms-control architecture when it comes up for renewal in 2021.

The conflict in Ukraine's east still simmers despite tentative progress in contacts between Russia and Ukraine during 2019. North Korea once again began testing missiles, but at year's end had so far not resumed tests of long-range systems. Terrorists continue to challenge security forces globally, as does conflict and instability in Africa and the Middle East and North Africa. Notably, the wars in Libya and in Yemen grind on. Meanwhile, while its territorial base might have been reduced, the Islamic State remains a threat. Scores of its fighters escaped from Kurdish-run jails in northern Syria in late 2019. This followed a US decision to withdraw military personnel from northern Syria, a Turkish incursion targeting Kurdish forces and also an advance in the north by Assad-regime forces. Nine years after the civil war began in Syria, and with Russia's help, the Assad regime is in the ascendant.

Defence spending

US dissatisfaction with NATO allies has for years been rooted in their low levels of defence spending, relative to Cold War and pre-financial-crisis levels. However, US exhortations to spend more have combined with changing threat perceptions in European states to bring about larger defence budgets. While Europe returned to defence-spending growth as early as 2015, total defence spending in Europe – when measured in real terms – in 2019 once again reached the levels observed when the financial crisis began in 2008. Overall, Europe's defence spending in 2019 rose by 4.2% compared with 2018.

These increases in Europe are part of an international trend. Global defence spending rose by 4.0% in real terms compared to 2018 data, when measured in constant 2015 dollars. This was the largest increase observed in ten years. In 2019, defence spending by both China and the US rose by 6.6% over 2018. In nominal terms, the US increase alone – at US$53.4bn – almost equalled the UK's entire 2019 defence budget of US$54.8bn.

NATO and Europe

Great-power competition continues to dominate Western defence policymaking and procurement. But there is less apparent unity, leadership or coordination than before in political responses, with national impulses increasingly prominent. One month before the December 2019 NATO summit in London, French President Macron claimed that the Alliance was 'brain dead' and seemed to cast doubt on the Article 5 commitment to collective-defence. Allies had, meanwhile, long looked nervously at US President Trump for his current view on this issue, and his comments at the summit seemed to offer little in the way of reassurance. Two out of the Alliance's three nuclear powers have now vacillated on the key issue of the collective-defence clause. Furthermore, November also saw NATO state Turkey mount joint patrols in northern Syria with Russian forces. Earlier, Ankara took delivery of elements of Russia's S-400 air-defence system.

Macron's answer to NATO's troubles was that Europe should be more militarily capable and that it should reopen a strategic dialogue with Russia. The French leader said that questions over US commitment should lead to a reassessment of 'what NATO is'. The commitment issue is generating the most concern. Both within NATO and beyond, and unlike in the past, the arrival of additional US personnel and equipment is not necessarily allaying allies' and partners' concerns about long-term US strategy, commitment and engagement, or wholly deterring opponents. The US continues to deploy personnel to Eastern Europe and in 2019 increased its deployments to the Gulf-region in response to Iranian activity. However, these did not effectively constrain Tehran, as shown in the September attack on Saudi oil facilities. And while these capabilities highlighted the range of military options open to the US, there was less discussion of strategy. Moreover, these deployments highlighted the challenge in maintaining a focus on the Asia-Pacific.

Regardless of allies' worries about Washington's commitment, they still have some way to go before they would be able to act effectively without US military assistance in anything but a relatively undemanding contingency. It is, for instance, unclear whether the current range of EU-level defence initiatives will significantly improve military capabilities in the near term. 2019 saw more projects agreed under the Permanent Structured Cooperation (PESCO) defence initiative. The real challenge, however, will not be in accumulating new projects, but instead in closing those that are not performing. Meanwhile, the French experience since 2013 in its military commitment in the Sahel – where it has not only deployed its own armed forces but also relied on allies and partners in areas where it is lacking, such as airlift support from the UK and US – underscored the limitations and dependencies of European NATO and EU member states.

It may transpire that Washington cannot always supply capabilities needed by allies and partners. States in the Gulf, for instance, may no longer be able to rely on US ISR to fill their own capability gaps as US security concerns deepen elsewhere. IISS analysis in 2019 indicated that European NATO members would have to invest between US$288bn and US$357bn to fill the gaps highlighted by a scenario where they would have to defend their territory without US support against state-level attack. Enablers are vital. EU members' tanker and tanker/transport aircraft numbered 49 in 2019, while the US figure was 555. Were a crisis to erupt that required rapid mobility of US equipment, for instance in the Asia-Pacific, it is highly likely that the US would look to move relevant enabling assets from where they are currently stationed.

Russia and China

These debates take place in an environment where potential adversaries continue to accelerate their military modernisation. The fortunes of Russia's Su-57 *Felon* multi-role fighter improved in May 2019 when President Putin increased the order in the current State Armament Programme from 16 to 76. It is also moving ahead with the development of faster and wholly new weapons. Its *Burevestnik* nuclear-powered and nuclear-armed cruise missile, and the *Status*-6 nuclear-armed long-range autonomous underwater vehicle, may have seen only halting progress, but hypersonic plans are firmer. The *Avangard* system (SS-19 *Stiletto* mod. 4) was on the brink of service entry at the end of 2019. The *Kinzhal* air-launched ballistic missile has been observed on MiG-31s, while Moscow has spoken of further integrating precision weapons on naval vessels. The '*Kalibr*-isation' of the fleet has been noted in recent years; Moscow is now discussing fitting to its naval vessels the 3M22 *Zircon* high-speed anti-ship cruise missile.

China's October 2019 military parade, marking the 70th anniversary of the People's Republic, highlighted the breadth of its military modernisation process and showcased systems designed to achieve military effect faster and at greater range than before. The DF-17 hypersonic glide vehicle was displayed at the anniversary parade. China's system is intermediate range, while Moscow's *Avangard* may be intercontinental. Concerns over China's military modernisation loom large in Washington's policy considerations, and they are driving many equipment and procurement decisions both in the US and elsewhere.

Systems like these pose additional challenges for air defences. They complicate early detection, target acquisition and successful intercept. Achieving all three is not impossible, though the number of targets that may arrive fast or slow, high or low, perhaps with signature-management features, means that investments will be needed in better radars, interceptors and command and control, all underpinned by ever-faster computing power and better coordination with partner countries. These weapons are being integrated in order to rapidly achieve destructive effect but perhaps also because this will help to outpace and undermine an enemy's decision-making cycle; this might, in turn, have implications for strategic stability.

Both China and Russia continue to modernise their conventional military forces. Moscow is improving its air-assault forces' mobility and striking power and also its artillery capabilities, among other areas. It is more closely integrating UAVs into its artillery find-fix-strike complex. China, meanwhile, stood up the first operational unit with its Chengdu J-20A combat aircraft, and has maintained recent progress in developing and fielding air-launched missiles. It also continues to build increasingly sophisticated naval vessels, which is an important factor motivating other Asian states to do the same. Both China and Russia aspire to improve their military capability by integrating emerging technologies such as artificial intelligence.

Today's challenges

In this environment of continuous, evolving and even accelerating competition, the response options for Western states might include integrating increasingly novel technologies or spending more to stay ahead. Alternatively, they could accept a levelling playing field as a new norm and adapt their strategies instead. This relates not just to conventional military power but also to cyber capability and the consistently contested information environment.

A related challenge is that of competitor states now using strategies to achieve effect by operating below the threshold of war. Examples include Russia's initial moves into Crimea and its denials over involvement in eastern Ukraine, its use of chemical weapons in the UK and its alleged election meddling. Iran's activities are another example. Its ability to conduct warfare through third parties has 'given Iran a strategic advantage over adversaries reliant on conventional capabilities', according to the IISS *Strategic Dossier* on Iran's networks of influence.

Capabilities routed through third parties, disinformation campaigns or kinetic actions that are denied outright are hard to tackle with conventional military responses. They place a premium not just on developing the right military and intelligence capabilities, but on boosting the adaptability and resilience of equipment and military forces and, more broadly, of societies and political decision-making. The same holds true when dealing with developments in new military or militarily-relevant technologies. In all cases, working effectively with partners, and making use of relevant international frameworks, have the potential to act as a force multiplier. However, while conflict still involves hard military power, it is now more diffused than before. It now involves a greater number of actors and more capabilities, some of which are not traditionally 'military', and clear outcomes in peace, war and the grey space between are, accordingly, less certain.

Domain trends

Defence economics

- Global defence spending continued to rebound in 2019, with real-terms growth rising by 4.0% this year (when compared with 2018 and measured in constant 2015 US dollars). This was the highest year-on-year increase observed in the past ten years. Total defence spending, excluding US foreign military financing programmes, reached US$1.73 trillion, when measured in current dollars, against US$1.67trn in 2018.
- In 2019, defence spending both in China and in the United States increased by 6.6%, when measured in real terms and compared to 2018. In nominal terms, the US increase alone (US$53.4 billion) almost equalled the United Kingdom's 2019 defence budget (US$54.8bn), while China's nominal increase (US$10.6bn) was just short of Taiwan's entire 2019 defence budget (US$10.9bn).
- After years of cuts, total defence spending in Europe, when measured in real terms, once again reached the levels seen before the financial crisis (US$277bn in 2008; US$289bn in 2019). This was an increase of 4.2%, when measured in real terms, compared to 2018. These spending increases are directed more and more towards procurements and research and development. Indeed, defence investments grew, as a share of total spending, from 19.8% in 2018 to 23.1% in 2019, for those countries where data is available.
- However, this increase in European spending was modest when measured in nominal dollar terms, rising from US$290bn to US$291bn, because the euro depreciated against the dollar over the year.
- When measured on a per capita basis, as well as in GDP terms, countries in the Middle East and North Africa spent the most on defence. In 2019, Oman spent over US$2,500 and Saudi Arabia more than US$2,300 per person on defence. That said, Australia, Norway, Singapore and the US are also in the top ten when spending is measured on a per capita basis. The UK, spending US$837 per person, is in 11th position.

Land

- States including Israel, the Netherlands, Russia, Turkey and the United States are increasingly seeking to integrate active-protection systems (APS) onto their armoured fighting vehicles, either as retrofits to existing designs or as integrated systems for future vehicles. The proliferation of highly capable man-portable anti-tank weapons has increased the demand for protection from this kind of threat in both low- and high-intensity conflicts. Many countries are looking to counter these weapons with APS. With many legacy platforms approaching their upper weight limits, these systems offer increased protection for relatively little weight gain, when compared to traditional armour.
- China, Russia and the US are all now at various stages of developing, testing and deploying truck-borne gun-howitzer systems. These are more easily transportable, including by air, than traditional tracked armoured systems, and offer integral mobility, potentially making them less vulnerable to counter-battery fire than their towed counterparts. This makes them particularly attractive to light- and medium-weight rapid-response units in need of fire support.
- China and Russia appeared to be in the process of deploying hypersonic glide-vehicles as 2019 drew to a close. The US is also expected to put its own hypersonic glide-vehicles and hypersonic cruise-missile systems into operational service in the early 2020s, and a number of other states are currently conducting research in this area. The performance characteristics of these systems further complicate an already demanding environment for missile defences.
- The relatively easy availability of uninhabited aerial vehicles (UAVs) for both state and non-state actors has led to renewed military interest in both hard- and soft-kill counter-UAV systems. Both Russia and the US have deployed systems to the Middle East to protect their facilities and/or vessels from attack and are likely to feed the lessons of their experiences into future development work.

Maritime

- Amphibious-warfare capabilities are again subject to close attention, especially in Asia. China is continuing to boost its capacity with more and larger vessels, Japan has established its amphibious rapid-deployment brigade and Australia is developing its navy as a task-group-focused force, centred on its landing helicopter docks. The United States, meanwhile, has issued a new operating concept and is looking to exploit new technologies and systems to enable integrated operations in contested environments.
- The increasing requirement to maintain long-range maritime presence has meant there is growing emphasis – notably in France and the United Kingdom – on forward presence and new crewing models to increase platform availability.
- There is growing concern, particularly among leading Western maritime nations, about the doctrinal, tactical and capability implications of 'hybrid' or 'grey zone' activities at sea. As a result, there is now emphasis on the requirement for maritime-domain-awareness and intelligence, surveillance and reconnaissance assets, including multi-mission aircraft and remote-sensing capabilities, not least to increase the prospect of attributing covert actions.

- Fifth-generation aerospace capabilities are being introduced into the maritime-aviation environment. The US Navy and US Marine Corps continue to experiment with the '*Lightning* carrier' concept of US Navy amphibious vessels operating F-35Bs, and the navy is preparing to introduce the F-35C. The UK is moving to operational sea trials prior to an initial operational deployment of its first new-generation aircraft carrier in 2021. Meanwhile, Japan and possibly South Korea are planning to introduce the F-35B onto their principal aviation-capable platforms.
- There is an emerging global trend towards the recapitalisation of anti-ship missile capabilities. This is driven by the age of some weapons in service and the fact that they are increasingly out-ranged and out-performed by competitor systems.

Aerospace

- The United States announced in 2019 it would end acquisition of the AIM-120 Advanced Medium Range Air-to-Air Missile (AMRAAM) by 2026. The successor, the Lockheed Martin AIM-260, is a response to aerospace developments in China and to a lesser extent Russia. Raytheon's AIM-120 has been the market standard in the West for active radar-guided air-to-air missiles (AAMs) for a quarter of a century.
- Crewed combat aircraft will likely be a part of air-force inventories for most of this century. Often termed sixth-generation platforms, the latest designs will notionally enter service from the mid-2030s onwards. Design considerations include platforms that can either be crewed or optionally crewed; have broad-band passive signature management, with the option of active stealth; integrated mission systems; and directed-energy payloads, along with adjunct uninhabited aerial vehicles (UAVs).
- From low-observable subsonic to Mach 5+ hypersonic weapons, cruise missiles pose an increasing challenge for air defences. Alongside missile defences, tactical combat aircraft are now seen as an element of the defensive architecture to counter cruise missiles.
- Air forces are re-examining assumptions about platform survivability. Key enablers, such as tankers and early-warning platforms – often based on large aircraft – are vulnerable to some air-to-air and surface-to-air missiles now in development. Similarly, the current generation of medium and large UAVs were not designed to be operated in defended airspace. Risk management might in the short term include changing tactics, but in the longer term, platform designs and capabilities will need to adjust in order to increase survivability.
- Active electronically scanned array (AESA) radars are increasingly being integrated onto combat aircraft in place of mechanically scanned radar. All next-generation combat aircraft now in test or development will use one or more AESA radars to provide their primary radio-frequency sensors. The advantages of AESA include increased detection ranges, improved resistance to countermeasures and improved reliability. In addition, many of the current generation of combat aircraft are re-equipping with AESA radars as part of mid-life upgrades and these radars are also being introduced on AAMs.

Cyber

- In June 2019, having called off a retaliatory airstrike, US President Donald Trump ordered a cyber attack on Iran's Islamic Revolutionary Guard Corps after Iran shot down a US uninhabited aerial vehicle on 19 June. Proportionality was likely a factor in the decision to employ cyber capabilities. These were again used by the US, in October, after Iran attacked Saudi Arabian oil facilities. The choice of cyber options may become more prominent as US armed forces expand cyber units at lower levels of command, implement the 2018 Cyber Deterrence Initiative and operate according to 'persistent engagement', which is intended to enable the US to 'build resilience, defend forward, and contest adversary activities in cyberspace'.
- An officer in the People's Liberation Army's Electronic Engineering Institute wrote that 'the ultimate purpose of information dominance operations is to influence or destroy an enemy's decision-making process'. Primary targets, the article continued, should include enemy command-and-control centres, communication nodes, radar stations and computer-network systems. However, China's 2019 defence white paper is not as fulsome as the 2015 white paper on the centrality of cyberspace as a new arena for international strategic competition, a decision perhaps influenced more by presentational considerations than by any weakening of the momentum towards military cyber power.
- India made progress during the year in establishing its new tri-service Defence Cyber Agency. In February, Singapore said that it would recruit 300 additional military cyber specialists, a year after it set up a Cyber Defence School in the armed forces. In November, it was reported that Malaysia would form a new Cyber Electromagnetic Command to lead cyber operations. These measures illustrate the catch-up or adaptation processes now under way in generating cyber capabilities.
- The head of Australia's Information Warfare Division, Major-General Marcus Thompson, raised on several occasions the role of the Australian Defence Force in defending the homeland in cyberspace. This reflects growing interest around the world by national armed forces in the adaptation processes needed, especially in terms of legal authorities, for a greater military role in homeland cyber defence.
- In May 2019, President Trump declared a national emergency in cyberspace. This executive order foreshadowed the possible termination on national-security grounds of ICT trade and technology transfers between the US and any country, should the administration declare that country to be an 'adversary'. This followed a decade of gradually escalating US pressure on China over national-security aspects of the ICT sector, especially against the Chinese firm Huawei Technologies.

Chapter One
China's armed forces: 'informatisation' and 'intelligentisation'

China's military modernisation has accelerated under President Xi Jinping. It is a central component of the 'China Dream', articulated by Xi in 2013. As part of this ambition, Xi has driven far-reaching reforms to the People's Liberation Army (PLA) that have changed defence structures and led to the integration of improved military equipment, and which Beijing says will generate 'world-class' military forces by 2049. Three terms appear often in recent Chinese military documentation: mechanisation (机械化), informatisation (信息化) and, more recently, intelligentisation (智能化). Although the PLA has not clearly defined these concepts in public, they have been developed over time in successive defence white papers and are useful in understanding not only China's motivations, progress and aspirations as it modernises its military forces, but also the PLA's views of contemporary and future conflict. Some of Beijing's efforts likely hinge on its capacity to introduce and exploit networked platforms, sensors and weapons that can support not only better and more integrated command-and-control (C2) systems but potentially also over-the-horizon targeting at extended ranges.

Developing thinking

China's military-modernisation process was motivated in part by its observation of the changes in modern warfare since its forces were last involved in major combat; this was in 1979, during the short war with Vietnam that principally involved ground forces. In particular, the 1991 First Gulf War against Iraq and, later, the 1999 NATO intervention in Kosovo provided the PLA with a clear example of how far it had fallen behind modern military forces. The PLA has also studied Soviet and Russian military modernisation.

The PLA had hitherto operated according to the strategy of 'People's War' and 'war under modern conditions'. However, the First Gulf War highlighted that modern technologies could be a force multiplier on the battlefield and that the PLA needed to boost the integration of its military systems and improve joint operations. Chinese thinking reflected this lesson shortly afterwards. Assessments were conducted and in early 1993 a new 'strategic guideline' was adopted by the PLA, indicating it would look to 'win local wars under modern high-technology conditions'.

The Kosovo intervention led to a study by China's National Defence University (NDU). This study, analysts noted, highlighted the centrality of 'information superiority' and paid close attention to how NATO forces used technology to suppress Serbia's command centre and telecommunications. China's 2004 defence white paper reflected the lessons drawn from Kosovo, and perhaps also Iraq in 2003. China's armed forces aspired, it said, to win 'local wars under informatised conditions', giving priority to 'building joint operational capabilities'. The assessment of the white paper was that information connects military domains and acts as a force multiplier but could also lead to more integrated force development.

China's 2015 defence white paper assessed that China's external environment was going through 'profound changes' and that threats were more diverse – and not necessarily local or indeed short term. China would, it said, take advantage of a period of strategic opportunity to build strong military forces. This white paper highlighted the increasing sophistication of long-range, precise, stealthy and uninhabited weapons and equipment, also noting that outer space and cyberspace were 'new commanding heights' in strategic competition. Ultimately, it noted, 'the form of war is accelerating its evolution to informatisation'.

In October 2017, Xi delivered a speech at the 19th Chinese Communist Party Congress in which he set out a timeline for the PLA to achieve its modernisation goals. By 2020, mechanisation should be 'basically achieved', 'information technology (IT) application' should also have progressed and strategic capabilities should have seen significant improvement. By 2035, he said, 'basic modernisation of our national defense and our forces' should be 'basically' complete, and at the same time the PLA should have modernised their 'theory, organisational structures, service personnel and weaponry'. By the middle of the next century (perhaps 2049, the 100th anniversary of the People's Republic), he said the PLA should have fully transformed into 'world-class' forces.

Modern warfare

Successive PLA studies and defence white papers indicate that China characterises modern warfare as a confrontation between opposing operational systems (作战体系). In a successful system-to-system confrontation (体系对抗), an adversary's operational system would either be destroyed or degraded such that it reduced military effectiveness. The 2015 defence white paper said that 'integrated combat forces' would be employed in order to 'prevail in system-vs-system operations featuring information dominance, precision strikes and joint operations'. The PLA, it asserted, must be prepared to confront opponents in multiple domains, including in space and cyberspace. Its targets included key elements of these operational systems, such as C2, reconnaissance and intelligence, as well as conventional equipment capabilities and their associated networks. The PLA's focus on integrated operations and potential targets, including enemy information and command systems, and acknowledgement of the growing importance of space and cyberspace, indicates not just that PLA thinking is still evolving, but that achieving information dominance remains a key objective.

This is core to the PLA's conception of future combat operations. Effective integrated operations

Terminology

Mechanisation: Analysts assess that the term 'mechanisation' refers broadly to ambitions to modernise and replace the PLA's legacy equipment across all services and branches, though with significant focus on the ground forces. It is also understood to be closely linked to the reorganisation of the PLA Army from 18 to 13 group armies, which was intended to improve quality and military efficiency.

Informatisation: The 2000 defence white paper stated that the PLA should transform from using 'semi-mechanised and mechanised weapon systems to automated and informatised systems'. By the time of the 2004 defence white paper, informatisation had 'become the key factor in enhancing the warfighting capability' of the PLA. According to the US Department of Defense (DoD), in its 2019 report on China's Military Power, the term 'informatisation' is 'roughly analogous to the U.S. military's concept of net-centric capability: a force's ability to use advanced IT and communications systems to gain operational advantage over an adversary'. China's view of informatised local wars was, the DoD said, 'defined by real-time, data-networked command and control (C2) and precision strike'.

According to PLA Strategic Support Force (SSF) personnel and the *Science of Military Strategy* publication, informatisation provides the PLA with military capabilities that allow it to 'leapfrog' the capabilities of currently technologically superior adversaries. Space-, cyber- and electromagnetic-warfare capacities have the potential to paralyse a high-tech enemy's 'operational system of systems' and undermine their command-level 'system of systems'.

However, the PLA also intends to harness these technologies to help it better collect, analyse, share and train with data and information. It aims to make 'basic progress' by 2020 by introducing additional information and communications technologies, including cyber capacities, across its theatre commands and forces, in order to improve information-enabled capabilities and to boost command, control and communications. Informatisation is also important to the PLA's efforts to improve its military education and training.

Intelligentisation: 'Intelligentisation' (智能化) is a newer concept. China's 2019 defence white paper said that 'intelligent warfare is on the horizon'. It is understood to be based on the premise that military systems will be enhanced by the integration of advanced automation, big data and artificial intelligence (AI). The use of big data has increasingly been highlighted in PLA debates as central to the development of more powerful platforms and systems enabled by AI. Some Chinese sources have also indicated that harnessing these technologies might provide a means by which to 'leapfrog' the capabilities of other military forces.

During a late 2019 forum on military big data, researchers from the Academy of Military Sciences (AMS) discussed aspects of the collection and processing of data, whether derived from reconnaissance, surveillance or intelligence, but also using data from geographic information systems and 'human social and cultural data and social media data'. As military forces try to integrate big data into their structures, they said, operations would increasingly be characterised by human–machine interaction, combinations of human–machine intelligence, data-centric analytical processing and, ultimately, independent decision-making and autonomous-attack capabilities. In short, 'the key to winning quickly is how to shorten the "OODA [observe, orient, decide, act] loop" and revolutionising C2'. However, while debates in China recognise that big data-driven research and development and AI-enabled technologies will result in the PLA's acquisition of 'smarter' and more autonomous platforms and systems, the AMS researchers emphasised that 'big data and AI technology cannot completely replace people and cannot change their decisive position in war'.

across the services will require accurate information on adversaries, while the PLA's own systems and forces have to improve their ability to not only gather more information but also process and disseminate it across all domains. The 2015 defence white paper said that the PLA would look to more efficiently use information resources, improve reconnaissance, early-warning and C2 systems, develop precision-strike capabilities and improve support systems: information systems will integrate operational forces and other elements and, the thinking goes, seamlessly link these with equipment platforms. Indeed, China could look to integrate its satellite reconnaissance and navigation data to enable over-the-horizon targeting. It might even consider developing what could be termed a 'reconnaissance-strike complex', integrating systems such as high-speed cruise missiles and high-speed reconnaissance UAVs (as shown in the 70th anniversary parade in 2019). Integrating capabilities in his way would help not only to deliver military strikes but also – if they were to target C2 nodes – to help achieve information superiority over an adversary.

Appropriate enabling structures

Successfully introducing these concepts will require persistent attention by senior decision-makers, including the PLA's Central Military Commission (CMC). This body was slimmed down in 2017 following the 19th Party Congress. Its four general departments were disbanded and reformed into 15 'functional sections'. This gave the PLA's top leadership direct control over the five new theatre commands and four military services, as well as the decision-making, executive and supervising authorities, in order to drive forward reforms and ensure Party loyalty. In addition, the commanders of the Navy, Air Force and Rocket Force were removed as CMC members and the Secretary of the Discipline Inspection Commission was added. The creation in 2015 of the Strategic Support Force, which reports directly to the CMC, has largely consolidated the PLA's space-, cyber-, electronic- and psychological-warfare capabilities. It is intended to improve readiness and create a more unified capability to prosecute complex multidimensional operations of the sort that might be seen in future conflicts. Moreover, the SSF also plays a support function across services and branches in theatre commands and looks to improve integration in relation to strategic-information operations. Other bodies, including within the Joint Staff Department, that were also tasked with C2 functions were slimmed down after the 2015 organisational reforms and, with some tasks shifted to the SSF, their precise responsibilities are currently unclear.

During Xi's presidency, military–civil fusion (军民融合) has been elevated to a national-level strategy, with a focus on leveraging public and private research and emerging technologies for future war fighting in the information and networked domains. The PLA has also restructured 67 universities and colleges into 37, in order to continue streamlining developments in strategic and disruptive technologies, as well as in military doctrine, strategy, joint operations and informatisation. In 2017, the PLA did not recruit any new students for its National Defence Student Programme. This began, in 1999, in over 115 civilian engineering, science and technology universities. The programme will cease to exist once the remaining students graduate in 2020.

Potential problems

Xi has on numerous occasions highlighted that the PLA has not yet reached its 2020 goals. Indeed, the 2019 defence white paper said that the PLA 'has yet to complete the task of mechanisation and is in urgent need of improving its informatisation'. That said, while mechanisation and informatisation are linked, they have different objectives, each with specific obstacles. For instance, though the navy and air force have benefited from significant investment in defence research and development and manufacturing in introducing newer-generation equipment, some information systems reportedly remain incompatible. Discussions in Chinese literature indicate that the level of standardisation of combat-management systems across the PLA remains low, as does the ability to share information across theatre commands and services. These sources say that informatisation is expected to improve C2 structures and ease the collection and sharing of data. It is perhaps also seen as important in improving decision-making within the PLA, potentially addressing what have been termed the 'five incapables' (五个不会): the inability of 'some' officers to judge situations, understand higher authorities' intentions, make operational decisions, deploy troops or deal with unexpected situations. While military experience in integrating networked capabilities has in some Western states enabled greater flexibility at lower levels of command, this has not been mirrored in the PLA. Communication between PLA decision-makers and subordinates is supposed to have been improved by the integration of new technologies, but there is little to suggest that informatisation has given the CMC the confidence to allow more independent decision-making at lower levels of command. Indeed, if anything, the CMC reforms in 2015 strengthened top-down decision-making, which is structured through Party Committees and Party Standing Committees at every level in the PLA and which are under increasing scrutiny from the Discipline Inspection Commissions. Meanwhile, it is not assured that the PLA will fully realise the benefits of organisational changes like the creation of the SSF. As analysts point out, integrating units such that their personnel, systems and military culture are wholly compatible can take time.

The PLA also faces challenges in recruiting and training highly qualified personnel capable of operating advanced equipment, while there is also competition from China's private technology sector. Better salaries have been offered, as have better benefits following military service, but these differ between officers and enlisted personnel. Reflecting growing concern in this area, a Ministry for Veterans Affairs was set up in 2018. Also, problems persist in improving military training, notwithstanding the introduction of online training and simulation tools, and continued trans-regional exercises designed to drive integration. Moreover, bringing recent graduates with high-tech expertise into the PLA has not proven an unalloyed success. As one source states, 'it is not easy for these professional technicians to adapt to the troops, and it is equally difficult for the force commanders to adapt to the new IT'. As well as acquiring new and information-enabled military equipment, training needs to improve so that China's troops can best exploit the capabilities of these systems.

Looking ahead

China's approach to future warfare and military modernisation seems to have heavily leveraged the lessons it observed when studying other modern militaries. Informatisation is similar to that of the US conception of network-centric warfare, utilising the employment of ICT-enabled modern weaponry and equipment, as well as improving C2. The PLA has focused on improving the capability and quantity of its precision-strike systems and its missiles, with emphasis on increased range and improved accuracy. It has pursued developments in the electromagnetic spectrum, in cyber and in space systems. In a way, the thoroughgoing ambition outlined for China's informatisation process reflects the PLA's understanding of its position relative to advanced Western militaries.

Discussions have been observed in China, in places such as the Academy of Military Sciences and the NDU, concerning the possible decentralisation of command structures and the potential degree of automation in future weapon systems. But while the drive for informatisation might have led the PLA to consider the need for greater flexibility in its decision-making and military-training requirements, Xi's tightened grip over the PLA has led to greater centralisation in the CMC. While the process of 'informatisation' may be improving PLA capabilities, in tandem with the development and introduction of more advanced military systems, this does not mean that the PLA is combat ready or that the benefits of informatisation are being felt rapidly. These concerns are borne out by what can be observed of the PLA's self-reflection as it goes through this process.

At the same time, the degree to which the integration of more intelligent capabilities, such as big data and AI, will influence and improve Chinese weapons developments remains unclear. Although concerns have arisen about the degree of automation in Chinese weapons systems, because of centralised decision-making, Chinese discussions seem to still anticipate having a human in the loop. It is possible that the initial benefits of intelligent capabilities may be felt more in areas such as logistics support and C2. It is not yet clear whether 'informatisation' and 'intelligentisation' will give the PLA a comparative advantage over potential adversaries, some of which are modernising in similar ways. As such, the PLA will be careful about the risk of introducing into its own systems the vulnerabilities it looks to exploit or target in others. This may explain reports of China's forces conducting exercises in a degraded electromagnetic environment. At the same time, while the PLA has looked to US performance in recent conflicts to inform its military-modernisation plans and objectives, it will in future likely also look towards the military-modernisation programmes of other Asian states that are looking to integrate emerging-technology developments into their military thinking, equipment and forces. For China, however, realising the full potential of these developments will likely take longer than was first envisaged.

Military use of the electromagnetic spectrum: the renewed focus on electronic warfare

Modern military forces and equipment capabilities are increasingly reliant on the electromagnetic spectrum (EMS) for strategic, operational and tactical situational awareness, as well as for communications and navigation. Radars on land, at sea, in the air and in space use radio-frequency (RF) emissions to detect and track targets. Armed forces, in turn, use RF transmissions to carry voice, data and imagery traffic to enhance their situational awareness and provide command-and-control (C2) functions. Meanwhile, satellite-RF transmissions provide the satellite-navigation (Global Navigation Satellite System, or GNSS) signals that are used by armed forces, and societies, for navigation and timing.

By the end of the Cold War, the United States and its allies had become accustomed to pre-eminence in the sophistication of their radar, communications and navigation systems. This was evident during US and NATO military interventions from the 1990s onwards. This pre-eminence was, if anything, the legacy of US military and civilian scientific and technological developments during the Second World War and the Cold War, and the post-war development by US allies of their own advanced military technologies. In contrast, reduced access to such technology hampered the development of similarly advanced materiel certainly in Russia but also elsewhere. Although Russia invested heavily in domestic military technology during the Cold War, reduced access to foreign innovation slowed its technical progress.

After the Cold War, Western military forces were in many cases focused on out-of-area operations, and were making ever-greater use of a generally uncontested EMS. Western armed forces increased their reliance on the EMS for situational awareness, including blue-force tracking, as well as for communications, reconnaissance, navigation and timing, and guidance and targeting data. At the same time, Western societies also deepened their dependence on the EMS. With only a limited number of threats to Western use of the EMS, few military capabilities were retained to tackle them. Moreover, tactics and procedures that would have been carefully adhered to during the Cold War, such as voice discipline and emission control, had become of reduced importance, while associated experience and skills faded. A German electronic-warfare officer, speaking about electronic warfare (EW) in the NATO context, observed that 'EW training in forces throughout NATO lost focus and EW skills atrophied'.

Challenging Western dominance

The growing reliance of US and allied militaries on the EMS was apparent to China, Russia and other states, including Iran and North Korea. Western military operations were studied, as were modern military means of harnessing the EMS to improve C2, situational awareness, intelligence, surveillance and reconnaissance (ISR), and targeting. As a result, these states embarked on programmes to improve their capacity to disrupt EMS use through electronic attack, as well as to themselves benefit from the EMS. They also started examining how to exploit the EMS to deliver cyber attacks, with potential targets including military-communications networks, radars and navigation systems, and civilian critical infrastructure.

However, these states are also deepening their reliance on the EMS. For example, Russian military modernisation over the past decade has seen the country invest in digital battle-management systems and advanced telecommunications and radars. The same holds true of China, which is engaged in a drive to improve its military 'informatisation', by developing network-centric capabilities, C2 and ISR, and more closely integrating into these structures the capabilities offered by increasingly modern military equipment. This exploitation of the EMS may present targeting opportunities for potential adversaries, who might exploit it to launch attacks, including by electronic means.

Russia's progress

In the decades prior to Russia's deployments to Ukraine (2014–) and Syria (2015–), its armed forces used EW to varying degrees during conflict in Chechnya in the 1990s and 2000s, as well as during its short war with Georgia in 2008. In Chechnya, it is thought that the gathering of communications intelligence (COMINT) on opposing forces, particularly in geo-locating sources of communications transmissions, was vital in finding and fixing enemy positions for targeting by artillery or airstrikes. In contrast, in Georgia Russian efforts to gather electronic intelligence (ELINT) on and direct jamming against ground-based air-surveillance and fire-control radars was said to have been poor, though this may have also been due to Georgian countermeasures.

Russia has since made efforts to regenerate its EW capabilities, and the deployments to Ukraine and Syria have provided an operational laboratory for the armed forces to refine and develop their EW doctrines. At the same time, they have to some extent offered a window to observe Russian capabilities. The US armed forces' Asymmetric Strategy Group, writing in the publicly available study of Russia's 'new generation warfare' (published 2015), said that Russia had observed, and looked to exploit, Western strategies. For instance, 'because of maneuver warfare's reliance on communication, Russia has invested heavily in Electronic Warfare systems which are capable of shutting down communications and signals across a broad spectrum'.

Russian EW in Ukraine was overtly offensive. Jamming helped sever Ukrainian military radio communications in Crimea, as Russia occupied and annexed that territory in early 2014. This was supported by the RB 314V *Leer*-3 uninhabited aerial vehicle (UAV)-equipped system, which was used to jam cellular networks, and the RP-377LA *Lorandit* COMINT system, which targeted high-frequency and very-/ultra-high-frequency communications. Jamming also affected the RF links used to control S-100 *Camcopter* UAVs assisting the Organisation for Security and Cooperation in Europe observation mission in Ukraine. Russia looked to integrate these capabilities to improve its 'reconnaissance-strike complex'. The Asymmetric Strategy Group stated that, in Ukraine, Russia used 'a sophisticated blend of Unmanned Aircraft Systems, electronic warfare jamming equipment, and long-range rocket artillery'.

In Syria, Russia's EW posture generally focused on force protection. The loss of a Russian Air Force Su-24M *Fencer* D combat aircraft to two Turkish Air Force F-16C fighters in November 2015 prompted Moscow to deploy additional EW systems. One month earlier, Russia had deployed the 1RL257 *Krasukha*-C4 jammer, which targets the X-band and Ku-band airborne radars typically used by combat aircraft and missiles, to protect Khmeimim air base in northern Syria. The *Krasukha*-C4 was supplemented by L-175V/VE *Container/Khibiny* and *Leer*-3 systems. The L-175V/VE jammer can be carried by Russian Air Force Su-30SM *Flanker*-H, Su-34 *Fullback* and Su-35 *Flanker* M combat aircraft.

Electronic warfare evolves

According to the US Department of Defense, in its Electronic Warfare Policy, updated in August 2018, electronic warfare includes the use of 'electromagnetic and directed energy to control the EMS or to attack the enemy'. NATO has a more elaborate explanation: it is 'a military action that exploits electromagnetic energy, both actively and passively, to provide situational awareness and create offensive and defensive effects'. It is warfare within the electromagnetic spectrum (EMS) and involves the military use of electromagnetic energy to prevent or reduce an enemy's effective use of the EMS, while protecting its use for friendly forces.

There are generally held to be three key components: protection (electronic countermeasures and counter-countermeasures), electronic attack (EA) and electronic support measures. The definition given by the DoD for EA is that it uses 'electromagnetic energy, directed energy, or anti-radiation weapons to attack personnel, facilities, or equipment with the intent of degrading, neutralizing, or destroying enemy combat equipment'.

Conducting effective EW missions may require tasking and/or the coordination of relevant assets on land, at sea and in the air or in space; it will involve knowledge of one's own C2 capability, communications and related data links, sensors and weapons – such as radars and lasers – and operating methods, such as jamming (including spoofing) and signals-intelligence collection. In turn, an awareness of adversary developments may drive development of offensive capability as much as it will spur better protection; it may also lead to better equipment design in terms of platforms (such as signature management, including through the integration of passive and perhaps even active stealth). Moreover, cyber and EW tools are more closely linked by digitisation. When EA first began to be used at significant scale, during the Second World War, it initially focused on the application of so-called 'noise jamming', with interference directed against an opponent's communications systems and radars. Recent years have seen jamming techniques increase in sophistication, such as the ability to manipulate transmissions to discretely jam radars. However, cyber effects can now be teamed with EW, such that EA acts as the conduit through which malign code can be introduced into an adversary's C2 or battle-management systems.

Leer-3 may have been deployed to support Syrian Army operations by jamming insurgent mobile phones. It may also have been used to deliver morale-sapping text messages to opposing forces. Reports have circulated of the Russian armed forces also deploying equipment such as the RB-301B *Borisoglebsk-2* COMINT system, which has also been used in the Ukraine theatre, and the *Repellent*-1 counter-UAV system, which is designed to interrupt the RF links between a UAV and its ground station. In June 2019, reports emerged that Israeli airspace had experienced GNSS jamming, possibly caused by Russian Army R-330Zh *Zhitel* systems being used to protect the Russian deployments at Khmeimim air base. Whether this jamming was deliberate, or an unintended consequence of operations, remains unclear.

Russian EW effects have also been observed in Europe. Moscow has been accused of using jamming against Norway and its Baltic neighbours. In March 2019, Oslo claimed that the Russian military had jammed GNSS signals in the country's north during NATO exercises in October–November 2018. Russia's earlier *Zapad* 2017 exercises saw EW used to prepare Russian forces for fighting in an electromagnetically contested environment. These EW efforts have not been performed in a vacuum. Operations in Ukraine and Syria showed that these form part of a wider strategy involving cyber attacks. Moscow has been accused of performing cyber attacks against Ukrainian critical infrastructure, and of targeting non-governmental organisations and opposition groups with cyber activity during its involvement in the Syrian conflict.

China

China is also overhauling its EW capabilities – perhaps even more so than Russia – as it modernises its armed forces. The US Department of Defense's (DoD's) 2018 China's Military Power report said that the People's Liberation Army (PLA) considered EW a key aspect of modern war and that 'its EW doctrine emphasizes using electromagnetic spectrum weapons to suppress or to deceive enemy electronic equipment. Potential EW victims include adversary systems operating in radio, radar, microwave, infrared, and optical frequency ranges, as well as adversarial computer and information systems.' Cyber actions, meanwhile, could attack an enemy's C2 system, with the potential to 'completely disrupt' these systems, thereby 'gaining battlefield superiority'. They would also be useful for other purposes including espionage. EW features in recent Chinese military exercises designed not only to improve the PLA's ability to use EW but also to enhance its capacity to operate in a contested electromagnetic environment. Its EW units routinely train, according to the DoD, in order to 'conduct jamming and anti-jamming operations against multiple communication and radar systems or GPS satellite systems in force-on-force exercises'. In 2019, meanwhile, reports that the accuracy of satellite-navigation systems was being degraded offshore Shanghai indicate growing Chinese capabilities, possibly in the civil sector as well as the armed forces.

NATO and the EW threat

GNSS jamming is of increasing concern to NATO member states, and they have been seeking to regenerate their EW capability and resilience. In its 2018 Electronic Warfare Policy, the Pentagon advised prioritising training 'in a congested and contested electromagnetic operational environment … both on live ranges and in training'.

The US is pursuing more jam-resistant Global Positioning System (GPS) satellite signals, while the US Army is looking at new navigational systems for

Table 1 **Selected Russian EW systems reported deployed to the Ukraine and Syrian theatres**

System	User	Estimated frequencies	Purpose
1RL257 *Krasukha*-C4	Army	8.5 gigahertz/GHz to 18GHz	Intended to jam airborne X-band and Ku-band radars
R-330Zh *Zhitel*	Army	1.1GHz to 1.6GHz	Designed to jam GNSS transmissions
RB-314V *Leer*-3	Army	800 megahertz/MHz to 2GHz	Used for the hacking/jamming of cell-phone transmissions and networks
L-175V/VE *Container/ Khibiny*	Aerospace Forces	2GHz to 18GHz/40GHz	Airborne ELINT/electronic-attack system for ground-based air surveillance and fire-control radars, and airborne fire-control radars
RB-301B *Borisoglebsk*-2	Army	30MHz to 3GHz	COMINT collection targeting very-/ultra-high-frequency land and air communications
Repellent-1	Army	300MHz to 6GHz	Possibly designed to disrupt air-to-ground/ground-to-air UAV communications, or to disrupt UAV GNSS
RP-377LA *Lorandit*	Army	3MHz to 3GHz	COMINT system designed to geolocate high-frequency and very-/ultra-high-frequency radio communications

its vehicles, incorporating Inertial Navigation Systems (INS) to reduce the reliance on GPS. Its M-1126 *Stryker* armoured infantry fighting vehicles are receiving the Mounted Assured Precision Navigation and Timing System (MAPS), which uses a GPS system teamed with an atomic clock to provide timing, an INS and an anti-spoofing GNSS antenna. The army is expected to roll out MAPS to other armoured vehicles, and also to develop a variant of the system to equip dismounted soldiers. The US Army has also overhauled its EW posture and was reportedly due to begin fielding new EW platoons in manoeuvre brigades in the second quarter of 2020.

The US Air Force is examining its posture to take account of the modern EW environment, as it looks to maintain what it calls the United States' strategic advantage. The air force is introducing systems such as the AGM-160C variant of the Miniature Air-Launched Decoy, which adds a radar jammer, and is upgrading its anti-radar AGM-88 air-to-surface missiles. However, some analysts have said that platform-protection priorities are still seen by the air force as key to mitigating the renewed EW threat, with this evident in the signature-management considerations observed in platform designs. The air force, it has been said, may have tactical jamming capability, but it also requires theatre-level capability – a capability it has not had since the EF-11A *Raven* electronic-warfare aircraft retired in 1998.

The US and NATO are also enhancing their cyber capabilities. After the shooting down by Iran of a US Navy BAMS-D reconnaissance UAV on 20 June 2019, US Cyber Command reportedly performed a cyber attack aimed at networked C2 systems controlling Iranian surface-to-air missile batteries.

Elsewhere in NATO, efforts are ongoing to enhance the abilities of allied forces and platforms to operate in electromagnetically contested areas. At the strategic and operational levels, the Alliance's Joint EW Core Staff (JEWCS) is drafting a new EW doctrine. It has also made important investments in NATO EW training and is overhauling its SIGINT capabilities via the NATO EW Database–Next Generation (NEDB-NG) initiative. This should improve the way member states analyse, store and share information, including on new EMS systems and associated platforms. Exercises practising and defending against EA are once more a frequent occurrence.

Steps are also being taken to fuse EW and cyber warfare. In 2018, for instance, the UK Ministry of Defence published its Cyber and Electromagnetic Activities Joint Doctrine Note, aimed at aligning the postures of the UK armed services, as well as with civilian agencies such as the GCHQ SIGINT organisation.

Platforms and weapons are also being designed to be resistant against EW and cyber threats. Low Probability of Interception/Detection waveforms transmitted by radar and communications systems can make it more difficult for SIGINT systems to detect and locate the source of transmissions, helping to prevent jamming and perhaps to protect against cyber attacks.

In the communications realm, analysts judge that lessons from Ukraine show that NATO communications are generally resilient against Russian jamming attempts. A small number of tactical radios equipped with NATO's Single Channel Ground and Airborne Radio System (SINCGARS) waveform were supplied to Ukraine. SINCGARS provides clear and protected communications between land forces, and SINCGARS radios were understood to have performed well despite Russian jamming activity. Over the longer term, the uptake of extremely high-frequency communications for tactical communications, which use bandwidths of 30–300 GHz, could result in systems that are difficult to jam due to their very narrow beamwidth; this makes them difficult to detect, locate and attack.

What next?

A number of potential adversary countries have closely studied recent Western military operations. After noting the reliance placed on the EMS by the US and its allies, they have taken steps to ensure that this can be challenged. At the same time, there has been growing recognition that cyber warfare can disrupt an adversary's military capabilities at the tactical and operational levels, and its socio-economic and political life at the strategic level. Indeed, electronic- and cyber-warfare disciplines are increasingly merging in the military context. NATO and partner nations have responded and refocused strategies in order to address their electromagnetic vulnerabilities, including improving their ability to operate in a degraded or denied EMS environment, at the same time as investing in electronic- and cyber-warfare capabilities. For major players – including China and Russia – an essential element of success will be not only how they improve their electromagnetic defences and resilience but also how they develop and exploit greater offensive capability as part of their military-modernisation plans.

The space domain: towards a regular realm of conflict?

In 2019, a series of announcements highlighted the growing importance of space for national security and defence. At its November 2019 foreign-ministers' meeting in Belgium, NATO declared space an 'operational domain' for the Alliance, three months after the United States activated US Space Command as a new, eleventh, combatant command. According to the US Department of Defense, the US 'faces serious and growing challenges to its freedom to operate in space'. China and Russia, it said, 'view counterspace capabilities as a means to reduce US and allied military effectiveness'.

Space is a critical aspect of everyday civilian, as well as military, activity. The technical and cost barriers to entry have reduced, enabling more countries to possess space assets. Many of these are dual use. More countries are relying on space to support and enhance their military operations, in turn providing an incentive for the development of counter-space and anti-satellite (ASAT) capabilities. Many of these resemble those developed by the Soviet Union and the US during the Cold War. One risk, some analysts argue, is that today there may be fewer deterrent effects to hold back the use of such capabilities, particularly if states look to employ these systems as part of sub-threshold activity.

This emergent acknowledgement that space is another domain of military competition and potential conflict raises numerous questions. These include how best to organise military space forces and how to protect or harden satellites against attack, while also developing the means to interfere with adversary assets. There are also questions relating to the rapid growth of private-sector space systems and how these may drive competition or be leveraged by armed forces. Another challenge is how to better integrate military space operations with operations in the air, on land, at sea and in cyberspace. Additionally, the prospect of offensive military action in space, or activity that targets uplinks, downlinks or ground stations, raises concerns about collateral damage to the global space services that underpin modern commercial and social life; how arms-control or confidence-building regimes could be used to limit the use of certain capabilities; and how to avoid misperceptions or mistakes that could risk confrontation or even conflict in space or on Earth.

Cold War heritage

The Russian (then-Soviet) and US space programmes have their roots in producing delivery vehicles for nuclear weapons, but this shifted, more or less contemporaneously, to include launching satellites. Increased Soviet air-defence capabilities drove the Eisenhower administration to develop satellites to bolster intelligence-collection activities. Although the Soviet Union achieved early public firsts with the *Sputnik* satellite (which reached orbit in October 1957 atop a modified ballistic missile) and the first human spaceflight (when Yuri Gagarin orbited on 12 April 1961 in *Vostok* 1), the classified US *Corona* reconnaissance-satellite programme first proved the national-security benefits to be had in exploiting space.

Moscow and Washington engaged in military competition in space throughout the Cold War. The 1967 Outer Space Treaty, the foundation of international space law, limited military space competition by outlawing the placement of nuclear weapons and other weapons of mass destruction in orbit and the establishment of military bases on the Moon, but also allowed for a wide range of other military space activities under the euphemism 'peaceful uses'. Initial ideas for crewed military space stations and orbital bombers soon gave way to more practical satellites that provided critical intelligence, surveillance and reconnaissance (ISR); communications; and positioning, navigation and timing (PNT) services from space. The military utility of these services drove both the Soviet Union and the US to also develop and deploy ground- and space-based ASAT capabilities. These weapons were never used in a military conflict, largely because the use of satellites to verify arms-control treaties and provide warning of nuclear attack deterred space attacks, for fear they would trigger a wider, possibly nuclear, confrontation.

Towards the end of the Cold War, the Reagan administration's public drive for its Strategic Defense Initiative (SDI) spurred a new round of international concern over military competition in space. There was increased concern that the militarisation of space might turn into the weaponisation of space, potentially including space-based systems that could be used to target installations on Earth. However, capabilities envisioned for SDI were not deployed before the Cold War came to an end.

Developing competition

The US was the dominant space power after the fall of the Soviet Union. Many Soviet-era Russian military space programmes faced budget cuts and, analysts understand, ASAT programmes were mothballed. For Washington, the value of space for supporting and enhancing military operations was proven in the 1990–91 First Gulf War and the 1999 bombing campaign in the former Yugoslavia. These drove increased military investment in space-based services and spurred their integration into air, land and maritime forces. In the late 1990s, the US armed forces drew up plans for broader efforts to achieve full-spectrum 'dominance' in space, but these lost momentum after 9/11 and the subsequent wars in Afghanistan and Iraq, in favour of using space capabilities to support and enhance those operations.

While the US was engaged in Afghanistan and Iraq, China and Russia began to increase their investment in national-security space capabilities. Both countries were embarked on military-modernisation programmes, learning lessons from US and Western operations as far back as the First Gulf War, and in Russia's case also rejuvenating some hitherto dormant military space projects with renewed funding streams. Some analysts understand this included moving some counter-space and ASAT programmes out of storage or developing new versions. It has been reported that the then-commander of Russia's space forces had said in 2010 that Russia was 'again developing inspection' and 'strike' satellites. Russia also embarked on a project to restore its GLONASS satellite-navigation constellation. For its part, China embarked on a wide-ranging programme to develop its own space-based capabilities for ISR, PNT and communications to support its national-security needs (launches began in 2000 for China's *Beidou* satellite-navigation system), as well as a suite of counter-space and ASAT capabilities of its own. China conducted multiple tests of ground-based ASAT weapons, including one in January 2007, using a direct-ascent missile, that destroyed one of its own weather satellites and resulted in several thousand pieces of orbital debris. (The US and Soviet Union had themselves carried out ASAT tests during the Cold War.)

During the 2010s, the US became increasingly concerned about the threats to its space capabilities. In 2013, the Obama administration compiled a National Intelligence Estimate of Russian and Chinese counter-space capabilities and reviewed the United States' space posture. This sparked several initiatives intended to reorganise national-security space capabilities and increase the resilience of US space assets to attack, and saw the first public discussions by senior military leaders about the possibility of space becoming a future domain of conflict. The Trump administration has continued this focus, with public statements about the inevitability of space as a war-fighting domain and impetus for a major reorganisation of US military space bureaucracy.

Diffusing space competition

With space becoming integral to future military competition and conflict, and as more countries invest in space-based capabilities to enhance their national-security interests, the tendency to seek counter-space and ASAT capabilities is now evident. Current conflicts in Syria and eastern Ukraine already feature the significant use of ground-based jamming and spoofing of satellite-navigation and satellite-communications systems as part of military operations. This has taken place elsewhere, as demonstrated by the 2016 jamming of satellite-navigation signals in South Korea, attributed to North Korea by the South, and reports in 2019 that satellite-navigation signals offshore Shanghai were being spoofed. Meanwhile, China and Russia have continued their ASAT testing and development programmes. Meanwhile, India tested its own direct-ascent ASAT weapon in March 2019 and some in the US have argued that it should also develop an offensive capability.

The types of counter-space capabilities being explored today are fundamentally the same as those developed during the Cold War. Russia's 51T6 *Gorgon* missile (part of the A-135 anti-ballistic-missile (ABM) system) was reported to have a latent direct-ascent ASAT capability, while it remains unclear if Russia's 14Ts033 *Nudol* (which might be associated with the A-235 ABM system) has a similar capability. As well as ground-, sea- or air-launched missiles used as direct-ascent weapons to destroy satellites in low-Earth orbit, interceptors placed in orbit could be used as co-orbital weapons, manoeuvring and rendezvousing with a target satellite to try and damage or destroy it. These interceptors could include manoeuvrable satellites. High-powered lasers and other types of directed-energy weapons could also be employed to temporarily blind or otherwise interfere with satellites, although physical destruction using a laser (particularly from a ground-based location) is, specialists assert, still some way off. More immediate threats, however, are the jamming of satellite radio-frequency transmissions and cyber attacks against ground-control stations, which could disrupt the military use of satellites during a conflict.

Protection and resilience
There is a continuing debate over how best to protect satellites from attack. Russia and the US were effectively deterred from targeting early-warning satellites during the Cold War by the risk of starting a nuclear war. The lack of hostile threats for most of the period since has meant that functionality became a prime design determinant for national-security satellites. This led to a focus on large, capable and expensive national-security satellites, with long development and replacement timelines. Some analysts have argued that developing offensive capabilities to threaten adversary satellites might itself deter potential attacks. That said, if a nation with such offensive capabilities is itself heavily reliant on space-enabled systems, it may be disinclined to take action that might in turn imperil these. Instead, a key strategy has been to increase the resilience of space capabilities by moving to new constellations of numerous smaller satellites, potentially spread across multiple orbits; using commercial or allied satellites; and generating operationally responsive space capabilities, so as to quickly reconstitute those constellations. For satellite applications where this is not feasible, the focus has been on enabling satellites to defend against attacks, perhaps with additional manoeuvring capabilities or on-board systems to confuse or interfere with targeting systems, or improved protection against threats including dazzling or jamming. Analysts understand that as part of the expansion of its military space functions, and stemming from concerns about potential on-orbit vulnerability, France is considering passive and active protection for its future satellites, as well as systems that could provide warning of an impending threat, thereby allowing defensive manoeuvres.

At the same time, some states are preparing to operate in environments where they no longer have assured access to space or assured data reliability from their space-based systems. More exercises have been observed in which GPS signals have been deliberately degraded, while it was reported in 2016 that the US Navy was reinstating celestial-navigation training amid fears of GPS degradation or spoofing. This is also significant for guided weapons, where there is renewed attention on hardening systems against electronic attack, as well as forms of redundancy, for instance in guidance systems that may be otherwise dependent on signals from space-based systems.

One critical contemporary feature that was not present during the Cold War is the involvement of the private sector. The *Apollo* programme and other major Cold War space programmes were government directed and funded (although they used contracted industry support), whereas today commercial companies are often engaged in their own space activities independent of governments. States are turning to commercial companies as a source of technological innovation that could be utilised for military applications and to provide core services, with the hoped-for benefit of releasing military budgets to fund military-specific capabilities.

Debates are also under way about how best to organise military space functions. While a range of countries have a military space function, these are often limited in scale, concerned with resilience or the management of space-enabled assets, and are attached or subordinate to larger organisations or services.

However, in recent years several states have moved to strengthen the integration of space and other military capabilities. In December 2015, China established its Strategic Support Force, combining electronic-warfare, space and cyber units, though analysts remain uncertain if this includes counter-space forces. Also in 2015, Russia established its Aerospace Forces, combining its previous air, air-defence and space units under the same command. France announced in August 2019 that it would elevate its existing Joint Space Command to a Space Command, under the renamed French Air and Space Forces. Meanwhile, the United Kingdom unveiled its Defence Space Strategy in mid-2019, announcing investments in space systems, including small-satellite development.

In the US, however, both Congress and the Trump administration have called for space to be separated out from the air force and put into a new military service. President Trump has insisted this be a separate

'Department of the Space Force', while the Pentagon and Congress seem to favour a semi-separate Space Force within the Department of the Air Force, similar to the relationship between the US Marine Corps and the US Navy. In 2018, Congress directed the re-establishment of US Space Command (USSPACECOM) to reassume the space-war-fighting function that had been carried out by US Strategic Command since the demise of the original USSPACECOM in 2002. In its new role, USSPACECOM will serve as a geographic combatant command, responsible for all military operations above 100 kilometres altitude and integrating military space capabilities into the planning and operations of other combatant commands. In December 2019, it was reported that (as part of the negotiations over the 2020 defence budget) US legislators agreed to establish a US Space Force as a separate military branch.

Unresolved issues

The increasing focus on space as a potential domain of military confrontation is also driving an awareness of the need to limit the effect that this could have on non-military space activities, as is the case with military activities in other domains. Analysts studying this challenge have posited a number of steps that could be considered, including the development of transparency and confidence-building measures that could help reduce the chances of accidents, mistakes or misperceptions that could trigger a confrontation, or worse, in space. Such measures could also be useful in helping to identify unusual actions or activities that could be, or could be a precursor to, a hostile attack against a satellite. Whether or not such an attack would amount to a use of force, possibly leading a state to invoke the right of self-defence, is a question being debated by military lawyers and academics, as are questions relating to the application of international humanitarian law and the law of armed conflict to military space operations. These debates become more complex if states look to employ military space capabilities that are below the threshold of conventional military activity.

There is also renewed interest in arms-control measures to mitigate the disastrous effect conflict in space could have on the civilian use of space services. In late 2018, the United Nations' First Committee continued its long-standing discussions regarding the potential for a rules-based order 'to securely govern' space. Russia and China highlighted their draft treaty (presented in 2008 and 2014), which is aimed at preventing the placement of weapons in space. The US position on China and Russia's proposals, as elaborated in the 2019 Worldwide Threat Assessment of the US Intelligence Community, is that they 'do not cover multiple issues connected to the ASAT weapons they are developing and deploying'. These shortcomings, according to the US, have allowed China and Russia to 'pursue space warfare capabilities while maintaining the position that space must remain weapons free'.

Space has become a critical part of the global economy and everyday life. It is essential to weather forecasting, climate monitoring, and maintaining global communications and transportation infrastructure. The widespread use of destructive space weapons that create persistent orbital debris or the indiscriminate jamming of civilian PNT signals could have consequences beyond their military purpose. As such, there are questions as to what potentially destructive space capabilities should be off limits, similar to discussions relating to cluster bombs, landmines, cyber warfare and similar capabilities in other domains.

A key difficulty is that many of these space capabilities are now generated not solely by and for governments but also by the private sector, with the same holding true of space-related research and development. Developing and maintaining a competitive advantage in space will in future likely involve greater cooperation between the public and private sectors. It will also mean generating more competition within the private sector to spur innovation and cost-effectiveness. Dependencies have also developed since the end of the Cold War – the US, for instance, is currently reliant on Russian engines and space-launch facilities for some of its major space requirements. If anything, the use of space-based assets has become so routine that reawakening their national-security relevance, or indeed informing populations of the extent of their dependence on space, is now a growing challenge for governments.

Chapter Two
Comparative defence statistics

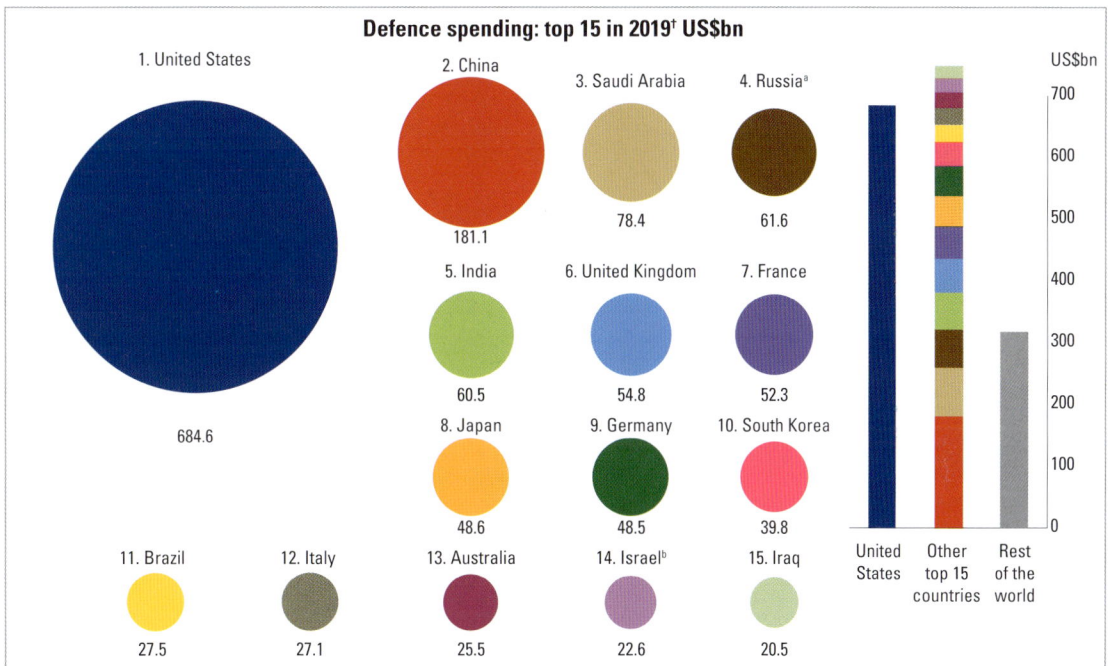

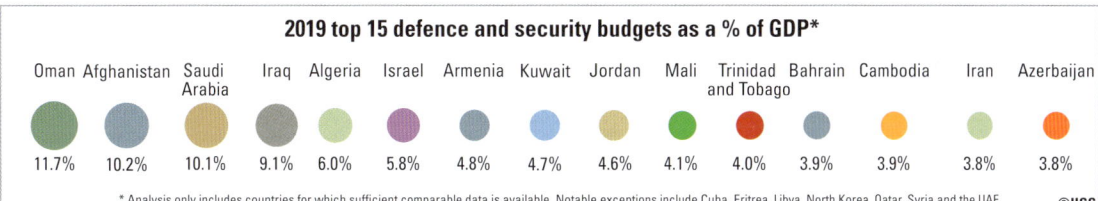

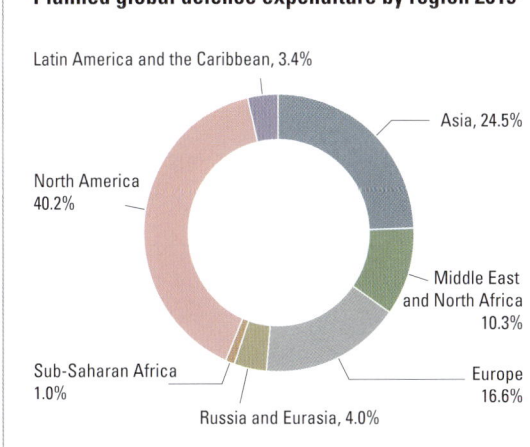

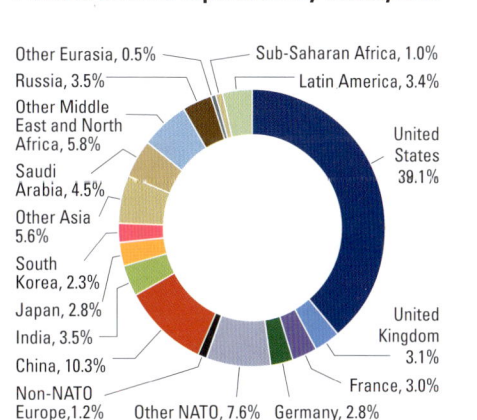

† At current prices and exchange rates

22 THE MILITARY BALANCE 2020

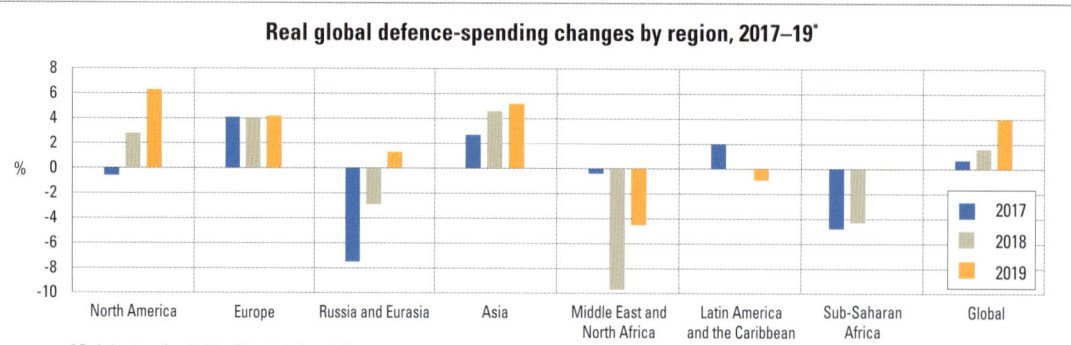

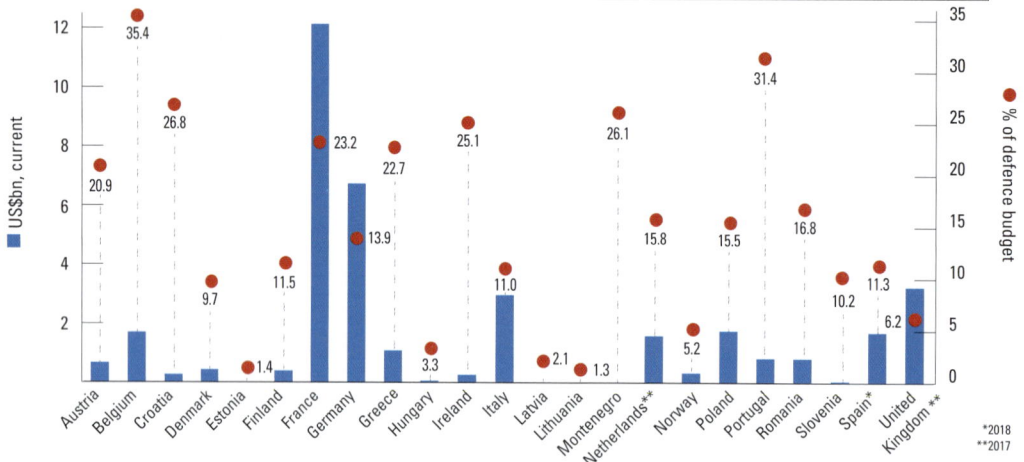

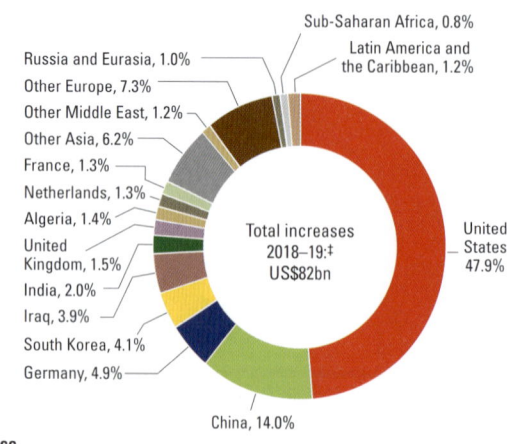

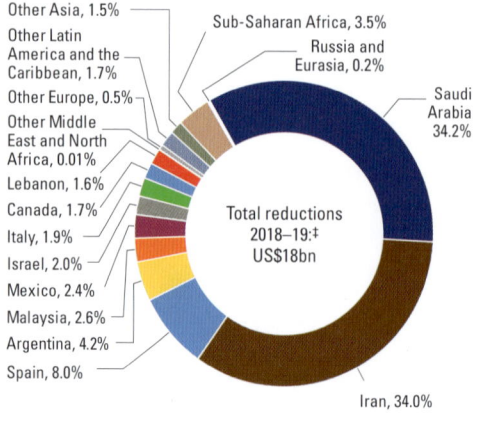

‡ At constant 2015 prices and exchange rates

High-speed helicopters: pushing the rotary limits

The speed ceiling for a conventional rotary-wing design is around 370 kilometres per hour (230 miles per hour). Almost since the advent of rotary flight, designers have been attempting to improve on this by combining lift rotors with either a rear propeller (the 'pusher' concept) or jet thrust combined with a stub wing to create a compound helicopter, thereby reducing the rotor's requirement to generate lift. One of the most well-known 'pusher' designs, which almost made it into service in the United States, was the late-1960s Lockheed AH-56A *Cheyenne* attack helicopter. An alternative approach is to use the propeller like a conventional rotor blade. However, this requires being able to move the propeller through 90 degrees, as employed in the only in-service tilt-rotor design, the Bell Boeing V-22 *Osprey*. There is now a renewed focus on the 'pusher' concept. US Army requirements are a catalyst for this in the military domain, with its Future Vertical Lift (FVL) project the design driver. However, both tilt-rotor and compound helicopter designs are being proposed to meet elements of the FVL programme. Bell's V-280 tilt-rotor is one option for the Future Long-Range Assault Aircraft, while the Sikorsky/Boeing S-97 *Raider* compound helicopter is a candidate for the Future Attack Reconnaissance Aircraft.

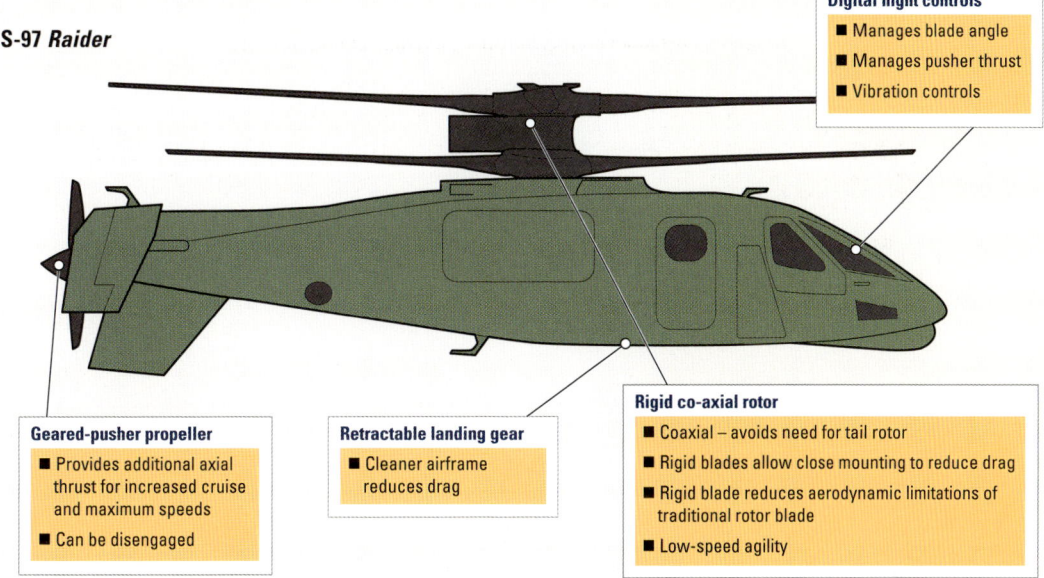

S-97 *Raider*

Digital flight controls
- Manages blade angle
- Manages pusher thrust
- Vibration controls

Geared-pusher propeller
- Provides additional axial thrust for increased cruise and maximum speeds
- Can be disengaged

Retractable landing gear
- Cleaner airframe reduces drag

Rigid co-axial rotor
- Coaxial – avoids need for tail rotor
- Rigid blades allow close mounting to reduce drag
- Rigid blade reduces aerodynamic limitations of traditional rotor blade
- Low-speed agility

Selected prototype compound helicopter and tilt-rotor designs, 1950s–1980s

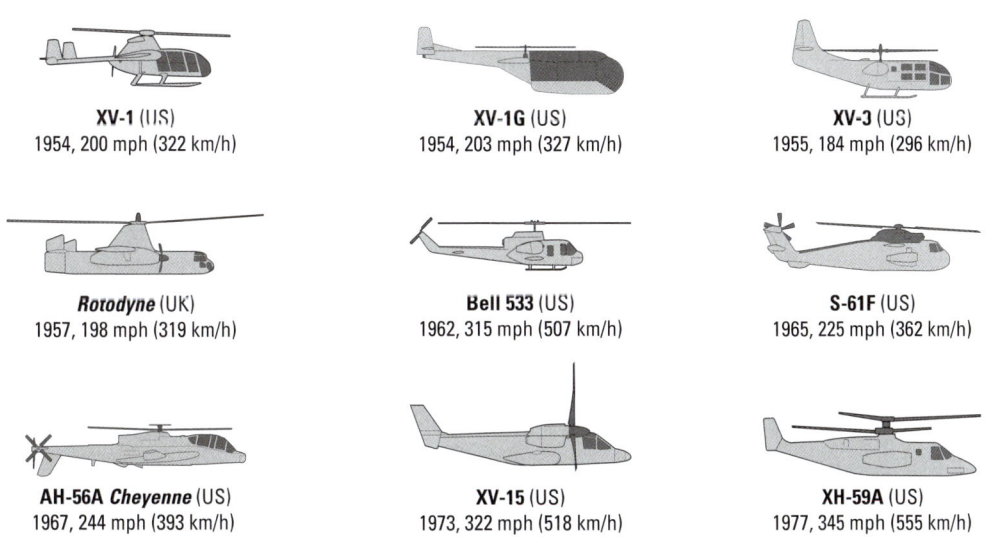

XV-1 (US)
1954, 200 mph (322 km/h)

XV-1G (US)
1954, 203 mph (327 km/h)

XV-3 (US)
1955, 184 mph (296 km/h)

Rotodyne (UK)
1957, 198 mph (319 km/h)

Bell 533 (US)
1962, 315 mph (507 km/h)

S-61F (US)
1965, 225 mph (362 km/h)

AH-56A *Cheyenne* (US)
1967, 244 mph (393 km/h)

XV-15 (US)
1973, 322 mph (518 km/h)

XH-59A (US)
1977, 345 mph (555 km/h)

© IISS

France's *Scorpion* armoured-vehicle-replacement programme

French military operations over recent decades have led the army to assess the likely character of future land warfare and the capabilities it needs. A key response from Paris has been the *Scorpion* combat system (*Synergie du COntact Renforcé par la Polyvalence et l'Info valorisatiON*). France sees the requirement for manoeuvre warfare platforms, networked together, that are as capable in dispersed operations at reach as they would be as part of a concentrated force. The new platforms are integrated by design around a common doctrine and linked by a common combat-in-formation system. Deliveries to the French Army of the *Scorpion* system's first elements, the VBMR *Griffon*, began in 2019. Belgium is also procuring the system for its ground forces.

European collaboration

As well as a vehicle purchase, Belgium and France are jointly developing the *Scorpion* doctrine, and a joint training programme has been established. Training has already taken place in the field and in synthetic environments. Both armies intend that *Scorpion*-equipped units are inter-operable down to section level. A May 2019 report by the French National Assembly said that *Scorpion* could set a template for other armies in Europe.

Operational concept

Combined Arms Tactical Formations

The *Scorpion* combat system is designed to facilitate combined-arms manoeuvre warfare. France's future *Scorpion*-equipped Combined Arms Tactical Formations will include 'Command', 'Discovery', 'Assault' and 'Logistics' echelons. France is looking to more closely integrate these elements both physically and in terms of their networked capability, in order to fuse these elements in a bid to enhance combat capability. *Jaguar* will be found in the Discovery echelon, operating far ahead of the main force and utilising such tactics as reconnaissance-by-contact, in order to assess and if required shape enemy dispositions so they can be better targeted by the Assault echelon. The VBCI IFV and *Leclerc* MBT will be located in the Assault echelon.

VBMR *Griffon* 6x6 wheeled armoured personnel carrier

Weight: 24.5 tonnes
Capacity: 2+8 soldiers
Versions: PAX carrier, command post, artillery observation, ambulance.
Main armament: 7.62 or 12.7 mm remotely operated turret
Deliveries: from 2019

Scorpion Combat Information System (CIS)

The *Scorpion* CIS networks troops, vehicles and weapons, and is also designed to process information from sensors installed on vehicles and other ground and air platforms. This capability is intended to allow distributed operations, so reducing the targeting options for adversaries, but enabling own forces to concentrate at speed when required. The CIS is also intended to generate information useful in reducing the logistical burden, including information on ammunition consumption, in order to lessen the cognitive workload on troops.

EBRC *Jaguar* reconnaissance vehicle

Weight: 25 tonnes
Main armaments: Cased Telescoped Armament 40 mm cannon, 7.62 mm remotely operated turret, two MMP anti-tank guided-missile launchers
Other equipment: with acoustic detonation-tracking system, laser warning detector
Deliveries: from 2021

Vehicle replacement plan

Other elements of the *Scorpion* programme include the multi-role VBMR-L *Serval* armoured vehicle, to be introduced from 2022, followed by modernised *Leclerc* main battle tanks and VBCI infantry fighting vehicles upgraded to *Scorpion* standard. However, the VBL reconnaissance vehicle replacement programme (VBAE) is expected to be initiated after 2025. The French Army plans to replace its 2,255 VAB APCs with 1,872 VBMR *Griffons* and 978 of the 2,000 VBMR-L *Serval* vehicles that the armed forces are due to receive. France's 247 AMX-10RC wheeled assault guns and its remaining 59 ERC-90 reconnaissance vehicles are due to be replaced with 300 EBRC *Jaguars*. In Belgium, the VBMR *Griffon* will replace the *Piranha*-III-C wheeled APC and *Dingo*-2 armoured utility vehicle, and the EBRC *Jaguar* will replace the *Piranha* III-C DF30 and DF90 IFVs.

Comparative defence statistics 25

China, Russia and the United States: surface-launched anti-ship missiles

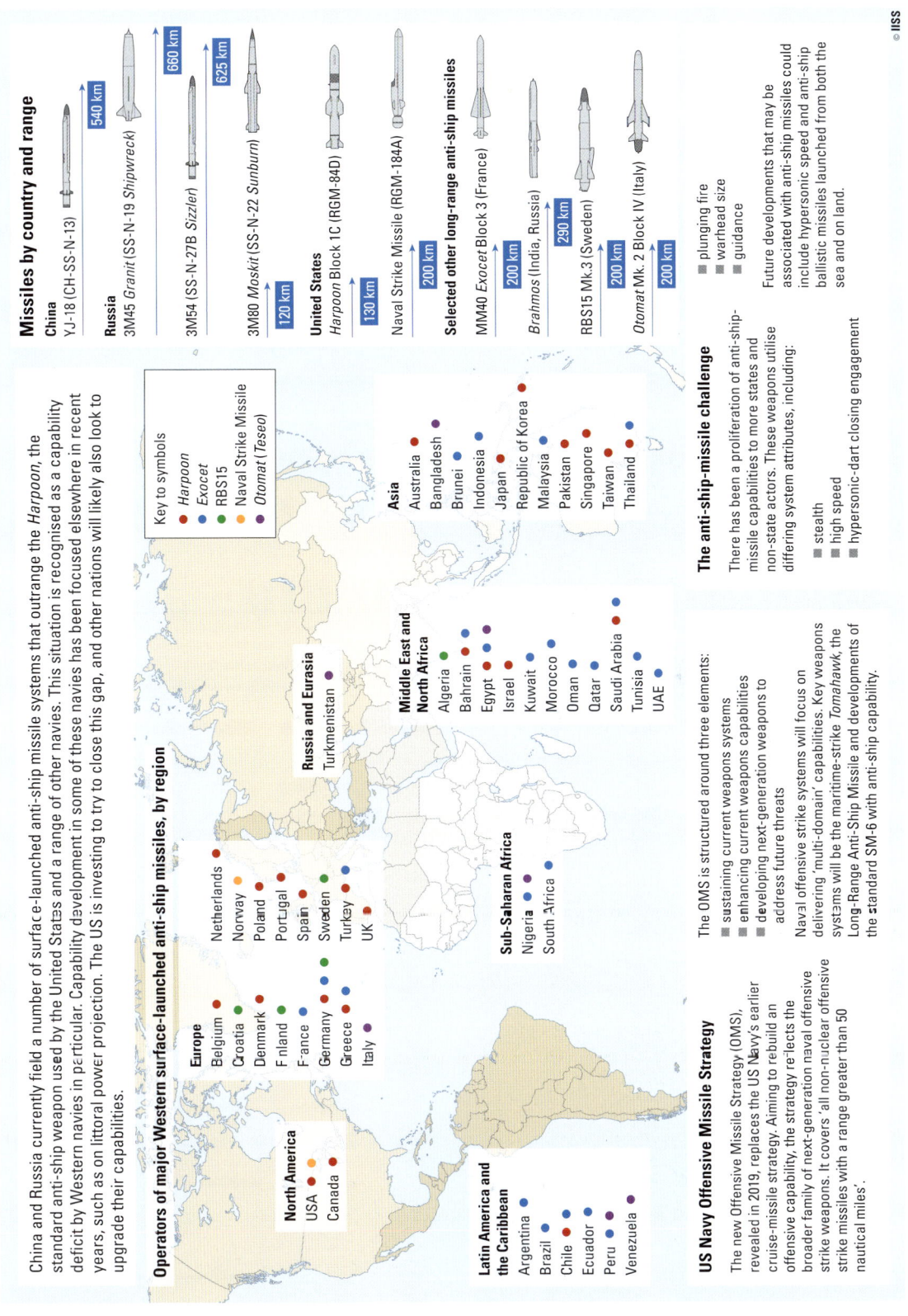

Key defence statistics

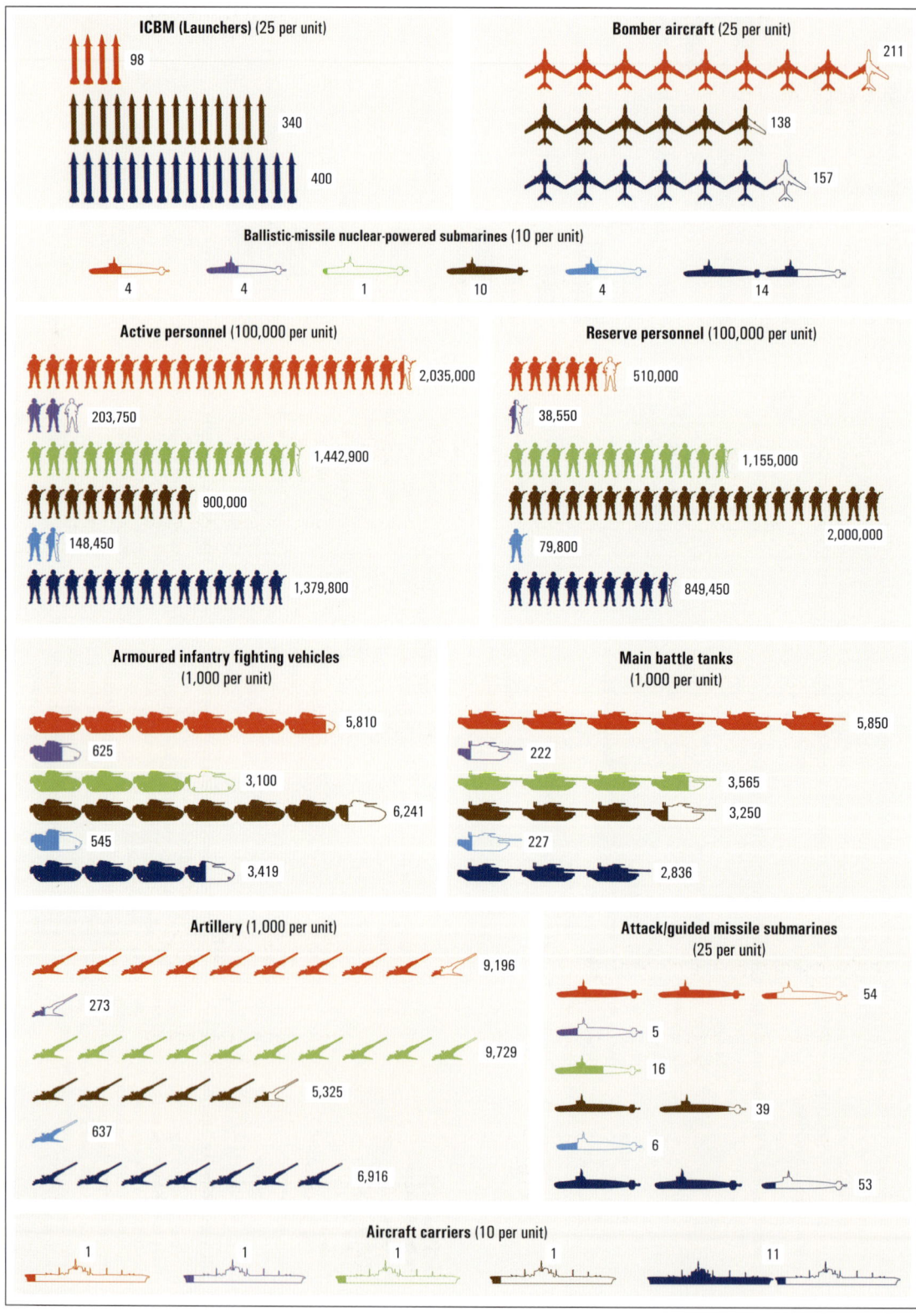

Comparative defence statistics

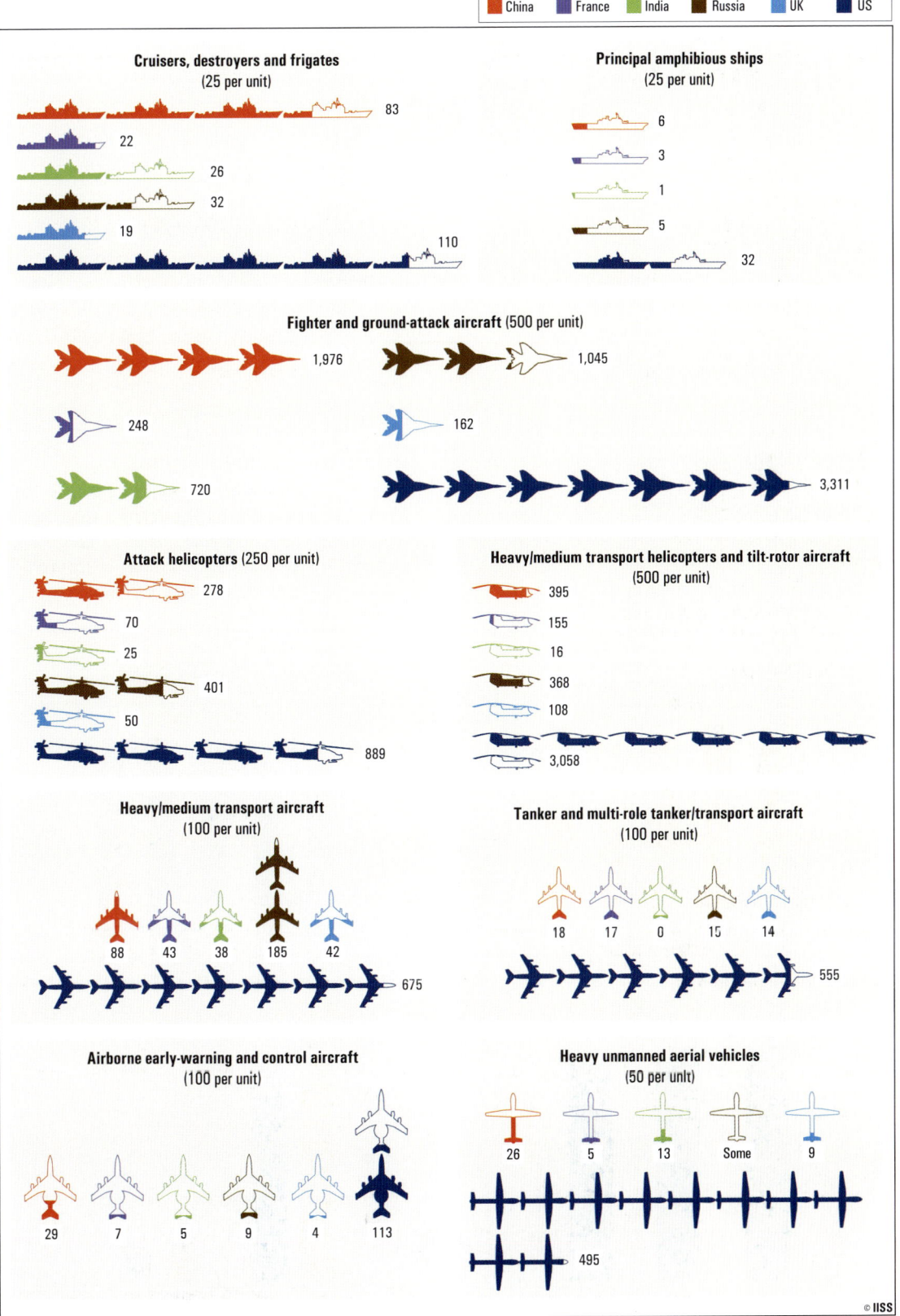

Chapter Three
North America

- The US Department of Defense saw two secretaries of defense and one acting secretary in the space of seven months, creating added uncertainties over policy direction and priorities.
- In August 2019, the US re-established a Space Command amid growing concern about the vulnerability of US space-based assets, and as a precursor to the creation of a US Space Force. Debates continue over the precise role of and ambition for such a force.
- Challenges over rebuilding readiness are vying with force-modernisation demands amid renewed focus on great-power competition. Rebuilding the reach and potency of offensive systems is key, such as with the army's Long-Range Precision Fires project and the navy's Offensive Missile Strategy.
- The planning guidance issued by the Commandant of the US Marine Corps said that it should no longer be bound by a goal of 38 large amphibious ships in light of the A2/AD challenge. This could significantly affect US Navy strategic planning and shipbuilding ambitions.
- The US Navy force structure remains under strain, including aircraft carriers but also submarines, as the navy, industry and legislators seek to mitigate a forecast fall in submarine numbers to the low 40s in the 2030s.
- The US Air Force continues to struggle to improve readiness. With the fleet ageing, planners are having to manage the demands of maintenance, modernisation and the introduction of new types, some with their own problems over initial readiness.
- Canada faces a long-term challenge in implementing its 2017 defence strategy, which detailed significant procurements both of combat aircraft, to replace the current F/A-18 fleet, and ship construction for the navy and coastguard. An initial hike in the budget has not been sustained so far.

US satellite holdings
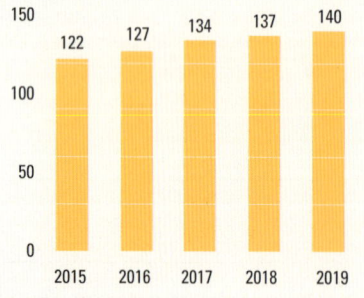

US Navy principal amphibious ships
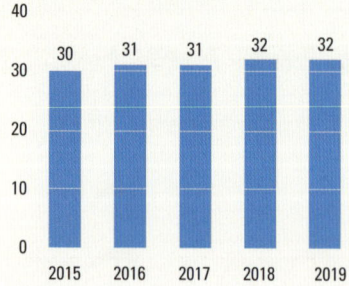

US tactical submarines
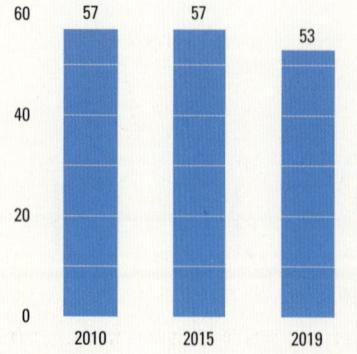

US Air Force active fixed-wing-aircraft inventories
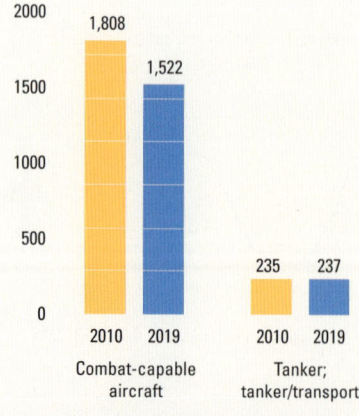

Regional defence policy and economics	30 ▶
Armed forces data section	43 ▶
Arms procurements and deliveries	61 ▶

US aircraft-carrier deployments and availability, mid-November 2019

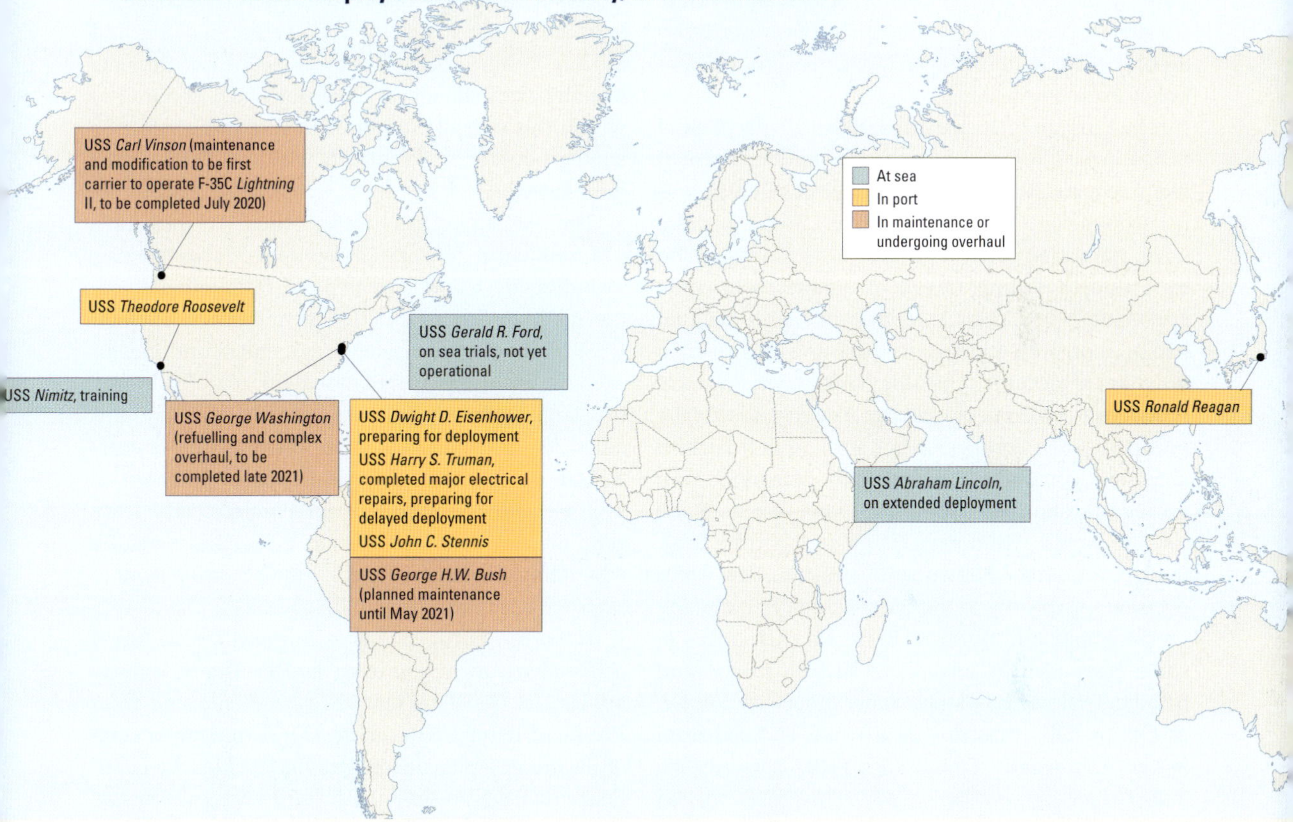

Legend:
- At sea
- In port
- In maintenance or undergoing overhaul

USS *Carl Vinson* (maintenance and modification to be first carrier to operate F-35C *Lightning* II, to be completed July 2020)

USS *Theodore Roosevelt*

USS *Nimitz*, training

USS *George Washington* (refuelling and complex overhaul, to be completed late 2021)

USS *Gerald R. Ford*, on sea trials, not yet operational

USS *Dwight D. Eisenhower*, preparing for deployment

USS *Harry S. Truman*, completed major electrical repairs, preparing for delayed deployment

USS *John C. Stennis*

USS *George H.W. Bush* (planned maintenance until May 2021)

USS *Ronald Reagan*

USS *Abraham Lincoln*, on extended deployment

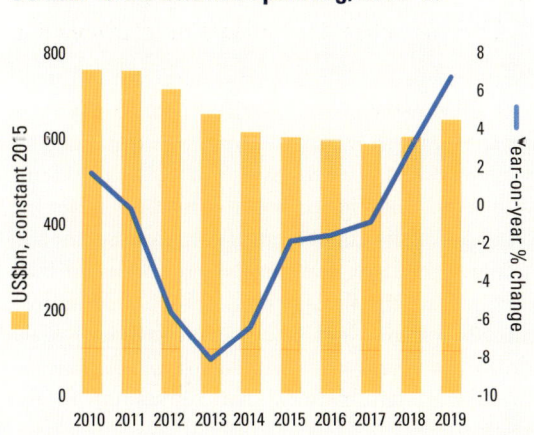

US real-terms defence spending, 2010–19

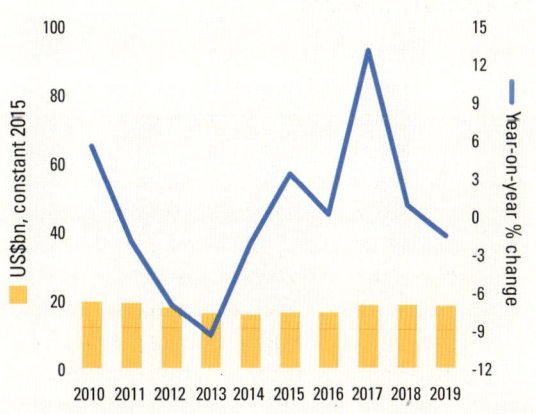

Canada real-terms defence spending, 2010–19

North America

UNITED STATES

Three years into the presidency of Donald Trump, US allies and partners continue to be disconcerted by aspects of the administration's defence- and foreign-policy decision-making.

Their certainty in the capabilities of the United States armed forces, its personnel and equipment likely remains strong, but confidence in White House decision-making was less certain. Two episodes have illustrated this. The first was the decision by President Trump to call off airstrikes on Iran, apparently when aircraft were already airborne, that had been organised in response to Iran's 19 June 2019 downing of a US BAMS-D uninhabited aerial vehicle (UAV) over the Strait of Hormuz. The second was the president's decision in October 2019, with a Turkish incursion looming, to withdraw US personnel from positions in northern Syria. (In December 2018, he said he would withdraw US troops from the area, though a number subsequently stayed.) The latter decision led directly to the unravelling of an already fragile situation in northern Syria: Kurdish forces in some cases resisted advancing Turkish troops and in others retreated; Islamic State, otherwise known as ISIS or ISIL, prisoners, meanwhile, escaped from Syrian Democratic Forces (SDF)-run jails; Russia and Turkey agreed joint patrols; the SDF opened negotiations with the Assad regime; and Russian and Syrian forces settled in abandoned US bases.

The apparent capricious nature of these decisions caused concern internationally. While they reflected the president's seeming aversion to new and enduring military activities, at least as of 2019, they also highlighted uncertainty over strategy and policy within an administration that has at the same time looked to pursue 'maximum pressure' campaigns against Iran and North Korea. While the administration's actions will concern partners who have long valued US reliability, and they may perhaps also embolden potential adversaries, they do not necessarily mean that Washington aims to limit its ability to conduct military operations globally. Nor indeed that it will actively dismantle the partnerships that have been at the core of its post-war defence relations – even if the White House's transactional approach to defence relations remains evident. However, there is perhaps more apparent detachment between White House policy decision-making and the day-to-day work of government, as departments like the Department of Defense (DoD) continue – within this overall environment – to implement the strategic-guidance documents with which they have been tasked.

The Pentagon has implemented Washington's commitment to Europe, its second priority theatre, including by the deployment of troops to Poland, the restructuring of NATO commands, a trilateral US–Finland–Sweden defence agreement and greater exercise commitments planned for 2020 (including the large *Defender Europe* exercise). Washington's allies, for their part, have supported the US over its allegation that Moscow was in material breach of its Intermediate-range Nuclear Forces (INF) Treaty commitments. At the same time, these allies also fully expect the US president to continue exhorting them to improve burden-sharing in defence.

However, European states' support for US forces and policies, including over the INF Treaty, did not appear to translate into reciprocal support from President Trump. Nor can the DoD's implementation of its strategy plans necessarily give allies the confidence that the president will fulfil US commitments if needed. This uncertainty is unsettling US allies in Europe and elsewhere. Indeed, it is unclear whether the White House views those allies as a strategic advantage or a burden. As a result, Washington risks missing strategically important opportunities both to align its allies to tackle a rising China and to benefit from allied assistance on security problems such as Iran and North Korea. These opportunities might have included drawing Europeans into the Trans-Pacific Partnership with the possibility of thereby improving consensus on the establishment of trade practices and standards; holding together P5+1 sanctions on Iran, while pressuring Tehran on its missile programmes and destabilising behaviour; and effecting a coalition for maritime security in the Strait of Hormuz beyond the few nations that signed up to the initiative.

Strategy documents

The 2017 National Security Strategy was notable for its clarion call about the return of great-power competition, the need to continue the United States' rebalance to the Pacific, and its assertion that while Washington took its political, economic and military advantages 'for granted', other nations were implementing plans to challenge the US. It also stated that US military advantages were shrinking. Indeed, when launching the subsequent National Defense Strategy (NDS) less than two months later, in January 2018, then-defense secretary James Mattis said that the United States' 'competitive advantage has eroded in every domain of warfare'. The congressionally mandated National Defense Strategy Commission validated those judgements in its November 2018 report, while censuring the DoD for underfunding and insufficient rigour in implementing the NDS, as well as criticising the document for leaving 'unanswered critical questions regarding how the United States will meet the challenges of a more dangerous world'.

Indeed, questions remain about the DoD's ability to deliver the priorities laid out in the NDS. Some of the architects of the strategy criticised associated documents that were meant to advance its implementation, such as the classified Chairman of the Joint Chiefs of Staff's National Military Strategy (NMS), which they did not think was aligned with the NDS. For example, some of those advocating a more exclusive focus on China see the NMS as reluctant to shed counter-insurgency capabilities and therefore as under-resourcing 'third offset' modernisation. Analysts consider it likely that the armed forces will have congressional support on the pace of implementation. At the same time, the prioritisation of military assets for the Indo-Pacific and Europe is to some degree dependent on demands in other theatres. Indeed, further attacks on Saudi Arabia may increase the demand for additional forces in the CENTCOM area of operations.

Nonetheless, the Pentagon continues to sharpen focus on what it terms the Indo-Pacific as its priority theatre. The Office of the Secretary of Defense established in June 2019 the position of a Deputy Assistant Secretary of Defense (DASD) for China, which had previously been the responsibility of the DASD for East Asian Affairs. The post was created, according to a Pentagon official, in order to 'drive alignment on China across the department as we carry out our National Defense Strategy and its implementation'. The new office was welcomed by some former officials: bilateral work on China was, it was said, enough for one person and the new office would allow the East Asia office to focus on alliance relations in the region. However, others cautioned that unless the DASD for China were carefully aligned with other regional offices, a separate office for China risked increasing departmental stovepipes.

The Pentagon's focus on its priority region was apparent in its 2019 Indo-Pacific Strategy Report, released as then-acting defense secretary Patrick Shanahan attended the 2019 IISS Shangri-La Dialogue in Singapore. It was intended, Shanahan said, to illustrate the regional implementation of the NDS. As the US modernised its forces, partners who 'bring interoperability to the table' may be at an advantage, and 'will be able to access' many of the technologies that the Pentagon is pursuing. Improved defence spending would also enable improved US military capabilities and postures in the region, including accelerating the forward presence of land forces and stationing 'some of our highest-end, most capable assets in the Indo-Pacific'.

The Pentagon also released an updated Arctic Strategy in June 2019. This reflected Chinese and Russian interest in the region and its importance to the US, including as 'a potential corridor for strategic competition'. Officials stressed that it was a strategy document rooted in the priorities of the 2018 NDS.

Implementing and funding strategies

The year 2019 saw three secretaries of defense in the US: James Mattis resigned and left office in February; Patrick Shanahan withdrew from consideration in June; and Mark Esper was confirmed in July. The turbulence generated by this turnover was steadied by the DoD's civil-servant corps and the armed forces, but the lack of leadership diminished the department's policy influence. White House selections for top DoD jobs perhaps suggest the president wants more muted voices and less expertise, possibly also reflecting White House confidence in its own decision-making: Trump was reported to have said in late 2017 that, when it came to foreign-policy decisions, 'I'm the only one that matters'. Indeed, some analysts have posited that Secretary Esper appears to concede policy decisions to the White House, focusing instead on elements more under the Pentagon's control such as the implementation of the NDS, the efficacy of spending, relations with US Congress and explaining DoD policies to the public. Congressional willingness to repair budget potholes created by the diversion of funds to border activities will be a test of the degree to which the Pentagon's budget can be insulated from the effects of presidential policies. Congress is challenging in court the administration's diversion of funding from congressionally authorised DoD spending.

By the Pentagon's own calculations, implementing the NDS requires a 3–5% annual spending increase. Though the DoD nominally received an increase of that level in 2018 and 2019, the administration's US$750-billion 2020 budget topline only represents a 1% increase when funds for non-DoD activities (principally border enforcement) are excluded and a decrease of 3% according to the Congressional Budget Office. Even before US$3.6bn was diverted from the defence budget to border activities, some budget analysts criticised the NDS for requiring 'either more investment or fewer demands on U.S. forces'.

Arms control

The New START treaty entered into force in 2011. It is intended to verifiably reduce and limit Russian and US strategic offensive armaments and, unless extended, it is due to expire in February 2021. The Trump administration's plans for extending the treaty include bringing China into the agreement. However, a Chinese foreign-ministry spokesman said in July 2019 that Beijing does not see 'right now … any conditions or basis for China to join the negotiation between the US and Russia'. Should the treaty expire in 2021, former officials reportedly said that this would cause the US to re-examine the modernisation plan for its nuclear triad, amid concern that this eventuality would mean 'there were no longer any constraints on the Russian programs'.

Meanwhile, the US finally withdrew from the INF Treaty in August 2019. Russia had not returned to compliance with the treaty, and Washington said that Moscow continued to field the SSC-8 *Screwdriver* ground-launched cruise missile. However, some observers held that the US decision was also rooted in the view that there were operational demands for US conventional missiles in the Pacific. Agreement by NATO allies in 2018 that Russia was in 'material breach' of its obligations under the treaty was a diplomatic victory for the Trump administration.

Space force

The president's proposal to create a separate space service is moving ahead. A separate command for the domain was established on 29 August 2019, separating space functions from US Strategic Command. However, both the (Democrat-controlled) House and (Republican-controlled) Senate rejected administration proposals to make space a separate military service, and Congress declined to revise Title 10 of the US code, which would have been necessary to create a new military service. The furthest Congress appears willing to go is to modify Title 10 so as to permit a space force as a constituent part of the air force.

Congress, defence and the White House

Objections to Congress's treatment of the president's proposal for a space force was only one of 39 administration objections to the 2020 National Defense Authorization Act. The White House threatened to veto the House version of the bill (in itself not an unusual occurrence) that would provide a budget of US$733bn and restrict funding for low-yield submarine-launched ballistic missiles and the transfer of prisoners to Guantanamo Bay. The House and Senate bills have a funding gap of US$17bn, but the central bone of contention remains the move by the president to obtain more funds for border enforcement and Republicans' support for this. Conference negotiations between the Senate and House Armed Services committees were under way at the time of writing.

However, a greater challenge than policy differences between the White House and Congress is the likelihood of Congress failing to reach agreement on a government spending bill. Although the president and Congress agreed a two-year US$2.7-trillion overall budget deal in August 2019, Congress did not make its deadline for appropriations legislation and was operating on a continuing resolution that extended the previous year's spending legislation until late November. The budget deal increases spending by roughly US$50bn each year and removes the requirement for a separate (always contentious) vote on increasing the debt ceiling. Yet Congress's acceptance of an annual US$1trn deficit led 123 Republicans to refuse their support.

Furthermore, the start of impeachment proceedings against the president by Congress may make the task of shielding the Pentagon from politicisation more difficult. For instance, the secretary of defense has to mediate between the White House and Congress on allowing congressional oversight of executive orders, which the White House maintains are a Commander in Chief's prerogative.

US Army

The US Army Strategy, published in late 2018, continued the army's shift from a focus on counter-insurgency to high-intensity conflict 'involving large-scale combat with Division and Corps-level maneuvers against near-peer competitors'. The strategy has four lines of effort: building readiness; modernisation; reform; and strengthening alliances and partnerships.

Building readiness for war and large-scale contingencies remains a key focus. In its posture statement in March 2019, the army reported that since 2016 it had increased the number of ready Brigade Combat Teams (BCTs) from 18 to 28, while readiness was up by 11%. At the same time, US$1.7bn was budgeted in fiscal years 2019 and 2020 to improve prepositioned equipment and supplies. The army also plans to staff its operational units to 105% of establishment strength by 2020 and has cut the number of non-deployable soldiers from 15% in 2015 to 6% in 2019, thereby making available thousands more personnel. Training is also receiving a boost, with more 'decisive action' rotations due at combat-training centres in fiscal year 2019. Additionally, recognising the challenges of high-intensity combat, the two Infantry BCTs have been converted into Armored BCTs; for one of these, it is understood the army had to draw equipment from its Korean Enduring Equipment Set. Meanwhile, the army has increased Infantry and Armor One Station Unit Training (basic training and elements of trade training) from 14 to 22 weeks and plans to increase training periods in other branches.

However, readiness challenges remain, particularly in recruiting to the desired end-strength. A strong US economy, coupled with low unemployment, is providing tough competition – the army was 6,500 people short of its 2018 personnel goal. It has since bolstered its recruiting efforts, adding 700 recruiters, expanding its online advertising and focusing on 22 cities. This approach worked in 2019; the army exceeded its goal, enlisting more than 68,000 new active-duty soldiers.

In July 2019, Army Futures Command reached full operational capability. It is responsible for providing unity of command for the army's modernisation efforts so that, as the Army Posture Statement has it, there is one commander for 'concept development, requirements determination, organizational design, science and technology research, and solution development'. The army's modernisation ambitions are reflected in its Army Reform Initiative. This effort reassigned funds from about 200 legacy programmes to 31 key modernisation efforts, particularly the army's top six priorities: long-range precision fires; next-generation combat vehicles; future vertical lift; army network; air and missile defence; and soldier lethality. These investments are bearing fruit, with new capabilities developing more rapidly than in the past; one example is the army's announcement that it will field a hypersonic-missile unit in 2023.

The army's main future concept is the U.S. Army in Multi-Domain Operations 2028 (version 1.5), published in December 2018. This looks to prepare the service, as part of a joint force, for the challenges posed particularly by China and Russia, both in competition and conflict. Key to the concept is the idea of integrating service capabilities, rather than simply synchronising them. Perhaps the central challenge to realising the potential of the concept is that the other armed services (and civilian agencies) will have to contribute capabilities the army does not control, and so far there does not seem to have been strong inter-service support for the army's efforts. There is no overarching joint concept to drive convergence, and the other services are developing their own operating approaches – for example the air force's Multi-Domain Command and Control concept. Furthermore, since the demise of the four-star US Joint Forces Command, joint concept-development capabilities have decreased. Nevertheless, the army is moving forward and has fielded an experimental multi-domain task force for the Pacific and is organising another for Europe.

The army is also trying to reform its processes in order to achieve efficiencies and reduce procurement and acquisition times. Several examples show the breadth of these efforts: the realignment of Installation Management Command under Army Materiel Command; the reform of contracting services; the implementation of an audit system across all army accounts by fiscal year 2022; and the reorganisation of medical capabilities, as the Department of Defense transitions medical-treatment facilities from the armed services to the Defense Health Agency.

The army also remains committed to strengthening alliances and partnerships. As well as its enduring and operational deployments abroad and a full exercise programme, a Security Force Assistance Command was established to oversee the army's new Security Force Assistance Brigades (SFABs). These are responsible for training, advising, assisting, enabling

Figure 1 M1 *Abrams* main battle tank: upgrade timeline, 1979–2019

The original M1 *Abrams* was the first third-generation main battle tank (MBT) introduced by the United States, gradually replacing the M60 A3 *Patton*. It introduced many modern features, and was the first series-produced US MBT to feature composite armour. It was designed in response to Soviet MBT developments, in particular the T-72 and T-64. It has served as the US Army's main MBT since 1980, with regular upgrades keeping it at the leading edge of armour development. It mounts a powerful gas-turbine engine and, from the M1A1 onwards, a 120 mm smoothbore gun. Defensive improvements have boosted the vehicle's survivability, while upgrades to the tank's main armament and fire-control system have enhanced its firepower. The *Abrams* is intended to serve through the 2020s, with a plan for its successor expected to be in place by 2023.

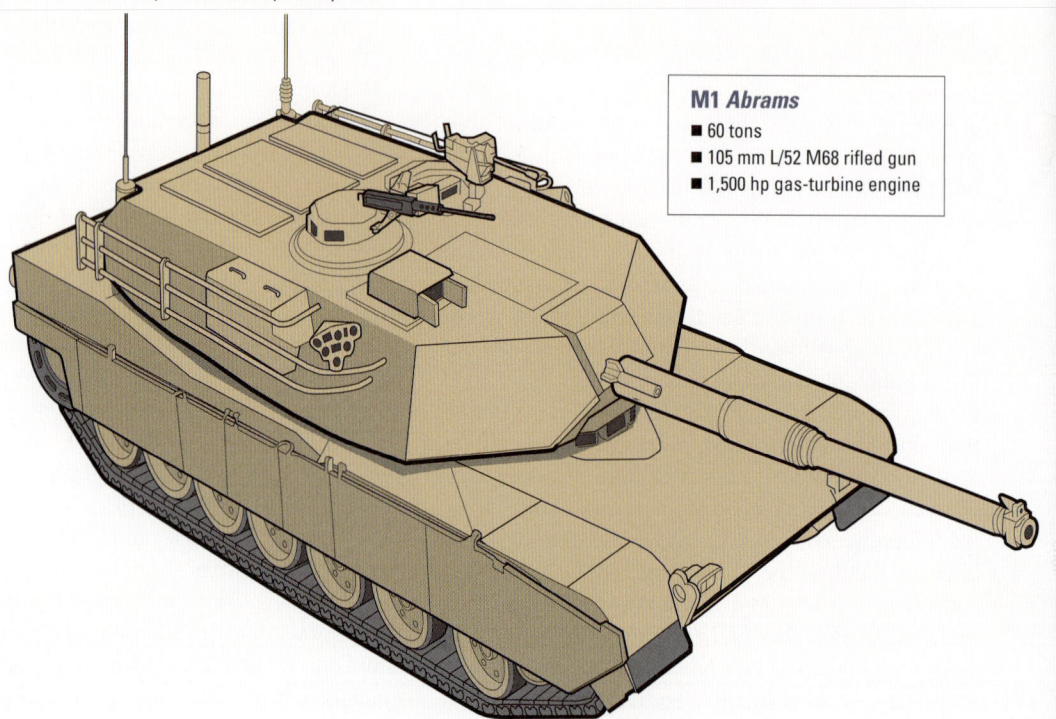

M1 *Abrams*
- 60 tons
- 105 mm L/52 M68 rifled gun
- 1,500 hp gas-turbine engine

M1A1
- 67 tons
- 120 mm L/44 M256 smoothbore gun
- Improved composite-armour package
- Improved gunner's sight
- Upgraded fire-control system
- Redesigned ammunition storage and blowout panels
- Additional turret-bustle storage rack
- Nuclear-biological-chemical overpressure system

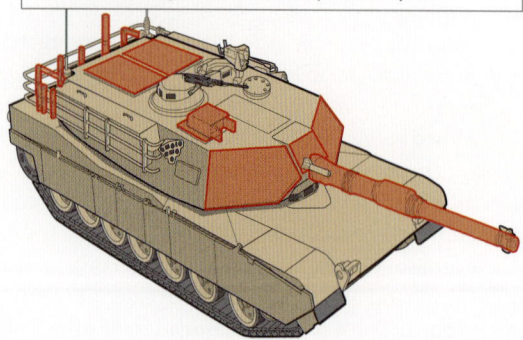

M1A2
- 70 tons
- Upgraded armour package including depleted-uranium elements
- Commander's independent thermal viewer with second-generation forward-looking infrared (FLIR)
- Further upgraded fire-control system
- Digital control systems
- Inertial navigation
- Improved commander's weapons station

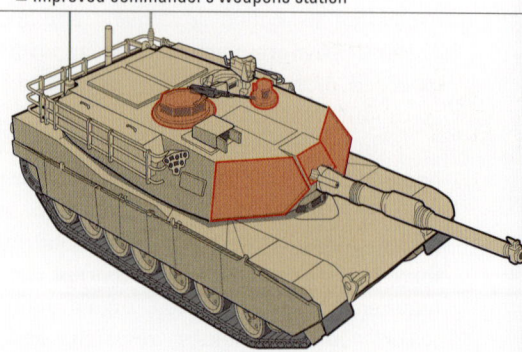

Modular protection upgrades

Trophy
- Modular active-protection system

Tank Urban Survival Kit II (TUSK II)
- Modular survivability upgrade
- Reactive armour tiles
- Gun shields for commander and loader
- Additional .50-calibre machine gun

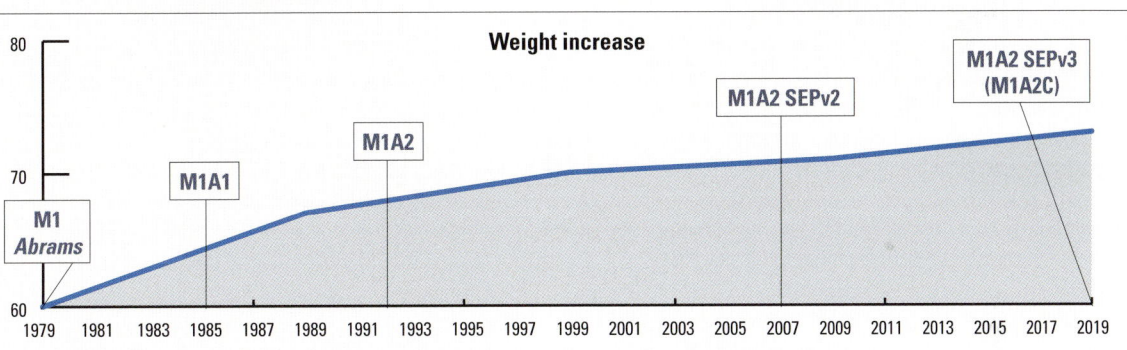

Weight increase

M1A2 SEPv2
- 71 tons
- Further upgraded armour package (second-generation depleted uranium)
- Common Remote Operated Weapons Station (CROWS) fitted as standard
- Improved fire control and optics for commander and gunner

M1A2 SEPv3 (M1A2C)
- 73 tons
- Further upgraded armour package (third-generation depleted uranium)
- Low-profile CROWS
- Ammunition data link for programmable rounds
- Third-generation forward-looking infrared commander's and gunner's optics
- Auxiliary power unit

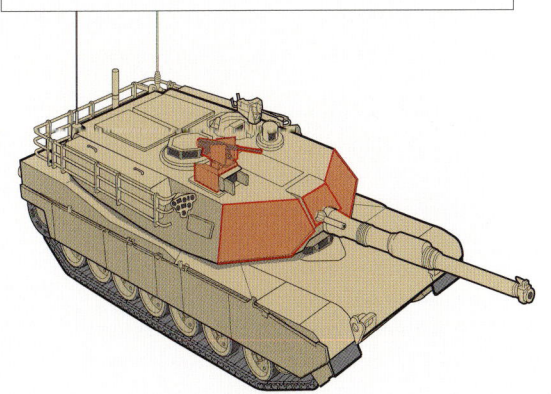
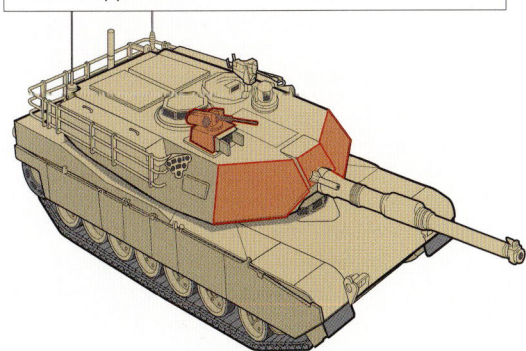

and accompanying allied and partner nations. The first of these, the 3rd SFAB, was formally activated in July 2019. The SFABs free other BCTs to focus on preparing for high-intensity combat, while retaining the capabilities gleaned from over a decade of counter-insurgency and irregular-warfare operations.

In summer 2019, the army saw significant leadership changes. Mark Esper became secretary

US Army Combat Training Centers

In 1980, the US Army activated the National Training Center (NTC) at Fort Irwin, California, to create realistic combined-arms training for battalion task forces and their controlling brigades, and to prepare them to fight and prevail against numerically superior Soviet forces. The NTC was the first of four centres that are now collectively known as the US Army Combat Training Centers (CTC) Program. The other CTCs are the Joint Readiness Training Center (JRTC) at Fort Polk, Louisiana; the Joint Multinational Readiness Center (JMTC), at Hohenfels, Germany; and the Mission Command Training Program (MCTP) at Fort Leavenworth, Kansas. The CTCs at Fort Irwin, Fort Polk and Hohenfels are located on large tracts of land that provide the space for army Brigade Combat Teams (BCTs) to conduct live-fire and combined-arms offensive and defensive operations, as well as urban operations. The CTCs also enable training in areas such as operating with degraded communications, simulated chemical and biological threats, cyber operations, and the integration of special forces and partner armed forces.

The NTC concept was developed by personnel from, among others, Army Training and Doctrine Command (TRADOC) and Army Forces Command (FORSCOM) in light of studies such as the 1978 Army Training Study. This document suggested that training needed to improve and that 'the Army had to be able to measure proficiency objectively and to verify that proficiency was translated into combat effectiveness'. According to the army, the CTCs are important because they 'build readiness by providing a crucible experience for units and leaders training in a complex and highly realistic DATE [decisive action training environment] under the most adverse conditions possible'.

The Fort Irwin NTC used the Multiple Integrated Laser Engagement System (MILES) to tackle the problem of how to replicate in exercises the effects of different weapons systems. MILES, originally introduced by the US Army in the late 1970s, was an instrumentation system that tracked units, vehicles and individuals with integrated video cameras and radio-monitoring stations. Now part of a suite of the Instrumentation, Training Aids, Devices, Simulators and Simulations (ITADSS) system, according to the army MILES is a laser system designed to 'adjudicate battlefield direct-fire effects'. More broadly, ITADSS enables the army to 'achieve instrumentation commonality and interoperability across the MCTCs [Maneuver Combat Training Centers] to achieve efficiencies of scale and support a standard data collection and dissemination capability for AARs [after-action reviews] and Army learning'.

Units also conduct live-fire training at the NTC and JRTC, but the real challenge is the simulated fight against the resident and well-trained opposing force (OPFOR). Originally modelled on the Soviet armed forces, the OPFOR is highly skilled and familiar with the terrain. Observer, coach, trainers (OCTs) are embedded in visiting units down to the platoon level. The OCTs are experienced soldiers and officers who are 'qualified to conduct an analysis of a unit and leader's performance while facilitating a meaningful AAR' and are 'critical to the success of the CTCs'. The NTC also originated the AAR process. At various stages in a CTC rotation, leaders of participating units are gathered and their performance subjected to rigorous critique by the OCTs.

After 9/11, the CTCs focused on preparing units for deployments to Afghanistan and Iraq, and the OPFOR adapted to resemble adversaries in those combat theatres. In recent years, however, the OPFOR has returned to imitating 'freethinking, realistic, hybrid threats under the most difficult conditions possible'. It was planned that there would be a total of 32 CTC rotations in fiscal year 2019, including '26 Decisive Action Training Environment rotations for Brigade Combat Teams and six other mission specific rotations'.

The MCTP, which began in 1988 with the Battle Command Training programme, provides exercises for Army Service Component Commands, Corps, Divisions, Functional/Multi-Functional Brigades and select Army National Guard BCTs. These exercises have a skilled OPFOR and OCTs, but also include retired general officers as senior mentors.

Since the NTC was created, the CTCs have provided adaptable, realistic environments to prepare US Army forces for combat, but they are still changing. For instance, with reports that MILES has limitations in replicating the full range of effects delivered by current equipment, the army is examining how it can develop future force-on-force live-training simulation aids. There are also challenges facing the CTCs, including cost and maintaining unit rotations. CTC exercises are expensive and there is a limit to how many rotations a CTC can execute each year.

of defense and General Mark Milley became the chairman of the US Joint Chiefs of Staff. Their tenures have marked a significant shift in direction for the army towards preparing for the challenges identified in the 2018 National Defense Strategy. Nevertheless, continuity seems to be ensured, as Esper and Milley are both succeeded by their deputies: Ryan McCarthy as secretary of the army and General James McConville as US Army chief of staff respectively.

US naval forces

The US Navy (USN) maintained a heightened tempo of freedom-of-navigation operations in the Asia-Pacific region in 2019. In May, it also accelerated the deployment of the USS *Abraham Lincoln* carrier strike group (CSG) to the US CENTCOM area of operation in response to increased tensions with Iran, while the newly re-established, North Atlantic-focused 2nd Fleet declared initial operating capability at the end of the same month. Also in May, the USS *Theodore Roosevelt* became the first US aircraft carrier to deploy to Alaska in a decade, as the navy continued to re-prioritise Arctic operations. There was also an enhanced tempo of deployments to the Black Sea.

Underscoring ongoing pressures on the carrier force, the USS *Harry S. Truman* CSG deployed in September as a surface action group but without the carrier itself. The *Truman* remained alongside in Norfolk with a major electrical failure and there was no other available carrier. Meanwhile, the operational debut of the navy's newest carrier, the USS *Gerald R. Ford*, could be further delayed by equipment problems, such as with the weapons elevators. Meanwhile, the USN's budget proposal to retire the *Truman* early in order to create financial headroom to invest in new remote systems was overturned by the White House, after controversy in Congress over the plan.

However, there have been significant developments in the troubled Littoral Combat Ship (LCS) programme. In July, the USS *Montgomery* became the first LCS to forward deploy in 19 months. In September, the USS *Gabrielle Giffords* became the first LCS to deploy with the Naval Strike Missile, part of an enhanced offensive and survivability package that will be applied to the rest of the fleet. Meanwhile, in June, the USN also finalised its requirements for the LCS's successor, the FFG(X) frigate programme, in a request for proposals to defence industry.

The USN commissioned the second of its new DDG-1000 *Zumwalt*-class destroyers, the USS *Michael Monsoor*, in January, while the USS *Zumwalt* itself began its first 'operational under way' in March. In May, the navy inaugurated its Surface Development Squadron, to be comprised of, and evaluate the capabilities of, the *Zumwalt*s and future unmanned surface platforms.

In 2019, the navy continued to work on a new force-structure assessment, which was due by the end of the year. As well as considering new threat analysis, the navy may decide that emerging technologies could modify its planned requirement for a 355-ship battle force, potentially adjusting the service's future requirements for surface combatants and sub-surface platforms.

Meanwhile, in July, the new commandant of the US Marine Corps (USMC) issued new planning guidance to integrate the USMC further into future naval operations, as a more maritime-focused force to support naval sea-control and sea-denial missions, rather than a land force supported by the navy. It underlined the requirement for more innovative stand-off capabilities, and notably placed a question mark over the long-standing force target of 38 large amphibious ships.

At the same time, as maritime-security requirements in the western Pacific evolve, the deployment of the US Coast Guard (USCG) cutter *Bertholf* to the region heralded Washington's intention to expand the coastguard's role there. Emphasising the service's increased focus on the Arctic, which it sees as an area of increasing geostrategic competition, the USCG unveiled its Arctic Strategic Outlook in April. In June, the USCG awarded a US$748-million contract for the design and construction of the first of its new heavy polar-security cutters, with three heavy and three medium icebreakers planned as part of the programme.

US Air Force

The United States Air Force (USAF) spent 2019 attempting to address concerns regarding its strength, operational tempo and agility, and also the age of its equipment.

In 2018, the USAF had produced a study entitled 'The Air Force We Need'. This document advocated an expansion from 312 to 386 operational squadrons by 2030. As of 2019, however, there was growing recognition that reaching this goal would be a challenge. Speaking to reporters after the Air Force Association's September conference, USAF Chief of Staff General David Goldfein said that achieving the 386-squadron target was 'not likely', though he maintained that the requirement remained valid.

Goldfein indicated that, partly to offset the shortfall in numbers, the USAF is looking to exploit increased multi-platform connectivity. This would see air, land, maritime and space systems integrated in a flexible and reactive fashion, in near-real time, in order to deliver the desired effect. This is intended to allow military commanders to rapidly blend disparate platforms and capabilities, though the extent to which this type of approach might be vulnerable to electronic countermeasures or cyber attack remains open to debate.

Squadron numbers

The requirement to grow the air force stems from the United States' 2018 National Defense Strategy, which said that 'long-term strategic competitions' with China and Russia were the Pentagon's principal priorities. Launching 'The Air Force We Need' in September 2018, then-secretary for the air force Heather Wilson said that the USAF was not just looking to increase operational-squadron numbers. The service was at the same time looking to improve readiness in its 204 'pacing squadrons' to an average of 80% readiness by 2022. These squadrons would be required in the first days of a war with a peer rival.

The USAF appears be adopting a dual-track approach in addressing the demands of a deteriorating security environment: continuing to pursue medium-term equipment recapitalisation and development, while trying to implement short-term improvements – but only if these do not undermine the first objective. These considerations became apparent in the debate over Wilson's decision to support the purchase of the Boeing F-15EX multi-role fighter as a near-term solution to the rapidly decreasing service life of the F-15C *Eagle*. Senior uniformed USAF personnel stressed that the F-15EX purchase should not come at the cost of cutting Lockheed Martin F-35A numbers. Funding for eight F-15EXs was included in the fiscal year 2020 budget, with the intention of acquiring an additional 72 by 2024.

The original plan was that the F-15C would be replaced by the Lockheed Martin F-22 *Raptor*, but repeated cuts to F-22 procurements meant that instead the *Eagle*'s service life had to be extended. F-22 acquisition numbers fell from an initial 750 to 381, and then 187 by 2009. Concern over the United States' aerospace defence-industrial base and the USAF's aim of supporting a second manufacturer capable of producing advanced combat aircraft contributed to the decision to acquire the F-15EX.

Fighter and bomber plan

In March 2020, the USAF is due to complete a report designed to address the Senate Armed Services Committee's request for an 'optimum' force structure to meet the challenge of peer rivals.

While the F-35A provides the air force with a multi-role combat aircraft, during 2019 the service continued to consider what it needed to meet its Next-Generation Air Dominance (NGAD) requirement. The NGAD project is notionally seen as a successor to the F-22 *Raptor* in providing the USAF with the capacity to contest and gain air superiority at any given time. The likelihood is that NGAD will include one or more new combat air platforms, crewed and otherwise, but the service is exploring the extent to which broad system-connectivity could be used to help deliver the required capability, rather than focusing only on new aircraft designs. It has also been considering ways to shorten the traditional decades-long combat-aircraft development cycle.

This renewed air-to-air threat is leading the air force to also examine its air-to-air weapons requirements. For instance, the Lockheed Martin AIM-260 Joint Advanced Tactical Missile, which is a partial successor to the Raytheon AIM-120 Advanced Medium-Range Air-to-Air Missile, was made public in mid-2019. The new missile is intended to enter service from 2022, while acquisition of the 'D' variant of the AIM-120 is scheduled to end in fiscal year 2026. There is limited detail regarding the performance or design of the AIM-260, although USAF officials have suggested it is intended to help address the threat potentially posed by the Chinese PL-15 medium-to-long-range air-to-air missile. The PL-15 was in service with the People's Liberation Army Air Force by the end of 2018.

There is more detail on the USAF's bomber road map, at least in terms of an airframe, if not numbers. The Northrop Grumman B-21 *Raider* is expected to be flown for the first time in December 2021. At least 100 of the type are to be acquired, although work is under way to try to increase this number through cost savings provided by the earlier-than-planned retirement of some B-1Bs. It is possible that the cost of addressing airframe-fatigue issues on the B-1B could be deemed prohibitive. However, while the USAF was looking at the early retirement of some B-1Bs it was also considering whether to extend the life of some tanker aircraft, as it continued to struggle with ongoing delays to the new Boeing KC-46A *Pegasus* tanker.

DEFENCE ECONOMICS

The 2020 budget request

The Department of Defense (DoD) 2020 budget request was intended to be a 'masterpiece', according to then-acting secretary of defense Patrick Shanahan. The budget would reflect the level and alignment of funding required by the 2018 National Defense Strategy (NDS), since that strategy was published too late to affect the 2019 DoD budget request. However, the White House cast doubt on this ambition. While the armed forces had been building the 2020 defence budget under the assumption that the overall topline for the discretionary 050 budgetary authority would be US$733 billion, President Donald Trump upended these plans in October 2018 with the announcement that the DoD would take a 5% cut with the rest of US federal agencies, reducing its 2020 request to US$700bn – a decrease from the fiscal year (FY) 2019 topline 050 level of US$716bn.

President Trump changed course after a December 2018 White House meeting with then-secretary of defense James Mattis, then-House Armed Services Committee chairman William Thornberry and Senate Armed Services Committee chairman James Inhofe. Following the meeting, Trump announced that the 2020 DoD topline would be US$750bn. Mattis and the two chairmen noted that this sum would meet the bare minimum of 3–5% real annual growth in the defence budget necessary to implement the findings of the NDS. This growth rate was endorsed by Mattis, then-chairman of the Joint Chiefs of Staff Joseph Dunford and the National Defense Strategy Commission (a bipartisan panel established by Congress to review the NDS). While a US$750bn 2020 topline budget was described by many as a strategy-driven figure, President Trump noted that the request would give him negotiating room to ensure that defence spending did not drop below the previously discussed level of US$733bn.

Budget components

With this US$750bn topline, the Pentagon delivered the 2020 budget request to Congress in March 2019. However, it included several non-defence items that made the actual topline lower, including US$3.2bn in military-construction funding for the prospective building of the southern border wall, US$3.2bn to backfill military-construction spending already used for the wall and over US$2bn in emergency disaster funding for military bases affected by hurricanes. This left the real DoD topline request at around US$741bn, or about 1.5% real-terms growth. (Although these figures refer to the US 'budget authority' request, the IISS uses annual outlays for its defence-budget figures; the request for this amounted to US$738bn for FY2020.)

As well as conflating funding of the southern border wall with DoD spending, the White House directed the DoD to move almost US$100bn of base defence spending into the Overseas Contingency Operations (OCO) account. In an effort to increase transparency, the department moved over entire accounts to the OCO, including significant procurement accounts dealing with munitions. However, this base-to-OCO transfer was rejected by Congress.

While the base-to-OCO move received a significant amount of attention, it was not a significant component of the budget. Instead, the element of the budget that was most aggressively touted by the DoD was the attempt to change the armed forces' investment strategy. This resulted in the largest-ever budget request for research, development, test and evaluation, at US$104bn. It also included offering to Congress several high-profile choices relating to equipment programmes.

Service choices

The US Army continues to prioritise for modernisation the 'big six' equipment projects: long-range precision fires; armoured-vehicle replacements; future vertical lift; networking efforts; air and missile defence; and soldier lethality.

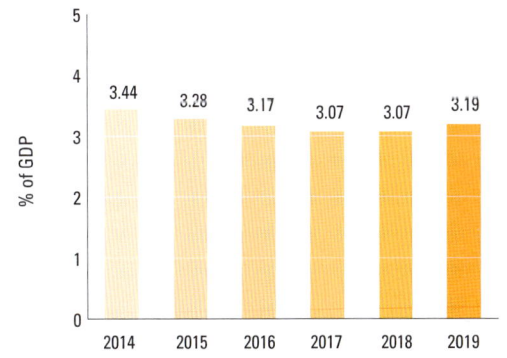

▼ Figure 2 **US defence expenditure** as % of GDP[1]

[1] Figures refer to the National Defense (050) Budget Function (Outlays) as a % of GDP

Table 2 **US National Defense Budget Function and other selected budgets, 2000, 2010–2020**

US$ in billions, current year dollars	National Defense Budget Function		Atomic Energy Defense Activities	Other Defense Activities	Total National Defense			Department of Homeland Security	Department of Veterans Affairs	Total Federal Government Outlays	Total Federal Budget Surplus/ Deficit
					Discretionary						
FY	BA	Outlay	BA	BA	BA	BA	Outlay	BA	BA		
2000	290.3	281.0	12.4	1.3	304.0	300.8	294.4	N/A	45.5	1,789.0	236.2
2010	695.6	666.7	18.2	7.3	721.2	714.1	693.5	45.4	124.3	3,457.1	-1,294.4
2011	691.5	678.1	18.5	7.0	717.0	710.1	705.6	41.6	122.8	3,603.1	-1,299.6
2012	655.4	650.9	18.3	7.7	681.4	669.6	677.9	45.9	124.0	3,526.6	-1,076.6
2013	585.2	607.8	17.5	7.4	610.2	600.4	633.4	61.9	136.0	3,454.9	-679.8
2014	595.7	577.9	18.4	8.2	622.3	606.2	603.5	44.1	165.7	3,506.3	-484.8
2015	570.8	562.5	19.0	8.5	598.4	585.9	589.7	45.3	160.5	3,691.8	-442.0
2016	595.7	565.4	20.1	8.3	624.1	606.8	593.4	46.0	163.3	3,852.6	-584.7
2017	626.2	568.9	21.4	8.7	656.3	634.1	598.7	62.3	178.8	3,981.6	-665.4
2018	694.5	600.7	23.3	9.0	726.8	700.9	631.2	103.0	181.8	4,109.0	-779.1
2019*	693.1	652.2	24.0	9.1	726.2	716.0	684.6	53.4	194.4	4,529.2	-1,091.5
2020*	728.0	704.3	24.8	9.0	761.8	750.0	737.9	69.2	216.2	4,745.6	-1,100.8

Notes

FY = Fiscal Year (1 October–30 September)
* (request)
[1] The National Defense Budget Function subsumes funding for the DoD, the Department of Energy Atomic Energy Defense Activities and some smaller support agencies (including Federal Emergency Management and Selective Service System). It does not include funding for International Security Assistance (under International Affairs), the Veterans Administration, the US Coast Guard (Department of Homeland Security), nor for the National Aeronautics and Space Administration (NASA). Funding for civil projects administered by the DoD is excluded from the figures cited here.

[2] Early in each calendar year, the US government presents its defence budget to Congress for the next fiscal year, which begins on 1 October. The government also presents its Future Years Defense Program (FYDP), which covers the next fiscal year plus the following five. Until approved by Congress, the budget is called the Budget Request; after approval, it becomes the Budget Authority (BA).

However, under the leadership of then-secretary of the army Mark Esper, the army attempted to make its modernisation plans budget-neutral by engaging in so-called 'night court' senior-level reviews of each army acquisition programme. This led to the saving of some US$25bn in five years for reinvestment in the big six priorities. The army's most controversial decisions included the cancellation of a planned upgrade to the CH-47 *Chinook* transport helicopter and reduced quantities of the Joint Light Tactical Vehicle and Armored Multi-Purpose Vehicle. As secretary of defense, Esper is expected to bring the same senior-level-review process to the entire DoD budget in the FY2021 budget request, a process he began with a review of defence-wide functions outside the military services.

The US Navy (USN) also attempted to make similar choices within its modernisation portfolio, though with less success. Controversially, the navy proposed to cancel the mid-life nuclear-core refuelling of the *USS Harry S. Truman* to generate savings to reinvest in new uninhabited surface vessels. Ostensibly, the decision to retire the *Truman* was made due to both budgetary and strategic considerations, as the navy tries to distribute its fleet to smaller, uninhabited vessels. However, after a poor reception in Congress, the White House itself announced the reversal of the *Truman* retirement decision.

The most significant decision made in the US Air Force (USAF) budget concerned legacy rather than new aircraft. The USAF decision to procure new F-15EXs to replace ageing F-15Cs was several years in the making, and the F-35A purchase rate remained constant from the previous year, with the service only requesting 48 of these aircraft despite widespread agreement among senior officials that an annual procurement rate of 72 F-35As was necessary to reduce the average age of the fighter fleet. Most other air-force acquisition programmes remained unchanged, except the Next-Generation Air Dominance (NGAD) programme, which was accelerated in the budget.

Some analysts consider that the 2020 budget fell short in meeting the administration's plans for missile defence, as outlined in the 2018 Missile Defense Review. The DoD intended to begin a project to develop a space-based satellite-sensor layer, expand Ground-Based Midcourse Defense and embark on novel boost-phase intercept programmes. However, the satellites did not appear in the 2020 budget, the new Redesigned Kill Vehicle for Ground-Based Interceptors was cancelled and boost-phase intercept efforts remain elusive. Indeed, the Missile Defense Agency topline actually fell between FY2019 and FY2020.

In contrast, the Pentagon and Congress have coalesced around several hypersonic-strike-weapon programmes, committing to more than US$10bn over five years across the US Army, USAF and USN.

The DoD pointed to improvements in military readiness throughout the rollout of its budget request, but nonetheless worrying trends began to emerge as the year progressed. For instance, the services did not meet then-secretary of defense Mattis's goal of reaching 80% mission availability for fighter aircraft. USN submarine maintenance and construction remains behind schedule – a hangover effect from the years of low spending due to sequestration. Although the army pointed to increases in readiness in its ground units, both the army and the navy reported that they had underfunded flying hours, and anonymous army-aviation units alleged that their readiness statistics had not been accurately presented to Congress.

The 2020 defence budget marked an inflection point in defence planning, as the Pentagon attempted to change course in its investments. However, hampered by the political disputes over the border wall and slowed down by the internal budget growth in entitlements and maintenance, the 2020 budget did not fully make up for the time and money lost under years of sequestration.

Bipartisan Budget Act of 2019

As FY2019 unfolded, the DoD saw on-time appropriations and readied its arguments about the 2020 budget for what it thought would be a largely receptive Congress. However, frustrated by his inability to secure funding for the border wall following a month-long partial government shutdown, President Trump exercised two measures to begin channelling border-wall funding through the Pentagon in early 2019.

In February 2019, before the 2020 DoD budget request was released, President Trump declared a national emergency regarding the southern US border. He then used an emergency military-construction authority called 'Section 2808' and announced his intention to divert US$3.6bn of the DoD's existing military-construction funds towards the border wall, and simultaneously exercised a second authority (Section 284) to move another US$2.5bn in DoD funding to border-wall construction – a total reduction of US$6.1bn from the DoD's FY2019 topline.

Congress, especially the Democrat-majority House, reacted strongly. Despite the existing two-year spending deal covering FY2018 and FY2019, there was concern that it would be impossible to reach a second two-year deal, leaving DoD funding flat in FY2020 and FY2021. Most problematically, several of the president's advisers are understood to believe that a full-year continuing resolution for FY2020 is the best funding strategy for the president. (These continue the previous years' funding levels in the absence of a new budget agreement.) In response to this uncertainty, Pentagon leaders provided Congress with an unprecedented level of detail about the effects that a full-year continuing resolution would have in FY2020, as the armed forces tried to realign to the priorities laid down in the NDS.

A partial deal agreed in July 2019 between the president and Speaker of the House Nancy Pelosi lifted the Budget Control Act spending caps for FY2020 and FY2021. However, given that the president had admitted that the US$750bn DoD topline was in his view a negotiating position, and with arguments continuing about the transfer of DoD funding to the border wall, Democrats were able to keep DoD spending far below the Pentagon's FY2020 budget request. The deal set the topline figure at US$738bn for FY2020 and US$740bn for FY2021; it also contained a one-time FY2020 OCO increase of about US$2bn. Depending on inflation, US$738bn roughly represents a 1% real-terms increase in DoD funding for FY2020, though US$740bn will represent a 1–2% decrease in 2021.

Over the past decade, the DoD has spent three years under continuing resolutions. Congress gave the DoD a brief respite through such measures as the underlying two-year Bipartisan Budget Agreement of 2018, and the armed forces began FY2019 with a real on-time appropriations bill. However, Senate appropriators had not passed any appropriations bills for FY2020, as a tactic to increase pressure for a budget deal. As a consequence, when lawmakers returned from their August recess in September 2019, they admitted that, despite possessing funding levels for FY2020, they would have to begin the year with a continuing resolution, including for the DoD.

Moreover, the budget deal, called the Bipartisan Budget Act of 2019, did not explicitly address the foremost concern for both President Trump and Speaker Pelosi: the border wall. Because of this, FY2020 funding could not be agreed until the two struck a deal on funding for the wall.

CANADA

Two years on from the publication of the Liberal government's 2017 defence-policy review, Canada's armed forces continue to maintain global deployments to fulfil Ottawa's alliance and peacekeeping ambitions. Though generally modest in scale, the deployments are notable for their scope. However, doubts remain over whether there are sufficient financial resources to deliver on Canada's capability and procurement plans.

Deployments

Canada maintains a frigate in European waters as part of *Operation Reassurance*, Canada's support to NATO, and in June 2019 took command of Standing NATO Maritime Group 2. Canada also leads the NATO Enhanced Forward Presence Battlegroup in Latvia and was due to deploy a new detachment of five CF-18 (F/A-18) *Hornet* combat aircraft to the NATO enhanced air-policing mission in Romania in autumn 2019. Canada also maintains 200 armed-forces members on six-month rotations supporting and training Ukrainian security forces. This commitment, called *Operation Unifier*, currently runs until March 2022. Meanwhile, Ottawa has also extended Canada's leadership of the NATO training and capacity-building mission in Iraq for a second year, until November 2020.

In August 2019, Canada completed a year-long operation to support the UN stabilisation mission in Mali. However, to support Ottawa's peacekeeping pledges, it was announced in August that the armed forces would embark on an operation centred on Uganda to support the UN missions in the Democratic Republic of the Congo and South Sudan with tactical airlift in the form of a CC-130J *Hercules* aircraft.

The government has made much of its ambition to be a security actor in the Asia-Pacific and again deployed two frigates to the region in 2019. The first, HMCS *Regina*, supported crucially by the recently acquired interim replenishment ship MV *Asterix*, deployed to the Arabian Sea during Canada's period in charge of Combined Task Force 150, supported UN sanctions operations against North Korea and participated in an exercise with the Japan Maritime Self-Defense Force in the South China Sea. In August, HMCS *Ottawa* took over the Pacific deployment role.

Equipment

Canada's procurement programme continues to experience difficulties. In July, the government issued a request for proposals in the latest phase of the search for a future fighter to replace its ageing CF-18 (F/A-18) *Hornet*s. The requirement is currently set at 88 new aircraft, to enter service from 2025. However, the Eurofighter *Typhoon* and Dassault *Rafale* have both been withdrawn from the competition, leaving three possible bidders – Boeing with the F/A-18E *Super Hornet*, Lockheed Martin with the F-35A and Saab with the *Gripen* E. In the meantime, the first of at least 18 second-hand Australian F/A-18s arrived in Canada in February and work then began to bring them to a similar configuration to the CF-18; the last is due to be delivered in 2021.

Meanwhile, in June, the Canadian Parliamentary Budget Office raised its estimate of the total cost of the new Canadian Surface Combatant programme by C$8 billion (US$6bn), to approximately C$70bn (US$53bn). This followed the selection in October 2018 of a design based on the BAE Systems Type-26 Global Combat Ship; the requirement is for 15 new vessels.

There were further delays in the plan to deliver the lead vessel in the new *Harry DeWolf* class of six Arctic/offshore patrol ships (AOPSs), although delivery of the first vessel and the launch of the second was expected in late 2019. However, the *Harry DeWolf* class has been criticised for being underequipped for its role, in terms of its weapons fit and its capacity to operate in thick ice. Nonetheless, to underscore Canada's increased focus on the Arctic, and under the umbrella of a national shipbuilding strategy, the government announced in May an investment of C$15.7bn (US$11.8bn) to regenerate the Canadian Coast Guard with the acquisition of two modified AOPSs and 16 multi-purpose vessels. This was followed by an announcement of plans for six new icebreakers. Canada has also announced a plan to modernise and enlarge its fleet of CH-149 *Cormorant* helicopters in order to continue providing search-and-rescue capabilities in the Arctic.

Canada CAN

Canadian Dollar $		2018	2019	2020
GDP	C$	2.22tr	2.30tr	
	US$	1.71tr	1.73tr	
per capita	US$	46,290	46,213	
Growth	%	1.9	1.5	
Inflation	%	2.2	2.0	
Def exp [a]	C$	29.0bn	29.6bn	
	US$	21.4bn	22.3bn	
Def bdgt [b]	C$	24.8bn	24.9bn	
	US$	19.1bn	18.7bn	
US$1= C$		1.296	1.327	

[a] NATO definition
[b] Department of National Defence and Veterans Affairs

Real-terms defence budget trend (US$bn, constant 2015)

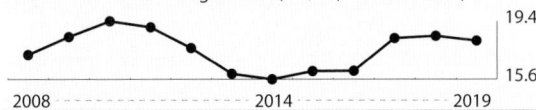

Population 36,136,376

Age	0–14	15–19	20–24	25–29	30–64	65 plus
Male	7.9%	2.8%	3.1%	3.5%	23.6%	8.7%
Female	7.5%	2.6%	2.9%	3.3%	23.2%	10.8%

Capabilities

Canada's armed forces are focused principally on territorial defence, as well as contributing important capabilities to international missions, principally through NATO. The 2017 defence review reaffirmed commitments to NATO, but also to modernising capabilities, including cyber power. The review promised to increase regular and reserve forces, with particular enhancements in the areas of cyber and intelligence. Canada's deployments, although relatively small scale, underscore a determination to maintain both international engagement and power-projection capability. Canada's leadership of a NATO battlegroup in Latvia highlights a continuing capability to deploy medium-sized land formations. It has also contributed to NATO's air-policing mission. Meanwhile, the deployments of frigates and submarines to the NATO theatre and the Pacific demonstrate continuing blue-water naval capabilities. The 2017 review pledged to finally deliver on a range of delayed procurements. It raised the target for a new-generation fighter to 88 aircraft, but a trade dispute with Boeing saw Canada turn to Australia to purchase second-hand F/A-18s to supplement its current fleet. Contenders for the long-term fighter replacement include the F/A-18E/F *Super Hornet*, the F-35A *Lightning* II and the *Gripen* E. In October 2018, the government selected the Lockheed Martin-led consortium and its BAE Systems Type-26 frigate design as the preferred bidder for Canada's future surface combatant. Canada maintains a well-developed range of mainly small and medium-sized defence firms. The strongest sector is in combat vehicles and components, though the government is using its latest naval procurements to establish a long-term national shipbuilding strategy.

ACTIVE 67,400 (Army 23,800 Navy 8,300 Air Force 12,000 Other 23,300) Paramilitary 4,500

RESERVE 35,600 (Army 25,600 Navy 4,600 Air 2,100 Other 3,300)

ORGANISATIONS BY SERVICE

Space
EQUIPMENT BY TYPE
SATELLITES • SPACE SURVEILLANCE 1 *Sapphire*

Army 23,800
FORCES BY ROLE
MANOEUVRE
  Mechanised
  1 (1st) mech bde gp (1 armd regt, 2 mech inf bn, 1 lt inf bn, 1 arty regt, 1 cbt engr regt, 1 log bn)
  2 (2nd & 5th) mech bde gp (1 armd recce regt, 2 mech inf bn, 1 lt inf bn, 1 arty regt, 1 cbt engr regt, 1 log bn)
COMBAT SUPPORT
  1 engr regt
  3 MP pl
AIR DEFENCE
  1 SAM regt
EQUIPMENT BY TYPE
ARMOURED FIGHTING VEHICLES
  MBT 82: 42 *Leopard* 2A4 (trg role); 20 *Leopard* 2A4M (upgraded); 20 *Leopard* 2A6M (52 *Leopard* 1C2 in store)
  RECCE ε120 LAV-25 *Coyote*
  IFV 550 LAV 6.0
  APC 443
    APC (T) 268: 235 M113; 33 M577 (CP)
    APC (W) 175 LAV *Bison* (incl 10 EW, 32 amb, 32 repair, 64 recovery)
  AUV 507: 7 *Cougar*; 500 TAPV
ENGINEERING & MAINTENANCE VEHICLES
  AEV 23: 5 *Buffalo*; 18 *Wisent* 2
  ARV 12 BPz-3 *Büffel*
ANTI-TANK/ANTI-INFRASTRUCTURE
  MSL • MANPATS TOW-2
  RCL 84mm *Carl Gustav*
ARTILLERY 287
  TOWED 163 105mm 126: 98 C3 (M101); 28 LG1 MkII; 155mm 37 M777
  MOR 124: 81mm 100; SP 81mm 24 LAV *Bison*
UNMANNED AERIAL VEHICLES • ISR • Light 5 RQ 21A *Blackjack*

Reserve Organisations 25,600

Canadian Rangers 5,250 Reservists
Provide a limited military presence in Canada's northern, coastal and isolated areas. Sovereignty, public-safety and surveillance roles

FORCES BY ROLE
MANOEUVRE
  Other
  5 (patrol) ranger gp (209 patrols)

Army Reserves 20,350 Reservists
Most units have only coy-sized establishments
FORCES BY ROLE
COMMAND
  10 bde gp HQ

MANOEUVRE
Reconnaissance
18 recce regt (sqn)
Light
51 inf regt (coy)
COMBAT SUPPORT
16 fd arty regt (bty)
3 indep fd arty bty
10 cbt engr regt (coy)
1 EW regt (sqn)
4 int coy
10 sigs regt (coy)
COMBAT SERVICE SUPPORT
10 log bn (coy)
3 MP coy

Royal Canadian Navy 8,300
EQUIPMENT BY TYPE
SUBMARINES • SSK 4:
4 *Victoria* (ex-UK *Upholder*) with 6 single 533mm TT with Mk 48 HWT (2 currently non-operational)
PRINCIPAL SURFACE COMBATANTS • FRIGATES • FFGHM 12:
12 *Halifax* with 2 quad lnchr with RGM-84L *Harpoon* Block II AShM, 2 8-cell Mk 48 mod 0 VLS with RIM-162C ESSM SAM, 2 twin SVTT Mk 32 mod 9 324mm ASTT with Mk 46 LWT, 1 Mk 15 *Phalanx* Block 1B CIWS, 1 57mm gun (capacity 1 SH-3 (CH-124) *Sea King* ASW hel)
MINE WARFARE
MINE COUNTERMEASURES • MCO 12 *Kingston* (also used in patrol role)
LOGISTICS AND SUPPORT 10
AORH 1 *Asterix* (*Resolve*) (capacity 2 CH-148 *Cyclone* ASW hel)
AX 9: AXL 8 *Orca*; AXS 1 *Oriole*

Reserves 4,600 reservists
24 units tasked with crewing 10 of the 12 MCOs, harbour defence & naval control of shipping

Royal Canadian Air Force (RCAF) 12,000
FORCES BY ROLE
FIGHTER/GROUND ATTACK
4 sqn with F/A-18A/B *Hornet* (CF-18AM/BM)
ANTI-SUBMARINE WARFARE
2 sqn with CH-148 *Cyclone*
MARITIME PATROL
2 sqn with P-3 *Orion* (CP-140 *Aurora*)
SEARCH & RESCUE/TRANSPORT
3 sqn with AW101 *Merlin* (CH-149 *Cormorant*); C-130H/H-30 (CC-130) *Hercules*
1 sqn with DHC-5 (CC-115) *Buffalo*
TANKER/TRANSPORT
1 sqn with A310/A310 MRTT (CC-150/CC-150T)
1 sqn with KC-130H
TRANSPORT
1 sqn with C-17A (CC-177) *Globemaster*
1 sqn with CL-600 (CC-144B)
1 sqn with C-130J-30 (CC-130) *Hercules*
1 (utl) sqn with DHC-6 (CC-138) *Twin Otter*
TRAINING
1 OCU sqn with F/A-18A/B *Hornet* (CF-18AM/BM)
1 OCU sqn with C-130H/H-30/J (CC-130) *Hercules*
1 OCU sqn with CH-148 *Cyclone*
1 OCU sqn with Bell 412 (CH-146 *Griffon*)
1 sqn with P-3 *Orion* (CP-140 *Aurora*)
TRANSPORT HELICOPTER
5 sqn with Bell 412 (CH-146 *Griffon*)
3 (cbt spt) sqn with Bell 412 (CH-146 *Griffon*)
1 (Spec Ops) sqn with Bell 412 (CH-146 *Griffon* – OPCON Canadian Special Operations Command)
1 sqn with CH-47F (CH-147F) *Chinook*
EQUIPMENT BY TYPE
AIRCRAFT 92 combat capable
FGA 78: 57 F/A-18A (CF-18AM) *Hornet*; 21 F/A-18B (CF-18BM) *Hornet*
ASW 14 P-3 *Orion* (CP-140M *Aurora*)
TKR/TPT 5: 2 A310 MRTT (CC-150T); 3 KC-130H
TPT 48: **Heavy** 5 C-17A (CC-177) *Globemaster* III; **Medium** 26: 7 C-130H (CC-130) *Hercules*; 2 C-130H-30 (CC-130) *Hercules*; 17 C-130J-30 (CC-130) *Hercules*; **Light** 10: 6 DHC-5 (CC-115) *Buffalo*; 4 DHC-6 (CC-138) *Twin Otter*;
PAX 7: 3 A310 (CC-150 *Polaris*); 4 CL-600 (CC-144B/C)
TRG 4 DHC-8 (CT-142)
HELICOPTERS
ASW 18 CH-148 *Cyclone* (4 more Block 2 hels delivered but not yet accepted)
MRH 68 Bell 412 (CH-146 *Griffon*)
TPT 29: **Heavy** 15 CH-47F (CH-147F) *Chinook*; **Medium** 14 AW101 *Merlin* (CH-149 *Cormorant*)
RADARS 53
AD RADAR • NORTH WARNING SYSTEM 47: 11 AN/FPS-117 (range 200nm); 36 AN/FPS-124 (range 80nm)
STRATEGIC 6: 4 Coastal; 2 Transportable
AIR-LAUNCHED MISSILES
AAM • IR AIM-9L *Sidewinder*
ARH AIM-120C AMRAAM
BOMBS
Laser-guided: GBU-10/GBU-12/GBU-16 *Paveway* II; GBU-24 *Paveway* III
INS/GPS-guided: GBU-31 JDAM; GBU-38 JDAM; GBU-49 *Enhanced Paveway* II

NATO Flight Training Canada
EQUIPMENT BY TYPE
AIRCRAFT
TRG 45: 26 T-6A *Texan* II (CT-156 *Harvard* II); 19 *Hawk* 115 (CT-155) (advanced wpns/tactics trg)

Contracted Flying Services – Southport
EQUIPMENT BY TYPE
AIRCRAFT
TPT • **Light** 7 Beech C90B *King Air*
TRG 11 G-120A
HELICOPTERS
MRH 9 Bell 412 (CH-146)
TPT • **Light** 7 Bell 206 *Jet Ranger* (CH-139)

Canadian Special Operations Forces Command 1,500

FORCES BY ROLE
SPECIAL FORCES
  1 SF regt (Canadian Special Operations Regiment)
  1 SF unit (JTF 2)
COMBAT SERVICE SUPPORT
  1 CBRN unit (Canadian Joint Incident Response Unit – CJIRU)
TRANSPORT HELICOPTER
  1 (spec ops) sqn, with Bell 412 (CH-146 *Griffon* – from the RCAF)
EQUIPMENT BY TYPE
NBC VEHICLES 4 LAV *Bison* NBC
HELICOPTERS • MRH 10 Bell 412 (CH-146 *Griffon*)

Canadian Forces Joint Operational Support Group

FORCES BY ROLE
COMBAT SUPPORT
  1 engr spt coy
  1 (close protection) MP coy
  1 (joint) sigs regt
COMBAT SERVICE SUPPORT
  1 (spt) log unit
  1 (movement) log unit

Paramilitary 4,500

Canadian Coast Guard 4,500

Incl Department of Fisheries and Oceans; all platforms are designated as non-combatant

EQUIPMENT BY TYPE
PATROL AND COASTAL COMBATANTS 72
  PSOH 1 *Leonard J Cowley*
  PSO 1 *Sir Wilfred Grenfell* (with hel landing platform)
  PCO 13: 2 *Cape Roger*; 1 *Gordon Reid*; 9 *Hero*; 1 *Tanu*
  PCC 1 *Harp*
  PBF 1 Response Boat-Medium (RB-M)
  PB 55: 1 *Post*; 1 *Quebecois*; 1 *Vakta*; 10 Type-300A; 36 Type-300B; 1 *S. Dudka*; 1 *Simmonds* (on loan from RCMP); 4 *Baie de Plaisance*
AMPHIBIOUS • LANDING CRAFT • UCAC 4 Type-400
LOGISTICS AND SUPPORT 35
  ABU 7
  AG 4
  AGB 16
  AGOS 8
HELICOPTERS • MRH 7 Bell 412EP • **TPT** 19: **Medium** 1 S-61; **Light** 18: 3 Bell 206L *Long Ranger*; 15 Bell 429

DEPLOYMENT

CYPRUS: UN • UNFICYP (*Operation Snowgoose*) 1
DEMOCRATIC REPUBLIC OF THE CONGO: UN • MONUSCO (*Operation Crocodile*) 8
EGYPT: MFO (*Operation Calumet*) 55; 1 MP team
IRAQ: *Operation Inherent Resolve* (*Impact*) 120; 1 SF trg gp; 1 med unit; **NATO** • NATO Mission Iraq 250; 1 hel flt with 3 Bell 412 (CH-146 *Griffon*) hel
KUWAIT: *Operation Inherent Resolve* (*Impact*) 1 A310 MRTT (C-150T); 2 C-130J-30 *Hercules* (CC-130J)
LATVIA: NATO • Enhanced Forward Presence (*Operation Reassurance*) 525; 1 mech inf bn HQ; 1 mech inf coy(+); 1 cbt spt coy; LAV 6.0; M777
MALI: UN • MINUSMA (*Operation Presence*) 5
MEDITERRANEAN SEA: NATO • SNMG 2: 1 FFGHM
MIDDLE EAST: UN • UNTSO (*Operation Jade*) 4
ROMANIA: NATO • Air Policing 135; 5 F/A-18A *Hornet* (CF-18)
SERBIA: NATO • KFOR • Joint Enterprise (*Operation Kobold*) 5
SOUTH SUDAN: UN • UNMISS (*Operation Soprano*) 11
UKRAINE: *Operation Unifier* 200

FOREIGN FORCES

United Kingdom BATUS 400; 1 trg unit; 1 hel flt with SA341 *Gazelle* AH1
United States 150

United States US

United States Dollar $		2018	2019	2020
GDP	US$	20.58tr	21.44tr	
per capita	US$	62,869	65,112	
Growth	%	2.9	2.4	
Inflation	%	2.4	1.8	
Def exp [a]	US$	672bn	730bn	
Def bdgt [b]	US$	631bn	685bn	738bn

[a] NATO definition

[b] National Defense Budget Function (50) Outlays. Includes DoD funding, as well as funds for nuclear-weapons-related activities undertaken by the Department of Energy. Excludes some military retirement and healthcare costs

Real-terms defence budget trend (US$bn, constant 2015)
755.7
581.6
2008   2014   2019

Population   331,883,986

Age	0–14	15–19	20–24	25–29	30–64	65 plus
Male	9.5%	3.2%	3.4%	3.7%	22.2%	7.3%
Female	9.1%	3.1%	3.2%	3.5%	22.7%	9.1%

Capabilities

The United States remains the world's most capable military power, with a unique ability to project power on a global basis. The Pentagon's 2018 National Defense Strategy refocused priorities on renewed 'great-power competition' and called for a reversal in reductions in the size of the joint force. A new Nuclear Posture Review backed the development of low-yield warheads and a nuclear-capable sea-launched cruise missile. A missile-defence review was published in January 2019 envisaging a number of new programmes and technologies, including space-based systems, to respond to a more challenging and evolving threat environment. In August 2019 the Pentagon established a new Space Command as a precursor to the creation of a space force, a White House plan that has fuelled debate over the best way to integrate space into national-security policy. The US is NATO's most capable member, and has defence-treaty obligations to, among others, Australia, the Philippines, Japan, South Korea and Thailand. The US maintains an all-volunteer force, including significant reserves, with high levels of training throughout all command and service levels. However, readiness remains a concern. Modernisation priorities include a renewal of strategic nuclear capabilities, including a new class of ballistic-missile submarine and a new long-range bomber, and a major recapitalisation of air assets across the services. In August 2019, the US withdrew from the Intermediate-range Nuclear Forces Treaty, and three weeks later conducted a ground-launched cruise-missile test. During 2019 the US Navy was carrying out a new force-structure assessment, which could adjust the long-term plan for a 355-ship combat fleet. The US also continues to actively develop its defensive and offensive cyber capabilities. The country has the strongest defence industry globally, with a dominant position in the international defence market, although a 2018 report to President Trump warned that key areas of the defence-industrial base were eroding, which could have consequences for the defence supply chain.

ACTIVE 1,379,800 (Army 481,750 Navy 337,100 Air Force 332,650 US Marine Corps 186,300 US Coast Guard 42,000)

RESERVE 849,450 (Army 524,700 Navy 102,250 Air Force 176,000 Marine Corps Reserve 39,000 US Coast Guard 7,500)

ORGANISATIONS BY SERVICE

US Strategic Command
HQ at Offutt AFB (NE). Five missions: US nuclear deterrent; missile defence; global strike; info ops; ISR

US Navy
EQUIPMENT BY TYPE
SUBMARINES • STRATEGIC • SSBN 14 *Ohio* with up to 20 UGM-133A *Trident* D-5/D-5LE nuclear SLBM, 4 single 533mm TT with Mk 48 ADCAP mod 6/7 HWT

US Air Force • Global Strike Command
FORCES BY ROLE
MISSILE
  9 sqn with LGM-30G *Minuteman* III
BOMBER
  5 sqn with B-52H *Stratofortress*
  2 sqn with B-2A *Spirit* (+1 ANG sqn personnel only)
EQUIPMENT BY TYPE
SURFACE-TO-SURFACE MISSILE LAUNCHERS
  ICBM • Nuclear 400 LGM-30G *Minuteman* III (1 Mk12A or Mk21 re-entry veh per missile)
AIRCRAFT
  BBR 66: 20 B-2A *Spirit*; 46 B-52H *Stratofortress*
AIR-LAUNCHED MISSILES
  ALCM • Nuclear AGM-86B

Strategic Defenses – Early Warning
North American Aerospace Defense Command (NORAD) – a combined US–CAN org

EQUIPMENT BY TYPE
RADAR
  NORTH WARNING SYSTEM 50: 14 AN/FPS-117 (range 200nm); 36 AN/FPS-124 (range 80nm)
  SOLID STATE PHASED ARRAY RADAR SYSTEM (SSPARS) 5: 2 AN/FPS-123 Early Warning Radar located at Cape Cod AFS (MA) and Clear AFS (AK); 3 AN/FPS-132 Upgraded Early Warning Radar located at Beale AFB (CA), Thule (GL) and Fylingdales Moor (UK)
  SPACETRACK SYSTEM 10: 1 AN/FPS-85 Spacetrack Radar at Eglin AFB (FL); 6 contributing radars at Cavalier AFS (ND), Clear (AK), Thule (GL), Fylingdales Moor (UK), Beale AFB (CA) and Cape Cod (MA); 3 Spacetrack Optical Trackers located at Socorro (NM), Maui (HI), Diego Garcia (BIOT)
  PERIMETER ACQUISITION RADAR ATTACK CHARACTERISATION SYSTEM (PARCS) 1 AN/FPQ-16 at Cavalier AFS (ND)
  DETECTION AND TRACKING RADARS 5 located at Kwajalein Atoll, Ascension Island, Australia, Kaena Point (HI), MIT Lincoln Laboratory (MA)
  GROUND BASED ELECTRO OPTICAL DEEP SPACE SURVEILLANCE SYSTEM (GEODSS) Socorro (NM), Maui (HI), Diego Garcia (BIOT)
STRATEGIC DEFENCES – MISSILE DEFENCES
  SEA-BASED: *Aegis* engagement cruisers and destroyers
  LAND-BASED: 40 ground-based interceptors at Fort Greely (AK); 4 ground-based interceptors at Vandenburg AFB (CA)

Space
EQUIPMENT BY TYPE
SATELLITES 140
  COMMUNICATIONS 45: 5 AEHF; 6 DSCS-III; 2 *Milstar*-I; 3 *Milstar*-II; 5 MUOS; 1 PAN-1 (P360); 5 SDS-III; 2 SDS-IV; 6 UFO; 10 WGS SV2
  NAVIGATION/POSITIONING/TIMING 31: 12 NAVSTAR Block IIF; 19 NAVSTAR Block IIR/IIRM
  METEOROLOGY/OCEANOGRAPHY 6 DMSP-5
  ISR 17: 5 FIA *Radar*; 5 Evolved Enhanced/Improved *Crystal* (visible and infrared imagery); 2 *Lacrosse* (*Onyx* radar imaging satellite); 1 NRO L-71; 1 NRO L-76; 1 ORS-1; 1 *TacSat*-4; 1 *TacSat*-6
  ELINT/SIGINT 27: 2 *Mentor* (advanced *Orion*); 3 Advanced *Mentor*; 4 *Mercury*; 1 NRO L-67; 1 *Trumpet*; 4 Improved *Trumpet*; 12 SBWASS (Space Based Wide Area Surveillance System; Naval Ocean Surveillance System)
  SPACE SURVEILLANCE 6: 4 GSSAP; 1 SBSS (Space Based Surveillance System); 1 ORS-5
  EARLY WARNING 8: 4 DSP; 4 SBIRS *Geo*-1

US Army 481,750

FORCES BY ROLE
Sqn are generally bn sized and tp are generally coy sized

COMMAND
3 (I, III & XVIII AB) corps HQ
1 (2nd) inf div HQ

SPECIAL FORCES
(see USSOCOM)

MANOEUVRE

Armoured
2 (1st Armd & 1st Cav) armd div (3 (1st–3rd ABCT) armd bde (1 armd recce sqn, 2 armd bn, 1 armd inf bn, 1 SP arty bn, 1 cbt engr bn, 1 CSS bn); 1 SP arty bde HQ; 1 log bde; 1 (hy cbt avn) hel bde)
1 (1st) inf div (2 (1st & 2nd ABCT) armd bde (1 armd recce sqn, 2 armd bn, 1 armd inf bn, 1 SP arty bn, 1 cbt engr bn, 1 CSS bn); 1 SP arty bde HQ; 1 log bde; 1 (cbt avn) hel bde)
1 (3rd) inf div (2 (1st & 2nd ABCT) armd bde (1 armd recce sqn, 2 armd bn, 1 armd inf bn, 1 SP arty bn, 1 cbt engr bn, 1 CSS bn); 1 lt inf bn; 1 SP arty bde HQ; 1 log bde; 1 (cbt avn) hel bde)

Mechanised
1 (4th) inf div (1 (3rd ABCT) armd bde (1 armd recce sqn, 2 armd bn, 1 armd inf bn, 1 SP arty bn, 1 cbt engr bn, 1 CSS bn); 1 (1st SBCT) mech bde (1 armd recce sqn, 3 mech inf bn, 1 arty bn, 1 cbt engr bn, 1 CSS bn); 1 (2nd IBCT) lt inf bde (1 recce sqn, 3 inf bn, 1 arty bn, 1 cbt engr bn, 1 CSS bn); 1 SP arty bde HQ; 1 log bde; 1 (hy cbt avn) hel bde)
1 (7th) inf div (2 (1st & 2nd SBCT, 2nd ID) mech bde (1 armd recce sqn, 3 mech inf bn, 1 arty bn, 1 cbt engr bn, 1 CSS bn))
1 (1st SBCT, 25th ID) mech bde (1 armd recce sqn, 3 mech inf bn, 1 arty bn, 1 cbt engr bn, 1 CSS bn)
2 (2nd & 3rd CR) mech bde (1 armd recce sqn, 3 mech sqn, 1 arty sqn, 1 cbt engr sqn, 1 CSS sqn)

Light
1 (10th Mtn) inf div (3 (1st–3rd IBCT) lt inf bde (1 recce sqn, 3 inf bn, 1 arty bn, 1 cbt engr bn, 1 CSS bn); 1 log bde; 1 (cbt avn) hel bde)
1 (25th) inf div (2 (2 & 3rd IBCT) inf bde (1 recce sqn, 2 inf bn, 1 arty bn, 1 cbt engr bn, 1 CSS bn); 1 log bde; 1 (cbt avn) hel bde)
3 (Sy Force Assist) inf bde(-)

Air Manoeuvre
1 (82nd) AB div (1 (1st AB BCT) AB bde (1 recce bn, 1 mech coy; 3 para bn, 1 arty bn, 1 cbt engr bn, 1 CSS bn); 2 (2nd & 3rd AB BCT) AB bde (1 recce bn, 3 para bn, 1 arty bn, 1 cbt engr bn, 1 CSS bn); 1 (cbt avn) hel bde; 1 log bde)
1 (101st) air aslt div (3 (1st–3rd AB BCT) AB bde (1 recce bn, 3 para bn, 1 arty bn, 1 cbt engr bn, 1 CSS bn); 1 (cbt avn) hel bde; 1 log bde)
1 (173rd AB BCT) AB bde (1 recce bn, 2 para bn, 1 arty bn, 1 cbt engr bn, 1 CSS bn)
1 (4th AB BCT, 25th ID) AB bde (1 recce bn, 2 para bn, 1 arty bn, 1 cbt engr bn, 1 CSS bn)

Other
1 (11th ACR) trg armd cav regt (OPFOR) (2 armd cav sqn, 1 CSS bn)

COMBAT SUPPORT
3 MRL bde (2 MRL bn)
1 MRL bde (5 MRL bn)
1 MRL bde (1 MRL bn)
4 engr bde
2 EOD gp (2 EOD bn)
10 int bde
2 int gp
4 MP bde
1 NBC bde
3 (strat) sigs bde
4 (tac) sigs bde

COMBAT SERVICE SUPPORT
2 log bde
3 med bde
1 tpt bde

ISR
1 ISR avn bde

HELICOPTER
2 (cbt avn) hel bde
1 (cbt avn) hel bde HQ

AIR DEFENCE
5 SAM bde

Reserve Organisations

Army National Guard 333,800 reservists
Normally dual-funded by DoD and states. Civil-emergency responses can be mobilised by state governors. Federal government can mobilise ARNG for major domestic emergencies and for overseas operations

FORCES BY ROLE

COMMAND
8 div HQ

SPECIAL FORCES
(see USSOCOM)

MANOEUVRE

Reconnaissance
1 armd recce sqn

Armoured
5 (ABCT) armd bde (1 armd recce sqn, 2 armd bn, 1 armd inf bn, 1 SP arty bn, 1 cbt engr bn, 1 CSS bn)

Mechanised
2 (SBCT) mech bde (1 armd recce sqn, 3 mech inf bn, 1 arty bn, 1 cbt engr bn, 1 CSS bn)

Light
14 (IBCT) lt inf bde (1 recce sqn, 3 inf bn, 1 arty bn, 1 cbt engr bn, 1 CSS bn)
6 (IBCT) lt inf bde (1 recce sqn, 2 inf bn, 1 arty bn, 1 cbt engr bn, 1 CSS bn)
1 (Sy Force Assist) inf bde(-)
4 lt inf bn

Air Manoeuvre
1 AB bn

COMBAT SUPPORT
8 arty bde
1 SP arty bn
8 engr bde

1 EOD regt
3 int bde
3 MP bde
1 NBC bde
2 (tac) sigs bde
18 (Mnv Enh) cbt spt bde
COMBAT SERVICE SUPPORT
9 log bde
17 (regional) log spt gp
HELICOPTER
8 (cbt avn) hel bde
5 (theatre avn) hel bde
AIR DEFENCE
3 SAM bde

Army Reserve 190,900 reservists
Reserve under full command of US Army. Does not have state-emergency liability of Army National Guard
FORCES BY ROLE
SPECIAL FORCES
(see USSOCOM)
COMBAT SUPPORT
4 engr bde
4 MP bde
2 NBC bde
2 sigs bde
3 (Mnv Enh) cbt spt bde
COMBAT SERVICE SUPPORT
9 log bde
11 med bde
HELICOPTER
2 (exp cbt avn) hel bde

Army Stand-by Reserve 700 reservists
Trained individuals for mobilisation
EQUIPMENT BY TYPE
ARMOURED FIGHTING VEHICLES
  MBT 2,389: 750 M1A1 SA *Abrams*; 1,605 M1A2 SEPv2 *Abrams*; 34+ M1A2C *Abrams* (in test) (ε3,300 more M1A1/A2 *Abrams* in store)
  ASLT 134 M1128 *Stryker* MGS
  RECCE 1,745: ε1,200 M3A2/A3 *Bradley*; 545 M1127 *Stryker* RV (ε800 more M3 *Bradley* in store)
  IFV 2,931: ε14 LAV-25; ε2,500 M2A2/A3 *Bradley*; 334 M7A3/SA BFIST (OP); 83 M1296 *Styker Dragoon*; (ε2,000 more M2 *Bradley* in store)
  APC 10,547
    APC (T) ε5,000 M113A2/A3 (ε8,000 more in store)
    APC (W) 2,613: 1,773 M1126 *Stryker* ICV; 348 M1130 *Stryker* CV (CP); 188 M1131 *Stryker* FSV (OP); 304 M1133 *Stryker* MEV (Amb)
    PPV 2,934: 2,633 *MaxxPro Dash*; 301 *MaxxPro* LWB (Amb)
  AUV 10,416+: 1,400+ JLTV; 2,900 M1117 ASV; 465 M1200 *Armored Knight* (OP); 5,651 M-ATV
ENGINEERING & MAINTENANCE VEHICLES
  AEV 531: 113 M1 ABV; 250 M9 ACE; 168 M1132 *Stryker* ESV
  ARV 1,195+: 360 M88A1; 835 M88A2 (ε1,000 more M88A1 in store); some M578
  VLB 60: 20 REBS; 40 *Wolverine* HAB
  MW 3+: *Aardvark* JSFU Mk4; some *Husky* 2G; 3+ *Hydrema* 910 MCV-2; M58/M59 MICLIC; M139; *Rhino*
  NBC VEHICLES 234 M1135 *Stryker* NBCRV
ANTI-TANK/ANTI-INFRASTRUCTURE
  MSL
    SP 1,133: 133 M1134 *Stryker* ATGM; ε1,000 M1167 HMMWV TOW
    MANPATS FGM-148 *Javelin*
  RCL 84mm *Carl Gustav*
ARTILLERY 5,444
  SP 155mm 998: 900 M109A6; 98 M109A7 (ε500 more M109A6 in store)
  TOWED 1,339: **105mm** 821 M119A2/3; **155mm** 518 M777A2
  MRL 227mm 600: 375 M142 HIMARS; 225 M270A1 MLRS
  MOR 2,507: **81mm** 990 M252; **120mm** 1,076 M120/M1064A3; **SP 120mm** 441 M1129 *Stryker* MC
SURFACE-TO-SURFACE MISSILE LAUNCHERS
  SRBM • Conventional MGM-140A/B ATACMS; MGM-168 ATACMS (All launched from M270A1 MLRS or M142 HIMARS MRLs)
AMPHIBIOUS 78
  PRINCIPAL AMPHIBIOUS SHIPS 8
    LSL 8 *Frank Besson* (capacity 24 *Abrams* MBT)
  LANDING CRAFT 70
    LCT 34 LCU 2000 (capacity 5 M1 *Abrams* MBT)
    LCM 36 LCM 8 (capacity either 1 M1 *Abrams* MBT or 200 troops)
AIRCRAFT
  ISR 39: 8 EMARSS-G; 4 EMARSS-V; 8 EMARSS-M; 19 RC-12X *Guardrail* (5 trg)
  ELINT 12: 4 EMARSS-S; 5 EO-5C ARL-M (COMINT/ELINT); 2 EO-5B ARL-C (COMINT); 1 TO-5C (trg)
  TPT 156: **Light** 152: 113 Beech A200 *King Air* (C-12 *Huron*); 28 Cessna 560 *Citation* (UC-35A/B); 11 SA-227 *Metro* (C-26E); **PAX** 4: 1 Gulfstream IV (C-20F); 2 Gulfstream V (C-37A); 1 Gulfstream G550 (C-37B)
  TRG 4 T-6D *Texan* II
HELICOPTERS
  ATK 714: 414 AH-64D *Apache*; 300 AH-64E *Apache*
  SAR 259: 19 HH-60L *Black Hawk*; 240 HH-60M *Black Hawk* (medevac)
  TPT 2,852: **Heavy** 450 CH-47F *Chinook*; **Medium** 1,914: 250 UH-60A *Black Hawk*; 914 UH-60L *Black Hawk*; 750 UH-60M *Black Hawk*; **Light** 488: 423 UH-72A *Lakota*; 65 UH-1H/V *Iroquois*
  TRG ε50 TH-67 *Creek*
UNMANNED AERIAL VEHICLES 388
  CISR • Heavy 152 MQ-1C *Gray Eagle*
  ISR • Medium 236 RQ-7B *Shadow*
AIR DEFENCE
  SAM 1,183+
    Long-range 480 MIM-104D/E/F *Patriot* PAC-2 GEM/PAC-2 GEM-T/PAC-3/PAC-3 MSE
    Short-range NASAMS
    Point-defence 703+: FIM-92 *Stinger*; 703 M1097 *Avenger*
  GUNS • Towed • 20mm *Phalanx* (LPWS)
MISSILE DEFENCE • Long-range 42 THAAD
AIR-LAUNCHED MISSILES
  ASM AGM-114K/L/M/N/R *Hellfire* II; APKWS

US Navy 337,100

Comprises 2 Fleet Areas, Atlantic and Pacific. 6 Fleets: 2nd – Atlantic; 3rd – Pacific; 4th – Caribbean, Central and South America; 5th – Arabian Sea, Persian Gulf, Red Sea; 6th – Mediterranean; 7th – Indian Ocean, East Asia, W. Pacific; plus Military Sealift Command (MSC); Naval Reserve Force (NRF). For Naval Special Warfare Command, see US Special Operations Command

EQUIPMENT BY TYPE
SUBMARINES 67
STRATEGIC • SSBN 14 *Ohio* opcon US STRATCOM with up to 20 UGM-133A *Trident* D-5/D-5LE nuclear SLBM, 4 single 533mm TT with Mk 48 ADCAP mod 6/7 HWT

TACTICAL 53
  SSGN 50:
    4 *Ohio* (mod) with 22 7-cell MAC VLS with UGM-109C/E *Tomahawk* Block III/IV LACM , 4 single 533mm TT with Mk 48 ADCAP mod 6/7 HWT
    7 *Los Angeles* Flight II with 1 12-cell VLS with UGM-109C/E *Tomahawk* Block III/IV LACM, 4 single 533mm TT with Mk 48 ADCAP mod 6/7 HWT
    22 *Los Angeles* Flight III with 1 12-cell VLS with UGM-109C/E *Tomahawk* Block III/IV LACM, 4 single 533mm TT with Mk 48 ADCAP mod 6/7 HWT
    10 *Virginia* Flight I/II with 1 12-cell VLS with UGM-109C/E *Tomahawk* Block III/IV LACM, 4 single 533mm TT with Mk 48 ADCAP mod 6/7 HWT
    7 *Virginia* Flight III with 2 6-cell VPT VLS with UGM-109C/E *Tomahawk* Block III/IV LACM, 4 single 533mm TT with Mk 48 ADCAP mod 6/7 HWT
  SSN 3 *Seawolf* with 8 single 660mm TT with UGM-109C/E *Tomahawk* Block III/IV LACM/Mk 48 ADCAP mod 6/7 HWT

PRINCIPAL SURFACE COMBATANTS 121
AIRCRAFT CARRIERS • CVN 11
  1 *Gerald R. Ford* with 2 octuple Mk 29 mod 5 GMLS with RIM-162D ESSM SAM, 2 Mk 49 mod 3 GMLS with RIM-116C RAM Block 2 SAM, 3 Mk 15 *Phalanx* Block 1B CIWS (typical capacity 75+ F/A-18E/F *Super Hornet* FGA ac; F-35C *Lightning* II FGA ac; E-2D *Hawkeye* AEW&C ac; EA-18G *Growler* EW ac; MH-60R *Seahawk* ASW hel; MH-60S *Knighthawk* MRH hel)
  10 *Nimitz* with 2 8-cell Mk29 GMLS with RIM-162 ESSM SAM, 2 Mk 49 GMLS with RIM-116 RAM Block 2 SAM, 3 Mk 15 *Phalanx* Block 1B CIWS (typical capacity 55 F/A-18 *Hornet* FGA ac; F-35C *Lightning* II FGA ac (IOC planned 02/2019); 4 EA-18G *Growler* EW ac; 4 E-2C/D *Hawkeye* AEW ac; 6 H-60 *Seahawk* hel)

CRUISERS • CGHM 24:
  22 *Ticonderoga* with *Aegis* Baseline 5/6/8/9 C2, 2 quad lnchr with RGM-84D *Harpoon* Block 1C AShM, 16 8-cell Mk 41 VLS (of which 2 only 5-cell and fitted with reload crane) with RGM-109C/E *Tomahawk* Block III/IV LACM/SM-2 Block III/IIIA/IIIB/IV SAM/SM-3 Block IA/B SAM/SM-6 Block I SAM, 2 triple SVTT Mk 32 324mm ASTT with Mk 54 LWT, 2 Mk 15 *Phalanx* Block 1B CIWS, 2 127mm guns (capacity 2 MH-60R *Seahawk*/MH-60S *Knight Hawk* hels)
  2 *Zumwalt* with 20 4-cell Mk 57 VLS with RGM-109C/E *Tomahawk* Block III/IV LACM/RIM-162 ESSM SAM/SM-2 Block IIIA SAM/ASROC A/S msl, 2 155mm guns (capacity 2 MH-60R *Seahawk* ASW hel or 1 MH-60R *Seahawk* ASW hel and 3 *Fire Scout* UAV)

DESTROYERS 67
  DDGHM 39 *Arleigh Burke* Flight IIA with *Aegis* Baseline 5/6/7/9 C2, 12 8-cell Mk 41 VLS with RGM-109C/E *Tomahawk* Block III/IV LACM/SM-2 Block III/IIIA/IIIB/IV SAM/SM-3 Block IA/B SAM/SM-6 Block I SAM/ASROC A/S msl, 2 triple SVTT Mk 32 324mm ASTT with Mk 54 LWT, 2 Mk 15 *Phalanx* Block 1B CIWS, 1 127mm gun (capacity 2 MH-60R *Seahawk*/MH-60S *Knight Hawk* hels)
  DDGM 28 *Arleigh Burke* Flight I/II with *Aegis* Baseline 5/9 C2, 2 quad lnchr with RGM-84D *Harpoon* Block 1C AShM, 12 8-cell Mk 41 VLS (of which 2 only 5-cell and fitted with reload crane) with RGM-109C/E *Tomahawk* Block III/IV LACM/SM-2 Block III/IIIA/IIIB/IV SAM/SM-3 Block IA/B SAM/SM-6 Block I SAM/ASROC A/S msl, 2 triple SVTT Mk 32 324mm ASTT with Mk 54 LWT, 2 Mk 15 *Phalanx* Block 1B CIWS (4 with 2 Mk 15 SeaRAM with RIM-116C RAM Block 2 instead of *Phalanx*), 1 127mm gun, 1 hel landing platform (of which one suffered major damage in collision in 2017)

FRIGATES 19
  FFGHM 1 *Independence* with 2 quad lnchr with NSM (RGM-184A) AShM, 1 11-cell SeaRAM lnchr with RIM-116C Block 2 SAM, 1 57mm gun (capacity 2 MH-60R/S *Seahawk* hel and 3 MQ-8 *Fire Scout* UAV)
  FFHM 18:
    9 *Freedom* with 1 21-cell Mk 49 lnchr with RIM-116C RAM Block 2 SAM, 1 57mm gun (capacity 2 MH-60R/S *Seahawk* hel or 1 MH-60 with 3 MQ-8 *Fire Scout* UAV)
    9 *Independence* with 1 11-cell SeaRAM lnchr with RIM-116C Block 2 SAM, 1 57mm gun (capacity 2 MH-60R/S *Seahawk* hel and 3 MQ-8 *Fire Scout* UAV)

PATROL AND COASTAL COMBATANTS 84
PCFG 10 *Cyclone* with 1 quad Mk 208 lnchr with BGM-176B *Griffin B* SSM
PCF 3 *Cyclone*
PBF 65: 12 Mk VI; 25 Combatant Craft Assault; 2 Combatant Craft Heavy; 25 Combatant Craft Medium Mk 1; 1 Coastal Command Boat
PBR 6 Riverine Command Boat

MINE WARFARE • MINE COUNTERMEASURES 11
MCO 11 *Avenger*

COMMAND SHIPS • LCC 2 *Blue Ridge* with 2 Mk 15 *Phalanx* Block 1B CIWS (capacity 3 LCPL; 2 LCVP; 700 troops; 1 med hel) (of which 1 vessel partially crewed by Military Sealift Command personnel)

AMPHIBIOUS
PRINCIPAL AMPHIBIOUS SHIPS 32
  LHA 1 *America* with 2 8-cell Mk 29 GMLS with RIM-162D ESSM SAM, 2 Mk 49 GMLS with RIM-116C RAM Block 2 SAM, 2 Mk 15 *Phalanx* Block 1B CIWS

(capacity 6 F-35B *Lightning* II FGA ac; 12 MV-22B *Osprey* tpt ac; 4 CH-53E *Sea Stallion* hel; 7 AH-1Z *Viper*/UH-1Y *Iroquois* hel; 2 MH-60 hel)

LHD 8 *Wasp* with 2 8-cell Mk 29 GMLS with RIM-7M/P *Sea Sparrow* SAM, 2 Mk 49 GMLS with RIM-116C RAM Block 2 SAM, 2 Mk 15 *Phalanx* Block 1B CIWS (capacity: 6 AV-8B *Harrier* II FGA or F-35B *Lightning* II FGA ac; 4 CH-53E *Sea Stallion* hel; 6 MV-22B *Osprey* tpt ac; 4 AH-1W/Z hel; 3 UH-1Y hel; 3 LCAC(L); 60 tanks; 1,687 troops)

LPD 11 *San Antonio* with 2 21-cell Mk 49 GMLS with RIM-116C RAM Block 2 SAM (capacity 2 CH-53E *Sea Stallion* hel or 2 MV-22 *Osprey*; 2 LCAC(L); 14 AAAV; 720 troops)

LSD 12:

4 *Harpers Ferry* with 2 Mk 49 GMLS with RIM-116C RAM Block 2 SAM, 2 Mk 15 *Phalanx* Block 1B CIWS (capacity 2 CH-53E *Sea Stallion* hel; 2 LCAC(L); 40 tanks; 500 troops)

8 *Whidbey Island* with 2 Mk 49 GMLS with RIM-116C RAM Block 2 SAM, 2 Mk 15 *Phalanx* Block 1B CIWS (capacity 2 CH-53E *Sea Stallion* hel; 4 LCAC(L); 40 tanks; 500 troops)

LANDING CRAFT 141

LCU 32 LCU 1610 (capacity either 1 M1 *Abrams* MBT or 350 troops)

LCM 8 LCM 8

LCP 33 Maritime Positioning Force Utility Boat (MPF-UB)

LCAC 68 LCAC(L) (capacity either 1 MBT or 60 troops (undergoing upgrade programme))

LOGISTICS AND SUPPORT 12

AFDL 1 *Dynamic*

AGOR 6 (all leased out): 2 *Ocean*; 3 *Thomas G. Thompson*; 1 *Kilo Moana*

ARD 2

AX 1 *Prevail*

ESB 1 *Lewis B. Puller* (capacity 4 MH-53/MH-60 hel)

UUV 1 *Cutthroat* (for testing)

Naval Reserve Forces 102,250

Selected Reserve 59,500

Individual Ready Reserve 42,750

Naval Inactive Fleet

Notice for reactivation:
60–90 days minimum (still on naval-vessel register)

EQUIPMENT BY TYPE
AMPHIBIOUS • LHA 3 *Tarawa*
LOGISTICS AND SUPPORT 4
  AOE 2 *Supply*
  ARS 2 *Safeguard*

Military Sealift Command (MSC)

Fleet Oiler (PM1)
EQUIPMENT BY TYPE
LOGISTICS AND SUPPORT 15
  AOR 15 *Henry J. Kaiser* with 1 hel landing platform

Special Mission (PM2)
EQUIPMENT BY TYPE
LOGISTICS AND SUPPORT 21
  AGM 3: 1 *Howard O. Lorenzen*; 1 *Invincible* (commercial operator); 1 Sea-based X-band Radar
  AGOR 6 *Pathfinder*
  AGOS 5: 1 *Impeccable* (commercial operator); 4 *Victorious*
  AGS 1 *Waters*
  ARC 1 *Zeus*
  AS 5 (long-term chartered, of which 1 *Dominator*, 4 *Arrowhead*)

Prepositioning (PM3)
EQUIPMENT BY TYPE
LOGISTICS AND SUPPORT 20
  AG 2: 1 *V Adm K.R. Wheeler*; 1 *Fast Tempo*
  AKR 10: 2 *Bob Hope*; 1 *Stockham*; 2 *Watson*
  AKRH 5 *2nd Lt John P. Bobo*
  ESB 1 *Lewis B. Puller* (capacity 4 MH-53 hel/4 MV-22 tiltrotor; 250 troops)
  ESD 2 *Montford Point*

Service Support (PM4)
EQUIPMENT BY TYPE
LOGISTICS AND SUPPORT 11
  AH 2 *Mercy* with 1 hel landing platform
  ARS 2 *Safeguard*
  AS 4: 1 *Carolyn Chouest*; 2 *Emory S Land*; 1 *Malama* (long-term chartered)
  ATF 3 *Powhatan*

Sealift (PM5)
(At a minimum of 4 days' readiness)
EQUIPMENT BY TYPE
LOGISTICS AND SUPPORT 25
  AOT 1 *Maersk Peary* (long-term chartered)
  AK 9: 3 *Sgt Matej Kocak*; 1 *1st Lt Harry L. Martin*; 1 *LCpl Roy M. Wheat*; 2 *LTC John U.D. Page*; 1 *Maj. Bernard F. Fisher*; 1 *CPT David I. Lyon*
  AKR 15: 5 *Bob Hope*; 2 *Gordon*; 2 *Shughart*; 6 *Watson*

Fleet Ordnance and Dry Cargo (PM6)
EQUIPMENT BY TYPE
LOGISTICS AND SUPPORT 16
  AOE 2 *Supply*
  AKEH 14 *Lewis and Clark*

Expeditionary Fast Transport (PM8)
EQUIPMENT BY TYPE
LOGISTICS AND SUPPORT 12
  AP 2 *Guam*
  EPF 10 *Spearhead*

Dry Cargo and Tankers
EQUIPMENT BY TYPE
LOGISTICS AND SUPPORT 9
  AK 4 (long-term chartered, of which 1 *Black Eagle*; 1 MV *Mohawk*; 1 *Sea Eagle*; 1 SLNC *Corsica*)
  AOT 5 (long-term chartered, of which 2 *Empire State*; 1 *Lawrence H. Gianella*; 1 SLNC *Pax*; 1 SLNC *Goodwill*)

US Maritime Administration (MARAD)

National Defense Reserve Fleet
EQUIPMENT BY TYPE
LOGISTICS AND SUPPORT 27
  AGOS 2 *General Rudder*
  AGM 2: 1 *Pacific Collector*; 1 *Pacific Tracker*
  AK 13: 2 *Cape Ann* (breakbulk); 1 *Cape Chalmers* (breakbulk); 2 *Cape Farewell*; 1 *Cape Fear*; 1 *Cape Girardeau*; 2 *Cape Jacob*; 1 *Cape May* (heavy lift); 1 *Cape Nome* (breakbulk); 1 *Del Monte* (breakbulk); 1 *Savannah*
  AOT 4: 3 *Paul Buck*; 1 *Petersburg*
  AP 4: 1 *Empire State VI*; 1 *Golden Bear*; 1 *Kennedy*; 1 *State of Maine*
  AX 2: 1 *Freedom Star*; 1 *Kings Pointer*

Ready Reserve Force
Ships at readiness up to a maximum of 30 days
EQUIPMENT BY TYPE
LOGISTICS AND SUPPORT 42
  ACS 6: 2 *Flickertail State*; 1 *Gopher State*; 3 *Keystone State*
  AK 2 *Wright* (breakbulk)
  AKR 33: 1 *Adm W.M. Callaghan*; 4 *Algol*; 4 *Cape Capella*; 1 *Cape Decision*; 4 *Cape Ducato*; 1 *Cape Edmont*; 1 *Cape Henry*; 2 *Cape Hudson*; 2 *Cape Knox*; 4 *Cape Island*; 1 *Cape Orlando*; 1 *Cape Race*; 1 *Cape Trinity*; 2 *Cape Trinity*; 2 *Cape Victory*; 2 *Cape Washington*
  AOT 1 *Petersburg*

Naval Aviation 98,600
10 air wg. Average air wing comprises 8 sqns: 4 with F/A-18; 1 with MH-60R; 1 with EA-18G; 1 with E-2C/D; 1 with MH-60S

FORCES BY ROLE
FIGHTER/GROUND ATTACK
  22 sqn with F/A-18E *Super Hornet*
  11 sqn with F/A-18F *Super Hornet*
  1 sqn with F-35C *Lightning* II
ANTI-SUBMARINE WARFARE
  11 sqn with MH-60R *Seahawk*
  3 ASW/ISR sqn with MH-60R *Seahawk*; MQ-8B *Fire Scout*
ELINT
  1 sqn with EP-3E *Aries* II
ELINT/ELECTRONIC WARFARE
  13 sqn with EA-18G *Growler*
MARITIME PATROL
  11 sqn with P-8A *Poseidon*
  1 sqn (forming) with P-8A *Poseidon*
AIRBORNE EARLY WARNING & CONTROL
  6 sqn with E-2C *Hawkeye*
  3 sqn with E-2D *Hawkeye*
COMMAND & CONTROL
  2 sqn with E-6B *Mercury*
MINE COUNTERMEASURES
  2 sqn with MH-53E *Sea Dragon*
TRANSPORT
  2 sqn with C-2A *Greyhound*
TRAINING
  1 (FRS) sqn with EA-18G *Growler*
  1 (FRS) sqn with C-2A *Greyhound*; E-2C/D *Hawkeye*; TE-2C *Hawkeye*
  1 sqn with E-6B *Mercury*
  2 (FRS) sqn with F/A-18C/D *Hornet*; F/A-18E/F *Super Hornet*
  1 (FRS) sqn with F-35C *Lightning* II
  1 (FRS) sqn with MH-53 *Sea Dragon*
  2 (FRS) sqn with MH-60S *Knight Hawk*; HH-60H *Seahawk*
  2 (FRS) sqn with MH-60R *Seahawk*
  1 sqn with P-3C *Orion*
  1 (FRS) sqn with P-3C *Orion*; P-8A *Poseidon*
  6 sqn with T-6A/B *Texan* II
  2 sqn with T-44C *Pegasus*
  5 sqn with T-45C *Goshawk*
  3 hel sqn with TH-57B/C *Sea Ranger*
  1 (FRS) UAV sqn with MQ-8B *Fire Scout*; MQ-8C *Fire Scout*
TRANSPORT HELICOPTER
  14 sqn with MH-60S *Knight Hawk*
  1 tpt hel/ISR sqn with MH-60S *Knight Hawk*; MQ-8B *Fire Scout*
ISR UAV
  1 sqn with MQ-4C *Triton*

EQUIPMENT BY TYPE
AIRCRAFT 981 combat capable
  FGA 716: 28 F-35C *Lightning* II; 10 F-16A *Fighting Falcon*; 4 F-16B *Fighting Falcon*; 5 F/A-18B *Hornet*; 60 F/A-18C *Hornet*; 25 F/A-18D *Hornet*; 310 F/A-18E *Super Hornet*; 274 F/A-18F *Super Hornet*
  ASW 107: 20 P-3C *Orion*; 87 P-8A *Poseidon*
  EW 158 EA-18G *Growler**
  ELINT 9 EP-3E *Aries* II
  AEW&C 82: 50 E-2C *Hawkeye*; 32 E-2D *Hawkeye*
  C2 16 E-6B *Mercury*
  TKR 3: 1 KC-130R *Hercules*; 1 KC-130T *Hercules*; 1 KC-130J *Hercules*
  TPT • Light 60: 4 Beech A200 *King Air* (C-12C *Huron*); 6 Beech A200 *King Air* (UC-12F *Huron*); 8 Beech A200 *King Air* (UC-12M *Huron*); 33 C-2A *Greyhound*; 2 DHC-2 *Beaver* (U-6A); 7 SA-227-BC *Metro* III (C-26D)
  TRG 581: 44 T-6A *Texan* II; 232 T-6B *Texan* II; 7 T-38C *Talon*; 55 T-44C *Pegasus*; 241 T-45C *Goshawk*; 2 TE-2C *Hawkeye*
HELICOPTERS
  ASW 269 MH-60R *Seahawk*
  MRH 260 MH-60S *Knight Hawk* (Multi Mission Support)
  MCM 28 MH-53E *Sea Dragon*
  ISR 3 OH-58C *Kiowa*
  TPT 13: **Heavy** 2 CH-53E *Sea Stallion*; **Medium** 3 UH-60L *Black Hawk*; **Light** 8: 5 UH-72A *Lakota*; 2 UH-1N *Iroquois*; 1 UH-1Y *Venom*
  TRG 119: 43 TH-57B *Sea Ranger*; 76 TH-57C *Sea Ranger*
UNMANNED AERIAL VEHICLES • ISR 106
  Heavy 56: 3 MQ-4C *Triton*; 20 MQ-8B *Fire Scout*; 29 MQ-8C *Fire Scout*; 4 RQ-4A *Global Hawk* (under evaluation

and trials); **Medium** 35 RQ-2B *Pioneer*; **Light** 15 RQ-21A *Blackjack*

AIR-LAUNCHED MISSILES
AAM • IR AIM-9M *Sidewinder*; **IIR** AIM-9X *Sidewinder* II; **SARH** AIM-7 *Sparrow* (being withdrawn); **ARH** AIM-120C-5/C-7/D AMRAAM
ASM AGM-65F *Maverick*; AGM-114B/K/M *Hellfire*; APKWS
AShM AGM-84D *Harpoon*; AGM-119A *Penguin* 3
ARM AGM-88B/C/E HARM/AARGM
ALCM • Conventional AGM-84E/H/K SLAM/SLAM-ER
BOMBS
Laser-guided: GBU-10/12/16 *Paveway* II; GBU-24 *Paveway* III
INS/GPS guided: GBU-31/32/38 JDAM; Enhanced *Paveway* II; GBU-54 Laser JDAM; AGM-154A/C/C-1 JSOW

Naval Aviation Reserve
FORCES BY ROLE
FIGHTER/GROUND ATTACK
 1 sqn with F/A-18C/D *Hornet*
ANTI-SUBMARINE WARFARE
 1 sqn with MH-60R *Seahawk*
ELECTRONIC WARFARE
 1 sqn with EA-18G *Growler*
MARITIME PATROL
 2 sqn with P-3C *Orion*
TRANSPORT
 6 log spt sqn with B-737-700 (C-40A *Clipper*)
 1 log spt sqn with Gulfstream IV (C-20G); Gulfstream V/G550 (C-37A/B)
 4 sqn with C-130T *Hercules*
 1 sqn with KC-130T *Hercules*
TRAINING
 2 (aggressor) sqn with F-5F/N *Tiger* II
 1 (aggressor) sqn with F/A-18C/D *Hornet*
TRANSPORT HELICOPTER
 1 sqn with MH-60S *Knight Hawk*
EQUIPMENT BY TYPE
AIRCRAFT 83 combat capable
 FTR 31: 2 F-5F *Tiger* II; 29 F-5N *Tiger* II
 FGA 35: 30 F/A-18C *Hornet*; 5 F/A-18D *Hornet*
 ASW 12 P-3C *Orion*
 EW 5 EA-18G *Growler**
 TKR 5 KC-130T *Hercules*
 TPT 40: **Medium** 18 C-130T *Hercules*; **PAX** 22: 17 B-737-700 (C-40A *Clipper*); 1 Gulfstream IV (C-20G); 1 Gulfstream V (C-37A); 3 Gulfstream G550 (C-37B)
HELICOPTERS
 ASW 7 MH-60R *Seahawk*
 MRH 11 MH-60S *Knight Hawk*
 MCM 7 MH-53E *Sea Dragon*

US Marine Corps 186,300
3 Marine Expeditionary Forces (MEF), 3 Marine Expeditionary Brigades (MEB), 7 Marine Expeditionary Units (MEU) drawn from 3 div. An MEU usually consists of a battalion landing team (1 SF coy, 1 lt armd recce coy, 1 recce pl, 1 armd pl, 1 amph aslt pl, 1 inf bn, 1 arty bty, 1 cbt engr pl), an aviation combat element (1 medium-lift sqn with attached atk hel, FGA ac and AD assets) and a composite log bn, with a combined total of about 2,200 personnel. Composition varies with mission requirements

FORCES BY ROLE
SPECIAL FORCES
 (see USSOCOM)
MANOEUVRE
 Reconnaissance
 3 (MEF) recce coy
 Amphibious
 1 (1st) mne div (2 armd recce bn, 1 recce bn, 1 tk bn, 2 mne regt (4 mne bn), 1 mne regt (3 mne bn), 1 amph aslt bn, 1 arty regt (3 arty bn, 1 MRL bn), 1 cbt engr bn, 1 EW bn, 1 int bn, 1 sigs bn)
 1 (2nd) mne div (1 armd recce bn, 1 recce bn, 1 tk bn, 3 mne regt (3 mne bn), 1 amph aslt bn, 1 arty regt (2 arty bn), 1 cbt engr bn, 1 EW bn, 1 int bn, 1 sigs bn)
 1 (3rd) mne div (1 recce bn, 1 inf regt (3 inf bn), 1 arty regt (2 arty bn), 1 cbt spt bn (1 armd recce coy, 1 amph aslt coy, 1 cbt engr coy), 1 EW bn, 1 int bn, 1 sigs bn)
COMBAT SERVICE SUPPORT
 3 log gp
EQUIPMENT BY TYPE
ARMOURED FIGHTING VEHICLES
 MBT 447 M1A1 *Abrams*
 IFV 488 LAV-25
 APC • APC (W) 207 LAV variants (66 CP; 127 log; 14 EW)
 AAV 1,200 AAV-7A1 (all roles)
 AUV 2,579+: 1,725 *Cougar*; 150+ JLTV; 704 M-ATV
ENGINEERING & MAINTENANCE VEHICLES
 AEV 42 M1 ABV
 ARV 185: 60 AAVRA1; 45 LAV-R; 80 M88A1/2
 MW 38 *Buffalo*; some *Husky* 2G
 VLB 6 Joint Aslt Bridge
ANTI-TANK/ANTI-INFRASTRUCTURE • MSL
 SP 106 LAV-AT
 MANPATS FGM-148 *Javelin*; FGM-172B SRAW-MPV; TOW
ARTILLERY 1,452
 TOWED 812: **105mm**: 331 M101A1; **155mm** 481 M777A2
 MRL 227mm 40 M142 HIMARS
 MOR 600: **81mm** 535 M252; **SP 81mm** 65 LAV-M; **120mm** (49 EFSS in store for trg)
UNMANNED AERIAL VEHCILES
 ISR • Light 100 BQM-147 *Exdrone*
AIR DEFENCE • SAM • Point-defence FIM-92 *Stinger*

Marine Corps Aviation 34,700
3 active Marine Aircraft Wings (MAW) and 1 MCR MAW
FORCES BY ROLE
FIGHTER
 1 sqn with F/A-18A++/C/C+ *Hornet*
 4 sqn with F/A-18C *Hornet*
 4 sqn with F/A-18D *Hornet*
FIGHTER/GROUND ATTACK
 5 sqn with AV-8B *Harrier* II

3 sqn with F-35B *Lightning* II
1 sqn with F-35C *Lightning* II (forming)
COMBAT SEARCH & RESCUE/TRANSPORT
1 sqn with Beech A200/B200 *King Air* (UC-12F/M *Huron)*; Beech 350 *King Air* (UC-12W *Huron*); Cessna 560 *Citation Ultra/Encore* (UC-35C/D); DC-9 *Skytrain* (C-9B *Nightingale*); Gulfstream IV (C-20G); HH-1N *Iroquois*
TANKER
3 sqn with KC-130J *Hercules*
TRANSPORT
14 sqn with MV-22B *Osprey*
2 sqn (forming) with MV-22B *Osprey*
TRAINING
1 sqn with AV-8B *Harrier* II; TAV-8B *Harrier*
1 sqn with F/A-18B/C/D *Hornet*
1 sqn with F-35B *Lightning* II
1 sqn with MV-22B *Osprey*
1 hel sqn with AH-1W *Cobra*; AH-1Z *Viper*; HH-1N *Iroquois*; UH-1Y *Venom*
1 hel sqn with CH-53E *Sea Stallion*
ATTACK HELICOPTER
1 sqn with AH-1W *Cobra*; UH-1Y *Venom*
6 sqn with AH-1Z *Viper*; UH-1Y *Venom*
TRANSPORT HELICOPTER
8 sqn with CH-53E *Sea Stallion*
1 (VIP) sqn with MV-22B *Osprey*; VH-3D *Sea King*; VH-60N *Presidential Hawk*
ISR UAV
3 sqn with RQ-21A *Blackjack*
AIR DEFENCE
2 bn with M1097 *Avenger*; FIM-92 *Stinger* (can provide additional heavy-calibre support weapons)
EQUIPMENT BY TYPE
AIRCRAFT 432 combat capable
  FGA 432: 80 F-35B *Lightning* II; 3 F-35C *Lightning* II; 16 F/A-18A++ *Hornet*; 7 F/A-18B *Hornet*; 107 F/A-18C *Hornet*; 2 F/A-18C+ *Hornet*; 92 F/A-18D *Hornet*; 109 AV-8B *Harrier* II; 16 TAV-8B *Harrier*
  TKR 45 KC-130J *Hercules*
  TPT 19: **Light** 16: 5 Beech A200/B200 *King Air* (UC-12F/M *Huron*); 5 Beech 350 *King Air* (C-12W *Huron*); 6 Cessna 560 *Citation Encore* (UC-35D); **PAX** 3: 2 DC-9 *Skytrain* (C-9B *Nightingale*); 1 Gulfstream IV (C-20G)
  TRG 3 T-34C *Turbo Mentor*
TILTROTOR • TPT 309 MV-22B *Osprey*
HELICOPTERS
  ATK 145: 20 AH-1W *Cobra*; 125 AH-1Z *Viper*
  SAR 4 HH-1N *Iroquois*
  TPT 286: **Heavy** 139: 138 CH-53E *Sea Stallion*; 1 CH-53K *King Stallion*; **Medium** 19: 8 VH-60N *Presidential Hawk* (VIP tpt); 11 VH-3D *Sea King* (VIP tpt); **Light** 128 UH-1Y *Venom*
UNMANNED AERIAL VEHICLES
  ISR • Light 80 RQ-21A *Blackjack*
AIR DEFENCE
  SAM • Point-defence FIM-92 *Stinger*; M1097 *Avenger*
AIR-LAUNCHED MISSILES
  AAM • IR AIM-9M *Sidewinder*; **IIR** AIM-9X *Sidewinder* II; **SARH** AIM-7P *Sparrow*; **ARH** AIM-120C AMRAAM
  ASM AGM-65E/F IR *Maverick*; AGM-114 *Hellfire*; AGM-176 *Griffin*; APKWS
  AShM AGM-84D *Harpoon*
  ARM AGM-88 HARM
  LACM AGM-84E/H/K SLAM/SLAM-ER
BOMBS
  Laser-guided GBU-10/12/16 *Paveway* II
  INS/GPS guided GBU-31 JDAM; AGM-154A/C/C-1 JSOW

Reserve Organisations

Marine Corps Reserve 39,000
FORCES BY ROLE
MANOEUVRE
  Reconnaissance
  2 MEF recce coy
  Amphibious
  1 (4th) mne div (1 armd recce bn, 1 recce bn, 2 mne regt (3 mne bn), 1 amph aslt bn, 1 arty regt (2 arty bn, 1 MRL bn), 1 cbt engr bn, 1 int bn, 1 sigs bn)
COMBAT SERVICE SUPPORT
  1 log gp

Marine Corps Aviation Reserve 12,000 reservists
FORCES BY ROLE
FIGHTER
  1 sqn with F/A-18A++ *Hornet*
TANKER
  1 sqn with KC-130J *Hercules*
  1 sqn with KC-130T *Hercules*
TRANSPORT
  2 sqn with MV-22B *Osprey*
TRAINING
  1 sqn with F-5F/N *Tiger* II
ATTACK HELICOPTER
  2 sqn with AH-1W *Cobra*; UH-1Y *Venom*
TRANSPORT HELICOPTER
  1 sqn with CH-53E *Sea Stallion*
ISR UAV
  1 sqn with RQ-21A *Blackjack*
EQUIPMENT BY TYPE
AIRCRAFT 27 combat capable
  FTR 12: 1 F-5F *Tiger* II; 11 F-5N *Tiger* II
  FGA 15 F/A-18A++ *Hornet*
  TKR 21: 9 KC-130J *Hercules*; 12 KC-130T *Hercules*
  TPT • Light 8: 2 Beech 350 *King Air* (UC-12W *Huron*); 2 Cessna 560 *Citation Ultra* (UC-35C); 4 Cessna 560 *Citation Encore* (UC-35D)
TILTROTOR • TPT 24 MV-22B *Osprey*
HELICOPTERS
  ATK 30 AH-1W *Cobra*
  TPT 29: **Heavy** 7 CH-53E *Sea Stallion*; **Light** 22 UH-1Y *Venom*
UNMANNED AERIAL VEHICLES
  ISR • Light 20 RQ-21A *Blackjack*

Marine Stand-by Reserve 700 reservists
Trained individuals available for mobilisation

US Coast Guard 42,000
9 districts (4 Pacific, 5 Atlantic)
EQUIPMENT BY TYPE
PATROL AND COASTAL COMBATANTS 340
  PSOH 25: 1 *Alex Haley*; 13 *Famous*; 3 *Hamilton*; 8 *Legend* with 1 Mk 15 *Phalanx* Block 1B CIWS, 1 57mm gun (capacity 2 MH-65 hel)
  PCO 48: 14 *Reliance* (with 1 hel landing platform); 34 *Sentinel* (Damen 4708)
  PCC 20 *Island*
  PBF 174 *Response Boat-Medium* (RB-M)
  PBI 73 *Marine Protector*
LOGISTICS AND SUPPORT 65
  ABU 52: 16 *Juniper*; 4 WLI; 14 *Keeper*; 18 WLR
  AGB 12: 9 *Bay*; 1 *Mackinaw*; 1 *Healy*; 1 *Polar* (1 *Polar* in reserve)
  AXS 1 *Eagle*

US Coast Guard Aviation
EQUIPMENT BY TYPE
AIRCRAFT
  SAR 20: 11 HC-130H *Hercules*; 9 HC-130J *Hercules*
  TPT 34: **Medium** 14 C-27J *Spartan*; **Light** 18 CN235-200 (HC-144A – MP role); **PAX** 2 Gulfstream V (C-37A)
HELICOPTERS
  SAR 146: 44 MH-60T *Jayhawk*; 102 AS366G1 (MH-65C/D) *Dauphin* II

US Air Force (USAF) 332,650
Almost the entire USAF (plus active-force ANG and AFR) is divided into 10 Aerospace Expeditionary Forces (AEF), each on call for 120 days every 20 months. At least 2 of the 10 AEFs are on call at any one time, each with 10,000–15,000 personnel, 90 multi-role ftr and bbr ac, 31 intra-theatre refuelling aircraft and 13 aircraft for ISR and EW missions

Global Strike Command (GSC)
2 active air forces (8th & 20th); 8 wg
FORCES BY ROLE
SURFACE-TO-SURFACE MISSILE
  9 ICBM sqn with LGM-30G *Minuteman* III
BOMBER
  4 sqn with B-1B *Lancer*
  2 sqn with B-2A *Spirit*
  5 sqn (incl 1 trg) with B-52H *Stratofortress*
COMMAND & CONTROL
  1 sqn with E-4B
TRANSPORT HELICOPTER
  3 sqn with UH-1N *Iroquois*

Air Combat Command (ACC)
2 active air forces (9th & 12th); 12 wg. ACC numbered air forces provide the air component to CENTCOM, SOUTHCOM and NORTHCOM
FORCES BY ROLE
FIGHTER
  3 sqn with F-22A *Raptor*
FIGHTER/GROUND ATTACK
  4 sqn with F-15E *Strike Eagle*
  3 sqn with F-16C/D *Fighting Falcon* (+6 sqn personnel only)
  3 sqn with F-35A *Lightning* II
GROUND ATTACK
  3 sqn with A-10C *Thunderbolt* II (+1 sqn personnel only)
ELECTRONIC WARFARE
  1 sqn with EA-18G *Growler* (personnel only – USN aircraft)
  2 sqn with EC-130H *Compass Call*
ISR
  2 sqn with E-8C J-STARS (personnel only)
  5 sqn with OC-135/RC-135/WC-135
  2 sqn with U-2S
AIRBORNE EARLY WARNING & CONTROL
  5 sqn with E-3B/C/G *Sentry*
COMBAT SEARCH & RESCUE
  2 sqn with HC-130J *Combat King* II
  2 sqn with HH-60G *Pave Hawk*
TRAINING
  1 sqn with A-10C *Thunderbolt* II
  1 sqn with E-3B/C *Sentry*
  2 sqn with F-15E *Strike Eagle*
  1 sqn with F-22A *Raptor*
  1 sqn with RQ-4A *Global Hawk*; TU-2S
  1 UAV sqn with MQ-9A *Reaper*
COMBAT/ISR UAV
  9 sqn with MQ-9A *Reaper*
ISR UAV
  2 sqn with EQ-4B/RQ-4B *Global Hawk*
  2 sqn with RQ-170 *Sentinel*
  1 sqn with RQ-180

Pacific Air Forces (PACAF)
Provides the air component of PACOM, and commands air units based in Alaska, Hawaii, Japan and South Korea. 3 active air forces (5th, 7th, & 11th); 8 wg
FORCES BY ROLE
FIGHTER
  2 sqn with F-15C/D *Eagle*
  2 sqn with F-22A *Raptor* (+1 sqn personnel only)
FIGHTER/GROUND ATTACK
  5 sqn with F-16C/D *Fighting Falcon*
  1 sqn with F-35A *Lightning* II (forming)
GROUND ATTACK
  1 sqn with A-10C *Thunderbolt* II
AIRBORNE EARLY WARNING & CONTROL
  2 sqn with E-3B/C *Sentry*
COMBAT SEARCH & RESCUE
  1 sqn with HH-60G *Pave Hawk*
TANKER
  1 sqn with KC-135R (+1 sqn personnel only)
TRANSPORT
  1 sqn with B-737-200 (C-40B); Gulfstream V (C-37A)
  2 sqn with C-17A *Globemaster*
  1 sqn with C-130J-30 *Hercules*
  1 sqn with Beech 1900C (C-12J); UH-1N *Huey*
TRAINING
  1 (aggressor) sqn with F-16C/D *Fighting Falcon*

United States Air Forces Europe (USAFE)
Provides the air component to both EUCOM and AFRICOM. 1 active air force (3rd); 5 wg
FORCES BY ROLE
FIGHTER
   1 sqn with F-15C/D *Eagle*
FIGHTER/GROUND ATTACK
   2 sqn with F-15E *Strike Eagle*
   3 sqn with F-16C/D *Fighting Falcon*
COMBAT SEARCH & RESCUE
   1 sqn with HH-60G *Pave Hawk*
TANKER
   1 sqn with KC-135R *Stratotanker*
TRANSPORT
   1 sqn with C-130J-30 *Hercules*
   2 sqn with Gulfstream V (C-37A); Learjet 35A (C-21A); B-737-700 (C-40B)

Air Mobility Command (AMC)
Provides strategic and tactical airlift, air-to-air refuelling and aeromedical evacuation. 1 active air force (18th); 12 wg and 1 gp
FORCES BY ROLE
TANKER
   4 sqn with KC-10A *Extender*
   1 sqn with KC-46A *Pegasus* (forming)
   8 sqn with KC-135R/T *Stratotanker* (+2 sqn with personnel only)
TRANSPORT
   1 VIP sqn with B-737-200 (C-40B); B-757-200 (C-32A)
   1 VIP sqn with Gulfstream V (C-37A)
   1 VIP sqn with VC-25 *Air Force One*
   2 sqn with C-5M *Super Galaxy*
   8 sqn with C-17A *Globemaster* III (+1 sqn personnel only)
   5 sqn with C-130J-30 *Hercules* (+1 sqn personnel only)
   1 sqn with Learjet 35A (C-21A)

Air Education and Training Command
1 active air force (2nd), 10 active air wg and 1 gp
FORCES BY ROLE
TRAINING
   1 sqn with C-17A *Globemaster* III
   1 sqn with C-130J-30 *Hercules*
   4 sqn with F-16C/D *Fighting Falcon*
   4 sqn with F-35A *Lightning* II
   1 sqn with KC-46A *Pegasus* (forming)
   1 sqn with KC-135R *Stratotanker*
   5 (flying trg) sqn with T-1A *Jayhawk*
   10 (flying trg) sqn with T-6A *Texan* II
   10 (flying trg) sqn with T-38C *Talon*
   5 UAV sqn with MQ-9A *Reaper*
EQUIPMENT BY TYPE
SURFACE-TO-SURFACE MISSILE LAUNCHERS
   ICBM • Nuclear 400 LGM-30G *Minuteman* III (1 Mk12A or Mk21 re-entry veh per missile)
AIRCRAFT 1,522 combat capable
   BBR 139: 61 B-1B *Lancer*; 20 B-2A *Spirit*; 58 B-52H *Stratofortress* (46 nuclear capable)
   FTR 271: 95 F-15C *Eagle*; 10 F-15D *Eagle*; 166 F-22A *Raptor*
   FGA 969: 211 F-15E *Strike Eagle*; 442 F-16C *Fighting Falcon*; 111 F-16D *Fighting Falcon*; 205 F-35A *Lightning* II
   ATK 143 A-10C *Thunderbolt* II
   EW 13 EC-130H *Compass Call*
   ISR 40: 2 E-9A; 4 E-11A; 2 OC-135B *Open Skies*; 26 U-2S; 4 TU-2S; 2 WC-135 *Constant Phoenix*
   ELINT 22: 8 RC-135V *Rivet Joint*; 9 RC-135W *Rivet Joint*; 3 RC-135S *Cobra Ball*; 2 RC-135U *Combat Sent*
   AEW&C 31: 11 E-3B *Sentry*; 3 E-3C *Sentry*; 17 E-3G *Sentry*
   C2 4 E-4B
   TKR 178: 22 KC-46A *Pegasus*; 126 KC-135R *Stratotanker*; 30 KC-135T *Stratotanker*
   TKR/TPT 59 KC-10A *Extender*
   CSAR 15 HC-130J *Combat King* II
   TPT 331: **Heavy** 182: 36 C-5M *Super Galaxy*; 146 C-17A *Globemaster* III; **Medium** 104 C-130J/J-30 *Hercules*; **Light** 23: 4 Beech 1900C (C-12J); 19 Learjet 35A (C-21A); **PAX** 22: 4 B-737-700 (C-40B); 4 B-757-200 (C-32A); 12 Gulfstream V (C-37A); 2 VC-25A *Air Force One*
   TRG 1,126: 178 T-1A *Jayhawk*; 443 T-6A *Texan* II; 505 T-38A/C *Talon*
HELICOPTERS
   CSAR 74 HH-60G *Pave Hawk*
   TPT • Light 62 UH-1N *Huey*
UNMANNED AERIAL VEHICLES 251
   CISR • Heavy 221 MQ-9A *Reaper*
   ISR • Heavy 51: 3 EQ-4B; 31 RQ-4B *Global Hawk*; ε10 RQ-170 *Sentinel*; ε7 RQ-180
AIR DEFENCE
   SAM • Point-defence FIM-92 *Stinger*
AIR-LAUNCHED MISSILES
   AAM • IR AIM-9M *Sidewinder*; **IIR** AIM-9X *Sidewinder* II; **SARH** AIM-7M *Sparrow*; **ARH** AIM-120C/D AMRAAM
   ASM AGM-65D/G *Maverick*; AGM-114 *Hellfire*; AGM-130A; AGM-176 *Griffin*; APKWS
   ALCM
      Nuclear AGM-86B (ALCM)
      Conventional AGM-86C (being withdrawn); AGM-86D (being withdrawn); AGM-158A JASSM; AGM-158B JASSM-ER
   ARM AGM-88B/C HARM
   EW MALD/MALD-J
BOMBS
   Laser-guided GBU 10/12/16 *Paveway* II, GBU-24 *Paveway* III; GBU-28
   INS/GPS guided GBU 31/32/38 JDAM; GBU-54 Laser JDAM; GBU-15 (with BLU-109 penetrating warhead or Mk84); GBU-39B Small Diameter Bomb (250lb); GBU 43B MOAB; GBU-57A/B MOP; Enhanced *Paveway* III

Reserve Organisations

Air National Guard 106,750 reservists
FORCES BY ROLE
BOMBER
   1 sqn with B-2A *Spirit* (personnel only)
FIGHTER
   5 sqn with F-15C/D *Eagle*
   1 sqn with F-22A *Raptor* (+1 sqn personnel only)

FIGHTER/GROUND ATTACK
  10 sqn with F-16C/D *Fighting Falcon*
  1 sqn with F-35A *Lightning* II (forming)
GROUND ATTACK
  4 sqn with A-10C *Thunderbolt* II
ISR
  1 sqn with E-8C J-STARS
COMBAT SEARCH & RESCUE
  1 sqn with HC-130P/N/J *Combat King/Combat King* II
  2 sqn with HC-130J *Combat King* II
  3 sqn with HH-60G *Pave Hawk*
TANKER
  1 sqn with KC-46A *Pegasus* (forming)
  16 sqn with KC-135R *Stratotanker* (+1 sqn personnel only)
  3 sqn with KC-135T *Stratotanker*
TRANSPORT
  1 sqn with B-737-700 (C-40C)
  6 sqn with C-17A *Globemaster* (+2 sqn personnel only)
  12 sqn with C-130H *Hercules*
  1 sqn with C-130H/LC-130H *Hercules*
  2 sqn with C-130J-30 *Hercules*
TRAINING
  1 sqn with C-130H *Hercules*
  1 sqn with F-15C/D *Eagle*
  4 sqn with F-16C/D *Fighting Falcon*
  1 sqn with MQ-9A *Reaper*
COMBAT/ISR UAV
  11 sqn with MQ-9A *Reaper*
EQUIPMENT BY TYPE
AIRCRAFT 576 combat capable
  FTR 157: 123 F-15C *Eagle*; 14 F-15D *Eagle*; 20 F-22A *Raptor*
  FGA 334: 288 F-16C *Fighting Falcon*; 44 F-16D *Fighting Falcon*; 2 F-35A *Lightning* II
  ATK 85 A-10C *Thunderbolt* II
  ISR 13 E-8C J-STARS
  ELINT 11 RC-26B *Metroliner*
  CSAR 14: 2 HC-130N *Combat King*; 3 HC-130P *Combat King*; 9 HC-130J *Combat King* II
  TKR 174: 2 KC-46A *Pegasus*; 148 KC-135R *Stratotanker*; 24 KC-135T *Stratotanker*
  TPT 206: **Heavy** 50 C-17A *Globemaster* III; **Medium** 153: 123 C-130H *Hercules*; 20 C-130J/J-30 *Hercules*; 10 LC-130H *Hercules*; **PAX** 3 B-737-700 (C-40C)
HELICOPTERS • **CSAR** 18 HH-60G *Pave Hawk*
UNMANNED AERIAL VEHICLES • **CISR** • **Heavy** 24 MQ-9A *Reaper*

Air Force Reserve Command 69,250 reservists
FORCES BY ROLE
BOMBER
  1 sqn with B-52H *Stratofortress* (personnel only)
FIGHTER
  2 sqn with F-22A *Raptor* (personnel only)
FIGHTER/GROUND ATTACK
  2 sqn with F-16C/D *Fighting Falcon* (+1 sqn personnel only)
  1 sqn with F-35A *Lightning* II (personnel only)
GROUND ATTACK
  1 sqn with A-10C *Thunderbolt* II (+2 sqn personnel only)
ISR
  1 (Weather Recce) sqn with WC-130J *Hercules*
AIRBORNE EARLY WARNING & CONTROL
  1 sqn with E-3B/C *Sentry* (personnel only)
COMBAT SEARCH & RESCUE
  1 sqn with HC-130N *Combat King*
  2 sqn with HH-60G *Pave Hawk*
TANKER
  4 sqn with KC-10A *Extender* (personnel only)
  1 sqn with KC-46A *Pegasus* (personnel only)
  7 sqn with KC-135R *Stratotanker* (+2 sqn personnel only)
TRANSPORT
  1 (VIP) sqn with B-737-700 (C-40C)
  2 sqn with C-5M *Super Galaxy* (+2 sqn personnel only)
  3 sqn with C-17A *Globemaster* (+9 sqn personnel only)
  6 sqn with C-130H *Hercules*
  1 sqn with C-130J-30 *Hercules*
  1 (Aerial Spray) sqn with C-130H *Hercules*
TRAINING
  1 (aggressor) sqn with A-10C *Thunderbolt* II; F-15C/E *Eagle*; F-16 *Fighting Falcon*; F-22A *Raptor* (personnel only)
  1 sqn with A-10C *Thunderbolt* II
  1 sqn with B-52H *Stratofortress*
  1 sqn with C-5M *Super Galaxy*
  1 sqn with F-16C/D *Fighting Falcon*
  5 (flying training) sqn with T-1A *Jayhawk*; T-6A *Texan* II; T-38C *Talon* (personnel only)
COMBAT/ISR UAV
  2 sqn with MQ-9A *Reaper* (personnel only)
ISR UAV
  1 sqn with RQ-4B *Global Hawk* (personnel only)
EQUIPMENT BY TYPE
AIRCRAFT 126 combat capable
  BBR 18 B-52H *Stratofortress*
  FGA 53: 49 F-16C *Fighting Falcon*; 4 F-16D *Fighting Falcon*
  ATK 55 A-10C *Thunderbolt* II
  ISR 10 WC-130J *Hercules* (Weather Recce)
  CSAR 6 HC-130N *Combat King*
  TKR 70 KC-135R *Stratotanker*
  TPT 104: **Heavy** 42: 16 C-5M *Super Galaxy*; 26 C-17A *Globemaster* III; **Medium** 58: 48 C-130H *Hercules*; 10 C-130J-30 *Hercules*; **PAX** 4 B-737-700 (C-40C)
HELICOPTERS • **CSAR** 16 HH-60G *Pave Hawk*

Civil Reserve Air Fleet
Commercial ac numbers fluctuate
AIRCRAFT • **TPT** 517 international (391 long-range and 126 short-range); 36 national

Air Force Stand-by Reserve 16,858 reservists
Trained individuals for mobilisation

US Special Operations Command (USSOCOM) 63,150; 6,550 (civilian)

Commands all active, reserve and National Guard Special Operations Forces (SOF) of all services based in CONUS

Joint Special Operations Command

Reported to comprise elite US SOF, including Special Forces Operations Detachment Delta ('Delta Force'), SEAL Team 6 and integral USAF support

US Army Special Operations Command 34,100

FORCES BY ROLE
SPECIAL FORCES
  5 SF gp (4 SF bn, 1 spt bn)
  1 ranger regt (3 ranger bn; 1 cbt spt bn)
COMBAT SUPPORT
  1 civil affairs bde (5 civil affairs bn)
  1 psyops gp (3 psyops bn)
  1 psyops gp (4 psyops bn)
COMBAT SERVICE SUPPORT
  1 (sustainment) log bde (1 sigs bn)
HELICOPTER
  1 (160th SOAR) hel regt (4 hel bn)
EQUIPMENT BY TYPE
ARMOURED FIGHTING VEHICLES
  APC • **APC (W)** 28: 16 M1126 *Stryker* ICV; 12 *Pandur*
  AUV 640 M-ATV
ARTILLERY 20
  MOR • **120mm** 20 XM905 EMTAS
HELICOPTERS
  MRH 51 AH-6M/MH-6M *Little Bird*
  TPT 141: **Heavy** 69 MH-47G *Chinook*; **Medium** 72 MH-60M *Black Hawk*
UAV
  CISR • **Heavy** 12 MQ-1C *Gray Eagle*
  ISR • **Light** 29: 15 XPV-1 *Tern*; 14 XPV-2 *Mako*
  TPT • **Heavy** 28 CQ-10 *Snowgoose*

Reserve Organisations

Army National Guard
FORCES BY ROLE
SPECIAL FORCES
  2 SF gp (3 SF bn)

Army Reserve
FORCES BY ROLE
COMBAT SUPPORT
  2 psyops gp
  4 civil affairs comd HQ
  8 civil affairs bde HQ
  32 civil affairs bn (coy)

US Navy Special Warfare Command 9,850

FORCES BY ROLE
SPECIAL FORCES
  8 SEAL team (total: 48 SF pl)
  2 SEAL Delivery Vehicle team

Reserve Organisations

Naval Reserve Force
FORCES BY ROLE
SPECIAL FORCES
  8 SEAL det
  10 Naval Special Warfare det
  2 Special Boat sqn
  2 Special Boat unit
  1 SEAL Delivery Vehicle det

US Marine Special Operations Command (MARSOC) 3,000

FORCES BY ROLE
SPECIAL FORCES
  1 SF regt (3 SF bn)
COMBAT SUPPORT
  1 int bn
COMBAT SERVICE SUPPORT
  1 spt gp

Air Force Special Operations Command (AFSOC) 16,200

FORCES BY ROLE
GROUND ATTACK
  1 sqn with AC-130J *Ghostrider*
  1 sqn with AC-130U *Spectre*
  1 sqn with AC-130W *Stinger* II
TRANSPORT
  4 sqn with CV-22B *Osprey*
  1 sqn with DHC-8; Do-328 (C-146A)
  2 sqn with MC-130H *Combat Talon*
  3 sqn with MC-130J *Commando* II
  3 sqn with PC-12 (U-28A)
TRAINING
  1 sqn with M-28 *Skytruck* (C-145A)
  1 sqn with CV-22A/B *Osprey*
  1 sqn with HC-130J *Combat King* II; MC-130J *Commando* II
  1 sqn with Bell 205 (TH-1H *Iroquois*)
  1 sqn with HH-60G *Pave Hawk*; UH-1N *Huey*
COMBAT/ISR UAV
  3 sqn with MQ-9 *Reaper*
EQUIPMENT BY TYPE
AIRCRAFT 34 combat capable
  ATK 34: 13 AC-130J *Ghostrider*; 9 AC-130U *Spectre*; 12 AC-130W *Stinger* II
  CSAR 3 HC-130J *Combat King* II
  TPT 102: **Medium** 54: 14 MC-130H *Combat Talon* II; 40 MC-130J *Commando* II; **Light** 48: 9 Do-328 (C-146A); 4 M-28 *Skytruck* (C-145A); 35 PC-12 (U-28A)
TILT-ROTOR 50 CV-22A/B *Osprey*
HELICOPTERS
  CSAR 3 HH-60G *Pave Hawk*
  TPT • **Light** 34: 28 Bell 205 (TH-1H *Iroquois*); 6 UH-1N *Huey*
UNMANNED AERIAL VEHICLES • CISR • **Heavy** 30 MQ-9 *Reaper*

Reserve Organisations

Air National Guard
FORCES BY ROLE
ELECTRONIC WARFARE
    1 sqn with C-130J *Hercules*/EC-130J *Commando Solo*
ISR
    1 sqn with Beech 350ER *King Air* (MC-12W *Liberty*)
TRANSPORT
    1 flt with B-737-200 (C-32B)
EQUIPMENT BY TYPE
AIRCRAFT
    EW 3 EC-130J *Commando Solo*
    ISR 13 Beech 350ER *King Air* (MC-12W *Liberty*)
    TPT 5: **Medium** 3 C-130J *Hercules*; **PAX** 2 B-757-200 (C-32B)

Air Force Reserve
FORCES BY ROLE
TRAINING
    1 sqn with AC-130U *Spectre* (personnel only)
    1 sqn with M-28 *Skytruck* (C-145A) (personnel only)
COMBAT/ISR UAV
    1 sqn with MQ-9 *Reaper* (personnel only)

DEPLOYMENT

AFGHANISTAN: NATO • *Operation Resolute Support* 8,475; 1 div HQ; 2 div HQ (fwd); 1 spec ops bn; 2 inf bde(-); 2 ARNG inf bn; 1 arty bty with M777A2; 1 ARNG MRL bty with M142 HIMARS; 1 EOD bn; 1 (cbt avn) hel bde with AH-64D *Apache*; CH-47F *Chinook*; UH-60M *Black Hawk*; 1 FGA sqn with F-16C *Fighting Falcon*; 1 atk sqn with A-10C *Thunderbolt* II; 1 EW sqn with EC-130H *Compass Call*; 1 ISR unit with RC-12X *Guardrail*; 1 tpt sqn with C-130J-30 *Hercules*; 1 CSAR sqn with HH-60G *Pave Hawk*; 1 CISR UAV sqn with MQ-9A *Reaper*; 1 ISR UAV unit with RQ-21A *Blackjack*
US Central Command • *Operation Freedom's Sentinel* 5,500

ARABIAN SEA: US Central Command • US Navy • 5th Fleet: 2 SSGN; 1 CVN; 2 CGHM; 2 DDGHM; **Combined Maritime Forces** • TF 53: 1 AE; 2 AKE; 1 AOH; 3 AO

ARUBA: US Southern Command • 1 Forward Operating Location

ASCENSION ISLAND: US Strategic Command • 1 detection and tracking radar at Ascension Auxiliary Air Field

AUSTRALIA: US Pacific Command • 1,500; 1 SEWS at Pine Gap; 1 comms facility at Pine Gap; 1 SIGINT stn at Pine Gap; US Strategic Command • 1 detection and tracking radar at Naval Communication Station Harold E Holt

BAHRAIN: US Central Command • 5,000; 1 HQ (5th Fleet); 1 ftr sqn(-) with 5 AV-8VB *Harrier* II; 1 ASW sqn with 5 P-8A *Poseidon*; 2 AD bty with MIM-104E/F *Patriot* PAC-2/-3

BELGIUM: US European Command • 1,050

BRITISH INDIAN OCEAN TERRITORY: US Strategic Command • 300; 1 Spacetrack Optical Tracker at Diego Garcia; 1 ground-based electro-optical deep space surveillance system (GEODSS) at Diego Garcia
US Pacific Command • 1 MPS sqn (MPS-2 with equipment for one MEB) at Diego Garcia with 2 AKRH; 3 AKR; 1 AKEH; 1 ESD; 1 naval air base at Diego Garcia, 1 support facility at Diego Garcia

BULGARIA: US European Command • 150; 1 armd inf coy with M1A2 SEPv2 *Abrams*; M2A3 *Bradley*

CAMEROON: US Africa Command • 300; MQ-1C *Gray Eagle*

CANADA: US Northern Command • 150

CENTRAL AFRICAN REPUBLIC: UN • MINUSCA 8

COLOMBIA: US Southern Command • 50

CUBA: US Southern Command • 1,000 (JTF-GTMO) at Guantánamo Bay

CURACAO: US Southern Command • 1 Forward Operating Location

DEMOCRATIC REPUBLIC OF THE CONGO: UN • MONUSCO 3

DJIBOUTI: US Africa Command • 4,700; 1 tpt sqn with C-130H/J-30 *Hercules*; 1 spec ops sqn with MC-130H/J; PC-12 (U-28A); 1 CSAR sqn with HH-60G *Pave Hawk*; 1 CISR UAV sqn with MQ-9A *Reaper*; 1 naval air base

EGYPT: MFO 454; elm 1 ARNG recce bn; 1 ARNG spt bn

EL SALVADOR: US Southern Command • 1 Forward Operating Location (Military, DEA, USCG and Customs personnel)

GERMANY: US Africa Command • 1 HQ at Stuttgart
US European Command • 38,750; 1 Combined Service HQ (EUCOM) at Stuttgart–Vaihingen
    US Army 23,750
    FORCES BY ROLE
        1 HQ (US Army Europe (USAREUR)) at Wiesbaden; 1 SF gp; 1 recce bn; 2 armd bn; 1 mech bde(-); 1 MRL bde (1 MRL bn); 1 fd arty bn; 1 (cbt avn) hel bde(-); 1 (cbt avn) hel bde HQ; 1 int bde; 1 MP bde; 1 sigs bde; 1 spt bde; 1 ARNG SAM bde(-); 1 (APS) armd bde eqpt set
    EQUIPMENT BY TYPE
        M1A2 SEPv2 *Abrams*; M2A3/M3A3 *Bradley*; M1296 *Stryker Dragoon*, M109A6; M777A2; AH-64D *Apache*; CH-47F *Chinook*; UH-60M *Black Hawk*; HH-60M *Black Hawk*
    US Navy 400
    USAF 13,150
    FORCES BY ROLE
        1 HQ (US Air Force Europe (USAFE)) at Ramstein AB; 1 HQ (3rd Air Force) at Ramstein AB; 1 ftr wg at Spangdahlem AB with 1 ftr sqn with 24 F-16C/D *Fighting Falcon*; 1 tpt wg at Ramstein AB with 14 C-130J-30 *Hercules*; 2 Gulfstream V (C-37A); 5 Learjet 35A (C-21A); 1 B-737-700 (C-40B)
    USMC 1,350

GREECE: US European Command • 1,000; 1 hel bn with AH-64D *Apache*; UH-60M *Black Hawk*; HH-60M *Black*

Hawk; 1 naval base at Makri; 1 naval base at Souda Bay; 1 air base at Iraklion

GREENLAND (DNK): US Strategic Command • 160; 1 AN/FPS-132 Upgraded Early Warning Radar and 1 Spacetrack Radar at Thule

GUAM: US Pacific Command • 8,150; 4 SSGN; 1 MPS sqn (MPS-3 with equipment for one MEB) with 2 AKRH; 4 AKR; 1 ESD; 1 AKEH; 1 bbr sqn with 6 B-52H *Stratofortress*; 1 tkr sqn with 12 KC-135R *Stratotanker*; 1 tpt hel sqn with MH-60S; 1 SAM bty with THAAD; 1 ISR UAV flt with 2 MQ-4C *Triton*; 1 air base; 1 naval base

HONDURAS: US Southern Command • 450; 1 avn bn with CH-47F *Chinook*; UH-60 *Black Hawk*

HUNGARY: US European Command • 200; 1 armd recce tp; M3A3 *Bradley*

IRAQ: US Central Command • *Operation Inherent Resolve* 6,000; 1 mech inf bde(-); 1 EOD pl; 1 atk hel sqn with AH-64E *Apache*

ISRAEL: US Strategic Command • 1 AN/TPY-2 X-band radar at Mount Keren

ITALY: US European Command • 12,750
US Army 4,200; 1 AB bde(-)
US Navy 4,000; 1 HQ (US Navy Europe (USNAVEUR)) at Naples; 1 HQ (6th Fleet) at Gaeta; 1 MP sqn with 4 P-8A *Poseidon* at Sigonella
USAF 4,350; 1 ftr wg with 2 ftr sqn with 21 F-16C/D *Fighting Falcon* at Aviano; 1 CSAR sqn with 8 HH-60G *Pave Hawk* at Aviano
USMC 200

JAPAN: US Pacific Command • 55,600
US Army 2,650; 1 corps HQ (fwd); 1 SF gp; 1 avn bn; 1 SAM bn
US Navy 20,950; 1 HQ (7th Fleet) at Yokosuka; 1 base at Sasebo; 1 base at Yokosuka

FORCES BY ROLE

3 FGA sqn at Iwakuni with 10 F/A-18E *Super Hornet*; 1 FGA sqn at Iwakuni with 10 F/A-18F *Super Hornet*; 2 EW sqn at Iwakuni/Misawa with 5 EA-18G *Growler*; 1 AEW&C sqn at Iwakuni with 5 E-2D *Hawkeye*; 2 ASW hel sqn at Atsugi with 12 MH-60R; 1 tpt hel sqn at Atsugi with 12 MH-60S

EQUIPMENT BY TYPE

1 CVN; 3 CGHM; 2 DDGHM; 9 DDGM (1 non-op); 1 LCC; 4 MCO; 1 LHD; 1 LPD; 2 LSD
USAF 12,550

FORCES BY ROLE

1 HQ (5th Air Force) at Okinawa – Kadena AB; 1 ftr wg at Misawa AB with (2 ftr sqn with 22 F-16C/D *Fighting Falcon*); 1 wg at Okinawa – Kadena AB with (2 ftr sqn with 27 F-15C/D *Eagle*; 1 ftr sqn with 14 F-22A *Raptor*; 1 tkr sqn with 15 KC-135R *Stratotanker*; 1 AEW&C sqn with 2 E-3B/C *Sentry*; 1 CSAR sqn with 10 HH-60G *Pave Hawk*); 1 tpt wg at Yokota AB with 10 C-130J-30 *Hercules*; 3 Beech 1900C (C-12J); 1 Spec Ops gp at Okinawa – Kadena AB with (1 sqn with 5 MC-130H *Combat Talon*; 1 sqn with 5 MC-130J *Commando*

II; 1 unit with 5 CV-22 *Osprey*); 1 ISR sqn with RC-135 *Rivet Joint*; 1 ISR UAV flt with 5 RQ-4A *Global Hawk*
USMC 19,450

FORCES BY ROLE

1 mne div; 1 mne regt HQ; 1 arty regt HQ; 1 recce bn; 1 mne bn; 1 amph aslt bn; 1 arty bn; 1 FGA sqn with 12 F/A-18C *Hornet*; 1 FGA sqn with 12 F/A-18D *Hornet*; 1 FGA sqn with 12 F-35B *Lightning* II; 1 tkr sqn with 15 KC-130J *Hercules*; 2 tpt sqn with 12 MV-22B *Osprey*

US Strategic Command • 1 AN/TPY-2 X-band radar at Shariki; 1 AN/TPY-2 X-Band radar at Kyogamisaki

JORDAN: US Central Command • *Operation Inherent Resolve* 2,300; 1 FGA sqn with 12 F-15E *Strike Eagle*; 1 CISR UAV sqn with 12 MQ-9A *Reaper*

KOREA, REPUBLIC OF: US Pacific Command • 28,500
US Army 19,200

FORCES BY ROLE

1 HQ (8th Army) at Seoul; 1 div HQ (2nd Inf) located at Tongduchon; 1 armd bde; 1 (cbt avn) hel bde; 1 MRL bde; 1 AD bde; 1 SAM bty with THAAD

EQUIPMENT BY TYPE

M1A2 SEPv2 *Abrams*; M2A2/M3A3 *Bradley*; M109A6; M270A1 MLRS; AH-64D *Apache*; CH-47F *Chinook*; UH-60L/M *Black Hawk*; MIM-104 *Patriot*; FIM-92A *Avenger*; 1 (APS) armd bde eqpt set
US Navy 250
USAF 8,800

FORCES BY ROLE

1 (AF) HQ (7th Air Force) at Osan AB; 1 ftr wg at Osan AB with (1 ftr sqn with 20 F-16C/D *Fighting Falcon*; 1 atk sqn with 24 A-10C *Thunderbolt* II); 1 ftr wg at Kunsan AB with (2 ftr sqn with 20 F-16C/D *Fighting Falcon*); 1 ISR sqn at Osan AB with U-2S
USMC 250

KUWAIT: US Central Command • 13,500; 1 ARNG armd bde(-); 1 USAR (cbt avn) hel bde; 1 spt bde; 1 tpt sqn with 12 MV-22B *Osprey*; 1 CISR UAV sqn with MQ-9A *Reaper*; 3 AD bty with MIM-104E/F *Patriot* PAC-2/-3; 1 (APS) armd bde set; 1 (APS) inf bde set

LIBYA: UN • UNSMIL 1

MALI: UN • MINUSMA 9

MARSHALL ISLANDS: US Strategic Command • 1 detection and tracking radar at Kwajalein Atoll

MEDITERRANEAN SEA: US European Command • US Navy • 6th Fleet: 1 SSGN; 4 DDGM; 1 LCC

MIDDLE EAST: UN • UNTSO 2

NETHERLANDS: US European Command • 400

NIGER: US Africa Command • 800; 1 ISR sqn with MQ-9A *Reaper*

NORWAY: US European Command • 1,400; 1 (USMC) MEU eqpt set; 1 (APS) SP 155mm arty bn set

NORTH SEA: NATO • SNMG1: 1 DDGHM

PERSIAN GULF: US Central Command • US Navy • 5th Fleet: 10 PCFG; 6 (Coast Guard) PCC

Combined Maritime Forces • CTF-152: 4 MCO; 1 ESB

PHILIPPINES: US Pacific Command • *Operation Pacific Eagle - Philippines* 200

POLAND: NATO • Enhanced Forward Presence 857; 1 ARNG armd bn with M1A1 AIM *Abrams*; M2A2 ODS *Bradley*; M109A6

US European Command • 2,000; 1 div HQ (fwd); 1 armd bde HQ; 1 armd cav sqn(-) with M1A2 SEPv2 *Abrams*; M3A3 *Bradley*; 1 SP arty bn with M109A7

PORTUGAL: US European Command • 250; 1 spt facility at Lajes

QATAR: US Central Command • 10,000: 1 ISR sqn with 4 RC-135 *Rivet Joint*; 1 ISR sqn with 4 E-8C JSTARS; 1 tkr sqn with 24 KC-135R/T *Stratotanker*; 1 tpt sqn with 4 C-17A *Globemaster*; 4 C-130H/J-30 *Hercules*; 2 AD bty with MIM-104E/F *Patriot* PAC-2/-3

US Strategic Command • 1 AN/TPY-2 X-band radar

ROMANIA: US European Command • 1,150; 1 armd inf bn HQ; 2 armd/armd inf coy with M1A2 SEPv2 *Abrams*; M2A3 *Bradley*; 1 tpt hel flt with UH-60M *Black Hawk*; 1 CISR UAV sqn with MQ-9A *Reaper*

SAUDI ARABIA: US Central Command • 2,000; 1 ftr sqn with 12 F-22A *Raptor*; 1 EW sqn with 5 EF-18G *Growler*; 1 SAM bty with MIM-104E/F *Patriot* PAC-2/-3

SERBIA: NATO • KFOR • *Joint Enterprise* 660; elm 1 ARNG inf bde HQ; 1 recce bn; 1 hel flt with UH-60

SINGAPORE: US Pacific Command • 200; 1 log spt sqn; 1 spt facility

SOMALIA: US Africa Command • 500

SOUTH SUDAN: UN • UNMISS 7

SPAIN: US European Command • 3,750; 1 air base at Morón; 1 naval base at Rota

SYRIA: US Central Command • *Operation Inherent Resolve* 1,500; 1 ARNG armd BG; 1 mne bn

THAILAND: US Pacific Command • 300

TURKEY: US European Command • 1,700; 1 tkr sqn with 14 KC-135; 1 ELINT flt with EP-3E *Aries* II; 1 air base at Incirlik; 1 support facility at Ankara; 1 support facility at Izmir

US Strategic Command • 1 AN/TPY-2 X-band radar at Kürecik

UKRAINE: JMTG-U 220 (trg mission)

UNITED ARAB EMIRATES: US Central Command • 5,500: 1 ftr sqn with 12 F-15C *Eagle*; 1 FGA sqn with 18 F-15E *Strike Eagle*; 1 FGA sqn with 12 F-35A *Lightning* II; 1 ISR sqn with 4 U-2; 1 AEW&C sqn with 4 E-3 *Sentry*; 1 tkr sqn with 12 KC-10A; 1 ISR UAV sqn with RQ-4 *Global Hawk*; 2 AD bty with MIM-104E/F *Patriot* PAC-2/-3

UNITED KINGDOM: US European Command • 9,500
FORCES BY ROLE
1 bbr flt at RAF Fairford with 4 B-52H *Stratofortress*; 1 ftr wg at RAF Lakenheath with 1 ftr sqn with 24 F-15C/D *Eagle*, 2 FGA sqn with 23 F-15E *Strike Eagle*; 1 ISR sqn at RAF Mildenhall with OC-135/RC-135; 1 tkr wg at RAF Mildenhall with 15 KC-135R/T *Stratotanker*; 1 spec ops gp at RAF Mildenhall with (1 sqn with 8 CV-22B *Osprey*; 1 sqn with 8 MC-130J *Commando* II)

US Strategic Command • 1 AN/FPS-132 Upgraded Early Warning Radar and 1 Spacetrack Radar at Fylingdales Moor

FOREIGN FORCES

Germany Air Force: trg units with 40 T-38 *Talon*; 69 T-6A *Texan* II; 24 *Tornado* IDS; • Missile trg at Fort Bliss (TX)

Netherlands 1 hel trg sqn with AH-64D *Apache*; CH-47D *Chinook*

Singapore Air Force: trg units with F-16C/D; 12 F-15SG; AH-64D *Apache*; 6+ CH-47D *Chinook* hel

Arms procurements and deliveries – North America

Significant events in 2019

FEBRUARY — F-35 IOC

The United States Navy (USN) declared that the F-35C combat aircraft had reached initial operational capability (IOC). This followed the US Marine Corps and US Air Force declaring that the F-35B and F-35A had reached IOC in 2015 and 2016 respectively. The F-35C is planned to deploy as part of the air wing on the USS *Carl Vinson* in 2021.

MARCH — BRADLEY RFP

The US issued a request for proposals for the Optionally Manned Fighting Vehicle. This is the US Army's third attempt to replace the *Bradley* Fighting Vehicle, which entered service in the 1980s. The army wants to reduce risk by acquiring a basic vehicle design 'off-the-shelf'. The US Army has already spent almost US$24 billion on two previous programmes before cancelling them and there is a growing need to replace the 40-year-old *Bradley* design.

AUGUST — HYPERSONIC WEAPONS

The US Army awarded Dynetics and Lockheed Martin two contracts totalling US$698.6 million to produce a first prototype battery of the ground-launched Long Range Hypersonic Weapon. The army wants to field a system with a basic combat capability by 2023. China, France, Japan and Russia are also developing hypersonic glide vehicles.

AUGUST — CANADA'S FIGHTERS

The United Kingdom's Ministry of Defence and Airbus Defence and Space withdrew the Eurofighter *Typhoon* from consideration in Canada's Future Fighter Capability Project, which is intended to replace Canada's F/A-18A/B *Hornet*s. Dassault withdrew the *Rafale* in late 2018. Canada identified a requirement to replace its *Hornet*s as far back as 2008 and selected the Lockheed Martin F-35 in 2010. This decision was then put on hold before the contest was relaunched in 2016. Concern has been expressed in the Canadian media that other competitors, such as Boeing with the F/A-18 *Super Hornet* and Saab with the *Gripen*, may also withdraw, effectively ending the competition. Canada expects to spend C$15–19bn (US$11.58–14.66bn) on the procurement.

SEPTEMBER — ARV

The US Navy stated that it had awarded contracts to two firms to develop a technology demonstrator for the US Marine Corps' Armored Reconnaissance Vehicle programme, which aims to replace the 1980s-era Light Armored Vehicle (LAV). General Dynamics Land Systems will design a vehicle using contemporary technologies, while SAIC will develop a vehicle that is based on technologies yet to fully mature. The marine corps is also extending the service life of its over 700 LAVs to the mid-2030s.

Table 3 US fixed-wing fighter-aircraft exports, 2010–Oct 2019

Country	Equipment	2010	2011	2012	2013	2014	2015	2016	2017	2018	Oct 2019
Australia	F-35A					2				8	6
Egypt	F-16C/D			7	20						
Indonesia	F-16C/D					5	4	5	4	2	
Iraq	F-16C/D						4	10	7	6	11
Israel	F-35I							2	7	5	4
Italy	F-16A/B			3							
Italy	F-35A							6*	2*	2*	1*
Italy	F-35B									1*	1*
Japan	F-35A							1	3 1*	5*	3*
Morocco	F-16C/D	3	13	6							
Netherlands	F-35A			1	1						7
Norway	F-35A						2	2	6	6	6
Pakistan	F-16C/D	14	14	1							
Saudi Arabia	F-15SA							4	26	19	16
Singapore	F-15SG	4		2				8			
South Korea	F-15K	2	2	3							
South Korea	F-35A									6	2
Turkey	F-16C/D			3	11						
Turkey	F-35A									2	2
United Arab Emirates	F-16E/F	3	3	1							
United Kingdom	F-35B			2	1			5	6	2	2
Total = 367		26	35	37	22	7	10	43	62	64	61

*Final assembly outside the US

Table 4 US: new-build armoured-vehicle programmes (in production)

First production contract date	Equipment	Type	Total quantity budgeted for (as of Nov 2019)	Total budgeted for (as of Nov 2019)	Prime contractor	Deliveries	Recipient service
Aug 2015	JLTV	Armoured utility vehicle	8,022	US$3.12bn	Oshkosh Defense	2016–ongoing	US Army
Aug 2015	JLTV	Armoured utility vehicle	2,515	US$1bn	Oshkosh Defense	2019–ongoing	US Marine Corps
Jun 2018	ACV 1.1	Amphibious-assault vehicle	56	US$324.17m	BAE Systems Land & Armaments	2020*	US Marine Corps
Oct 2018	JLTV	Armoured utility vehicle	11	US$66.58m	Oshkosh Defense	2019*	US Navy
Feb 2019	AMPV	Tracked armoured personnel carrier	328	US$1.23bn	BAE Systems Land & Armaments	2020*	US Army

* Planned

Figure 3 US Navy Littoral Combat Ship programme

The Littoral Combat Ship (LCS) programme began in 2001. The US Navy wanted a class of over 50 ships designed to operate in coastal shallow waters and perform anti-submarine-warfare, mine-countermeasures and surface-warfare missions. In a novel acquisition process, the navy would trial two classes of prototype 'seaframes' before deciding which to pursue for full-rate production. It would also develop mission packages for each role that could be changed depending on the required task. Increased automation and greater reliance on shore-based logistics would also enable a smaller crew. The plan was that three crews would rotate between two ships, with one of these forward-deployed and the other training or working-up (the 3-2-1 plan).

Freedom class (LCS 1)

Independence class (LCS 2)

Troubled status
However, by the end of 2019 only 19 LCSs were in service. The plan is to now build 35 hulls. In 2007, the navy cancelled its cost-plus contract with Lockheed Martin for its second vessel (LCS 3), as well as several others budgeted with the firm and General Dynamics, due to the expected price more than doubling to around US$350 million. The navy, General Dynamics and Lockheed Martin later agreed two fixed-price contracts worth US$433.69m for LCS 3 and LCS 4. In late 2010, the navy decided to buy both the *Freedom*- and *Independence*-class designs. The argument was that reduced seaframe costs allowed both to be procured; the navy could therefore obtain ships more rapidly; and that it would improve investment in the naval-shipbuilding sector. However, both Congress and government auditors said that operating two different ship classes would lead to higher maintenance, training and upgrade costs. Meanwhile, all three mission packages are behind schedule and, although the surface-warfare package achieved initial operating capability (IOC) in 2014, this was in part because the navy temporarily reduced the minimum requirements. All three mission packages are due to reach IOC in 2021.

The future
A programme review in 2016 saw the 3-2-1 crew plan replaced. Each LCS would have two crews (Blue/Gold) that would rotate, as in the submarine service. A mission package would be attached to each LCS, which would then be grouped into a surface division, based on their common role.
The LCS programme is at a crucial point. The final *Oliver Hazard Perry*-class frigate was retired in 2015 and the 11 *Avenger*-class mine-countermeasure vessels are approximately 25–30 years old. At the same time, reflecting current concerns, the navy is planning to build a larger, more heavily armed and more expensive FFG(X) frigate. But in the meantime, the navy needs the LCS to begin operating with its forward-deployed fleets.

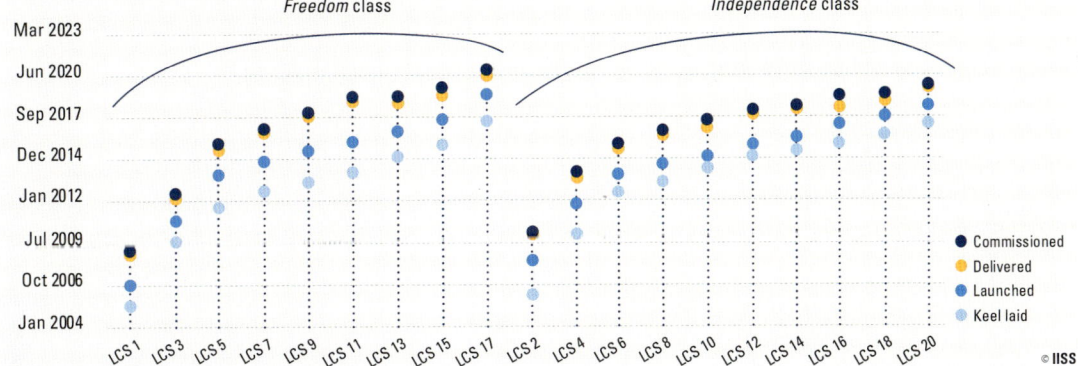

Littoral Combat Ship: commissioned vessels' production rate

Table 5 Littoral Combat Ship programme: planned and achieved IOC dates

System	Planned initial operational capability	Achieved initial operational capability
Freedom-class (LCS 1) seaframe	2007	2014
Independence-class (LCS 2) seaframe	2008	2015
Mine-countermeasures mission package	2008	2021*
Surface-warfare mission package (surface-to-surface missile capability)	2010 (2011)	2014 (2019)
Anti-submarine-warfare mission package	2010	2020*

* Planned

Chapter Four
Europe

- Against the objections of the US and other NATO allies, Turkey decided to purchase Russia's S-400 air-defence system. As a result, the US halted Turkey's participation in the F-35 combat-aircraft programme. Turkey's incursion into northeast Syria, following the US withdrawal, increased military friction between Washington and Ankara. By November, Turkish forces were organising joint patrols in northern Syria with Russian personnel.
- In September 2019, the new NATO Joint Support and Enabling Command (JSEC) reached initial operating capability. Located in Ulm, Germany, JSEC is to coordinate the movement of allied forces and supplies within Europe.
- NATO continued to operationalise its 'Four 30s' readiness initiative. This is to allow the Alliance to deploy 30 battalions, 30 air squadrons and 30 combat ships to NATO within 30 days.
- Europe once again spent just under US$290 billion on defence in 2019, in real terms. This marked a return to the level seen before the financial crisis; the last time the region's budgets exceeded this figure in real terms was in 2009. Nominal spending in 2019 was US$291bn.
- EU officials continued to work for a more coordinated approach to security policy and defence capability. Principal initiatives are the Capability Development Plan, the Coordinated Annual Review on Defence, the European Defence Fund and Permanent Structured Cooperation. However, European capability gaps are unlikely to close within the next decade. Moreover, some would considerably widen after Brexit.
- There were signs of increasing European defence-industrial cooperation. France's Naval Group and Italy's Fincantieri agreed to combine research and development activities. France and Germany are collaborating on a new tank programme and Rheinmetall bought a controlling share in BAE UK's armoured-vehicle business. Separate UK and Franco-German programmes for new fighter aircraft have both embraced international partners.

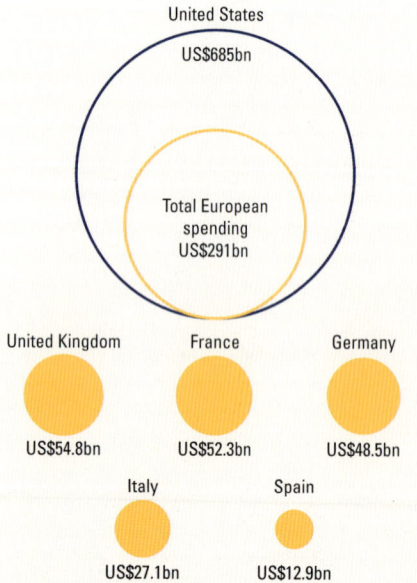

Europe defence spending, 2019 – top 5

- United States US$685bn
- Total European spending US$291bn
- United Kingdom US$54.8bn
- France US$52.3bn
- Germany US$48.5bn
- Italy US$27.1bn
- Spain US$12.9bn

Active military personnel – top 10
(15,000 per unit)

Turkey	355,200
France	203,750
Germany	181,400
Italy	165,500
United Kingdom	148,450
Greece	143,850
Poland	123,700
Spain	120,350
Romania	69,600
Netherlands	35,400

Global total 19,852,000
Regional total 1,962,000

Regional defence policy and economics 66 ▶
Armed forces data section 86 ▶
Arms procurements and deliveries 163 ▶

NATO Enhanced Forward Presence: personnel numbers, 2019

Estonia
United Kingdom – 800
France – 330
Denmark – 3
(Czech Republic –
Baltic Air Policing)

Latvia
Canada – 525
Spain – 350
Poland – 175
Italy – 166
Slovakia – 152
Czech Republic – 55
Slovenia – 33
Albania – 21
Montenegro – 10

Poland
United States – 857
United Kingdom – 140
Romania – 120
Croatia – 80

Lithuania
Germany – 560
Belgium – 262 (Baltic Air Policing)
Netherlands – 270
Norway – 120
Czech Republic – 35
(Denmark – Baltic Air Policing)

© IISS

Ground-based air defence: Soviet- and Russian-origin surface-to-air-missile systems still in service

Long range
- S-200 (SA-5 *Gammon*) Bulgaria, Poland
- S-300 (SA-10 *Grumble*) Bulgaria, Greece, Slovakia

Medium range
- S-75 (SA-2 *Guideline*) Romania

Short range
- 2K12 *Kub* (SA-6 *Gainful*) Bulgaria, Czech Republic, Hungary, Poland, Slovakia
- S-125 (SA-3 *Goa*) Bulgaria, Poland
- 9K33 *Osa* (SA-8 *Gecko*) Bulgaria, Greece, Romania, Poland
- 9K331 *Tor*-M1 (SA-15 *Gauntlet*) Greece

Point-defence
- 9K31 *Strela*-1 (SA-9 *Gaskin*) Croatia
- 9K35 *Strela*-10 (SA-13 *Gopher*) Croatia, Czech Republic

Selected EU 27 and UK military capabilities, 2019

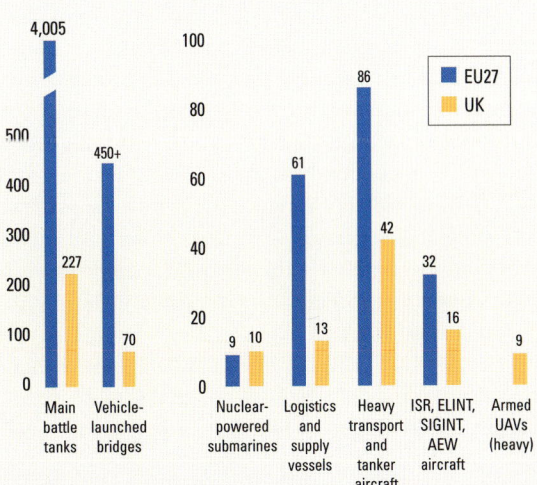

EU27 / UK

- Main battle tanks: 4,005 / 227
- Vehicle-launched bridges: 450+ / 70
- Nuclear-powered submarines: 9 / 10
- Logistics and supply vessels: 61 / 13
- Heavy transport and tanker aircraft: 86 / 42
- ISR, ELINT, SIGINT, AEW aircraft: 32 / 16
- Armed UAVs (heavy): 0 / 9

Europe

On 2 August 2019, the United States withdrew from the Intermediate-range Nuclear Forces (INF) Treaty. This came only a few weeks after NATO Secretary-General Jens Stoltenberg, speaking at the Aspen Security Forum, had called the accord a 'cornerstone of arms control in Europe'. Agreed between the US and the Soviet Union in 1987, the INF Treaty eliminated all conventional and nuclear-armed ground-launched ballistic and cruise missiles with ranges of 500–5,500 kilometres. Its demise sharpened European perceptions about the uncertain state of regional security.

The United States' withdrawal capped a five-year period during which it alleged that Russia had breached the treaty. Washington said that Moscow had developed and then fielded a non-compliant missile, identified as the 9M729 (SSC-8 *Screwdriver*). The allegation, first made in the July 2014 'Compliance Report' of the US Bureau of Arms Control and Verification, has been consistently denied by Moscow. Speaking to the US House Armed Services Committee in 2015, Rose Gottemoeller, then the under secretary for arms control and international security, said that the US had information in 2011 that Russia was violating the treaty. Indeed, this led the US to re-examine earlier data and then conclude that Russia had started testing a ground-launched cruise missile (GLCM) in 2008.

In October 2018, US President Donald Trump said that he wanted to terminate the INF Treaty, and on 4 December Secretary of State Mike Pompeo declared Russia to be in material breach of the treaty, an assessment that all NATO member states backed publicly the same day. On 2 February 2019, Pompeo announced that the US would suspend its INF obligations and that it intended to withdraw, so starting a six-month countdown that ended on 2 August. Choosing not to return to compliance with its INF obligations, open-source information indicated that Russia had at that point deployed the 9M729 with four battalions – in Elansky, Kapustin Yar (training), Mozdok and Shuya.

The demise of the INF Treaty generated two significant concerns. The first was that intermediate-range missiles might proliferate, particularly in Asia, where China's missile arsenal predominantly consists of INF-range systems and where the US has declared that it might wish to deploy such weapons. The second was there might be procurement in Europe of such systems absent the restraining influence of the INF Treaty. The 9M729 is seen as particularly destabilising because it is a road-mobile system, meaning that the launch vehicle and its cruise missiles could be hard to detect. Furthermore, the missiles could be armed with either conventional or nuclear warheads, so discerning the payload of an incoming missile might pose problems. With a possibility of reduced warning time, for instance due to the system's flight profile and location, and uncertainty about its warhead, NATO said that the 9M729 might lower 'the threshold for nuclear conflict'.

NATO's response and arms control

Three schools of thought have emerged regarding how NATO should respond to this deteriorating security environment. One, without widespread support, is that the US should itself deploy nuclear-capable GLCMs in Europe. The 2018 US Nuclear Posture Review suggested research and development work on conventional GLCMs was already under way. Indeed, the Arms Control Association reported in May 2019 that the Trump administration had requested in its 2020 defence budget nearly US$100 million to develop three missile systems that would exceed INF range limits, including a land-based cruise missile. In August 2019, the US tested a conventionally configured GLCM that exceeded the INF Treaty's lower range threshold. Earlier, in February 2019, US ambassador to NATO Kay Bailey Hutchison declared in an interview with the German media that the US was not considering deploying a nuclear system in Europe and that it was focusing on conventional weapons.

Some German politicians briefly considered a new dual-track decision – modelled on the 1979 choice to deploy medium-range nuclear weapons in Europe while also offering arms-control talks to the Soviet Union – while Polish Minister of Foreign Affairs Jacek Czaputowicz was reported to have initially made some ambiguous statements about the desirability of US nuclear weapons in Europe. Nonetheless, as of the end of 2019, it seemed unlikely that European NATO member states would wish to host US nuclear GLCMs. NATO Secretary-General Stoltenberg clarified the Alliance position in July: 'We will not mirror what Russia is doing, meaning that we will not deploy, we don't have an intention of deploying new ground-launched nuclear missiles in Europe.' Any change to this position would most likely take place at the NATO level, requiring unanimity, rather than through a bilateral agreement between the US and a European ally.

NATO's position is that it does not need to match Russia's actions in order to maintain a credible deterrence and defence posture. Instead, it is looking to build stronger conventional forces, improve readiness and consider new arms-control measures. The Alliance is also considering the adaptation and potential modernisation of missile-defence systems in Europe. Analysts considered that the Alliance might generate options for this in time for the December 2019 leaders' meeting in London. These were thought to include upgrades to existing missile-defence systems – such as new radars, software and interceptors – that would enable states to better counter the challenge posed by Russia's intermediate-range cruise missiles, for which current systems are not necessarily optimised. Alternatively, NATO could consider deploying new systems designed from the outset to take such capabilities into account. However, any upgrade or expansion of NATO's missile-defence architecture would likely trigger a negative reaction in Moscow.

Russia's missile development has led the security concerns of many NATO member states to coalesce. While this could be seen as a useful starting point for an Alliance response, it does not necessarily lead to a coherent arms-control agenda. The debate in Germany included one proposal that would effectively ask Moscow to move the offending missile systems further east. Putting NATO territory out of reach of the 9M729 would, the argument went, constitute a confidence-building measure from which other measures might flow. However, critics argued that the system's inherent mobility was the principal flaw with this idea – keeping track of the launchers would be problematic.

Other ideas included expanding the INF Treaty's provisions to other countries, including China, so moving away from the treaty's bilateral approach, which neither Russia nor the US saw as satisfactory. However, it remains difficult to envisage how Beijing would be motivated (at least in the short to medium term) to agree to a conversation that would result in 80–90% of its missile force being dismantled. Another option, instead of expanding geographic coverage, might be to increase the functional scope of a future treaty, and by doing so look to include more, or even all, nuclear systems in an arms-control framework. An idea promoted by then NATO deputy secretary-general Rose Gottemoeller is the 'freedom to mix' approach. As Gottemoeller explained in a speech at the University of Oslo on 9 September 2019, this would allow 'a party to an arms control treaty … to decide just how many weapons systems of a certain type he wants to deploy within a certain negotiated ceiling, choosing not to deploy other weapons … So it would have the freedom to mix within the overall limit', enabling a posture driven by national circumstance and threat perceptions. Such an approach, Gottemoeller continued, could be extended to new systems entering service, such as hypersonic glide vehicles.

NATO leaders' meeting

NATO's December 2019 leaders' meeting was expected to be concerned with the continuing adaptation of the Alliance's command structure, as well as the NATO Readiness Initiative. On 17 September 2019, the new NATO Joint Support and Enabling Command (JSEC) reached initial operating capability (IOC). Located in Ulm, Germany, JSEC is one of two new commands agreed at NATO's February 2018 defence ministerial and is intended to enable the fast, coordinated and secure movement of allied personnel and assets within Europe. According to planners, JSEC has the capacity to grow from its peacetime establishment of some 160 posts to about 600 in crisis situations. The second new command, the Joint Force Command Norfolk (JFCNF, in Norfolk, Virginia), was also scheduled to reach IOC by the end of 2019. Both commands are due to reach full operating capability in 2021.

Alliance leaders were also likely to review progress made on the NATO Readiness Initiative, agreed in June 2018 and also known as the 'four 30s'. This is a framework for allies to provide, by 2020, 30 battalions, 30 combat air squadrons and 30 combat vessels at 30-day readiness. All allies are required to contribute but, according to NATO officials, there were still gaps at the end of 2019 and more work was needed in 2020 to meet the schedule.

The Alliance is likely to focus more in future on the implications of China's economic rise and its growing global security and defence footprint. Stoltenberg said in August 2019 that 'great power competition is global, [and] affects us all'. As such, NATO was due to conduct a review of the risks and vulnerabilities that China's policies and postures might pose for the Alliance.

At NATO's mid-November 2019 foreign ministers' meeting, member states discussed some of these issues in advance of the December summit, and also agreed to recognise space as a new operational domain, in addition to air, land, sea and cyber. This would allow, said Stoltenberg, 'NATO planners to make requests for Allies to provide capabilities and services – such as hours of satellite communications or data for imagery'.

Meanwhile, burden sharing across the Alliance has not improved greatly, even if European NATO members in aggregate were in 2019 spending more on defence than the previous year and many had plans to spend yet more in the near term. At the time of writing, member states were expecting the US administration, and President Trump personally, to use the leaders' meeting to drive home this point; what was uncertain was how this message would be delivered and the effect it might have on Alliance relations.

NATO cohesion had already been challenged by Turkey's decision to proceed with the purchase of Russia's S-400 air-defence system against the explicit objections of the US and other NATO allies. As a result, the US decided in July to halt Turkey's participation in the F-35 combat-aircraft programme. In order to contain the diplomatic fallout, NATO has stressed other aspects of Turkey's involvement in NATO, but even Stoltenberg admitted that 'what matters for NATO is interoperability and the S-400 system [purchased by Turkey] will not be interoperable with NATO'. In April, Turkey's Minister of Foreign Affairs Mevlüt Cavuşoğlu said that 'Turkey doesn't have to choose between Russia or any others. And we don't see our relations with Russia as an alternative to our relations with others. And nobody, neither West nor Russia, should or can ask us to choose.' There is some concern in the Alliance that the Turkish government may be considering its relationships with NATO allies and Russia in terms of balancing, and perhaps even equivalence.

EU security and defence

The surprise nomination of former German defence minister Ursula von der Leyen as president of the European Commission raised expectations for further progress on the European Union's security and defence agenda. As defence minister, von der Leyen was a vocal supporter of closer European defence collaboration and considered mechanisms such as the Coordinated Annual Review on Defence (CARD), the European Defence Fund (EDF) and Permanent Structured Cooperation (PESCO) as building blocks towards a European security and defence union.

When presenting her team of designated commissioners in September, von der Leyen suggested the new Commission would play an explicit geopolitical role and would seek to be a 'guardian of multilateralism'. In the political guidelines she presented to the European Parliament, von der Leyen argued that the EU needed 'further bold steps in the next five years towards a genuine European Defence Union' through closer European defence collaboration. Von der Leyen indicated that she would seek to boost the EDF, a financial instrument controlled by the Commission and designed to support defence research, development and capability development. The portfolio of the Commissioner for the Internal Market included a new Directorate-General for Defence Industry and Space. In her 'mission letter' from 10 September 2019, von der Leyen clarified the Commissioner would be responsible for the EDF and should focus on 'building an open and competitive European defence equipment market'.

Between 2016 and 2019, the EU established the conceptual basis for a defence-planning process that would assist member states in meeting their military-capability goals. Its principal elements are the Capability Development Plan (CDP), CARD, the EDF and PESCO. The challenge for the EU, and the European Defence Agency (EDA) in particular, is to make sure that the conceptual construct designed in Brussels becomes established in national processes, where decisions about defence investments and military-capability development will ultimately be made. But important too will be how the EU looks to ensure the organisational coherence of all these defence-cooperation tools. Currently, some are managed by the EDA, which as an executive agency reports to the European Council and member states, and others – such as the EDF – are managed by the Commission. The European Parliament is, in addition,

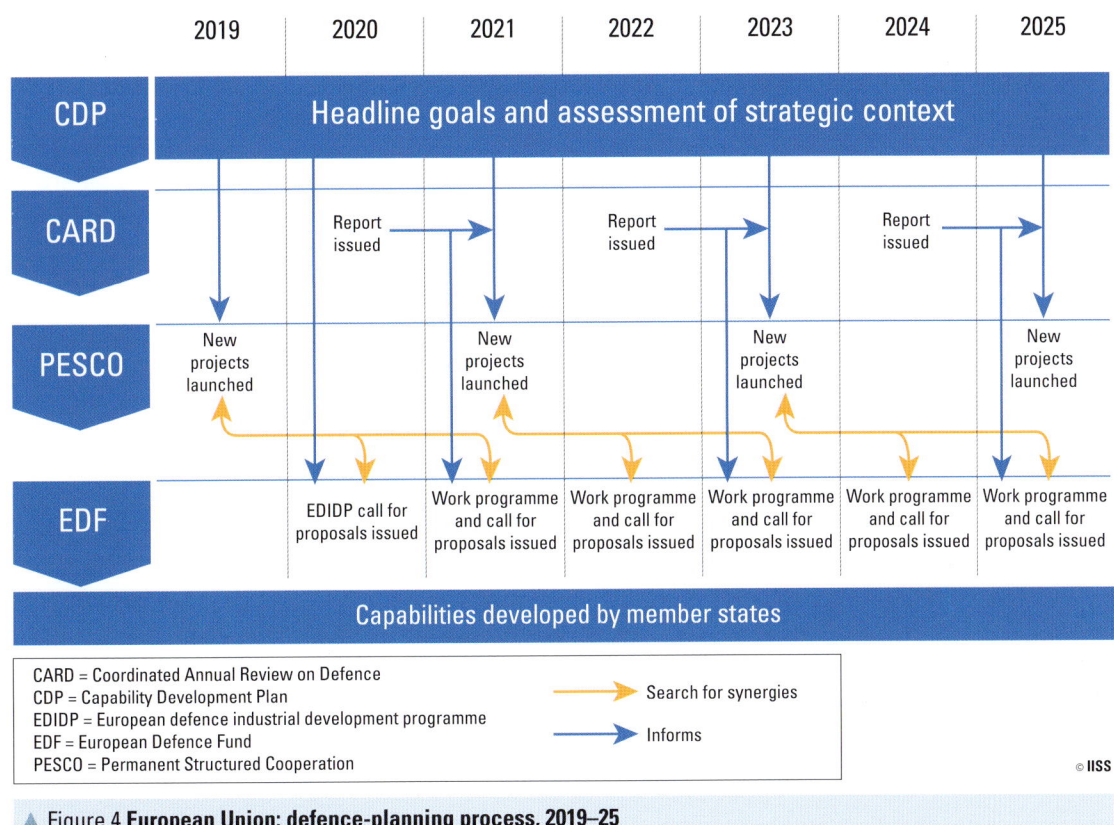

Figure 4 **European Union: defence-planning process, 2019–25**

seeking to boost its role in terms of parliamentary oversight and scrutiny.

One issue that emerged during this process was that the EU's level of ambition is no longer limited to its Common Security and Defence Policy (CSDP), under which the EU has conducted more than 30 crisis-management missions since the CSDP became operational in 2003. Elements of both the 2009 Treaty of Lisbon and the 2016 EU Global Strategy have also found their way into the CDP, but these are currently not adequately reflected in the EU's military level of ambition. These include the 'mutual assistance' and 'mutual solidarity' clauses of the Treaty of Lisbon and the ambition – reflected in the EU's Global Strategy – that the EU should protect its territory and citizens; this at least raises the question of whether this means full-spectrum defence tasks.

As EU member states press ahead with initiatives such as PESCO, attention also needs to be paid to the link between the EU's political–strategic guidance and the military concepts intended to underpin it. There is otherwise a risk that a disconnect might emerge to undermine these carefully designed processes. Already, EU member states face significant capability shortfalls against the declared level of military ambition. The EU Military Staff has assessed that closing this gap requires a phased approach. Until the mid-2020s, the effort is only focused on the most likely military and security scenarios, with work on more challenging scenarios expected to be tackled between the mid-2020s and the early 2030s. Indeed, current modernisation and spending trends make it unlikely that EU member states will be able to close their capability gaps within the next decade.

DEFENCE ECONOMICS

Macroeconomics

Economic growth in Europe slowed down in 2019. The International Monetary Fund (IMF) projected that growth in the eurozone would be 1.2% in 2019, down from 1.9% in 2018. The rate in emerging and developing European countries was expected to be 1.8% in 2019, after growth of 3.9% in 2017 and 3.1% in 2018. The deceleration in the United Kingdom was less acute, but growth nonetheless slowed from 1.8%

in 2017 to 1.4% in 2018 and 1.2% in 2019. According to the Organisation for Economic Co-operation and Development (OECD), trade tensions are reducing global growth; they can raise tariffs and disrupt supply chains, affecting confidence and investments. In the eurozone, this is troubling Germany and Italy in particular, where GDP growth in 2019 was respectively 0.5% and 0.0%. With strong industrial and export-oriented economies, these two countries have proven more vulnerable to trade disputes that reduce demand for their exports. Meanwhile, the Turkish economy grew by only 0.2%, which had the effect of slowing overall growth in the IMF's 'Emerging and Developing Europe' grouping. Recession in Turkey was ascribed principally to financial-market pressures in 2018, when the local currency depreciated sharply, which in turn led to high levels of inflation (15.7% in 2019).

Mounting global commercial uncertainties and signs of weaknesses in the eurozone, combined with a long period of low inflation, led the European Central Bank (ECB) to lower interest rates and resume its quantitative-easing policy in a bid to stimulate eurozone economies. The ECB now foresees interest rates staying low until mid-2020. The UK's halting exit from the European Union contributed to the overall sense of regional economic uncertainty and hampered investment. Should the UK end up trading with the EU under World Trade Organization terms, the OECD said that Spain and Denmark, the Netherlands and Belgium, and Ireland would be most exposed, with GDP growth in these states projected to decline by 0.5–0.75%, 0.75–1% and 1.5% respectively.

Defence-budget trends

After successive years of rising defence budgets, Europe spent US$289 billion on defence in 2019, in real terms. However, this just marked a return to the level seen before the financial crisis; the last time the region's budgets exceeded the US$280bn mark in real terms was 2009 (see Figure 5).

Germany was largely responsible for the rise in European defence spending. The region's defence spending increased by US$11.5bn in constant (2015) US dollars, with Germany accounting for over a third of this. Nonetheless, even with this increase, Germany still fell US$28.7bn short of the NATO target of aiming to spend 2% of GDP on defence.

Defence spending was projected to increase strongly in Central Europe, rising by 9.0% in constant US dollars in 2019 when compared with 2018. Meanwhile, defence outlays increased by 6.6% in Northern Europe and by 2.9% in Western Europe. In contrast, defence spending fell by 3.0% in Southern Europe, largely because of reductions in Italy and Spain.

Many NATO countries have outlined plans to increase defence spending. This comes amid a changed security environment in Europe, with many European states perceiving a renewed security challenge from Russia and with the United States pressuring them for greater burden sharing over defence. It was in 2014, at NATO's summit in Wales, that member states pledged to aim to move towards the guideline of spending 2% of GDP on defence by 2024. The year 2019 marked the halfway point towards that goal. A year before, in August 2018, NATO's Brussels Summit Declaration said that

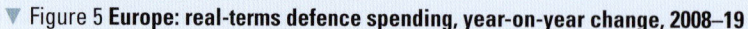

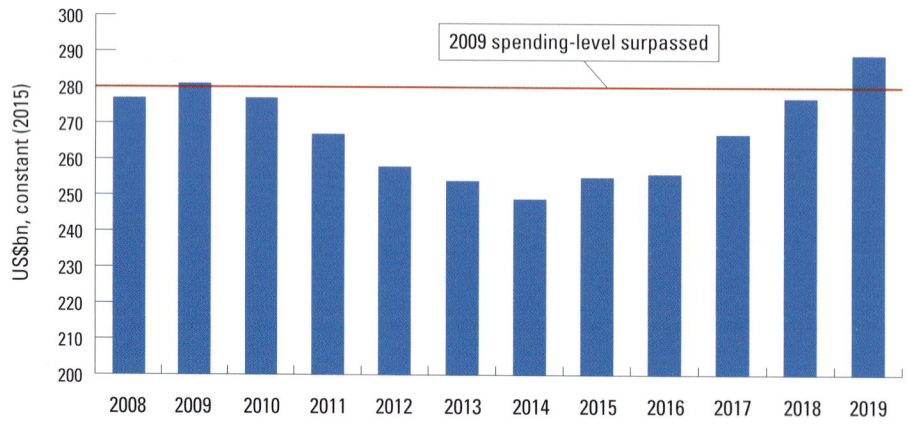

Figure 5 **Europe: real-terms defence spending, year-on-year change, 2008–19**

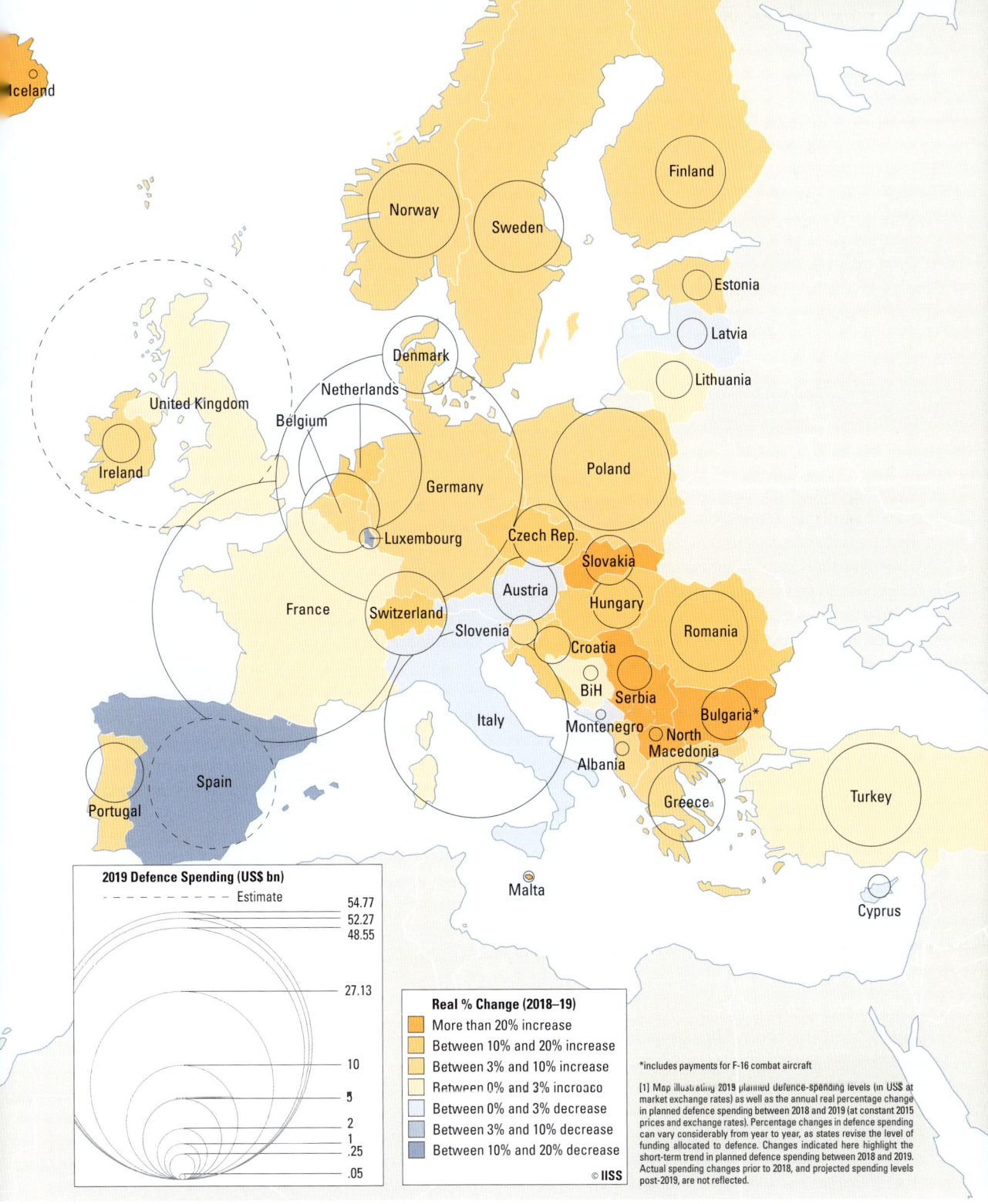

▲ Map 1 **Europe regional defence spending**[1]

Sub-regional groupings referred to in defence economics text: Central Europe (Austria, Czech Republic, Germany, Hungary, Poland, Slovakia and Switzerland), Northern Europe (Denmark, Estonia, Finland, Latvia, Lithuania, Norway and Sweden), Southern Europe (Cyprus, Greece, Italy, Malta, Portugal and Spain), Southeastern Europe (Bulgaria, Romania and Turkey), the Balkans (Albania, Bosnia-Herzegovina, Croatia, North Macedonia, Montenegro, Serbia and Slovenia) and Western Europe (Belgium, France, Iceland, Ireland, Luxembourg, the Netherlands and the United Kingdom).

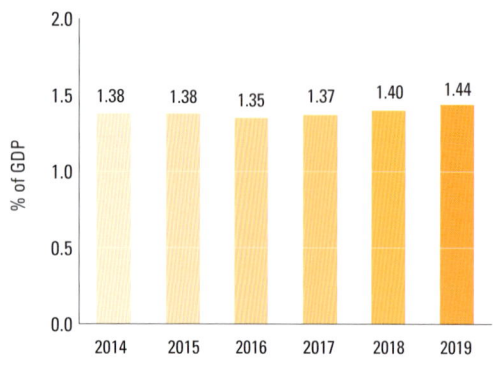

▲ Figure 6 **Europe regional defence expenditure** as % of GDP

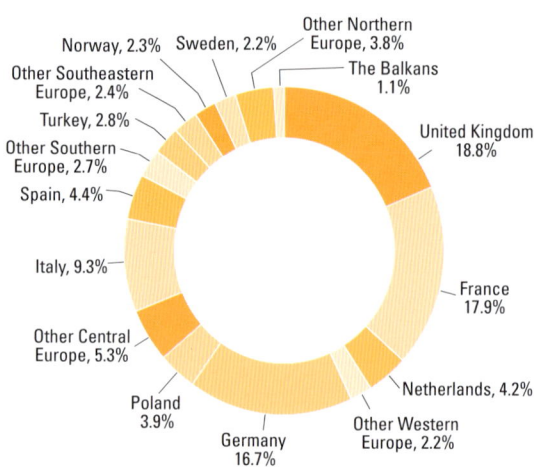

Other Western Europe – Belgium, Iceland, Ireland, Luxembourg
Other Central Europe – Austria, Czech Republic, Hungary, Slovakia, Switzerland
Other Northern Europe – Denmark, Estonia, Finland, Latvia, Lithuania
Other Southern Europe – Cyprus, Malta, Portugal
The Balkans – Albania, Bosnia-Herzegovina, Croatia, North Macedonia, Montenegro, Serbia, Slovenia
Other Southeastern Europe – Bulgaria, Romania

© IISS

▲ Figure 7 **Europe defence spending by country and sub-region, 2019**

'two-thirds of Allies have national plans in place to spend 2% of their Gross Domestic Product on defence by 2024'. While that might be the case, and the spending trajectory might be upwards, there is still some way to go for states to reach the target by 2024.

In March 2018, the Czech Republic committed to meet the 2% target by the agreed date, which would see its defence budget rise from US$2.94bn in 2019 to US$6.43bn in 2024. Estonia already meets the 2% target, and vowed to keep it as a baseline in its 2020–23 defence plan. The Netherlands' 2020 budget forecasts that defence spending will reach €11.6bn (US$13.4bn) by 2024, up from €10.8bn (US$12.1bn) in 2019, but still far from the NATO target at only 1.2%. Poland, meanwhile, said it would reach 2.5% of GDP by 2030.

Non-NATO European countries followed suit. Sweden's Defence Commission (a cross-party parliamentary committee advising on future defence-policy plans) recommended in 2017 that the country's defence spending should reach 1.5% of GDP by 2025, with annual increases of SEK5bn (US$540 million) between 2022 and 2025. These spending plans will be financed by a new bank tax, supported by an August 2019 agreement between the Social Democrat–Green ruling coalition and the Centre and Liberal opposition parties.

European states' desire to show progress towards the 2% target has led some to adapt their reporting systems to match NATO's definition of defence expenditure. The NATO definition encompasses broader defence-related expenses, rather than simply reflecting defence-ministry budgets. For reasons of transparency, some countries explain the differences observed between their national definitions of defence spending and what they report to NATO. For instance, Denmark in 2019 clarified that in its report to NATO it added to its calculations defence revenue, healthcare for defence personnel, civilian training, pensions and UN peacekeeping operations. Bulgaria specified that it includes transfers to public military high schools, but not pensions – the only NATO country not to do this. Each year, Italy publishes a discussion of defence-spending definitions, comparing its own calculations with how it reports to various institutions, including the IISS. It explains how some funds for military procurement come from the Ministry of Economic Development, while some funds for military missions are allocated by the Ministry of Economy and Finance. Such precision enables a better understanding of potential data discrepancies between different organisations.

It is likely that most countries adjusting their definitions of defence spending do so with the objective of showing that they are moving closer to the 2%-of-GDP target. However, the French government has vowed to reach 2% by 2025 without including pensions, even though these fall within the NATO definition.

Defence procurements

A key element in NATO's spending plans is to increase the proportion dedicated to major equipment, including related research and development. In Central and Southeastern Europe, the focus is on replacing Soviet-era equipment. In late 2018, Hungary signed contracts for equipment including new helicopters and second-hand main battle tanks. In February 2019, Poland reported on its Technical Modernisation Programme (TMP) 2017–26, which noted plans to procure combat aircraft, attack helicopters and short-range air-defence systems as key priorities. Warsaw released a new TMP in October. And Romania, which plans to increase its defence budget by 21.8% between 2018 and 2019 (in local currency terms), announced in July 2019 that it would boost its naval capabilities with four French *Gowind* frigates. As part of the same deal, with France's Naval Group and local firm Santierul Naval Constanta, Romania intends to also modernise its ex-UK Type-22 frigates and to build a maintenance centre and a training centre. Poland and Romania are also looking to increase the range of their ground forces' strike capability and plan to introduce HIMARS launchers with GMLRS and ATACMS missiles; both countries are also improving their air-defence systems with the procurement of *Patriot*.

In summer 2019 Bulgaria moved to purchase F-16 fighter aircraft to replace its Soviet-era MiG-29s, while Slovakia selected the F-16 in 2018. Aiming instead for the latest generation of combat aircraft, Poland's bid to procure the F-35 (32 aircraft) was approved

Southeastern Europe: combat-aircraft recapitalisation

States in Southeastern Europe are looking to recapitalise their ageing fixed-wing combat-aircraft inventories, following years of limited defence investments and amid concerns over the trajectory of European security developments. All four states are considering the acquisition of F-16 variants. In the region, Serbia is the exception to this procurement trend; Belgrade is taking delivery of MiG-29 *Fulcrum*s from Russia.

In 2013, **Romania** signed for 12 surplus Portuguese F-16s, which reportedly included a mid-life upgrade by Portuguese aviation firm OGMA valued at €628 million (US$834.07m). By 2017, these F-16s had joined the 53rd Fighter Squadron at Fetesti, replacing the obsolete MiG-21 *Lancer*. In July 2019, Romania's parliament approved the purchase of a second batch of five ex-Portuguese F-16s, so that a squadron of 17 aircraft could be generated. A new contract was expected in 2019. Romania has also been mentioned in the context of a potential future F-35 *Lightning* II order, though any ambitions in this area may be constrained by the country's budgetary situation.

Similarly, **Bulgaria's** combat-aircraft fleet comprises Soviet-era airframes that present an ever-more challenging maintenance task. In July 2019, the government approved a draft agreement with the United States to replace Bulgaria's MiG-29s with eight F-16C/D Block 70/72s. The US Defence Security Cooperation Agency said a month earlier that this was worth an estimated US$1.67 billion, should all options be exercised. Though Bulgaria's president blocked the deal in July 2019, citing concerns over prices, warranties, delivery times, penalties and indemnities, this was overturned by parliament later that month. In August Bulgaria transferred the first funds as part of the contract. If all options are exercised, the complete contract would also include 16 AMRAAM and 24 AIM-9X air-to-air missiles, bombs and laser-guided tail kits.

Croatia's MiG-21s, though partly refurbished and upgraded in 2014–15, are nearing the end of their service life. Croatia has been discussing the acquisition from Israel of 12 F-16s, though Israel was unable to secure US approval for the sale. As of early 2019, Croatia was understood to be examining the option of either procuring six new F-16s from the US or opting for Sweden's JAS 39 *Gripen*.

Serbia, meanwhile, has chosen to buy second-hand Russian and Belarusian MiG-29s. Serbia has received six MiG-29s (two in the -UB variant) from Moscow, reportedly at no cost, as well as four MiG-29Cs from Minsk. The procurement of Russian equipment underlines the two countries' good bilateral relations. Although Serbia aspires to European Union membership and is a member of NATO's Partnership for Peace Programme, it is not pursuing NATO membership.

In December 2018, **Greece** signed an agreement with Lockheed Martin to upgrade 84 of its F-16s to the V variant. The contract, worth US$996.8m (€843.7m), is scheduled to be completed by June 2027. The first two aircraft will be upgraded at Lockheed Martin's Fort Worth plant in Texas, with the remainder modernised by Hellenic Aerospace Industry at its Tanagra facility in Greece. Athens has also sent a letter of request to Lockheed Martin concerning the price and availability for 25–30 F-35 *Lightning* IIs.

in 2019 by the US Defense Security Cooperation Agency. These will replace Poland's MiG-29s and Su-22s. Turkey, however, may be heading in the opposite direction. Following Ankara's decision to procure the Russian S-400 air-defence system, the US suspended Turkey from the F-35 programme, with US Secretary of Defense Mark Esper saying that Turkey would only be allowed to rejoin if all S-400 elements were removed. Not only does this affect Turkish defence companies that participated in the aircraft's global supply chain and maintenance network, it also affects the Turkish Air Force's future fleet plans. However, Ankara could turn to Moscow for the supply of modern combat-aircraft platforms, potentially the Su-57 but perhaps more likely the Su-35.

Defence industry

While European aerospace firms began to consolidate in the early 2000s, the same did not happen in the naval and land sectors, with national champions still found in various European countries. Yet there have been recent indications that rationalisation is starting to take place in these sectors as well.

In the naval sphere, France's Naval Group and Italy's Fincantieri signed a joint-venture agreement in June 2019 to combine their research and development activities and offer joint programmes to international customers. The new entity will be named 'Naviris'. In the land domain, France's Nexter and Germany's Krauss-Maffei Wegmann have operated since 2015 as the KNDS group. Although the two companies still work as separate entities, KNDS forms the basis for more integrated activities in the longer term. In early 2019, German company Rheinmetall signalled its interest in acquiring at least a 50% stake in KNDS, a move that would further consolidate the sector. However, it is unclear whether this would be welcome in Paris, as the German firm would then become the largest stakeholder in the holding. Rheinmetall also deepened ties with the UK in 2019, purchasing a 55% stake in BAE Systems' combat-vehicle unit. This entity was transformed into Rheinmetall BAE Systems Land – a joint venture between the two groups. As a result, armoured-vehicle-manufacturing capabilities in the UK are now foreign-owned, although BAE itself retains manufacturing activities in this sector in Sweden and the US.

In the aerospace arena, further cooperation activity in 2019 was driven more by governments than industry, principally through two major next-generation combat-aircraft programmes. At the Paris Air Show, Spain formally joined France and Germany in the Future Combat Air System (FCAS), with the

Table 6 **European aerospace industry: participation in combat-aircraft programmes, 2019**

Company	Country base	F-35	FCAS	Tempest	Rafale	Gripen	Eurofighter Typhoon	Total number of projects per company
BAE Systems	UK	x		x			x	3
Leonardo	Italy	x		x			x	3
MBDA	UK France	x	x	x	x	x	x	6
Dassault	France		x		x			2
Saab	Sweden			x		x		2
Airbus	France Germany Italy Spain	x	x				x	3
MTU	Germany		x				x	2
Safran	France		x		x			2
Rolls-Royce	UK	x		x			x	3
Indra	Spain		x				x	2
Thales	France UK	x	x	x	x	x	x	6
Total number of companies per project		6	7	6	4	3	8	

firm Indra, which remains involved in Eurofighter, taking the defence-industrial lead on the Spanish side. Meanwhile, Italy officially joined the UK's *Tempest* project as a partner at the 2019 Defence Security and Equipment International exhibition in London. Earlier in the year, Sweden had also expressed its interest in the British project. At the same time, Europe's manufacturers have benefited from the increased number of aerospace programmes, including the US-led F-35.

While these projects tie the UK to some of its neighbours for decades to come, unless special arrangements are reached in the UK's departure from the EU, the country will miss out on the EU's initiatives for increased defence-industrial cooperation in Europe. The Permanent Structured Cooperation (PESCO) framework already includes 34 projects adopted in 2018, and a new list of 13 projects in 2019. This is fewer than in the first two PESCO rounds (17 projects each), but the list incorporates more ambitious programmes, such as the European Patrol Corvette, led by France and Italy, and the Timely Warning and Interception with Space-based TheatER surveillance (TWISTER) project, which promotes a European self-standing ability to contribute to NATO ballistic-missile defence. France is the coordinating nation for this project; Finland, Italy, the Netherlands and Spain are the other project members.

Earlier in the year, the European Commission launched its first call for defence-industrial and research projects, releasing €500m (US$562m) for 2019 and 2020. More than 25% of this first injection of EU funds will go to the Eurodrone (€100m, or US$112m) and European Secure Software-defined Radio projects (€37m, or US$42m). The remainder will support areas such as counter uninhabited aerial vehicle systems, cyber situational awareness, maritime-surveillance capabilities and next-generation ground-based precision-strike capabilities. EU defence-industrial cooperation efforts culminated in 2019 with the announcement of a Directorate General for Defence, Industry and Space (included in the portfolio of the Commissioner for the Internal Market, alongside industrial and digital policies). A principal role of this new directorate will be to supervise the future European Defence Fund (EDF). The EDF's funding will be channelled through the EU's next financial framework (for 2021–27), though at the time of writing this had yet to be voted through by the European Parliament.

GERMANY

Many observers in Berlin were surprised when in July 2019 defence minister Ursula von der Leyen was proposed as candidate for the position of president of the European Commission (a job she assumed from November onwards). Christian Democratic Union (CDU) chair Annegret Kramp-Karrenbauer was appointed as her successor. Following cuts to defence spending and force structures decided under her predecessors, von der Leyen was judged as having struggled to make progress in preparing the German armed forces for a future in which they would have to rebuild their capabilities for territorial and collective defence.

The armed forces have started to address the post-2014 shift in European security and defence priorities and are operating under defence planning and policy guidance that assumes NATO collective defence will be the dominant mission set. Having previously tried to turn itself into a lighter and more mobile force to support international crisis-management operations – often at significant distances – the Bundeswehr is now attempting to return to a posture where it can effectively defend NATO territory against an attack by a state-based adversary. In its national planning documents, and in communications with NATO, Germany anticipates that it will provide a fully equipped and certified NATO Very High Readiness Joint Task Force (VJTF) brigade by 2023; a modernised, digitised and reinforced armoured division by 2027; and three combat-capable divisions by 2032.

However, in order to achieve these objectives, Germany's defence establishment needs to address critical challenges relating to defence spending, personnel, readiness and procurement. If the current coalition government (CDU, Christian Social Union and Social Democratic Party (SPD)) survives, these issues will dominate Kramp-Karrenbauer's term as much as they did that of her predecessor.

Defence spending

Von der Leyen took over the defence portfolio in December 2013. In 2014, the defence budget stood at €32.4 billion (US$43.1bn and 1.1% of GDP) and rose in 2019 to €43.2bn (US$48.5bn and 1.26% of GDP). This represents a 23% real-terms increase. There was, over this period, a small increase in the share of defence-investment spending; von der Leyen's initial priorities seemed focused on recruitment and retention. Furthermore, current government budget-planning documents suggest that defence spending will stall after 2020 and might even decline towards the end of the current five-year planning horizon.

Kramp-Karrenbauer has stated unequivocally that she is seeking 1.5% of GDP as the defence-spending target by 2024 and has clarified that the German government has plans to move towards 2% of GDP by 2031. However, this target does not have the support of the SPD. Nonetheless, against the backdrop of a relatively poor economic outlook for Germany, the defence minster's statements have confirmed government policy and reiterated the commitment to NATO's 2014 defence-investment pledge.

Personnel and equipment

Active-service personnel numbers stood at 181,550 in 2014, dipping to the lowest post-war level in 2016 at 176,000 before recovering in 2019 to 182,000, just above the 2014 level. The government recognises that the force structure needs to expand in light of Germany's ambitious plans but is grappling with recruitment and retention issues. To address this, Berlin launched a new strategy in October 2019, designed to create a more flexible reserve cadre that can rapidly respond to territorial and collective-defence tasks. One motivating factor is the requirement to mobilise significant additional personnel in a defence contingency, and as such one provision is that all those leaving active service will be available for reserve duty for a period of six years, even though any duties for these regular reservists would likely remain voluntary. The concept foresees that reserve units would be equipped like regular units.

Germany also needs to take important acquisition decisions. Its heavy transport helicopters and *Tornado* aircraft are due for replacement; some of the latter underpin Germany's nuclear-weapons role in NATO. Long-standing requirements for air and missile defence, as well as a number of naval vessels, require key decisions after delays. Meanwhile, work with France on the Future Combat Air System (FCAS) and Major Ground Combat System, which is meant to modernise France's and Germany's fleets of main battle tanks, is in its early stages. Funds for a 24-month FCAS concept study were allocated in February 2019.

However, Germany's attractiveness as a collaborative procurement partner in Europe dipped throughout 2019, when both France and the United Kingdom expressed concerns about Germany's restrictive arms-exports policy. This policy had prevented companies based in France and the UK from exporting equipment to countries involved in the Yemen campaign. Perhaps most importantly, from the Bundeswehr's perspective, current budget-planning parameters do not seem to provide enough financial resources to support the identified procurement priorities.

Readiness and availability

The Bundeswehr's readiness crisis will likely prove to be the area where its spending, personnel and acquisition challenges will coalesce. This crisis is affecting all services. Germany is one of four lead nations in NATO's enhanced forward presence deployment in Eastern Europe, it regularly leads the land component of NATO's VJTF, and it maintains other deployments in the EU, NATO and United Nations frameworks. Indeed, when Germany is under pressure for its low level of defence spending compared to NATO's 2%-of-GDP benchmark, officials try to portray Berlin's contribution in a more positive light by suggesting that capabilities and commitments are more important output measures. The readiness crisis, however, throws this into sharp relief.

In June 2019, *Der Spiegel* magazine reported on leaked documents from the German Navy, assessing that a maintenance and repair backlog means it might not be able to meet operational and NATO commitments after 2021. Then, in early August, it emerged that only just over half of Bundeswehr pilots were considered combat ready by NATO standards. These problems are the result of persistent underfunding and force-structure reductions, including some outsourcing of military maintenance, repair and overhaul capacity. Fixing these problems will take time, as will rebuilding capabilities that were cut entirely. In 2014, Germany started to regenerate a limited amphibious-assault capability in the form of the Seebatallion. In 2020, it hopes that part of the Seebatallion, following extensive training and exercises with the Dutch Korps Mariniers, will be certified for the Amphibious Task Group the Netherlands has offered to NATO.

The NATO Readiness Initiative, agreed at the NATO summit in 2018, is intended to generate firm commitments from member states by 2020. However, it might well serve as an inflection point for Germany; Berlin will be expected to make a contribution befitting its political and economic weight.

Rebuilding the Bundeswehr for territorial and collective-defence tasks remains a work in progress.

Defence-planning documents have been drawn up and a path has been charted. However, tackling all of these challenges will take time and will require more money than is currently made available in the German budget. Consequently, the new defence minister may have little choice but to continue the work started by her predecessor.

POLAND

Poland transformed its armed forces after it joined NATO in 1999. The 20-year period to 2019 saw Polish forces take part in expeditionary operations, including in Afghanistan and Iraq, while Warsaw also started investing in a range of modern military capabilities. Russia's seizure of Crimea in 2014, and its subsequent military action in eastern Ukraine, began a transformation in European security affairs. Concern over Moscow's actions has long been felt most acutely by NATO's eastern members. Warsaw has been in the forefront as NATO adapted in response, and Poland has hosted forces from the United States and other NATO allies since 2017. Meanwhile, bilateral strategic cooperation with the US received a boost in 2019 with an agreement to deploy additional US force elements on a continuous rotational basis.

Defence policy

Poland's strategic culture and history strongly influence its defence thinking. This includes Central and Eastern Europe's place as both a target of and a barrier against Russian expansionism, and a widely held view that the US is the only power that can effectively deter and defend the region against Moscow. Warsaw perceives that European allies would have only limited willingness to risk escalation with Russia.

The possibility of a military confrontation with Russia has been Poland's main security concern since the end of the Cold War. Overall, however, such a confrontation was considered unlikely, and this view guided the transformation of Poland's armed forces. They were reduced from a conscript-based force of 312,000 in 1991 to an all-volunteer force of around 120,000 in 2008. Many units were dissolved, legacy platforms scrapped, and some infrastructure was converted to civilian use and then privatised. At the same time, Poland's growing engagement in European Union and NATO operations required it to increase the deployability of its forces and adjust military education and training.

This situation changed after 2014. The number of Polish opinion-poll respondents seeing an imminent threat to Polish independence sharply increased after the annexation of Crimea, from only 15% in December 2013 to almost 50% in April 2014. Since then, the figure has stayed at around 40%. Among Poland's political elites, Russia is seen as a long-term security challenge, and differences on the issue between the major political groups are generally over the likelihood of a military stand-off with Moscow.

One scenario understood to inform Poland's defence planning assumes that Russia could use its local military superiority on NATO's eastern flank to accomplish a quick win. In this case, Russia's strategic goals are considered to include establishing 'facts on the ground' and then compelling a new political and legal order in Europe that accepts Moscow's sphere of influence in Central and Eastern Europe. Russia's 'anti-access/area-denial' capabilities, including short- and intermediate-range ballistic-missile systems and air- and coastal-defence systems, are seen in Poland as giving Russia time and space advantages that may prevent NATO from moving in the reinforcements necessary to blunt a Russian offensive and regain lost territory. At the same time, Poland remains concerned with the possibility of non-traditional Russian actions, including cyber attacks, information operations, and criminal and covert activities, aimed at destabilising the eastern flank while also widening and exploiting divisions in NATO.

The government instigated a Strategic Defence Review in 2016, and in May 2017 published a National Defence Concept. This updated Warsaw's analysis of its security environment and alliance policy, providing a vision of its armed forces in the year 2032. The Defence Concept identifies the 'Aggressive Policy of the Russian Federation' as the country's main threat. According to the document, Russia seeks to dismantle the current international order and establish a 'concert of powers' system akin to that in early nineteenth-century Europe. To achieve this, the document says, Moscow is ready to use force, threats and coercion. Russia is described as having developed hybrid-warfare methods and modernised its armed forces in order to reinforce its local advantage over NATO. Other threats noted in the Defence Concept include instability in the post-Soviet space and Europe's southern neighbourhood; terrorism; and the erosion of EU and NATO solidarity.

The document's underlying assumption is that deterrence and territorial defence are the armed forces' principal priorities. They should also be capable of playing a 'unifying' role in NATO operations in the eastern flank, providing the necessary host-nation support to enable the swift reception, staging, onward movement and integration of Alliance forces. Contributing to expeditionary missions remains a stated goal, though at the end of the list, and as long as these do not reduce national-defence capability. Moreover, Poland's current deployments may indicate a reduced level of ambition when it comes to expeditionary operations: a decade ago Poland deployed over 3,500 troops abroad; in 2019 the figure was around 1,300.

Alliance relationships

NATO's position as the cornerstone of Poland's alliance policy was reinforced in 2014–18 as the organisation overhauled its operational planning, command structures, exercises and capabilities, primarily to strengthen its deterrent capabilities towards Russia. The Alliance's deployment in 2017 of four multinational battlegroups to Estonia, Latvia, Lithuania and Poland (each about 1,000 strong) meant it was finally seen in Warsaw as providing the kind of security guarantee against Russia that previously, according to some, it had failed to deliver. Before then, NATO had only a light footprint on the eastern flank.

However, the bilateral partnership with the US dominates Poland's alliance policy. In 2017, US Armored Brigade Combat Teams began rotational deployments to Poland, and the US became lead nation for the Poland-based NATO battlegroup, with a contingent of about 800 troops. A series of bilateral exercises followed, together with additional US deployments including a Combat Aviation Brigade (CAB) to Powidz Airbase and in 2019 an MQ-9 *Reaper* uninhabited aerial vehicle (UAV) detachment to Miroslawiec Airbase. US deployments had been overseen by Mission Command Element (MCE), a division-level headquarters based in Poznan, while a Combat Sustainment Support (CSS) unit at Powidz worked with other units to expand the facilities there, including as a location for US Army prepositioned stocks.

Polish political leaders have advocated a more permanent US military presence in the country – the name 'Fort Trump' was even suggested by President Andrzej Duda in September 2018. Bilateral discussions led to the establishment of a framework for the continuous rotational presence of US forces and the deployment of larger units in times of crisis. Two joint declarations signed in June and September 2019 specified that a Divisional Headquarters (Forward) would be established in place of the MCE, together with an area-support group in Poznan and a joint Combat Training Centre in Drawsko Pomorskie. (The Divisional Headquarters (Forward) took on the MCE's role in October 2019.) In addition, a US Air Force APOD (air-port of debarkation) will be set up at the existing Wroclaw-Strachowice Airbase, which will be expanded. The cost of all infrastructure investments, some yet unspecified, will be borne by Poland.

In addition, the MQ-9 *Reaper* UAV detachment will be moved to Lask, while a US special-operations forces (SOF) facility will be established in Lubliniec, home of one of Poland's special-forces units. The US Army's CAB and CSS will remain based at Powidz, with the addition of a small SOF element. The US is also poised to complete the delayed *Aegis* Ashore missile-defence site in Redzikowo in 2020.

Meanwhile, Warsaw is concerned that the EU's Permanent Structured Cooperation (PESCO) might have an adverse effect on NATO if it leads to duplication of effort or competition for resources. Warsaw instead stresses the EU's potential in boosting European defence-capability development, addressing hybrid threats and improving military mobility. Two years after its launch, Poland is participating in ten of the 34 PESCO programmes (including military mobility, logistic hubs, an uninhabited ground system, harbour and littoral surveillance, software-defined radio, cyber-defence rapid-reaction teams, and autonomous maritime counter-mine systems) and at the time of writing was set to launch its own PESCO project with Hungary. Poland is calling for PESCO to be opened to non-EU NATO members, with a view to cooperation with the US and, after Brexit, the United Kingdom.

The first meeting of the 'Bucharest Nine' (Bulgaria, the Czech Republic, Estonia, Hungary, Latvia, Lithuania, Poland, Romania and Slovakia) took place in late 2015. Warsaw's aim is to make this a primary vehicle to coordinate its policy in NATO with regional partners. At the same time, practical military cooperation has been developed through the Visegrad (V4) Group (the Czech Republic, Hungary, Poland and Slovakia). A V4 EU battlegroup was on standby in the second half of 2019 and a common logistics headquarters is being prepared.

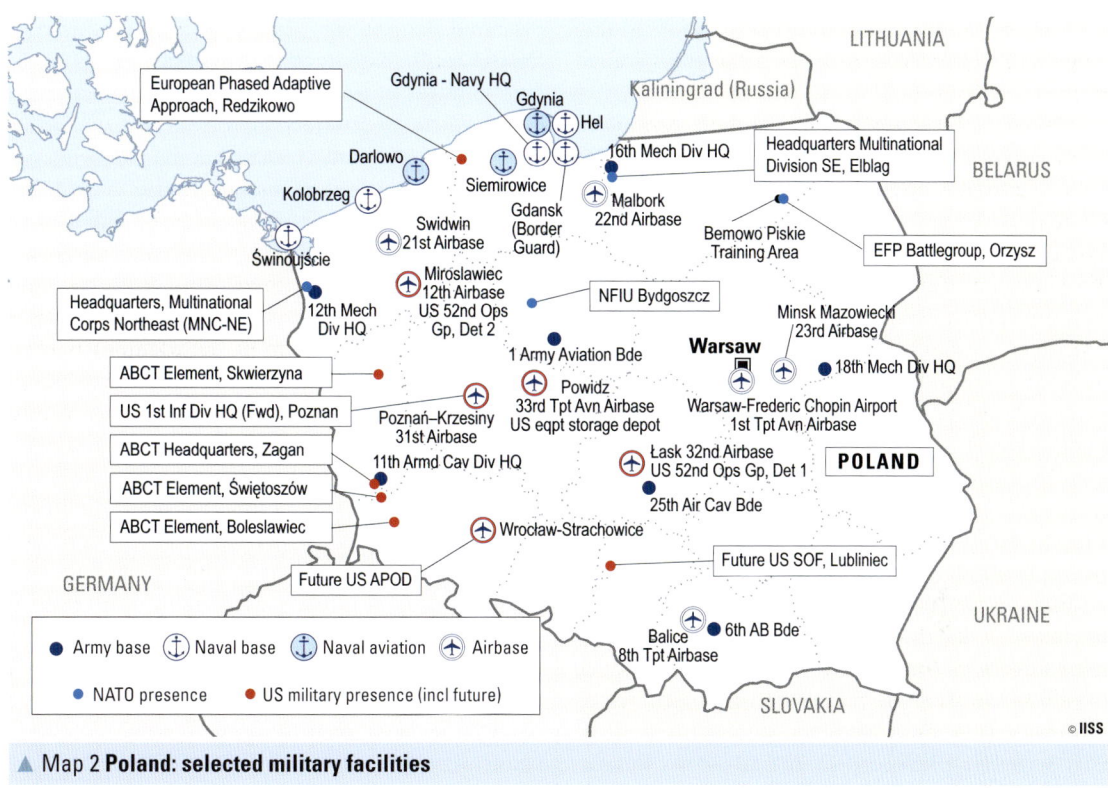

Map 2 **Poland: selected military facilities**

Transforming the force

Poland's Territorial Defence Force (TDF) became a new service branch in 2017. Tasked with augmenting regular forces in countering hybrid-warfare or irregular activities, the TDF is a response to worries about Russia, as well as an additional source of disaster-relief assistance in peacetime. Comprising mainly volunteers, its personnel combine their civilian careers with limited military service of a minimum of two days twice a month and an annual two-week camp. The TDF is planned to be 53,000 strong at full strength, and each of Poland's 17 regions is due to have a lightly armed TDF brigade; Masovia, containing Warsaw, will have two. The TDF was reported at a strength of around 21,000 in late 2019.

There have been changes to the regular forces' conditions of service in order to try to improve recruitment and retention, such as by waiving time limits that had previously led some soldiers to leave if they had been passed over for promotion. More reforms were launched after the 2017 Defence Concept. In 2018, the General Staff resumed operational command and control over all branches (except the TDF). Plans for a 2,000-strong cyber-defence force were also unveiled in 2019. Centralised within the defence ministry, this force is due to be operational before 2025. A cyber component was also set up in the TDF in 2019.

The military presence in the east has also been strengthened. A fourth mechanised division, based in the northeastern city of Siedlce, has been set up and is planned to be at full strength by 2026. Moreover, Poland's active-personnel strength, including the TDF, is planned to increase to around 200,000 by 2026. And modern land platforms, such as *Leopard* 2 main battle tanks (MBTs), have been moved to eastern-based units.

Force modernisation

Poland's armed forces continue to rely in general on legacy Soviet-era systems, despite some modern Western additions. The air force operates the F-16 Block 52+ combat aircraft integrated with weapons including the AGM-158 Joint Air-to-Surface Standoff Missile (also in an Extended Range variant). Airlift is enabled by C295M, C-130E *Hercules* and C-17 *Globemaster* IIIs, the latter through NATO's Strategic Airlift Capability programme. Some of the remaining Soviet-era airframes have undergone limited modernisation but all the MiG-29s are reportedly grounded following a series of accidents, while the upgraded Su-22M4s have only limited combat capability.

The army boasts only two modern armoured-vehicle types: second-hand *Leopard* 2A4/5 MBTs acquired from Germany (142 A4s are planned to be modernised to 'PL' standard by the end of 2020) and 8x8 *Rosomak* infantry fighting vehicles (IFVs). The newest additions (from 2017) are 155 mm *Krab* self-propelled howitzers and 120 mm *Rak* mortars (integrated on *Rosomak*). The remaining fleet includes Soviet-era tanks, including the PT-91M (a Polish T-72 variant) and the T-72M1 (312 are due to undergo limited modernisation by 2025 in the Bumar-Labedy plant in Gliwice), as well as legacy IFVs including the BMP-1 and BRDM-2. Air mobility and close air support are provided by legacy Mi-24 and Mi-8/17 helicopters, both long due for replacement.

The navy has suffered protracted underinvestment. Its most modern vessels are the *Kormoran* II minehunters, two more of which will enter service by 2022, and a single Slazak patrol vessel, which has been in development since the early 2000s and was originally planned as a corvette. Two *Pulaski*-class (ex-*Oliver Hazard Perry*) frigates donated by the US require ongoing maintenance and costly upgrades. These are supported by RBS15-missile-equipped *Orkan*-class patrol boats. Sub-surface capability is limited to the single post-Soviet *Kilo*-class submarine and two ex-Norwegian *Kobben*-class boats troubled with end-of-life wear and lack of spares. Consequently, the navy's Coastal Missile Unit, equipped with Kongsberg's Naval Strike Missile, takes on most coastal-defence tasks.

Technical Modernization Programme

A new Technical Modernization Programme (TMP) was unveiled in October 2019, after the February update to the earlier TMP. Enabled by a zł524 billion (US$133bn) budget line for 2021–35, the programme's priorities are air and missile defence, long-range precision fires and a fifth-generation fighter aircraft. The TMP also introduced a dedicated programme for intelligence, surveillance and reconnaissance, both space-based (satellites and micro-satellites) and airborne (inhabited and uninhabited platforms).

In May 2019, Poland formally asked the US about the availability and price of a batch of 32 F-35A combat aircraft under the Foreign Military Sales (FMS) scheme. The sale was approved by the US in September 2019, with a US$6.5bn price tag and a projected first delivery date of 2026; this is seen in Poland as the basis for further negotiations. Poland also aims to acquire the 'loyal wingman' system for its F-35s; the production version of the XQ-58A *Valkyrie* uninhabited combat aerial vehicle has been mentioned as a possibility in this regard. An unspecified number of additional F-16s will also be acquired to make up for the old MiGs and Sukhois.

Poland is also acquiring two *Patriot* air- and missile-defence batteries under FMS. Four firing units are planned for delivery by 2022 at a cost of US$4.75bn. The second phase of this *Wisla* medium-range air-defence programme is planned to include an even larger contract for six batteries, equipped with a new 360-degree radar, an Integrated Battle Command System and *SkyCeptor* missiles. The *Narew* short-range air-defence programme is still a priority, but there are as yet no details concerning dates and financing. Rocket-artillery capabilities will improve on completion of the February 2019 US$414 million FMS contract for 20 M-142 HIMARS launchers, together with a mix of Army Tactical Missile System (ATACMS) and shorter-range Guided Multiple Launch Rocket System (GMLRS) missiles. These are to be delivered by 2023.

Both the plan to replace more than 30 Mi-24 attack helicopters (*Kruk*) and the planned acquisition of three submarines with cruise-missile capability (*Orka*) appeared in the new TMP. There is now the suggestion that these may move more rapidly than their hitherto very limited progress. The latter programme will involve a 'bridging' stage with the acquisition of a second-hand boat (or boats) to sustain underwater capability until the new vessels arrive. Meanwhile, debate over the operational utility of a frigate-size vessel in the Baltic Sea was judged as responsible for the halt in negotiations on the acquisition of former Australian frigates. The new TMP plans for two *Miecznik*-class coastal-defence vessels and six smaller *Murena*-class missile cutters.

Defence budget

Poland's defence budget has grown steadily over the last 20 years. Sustained resource allocations have been made possible by the Act on the Technical Modernisation of the Armed Forces, which from 2002 placed a legal obligation on the government to allocate at least 1.95% of GDP to national defence in each annual budget, based on the preceding year's output. To respond to both the need to fund the modernisation and transformation plan and US calls for fairer burden-sharing in NATO, the bar was set at 2% of GDP in 2015 and increased in 2017 with the aim of reaching 2.5% of GDP in 2030. The basis for this calculation will now be the upcoming year's projected output.

Defence expenditure in 2019 was set at zł45.4bn (US$11.4bn) – 3% more in real terms than in the preceding year and more than three times as much as the 2002 figure of zł14.5bn (US$3.55bn). While defence investments have risen, from 12.5% in 2002 to 31.4% in 2019, personnel costs have in contrast fallen from 54% in 2002 to around 46% in 2019, including salaries and pensions.

Defence industry

Poland's defence industry comprises three distinct groups. The first consists of a small number of formerly state-owned companies that were privatised after 2000 and became subsidiaries of the world's aerospace primes: PZL Warszawa Okecie (an Airbus subsidiary), PZL-Swidnik (Leonardo) and PZL Mielec (Lockheed Martin). Their products range from platforms (such as S-70i helicopters) to components (C295M and A400M parts) and subsystems. Independent firms form the second group, specialising mainly in military electronics.

The third and largest group consists of state-owned companies. Following a series of failed consolidation attempts, the Polish Armaments Group (Polska Grupa Zbrojeniowa, or PGZ) was launched in 2014 as Poland's national-defence champion. This pool of more than 60 individual firms has 17,500 employees and covers land systems, munitions, military electronics and naval platforms, producing a wide range of products, including small arms, artillery and surveillance radars, very-short-range air-defence systems, armoured vehicles and naval surface combatants. The firms have significant assets at their disposal, including substantial production facilities, research laboratories and test ranges, yet they suffer from having a relatively ageing technological base. With arms sales of around US$1.32bn in 2017, PGZ lags behind other European primes. And it has not exported a platform, or a complete weapon system, in more than a decade.

Some analysts consider that the group's firms will remain largely uncompetitive at the European level unless they are restructured and provided with modern technology. Offsets linked to major programmes with the US, including air and missile defence and long-range fires, are seen as a key means by which technology transfer can take place, as well as being a way of enhancing skills in Poland's defence industries. It is expected that US primes will share some technologies with Polish firms, which as a result will develop the capacity not only to maintain and service US systems, but also to join the US companies' global supply chains. Accessing European Defence Fund money may be more difficult, however: Poland has never participated in a European collaborative armament programme.

Modernising the defence-acquisition process is another challenge. The process is widely criticised in Poland for its complexity and the large number of stakeholders, which increases the risk that programme management becomes overly cumbersome. A central armaments agency has been proposed to alleviate these problems, though no formal procedure to establish one has ever been completed. However, a small step has been taken towards a longer-term vision with the decision to extend Poland's capability-planning timeline from ten to 15 years.

TURKEY

In late 2019, the Turkish Armed Forces (TAF) were facing the prospect of persistent commitments in Syria and northern Iraq. At the same time, they were trying to adapt to personnel reductions following changes to the conscription system, as well as disruption caused by continuing purges of officers accused of complicity in the attempted coup of July 2016.

On 25 June, President Recep Tayyip Erdogan ratified a new law that reduced the length of compulsory military service from 12 to six months. On payment of a fee, compulsory service can be reduced further to one month of basic training. The changes were expected to reduce the overall size of the armed forces by around 35%, as part of Turkey's long-term plan to create compact and fully professional armed forces. However, it was unclear whether the reforms would leave sufficient personnel for the armed forces' needs. Although most offensive military operations are now conducted by units staffed with professional soldiers, conscripts are still extensively used in defensive and support roles, including against the Kurdistan Workers' Party (PKK) in the predominantly Kurdish southeast of Turkey.

The overall reduction in the size of the armed forces has been accompanied by a contraction in the officer corps. By late 2019, more than 17,500 officers had been dismissed from the military since July

2016. Although many of the officers were known to be hardline secularists, many were accused of being sympathisers of the exiled former Islamic cleric Fethullah Gulen, who according to the Turkish authorities masterminded the failed coup. The effect on officer morale of these continuing purges was exacerbated by the widespread suspicion that promotions and appointments were increasingly politicised, with outspoken supporters of Erdogan fast-tracked for promotion.

There was also unease at what were regarded as Erdogan's attempts to assert his authority over the armed forces. In 2018, Erdogan began appointing senior officers to posts normally assigned to those of a lower rank. When he did the same during the annual round of appointments in August 2019, four one-star generals and one two-star general requested early retirement rather than take up their new posts. In addition, Erdogan refused to appoint any new four-star generals, leaving the number at seven, compared with 16 in 2016. Erdogan also appointed three-star generals to command three of Turkey's four armies, positions that had previously always been held by four-star generals.

There were also, analysts understand, concerns in the officer corps about Erdogan's policies in Syria, where members of the armed forces were deployed alongside what Ankara terms the Syrian National Army (including many former members of extremist Islamist rebel groups), and his support for closer defence–industrial ties with Russia. Unlike a decade earlier, when major procurement decisions were effectively made by the armed forces, the decision to purchase two S-400 air-defence systems from Russia was made by the president without detailed consultation with the armed forces about the possible technical and strategic repercussions. After elements of the S-400 system began to arrive in Turkey in August 2019, the United States responded by suspending Turkey's participation in the F-35 combat-aircraft production programme and blocking any sales to Ankara. The decision was a blow to the armed forces, whose plans for Turkey's future air-combat capabilities had been based on the expected purchase of 100 F-35s. Nor did many in the armed forces share Erdogan's publicly expressed confidence that the gap could be filled by purchases of Su-57s from Russia – though the Su-35 may be more likely – or that Turkey could develop a fifth-generation fighter of its own.

At the time of writing, it was still unclear whether the S-400 purchase would trigger additional US sanctions against Ankara, such as under the Countering America's Adversaries Through Sanctions Act. However, there were military concerns about the repercussions for both future purchases and the supply of spare parts for US-made assets already in the inventory.

Turkey's suspension from the F-35 programme was also a major setback for the development of the country's growing defence industry, which was already likely to struggle to achieve Erdogan's target of supplying 75% of the armed forces' equipment needs and generating US$10.2 billion in exports by 2023. Nevertheless, this goal is likely to remain one of Erdogan's priority focus areas, with emphasis on defence sales to other Muslim countries.

UNITED KINGDOM

The United Kingdom's Ministry of Defence (MoD) will likely continue to struggle to fund its current capabilities, arrest a decline in personnel numbers and manage the risk to its equipment-modernisation plans, even with the increase of £2.2 billion (US$2.8bn) over two years that came with the 2019 defence budget.

British defence policy remains based on the requirement to use its forces to project stability abroad in order to reduce direct threats to the UK. This requires military commitments to NATO, counter-terrorism operations abroad and supporting Gulf security. There have been additional deployments to the Asia-Pacific in recent years and there is also increased emphasis on the military's role in countering 'hybrid' challenges. The armed forces are still regenerating capabilities that were drawn down after the 2010 Strategic Defence and Security Review (SDSR), such as aircraft carriers and maritime patrol, at the same time as receiving modern platforms such as *Ajax* scout vehicles, the recently ordered *Boxer* armoured personnel carrier and the F-35 combat aircraft. In December 2018, the MoD published an interim Modernising Defence Programme, which increased expenditure on readiness and emerging technology, such as uninhabited and autonomous systems.

Nonetheless, while the armed forces remain overall relatively well balanced between combat, combat-support and logistic-support functions, some key capabilities – such as armoured warfare and air defence – remain close to critical mass. Furthermore, the MoD is increasingly conscious of the UK's dearth

Figure 8 UK future combat-aircraft concept

In 2005, the United Kingdom's Ministry of Defence did not think it would require a crewed combat aircraft beyond the Eurofighter *Typhoon* or the Lockheed Martin F-35 *Lightning* II. A decade later, as part of the 2015 Strategic Defence and Security Review, it provided funding for the Future Combat Air System Technology Initiative (FCAS TI). This effort was, at the very least, a placeholder intended to allow the UK to be able to decide by around the turn of the decade its approach to future combat-aircraft needs. In July 2018, the Ministry of Defence (MoD) published the Combat Air Strategy, presented 'Team *Tempest*' (BAE Systems, Leonardo, MBDA and Rolls-Royce) and unveiled a concept model of a comparatively large next-generation twin-engine, low-observable crewed combat aircraft. The concept phase of FCAS TI is planned to run until the end of 2020, providing the MoD with the basis for a procurement approach to meet its combat-aircraft needs beyond 2035. Sweden and Italy, from July and September 2019 respectively, are partnering with the UK on elements of the present phase of the project. France, Germany and Spain are working on a rival Next-Generation Fighter design slated to begin entering service around 2040.

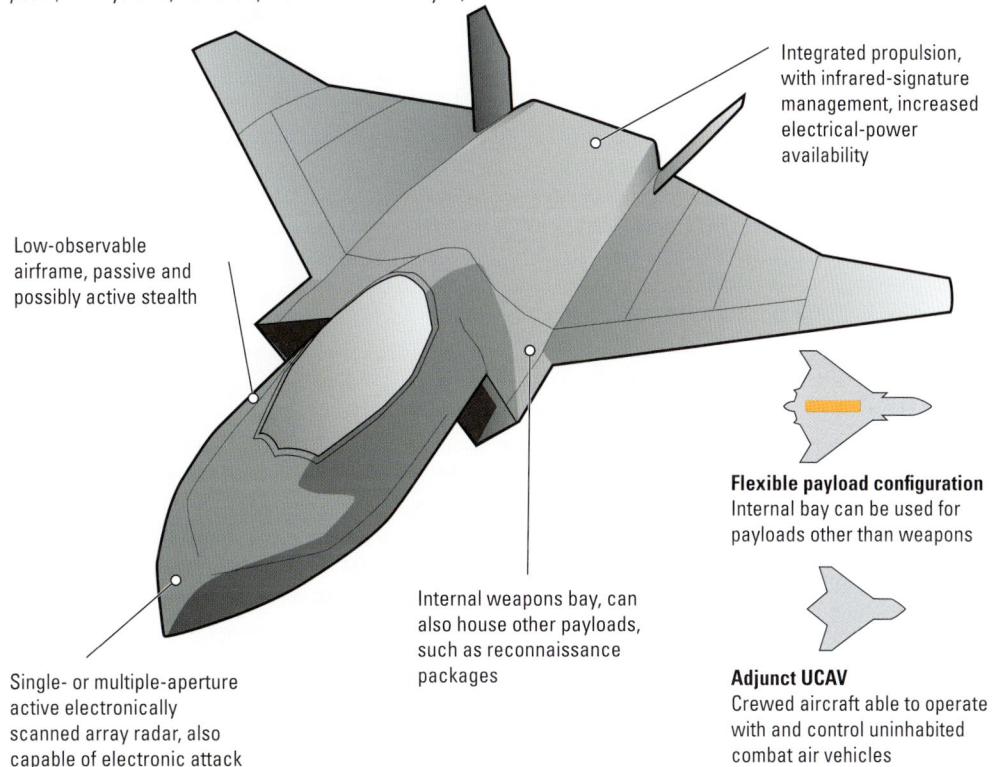

- Integrated propulsion, with infrared-signature management, increased electrical-power availability
- Low-observable airframe, passive and possibly active stealth
- Flexible payload configuration: Internal bay can be used for payloads other than weapons
- Internal weapons bay, can also house other payloads, such as reconnaissance packages
- Adjunct UCAV: Crewed aircraft able to operate with and control uninhabited combat air vehicles
- Single- or multiple-aperture active electronically scanned array radar, also capable of electronic attack

Weapons

European weapons manufacturer MBDA is exploring a range of air-to-air and air-to-surface weapons concepts as part of Team *Tempest*. As well as kinetic systems, short-range laser weapons may also feature. As with other elements of the programme, baseline systems could be drawn from the *Typhoon*, such as the *Meteor* extended-range air-to-air missile, or the *Storm Shadow* cruise missile.

Existing systems

Storm Shadow

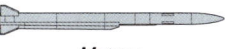
Meteor

Development or concept phase

Low-observable/very-low-observable and high-speed cruise-missile options

SPEAR 3
Stand-off missile with increased load out and escort jammers

Increased load-out of within visual range, radio-frequency and imaging infrared missiles

Self-defence and air-to-ground micro-missile

© IISS

of missile-defence capability. Though there has been progress towards the 'Joint Force 2025' plan envisaged in the 2015 SDSR – particularly in the delivery of new equipment – risks include the continuing personnel shortfall and the fact that some key equipment programmes, such as modernisation of *Challenger* tanks and *Warrior* infantry fighting vehicles, had yet to be fully contracted at the time of writing.

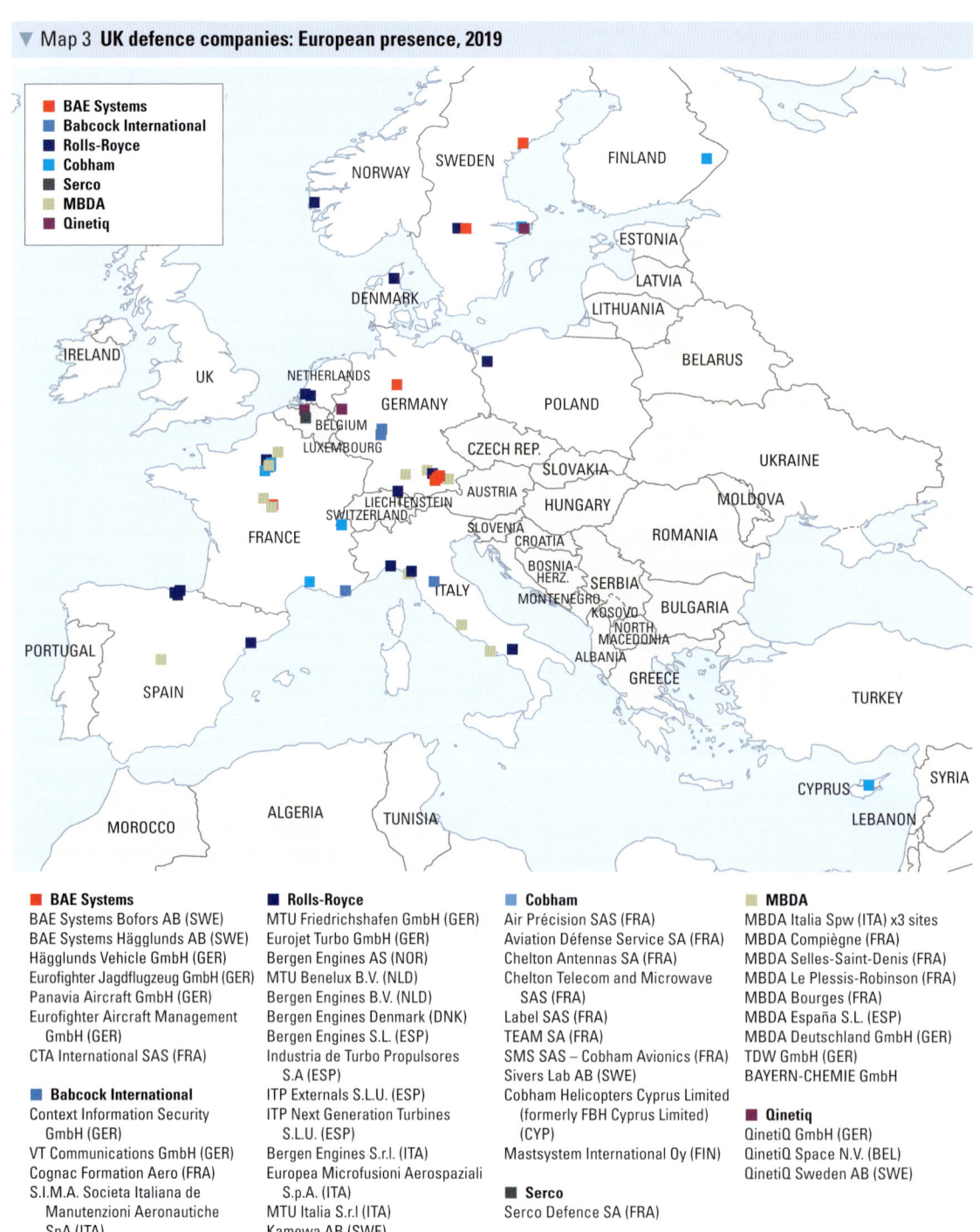

Map 3 **UK defence companies: European presence, 2019**

BAE Systems
BAE Systems Bofors AB (SWE)
BAE Systems Hägglunds AB (SWE)
Hägglunds Vehicle GmbH (GER)
Eurofighter Jagdflugzeug GmbH (GER)
Panavia Aircraft GmbH (GER)
Eurofighter Aircraft Management GmbH (GER)
CTA International SAS (FRA)

Babcock International
Context Information Security GmbH (GER)
VT Communications GmbH (GER)
Cognac Formation Aero (FRA)
S.I.M.A. Societa Italiana de Manutenzioni Aeronautiche SpA (ITA)

Rolls-Royce
MTU Friedrichshafen GmbH (GER)
Eurojet Turbo GmbH (GER)
Bergen Engines AS (NOR)
MTU Benelux B.V. (NLD)
Bergen Engines B.V. (NLD)
Bergen Engines Denmark (DNK)
Bergen Engines S.L. (ESP)
Industria de Turbo Propulsores S.A (ESP)
ITP Externals S.L.U. (ESP)
ITP Next Generation Turbines S.L.U. (ESP)
Bergen Engines S.r.l. (ITA)
Europea Microfusioni Aerospaziali S.p.A. (ITA)
MTU Italia S.r.l (ITA)
Kamewa AB (SWE)
MTU France S.A.S (FRA)
MTU Polska Sp. z o.o. (POL)

Cobham
Air Précision SAS (FRA)
Aviation Défense Service SA (FRA)
Chelton Antennas SA (FRA)
Chelton Telecom and Microwave SAS (FRA)
Label SAS (FRA)
TEAM SA (FRA)
SMS SAS – Cobham Avionics (FRA)
Sivers Lab AB (SWE)
Cobham Helicopters Cyprus Limited (formerly FBH Cyprus Limited) (CYP)
Mastsystem International Oy (FIN)

Serco
Serco Defence SA (FRA)

MBDA
MBDA Italia Spw (ITA) x3 sites
MBDA Compiègne (FRA)
MBDA Selles-Saint-Denis (FRA)
MBDA Le Plessis-Robinson (FRA)
MBDA Bourges (FRA)
MBDA España S.L. (ESP)
MBDA Deutschland GmbH (GER)
TDW GmbH (GER)
BAYERN-CHEMIE GmbH

Qinetiq
QinetiQ GmbH (GER)
QinetiQ Space N.V. (BEL)
QinetiQ Sweden AB (SWE)

© IISS

Funding difficulties

Meanwhile, the MoD's finances still present considerable problems. At the end of 2018, the National Audit Office (NAO) assessed that there was a £7bn (US$9.4bn) shortfall between the estimated cost of the Defence Equipment Plan and the allocated funding; the NAO predicted that this gap could widen to £14.8bn (US$19.8bn) if all potential risks materialised. Of the £2.2bn (US$2.8bn) budget increase in 2019 – comprising £300 million (US$377m) for fiscal year 2019–20 and £1.9bn (US$2.4bn) for 2020–21, over 30% (£700m, or US$879m) was earmarked for MoD pensions. Most of the remainder (£1.2bn, or US$1.5bn) is intended to support the modernisation programme.

The successful delivery of new equipment on time and on budget is not assured, with the ministry's finance director stating that 'we are facing severe financial challenges within the Equipment Programme'. Indeed, the July 2019 independent Major Projects Review assessed that of 33 major defence-modernisation programmes, only three were graded green, with 12 graded amber or red. Many programmes at risk form part of Joint Force 2025, including the *Warrior* armoured-vehicle upgrade, future satellites, the P-8 *Poseidon* maritime-patrol aircraft and *Protector* uninhabited aerial vehicles. If the additional level of funding allocated in 2019 is not sustained after 2021, or if wider economic challenges affect the defence budget, there may be increased risk for those equipment-modernisation programmes that have not yet been funded, such as full modernisation of ageing armoured vehicles and artillery.

Personnel problems

The personnel strength of the British armed forces continues to decrease, with an overall deficit of 7.6% in 2019, compared with 6.2% the previous year. Although recruitment initiatives continue, shortages remain in key specialist areas, including 18% of required Royal Air Force (RAF) pilots. The MoD routinely claims that it has enough personnel to meet operational requirements, and in the event of a large-scale operation, such as a NATO Article 5 contingency, the army could probably draw on its reserves to bring its units to full strength. But the Royal Navy and RAF, with smaller reserves, might find it more problematic to generate the necessary personnel for a large-scale operation.

Albania ALB

Albanian Lek		2018	2019	2020
GDP	lek	1.63tr	1.71tr	
	US$	15.1bn	15.4bn	
per capita	US$	5,239	5,373	
Growth	%	4.1	3.0	
Inflation	%	2.0	1.8	
Def exp [a]	lek	19.0bn	21.7bn	
	US$	176m	196m	
Def bdgt [b]	lek	14.3bn	15.7bn	20.9bn
	US$	133m	142m	
FMA (US)	US$	0m	0m	0m
US$1=lek		107.99	110.61	

[a] NATO definition
[b] Excludes military pensions

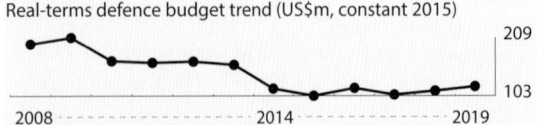
Real-terms defence budget trend (US$m, constant 2015)

Population 3,066,126

Ethnic groups: Albanian 82.6%; Greek 0.9%; Romani 0.3%; Macedonian 0.2%; other or unspecified 15.7%

Age	0–14	15–19	20–24	25–29	30–64	65 plus
Male	9.3%	3.8%	4.6%	4.8%	21.0%	5.9%
Female	8.4%	3.4%	4.3%	4.6%	23.1%	6.7%

Capabilities

Principal missions for Albania's armed forces include territorial defence, internal security, disaster-relief tasks, and small-scale peacekeeping or training deployments. Tirana is looking to improve the operational readiness of its infantry battalion in order to fulfil obligations to NATO, which it joined in 2009. Other priorities include improving border management and information sharing to prevent transnational crime and terrorism. Greece and Italy police Albania's airspace. Albania contributes to EU missions but does not possess an independent expeditionary capability. Most Soviet-era equipment has been sold. Limited defence modernisation under the Long-term Development Plan 2016–25 is proceeding, but progress has so far been restricted to small numbers of helicopters. However, the contract for the purchase of the Integrated Surveillance System for Albanian Airspace was approved in November 2017. The navy is expected to receive upgrades to vessels that have been or still are deployed in the Aegean Sea. In late 2018, the prime minister announced that NATO will invest US$51 million to modernise the Kucove air base, using this location for regional surveillance requirements. Albania has little in the way of domestic defence industry, with no ability to design and manufacture modern military platforms. Nevertheless, the country has some publicly owned defence companies that are capable of producing small arms, explosives and ammunition.

ACTIVE 8,000 (Land Force 3,000 Naval Force 650 Air Force 550 Other 3,800)

ORGANISATIONS BY SERVICE

Land Force 3,000
FORCES BY ROLE
SPECIAL FORCES
  1 SF bn
  1 cdo bn
MANOEUVRE
  Light
  3 lt inf bn
COMBAT SUPPORT
  1 mor bty
  1 NBC coy
EQUIPMENT BY TYPE
ARMOURED FIGHTING VEHICLES
  APC • PPV 40 *Maxxpro Plus*
ARTILLERY • MOR 93: **82mm** 81; **120mm** 12

Naval Force 650
EQUIPMENT BY TYPE
PATROL AND COASTAL COMBATANTS • PBF 5
Archangel

Coast Guard
EQUIPMENT BY TYPE
PATROL AND COASTAL COMBATANTS 22
  PB 9: 4 *Iluria* (Damen Stan Patrol 4207); 3 Mk3 *Sea Spectre*; 2 (other)
  PBR 13: 4 Type-227; 1 Type-246; 1 Type-303; 7 Type-2010

Air Force 550
EQUIPMENT BY TYPE
HELICOPTERS
  TPT 27: **Medium** 4 AS532AL *Cougar*; **Light** 23: 1 AW109; 5 Bell 205 (AB-205); 7 Bell 206C (AB-206C); 8 Bo-105; 2 H145

Regional Support Brigade 700
FORCES BY ROLE
COMBAT SUPPORT
  1 cbt spt bde (1 engr bn, 1 (rescue) engr bn, 1 CIMIC det)

Military Police
FORCES BY ROLE
COMBAT SUPPORT
  1 MP bn
EQUIPMENT BY TYPE
ARMOURED FIGHTING VEHICLES
  AUV 8 IVECO LMV

Logistics Brigade 1,200
FORCES BY ROLE
COMBAT SERVICE SUPPORT
  1 log bde (1 tpt bn, 2 log bn)

DEPLOYMENT

AFGHANISTAN: NATO • *Operation Resolute Support* 135
BOSNIA-HERZEGOVINA: EU • EUFOR • *Operation Althea* 1
LATVIA: NATO • Enhanced Forward Presence 21; 1 EOD pl
MALI: EU • EUTM Mali 4
MEDITERRANEAN SEA: NATO • SNMG 2; 1 PB
SERBIA: NATO • KFOR 29
SOUTH SUDAN: UN • UNMISS 2

Austria AUT

Euro €		2018	2019	2020
GDP	€	386bn	399bn	
	US$	456bn	448bn	
per capita	US$	51,344	50,023	
Growth	%	2.7	1.6	
Inflation	%	2.1	1.5	
Def bdgt [a]	€	2.87bn	2.89bn	3.04bn
	US$	3.39bn	3.25bn	
US$1=€		0.85	0.89	

[a] Includes military pensions

Real-terms defence budget trend (US$bn, constant 2015)
3.09
2.55
2008 — 2014 — 2019

Population 8,828,456

Age	0–14	15–19	20–24	25–29	30–64	65 plus
Male	7.2%	2.5%	2.9%	3.4%	24.5%	8.6%
Female	6.8%	2.4%	2.8%	3.3%	24.7%	11.1%

Capabilities

Austria remains constitutionally non-aligned, but is an EU member and actively engaged in the Common Security and Defence Policy. Defence-policy objectives are based on the 2013 National Security Strategy, the 2014 Defence Strategy and the 2015 Military Strategy, including providing military capabilities to maintain sovereignty and territorial integrity, to enable military assistance to the civil authorities and to participate in crisis-management missions abroad. A 2017 defence plan included structural changes at the operational and tactical command-and-control level; Vienna is also planning to boost its rapid-response capability and to stand up new Jäger battalions. In addition, army brigades will specialise according to roles, such as rapid response, mechanised (heavy), air-mobile (light) and mountain warfare. Initial steps were taken in 2017 but implementation appears incomplete. While not a NATO member, Austria joined NATO's Partnership for Peace framework in 1995 and has since participated in NATO-led crisis-management operations. In April 2018, the government announced modest budget increases to support training and exercises but a report published by the chief of the general staff in 2019 pointed to a substantial investment backlog, risking the armed forces' ability to perform basic territorial-defence tasks. A September 2019 report from the defence ministry defined a recapitalisation need for the Bundesheer of €16bn by 2030. The level of ambition for crisis response is to be able to deploy and sustain a minimum (on average) of 1,100 troops. The ministry's September 2019 report also called for Austria's *Typhoon* aircraft fleet to be upgraded on cost grounds, rather than replacing the airframes. Protected mobility is a modernisation priority, and delivery of a range of armoured vehicles began in 2019. Austria's defence-industrial base is comprised of some 100 companies with significant niche capabilities and international ties in the areas of weapons and ammunitions, communications equipment and vehicles.

ACTIVE 22,850 (Land Forces 12,850 Air 2,750 Support 7,250)
Conscript liability 6 months recruit trg, 30 days reservist refresher trg for volunteers; 120–150 days additional for officers, NCOs and specialists. Authorised maximum wartime strength of 55,000

RESERVE 143,800 (Joint structured 31,200; Joint unstructured 112,600)
Some 12,000 reservists a year undergo refresher trg in tranches

ORGANISATIONS BY SERVICE

Land Forces 12,850
FORCES BY ROLE
MANOEUVRE
  Armoured
    1 (4th) armd inf bde (1 recce/SP arty bn, 1 tk bn, 2 armd inf bn, 1 spt bn)
  Mechanised
    1 (3rd) mech inf bde (1 recce/SP arty bn, 2 mech inf bn, 1 mot inf bn; 1 cbt engr bn, 1 spt bn)
  Light
    1 (7th) lt inf bde (1 recce bn, 3 inf bn, 1 cbt engr bn, 1 spt bn)
    1 (6th) mtn inf bde (3 mtn inf bn, 1 cbt engr bn, 1 spt bn)
EQUIPMENT BY TYPE
ARMOURED FIGHTING VEHICLES
  MBT 56 *Leopard* 2A4
  AIFV 112 *Ulan*
  APC 115
    APC (T) 32 BvS-10
    APC (W) 83: 78 *Pandur*; 5 *Pandur* EVO
  AUV 236: 108 *Dingo* 2; 128 IVECO LMV
ENGINEERING & MAINTENANCE VEHICLES
  ARV 34: 24 4KH7FA-SB *Greif*; 10 M88A1
NBC VEHICLES 12 *Dingo* 2 AC NBC
ANTI-TANK/ANTI-INFRASTRUCTURE
  MSL • **MANPATS** *Bill* 2 (PAL 2000)
ARTILLERY 114
  SP 155mm 48 M109A5ÖE
  MOR 120mm 66 sGrW 86 (10 more in store)

Air Force 2,750
The Air Force is part of Joint Forces Comd and consists of 2 bde; Air Support Comd and Airspace Surveillance Comd
FORCES BY ROLE
FIGHTER
  2 sqn with *Typhoon*

ISR
  1 sqn with PC-6B *Turbo Porter*
TRANSPORT
  1 sqn with C-130K *Hercules*
TRAINING
  1 trg sqn with Saab 105Oe*
  1 trg sqn with PC-7 *Turbo Trainer*
TRANSPORT HELICOPTER
  2 sqn with Bell 212 (AB-212)
  1 sqn with OH-58B *Kiowa*
  1 sqn with S-70A *Black Hawk*
  2 sqn with SA316/SA319 *Alouette* III
AIR DEFENCE
  2 bn
  1 radar bn

EQUIPMENT BY TYPE
AIRCRAFT 27 combat capable
  FTR 15 Eurofighter *Typhoon* Tranche 1
  TPT 11: **Medium** 3 C-130K *Hercules*; **Light** 8 PC-6B *Turbo Porter*
  TRG 28: 12 PC-7 *Turbo Trainer*; 12 Saab 105Oe*; 4 DA40NG
HELICOPTERS
  MRH 19 SA316/SA319 *Alouette* III
  ISR 10 OH-58B *Kiowa*
  TPT 32: **Medium** 9 S-70A-42 *Black Hawk*; **Light** 23 Bell 212 (AB-212)
AIR DEFENCE
  SAM • Point-defence *Mistral*
  GUNS 35mm 24 GDF-005 (6 more in store)
AIR-LAUNCHED MISSILES • AAM • IIR IRIS-T

Special Operations Forces
FORCES BY ROLE
SPECIAL FORCES
  2 SF gp
  1 SF gp (reserve)

Support 6,950
Support forces comprise Joint Services Support Command and several agencies, academies and schools

DEPLOYMENT
AFGHANISTAN: NATO • *Operation Resolute Support* 16
BOSNIA-HERZEGOVINA: EU • EUFOR • *Operation Althea* 344; 1 inf bn HQ; 2 inf coy; 1 hel unit
CYPRUS: UN • UNFICYP 3
LEBANON: UN • UNIFIL 185; 1 log coy
MALI: EU • EUTM Mali 47; **UN •** MINUSMA 2
MIDDLE EAST: UN • UNTSO 5
SERBIA: NATO • KFOR 330; 2 mech inf coy; 1 log coy
WESTERN SAHARA: UN • MINURSO 5

Belgium BEL

Euro €		2018	2019	2020
GDP	€	451bn	461bn	
	US$	532bn	518bn	
per capita	US$	46,696	45,176	
Growth	%	1.4	1.2	
Inflation	%	2.3	1.5	
Def exp [a]	€	4.10bn	4.30bn	
	US$	4.84bn	4.83bn	
Def bdgt [b]	€	4.10bn	4.30bn	4.77bn
	US$	4.84bn	4.83bn	
US$1=€		0.85	0.89	

[a] NATO definition
[b] Includes military pensions

Real-terms defence budget trend (US$bn, constant 2015)

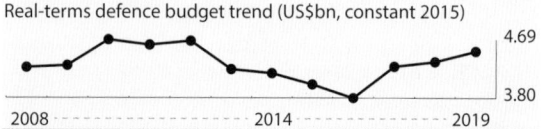

Population 11,647,253

Age	0–14	15–19	20–24	25–29	30–64	65 plus
Male	8.8%	2.8%	2.9%	3.3%	23.2%	8.3%
Female	8.4%	2.7%	2.8%	3.2%	23.0%	10.7%

Capabilities

In July 2016, the government published its strategic vision for defence up to 2030. Brussels intends to stabilise Belgium's defence effort and then provide for growth after 2020. It also envisages a reduced personnel component of around 25,000. However, a large number of impending service retirements means that a gradual increase in recruitment is planned. Belgium also continues to pursue high readiness levels and deployable niche capabilities. NATO membership is central to defence policy, as are the EU and the UN. Troops have been deployed to support police counter-terrorism efforts. Due to its limited force size, Belgium often collaborates with neighbours and has committed with Denmark and the Netherlands to form a composite combined special-operations command. Belgium can deploy forces for a small-scale overseas operation and maintains overseas deployments on EU and UN missions. The government is investing in short-term requirements related to aircraft readiness, personal equipment and land-forces vehicles. As part of the defence plan, the government envisages launching five investment projects for fighter aircraft, frigates, mine-countermeasures vessels (to be procured jointly with the Netherlands), UAVs and land-combat vehicles. The army has ordered French *Griffon* and *Jaguar* wheeled armoured vehicles for its motorised brigade. The air force has selected the F-35 to replace its F-16s and is to procure MQ-9B *Sky Guardian* UAVs. Belgium has an advanced, export-focused defence industry, focusing on components and subcontracting, though in FN Herstal it has one of the world's largest manufacturers of small arms.

ACTIVE 26,300 (Army 9,750 Navy 1,400 Air 5,500 Medical Service 1,250 Joint Service 8,400)

RESERVE 5,100

ORGANISATIONS BY SERVICE

Land Component 9,750
FORCES BY ROLE
SPECIAL FORCES
1 spec ops regt (1 SF gp, 1 cdo bn, 1 para bn, 1 sigs gp)
MANOEUVRE
Mechanised
1 mech bde (1 ISR bn; 3 mech bn; 2 lt inf bn; 1 arty bn; 2 engr bn; 2 sigs gp; 2 log bn)
COMBAT SUPPORT
1 EOD unit
1 MP coy
COMBAT SERVICE SUPPORT
1 log bn
EQUIPMENT BY TYPE
ARMOURED FIGHTING VEHICLES
ASLT 18 *Piranha* III-C DF90
RECCE 36 *Pandur Recce*
IFV 19 *Piranha* III-C DF30
APC • APC (W) 78: 64 *Piranha* III-C; 14 *Piranha* III-PC (CP)
AUV 656: 220 *Dingo* 2 (inc 52 CP); 436 IVECO LMV
ENGINEERING & MAINTENANCE VEHICLES
AEV 14: 6 Pionierpanzer 2 *Dachs*; 8 *Piranha* III-C
ARV 13: 4 *Pandur*; 9 *Piranha* III-C
VLB 4 *Leguan*
ANTI-TANK/ANTI-INFRASTRUCTURE
MSL • MANPATS *Spike*-MR
ARTILLERY 60
TOWED **105mm** 14 LG1 MkII
MOR 46: **81mm** 14 Expal; **120mm** 32 RT-61

Naval Component 1,400
EQUIPMENT BY TYPE
PRINCIPAL SURFACE COMBATANTS 2
FRIGATES • FFGHM 2 *Leopold* I (ex-NLD *Karel Doorman*) with 2 quad lnchr with RGM-84 *Harpoon* AShM, 1 16-cell Mk 48 mod 1 VLS with RIM-7P *Sea Sparrow* SAM, 2 twin SVTT Mk 32 324mm ASTT with Mk 46 LWT, 1 *Goalkeeper* CIWS, 1 76mm gun (capacity 1 med hel)
PATROL AND COASTAL COMBATANTS
PCC 2 *Castor*
MINE WARFARE • MINE COUNTERMEASURES
MHC 5 *Flower* (*Tripartite*)
LOGISTICS AND SUPPORT 3
AGFH 1 *Godetia* (log spt/comd) (capacity 1 *Alouette* III)
AGOR 1 *Belgica* (owned by BELSPO, managed by RBINS)
AXS 1 *Zenobe Gramme*

Naval Aviation
(part of the Air Component)
EQUIPMENT BY TYPE
HELICOPTERS
ASW 4 NH90 NFH
MRH 3 SA316B *Alouette* III

Air Component 5,500
FORCES BY ROLE
FIGHTER/GROUND ATTACK/ISR
4 sqn with F-16AM/BM *Fighting Falcon*
SEARCH & RESCUE
1 sqn with NH90 NFH
TRANSPORT
1 sqn with A321; ERJ-135 LR; ERJ-145 LR; *Falcon* 900B
1 sqn with C-130H *Hercules*
TRAINING
1 OCU sqn with F-16AM/BM *Fighting Falcon*
1 sqn with SF-260D/M
1 BEL/FRA unit with *Alpha Jet**
1 OCU unit with AW109
TRANSPORT HELICOPTER
2 sqn with AW109 (ISR)
ISR UAV
1 sqn with RQ-5A *Hunter* (B-*Hunter*)
EQUIPMENT BY TYPE
AIRCRAFT 72 combat capable
FTR 54: 45 F-16AM *Fighting Falcon*; 9 F-16BM *Fighting Falcon*
TPT 14: **Medium** 8 C-130H *Hercules*; **Light** 3: 2 ERJ-135 LR; 1 ERJ-145 LR; **PAX** 3: 1 A321; 2 *Falcon* 7X
TRG 50: 18 *Alpha Jet**; 9 SF-260D; 23 SF-260M
HELICOPTERS
ASW 4 NH90 NFH opcon Navy
MRH 3 SA316B *Alouette* III opcon Navy
TPT 17: **Medium** 4 NH90 TTH; **Light** 13 AW109 (ISR) (7 more in store)
UNMANNED AERIAL VEHICLES
ISR • **Heavy** 12 RQ-5A *Hunter* (B-*Hunter*) (1 more in store)
AIR-LAUNCHED MISSILES
AAM • **IR** AIM-9M *Sidewinder*; **IIR** AIM-9X *Sidewinder* II; **ARH** AIM-120B AMRAAM
BOMBS
Laser-guided: GBU-10/GBU-12 *Paveway* II; GBU-24 *Paveway* III
INS/GPS guided: GBU-31 JDAM; GBU-38 JDAM; GBU-54 Laser JDAM (dual-mode)

Medical Service 1,250
FORCES BY ROLE
COMBAT SERVICE SUPPORT
4 med unit
1 fd hospital
EQUIPMENT BY TYPE
ARMOURED FIGHTING VEHICLES
APC • APC (W) 10: 4 *Pandur* (amb); 6 *Piranha* III-C (amb)
AUV 10 *Dingo* 2 (amb)

DEPLOYMENT

AFGHANISTAN: NATO • *Operation Resolute Support* 83

DEMOCRATIC REPUBLIC OF THE CONGO: UN • MONUSCO 2

FRANCE: NATO • Air Component 28 *Alpha Jet* located at Cazaux/Tours

IRAQ: *Operation Inherent Resolve* 5

LITHUANIA: NATO • Enhanced Forward Presence 262; 1 mech inf coy(+); *Piranha* III-C; *Pirahna* III-C DF30; *Piranha* III-C DF90 • Baltic Air Policing 4 F-16AM *Fighting Falcon*

MALI: EU • EUTM Mali 15; **UN** • MINUSMA 38

MIDDLE EAST: UN • UNTSO 1

NIGER: METT *Maradi* 41 (trg)

FOREIGN FORCES

United States US European Command: 1,050

Bosnia-Herzegovina BIH

Convertible Mark		2018	2019	2020
GDP	mark	33.4bn	34.9bn	
	US$	20.2bn	20.1bn	
per capita	US$	5,755	5,742	
Growth	%	3.6	2.8	
Inflation	%	1.4	1.1	
Def bdgt	mark	284m	289m	288m
	US$	171m	167m	
FMA (US)	US$	0m	0m	0m
US$1=mark		1.66	1.73	

Real-terms defence budget trend (US$m, constant 2015)

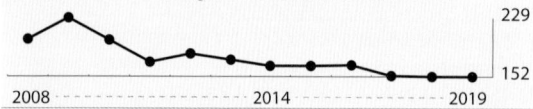

Population 3,843,037

Ethnic groups: Bosniac 50.1%; Serb 30.7%; Croat 15.4%; other or unspecified 3.7%

Age	0–14	15–19	20–24	25–29	30–64	65 plus
Male	6.8%	2.5%	3.2%	3.4%	26.6%	6.2%
Female	6.4%	2.4%	3.0%	3.2%	27.0%	9.4%

Capabilities

The armed forces' primary goals are to defend territorial integrity and contribute to peacekeeping missions and civilian-support operations. Bosnia-Herzegovina joined NATO's Partnership for Peace in 2006 and a Membership Action Plan was presented in 2010. Its aspiration to join NATO has been delayed due to unresolved defence-property issues. The country is reforming its armed forces and modernising its equipment in accordance with its Defence Review, Development and Modernisation Plan for 2017–27 and its NATO aspirations. The armed forces are professional and represent all three ethnic groups. However, low salaries likely negatively affect recruitment and retention. Bosnia-Herzegovina contributes to NATO missions and has deployed personnel to *Operation Resolute Support* in Afghanistan, but the armed forces have no capacity to independently deploy and self-sustain beyond national borders. The inventory comprises mainly ageing Soviet-era equipment, though some new helicopters have been procured from the US. Bosnia-Herzegovina has little in the way of a domestic defence industry, with only the capability to produce small arms, ammunition and explosives.

ACTIVE 10,500 (Armed Forces 10,500)

ORGANISATIONS BY SERVICE

Armed Forces 10,500

1 ops comd; 1 spt comd

FORCES BY ROLE
MANOEUVRE
  Light
  3 inf bde (1 recce coy, 3 inf bn, 1 arty bn)
COMBAT SUPPORT
  1 cbt spt bde (1 tk bn, 1 engr bn, 1 EOD bn, 1 int bn, 1 MP bn, 1 CBRN coy, 1 sigs bn)
COMBAT SERVICE SUPPORT
  1 log comd (5 log bn)
EQUIPMENT BY TYPE
ARMOURED FIGHTING VEHICLES
  MBT 45 M60A3
  APC • APC (T) 20 M113A2
ENGINEERING & MAINTENANCE VEHICLES
  VLB MTU
  MW *Bozena*
ANTI-TANK/ANTI-INFRASTRUCTURE • MSL
  SP 60: 8 9P122 *Malyutka*; 9 9P133 *Malyutka*; 32 BOV-1; 11 M-92
  MANPATS 9K11 *Malyutka* (AT-3 *Sagger*); 9K111 *Fagot* (AT-4 *Spigot*); 9K115 *Metis* (AT-7 *Saxhorn*); HJ-8; *Milan*
ARTILLERY 224
  TOWED 122mm 100 D-30
  MRL 122mm 24 APRA-40
  MOR 120mm 100 M-75

Air Force and Air Defence Brigade 800

FORCES BY ROLE
HELICOPTER
  1 sqn with Bell 205; Mi-8MTV *Hip*; Mi-17 *Hip* H
  1 sqn with Mi-8 *Hip*; SA-342H/L *Gazelle* (HN-42/45M)
AIR DEFENCE
  1 AD bn
EQUIPMENT BY TYPE
AIRCRAFT
  FGA (7 J-22 *Orao* in store)
  ATK (6 J-1 (J-21) *Jastreb*; 3 TJ-1(NJ-21) *Jastreb* all in store)
  ISR (2 RJ-1 (IJ-21) *Jastreb** in store)
  TRG (1 G-4 *Super Galeb* (N-62)* in store)
HELICOPTERS
  MRH 13: 4 Mi-8MTV *Hip*; 1 Mi-17 *Hip* H; 1 SA-341H *Gazelle* (HN-42); 7 SA-342L *Gazelle* (HN-45M)
  TPT 21: **Medium** 8 Mi-8 *Hip* **Light** 13 Bell 205 (UH-1H *Iroquois*)
  TRG 1 Mi-34 *Hermit*
AIR DEFENCE
  SAM
    Short-range 20 2K12 *Kub* (SA-6 *Gainful*)
    Point-defence 9K34 *Strela*-3 (SA-14 *Gremlin*); 9K310 *Igla*-1 (SA-16 *Gimlet*)
  GUNS • TOWED 40mm 47: 31 L/60, 16 L/70

DEPLOYMENT

AFGHANISTAN: NATO • *Operation Resolute Support* 68
CENTRAL AFRICAN REPUBLIC: EU • EUTM RCA 2
DEMOCRATIC REPUBLIC OF THE CONGO: UN • MONUSCO 3
MALI: UN • MINUSMA 2

FOREIGN FORCES

Part of EUFOR – *Operation Althea* unless otherwise stated
Albania 1
Austria 344; 1 inf bn HQ; 2 inf coy
Bulgaria 11
Chile 15
Czech Republic 2
Greece 2
Hungary 164; 1 inf coy
Ireland 5
Italy 5
Macedonia, North 3
Poland 25
Romania 35
Slovakia 41
Slovenia 10
Spain 2
Switzerland 21
Turkey 249; 1 inf coy
United Kingdom 2

Bulgaria BLG

Bulgarian Lev L		2018	2019	2020
GDP	L	108bn	115bn	
	US$	65.2bn	66.3bn	
per capita	US$	9,314	9,518	
Growth	%	3.1	3.7	
Inflation	%	2.6	2.5	
Def exp [a]	L	1.59bn	3.72bn	
	US$	962m	2.13bn	
Def bdgt [b]	L	1.59bn	3.61bn	1.98bn
	US$	959m	2.07bn	
FMA (US)	US$	0m	0m	0m
US$1=L		1.66	1.74	

[a] NATO definition
[b] Excludes military pensions

Real-terms defence budget trend (US$m, constant 2015)

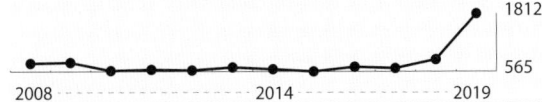

Population	7,012,640					
Age	0–14	15–19	20–24	25–29	30–64	65 plus
Male	7.5%	2.5%	2.4%	3.1%	25.3%	8.0%
Female	7.1%	2.3%	2.2%	2.8%	25.1%	11.8%

Capabilities

The armed forces' main priority is defending state sovereignty and territorial integrity. Bulgaria is in the process of implementing the Programme for the Development of the Defence Capabilities of the Bulgarian Armed Forces 2020. In March 2018, the National Assembly adopted a new National Security Strategy that includes cyber and transportation security for the first time, while attention was also paid to hybrid threats. A NATO member, Bulgaria enjoys close ties with the US. With only limited numbers of combat aircraft itself, Bulgaria's airspace is protected by NATO's Air Policing Mission. It has reached several bilateral defence-cooperation agreements with regional states. Sofia has increased the military retirement age and reduced the maximum age for recruitment in an attempt to cope with personnel shortages. Training is prioritised for those units intended for international operations and those with certain readiness levels declared to NATO and the EU. Bulgaria regularly trains and exercises with NATO partners and regional allies. The country contributes to NATO and EU missions but has little logistics-support capability. Despite long-term plans for reform, the armed forces still rely heavily on ageing Soviet-era equipment. However, in July 2019, Bulgaria approved the purchase of F-16 Block 70 fighter aircraft to replace its MiG-29s. There are also plans to acquire core combat capabilities to enable the formation of battalion battlegroups within the mechanised brigades. The navy is prioritising the procurement of a multi-purpose patrol vessel and the modernisation of its frigates to boost its presence in the Black Sea. Bulgaria's defence industry exports small arms but has limited capacity to design and manufacture platforms.

ACTIVE 36,950 (Army 17,000 Navy 4,450 Air 8,500 Central Staff 7,000)

RESERVE 3,000 (Joint 3,000)

ORGANISATIONS BY SERVICE

Army 16,300
FORCES BY ROLE
MANOEUVRE
  Reconnaissance
  1 recce bn
  Mechanised
  2 mech bde (4 mech inf bn, 1 SP arty bn, 1 cbt engr bn, 1 log bn, 1 SAM bn)
  Light
  1 mtn inf regt
COMBAT SUPPORT
  1 arty regt (1 fd arty bn, 1 MRL bn)
  1 engr regt (1 cbt engr bn, 1 ptn br bn, 1 engr spt bn)
  1 NBC bn
COMBAT SERVICE SUPPORT
  1 log regt
EQUIPMENT BY TYPE
ARMOURED FIGHTING VEHICLES
  MBT 90 T-72M1/M2†
  IFV 160: 90 BMP-1; 70 BMP-23
  APC 120
    APC (T) 100 MT-LB
    APC (W) 20 BTR-60
  AUV 44: 17 M1117 ASV; 27 Plasan *Sandcat*
ENGINEERING & MAINTENANCE VEHICLES
  AEV MT-LB

ARV T-54/T-55; MTP-1; MT-LB
VLB BLG67; TMM
ANTI-TANK/ANTI-INFRASTRUCTURE
MSL
SP 24 9P148 *Konkurs* (AT-5 *Spandrel*)
MANPATS 9K111 *Fagot* (AT-4 *Spigot*); 9K111-1 *Konkurs* (AT-5 *Spandrel*); (9K11 *Malyutka* (AT-3 *Sagger*) in store)
GUNS 126: **85mm** (150 D-44 in store); **100mm** 126 MT-12
ARTILLERY 176
SP **122mm** 48 2S1
TOWED **152mm** 24 D-20
MRL **122mm** 24 BM-21
MOR **120mm** ε80 *Tundza/Tundza Sani*
SURFACE-TO-SURFACE MISSILE LAUNCHERS
SRBM • **Conventional** 9K79 *Tochka* (SS-21 *Scarab*)
AIR DEFENCE
SAM • **Point-defence** 9K32 *Strela* (SA-7 *Grail*)‡; 24 9K33 *Osa* (SA-8 *Gecko*)
GUNS 400
SP **23mm** ZSU-23-4
TOWED **23mm** ZU-23-2; **57mm** S-60

Navy 3,450
EQUIPMENT BY TYPE
PRINCIPAL SURFACE COMBATANTS • FRIGATES • 4
FFM 3 *Drazki* (ex-BEL *Wielingen*) with 1 octuple Mk 29 GMLS with RIM-7P *Sea Sparrow* SAM, 2 single 533mm ASTT with L5 mod 4 HWT, 1 sextuple Bofors ASW Rocket Launcher System 375mm A/S mor, 1 100mm gun (Fitted for but not with 2 twin lnchr with MM38 *Exocet* AShM)
FF 1 *Smeli* (ex-FSU *Koni*) with 2 RBU 6000 *Smerch* 2 A/S mor, 2 twin 76mm guns
PATROL AND COASTAL COMBATANTS 3
PCFG 1 *Molnya*† (ex-FSU *Tarantul* II) with 2 twin lnchr with P-22 (SS-N-2C *Styx*) AShM, 2 AK630M CIWS, 1 76mm gun
PCT 2 *Reshitelni* (ex-FSU *Pauk* I) with 4 single 406mm TT, 2 RBU 1200 *Uragan* A/S mor, 1 76mm gun
MINE COUNTERMEASURES 7
MHC 1 *Tsibar* (Tripartite – ex-BEL *Flower*)
MSC 3 *Briz* (ex-FSU *Sonya*)
MSI 3 *Olya* (ex-FSU) (3 more non-operational)
AMPHIBIOUS 1
LCM 1 *Vydra* (capacity either 3 MBT or 200 troops)
LOGISTICS AND SUPPORT 8: 2 **AGS**; 2 **AOL**; 1 **ARS**; 2 **ATF**; 1 **AX**

Naval Aviation
EQUIPMENT BY TYPE
HELICOPTERS • ASW 2 AS565MB *Panther*

Air Force 6,700
FORCES BY ROLE
FIGHTER/ISR
1 sqn with MiG-29A/UB *Fulcrum*
TRANSPORT
1 sqn with An-30 *Clank*; C-27J *Spartan*; L-410UVP-E; PC-12M
TRAINING
1 sqn with L-39ZA *Albatros**
1 sqn with PC-9M
ATTACK HELICOPTER
1 sqn with Mi-24D/V *Hind* D/E
TRANSPORT HELICOPTER
1 sqn with AS532AL *Cougar*; Bell 206 *Jet Ranger*; Mi-17 *Hip* H
EQUIPMENT BY TYPE
AIRCRAFT 21 combat capable
FTR 15: 12 MiG-29A *Fulcrum*†; 3 MiG-29UB *Fulcrum*†
FGA (Some MiG-21bis *Fishbed*/MiG-21UM *Mongol* B in store)
ISR 1 An-30 *Clank*
TPT 7: **Medium** 3 C-27J *Spartan*; **Light** 4: 1 An-2T *Colt*; 2 L-410UVP-E; 1 PC-12M
TRG 12: 6 L-39ZA *Albatros**; 6 PC-9M (basic)
HELICOPTERS
ATK 6 Mi-24D/V *Hind* D/E
MRH 5 Mi-17 *Hip* H
TPT 18: **Medium** 12 AS532AL *Cougar*; **Light** 6 Bell 206 *Jet Ranger*
UNMANNED AERIAL VEHICLES • EW *Yastreb*-2S
AIR DEFENCE
SAM
Long-range S-200 (SA-5 *Gammon*); S-300P (SA-10 *Grumble*)
Short-range S-125 *Pechora* (SA-3 *Goa*); 2K12 *Kub* (SA-6 *Gainful*)
AIR-LAUNCHED MISSILES
AAM • **IR** R-3 (AA-2 *Atoll*)‡ R-73 (AA-11A *Archer*)
SARH R-27R (AA-10 *Alamo* A)
ASM Kh-29 (AS-14 *Kedge*); Kh-25 (AS-10 *Karen*)

Special Forces
FORCES BY ROLE
SPECIAL FORCES
1 spec ops bde (1 SF bn, 1 para bn)

DEPLOYMENT
AFGHANISTAN: NATO • *Operation Resolute Support* 159
BOSNIA-HERZEGOVINA: EU • EUFOR • *Operation Althea* 11
MALI: EU • EUTM Mali 5
SERBIA: NATO • KFOR 22

FOREIGN FORCES
United States US European Command: 150; 1 armd inf coy; M1A2 SEPv2 *Abrams*; M2A3 *Bradley*

Croatia CRO

Croatian Kuna k		2018	2019	2020
GDP	k	382bn	401bn	
	US$	60.8bn	60.7bn	
per capita	US$	14,870	14,950	
Growth	%	2.6	3.0	
Inflation	%	1.5	1.0	
Def exp [a]	k	6.07bn	6.68bn	
	US$	966m	1.01bn	
Def bdgt [b]	k	6.06bn	6.94bn	7.27bn
	US$	966m	1.05bn	
US$1=k		6.28	6.60	

[a] NATO definition
[b] Includes military pensions

Real-terms defence budget trend (US$m, constant 2015)

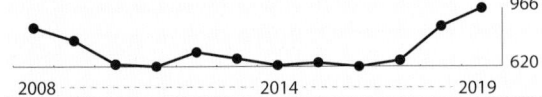

Population 4,248,989

Ethnic groups: Croat 90.4%; Serb 4.3%; Bosniac 0.7%; Italian 0.4%; Hungarian 0.3%; other or unspecified 3.9%

Age	0–14	15–19	20–24	25–29	30–64	65 plus
Male	7.3%	2.5%	3.1%	3.0%	24.0%	8.3%
Female	6.9%	2.4%	2.9%	2.9%	24.5%	12.2%

Capabilities

Principal tasks for the armed forces include defending national sovereignty and territorial integrity as well as tackling terrorism and contributing to international peacekeeping missions. Croatia joined NATO in 2009, having reformed its armed forces to create a small professional force. There have been recent moves to improve conditions of service. Economic challenges have delayed further defence modernisation. Zagreb has defence-cooperation agreements with Bosnia-Herzegovina, Hungary and Romania, and personnel frequently train with regional and international allies. Croatia participates in NATO and EU missions, including in Afghanistan. The inventory is almost entirely composed of ageing Soviet-era equipment. Modernisation objectives include the acquisition of helicopters. However, the replacement process for Croatia's MiG-21 fighter aircraft had to be restarted following US objections to the proposed sale of second-hand, upgraded Israeli F-16s. Croatia has a small defence industry, focused on small arms, ammunition, explosives and naval systems.

ACTIVE 15,200 (Army 10,750 Navy 1,300 Air 1,300 Joint 1,850) **Paramilitary 3,000**

Conscript liability Voluntary conscription, 8 weeks

RESERVE 18,350 (Army 18,350)

ORGANISATIONS BY SERVICE

Joint 1,850 (General Staff)
FORCES BY ROLE
SPECIAL FORCES
 1 SF bn

Army 10,750
FORCES BY ROLE
MANOEUVRE
 Armoured
  1 armd bde (1 tk bn, 1 armd bn, 2 armd inf bn, 1 SP arty bn, 1 ADA bn, 1 cbt engr bn)
 Light
  1 mot inf bde (2 mech inf bn, 2 mot inf bn, 1 fd arty bn, 1 ADA bn, 1 cbt engr bn)
 Other
  1 inf trg regt
COMBAT SUPPORT
 1 arty/MRL regt
 1 engr regt
 1 NBC bn
 1 sigs regt
COMBAT SERVICE SUPPORT
 1 log regt
AIR DEFENCE
 1 ADA regt
EQUIPMENT BY TYPE
ARMOURED FIGHTING VEHICLES
 MBT 75 M-84
 IFV 102 M-80
 APC 198
  APC (T) 14: 11 BTR-50; 3 OT M-60
  APC (W) 132: 6 BOV-VP; 126 Patria AMV (incl variants)
 PPV 52: 32 Maxxpro Plus; 20 RG-33 HAGA (amb)
 AUV 172: 10 IVECO LMV; 162 M-ATV
ENGINEERING & MAINTENANCE VEHICLES
 ARV 22: 12 JVBT-55A; 1 M-84AI; 1 WZT-2; 2 WZT-3; 6 Maxxpro Recovery
 VLB 5 MT-55A
 MW 4 MV-4
ANTI-TANK/ANTI-INFRASTRUCTURE • MSL
 SP 20 BOV-1
 MANPATS 9K11 Malyutka (AT-3 Sagger); 9K111 Fagot (AT-4 Spigot); 9K111-1 Konkurs (AT-5 Spandrel); 9K115 Metis (AT-7 Saxhorn)
ARTILLERY 167
 SP 20: **122mm** 8 2S1 Gvozdika; **155mm** 12 PzH 2000
 TOWED 122mm 20 D 30
 MRL 122mm 27: 6 M91 Vulkan; 21 BM-21 Grad
 MOR 100: **82mm** 54 LMB M96; **120mm** 46 M-75/UBM 52
AIR DEFENCE
 SAM • Point-defence 9 9K35 Strela-10M3 (SA-13 Gopher); 9K310 Igla-1 (SA-16 Gimlet)
 GUNS SP 20mm 33 BOV-3 SP

Navy 1,300
Navy HQ at Split
EQUIPMENT BY TYPE
PATROL AND COASTAL COMBATANTS 5
 PCFG 1 Končar with 2 twin lnchr with RBS15B Mk I AShM, 1 AK630 CIWS, 1 57mm gun
 PCG 4:
  2 Kralj with 4 single lnchr with RBS15B Mk I AShM, 1 AK630 CIWS, 1 57mm gun (with minelaying capability)

2 *Vukovar* (ex-FIN *Helsinki*) with 4 single lnchr with RBS15B Mk I AShM, 1 57mm gun
MINE WARFARE • MINE COUNTERMEASURES • MHI 1 *Korcula*
AMPHIBIOUS • LANDING CRAFT 5:
  LCT 2 *Cetina* (with minelaying capability)
  LCVP 3: 2 Type-21; 1 Type-22
LOGISTICS AND SUPPORT • AKL 1
COASTAL DEFENCE • AShM 3 RBS15K

Marines
FORCES BY ROLE
MANOEUVRE
  Amphibious
    1 indep mne coy

Coast Guard
FORCES BY ROLE
Two divisions, headquartered in Split (1st div) and Pula (2nd div)
EQUIPMENT BY TYPE
PATROL AND COASTAL COMBATANTS • PB 5: 4 *Mirna*; 1 *Omiš*
LOGISTICS AND SUPPORT
  AKL 1 PT-71
  AX 2

Air Force and Air Defence 1,300
FORCES BY ROLE
FIGHTER/GROUND ATTACK
  1 (mixed) sqn with MiG-21bis/UMD *Fishbed*
TRANSPORT
  1 sqn with An-32 *Cline*
TRAINING
  1 sqn with PC-9M; Z-242L
  1 hel sqn with Bell 206B *Jet Ranger* II
TRANSPORT HELICOPTER
  2 sqn with Mi-8MTV *Hip* H; Mi-8T *Hip* C; Mi-171Sh
EQUIPMENT BY TYPE
AIRCRAFT 11 combat capable
  FGA 11: 8 MiG-21bis *Fishbed*; 3 MiG-21UMD *Fishbed*
  TPT • Light (2 An-32 *Cline* in store)
  TRG 22: 17 PC-9M; 5 Z-242L
HELICOPTERS
  MRH 27: 11 Mi-8MTV *Hip* H; 16 OH-58D *Kiowa Warrior*
  TPT 21: Medium 13: 3 Mi-8T *Hip* C; 10 Mi-171Sh; Light 8 Bell 206B *Jet Ranger* II
UNMANNED AERIAL VEHICLES
  ISR • Medium *Hermes* 450
AIR DEFENCE • SAM
  Point-defence 9K31 *Strela*-1 (SA-9 *Gaskin*); 9K34 *Strela*-3 (SA-14 *Gremlin*); 9K310 *Igla*-1 (SA-16 *Gimlet*)
AIR-LAUNCHED MISSILES
  AAM • IR R-3S (AA-2 *Atoll*)‡; R-60; R-60MK (AA-8 *Aphid*)
  ASM AGM-114 *Hellfire*

Special Forces Command
FORCES BY ROLE
SPECIAL FORCES
  2 SF gp

Paramilitary 3,000
Police 3,000 armed

DEPLOYMENT
AFGHANISTAN: NATO • Operation Resolute Support 110
INDIA/PAKISTAN: UN • UNMOGIP 9
LEBANON: UN • UNIFIL 1
POLAND: NATO • Enhanced Forward Presence 80; 1 MRL bty with M91 *Vulkan*
SERBIA: NATO • KFOR 38; 1 hel unit with Mi-8 *Hip*
WESTERN SAHARA: UN • MINURSO 7

Cyprus CYP

Euro €		2018	2019	2020
GDP	€	20.7bn	21.6bn	
	US$	24.5bn	24.3bn	
per capita	US$	28,341	27,720	
Growth	%	3.9	3.1	
Inflation	%	0.8	0.7	
Def bdgt	€	365m	359m	355m
	US$	431m	403m	
US$1=€		0.85	0.89	

Real-terms defence budget trend (US$m, constant 2015)

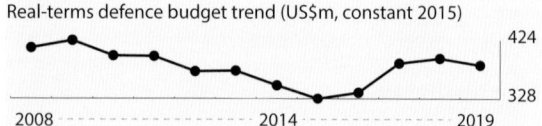

Population 1,252,147

Age	0–14	15–19	20–24	25–29	30–64	65 plus
Male	8.0%	2.9%	4.0%	4.7%	25.9%	5.5%
Female	7.6%	2.5%	3.3%	3.9%	24.4%	7.2%

Capabilities

The National Guard is focused on protecting the island's territorial integrity and sovereignty, and safeguarding Cyprus's EEZ. Its main objective is to deter any Turkish incursion, and to provide enough opposition until military support can be provided by Greece, its primary ally. Cyprus has been enhancing its defence cooperation with Greece, including on cyber defence. Nicosia has also pledged deeper military ties with Israel, while France has renewed and enhanced its defence-cooperation agreement with Cyprus. In 2018 Cyprus also signed a memorandum of understanding on enhancing defence and security cooperation with the UK. Having reduced conscript liability in 2016, Nicosia began recruiting additional contract-service personnel, as part of the effort to modernise and professionalise its forces. Cyprus exercises with several international partners, most notably France, Greece and Israel. External deployments have been limited to some officers joining EU and UN missions. Cyprus has little logistics capability to support operations abroad. Equipment comprises a mix of Soviet-era and modern European systems. The defence minister announced in 2019 the intention to introduce an eight-year military-modernisation programme that would also involve a higher defence budget. Cyprus has little in the way of a domestic defence industry, with no ability to design and manufacture modern equipment. However, the government is looking for opportunities to cooperate with defence firms in Greece.

ACTIVE 15,000 (National Guard 15,000)
Paramilitary 750
Conscript liability 14 months

RESERVE 50,000 (National Guard 50,000)
Reserve service to age 50 (officers dependent on rank; military doctors to age 60)

ORGANISATIONS BY SERVICE

National Guard 15,000 (incl conscripts)
FORCES BY ROLE
SPECIAL FORCES
  1 comd (regt) (1 SF bn)
MANOEUVRE
  Armoured
    1 lt armd bde (2 armd bn, 1 armd inf bn)
  Mechanised
    4 (1st, 2nd, 6th & 7th) mech bde
  Light
    1 (4th) lt inf bde
    2 (2nd & 8th) lt inf regt
COMBAT SUPPORT
  1 arty comd (8 arty bn)
COMBAT SERVICE SUPPORT
  1 (3rd) spt bde
EQUIPMENT BY TYPE
ARMOURED FIGHTING VEHICLES
  MBT 134: 82 T-80U; 52 AMX-30B2
  RECCE 69 EE-9 *Cascavel*
  IFV 43 BMP-3
  APC 294
    APC (T) 168 *Leonidas*
    APC (W) 126 VAB (incl variants)
  AUV 8 BOV M16 *Milos*
ENGINEERING & MAINTENANCE VEHICLES
  ARV 3: 2 AMX-30D; 1 BREM-1
ANTI-TANK/ANTI-INFRASTRUCTURE
  MSL
    SP 33: 15 EE-3 *Jararaca* with *Milan*; 18 VAB with HOT
    MANPATS *Milan*
  RCL 106mm 144 M40A1
  GUNS • TOWED 100mm 20 M-1944
ARTILLERY 434
  SP 155mm 26+: 12 Mk F3; 2+ NORA B-52; 12 *Zuzana*
  TOWED 84: 105mm 72 M-56; 155mm 12 TR-F-1
  MRL 22. 122mm 4 BM-21; 128mm 18 M-63 *Plamen*
  MOR 302: 81mm 170 E-44 (70+ M1/M9 in store); 107mm 20 M2/M30; 120mm 112 RT61
AIR DEFENCE
  SAM
    Medium-range 4 9K37M1 *Buk* M1-2 (SA-11 *Gadfly*)
    Short-range 18: 12 *Aspide*; 6 9K331 *Tor*-M1 (SA-15 *Gauntlet*)
    Point-defence *Mistral*
  GUNS • TOWED 60: 20mm 36 M-55; 35mm 24 GDF-003 (with *Skyguard*)

Maritime Wing
FORCES BY ROLE
COMBAT SUPPORT
  1 (coastal defence) AShM bty with MM40 *Exocet* AShM
EQUIPMENT BY TYPE
PATROL AND COASTAL COMBATANTS 6
  PCC 2: 1 *Alasia* (ex-OMN *Al Mabrukha*) with 1 hel landing platform; 1 OPV 62 (ISR *Sa'ar* 4.5 derivative)
  PBF 4: 2 Rodman 55; 2 *Vittoria*
COASTAL DEFENCE • AShM 3 MM40 *Exocet*

Air Wing EQUIPMENT BY TYPE
AIRCRAFT
  TPT • Light 1 BN-2B *Islander* TRG 1 PC-9
HELICOPTERS
  ATK 11 Mi-35P *Hind* E
  MRH 7: 3 AW139 (SAR); 4 SA342L1 *Gazelle* (with HOT for anti-armour role)
  TPT • Light 2 Bell 206L3 *Long Ranger*

Paramilitary 750+

Armed Police 500+
FORCES BY ROLE
MANOEUVRE
  Other
    1 (rapid-reaction) paramilitary unit
EQUIPMENT BY TYPE
ARMOURED FIGHTING VEHICLES
  APC • APC (W) 2 VAB VTT
HELICOPTERS • MRH 4: 2 AW139; 2 Bell 412SP

Maritime Police 250
EQUIPMENT BY TYPE
PATROL AND COASTAL COMBATANTS 10
  PBF 5: 2 *Poseidon*; 1 *Shaldag*; 2 *Vittoria*
  PB 5 SAB-12

DEPLOYMENT
LEBANON: UN • UNIFIL 2

FOREIGN FORCES
Argentina UNFICYP 243; 2 inf coy; 1 hel flt
Australia UNFICYP 3
Austria UNFICYP 3
Brazil UNFICYP 2
Canada UNFICYP 1
Chile UNFICYP 12
Ghana UNFICYP 1
Greece Army: 950; ε200 (officers/NCO seconded to Greek-Cypriot National Guard)
Hungary UNFICYP 13
India UNFICYP 1
Pakistan UNFICYP 1
Paraguay UNFICYP 12
Serbia UNFICYP 3
Slovakia UNFICYP 240; 1 inf coy; 1 engr pl

United Kingdom 2,260; 2 inf bn; 1 hel sqn with 4 Bell 412 *Twin Huey* • *Operation Inherent Resolve* (*Shader*) 500: 1 FGA sqn with 8 *Tornado* GR4; 6 *Typhoon* FGR4; 2 *Sentinel* R1; 1 A330 MRTT *Voyager* KC3; 2 C-130J *Hercules* • UNFICYP (*Operation Tosca*) 257: 1 log coy (inf role)

TERRITORY WHERE THE GOVERNMENT DOES NOT EXERCISE EFFECTIVE CONTROL

Data here represents the de facto situation on the northern section of the island. This does not imply international recognition as a sovereign state.

Capabilities

ACTIVE 3,000 (Army 3,000) **Paramilitary 150**
Conscript liability 15 months

RESERVE 15,000
Reserve liability to age 50

ORGANISATIONS BY SERVICE

Army ε3,000
FORCES BY ROLE
MANOEUVRE
  Light
    5 inf bn
    7 inf bn (reserve)
EQUIPMENT BY TYPE
ANTI-TANK/ANTI-INFRASTRUCTURE
  MSL • MANPATS *Milan*
  RCL • **106mm** 36
ARTILLERY • MOR • **120mm** 73

Paramilitary

Armed Police ε150
FORCES BY ROLE
SPECIAL FORCES
  1 (police) SF unit

Coast Guard
PATROL AND COASTAL COMBATANTS 6
  PCC 5: 2 SG45/SG46; 1 *Rauf Denktash*; 2 US Mk 5
  PB 1

FOREIGN FORCES

TURKEY
Army ε33,800
  FORCES BY ROLE
  1 corps HQ; 1 SF regt; 1 armd bde; 2 mech inf div; 1 mech inf regt; 1 arty regt; 1 avn comd
  EQUIPMENT BY TYPE
  ARMOURED FIGHTING VEHICLES
    MBT ε342: ε300 M48A5T1; 42 *Leopard* 2A4
    IFV 147 ACV AIFV

  APC • APC (T) 492: 106 ACV AAPC (incl variants); 386 M113 (incl variants)
  ANTI-TANK/ANTI-INFRASTRUCTURE
    MSL
      SP 60 ACV TOW
      MANPATS *Milan*
    RCL **106mm** 219 M40A1
  ARTILLERY 643
    SP **155mm** 194: 30 M44T; 144 M52T1; 20 T-155 *Firtina*
    TOWED 84: **105mm** 36 M101A1; **155mm** 36 M114A2; **203mm** 12 M115
    MRL **122mm** 9 T-122
    MOR 376: **81mm** 171; **107mm** 70 M30; **120mm** 135 HY-12
  PATROL AND COASTAL COMBATANTS 1 PB
  AIRCRAFT • TPT • Light 3 Cessna 185 (U-17)
  HELICOPTERS • TPT 3 Medium 2 AS532UL *Cougar* Light 1 Bell 205 (UH-1H *Iroquois*)
  AIR DEFENCE
    SAM Point-defence FIM-92 *Stinger*
    GUNS • TOWED 150: **20mm** 122: 44 Rh 202; 78 GAI-D01; **35mm** 28 GDF-003

Czech Republic CZE

Czech Koruna Kc		2018	2019	2020
GDP	Kc	5.33tr	5.60tr	
	US$	245bn	247bn	
per capita	US$	23,113	23,214	
Growth	%	3.0	2.5	
Inflation	%	2.2	2.6	
Def exp [a]	Kc	59.8bn	66.7bn	
	US$	2.75bn	2.94bn	
Def bdgt [b]	Kc	58.9bn	66.7bn	75.5bn
	US$	2.71bn	2.94bn	
US$1=Kc		21.73	22.70	

[a] NATO definition
[b] Includes military pensions

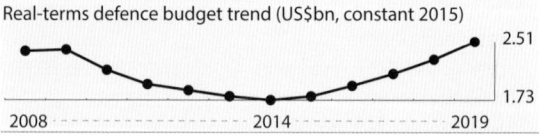
Real-terms defence budget trend (US$bn, constant 2015)

Population 10,695,547

Age	0–14	15–19	20–24	25–29	30–64	65 plus
Male	7.8%	2.3%	2.4%	3.2%	25.1%	8.3%
Female	7.4%	2.2%	2.3%	3.0%	24.4%	11.5%

Capabilities

The 2015 national-security strategy states that NATO is central to Czech security, while the 2017 defence strategy points to Russian assertiveness, an arc of instability to the south and southeast of Europe and information warfare, including cyber attacks, as core security challenges. In February 2017, the Czech Republic signed a letter of intent with Germany to affiliate the 4th Czech Rapid Deployment Brigade with the 10th German Armoured Division under NATO's Framework Nations Concept. In the same year, a bilateral agreement with Slovakia addressed mutual air-defence issues. It was announced in 2018 that the two countries will cooperate on procurement tenders. The government plans to increase personnel numbers and adopted an Active Reserve Law in 2016, which aims to incentivise engagement in the reserves. However, recruitment and retention remains a challenge. The armed forces are able to deploy on a variety of international crisis-management operations, including NATO's Enhanced Forward Presence in the Baltic states, participating in Baltic Air Policing and contributing to NATO's Very High Readiness Joint Task Force. The defence ministry announced plans at the end of 2017 to upgrade existing military training and simulation facilities by 2025. The government is trying to replace legacy equipment in order to both modernise the armed forces and reduce dependence on Russia for spare parts and services. Modernisation priorities include infantry fighting vehicles, self-propelled howitzers, multi-role helicopters, transport aircraft, short-range air-defence systems and UAVs. The defence-industrial base includes development and manufacturing capability, in particular relating to small arms, vehicles, and training and light attack aircraft. The holding company Czechoslovak Group brings together several companies across the munitions, vehicles and aerospace sectors.

ACTIVE 21,750 (Army 12,250 Air 5,850 Other 3,650)

ORGANISATIONS BY SERVICE

Army 12,250
FORCES BY ROLE
MANOEUVRE
  Reconnaissance
  1 ISR/EW regt (1 recce bn, 1 EW bn)
  Armoured
  1 (7th) mech bde (1 tk bn, 2 armd inf bn, 1 mot inf bn)
  Mechanised
  1 (4th) rapid reaction bde (2 mech inf bn, 1 mot inf bn, 1 AB bn)
COMBAT SUPPORT
  1 (13th) arty regt (2 arty bn)
  1 engr regt (2 engr bn, 1 EOD bn)
  1 CBRN regt (2 CBRN bn)
COMBAT SERVICE SUPPORT
  1 log regt (2 log bn, 1 maint bn)

Active Reserve
FORCES BY ROLE
COMMAND
  14 (territorial defence) comd
MANOEUVRE
  Armoured
  1 armd coy
  Light
  14 inf coy (1 per territorial comd) (3 inf pl, 1 cbt spt pl, 1 log pl)
EQUIPMENT BY TYPE
ARMOURED FIGHTING VEHICLES
  MBT 30 T-72M4CZ (89 T-72 in store)
  RECCE 34 BPzV *Svatava*
  IFV 227: 120 BMP-2; 107 *Pandur* II (incl variants); (98 BMP-1; 65 BMP-2 all in store)
  APC
    APC (T) (17 OT-90 in store)
  AUV 21 *Dingo* 2; IVECO LMV

ENGINEERING & MAINTENANCE VEHICLES
  ARV 13+: 10 VPV-ARV (12 more in store); VT-55A; 3 VT-72M4
  VLB 6 MT-55A (3 more in store)
  MW *Bozena* 5; UOS-155 *Belarty*
NBC VEHICLES BRDM-2RCH
ANTI-TANK/ANTI-INFRASTRUCTURE
  MSL • MANPATS 9K111-1 *Konkurs* (AT-5 *Spandrel*); FGM-148 *Javelin*; *Spike*-LR
  RCL 84mm *Carl Gustaf*
ARTILLERY 96
  SP 152mm 48 M-77 *Dana* (38 more in store)
  MOR 48: **120mm** 40 M-1982; (45 more in store); **SP 120mm** 8 SPM-85

Air Force 5,850
Principal task is to secure Czech airspace. This mission is fulfilled within NATO Integrated Extended Air Defence System (NATINADS) and, if necessary, by means of the Czech national reinforced air-defence system. The air force also provides CAS for army SAR, and performs a tpt role

FORCES BY ROLE
FIGHTER/GROUND ATTACK
  1 sqn with *Gripen* C/D
  1 sqn with L-159 ALCA; L-159T1*
TRANSPORT
  2 sqn with A319CJ; C295M; CL-601 *Challenger*; L-410 *Turbolet*; Yak-40 *Codling*
TRAINING
  1 sqn with L-159 ALCA; L-159T1*; L-159T2*
ATTACK HELICOPTER
  1 sqn with Mi-24/Mi-35 *Hind*
TRANSPORT HELICOPTER
  1 sqn with Mi-17 *Hip* H; Mi-171Sh
  1 sqn with Mi-8 *Hip*; Mi-17 *Hip* H; PZL W-3A *Sokol*
AIR DEFENCE
  1 (25th) SAM regt (2 AD gp)
EQUIPMENT BY TYPE
AIRCRAFT 38 combat capable
  FGA 14: 12 *Gripen* C; 2 *Gripen* D
  ATK 16 L-159 ALCA
  TPT 15: **Light** 12: 4 C295M; 6 L-410 *Turbolet*; 2 Yak-40 *Codling*; **PAX** 3: 2 A319CJ; 1 CL-601 *Challenger*
  TRG 8: 5 L-159T1*; 3 L-159T2*
HELICOPTERS
  ATK 17: 7 Mi-24 *Hind* D; 10 Mi-35 *Hind* E
  MRH 5 Mi-17 *Hip* H
  TPT • Medium 30: 4 Mi-8 *Hip*; 16 Mi-171Sh; 10 PZL W3A *Sokol*
AIR DEFENCE • SAM
  Point-defence 9K35 *Strela*-10 (SA-13 *Gopher*); 9K32 *Strela*-2‡ (SA-7 *Grail*) (available for trg RBS-70 gunners); RBS-70
AIR-LAUNCHED MISSILES
  AAM • IR AIM-9M *Sidewinder*; **ARH** AIM-120C-5 AMRAAM
BOMBS
  Laser-guided: GBU *Paveway*

Other Forces 3,650
FORCES BY ROLE
SPECIAL FORCES
  1 SF gp
MANOEUVRE
  Other
  1 (presidential) gd bde (2 bn)
  1 (honour guard) gd bn (2 coy)
COMBAT SUPPORT
  1 int gp
  1 (central) MP comd
  3 (regional) MP comd
  1 (protection service) MP comd

DEPLOYMENT

AFGHANISTAN: NATO • *Operation Resolute Support* 334
BOSNIA-HERZEGOVINA: EU • EUFOR • *Operation Althea* 2
CENTRAL AFRICAN REPUBLIC: UN • MINUSCA 3
DEMOCRATIC REPUBLIC OF THE CONGO: UN • MONUSCO 2
EGYPT: MFO 18; 1 C295M
ESTONIA: NATO • Baltic Air Policing 4 *Gripen* C
IRAQ: *Operation Inherent Resolve* 30
LATVIA: NATO • Enhanced Forward Presence 55; 1 mor pl
LITHUAINA: NATO • Enhanced Forward Presence 35; 1 EW unit
MALI: EU • EUTM Mali 120; UN • MINUSMA 7
SERBIA: NATO • KFOR 9; UN • UNMIK 2
SYRIA/ISRAEL: UN • UNDOF 3

Denmark DNK

Danish Krone kr		2018	2019	2020
GDP	kr	2.22tr	2.30tr	
	US$	352bn	347bn	
per capita	US$	60,897	59,795	
Growth	%	1.5	1.7	
Inflation	%	0.7	1.3	
Def exp [a]	kr	28.8bn	30.4bn	
	US$	4.56bn	4.59bn	
Def bdgt [b]	kr	28.8bn	30.4bn	32.2bn
	US$	4.56bn	4.59bn	
US$1=kr		6.31	6.62	

[a] NATO definition
[b] Includes military pensions

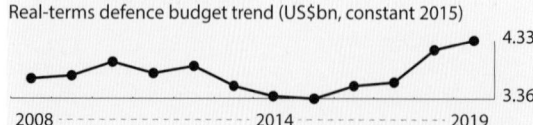
Real-terms defence budget trend (US$bn, constant 2015)

Population	5,841,522					
Age	0–14	15–19	20–24	25–29	30–64	65 plus
Male	8.5%	3.1%	3.4%	3.5%	22.4%	9.0%
Female	8.0%	2.9%	3.2%	3.3%	22.1%	10.6%

Capabilities

Danish military capabilities remain compact but effective despite pressures on spending and deployments. In the foreign- and security-policy strategy 2019–20, released at the end of 2018, the government expressed its concerns about an aggressive Russia, instability in the Middle East and cyber attacks. Earlier, the government issued a defence agreement for 2018–23, envisaging increased defence spending to deal with a deteriorating security environment. In particular, it is intended to strengthen deterrence, cyber defence and Denmark's role in international operations, as well as the armed forces' ability to support civilian authorities in national-security tasks. Denmark plans to set up a heavy brigade with ground-based air-defence capabilities and a light infantry battalion to take on patrol and guard tasks in support of the police. Denmark also intends to strengthen naval air defence, as well as anti-submarine-warfare capabilities. Ties to NATO, NORDEFCO and other regional neighbours have increased. A joint declaration, aimed at deterring Russia, was signed in April 2015 with other Nordic states. Denmark is an EU member but has opted out of military cooperation under the Common Security and Defence Policy. The new defence agreement foresees that national service is retained and that the annual conscript intake should rise. In June 2016, it was confirmed that the F-35A would replace the country's ageing F-16AM/BM fleet, though the strain of transitioning to the new platform might temporarily reduce Denmark's ability to contribute to NATO Air Policing tasks. Industrial support from Terma, Denmark's largest defence company, may have been important to the F-35 procurement decision, as some key sub-components and composites are produced by the firm. The defence-industrial base is focused on exports to Europe and North America and is mainly active in defence electronics and the design and manufacture of components and subsystems.

ACTIVE 14,500 (Army 7,100 Navy 2,250 Air 3,000 Joint 2,150)
Conscript liability 4–12 months, most voluntary

RESERVES 44,000 (Army 34,200 Navy 5,300 Air Force 4,500)

ORGANISATIONS BY SERVICE

Army 7,100
Div and a bde HQ in transformation into operational formations
FORCES BY ROLE
COMMAND
  1 (MND-N) div HQ
MANOEUVRE
  Mechanised
  1 (1st) mech bde (1 ISR bn, 3 mech inf bn, 1 SP arty bn, 1 cbt engr bn, 1 sigs bn, 1 log bn)
  1 (2nd) mech bde (1 recce bn, 1 tk bn, 1 lt inf bn)
COMBAT SUPPORT
  1 CBRN/construction bn
  1 EOD bn
  1 int bn
  1 MP bn
  2 sigs bn
COMBAT SERVICE SUPPORT
  1 log bn
  1 maint bn
  1 spt bn

AIR DEFENCE
1 AD bn
EQUIPMENT BY TYPE
ARMOURED FIGHTING VEHICLES
MBT 44: 43 *Leopard* 2A5 (to be upgraded to 2A7); 1 *Leopard* 2A7
IFV 44 CV9035 MkIII
APC 233
APC (T) 125 M113 (incl variants)
APC (W) 108: 79 *Piranha* III (incl variants); 29 *Piranha* V
AUV 120: 84 *Eagle* IV; 36 *Eagle* V
ENGINEERING & MAINTENANCE VEHICLES
AEV 6 *Wisent*
ARV 10 BPZ-2
VLB 9 *Biber*
ANTI-TANK/ANTI-INFRASTRUCTURE
RCL 84mm *Carl Gustav*
ARTILLERY 32
SP 155mm 12 M109A3 (being replaced by CAESAR)
MOR • TOWED 120mm 20 Soltam K6B1
AIR DEFENCE • SAM • Point-defence FIM-92 *Stinger*

Navy 2,250
EQUIPMENT BY TYPE
PRINCIPAL SURFACE COMBATANTS 3
DESTROYERS • DDGHM 3 *Iver Huitfeldt* with 4 quad lnchr with RGM-84L *Harpoon* Block II AShM, 4 8-cell Mk 41 VLS (to be fitted with SAM), 2 12-cell Mk 56 VLS with RIM-162B ESSM SAM, 2 twin 324mm TT with MU90 LWT, 1 *Millennium* CIWS, 2 76mm guns (capacity 1 med hel)
PATROL AND COASTAL COMBATANTS 13
PSOH 4 *Thetis* 1 76mm gun (capacity 1 MH-60R *Seahawk*)
PSO 3 *Knud Rasmussen* with 1 76mm gun, 1 hel landing platform
PCC 6 *Diana*
MINE WARFARE • MINE COUNTERMEASURES 6
MCI 4 MSF MK-I
MSD 2 *Holm*
LOGISTICS AND SUPPORT 11
ABU 2 (primarily used for MARPOL duties)
AE 1 *Sleipner*
AG 2 *Absalon* (flexible support ships) with 4 quad lnchr with RGM-84L *Harpoon* Block II AShM, 3 12-cell Mk 56 VLS with RIM-162B ESSM SAM, 2 twin 324mm TT with MU90 LWT, 2 *Millennium* CIWS, 1 127mm gun (capacity 2 AW101 *Merlin*; 2 LCP, 7 MBT or 40 vehicles; 130 troops)
AGS 2 *Holm*
AKL 2 *Seatruck*
AXS 2 *Svanen*

Air Force 3,000
Tactical Air Command
FORCES BY ROLE
FIGHTER/GROUND ATTACK
2 sqn with F-16AM/BM *Fighting Falcon*
ANTI-SUBMARINE WARFARE
1 sqn with MH-60R *Seahawk*
SEARCH & RESCUE/TRANSPORT HELICOPTER
1 sqn with AW101 *Merlin*
1 sqn with AS550 *Fennec* (ISR)
TRANSPORT
1 sqn with C-130J-30 *Hercules*; CL-604 *Challenger* (MP/VIP)
TRAINING
1 unit with MFI-17 *Supporter* (T-17)
EQUIPMENT BY TYPE
AIRCRAFT 44 combat capable
FTR 44: 34 F-16AM *Fighting Falcon*; 10 F-16BM *Fighting Falcon* (30 operational)
TPT 8: **Medium** 4 C-130J-30 *Hercules*; **PAX** 4 CL-604 *Challenger* (MP/VIP)
TRG 27 MFI-17 *Supporter* (T-17)
HELICOPTERS
ASW 9 MH-60R *Seahawk*
SAR 8 AW101 *Merlin*
MRH 8 AS550 *Fennec* (ISR) (4 more non-operational)
TPT • **Medium** 6 AW101 *Merlin*
AIR-LAUNCHED MISSILES
AAM • **IR** AIM-9L *Sidewinder*; **IIR** AIM-9X *Sidewinder* II; **ARH** AIM-120B AMRAAM
ASM AGM-65 *Maverick*
BOMBS
Laser-guided EGBU-12/GBU-24 *Paveway* II/III
INS/GPS guided GBU-31 JDAM

Control and Air Defence Group
1 Control and Reporting Centre, 1 Mobile Control and Reporting Centre. 4 Radar sites

Special Operations Command
FORCES BY ROLE
SPECIAL FORCES
1 SF unit
1 diving unit

Reserves

Home Guard (Army) 34,300 reservists (to age 50)
FORCES BY ROLE
MANOEUVRE
Light
2 regt cbt gp (3 mot inf bn, 1 arty bn)
5 (local) def region (up to 2 mot inf bn)

Home Guard (Navy) 5,300 reservists (to age 50)
EQUIPMENT BY TYPE
PATROL AND COASTAL COMBATANTS 30
PB 30: 17 MHV800; 1 MHV850; 12 MHV900

Home Guard (Air Force) 4,750 reservists (to age 50)

Home Guard (Service Corps) 1,350 reservists

DEPLOYMENT
AFGHANISTAN: NATO • *Operation Resolute Support* 155
BALTIC SEA: NATO • SNMCMG 1: 1 PSOH
ESTONIA: NATO • Enhanced Forward Presence 3

IRAQ: *Operation Inherent Resolve* 190; 1 SF gp; 1 trg team
KUWAIT: *Operation Inherent Resolve* 20
LITHUANIA: NATO • Baltic Air Policing 4 F-16AM *Fighting Falcon*
MALI: UN • MINUSMA 2
MIDDLE EAST: UN • UNTSO 11
SERBIA: NATO • KFOR 35
SOUTH SUDAN: UN • UNMISS 10
UNITED ARAB EMIRATES: *Operation Inherent Resolve* 20

Estonia EST

Euro €		2018	2019	2020
GDP	€	26.0bn	27.6bn	
	US$	30.8bn	31.0bn	
per capita	US$	23,330	23,524	
Growth	%	4.8	3.2	
Inflation	%	3.4	2.5	
Def Exp [a]	€	514m	586m	
	US$	607m	658m	
Def bdgt [b]	€	546m	615m	627m
	US$	645m	691m	
FMA (US)	US$	8m	0m	5m
US$1=€		0.85	0.89	

[a] NATO definition
[b] Includes military pensions

Real-terms defence budget trend (US$m, constant 2015)

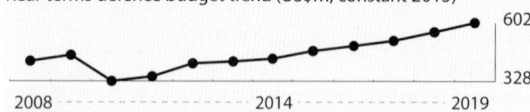

Population 1,236,641

Ethnic groups: Estonian 70%; Russian 25%; Ukranian 1.7%; Belarusian 1%; other or unspecified 2.3%

Age	0–14	15–19	20–24	25–29	30–64	65 plus
Male	8.4%	2.3%	2.2%	3.0%	23.8%	7.1%
Female	7.9%	2.2%	2.1%	2.8%	24.7%	13.5%

Capabilities

Estonia has small active armed forces and is reliant on NATO membership as a security guarantor. Security policy is predicated on the goals of ensuring sovereignty and territorial integrity, and there is concern over Russian security policy and military activity. The government's 2017–26 National Defence Development Plan (NDDP) reflects the worsening security environment in the Baltic region. The active armed forces are supplemented by a reserve component. In June 2018, Estonia joined the French-inspired European Intervention Force. A NATO battlegroup based in Estonia became operational in mid-2017 as part of the Alliance's Enhanced Forward Presence. The country's Amari air base hosts a NATO Baltic Air Policing detachment. Estonia is also a member of the UK-led multinational Joint Expeditionary Force. Cyber security is a strength, and Tallinn hosts NATO's Cybersecurity Centre of Excellence. The NDDP notes a desire to increase the annual conscript intake and the total number of active personnel. There is very limited organic capability to deploy beyond borders, though Estonian forces take part in EU, NATO and UN missions abroad on a small scale. The NDDP identifies the need for additional armoured mobility and armoured firepower, anti-armour weapons and increased munitions stocks. The country has a niche defence-industrial capability, including ship repair and digital systems.

ACTIVE 6,700 (Army 3,900 Navy 300 Air 400 Other 2,100) Defence League 15,800
Conscript liability 8 or 11 months (depending on specialisation; conscripts cannot be deployed)

RESERVE 12,000 (Joint 12,000)

ORGANISATIONS BY SERVICE

Army 1,500; 2,400 conscript (total 3,900)
4 def region. All units except one inf bn are reserve based
FORCES BY ROLE
MANOEUVRE
  Mechanised
  1 (1st) bde (1 recce coy, 1 armd inf bn; 2 mech inf bn, 1 arty bn, 1 AT coy, 1 cbt engr bn, 1 spt bn, 1 AD bn)
  Light
  1 (2nd) inf bde (1 recce coy, 3 inf bn, 1 arty bn, 1 AT coy, 1 cbt engr bn, 1 spt bn, 1 AD bn)

Defence League 15,800
15 Districts
EQUIPMENT BY TYPE
ARMOURED FIGHTING VEHICLES
  IFV 44 CV9035EE (incl 2 CP)
  APC • APC (W) 136: 56 XA-180 *Sisu*; 80 XA-188 *Sisu*
ENGINEERING & MAINTENANCE VEHICLES
  AEV 2 Pioneerpanzer 2 *Dachs*
  ARV 2 BPz-2
  VLB 2 *Biber*
ANTI-TANK/ANTI-INFRASTRUCTURE
  MSL • MANPATS FGM-148 *Javelin*; Milan
  RCL 84mm *Carl Gustav*; 90mm PV-1110
ARTILLERY 165
  TOWED 42: 122mm 18 D-30 (H 63); 155mm 24 FH-70
  MOR 123: 81mm 60 B455/NM 95/M252; 120mm 63 2B11/M/41D
AIR DEFENCE
  SAM • Point-defence *Mistral*
  GUNS • TOWED 23mm ZU-23-2

Navy 200; 100 conscript (total 300)
EQUIPMENT BY TYPE
MINE WARFARE • MINE COUNTERMEASURES 4
  MCCS 1 *Tasuja* (ex-DNK *Lindormen*)
  MHC 3 *Admiral Cowan* (ex-UK *Sandown*) (1 in refit)

Air Force 400
FORCES BY ROLE
TRANSPORT
  1 sqn with An-2 *Colt*
TRANSPORT HELICOPTER
  1 sqn with R-44 *Raven* II

EQUIPMENT BY TYPE
AIRCRAFT • TPT • Light 3: 2 An-2 *Colt*; 1 M-28 *Skytruck*
HELICOPTERS • TPT • Light 4 R-44 *Raven* II

Other 1,400; 700 conscript (total 2,100)
Includes Cyber Command, Support Command and Special Operations Forces
FORCES BY ROLE
SPECIAL FORCES
  1 spec ops bn
COMBAT SUPPORT
  2 MP coy
COMBAT SERVICE SUPPORT
  1 log bn

Paramilitary

Border Guard
The Estonian Border Guard is subordinate to the Ministry of the Interior. Air support is provided by the Estonian Border Guard Aviation Corps
EQUIPMENT BY TYPE
PATROL AND COASTAL COMBATANTS 13
  PCO 2: 1 *Kati*; 1 *Kindral Kurvits*
  PCC 1 *Kou* (FIN *Silma*)
  PB 10: 1 *Pikker*; 1 *Raju* (Baltic 4500WP); 1 *Valve*; 8 (other)
AMPHIBIOUS • LANDING CRAFT • LCU 3
LOGISTICS & SUPPORT • AGF 1 *Balsam*
AIRCRAFT • TPT • Light 2 L-410
HELICOPTERS • MRH 3 AW139

DEPLOYMENT

AFGHANISTAN: NATO • *Operation Resolute Support* 42

IRAQ: *Operation Inherent Resolve* 10 **• NATO** Mission Iraq 5

LEBANON: UN • UNIFIL 1

MALI: *Operation Barkhane* 50; **EU •** EUTM Mali 10; **UN •** MINUSMA 3

MIDDLE EAST: UN • UNTSO 3

FOREIGN FORCES
All **NATO** Enhanced Forward Presence unless stated
Denmark 3
Czech Republic NATO Baltic Air Policing 4 *Gripen* C
France 330; 1 armd inf coy(+)
United Kingdom 800; 1 armd regt HQ; 1 tk sqn, 1 armd inf coy (+); 1 cbt engr coy

Finland FIN

Euro €		2018	2019	2020
GDP	€	232bn	239bn	
	US$	274bn	270bn	
per capita	US$	49,738	48,869	
Growth	%	1.7	1.2	
Inflation	%	1.2	1.2	
Def bdgt [a]	€	3.18bn	3.55bn	3.58bn
	US$	3.76bn	4.00bn	
US$1=€		0.85	0.89	

[a] Includes military pensions

Real-terms defence budget trend (US$bn, constant 2015)

3.77
3.07

2008 2014 2019

Population 5,555,154

Age	0–14	15–19	20–24	25–29	30–64	65 plus
Male	8.4%	2.7%	2.9%	3.3%	22.4%	9.6%
Female	8.0%	2.6%	2.8%	3.1%	21.9%	12.3%

Capabilities

Finland's armed forces are primarily focused on territorial defence. The country's long border with Russia has focused attention on Russia's military capabilities and plans. The 2017 Defence Report argues that changes in the security environment have increased the demands on the armed forces and stresses that financial constraints are forcing trade-offs between long-term procurement plans and operational readiness. An EU member state, Finland's principal multilateral defence relationships include NORDEFCO and the Northern Group, as well as strong bilateral cooperation with Sweden and the US; it is building close ties with NATO short of membership. In 2017, Finland joined a multinational cooperation programme for air-to-ground precision-guided munitions set up by a group of NATO member states. The country participates in UN peacekeeping missions and contributes to NATO operations and the international counter-ISIS coalition. Legislation limits the number of personnel deployed on international crisis-management operations to an upper ceiling of 2,000 troops. In 2015, the air force launched the HX Fighter Programme to replace its F/A-18s. A request for quotations was issued in April 2018 and the replacement aircraft is expected to be selected in 2021. Under Finland's Squadron 2020 programme, the navy will replace patrol boats and minelayers with corvette-sized vessels capable of operating in shallow water and cold weather. Finland's defence industry consists largely of privately owned SMEs, concentrating on niche products for international markets, but it also features some internationally competitive larger companies producing wheeled armoured vehicles and turreted mortar systems.

ACTIVE 21,500 (Army 15,300 Navy 3,500 Air 2,700)
Paramilitary 2,700
Conscript liability 165, 255 or 347 days (latter for NCOs, officers or those on 'especially demanding' duties)

RESERVE 216,000 (Army 170,000 Navy 20,000 Air 26,000) **Paramilitary 11,500**
18,000 reservists a year do refresher training: total obligation 80 days (150 for NCOs, 200 for officers) between conscript service and age 50 (NCOs and officers to age 60)

ORGANISATIONS BY SERVICE

Army 5,000; 10,300 conscript (total 15,300)

FORCES BY ROLE
Finland's army maintains a mobilisation strength of about 285,000. In support of this requirement, two conscription cycles, each for about 13,500 conscripts, take place each year. After conscript training, reservist commitment is to the age of 60. Reservists are usually assigned to units within their local geographical area. All service appointments or deployments outside Finnish borders are voluntary for all members of the armed services. All brigades are reserve based

Reserve Organisations 170,000

FORCES BY ROLE
SPECIAL FORCES
 1 SF bn
MANOEUVRE
 Armoured
  2 armd BG (regt)
 Mechanised
  2 (Karelia & Pori Jaeger) mech bde
 Light
  3 (Jaeger) bde
  6 lt inf bde
COMBAT SUPPORT
 1 arty bde
 1 AD regt
 7 engr regt
 3 sigs bn
COMBAT SERVICE SUPPORT
 Some log unit
HELICOPTER
 1 hel bn

EQUIPMENT BY TYPE
ARMOURED FIGHTING VEHICLES
 MBT 100 *Leopard* 2A6 (100 *Leopard* 2A4 in store)
 IFV 212: 110 BMP-2/-2MD; 102 CV9030FIN
 APC 613
  APC (T) 142: 40 MT-LBu; 102 MT-LBV
  APC (W) 471: 260 XA-180/185 *Sisu*; 101 XA-202 *Sisu* (CP); 48 XA-203 *Sisu*; 62 AMV (XA-360)
ENGINEERING & MAINTENANCE VEHICLES
 ARV 27: 15 MTP-LB; 12 VT-55A
 VLB 27: 12 BLG-60M2; 6 *Leopard* 2S; 9 SISU *Leguan*
 MW 6+: *Aardvark* Mk 2; KMT T-55; 6 *Leopard* 2R CEV; RA-140 DS
ANTI-TANK/ANTI-INFRASTRUCTURE
 MSL • MANPATS NLAW; *Spike*-MR; *Spike*-LR
ARTILLERY 699
 SP 122mm 40: 4 K9 *Thunder*; 36 2S1 *Gvozdika* (PsH 74)
 TOWED 324: **122mm** 234 D-30 (H 63); **130mm** 36 M-46 (K 54); **155mm** 54 K 83/GH-52 (K 98)
 MRL 56: **122mm** 34 RM-70; **227mm** 22 M270 MLRS
 MOR 279+: **81mm** Krh/71; **120mm** 261 Krh/92; **SP 120mm** 18 XA-361 AMOS
HELICOPTERS
 MRH 7: 5 Hughes 500D; 2 Hughes 500E
 TPT • Medium 20 NH90 TTH

UNMANNED AERIAL VEHICLES
 ISR
  Medium 11 ADS-95 *Ranger*
AIR DEFENCE
 SAM
  Short-range 44: 20 *Crotale* NG (ITO 90); 24 NASAMS II FIN (ITO 12)
  Point-defence 16+: 16 ASRAD (ITO 05); FIM-92 *Stinger* (ITO 15); RBS 70 (ITO 05/05M)
 GUNS 407+: **23mm** ItK 95/ZU-23-2 (ItK 61); **35mm** GDF-005 (ItK 88); **SP 35mm** 7 *Leopard* 2 ITK *Marksman*

Navy 1,600; 1,900 conscript (total 3,500)

FORCES BY ROLE
Naval Command HQ located at Turku; with two subordinate Naval Commands (Gulf of Finland and Archipelago Sea); 1 Naval bde; 3 spt elm (Naval Materiel Cmd, Naval Academy, Naval Research Institute)

EQUIPMENT BY TYPE
PATROL AND COASTAL COMBATANTS 20
 PCGM 4 *Hamina* with 4 RBS15 Mk3 (MTO-85M) AShM, 1 8-cell VLS with *Umkhonto*-IR (ITO2004) SAM, 1 57mm gun
 PBF 12 *Jehu* (U-700) (capacity 24 troops)
 PBG 4 *Rauma* with 6 RBS15 Mk3 (MTO-85M) AShM
MINE WARFARE 15
 MINE COUNTERMEASURES 10
  MCC 3 *Katanpää*
  MSI 7: 4 *Kiiski*; 3 *Kuha*
 MINELAYERS • ML 5:
  2 *Hameenmaa* with 1 8-cell VLS with *Umkhonto*-IR (ITO2004) SAM, 2 RBU 1200 *Uragan* A/S mor, 1 57mm gun (can carry up to 100–120 mines)
  3 *Pansio* with 50 mines
AMPHIBIOUS • LANDING CRAFT 51
 LCM 1 *Kampela*
 LCP 50
LOGISTICS AND SUPPORT 7
 AG 3: 1 *Louhi*; 2 *Hylje*
 AX 4: 3 *Fabian Wrede*; 1 *Lokki*

Coastal Defence

FORCES BY ROLE
 MANOEUVRE Amphibious
  1 mne bde
 COMBAT SUPPORT
  1 cbt spt bde (1 AShM bty)
EQUIPMENT BY TYPE
COASTAL DEFENCE
 AShM 4 RBS15K
 ARTY • 130mm 30 K-53tk (static)
ANTI-TANK/ANTI-INFRASTRUCTURE
 MSL • MANPATS *Spike* (used in AShM role)

Air Force 1,950; 750 conscript (total 2,700)

3 Air Comds: Satakunta (West), Karelia (East), Lapland (North)

FORCES BY ROLE
FIGHTER/GROUND ATTACK
 3 sqn with F/A-18C/D *Hornet*

ISR
1 (survey) sqn with Learjet 35A
TRANSPORT
1 flt with C295M
4 (liaison) flt with PC-12NG
TRAINING
1 sqn with *Hawk* Mk50/51A/66* (air-defence and ground-attack trg)
1 unit with G-115EA
EQUIPMENT BY TYPE
AIRCRAFT 107 combat capable
 FGA 62: 55 F/A-18C *Hornet*; 7 F/A-18D *Hornet*
 MP 1 F-27-400M
 ELINT 1 C295M
 TPT • **Light** 10: 2 C295M; 3 Learjet 35A (survey; ECM trg; tgt-tow); 5 PC-12NG
 TRG 73: 28 G-115EA; 29 *Hawk* Mk50/51A*; 16 *Hawk* Mk66*
AIR-LAUNCHED MISSILES
 AAM • IR AIM-9 *Sidewinder*; IIR AIM-9X *Sidewinder*
 ARH AIM-120C AMRAAM
 LACM **Conventional** AGM-158 JASSM
BOMBS
 INS/GPS-guided GBU-31 JDAM; AGM-154C JSOW

Paramilitary

Border Guard 2,700
Ministry of Interior. 4 Border Guard Districts and 2 Coast Guard Districts
FORCES BY ROLE
MARITIME PATROL
 1 sqn with Do-228 (maritime surv); AS332 *Super Puma*; Bell 412 (AB-412) *Twin Huey*; Bell 412EP (AB-412EP) *Twin Huey*;AW119KE *Koala*
EQUIPMENT BY TYPE
PATROL AND COASTAL COMBATANTS 45
 PSO 1 *Turva* with 1 hel landing platform
 PCC 3: 2 *Tursas*; 1 *Merikarhu*
 PB 41
AMPHIBIOUS • LANDING CRAFT • UCAC 6
AIRCRAFT • TPT • Light 2 Do-228
HELICOPTERS
 MRH 5: 3 Bell 412 (AB-412) *Twin Huey*; 2 Bell 412EP (AB-412EP) *Twin Huey*
 TPT 9: **Medium** 5 AS332 *Super Puma*; **Light** 4 AW119KE *Koala*

Reserve 11,500 reservists on mobilisation

DEPLOYMENT

AFGHANISTAN: NATO • *Operation Resolute Support* 67
IRAQ: *Operation Inherent Resolve* 80; 1 trg team; **NATO** • NATO Mission Iraq 1
LEBANON: UN • UNIFIL 198; 1 maint coy
MALI: EU • EUTM Mali 3; **UN** • MINUSMA 4
MIDDLE EAST: UN • UNTSO 15
SERBIA: NATO • KFOR 20; **UN** • UNMIK 1
SOMALIA: EU • EUTM Somalia 10

France FRA

Euro €		2018	2019	2020
GDP	€	2.35tr	2.41tr	
	US$	2.78tr	2.71tr	
per capita	US$	42,953	41,761	
Growth	%	1.7	1.2	
Inflation	%	2.1	1.2	
Def exp [a]	€	42.7bn	44.4bn	
	US$	50.5bn	49.8bn	
Def bdgt [b]	€	45.0bn	46.5bn	48.1bn
	US$	53.2bn	52.3bn	
US$1=€		0.85	0.89	

[a] NATO definition
[b] Includes pensions

Real-terms defence budget trend (US$bn, constant 2015)

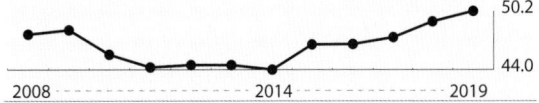

Population	67,611,479					
Age	0–14	15–19	20–24	25–29	30–64	65 plus
Male	9.4%	3.1%	3.0%	3.0%	21.8%	8.7%
Female	9.0%	3.0%	2.8%	2.9%	22.0%	11.4%

Capabilities

France maintains globally deployed forces that are also engaged on enduring operations in Africa. The 2017 Strategic Review reiterated operational commitments in sub-Saharan Africa and the Middle East, as well as a continued presence in the Asia-Pacific. The Programme Budget Law for 2019–25 set out defence-budget increases to support these goals. France plays a leading military role in the EU, NATO and the UN. In 2018, Paris launched the European Intervention Initiative, joined by 11 other European countries, intended to foster a common strategic culture and develop the ability to jointly deploy quickly in case of crises. France is also expanding its capabilities in non-traditional domains, having set up a space command, developed a space strategy and formalised a cyber-offensive doctrine. Deployments abroad have demonstrated the ability to support expeditionary forces independently; however, the more recent focus on domestic security has reduced training levels and limited the ability to deploy more troops overseas. Some strategic military air-transport requirements are dependent on allies and external contractors. The high operational tempo has increased the stress on equipment. The Programme Budget Law seeks to remedy this with a budget increase for maintenance, reform of aerospace maintenance, and accelerated modernisation of multi-role tanker-transport and refuelling aircraft. France has a sophisticated defence industry, exemplified by companies such as Dassault, MBDA and Nexter, with most procurements undertaken domestically and strong exports. However, President Macron has called for increased European defence-industrial cooperation. France is also seeking to invest in future technologies and supports start-ups and innovation in the defence domain.

ACTIVE 203,750 (Army 114,850 Navy 35,100 Air 40,500, Other Staffs 13,300) Paramilitary 100,500

RESERVE 38,550 (Army 22,750 Navy 6,000 Air 5,700 Other Staffs 4,100) Paramilitary 30,300

ORGANISATIONS BY SERVICE

Strategic Nuclear Forces

Navy 2,200
EQUIPMENT BY TYPE
SUBMARINES • STRATEGIC • SSBN 4
  4 *Le Triomphant* with 16 M51 SLBM with 6 TN-75 nuclear warheads, 4 single 533mm TT with SM39 *Exocet* AShM/F17 mod 2 HWT
AIRCRAFT • FGA 20 *Rafale* M F3 with ASMPA msl

Air Force 1,800

Air Strategic Forces Command
FORCES BY ROLE
STRIKE
  1 sqn with *Rafale* B with ASMPA msl
  1 sqn with *Rafale* B with ASMPA msl (forming)
TANKER
  1 sqn with C-135FR; KC-135 *Stratotanker*
EQUIPMENT BY TYPE
AIRCRAFT 20 combat capable
  FGA 20 *Rafale* B
  TKR/TPT 11 C-135FR
  TKR 3 KC-135 *Stratotanker*

Paramilitary

Gendarmerie 40

Space
EQUIPMENT BY TYPE
SATELLITES 7
  COMMUNICATIONS 3: 2 *Syracuse*-3 (designed to integrate with UK *Skynet* & ITA *Sicral*); 1 *Athena-Fidus* (also used by ITA)
  ISR 4: 2 *Helios* (2A/2B); 2 *Pleiades*

Army 114,850
Regt and BG normally bn size
FORCES BY ROLE
COMMAND
  1 corps HQ (CRR-FR)
  2 div HQ
MANOEUVRE
  Reconnaissance
  1 recce regt
  Armoured
  1 (2nd) armd bde (2 tk regt, 3 armd inf regt, 1 SP arty regt, 1 engr regt)
  1 (7th) armd bde (1 tk regt, 1 armd BG, 3 armd inf regt, 1 SP arty regt, 1 engr regt)
  1 armd BG (UAE)
  Mechanised
  1 (6th) lt armd bde (2 armd cav regt, 1 armd inf regt, 1 mech inf regt, 1 mech inf regt, 1 SP arty regt, 1 engr regt)
  1 (FRA/GER) mech bde (1 armd cav regt, 1 mech inf regt)
  1 mech regt (Djibouti)
  Light
  1 (27th) mtn bde (1 armd cav regt, 3 mtn inf regt, 1 arty regt, 1 engr regt)
  3 inf regt (French Guiana & French West Indies)
  1 inf regt (New Caledonia)
  1 inf bn (Côte d'Ivoire)
  1 inf coy (Mayotte)
  Air Manoeuvre
  1 (11th) AB bde (1 armd cav regt, 4 para regt, 1 arty regt, 1 engr regt, 1 spt regt)
  1 AB regt (La Réunion)
  1 AB bn (Gabon)
  Amphibious
  1 (9th) amph bde (2 armd cav regt, 1 armd inf regt, 2 mech inf regt, 1 SP arty regt, 1 engr regt)
  Other
  4 SMA regt (French Guiana, French West Indies & Indian Ocean)
  3 SMA coy (French Polynesia, Indian Ocean & New Caledonia)
COMBAT SUPPORT
  1 MRL regt
  2 engr regt
  2 EW regt
  1 int bn
  1 CBRN regt
  5 sigs regt
COMBAT SERVICE SUPPORT
  5 tpt regt
  1 log regt
  1 med regt
  3 trg regt
HELICOPTER
  1 (4th) hel bde (3 hel regt)
ISR UAV
  1 UAV regt
AIR DEFENCE
  1 SAM regt

Special Operation Forces 2,200
FORCES BY ROLE
SPECIAL FORCES
  2 SF regt
HELICOPTER
  1 hel regt

Reserves 22,750 reservists
Reservists form 79 UIR (Reserve Intervention Units) of about 75 to 152 troops, for 'Proterre' – combined land projection forces bn, and 23 USR (Reserve Specialised Units) of about 160 troops, in specialised regt
EQUIPMENT BY TYPE
ARMOURED FIGHTING VEHICLES
  MBT 222 *Leclerc*

ASLT 247 AMX-10RC
RECCE 1,483: 59 ERC-90F4 *Sagaie*; 1,424 VBL/VB2L
IFV 625: 515 VBCI VCI; 110 VBCI VPC (CP)
APC 2,345
   APC (T) 53 BvS-10
   APC (W) 2,279: 24 VBMR *Griffon*; 2,190 VAB; 65 VAB VOA (OP)
   PPV 13 *Aravis*
ENGINEERING & MAINTENANCE VEHICLES
   AEV 50 AMX-30EBG
   ARV 47+: 30 AMX-30D; 17 *Leclerc* DNG; VAB-EHC
   VLB 67: 39 EFA; 18 PTA; 10 SPRAT
   MW 24+: AMX-30B/B2; 4 *Buffalo*; 20 *Minotaur*
NBC VEHICLES 40 VAB NRBC
ANTI-TANK/ANTI-INFRASTRUCTURE • MSL
   SP 110 VAB *Milan*
   MANPATS *Eryx*; FGM-148 *Javelin*; *Milan*; MMP
ARTILLERY 265+
   SP 155mm 109: 32 AU-F-1; 77 CAESAR
   TOWED 155mm 12 TR-F-1
   MRL 227mm 13 M270 MLRS
   MOR 131+: **81mm** LLR 81mm; **120mm** 131 RT-F-1
AIRCRAFT • TPT • Light 13: 5 PC-6B *Turbo Porter*; 5 TBM-700; 3 TBM-700B
HELICOPTERS
   ATK 66: 29 *Tiger* HAP; 37 *Tiger* HAD
   MRH 105: 18 AS555UN *Fennec*; 87 SA341F/342M *Gazelle* (all variants)
   TPT 155: **Heavy** 8 H225M *Caracal* (CSAR); **Medium** 112: 26 AS532UL *Cougar*; 2 EC225LP *Super Puma*; 38 NH90 TTH; 46 SA330 *Puma*; **Light** 35 H120 *Colibri* (leased)
UNMANNED AERIAL VEHICLES
   ISR • Medium 23 SDTI (*Sperwer*)
AIR DEFENCE • SAM • Point-defence *Mistral*

Navy 35,100
EQUIPMENT BY TYPE
SUBMARINES 9
   STRATEGIC • SSBN 4:
     4 *Le Triomphant* opcon Strategic Nuclear Forces with 16 M51 SLBM with 6 TN-75 nuclear warheads, 4 single 533mm TT with SM39 *Exocet* AShM/F17 mod 2 HWT
   TACTICAL • SSN 5:
     5 *Rubis* with 4 single 533mm TT with SM39 *Exocet* AShM/F17 mod 2 HWT
PRINCIPAL SURFACE COMBATANTS 23
   AIRCRAFT CARRIERS 1
     CVN 1 *Charles de Gaulle* with 4 *Sylver* A43 8-cell VLS with *Aster* 15 SAM, 2 sextuple *Sadral* lnchr with *Mistral* SAM (capacity 30 *Rafale* M fga ac, 2 E-2C *Hawkeye* AEW&C ac, 8 AS365 *Dauphin*/NH90 NFH hel)
   DESTROYERS • DDGHM 11:
     1 *Cassard* with 2 quad lnchr with MM40 *Exocet* Block 2 AShM, 1 Mk 13 GMLS with SM-1MR Block VI SAM, 2 sextuple *Sadral* lnchr with *Mistral* SAM, 2 single 533mm ASTT with L5 mod 4 HWT, 1 100mm gun (capacity 1 AS565SA *Panther* ASW hel)
     2 *Forbin* with 2 quad lnchr with MM40 *Exocet* Block 3 AShM, 4 8-cell *Sylver* A50 VLS with *Aster* 30 SAM, 2 8-cell *Sylver* A50 VLS with *Aster* 15 SAM, 2 twin 324mm ASTT with MU90 LWT, 2 76mm gun (capacity 1 NH90 TTH hel)
     2 *Georges Leygues* (mod) with 2 quad lnchr with MM40 *Exocet* AShM, 1 octuple lnchr with *Crotale* SAM, 2 twin *Simbad* lnchr with *Mistral* SAM, 2 single 324mm ASTT with MU90 LWT, 1 100mm gun (capacity 2 *Lynx* hel)
     4 *Aquitaine* (FREMM ASM) with 2 8-cell *Sylver* A70 VLS with MdCN (SCALP Naval) LACM, 2 quad lnchr with MM40 *Exocet* Block 3 AShM, 2 8-cell *Sylver* A43 VLS with *Aster* 15 SAM, 2 twin B-515 324mm ASTT with MU90 LWT, 1 76mm gun (capacity 1 NH90 NFH hel)
     1 *Aquitaine* (FREMM ASM) with 2 8-cell *Sylver* A70 VLS with MdCN (SCALP Naval) LACM, 2 quad lnchr with MM40 *Exocet* Block 3 AShM, 2 8-cell *Sylver* A50 VLS with *Aster* 15 SAM (*Aster* 30 to be fitted), 2 twin B-515 324mm ASTT with MU90 LWT, 1 76mm gun (capacity 1 NH90 NFH hel)
     1 *Aquitaine* (FREMM ASM) with 2 8-cell *Sylver* A70 VLS with MdCN (SCALP Naval) LACM, 2 quad lnchr with MM40 *Exocet* Block 3 AShM, 2 8-cell *Sylver* A50 VLS with *Aster* 15 SAM/*Aster* 30 SAM, 2 twin B-515 324mm ASTT with MU90 LWT, 1 76mm gun (capacity 1 NH90 NFH hel)
   FRIGATES • FFGHM 11:
     6 *Floreal* with 2 single lnchr with MM38 *Exocet* AShM, 1 twin *Simbad* lnchr with *Mistral* SAM, 1 100mm gun (capacity 1 AS565SA *Panther* hel)
     5 *La Fayette* with 2 quad lnchr with MM40 *Exocet* Block 3 AShM, 1 octuple lnchr with *Crotale* SAM (space for fitting 2 8-cell VLS lnchr for *Aster* 15/30), 1 100mm gun (capacity 1 AS565SA *Panther*/SA321 *Super Frelon* hel)
PATROL AND COASTAL COMBATANTS 22
   FSM 7 *D'Estienne d'Orves* with 1 twin *Simbad* lnchr with *Mistral* SAM, 2 twin 533mm ASTT, 1 100mm gun
   PSO 4 *d'Entrecasteaux* with 1 hel landing platform
   PCC 5: 2 *L'Audacieuse*; 3 *Flamant*
   PCO 6: 3 *La Confiance*, 1 *Lapérouse*; 1 *Le Malin*; 1 *Fulmar*
MINE WARFARE • MINE COUNTERMEASURES 17
   MCD 4 *Vulcain*
   MHC 3 *Antarès*
   MHO 10 *Éridan*
AMPHIBIOUS
   PRINCIPAL AMPHIBIOUS SHIPS 3
     LHD 3 *Mistral* with 2 twin *Simbad* lnchr with *Mistral* SAM (capacity up to 16 NH90/SA330 *Puma*/AS532 *Cougar*/*Tiger* hel; 2 LCAC or 4 LCM; 13 MBTs; 50 AFVs; 450 troops)
   LANDING CRAFT 38
     LCT 4 EDA-R
     LCM 9 CTM
     LCVP 25
LOGISTICS AND SUPPORT 35
   ABU 1 *Telenn Mor*
   AG 2 *Chamois*
   AGE 2: 1 *Corraline*; 1 *Lapérouse* (used as trials ships for mines and divers)

AGI 1 *Dupuy de Lome*
AGM 1 *Monge*
AGOR 2: 1 *Pourquoi pas?* (used 150 days per year by Ministry of Defence; operated by Ministry of Research and Education otherwise); 1 *Beautemps-beaupré*
AGS 3 *Lapérouse*
AORH 3 *Durance* with 3 twin *Simbad* lnchr with *Mistral* SAM (capacity 1 SA319 *Alouette* III/AS365 *Dauphin/Lynx*)
ATF 2 *Malabar*
ATS 4 *Loire* (BSAH)
AXL 10: 8 *Léopard*; 2 *Glycine*
AXS 4: 2 *La Belle Poule*; 2 other

Naval Aviation 6,500
FORCES BY ROLE
STRIKE/FIGHTER/GROUND ATTACK
  2 sqn with *Rafale* M F3
  1 sqn with *Rafale* M F3/F3-R
ANTI-SURFACE WARFARE
  1 sqn with AS565SA *Panther*
ANTI-SUBMARINE WARFARE
  2 sqn (forming) with NH90 NFH
  1 sqn with *Lynx* Mk4
MARITIME PATROL
  2 sqn with *Atlantique* 2
  1 sqn with *Falcon* 20H *Gardian*
  1 sqn with *Falcon* 50MI
AIRBORNE EARLY WARNING & CONTROL
  1 sqn with E-2C *Hawkeye*
SEARCH & RESCUE
  1 sqn with AS365N/F *Dauphin* 2
TRAINING
  1 sqn with EMB 121 *Xingu*
  1 unit with SA319B *Alouette* III
  1 unit with *Falcon* 10MER
  1 unit with CAP 10M
EQUIPMENT BY TYPE
AIRCRAFT 54 combat capable
  FGA 42: 41 *Rafale* M F3; 1 *Rafale* M F3-R
  ASW 12 *Atlantique* 2 (10 more in store)
  AEW&C 3 E-2C *Hawkeye*
  SAR 8 *Falcon* 50MS
  TPT 25: **Light** 10 EMB-121 *Xingu*; **PAX** 15: 6 *Falcon* 10MER; 5 *Falcon* 20H *Gardian*; 4 *Falcon* 50MI
  TRG 6 CAP 10M
HELICOPTERS
  ASW 36: 14 *Lynx* Mk4; 22 NH90 NFH
  MRH 43: 9 AS365N/F/SP *Dauphin* 2; 2 AS365N3; 16 AS565SA *Panther*; 16 SA319B *Alouette* III
AIR-LAUNCHED MISSILES
  AAM • **IR** R-550 *Magic* 2; **IIR** *Mica* IR; **ARH** *Mica* RF
  ASM AASM; AS-30L
  AShM AM39 *Exocet*
  LACM Nuclear ASMPA
BOMBS
  Laser-guided: GBU-12 *Paveway* II

Marines 2,000

Commando Units 550
FORCES BY ROLE
MANOEUVRE
  Reconnaissance
    1 recce gp
  Amphibious
    2 aslt gp
    1 atk swimmer gp
    1 raiding gp
COMBAT SUPPORT
  1 cbt spt gp
COMBAT SERVICE SUPPORT
  1 spt gp

Fusiliers-Marin 1,450
FORCES BY ROLE
MANOEUVRE
  Other
    2 sy gp
    7 sy coy

Reserves 6,000 reservists

Air Force 40,500
FORCES BY ROLE
STRIKE
  1 sqn with *Rafale* B with ASMPA msl
  1 sqn with *Rafale* B with ASMPA msl (forming)
SPACE
  1 (satellite obs) sqn
FIGHTER
  1 sqn with *Mirage* 2000-5
  1 sqn with *Mirage* 2000B/C
FIGHTER/GROUND ATTACK
  3 sqn with *Mirage* 2000D
  1 (composite) sqn with *Mirage* 2000-5/D (Djibouti)
  2 sqn with *Rafale* B/C
  1 sqn with *Rafale* B/C (UAE)
ELECTRONIC WARFARE
  1 flt with C-160G *Gabriel* (ESM)
AIRBORNE EARLY WARNING & CONTROL
  1 (Surveillance & Control) sqn with E-3F *Sentry*
SEARCH & RESCUE/TRANSPORT
  4 sqn with C-160R *Transall*; CN235M; SA330 *Puma*; AS555 *Fennec* (Djibouti, French Guiana, Gabon, Indian Ocean & New Caledonia)
TANKER
  1 sqn with A330 MRTT
  1 sqn with C-135FR; KC-135 *Stratotanker*
TANKER/TRANSPORT
  2 sqn with C-160R *Transall*
TRANSPORT
  1 sqn with A310-300; A330; A340-200 (on lease)
  1 sqn with A400M; KC-130J *Hercules*
  1 sqn with C-130H/H-30 *Hercules*; C-160R *Transall*
  1 sqn with C-130H/H-30/J-30 *Hercules*
  2 sqn with CN235M
  1 sqn with *Falcon* 7X (VIP); *Falcon* 900 (VIP); *Falcon* 2000

3 flt with TBM-700A
1 (mixed) gp with C-160 *Transall*; DHC-6-300 *Twin Otter*
TRAINING
1 OCU sqn with *Mirage* 2000D
1 OCU sqn with *Rafale* B/C
1 OCU sqn with SA330 *Puma*; AS555 *Fennec*
1 OCU unit with C-160 *Transall*
1 (aggressor) sqn with *Alpha Jet**
4 sqn with *Alpha Jet**
3 sqn with Grob G120A-F; TB-30 *Epsilon*
1 sqn with EMB-121
TRANSPORT HELICOPTER
2 sqn with AS555 *Fennec*
2 sqn with AS332C/L *Super Puma*; SA330 *Puma*; H225M
ISR UAV
1 sqn with MQ-9A *Reaper*
AIR DEFENCE
3 sqn with *Crotale* NG; SAMP/T
1 sqn with SAMP/T
EQUIPMENT BY TYPE
SATELLITES *see* Space
AIRCRAFT 284 combat capable
FTR 41: 35 *Mirage* 2000-5/2000C; 6 *Mirage* 2000B
FGA 166: 66 *Mirage* 2000D; 52 *Rafale* B; 48 *Rafale* C
ELINT 2 C-160G *Gabriel* (ESM)
AEW&C 4 E-3F *Sentry*
TKR 4: 1 KC-130J *Hercules*; 3 KC-135 *Stratotanker*
TKR/TPT 13: 2 A330 MRTT; 11 C-135FR
TPT 125: **Heavy** 15 A400M; **Medium** 28: 5 C-130H *Hercules*; 9 C-130H-30 *Hercules*; 2 C-130J-30 *Hercules*; 12 C-160R *Transall*; **Light** 70: 19 CN235M-100; 8 CN235M-300; 5 DHC-6-300 *Twin Otter*; 23 EMB-121 *Xingu*; 15 TBM-700; **PAX** 12: 3 A310-300; 1 A330; 2 A340-200 (on lease); 2 *Falcon* 7X; 2 *Falcon* 900 (VIP); 2 *Falcon* 2000
TRG 157: 77 *Alpha Jet**; 18 Grob G120A-F (leased); 25 TB-30 *Epsilon* (incl many in storage); 17 PC-21; 13 SR20 (leased); 7 SR22 (leased)
HELICOPTERS
MRH 37 AS555 *Fennec*
TPT 35: **Heavy** 10 H225M *Caracal*; **Medium** 25: 1 AS332C *Super Puma*; 4 AS332L *Super Puma*; 20 SA330B *Puma*
UNMANNED AERIAL VEHICLES
CISR • **Heavy** 5 MQ-9A *Reaper* (unarmed)
AIR DEFENCE • SAM **Long-range** 40 SAMP/T; **Short-range** 24 *Crotale* NG
AIR-LAUNCHED MISSILES
AAM • **IR** R-550 *Magic* 2; **IIR** *Mica* IR; **ARH** *Mica* RF
ASM AASM; AS-30L; *Apache*
LACM
Nuclear ASMPA
Conventional SCALP EG
BOMBS • **Laser-guided**: GBU-12 *Paveway* II

Security and Intervention Brigade
FORCES BY ROLE
SPECIAL FORCES
3 SF gp

MANOEUVRE
Other
24 protection units
30 (fire fighting and rescue) unit

Reserves 5,700 reservists

Paramilitary 100,500

Gendarmerie 100,500; 30,300 reservists
EQUIPMENT BY TYPE
ARMOURED FIGHTING VEHICLES
APC • **APC (W)** 82 VXB-170 (VBRG-170); VAB
ARTILLERY • **MOR 81mm** some
PATROL AND COASTAL COMBATANTS 38
PB 38: 2 *Athos*; 4 *Géranium*; 24 VCSM; 8 VSMP
HELICOPTERS • TPT • **Light** 60: 25 AS350BA *Ecureuil*; 20 H135; 15 H145

DEPLOYMENT
ARABIAN SEA: Combined Maritime Forces • CTF-150: 1 DDGHM; 1 FFGHM

BURKINA FASO: *Operation Barkhane* 250; 1 SF gp; 1 Tiger; 2 AS532UL *Cougar*; 2 H225M; 3 SA342 *Gazelle*

CENTRAL AFRICAN REPUBLIC: 160; **EU** • EUTM RCA 40
UN • MINUSCA 9

CHAD: *Operation Barkhane* 1,500; 1 mech inf BG; 1 FGA det with 4 *Mirage* 2000D; 1 tpt det with 1 C-130H; 2 CN235M; 1 UAV det with 1 MQ-9A *Reaper*

CÔTE D'IVOIRE: 950; 1 (Marine) inf bn; 2 SA330 *Puma*; 1 SA342 *Gazelle*

DEMOCRATIC REPUBLIC OF THE CONGO: UN • MONUSCO 3

DJIBOUTI: 1,450; 1 (Marine) combined arms regt with (2 recce sqn, 2 inf coy, 1 arty bty, 1 engr coy); 1 hel det with 2 SA330 *Puma*; 2 SA342 *Gazelle*; 1 LCM; 1 FGA sqn with 4 *Mirage* 2000-5; 1 SAR/tpt sqn with 1 CN235M; 2 SA330 *Puma*

EGYPT: MFO 1

ESTONIA: 330, 1 armd inf coy(+)

FRENCH GUIANA: 2,100: 1 (Foreign Legion) inf regt; 1 (Marine) inf regt; 1 SMA regt; 2 PCO; 1 tpt sqn with 3 CN235M; 5 SA330 *Puma*; 4 AS555 *Fennec*; 3 gendarmerie coy; 1 AS350BA *Ecureuil*; 1 H145

FRENCH POLYNESIA: 1,180: 1 SMA coy; 1 naval HQ at Papeete; 1 FFGHM; 1 PSO; 1 PCO; 1 AFS; 3 *Falcon* 200 *Gardian*; 1 SAR/tpt sqn with 2 CN235M

FRENCH WEST INDIES: 1,000; 1 (Marine) inf regt; 2 SMA regt; 2 FFGHM; 1 AS565SA *Panther*; 1 SA319 *Alouette* III; 1 naval base at Fort de France (Martinique); 4 gendarmerie coy; 1 PCO; 1 PB; 2 AS350BA *Ecureuil*

GABON: 350; 1 AB bn

GERMANY: 2,000 (incl elm Eurocorps and FRA/GER bde); 1 (FRA/GER) mech bde (1 armd cav regt, 1 mech inf regt)

GULF OF GUINEA: *Operation Corymbe* 1 AORH

INDIAN OCEAN: 2,000 (incl La Réunion and TAAF); 1 (Marine) para regt; 1 (Foreign Legion) inf coy; 1 SMA regt; 1 SMA coy; 2 FFGHM; 1 PCO; 1 LCM; 1 naval HQ at Port-des-Galets (La Réunion); 1 naval base at Dzaoudzi (Mayotte); 1 Falcon 50M; 1 SAR/tpt sqn with 2 CN235M; 5 gendarmerie coy; 1 SA319 *Alouette* III

IRAQ: *Operation Inherent Resolve* (*Chammal*) 400; 1 SF gp

JORDAN: *Operation Inherent Resolve* (*Chammal*) 8 *Rafale* F3; 1 *Atlantique* 2

LEBANON: UN • UNIFIL 670; 1 mech inf bn(-); 1 maint coy; VBL; VBCI; VAB; *Mistral*

MALI: *Operation Barkhane* 1,750; 1 mech inf BG; 1 log bn; 1 tpt unit with 1 CN235M; 1 hel unit with 4 *Tiger*; 7 NH90 TTH; 4 SA342 *Gazelle*; EU • EUTM Mali 13; UN • MINUSMA 25

NEW CALEDONIA: 1,660; 1 (Marine) mech inf regt; 1 SMA coy; 6 ERC-90F1 *Lynx*; 1 FFGHM; 1 PSO; 2 PCC; 1 base with 2 *Falcon* 200 *Gardian* at Nouméa; 1 tpt unit with 2 CN235 MPA; 3 SA330 *Puma*; 4 gendarmerie coy; 2 AS350BA *Ecureuil*

NIGER: *Operation Barkhane* 500; 1 FGA det with 4 *Mirage* 2000D; 1 tkr/tpt det with 1 C-135FR; 1 C-160R *Transall*; 1 UAV det with 2 MQ-9A *Reaper*

QATAR: *Operation Inherent Resolve* (*Chammal*) 1 E-3F *Sentry*

SENEGAL: 350; 1 *Falcon* 50MI

SYRIA: *Operation Inherent Resolve* (*Chammal*) 1 SF unit

UNITED ARAB EMIRATES: 650: 1 armd BG (1 tk coy, 1 arty bty); *Leclerc*; CAESAR; •: *Operation Inherent Resolve* (*Chammal*); 1 FGA sqn with 6 *Rafale* F3

WESTERN SAHARA: UN • MINURSO 3

FOREIGN FORCES

Belgium 28 *Alpha Jet* trg ac located at Cazaux/Tours
Germany 400 (GER elm Eurocorps)
Singapore 200; 1 trg sqn with 12 M-346 *Master*

Germany GER

Euro €		2018	2019	2020
GDP	€	3.34tr	3.44tr	
	US$	3.95tr	3.86tr	
per capita	US$	47,662	46,564	
Growth	%	1.5	0.5	
Inflation	%	1.9	1.5	
Def exp [a]	€	42.1bn	47.9bn	
	US$	49.8bn	53.8bn	
Def bdgt [b]	€	38.5bn	43.2bn	44.9bn
	US$	45.5bn	48.5bn	
US$1=€		0.85	0.89	

[a] NATO definition
[b] Includes military pensions

Real-terms defence budget trend (US$bn, constant 2015)
45.2 / 36.1 / 2008–2014–2019

Population	80,313,272					
Age	0–14	15–19	20–24	25–29	30–64	65 plus
Male	6.6%	2.4%	2.7%	3.0%	24.5%	10.0%
Female	6.3%	2.3%	2.6%	2.9%	24.3%	12.7%

Capabilities

The 2016 defence white paper committed Germany to a leadership role in European defence. It also emphasised the importance of NATO and the need for the armed forces to contribute to collective-defence tasks. The 2018 Konzeption der Bundeswehr underlines that collective- and territorial-defence tasks will drive current military-modernisation efforts and are of equal standing with international crisis-management operations. The key implication for defence modernisation is that Germany will need to invest in readiness and return to fully equipping operational units, after having experimented in recent years with rotating equipment among units depending on their deployment or training demands. Germany is aligning its defence-planning process with capability goals derived from multinational guidance. Berlin has been a key sponsor of the Framework Nations Concept and in the EU led the drive to implement Permanent Structured Cooperation on defence. Close military cooperation has been established, including the affiliation of units, with the Czech Republic, France, the Netherlands and Romania. The defence ministry has announced the objective of increasing authorised active force numbers but this will be challenging, given recruitment and retention problems after conscription was suspended in 2011. The armed forces are also struggling to improve their readiness levels in light of increasing demands on NATO's eastern flank. In 2019, Germany was the lead nation for NATO's Very High Readiness Joint Task Force land component. Shortages of spare parts and maintenance problems are reported in all three services. Germany's defence-industrial base is able to design and manufacture equipment to meet requirements across all military domains, with strengths in land and naval systems. The government is pursuing a policy of closer defence-industrial cooperation in Europe.

ACTIVE 181,400 (Army 62,150 Navy 16,350 Air 27,750 Joint Support Service 27,600 Joint Medical Service 19,900 Cyber 13,150 Other 14,500)

Conscript liability Voluntary conscription only. Voluntary conscripts can serve up to 23 months

RESERVE 29,200 (Army 6,700 Navy 1,200 Air 3,300 Joint Support Service 11,800 Joint Medical Service 3,400 Cyber 1,150 Other 1,650)

ORGANISATIONS BY SERVICE

Space
EQUIPMENT BY TYPE
SATELLITES 7
  COMMUNICATIONS 2 COMSATBw (1 & 2)
  ISR 5 SAR-*Lupe*

Army 62,150
FORCES BY ROLE
COMMAND
  elm 2 (1 GNC & MNC NE) corps HQ
MANOEUVRE
  Armoured
  1 (1st) armd div (1 (9th) armd bde (1 armd recce bn, 1 tk bn, 2 armd inf bn, 1 lt inf bn, 1 cbt engr bn, 1 spt bn); 1 (21st) armd bde (1 armd recce bn, 1 tk bn, 1 armd inf bn, 1 lt inf bn, 1 cbt engr bn, 1 spt bn); 1 (41st) mech inf bde (1 armd recce bn, 2 armd inf bn, 1 lt inf bn, 1 cbt engr bn, 1 sigs coy, 1 spt bn); 1 tk bn (for NLD 43rd Bde); 1 SP arty bn; 1 sigs coy)
  1 (10th) armd div (1 (12th) armd bde (1 armd recce bn, 1 tk bn, 2 armd inf bn, 1 cbt engr bn, 1 sigs coy, 1 spt bn); 1 (37th) mech inf bde (1 armd recce bn, 1 tk bn, 2 armd inf bn, 1 engr bn, 1 sigs coy, 1 spt bn); 1 (23rd) mtn inf bde (1 recce bn, 3 mtn inf bn, 1 cbt engr bn, 1 spt bn); 1 SP arty bn; 1 SP arty trg bn; 2 mech inf bn (GER/FRA bde); 1 arty bn (GER/FRA bde); 1 cbt engr coy (GER/FRA bde); 1 spt bn (GER/FRA bde))
  Air Manoeuvre
  1 (rapid reaction) AB div (1 SOF bde (2 SOF bn); 1 AB bde (2 recce coy, 2 para regt, 2 cbt engr coy); 1 atk hel regt; 2 tpt hel regt; 1 sigs coy)

EQUIPMENT BY TYPE
ARMOURED FIGHTING VEHICLES
  MBT 245: 225 *Leopard* 2A5/A6; 19 *Leopard* 2A7; 1 *Leopard* 2A7V (78 *Leopard* 2A4/A5/A6 in store)
  RECCE 169 *Fennek* (incl 14 engr recce, 14 fires spt)
  IFV 651: 383 *Marder* 1A3/A4/A5; 268 *Puma*
  APC 807
    APC (T) 227: 65 Bv-206S; 162 M113 (inc variants)
    APC (W) 580: 221 *Boxer* (inc variants); 359 TPz-1 *Fuchs* (inc variants)
  AUV 683: 247 *Dingo* 2; 363 *Eagle* IV/V; 73 *Wiesel* 1 Mk20 (with 20mm gun)
ENGINEERING & MAINTENANCE VEHICLES
  AEV 42 *Dachs*
  ARV 134: 89 BPz-2 1; 45 BPz-3 *Büffel*
  VLB 54: 22 *Biber*; 2 *Leopard* 2 with *Leguan*; 30 M3
  MW 24 *Keiler*
NBC VEHICLES 8 TPz-1 *Fuchs* NBC
ANTI-TANK/ANTI-INFRASTRUCTURE • MSL
  SP 102 *Wiesel* with TOW
  MANPATS *Milan*; *Spike*-LR (MELLS)
ARTILLERY 252
  SP 155mm 121 PzH 2000
  MRL 227mm 41 M270 MLRS
  MOR 90: **120mm** 60 Tampella; **SP 120mm** 30 M113 with Tampella
HELICOPTERS
  ATK 53 *Tiger*
  TPT 126: **Medium** 72 NH90; **Light** 54: 41 Bell 205 (UH-1D *Iroquois*); 13 H135
UNMANNED AERIAL VEHICLES
  ISR 128: **Medium** 44 KZO; **Light** 84 LUNA

Navy 16,350
EQUIPMENT BY TYPE
SUBMARINES • TACTICAL • SSK 6:
  6 Type-212A (of which 3 non-operational) with 6 single 533mm TT with DM2A4 HWT
PRINCIPAL SURFACE COMBATANTS 15
  DESTROYERS • DDGHM 8:
    4 *Brandenburg* (F123) with 2 twin lnchr with MM38 *Exocet* AShM, 2 8-cell Mk 41 VLS with RIM-7P *Sea Sparrow* SAM, 2 Mk 49 GMLS with RIM-116 RAM SAM, 2 twin SVTT Mk 32 324mm ASTT with Mk 46 LWT, 1 76mm gun (capacity 2 *Sea Lynx* Mk88A hel)
    3 *Sachsen* (F124) with 2 quad lnchr with RGM-84C *Harpoon* Block 1B AShM, 4 8-cell Mk 41 VLS with SM-2 Block IIIA SAM/RIM-162B ESSM SAM, 2 21-cell Mk 49 GMLS with RIM-116 RAM SAM, 2 triple SVTT Mk 32 324mm ASTT with MU90 LWT, 1 76mm gun (capacity; 2 *Sea Lynx* Mk88A hel)
    1 *Baden-Württemberg* (F125) with 2 quad lnchr with RGM-84C *Harpoon* Block 1B AShM, 2 21-cell Mk 49 GMLS with RIM-116C RAM Block 2 SAM, 1 127mm gun (Capacity 2 NH90 hel)
  FRIGATES 7
    FFGHM 2 *Bremen* (F122) with 2 quad lnchr with RGM-84C *Harpoon* Block 1B AShM, 1 octuple Mk 29 GMLS with RIM-7P *Sea Sparrow* SAM, 2 21-cell Mk 49 GMLS with RIM-116 RAM SAM, 2 twin SVTT Mk 32 324mm ASTT with Mk 46 LWT, 1 76mm gun (capacity 2 *Sea Lynx* Mk88A hel)
    FFGM 5 *Braunschweig* (K130) with 2 twin lnchr with RBS15 Mk3 AShM, 2 21-cell Mk 49 GMLS with RIM-116 RAM SAM, 1 76mm gun, 1 hel landing platform
MINE WARFARE • MINE COUNTERMEASURES 19
  MHO 10 *Frankenthal* (2 used as diving support)
  MSO 2 *Ensdorf*
  MSD 7 *Seehund*
AMPHIBIOUS • LCU 1 Type-520
LOGISTICS AND SUPPORT 22
  AG 4: 2 *Schwedeneck* (Type-748); 2 *Stollergrund* (Type-745)
  AGI 3 *Oste* (Type-423)
  AGOR 1 *Planet* (Type-751)
  AOR 6 *Elbe* (Type-404) with 1 hel landing platform (2 specified for PFM support; 1 specified for SSK support; 3 specified for MHO/MSO support)
  AORH 3 *Berlin* (Type-702) (fitted for but not with RIM-116 RAM SAM) (capacity 2 *Sea King* Mk41 hel)

AOT 2 *Rhön* (Type-704)
APB 2: 1 *Knurrhahn*; 1 *Ohre*
AXS 1 *Gorch Fock*

Naval Aviation 2,000
EQUIPMENT BY TYPE
AIRCRAFT 8 combat capable
  ASW 8 AP-3C *Orion*
  TPT • Light 2 Do-228 (pollution control)
HELICOPTERS
  ASW 22 *Lynx* Mk88A
  SAR 20: 19 *Sea King* Mk41; 1 NH90 NFH (*Sea Lion*)

Naval Special Forces Command
FORCES BY ROLE
SPECIAL FORCES
  1 SF coy

Sea Battalion
FORCES BY ROLE
MANOEUVRE
  Amphibious
    1 mne bn

Air Force 27,750
FORCES BY ROLE
FIGHTER
  3 wg (2 sqn with Eurofighter *Typhoon*)
FIGHTER/GROUND ATTACK
  1 wg (2 sqn with *Tornado* IDS)
  1 wg (2 sqn with Eurofighter *Typhoon* (multi-role))
ISR
  1 wg (1 ISR sqn with *Tornado* ECR/IDS; 2 UAV sqn with *Heron*)
TANKER/TRANSPORT
  1 (special air mission) wg (3 sqn with A310 MRTT; A319; A340; AS532U2 *Cougar* II; *Global* 5000)
TRANSPORT
  1 wg (total: 1 sqn with C-160D *Transall*)
  1 wg (3 sqn (forming) with A400M *Atlas*)
TRAINING
  1 sqn located at Holloman AFB (US) with *Tornado* IDS
  1 unit (ENJJPT) located at Sheppard AFB (US) with T-6 *Texan* II; T-38A
  1 hel unit located at Fassberg
TRANSPORT HELICOPTER
  1 tpt hel wg (3 sqn with CH-53G/GA/GE/GS *Stallion*; 1 sqn with H145M)
AIR DEFENCE
  1 wg (3 SAM gp) with MIM-104C/F *Patriot* PAC-2/3
  1 AD gp with ASRAD *Ozelot*; C-RAM *Mantis* and trg unit
  1 AD trg unit located at Fort Bliss (US) with MIM-104C/F *Patriot* PAC-2/3
  3 (tac air ctrl) radar gp

Air Force Regiment
FORCES BY ROLE
MANOEUVRE
  Other
    1 sy regt

EQUIPMENT BY TYPE
AIRCRAFT 228 combat capable
  FTR 140 Eurofighter *Typhoon*
  ATK 68 *Tornado* IDS
  ATK/EW 20 *Tornado* ECR*
  TKR/TPT 4 A310 MRTT
  TPT 57: **Heavy** 31 A400M; **Medium** 17 C-160D *Transall*;
  PAX 9: 1 A321; 2 A340 (VIP); 2 A319; 4 *Global* 5000
  TRG 109: 69 T-6A *Texan* II, 40 T-38A
HELICOPTERS
  MRH 15 H145M
  TPT 73: **Heavy** 70 CH-53G/GA/GS/GE *Stallion*; **Medium** 3 AS532U2 *Cougar* II (VIP)
UNMANNED AERIAL VEHICLES • ISR • Heavy 8 *Heron* 1
AIR DEFENCE
  SAM
    Long-range 30 MIM-104C/F *Patriot* PAC-2/PAC-3
    Point-defence 20 ASRAD *Ozelot* (with FIM-92 *Stinger*)
  GUNS 35mm 12 C-RAM *Mantis*
AIR-LAUNCHED MISSILES
  AAM • IR AIM-9L/Li *Sidewinder*; **IIR** IRIS-T; **ARH** AIM-120B AMRAAM
  LACM *Taurus* KEPD 350
  ARM AGM-88B HARM
BOMBS
  Laser-guided GBU-24 *Paveway* III, GBU-54 JDAM

Joint Support Service 27,600
FORCES BY ROLE
COMBAT SUPPORT
  3 MP regt
  2 NBC bn
COMBAT SERVICE SUPPORT
  6 log bn
  1 spt regt
EQUIPMENT BY TYPE
ARMOURED FIGHTING VEHICLES
  AUV 451: 206 *Dingo* 2; 245 *Eagle* IV/V
ENGINEERING & MAINTENANCE VEHICLES
  ARV 59: 29 BPz-2; 30 BPz-3 *Büffel*
NBC VEHICLES 35 TPz-1 *Fuchs* A6/A7/A8 NBC

Joint Medical Services 19,900
FORCES BY ROLE
COMBAT SERVICE SUPPORT
  4 med regt
EQUIPMENT BY TYPE
ARMOURED FIGHTING VEHICLES
  APC • APC (W) 109: 72 *Boxer* (amb); 37 TPz-1 *Fuchs* (amb)
  AUV 42 *Eagle* IV/V (amb)

Cyber & Information Command 13,150
FORCES BY ROLE
COMBAT SUPPORT
  4 EW bn
  6 sigs bn

DEPLOYMENT

AFGHANISTAN: NATO • *Operation Resolute Support* 1,300; 1 bde HQ; 1 recce bn; 1 hel flt with CH-53; 1 UAV flt with 3 *Heron* 1 UAV

BALTIC SEA: NATO • SNMCMG 1: 1 MHO

DJIBOUTI: EU • *Operation Atalanta* 1 AP-3C *Orion*

ESTONIA: NATO • Baltic Air Policing 6 Eurofighter *Typhoon*

FRANCE: 400 (incl GER elm Eurocorps)

IRAQ: *Operation Inherent Resolve* 150 (trg spt)

JORDAN: *Operation Inherent Resolve* 280; 4 *Tornado* ECR; 1 A310 MRTT

LEBANON: UN • UNIFIL 182; 1 FFGM

LIBYA: UN • UNISMIL 2

LITHUANIA: NATO • Enhanced Forward Presence 560; 1 armd inf bn HQ; 1 armd inf coy(+) with *Leopard* 2A6; *Marder*; *Boxer*

MALI: EU • EUTM Mali 174; **UN** • MINUSMA 370; 1 sy coy; 1 int coy; 1 UAV sqn

MEDITERRANEAN SEA: NATO • SNMG 2: 1 DDGHM

NIGER: *Operation Barkhane* 2 C-160 *Transall*

POLAND: 95 (GER elm MNC-NE)

SERBIA: NATO • KFOR 70

SOUTH SUDAN: UN • UNMISS 14

UNITED STATES: Trg units with 40 T-38 *Talon*; 69 T-6A *Texan II* at Goodyear AFB (AZ)/Sheppard AFB (TX);NAS Pensacola (FL); Fort Rucker (AL); Missile trg at Fort Bliss (TX)

WESTERN SAHARA: UN • MINURSO 3

FOREIGN FORCES

France 2,000; 1 (FRA/GER) mech bde (1 armd cav regt, 1 mech inf regt)

United Kingdom 185

United States

US Africa Command: Army; 1 HQ at Stuttgart

US European Command: 38,750; 1 combined service HQ (EUCOM) at Stuttgart-Vaihingen

Army 23,750; 1 HQ (US Army Europe (USAREUR) at Wiesbaden; 1 div HQ (fwd); 1 SF gp; 1 recce bn; 2 armd bn; 1 mech bde(-); 1 fd arty bn; 1 MRL bde (1 MRL bn)1 (cbt avn) hel bde(-); 1 (cbt avn) hel bde HQ; 1 int bde; 1 MP bde; 1 sigs bde; 1 spt bde; 1 ARNG SAM bde(-); 1 (APS) armd bde eqpt set; M1A2 SEPv2 *Abrams*; M2A2 *Bradley*; *Stryker Dragoon*; M109A6, M119A3; M777A2; AH-64D *Apache*; CH-47F *Chinook*; UH-60L/M *Black Hawk*; HH-60M *Black Hawk*; M1097 *Avenger*

Navy 500

USAF 13,150; 1 HQ (US Airforce Europe (USAFE)) at Ramstein AB; 1 HQ (3rd Air Force) at Ramstein AB; 1 ftr wg at Spangdahlem AB with 1 ftr sqn with 24 F-16CJ *Fighting Falcon*; 1 airlift wg at Ramstein AB with 14 C-130J-30 *Hercules*; 2 Gulfstream V (C-37A); 5 Learjet 35A (C-21A); 1 B-737-700 (C-40B)

USMC 1,350

Greece GRC

Euro €		2018	2019	2020
GDP	€	185bn	190bn	
	US$	218bn	214bn	
per capita	US$	20,317	19,974	
Growth	%	1.9	2.0	
Inflation	%	0.8	0.6	
Def exp [a]	€	4.56bn	4.32bn	
	US$	5.39bn	4.87bn	
Def bdgt [b]	€	4.11bn	4.29bn	4.36bn
	US$	4.86bn	4.83bn	
US$1=€		0.85	0.89	

[a] NATO definition
[b] Includes military pensions

Real-terms defence budget trend (US$bn, constant 2015)

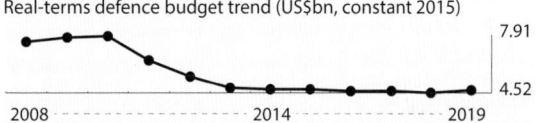

Population	10,752,626					
Age	0–14	15–19	20–24	25–29	30–64	65 plus
Male	7.0%	2.5%	2.5%	2.6%	24.8%	9.4%
Female	6.6%	2.3%	2.4%	2.6%	25.3%	12.0%

Capabilities

Greece's 2014 National Military Strategy identifies the country's principal defence objectives as safeguarding sovereignty and territorial integrity. The armed forces would also be expected to support Cyprus in the event of a conflict. The Force Structure 2013–27 document set out plans to make the armed forces more flexible, rapidly deployable and cost-effective. Greece is a NATO member and leads an EU battlegroup. In recent years, defence-cooperation agreements have been signed with Cyprus, Egypt and Israel. In 2018, talks began on an enhanced US presence in the country and elements of US Combat Aviation Brigades have deployed to Greece for training. The Mutual Defense Cooperation Agreement is the cornerstone of US–Greece defence cooperation and provides for a naval-support facility and an airfield at Souda Bay in Crete. The armed forces still include a significant number of conscripts but the majority of personnel are now regulars and Athens is looking to move to a fully professional force. However, financial difficulties and widespread abuse of the deferment process have slowed plans. Training levels are reportedly good, with a focus by the armed forces on joint operational training. Greece's deployments involve limited numbers of personnel and focus on the near abroad, although the country contributes to EU, NATO and UN missions. Procurement priorities include multi-purpose frigates and a new combat aircraft. Greece has an extensive defence industry focused on the domestic market, capable of manufacturing and developing naval vessels, subsystems, ammunition and small arms.

ACTIVE 143,850 (Army 93,500 Navy 16,800 Air 21,950 Joint 11,600) **Paramilitary 4,000**

Conscript liability 9 months for all services

RESERVE 221,600 (Army 181,500 Navy 6,100 Air 34,000)

ORGANISATIONS BY SERVICE

Army 48,500; 45,000 conscripts (total 93,500)

Units are manned at 3 different levels – Cat A 85% fully ready, Cat B 60% ready in 24 hours, Cat C 20% ready in 48 hours (requiring reserve mobilisation). 3 military regions

FORCES BY ROLE
COMMAND
  2 corps HQ (incl NRDC-GR)
  1 armd div HQ
  3 mech inf div HQ
  1 inf div HQ
SPECIAL FORCES
  1 SF comd
  1 cdo/para bde
MANOEUVRE
  Reconnaissance
  4 recce bn
  Armoured
  4 armd bde (2 armd bn, 1 mech inf bn, 1 SP arty bn)
  Mechanised
  10 mech inf bde (1 armd bn, 2 mech bn, 1 SP arty bn)
  Light
  2 inf regt
  Air Manoeuvre
  1 air mob bde
  1 air aslt bde
  Amphibious
  1 mne bde
COMBAT SUPPORT
  2 MRL bn
  3 AD bn (2 with I-*Hawk*, 1 with *Tor* M1)
  3 engr regt
  2 engr bn
  1 EW regt
  10 sigs bn
COMBAT SERVICE SUPPORT
  1 log corps HQ
  1 log div (3 log bde)
HELICOPTER
  1 hel bde (1 hel regt with (2 atk hel bn), 2 tpt hel bn, 4 hel bn)

EQUIPMENT BY TYPE
ARMOURED FIGHTING VEHICLES
  MBT 1,228: 170 *Leopard* 2A6HEL; 183 *Leopard* 2A4; 500 *Leopard* 1A4/5; 375 M48A5
  RECCE 242 VBL
  IFV 188 BMP-1
  APC • APC (T) 2,407: 86 *Leonidas* Mk1/2; 2,108 M113A1/A2; 213 M577 (CP)
ENGINEERING & MAINTENANCE VEHICLES
  ARV 261: 12 *Büffel*; 43 BPz-2; 94 M88A1; 112 M578
  VLB 12+: 12 *Biber*; *Leguan*
  MW *Giant Viper*
ANTI-TANK/ANTI-INFRASTRUCTURE
  MSL
    SP 557: 195 HMMWV with 9K135 *Kornet*-E (AT-14 Spriggan); 362 M901
    MANPATS 9K111 *Fagot* (AT-4 *Spigot*); *Milan*; TOW
  RCL 581+: **84mm** *Carl Gustav*; **90mm** EM-67; **SP 106mm** 581 M40A1
ARTILLERY 3,609
  SP 587: **155mm** 442: 418 M109A1B/A2/A3GEA1/A5; 24 PzH 2000; **203mm** 145 M110A2
  TOWED 557: **105mm** 351: 333 M101; 18 M-56; **155mm** 206 M114
  MRL 145: **122mm** 109 RM-70; **227mm** 36 M270 MLRS
  MOR 2,320: **81mm** 1,700; **107mm** 620 M30 (incl 231 SP)
SURFACE-TO-SURFACE MISSILE LAUNCHERS
  SRBM • Conventional MGM-140A ATACMS (launched from M270 MLRS)
AIRCRAFT • TPT • Light 18: 1 Beech 200 *King Air* (C-12C) 2 Beech 200 *King Air* (C-12R/AP *Huron*); 15 Cessna 185 (U-17A/B)
HELICOPTERS
  ATK 28: 19 AH-64A *Apache*; 9 AH-64D *Apache*
  MRH 60 OH-58D *Kiowa Warrior*
  TPT 141: **Heavy** 25: 19 CH-47D *Chinook*; 6 CH-47SD *Chinook*; **Medium** 14 NH90 TTH; **Light** 102: 88 Bell 205 (UH-1H *Iroquois*); 14 Bell 206 (AB-206) *Jet Ranger*
UNMANNED AERIAL VEHICLES
  ISR • Medium 4 *Sperwer*
AIR DEFENCE
  SAM 155
    Medium-range 42 MIM-23B I-*Hawk*
    Short-range 21 9K331 *Tor*-M1 (SA-15 *Gauntlet*)
    Point-range 92+: 38 9K33 *Osa*-M (SA-8B *Gecko*); 54 ASRAD HMMWV; FIM-92 *Stinger*
  GUNS • TOWED 727: **20mm** 204 Rh 202; **23mm** 523 ZU-23-2

National Guard 38,000 reservists

Internal security role

FORCES BY ROLE
MANOEUVRE
  Light
  1 inf div
  Air Manoeuvre
  1 para regt
COMBAT SUPPORT
  8 arty bn
  4 AD bn
HELICOPTER
  1 hel bn

Navy 14,200; 2,600 conscript (total 16,800)

EQUIPMENT BY TYPE
SUBMARINES • TACTICAL • SSK 11:
  3 *Poseidon* (GER Type-209/1200) with 8 single 533mm TT with SUT HWT
  1 *Poseidon* (GER Type-209/1200) (modernised with AIP technology) with 8 single 533mm TT with UGM-84C *Harpoon* Block 1B AShM/SUT HWT
  3 *Glavkos* (GER Type-209/1100) with 8 single 533mm TT with UGM-84C *Harpoon* Block 1B AShM/SUT HWT
  4 *Papanikolis* (GER Type-214) with 8 single 533mm TT with UGM-84C *Harpoon* Block 1B AShM/SUT HWT

PRINCIPAL SURFACE COMBATANTS 13
    FRIGATES • FFGHM 13:
        4 *Elli* Batch I (ex-NLD *Kortenaer* Batch 2) with 2 quad lnchr with RGM-84C/G *Harpoon* Block 1B/G AShM, 1 octuple Mk 29 GMLS with RIM-7M/P *Sea Sparrow* SAM, 2 twin SVTT Mk 32 mod 9 324mm ASTT with Mk 46 mod 5 LWT, 1 Mk 15 *Phalanx* CIWS, 1 76mm gun (capacity 2 Bell 212 (AB-212) hel or 1 S-70B *Seahawk* hel)
        2 *Elli* Batch II (ex-NLD *Kortenaer* Batch 2) with 2 quad lnchr with RGM-84C/G *Harpoon* Block 1B/G AShM, 1 octuple Mk 29 GMLS with RIM-7M/P *Sea Sparrow* SAM, 2 twin SVTT Mk 32 mod 9 324mm ASTT with Mk 46 mod 5 LWT, 1 Mk 15 *Phalanx* CIWS, 2 76mm gun (capacity 2 Bell 212 (AB-212) hel or 1 S-70B *Seahawk* hel)
        3 *Elli* Batch III (ex-NLD *Kortenaer* Batch 2) with 2 quad lnchr with RGM-84C/G *Harpoon* Block 1B/G AShM, 1 octuple Mk 29 lnchr with RIM-7P *Sea Sparrow* SAM, 2 twin SVTT Mk 32 mod 9 324mm ASTT with Mk 46 LWT, 1 Mk 15 *Phalanx* CIWS, 1 76mm gun (capacity 2 Bell 212 (AB-212) hel)
        4 *Hydra* (GER MEKO 200) with 2 quad lnchr with RGM-84G *Harpoon* Block 1G AShM, 1 16-cell Mk 48 mod 2 VLS with RIM-162C ESSM SAM, 2 triple SVTT Mk 32 mod 5 324mm ASTT with Mk 46 LWT, 2 Mk 15 *Phalanx* CIWS, 1 127mm gun (capacity 1 S-70B *Seahawk* ASW hel)
PATROL AND COASTAL COMBATANTS 33
    CORVETTES • FSGM 5 *Roussen* (*Super Vita*) with 2 quad lnchr with MM40 *Exocet* Block 2/3 AShM, 1 21-cell Mk 49 GMLS with RIM-116 RAM SAM, 1 76mm gun
    PCFG 8:
        3 *Kavaloudis* (FRA *La Combattante* IIIB) with 2 twin lnchr with RGM-84C *Harpoon* Block 1B AShM, 2 single 533mm TT with SST-4 HWT, 2 76mm gun
        1 *Laskos* (FRA *La Combattante* III) with 4 MM38 *Exocet* AShM, 2 single 533mm TT with SST-4 HWT, 2 76mm gun
        3 *Laskos* (FRA *La Combattante* III) with 2 twin lnchr with RGM-84C *Harpoon* Block 1B AShM, 2 single 533mm TT with SST-4 HWT, 2 76mm gun
        1 *Votsis* (ex-GER *Tiger*) with 2 twin lnchr with RGM-84C *Harpoon* AShM, 1 76mm gun
    PCFT 2:
        2 *Kavaloudis* (FRA *La Combattante* IIIB) with 2 single 533mm TT with SST-4 HWT, 2 76mm gun
    PCF 2:
        2 *Votsis* (ex-GER *Tiger*) with 1 76mm gun
    PCO 8:
        2 *Armatolos* (DNK *Osprey*) with 1 76mm gun
        2 *Pirpolitis* with 1 76mm gun
        4 *Machitis* with 1 76mm gun
    PB 8: 4 *Andromeda* (NOR *Nasty*); 2 *Stamou*; 2 *Tolmi*
MINE COUNTERMEASURES 4
    MHO 4: 2 *Evropi* (ex-UK *Hunt*); 2 *Evniki* (ex-US *Osprey*)
AMPHIBIOUS
    LANDING SHIPS • LST 5:
        5 *Chios* (capacity 4 LCVP; 300 troops) with 1 76mm gun, 1 hel landing platform

LANDING CRAFT 15
    LCU 5
    LCA 7
    LCAC 3 *Kefallinia* (*Zubr*) with 2 AK630 CIWS (capacity either 3 MBT or 10 APC (T); 230 troops)
LOGISTICS AND SUPPORT 25
    ABU 2
    AG 2 *Pandora*
    AGOR 1 *Naftilos*
    AGS 2: 1 *Stravon*; 1 *Pytheas*
    AOR 2 *Axios* (ex-GER *Luneburg*)
    AORH 1 *Prometheus* (ITA *Etna*) with 1 Mk 15 *Phalanx* CIWS
    AOT 4 *Ouranos*
    AWT 6 *Kerkini*
    AXS 5

Coastal Defence

EQUIPMENT BY TYPE
COASTAL DEFENCE • AShM 2 MM40 *Exocet*

Naval Aviation

FORCES BY ROLE
ANTI-SUBMARINE WARFARE
    1 div with S-70B *Seahawk*; Bell 212 (AB-212) ASW
EQUIPMENT BY TYPE
AIRCRAFT 1 combat capable
    ASW 1 P-3B *Orion* (4 P-3B *Orion* in store undergoing modernisation)
HELICOPTERS
    ASW 18: 7 Bell 212 (AB-212) ASW; 11 S-70B *Seahawk*
AIR-LAUNCHED MISSILES
    ASM AGM-114 *Hellfire*
    AShM AGM-119 *Penguin*

Air Force 18,800; 3,150 conscripts (total 21,950)

Tactical Air Force

FORCES BY ROLE
FIGHTER/GROUND ATTACK
    1 sqn with F-4E *Phantom* II
    3 sqn with F-16CG/DG Block 30/50 *Fighting Falcon*
    3 sqn with F-16CG/DG Block 52+ *Fighting Falcon*
    2 sqn with F-16C/D Block 52+ ADV *Fighting Falcon*
    1 sqn with *Mirage* 2000-5EG/BG Mk2
    1 sqn with *Mirage* 2000EG/BG
AIRBORNE EARLY WARNING
    1 sqn with EMB-145H *Erieye*
EQUIPMENT BY TYPE
AIRCRAFT 230 combat capable
    FGA 230: 34 F-4E *Phantom* II; 69 F-16CG/DG Block 30/50 *Fighting Falcon*; 55 F-16CG/DG Block 52+; 30 F-16 C/D Block 52+ ADV *Fighting Falcon*; 19 *Mirage* 2000-5EG Mk2; 5 *Mirage* 2000-5BG Mk2; 16 *Mirage* 2000EG; 2 *Mirage* 2000BG
    AEW 4 EMB-145AEW (EMB-145H) *Erieye*
AIR-LAUNCHED MISSILES
    AAM • IR AIM-9L/P *Sidewinder*; R-550 *Magic* 2; **IIR** IRIS-T; *Mica* IR; **ARH** AIM-120B/C AMRAAM; *Mica* RF
    ASM AGM-65A/B/G *Maverick*

LACM SCALP EG
AShM AM39 *Exocet*
ARM AGM-88 HARM
BOMBS
Electro-optical guided: GBU-8B HOBOS
Laser-guided: GBU-10/12/16 *Paveway* II; GBU-24 *Paveway* III; GBU-50 *Enhanced Paveway* II
INS/GPS-guided GBU-31 JDAM; AGM-154C JSOW

Air Defence
FORCES BY ROLE
AIR DEFENCE
6 sqn/bty with MIM-104A/B/D *Patriot/Patriot* PAC-1 SOJC/*Patriot* PAC-2 GEM
2 sqn/bty with S-300PMU-1 (SA-10C *Grumble*)
12 bty with *Skyguard*/RIM-7 *Sparrow*/guns; *Crotale* NG/GR; *Tor*-M1 (SA-15 *Gauntlet*)
EQUIPMENT BY TYPE
AIR DEFENCE
SAM
Long-range 48: 36 MIM-104A/B/D *Patriot/Patriot* PAC-1 SOJC/PAC-2 GEM; 12 S-300PMU-1 (SA-10C *Grumble*)
Short-range 33: 9 *Crotale* NG/GR; 4 9K331 *Tor*-M1 (SA-15 *Gauntlet*); 20 RIM-7M *Sparrow* with *Skyguard*
GUNS 59: 20mm some Rh-202; 30mm 35+ *Artemis*-30; 35mm 24 GDF-005 with *Skyguard*

Air Support Command
FORCES BY ROLE
SEARCH & RESCUE/TRANSPORT HELICOPTER
1 sqn with AS332C *Super Puma* (SAR/CSAR)
1 sqn with AW109; Bell 205A (AB-205A) (SAR); Bell 212 (AB-212 - VIP, tpt)
TRANSPORT
1 sqn with C-27J *Spartan*
1 sqn with C-130B/H *Hercules*
1 sqn with EMB-135BJ *Legacy*; ERJ-135LR; Gulfstream V
EQUIPMENT BY TYPE
AIRCRAFT
TPT 26: Medium 23: 8 C-27J *Spartan*; 5 C-130B *Hercules*; 10 C-130H *Hercules*; Light 2: 1 EMB-135BJ *Legacy*; 1 ERJ-135LR; PAX 1 Gulfstream V
HELICOPTERS
TPT 31: Medium 12 AS332C *Super Puma*; Light 19: 12 Bell 205A (AB-205A) (SAR); 4 Bell 212 (AB-212) (VIP, Tpt); 3 AW109

Air Training Command
FORCES BY ROLE
TRAINING
2 sqn with T-2C/E *Buckeye*
2 sqn with T-6A/B *Texan* II
1 sqn with P2002JF; T-41D
EQUIPMENT BY TYPE
AIRCRAFT • TRG 103: 12 P2002JF; 28 T-2C/E *Buckeye*; 20 T-6A *Texan* II; 25 T-6B *Texan* II; 18 T-41D

Paramilitary
Coast Guard and Customs 4,000
EQUIPMENT BY TYPE
PATROL AND COASTAL COMBATANTS 124:
PCC 3
PCO 1 *Gavdos* (Damen 5009)
PBF 54
PB 66
AIRCRAFT • TPT • Light 4: 2 Cessna 172RG *Cutlass*; 2 TB-20 *Trinidad*
HELICOPTERS
SAR: 3 AS365N3

DEPLOYMENT
AFGHANISTAN: NATO • Operation Resolute Support 11
BOSNIA-HERZEGOVINA: EU • EUFOR • Operation Althea 2
CYPRUS: Army 950 (ELDYK army); ε200 (officers/NCOs seconded to Greek-Cypriot National Guard) (total 1,150); 1 mech bde (1 armd bn, 2 mech inf bn, 1 arty bn); 61 M48A5 MOLF MBT; 80 *Leonidas* APC; 12 M114 arty; 6 M110A2 arty
IRAQ: NATO • NATO Mission Iraq 1
LEBANON: UN • UNIFIL 146; 1 FFGHM
MALI: EU • EUTM Mali 2
MEDITERRANEAN SEA: NATO • SNMG 2: 1 FFGHM
SERBIA: NATO • KFOR 111; 1 inf coy

FOREIGN FORCES
United States US European Command: 1,000; 1 hel bn with AH-64D *Apache*; UH-60M *Black Hawk*; HH-60M *Black Hawk*; 1 naval base at Makri; 1 naval base at Soudha Bay; 1 air base at Iraklion

Hungary HUN

Hungarian Forint f		2018	2019	2020
GDP	f	42.1tr	45.3tr	
	US$	161bn	170bn	
per capita	US$	16,484	17,463	
Growth	%	4.9	4.6	
Inflation	%	2.8	3.4	
Def exp [a]	f	484bn	553bn	
	US$	1.85bn	2.08bn	
Def bdgt [b]	f	450bn	530bn	616bn
	US$	1.72bn	1.99bn	
US$1=f		261.03	266.00	

[a] NATO definition
[b] Includes military pensions

Real-terms defence budget trend (US$bn, constant 2015)

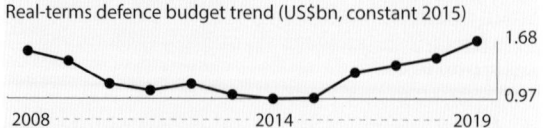

Population 9,799,351

Age	0–14	15–19	20–24	25–29	30–64	65 plus
Male	7.5%	2.6%	2.8%	3.2%	23.8%	7.6%
Female	7.1%	2.5%	2.7%	3.1%	24.6%	12.4%

Capabilities

Hungary published a National Security Strategy and National Military Strategy in 2012. Territorial defence and the ability to participate in NATO and other international operations are central tenets of the military strategy, including the medium-term aim of having forces capable of taking part in high-intensity operations. Hungary is also implementing the Zrínyi 2026 national-defence and armed-forces modernisation plan, announced in December 2016. Hungary coordinates policy with the other member states of the Visegrád Group, including on defence, and hosts the NATO Centre of Excellence for Military Medicine. At the end of 2018, legislation increased the authorised number of active personnel by 8,000 and separated the armed forces' command from the ministry of defence. The armed forces participate in international crisis-management missions, notably in Afghanistan, the Balkans and Iraq, but have very limited organic capacity to deploy forces beyond national borders. Increasing migration pressure has involved the armed forces in internal border-control operations, assisting national police forces. Announced equipment-modernisation priorities focus on individual-soldier equipment and fixed- and rotary-wing aircraft. In 2019, the government announced that it had raised the level of ambition for the maximum number of Hungarian soldiers deployed on international missions from 1,000 to 1,200. While the air-force-related elements of Zrínyi 2026 had been a focus of attention, at the end of 2018 the ministry also initiated procurement activities in the land domain, including for main battle tanks and self-propelled artillery. Hungary's defence-industrial base is limited, though the defence ministry set up an inter-ministerial working group to boost domestic capacity in the small-arms sector.

ACTIVE 27,800 (Army 10,450 Air 5,750 Joint 11,600)
Paramilitary 12,000
RESERVE 20,000

ORGANISATIONS BY SERVICE

Hungary's armed forces have reorganised into a joint force

Land Component 10,450 (incl riverine element)

FORCES BY ROLE
SPECIAL FORCES
  1 SF regt
MANOEUVRE
  Reconnaissance
  1 ISR regt
  Mechanised
  1 (5th) mech inf bde (3 mech inf bn, 1 cbt engr coy, 1 sigs coy, 1 log bn)
  1 (25th) mech inf bde (1 tk bn; 2 mech inf bn, 1 arty bn, 1 AT bn, 1 log bn)
COMBAT SUPPORT
  1 engr regt
  1 EOD/rvn regt
  1 CBRN bn
  1 sigs regt
COMBAT SERVICE SUPPORT
  1 log regt

EQUIPMENT BY TYPE
ARMOURED FIGHTING VEHICLES
  MBT 44 T-72M1
  IFV 120 BTR-80A
  APC 272
    APC (W) 260 BTR-80
    PPV 12 Maxxpro Plus
ENGINEERING & MAINTENANCE VEHICLES
  AEV BAT-2
  ARV VT-55A
  VLB BLG-60; MTU; TMM
NBC VEHICLES 24+: 24 K90 CBRN Recce; PSZH-IV CBRN Recce
ANTI-TANK/ANTI-INFRASTRUCTURE
  MSL • MANPATS 9K111 *Fagot* (AT-4 *Spigot*); 9K111-1 *Konkurs* (AT-5 *Spandrel*)
ARTILLERY 31
  TOWED 152mm 31 D-20
  MOR 82mm
PATROL AND COASTAL COMBATANTS • PBR 2
MINE COUNTERMEASURES • MSR 4 *Nestin*

Air Component 5,750

FORCES BY ROLE
FIGHTER/GROUND ATTACK
  1 sqn with *Gripen* C/D
TRANSPORT
  1 sqn with An-26 *Curl*
TRAINING
  1 sqn with Z-143LSi; Z-242L
ATTACK HELICOPTER
  1 sqn with Mi-24 *Hind*
TRANSPORT HELICOPTER
  1 sqn with Mi-8 *Hip*; Mi-17 *Hip* H
AIR DEFENCE
  1 SAM regt (9 bty with *Mistral*; 3 bty with 2K12 *Kub* (SA-6 *Gainful*))
  1 radar regt

EQUIPMENT BY TYPE
AIRCRAFT 14 combat capable
  FGA 14: 12 *Gripen* C; 2 *Gripen* D
  TPT 6: Light 4 An-26 *Curl*; PAX 2 A319
  TRG 4: 2 Z-143LSi; 2 Z-242L
HELICOPTERS
  ATK 11: 3 Mi-24D *Hind* D; 6 Mi-24V *Hind* E; 2 Mi-24P *Hind* F
  MRH 9: 2 H145M; 7 Mi-17 *Hip* H
  TPT • Medium 3 Mi-8 *Hip* (10 in store)
AIR DEFENCE
  SAM • Point-defence 16 2K12 *Kub* (SA-6 *Gainful*); *Mistral*
AIR-LAUNCHED MISSILES
  AAM • IR AIM-9 *Sidewinder*; SARH R-27 (AA-10 *Alamo* A); ARH AIM-120C AMRAAM
  ASM AGM-65 *Maverick*; 3M11 *Falanga* (AT-2 *Swatter*); 9K114 *Shturm*-V (AT-6 *Spiral*)
  BOMBS • Laser-guided *Paveway* II

Paramilitary 12,000

Border Guards 12,000 (to reduce)

Ministry of Interior

FORCES BY ROLE
MANOEUVRE
Other
1 (Budapest) paramilitary district (7 rapid reaction coy)
11 (regt/district) paramilitary regt
EQUIPMENT BY TYPE
ARMOURED FIGHTING VEHICLES
APC • APC (W) 68 BTR-80

DEPLOYMENT

AFGHANISTAN: NATO • *Operation Resolute Support* 93
BOSNIA-HERZEGOVINA: EU • *Operation Althea* 164; 1 inf coy
CENTRAL AFRICAN REPUBLIC: UN • MINUSCA 1
CYPRUS: UN • UNFICYP 13
IRAQ: *Operation Inherent Resolve* 170
LEBANON: UN • UNIFIL 2
MALI: EU • EUTM Mali 7
SERBIA: NATO • KFOR 411; 1 inf coy (KTM)
WESTERN SAHARA: UN • MINURSO 7

FOREIGN FORCES
United States US European Command: 200; 1 armd recce tp; M3A3 *Bradley*

Iceland ISL

Icelandic Krona Kr		2018	2019	2020
GDP	Kr	2.81tr	2.93tr	
	US$	26.0bn	23.9bn	
per capita	US$	74,515	67,037	
Growth	%	4.8	0.8	
Inflation	%	2.7	2.8	
Sy Bdgt [a]	Kr	4.28bn	6.75bn	7.07bn
	US$	39.5m	55.1m	
US$1=Kr		108.30	122.54	

[a] Coast Guard budget

Real-terms defence budget trend (US$m, constant 2015)

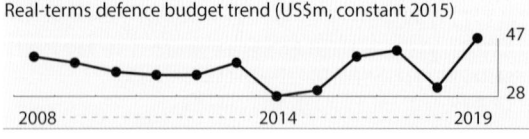

Population 347,183

Age	0–14	15–19	20–24	25–29	30–64	65 plus
Male	10.4%	3.2%	3.4%	3.7%	22.3%	7.1%
Female	10.0%	3.2%	3.3%	3.6%	22.0%	8.0%

Capabilities
Iceland is a NATO member but maintains only a coastguard service. In 2016, the country established a National Security Council to implement and monitor security policy. The coastguard controls the NATO Iceland Air Defence System, as well as a NATO Control and Reporting Centre that feeds into NATO air- and missile-defence and air-operations centres. Increased Russian air and naval activities in the Atlantic and close to NATO airspace have led to complaints from Iceland. Iceland considers its bilateral defence agreement with the US as an important pillar of its security policy and also participates in the security-policy dialogue of NORDEFCO. Iceland hosts NATO and regional partners for exercises, transits and naval task groups, as well as the Icelandic Air Policing mission. Despite there being no standing armed forces, Iceland makes financial contributions and on occasion deploys civilian personnel to NATO missions. In late 2016, following a joint declaration in June that year, the US Navy began operating P-8 *Poseidon* maritime-patrol aircraft from Keflavik air base. In summer 2019, it was reported that related upgrade projects would include accommodation, dangerous-cargo handling facilities and runway extensions to enable tanker operations, though these had yet to begin.

ACTIVE NIL Paramilitary 250

ORGANISATIONS BY SERVICE

Paramilitary

Iceland Coast Guard 250
EQUIPMENT BY TYPE
PATROL AND COASTAL COMBATANTS 3
PSOH 2 *Aegir*
PSO 1 *Thor*
LOGISTICS AND SUPPORT • AGS 1 *Baldur*
AIRCRAFT • **TPT** • **Light** 1 DHC-8-300 (MP)
HELICOPTERS
TPT • **Medium** 2 H225 (leased)

FOREIGN FORCES
Iceland Air Policing: Aircraft and personnel from various NATO members on a rotating basis

Ireland IRL

Euro €		2018	2019	2020
GDP	€	324bn	343bn	
	US$	383bn	385bn	
per capita	US$	78,335	77,771	
Growth	%	8.3	4.3	
Inflation	%	0.7	1.2	
Def bdgt [a]	€	946m	994m	1.04bn
	US$	1.12bn	1.12bn	
US$1=€		0.85	0.89	

[a] Includes military pensions and capital expenditure

Real-terms defence budget trend (US$bn, constant 2015)

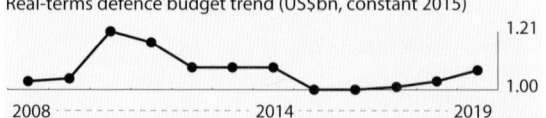

Population 5,123,219

Age	0–14	15–19	20–24	25–29	30–64	65 plus
Male	10.9%	3.1%	3.0%	3.0%	23.7%	6.3%
Female	10.4%	3.0%	2.9%	3.0%	23.5%	7.3%

Capabilities

The armed forces' core mission is defending the state against armed aggression, although a 2015 white paper broadened the scope of the national-security risk assessment beyond traditional military and paramilitary threats. It listed inter- and intra-state conflict, cyber attacks, terrorism, emergencies and natural disasters, among others. A white paper update was under way in 2019. The army maintains substantial EOD capabilities. Ireland is active in EU defence cooperation and continues to contribute to multinational operations. Its forces are well trained for their roles. Ireland is also working to establish a specialist reserve with relevant professional qualifications. It has sufficient logistic capability to sustain its UN deployments but has no strategic-airlift capacity. After the 2015 white paper, Dublin identified a large number of defence projects to be completed over a ten-year period. Key priorities include a mid-life upgrade for the army's *Piranha* armoured personnel carriers, EOD robots and UAVs. Other stated priorities include new armoured vehicles, new aircraft, naval-vessel refits, training facilities and upgrades to military facilities. A planned rise in the 2020 defence budget may be intended to help boost military pay, naval refits and armoured-vehicle modernisation plans. Ireland has a small, specialist defence industry focused on areas including drive-train technologies for land systems.

ACTIVE 8,650 (Army 7,000 Navy 950 Air 700)

RESERVE 4,050 (Army 3,850 Navy 200)

ORGANISATIONS BY SERVICE

Army 7,000
FORCES BY ROLE
SPECIAL FORCES
  1 ranger coy
MANOEUVRE
  Reconnaissance
  1 armd recce sqn
  Mechanised
  1 mech inf coy
  Light
  1 inf bde (1 cav recce sqn, 4 inf bn, 1 arty regt (3 fd arty bty, 1 AD bty), 1 fd engr coy, 1 sigs coy, 1 MP coy, 1 tpt coy)
  1 inf bde (1 cav recce sqn, 3 inf bn, 1 arty regt (3 fd arty bty, 1 AD bty), 1 fd engr coy, 1 sigs coy, 1 MP coy, 1 tpt coy)
EQUIPMENT BY TYPE
ARMOURED FIGHTING VEHICLES
  RECCE 6 *Piranha* IIIH 30mm
  APC 101
    APC (W) 74: 56 *Piranha* III; 18 *Piranha* IIIH
    PPV 27 RG-32M
ANTI-TANK/ANTI-INFRASTURCTURE
  MSL • MANPATS FGM-148 *Javelin*
  RCL 84mm *Carl Gustav*
ARTILLERY 131
  TOWED • 105mm 23: 17 L118 Light Gun; 6 L119 Light Gun
  MOR 108: **81mm** 84 Brandt; **120mm** 24 Ruag M87
AIR DEFENCE
  SAM • Point-defence RBS-70
  GUNS • TOWED 40mm 32 L/70 with 8 *Flycatcher*

Reserves 3,850 reservists
FORCES BY ROLE
MANOEUVRE
  Reconnaissance
  1 (integrated) armd recce sqn
  2 (integrated) cav sqn
  Mechanised
  1 (integrated) mech inf coy
  Light
  14 (integrated) inf coy
COMBAT SUPPORT
  4 (integrated) arty bty
  2 engr gp
  2 MP coy
  3 sigs coy
COMBAT SERVICE SUPPORT
  2 med det
  2 tpt coy

Naval Service 950
EQUIPMENT BY TYPE
PATROL AND COASTAL COMBATANTS 7
  PSOH (1 *Eithne* (in reserve since mid-2019 due to crew shortage) with 1 57mm gun)
  PSO 6: 2 *Roisin* with 1 76mm gun; 4 *Samuel Beckett* with 1 76mm gun
  PCO 1 *Orla* (ex-UK *Peacock*) with 1 76mm gun (1 more in reserve since mid-2019 due to crew shortage)
LOGISTICS AND SUPPORT • AXS 2

Air Corps 700
2 ops wg; 2 spt wg; 1 trg wg; 1 comms and info sqn
EQUIPMENT BY TYPE
AIRCRAFT
  MP 2 CN235 MPA
  TPT • Light 1 Learjet 45 (VIP)
  TRG 8 PC-9M
HELICOPTERS:
  MRH 6 AW139
  TPT • Light 2 H135 (incl trg/medevac)

DEPLOYMENT

BOSNIA-HERZEGOVINA: EU • EUFOR • *Operation Althea* 5

DEMOCRATIC REPUBLIC OF THE CONGO: UN • MONUSCO 3

LEBANON: UN • UNIFIL 461; 1 mech inf bn(-)

MALI: EU • EUTM Mali 20

MIDDLE EAST: UN • UNTSO 12

SERBIA: NATO • KFOR 12

SYRIA/ISRAEL: UN • UNDOF 126; 1 inf coy

WESTERN SAHARA: UN • MINURSO 3

Italy ITA

Euro €		2018	2019	2020
GDP	€	1.76tr	1.77tr	
	US$	2.08tr	1.99tr	
per capita	US$	34,321	32,947	
Growth	%	0.9	0.0	
Inflation	%	1.2	0.7	
Def exp [a]	€	21.2bn	21.4bn	
	US$	25.0bn	24.0bn	
Def bdgt [b]	€	24.3bn	24.2bn	
	US$	28.7bn	27.1bn	
US$1=€		0.85	0.89	

[a] NATO definition
[b] Includes military pensions

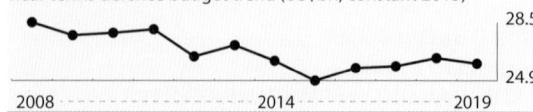

Real-terms defence budget trend (US$bn, constant 2015)

Population	62,334,799					
Age	0–14	15–19	20–24	25–29	30–64	65 plus
Male	6.9%	2.4%	2.4%	2.7%	24.4%	9.4%
Female	6.6%	2.3%	2.4%	2.7%	25.3%	12.4%

Capabilities

Italy is concerned by security challenges in the Euro-Atlantic environment, as well as from Europe's southern flank. The 2019–21 defence plan, building on the 2015 defence white paper and the 2017–19 defence plan, outlined the goal to reduce personnel numbers and improve joint activity between the services. Italy has taken part in NATO's air-policing missions in the Baltic states, Iceland and Romania and since early 2017 has deployed to Latvia as part of the Enhanced Forward Presence. The EUNAVFOR-MED force is headquartered in Rome, while the US Navy 6th Fleet is based in Naples. The country takes part in and hosts NATO and other multinational exercises and continues to support NATO, EU and UN operations abroad. However, Italy is planning to gradually reduce its presence overseas to focus on Europe's southern flank. Italy's logistics capability is enabled by a fleet of medium transport aircraft and tankers. The white paper detailed capability-enhancement programmes including upgrades to main battle tanks and procurement of armoured fighting vehicles, counter-UAV systems and electronic-warfare capabilities. The expected retirement of much of the naval fleet has triggered a long-term replacement plan; funds are still being allocated for the FREMM frigate programme. F-35As have been ordered for the air force (and F-35Bs for naval aviation). Italy has an advanced defence industry, producing equipment across all the domains, with particular strengths in shipbuilding and aircraft and helicopter manufacturing. The country hosts Europe's F-35 final assembly and check-out facility at Cameri. Italy takes part in European defence-industrial cooperation projects, including PESCO projects.

ACTIVE 165,500 (Army 96,700 Navy 28,850 Air 39,950) **Paramilitary 175,750**

RESERVES 18,300 (Army 13,400 Navy 4,900)

ORGANISATIONS BY SERVICE

Space
EQUIPMENT BY TYPE
SATELLITES 9
 COMMUNICATIONS 4: 1 *Athena-Fidus* (also used by FRA); 3 *Sicral*
 ISR 5: 4 *Cosmo* (*Skymed*); 1 OPSAT-3000

Army 96,700
Regt are bn sized
FORCES BY ROLE
COMMAND
 1 (NRDC-ITA) corps HQ (1 spt bde, 1 sigs regt, 1 spt regt)
MANOEUVRE
 Mechanised
 1 (*Vittorio Veneto*) div (1 (*Ariete*) armd bde (1 cav regt, 2 tk regt, 1 mech inf regt, 1 SP arty regt, 1 cbt engr regt, 1 log regt); 1 (*Pozzuolo del Friuli*) cav bde (1 cav regt, 1 amph regt, 1 arty regt, 1 cbt engr regt, 1 log regt); 1 (*Folgore*) AB bde (1 cav regt, 3 para regt, 1 arty regt, 1 cbt engr regt, 1 log regt); 1 (*Friuli*) air mob bde (1 air mob regt, 2 avn regt))
 1 (*Acqui*) div (1 (*Pinerolo*) mech bde (1 tk regt, 3 mech inf regt, 1 SP arty regt, 1 cbt engr regt, 1 log regt); 1 (*Granatieri*) mech bde (1 cav regt, 1 mech inf regt); 1 (*Garibaldi Bersaglieri*) mech bde (1 cav regt, 1 tk regt, 2 mech inf regt, 1 SP arty regt, 1 cbt engr regt, 1 log regt); 1 (*Aosta*) mech bde (1 cav regt, 3 mech inf regt, 1 SP arty regt, 1 cbt engr regt, 1 log regt); 1 (*Sassari*) lt mech bde (3 mech inf regt, 1 cbt engr regt, 1 log regt))
 Mountain
 1 (*Tridentina*) mtn div (2 mtn bde (1 cav regt, 3 mtn inf regt, 1 arty regt, 1 mtn cbt engr regt, 1 spt bn, 1 log regt))
COMBAT SUPPORT
 1 arty comd (1 arty regt, 1 MRL regt, 1 NBC regt)
 1 AD comd (3 SAM regt)
 1 engr comd (2 engr regt, 1 ptn br regt, 1 CIMIC regt)
 1 EW/sigs comd (1 EW/ISR bde (1 EW regt, 1 int regt, 1 STA regt); 1 sigs bde with (7 sigs regt))
COMBAT SERVICE SUPPORT
 1 log comd (3 log regt, 4 med unit)
HELICOPTER
 1 hel bde (3 hel regt)
EQUIPMENT BY TYPE
ARMOURED FIGHTING VEHICLES
 MBT 200 C1 *Ariete*
 ASLT 259 B1 *Centauro*
 IFV 432: 200 VCC-80 *Dardo*; 232 VBM 8×8 *Freccia* (incl 4 amb 20 CP and 36 with *Spike*-LR)
 APC 828
  APC (T) 361: 245 Bv-206; 116 M113 (incl variants)
  APC (W) 428: 151 *Puma* 4×4; 277 *Puma* 6×6
 PPV 39 VTMM
 AUV 10 *Cougar*; IVECO LMV
 AAV 15: 14 AAVP-7; 1 AAVC-7

ENGINEERING & MAINTENANCE VEHICLES
 AEV 40 *Dachs*; M113
 ARV 138: 137 BPz-2; 1 AAVR-7
 VLB 64 *Biber*
 MW 9: 6 *Buffalo*; 3 *Miniflail*
 NBC VEHICLES 14: 5 VBR NBC; 9 VBR NBC Plus
ANTI-TANK/ANTI-INFRASTRUCTURE
 MSL • MANPATS *Spike*
ARTILLERY 908
 SP **155mm** 69 PzH 2000
 TOWED 188: **105mm** 25 Oto Melara Mod 56; **155mm** 163 FH-70
 MRL **227mm** 22 MLRS
 MOR 629: **81mm** 283 Expal; **120mm** 325: 183 Brandt; 142 RT-61 (RT-F1) SP **120mm** 21 VBM 8×8 *Freccia*
AIRCRAFT • TPT • Light 6: 3 Do-228 (ACTL-1); 3 P-180 *Avanti*
HELICOPTERS
 ATK 36 AW129CBT *Mangusta*
 MRH 14 Bell 412 (AB-412) *Twin Huey*
 TPT 135: **Heavy** 15 CH-47F *Chinook*; (12 CH-47C *Chinook* in store) **Medium** 39 NH90 TTH (UH-90); **Light** 81: 8 AW109; 32 Bell 205 (AB-205); 28 Bell 206 *Jet Ranger* (AB-206); 13 Bell 212 (AB-212)
AIR DEFENCE
 SAM
  Long-range 20 SAMP/T
  Short-range 32 *Aspide* with *Skyguard*
  Point-defence FIM-92 *Stinger*
 AIR-LAUNCHED MISSILES
  ASM *Spike*-ER

Navy 28,850
EQUIPMENT BY TYPE
SUBMARINES • TACTICAL • SSK 8:
 4 *Pelosi* (imp *Sauro*, 3rd and 4th series) with 6 single 533mm TT with A184 mod 3 HWT
 4 *Salvatore Todaro* (Type-212A) with 6 single 533mm TT with *Black Shark* HWT
PRINCIPAL SURFACE COMBATANTS 19
 AIRCRAFT CARRIERS • CVS 2:
  1 *Cavour* with 4 8-cell *Sylver* A43 VLS with *Aster* 15 SAM, 2 76mm guns (capacity mixed air group of 20 AV-8B *Harrier* II; AW101 *Merlin*; NH90; Bell 212)
  1 *G. Garibaldi* with 2 octuple *Albatros* lnchr with *Aspide* SAM, 2 triple 324mm ASTT with Mk 46 LWT (capacity mixed air group of 18 AV-8B *Harrier* II; AW101 *Merlin*; NH90; Bell 212)
 DESTROYERS • DDGIIM 12.
  2 *Andrea Doria* with 2 quad lnchr with *Otomat* (*Teseo*) Mk2A AShM, 6 8-cell *Sylver* A50 VLS with *Aster* 15/*Aster* 30 SAM, 2 single B-515 324mm ASTT with MU90 LWT, 3 76mm guns (capacity 1 AW101 *Merlin*/NH90 hel)
  2 *Luigi Durand de la Penne* (ex-*Animoso*) with 2 quad lnchr with *Otomat* (*Teseo*) Mk2A AShM/*Milas* A/S msl, 1 Mk 13 mod 4 GMLS with SM-1MR Block VI SAM, 1 octuple *Albatros* lnchr with *Aspide* SAM, 2 triple B-515 324mm ASTT with Mk 46 LWT, 1 127mm gun, 3 76mm guns (capacity 1 NH90 or 2 Bell 212 (AB-212) hel)
  4 *Bergamini* (GP) with 2 quad lnchr with *Otomat* (*Teseo*) Mk2A AShM, 2 8-cell *Sylver* A50 VLS with *Aster* 15/*Aster* 30 SAM, 2 triple B-515 324mm ASTT with MU90 LWT, 1 127mm gun, 1 76mm gun (capacity 2 AW101/NH90 hel)
  4 *Bergamini* (ASW) with 2 twin lnchr with *Otomat* (*Teseo*) Mk2A AShM, 2 twin lnchr with MILAS A/S msl, 2 8-cell *Sylver* A50 VLS with *Aster* 15/*Aster* 30 SAM, 2 triple B-515 324mm ASTT with MU90 LWT, 2 76mm gun (capacity 2 AW101/NH90 hel)
 FRIGATES • FFGHM 5 *Maestrale* with 4 single lnchr with *Otomat* (*Teseo*) Mk2 AShM, 1 octuple *Albatros* lnchr with *Aspide* SAM, 2 triple SVTT Mk 32 324mm ASTT with Mk 46 LWT, 1 127mm gun (capacity 1 NH90 or 2 Bell 212 (AB-212) hel)
PATROL AND COASTAL COMBATANTS 14
 PSOH 10:
  4 *Cassiopea* with 1 76mm gun (capacity 1 Bell 212 (AB-212) hel)
  4 *Comandante Cigala Fuligosi* with 1 76mm gun (capacity 1 Bell 212 (AB-212)/NH90 hel)
  2 *Sirio* (capacity 1 Bell 212 (AB-212) or NH90 hel)
 PB 4 *Esploratore*
MINE WARFARE • MINE COUNTERMEASURES 10
 MHO 10: 8 *Gaeta*; 2 *Lerici*
AMPHIBIOUS
 PRINCIPAL AMPHIBIOUS SHIPS 3
  LHD 3:
   2 *San Giorgio* (capacity 3-4 AW101/NH90/Bell 212; 3 LCM 2 LCVP; 30 trucks; 36 APC (T); 350 troops)
   1 *San Giusto* with 1 76mm gun (capacity 2 AW101 *Merlin*/ NH90/Bell 212; 3 LCM 2 LCVP; 30 trucks; 36 APC (T); 350 troops)
 LANDING CRAFT 24: 15 **LCVP**; 9 **LCM**
LOGISTICS AND SUPPORT 56
 ABU 5 *Ponza*
 AFD 9
 AGE 3: 1 *Leonardo* (coastal); 1 *Raffaele Rosseti*; 1 *Vincenzo Martellota*
 AGI 1 *Elettra*
 AGOR 1 *Alliance*
 AGS 3: 1 *Ammiraglio Magnaghi* with 1 hel landing platform; 2 *Aretusa* (coastal)
 AKSL 6 *Gorgona*
 AORH 3: 1 *Etna* with 1 76mm gun (capacity 1 AW101/NH90/Bell 212 hel); 2 *Stromboli* with 1 76mm gun (capacity 1 AW101/NH90 hel)
 AOT 4 *Panarea*
 ARSH 1 *Anteo* (capacity 1 Bell 212 (AB-212) hel)
 ATS 6 *Ciclope*
 AWT 3: 1 *Bormida*; 2 *Simeto*
 AXL 3 *Aragosta*
 AXS 8: 1 *Amerigo Vespucci*; 5 *Caroly*; 1 *Italia*; 1 *Palinuro*

Naval Aviation 2,200
FORCES BY ROLE
FIGHTER/GROUND ATTACK
 1 sqn with AV-8B *Harrier* II; TAV-8B *Harrier* II

ANTI-SUBMARINE WARFARE/TRANSPORT
5 sqn with AW101 ASW *Merlin*; Bell 212 ASW (AB-212AS); Bell 212 (AB-212); NH90 NFH
MARITIME PATROL
1 flt with P-180
AIRBORNE EARLY WANRING & CONTROL
1 flt with AW101 AEW *Merlin*
EQUIPMENT BY TYPE
AIRCRAFT 18 combat capable
  FGA 18: 14 AV-8B *Harrier* II; 2 TAV-8B *Harrier* II; 2 F-35B *Lightning* II
  MP 3 P-180
HELICOPTERS
  ASW 47: 10 AW101 ASW *Merlin*; 9 Bell 212 ASW; 28 NH90 NFH (SH-90)
  AEW 4 AW101 AEW *Merlin*
  TPT 15: **Medium** 11: 8 AW101 *Merlin*; 3 NH90 MITT (MH-90); **Light** 4 Bell 212 (AB-212)
AIR-LAUNCHED MISSILES
  AAM • **IR** AIM-9L *Sidewinder*; **ARH** AIM-120 AMRAAM
  ASM AGM-65 *Maverick*
  AShM *Marte* Mk 2/S

Marines 3,000
FORCES BY ROLE
MANOEUVRE
Amphibious
1 mne regt (1 recce coy, 2 mne bn, 1 log bn)
1 (boarding) mne regt (2 mne bn)
1 landing craft gp
Other
1 sy regt (3 sy bn)
EQUIPMENT BY TYPE
ARMOURED FIGHTING VEHICLES
  APC (T) 27: 24 VCC-1; 3 VCC-2
  AAV 17: 15 AAVP-7; 2 AAVC-7
ENGINEERING & MAINTENANCE VEHICLES
  ARV 1 AAVR-7
ANTI-TANK/ANTI-INFRASTRUCTURE
  MSL• **MANPATS** *Milan*; *Spike*
ARTILLERY
  MOR 32: **81mm** 18 Brandt; **120mm** 10 Brandt; **SP 120mm** 4 M106
AIR DEFENCE • **SAM** • **Point-defence** FIM-92 *Stinger*

Air Force 39,950
FORCES BY ROLE
FIGHTER
4 sqn with Eurofighter *Typhoon*
FIGHTER/GROUND ATTACK
1 sqn with AMX *Ghibli*
1 (SEAD/EW) sqn with *Tornado* ECR
2 sqn with *Tornado* IDS
1 sqn with F-35A *Lightning* II
FIGHTER/GROUND ATTACK/ISR
1 sqn with AMX *Ghibli*
MARITIME PATROL
1 sqn (opcon Navy) with ATR-72MP (P-72A)
TANKER/TRANSPORT
1 sqn with KC-767A
COMBAT SEARCH & RESCUE
1 sqn with AB-212 ICO
SEARCH & RESCUE
1 wg with AW139 (HH-139A); Bell 212 (HH-212); HH-3F *Pelican*
TRANSPORT
2 (VIP) sqn with A319CJ; AW139 (VH-139A); *Falcon* 50; *Falcon* 900 *Easy*; *Falcon* 900EX; SH-3D *Sea King*
2 sqn with C-130J/C-130J-30/KC-130J *Hercules*
1 sqn with C-27J *Spartan*
1 (calibration) sqn with P-180 *Avanti*/Gulfstream G550 CAEW
TRAINING
1 OCU sqn with Eurofighter *Typhoon*
1 sqn with MB-339PAN (aerobatic team)
1 sqn with MD-500D/E (NH-500D/E)
1 OCU sqn with *Tornado*
1 OCU sqn with AMX-T *Ghibli*
1 sqn with MB-339A
1 sqn with M-346
1 sqn with SF-260EA, 3 P2006T (T-2006A)
ISR UAV
1 sqn with MQ-9A *Reaper*; RQ-1B *Predator*
AIR DEFENCE
2 bty with *Spada*
EQUIPMENT BY TYPE
AIRCRAFT 220 combat capable
  FTR 93 Eurofighter *Typhoon*
  FGA 50: 31 AMX *Ghibli*; 8 AMX-T *Ghibli*; 11 F-35A *Lightning* II
  ATK 34 *Tornado* IDS
  ATK/EW 15 *Tornado* ECR*
  MP 3 ATR-72MP (P-72A)
  SIGINT 1 Beech 350 *King Air*
  AEW&C 2 Gulfstream G550 CAEW
  TKR/TPT 6: 4 KC-767A; 2 KC-130J *Hercules*
  TPT 74: **Medium** 30: 8 C-130J *Hercules*; 10 C-130J-30 *Hercules*; 12 C-27J *Spartan*; **Light** 37: 17 P-180 *Avanti*; 20 S-208 (liaison); **PAX** 7: 2 A319CJ; 2 *Falcon* 50 (VIP); 2 *Falcon* 900 *Easy*; 1 *Falcon* 900EX (VIP)
  TRG 111: 20 M-346; 21 MB-339A; 28 MB-339CD*; 16 MB-339PAN (aerobatics); 26 SF-260EA
HELICOPTERS
  MRH 54: 13 AW139 (HH-139A/VH-139A); 2 MD-500D (NH-500D); 39 MD-500E (NH-500E)
  CSAR 7 AW101 (HH-101A)
  SAR 12 HH-3F *Pelican*
  TPT 31: **Medium** 2 SH-3D *Sea King* (liaison/VIP); **Light** 29 Bell 212 (HH-212)/AB-212 ICO
UNMANNED AERIAL VEHICLES • **ISR** • **Heavy** 12: 6 MQ-9A *Reaper*; 6 RQ-1B *Predator*
AIR DEFENCE • **SAM** • **Short** SPADA
AIR-LAUNCHED MISSILES
  AAM • **IR** AIM-9L *Sidewinder*; **IIR** IRIS-T; **ARH** AIM-120B AMRAAM
  ARM AGM-88 HARM
  LACM SCALP EG/*Storm Shadow*
BOMBS
  Laser-guided/GPS: Enhanced *Paveway* II; Enhanced *Paveway* III

Joint Special Forces Command (COFS)

Army
FORCES BY ROLE
SPECIAL FORCES
1 SF regt (9th *Assalto paracadutisti*)
1 STA regt
1 ranger regt (4th *Alpini paracadutisti*)
COMBAT SUPPORT
1 psyops regt
TRANSPORT HELICOPTER
1 spec ops hel regt

Navy (COMSUBIN)
FORCES BY ROLE
SPECIAL FORCES
1 SF gp (GOI)
1 diving gp (GOS)

Air Force
FORCES BY ROLE
SPECIAL FORCES
1 wg (sqn) (17th *Stormo Incursori*)

Paramilitary

Carabinieri
FORCES BY ROLE
SPECIAL FORCES
1 spec ops gp (GIS)

Paramilitary 175,750

Carabinieri 107,650
The Carabinieri are organisationally under the MoD. They are a separate service in the Italian Armed Forces as well as a police force with judicial competence

Mobile and Specialised Branch
FORCES BY ROLE
MANOEUVRE
Other
1 (mobile) paramilitary div (1 bde (1st) with (1 horsed cav regt, 11 mobile bn); 1 bde (2nd) with (1 (1st) AB regt, 2 (7th & 13th) mobile regt))
HELICOPTER
1 hel gp
EQUIPMENT BY TYPE
ARMOURED FIGHTING VEHICLES
APC • APC (T) 3 VCC-2
PATROL AND COASTAL COMBATANTS • PB 69
AIRCRAFT • TPT • Light: 1 P-180 *Avanti*
HELICOPTERS
MRH 24 Bell 412 (AB-412)
TPT • Light 19 AW109

Customs 68,100
(Servizio Navale Guardia Di Finanza)
EQUIPMENT BY TYPE
PATROL AND COASTAL COMBATANTS 177

PCF 1 *Antonio Zara*
PBF 144: 19 *Bigliani*; 22 *Corrubia*; 9 *Mazzei*; 62 V-2000; 32 V-5000/V-6000
PB 32: 24 *Buratti*; 8 *Meatini*
LOGISTICS AND SUPPORT • AX 1 *Giorgio Cini*
AIRCRAFT
MP 4 ATR-42-500MP
TPT • Light 2 P-180 *Avanti*
HELICOPTERS
TPT • Light 30: 14 AW139; 1 AW169M; 15 Bell 412HP *Twin Huey*

DEPLOYMENT

AFGHANISTAN: NATO • *Operation Resolute Support* 895; 1 mech inf bde HQ; 1 mech inf regt(-); 1 hel regt(-); AW129 *Mangusta*; NH90; RQ-7

BLACK SEA: NATO • SNMCMG 2: 1 MHO; 1 AORH

BOSNIA-HERZEGOVINA: EU • EUFOR • *Operation Althea* 5

CENTRAL AFRICAN REPUBLIC: EU • EUTM RCA 3

DJIBOUTI: 88

EGYPT: MFO 77; 3 PB

GULF OF ADEN & INDIAN OCEAN: EU • *Operation Atalanta* 1 DDGHM

INDIA/PAKISTAN: UN • UNMOGIP 2

IRAQ: *Operation Inherent Resolve* (*Prima Parthica*) 600; 1 inf regt; 1 trg unit; 1 hel sqn with 4 NH90; NATO • NATO Mission Iraq 12

KUWAIT: *Operation Inherent Resolve* (*Prima Parthica*) 250; 4 Eurofighter *Typhoon*; 2 MQ-9A *Reaper*; 1 KC-767A

LATVIA: NATO • Enhanced Forward Presence 166; 1 armd inf coy with C1 *Ariete*; VCC-80 *Dardo*

LEBANON: UN • UNIFIL 1,066; 1 mech bde HQ; 1 mech inf bn; 1 MP coy; 1 hel bn

LIBYA: MIASIT 300

MALI: EU • EUTM Mali 7; UN • MINUSMA 2

NIGER: MISIN 96

SERBIA: NATO • KFOR 542; 1 mtn inf BG HQ; 1 Carabinieri unit

SOMALIA: EU • EUTM Somalia 128

TURKEY: NATO • *Operation Active Fence* 130; 1 SAM bty with SAMP/T

UNITED ARAB EMIRATES: 113; 1 tpt flt with 2 C-130J *Hercules*

WESTERN SAHARA: UN • MINURSO 2

FOREIGN FORCES

United States US European Command: 12,750
Army 4,200; 1 AB IBCT(-)
Navy 4,000; 1 HQ (US Navy Europe (USNAVEUR)) at Naples; 1 HQ (6th Fleet) at Gaeta; 1 ASW Sqn with 4 P-8A *Poseidon* at Sigonella

USAF 4,350; 1 ftr wg with 2 ftr sqn with 21 F-16C/D *Fighting Falcon* at Aviano; 1 CSAR sqn with 8 HH-60G *Pave Hawk*
USMC 200

Latvia LVA

Euro €		2018	2019	2020
GDP	€	29.5bn	31.2bn	
	US$	34.9bn	35.0bn	
per capita	US$	18,033	18,172	
Growth	%	4.8	2.8	
Inflation	%	2.6	3.0	
Def exp [a]	€	613m	634m	
	US$	724m	712m	
Def bdgt [b]	€	613m	634m	663m
	US$	724m	712m	
FMA (US)	US$	8m	0m	5m
US$1= €		0.85	0.89	

[a] NATO definition
[b] Includes military pensions

Real-terms defence budget trend (US$m, constant 2015)
635
231
2008 · · · · · · · · · · · 2014 · · · · · · · · · · · 2019

Population   1,902,424

Ethnic groups: Latvian 62%; Russian 27%; Belarusian 3%; Polish 2.2%

Age	0–14	15–19	20–24	25–29	30–64	65 plus
Male	7.8%	2.4%	2.3%	3.3%	23.7%	6.7%
Female	7.4%	2.2%	2.1%	3.1%	25.4%	13.5%

Capabilities

Latvia has small armed forces focused on maintaining national sovereignty and territorial integrity but the country depends on NATO membership as a security guarantor. Russia is Latvia's overriding security concern, which in general drives security policy. The 2016 State Defence Concept set defence-strategic principles, priorities and activities. That same year, a National Armed Forces Development plan 2016–28 illustrated a capabilities-based planning process. Principal tasks are to improve early warning, detection and situational awareness, to increase combat readiness and to enhance the ability to counter hybrid threats. The armed forces are volunteer-based, although the option of moving to conscription was discussed, and rejected, in 2017. There are plans to improve combat readiness. Latvia has no requirement and therefore no capacity to independently deploy and sustain forces beyond its national boundaries, although the armed forces have taken part in a range of NATO operations, and EU civilian and military missions. Capability-development projects include military engineering, special operations, mechanised infantry, air defence, air surveillance and the National Guard. Acquisition requirements include self-propelled howitzers, CVR(T) and ATGW systems. Latvia has only niche defence-industrial capability, with cyber security a focus. An updated cyber-security strategy was approved in September 2019.

ACTIVE 6,900 (Army 1,500 Navy 500 Air 500 Joint Staff 3,500 National Guard 900)

RESERVE 10,500 (National Guard 7,500; Other 3,000)

ORGANISATIONS BY SERVICE

Joint 3,300
FORCES BY ROLE
SPECIAL FORCES
1 SF unit
COMBAT SUPPORT
1 MP bn

Army 1,500
FORCES BY ROLE
MANOEUVRE
Mechanised
1 mech inf bde (2 mech inf bn, 1 SP arty bn, 1 cbt spt bn HQ, 1 CSS bn HQ)

National Guard 600; 7,750 part-time (8,350 total)
FORCES BY ROLE
MANOEUVRE
Light
1 (2nd) inf bde (4 inf bn; 1 engr bn)
3 (1st, 3rd & 4th) inf bde (3 inf bn; 1 sy bn; 1 spt bn)
COMBAT SUPPORT
1 cyber unit
1 NBC coy
1 psyops pl
EQUIPMENT BY TYPE
ARMOURED FIGHTING VEHICLES
MBT 3 T-55 (trg)
RECCE 99 FV107 *Scimitar* (incl variants)
ANTI-TANK/ANTI-INFRASTRUCTURE
MANPATS *Spike*-LR
RCL 84mm *Carl Gustav*; 90mm 130 Pvpj 1110
ARTILLERY 123
SP 155mm 47 M109A5ÖE
TOWED 100mm 23 K-53
MOR 53: 81mm 28 L16; 120mm 25 M120

Navy 500 (incl Coast Guard)
Naval Forces Flotilla separated into an MCM squadron and a patrol-boat squadron. LVA, EST and LTU have set up a joint naval unit, BALTRON, with bases at Liepaja, Riga, Ventspils (LVA), Tallinn (EST), Klaipeda (LTU). Each nation contributes 1–2 MCMVs
EQUIPMENT BY TYPE
PATROL AND COASTAL COMBATANTS 5
PB 5 *Skrunda* (GER *Swath*)
MINE WARFARE • MINE COUNTERMEASURES 6
MHO 5 *Imanta* (ex-NLD *Alkmaar/Tripartite*)
MCCS 1 *Vidar* (ex-NOR)
LOGISTICS AND SUPPORT 1
AXL 1 *Varonis* (comd and spt ship, ex-NLD)

Coast Guard
Under command of the Latvian Naval Forces
EQUIPMENT BY TYPE
PATROL AND COASTAL COMBATANTS
PB 6: 1 *Astra*; 5 KBV 236 (ex-SWE)

Air Force 500
Main tasks are airspace control and defence, maritime and land SAR and air transportation
FORCES BY ROLE
TRANSPORT
1 (mixed) tpt sqn with An-2 *Colt*; Mi-17 *Hip* H; PZL Mi-2 *Hoplite*
AIR DEFENCE
1 AD bn
1 radar sqn (radar/air ctrl)
AIRCRAFT • TPT • Light 4 An-2 *Colt*
HELICOPTERS
MRH 4 Mi-17 *Hip* H
TPT • Light 2 PZL Mi-2 *Hoplite*
AIR DEFENCE
SAM • **Point-defence** FIM-92 *Stinger*; RBS-70
GUNS • **TOWED 40mm** 24 L/70

Paramilitary

State Border Guard
EQUIPMENT BY TYPE
PATROL AND COASTAL COMBATANTS
PB 3: 1 *Valpas* (ex-FIN); 1 *Lokki* (ex-FIN); 1 *Randa*
HELICOPTERS
TPT • Light 4: 2 Bell 206B (AB-206B) *Jet Ranger* II; 2 AW109E *Power*

DEPLOYMENT
AFGHANISTAN: NATO • *Operation Resolute Support* 40
BALTIC SEA: NATO • SNMCMG 1: 1 MHO
IRAQ: *Operation Inherent Resolve* 6
MALI: EU • EUTM Mali 3; **UN •** MINUSMA 9

FOREIGN FORCES
All **NATO** Enhanced Forward Presence unless stated
Albania 21; 1 EOD pl
Canada 525; 1 mech inf bn HQ; 1 mech inf coy(+);l 1 cbt spt coy
Czech Republic 55; 1 mor pl
Italy 166; 1 armd inf coy
Montenegro 10
Poland 175; 1 tk coy
Slovakia 152; 1 mech inf coy
Slovenia 33; 1 engr pl
Spain 350; 1 armd inf coy(+)

Lithuania LTU

Euro €		2018	2019	2020
GDP	€	45.1bn	47.8bn	
	US$	53.3bn	53.6bn	
per capita	US$	18,994	19,267	
Growth	%	3.5	3.4	
Inflation	%	2.5	2.3	
Def exp [a]	€	895m	968m	
	US$	1.06bn	1.09bn	
Def bdgt [b]	€	895m	948m	1.02bn
	US$	1.06bn	1.07bn	
FMA (US)	US$	8m	0m	5m
US$1=€		0.85	0.89	

[a] NATO definition
[b] Includes military pensions

Real-terms defence budget trend (US$m, constant 2015)

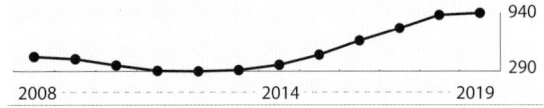

Population 2,762,485

Ethnic groups: Lithuanian 84.2%; Polish 6.6%; Russian 5.8%; Belarusian 1.2%

Age	0–14	15–19	20–24	25–29	30–64	65 plus
Male	7.8%	2.5%	2.9%	3.3%	22.8%	6.8%
Female	7.4%	2.4%	2.6%	3.1%	25.0%	13.3%

Capabilities

Lithuania's small armed forces focus on maintaining territorial integrity and national sovereignty but the country relies on NATO membership for its security. Like the other Baltic states, it is reliant on NATO's air-policing deployment for a combat-aircraft capacity. Russia is the country's predominant security concern, and this shapes Lithuanian defence policy. In January 2017, Lithuania adopted a new National Security Strategy, reflecting the worsening regional security environment. Better combat readiness is an objective and the mobilisation system is being reformed. Compulsory military service was reintroduced in 2015. Reforms to defence planning and acquisition management came into force in 2018. There is increased attention to communications security. Lithuania has a limited medium-airlift capability, for use in supporting its forces on multinational deployed operations. It takes an active part in NATO and EU operations. The country is purchasing the NASAMS SAM system to improve its ground-based air defences. Lithuania has a small defence-industrial base, with niche capabilities, for instance in helicopter support and maintenance.

ACTIVE 20,650 (Army 12,900 Navy 700 Air 1,350 Other 5,700) **Paramilitary 15,500**
Conscript liability 9 months

RESERVE 6,700 (Army 6,700)

ORGANISATIONS BY SERVICE

Army 7,650; 5,250 active reserves (total 12,900)

FORCES BY ROLE
MANOEUVRE
  Mechanised
    1 (1st) mech bde (1 recce coy, 4 mech inf bn, 1 arty bn)
  Light
    1 (2nd) mot inf bde (3 mot inf bn, 1 arty bn)
COMBAT SUPPORT
  1 engr bn
COMBAT SERVICE SUPPORT
  1 trg regt
EQUIPMENT BY TYPE
ARMOURED FIGHTING VEHICLES
  IFV 4 Boxer (Vilkas) (in test; incl 2 trg)
  APC • APC (T) 256: 234 M113A1; 22 M577 (CP)
ENGINEERING & MAINTENANCE VEHICLES
  AEV 8 MT-LB
  ARV 6: 2 BPz-2; 4 M113
ANTI-TANK/ANTI-INFRASTRUCTURE
  MSL
    SP 10 M1025A2 HMMWV with FGM-148 Javelin
    MANPATS FGM-148 Javelin
  RCL 84mm Carl Gustav
ARTILLERY 91
  SP 16 PzH 2000
  TOWED 105mm 18 M101
  MOR 57: 120mm 42: 20 2B11; 22 M/41D; SP 120mm 15 M113 with Tampella
AIR DEFENCE • SAM • Point-defence GROM

Reserves

National Defence Voluntary Forces 5,250 active reservists
FORCES BY ROLE
MANOEUVRE
  Other
    6 (territorial) def unit

Navy 700

LVA, EST and LTU established a joint naval unit, BALTRON, with bases at Liepaja, Riga, Ventpils (LVA), Tallinn (EST), Klaipeda (LTU)
EQUIPMENT BY TYPE
PATROL AND COASTAL COMBATANTS 4
  PCC 4 Zemaitis (ex-DNK Flyvefisken) with 1 76mm gun
MINE WARFARE • MINE COUNTERMEASURES 4
  MHC 3: 1 Sūduvis (ex-GER Lindau); 2 Skulvis (ex-UK Hunt)
  MCCS 1 Jotvingis (ex-NOR Vidar)
LOGISTICS AND SUPPORT • AAR 1 Šakiai

Air Force 1,350

FORCES BY ROLE
AIR DEFENCE
  1 AD bn
EQUIPMENT BY TYPE
AIRCRAFT
  TPT 6: Medium 3 C-27J Spartan; Light 3: 1 Cessna 172RG; 2 L-410 Turbolet
HELICOPTERS
  MRH 3 AS365M3 Dauphin (SAR)
  TPT • Medium 3 Mi-8 Hip (tpt/SAR)
AIR DEFENCE • SAM • Point-defence FIM-92 Stinger; RBS-70

Special Operation Force

FORCES BY ROLE
SPECIAL FORCES
  1 SF gp (1 CT unit; 1 Jaeger bn, 1 cbt diver unit)

Logistics Support Command 1,400

FORCES BY ROLE
COMBAT SERVICE SUPPORT
  1 log bn

Training and Doctrine Command 1,500

FORCES BY ROLE
COMBAT SERVICE SUPPORT
  1 trg regt

Other Units 2,600

FORCES BY ROLE
COMBAT SUPPORT
  1 MP bn

Paramilitary 15,500

Riflemen Union 12,000

State Border Guard Service 3,300

Ministry of Interior
EQUIPMENT BY TYPE
PATROL AND COASTAL COMBATANTS • PB 3: 1 Lokki (ex-FIN); 1 KBV 041 (ex-SWE); 1 Bakauskas (Baltic Patrol 2700)
AMPHIBIOUS • LANDING CRAFT • UCAC 2 Christina (Griffon 2000)
AIRCRAFT • TPT • Light 1 Cessna 172RG
HELICOPTERS • TPT • Light 5: 1 BK-117 (SAR); 2 H120 Colibri; 2 H135

DEPLOYMENT

AFGHANISTAN: NATO • Operation Resolute Support 50
CENTRAL AFRICAN REPUBLIC: EU • EUTM RCA 2
IRAQ: Operation Inherent Resolve 6; **NATO** • NATO Mission Iraq 9
MALI: EU • EUTM Mali 2; **UN** • MINUSMA 37
SERBIA: NATO • KFOR 1
UKRAINE: JMTG-U 26

FOREIGN FORCES

All **NATO** Enhanced Forward Presence unless stated
Belgium 262; 1 mech inf coy • **NATO** Baltic Air Policing 4 F-16AM Fighting Falcon
Czech Republic 35; 1 EW unit

Denmark NATO Baltic Air Policing 4 F-16AM *Fighting Falcon*
Germany 560; 1 armd inf bn HQ; 1 armd inf coy(+)
Netherlands 270; 1 armd inf coy
Norway 120; 1 armd inf coy

Luxembourg LUX

Euro €		2018	2019	2020
GDP	€	58.9bn	61.6bn	
	US$	69.6bn	69.5bn	
per capita	US$	115,536	113,196	
Growth	%	2.6	2.6	
Inflation	%	2.0	1.7	
Def exp [a]	€	301m	346m	
	US$	356m	390m	
Def bdgt	€	341m	305m	341m
	US$	403m	344m	
US$1=€		0.85	0.89	

[a] NATO definition

Real-terms defence budget trend (US$m, constant 2015)

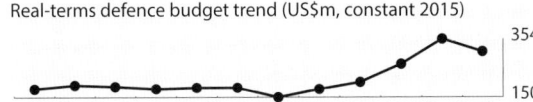

Population 617,185

Age	0–14	15–19	20–24	25–29	30–64	65 plus
Male	8.6%	2.9%	3.2%	3.7%	25.1%	6.9%
Female	8.1%	2.8%	3.0%	3.5%	23.9%	8.4%

Capabilities

Luxembourg maintains a limited military capability to participate in European collective security and crisis management. Defence Guidelines for 2025 and Beyond were published at the end of 2017. They contain strong statements of support for NATO and EU security policy and contributions to international missions. They also outline ambitious modernisation plans, including a reorganisation of the army, which will take on joint responsibilities, including for ISR, a new air component and a military cyber cell. Luxembourg has contributed troops to the multinational battlegroup in Lithuania as part of NATO's Enhanced Forward Presence. It is part of the European Multi-Role Tanker Transport Fleet programme, partially funding one A330 MRTT, but the Belgian and Dutch air forces are responsible for policing Luxembourg's airspace. Sustaining the army's personnel strength depends on better recruiting and retention and being able to recruit from other EU states. A review is under way, examining a specialised reserve of civilian experts. The defence guidelines envisage considerable equipment improvements and cooperative development of UAV capabilities with Belgium and the Netherlands. Ambitions for the new air component include tactical-airlift and medical-evacuation capabilities. There is a small but advanced space industry and some foreign defence firms have a presence, but the country is otherwise reliant on imports. A strategy for defence industry, innovation and research is to be developed as part of the new defence guidelines.

ACTIVE 900 (Army 900) **Paramilitary 600**

ORGANISATIONS BY SERVICE

Army 900
FORCES BY ROLE
MANOEUVRE
  Reconnaissance
  2 recce coy (1 to Eurocorps/BEL div, 1 to NATO pool of deployable forces)
EQUIPMENT BY TYPE
ARMOURED FIGHTING VEHICLES
  AUV 48 *Dingo* 2
ANTI-TANK/ANTI-INFRASTRUCTURE
  MSL • MANPATS NLAW; TOW
ARTILLERY • MOR 81mm 6

Paramilitary 600
  Gendarmerie 600

DEPLOYMENT

AFGHANISTAN: NATO • *Operation Resolute Support* 2
MALI: EU • EUTM Mali 2
MEDITERRANEAN SEA: EU • EUNAVFOR MED 2 *Merlin* IIIC (leased)

Macedonia, North MKD

Macedonian Denar d		2018	2019	2020
GDP	d	660bn	695bn	
	US$	12.7bn	12.7bn	
per capita	US$	6,100	6,096	
Growth	%	2.7	3.2	
Inflation	%	1.5	1.3	
Def bdgt	d	6.50bn	8.31bn	
	US$	125m	152m	
US$1=d		52.12	54.82	

Real-terms defence budget trend (US$m, constant 2015)

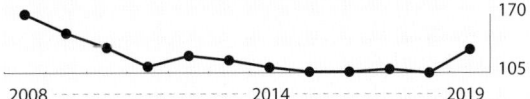

Population 2,122,693

Ethnic groups: Macedonian 64.2%; Albanian 25.2%; Turkish 3.9%; Romani 2.7%; Serb 1.8%; Bosniac 0.9%

Age	0–14	15–19	20–24	25–29	30–64	65 plus
Male	8.4%	3.1%	3.7%	3.7%	25.0%	6.0%
Female	7.8%	2.9%	3.4%	3.5%	24.7%	7.8%

Capabilities

The armed forces' primary goals are safeguarding the state's territorial integrity and sovereignty, as well as contributing to operations under the EU, NATO and UN umbrellas. A strategic defence review was released in 2018, which set out aims to optimise, reorganise and modernise the armed forces into a small, modern and flexible force. The review's 'Future armed forces 2028' concept calls for changes in the armed forces' structure, the consolidation of commands and headquarters, and a reorganised defence ministry. Following the agreement to resolve the dispute with Greece over the country's name, the accession protocol for NATO membership was signed in February 2019. The armed forces are fully professional and the country aims to train all units, particularly those with deployable capability, to NATO standards. A number of units are earmarked for participation in NATO-led operations. Skopje contributes to EU, NATO and UN missions, with personnel deployed to *Operation Resolute Support* in Afghanistan. Participation in international peacekeeping missions has increased logistics capability. The country has modest maritime and air wings and relies on Soviet-era equipment. A 2014–23 modernisation plan is intended to update equipment to NATO standards, but progress has been limited. Among the priorities identified are the procurement of air-defence missile batteries and medium- and long-range anti-armour systems. There is little in the way of a domestic defence industry, with no ability to design and manufacture modern equipment.

ACTIVE 8,000 (Army 8,000) Paramilitary 7,600

RESERVE 4,850

ORGANISATIONS BY SERVICE

Army 8,000
FORCES BY ROLE
SPECIAL FORCES
  1 SF regt (1 SF bn, 1 Ranger bn)
MANOEUVRE
  Mechanised
  1 mech inf bde (1 tk bn, 4 mech inf bn, 1 arty bn, 1 engr bn, 1 NBC coy)
COMBAT SUPPORT
  1 MP bn
  1 sigs bn
COMBAT SERVICE SUPPORT
  1 log bde (3 log bn)

Reserves
  FORCES BY ROLE
    MANOEUVRE *Light*
    1 inf bde
EQUIPMENT BY TYPE
ARMOURED FIGHTING VEHICLES
  MBT 31 T-72A
  RECCE 10 BRDM-2
  IFV 11: 10 BMP-2; 1 BMP-2K (CP)
  APC 202
    APC (T) 47: 9 *Leonidas*; 28 M113; 10 MT-LB
    APC (W) 155: 57 BTR-70; 12 BTR-80; 2 *Cobra*; 84 TM-170 *Hermelin*
ANTI-TANK/ANTI-INFRASTRUCTURE
  MSL • MANPATS *Milan*
  RCL 57mm; **82mm** M60A
ARTILLERY 126
  TOWED 70: **105mm** 14 M-56; **122mm** 56 M-30 M-1938
  MRL 17: **122mm** 6 BM-21; **128mm** 11
  MOR 39: **120mm** 39

Marine Wing
EQUIPMENT BY TYPE
PATROL AND COASTAL COMBATANTS • PB 2
Botica

Aviation Brigade
FORCES BY ROLE
TRAINING
  1 flt with Z-242; Bell 205 (UH-1H *Iroquois*)
ATTACK HELICOPTER
  1 sqn with Mi-24K *Hind* G2; Mi-24V *Hind* E
TRANSPORT HELICOPTER
  1 sqn with Mi-8MTV *Hip*; Mi-17 *Hip* H
AIR DEFENCE
  1 AD bn
EQUIPMENT BY TYPE
AIRCRAFT
  TPT • Light 1 An-2 *Colt*
  TRG 5 Z-242
HELICOPTERS
  ATK 4 Mi-24V *Hind* E (10: 2 Mi-24K *Hind* G2; 8 Mi-24V *Hind* E in store)
  MRH 6: 4 Mi-8MTV *Hip*; 2 Mi-17 *Hip* H
  TPT • Light 2 Bell 205 (UH-1H *Iroquois*)
AIR DEFENCE
  SAM • Point-defence 8 9K35 *Strela*-10 (SA-13 *Gopher*); 9K310 *Igla*-1 (SA-16 *Gimlet*)
  GUNS 40mm 36 L/60

Paramilitary

Police 7,600 (some 5,000 armed)
incl 2 SF units
EQUIPMENT BY TYPE
ARMOURED FIGHTING VEHICLES
  APC • APC (T) M113; **APC (W)** BTR-80; TM-170 *Heimlin*
  AUV *Ze'ev*
HELICOPTERS
  MRH 1 Bell 412EP *Twin Huey*
  TPT • Light 2: 1 Bell 206B (AB-206B) *Jet Ranger* II; 1 Bell 212 (AB-212)

DEPLOYMENT

AFGHANISTAN: NATO • *Operation Resolute Support* 47
BOSNIA-HERZEGOVINA: EU • EUFOR • *Operation Althea* 3
LEBANON: UN • UNIFIL 2

Malta MLT

Euro €		2018	2019	2020
GDP	€	12.3bn	13.2bn	
	US$	14.6bn	14.9bn	
per capita	US$	30,609	30,650	
Growth	%	6.8	5.1	
Inflation	%	1.7	1.7	
Def bdgt [a]	€	59.1m	74.7m	71m
	US$	69.9m	83.9m	
US$1=€		0.85	0.89	

[a] Excludes military pensions

Real-terms defence budget trend (US$m, constant 2015)

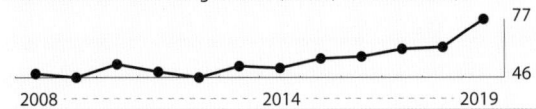

Population 453,319

Age	0–14	15–19	20–24	25–29	30–64	65 plus
Male	7.4%	2.4%	3.1%	3.8%	24.1%	9.5%
Female	6.9%	2.3%	2.8%	3.4%	22.9%	11.4%

Capabilities

The principal roles for the armed forces are maintaining external security and support for civil emergencies and to the police. There is also focus on maritime security in the Mediterranean. Malta is neutral but is a member of NATO's Partnership for Peace programme. The country also participates in bilateral and multilateral exercises. Although deployment capacity is limited, Malta has contributed to European missions. Italy has assisted Malta in meeting some security requirements, including air surveillance, while the European Internal Security Fund is funding some modernisation. Although there is some shipbuilding and ship-repair activity and a small aviation-maintenance industry, none are defence-specific and Malta relies on imports to equip its armed forces.

ACTIVE 1,750 (Armed Forces 1,750)

RESERVE 180 (Volunteer Reserve Force 60 Individual Reserve 120)

ORGANISATIONS BY SERVICE

Armed Forces of Malta 1,950
FORCES BY ROLE
SPECIAL FORCES
 1 SF unit
MANOEUVRE
 Light
 1 (1st) inf regt (3 inf coy, 1 cbt spt coy)
COMBAT SUPPORT
 1 (3rd) cbt spt regt (1 cbt engr sqn, 1 EOD sqn, 1 maint sqn)
COMBAT SERVICE SUPPORT
 1 (4th) CSS regt (1 CIS coy, 1 sy coy)
EQUIPMENT BY TYPE
ARTILLERY • MOR 81mm L16
AIR DEFENCE • GUNS 14.5mm 1 ZPU-4

Maritime Squadron 300
Organised into 5 divisions: offshore patrol; inshore patrol; rapid deployment and training; marine engineering; and logistics
EQUIPMENT BY TYPE
PATROL AND COASTAL COMBATANTS 8
 PCO 1 *Emer*
 PCC 1 *Diciotti* with 1 hel landing platform
 PB 6: 4 Austal 21m; 2 *Marine Protector*
LOGISTICS AND SUPPORT 2
 AAR 2 *Cantieri Vittoria*

Air Wing
1 base party. 1 flt ops div; 1 maint div; 1 integrated log div; 1 rescue section
EQUIPMENT BY TYPE
AIRCRAFT
 TPT • Light 5: 3 Beech 200 *King Air* (maritime patrol); 2 BN-2B *Islander*
 TRG 3 *Bulldog* T MK1
HELICOPTERS
 MRH 6: 3 AW139 (SAR); 3 SA316B *Alouette* III

DEPLOYMENT

LEBANON: UN • UNIFIL 11

Montenegro MNE

Euro €		2018	2019	2020
GDP	€	4.62bn	4.81bn	
	US$	5.46bn	5.42bn	
per capita	US$	8,763	8,704	
Growth	%	4.9	3.0	
Inflation	%	2.6	1.1	
Def exp [a]	€	64m	81m	
	US$	76m	91m	
Def bdgt [b]	€	67.0m	65.9m	64.7m
	US$	79.1m	74.3m	
FMA (US)	US$	0m	0m	0m
US$1=€		0.85	0.89	

[a] NATO definition
[b] Includes military pensions

Real-terms defence budget trend (US$m, constant 2015)

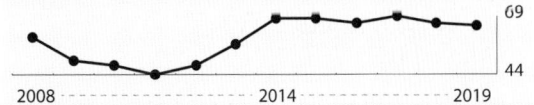

Population 612,107

Ethnic groups: Montenegrin 45%; Serb 28.7%; Bosniac 8.6%; Albanian 4.9%; Croat 1%

Age	0–14	15–19	20–24	25–29	30–64	65 plus
Male	9.4%	3.4%	3.3%	3.2%	23.3%	6.7%
Female	8.7%	3.2%	3.1%	3.0%	23.9%	8.8%

Capabilities

According to its defence strategy, Montenegro intends to develop an integrated defence system, capable of defending and preserving independence, sovereignty and national territory. However, the principal concern of the authorities is integrating Montenegro into the collective security system of NATO as well as the EU. A NATO member since 2017, Montenegro has accepted NATO's capability targets and has been aligning its defence-planning process with NATO standards. Defence agreements have in recent years been signed with Croatia, Slovenia and Poland. Reform and professionalism of the armed forces has been slow, and developments have been focused on structural issues around improving recruitment, outflow and professional development. The armed forces are not designed to have an expeditionary capability, and as such have little logistics capability to support deployments beyond national borders. Nevertheless, personnel have deployed to Afghanistan with NATO, affording them valuable experience. Podgorica intends to replace ageing Soviet-era equipment. Procurement priorities include light and medium helicopters and light armoured vehicles as well as improved communications capacities according to NATO standards. Future plans include the formation of a SOF unit and an intelligence unit in the land forces. The country's defence industry is capable of producing small arms and ammunition.

ACTIVE 2,350 (Army 1,275 Navy 350 Air Force 225 Other 500) **Paramilitary 10,100**

ORGANISATIONS BY SERVICE

Army 1,275
FORCES BY ROLE
MANOEUVRE
  Reconnaissance
    1 recce coy
  Light
    1 mot inf bn
COMBAT SUPPORT
  1 MP coy
  1 sigs coy
COMBAT SERVICE SUPPORT
  1 log bn
EQUIPMENT BY TYPE
ARMOURED FIGHTING VEHICLES
  APC • APC (W) 8 BOV-VP M-86
ANTI-TANK/ANTI-INFRASTRUCTURE
  SP 9 BOV-1
  MSL • MANPATS 9K111 *Fagot* (AT-4 *Spigot*); 9K111-1 *Konkurs* (AT-5 *Spandrel*)
ARTILLERY 135
  TOWED 122mm 12 D-30
  MRL 128mm 18 M-63/M-94 *Plamen*
  MOR 105: 82mm 73; 120mm 32

Navy 350
1 Naval Cmd HQ with 4 operational naval units (patrol boat; coastal surveillance; maritime detachment; and SAR) with additional sigs, log and trg units with a separate coastguard element. Some listed units are in the process of decommissioning
EQUIPMENT BY TYPE
PATROL AND COASTAL COMBATANTS 5
  PSO 1 *Kotor* with 1 twin 76mm gun (1 further vessel in reserve)
  PCF 2 *Rade Končar*†
  PB 2 *Mirna* (Type-140) (Police units)
LOGISTICS AND SUPPORT 1
  AXS 1 *Jadran*†

Air Force 225
Golubovci (Podgorica) air base under army command
FORCES BY ROLE
TRAINING
  1 (mixed) sqn with G-4 *Super Galeb*; Utva-75 (none operational)
TRANSPORT HELICOPTER
  1 sqn with SA341/SA342L *Gazelle*
EQUIPMENT BY TYPE
AIRCRAFT • TRG (4 G-4 *Super Galeb* non-operational; 4 Utva-75 non-operational)
HELICOPTERS
  MRH 13 SA341/SA342L (HN-45M) *Gazelle*
  TPT • **Medium** 1 Bell 412EP *Twin Huey*

Paramilitary ε10,100

Montenegrin Ministry of Interior Personnel ε6,000

Special Police Units ε4,100

DEPLOYMENT
AFGHANISTAN: NATO • *Operation Resolute Support* 27
LATVIA: NATO • Enhanced Forward Presence 10
MALI: EU • EUTM Mali 1
SERBIA: NATO • KFOR 2
WESTERN SAHARA: UN • MINURSO 1

Multinational Organisations

Capabilities
The following represent shared capabilities held by contributors collectively rather than as part of national inventories

ORGANISATIONS BY SERVICE

NATO AEW&C Force
Based at Geilenkirchen (GER). Original participating countries (BEL, CAN, DNK, GER, GRC, ITA, NLD, NOR, PRT, TUR, US) have been subsequently joined by 5 more (CZE, ESP, HUN, POL, ROM)
FORCES BY ROLE
AIRBORNE EARLY WARNING & CONTROL
  1 sqn with B-757 (trg); E-3A *Sentry* (NATO standard)
EQUIPMENT BY TYPE
AIRCRAFT
  AEW&C 16 E-3A *Sentry* (NATO standard)
  TPT • PAX 1 B-757 (trg)

Strategic Airlift Capability

Heavy Airlift Wing based at Papa air base (HUN). 12 participating countries (BLG, EST, FIN, HUN, LTU, NLD, NOR, POL, ROM, SVN, SWE, USA)

EQUIPMENT BY TYPE
AIRCRAFT • TPT • **Heavy** 3 C-17A *Globemaster* III

Strategic Airlift Interim Solution

Intended to provide strategic-airlift capacity pending the delivery of A400M aircraft by leasing An-124s. 14 participating countries (BEL, CZE, FIN, FRA, GER, GRC, HUN, LUX, NOR, POL, SVK, SVN, SWE, UK)

EQUIPMENT BY TYPE
AIRCRAFT • TPT • **Heavy** 2 An-124-100 (4 more available on 6–9 days' notice)

Netherlands NLD

Euro €		2018	2019	2020
GDP	€	774bn	803bn	
	US$	915bn	902bn	
per capita	US$	53,228	52,368	
Growth	%	2.6	1.8	
Inflation	%	1.6	2.5	
Def exp [a]	€	9.46bn	11.2bn	
	US$	10.9bn	12.3bn	
Def bdgt [b]	€	9.53bn	10.8bn	11.0bn
	US$	11.3bn	12.1bn	
US$1=€		0.85	0.89	

[a] NATO definition
[b] Includes military pensions

Real-terms defence budget trend (US$bn, constant 2015)

Population	17,216,476					
Age	0–14	15–19	20–24	25–29	30–64	65 plus
Male	8.3%	3.0%	3.1%	3.3%	23.0%	8.8%
Female	7.9%	2.9%	3.0%	3.2%	23.0%	10.6%

Capabilities

The 2018 defence review tasks the armed forces with territorial defence and supporting national civil authorities with law enforcement, disaster relief and humanitarian assistance. Dutch forces have increasingly integrated with NATO allies, particularly Germany. The army contributes to a Dutch–German tank battalion and its mechanised and air mobile brigades are integral formations within German divisions. There is also cooperation and integration with the German armed forces in the air and naval domains. The Netherlands has air-policing agreements with France, Belgium and Luxembourg and is a member of the UK-led Joint Expeditionary Force. The Netherlands, Belgium and Denmark have committed to forming a composite special-operations command. Dutch forces are fully professional and well trained and the Netherlands can deploy and sustain a medium-scale force for a single operation, or a small-scale joint force for an extended period. The Netherlands makes significant contributions to NATO and EU military operations globally. The country has a modern European- and US-sourced equipment inventory. An agreement is in place with Belgium on the joint acquisition of new frigates and minehunters, while the air force is acquiring F-35 combat aircraft and MQ-9 *Reaper* UAVs. The Netherlands is part of the programme for a multinational NATO unit of A330 transport/tanker aircraft. The country has an advanced domestic defence industry focusing on armoured vehicles, naval ships and air-defence systems, but also hosts a range of international aerospace-company subsidiaries. Damen Schelde Naval Shipbuilding exports frigates, corvettes and fast-attack craft, while DutchAero manufactures engine components for the F-35. The country also collaborates with Germany on the *Boxer* and *Fennek* armoured vehicles.

ACTIVE 35,400 (Army 18,850 Navy 8,500 Air 8,050) Military Constabulary 5,900
RESERVE 4,500 (Army 4,000 Navy 80 Air 420) Military Constabulary 160 Reserve liability to age 35 for soldiers/sailors, 40 for NCOs, 45 for officers

ORGANISATIONS BY SERVICE

Army 18,850
FORCES BY ROLE
COMMAND
 elm 1 (1 GNC) corps HQ
SPECIAL FORCES
 4 SF coy
MANOEUVRE
 Reconnaissance
 1 ISR bn (2 armd recce sqn, 1 EW coy, 2 int sqn, 1 UAV bty)
 Mechanised
 1 (43rd) mech bde (1 armd recce sqn, 2 armd inf bn, 1 engr bn, 1 maint coy, 1 med coy)
 1 (13th) mech bde (1 recce sqn, 2 mech inf bn, 1 engr bn, 1 maint coy, 1 med coy)
 Air Manoeuvre
 1 (11th) air mob bde (3 air mob inf bn, 1 engr coy, 1 med coy, 1 supply coy, 1 maint coy)
COMBAT SUPPORT
 1 SP arty bn (3 SP arty bty)
 1 AD comd (1 AD sqn; 1 AD bty)
 1 CIMIC bn
 1 engr bn
 2 EOD coy 1 (CIS) sigs bn 1 CBRN coy
COMBAT SERVICE SUPPORT
 1 med bn
 5 fd hospital
 3 maint coy
 2 tpt bn

Reserves 2,700 reservists

National Command
Cadre bde and corps tps completed by call-up of reservists (incl Territorial Comd)
FORCES BY ROLE
MANOEUVRE
 Light
 3 inf bn (could be mobilised for territorial def)

EQUIPMENT BY TYPE
ARMOURED FIGHTING VEHICLES
  RECCE 197 *Fennek*
  IFV 117 CV9035NL (32 more in store)
  APC • APC (W) 200 *Boxer* (8 driver trg; 52 amb; 36 CP; 92 engr; 12 log)
  AUV 248: 98 *Bushmaster* IMV; 150 *Fennek*
ENGINEERING & MAINTENANCE VEHICLES
  AEV 10: *Dachs*; 10 *Kodiak*
  ARV 25+: BPz-2; 25 BPz-3 *Büffel*
  VLB 17: 13 *Leopard* 1 with *Legaun*; 4 MLC70 with *Leguan*
  MW *Bozena*
NBC VEHICLES 6 TPz-1 *Fuchs* NBC
ANTI-TANK/ANTI-INFRASTRUCTURE • MSL
  MANPATS *Spike*-MR
ARTILLERY 119:
  SP 155mm 18 PzH 2000 (38 more in store)
  MOR 101: **81mm** 83 L16/M1; **120mm** 18 Brandt
AIR DEFENCE • SAM
  Long-range 18 MIM-104D/F *Patriot* PAC-2 GEM/PAC-3 (TMD capable)
  Short-range 6 NASAMS II
  Point-defence 18+: FIM-92 *Stinger*; 18 *Fennek* with FIM-92 *Stinger*

Navy 8,500 (incl Marines)
EQUIPMENT BY TYPE
SUBMARINES • TACTICAL • SSK 4 *Walrus* with 4 single 533mm TT with Mk 48 ADCAP mod 7 HWT
PRINCIPAL SURFACE COMBATANTS 6
  DESTROYERS • DDGHM 4:
    3 *De Zeven Provinciën* with 2 quad lnchr with RGM-84C *Harpoon* Block 1B AShM, 5 8-cell Mk 41 VLS with SM-2 Block IIIA/RIM-162B ESSM SAM, 2 twin SVTT Mk 32 324mm ASTT with Mk 46 LWT, 1 *Goalkeeper* CIWS, 1 127mm gun (capacity 1 NH90 hel)
    1 *De Zeven Provinciën* with 2 quad lnchr with RGM-84C *Harpoon* Block 1B AShM, 5 8-cell Mk 41 VLS with SM-2 Block IIIA/RIM-162B ESSM SAM, 2 twin SVTT Mk 32 324mm ASTT with Mk 46 LWT, 2 *Goalkeeper* CIWS, 1 127mm gun (capacity 1 NH90 hel)
  FRIGATES • FFGHM
    2 *Karel Doorman* with 2 quad lnchr with RGM-84C *Harpoon* Block 1B AShM, 1 16-cell Mk 48 mod 1 VLS with RIM-7P *Sea Sparrow* SAM, 2 twin SVTT Mk 32 324mm ASTT with Mk 46 LWT, 1 *Goalkeeper* CIWS, 1 76mm gun (capacity 1 NH90 hel)
PATROL AND COASTAL COMBATANTS
  PSOH 4 *Holland* with 1 76mm gun (capacity 1 NH90 hel)
MINE WARFARE • MINE COUNTERMEASURES
  MHO 6 *Alkmaar* (*Tripartite*)
AMPHIBIOUS
  PRINCIPAL AMPHIBIOUS SHIPS • LPD 2:
    1 *Rotterdam* with 2 *Goalkeeper* CIWS (capacity 6 NH90/AS532 *Cougar* hel; either 6 LCVP or 2 LCM and 3 LCVP; either 170 APC or 33 MBT; 538 troops)
    1 *Johan de Witt* with 2 *Goalkeeper* CIWS (capacity 6 NH90 hel or 4 AS532 *Cougar* hel; either 6 LCVP or 2 LCM and 3 LCVP; either 170 APC or 33 MBT; 700 troops)
  LANDING CRAFT 17
    LCU 5 LCU Mk II
    LCVP 12 Mk5
LOGISTICS AND SUPPORT 8
  AFSH 1 *Karel Doorman* with 2 *Goalkeeper* CIWS (capacity 6 NH90/AS532 *Cougar* or 2 CH-47F *Chinook* hel; 2 LCVP)
  AGS 2 *Snellius*
  AK 1 *Pelikaan*
  AOT 1 *Patria*
  AS 1 *Mercuur*
  AXL 1 *Van Kingsbergen*
  AXS 1 *Urania*

Marines 2,650
FORCES BY ROLE
SPECIAL FORCES
  1 SF gp (1 SF sqn, 1 CT sqn)
MANOEUVRE
  Amphibious
  2 mne bn
  1 amph aslt gp
COMBAT SERVICE SUPPORT
  1 spt gp (coy)
EQUIPMENT BY TYPE
ARMOURED FIGHTING VEHICLES
  APC • APC (T) 152: 87 Bv-206D; 65 BvS-10 *Viking*
ENGINEERING & MAINTENANCE VEHICLES
  ARV 4 BvS-10; 4 BPz-2
  MED 4 BvS-10
ANTI-TANK/ANTI-INFRASTRUCTURE
  MSL • MANPATS *Spike*-MR
ARTILLERY • MOR 81mm 12 L16/M1
AIR DEFENCE • SAM • Point-defence FIM-92 *Stinger*

Air Force 8,050
FORCES BY ROLE
FIGHTER/GROUND ATTACK
  3 sqn with F-16AM/BM *Fighting Falcon*
ANTI-SUBMARINE WARFARE/SEARCH & RESCUE
  1 sqn with NH90 NFH
TANKER/TRANSPORT
  1 sqn with C-130H/H-30 *Hercules*
  1 sqn with KDC-10; Gulfstream IV
TRAINING
  1 OEU sqn with F-35A *Lightning* II
  1 sqn with PC-7 *Turbo Trainer*
  1 hel sqn with AH-64D *Apache*; CH-47D *Chinook* (based at Fort Hood, TX)
ATTACK HELICOPTER
  1 sqn with AH-64D *Apache*
TRANSPORT HELICOPTER
  1 sqn with AS532U2 *Cougar* II
  1 sqn with CH-47D/F *Chinook*
EQUIPMENT BY TYPE
AIRCRAFT 70 combat capable
  FTR 61 F-16AM/BM *Fighting Falcon*
  FGA 9 F-35A *Lightning* II (in test)

TKR 2 KDC-10
TPT 5: **Medium** 4: 2 C-130H *Hercules*; 2 C-130H-30 *Hercules*; **PAX** 1 Gulfstream IV
TRG 13 PC-7 *Turbo Trainer*
HELICOPTERS
ATK 28 AH-64D *Apache*
ASW 12 NH90 NFH
TPT 33: **Heavy** 17: 11 CH-47D *Chinook*; 6 CH-47F *Chinook*; **Medium** 16: 8 AS532U2 *Cougar* II; 8 NH90 TTH
AIR-LAUNCHED MISSILES
AAM • IR AIM-9L/M *Sidewinder*; IIR AIM-9X *Sidewinder* II; ARH AIM-120B AMRAAM
ASM AGM-114K *Hellfire*; AGM-65D/G *Maverick*
BOMBS
Laser-guided GBU-10/GBU-12 *Paveway* II; GBU-24 *Paveway* III (all supported by LANTIRN)
INS/GPS guided GBU-39 Small Diameter Bomb

Paramilitary

Royal Military Constabulary 5,900
Subordinate to the Ministry of Defence, but performs most of its work under the authority of other ministries
FORCES BY ROLE
MANOEUVRE
  Other
    5 paramilitary district (total: 28 paramilitary unit)
EQUIPMENT BY TYPE
ARMOURED FIGHTING VEHICLES
APC • **APC (W)** 24 YPR-KMar

DEPLOYMENT

AFGHANISTAN: NATO • *Operation Resolute Support* 160
BALTIC SEA: NATO • SNMCMG 1: 1 MHO
IRAQ: *Operation Inherent Resolve* 60; 2 trg unit; **NATO** • NATO Mission Iraq 2
LEBANON: UN • UNIFIL 1
LITHUANIA: NATO • Enhanced Forward Presence 270; 1 mech inf coy
MALI: UN • MINUSMA 4; **EU** • EUTM Mali 1
MIDDLE EAST: UN • UNTSO 12
NORTH SEA: NATO • SNMG 1: 1 FFGHM
SYRIA/ISRAEL: UN • UNDOF 2
UNITED STATES: 1 hel trg sqn with AH-64D *Apache*; CH-47D *Chinook* based at Fort Hood (TX)

FOREIGN FORCES
United States US European Command: 400

Norway NOR

Norwegian Kroner kr		2018	2019	2020
GDP	kr	3.53tr	3.66tr	
	US$	434bn	418bn	
per capita	US$	81,550	77,975	
Growth	%	1.3	1.9	
Inflation	%	2.8	2.3	
Def exp [a]	kr	61.3bn	66.1bn	
	US$	7.54bn	7.55bn	
Def bdgt [b]	kr	54.9bn	58.9bn	61.0bn
	US$	6.76bn	6.72bn	
US$1=kr		8.13	8.76	

[a] NATO definition
[b] Includes military pensions

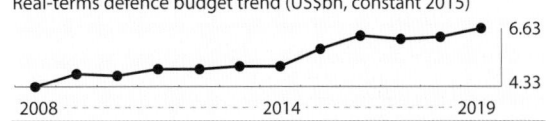
Real-terms defence budget trend (US$bn, constant 2015)

Population	5,421,399					
Age	0–14	15–19	20–24	25–29	30–64	65 plus
Male	9.2%	3.0%	3.3%	3.6%	23.5%	8.0%
Female	8.8%	2.8%	3.1%	3.4%	22.2%	9.2%

Capabilities

Norway sustains small but well-equipped and highly trained armed forces. Territorial defence is at the heart of security policy. The Long Term Defence Plan, published in 2016, said that the armed forces needed further adjustments to address evolving security challenges at home and abroad. In October 2017, the defence ministry announced measures to strengthen capability in the High North. A US Marine Corps contingent has deployed to Vaernes, on a rotational basis, since January 2017. In August 2018, this was extended for up to five years and a second location at Setermonden added. The US had planned to invest, through its European Deterrence Initiative (EDI), in infrastructure upgrades at Rygge Air Station to enable reinforcements in case of conflict. Some of these investments have been put in doubt by funding cuts to the EDI announced by the US in September 2019. Norway is not an EU member, but it signed a cooperation agreement with the European Defence Agency in 2006. At any one time, around one-third of troops are conscripts. Senior officers reportedly expressed concerns in 2019 that Norway's force structure was too small for defence requirements. A report by the Norwegian chief of defence published in October 2019 argued that in order to address the challenging security situation, the number of combat units in all services should increase. Norway maintains a small presence in a range of international crisis-management missions. Equipment recapitalisation is ongoing. Norway's first F-35A arrived in late 2017 and the government announced that it would procure four submarines as part of a strategic partnership with Germany. Large procurements will stretch budgets, with the F-35 alone reportedly taking up 27% of all procurement spending between 2019 and 2026. In June 2018, it was announced that a planned upgrade to Norway's main-battle-tank fleet would be abandoned until the mid-2020s; current budget forecasts foresee funding being made available for this purpose in 2025/26. Norway has an advanced and diverse defence-industrial base with a high percentage of SMEs and a mix of private and state-owned companies.

ACTIVE 23,250 (Army 8,100 Navy 3,900 Air 3,600 Central Support 7,000 Home Guard 650)

Conscript liability 19 months maximum. Conscripts first serve 12 months from 19–28, and then up to 4–5 refresher training periods until age 35, 44, 55 or 60 depending on rank and function. Conscription was extended to women in 2015

RESERVE 40,000 (Home Guard 40,000)

Readiness varies from a few hours to several days

ORGANISATIONS BY SERVICE

Army 3,700; 4,400 conscript (total 8,100)

The armoured infantry brigade – Brigade North – trains new personnel of all categories and provides units for international operations. At any time around one-third of the brigade will be trained and ready to conduct operations. The brigade includes one high-readiness armoured battalion (Telemark Battalion) with combat support and combat service support units on high readiness

FORCES BY ROLE
MANOEUVRE
  Reconnaissance
  1 ISR bn
  1 (GSV) bn (1 (border) recce coy, 1 ranger coy, 1 spt coy, 1 trg coy)
  Armoured
  1 armd inf bde (2 armd bn, 1 lt inf bn, 1 arty bn, 1 engr bn, 1 MP coy, 1 CIS bn, 1 spt bn, 1 med bn)
  Light
  1 lt inf bn (His Majesty The King's Guards)
EQUIPMENT BY TYPE
ARMOURED FIGHTING VEHICLES
  MBT 36 *Leopard* 2A4
  RECCE 46: 21 CV9030; 25 HMT *Extenda*
  IFV 91: 76 CV9030N; 15 CV9030N (CP)
  APC 390
    APC (T) 315 M113 (incl variants)
    APC (W) 75 XA-186 *Sisu*/XA-200 *Sisu*
  AUV 140: 20 *Dingo* 2; 120 IVECO LMV (50 more in store)
ENGINEERING & MAINTENANCE VEHICLES
  AEV 24: 16 CV90 STING; 8 M113 AEV
  ARV 9: 6 BPz-2; 3 *Wisent*-2
  VLB 35: 26 *Leguan*; 9 *Leopard* 1
  MW 9 910 MCV-2
NBC VEHICLES 6 TPz-1 *Fuchs* NBC
ANTI-TANK/ANTI-INFRASTRUCTURE
  MANPATS FGM-148 *Javelin*
  RCL 84mm *Carl Gustav*
ARTILLERY 169
  SP 155mm 26: 2 K9 *Thunder*; 24 M109A3GN
  MOR 143: 81mm 115 L16; SP 81mm 28: 16 CV9030; 12 M125A2

Navy 2,100; 1,800 conscripts (total 3,900)

Joint Command – Norwegian National Joint Headquarters. The Royal Norwegian Navy is organised into four elements under the command of the chief of staff of the Navy: the naval units (*Marinen*), the naval academy (KNM *Harald Haarfagre*), the navy medical branch and the Coast Guard (*Kystvakten*)

FORCES BY ROLE
MANOEUVRE
  Reconnaissance
  1 ISR coy (Coastal Rangers)
COMBAT SUPPORT
  1 EOD pl
EQUIPMENT BY TYPE
SUBMARINES • TACTICAL • SSK 6 *Ula* with 8 single 533mm TT with *SeaHake* (DM2A3) HWT
PRINCIPAL SURFACE COMBATANTS 4
  DESTROYERS • DDGHM 4 *Fridtjof Nansen* with *Aegis* C2 (mod), 2 quad lnchr with NSM AShM, 1 8-cell Mk 41 VLS with RIM-162A ESSM SAM, 2 twin 324mm ASTT with *Sting Ray* mod 1 LWT, 1 76mm gun (capacity 1 NH90 hel)
PATROL AND COASTAL COMBATANTS 12:
  PCFG 6 *Skjold* with 8 single lnchr with NSM AShM, 1 76mm gun
  PBF 6 CB90N (capacity 20 troops)
MINE WARFARE • MINE COUNTERMEASURES 4:
  MSC 2 *Alta* with 1 twin *Simbad* lnchr with *Mistral* SAM
  MHC 2 *Oksoy* with 1 twin *Simbad* lnchr with *Mistral* SAM
LOGISTICS AND SUPPORT 6
  AGI 1 *Marjata* IV
  AGS 2: 1 *HU Sverdrup* II; 1 *Eger* (*Marjata* III) with 1 hel landing platform
  AORH 1 *Maud* (BMT *Aegir*) (capacity 2 med hel)
  AXL 2 *Reine*

Coast Guard

EQUIPMENT BY TYPE
PATROL AND COASTAL COMBATANTS 13
  PSOH 3 *Nordkapp* with 1 57mm gun (capacity 1 med tpt hel)
  PSO 5: 3 *Barentshav*; 1 *Harstad*; 1 *Svalbard* with 1 57mm gun, 1 hel landing platform
  PCC 5 *Nornen*

Air Force 2,600 ; 1,000 conscript (total 3,600)

Joint Command – Norwegian National HQ

FORCES BY ROLE
FIGHTER/GROUND ATTACK
  1 sqn with F-16AM/BM *Fighting Falcon*
  1 sqn with F-35A *Lightning* II (forming)
MARITIME PATROL
  1 sqn with P-3C *Orion*; P-3N *Orion* (pilot trg)
ELECTRONIC WARFARE
  1 sqn with *Falcon* 20C (EW, Flight Inspection Service)
SEARCH & RESCUE
  1 sqn with *Sea King* Mk43B; AW101
TRANSPORT
  1 sqn with C-130J-30 *Hercules*
TRAINING
  1 sqn with MFI-15 *Safari*
TRANSPORT HELICOPTER
  2 sqn with Bell 412SP *Twin Huey*
  1 sqn with NH90 (forming)

AIR DEFENCE
1 bn with NASAMS II
EQUIPMENT BY TYPE
AIRCRAFT 62 combat capable
FTR 35: 30 F-16AM *Fighting Falcon*; 5 F-16BM *Fighting Falcon*
FGA 22 F-35A *Lightning* II
ASW 5: 4 P-3C *Orion*; 1 P-3N *Orion* (pilot trg)
EW 2 *Falcon* 20C
TPT • Medium 4 C-130J-30 *Hercules*
TRG 16 MFI-15 *Safari*
HELICOPTERS
ASW 8 NH90 NFH
SAR 17: 5 AW101; 12 *Sea King* Mk43B
MRH 18: 6 Bell 412HP; 12 Bell 412SP
AIR DEFENCE
SAM • Short-range NASAMS II
AIR-LAUNCHED MISSILES
AAM • IR AIM-9L *Sidewinder*; IIR AIM-9X *Sidewinder* II; IRIS-T; ARH AIM-120B AMRAAM; AIM-120C AMRAAM
BOMBS
Laser-guided EGBU-12 *Paveway* II
INS/GPS guided JDAM

Special Operations Command (NORSOCOM)
FORCES BY ROLE
SPECIAL FORCES
1 (armed forces) SF comd (2 SF gp)
1 (navy) SF comd (1 SF gp)

Central Support, Administration and Command 6,150; 850 conscripts (total 7,000)
Central Support, Administration and Command includes military personnel in all joint elements and they are responsible for logistics and CIS in support of all forces in Norway and abroad

Home Guard 650 (40,000 reserves)
The Home Guard is a separate organisation, but closely cooperates with all services. The Home Guard is organised in 11 Districts with mobile Rapid Reaction Forces (3,000 troops in total) as well as reinforcements and follow-on forces (37,000 troops in total)
EQUIPMENT BY TYPE
PATROL AND COASTAL COMBATANTS • PB 11: 4 *Harek*; 2 *Gyda*; 5 *Alusafe* 1290

DEPLOYMENT
AFGHANISTAN: NATO • *Operation Resolute Support* 54
BALTIC SEA: NATO • SNMCMG 1: 1 MSC
EGYPT: MFO 3
IRAQ: *Operation Inherent Resolve* 60; 1 trg unit; NATO • NATO Mission Iraq 2
JORDAN: *Operation Inherent Resolve* 20
LITHUANIA: NATO • Enhanced Forward Presence 120; 1 armd inf coy
MALI: UN • MINUSMA 91; 1 tpt flt with 1 C-130J
MIDDLE EAST: UN • UNTSO 13
NORTH SEA: NATO • SNMG 1: 1 DDGHM
SERBIA: NATO • KFOR 2
SOUTH SUDAN: UN • UNMISS 17

FOREIGN FORCES
United States US European Command: 1,400; 1 mne bn; 1 (USMC) MEU eqpt set; 1 (APS) 155mm SP Arty bn eqpt set

Poland POL

Polish Zloty z		2018	2019	2020
GDP	z	2.12tr	2.26tr	
	US$	586bn	566bn	
per capita	US$	15,426	14,902	
Growth	%	5.1	4.0	
Inflation	%	1.6	2.4	
Def exp [a]	z	42.8bn	45.1bn	
	US$	11.9bn	11.3bn	
Def bdgt [b]	z	42.9bn	45.4bn	50.4bn
	US$	11.9bn	11.4bn	
US$1=z		3.61	3.99	

[a] NATO definition

[b] Includes military pensions

Real-terms defence budget trend (US$bn, constant 2015)

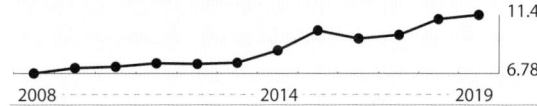

Population 38,356,121

Age	0–14	15–19	20–24	25–29	30–64	65 plus
Male	7.6%	2.4%	2.7%	3.4%	25.0%	7.2%
Female	7.2%	2.3%	2.6%	3.2%	25.4%	10.9%

Capabilities

Territorial defence and NATO membership are central pillars of Poland's defence policy. The primary focus of the 2017–32 defence concept is to prepare the armed forces to provide a deterrent against Russian aggression. Russia is characterised as a direct threat to Poland and to a stable international order. The government continues to pursue a goal of permanently stationing US troops in the country. Security and defence cooperation also takes place through the Visegrad Group. There are also defence ties through the Bucharest Nine, which brings together NATO's eastern-flank countries. Warsaw has also established a fund to bolster its neighbours' defence-modernisation ambitions. The 2017–32 defence concept defines an ambition to restore divisions as tactical combat units, rather than administrative units. Recruitment is under way for the Territorial Defence Force, which was launched in 2017. Poland has some capacity to independently deploy forces beyond national borders. Defence-acquisition reform is planned but a national armaments strategy has yet to be released. A new armaments agency, intended to consolidate responsibilities and establish stronger control over programmes, has been proposed but so far has not materialised. Poland intends to build up its own anti-access/area-denial capacity and in the 2017 Defence Concept expressed an interest in research into emerging technologies. A technical-modernisation plan, covering the period 2021 to 2035, was released in October 2019, which extended the planning horizon from ten to 15 years. Warsaw continues plans to strengthen its domestic defence-industrial base, much of which is now consolidated in the state-owned holding company PGZ, using technology transfers and international partnering. Beyond PGZ, several international defence primes have subsidiaries in Poland.

ACTIVE 123,700 (Army 80,000 Navy 7,000 Air Force 16,500 Special Forces 3,500 Territorial 3,200 Joint 13,500) Paramilitary 73,400

ORGANISATIONS BY SERVICE

Army 61,200
FORCES BY ROLE
COMMAND
  elm 1 (MNC NE) corps HQ
MANOEUVRE
  Reconnaissance
  3 recce regt
  Armoured
  1 (11th) armd cav div (2 armd bde, 1 mech bde, 1 arty regt)
  Mechanised
  1 (12th) mech div (2 mech bde, 1 (coastal) mech bde, 1 arty regt)
  1 (16th) mech div (1 armd bde, 2 mech bde, 1 arty regt, 1 AT regt)
  1 (18th) mech div (1 armd bde, 2 mech bde, 1 log regt)
  Air Manoeuvre
  1 (6th) AB bde (3 para bn)
  1 (25th) air cav bde (3 air cav bn, 2 tpt hel bn, 1 (casevac) med unit)
COMBAT SUPPORT
  2 engr regt
  1 ptn br regt
  2 chem def regt
COMBAT SUPPORT
  2 log bde
HELICOPTER
  1 (1st) hel bde (2 atk hel sqn with Mi-24D/V *Hind* D/E, 1 CSAR sqn with Mi-24V *Hind* E; PZL W-3PL *Gluszec*; 2 ISR hel sqn with Mi-2URP; 2 hel sqn with Mi-2)
AIR DEFENCE
  3 AD regt
EQUIPMENT BY TYPE
ARMOURED FIGHTING VEHICLES
  MBT 606: 142 *Leopard* 2A4 (being upgraded to 2PL); 105 *Leopard* 2A5; 232 PT-91 *Twardy*; 127 T-72A/T-72M1 (257 more in store)
  RECCE 407: 282 BRDM-2; 38 BWR; 87 BRDM-2 R5
  IFV 1,611: 1,252 BMP-1; 359 *Rosomak* IFV
  APC 368
    APC (T) 6 WDSz (OP)
    APC (W) 332: 300 *Rosomak* APC (incl variants); 32 AWD RAK (CP)
    PPV 30 *Maxxpro*

AUV 85: 40 *Cougar* (on loan from US); 45 M-ATV
ENGINEERING & MAINTENANCE VEHICLES
  AEV 94+: IWT; 65 MT-LB AEV; 21 *Rosomak* WRT; 8 MID *Bizon*
  ARV 122: 28 BPz-2; 68 MT-LB ARV; 26 WZT-3M
  VLB 121: 4 *Biber*; 107 BLG67M2; 10 MS-20 *Daglezja*
  MW 22: 14 *Bozena* 4; 4 ISM *Kroton*; 4 *Kalina* SUM
ANTI-TANK/ANTI-INFRASTRUCTURE
  MSL • MANPATS 9K11 *Malyutka* (AT-3 *Sagger*); 9K111 *Fagot* (AT-4 *Spigot*); *Spike*-LR
ARTILLERY 836
  SP 419: **122mm** 260 2S1 *Gvozdika*; **152mm** 111 M-77 *Dana*; **155mm** 48 *Krab*
  MRL 122mm 197: 93 BM-21; 29 RM-70; 75 WR-40 *Langusta*
  MOR 220: **120mm** 156: 14 2B11; 142 M120; **SP 120mm** 64 SMK120 RAK
HELICOPTERS
  ATK 28 Mi-24D/V *Hind* D/E
  MRH 64: 7 Mi-8MT *Hip*; 3 Mi-17 *Hip* H; 1 Mi-17AE *Hip* (aeromedical); 5 Mi-17-1V *Hip*; 16 PZL Mi-2URP *Hoplite*; 24 PZL W-3W/WA *Sokol*; 8 PZL W-3PL *Gluszec* (CSAR)
  TPT 34: **Medium** 9: 7 Mi-8T *Hip*; 2 PZL W-3AE *Sokol* (aeromedical); **Light** 25 PZL Mi-2 *Hoplite*
AIR DEFENCE
  SAM
    Short-range 20 2K12 *Kub* (SA-6 *Gainful*)
    Point-defence 185+: 64 9K33 *Osa*-AK (SA-8 *Gecko*); 20 ZSU-23-4MP *Biala*; GROM; 72 ZUR-23-2KG *Jodek*-G; *Piorun*; 29 *Poprad*
  GUNS 260
    SP 23mm 8 ZSU-23-4
    TOWED 23mm 252 ZU-23-2

Navy 7,000
EQUIPMENT BY TYPE
SUBMARINES • TACTICAL 3
  SSK 3:
    2 *Sokol* (ex-NOR Type-207) with 8 single 533mm TT with Torped 613 HWT
    1 *Orzel* (ex-FSU *Kilo*) with 6 single 533mm TT each with 53-65KE HWT/TEST-71ME (currently non-operational; has been in refit since 2014; damaged by fire in 2017)
PRINCIPAL SURFACE COMBATANTS 2
  FRIGATES • FFGHM 2 *Pulaski* (ex-US *Oliver Hazard Perry*) with 1 Mk 13 GMLS with RGM-84G *Harpoon* Block 1G AShM/SM-1MR Block VI SAM, 2 triple SVTT Mk 32 324mm ASTT with MU90 LWT, 1 Mk 15 *Phalanx* CIWS, 1 76mm gun (capacity 2 SH-2G *Super Seasprite* ASW hel) (1 vessel used as training ship)
PATROL AND COASTAL COMBATANTS 4
  CORVETTES • FSM 1 *Kaszub* with 2 quad lnchr with 9K32 *Strela*-2 (SA-N-5 *Grail*) SAM, 2 twin 533mm ASTT with SET-53 HWT, 2 RBU 6000 *Smerch* 2 A/S mor, 1 76mm gun
  PCFGM 3:
    3 *Orkan* (ex-GDR *Sassnitz*) with 1 quad lnchr with RBS15 Mk3 AShM, 1 quad lnchr (manual aiming)

with 9K32 *Strela*-2M (SA-N-5 *Grail*) SAM, 1 AK630 CIWS, 1 76mm gun
MINE WARFARE • MINE COUNTERMEASURES 22
  MCCS 1 *Kontradmiral Xawery Czernicki*
  MCO 1 *Kormoran* II
  MHO 3 *Krogulec*
  MSI 17: 1 *Goplo*; 12 *Gardno*; 4 *Mamry*
AMPHIBIOUS 8
  LANDING SHIPS • LSM 5 *Lublin* (capacity 9 tanks; 135 troops)
  LANDING CRAFT • LCU 3 *Deba* (capacity 50 troops)
LOGISTICS AND SUPPORT 20
  AGI 2 *Moma*
  AGS 8: 2 *Heweliusz*; 4 *Wildcat* 40; 2 (coastal)
  AORL 1 *Baltyk*
  AOL 1 *Moskit*
  ARS 4: 2 *Piast*; 2 *Zbyszko*
  ATF 2
  AX 1 *Wodnik* with 1 twin AK230 CIWS
  AXS 1 *Iskra*
COASTAL DEFENCE • AShM 12 NSM

Naval Aviation 1,300
FORCES BY ROLE
ANTI SUBMARINE WARFARE/SEARCH & RESCUE
  1 sqn with Mi-14PL *Haze* A; Mi-14PL/R *Haze* C
  1 sqn with PZL W-3RM *Anakonda*; SH-2G *Super Seasprite*
MARITIME PATROL
  1 sqn with An-28RM; An-28E
TRANSPORT
  1 sqn with An-28TD; M-28B TD *Bryza*
  1 sqn with An-28TD; M-28B; Mi-17 *Hip* H; PZL Mi-2 *Hoplite*; PZL W-3T; 1 PZL W-3A
EQUIPMENT BY TYPE
AIRCRAFT
  MP 10: 8 An-28RM *Bryza*; 2 An-28E *Bryza*
  TPT • Light 4: 2 An-28TD *Bryza*; 2 M-28B TD *Bryza*
  HELICOPTERS ASW 11: 7 Mi-14PL *Haze*; 4 SH-2G *Super Seasprite*
  MRH 1 Mi-17 *Hip* H
  SAR 8: 2 Mi-14PL/R *Haze* C; 4 PZL W-3RM *Anakonda*; 2 PZL W-3WA RM *Anakonda*
  TPT • Light 7: 4 PZL Mi-2 *Hoplite*; 1 PZL W-3A; 2 PZL-W-3T

Air Force 16,500
FORCES BY ROLE
FIGHTER
  2 sqn with MiG-29A/UB *Fulcrum*
FIGHTER/GROUND ATTACK
  3 sqn with F-16C/D Block 52+ *Fighting Falcon*
FIGHTER/GROUND ATTACK/ISR
  2 sqn with Su-22M-4 *Fitter*
SEARCH AND RESCUE
  1 sqn with Mi-2; PZL W-3 *Sokol*
TRANSPORT
  1 sqn with C-130E; PZL M-28 *Bryza*
  1 sqn with C295M; PZL M-28 *Bryza*

TRAINING
  1 sqn with PZL-130 *Orlik*
  1 sqn with TS-11 *Iskra*
  1 hel sqn with SW-4 *Puszczyk*
TRANSPORT HELICOPTER
  1 (Spec Ops) sqn with Mi-17 *Hip* H
  1 (VIP) sqn with Mi-8; W-3WA *Sokol*
AIR DEFENCE
  1 bde with S-125 *Neva* SC (SA-3 *Goa*); S-200C *Vega* (SA-5 *Gammon*)
EQUIPMENT BY TYPE
AIRCRAFT 95 combat capable
  FTR 29: 22 MiG-29A *Fulcrum*; 7 MiG-29UB *Fulcrum*
  FGA 66: 36 F-16C Block 52+ *Fighting Falcon*; 12 F-16D Block 52+ *Fighting Falcon*; 12 Su-22M4 *Fitter*; 6 Su-22UM3K *Fitter*
  TPT 46: **Medium** 5 C-130E *Hercules*; **Light** 39: 16 C295M; 23 M-28 *Bryza* TD; **PAX** 2: 1 Gulfstream G550; 1 737-800
  TRG 68: 8 M-346; 28 PZL-130 *Orlik*; 32 TS-11 *Iskra*
HELICOPTERS
  MRH 8 Mi-17 *Hip* H
  TPT 69: **Medium** 29: 9 Mi-8 *Hip*; 10 PZL W-3 *Sokol*; 10 PZL W-3WA *Sokol* (VIP); **Light** 40: 16 PZL Mi-2 *Hoplite*; 24 SW-4 *Puszczyk* (trg)
AIR DEFENCE • SAM
  Long-range 1 S-200C *Vega* (SA-5 *Gammon*)
  Short-range 17 S-125 *Neva* SC (SA-3 *Goa*)
AIR-LAUNCHED MISSILES
  AAM • IR R-60 (AA-8 *Aphid*); R-73 (AA-11A *Archer*); AIM-9 *Sidewinder*; R-27T (AA-10B *Alamo*); **IIR** AIM-9X *Sidwinder* II; **ARH** AIM-120C AMRAAM
  ASM AGM-65J/G *Maverick*; Kh-25 (AS-10 *Karen*); Kh-29 (AS-14 *Kedge*)
  LACM Conventional AGM-158 JASSM

Special Forces 3,500
FORCES BY ROLE
SPECIAL FORCES
  3 SF units (GROM, FORMOZA & cdo)
COMBAT SUPPORT/
  1 cbt spt unit (AGAT)
COMBAT SERVICE SUPPORT
  1 spt unit (NIL)

Territorial Defence Forces 3,200 (plus 18,500 reservists)
FORCES BY ROLE
MANOEUVRE
  Other
  13 sy bde
  4 sy bde (forming)

Paramilitary 73,400

Border Guards 14,300
Ministry of Interior

Maritime Border Guard 3,700
EQUIPMENT BY TYPE
PATROL AND COASTAL COMBATANTS 18
  PCC 2 *Kaper*

PBF 6: 2 *Straznik*; 4 IC16M
PB 10: 2 *Wisloka*; 2 *Baltic* 24; 1 Project MI-6
AMPHIBIOUS • LANDING CRAFT • UCAC 2 *Griffon* 2000TDX

Prevention Units (Police) 59,100
Anti-terrorist Operations Bureau n.k.
Ministry of Interior

DEPLOYMENT

AFGHANISTAN: NATO • *Operation Resolute Support* 354
BOSNIA-HERZEGOVINA: EU • EUFOR • *Operation Althea* 25
CENTRAL AFRICAN REPUBLIC: EU • EUTM RCA 1
DEMOCRATIC REPUBLIC OF THE CONGO: UN • MONUSCO 2
IRAQ: *Operation Inherent Resolve* 150; **NATO** • NATO Mission Iraq 65
LATVIA: NATO • Enhanced Forward Presence 175; 1 tk coy
ROMANIA: NATO • MNB-SE 230; 1 mech inf coy; *Rosomak*
SERBIA: NATO • KFOR 246; 1 inf coy; **UN** • UNMIK 1
SOUTH SUDAN: UN • UNMISS 1
UKRAINE: JMTG-U 40

FOREIGN FORCES

All NATO Enhanced Forward Presence unless stated
Croatia 80; 1 MRL bty with M91 *Vulkan*
Germany MNC-NE corps HQ: 95
Romania 120; 1 ADA bty
United Kingdom 140; 1 recce sqn
United States: 857; 1 ARNG armd bn with M1A1 AIM *Abrams*; M2A2 ODS *Bradley*; M109A6 • *Operation Atlantic Resolve* 2,000; 1 div HQ (fwd); 1 armd bde HQ; 1 armd cav sqn(-); 1 SP arty bn; M1A2 SEPv2 *Abrams*; M3A3 *Bradley*; M109A7

Portugal PRT

Euro €		2018	2019	2020
GDP	€	204bn	210bn	
	US$	241bn	236bn	
per capita	US$	23,437	23,031	
Growth	%	2.4	1.9	
Inflation	%	1.2	0.9	
Def exp [a]	€	2.87bn	3.16bn	
	US$	3.40bn	3.55bn	
Def bdgt	€	2.18bn	2.39bn	
	US$	2.57bn	2.68bn	
US$1=€		0.85	0.89	

[a] NATO definition

Real-terms defence budget trend (US$bn, constant 2015)

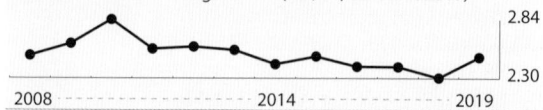

Population	10,328,384					
Age	0–14	15–19	20–24	25–29	30–64	65 plus
Male	7.1%	2.8%	2.8%	2.8%	23.7%	8.2%
Female	6.7%	2.7%	2.6%	2.7%	25.5%	12.4%

Capabilities

Principal tasks for Portugal's all-volunteer armed forces are homeland defence, maritime security, multinational operations and responding to humanitarian disasters. The 2013 strategic review set out key defence tasks and envisaged a reduction in army strength and organisational change dividing the services into immediate reaction forces, permanent defence forces and modular forces. Investment plans support Portugal's ambition to field rapid-reaction and maritime-surveillance capabilities for territorial defence and multinational operations. A new military programme law for 2019–30 was approved by parliament, funding the acquisition of five KC-390 aircraft, six offshore-patrol vessels, a replenishment tanker and a multi-purpose logistics ship, as well as cyber-defence and soldier-combat systems. Portugal is an active member of NATO, and NATO's new cyber-security academy has been built there. It also contributes to EU military structures. There is a close relationship with former dependencies and with the US, which operates out of Lajes air base. All three services have programmes for the modernisation and sustainment of existing equipment platforms. There is an active defence industry, though principally in relation to shipbuilding, broader maintenance tasks and the manufacture of components, and small arms and light weapons.

ACTIVE 27,250 (Army 13,700 Navy 7,650 Air 5,900)
Paramilitary 24,700

RESERVE 211,700 (Army 210,000 Navy 1,000, Air Force 700)
Reserve obligation to age 35

ORGANISATIONS BY SERVICE

Army 13,700
5 territorial comd (2 mil region, 1 mil district, 2 mil zone)

FORCES BY ROLE
SPECIAL FORCES
1 SF bn
MANOEUVRE
Reconnaissance
1 ISR bn
Mechanised
1 mech bde (1 cav tp, 1 tk regt, 1 mech inf bn, 1 arty bn, 1 AD bty, 1 engr coy, 1 sigs coy, 1 spt bn)
1 (intervention) bde (1 cav tp, 1 recce regt, 2 mech inf bn, 1 arty bn, 1 AD bty, 1 engr coy, 1 sigs coy, 1 spt bn)
Air Manoeuvre
1 (rapid reaction) bde (1 cav tp, 1 cdo bn, 2 para bn, 1 arty bn, 1 AD bty, 1 engr coy, 1 sigs coy, 1 spt bn)
Other
1 (Azores) inf gp (2 inf bn, 1 AD bty)
1 (Madeira) inf gp (1 inf bn, 1 AD bty)
COMBAT SUPPORT
1 STA bty
1 engr bn (1 construction coy; 1 EOD unit; 1 ptn br coy; 1 CBRN coy)
1 EW coy
1 MP bn
1 psyops unit
1 CIMIC coy (joint)
1 sigs bn
COMBAT SERVICE SUPPORT
1 maint coy
1 log coy
1 tpt coy
1 med unit
AIR DEFENCE
1 AD bn

Reserves 210,000
FORCES BY ROLE
MANOEUVRE
Light
3 (territorial) def bde (on mobilisation)
EQUIPMENT BY TYPE
ARMOURED FIGHTING VEHICLES
MBT 37 *Leopard* 2A6
RECCE 25: 9 V-150 *Chaimite*; 16 VBL
IFV 30 *Pandur* II MK 30mm
APC 397
  APC (T) 239: 176 M113A1; 14 M113A2; 49 M577A2 (CP)
  APC (W) 158: 12 V-200 *Chaimite*; 146 *Pandur* II (incl variants)
ENGINEERING & MAINTENANCE VEHICLES
AEV M728
ARV 13: 6 M88A1, 7 *Pandur* II ARV
VLB M48
ANTI-TANK/ANTI-INFRASTRUCTURE
MSL
  SP 26: 17 M113 with TOW; 4 M901 with TOW; 5 *Pandur* II with TOW
  MANPATS *Milan*; TOW
RCL • **84mm** *Carl Gustav*; **106mm** 45 M40A1

ARTILLERY 320
SP **155mm** 24: 6 M109A2; 18 M109A5
TOWED 62: **105mm** 39: 17 L119 Light Gun; 21 M101A1; **155mm** 24 M114A1
MOR 234: **81mm** 143; SP **81mm** 12: 2 M125A1; 10 M125A2; **107mm** 11 M30; SP **107mm** 18: 3 M106A1; 15 M106A2; **120mm** 50 Tampella
AIR DEFENCE
SAM • Point-defence 20+: 1 M48A2 *Chaparral*; 19 M48A3 *Chaparral*; FIM-92 *Stinger*
GUNS • TOWED **20mm** 20 Rh 202

Navy 7,600 (incl 960 Marines)
EQUIPMENT BY TYPE
SUBMARINES • TACTICAL • SSK 2 *Tridente* (GER Type-214) with 8 533mm TT with UGM-84L *Harpoon* Block II AShM/*Black Shark* HWT
PRINCIPAL SURFACE COMBATANTS 5
FRIGATES • FFGHM 5:
  2 *Bartolomeu Dias* (ex-NLD *Karel Doorman*) with 2 quad lnchr with RGM-84C *Harpoon* Block 1B AShM, 1 16-cell Mk 48 mod 1 VLS with RIM-7M *Sea Sparrow* SAM, 2 SVTT Mk 32 twin 324mm ASTT with Mk 46 LWT, 1 *Goalkeeper* CIWS, 1 76mm gun (capacity 1 *Lynx* Mk95 (*Super Lynx*) hel)
  3 *Vasco Da Gama* with 2 quad lnchr with RGM-84C *Harpoon* Block 1B AShM, 1 octuple Mk 29 GMLS with RIM-7M *Sea Sparrow* SAM, 2 SVTT Mk 32 triple 324mm ASTT with Mk 46 LWT, 1 Mk 15 *Phalanx* Block 1B CIWS, 1 100mm gun (capacity 2 *Lynx* Mk95 (*Super Lynx*) hel)
PATROL AND COASTAL COMBATANTS 21
CORVETTES • FS 2:
  1 *Baptista de Andrade* with 1 100mm gun, 1 hel landing platform
  1 *Joao Coutinho* with 1 twin 76mm gun, 1 hel landing platform
PSO 4 *Viana do Castelo* with 1 hel landing platform
PCC 5: 1 *Cacine*; 4 *Tejo* (ex-DNK *Flyvisken*)
PBR 10: 5 *Argos*; 4 *Centauro*; 1 *Rio Minho*
LOGISTICS AND SUPPORT 11
AGS 4: 2 *D Carlos* I (ex-US *Stalwart*); 2 *Andromeda*
AORL 1 *Bérrio* (ex-UK *Rover*) with 1 hel landing platform (for medium hel)
AXS 6: 1 *Sagres*; 1 *Creoula*; 1 *Polar*; 2 *Belatrix*; 1 *Zarco*

Marines 950
FORCES BY ROLE
SPECIAL FORCES
1 SF det
MANOEUVRE
Light
1 lt inf bn
COMBAT SUPPORT
1 mor coy
1 MP coy
EQUIPMENT BY TYPE
ANTI-TANK/ANTI-INFRASTRUCTURE
MSL • MANPATS *Milan*; TOW
RCL • **84mm** *Carl Gustav*;
ARTILLERY • MOR 30+: **81mm** some; **120mm** 30

Naval Aviation
EQUIPMENT BY TYPE
HELICOPTERS • ASW 5 *Lynx* Mk95 (*Super Lynx*)

Air Force 5,900
FORCES BY ROLE
FIGHTER/GROUND ATTACK
  2 sqn with F-16AM/BM *Fighting Falcon*
MARITIME PATROL
  1 sqn with P-3C *Orion*
ISR/TRANSPORT
  1 sqn with C295M
COMBAT SEARCH & RESCUE
  1 sqn with with AW101 *Merlin*
TRANSPORT
  1 sqn with C-130H/C-130H-30 *Hercules*
  1 sqn with *Falcon* 50
TRAINING
  1 sqn with AW119 *Koala* (forming)
  1 sqn with TB-30 *Epsilon*
EQUIPMENT BY TYPE
AIRCRAFT 35 combat capable
  FTR 30: 26 F-16AM *Fighting Falcon*; 4 F-16BM *Fighting Falcon*
  ASW 5 P-3C *Orion*
  ISR: 7: 5 C295M (maritime surveillance), 2 C295M (photo recce)
  TPT 13: **Medium** 5: 2 C-130H *Hercules*; 3 C-130H-30 *Hercules* (tpt/SAR); **Light** 5 C295M; **PAX** 3 *Falcon* 50 (tpt/VIP)
  TRG 16 TB-30 *Epsilon*
HELICOPTERS
  MRH 6 SA316 *Alouette* III (trg, utl)
  TPT 15: **Medium** 12 AW101 *Merlin* (6 SAR, 4 CSAR, 2 fishery protection); **Light** 3 AW119 *Koala*
AIR-LAUNCHED MISSILES
  AAM • IR AIM-9L/I *Sidewinder*; ARH AIM-120C AMRAAM
  ASM AGM-65A *Maverick*
  AShM AGM-84A *Harpoon*
BOMBS
  Laser-guided/GPS GBU-49 *Enhanced Paveway* II
  INS/GPS guided GBU-31 JDAM

Paramilitary 24,700

National Republican Guard 24,700
EQUIPMENT BY TYPE
PATROL AND COASTAL COMBATANTS 32
  PBF 12
  PB 20
HELICOPTERS • MRH 7 SA315 *Lama*

DEPLOYMENT
AFGHANISTAN: NATO • Operation Resolute Support 214
CENTRAL AFRICAN REPUBLIC: EU • EUTM RCA 45; UN • MINUSCA 188; 1 AB coy
IRAQ: Operation Inherent Resolve 34
MALI: EU • EUTM Mali 11; UN • MINUSMA 2
NORTH SEA: NATO • SNMG 1: 1 FFGHM
SERBIA: NATO • KFOR 3
SOMALIA: EU • EUTM Somalia 4

FOREIGN FORCES
United States US European Command: 250; 1 spt facility at Lajes

Romania ROM

New Lei		2018	2019	2020
GDP	lei	944bn	1.03tr	
	US$	240bn	244bn	
per capita	US$	12,270	12,483	
Growth	%	4.1	4.0	
Inflation	%	4.6	4.2	
Def exp [a]	lei	17.2bn	20.9bn	
	US$	4.36bn	4.96bn	
Def bdgt [b]	lei	17.2bn	20.9bn	22.0bn
	US$	4.36bn	4.96bn	
FMA (US)	US$	0m	0m	0m
US$1=lei		3.94	4.22	

[a] NATO definition
[b] Includes military pensions

Real-terms defence budget trend (US$bn, constant 2015)

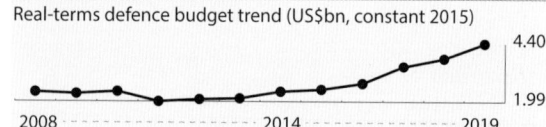

Population	21,381,356					
Age	0–14	15–19	20–24	25–29	30–64	65 plus
Male	7.3%	2.6%	2.7%	3.1%	25.9%	6.9%
Female	6.9%	2.4%	2.6%	3.0%	26.2%	10.2%

Capabilities

Romania's armed forces are structured around territorial defence, support to NATO and EU missions and contributing to regional and global stability and security. Principal security threats include, according to the National Defence Strategy 2015–19 and the 2016 Military Strategy, Russia's increased presence in the Black Sea, hybrid warfare, cyber attacks and terrorism. The government has stated the intention to strengthen operational capabilities and develop its partnerships and cooperation with other NATO and EU members, and there is an ongoing programme to modernise and upgrade the armed forces to meet NATO standards. Bucharest has signed defence-cooperation agreements with regional allies. Nevertheless, it places a great value on its strategic partnership with the US. Romania hosts the *Aegis* Ashore ballistic-missile-defence system at Deveselu. Romania trains widely with its NATO and regional allies and contributes to EU and NATO missions. The inventory is mainly composed of ageing Soviet-era equipment, which is seen as a factor limiting capability. Acquisition plans include armoured vehicles, air-defence radars, surface-to-air missiles and corvettes. The acquisition of additional second-hand F-16s will enhance Romania's air capabilities. Romania was once a significant weapons exporter, yet since 1989 the country's defence industry has struggled. Current production focuses on small arms and ammunition. However, Bucharest is looking to boost the industry through offset agreements and technology transfers.

ACTIVE 69,600 (Army 35,800 Navy 6,600 Air 10,700 Joint 16,500) Paramilitary 57,000

RESERVE 53,000 (Joint 53,000)

ORGANISATIONS BY SERVICE

Army 35,800

Readiness is reported as 70–90% for NATO-designated forces (1 div HQ, 1 mech bde, 1 inf bde & 1 mtn inf bde) and 40–70% for other forces

FORCES BY ROLE
COMMAND
  2 div HQ (2nd & 4th)
  elm 1 div HQ (MND-SE)
SPECIAL FORCES
  1 SF bde (2 SF bn, 1 para bn, 1 log bn)
MANOEUVRE
  Reconnaissance
  1 recce bde
  2 recce regt
  Mechanised
  5 mech bde (1 tk bn, 2 mech inf bn, 1 arty bn, 1 AD bn, 1 log bn)
  Light
  1 (MNB-SE) inf bde (3 inf bn, 1 arty bn, 1 AD bn, 1 log bn)
  2 mtn inf bde (3 mtn inf bn, 1 arty bn, 1 AD bn, 1 log bn)
COMBAT SUPPORT
  1 MRL bde (3 MRL bn, 1 STA bn, 1 log bn)
  2 arty regt
  1 engr bde (4 engr bn, 1 ptn br bn, 1 log bn)
  2 engr bn
  3 sigs bn
  1 CIMIC bn
  1 MP bn
  3 CBRN bn
COMBAT SERVICE SUPPORT
  3 spt bn
AIR DEFENCE
  3 AD regt
EQUIPMENT BY TYPE
ARMOURED FIGHTING VEHICLES
  MBT 400: 243 T-55AM; 103 TR-85; 54 TR-85 M1
  IFV 142: 41 MLI-84 (incl CP); 101 MLI-84M *Jderul*
  APC 753
    APC (T) 76 MLVM
    APC (W) 617: 69 B33 TAB *Zimbru*; 31 *Piranha* III; 10 *Piranha* V; 354 TAB-71 (incl variants); 153 TAB-77 (incl variants)
    PPV 60 *Maxxpro*
  AUV 382 TABC-79 (incl variants)
ENGINEERING & MAINTENANCE VEHICLES
  ARV 55: 3 MLI-84M TEHEVAC; 8 TERA-71L; 44 TERA-77L
  VLB 43 BLG-67
NBC VEHICLES 109 RCH-84

ANTI-TANK/ANTI-INFRASTRUCTURE
  MSL
    SP 134: 12 9P122 *Malyutka* (AT-3 *Sagger*); 74 9P133 *Malyutka* (AT-3 *Sagger*); 48 9P148 *Konkurs* (AT-5 *Spandrel*)
    MANPATS *Spike*-LR
  GUNS
    SP 100mm (23 SU-100 in store)
    TOWED 100mm 218 M-1977
ARTILLERY 1,118
  SP 122mm 40: 6 2S1; 34 Model 89
  TOWED 447: **122mm** 96 (M-30) M-1938 (A-19); **152mm** 351: 247 M-1981; 104 M-1985
  MRL 122mm 188: 134 APR-40; 54 LAROM
  MOR 443: **SP 82mm** 177: 92 TAB-71AR; 85 TABC-79AR; **120mm** 266 M-1982
AIR DEFENCE
  SAM
    Short-range 54: 38 2K12 *Kub* (SA-6 *Gainful*); 16 9K33 *Osa* (SA-8 *Gecko*)
    Point-defence 48 CA-95
  GUNS 65
    SP 35mm 41 *Gepard*
    TOWED 14.5mm ZPU-2; **35mm** 24 GDF-003; **57mm** S-60

Navy 6,600

EQUIPMENT BY TYPE
PRINCIPAL SURFACE COMBATANTS 3
  DESTROYERS 3
    DDGH 1 *Marasesti* with 4 twin lnchr with P-22 (SS-N-2C *Styx*) AShM, 2 triple 533mm ASTT with 53–65 HWT, 2 RBU 6000 *Smerch* 2 A/S mor, 4 AK630M CIWS, 2 twin 76mm guns (capacity 2 SA-316 (IAR-316) *Alouette* III hel)
    DDH 2 *Regele Ferdinand* (ex-UK Type-22), with 2 triple STWS Mk.2 324mm TT, 1 76mm gun (capacity 1 SA330 (IAR-330) *Puma*)
PATROL AND COASTAL COMBATANTS 24
  CORVETTES 4
    FSH 2 *Tetal* II with 2 twin 533mm ASTT with SET-53M HWT, 2 RBU 6000 *Smerch* 2 A/S mor, 2 AK630 CIWS, 1 76mm gun (capacity 1 SA316 (IAR-316) *Alouette* III hel)
    FS 2 *Tetal* I with 2 twin 533mm ASTT with SET-53M HWT, 2 RBU 2500 *Smerch* 1 A/S mor, 2 AK230 CIWS, 2 twin 76mm guns
  PCFG 3 *Zborul* with 2 twin lnchr with P-22 (SS-N-2C *Styx*) AShM, 2 AK630 CIWS, 1 76mm gun
  PCFT 3 *Naluca* with 4 single 533mm ASTT
  PCR 8:
    5 *Brutar* II with 2 BM-21 MRL, 1 100mm gun
    3 *Kogalniceanu* with 2 BM-21 MRL, 2 100mm guns
  PBR 6 VD141 (ex-MSR now used for river patrol)
MINE WARFARE 11
  MINE COUNTERMEASURES 10
    MSO 4 *Musca* with 2 RBU 1200 *Uragan* A/S mor, 2 AK230 CIWS
    MSR 6 VD141
  MINELAYERS • ML 1 *Corsar* with up to 120 mines, 2 RBU 1200 *Uragan* A/S mor, 2 AK230 CIWS

LOGISTICS AND SUPPORT 8

AE 2 *Constanta* with 2 RBU 1200 *Uragan* A/S mor, 2 AK230 CIWS, 2 twin 57mm guns
AGOR 1 *Corsar*
AGS 2: 1 *Emil Racovita*; 1 *Catuneanu*
AOL 1 *Tulcea*
ATF 1 *Grozavu*
AXS 1 *Mircea*

Naval Infantry

FORCES BY ROLE
MANOEUVRE
Light
 1 naval inf regt

EQUIPMENT BY TYPE
ARMOURED FIGHTING VEHICLES
 AUV 14: 11 ABC-79M; 3 TABC-79M

Air Force 10,700

FORCES BY ROLE
FIGHTER
 2 sqn with MiG-21 *Lancer* C
FIGHTER GROUND ATTACK
 1 sqn (forming) with with F-16AM/BM *Fighting Falcon*
GROUND ATTACK
 1 sqn with IAR-99 *Soim*
TRANSPORT
 1 sqn with An-30 *Clank*; C-27J *Spartan*
 1 sqn with C-130B/H *Hercules*
TRAINING
 1 sqn with IAR-99 *Soim**
 1 sqn with SA316B *Alouette* III (IAR-316B); Yak-52 (Iak-52)
TRANSPORT HELICOPTER
 2 (multi-role) sqn with IAR-330 SOCAT *Puma*
 3 sqn with SA330 *Puma* (IAR-330)
AIR DEFENCE
 1 AD bde
COMBAT SERVICE SUPPORT
 1 engr spt regt

EQUIPMENT BY TYPE
AIRCRAFT 56 combat capable
 FTR 12: 8 F-16AM *Fighting Falcon*; 4 F-16BM *Fighting Falcon*
 FGA 24: 6 MiG-21 *Lancer* B; 18 MiG-21 *Lancer* C
 ISR 2 An-30 *Clank*
 TPT • **Medium** 12: 7 C-27J *Spartan*; 4 C-130B *Hercules*; 1 C-130H *Hercules*
 TRG 32: 10 IAR-99*; 10 IAR-99C *Soim**; 12 Yak-52 (Iak-52)
HELICOPTERS
 MRH 30: 22 IAR-330 SOCAT *Puma*; 8 SA316B *Alouette* III (IAR-316B)
 TPT • **Medium** 36: 21 SA330L *Puma* (IAR-330L); 15 SA330M *Puma* (IAR-330M)
AIR DEFENCE • SAM • Medium-range 13: 5 S-75M3 *Volkhov* (SA-2 *Guideline*); 8 MIM-23 *Hawk* PIP III
AIR-LAUNCHED MISSILES
 AAM • **IR** AIM-9M *Sidewinder*; R-73 (AA-11 *Archer*); R-550 *Magic* 2; *Python* 3 **ARH** AIM-120C AMRAAM
 ASM *Spike*-ER
BOMBS
 Laser-guided GBU-12 *Paveway*
 INS/GPS guided GBU-38 JDAM

Paramilitary ε57,000

Gendarmerie ε57,000
Ministry of Interior

DEPLOYMENT

AFGHANISTAN: NATO • *Operation Resolute Support* 797; 1 inf bn
BOSNIA-HERZEGOVINA: EU • EUFOR • *Operation Althea* 35
CENTRAL AFRICAN REPUBLIC: EU • EUTM RCA 13
DEMOCRATIC REPUBLIC OF THE CONGO: UN • MONUSCO 10
INDIA/PAKISTAN: UN • UNMOGIP 2
IRAQ: *Operation Inherent Resolve* 10; NATO • NATO Mission Iraq 4
MALI: EU • EUTM Mali 1; UN • MINUSMA 18
POLAND: NATO • Enhanced Forward Presence 120; 1 ADA bty
SERBIA: NATO • KFOR 57; UN • UNMIK 1
SOMALIA: EU • EUTM Somalia 1
SOUTH SUDAN: UN • UNMISS 6

FOREIGN FORCES

Canada NATO Air Policing: 135; 5 F/A-18A *Hornet* (CF-18)
Poland NATO MNB-SE 230; 1 mech inf coy; *Rosomak*
United States US European Command: 1,150; 1 armd inf bn HQ; 2 armd/armd inf coy; M1A2 SEPv2 *Abrams*; M2A3 *Bradley*; 1 tpt hel flt with 5 UH-60L *Black Hawk*; 1 CISR UAV sqn with MQ-9A *Reaper*

Serbia SER

Serbian Dinar d		2018	2019	2020
GDP	d	5.06tr	5.41tr	
	US$	50.5bn	51.5bn	
per capita	US$	7,223	7,398	
Growth	%	4.3	3.5	
Inflation	%	2.0	2.2	
Def bdgt	d	70.5bn	95.1bn	
	US$	704m	906m	
US$1=d		100.17	104.96	

Real-terms defence budget trend (US$m, constant 2015)

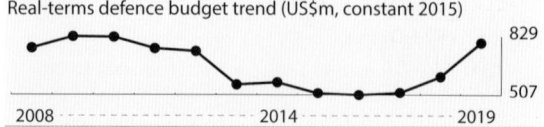

Population 7,045,162

Ethnic groups: Serb 83.3%; Hungarian 3.35%; Romani 2.05%; Bosniac 2.02%; Croat 0.8%

Age	0–14	15–19	20–24	25–29	30–64	65 plus
Male	7.3%	2.8%	2.9%	3.2%	24.4%	8.1%
Female	6.9%	2.6%	2.8%	3.0%	24.6%	11.4%

Capabilities

Serbia's armed forces focus on territorial defence, internal security and limited support to peacekeeping missions. According to the 2018 draft security strategy, key threats include separatism, religious and political extremism, and further international recognition of Kosovo. The armed forces are modernising to address long-term capability shortfalls and personnel shortages. Priorities include procurements; improving availability, maintenance and readiness levels; and bolstering air-defence systems. Serbia has agreed to deepen cooperation with NATO through an Individual Partnership Action Plan, though Belgrade does not aspire to join the Alliance. Serbia also maintains a close relationship with Russia, which in recent years has transferred military equipment to Serbia. The armed forces have reduced in size over the last decade, though annual recruitment goals are not being met. The armed forces also lack skilled technicians to operate and maintain advanced systems and suffer from a shortage of pilots. Serbia mostly trains with its Balkan neighbours, as well as Belarus, Russia and NATO countries. Serbia contributes to EU, OSCE and UN peacekeeping missions. Serbia's defence industry focuses on missile and artillery systems, and small arms and ammunition, but the country is reliant on external suppliers for major platforms. Serbia continues to develop its defence industry with a focus on the aerospace industry.

ACTIVE 28,150 (Army 13,250 Air Force and Air Defence 5,100 Training Command 3,000 Guards 1,600 Other MoD 5,200) Paramilitary 3,700
Conscript liability 6 months (voluntary)

RESERVE 50,150

ORGANISATIONS BY SERVICE

Army 13,250
FORCES BY ROLE
SPECIAL FORCES
1 SF bde (1 CT bn, 1 cdo bn, 1 para bn)
MANOEUVRE
  Mechanised
  1 (1st) bde (1 tk bn, 2 mech inf bn, 1 inf bn, 1 SP arty bn, 1 MRL bn, 1 AD bn, 1 engr bn, 1 log bn)
  3 (2nd, 3rd & 4th) bde (1 tk bn, 2 mech inf bn, 2 inf bn, 1 SP arty bn, 1 MRL bn, 1 AD bn, 1 engr bn, 1 log bn)
COMBAT SUPPORT
1 (mixed) arty bde (4 arty bn, 1 MRL bn, 1 spt bn)
2 ptn bridging bn
1 NBC bn
1 sigs bn
2 MP bn

Reserve Organisations
FORCES BY ROLE
MANOEUVRE
  Light
  8 (territorial) inf bde
EQUIPMENT BY TYPE
ARMOURED FIGHTING VEHICLES
  MBT 212: 199 M-84; 13 T-72
  RECCE 56: 46 BRDM-2; 10 BRDM-2M
  IFV 329: 323 M-80; 6 *Lazar*-3
  APC 89
    APC(T) 44: 12 BTR-50 (CP); 32 MT-LB (CP)
    APC (W) 45: 39 BOV-VP M-86; 6 *Lazar*-3
  AUV BOV M16 *Milos*
ENGINEERING & MAINTENANCE VEHICLES
  AEV IWT
  ARV M84A1; T-54/T-55
  VLB MT-55; TMM
ANTI-TANK/ANTI-INFRASTRUCTURE
  MSL
    SP 48 BOV-1 (M-83) with 9K11 *Malyutka* (AT-3 *Sagger*)
    MANPATS 9K11 *Malyutka* (AT-3 *Sagger*); 9K111 *Fagot* (AT-4 *Spigot*)
  RCL 90mm 6 M-79
ARTILLERY 449
  SP 73+: 122mm 67 2S1 *Gvozdika*; 155mm 6+ B-52 NORA
  TOWED 132: 122mm 78 D-30; 130mm 18 M-46; 152mm 36 M-84 NORA-A
  MRL 81: 128mm 78: 18 M-63 *Plamen*; 60 M-77 *Organj*; 262mm 3 M-87 *Orkan*
  MOR 163: 82mm 106 M-69; 120mm 57 M-74/M-75
AIR DEFENCE
  SAM
    Short-range 77 2K12 *Kub* (SA-6 *Gainful*);
    Point-defence 17+: 12 9K31M *Strela*-1M (SA-9 *Gaskin*); 5 9K35M *Strela*-10M; 9K32M *Strela*-2M (SA-7B *Grail*)‡; *Šilo* (SA-16 *Gimlet*)
  GUNS • TOWED 40mm 36 Bofors L/70

River Flotilla

The Serbian–Montenegrin navy was transferred to Montenegro upon independence in 2006, but the Danube flotilla remained in Serbian control. The flotilla is subordinate to the Land Forces

EQUIPMENT BY TYPE
PATROL AND COASTAL COMBATANTS 5
  PBR 5: 3 Type-20; 2 others
MINE WARFARE • MINE COUNTERMEASURES 4
  MSI 4 *Nestin* with 1 quad lnchr with 9K32 *Strela*-2M (SA-N-5 *Grail*) SAM
AMPHIBOUS • LANDING CRAFT • LCVP 5 Type-22
LOGISTICS AND SUPPORT 2
  AGF 1 *Kozara*
  AOL 1

Air Force and Air Defence 5,100
FORCES BY ROLE
FIGHTER
  1 sqn with MiG-21bis *Fishbed*; MiG-29 *Fulcrum*
FIGHTER/GROUND ATTACK
  1 sqn with G-4 *Super Galeb**; J-22 *Orao*
ISR
  2 flt with IJ-22 *Orao* 1*; MiG-21R *Fishbed* H*
TRANSPORT
  1 sqn with An-2; An-26; Do-28; Yak-40 (Jak-40); 1 PA-34 *Seneca* V
TRAINING
  1 sqn with G-4 *Super Galeb** (adv trg/light atk); SA341/342 *Gazelle*; Utva-75 (basic trg)
ATTACK HELICOPTER
  1 sqn with SA341H/342L *Gazelle*; (HN-42/45); Mi-24 *Hind*

TRANSPORT HELICOPTER
2 sqn with Mi-8 *Hip*; Mi-17 *Hip* H; Mi-17V-5 *Hip*
AIR DEFENCE
1 bde (5 bn (2 msl, 3 SP msl) with S-125 *Neva* (SA-3 *Goa*); 2K12 *Kub* (SA-6 *Gainful*); 9K32 *Strela*-2 (SA-7 *Grail*); 9K310 *Igla*-1 (SA-16 *Gimlet*))
2 radar bn (for early warning and reporting)
COMBAT SUPPORT
1 sigs bn
COMBAT SERVICE SUPPORT
1 maint bn
EQUIPMENT BY TYPE
AIRCRAFT 63 combat capable
  FTR 13+ : 2+ MiG-21bis *Fishbed*; 2+ MiG-21UM *Mongol* B; 5 MiG-29 *Fulcrum*; 4 MiG-29UB *Fulcrum*
  FGA 17 J-22 *Orao* 1
  ISR 12: 10 IJ-22R *Orao* 1*; 2 MiG-21R *Fishbed* H*
  TPT • Light 10: 1 An-2 *Colt*; 4 An-26 *Curl*; 2 Do-28 *Skyservant*; 2 Yak-40 (Jak-40); 1 PA-34 *Seneca* V
  TRG 46: 21 G-4 *Super Galeb**; 11 Utva-75; 14 *Lasta* 95
HELICOPTERS
  ATK 2 Mi-24 *Hind*
  MRH 53: 1 H145M; 1 Mi-17 *Hip* H; 2 Mi-17V-5 *Hip*; 2 SA341H *Gazelle* (HI-42); 34 SA341H *Gazelle* (HN-42)/ SA342L *Gazelle* (HN-45); 13 SA341H *Gazelle* (HO-42)/ SA342L1 *Gazelle* (HO-45)
  TPT • Medium 8 Mi-8T *Hip* (HT-40)
AIR DEFENCE
  SAM
    Short-range 15: 6 S-125 *Pechora* (SA-3 *Goa*); 9 2K12 *Kub* (SA-6 *Gainful*)
    Point-defence 9K32 *Strela*-2 (SA-7 *Grail*)‡; 9K310 *Igla*-1 (SA-16 *Gimlet*)
  GUNS • TOWED 40mm 24 *Bofors* L/70
AIR-LAUNCHED MISSILES
  AAM • IR R-60 (AA-8 *Aphid*)
  ASM AGM-65 *Maverick*; A-77 *Thunder*

Guards 1,600
FORCES BY ROLE
MANOEUVRE
  Other
    1 (ceremonial) gd bde (1 gd bn, 1 MP bn, 1 spt bn)

Paramilitary 3,700

Gendarmerie 3,700
EQUIPMENT BY TYPE
ARMOURED FIGHTING VEHICLES
  APC • APC (W) 24: 12 *Lazar*-3; 12 BOV-VP M-86
  AUV BOV M16 *Milos*

DEPLOYMENT

CENTRAL AFRICAN REPUBLIC: EU • EUTM RCA 7; **UN** • MINUSCA 77; 1 med coy
CYPRUS: UN • UNFICYP 3
DEMOCRATIC REPUBLIC OF THE CONGO: UN • MONUSCO 1
LEBANON: UN • UNIFIL 177; 1 mech inf coy
MALI: EU • EUTM Mali 3
MIDDLE EAST: UN • UNTSO 2
SOMALIA: EU • EUTM Somalia 6

TERRITORY WHERE THE GOVERNMENT DOES NOT EXERCISE EFFECTIVE CONTROL

Data here represents the de facto situation in Kosovo. This does not imply international recognition as a sovereign state. In February 2008, Kosovo declared itself independent. Serbia remains opposed to this, and while Kosovo has not been admitted to the United Nations, a number of states have recognised Kosovo's self-declared status.

Kosovo Security Force 2,500; reserves 800

The Kosovo Security Force (KSF) was formed in January 2009 as a non-military organisation with responsibility for crisis response, civil protection and EOD. In 2017, a proposal by Pristina to establish an army was opposed by Russia, Serbia, the US and NATO. Legislation to this effect was passed by Pristina in October 2018. In December, NATO said that should the KSF's mandate evolve, it would have to examine its level of engagement with the force. The KSF is armed with small arms and light vehicles only.

FOREIGN FORCES

All under Kosovo Force (KFOR) command unless otherwise specified
Albania 29
Armenia 41
Austria 330; 2 mech inf coy; 1 log coy
Bulgaria 22
Canada 5
Croatia 38; 1 hel flt with Mi-8
Czech Republic 9 • UNMIK 2 obs
Denmark 35
Finland 20 • UNMIK 1 obs
Germany 70
Greece 111; 1 inf coy
Hungary 411; 1 inf coy (KTM)
Ireland 12
Italy 542; 1 mtn inf BG HQ; 1 Carabinieri unit
Lithuania 1
Moldova 41 • UNMIK 1 obs
Montenegro 2
Norway 2
Poland 246; 1 inf coy • UNMIK 1 obs
Portugal 3
Romania 57 • UNMIK 1 obs
Slovenia 242; 1 mot inf coy; 1 MP unit; 1 hel unit
Sweden 4
Switzerland 165; 1 inf coy; 1 engr pl; 1 hel flt with AS332
Turkey 244; 1 inf coy • UNMIK 1 obs
Ukraine 40 • UNMIK 2 obs
United Kingdom 23
United States 660; elm 1 ARNG inf bde HQ; 1 recce bn; 1 hel flt with UH-60

Slovakia SVK

Euro €		2018	2019	2020
GDP	€	90.2bn	94.9bn	
	US$	107bn	107bn	
per capita	US$	19,579	19,548	
Growth	%	4.1	2.6	
Inflation	%	2.5	2.6	
Def exp [a]	€	1.10bn	1.67bn	
	US$	1.30bn	1.87bn	
Def bdgt	€	1.10bn	1.66bn	1.86bn
	US$	1.30bn	1.87bn	
US$1=€		0.85	0.89	

[a] NATO definition

Real-terms defence budget trend (US$m, constant 2015)

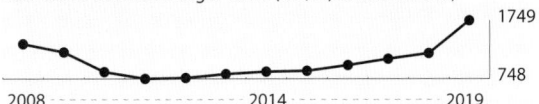

1749 / 748 / 2008 / 2014 / 2019

Population	5,443,336					
Age	0–14	15–19	20–24	25–29	30–64	65 plus
Male	7.8%	2.5%	2.8%	3.5%	25.6%	6.5%
Female	7.4%	2.4%	2.6%	3.3%	25.8%	10.0%

Capabilities

Slovakia is trying to modernise its armed forces and replace obsolete equipment while contributing to international crisis-management missions. A defence white paper in September 2016 set out security priorities and a plan to increase defence capabilities. In 2017, the government approved a new defence strategy, a new military strategy and a Long-Term Defence Development Plan. A NATO and EU member state, Slovakia cooperates closely with the Visegrád Group framework. Bratislava has signed an agreement to enable air policing and closer integration of air-defence capabilities. After amending the law on conscription in 2017, Slovakia began to implement its Active Reserves pilot project in order to help address shortfalls in specialist capacities, including in engineering. Results of the pilot project fell short of expectations, and Slovakia passed legislation in early 2018 to improve the training conditions for active reservists from mid-2018 onwards. Slovakia has committed to deploying a company-sized unit to NATO's Enhanced Forward Presence and has also contributed to EU operations and UN peacekeeping missions. Bratislava has begun to replace its small fighter and rotary-wing-transport fleets. Coinciding with the July 2018 NATO summit, the government announced it had selected the F-16, with delivery due between 2022 and 2024. There are also ambitions to replace land equipment and improve the level of technology in the armed forces. Part of Slovakia's defence-industrial base is organised within the state-controlled holding company DMD Group, including KONSTRUKTA Defence, which produces land systems. Other companies focus on maintenance, repair and overhaul services.

ACTIVE 15,850 (Army 6,250 Air 3,950 Central Staff 2,550 Support and Training 3,100)

ORGANISATIONS BY SERVICE

Central Staff 2,550

FORCES BY ROLE
SPECIAL FORCES
  1 (5th) spec ops bn

Army 6,250
FORCES BY ROLE
MANOEUVRE
  Armoured
    1 (2nd) armd bde (1 recce bn, 1 tk bn, 2 armd inf bn, 1 mot inf bn, 1 mixed SP arty bn)
  Mechanised
    1 (1st) mech bde (3 armd inf bn, 1 MRL bn, 1 engr bn, 1 NBC bn)
COMBAT SUPPORT
  1 MP bn
COMBAT SERVICE SUPPORT
  1 spt bde (2 log bn, 1 maint bn, 1 spt bn)
EQUIPMENT BY TYPE
ARMOURED FIGHTING VEHICLES
  MBT 30 T-72M
  RECCE 18 BPsVI
  IFV 249: 148 BMP-1; 91 BMP-2; 10 BVP-M
  APC 101+
    APC (T) 72 OT-90
    APC (W) 22: 7 OT-64; 15 Tatrapan (6×6)
    PPV 7+ RG-32M
  AUV IVECO LMV
ENGINEERING & MAINTENANCE VEHICLES
  ARV MT-55; VT-55A; VT-72B; WPT-TOPAS
  VLB AM-50; MT-55A
  MW Bozena; UOS-155 Belarty
ANTI-TANK/ANTI-INFRASTRUCTURE
  SP 9S428 with Malyutka (AT-3 Sagger) on BMP-1; 9P135 Fagot (AT-4 Spigot) on BMP-2; 9P148 Konkurs (AT-5 Spandrel) on BRDM-2
  MANPATS 9K11 Malyutka (AT-3 Sagger); 9K111-1 Konkurs (AT-5 Spandrel)
  RCL 84mm Carl Gustav
ARTILLERY 49
  SP 19: **152mm** 3 M-77 Dana; **155mm** 16 M-2000 Zuzana
  MRL 30: **122mm** 4 RM-70; **122/227mm** 26 RM-70/85 MODULAR
AIR DEFENCE
  SAM • Point-defence 9K310 Igla-1 (SA-16 Gimlet)

Air Force 3,950
FORCES BY ROLE
FIGHTER
  1 sqn with MiG-29AS/UBS Fulcrum
TRANSPORT
  1 flt with C-27J Spartan
  1 flt with L-410FG/T/UVP Turbolet
TRANSPORT HELICOPTER
  1 sqn with Mi-8 Hip; Mi-17 Hip H
  1 sqn with PZL MI-2 Hoplite
TRAINING
  1 sqn with L-39CM/ZA/ZAM Albatros*
AIR DEFENCE
  1 bde with 2K12 Kub (SA-6 Gainful); S-300PMU (SA-10 Grumble)

EQUIPMENT BY TYPE

AIRCRAFT 23 combat capable
  FTR 11: 9 MiG-29AS *Fulcrum*; 2 MiG-29UBS *Fulcrum*;
  TPT 10: **Medium** 2 C-27J *Spartan*; **Light** 8: 2 L-410FG *Turbolet*; 2 L-410T *Turbolet*; 4 L-410UVP *Turbolet*
  TRG 12: 6 L-39CM *Albatros**; 5 L-39ZA *Albatros**; 1 L-39ZAM *Albatros**

HELICOPTERS
  ATK (15: 5 Mi-24D *Hind* D; 10 Mi-24V *Hind* E all in store)
  MRH 13 Mi-17 *Hip* H
  TPT 9: **Medium** 3: 1 Mi-8 *Hip*; 2 UH-60M *Black Hawk* **Light** 6 PZL MI-2 *Hoplite*

AIR DEFENCE • SAM
  Long-range S-300PMU (SA-10 *Grumble*)
  Short-range 2K12 *Kub* (SA-6 *Gainful*)

AIR-LAUNCHED MISSILES
  AAM • IR R-60 (AA-8 *Aphid*); R-73 (AA-11A *Archer*)
  SARH R-27R (AA-10A *Alamo*)
  ASM S5K/S5KO (57mm rockets); S8KP/S8KOM (80mm rockets)

DEPLOYMENT

AFGHANISTAN: NATO • *Operation Resolute Support* 33

BOSNIA-HERZEGOVINA: EU • EUFOR • *Operation Althea* 41

CYPRUS: UN • UNFICYP 240; 2 inf coy; 1 engr pl

IRAQ: NATO • NATO Mission Iraq 42

LATVIA: NATO • Enhanced Forward Presence 152; 1 mech inf coy

MIDDLE EAST: UN • UNTSO 2

Slovenia SVN

Euro €		2018	2019	2020
GDP	€	45.8bn	48.2bn	
	US$	54.1bn	54.2bn	
per capita	US$	26,146	26,170	
Growth	%	4.1	2.9	
Inflation	%	1.7	1.8	
Def exp [a]	€	463m	508m	
	US$	547m	570m	
Def bdgt [b]	€	503m	561m	530m
	US$	594m	630m	
US$1=€		0.85	0.89	

[a] NATO definition
[b] Includes military pensions

Real-terms defence budget trend (US$m, constant 2015)

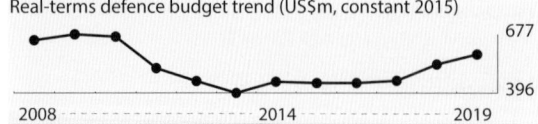

Population 2,102,538

Ethnic groups: Slovenian 83%; Serb 2%; Croat 1.8%; Bosniac 1%; other or unspecified 12.2%

Age	0–14	15–19	20–24	25–29	30–64	65 plus
Male	7.6%	2.3%	2.4%	2.7%	26.0%	8.9%
Female	7.2%	2.1%	2.2%	2.5%	24.2%	11.8%

Capabilities

Since joining NATO and the EU in 2004, territorial defence and the ability to take part in peace-support operations have been central to Slovenia's defence strategy. The defence ministry completed a Strategic Defence Review in December 2016. Its core conclusion was that the goals of the previous 2009 review had been missed and that capability development had stalled at a time when Europe's security environment had deteriorated. Underfunding and bureaucratic failure to implement the policy guidelines were singled out as key reasons. The main development goal to 2023 has been defined as the formation and equipping of two battalion-sized battlegroups. Doctrine will also be reviewed. Slovenia acts as the framework nation for the NATO Mountain Warfare Centre of Excellence. Because its small air wing is not equipped to provide air policing, Italy and Hungary currently provide this capability under NATO arrangements. The country contributes to EU, NATO and UN operations and exercises with other member states. Recruitment and retention continues to be a challenge. Slovenia participates in NATO's Enhanced Forward Presence, where it contributes to the Canadian-led battlegroup in Latvia. Continuing resource challenges mean that significant modernisation steps seem unlikely during the current Medium-Term Defence Programme to 2020. Slovenia's defence industry relies heavily on exports for its revenue and focuses on individual solider equipment, small arms and ammunition, and CBRN protection and detection.

ACTIVE 7,250 (Army 7,250)

RESERVE 1,200 (Army 1,200)

ORGANISATIONS BY SERVICE

Army 7,250

FORCES BY ROLE
Regt are bn sized
SPECIAL FORCES
  1 SF unit (1 spec ops coy, 1 CSS coy)
MANOEUVRE
  Mechanised
  1 (1st) mech inf bde (1 mech inf regt, 1 mtn inf regt, 1 cbt spt bn (1 ISR coy, 1 arty bty, 1 engr coy, 1 MP coy, 1 CBRN coy, 1 sigs coy, 1 SAM bty))
  1 (72nd) mech inf bde (2 mech inf regt, 1 cbt spt bn (1 ISR coy, 1 arty bty, 1 engr coy, 1 MP coy, 1 CBRN coy, 1 sigs coy, 1 SAM bty))
COMBAT SUPPORT
  1 EW coy
COMBAT SERVICE SUPPORT
  1 log bde (1 log regt, 1 maint regt (1 tk coy), 1 med regt)

Reserves

FORCES BY ROLE
MANOEUVRE
  Mountain
  2 inf regt (territorial – 1 allocated to each inf bde)

EQUIPMENT BY TYPE
ARMOURED FIGHTING VEHICLES
  MBT 14 M-84 (trg role) (32 more in store)

APC 115+:
APC (W) 115: 85 *Pandur* 6×6 (*Valuk*); 30 Patria 8×8 (*Svarun*)
PPV *Cougar* 6×6 JERRV
ENGINEERING & MAINTENANCE VEHICLES
ARV VT-55A
VLB MT-55A
NBC VEHICLES 10 *Cobra* CBRN
ANTI-TANK/ANTI-INFRASTRUCTURE
MSL • MANPATS *Spike* MR/LR
ARTILLERY 68
TOWED • **155mm** 18 TN-90
MOR 50+: **82mm** M-69; **120mm** 50 MN-9/M-74
AIR DEFENCE • SAM • Point-defence 9K338 *Igla*-S (SA-24 *Grinch*)

Army Maritime Element 130
FORCES BY ROLE
SPECIAL FORCES
1 SF unit
EQUIPMENT BY TYPE
PATROL AND COASTAL COMBATANTS 2
PCC 1 *Triglav* III (RUS *Svetlyak*)
PBF 1 *Super Dvora* MkII

Air Element 590
FORCES BY ROLE
TRANSPORT
1 sqn with *Falcon* 2000EX; L-410 *Turbolet*; PC-6B *Turbo Porter*;
TRAINING
1 unit with Bell 206 *Jet Ranger* (AB-206); PC-9M*; Z-143L; Z-242L
TRANSPORT HELICOPTER
1 sqn with AS532AL *Cougar*; Bell 412 *Twin Huey*
COMBAT SERVICE SUPPORT
1 maint sqn
EQUIPMENT BY TYPE
AIRCRAFT 9 combat capable
TPT 4: **Light** 3: 1 L-410 *Turbolet*; 2 PC-6B *Turbo Porter*
PAX 1 *Falcon* 2000EX
TRG 19: 9 PC-9M*; 2 Z-143L; 8 Z-242L
HELICOPTERS
MRH 8: 5 Bell 412EP *Twin Huey*; 2 Bell 412HP *Twin Huey*; 1 Bell 412SP *Twin Huey* (some armed)
TPT 8: **Medium** 4 AS532AL *Cougar*; **Light** 4 Bell 206 *Jet Ranger* (AB-206)

DEPLOYMENT
AFGHANISTAN: NATO • *Operation Resolute Support* 8
BOSNIA-HERZEGOVINA: EU • EUFOR • *Operation Althea* 10
IRAQ: *Operation Inherent Resolve* 6
LATVIA: NATO • Enhanced Forward Presence 33; 1 engr pl
LEBANON: UN • UNIFIL 15
MALI: EU • EUTM Mali 8
MIDDLE EAST: UN • UNTSO 3
SERBIA: NATO • KFOR 242; 1 mot inf coy; 1 MP unit; 1 hel unit

Spain ESP

Euro €		2018	2019	2020
GDP	€	1.21tr	1.24tr	
	US$	1.43tr	1.40tr	
per capita	US$	30,733	29,961	
Growth	%	2.6	2.2	
Inflation	%	1.7	0.7	
Def exp [a]	€	11.2bn	11.5bn	
	US$	13.2bn	12.9bn	
Def bdgt [b]	€	12.7bn	ε11.5bn	
	US$	15.1bn	ε12.9bn	
US$1=€		0.85	0.89	

[a] NATO definition
[b] Includes military pensions

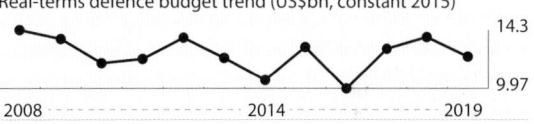
Real-terms defence budget trend (US$bn, constant 2015)

Population 49,683,254

Age	0–14	15–19	20–24	25–29	30–64	65 plus
Male	7.8%	2.6%	2.5%	2.8%	25.9%	7.9%
Female	7.4%	2.4%	2.3%	2.6%	25.5%	10.5%

Capabilities

The 2017 National Security Strategy indicated that Spain's defence policy was global in scope, though concerned by threats emanating from the Middle East and sub-Saharan Africa. The army reviewed its force structure in 2015, which resulted in a reorganisation into multipurpose brigades with heavy, medium and light capabilities, optimised for deployable operations. Spain is a member of NATO, continues to support NATO, EU and UN operations abroad, and hosts one of NATO's two Combined Air Operations Centres. The armed forces are well trained and there is a routine exercise programme for both domestic and multinational exercises. The country's equipment and logistic-support capability appears to be sufficient to meet its national commitments and contribution to NATO operations and exercises. In early 2018, Spain launched an equipment-modernisation plan, with funding for the modernisation of army *Chinook* helicopters, for the S-80 submarine programme and for military-communications satellites. Spain's defence industry manufactures across all domains and exports globally. Navantia is the principal, state-owned, shipbuilding firm. The industry is largely integrated within the European defence-industrial manufacturing base.

ACTIVE 120,350 (Army 69,250 Navy 20,100 Air 19,350 Joint 11,650) **Paramilitary 75,800**

RESERVE 15,150 (Army 9,200 Navy 2,900 Air 2,350 Other 700)

ORGANISATIONS BY SERVICE

Space
EQUIPMENT BY TYPE
SATELLITES 3

COMMUNICATIONS 2: 1 *Spainsat*; 1 *Xtar-Eur*
ISR 1 *Paz*

Army 69,250

The Land Forces High Readiness HQ Spain provides one NATO Rapid Deployment Corps HQ (NRDC-ESP)

FORCES BY ROLE
COMMAND
1 corps HQ (CGTAD/NRDC-ESP) (1 int regt, 1 MP bn)
2 div HQ

SPECIAL FORCES
1 comd (4 spec ops bn, 1 int coy, 1 sigs coy, 1 log bn)

MANOEUVRE
Reconnaissance
1 armd cav regt (2 armd recce bn)

Mechanised
2 (10th & 11th) mech bde (1 armd regt (1 armd recce bn, 1 tk bn), 1 mech inf regt (1 armd inf bn, 1 mech inf bn), 1 lt inf bn, 1 SP arty bn, 1 AT coy, 1 AD coy, 1 engr bn, 1 int coy, 1 NBC coy, 1 sigs coy, 1 log bn)
1 (12th) mech bde (1 armd regt (1 armd recce bn, 1 tk bn), 1 mech inf regt (1 armd inf bn, 1 mech inf bn), 1 SP arty bn, 1 AT coy, 1 AD coy, 1 engr bn, 1 int coy, 1 NBC coy, 1 sigs coy, 1 log bn)
1 (1st) mech bde (1 armd regt (1 armd recce bn, 1 tk bn), 1 mech inf regt (1 armd inf bn, 1 mtn inf bn), 2 mtn inf bn, 1 SP arty bn, 1 AT coy, 1 AD coy, 1 engr bn, 1 int coy, 1 NBC coy, 1 sigs coy, 1 log bn)
2 (2nd/La Legion & 7th) lt mech bde (1 armd recce bn, 1 mech inf regt (2 mech inf bn), 1 lt inf bn, 1 fd arty bn, 1 AT coy, 1 AD coy, 1 engr bn, 1 int coy, 1 NBC coy, 1 sigs coy, 1 log bn)

Air Manoeuvre
1 (6th) bde (1 recce bn, 2 para bn, 1 lt inf bn, 1 fd arty bn, 1 AT coy, 1 AD coy, 1 engr bn, 1 int coy, 1 NBC coy, 1 sigs coy, 1 log bn)

Other
1 (Canary Islands) comd (1 lt inf bde (2 mech inf regt (1 mech inf bn), 1 lt inf regt (1 lt inf bn)), 1 fd arty regt, 1 AT coy, 1 engr bn, 1 int coy, 1 NBC coy, 1 sigs coy, 1 log bn); 1 spt hel bn; 1 AD regt)
1 (Balearic Islands) comd (1 inf regt)
2 (Ceuta and Melilla) comd (1 recce regt, 1 mech inf bn, 1 inf bn, 1 arty regt, 1 engr bn, 1 sigs coy, 1 log bn)

COMBAT SUPPORT
1 arty comd (1 arty regt; 1 MRL regt; 1 coastal arty regt)
1 engr comd (2 engr regt, 1 bridging regt)
1 EW/sigs bde (2 EW regt, 3 sigs regt)
1 NBC regt
1 CIMIC bn

COMBAT SERVICE SUPPORT
1 log bde (5 log regt; 1 tpt regt)
1 med bde (1 log unit, 2 med regt, 1 fd hospital unit)

HELICOPTER
1 hel comd (1 atk hel bn, 2 spt hel bn, 1 tpt hel bn, 1 sigs bn, 1 log unit (1 spt coy, 1 supply coy))

AIR DEFENCE
1 AD comd (3 SAM regt, 1 sigs unit)

EQUIPMENT BY TYPE
ARMOURED FIGHTING VEHICLES
MBT 327: 108 *Leopard* 2A4; 219 *Leopard* 2E
ASLT 84 B1 *Centauro*
RECCE 187 VEC-M1
IFV 227: 206 *Pizarro*; 21 *Pizarro* (CP)
APC 895
 APC (T) 473: 20 Bv-206S; 453 M113 (incl variants)
 APC (W) 312 BMR-600/BMR-600M1
PPV 110 RG-31
AUV 260 IVECO LMV

ENGINEERING & MAINTENANCE VEHICLES
AEV 34 CZ-10/25E
ARV 72: 16 *Leopard* REC; 1 AMX-30; 3 BMR REC; 4 *Centauro* REC; 14 *Maxxpro* MRV; 12 M113; 22 M47
VLB 16: 1 M47; 15 M60
MW 6 *Husky* 2G

ANTI-TANK/ANTI-INFRASTRUCTURE
MSL • MANPATS *Spike*-LR; TOW

ARTILLERY 1,560
SP 155mm 96 M109A5
TOWED 281: **105mm** 217: 56 L118 Light Gun; 161 Model 56 pack howitzer; **155mm** 64 SBT 155/52 SIAC
MOR 1,183: **81mm** 777; **SP 81mm** 4 VAMTAC with Cardom 81mm; **120mm** 402

COASTAL DEFENCE • ARTY 155mm 19 SBT 155/52 APU SBT V07

HELICOPTERS
ATK 21: 6 *Tiger* HAP-E; 15 *Tiger* HAD-E
TPT 90: **Heavy** 17 CH-47D *Chinook* (HT-17D); **Medium** 46: 16 AS332B *Super Puma* (HU-21); 12 AS532UL *Cougar*; 6 AS532AL *Cougar*; 12 NH90 TTH; **Light** 27: 6 Bell 205 (HU-10B *Iroquois*); 5 Bell 212 (HU.18); 16 H135 (HE.26/HU.26)

UAV • ISR • Medium 6: 2 *Searcher* MkII-J (PASI); 4 *Searcher* MkIII (PASI)

AIR DEFENCE
SAM
 Long-range 18 MIM-104C *Patriot* PAC-2 • **Medium-range** 38 MIM-23B I-*Hawk* Phase III • **Short-range** 21: 8 NASAMS; 13 *Skyguard/Aspide* • **Point-defence** *Mistral*
GUNS • TOWED 35mm 67: 19 GDF-005; 48 GDF-007

Navy 20,100 (incl Naval Aviation and Marines)

EQUIPMENT BY TYPE
SUBMARINES • TACTICAL • SSK 3:
3 *Galerna* with 4 single 533mm TT with F17 mod 2 HWT

PRINCIPAL SURFACE COMBATANTS 11
DESTROYERS • DDGHM 5:
5 *Alvaro de Bazan* with *Aegis* Baseline 5 C2, 2 quad lnchr with RGM-84L *Harpoon* Block II AShM, 6 8-cell Mk 41 VLS with SM-2 Block IIIA/RIM-162B ESSM SAM, 2 SVTT Mk 32 mod 9 SVTT twin 324mm ASTT with Mk 46 mod 5 LWT, 1 127mm gun (capacity 1 SH-60B *Seahawk* ASW hel)

FRIGATES • FFGHM 6:
6 *Santa Maria* with 1 Mk 13 GMLS with RGM-84C *Harpoon* Block 1B AShM/SM-1MR Block VI SAM, 2 SVTT Mk 32 triple 324mm ASTT with Mk 46 mod 5 LWT, 1 *Meroka* mod 2B CIWS, 1 76mm gun (capacity 2 SH-60B *Seahawk* ASW hel)

AMPHIBIOUS
PRINCIPAL AMPHIBIOUS SHIPS 3:
LHD 1 *Juan Carlos* I (capacity 18 hel or 10 AV-8B FGA ac; 4 LCM-1E; 42 APC; 46 MBT; 900 troops)
LPD 2 *Galicia* (capacity 6 Bell 212 or 4 SH-3D *Sea King* hel; 4 LCM or 2 LCM & 8 AAV; 130 APC or 33 MBT; 540 troops)
LANDING CRAFT 12
LCM 12 LCM 1E
LOGISTICS AND SUPPORT 2
AORH 2: 1 *Patino* (capacity 3 Bell 212 or 2 SH-3D *Sea King* hel); 1 *Cantabria* (capacity 3 Bell 212 or 2 SH-3D *Sea King* hel)

Maritime Action Force
EQUIPMENT BY TYPE
PATROL AND COASTAL COMBATANTS 23
PSOH 6 *Meteoro* (*Buques de Accion Maritima*) with 1 76mm gun
PSO 5:
3 *Alboran* each with 1 hel landing platform
2 *Descubierta* with 1 76mm gun
PCO 4 *Serviola* with 1 76mm gun
PCC 3 *Anaga* with 1 76mm gun
PB 4: 2 P-101; 2 *Toralla*
PBR 1 *Cabo Fradera*
MINE WARFARE • MINE COUNTERMEASURES 6
MHO 6 *Segura*
LOGISTICS AND SUPPORT 29
AGI 1 *Alerta*
AGOR 2 (with ice-strengthened hull, for polar research duties in Antarctica)
AGS 3: 2 *Malaspina*; 1 *Castor*
AK 2: 1 *Martin Posadillo* with 1 hel landing platform; 1 *El Camino Español*
AP 1 *Contramaestre Casado* with 1 hel landing platform
ASR 1 *Neptuno*
ATF 3: 1 *Mar Caribe*; 1 *Mahon*; 1 *La Grana*
AXL 8: 4 *Contramaestre*; 4 *Guardiamarina*
AXS 8

Naval Aviation 850
FORCES BY ROLE
FIGHTER/GROUND ATTACK
1 sqn with AV-8B *Harrier* II Plus
ANTI-SUBMARINE WARFARE
1 sqn with SH-60B/F *Seahawk*
TRANSPORT
1 (liaison) sqn with Cessna 550 *Citation* II; Cessna 650 *Citation* VII
TRAINING
1 sqn with Hughes 500MD8
1 flt with TAV-8B *Harrier*
TRANSPORT HELICOPTER
1 sqn with Bell 212 (HU-18)
1 sqn with SH-3D *Sea King*
EQUIPMENT BY TYPE
AIRCRAFT 13 combat capable
FGA 13: 8 AV-8B *Harrier* II Plus; 4 AV-8B *Harrier* II (upgraded to II Plus standard); 1 TAV-8B *Harrier* (on lease from USMC)

TPT • Light 4: 3 Cessna 550 *Citation* II; 1 Cessna 650 *Citation* VII
HELICOPTERS
ASW 20: 6 SH-3D *Sea King* (tpt); 12 SH-60B *Seahawk*; 2 SH-60F *Seahawk*
MRH 9 Hughes 500MD
TPT • Light 7 Bell 212 (HA-18)
AIR-LAUNCHED MISSILES
AAM • IR AIM-9L *Sidewinder*; ARH AIM-120 AMRAAM
ASM AGM-65G *Maverick*
AShM AGM-119 *Penguin*

Marines 5,350
FORCES BY ROLE
SPECIAL FORCES
1 spec ops bn
MANOEUVRE
Amphibious
1 mne bde (1 recce unit, 1 mech inf bn, 2 inf bn, 1 arty bn, 1 log bn)
Other
1 sy bde (5 mne garrison gp)
EQUIPMENT BY TYPE
ARMOURED FIGHTING VEHICLES
MBT 2 M60A3TTS
APC • APC (W) 34: 32 *Piranha* IIIC; 1 *Piranha* IIIC (amb); 1 *Piranha* IIIC EW (EW)
AAV 18: 16 AAV-7A1/AAVP-7A1; 2 AAVC-7A1 (CP)
ENGINEERING & MAINTENANCE VEHICLES
AEV 4 *Piranha* IIIC
ARV 3: 1 AAVR-7A1; 1 M88; 1 *Piranha* IIIC
ARTILLERY 30
SP 155mm 6 M109A2
TOWED 105mm 24 Model 56 pack howitzer
ANTI-TANK/ANTI-INFRASTRUCTURE
MSL • MANPATS Spike-LR; TOW-2
AIR DEFENCE • SAM • Point-defence Mistral

Air Force 19,350
The Spanish Air Force is organised in 3 commands – General Air Command, Combat Air Command and Canary Islands Air Command
FORCES BY ROLE
FIGHTER
2 sqn with Eurofighter *Typhoon*
FIGHTER/GROUND ATTACK
5 sqn with F/A-18A/B MLU *Hornet* (EF-18A/B MLU)
MARITIME PATROL
1 sqn with P-3A/M *Orion*
ISR
1 sqn with Beech C90 *King Air*
1 sqn with Cessna 550 *Citation* V; CN235 (TR-19A)
ELECTRONIC WARFARE
1 sqn with C-212 *Aviocar*; *Falcon* 20D
SEARCH & RESCUE
1 sqn with AS332B/B1 *Super Puma*; CN235 VIGMA
1 sqn with AS332B *Super Puma*; CN235 VIGMA; H215 (AS332C1) *Super Puma*
1 sqn with C-212 *Aviocar*; CN235 VIGMA

TANKER/TRANSPORT
　1 sqn with KC-130H *Hercules*
TRANSPORT
　1 VIP sqn with A310; *Falcon* 900
　1 sqn with C-130H/H-30 *Hercules*; A400M
　1 sqn with C-212 *Aviocar*
　2 sqn with C295
　1 sqn with CN235
TRAINING
　1 OCU sqn with Eurofighter *Typhoon*
　1 OCU sqn with F/A-18A/B (EF-18A/B MLU) *Hornet*
　1 sqn with Beech F33C *Bonanza*
　2 sqn with C-101 *Aviojet*
　1 sqn with C-212 *Aviocar*
　1 sqn with T-35 *Pillan* (E-26)
　2 (LIFT) sqn with F-5B *Freedom Fighter*
　1 hel sqn with H120 *Colibri*
　1 hel sqn with S-76C
TRANSPORT HELICOPTER
　1 sqn with AS332M1 *Super Puma*; AS532UL *Cougar* (VIP)
EQUIPMENT BY TYPE
AIRCRAFT 174 combat capable
　FTR 87: 68 Eurofighter *Typhoon*; 19 F-5B *Freedom Fighter*
　FGA 84: 20 F/A-18A *Hornet* (EF-18A); 52 EF-18A MLU; 12 EF-18B MLU
　ASW 3 P-3M *Orion*
　MP 8 CN235 VIGMA
　ISR 2 CN235 (TR-19A)
　EW 3: 1 C-212 *Aviocar* (TM.12D); 2 *Falcon* 20D
　TKR 5 KC-130H *Hercules*
　TPT 78: **Heavy** 5 A400M; **Medium** 7: 6 C-130H *Hercules*; 1 C-130H-30 *Hercules*; **Light** 58: 3 Beech C90 *King Air*; 22 Beech F33C *Bonanza*; 10 C-212 *Aviocar* (incl 9 trg); 12 C295; 8 CN235; 3 Cessna 550 *Citation* V (ISR); **PAX** 8: 2 A310; 1 B-707; 5 *Falcon* 900 (VIP)
　TRG 96: 60 C-101 *Aviojet*; 36 T-35 *Pillan* (E-26)
HELICOPTERS
　TPT 41: **Medium** 19: 9 AS332B/B1 *Super Puma*; 4 AS332M1 *Super Puma*; 4 H215 (AS332C1) *Super Puma*; 2 AS532UL *Cougar* (VIP); **Light** 22: 14 H120 *Colibri*; 8 S-76C
AIR DEFENCE • SAM
　Short-range *Skyguard/Aspide*
　Point-defence *Mistral*
AIR-LAUNCHED MISSILES
　AAM • IR AIM-9L/JULI *Sidewinder*; **IIR** IRIS-T; **SARH** AIM-7P *Sparrow*; **ARH** AIM-120B/C AMRAAM
　ARM AGM-88B HARM
　ASM AGM-65G *Maverick*
　AShM AGM-84D *Harpoon*
　LACM Taurus KEPD 350
BOMBS
　Laser-guided: GBU-10/12/16 *Paveway* II; GBU-24 *Paveway* III; EGBU-16 *Paveway* II; BPG-2000
　INS/GPS guided: GBU-38 JDAM

Emergencies Military Unit (UME) 3,500

FORCES BY ROLE
COMMAND
　1 div HQ
MANOEUVRE
　Other
　　5 Emergency Intervention bn
　　1 Emergency Support and Intervention regt
COMBAT SUPPORT
　1 sigs bn
HELICOPTER
　1 hel bn opcon Army

Paramilitary 75,800

Guardia Civil 75,800

17 regions, 54 Rural Comds
FORCES BY ROLE
SPECIAL FORCES
　8 (rural) gp
MANOEUVRE
　Other
　　15 (traffic) sy gp
　　1 (Special) sy bn
EQUIPMENT BY TYPE
PATROL AND COASTAL COMBATANTS 64
　PSO 1 with 1 hel landing platform
　PCC 2
　PBF 34
　PB 27
AIRCRAFT • TPT • Light 2 CN235-300
HELICOPTERS
　MRH 20: 2 AS653N3 *Dauphin*; 18 Bo-105ATH
　TPT • Light 21: 8 BK-117; 13 H135

DEPLOYMENT

AFGHANISTAN: NATO • *Operation Resolute Support* 66

BLACK SEA: NATO • SNMCMG 2: 1 MHO

BOSNIA-HERZEGOVINA: EU • EUFOR • *Operation Althea* 2

CENTRAL AFRICAN REPUBLIC: EU • EUTM RCA 5

DJIBOUTI: EU • *Operation Atalanta* 1 P-3M *Orion*

GABON: *Operation Barkhane* 45; 1 C295M

GULF OF ADEN & INDIAN OCEAN: EU • *Operation Atalanta* 1 FFGHM

IRAQ: *Operation Inherent Resolve* 500; 2 trg unit; 1 hel unit with CH-47D *Chinook*; AS532 *Cougar*; **NATO •** NATO Mission Iraq 70

LATVIA: NATO • Enhanced Forward Presence 350; 1 armd inf coy(+)

LEBANON: UN • UNIFIL 635; 1 mech bde HQ; 1 mech inf bn(-); 1 engr coy; 1 sigs coy

MALI: EU • EUTM Mali 200

MEDITERRANEAN SEA: NATO • SNMG 2: 1 DDGHM;1 AORH

SENEGAL: *Operation Barkhane* 60; 1 C-130H *Hercules*

SOMALIA: EU • EUTM Somalia 20

TURKEY: NATO • *Operation Active Fence* 149; 1 SAM bty with MIM-104C *Patriot* PAC-2

FOREIGN FORCES

United States US European Command: 3,750; 1 air base at Morón; 1 naval base at Rota

Sweden SWE

Swedish Krona Skr		2018	2019	2020
GDP	Skr	4.83tr	4.99tr	
	US$	556bn	529bn	
per capita	US$	54,356	51,242	
Growth	%	2.3	0.9	
Inflation	%	2.0	1.7	
Def bdgt	Skr	53.8bn	60.3bn	64.8bn
	US$	6.19bn	6.38bn	
US$1=Skr		8.69	9.44	

Real-terms defence budget trend (US$bn, constant 2015)

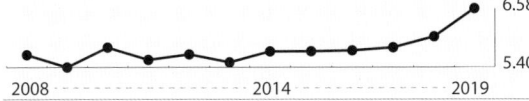

Population	10,121,794					
Age	0–14	15–19	20–24	25–29	30–64	65 plus
Male	9.1%	2.8%	2.9%	3.6%	22.2%	9.5%
Female	8.6%	2.6%	2.8%	3.5%	21.7%	11.0%

Capabilities

Sweden's armed forces remain configured for territorial defence and there has been growing concern at Russian military activity in the Baltic area. There has also been a focus on increasing cooperation with neighbours and NATO in recent years. The 2016–20 defence bill set out the aims of strengthening operational capabilities and deepening multilateral and bilateral defence relationships. Sweden decided to relocate its service staffs from Stockholm to other locations in 2019 in order to provide better protection. There are plans to increase defence ties with the UK and the US. In July 2019, Sweden joined the UK-led *Tempest* future-combat-aircraft programme. Concerns over readiness levels have led to greater cooperation with NATO and NORDEFCO. In May 2018, Sweden, Finland and the US signed a statement of intent to develop closer cooperation on exercises and interoperability. Readiness, exercises and training, as well as cyber defence, are spending priorities. Amid recruitment challenges, Sweden announced in March 2017 that it would reinstate conscription from January 2018. Sweden has started to re-garrison the island of Gotland. Readiness challenges in the air force triggered a discussion about extending the service life of the JAS-39C *Gripen* Cs beyond their intended 2026 retirement date, not least since the air force was slated to receive a lower number of JAS-39Es than requested. In August 2018, Sweden proceeded with the acquisition of the *Patriot* air-defence system. The country's export-oriented defence industry is privately owned and capable of meeting most of the armed forces' equipment needs, including for advanced combat aircraft and conventional submarines.

ACTIVE 15,150 (Army 6,850 Navy 2,100 Air 2,700 Other 3,500) **Voluntary Auxiliary Organisations 21,200**

Conscript liability 4–11 months, depending on branch (selective conscription; 4,000 in total, gender neutral)

RESERVE 10,000

ORGANISATIONS BY SERVICE

Army 6,850

The army has been transformed to provide brigade-sized task forces depending on the operational requirement

FORCES BY ROLE
COMMAND
  2 bde HQ
MANOEUVRE
  Reconnaissance
  1 recce bn
  Armoured
  5 armd bn
  1 armd BG
  Mechanised
  1 mech bn
  Light
  1 mot inf bn
  1 lt inf bn
  Air Manoeuvre
  1 AB bn
  Other
  1 sy bn
COMBAT SUPPORT
  2 arty bn
  2 engr bn
  2 MP coy
  1 CBRN coy
COMBAT SERVICE SUPPORT
  1 tpt coy
AIR DEFENCE
  2 AD bn

Reserves

FORCES BY ROLE
MANOEUVRE
  Other
  40 Home Guard bn
EQUIPMENT BY TYPE
ARMOURED FIGHTING VEHICLES
  MBT 120 *Leopard* 2A5 (Strv 122)
  IFV 396: 354 CV9040 (Strf 9040; incl CP); 42 Epbv 90 (OP)
  APC 1,083
    APC (T) 408: 258 Pbv 302; 150 BvS-10 MkII
    APC (W) 315: 34 XA-180 *Sisu* (Patgb 180); 20 XA-202 *Sisu* (Patgb 202); 148 XA-203 *Sisu* (Patgb 203); 113 Patria AMV (XA-360/Patgb 360)
  PPV 360 RG-32M
ENGINEERING & MAINTENANCE VEHICLES
  AEV 6 Pionierpanzer-3 *Kodiak* (Ingbv 120)
  ARV 40: 14 Bgbv 120; 26 Bgbv 90
  VLB 3 Brobv 120
  MW 33+: *Aardvark* Mk2; 33 Area Clearing System
ANTI-TANK/ANTI-INFRASTRUCTURE
  MSL • MANPATS NLAW; RBS-55
  RCL 84mm *Carl Gustav*
ARTILLERY 309
  SP 155mm 23 *Archer*
  MOR 286; 81mm 201 M/86; 120mm 81 M/41D SP 120mm 4 CV90 *Mjolnir* (Gkpbv 90)

AIR DEFENCE
SAM
Medium-range MIM-23B *Hawk* (RBS-97)
Short-range 8 IRIS-T SLS (RBS-98); RBS-23 BAMSE
Point-defence RBS-70
GUNS • SP 40mm 30 Lvkv 90

Navy 1,250; 850 Amphibious (total 2,100)
EQUIPMENT BY TYPE
SUBMARINE • TACTICAL • SSK 5:
  1 *Gotland* (AIP fitted) with 2 single 400mm TT with Torped 431 LWT/Torped 451 LWT, 4 single 533mm TT with Torped 613 HWT/Torped 62 HWT
  2 *Gotland* mod (AIP fitted) with 2 single 400mm TT with Torped 431 LWT/Torped 451 LWT, 4 single 533mm TT with Torped 613 HWT/Torped 62 HWT
  2 *Sodermanland* (AIP fitted) with 3 single 400mm TT with Torped 431 LWT/Torped 451 LWT, 6 single 533mm TT with Torped 613 HWT/Torped 62 HWT
PATROL AND COASTAL COMBATANTS 145
  CORVETTES • FSG 5 *Visby* with 8 RBS15 Mk2 AShM, 4 single 400mm ASTT with Torped 45 LWT, 1 57mm gun, 1 hel landing platform
  PCGT 4:
    2 *Göteborg* with 4 twin lnchr with RBS15 Mk2 AShM, 4 single 400mm ASTT with Torped 431 LWT, 1 57mm gun
    2 *Stockholm* with 4 twin lnchr with RBS15 Mk2 AShM, 4 single 400mm ASTT with Torped 431 LWT, 1 57mm gun
  PBF 128: 100+ Combat Boat 90H (capacity 18 troops); 27 Combat Boat HS (capacity 18 troops); 1 Combat Boat 90HSM (capacity 18 troops)
  PB 8 *Tapper* (Type 80)
MINE WARFARE • MINE COUNTERMEASURES 7
  MCC 5 *Koster*
  MCD 2 *Spårö* (*Styrsö* mod)
AMPHIBIOUS • LANDING CRAFT 11
  LCVP 8 *Trossbat*
  LCAC 3 *Griffon* 8100TD
LOGISTICS AND SUPPORT 15
  AG 2: 1 *Carlskrona* with 1 hel landing platform (former ML); 1 *Trosso* (spt ship for corvettes and patrol vessels but can also be used as HQ ship)
  AGF 2 *Ledningsbåt* 2000
  AGI 1 *Orion*
  AKL 1 *Loke*
  ARS 2: 1 *Belos* III; 1 *Furusund* (former ML)
  AX 5 *Altair*
  AXS 2: 1 *Falken*; 1 *Gladan*

Amphibious 850
FORCES BY ROLE
MANOEUVRE
  Amphibious
    1 amph bn
EQUIPMENT BY TYPE
ARTILLERY • MOR 81mm 12 M/86
COASTAL DEFENCE • AShM 8 RBS-17 *Hellfire*

Coastal Defence
FORCES BY ROLE
COASTAL DEFENCE
  1 AShM bty with RBS-15
EQUIPMENT BY TYPE
COASTAL DEFENCE • AShM RBS-15

Air Force 2,700
FORCES BY ROLE
FIGHTER/GROUND ATTACK/ISR
  6 sqn with JAS 39C/D *Gripen*
TRANSPORT/ISR/AEW&C
  1 sqn with C-130H *Hercules* (Tp-84); KC-130H *Hercules* (Tp-84); Gulfstream IV SRA-4 (S-102B); S-100B/D *Argus*
TRAINING
  1 unit with Sk-60
AIR DEFENCE
  1 (fighter control and air surv) bn
EQUIPMENT BY TYPE
AIRCRAFT 96 combat capable
  FGA 96 JAS 39C/D *Gripen*
  ELINT 2 Gulfstream IV SRA-4 (S-102B)
  AEW&C 3: 1 S-100B *Argus*; 2 S-100D *Argus*
  TKR 1 KC-130H *Hercules* (Tp-84)
  TPT 8: **Medium** 5 C-130H *Hercules* (Tp-84); **Light** 2 Saab 340 (OS-100A/Tp-100C); **PAX** 1 Gulfstream 550 (Tp-102D)
  TRG 67 Sk-60W
UNMANNED AERIAL VEHICLES
  ISR • Medium 8 RQ-7 *Shadow* (AUV 3 *Örnen*)
AIR-LAUNCHED MISSILES
  ASM AGM-65 *Maverick* (RB-75)
  AShM RB-15F
  AAM • IR AIM-9L *Sidewinder* (RB-74); **IIR** IRIS-T (RB-98); **ARH** AIM-120B AMRAAM (RB-99); *Meteor*
BOMBS
  Laser-Guided GBU-12 *Paveway* II
  INS/GPS guided GBU-39 Small Diameter Bomb

Armed Forces Hel Wing
FORCES BY ROLE
TRANSPORT HELICOPTER
  3 sqn with AW109 (Hkp 15A); AW109M (Hkp-15B); NH90 (Hkp-14) (SAR/ASW); UH-60M *Black Hawk* (Hkp-16)
EQUIPMENT BY TYPE
HELICOPTERS
  ASW 9 NH90 ASW (Hkp-14)
  TPT 44: **Medium** 24: 15 UH-60M *Black Hawk* (Hkp-16); 9 NH90 TTH (Hkp-14); **Light** 20: 12 AW109 (Hkp-15A); 8 AW109M (Hkp-15B)

Special Forces
FORCES BY ROLE
SPECIAL FORCES
  1 spec ops gp
COMBAT SUPPORT
  1 cbt spt gp

Other 3,500
Includes staff, logisitics and intelligence personnel
FORCES BY ROLE
COMBAT SUPPORT
1 EW bn
1 psyops unit
COMBAT SERVICE SUPPORT
2 log bn
1 maint bn
4 med coy
1 tpt coy

DEPLOYMENT

AFGHANISTAN: NATO • *Operation Resolute Support* 25
CENTRAL AFRICAN REPUBLIC: EU • EUTM RCA 9
DEMOCRATIC REPUBLIC OF THE CONGO: UN • MONUSCO 2
INDIA/PAKISTAN: UN • UNMOGIP 5
IRAQ: *Operation Inherent Resolve* 66; **NATO** NATO Mission Iraq 1
KOREA, REPUBLIC OF: NNSC • 5 obs
MALI: EU • EUTM Mali 6; **UN** • MINUSMA 240; 1 int coy
MIDDLE EAST: UN • UNTSO 5
SERBIA: NATO • KFOR 4
SOMALIA: EU • EUTM Somalia 9
SOUTH SUDAN: UN • UNMISS 2
WESTERN SAHARA: UN • MINURSO 2

Switzerland CHE

Swiss Franc fr		2018	2019	2020
GDP	fr	690bn	707bn	
	US$	706bn	715bn	
per capita	US$	83,162	83,717	
Growth	%	2.8	0.8	
Inflation	%	0.9	0.6	
Def bdgt [a]	fr	4.71bn	5.31bn	5.37bn
	US$	4.81bn	5.37bn	
US$1=fr		0.98	0.99	

[a] Includes military pensions

Real-terms defence budget trend (US$bn, constant 2015)

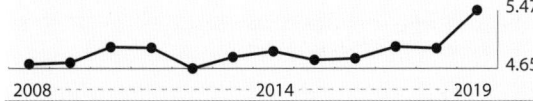

Population 8,348,737

Age	0–14	15–19	20–24	25–29	30–64	65 plus
Male	7.9%	2.6%	2.8%	3.2%	24.7%	8.2%
Female	7.4%	2.4%	2.7%	3.2%	24.6%	10.3%

Capabilities

The conscript-based armed forces are postured for territorial defence and limited participation in international peace-support operations. The government has begun to reduce its armed forces, reflecting an assessment that in the militia-based system not all personnel would realistically be available for active service. With permanent neutrality a core feature of foreign and security policy, Switzerland is not a member of any alliances, although it joined NATO's Partnership for Peace programme in 1996 and on occasion contributes to NATO- and EU-led operations alongside its engagement in UN or OSCE missions. Switzerland does not participate in combat operations for peace-enforcement purposes and its deployments are limited in size. The 2016 armed-forces development plan emphasises improvements in readiness, training and equipment, and is meant to be implemented by the end of 2022. The approach to readiness is changing to a flexible model in which different units are called up for active service gradually and on different timelines. Plans to replace F-5 *Tiger* II combat aircraft with the *Gripen* were scrapped after a national referendum rejected the proposal in May 2014. With Switzerland's air-policing capabilities diminished, in July 2018 the government relaunched its attempt to procure a new combat aircraft. The multi-stage selection process is expected to be completed by the end of 2020 and now includes replacement of the F/A-18 *Hornet*, which will be life-extended through to 2030. In spring 2019, the government declared that the life-extension programme was behind schedule, further reducing availability. The fighter-acquisition programme was capped at CHF6 billion in May 2019 and has been separated from the ground-based air-defence procurement. Previously both programmes were linked. Other priorities include upgrades to Switzerland's air-surveillance systems and transport helicopters. Switzerland's defence industry has limited design and manufacturing capabilities, with recognised capacity in the land-vehicles sector, which has links to North American companies.

ACTIVE 21,450 (Armed Forces 21,450)
Conscript liability 260–600 compulsory service days depending on rank. 18 or 23 weeks' training (depending on branch) generally at age 20, followed by 6 refresher trg courses (3 weeks each). Alternative service available

RESERVE 134,800

Civil Defence 73,000 (51,000 Reserve)

ORGANISATIONS BY SERVICE

Armed Forces 2,950 active; 18,500 conscript (21,450 total)

Operations Command 72,600 on mobilisation

4 Territorial Regions. With the exception of military police all units are non-active

FORCES BY ROLE
COMMAND
4 regional comd
SPECIAL FORCES
2 SF bn
MANOEUVRE
Armoured
2 (1st & 11th) bde (1 recce bn, 1 tk bn, 2 armd inf bn, 1 SP arty bn, 1 engr bn, 1 sigs bn)

Mechanised
1 (4th) bde (2 recce bn, 2 SP arty bn, 1 ptn br bn)
Light
10 inf bn
7 mtn inf bn
1 mtn inf unit
COMBAT SUPPORT
4 engr bn
4 MP bn
1 NBC bn
1 int unit
COMBAT SUPPORT
4 engr rescue bn
EQUIPMENT BY TYPE
ARMOURED FIGHTING VEHICLES
MBT 134 Leopard 2 (Pz-87 Leo)
IFV 186: 154 CV9030CH; 32 CV9030 (CP)
APC 914
APC (T) 238 M113A2 (incl variants)
APC (W) 676: 346 Piranha II; 330 Piranha I/II/IIIC (CP)
AUV 441 Eagle II
ENGINEERING & MAINTENANCE VEHICLES
AEV 12 Kodiak
ARV 25 Büffel
MW 46: 26 Area Clearing System; 20 M113A2
NBC VEHICLES 12 Piranha IIIC CBRN
ANTI-TANK/ANTI-INFRASTRUCTURE
MSL • SP 106 Piranha I TOW-2
ARTILLERY 433
SP 155mm 133 M109 KAWEST
MOR • 81mm 300 Mw-72
PATROL AND COASTAL COMBATANTS • PBR 11 Aquarius
AIR DEFENCE • SAM • Point-defence FIM-92 Stinger

Air Force 17,200 on mobilisation
FORCES BY ROLE
FIGHTER
3 sqn with F-5E/F Tiger II
3 sqn with F/A-18C/D Hornet
TRANSPORT
1 sqn with Beech 350 King Air; DHC-6 Twin Otter; PC-6 Turbo Porter; PC-12
1 VIP Flt with Beech 1900D; Cessna 560XL Citation; Falcon 900EX
TRAINING
1 sqn with PC-7CH Turbo Trainer; PC-21
1 sqn with PC-9 (tgt towing)
1 OCU Sqn with F-5E/F Tiger II
TRANSPORT HELICOPTER
6 sqn with AS332M Super Puma; AS532UL Cougar; H135M
ISR UAV
1 sqn with ADS 95 Ranger
EQUIPMENT BY TYPE
AIRCRAFT 56 combat capable
FTR 26: 21 F-5E Tiger II; 5 F-5F Tiger II
FGA 30: 25 F/A-18C Hornet; 5 F/A-18D Hornet
TPT 22: Light 21: 1 Beech 350 King Air; 1 Beech 1900D; 1 Cessna 560XL Citation; 1 DHC-6 Twin Otter; 15 PC-6 Turbo Porter; 1 PC-6 (owned by armasuisse, civil registration); 1 PC-12 (owned by armasuisse, civil registration); PAX 1 Falcon 900EX
TRG 41: 27 PC-7CH Turbo Trainer; 6 PC-9; 8 PC-21
HELICOPTERS
MRH 20 H135M
TPT • Medium 25: 15 AS332M Super Puma; 10 AS532UL Cougar
UNMANNED AERIAL VEHICLES
ISR • Medium 16 ADS 95 Ranger (4 systems)
AIR-LAUNCHED MISSILES • AAM • IR AIM-9P Sidewinder; IIR AIM-9X Sidewinder II; ARH AIM-120B/C-7 AMRAAM

Ground Based Air Defence (GBAD)
GBAD assets can be used to form AD clusters to be deployed independently as task forces within Swiss territory
EQUIPMENT BY TYPE
AIR DEFENCE
SAM • Point Rapier; FIM-92 Stinger
GUNS 35mm Some GDF-003/-005 with Skyguard

Armed Forces Logistic Organisation 9,650 on mobilisation
FORCES BY ROLE
COMBAT SERVICE SUPPORT
1 log bde (6 log bn; 1 tpt bn; 6 med bn)

Command Support Organisation 11,150 on mobilisation
FORCES BY ROLE
COMBAT SERVICE SUPPORT
1 spt bde

Training Command 37,350 on mobilisation
COMBAT SERVICE SUPPORT
5 trg unit

Civil Defence 73,000 (51,000 Reserve)
(not part of armed forces)

DEPLOYMENT

BOSNIA-HERZEGOVINA: EU • EUFOR • Operation Althea 21
DEMOCRATIC REPUBLIC OF THE CONGO: UN • MONUSCO 1
INDIA/PAKISTAN: UN • UNMOGIP 3
KOREA, REPUBLIC OF: NNSC • 5 officers
MALI: UN • MINUSMA 4
MIDDLE EAST: UN • UNTSO 12
SERBIA: NATO • KFOR 165 (military volunteers); 1 inf coy; 1 engr pl; 1 hel flt with AS332M Super Puma
SOUTH SUDAN: UN • UNMISS 1
WESTERN SAHARA: UN • MINURSO 1

Turkey TUR

New Turkish Lira L		2018	2019	2020
GDP	L	3.72tr	4.27tr	
	US$	771bn	744bn	
per capita	US$	9,405	8,958	
Growth	%	2.8	0.2	
Inflation	%	16.3	15.7	
Def exp [a]	L	68.3bn	79.4bn	
	US$	14.1bn	13.8bn	
Def bdgt [b]	L	40.5bn	46.6bn	
	US$	8.38bn	8.10bn	
US$1=L		4.83	5.74	

[a] NATO definition
[b] Includes funding for Undersecretariat of Defence Industries

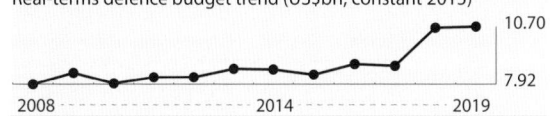
Real-terms defence budget trend (US$bn, constant 2015)

Population 81,648,103

Age	0–14	15–19	20–24	25–29	30–64	65 plus
Male	12.2%	4.1%	3.9%	3.9%	22.6%	3.6%
Female	11.6%	3.9%	3.8%	3.7%	22.2%	4.5%

Capabilities

Turkey has large, well-equipped armed forces that are primarily structured for national defence. Much recent activity has focused on internal security and cross-border operations in response to the continuing war in Syria. The Turkish Armed Forces 2033 Strategic Plan aims to modernise military equipment and the force structure. According to government officials, terrorism is the main security threat. Turkey is a NATO member and has provided access to its airspace and facilities for operations in Iraq and Syria. However, relationships with NATO allies have come under pressure as a result of Ankara's decision to procure the Russian-made S-400 air-defence system and launch offensive operations in northern Syria in October 2019. Deliveries on the S-400 contract began in 2019 and as a result the US government terminated Turkey's participation in the F-35 programme in July. Following the attempted coup in July 2016, Ankara dismissed large numbers of officers from its armed forces, with the loss of experienced personnel affecting both operational effectiveness and training levels, especially in the air force. The armed forces train regularly, including with NATO allies. Turkish statements have indicated an intention to enhance its presence in Cyprus, possibly including a naval base in the northern part of the Island. Equipment is mostly sourced from national firms. Ankara signed a contract with manufacturer BMC in 2018 for the production of a first batch of the *Altay* main battle tank, a much delayed project, and prototype testing is scheduled to begin in 2020. Turkey is also developing a domestic fighter aircraft but is dependent on collaboration with external defence companies for the implementation of this project. Under new laws, the president has authority over defence procurement and control over Turkey's top defence companies. Turkey has signed defence cooperation agreements with a focus on exports and technology transfer, in an effort to boost its national defence industry and achieve defence-industrial autonomy.

ACTIVE 355,200 (Army 260,200 Navy 45,000 Air 50,000) **Paramilitary 156,800**
Conscript liability 12 months (5.5 months for university graduates; 21 days for graduates with exemption) (reducing to 6 months)

RESERVE 378,700 (Army 258,700 Navy 55,000 Air 65,000)
Reserve service to age 41 for all services

ORGANISATIONS BY SERVICE

Space
EQUIPMENT BY TYPE
SATELLITES • ISR 2 *Gokturk*-1/2

Army ε260,200 (including conscripts)
FORCES BY ROLE
COMMAND
 4 army HQ
 9 corps HQ
SPECIAL FORCES
 8 cdo bde
 1 mtn cdo bde
 1 cdo regt
MANOEUVRE
 Armoured
 1 (52nd) armd div (2 armd bde, 1 mech bde)
 7 armd bde
 Mechanised
 2 (28th & 29th) mech div
 14 mech inf bde
 Light
 1 (23rd) mot inf div (3 mot inf regt)
 7 mot inf bde
COMBAT SUPPORT
 2 arty bde
 1 trg arty bde
 6 arty regt
 2 engr regt
AVIATION
 4 avn regt
 4 avn bn
EQUIPMENT BY TYPE
ARMOURED FIGHTING VEHICLES
 MBT 2,379: 316 *Leopard* 2A4; 170 *Leopard* 1A4; 227 *Leopard* 1A3; 100 M60A1; 650 M60A3; 166 M60T; 750 M48A5 T2 (2,000 M48A5 T1 in store)
 RECCE ε250 *Akrep*
 IFV 645 ACV AIFV
 APC 5,196
  APC (T) 3,636: 823 ACV AAPC; 2,813 M113/M113A1/M113A2
  PPV 1,560: 360 *Edjer Yaclin* 4×4; ε650 *Kirpi*; 320 *Kirpi*-2; 230 *Vuran*
 AUV 882: 800+ *Cobra*; 82 *Cobra* II
ENGINEERING & MAINTENANCE VEHICLES
 AEV 12+: AZMIM; 12 M48; M113A2T2
 ARV 150: 12 *Leopard* 1; 105 M48T5; 33 M88A1
 VLB 88: 36 *Leguan*; 52 Mobile Floating Assault Bridge
 MW 4+: 4 *Husky* 2G; *Tamkar*; *Bozena*

ANTI-TANK/ANTI-INFRASTRUCTURE
  MSL
    SP 365 ACV TOW
    MANPATS 9K135 Kornet-E (AT-14 Spriggan); Eryx; FGM-148 Javelin; Milan
  RCL 106mm M40A1
ARTILLERY 7,833+
  SP 1,080: **155mm** 825: ε150 M44T1; 365 M52T (mod); ε310 T-155 Firtina; **175mm** 36 M107; **203mm** 219 M110A2
  TOWED 794+: **105mm** 75+ M101A1; **155mm** 557: 517 M114A1/M114A2; 40 Panter; **203mm** 162 M115
  MRL 146+: **107mm** 48; **122mm** ε36 T-122; **227mm** 12 M270 MLRS; **302mm** 50+ TR-300 Kasirga (WS-1)
  MOR 5,813+
    SP 1,443+: **81mm**; **107mm** 1,264 M106; **120mm** 179
    TOWED 4,370: **81mm** 3,792; **120mm** 578
SURFACE-TO-SURFACE MISSILE LAUNCHERS
  SRBM • **Conventional** Bora; MGM-140A ATACMS (launched from M270 MLRS); J-600T Yildrim (B-611/CH-SS-9 mod 1)
AIRCRAFT
  ISR 5 Beech 350 King Air
  TPT • **Light** 8: 5 Beech 200 King Air; 3 Cessna 421
  TRG 49: 45 Cessna T182; 4 T-42A Cochise
HELICOPTERS
  ATK 86: 18 AH-1P Cobra; 12 AH-1S Cobra; 5 AH-1W Cobra; 4 TAH-1P Cobra; 9 T129A; 38 T129B
  MRH 28 Hughes 300C
  TPT 227+: **Heavy** 11 CH-47F Chinook; **Medium** 77+: 29 AS532UL Cougar; 48+ S-70A Black Hawk; **Light** 139: 12 Bell 204B (AB-204B); ε43 Bell 205 (UH-1H Iroquois); 64 Bell 205A (AB-205A); 20 Bell 206 Jet Ranger
UNMANNED AERIAL VEHICLES
  CISR • **Medium** 33 Bayraktar TB2
  ISR • **Heavy** Falcon 600/Firebee; **Medium** CL-89; Gnat; **Light** Harpy
AIR DEFENCE
  SAM • **Point-defence** 148+: 70 Altigan PMADS octuple Stinger lnchr, 78 Zipkin PMADS quad Stinger lnchr; FIM-92 Stinger
  GUNS 1,664
    SP 35mm 13+ Korkut
    TOWED 1,362: **20mm** 439 GAI-D01/Rh-202; **35mm** 120 GDF-001/-003; **40mm** 803 L/60/L/70
AIR-LAUNCHED MISSILES
  ASM Mizrak-U (UMTAS)
BOMBS
  Laser-guided MAM-L; MAM-C

Navy ε45,000 (including conscripts)
EQUIPMENT BY TYPE
SUBMARINES • **TACTICAL** • **SSK** 12:
  4 Atilay (GER Type-209/1200) with 8 single 533mm ASTT with SST-4 HWT
  4 Preveze (GER Type-209/1400) (MLU ongoing) with 8 single 533mm ASTT with UGM-84 Harpoon AShM/Mk 24 Tigerfish mod 2 HWT/SeaHake mod 4 (DM2A4) HWT
  4 Gür (GER Type-209/1400) with 8 single 533mm ASTT with UGM-84 Harpoon AShM/Mk 24 Tigerfish mod 2 HWT/SeaHake mod 4 (DM2A4) HWT
PRINCIPAL SURFACE COMBATANTS 20
  FRIGATES • **FFGHM** 20:
    4 Barbaros (mod GER MEKO 200) with 2 quad lnchr with RGM-84C Harpoon Block 1B AShM, 2 8-cell Mk 41 VLS with RIM-162B ESSM SAM, 2 SVTT Mk 32 triple 324mm ASTT with Mk 46 LWT, 3 Sea Zenith CIWS, 1 127mm gun (capacity 1 Bell 212 (AB-212) hel)
    4 Gabya (ex-US Oliver Hazard Perry class) with 1 Mk 13 GMLS with RGM-84C Harpoon Block 1B AShM/SM-1MR Block VI SAM, 1 8-cell Mk 41 VLS with RIM-162B ESSM SAM, 2 SVTT Mk 32 triple 324mm ASTT with Mk 46 LWT, 1 Mk 15 Phalanx Block 1B CIWS, 1 76mm gun (capacity 1 S-70B Seahawk/AB-212 ASW hel)
    4 Gabya (ex-US Oliver Hazard Perry class) with 1 Mk 13 GMLS with RGM-84C Harpoon Block 1B AShM/SM-1MR Block VI SAM, 2 SVTT Mk 32 triple 324mm ASTT with Mk 46 LWT, 1 Mk 15 Phalanx Block 1B CIWS, 1 76mm gun (capacity 1 S-70B Seahawk/AB-212 ASW hel)
    4 Yavuz (GER MEKO 200TN) with 2 quad lnchr with RGM-84C Harpoon Block 1B AShM, 1 octuple Mk 29 GMLS with RIM-7M Sea Sparrow SAM, 2 SVTT Mk 32 triple 324mm ASTT with Mk 46 LWT, 3 Sea Zenith CIWS, 1 127mm gun (capacity 1 Bell 212 (AB-212) hel)
    4 Ada with 2 quad lnchr with RGM-84C Harpoon Block 1B AShM, 1 Mk 49 21-cell lnchr with RIM-116 SAM, 2 SVTT Mk 32 twin 324mm ASTT with Mk 46 LWT, 1 76mm gun (capacity 1 S-70B Seahawk hel)
PATROL AND COASTAL COMBATANTS 41:
  CORVETTES • **FSGM** 6:
    6 Burak (ex-FRA d'Estienne d'Orves) with 2 single lnchr with MM38 Exocet AShM, 4 single 324mm ASTT with Mk 46 LWT, 1 Creusot-Loire Mk 54 A/S mor, 1 100mm gun
  PCFG 19:
    4 Dogan (GER Lurssen-57) with 2 quad lnchr with RGM-84C Harpoon Block 1B AShM, 1 76mm gun
    9 Kilic with 2 quad lnchr with RGM-84C Harpoon Block 1B AShM, 1 76mm gun
    4 Rüzgar (GER Lurssen-57) with 2 quad lnchr with RGM-84C Harpoon Block 1B AShM, 1 76mm gun
    2 Yildiz with 2 quad lnchr with RGM-84C Harpoon Block 1B AShM, 1 76mm gun
  PCC 16 Tuzla
MINE WARFARE • **MINE COUNTERMEASURES** 15:
  MHO 11: 5 Engin (FRA Circe); 6 Aydin
  MSC 4 Seydi (US Adjutant)
AMPHIBIOUS
  LANDING SHIPS • **LST** 5:
    2 Bayraktar with 2 Mk 15 Phalanx Block 1B CIWS, 1 hel landing platform (capacity 20 MBT; 250 troops)
    1 Osman Gazi with 1 Mk 15 Phalanx CIWS (capacity 4 LCVP; 17 tanks; 980 troops) (with 1 hel landing platform)

2 *Sarucabey* with 1 Mk 15 *Phalanx* CIWS (capacity 11 tanks; 600 troops) (with 1 hel landing platform)
LANDING CRAFT 30
  LCT 21: 2 C-120/130; 11 C-140; 8 C-151
  LCM 9: 1 C-310; 8 LCM 8
LOGISTICS AND SUPPORT 35
  ABU 2: 1 AG5; 1 AG6 with 1 76mm gun
  AGS 2: 1 *Cesme* (ex-US *Silas Bent*); 1 *Cubuklu*
  AOR 2 *Akar* with 1 Mk 15 *Phalanx* CIWS, 1 hel landing platform
  AOT 2 *Burak*
  AOL 1 *Gurcan*
  AP 1 *Iskenderun*
  ASR 3: 1 *Alemdar* with 1 hel landing platform; 2 *Isin* II
  ATF 9: 1 *Akbas*; 1 *Degirmendere*; 1 *Gazal*; 1 *Inebolu*; 5 *Onder*
  AWT 3 *Sogut*
  AXL 8
  AX 2 *Pasa* (ex-GER *Rhein*)

Marines 3,000
FORCES BY ROLE
MANOEUVRE
  Amphibious
    1 mne bde (3 mne bn; 1 arty bn)

Naval Aviation
FORCES BY ROLE
ANTI-SUBMARINE WARFARE
  2 sqn with Bell 212 ASW (AB-212 ASW); S-70B *Seahawk*
  1 sqn with ATR-72-600; CN235M-100; TB-20 *Trinidad*
EQUIPMENT BY TYPE
AIRCRAFT 4 combat capable
  ASW 4 ATR-72-600
  MP 6 CN235M-100
  TPT • **Light** 7: 2 ATR-72-600; 5 TB-20 *Trinidad*
HELICOPTERS
  ASW 29: 11 Bell 212 ASW (AB-212 ASW); 18 S-70B *Seahawk*
UNMANNED AERIAL VEHICLES 7
  CISR 7: **Heavy** 3 ANKA-S; **Medium** 4 *Bayraktar* TB2

Air Force ε50,000
2 tac air forces (divided between east and west)
FORCES BY ROLE
FIGHTER/GROUND ATTACK
  1 sqn with F-4E *Phantom* 2020
  8 sqn with F-16C/D *Fighting Falcon*
ISR
  1 sqn with F-16C/D *Fighting Falcon*
  1 unit with *King Air* 350
AIRBORNE EARLY WARNING & CONTROL
  1 sqn (forming) with B-737 AEW&C
EW
  1 unit with CN235M EW
SEARCH & RESCUE
  1 sqn with AS532AL/UL *Cougar*
TANKER
  1 sqn with KC-135R *Stratotanker*
TRANSPORT
  1 sqn with A400M; C-160D *Transall*
  1 sqn with C-130B/E/H *Hercules*
  1 (VIP) sqn with Cessna 550 *Citation* II (UC-35); Cessna 650 *Citation* VII; CN235M; Gulfstream 550
  3 sqn with CN235M
  10 (liaison) flt with Bell 205 (UH-1H *Iroquois*); CN235M
TRAINING
  1 sqn with F-16C/D *Fighting Falcon*
  1 sqn with F-5A/B *Freedom Fighter*; NF-5A/B *Freedom Fighter*
  1 sqn with SF-260D
  1 sqn with KT-1T
  1 sqn with T-38A/M *Talon*
  1 sqn with T-41D *Mescalero*
AIR DEFENCE
  4 bn with S-400 (SA-21 *Growler*)
  4 sqn with MIM-14 *Nike Hercules*
  2 sqn with *Rapier*
  8 (firing) unit with MIM-23 *Hawk*
MANOEUVRE
  Air Manoeuvre
    1 AB bde

EQUIPMENT BY TYPE
AIRCRAFT 310 combat capable
  FTR 27: 17 NF-5A *Freedom Fighter*; 10 NF-5B *Freedom Fighter* (48 F-5s being upgraded as LIFT)
  FGA 283: 19 F-4E *Phantom* 2020; 27 F-16C *Fighting Falcon* Block 30; 162 F-16C *Fighting Falcon* Block 50; 14 F-16C *Fighting Falcon* Block 50+; 8 F-16D Block 30 *Fighting Falcon*; 33 F-16D *Fighting Falcon* Block 50; 16 F-16D *Fighting Falcon* Block 50+; 4 F-35A *Lightning* II (in US)
  ISR 6: 5 Beech 350 *King Air*; 1 C-160D *Transall*
  EW 2+ CN235M EW
  AEW&C 4 B-737 AEW&C
  TKR 7 KC-135R *Stratotanker*
  TPT 90: **Heavy** 9 A400M; **Medium** 31: 6 C-130B *Hercules*; 12 C-130E *Hercules*; 1 C-130H *Hercules*; 12 C-160D *Transall*; **Light** 49: 2 Cessna 550 *Citation* II (UC-35 - VIP); 2 Cessna 650 *Citation* VII; 45 CN235M; **PAX** 1 Gulfstream 550
  TRG 168: 33 SF-260D; 70 T-38A/M *Talon*; 25 T-41D *Mescalero*; 40 KT-1T
HELICOPTERS
  TPT 35: **Medium** 20: 6 AS532AL *Cougar* (CSAR); 14 AS532UL *Cougar* (SAR); **Light** 15 Bell 205 (UH-1H *Iroquois*)
UNMANNED AERIAL VEHICLES 35+
  CISR • **Heavy** 14 ANKA-S
  ISR 27+: **Heavy** 9+: some ANKA; 9 *Heron*; **Medium** 18 *Gnat* 750
AIR DEFENCE
  SAM
    Long-range MIM-14 *Nike Hercules*; 32 S-400 (SA-21 *Growler*)
    Medium-range MIM-23 *Hawk*
    Point-defence *Rapier*
AIR-LAUNCHED MISSILES
  AAM • **IR** AIM-9S *Sidewinder*; *Shafrir* 2(‡); **IIR** AIM-9X *Sidewinder* II; **SARH** AIM-7E *Sparrow*; **ARH** AIM-120A/B AMRAAM

ARM AGM-88A HARM
   ASM AGM-65A/G *Maverick; Popeye* I
   LACM Coventional AGM-84K SLAM-ER
BOMBS
   Electro-optical guided GBU-8B HOBOS (GBU-15)
   INS/GPS guided AGM-154A JSOW; AGM-154C JSOW
   Laser-guided MAM-C; MAM-L; *Paveway* I; *Paveway* II

Paramilitary 156,800

Gendarmerie 152,100
Ministry of Interior; Ministry of Defence in war
FORCES BY ROLE
SPECIAL FORCES
   1 cdo bde
MANOEUVRE
   Other
   1 (border) paramilitary div
   2 paramilitary bde
EQUIPMENT BY TYPE
ARMOURED FIGHTING VEHICLES
   RECCE *Akrep*
   APC 560+
      APC (W) 560: 535 BTR-60/BTR-80; 25 *Condor*
      PPV *Edjer Yaclin* 4×4; *Kirpi*
   AUV *Cobra; Cobra* II
AIRCRAFT
   ISR Some O-1E *Bird Dog*
   TPT • Light 2 Do-28D
HELICOPTERS
   ATK 6 T129B
   MRH 19 Mi-17 *Hip* H
   TPT 35: Medium 12 S-70A *Black Hawk*; Light 23: 8 Bell 204B (AB-204B); 6 Bell 205A (AB-205A); 8 Bell 206A (AB-206A) *Jet Ranger*; 1 Bell 212 (AB-212)
UNMANNED AERIAL VEHICLES
   CISR 16: Heavy 4 *Anka*-S; Medium 12 *Bayraktar* TB2
BOMBS
   Laser-guided MAM-L; MAM-C

Coast Guard 4,700
EQUIPMENT BY TYPE
PATROL AND COASTAL COMBATANTS 104
   PSOH 4 *Dost*
   PBF 60
   PB 40
AIRCRAFT • MP 3 CN235 MPA
HELICOPTERS • MRH 8 Bell 412EP (AB-412EP – SAR)

DEPLOYMENT

AFGHANISTAN: NATO • *Operation Resolute Support* 579; 1 mot inf bn(-)

BLACK SEA: NATO • SNMCMG 2: 1 MHO

BOSNIA-HERZEGOVINA: EU • EUFOR • *Operation Althea* 249; 1 inf coy

CYPRUS (NORTHERN): ε33,800; 1 army corps HQ; 1 SF regt; 1 armd bde; 2 mech inf div; 1 mech inf regt; 1 arty regt; 1 avn comd; 287 M48A5T2; 147 ACV AIFV; 106 ACV AAPC (incl variants); 386 M113 (incl variants); 36 M101A1; 36 M114A2; 12 M115; 30 M44T; 144 M52T1; 9 T-122; 171 81mm mor; 70 M30; 135 HY-12; *Milan*; 60 ACV TOW; 219 M40A1; FIM-92 *Stinger*; 44 Rh 202; 78 GAI-D01; 16 GDF-003; 3 Cessna 185 (U-17); 2 AS532UL *Cougar*; 1 Bell 205 (UH-1H *Iroquois*); 1 PB

IRAQ: Army: 1,000; 1 cdo unit; NATO • NATO Mission Iraq up to 30

LEBANON: UN • UNIFIL 85; 1 PCFG

MEDITERRANEAN SEA: NATO • SNMG 2: 1 FFGHM

QATAR: Army: 300 (trg team); 1 mech inf coy; 1 arty unit; 12+ ACV AIFV/AAPC; 2 T-155 *Firtina*

SERBIA: NATO • KFOR 244; 1 inf coy
UN • UNMIK 1

SOMALIA: 200 (trg team); UN • UNSOM 1

SYRIA: ε1,000; some cdo units; 2 armd BG; 1 SAM unit; 1 gendarmerie unit

FOREIGN FORCES

Italy *Active Fence*: 130; 1 SAM bty with SAMP/T
Spain *Active Fence*: 149; 1 SAM bty with MIM-104C *Patriot* PAC-2
United States US European Command: 1,700; 1 tkr sqn with 14 KC-135; 1 ELINT flt with EP-3E *Aries* II; 1 spt facility at Izmir; 1 spt facility at Ankara; 1 air base at Incirlik • US Strategic Command: 1 AN/TPY-2 X-band radar at Kürecik

United Kingdom UK

British Pound £		2018	2019	2020
GDP	£	2.12tr	2.18tr	
	US$	2.83tr	2.74tr	
per capita	US$	42,580	41,030	
Growth	%	1.4	1.2	
Inflation	%	2.5	1.8	
Def exp [a]	£	45.2bn	46.9bn	
	US$	60.4bn	58.8bn	
Def bdgt [b]	£	41.9bn	ε43.6bn	
	US$	56.0bn	ε54.8bn	
US$1=£		0.75	0.80	

[a] NATO definition

[b] Includes total departmental expenditure limits; costs of military operations; and external income earned by the MoD

Real-terms defence budget trend (US$bn, constant 2015)

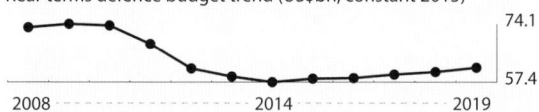

Population	65,436,510					
Age	0–14	15–19	20–24	25–29	30–64	65 plus
Male	9.0%	2.8%	3.1%	3.5%	23.1%	8.2%
Female	8.6%	2.7%	3.0%	3.3%	22.5%	10.1%

Capabilities

The 2018 National Security Capability Review highlighted a range of security challenges, including state-based threats and terrorism. UK defence policy is based on using the armed forces to reduce direct threats by projecting stability abroad. Principal defence priorities are counter-terrorism and contributing to the counter-ISIS coalition and NATO tasks, including in Afghanistan and in Eastern Europe. Joint Forces Command comprises key joint force elements, such as special-forces and military cyber capabilities. It is to be upgraded to become 'Strategic Command'. Britain retains well-trained, rapidly deployable armed forces with a wide range of capabilities, combat ethos and sufficient strategic lift to deploy forces for small- and medium-scale operations. A Modernising Defence Programme reported in late 2018, promising extra investment in modernisation and advanced technology. Equipment modernisation continues, but the defence budget is under pressure because of the fall in the value of the pound, cost growth of major equipment programmes and the difficulty of achieving savings targets. A defence-budget increase announced in September 2019 will alleviate, but not eliminate, these risks to the delivery of the modernised 'Joint Force 2025'. The US is the country's closest military ally. There is also a close intelligence relationship with the 'Five Eyes' nations and a growing military partnership with France. The UK has decided to retain military forces in Germany and leads the Combined Joint Expeditionary Force partnership. There is a naval base in Bahrain and a training and logistics base in Oman. The UK continues to support the FPDA in Southeast Asia. Expeditionary logistic capability meets policy requirements, but peacetime logistic support within the UK is dependent on contractors. The country's sophisticated defence industry is a world leader in defence exports but cannot meet all of the UK's requirements.

ACTIVE 148,450 (Army 83,500 Navy 32,450 Air 32,500)

RESERVE 79,800 (Regular Reserve 43,150 (Army 29,450, Navy 6,100, Air 7,600); Volunteer Reserve 34,600 (Army 27,450, Navy 3,900, Air 3,250); Sponsored Reserve 2,050)

Includes both trained and those currently under training within the Regular Forces, excluding university cadet units

ORGANISATIONS BY SERVICE

Strategic Forces 1,000

Royal Navy
EQUIPMENT BY TYPE
SUBMARINES • STRATEGIC • SSBN 4:
  4 *Vanguard* with 16 UGM-133A *Trident* II D-5/D-5LE nuclear SLBM, 4 533mm TT with *Spearfish* HWT (each boat will not deploy with more than 40 warheads, but each missile could carry up to 12 MIRV; some *Trident* D-5 capable of being configured for sub-strategic role)
MSL • SLBM • Nuclear 48 UGM-133A *Trident* II D-5 (fewer than 160 declared operational warheads)

Royal Air Force
EQUIPMENT BY TYPE
RADAR • STRATEGIC 1 Ballistic Missile Early Warning System (BMEWS) at Fylingdales Moor

Space
EQUIPMENT BY TYPE
SATELLITES • COMMUNICATIONS 8: 1 NATO-4B; 3 *Skynet*-4; 4 *Skynet*-5

Army 80,400; 3,100 Gurkhas (total 83,500)

Regt normally bn size. Many cbt spt and CSS regt and bn have reservist sub-units

FORCES BY ROLE
COMMAND
  1 (ARRC) corps HQ
MANOEUVRE
  Armoured
  1 (3rd) armd div (3 armd inf bde (1 armd recce regt, 1 tk regt, 2 armd inf bn, 1 mech inf bn); 1 arty bde (2 SP arty regt, 1 MRL regt, 2 fd arty regt); 3 cbt engr regt; 1 sigs regt; 1 log bde (3 MP regt; 5 log regt; 3 maint regt; 3 med regt); 2 AD regt)
  Light
  1 (1st) lt inf div (2 (4th & 51st) inf bde (1 recce regt, 1 lt mech inf bn; 1 lt inf bn); 1 (7th) inf bde (1 recce regt, 3 lt inf bn); 1 (11th) inf bde (2 lt inf bn); 1 engr bde (1 cbt engr regt, 1 CBRN regt, 2 EOD regt, 1 (MWD) EOD search regt, 1 engr regt, 1 (air spt) engr regt, 1 log regt); 1 log bde (2 log regt; 2 maint bn; 1 med regt); 1 log bde (3 log regt; 1 maint regt); 1 med bde (3 fd hospital))

1 (38th) inf bde (1 lt inf bn)
1 (160th) inf bde (2 lt inf bn)
2 inf bn (London)
1 inf bn (Brunei)
Air Manoeuvre
1 (16th) air aslt bde (1 recce pl, 2 para bn, 1 air aslt bn, 1 fd arty regt, 1 cbt engr regt, 1 log regt, 1 med regt)
COMBAT SUPPORT
1 (6th) cbt spt div (1 (Spec Inf Gp) inf bde(-) (5 inf bn(-)); 1 ISR bde (1 STA regt, 1 EW regt, 3 int bn, 1 ISR UAV regt); 1 (77th) info ops bde (3 info ops gp, 1 spt gp, 1 engr spt/log gp) 1 sigs bde (6 sigs regt); 1 sigs bde (2 sigs regt; 1 (ARRC) sigs bn)
1 (geographic) engr regt

Reserves

Army Reserve 27,450 reservists

The Army Reserve (AR) generates individuals, sub-units and some full units. The majority of units are subordinate to regular-formation headquarters and paired with one or more regular units

FORCES BY ROLE
MANOEUVRE
  Reconnaissance
  3 recce regt
  Armoured
  1 armd regt
  Light
  15 lt inf bn
  Air Manoeuvre
  1 para bn
COMBAT SUPPORT
  3 arty regt
  1 STA regt
  1 MRL regt
  3 engr regt
  1 EOD regt
  4 int bn
  4 sigs regt
COMBAT SERVICE SUPPORT
  11 log regt
  3 maint regt
  3 med regt
  9 fd hospital
AIR DEFENCE
  1 AD regt
EQUIPMENT BY TYPE
ARMOURED FIGHTING VEHICLES
  MBT 227 *Challenger* 2
  RECCE 616: 3 *Ajax* (in test); 197 *Jackal*; 110 *Jackal* 2; 130 *Jackal* 2A; 145 FV107 *Scimitar*; 31 *Scimitar* Mk2
  IFV 388+: 388 FV510 *Warrior*; FV511 *Warrior* (CP); FV514 *Warrior* (OP); FV515 *Warrior* (CP)
  APC 809
    APC (T) 413: 3 *Ares* (in test); 1 *Athena* (CP – in test); 409 FV430 *Bulldog* (incl variants)
    PPV 396 *Mastiff* (6×6)

  AUV 1,262: 399 *Foxhound*; 252 FV103 *Spartan* (incl variants); 23 *Spartan* Mk2 (incl variants); 396 *Panther* CLV; 168 *Ridgback*
ENGINEERING & MAINTENANCE VEHICLES
  AEV 92: 60 *Terrier*; 32 *Trojan*
  ARV 286: 1 *Apollo* (in test); 1 *Atlas* (in test); 80 *Challenger* ARRV; 30 FV106 *Samson*; 28 *Samson* Mk2; 105 FV512 *Warrior*; 41 FV513 *Warrior*
  MW 64 *Aardvark*
  VLB 70: 37 M3; 33 *Titan*
NBC VEHICLES 8 TPz-1 *Fuchs* NBC
ANTI-TANK/ANTI-INFRASTRUCTURE • MSL
  SP *Exactor*-2 (*Spike* NLOS)
  MANPATS FGM-148 *Javelin*; NLAW
ARTILLERY 598
  SP 155mm 89 AS90
  TOWED 105mm 114 L118 Light Gun
  MRL 227mm 35 M270B1 MLRS
  MOR 81mm 360 L16A1
AMPHIBIOUS • LCM 3 Ramped Craft Logistic
AIR DEFENCE • SAM
  Point-defence 74: 60 FV4333 *Stormer* with *Starstreak*; 14 *Rapier* FSC; *Starstreak* (LML)

Joint Helicopter Command

Tri-service joint organisation including Royal Navy, Army and RAF units

Army

FORCES BY ROLE
ISR
  1 regt (1 sqn with SA341B *Gazelle* AH1)
ATTACK HELICOPTER
  1 regt (2 sqn with AH-64D *Apache*; 1 trg sqn with AH-64D *Apache*)
  1 regt (2 sqn with AH-64D *Apache*)
HELICOPTER
  1 regt (2 sqn with AW159 *Wildcat* AH1; 1 trg sqn with AW159 *Wildcat* AH1)
  1 (spec ops) sqn with AS365N3; SA341B *Gazelle* AH1
  1 flt with Bell 212 (Brunei)
  1 flt with SA341B *Gazelle* AH1 (Canada)
TRAINING
  1 hel regt (1 sqn with AH-64D *Apache*; 1 sqn with AS350B *Ecureuil*; 1 sqn with Bell 212; *Lynx* AH9A; SA341B *Gazelle* AH1)
ISR UAV
  1 ISR UAV regt
COMBAT SERVICE SUPPORT
  1 maint regt

Army Reserve

FORCES BY ROLE
HELICOPTER
  1 hel regt (4 sqn personnel only)

Royal Navy
FORCES BY ROLE
ATTACK HELICOPTER
1 lt sqn with AW159 *Wildcat* AH1
TRANSPORT HELICOPTER
2 sqn with AW101 *Merlin* HC3/3A/3i

Royal Air Force
FORCES BY ROLE
TRANSPORT HELICOPTER
3 sqn with CH-47D/SD/F *Chinook* HC3/4/4A/6
2 sqn with SA330 *Puma* HC2
TRAINING
1 OCU sqn with CH-47D/SD/F *Chinook* HC3/4/4A/6; SA330 *Puma* HC2
EQUIPMENT BY TYPE
AIRCRAFT • TPT • Light 12:
HELICOPTERS
  ATK 50 AH-64D *Apache*
  MRH 66: 5 AS365N3; 34 AW159 *Wildcat* AH1; 27 SA341B *Gazelle* AH1
  TPT 122: **Heavy** 60: 38 CH-47D *Chinook* HC4/4A; 7 CH-47SD *Chinook* HC3; 1 CH-47SD *Chinook* HC5; 14 CH-47F *Chinook* HC6; **Medium** 48: 25 AW101 *Merlin* HC3/3A/3i; 23 SA330 *Puma* HC2; **Light** 14: 9 AS350B *Ecureuil*; 5 Bell 212
UNMANNED AERIAL VEHICLES • ISR • Medium 7 *Watchkeeper* (37+ more in store)

Royal Navy 32,450
EQUIPMENT BY TYPE
SUBMARINES 10
  STRATEGIC • SSBN 4:
    4 *Vanguard*, opcon Strategic Forces with 16 UGM-133A *Trident* II D-5/D-5LE nuclear SLBM, 4 single 533mm TT with *Spearfish* HWT (each boat will not deploy with more than 40 warheads, but each missile could carry up to 12 MIRV; some *Trident* D-5 capable of being configured for sub-strategic role)
  TACTICAL • SSN 6:
    3 *Trafalgar* with 5 single 533mm TT with UGM-109E *Tomahawk* Block IV LACM/*Spearfish* HWT
    3 *Astute* with 6 single 533mm TT with UGM-109E *Tomahawk* Block IV LACM/*Spearfish* HWT
PRINCIPAL SURFACE COMBATANTS 20
  AIRCRAFT CARRIERS • CV 1
    1 *Queen Elizabeth* (to be fitted with 3 Mk 15 *Phalanx* Block 1B CIWS) (future capacity 24 F-35B *Lightning* II, 14 *Merlin* HM2/*Wildcat* HMA2/CH-47 *Chinook* hel) (in trials; second of class to commission Dec 2019)
  DESTROYERS 6
    DDGHM 3 *Daring* (Type-45) with 2 quad lnchr with RGM-84D *Harpoon* Block 1C AShM, 6 8-cell *Sylver* A50 VLS with *Aster* 15/30 (*Sea Viper*) SAM, 2 Mk 15 *Phalanx* Block 1B CIWS, 1 114mm gun (capacity 1 AW159 *Wildcat*/AW101 *Merlin* hel)
    DDHM 3 *Daring* (Type-45) with 6 8-cell *Sylver* A50 VLS with *Aster* 15/30 (*Sea Viper*) SAM, 2 Mk 15 *Phalanx* Block 1B CIWS, 1 114mm gun (capacity 1 AW159 *Wildcat*/AW101 *Merlin* hel)
  FRIGATES • FFGHM 13:
    8 *Duke* (Type-23) with 2 quad lnchr with RGM-84D *Harpoon* Block 1C AShM, 1 32-cell VLS with *Sea Wolf* SAM, 2 twin 324mm ASTT with *Sting Ray* LWT, 1 114mm gun (capacity either 2 AW159 *Wildcat* or 1 AW101 *Merlin* hel)
    5 *Duke* (Type-23) with 2 quad lnchr with RGM-84D *Harpoon* Block 1C AShM, 1 32-cell VLS with *Sea Ceptor* SAM, 2 twin 324mm ASTT with *Sting Ray* LWT, 1 114mm gun (capacity either 2 AW159 *Wildcat* or 1 AW101 *Merlin* hel)
PATROL AND COASTAL COMBATANTS 23
  PSO 5: 2 *River* Batch 1; 1 *River* Batch 1 (mod) with 1 hel landing platform; 2 *River* Batch 2 with 1 hel landing platform
  PBI 18: 16 *Archer* (trg); 2 *Scimitar*
MINE WARFARE • MINE COUNTERMEASURES 13
  MCO 6 *Hunt* (incl 4 mod *Hunt*)
  MHC 7 *Sandown* (1 additional decommissioned and used in trg role)
AMPHIBIOUS
  PRINCIPAL AMPHIBIOUS SHIPS 2
    LPD 2 *Albion* with 2 Mk 15 *Phalanx* Block 1B CIWS (capacity 2 med hel; 4 LCU or 2 LCAC; 4 LCVP; 6 MBT; 300 troops) (of which 1 at extended readiness)
LOGISTICS AND SUPPORT 4
  AGB 1 *Protector* with 1 hel landing platform
  AGS 3: 1 *Scott*; 2 *Echo* (all with 1 hel landing platform)

Royal Fleet Auxiliary
Support and miscellaneous vessels are mostly manned and maintained by the Royal Fleet Auxiliary (RFA), a civilian fleet owned by the UK MoD, which has approximately 1,900 personnel with type comd under Fleet Commander
AMPHIBIOUS • PRINCIPAL AMPHIBIOUS SHIPS 3
  LSD 3 *Bay* (capacity 4 LCU; 2 LCVP; 24 CR2 *Challenger* 2 MBT; 350 troops)
LOGISTICS AND SUPPORT 14
  AOEH 4 *Tide* (capacity 1 AW159 *Wildcat*/AW101 *Merlin* hel)
  AORH 3: 2 *Wave*; 1 *Fort Victoria* with 2 Mk 15 *Phalanx* Block 1B CIWS
  AFSH 2 *Fort Rosalie*
  AG 1 *Argus* (aviation trg ship with secondary role as primarily casualty-receiving ship)
  AKR 4 *Point* (not RFA manned)

Naval Aviation (Fleet Air Arm) 4,900
FORCES BY ROLE
ANTI-SUBMARINE WARFARE
3 sqn with AW101 ASW *Merlin* HM2
2 sqn with AW159 *Wildcat* HMA2

AIRBORNE EARLY WARNING
1 sqn with Merlin HM2 Crowsnest (forming)
TRAINING
1 sqn with Beech 350ER King Air
1 sqn with G-115
1 sqn with Hawk T1
EQUIPMENT BY TYPE
AIRCRAFT
TPT • Light 4 Beech 350ER King Air (Avenger)
TRG 17: 5 G-115; 12 Hawk T1
HELICOPTERS
ASW 58: 28 AW159 Wildcat HMA2; 30 AW101 ASW Merlin HM2

Royal Marines 6,600
FORCES BY ROLE
MANOEUVRE
Amphibious
1 (3rd Cdo) mne bde (2 mne bn; 2 sy bn; 1 amph aslt sqn; 1 (army) arty regt; 1 (army) engr regt; 1 ISR gp (1 EW sqn; 1 cbt spt sqn; 1 sigs sqn; 1 log sqn), 1 log regt)
1 landing craft sqn opcon Royal Navy
EQUIPMENT BY TYPE
ARMOURED FIGHTING VEHICLES
APC (T) 99 BvS-10 Mk2 Viking
ANTI-TANK/ANTI-INFRASTRUCTURE
MSL • MANPATS FGM-148 Javelin
ARTILLERY 39
TOWED 105mm 12 L118 Light Gun
MOR 81mm 27 L16A1
PATROL AND COASTAL COMBATANTS • PB 2
Island
AMPHIBIOUS • LANDING CRAFT 30
LCU 10 LCU Mk10 (capacity 4 Viking APC or 120 troops)
LCVP 16 LCVP Mk5B (capacity 35 troops)
UCAC 4 Griffon 2400TD
AIR DEFENCE • SAM • Point-defence Starstreak

Royal Air Force 32,500
FORCES BY ROLE
FIGHTER
2 sqn with Typhoon FGR4/T3
FIGHTER/GROUND ATTACK
3 sqn with Typhoon FGR4/T3
2 sqn with Typhoon FGR4/T3 (forming)
1 sqn with F-35B Lightning II
ANTI-SUBMARINE WARFARE
1 sqn with P-8A Poseidon MRA Mk1 (forming)
ISR
1 sqn with Sentinel R1
1 sqn with Shadow R1
1 sqn with BN-2 Defender/Islander
ELINT
1 sqn with RC-135W Rivet Joint
AIRBORNE EARLY WARNING & CONTROL
1 sqn with E-3D Sentry
SEARCH & RESCUE
1 sqn with Bell 412EP Griffin HAR-2
TANKER/TRANSPORT
2 sqn with A330 MRTT Voyager KC2/3
TRANSPORT
1 (comms) sqn with AW109E/SP; BAe-146
1 sqn with A400M Atlas
1 sqn with C-17A Globemaster
3 sqn with C-130J/J-30 Hercules
TRAINING
1 OCU sqn with F-35B Lightning II (forming)
1 OCU sqn with Typhoon
1 OCU sqn with E-3D Sentry; Sentinel R1; RC-135W Rivet Joint
1 sqn with Beech 200 King Air
1 sqn with Hawk T1/1A/1W*
2 sqn with Hawk T2
1 sqn with T-6C Texan II
2 sqn with Tutor
COMBAT/ISR UAV
2 sqn with MQ-9A Reaper
EQUIPMENT BY TYPE
AIRCRAFT 222 combat capable
FGA 162: 18 F-35B Lightning II; 138 Typhoon FGR4; 6 Typhoon T3
ASW 1 P-8A Poseidon MRA Mk1
ISR 9: 4 Sentinel R1; 5 Shadow R1
ELINT 3 RC-135W Rivet Joint
AEW&C 4 E-3D Sentry
TKR/TPT 14 A330 MRTT Voyager KC2/3
TPT 65: **Heavy** 28: 20 A400M Atlas; 8 C-17A Globemaster; **Medium** 14: 1 C-130J Hercules; 13 C-130J-30 Hercules; **Light** 19: 5 Beech 200 King Air (on lease); 2 Beech 200GT King Air (on lease); 9 BN-2T-4S Defender; 3 BN-2 Islander R1; **PAX** 4 BAe-146 CC2/C3
TRG 165: 5 EMB-500 Phenom 100; 91 G-115E Tutor; 28 Hawk T2*; 31 Hawk T1/1A/1W* (ε34 more in store); 10 T-6C Texan II
HELICOPTERS
MRH 5: 1 AW139; 4 Bell 412EP Griffin HAR-2
TPT • Light 3: 2 AW109E; 1 AW109SP
UNMANNED AERIAL VEHICLES
CISR • Heavy 9 MQ-9A Reaper
AIR-LAUNCHED MISSILES
AAM • IR AIM-9L/L(I) Sidewinder; **IIR** ASRAAM; **ARH** AIM-120C-5 AMRAAM; Meteor
ASM AGM-114 Hellfire; Brimstone; Dual-Mode Brimstone; Brimstone II
LACM Storm Shadow
BOMBS
Laser/GPS-guided GBU-10 Paveway II; GBU-24 Paveway III; Enhanced Paveway II/III; Paveway IV

Royal Air Force Regiment
FORCES BY ROLE
MANOEUVRE
Other
6 sy sqn

Tri-Service Defence Helicopter School

FORCES BY ROLE
TRAINING
  1 hel sqn with Bell 412EP *Griffin* HT1
  2 hel sqn with AS350B *Ecureuil*
EQUIPMENT BY TYPE
HELICOPTERS
  MRH 11 Bell 412EP *Griffin* HT1
  TPT • Light 27: 25 AS350B *Ecureuil*; 2 AW109E

Volunteer Reserve Air Forces

(Royal Auxiliary Air Force/RAF Reserve)
MANOEUVRE
  Other
    5 sy sqn
COMBAT SUPPORT
  2 int sqn
COMBAT SERVICE SUPPORT
  1 med sqn
  1 (air movements) sqn
  1 (HQ augmentation) sqn
  1 (C-130 Reserve Aircrew) flt

UK Special Forces

Includes Royal Navy, Army and RAF units
FORCES BY ROLE
SPECIAL FORCES
  1 (SAS) SF regt
  1 (SBS) SF regt
  1 (Special Reconnaissance) SF regt
  1 SF BG (based on 1 para bn)
AVIATION
  1 wg (includes assets drawn from 3 Army hel sqn, 1 RAF tpt sqn and 1 RAF hel sqn)
COMBAT SUPPORT
  1 sigs regt

Reserve

FORCES BY ROLE
SPECIAL FORCES
  2 (SAS) SF regt
EQUIPMENT BY TYPE
ARMOURED FIGHTING VEHICLES
  AUV 24 *Bushmaster* IMV
ANTI-TANK/ANTI-INFRASTRUCTURE • MSL
  MANPATS FGM-148 *Javelin*; NLAW

DEPLOYMENT

AFGHANISTAN: NATO • *Operation Resolute Support* 1,100; 1 inf bn(+); 1 hel flt with 3 *Puma* HC2

ARABIAN SEA: Combined Maritime Forces • 1 FFGHM

ASCENSION ISLAND: 20

ATLANTIC (NORTH)/CARIBBEAN: 1 LSD

ATLANTIC (SOUTH): 1 PSO

BAHRAIN: 160; 1 naval base

BALTIC SEA: NATO • SNMCMG 1: 1 MHO

BELIZE: BATSUB 12

BOSNIA-HERZEGOVINA: EU • EUFOR • *Operation Althea* 2

BRITISH INDIAN OCEAN TERRITORY: 40; 1 navy/marine det

BRUNEI: 1,000; 1 (Gurkha) lt inf bn; 1 jungle trg centre; 1 hel flt with 3 Bell 212

CANADA: BATUS 370; 1 trg unit; 1 hel flt with SA341 *Gazelle* AH1

CYPRUS: 2,260; 2 inf bn; 1 SAR sqn with 4 Bell 412 *Griffin* HAR-2; 1 radar (on det); *Operation Shader* 500: 1 FGA sqn with 6 *Tornado* GR4; 6 *Typhoon* FGR4; 2 *Sentinel* R1; 1 E-3D *Sentry*; 1 A330 MRTT *Voyager* KC3; 2 C-130J *Hercules*; UN • UNFICYP (*Operation Tosca*) 257; 1 log coy (inf role)

DEMOCRATIC REPUBLIC OF THE CONGO: UN • MONUSCO (*Operation Percival*) 3

EGYPT: MFO 2

ESTONIA: NATO • Enhanced Forward Presence (*Operation Cabrit*) 800; 1 armd regt HQ; 1 tk sqn; 1 armd inf coy(+); 1 cbt engr coy

FALKLAND ISLANDS: 1,200: 1 inf coy(+); 1 sigs unit; 1 AD det with *Rapier*; 1 PSO; 1 ftr flt with 4 *Typhoon* FGR4; 1 tkr/tpt flt with 1 A330 MRTT *Voyager*; 1 A400M; 1 hel flt with 2 *Chinook*

GERMANY: 185

GIBRALTAR: 570 (incl Royal Gibraltar regt); 2 PB

IRAQ: *Operation Shader* 400; 2 inf bn(-); 1 engr sqn(-)

KENYA: BATUK 350; 1 trg unit

KUWAIT: *Operation Shader* 50; 1 CISR UAV sqn with 8 MQ-9A *Reaper*

LIBYA: UN • UNSMIL (*Operation Tramal*) 1

MALI: *Operation Barkhane* 90; 1 hel flt with 3 *Chinook* HC5; EU • EUTM Mali 8; UN • MINUSMA (*Operation Newcombe*) 2

NEPAL: 60 (Gurkha trg org)

NIGERIA: 80 (trg team)

OMAN: 90

PERSIAN GULF: *Operation Kipion* 1 DDHM; 2 MCO; 2 MHC; 1 LSD

POLAND: NATO • Enhanced Forward Presence 140; 1 recce sqn

SERBIA: NATO • KFOR 23

SOMALIA: EU • EUTM Somalia 3; UN • UNSOM (*Operation Praiser*) 3; UN • UNSOS (*Operation Catan*) 13

SOUTH SUDAN: UN • UNMISS (*Operations Trenton & Vogul*) 299; 1 engr coy

UKRAINE: *Operation Orbital* 53 (trg team)

UNITED ARAB EMIRATES: 200; 1 tpt/tkr flt with C-17A *Globemaster*; A400M *Atlas*; A330 MRTT *Voyager* (on rotation)

FOREIGN FORCES

United States
US European Command: 9,500; 1 bbr flt at RAF Fairford with 4 B-52H *Stratofortress*; 1 ftr wg at RAF Lakenheath (1 ftr sqn with 24 F-15C/D *Eagle*, 2 FGA sqn with 23 F-15E *Strike Eagle*); 1 ISR sqn at RAF Mildenhall with OC-135/RC-135; 1 tkr wg at RAF Mildenhall with 15 KC-135R/T *Stratotanker*; 1 spec ops gp at RAF Mildenhall (1 sqn with 8 CV-22B *Osprey*; 1 sqn with 8 MC-130J *Commando* II) • US Strategic Command: 1 AN/FPS-132 Upgraded Early Warning Radar and 1 *Spacetrack* radar at Fylingdales Moor

Arms procurements and deliveries – Europe

Significant events in 2019

JANUARY — RBSL JOINT VENTURE

BAE Systems sold 55% of its UK-based armoured-vehicles business to Germany's Rheinmetall in order to establish a new joint venture called Rheinmetall BAE Systems Land (RBSL). RBSL's ARTEC *Boxer* has been selected for the UK's Mechanised Infantry Vehicle programme, though it is unclear whether the two companies will now cooperate on a joint proposal for the *Challenger* 2 main battle tank Life Extension Programme or continue offering separate bids. In future, RBSL will likely compete with General Dynamics UK in future UK armoured-vehicle competitions.

MAY — FRANCE ARMS SALES

Belgium signed a €1.5 billion (US$1.72bn) agreement with France for 60 *Jaguar* and 382 *Griffon* armoured vehicles. This is the first time France has sold military equipment to another country under its new 'Foreign Military Sales (FMS)' type system, and will see Belgium and France cooperate closely on doctrine, training and maintenance. A number of armed forces have for decades acquired defence equipment and services through the United States' FMS programme. This allows states to acquire equipment that is in service with the US armed forces, thereby lowering unit costs, and enjoy a closer relationship with the US military in terms of training, doctrine and interoperability. France is trying to emulate this programme to boost exports and improve relations with other countries.

JUNE — POSEIDON PROJECT

France's Naval Group and Italy's Fincantieri, the largest naval shipbuilders in Europe, signed an agreement setting out the terms of a 50/50 joint venture known as the *Poseidon* project. The two companies and their respective governments hope that the joint venture will enable the two firms to better compete against other shipyards, including in the market for medium to large frigates.

SEPTEMBER — COMBAT AIR TIE-UPS

The United Kingdom signed a statement of intent with Italy to work together on future combat air capabilities. This agreement follows a memorandum of understanding signed with Sweden in July enabling up to ten years of work on combat air development and acquisition. Neither agreement commits those countries to acquire any particular systems, but both Italy and Sweden are seen as potential partners for the UK's *Tempest* next-generation combat aircraft. The UK is currently investing £2bn (US$2.59bn) in the Future Combat Air System Technology Initiative, which is led by a consortium of British companies.

SEPTEMBER — POLISH ACQUISITIONS

The US State Department approved the sale of 32 F-35A combat aircraft to Poland for a total estimated cost of US$6.5bn. Negotiations are ongoing. This is Poland's second major equipment acquisition from the US in as many years. In 2018 Poland signed an agreement worth US$4.75bn for the *Patriot* missile-defence system. These programmes highlight both the pace of Polish military modernisation and the country's desire to invest in its relationship with the US.

Figure 9 Europe: long-range surface-to-air missile (LR-SAM) system modernisation

Increased numbers of advanced fighter aircraft and ballistic and cruise missiles on Europe's periphery have encouraged some European states to recapitalise their upper-tier ground-based air-defence (GBAD) systems. In 2003, France and Italy contracted Eurosam (a Thales–MBDA joint venture) to deliver the SAMP/T. This system uses the *Aster* 30 surface-to-air missile (SAM). Both countries are now modernising SAMP/T and co-developing a new missile variant, the *Aster* 30 Block 1NT, intended to generate a counter medium-range ballistic-missile capability. Other countries have opted to acquire the US *Patriot* system, the first version of which entered service with the US Army in the early 1980s. The latest version of *Patriot* includes two missiles: the long-range PAC-2 GEM-T, designed to defeat fighter aircraft, and the shorter-range PAC-3 MSE, intended to defeat cruise missiles and short-range ballistic missiles. Turkey's acquisition of the Russian S-400 system led to its suspension from the F-35 combat-aircraft programme. Ankara says that the S-400 is an interim solution until it can manufacture its own SAM system. Turkey's long-running T-LORAMIDS programme resulted in a definition-study contract being awarded to Aselsan, Eurosam and Roketsan in 2018. The current status of this project is unclear.

Patriot launcher

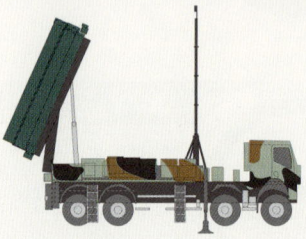

SAMP/T launcher

Table 7 European countries operating LR-SAM systems introduced in the 1980s or earlier

Country	System	System introduction	Notes
Bulgaria	S-200 (SA-5 *Gammon*)	1960s	
	S-300PMU (SA-10 *Grumble*)	1980s	
Germany	*Patriot* PAC-2 GEM; PAC-3	1980s; 2000s	To be replaced by Medium Extended Air Defense System (MEADS)
Greece	S-300PMU1 (SA-20 *Gargoyle*)	1980s	Transferred from Cyprus in the 1990s
	Patriot PAC-1; PAC-2	1980s; 1990s	
	MIM-23B I-*Hawk*	1970s	
Netherlands	*Patriot* PAC-2 GEM; PAC-3	1980s; 2000s	Upgrade programme ongoing
Romania	S-75M3 *Volkhov* (SA-2 *Guideline*)	1970s	
	MIM-23 *Hawk* PIP III	1980s	
Slovakia	S-300PMU (SA-10 *Grumble*)	1980s	Inherited from Czechoslovakia
Spain	*Patriot* PAC-2	1980s	Acquired from Germany in mid-2000s
	MIM-23B I-*Hawk* Phase III	1980s	

Table 8 European LR-SAM programmes with production contracts

Country	System	Quantity	Date	Value	Prime contractor	Deliveries
France	SAMP/T	10 bty	2003	€1.34bn (US$1.52bn)	M Eurosam	2007–16
Italy	SAMP/T	5 bty	2003	€860m (US$972.32m)	M Eurosam	2007–14
Turkey	S-400 (SA-21 *Growler*)	8 bty	2017	US$2.5bn	Almaz-Antey	2019–ongoing
Romania	*Patriot* configuration 3+	7 bty	2017	est. US$3.9bn	Raytheon	2019–n.k.*
Poland	*Patriot* configuration 3+	2 bty	2018	US$4.75bn	Raytheon	2022–24*
Sweden	*Patriot* configuration 3+	4 bty	2018	est. US$3.2bn	Raytheon	2021–22*

* Planned; bty - battery; M - multinational

Figure 10 ARTEC *Boxer* modular wheeled armoured vehicle

In the 1990s, a number of European armed forces began to develop new wheeled armoured vehicles to replace ageing platforms, intending to generate new vehicles capable of rapid deployment. Germany began work on a new vehicle concept in 1990 and in 1994 agreed to work with France on a common design. The United Kingdom joined this project in the mid-1990s looking to fulfil its Multi-Role Armoured Vehicle (MRAV) programme. However, in 1999 France left the programme, subsequently introducing 600 domestically produced VBCIs. The Netherlands joined the programme in 2001 and the following year Germany's first prototype, now called *Boxer*, was delivered. The UK left the project seven months later when it cancelled MRAV. Other Western countries, such as Belgium and more recently Denmark and Romania, opted instead to acquire modern variants of the Mowag *Piranha* design. (This Swiss firm has since 2004 been part of General Dynamics European Land Systems.) The United States bought 4,500 vehicles of this *Piranha* design, calling it *Stryker*.

Boxer consists of two components: the 8x8 vehicle and a mission module. Currently there are approximately 12 different variants on order and more are under development, including bridge-laying and artillery modules. The platform design is intended to allow for rapid reconfiguration for new missions, though this requires a logistics infrastructure in order to swap mission modules, a fact that has limited the *Boxer*'s deployability. Partly to address this problem, the German company FFG has advertised a variant fitted with a crane, though this has yet to be ordered. Despite France fielding the VBCI more rapidly than Germany managed with *Boxer*, the German-Dutch vehicle has so far proven more successful on the export market; it has been ordered or selected by four other countries. One of these is the UK which in 2019 rejoined the programme and signed the largest *Boxer* contract to date for 523 vehicles.

© IISS

Table 9 *Boxer* new-build production contracts

Contract date	Customer	Quantity	Original value	Variants ordered	Deliveries
Dec 2006	Germany	272	€958.33m (US$1.06bn) (includes R&D costs)	4	2009–16
Dec 2006	Netherlands	200	€737m (US$925.37m) (includes R&D costs)	6	2013–18
Dec 2015	Germany	131 (A2 variant)	€476m (US$528.18m)	1	2017–ongoing
Aug 2016	Lithuania	91 (IFV variant)	€385.6m (US$430.51m)	2	2017–ongoing
Aug 2018	Australia	211	A$5.2bn (US$4.11bn)	7	2019–26*
Nov 2019	United Kingdom	523	£2.8bn (US$3.63bn)	4	2022*–n.k.
	Total	**1,428**	**US$10.68bn**		

* Planned

Table 10 Countries that have selected *Boxer*

Date of selection	Customer	Quantity	Value	Notes
Feb 2018	Slovenia	48	€306m (US$361.53m)	Contract on hold pending review

Chapter Five
Russia and Eurasia

- The year 2020 was meant to end a decade in which the Russian Army had started to field a significant number of T-14 *Armata* main battle tanks in front-line units. However, by the end of 2019 none had entered operational service. Development and production challenges are contributory factors, as is cost, and instead the army has resumed upgrades to armour already in service, in particular the T-72B3 mod. and the T-80BVM.

- Russia's president announced during the June 2019 Army Military Show that 76 Sukhoi Su-57 *Felon* multi-role fighters were to be delivered by the end of 2027. When it was finalised at the end of 2017, the State Armament Programme to 2027 only covered the manufacture of up to a further 16 of the aircraft in the early 2020s. Around 60 *Felons* were originally to have been delivered by the conclusion of the 2020 State Armament Programme; realising this ambition was difficult even when the plan was drafted in 2010.

- Moscow continued during 2019 to pursue a number of nuclear-delivery systems intended to defeat US missile defences, including some beyond New START definitions. These included the *Burevestnik* (SSC-X-9 *Skyfall*) nuclear-powered, nuclear-armed long-endurance cruise missile, despite a series of test failures. While the *Burevestnik* remained some way from service entry, the *Avangard* hypersonic boost-glide programme was on the brink of entering the inventory. The MiG-31K variant of the *Foxhound* modified to carry the *Kinzhal* air-launched ballistic missile was also near to service entry as 2019 concluded. The *Status-6*/*Poseidon* nuclear-armed, nuclear-powered autonomous underwater vehicle remains in development.

- Most Eurasian states continue to rely on ageing Soviet-era combat aircraft that are only slowly being replaced with more capable types. Belarus will become the second regional export operator of the Su-30SM *Flanker* H alongside Kazakhstan with the delivery due by the end of 2019 of the first four of 12 on order. A number of countries continue to operate early-model MiG-29 *Fulcrum* and Su-27 *Flanker* B aircraft in the fighter role including Belarus, Kazakhstan and Uzbekistan.

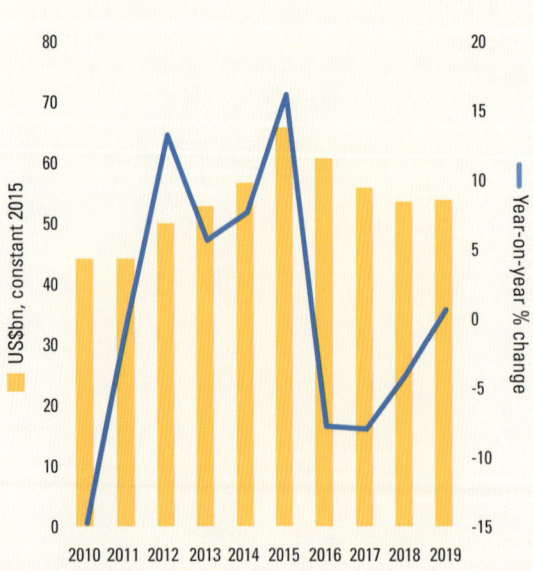

Russia real-terms total military expenditure, 2010–19 (US$bn, constant 2015)

Active military personnel – top 10
(25,000 per unit)

- Russia 900,000
- Ukraine 209,000
- Azerbaijan 66,950
- Uzbekistan 48,000
- Belarus 45,350
- Armenia 44,800
- Kazakhstan 39,000
- Turkmenistan 36,500
- Georgia 20,650
- Kyrgyzstan 10,900

Global 19,852,
Regional 1,435,000

Regional defence policy and economics 168 ▶
Armed forces data section 183 ▶
Arms procurements and deliveries 217 ▶

Russia's new strategic-weapons development, 1980–2025

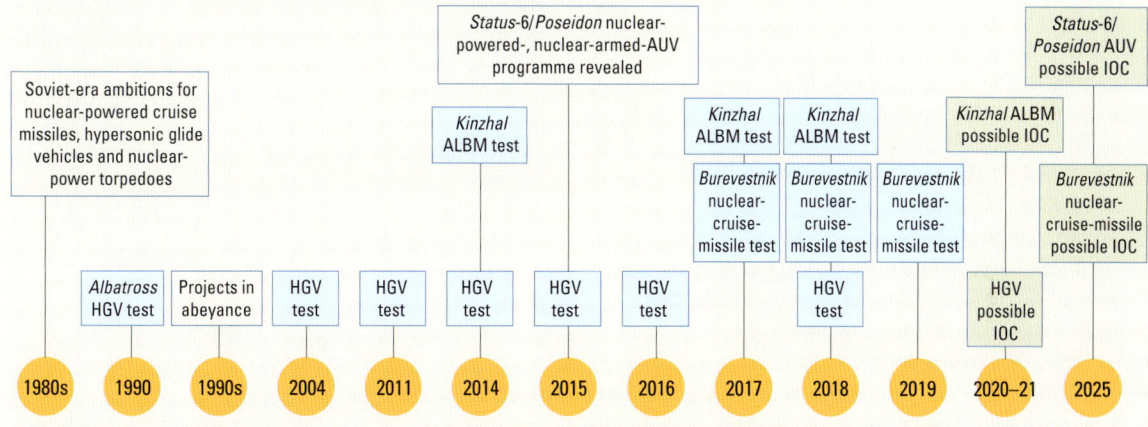

ALBM: air-launched ballistic missile; AUV: autonomous underwater vehicle; HGV: hypersonic glide vehicle; IOC: initial operating capability

Russian main battle tanks: acquisition, upgrade and total numbers, 2019*

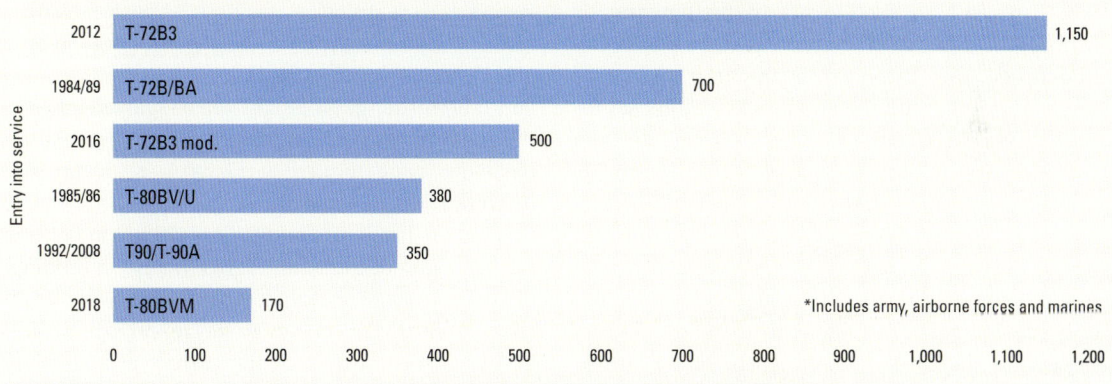

*Includes army, airborne forces and marines

Su-57 *Felon* multi-role combat aircraft: notional build-up of inventory numbers

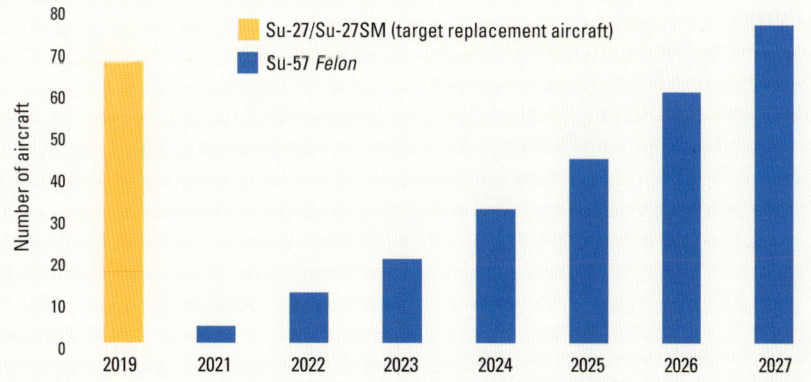

Russia and Eurasia

Russia's military-modernisation process continues to lead to the introduction of new equipment and reshaped military formations and defence organisations, though familiar problems persist, including some aspects of defence production. Though there had earlier been various reform aspirations, the process began in earnest some 11 years ago under then-defence minister Anatoly Serdyukov, after flaws were exposed by the August 2008 war in Georgia. Elements of the new approach were reshaped following the appointment of Defence Minister Sergei Shoigu in November 2012. Chief of the General Staff General Valery Gerasimov was appointed around the same time.

The successor to the State Armament Programme (GPV) 2020, GPV 2027, was finally agreed in late 2017. It should have been agreed before then, and should have covered the period to 2025, but it was delayed by economic difficulties. According to GPV 2020, the share of 'modern' weapons in Russia's armed forces should have risen to 70% by the time it ends in 2020 (the meaning of 'modern' remains somewhat ill-defined). But this year is important in other respects. It will mark the end of a key target set for the recruitment of contract soldiers. Meanwhile, both classified and public strategic-planning documents are due to be reviewed, such as the National Security Strategy, Military Doctrine, Maritime Doctrine and Arctic Doctrine. As such, it is possible that in 2020 or 2021 announcements will be made indicating not only Russia's policy priorities but also new long-term targets for the further development of the armed forces.

Policy and strategy

Changes have already been announced to Russia's National Security Strategy, in order to more closely align it with a new version of Russia's Strategy for Social and Economic Development. Updates to planning documents in 2020 will likely also reflect Russia's views of the international security situation, including strategic relations with the United States.

Russia publicly blames the US for the collapse of the Intermediate-range Nuclear Forces (INF) Treaty, while continuing to deny that it has developed and deployed a ground-launched cruise missile (GLCM) in violation of the treaty, as Washington and its NATO allies assert. In January 2019, Moscow staged a briefing during which a system was displayed labelled as '9M729' – the weapon that NATO associates with Russia's GLCM and to which it has assigned the reporting name SSC-8 *Screwdriver*. However, it remains unclear whether the system displayed was indeed the 9M729, since all that was shown was a launch canister and what authorities claimed was the associated launch vehicle. Nonetheless, Moscow did not make a concerted effort to maintain the treaty. Some Russian analysts argue that Moscow sees short- and medium-range missiles as useful assets not only in the European theatre, but also for counteracting potential threats in Russia's Far East. At a September 2019 meeting in Vladivostok, President Vladimir Putin said that Russia would quickly develop GLCM systems in response to the test of such a system by the US, though Washington asserts that Russia began testing such a system as far back as 2008. Moscow said it would not deploy INF-range GLCMs 'in any given region until US-made intermediate-range and shorter-range missiles are deployed there'. IISS assessments indicate that the first four 9M729 battalions were located at Elansky, Kapustin Yar (training), Mozdok and Shuya.

Moscow has indicated that it is willing to discuss the extension of the New START treaty on limiting offensive strategic weapons, which is due to expire in 2021. Defence Minister Shoigu was reported as saying in late October 2019 that the current arrangement could be extended in parallel to discussions on an improved regime. Moreover, while the foreign ministry said in early November that it would now be difficult to agree a new treaty (presumably given the negotiating time involved), it also said that even an extension of the existing treaty 'would need at least six months' due to legislative schedules. Russia has indicated, with reference to US wishes to widen the scope of new arms-control mechanisms to include China, that it respects Beijing's position not to engage in trilateral disarmament talks. Another US concern is that New START only deals with certain types of nuclear-delivery systems and that technologies have changed since it was signed. Moscow, for its part, reportedly welcomes a more multilateral approach but also advocates including a wider range of systems, such as those associated with missile defence and 'prompt global strike'. Meanwhile, a Russian foreign-ministry official said in November 2019 that Russia's (developmental) RS-28 *Sarmat* intercontinental ballistic missile (ICBM) and *Avangard* hypersonic glide vehicle fall within the scope of the current treaty. *Sarmat* is an ICBM and therefore accountable. *Avangard* falls within the scope of the treaty, as it uses the RS-18 (SS-19) ICBM as its booster. In November, Russia formally showed the *Avangard* system to US inspectors, in accordance with treaty provisions. Other developmental systems such as the *Poseidon* nuclear-powered and nuclear-capable uninhabited underwater vehicle (UUV) or the *Burevestnik* (SSC-X-9 *Skyfall*) nuclear-powered cruise missile would fall outside the current treaty. On 1 November, the deputy director of the Russian foreign ministry's Non-Proliferation and Arms Control Department reiterated that these two systems – and the *Kinzhal* hypersonic missile – fall outside the New START treaty, and that according to Moscow, 'limitation of these kinds of systems will require new agreements'.

Perhaps the most significant development in Moscow's foreign-military cooperation in 2019 was with NATO member Turkey, rather than with a traditional partner. Despite long-standing disagreement over the future of the Assad regime in Syria and indeed over Russia's presence in the country (with recent history including the downing by a Turkish F-16 of a Russian Su-24 in 2015), the two countries exploited the United States' withdrawal from positions in northern Syria to advance their interests there. Turkey launched a cross-border incursion (that it was already planning) against Kurdish forces and Russian personnel were filmed in former US bases. By November 2019, Russia was mounting joint military patrols, in Syria, with a NATO member state. Turkey's agreement to buy the Russian S-400 air-defence system had earlier complicated NATO Alliance politics. It led to Turkey being refused the US *Patriot* air-defence system and ejected from the F-35 combat-aircraft programme.

Turkey's President Recep Tayyip Erdogan, when visiting the 27 August–1 September 2019 MAKS air show in Russia, became the first foreign leader to see the cockpit of the Su-57 *Felon* combat aircraft. However, though speculation subsequently arose that Turkey might look to purchase the *Felon*, should a combat-aircraft deal materialise, analysts consider that a more likely contender would be the Su-35. Erdogan's appearance was perhaps intended more as a message that the two nations were willing to work together more closely in the military sphere.

Personnel

The proportion and overall number of conscripts in Russia's armed forces continues to decline, falling from 307,000 in 2016 to 260,500 in 2018. At the same time, the number of professional contract service personnel rose from 384,000 in 2018 (the plan had earlier been to reach this target in 2016) to 393,800 in 2019. The target of 400,000 professional personnel by 2020 was mentioned by Gerasimov in a March 2019 speech to the Academy of Military Sciences. The plan now is that this figure rises to 475,600 by 2025. This illustrates, if anything, the ambiguity that persists over long-term personnel targets, and that the planned increase in contract strength has slowed. This is seen by some analysts as a causal factor for the rise observed in the spring 2019 draft – at 135,000, this was 7,000 higher than the spring draft from 2018. The autumn drafts in 2018 and 2019 were approximately the same (132,500 vs 132,000). The initial plan, back in 2014, was to recruit 499,200 contract personnel by 2020. This was subsequently changed to 425,000 before the most recent adjustment.

Moreover, accurately discerning the composition of the total number of contract personnel is also problematic. Some reports indicate that the declared number of contract servicemen might include warrant officers, as well as contract non-commissioned officers and privates. Other analysts point to caveats that might need to be applied in drawing conclusions about overall combat capability from rising contract-personnel totals. Not all these contractors are long-term professionals; some might be on short-service contracts, as there is an option for a two-year term of service. Meanwhile, the defence minister reportedly said in September that conscription should continue: it is seen as a useful strategic reserve and a feeder for the recruitment of contract service personnel.

The requirement to recruit and retain contract personnel led to the first significant increase in armed forces' pay for five years. From 1 September 2019, it was planned that private soldiers on the first year of their contract would receive around 32,000–34,000 roubles (US$480–510) per month, depending on their trade, with sergeants due to be paid around 41,000 roubles (US$616) per month. Wages are due to be index-linked for those who have already served for several years. Nonetheless, military pay will likely remain lower than the national average and, even with additional benefits – such as improved housing and relative pay differentials depending on the hardship of the posting – military service remains attractive mainly to those from economically disadvantaged and rural regions.

Dispositions and deployments

At the 2019 Moscow Conference on International Security, Gerasimov said that Russia viewed the reinforcement of its Western and Southern Military Districts as a priority, citing NATO's 'Four 30s' readiness initiative as the principal motivating factor. That said, there is nothing new in transferring forces between regions and standing up units. In recent years, a number of bases have been constructed close to the border with Ukraine and formations established there, such as the 20th Combined Arms Army at Voronezh. In 2019, Russia bolstered its forces and equipment in Crimea, principally because it had made significant progress in forming units further north, near the land border with Ukraine.

There has been further consolidation of forces close to the border with Ukraine. A separate tank battalion in the 144th Motor-Rifle Division of the 20th Combined Arms Army has been enlarged to regimental size, becoming the 59th Tank Regiment at Yelna. The 144th Motor-Rifle Division's second Motor-Rifle Regiment, the 254th, was formed at Klintsky, bringing the division close to initial operating capability. Meanwhile, a coastal-defence battalion in Crimea re-equipped with the shore-based *Bal* (SSC-6 *Sennight*) anti-ship missile system. At the same time, Russia has increased the frequency and complexity of its military exercises in Crimea. Strike scenarios against surface ships in the Black Sea have been practised, as well as defensive scenarios including cruise-missile strikes on the peninsula. Plans were again reiterated in early October to build a *Voronezh*-SM early-warning radar at Sevastopol.

The end of 2019 was due to see the navy's Northern Fleet transform into a new administrative formation akin to that of a Military District. The date traditionally associated with changes of this nature has been 1 December. The fleet had previously been

▼ Map 4 **Russia: military bases abroad and in disputed territories**

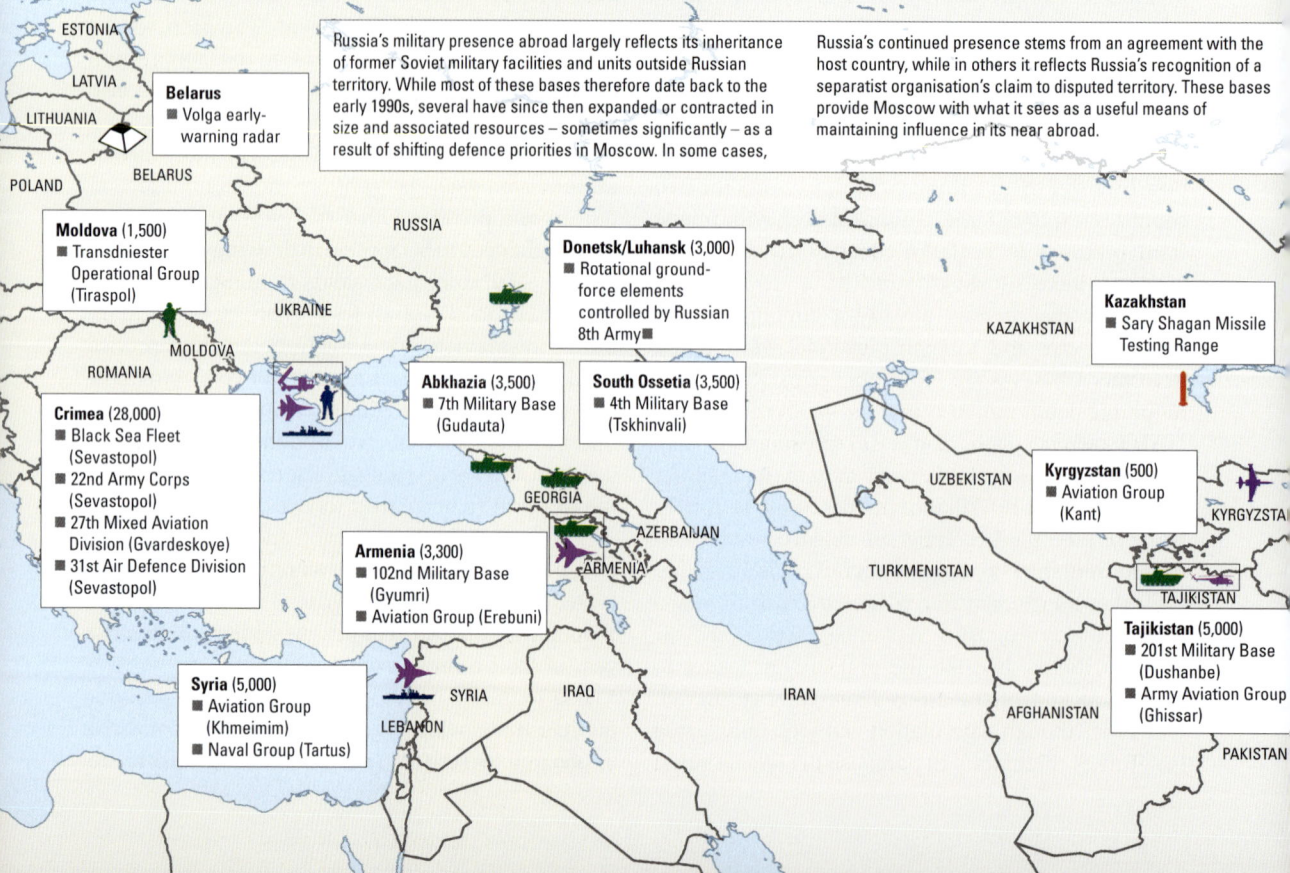

transformed, in 2014, into a Joint Strategic Command (OSK); however, reports in mid-2019 indicated that the change to OSK status had been 'experimental'. Nonetheless, the move indicates the continuing importance of the Arctic to Russia. The reshaped Northern Fleet will have responsibility for Russia's entire Arctic territory, as well as the Northern Sea Route.

Russia is still upgrading its bases in the region. A concrete all-season runway is being built at a base in the Franz Josef archipelago and construction began in 2019 at sites intended for a new Northern Fleet air-defence division; the area of responsibility for this formation will include parts of the Northern Sea Route (from Novaya Zemlya to Chukotka). Its main base will be at Tiksi. More generally, plans to equip the Northern Fleet and associated units with new equipment continue, including some bespoke variants such as the *Tor*-M2DT air-defence system. However, reactivating significant Russian military capability in the Arctic has proven slower than planned, not least because of the challenges posed by the environment. There have also been reports of capability improvements in Kaliningrad, including to armour, air defence, electronic warfare and rocket artillery, while the majority of air-force-pilot graduates were this year sent there in order to improve staffing in Kaliningrad-based air-force units.

New weapons and research and development

The new strategic systems announced by President Putin in 2018 were already at an advanced stage of development when the announcement was made. Further progress has been made, but there have also been evident problems.

Tests of the *Burevestnik* (SSC-X-9 *Skyfall*) missile resumed in 2019. However, US sources indicate that nearly all the test launches failed. In August 2019, an accident occurred when a team was recovering wreckage from a previous missile test. Seven people were killed and there was localised radiation contamination. It is not surprising that the defence ministry has not elaborated on the nature of the problem, but it has said that further design development will take place before testing resumes.

Development of the *Avangard* glide vehicle is, however, more advanced. At least officially, development is complete and series production has begun. The weapon was successfully tested in December 2018, being launched from an RS-18 (SS-19) ICBM. It was announced that the first of these missiles with the *Avangard* glide vehicle will be deployed by the end of 2019. Russian analysts understand, based on unofficial data, that GPV 2027 includes equipping two RS-18 (SS-19) regiments. It is possible that the *Avangard* could also be fitted to other launch platforms, such as the RS-28 *Sarmat* ICBM that is currently under development.

Meanwhile, an experimental squadron of MiG-31K aircraft equipped with *Kinzhal* hypersonic missiles reportedly made more than 400 flights over the Caspian and Black seas in 2018, while the first *Peresvet* laser systems have been on trial combat duty since the end of 2018 with two divisions of the Strategic Rocket Forces. It is unclear whether these are operated by troops from the Strategic Rocket Forces or by air-force personnel, but Russian analysts understand that a *Peresvet* training centre is being built at the Russian Federal Nuclear Centre at Sarov. In February 2019, range trials were reported completed on the *Poseidon* UUV, and two months later the much-modified Project 09852 *Oscar* II-class submarine *Belgorod* was launched. This may be the first delivery platform for *Poseidon*.

2019 also saw construction continue at the Era military-technology park at Anapa on the Black Sea coast. Six additional research disciplines were also announced, including the development of weapons with novel physical principles (such as lasers and plasma), small satellites, geo-information systems and work on the use of artificial intelligence for military purposes.

Ground forces and Airborne Forces

Reports indicate that Russia's ground forces have formed a standing combat-ready fighting core consisting exclusively of professional servicemen. Their precise readiness level, however, remains uncertain. In March 2019, Defence Minister Shoigu that that this combat core consists of 136 battalion tactical groups (BTGs), including Airborne Forces (VDV) units. (This is out of a total of around 200 BTGs that may include, analysts understand, naval infantry and coastal-defence forces.)

The original plan was that each ground-forces regiment or brigade would be capable of forming two BTGs of contract service personnel and one comprising conscripts. However, the conscript formations tended to be understaffed, while experience indicated that on some postings the

Uninhabited aerial vehicles (UAVs)

The Russian armed forces have maintained their focus on deriving greater capability from UAVs. The *Iskander* missile brigades are reported to now maintain subordinate organic UAV formations, equipped with quadcopters for force-protection tasks and *Orlan*-10s for target-acquisition and battle-damage assessment.

The armed forces continue to integrate the lessons of operations in Syria. In 2019, Russian analysts said that there was emphasis on improving interoperability between artillery and UAVs, and between UAVs and fixed-wing and rotary-wing aviation. One aspiration was to further reduce the time between target acquisition and engagement. *Orlan* and *Forpost* UAV teams, analysts understand, now have as standard tasks not only target acquisition but also battle-damage assessment and adjusting artillery fire. At the same time, the Syria mission has also led to greater focus on countering adversary use of UAVs.

Meanwhile, there was further development of the Aerospace Forces' first large uninhabited combat air vehicle in 2019, with the first flight of the 20-tonne S-70 *Okhotnik*. A modernised six-tonne *Altius* UAV also took to the air, with this variant fitted with a satellite-communications link. Precision-guided weapons for these systems are in test. It was reported that the *Tsentr*-2019 exercise involved UAVs working as independent 'strike groups', with targets including headquarters and command posts, air-defence systems, transport infrastructure and enemy reserves' avenues of approach, though it was not reported that UAV systems were armed during these experiments. An additional order has been announced for *Forpost*-M UAVs, improved in light of the Syria experience, though due to the import-substitution programme it has been specified that this can contain only Russian components.

conscript battalion risked losing its officers and contract soldiers to the contract battalions, with the conscript formation remaining on tasks including garrison duties.

The ground forces are also attempting to improve their air mobility. In December 2018, experimental plans were announced to allocate to every motor-rifle brigade and regiment in the Southern Military District – as well as to each naval infantry unit – one company trained in helicopter insertion and also in ground-combat tasks independent of a main force but supported by helicopters.

The VDV has been conducting similar experiments. The 31st Guards Air Assault Brigade in Ulyanovsk has been designated as a 'new type' brigade, intended for deployment by helicopter rather than by fixed-wing aircraft, with organic assets planned to include transport, attack and reconnaissance helicopters. At Russia's *Tsentr*-2019 exercise, Shoigu said that tests with this air-mobile experiment had been successful, operating in a battalion-sized air-mobile operation, in comparison to the company-sized operation seen at *Vostok*-2018. However, a principal problem is the lack of sufficient helicopters in the Aerospace Forces' inventory for the requirements of ground forces and VDV units. There are not enough to simultaneously support more than a few air-mobile units. The plan is to purchase another 300 helicopters under GPV 2027, but given competing demands for various helicopter types, it is unclear whether this will be enough to enable the formation of significant numbers of 'new type' air-mobile units in the ground forces and VDV.

Meanwhile, the VDV continues to expand. A third air-assault formation, the 237th Air Assault Regiment, has been added to the Pskov-based 76th Air Assault Division. Previously, divisions only had two regiments. Additionally, reports in 2019 indicated that the 76th and 7th Air Assault Divisions would, along with the 56th Air Assault Brigade, be reinforced with tank battalions. While this would increase their firepower, the timescale for this change, and how the resulting transport requirement would be met, remained unclear. It was also reported that at *Tsentr*-2019 the VDV had conducted a regimental-sized airborne landing for the first time since *Zapad*-1981.

All former *Tochka*-U missile brigades have now re-equipped with the *Iskander* missile system, though it is unclear whether the one wholly new *Iskander* brigade that was due to form under a 2017 contract has yet stood up.

Aerospace Forces

Air-force equipment-recapitalisation plans were boosted in 2019 by a presidential announcement revising acquisition plans for the Su-57 *Felon* multi-role combat aircraft. It is now planned that 76 of these aircraft will be purchased under GPV 2027, rather than the previously planned 16. These increased numbers would be sufficient to equip three full aviation regiments (six squadrons) with Su-57s. This increased purchase would be enabled, the president said, by a 20% reduction in unit costs (the plan is likely that this larger order will generate the reduction). Up to now, the air force had to rely on upgrading Soviet-era designs in order to sustain its combat inventory.

This change of direction is significant in two ways. Not only will the Su-57 provide the Aerospace Forces with its first 'stealthy' multi-role fighter, allowing it to narrow the capability gap with the US, but the revised order calls into question how many more Su-35S *Flanker* M fighter/ground-attack aircraft will be purchased.

Russia's efforts to refresh its tactical combat-aircraft inventory have often been hampered by a lack of realism or adequate funding, or both. In 2010, Moscow's aim was to buy more than 200 Su-57s by 2025. However, this ambition was stymied by the knock-on effect of the collapse in oil prices in 2014. Even so, when GPV 2020 first appeared the plan was to order 60 aircraft, with at least a further 140 to be included in the next armament programme, for delivery by 2025.

The air force is also receiving a small number of MiG-35s. This is a further upgrade of the MiG-29 *Fulcrum* fighter. The first two of an initial order of six were delivered in mid-2019 and a follow-on order is under discussion. That said, the MiG-35 buy may be motivated as much by a desire to boost the aircraft's export prospects as it is by an air-force requirement.

By the end of 2019, nearly all the air force's operational MiG-31 *Foxhound* fighter units had re-equipped with the MiG-31BM *Foxhound* C. While a successor to the *Foxhound* has been mentioned (termed the PAK-DP fighter requirement), near-term development appears unlikely due to budgetary limitations and other priorities.

Test flights of prototypes of the Tu-160M2 *Blackjack* and Tu-22M3M *Backfire* bombers bookended 2018. Both are intended to eventually upgrade existing airframes, but the *Blackjack* programme also includes new-build aircraft. Work is under way at Kazan on two *Blackjack* modifications: the Tu-160M1 and the Tu-160M2. The latter will be the baseline for the new-build Tu-160. The Tu-160M1 standard included the integration of the Kh-101/102 (AS-23A/B *Kodiak*) family of conventional and nuclear land-attack cruise missiles. The first new Tu-160M is due to be ready for initial flight tests by December 2020. There has been no contract signed yet for a subsequent batch, though the plan announced in December 2017 was to build up to 50 of these aircraft.

Upgrades to existing *Blackjack*s, and the decision to restart production, have raised questions over the future of the PAK-DA future bomber project. Nonetheless, it was confirmed in August 2019 that a contract had been signed for research and development work. PAK-DA will be a subsonic flying-wing design, featuring signature-management technology. There is as yet no production contract and no information on the number Russia may eventually acquire.

Modernisation plans have been announced for some aircraft types, based on lessons from the Syria deployment. Contracts were signed in 2019 for the modernisation of the Su-34, principally to improve its avionics and electronic-warfare systems and to integrate additional air-to-surface weapons, and for 98 of the newly modernised Mi-28NM attack helicopters. A contract is expected in 2020 for a similar number of modified Ka-52M helicopters, though how many are ordered may depend on the number of other helicopter orders under GPV 2027 (such as Mi-8s and Mi-26s).

Guided weapons

Russia's Tactical Missile Corporation (KTRV) is benefiting from the air force's renewed investment in air-launched weapons. Upgraded versions of the R-73 (AA-11A *Archer*) and R-77 (AA-12A *Adder*) air-to-air missiles (AAMs) are now being manufactured and in June 2019 a production contract was placed for the K-77M (AA-X-12C). The R-37M (AA-13A *Axehead*) long-range AAM is in production and in service with the air force.

The initial upgrade to the basic R-77, the R-77-1 (AA-12B *Adder*), entered service with the air force in 2015, with the missile first seen in public on Su-35S *Flanker* M aircraft deployed in Syria. Offered for export as the RVV-MD, it has already been delivered to China as part of the Su-35 sale.

Russia's intervention in Syria has given KTRV an opportunity to assess the combat performance of some its weapons, particularly Raduga's Kh-555 (AS-22 *Kluge*) and Kh-101 (AS-23A *Kodiak*) long-range land-attack cruise missiles. Raduga is one of Russia's three cruise-missile designers, and is part of KTRV, as is NPO Mashinostroyenia. The third, Novator, is part of the Almaz-Antey company. The

Russia's guided-weapons sector is located predominantly in Moscow or in the Moscow region, reflecting its Soviet heritage. There are two main conglomerates active in the field. The Tactical Missile Corporation (KTRV) focuses primarily on air-launched systems, while Almaz-Antey is generally concerned with surface-to-air systems. Both groups also have subsidiaries that produce anti-ship cruise missiles: NPO Mashinostroyenia (KTRV) and Novator (Almaz-Antey).

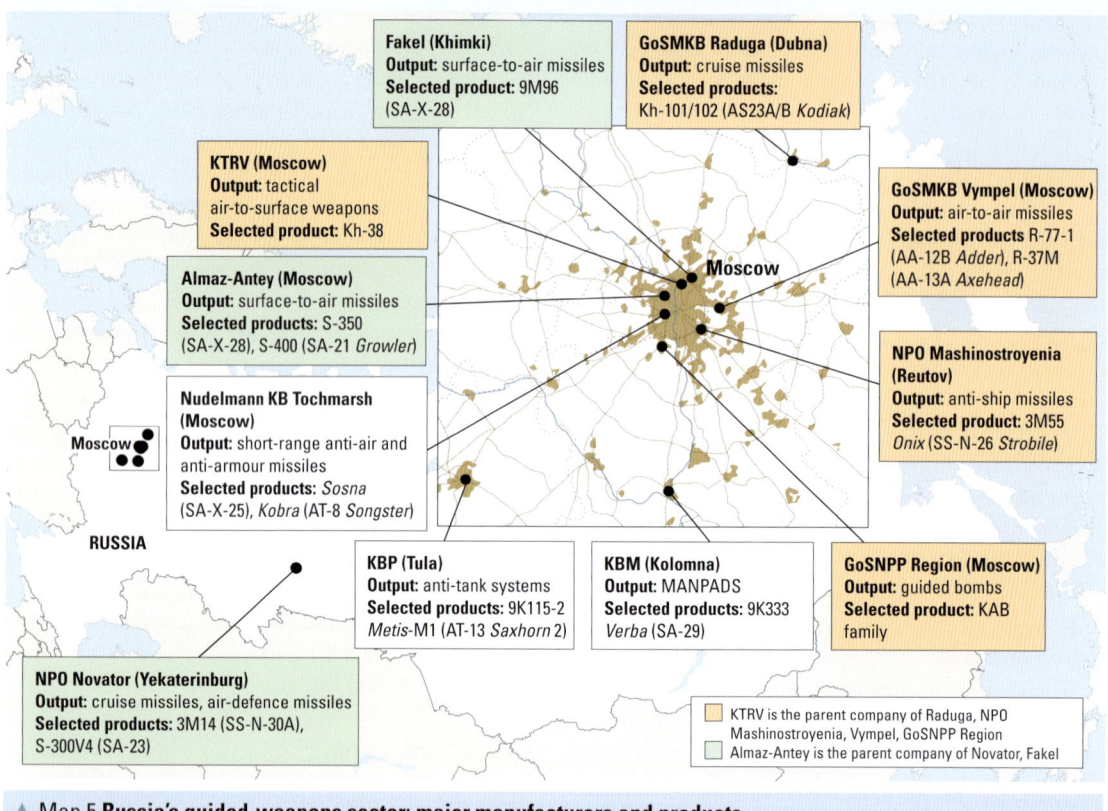

▲ Map 5 **Russia's guided-weapons sector: major manufacturers and products**

naval 3M14 (SS-N-30A) land-attack cruise missile, manufactured by Novator, has also been used in the Syria campaign.

The Russian Air Force has used comparatively few tactical air-to-surface missiles in Syria. While aircraft have been observed carrying the Kh-27 (AS-12 *Kegler*) and the Kh-29 (AS-14 *Kedge*), iron bombs and rockets were a far more common payload. KTRV is working on the Kh-38 family of weapons as a replacement for the Kh-27 and Kh-29, and the Kh-38 semi-active-laser variant has reportedly completed state testing. The Kh-35U upgrade of the Kh-35 (AS-20 *Kayak*) was also seen in theatre, although the reason for its deployment was unclear.

There is a renewed emphasis on introducing into service more precision-guided tactical weapons. Along with the Kh-38 family, the air force was due to receive at least two types of precision-guided glide bombs from the beginning of 2020.

Navy

Russia's maritime capacity in 2019 presented a mixed picture: there was further development in terms of smaller but well-armed surface platforms and at the same time a reassertion of global deployment aspirations. There was also mixed progress for Russia's most potent naval arm, the submarine service. Shipbuilding output overall remains limited. In addition, the October 2018 accident involving the floating dock used for the refit of the aircraft carrier *Admiral Kuznetsov* resulted in damage to the ship. Replacing the dock means that the planned refit will now be completed no earlier than 2021; reports indicate that Russia is looking to combine two dry docks at the 35th Ship Repair Plant in Murmansk (the accident occurred, in Murmansk, at the 82nd Ship Repair Plant) in order to accommodate the vessel.

Problems continue with the construction of large surface ships. Russia's major military shipyards are

Map 6 Selected maritime capabilities in the Caspian Sea

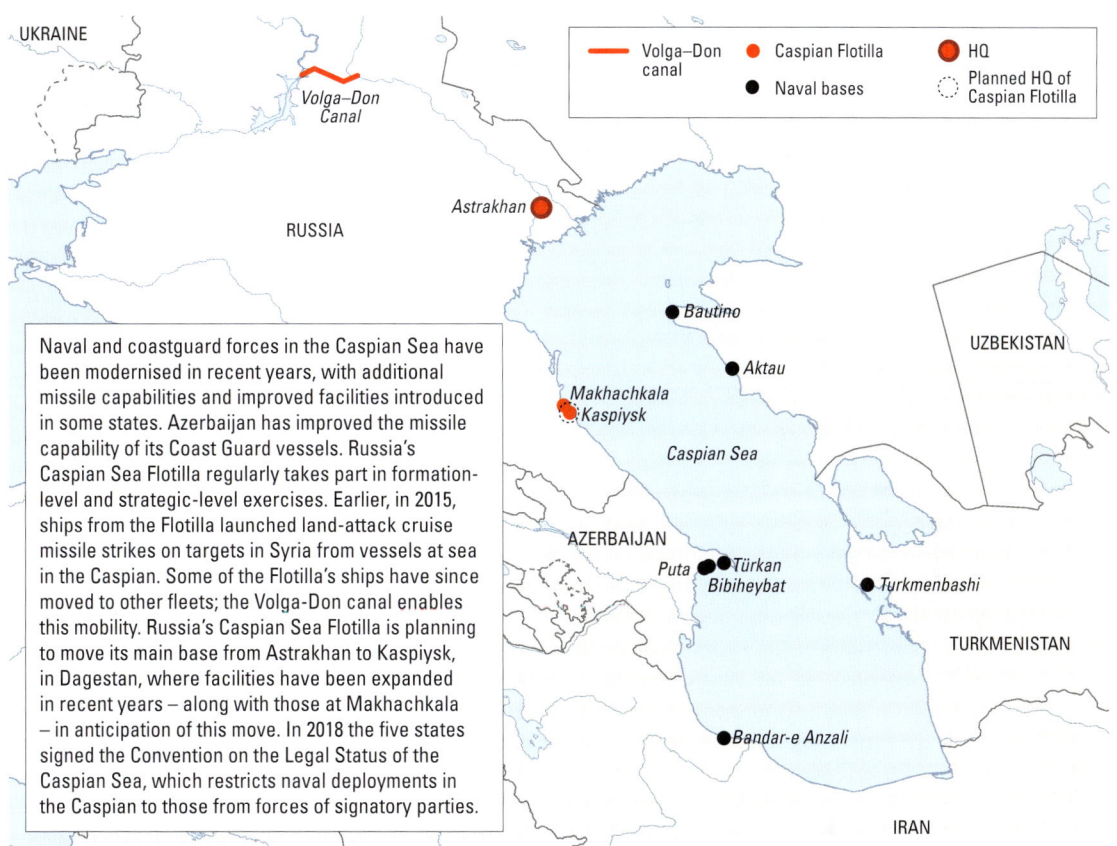

Naval and coastguard forces in the Caspian Sea have been modernised in recent years, with additional missile capabilities and improved facilities introduced in some states. Azerbaijan has improved the missile capability of its Coast Guard vessels. Russia's Caspian Sea Flotilla regularly takes part in formation-level and strategic-level exercises. Earlier, in 2015, ships from the Flotilla launched land-attack cruise missile strikes on targets in Syria from vessels at sea in the Caspian. Some of the Flotilla's ships have since moved to other fleets; the Volga–Don canal enables this mobility. Russia's Caspian Sea Flotilla is planning to move its main base from Astrakhan to Kaspiysk, in Dagestan, where facilities have been expanded in recent years – along with those at Makhachkala – in anticipation of this move. In 2018 the five states signed the Convention on the Legal Status of the Caspian Sea, which restricts naval deployments in the Caspian to those from forces of signatory parties.

Naval and paramilitary frigates, corvettes and patrol vessels, as of Nov 2019

Type	Quantity	Anti-Ship and Cruise Missiles
Azerbaijan		
FS	1	
PSO	2	
PCG	4	Spike NLOS SSM
PCC	3	
PB/PBF (navy and coastguard)	19	
Iran		
PCFG	3	C-802 (CH-SS-N-6) AShM
PB	6	
Kazakhstan		
PCGM	3	Barrier-VK SSM
PCC	1	
PB/PBF (navy and coastguard)	31	

Type	Quantity	Anti-Ship and Cruise Missiles
Russia		
FFGM	1	3M24 Uran (SS-N-25 Switchblade) AShM
FFGM	1	Kalibr dual-capable cruise-missile family
FSGM	1	Kalibr dual-capable cruise-missile family
FSM	3	
PCFG	1	P-27 Termit-R (SS-N-2D Styx) AShM
PCO (coastguard)	1	
PCC	7	
PB/PBF (navy and coastguard)	22	
Turkmenistan		
PCFG	2	3M24E Uran-E (SS-N-25 Switchblade) AShM
PCGM (navy and coastguard)	10	Otomat AShM
PBFG (coastguard)	6	Marte Mk2/N AShM
PB/PBF (coastguard)	19	

FS – corvette **PCG** – guided-missile patrol craft **PCO** – offshore patrol craft **PCC** – coastal patrol craft **PCGM** – guided-missile patrol craft with surface-to-air missiles **PB/PBF** – patrol boat, fast patrol boat **PCFGM** – fast guided-missile patrol craft **FFGM** – guided-missile frigate with surface-to-air missiles **PSO** – Offshore patrol ship **FSM** – Corvette with surface-to-air missiles **PBFG** – Fast patrol boat with guided missiles

mostly ageing and they are generally inadequate for building major naval combatants. Plans to boost the country's shipbuilding capacity are falling behind, although a new construction hall at Severnaya Verf suitable for vessels of the size of destroyers and helicopter carriers was due to be completed by the end of 2020.

Nevertheless, in December 2018, the Project 22800 corvette *Mytishchi* entered service. This is the first of what Russia designates as its *Karakurt* class. A sixth Project 20380 frigate, called *Steregushchiy* in Russian service, was commissioned the same month (the last five of these are equipped with the 3K96-3 *Redut* (SA-N-28) air-defence system). The first Project 20385 (NATO designation *Gremyashchiy* class) frigate made its public debut at the St Petersburg naval review at the end of July 2019 and was expected to enter service later in 2019, with a second probably not far behind.

At the same time, Russia continues with its plans and aspirations to distribute an extended range of guided weapons to its vessels. The equipping of various ships with the 3M14 (SS-N-30A) cruise missile has been observed, as has the operational employment of these weapons from some ships and submarines, but in 2019 there was reporting that Russia may be looking to also fit the 3M22 *Zircon* high-speed anti-ship cruise missile, or a variant of it, to surface ships and submarines. This weapon has a reported speed of around Mach 6. The Project 22350 destroyer *Admiral Gorshkov* and a *Yasen*-M submarine, as well as a Project 22800 corvette, have been reported as associated with tests or potential tests of *Zircon*. The means of launching any naval variant of *Zircon*, such as whether it will be capable of launching from the current series UKSK universal vertical-launch system, or perhaps slant-launch, remains unclear.

Defence Minister Shoigu has stated that Moscow does not intend to give up its blue-water presence and will continue to support the core of an ocean-going fleet. In 2018, the first *Ocean Shield* exercise took place, comprising a mixed group of expeditionary forces from various Russian fleet groups in the Mediterranean Sea. In 2019, it was repeated in the Baltic, with forces then deploying into the Norwegian Sea. It was announced that these exercises will continue each year. Deployments of this nature could pose a challenge to NATO operating assumptions. In addition, the new Project 22350 destroyer *Admiral Gorshkov* led a small flotilla from the Northern Fleet in a global deployment, visiting the Mediterranean and the Indian Ocean, then China, before returning via the eastern Pacific and the Panama Canal, and making a visit to Cuba.

Two more Project 22350 vessels were laid down in 2019. Officially, problems relating to the ships' *Poliment-Redut* (SA-N-28) air-defence system and substitution of their Ukrainian-manufactured engines have been resolved. Meanwhile, construction has started on two modified Project 11711 landing platform docks.

Four nuclear-powered and two diesel-electric submarines are planned to be handed over to the navy in 2020. A contract was signed at the Army 2019 defence exhibition for two more *Yasen*-M-class submarines, bringing the total number of that class to nine, though the commissioning of the first *Yasen*-M boat appeared to have been further delayed by technical problems. April 2019 saw the launch of the large modified *Oscar* II-class submarine *Belgorod*, which is set to be a mother-ship for special-mission capabilities including the *Poseidon* nuclear-powered and nuclear-capable UUV. The navy is due to receive the second delivery platform for the *Poseidon* UUV, the Project 09851 boat *Khabarovsk*, by the end of 2022. It is reported that *Khabarovsk* may be equipped with six *Poseidon* UUVs, but the 2022 launch date may be optimistic given the challenges experienced by Russia's shipbuilding sector. In July 2019 a fire, reportedly on the *Losharik* nuclear-powered submersible, killed 14 people including a number of senior officers. Although the boat was recovered, it will require refit and modernisation, which is due to take place at Zvezdochka shipyard.

Strategic Rocket Forces

The Strategic Rocket Forces still set the pace in the armed forces' modernisation. It was reported that this service had in 2018 already attained the overall Russian armed forces' target of having 70% percent of new equipment in service by 2020. The plan is to equip three regiments with road-mobile RS-24 *Yars* (SS-27 mod 2) missiles before 2021. The Strategic Rocket Forces also plan to deliver two RS-24s for silo-basing with the 28th Guards Missile Division, and to start re-equipping (on an experimental basis) one regiment of the 13th Guards Missile Division at Dombarovsky with the *Avangard* hypersonic glide vehicle.

The test period for the *Sarmat* heavy liquid-fuelled ICBM has been changed. 'Pop-up' tests were completed in 2018 and engine ground-tests took place in 2019. Full test launches are now planned to take place no later than the end of 2020. Until *Sarmat* enters service in large numbers, the main launch vehicle for hypersonic glide vehicles will be the RS-18 (SS-19 *Stiletto*), which will likely see its service life extended.

Russia and future conflict

Since 2014, Russia has made increasingly visible use of its armed forces as a tool of national policy. Its military actions in Ukraine surprised transatlantic leaders, even though Russia had used military force before, in Georgia in 2008. John Kerry, the then US secretary of state, called Russia's occupation of Crimea a 'stunningly wilful choice'. Moscow's actions led to speculation about how its leadership was 'reinventing war' and assessments about how Russian ways of war were evolving. Some of the more prominent of these, arguing that Russia was waging a form of 'hybrid war', emerged after Crimea was annexed, and after a retrospective reading of a 2013 article signed by General Valery Gerasimov, then newly appointed as Russia's chief of the general staff. Entitled 'The Value of Science is in the Foresight: New Challenges Demand Rethinking in the Forms and Methods of Carrying out Combat Operations', this piece appeared in the 27 February 2013 edition of the *Military Industrial Courier*. Commentators introduced a range of catchy epithets – some coined by Western authors, others picked from the discussion among Russian sources – such as 'war in the grey zone', 'non-linear war' or 'new generation war', generally labelled as the so-called 'Gerasimov doctrine'. These views have remained prominent, updated with 'new' or '2.0' following another speech by Gerasimov in March 2019.

This emphasis may derive from Western strategists' judgement that Russia is obliged to compete in indirect, asymmetric ways since it could not hope to win a direct conventional confrontation with NATO states. According to General Sir Nick Carter, the United Kingdom's chief of defence staff, speaking in 2018, countries like China and Russia had been studying Western states' strengths and weaknesses and had become 'masters at exploiting the seams between peace and war'. Moscow would operate below the threshold of conventional war, weaponising a range of tools to pose a strategic challenge. These tools include, but are not limited to, energy supplies, corruption, assassination, disinformation and propaganda, and the use of proxies, including private military companies (PMCs). This is understood as a new Russian way of war that corresponds to 'measures short of war', and a preference for the manipulation of adversaries, avoiding military violence.

However, as specialists have pointed out, in the Russian debate there is no formulation resembling the 'Gerasimov doctrine'. Moreover, giving too much weight to terms such as 'new generation war' may also hinder an accurate understanding of Russian views of contemporary conflict. These do reflect a changing security environment and non-conventional capacities, but also reflect significant focus on the use of combat power.

Russian debate on future conflict

There was some discussion in Russia in 2013 about 'new generation war', but since then Russian practitioners and observers have tended to use the term 'new type' warfare. This is an important distinction in Russian military theory, given the extensive and long-running debates about the changing character of war, including the idea of 'sixth generation' warfare referenced by Major-General Vladimir Slipchenko following *Operation Desert Storm* in 1991. However, even though the term 'hybrid warfare' does exist in the Russian debate, it is used in reference to Western forms of war and how contemporary warfare more generally is evolving, not as some form of particularly Russian reinvention of war. Gerasimov himself noted, again in the *Military Industrial Courier* but in March 2017, that while 'so-called hybrid methods' are an important feature of international competition, it is 'premature' to classify 'hybrid warfare' as a type of military conflict, as US theorists do.

Indeed, rather than implementing 'measures short of war', there is evidence that Russia's leaders have sought to enhance national readiness, as illustrated by the many exercises that bring together all elements of the state and move the country onto a war footing. These exercises – including the *Vostok*, *Tsentr*, *Kavkaz* and *Zapad* series of strategic-level drills – seek to prepare Russia for fighting in a large-scale war. Furthermore, as is evident from the battlefields in Ukraine and Syria, while it may be considered preferable to achieve aims non-violently, this remains a theoretical ideal and the considerable weight of combat firepower is still a prominent feature of Russian conceptions of war fighting. Indeed, the scale of Russia's combat deployment has regularly been announced by the Russian leadership, particularly with reference to operations in Syria. It is more appropriate to think, therefore, not in terms of Russian 'measures short of war', but perhaps instead in terms of Russian 'measures of war'.

Continuity and change

Contemporary Russian views of conflict reflect both established and novel factors. They are the consequence of the blending of tradition – including Russia's history and its political, military and social structures inherited from the former Soviet Union – and the results of the extensive military-modernisation and reform process ongoing since the late 2000s. This has been characterised by a thoroughgoing, decade-long re-equipment programme, including organisational reform and increased exercises, interlaced with experience gained from foreign deployments.

An essential element in Russia's conception of contemporary conflict is the traditional importance of military science and the attempt to understand the changing character of war – and indeed to be able to forecast where and in what form war might in future occur – as well as to prepare the range of military structures and methods, such as doctrine and tactics, needed to employ the relevant forces. Indeed, this emphasis on military science runs throughout not only Gerasimov's 2013 article, but also some of those signed by him subsequently, as well as those by other senior figures. This points to the ongoing influence of prominent historical Russian and Soviet military thinkers, as well as Russian history, particularly the Second World War. Nonetheless, there is foreign influence, not only through Clausewitzian tradition, but also because Russia is actively seeking contemporary experience and expertise from abroad. For instance, between 2010 and 2012 Russian scientific teams were tasked with exploring foreign approaches to defence innovation and the exploitation of emerging technologies, in order to provide an assessment and recommendations drawing on leading international examples.

The intellectual foundation provided by military science underpins a range of practical results, including the creation of new units and the establishment of links to non-state organisations. Gerasimov has noted, for example, that the conflicts at the end of the twentieth century and those at the start of the twenty-first century differ in the balance of participants and weaponry used, as well as in the different types of forces and methods employed, such as 'joint teams of private military companies … and armed formations from the opposition' within a state. He reiterated this view in 2019, stating that 'wars are expanding and their contents significantly changing' and include attempts to destabilise the internal security of a state, including through the active use of the 'protest potential of a fifth column'. The number of participants is therefore increasing to include not only armed forces, but also various non-state groups, PMCs and 'self-proclaimed quasi states'.

This illustrates the view in Moscow that there are blurred lines between both peace and war and indeed between front lines and rear areas. It has led Russia's leadership to emphasise the need for effective territorial defence, in turn leading to shifts in the Russian security and defence landscape. The establishment in 2016 of the National Guard, also known as Rosgvardia, is an important example. The National Guard brings together Russia's interior troops and a range of other specialist forces, including riot police, and its remit ranges from the management of civil disobedience and protest to protecting strategic sites and addressing the potential challenge of well-armed insurgent forces.

Moscow's assessment that non-state groups with various roles are a feature of war is not new; it has sought to enhance its capacity by employing such groups to its own advantage, to enhance domestic security and to expand Russian influence abroad. In this respect, the activities of Russian PMCs in sub-Saharan Africa and Syria have received much attention. But the (re-)emergence of other non-state groups is also noteworthy in illustrating Moscow's attempt to enhance Russian territorial defence. Indeed, a number of paramilitary, militia-type organisations – including the Cossacks and other military-patriotic and sporting clubs – have emerged to play a role in forging patriotic social consensus, law enforcement, and martial-arts and military-style youth-training activities, such as urban warfare, anti-protest training and the control of public spaces. Taken together, non-state groups like these offer Moscow a number of advantages. They are useful as a comparatively cost-effective and flexible tool, potentially useful in a range of contingencies, and for their deployability, including to trouble spots abroad, combined with plausible deniability.

Nonetheless, the armed forces remain central to contemporary Russian conceptions of conflict. As Gerasimov has often noted, while the principle of warfare may have evolved to include non-military measures, the armed forces retain a 'decisive role'. This is not only because military force can be used when goals cannot be achieved by non-military means, but because Russia's opponents are seen as preparing to wage war using precision-guided munitions. For this reason, Gerasimov said in 2019, Russia's armed forces 'must be ready to conduct wars and armed conflicts of a new type using classical … methods of action'. Indeed, Gerasimov has underlined this during his tenure as chief of the general staff, repeatedly emphasising that military actions are becoming more dynamic and that new possibilities in command and control have strengthened the role of mobile, mixed groups of forces acting in a single information space. This offers the grounds to develop groups of forces for a 'strategy of limited action', in which Russia generates self-sufficient, highly mobile formations and a 'unified system of integrated forces', as well as the means to detect targets and deliver military strikes in real time.

Russian views of warfare have evolved considerably even since the Russo-Georgian war of 2008, with important consequences for force development and posture. The Russian defence and security landscape is changing in response and the shifting balance between military and non-military resources to achieve political ends is often referenced by senior officials. But at the same time, the role of the armed forces in ensuring Russian security is being reinforced. As such, conventional combat remains a central element in Russia's contemporary conception of conflict, with an emphasis on long-range precision strike and massed artillery fire, enhanced by new technology developments, including uninhabited systems and better command and control, and exploited by high-mobility forces.

DEFENCE ECONOMICS

Defence spending

Russia's total military expenditure in 2019 reverted to a more typical growth rate, with the share of spending falling to about 3.76% of GDP. This followed a period of sustained funding dedicated to improving military modernisation and weaponry in 2011–16. This has taken place within the context of an economy that is growing at only a modest pace: 0.3% in 2016, 1.6% in 2017, 2.3% in 2018 and an expected 1.1% in 2019. According to the International Monetary Fund, growth in 2020 will be 1.87%, rising to 2.05% in 2021 and 2022. Initial indications are that spending on 'national defence' (the budget chapter devoted to the defence ministry's military spending) in 2020 will be 3,056 billion roubles (US$44.2bn) – slightly less in nominal terms than in the 2019 budget.

Meanwhile, the structure of military spending has experienced change. In the state defence order, the share of total spending on procurement, modernisation, weapon repair and research and development (R&D) has been declining steadily from a peak of nearly 60% in 2015 to around 50% in 2019, while spending on pay and conditions, as well as defence infrastructure, has increased. In addition, there is still relatively high funding for defence-industry modernisation, the development of advanced materials and import-substitution measures.

As in 2017, the defence ministry in 2018 withheld some payments for deliveries under the state defence

Table 11 **Russian defence expenditure as % of GDP**

Year	'National Defence'			Total military expenditure[1]		
	Roubles (trillion)	US$ (billion)	% of GDP	Roubles (trillion)	US$ (billion)	% of GDP
2019	3.211	48.2	2.94	4.105	61.6	3.76
2018	2.830	45.2	2.72	3.928	62.7	3.78
2017	2.666[2]	45.7	2.89	3.712	63.7	4.03[2]
2016	2.982[2]	44.4	3.47	3.831	57.0	4.45[2]
2015	3.181	51.9	3.83	4.026	65.7	4.85
2014	2.479	64.5	3.14	3.222	83.9	4.08
2013	2.106	66.1	2.88	2.783	87.4	3.82
2012	1.812	58.3	2.66	2.482	79.9	3.68
2011	1.516	51.6	2.52	2.028	69.0	3.37

1. According to NATO definition.
2. Excluding a one-off payment to reduce accumulated debts of defence-industry enterprises under the scheme of state-guaranteed credits.

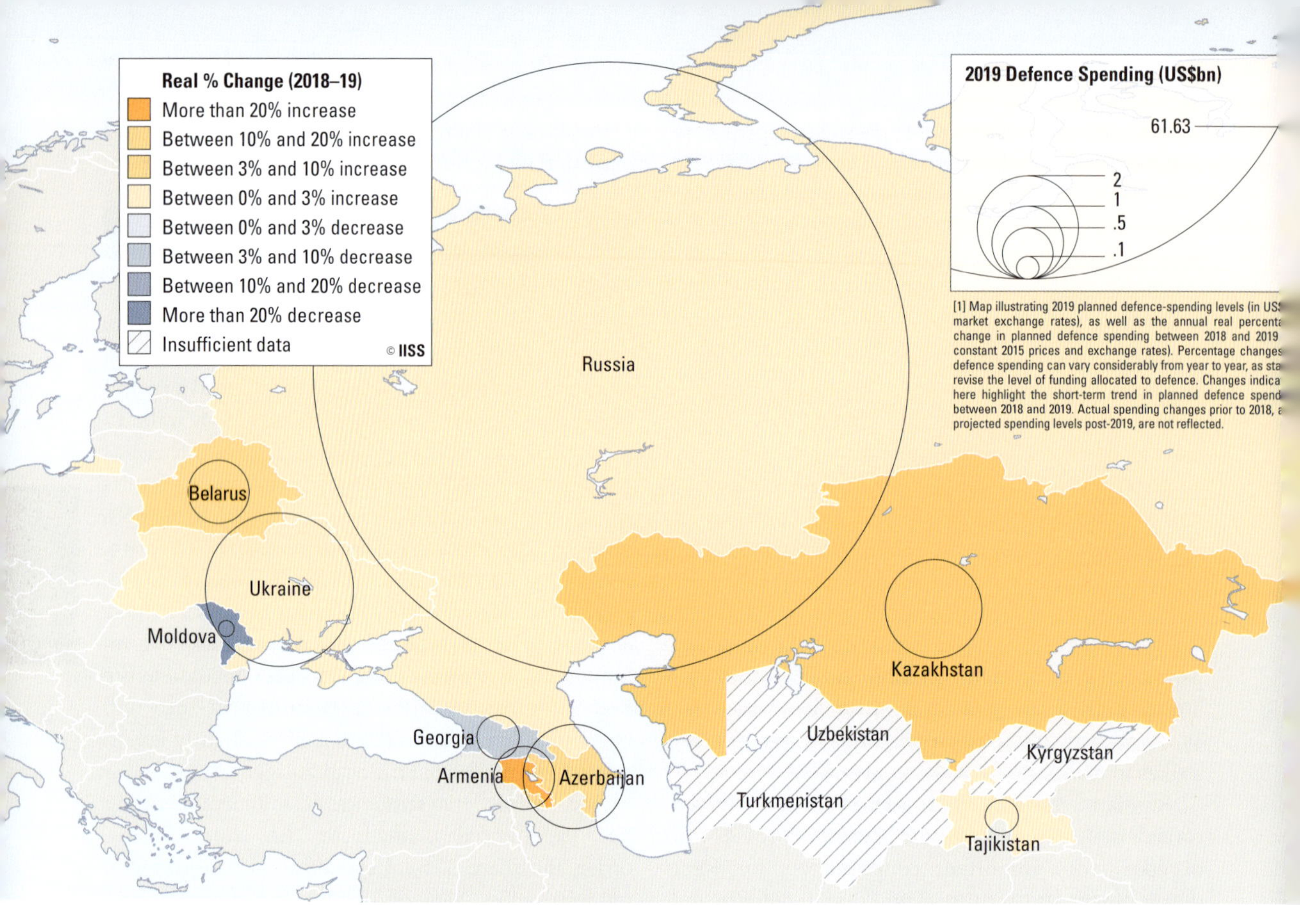

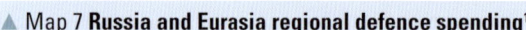

▲ Map 7 **Russia and Eurasia regional defence spending**[1]

▲ Figure 11 **Russia: estimated total military expenditure** as % of GDP

order until procurement and R&D contracts had been fully implemented. This resulted in an underspend in the budget allocation for 'national defence' and extra spending in spring 2019 as contracts were completed. This appears to have become a regular practice and analysts assess that in doing so the defence ministry is hoping that contract discipline will improve, in time leading to a steady diminution in the volume of delayed payments.

Weapons procurements

The final year in the State Armament Programme (GPV), which started in 2011, is 2020. This programme's main goal was to improve by 2020 the share of 'modern' weapons in active service units to at least 70%. The defence industry is now working to a new GPV to 2027, which started in 2018. GPV 2027 envisages that equipment will now be replaced at a more modest rate, though maintaining the 70% share throughout the period and beyond. According to the defence ministry, the actual share of modern weapons was 61.5% by the end of 2018 and it was expected to reach 67% by the end of 2019. It was forecast that the nuclear triad as a whole would have 85% modern systems, the air force 65%, the navy 64% and ground forces 51% by the end of 2019.

Overall, analysts estimate that around 60% of the equipment targets under GPV 2020 have been met. The construction of new submarines has proven more difficult than envisaged – although in 2020 as many as six may enter service – and the construction of surface combatants has been hampered by sanctions, ending the supply of power units from Germany and Ukraine. There is an active import-substitution programme but it will take a further two to three years to reach an acceptable level of domestic supply.

Defence industry

The most significant organisational change in Russia's defence industry was the start, in 2019, of the incorporation of United Aircraft Corporation (UAC) into the Rostec state corporation. It is reported that the process will be completed in 2020. The merger gives Rostec control of the entire aviation industry. The aviation cluster within Rostec will consist of a restructured UAC, Russian Helicopters, United Engine Corporation and Concern Radio-electronic Technology, with total annual sales exceeding 1 trillion roubles (US$14.5bn). Meanwhile, the space and missile industry, now under the Roscosmos state corporation, is undergoing a major restructuring programme, with the aim of achieving greater efficiency, more innovation and higher quality manufacturing in order to reduce the number of space-launch failures.

The defence industry's military output is now declining and civilian activities have become the principal source of growth. The aviation industry experienced the most rapid rate of decline of military production in 2018 and the first half of 2019. When this sector was at peak production, in order to meet the goals of GPV 2020, military-aviation output was up to 100 aircraft and up to 90 helicopters annually; the rate has now fallen to 50–60 and 30–40 respectively. These developments pose a challenge for the defence industry, if output and employment are to be sustained.

The accumulation of debt by the defence industry, now totalling up to 2trn roubles (US$30bn), is a serious problem. This has been caused by firms having to resort to credit because the defence ministry pays for new weapons only after they have been delivered and, over recent years, the volume of advance payments has been reduced. Commercial banks charge high rates of interest, often far in excess of 10%, but defence managers are also partly to blame as they reportedly set prices too low and underestimate costs in order to secure contracts. The defence ministry has been pursuing a tough financial policy and often does not compensate for cost overruns. Deputy Prime Minister Yuri Borisov, who is responsible for oversight of the defence industry, has called for 600–700bn roubles (US$9–10.5bn) of relief derived from the defence budget, but the finance ministry has rejected the appeal. It is not clear how this issue will be resolved but it cannot be ruled out that an amended version of the 2019 budget or the 2020 budget will include a substantial debt-resettlement allocation, as it did in 2016; however, that only related to state-guaranteed credits, not normal bank credit.

Defence-industry diversification

Diversification is now a priority task for Russia's defence industry, with the volume of spending on the state defence order beginning to decline and little prospect that its growth rate will pick up in the near term. Diversification was discussed by President Putin in September 2016 and basic targets have already been agreed. The civilian share of defence-industrial output is planned to rise from 17% in 2020 to 30% in 2025 and 50% by 2030. In 2019, the reported share reached over 20% and civilian output is now growing more rapidly than military output. Defence companies are expected to develop and manufacture

Table 12 **Russia's defence industry: annual percentage change of industrial output**[1]

	2011	2012	2013	2014	2015	2016	2017	2018
Total output	5.8	5.8	13.9	15.5	12.9	10.7	3.4	-2.5
Total military output	5.8	13.1	17.8	20.1	19.7	9.5	8.2	-10.8
By branch								
Aviation	9	12.3	17.2	18.3	5.2	9	11.7	-12.7
Missile space	10.6	11.8	15.3	8.6	8.9	-0.9	8.3	-4.1
Ground forces	17.1	7	2.8	5.2	-2.6	10.1	6.5	1.6
Munitions	2.5	7.6	9.1	14	22.3	14.4	-6	2.7
Shipbuilding	-13.2	-7.8	1.4	40.7	14.7	3.9	10.9	1.5
Radio-electronics[2]	9.9	17.1	29.5	19.9	33	18.5	-11.2	8.8

1. Excludes nuclear industry
2. Includes air-defence-system development and manufacture

high-technology civilian goods, selling both at home and abroad. There appears to be confidence in some large industrial actors that the targets can be met, notably Rostec, which already has some diversified companies with considerable experience of non-military work. But in other sectors, the need to diversify is giving rise to considerable concern, with mounting demands for budgetary and other state support.

There is now considerable emphasis on the role the defence industry could play in meeting the goals of the 'national programmes', which are seen in Russia as a means of boosting economic growth, and improving the provision of health, education and welfare and the development of the country's transport system and infrastructure. The Ministry of Industry and Trade estimates that during 2019–24 the defence industry will produce civil goods for national projects to a value of 2.2trn roubles (US$33bn), especially goods for the digital economy, and Russia's health, education and transport programmes. Industry has been asked to submit proposals for new products that will meet the needs of these state programmes and then compete for federal and regional budget funding and possible medium- and long-term 'credits'. In order to boost demand, credits will also be granted to the customers of these new products. More contentious is a proposal by the Ministry of Industry and Trade that customers will be obliged to purchase from domestic producers, above all defence-industrial enterprises, with limited access to imports. Some official agencies, notably the Anti-monopoly Service, are opposed to this proposal and it may not gain government backing. According to Borisov, a state programme for diversification may be set out and approved along with the next GPV.

Arms exports

In 2018, Russia's military exports totalled almost US$16bn, including US$13.7bn by state intermediary Rosoboronexport, with an overall portfolio of orders in June 2019 of US$54bn. The share of air-defence systems in the portfolio has increased to 20%, compared with 15% in 2017. This trend is set to continue, given the strong interest in Russian air-defence systems, including the S-400. There is little evidence that pressure from the United States, or even the imposition of sanctions designed to persuade states not to purchase weapons from Russia, has had much impact, although in some cases it may be delaying the implementation of contracts that have been agreed in principle. Delivery to Turkey of the S-400 has started and it may be operational there in early in 2020. With Turkey ejected from the F-35 combat-aircraft programme, there is speculation that either the Su-35 or Su-57 could be imported from Russia. Analysts see that progress in this regard would be more likely with the Su-35. India concluded a US$5.43bn contract for the S-400 in October 2018 and is expected to start receiving the system in 2020. However, US pressure is leading to the reduced use of the US dollar in Russian arms sales, with growth in settlement in national currencies and resort to diverse offset agreements.

Armenia ARM

Armenian Dram d		2018	2019	2020
GDP	d	6.01tr	6.54tr	
	US$	12.4bn	13.4bn	
per capita	US$	4,188	4,528	
Growth	%	5.2	6.0	
Inflation	%	2.5	1.7	
Def bdgt [a]	d	248bn	313bn	
	US$	513m	644m	
FMA (US)	US$	0m	0m	0m
US$1=d		482.99	486.54	

[a] Includes imported military equipment, excludes military pensions

Real-terms defence budget trend (US$m, constant 2015)

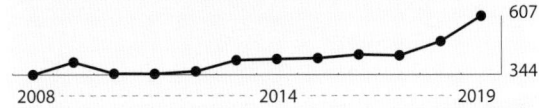

Population	3,030,288					
Age	0–14	15–19	20–24	25–29	30–64	65 plus
Male	9.9%	3.0%	3.3%	4.1%	23.5%	4.9%
Female	8.8%	2.6%	3.1%	4.1%	25.5%	7.2%

Capabilities

The armed forces' main focus is territorial defence, given continuing tensions with neighbouring Azerbaijan over Nagorno-Karabakh. In early 2018, a Modernisation Programme was released for the period 2018–24. Despite economic constraints, the document outlined the ambitious goal of reorganising the command structure and modernising the equipment inventory. The programme includes sections on cyber- and information-domain capabilities. Armenia is a member of the CSTO and maintains close defence ties with Russia, centred on equipment-procurement, technical-advice and personnel-training programmes. Military doctrine remains influenced by Russian thinking. Armenia is also engaged in a NATO Individual Partnership Action Plan. Conscription continues, but there is a growing cohort of professional officers. The armed forces have deployed on NATO and UN missions in Afghanistan, Kosovo and Lebanon, providing learning opportunities. Personnel train regularly and take part in annual CSTO exercises and with Russia in bilateral drills. Equipment is mainly of Russian origin. Agreements have been reached in recent years to purchase modern Russian systems. Serviceability and maintenance of mainly ageing aircraft have been a problem for the air force. There is some capacity to manufacture defence equipment for the domestic market, including electro-optics, light weapons and UAVs, but Armenia is reliant on Russia for other equipment platforms and systems.

ACTIVE 44,800 (Army 41,850 Air/AD Aviation Forces (Joint) 1,100 other Air Defence Forces 1,850)
Paramilitary 4,300
Conscript liability 24 months

RESERVE
Some mobilisation reported, possibly 210,000 with military service within 15 years

ORGANISATIONS BY SERVICE

Army 22,900; 18,950 conscripts (total 41,850)
FORCES BY ROLE
SPECIAL FORCES
  1 SF bde
MANOEUVRE
  Mechanised
  1 (1st) corps (1 recce bn, 1 tk bn, 2 MR regt, 1 maint bn)
  1 (2nd) corps (1 recce bn, 1 tk bn, 2 MR regt, 1 lt inf regt, 1 arty bn)
  1 (3rd) corps (1 recce bn, 1 tk bn, 4 MR regt, 1 lt inf regt, 1 arty bn, 1 MRL bn, 1 sigs bn, 1 maint bn)
  1 (4th) corps (4 MR regt; 1 SP arty bn; 1 sigs bn)
  1 (5th) corps (with 2 fortified areas) (1 MR regt)
  Other
  1 indep MR trg bde
COMBAT SUPPORT
  1 arty bde
  1 MRL bde
  1 AT regt
  1 AD bde
  2 AD regt
  2 (radiotech) AD regt
  1 engr regt
EQUIPMENT BY TYPE
ARMOURED FIGHTING VEHICLES
  MBT 109: 3 T-54; 5 T-55; 101 T-72A/B
  RECCE 12 BRM-1K (CP)
  IFV 231: 75 BMP-1; 6 BMP-1K (CP); 150 BMP-2
  APC • APC (W) 130: 8 BTR-60; 100 BTR-60 look-a-like; 18 BTR-70; 4 BTR-80
ENGINEERING & MAINTENANCE VEHICLES
  AEV MT-LB
  ARV BREhM-D; BREM-1
ANTI-TANK/ANTI-INFRASTRUCTURE
  MSL • SP 22+: 9 9P148 *Konkurs* (AT-5 *Spandrel*); 13 9P149 *Shturm* (AT-6 *Spiral*); 9K129 *Kornet-E* (AT-14 *Spriggan*)
ARTILLERY 232
  SP 28: **122mm** some 2S1 *Gvozdika*; **152mm** 28 2S3 *Akatsiya*
  TOWED 131: **122mm** 69 D-30; **152mm** 62: 26 2A36 *Giatsint-B*; 2 D-1; 34 D-20
  MRL 60: **122mm** ε50 BM-21 *Grad*; **273mm** 4 WM-80; **300mm** 6 9A52 *Smerch*
  MOR 120mm 12 M120
SURFACE-TO-SURFACE MISSILE LAUNCHERS
  SRBM • Conventional 16: 8 9K72 *Elbrus* (SS-1C *Scud B*); 4 9K79 *Tochka* (SS-21 *Scarab*); 4 9K720 *Iskander*-E
UNMANNED AERIAL VEHICLES
  ISR • Light 15 *Krunk*
AIR DEFENCE
  SAM
    Medium-range 2K11 *Krug* (SA-4 *Ganef*); S-75 *Dvina* (SA-2 *Guideline*); 9K37M *Buk*-M1 (SA-11 *Gadfly*)
    Short-range 2K12 *Kub* (SA-6 *Gainful*); S-125 *Pechora* (SA-3 *Goa*)
    Point-defence 9K33 *Osa* (SA-8 *Gecko*); 9K310 *Igla*-1 (SA-16 *Gimlet*); 9K38 *Igla* (SA-18 *Grouse*); 9K333 *Verba*;

9K338 *Igla*-S (SA-24 *Grinch*)
GUNS
 SP 23mm ZSU-23-4
 TOWED 23mm ZU-23-2

Air and Air Defence Aviation Forces 1,100
1 Air & AD Joint Command
FORCES BY ROLE
GROUND ATTACK
 1 sqn with Su-25/Su-25UBK *Frogfoot*
EQUIPMENT BY TYPE
AIRCRAFT 14 combat capable
 ATK 14: 13 Su-25 *Frogfoot*; 1 Su-25UBK *Frogfoot*
 TPT 4: Heavy 3 Il-76 *Candid*; **PAX** 1 A319CJ
 TRG 14: 4 L-39 *Albatros*; 10 Yak-52
HELICOPTERS
 ATK 7 Mi-24P *Hind*
 ISR 4: 2 Mi-24K *Hind*; 2 Mi-24R *Hind* (cbt spt)
 MRH 10 Mi-8MT (cbt spt)
 C2 2 Mi-9 *Hip* G (cbt spt)
 TPT • Light 7 PZL Mi-2 *Hoplite*
AIR DEFENCE • SAM • Long-range S-300PT (SA-10 *Grumble*); S-300PS (SA-10 *Grumble*)

Paramilitary 4,300

Police
FORCES BY ROLE
MANOEUVRE
 Other
  4 paramilitary bn
EQUIPMENT BY TYPE
ARMOURED FIGHTING VEHICLES
 RECCE 5 BRM-1K (CP)
 IFV 45: 44 BMP-1; 1 BMP-1K (CP)
 APC • APC (W) 24 BTR-60/BTR-70/BTR-152
 ABCV 5 BMD-1

Border Troops
Ministry of National Security
EQUIPMENT BY TYPE
ARMOURED FIGHTING VEHICLES
 RECCE 3 BRM-1K (CP)
 IFV 35 BMP-1
 APC • APC (W) 23: 5 BTR-60; 18 BTR-70
 ABCV 5 BMD-1

DEPLOYMENT
AFGHANISTAN: NATO • *Operation Resolute Support* 121
LEBANON: UN • UNIFIL 33
SERBIA: NATO • KFOR 41

FOREIGN FORCES
Russia 3,300: 1 mil base with (1 MR bde; 74 T-72; 80 BMP-1; 80 BMP-2; 12 2S1; 12 BM-21); 1 ftr sqn with 18 MiG-29 *Fulcrum*; 1 hel sqn with 8 Mi-24P *Hind*; 4 Mi-8MT *Hip*; 2 SAM bty with S-300V (SA-12 *Gladiator/Giant*); 1 SAM bty with 2K12 *Kub* (SA-6 *Gainful*)

Azerbaijan AZE

Azerbaijani New Manat m		2018	2019	2020
GDP	m	79.8bn	80.2bn	
	US$	46.9bn	47.2bn	
per capita	US$	4,722	4,689	
Growth	%	1.0	2.7	
Inflation	%	2.3	2.8	
Def bdgt [a]	m	2.91bn	3.04bn	
	US$	1.71bn	1.79bn	
US$1=m		1.70	1.70	

[a] Official defence budget. Excludes a significant proportion of procurement outlays

Real-terms defence budget trend (US$bn, constant 2015)

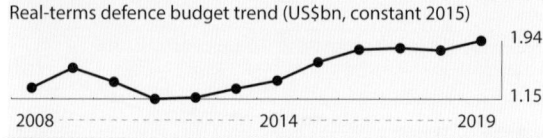

Population	10,128,025					
Age	0–14	15–19	20–24	25–29	30–64	65 plus
Male	12.2%	3.3%	3.8%	4.8%	22.7%	2.7%
Female	10.8%	2.9%	3.4%	4.6%	24.4%	4.3%

Capabilities

The armed forces' principal focus is territorial defence, in light of continuing tensions with neighbouring Armenia over Nagorno-Karabakh. Azerbaijan maintains a defence relationship with NATO, concluding in 2019 a fifth cycle of its NATO Individual Partnership Action Plan. Azerbaijan is looking to deepen ties with Belarus, Serbia, the UK and the US through military-cooperation agreements. Defence cooperation with Moscow is focused on equipment procurement and technical advice. Readiness within Azerbaijan's conscript-based armed services varies between units. Azerbaijan has taken part in multilateral exercises and its forces have trained with Turkish troops in bilateral drills. The armed forces have little expeditionary capability though they contribute to NATO's *Resolute Support* mission in Afghanistan. Defence modernisation and procurement has been a focus in the past decade, to replace the ageing inventory of mainly Soviet-era equipment. The air force in particular suffers from maintenance problems. Recent orders include for air-defence and artillery systems and wheeled and tracked armoured vehicles, predominantly of Russian origin. Azerbaijan's limited but growing defence-industrial capabilities are centred on the Ministry of Defence Industry, which manages and oversees the production of small arms and light weapons. While the country is reliant on external suppliers for major defence-equipment platforms and systems, some defence companies have started to export to foreign markets.

ACTIVE 66,950 (Army 56,850 Navy 2,200 Air 7,900)
Paramilitary 15,000
Conscript liability 18 months (12 for graduates)

RESERVE 300,000
Some mobilisation reported; 300,000 with military service within 15 years

ORGANISATIONS BY SERVICE

Army 56,850
FORCES BY ROLE
COMMAND
  5 corps HQ
MANOEUVRE
  Mechanised
    4 MR bde
  Light
    19 MR bde
  Other
    1 sy bde
COMBAT SUPPORT
  1 arty bde
  1 arty trg bde
  1 MRL bde
  1 AT bde
  1 engr bde
  1 sigs bde
COMBAT SERVICE SUPPORT
  1 log bde
EQUIPMENT BY TYPE
ARMOURED FIGHTING VEHICLES
  MBT 439: 95 T-55; 244 T-72A/AV/B; 100 T-90S
  RECCE 15 BRM-1
  IFV 216: 43 BMP-1; 33 BMP-2; 88 BMP-3; 7 BTR-80A; 45+ BTR-82A
  APC 568
    APC (T) 336 MT-LB
    APC (W) 142: 10 BTR-60; 132 BTR-70
    PPV 90: 45 *Marauder*; 45 *Matador*
  AUV 65+: 35 *Cobra*; 30+ *Sand Cat*
  ABCV 20 BMD-1
ENGINEERING & MAINTENANCE VEHICLES
  AEV IMR-2; MT-LB
  ARV BREM-L *Brelianka*
  MW *Bozena*; GW-3 (minelayer)
ANTI-TANK/ANTI-INFRASTRUCTURE
  SP 10 9P157-2 *Khrizantema*-S (AT-15 *Springer*)
  MSL • MANPATS 9K11 *Malyutka* (AT-3 *Sagger*); 9K111 *Fagot* (AT-4 *Spigot*); 9K111-1 *Konkurs* (AT-5 *Spandrel*); 9K115 *Metis* (AT-7 *Saxhorn*); *Spike*-LR
ARTILLERY 598
  SP 96: **122mm** 46 2S1 *Gvozdika*; **152mm** 33: 6 2S3 *Akatsiya*; 18 2S19 *Msta*-S; 9 M-77 *Dana*; **155mm** 5 ATMOS 2000; **203mm** 12 2S7 *Pion*
  TOWED 207: **122mm** 129 D-30; **130mm** 36 M-46; **152mm** 42: 18 2A36 *Giatsint*-B; 24 D-20
  GUN/MOR 120mm 36: 18 2S9 NONA-S; 18 2S31 *Vena*
  MRL 147: **122mm** 60+: 43 BM-21 *Grad*; 9+ IMI *Lynx*; 8 RM-70 *Vampir*; **128mm** 12 RAK-12; **220mm** 18 TOS-1A; **300mm** 36: 30 9A52 *Smerch*; 6+ *Polonez*; **302mm** 21 T-300 *Kasirga*
  MOR 120mm 112: 5 *Cardom*; 107 M-1938 (PM-38)
SURFACE-TO-SURFACE MISSILE LAUNCHERS
  SRBM • Conventional 6: 2 IAI LORA; ε4 9K79 *Tochka* (SS-21 *Scarab*)

UNMANNED AERIAL VEHICLES
  ISR • Medium 3 *Aerostar*
AIR DEFENCE
  SAM
    Medium-range 2K11 *Krug* (SA-4 *Ganef*)
    Point-defence 9K33 *Osa* (SA-8 *Gecko*); 9K35 *Strela*-10 (SA-13 *Gopher*); 9K32 *Strela* (SA-7 *Grail*)‡; 9K34 *Strela*-3 (SA-14 *Gremlin*); 9K310 *Igla*-1 (SA-16 *Gimlet*); 9K338 *Igla*-S (SA-24 *Grinch*)
  GUNS
    SP 23mm ZSU-23-4
    TOWED 23mm ZU-23-2

Navy 2,200
EQUIPMENT BY TYPE
PATROL AND COASTAL COMBATANTS 12
  CORVETTES • FS 1 *Kusar* (ex-FSU *Petya II*) with 2 RBU 6000 *Smerch* 2 A/S mor, 2 twin 76mm gun
  PSO 2: 1 *Luga* (*Wodnik* 2) (FSU Project 888; additional trg role); 1 *Neftegaz* (Project B-92) (ex-Coast Guard)
  PCC 3: 2 *Petrushka* (FSU UK-3; additional trg role); 1 *Shelon* (ex-FSU Project 1388M)
  PB 3: 1 *Araz* (ex-TUR AB 25); 1 *Bryza* (ex-FSU Project 722); 1 *Poluchat* (ex-FSU Project 368)
  PBF 3 *Stenka*
MINE WARFARE • MINE COUNTERMEASURES 4
  MHC 4: 2 *Korund* (*Yevgenya*) (Project 1258); 2 *Yakhont* (FSU *Sonya*)
AMPHIBIOUS 6
  LSM 3: 1 *Polnochny A* (FSU Project 770) (capacity 6 MBT; 180 troops); 2 *Polnochny B* (FSU Project 771) (capacity 6 MBT; 180 troops)
  LCM 3: 2 T-4 (FSU); 1 *Vydra*† (FSU) (capacity either 3 MBT or 200 troops)
LOGISTICS AND SUPPORT • AGS 1 (FSU Project 10470)

Air Force and Air Defence 7,900
FORCES BY ROLE
FIGHTER
  1 sqn with MiG-29 *Fulcrum*; MiG-29UB *Fulcrum*
FIGHTER/GROUND ATTACK
  1 regt with Su-24 *Fencer*; Su-25 *Frogfoot*; Su-25UB *Frogfoot* B
TRANSPORT
  1 sqn with An-12 *Cub*; Yak-40 *Codling*
TRAINING
  1 sqn with L-39 *Albatros*
ATTACK/TRANSPORT HELICOPTER
  1 regt with Ka-32 *Helix* C; Mi-8 *Hip*; Mi-24 *Hind*; PZL Mi-2 *Hoplite*
EQUIPMENT BY TYPE
AIRCRAFT 36 combat capable
  FTR 15: 13 MiG-29 *Fulcrum*; 2 MiG-29UB *Fulcrum*
  ATK 21: 2 Su-24 *Fencer*†; 16 Su-25 *Frogfoot*; 3 Su-25UB *Frogfoot* B
  TPT 4: **Medium** 1 An-12 *Cub*; **Light** 3 Yak-40 *Codling*
  TRG 15: 12 L-39 *Albatros*; 3+ *Super Mushshak*
HELICOPTERS
  ATK 26 Mi-24 *Hind*
  MRH: 20+ Mi-17-IV *Hip*

TPT 24: **Medium** 17: 1 Bell 412; 3 Ka-32 *Helix* C; 13 Mi-8 *Hip* **Light** 7 PZL Mi-2 *Hoplite*
UAV • **ISR** 16: **Heavy** 1 *Heron*; **Medium** 15: 4 *Aerostar*; 10+ *Hermes* 450; 1 *Hermes* 900
AIR DEFENCE • SAM
  Long-range S-200 *Vega* (SA-5 *Gammon*); S-300PM/PMU2
  Medium-range S-75 *Dvina* (SA-2 *Guideline*); 9K37M *Buk*-M1 (SA-11 *Gadfly*); *Buk*-MB; S-125-2TM *Pechora*-2TM (SA-26)
  Short-range *Abisr*
AIR-LAUNCHED MISSILES
  AAM • **IR** R-60 (AA-8 *Aphid*); R-73 (AA-11A *Archer*) **IR/SARH** R-27 (AA-10 *Alamo*)
  ASM *Barrier*-V

Paramilitary ε15,000

State Border Service ε5,000
Ministry of Internal Affairs
EQUIPMENT BY TYPE
ARMOURED FIGHTING VEHICLES
  IFV 168 BMP-1/BMP-2
  APC • **APC (W)** 19 BTR-60/70/80
ARTILLERY • **MRL 122mm** 3 T-122
HELICOPTERS • **ATK** 24 Mi-35M *Hind*
UNMANNED AERIAL VEHICLES
  ISR • **Medium** *Hermes* 900

Coast Guard
The Coast Guard was established in 2005 as part of the State Border Service
EQUIPMENT BY TYPE
PATROL AND COASTAL COMBATANTS 17
  PCG 4 *Sa'ar* 62 with 1 8-cell *Typhoon* MLS-NLOS lnchr with *Spike* NLOS SSM, 1 hel landing platform
  PBF 9: 1 *Osa* II (FSU Project 205); 6 *Shaldag* V; 2 Silver Ships 48ft
  PB 4: 2 Baltic 150; 1 *Point* (US); 1 *Grif* (FSU *Zhuk*)
LOGISTICS AND SUPPORT 5
  ARS 1 *Iva* (FSU *Vikhr*)
  ATF 4 *Neftegaz* (Project B-92) (also used for patrol duties)

Internal Troops 10,000+
Ministry of Internal Affairs
EQUIPMENT BY TYPE
ARMOURED FIGHTING VEHICLES
  APC • **APC (W)** 7 BTR-60/BTR-70/BTR-80

DEPLOYMENT

AFGHANISTAN: NATO • *Operation Resolute Support* 120

TERRITORY WHERE THE GOVERNMENT DOES NOT EXERCISE EFFECTIVE CONTROL

Nagorno-Karabakh was part of Azerbaijan, but mostly populated by ethnic Armenians. In 1988, when inter-ethnic clashes between Armenians and Azeris erupted in Azerbaijan, the local authorities declared their intention to secede and join Armenia. Baku rejected this and armed conflict erupted. A ceasefire was brokered in 1994; since then, Armenia has controlled most of Nagorno-Karabakh. While Armenia provides political, economic and military support to Nagorno-Karabakh, the region has declared itself independent – although this has not been recognised by any other state, including Armenia. Baku claims Nagorno-Karabakh and the occupied territories as part of Azerbaijan. Data presented here represents an assessment of the de facto situation.

Nagorno-Karabakh

Available estimates vary with reference to military holdings in Nagorno-Karabakh. Main battle tanks are usually placed at around 200–300 in number, with similar numbers for other armoured combat vehicles and artillery pieces, and small numbers of helicopters. Overall personnel-strength estimates are between 18,000 and 20,000. Some of the equipment listed may belong to Armenian forces.
EQUIPMENT BY TYPE
ARMOURED FIGHTING VEHICLES
  MBT T-72
  RECCE BRDM-2
  IFV BMP-1; BMP-2
ANTI-TANK/ANTI-INFRASTRUCTURE
  MSL
    SP 9P148 *Konkurs* (AT-5 *Spandrel*); 9P149 *Shturm* (AT-6 *Spiral*)
    MANPATS 9K111-1 *Konkurs* (AT-5 *Spandrel*)
  RCL **73mm** SPG-9
ARTILLERY 232
  SP 122mm 2S1 *Gvozdika*; **152mm** 2S3 *Akatsiya*
  TOWED 122mm D-30; **152mm** 2A36 *Giatsint*-B; D-20
  MRL 122mm BM-21 *Grad*; **273mm** WM-80
  MOR 120mm M-74/M-75
SURFACE-TO-SURFACE MISSILE LAUNCHERS
  SRBM • **Conventional** 9K72 *Elbrus* (SS-1C *Scud* B)
HELICOPTERS
  ATK 5 Mi-24 *Hind*
  MRH 5 Mi-8MT *Hip*
AIR DEFENCE
  SAM
    Medium-range 2K11 *Krug* (SA-4 *Ganef*); S-75 *Dvina* (SA-2 *Guideline*)
    Short-range 2K12 *Kub* (SA-6 *Gainful*); S-125 *Pechora* (SA-3 *Goa*)
    Point-defence 9K33 *Osa* (SA-8 *Gecko*); 9K310 *Igla*-1 (SA-16 *Gimlet*); 9K38 *Igla* (SA-18 *Grouse*)
  GUNS
    SP 23mm ZSU-23-4
    TOWED 23mm ZU-23-2

Belarus BLR

Belarusian Ruble r		2018	2019	2020
GDP	r	122bn	131bn	
	US$	59.6bn	62.6bn	
per capita	US$	6,283	6,604	
Growth	%	3.1	1.5	
Inflation	%	4.9	5.4	
Def bdgt	r	1.22bn	1.36bn	
	US$	599m	650m	
US$1=r		2.04	2.10	

Real-terms defence budget trend (US$m, constant 2015)

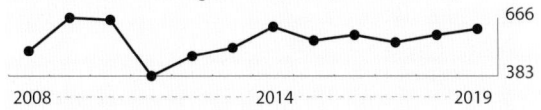

666
383
2008 — 2014 — 2019

Population	9,503,591					
Age	0–14	15–19	20–24	25–29	30–64	65 plus
Male	8.2%	2.4%	2.6%	3.5%	24.8%	5.0%
Female	7.8%	2.3%	2.4%	3.3%	27.2%	10.5%

Capabilities

Located between Russia and NATO European members, the main task of Belarus's armed forces is maintaining territorial integrity. The country's latest military doctrine was approved in July 2016, and identified as security challenges 'hybrid methods' and 'colour revolutions'. It also called for smaller, more mobile forces with improved counter-terrorism capabilities. Belarus is a member of the CSTO. Russia remains the country's principal defence partner, though Minsk has also looked to improve defence cooperation with China and Turkey. The forces remain conscript-based and train regularly with other CSTO partners. There has been increased emphasis on the training of territorial-defence troops to allow them to better operate with the regular forces. There is a small heavy-airlift fleet that could be supplemented by civil transport aircraft, and Minsk has a special-forces brigade trained for the air-assault role. There is no requirement to independently deploy and sustain the armed forces, but they could do so as a part of the CSTO. Russia continues to be Minsk's main defence-equipment supplier. In recent years, Belarus has received air-defence systems and advanced combat-trainer/light-attack aircraft from Moscow. The first Su-30SM *Flanker* H multi-role fighter aircraft were delivered from Russia in late 2019. The local defence industry manufactures vehicles, guided weapons and electronic-warfare systems, among other equipment. However, there is no capacity to design or manufacture modern combat aircraft. The sector also undertakes upgrade work for foreign customers.

ACTIVE 45,350 (Army 10,700 Air 11,750 Special Operations Forces 5,900 Joint 17,000) **Paramilitary 110,000**

Conscript liability 18 months; 12 months for graduates (alternative service option)

RESERVE 289,500 (Joint 289,500 with mil service within last 5 years)

ORGANISATIONS BY SERVICE

Army 10,700

FORCES BY ROLE
COMMAND
  2 comd HQ (West & North West)
MANOEUVRE
  Mechanised
  2 mech bde
  2 mech bde(-)
COMBAT SUPPORT
  2 arty bde
  1 engr bde
  1 engr regt

EQUIPMENT BY TYPE
ARMOURED FIGHTING VEHICLES
  MBT 532: 517 T-72B; 15 T-72B3 mod
  RECCE 132 BRM-1; *Cayman* BRDM
  IFV 932 BMP-2
  APC • APC (T) 58 MT-LB
  AUV 8 CS/VN3B mod; GAZ *Tigr*
ENGINEERING & MAINTENANCE VEHICLES
  AEV BAT-2; IMR-2; MT-LB
  VLB 24: 20 MTU-20; 4 MT-55A
  MW UR-77
NBC VEHICLES BRDM-2RKhB; RKhM-4; RKhm-K
ANTI-TANK/ANTI-INFRASTRUCTURE • MSL
  SP 160: 75 9P148 *Konkurs*; 85 9P149 *Shturm*
  MANPATS 9K111 *Fagot* (AT-4 *Spigot*); 9K111-1 *Konkurs* (AT-5 *Spandrel*); 9K115 *Metis* (AT-7 *Saxhorn*)
ARTILLERY 583
  SP 333: **122mm** 125 2S1 *Gvozdika*; **152mm** 208: 125 2S3 *Akatsiya*; 71 2S5; 12 2S19 *Msta-S*
  TOWED 152mm 72 2A65 *Msta-B*
  MRL 164: **122mm** 128 BM-21 *Grad*; **220mm** 36 9P140 *Uragan*
  MOR 120mm 14 2S12
AIR DEFENCE
  SAM Point-defence 2K22 *Tunguska* (SA-19 *Grison*)
  GUNS • SP 23mm ZU-23-2 (tch)

Air Force and Air Defence Forces 11,750

FORCES BY ROLE
FIGHTER
  2 sqn with MiG-29/S/UB *Fulcrum*
GROUND ATTACK
  2 sqn with Su-25K/UBK *Frogfoot* A/B
TRANSPORT
  1 base with An-12 *Cub*; An-24 *Coke*; An-26 *Curl*; Il-76 *Candid*; Tu-134 *Crusty*
TRAINING
  Some sqn with L-39 *Albatros*
ATTACK HELICOPTER
  Some sqn with Mi-24 *Hind*
TRANSPORT HELICOPTER
  Some (cbt spt) sqn with Mi-8 *Hip*; Mi-8MTV-5 *Hip*; Mi-26 *Halo*

EQUIPMENT BY TYPE
AIRCRAFT 70 combat capable
  FTR 34: 28 MiG-29 *Fulcrum*/MiG-29S *Fulcrum* C; 6 MiG-29UB *Fulcrum* B
  FGA 2 Su-30SM *Flanker* H; (21 Su-27/UB *Flanker* B/C non-operational/stored)
  ATK 22 Su-25K/UBK *Frogfoot* A/B
  TPT 8: **Heavy** 2 Il-76 *Candid* (+9 civ Il-76 available for mil use); **Light** 6: 1 An-24 *Coke*; 4 An-26 *Curl*; 1 Tu-134 *Crusty*
  TRG 12+: Some L-39 *Albatros*; 12 Yak-130 *Mitten**
HELICOPTERS
  ATK 12 Mi-24 *Hind*
  TPT 26: **Heavy** 6 Mi-26 *Halo*; **Medium** 20: 8 Mi-8 *Hip*; 12 Mi-8MTV-5 *Hip*
AIR-LAUNCHED MISSILES
  AAM • IR R-60 (AA-8 *Aphid*); R-73 (AA-11A *Archer*)
  SARH R-27R (AA-10 *Alamo* A)
  ASM Kh-25 (AS-10 *Karen*); Kh-29 (AS-14 *Kedge*)
  ARM Kh-58 (AS-11 *Kilter*) (likely WFU)

Air Defence
AD data from Uzal Baranovichi EW radar
FORCES BY ROLE
AIR DEFENCE
  1 bde S-300PS (SA-10 *Grumble*)
  3 regt with S-300PS (SA-10 *Grumble*)
  1 bde with 9K37 *Buk* (SA-11 *Gadfly*); 9K332 *Tor-M2E* (SA-15 *Gauntlet*)
  1 regt with 9K322 *Tor-M2E*
  2 regt with 9K33 *Osa* (SA-8 *Gecko*)
EQUIPMENT BY TYPE
AIR DEFENCE • SAM
  Long-range S-300PS (SA-10 *Grumble*)
  Medium-range 9K37 *Buk* (SA-11 *Gadfly*)
  Short-range 17 9K332 *Tor-M2E* (SA-15 *Gauntlet*)
  Point-defence 9K33 *Osa* (SA-8 *Gecko*); 9K35 *Strela*-10 (SA-13 *Gopher*)

Special Operations Command 5,900
FORCES BY ROLE
SPECIAL FORCES
  1 SF bde
MANOEUVRE
  Mechanised
  2 mech bde
EQUIPMENT BY TYPE
ARMOURED FIGHTING VEHICLES
  APC • APC (W) 185: 32 BTR-70M1; 153 BTR-80
ARTILLERY 42
  TOWED 122mm 24 D-30
  GUN/MOR • TOWED 120mm 18 2B23 NONA-M1
ANTI-TANK/ANTI-INFRASTRUCTURE • MSL
  MANPATS 9K111 *Fagot* (AT-4 *Spigot*); 9K111-1 *Konkurs* (AT-5 *Spandrel*); 9K115 *Metis* (AT-7 *Saxhorn*)

Joint 17,000 (Centrally controlled units and MoD staff)
FORCES BY ROLE
SURFACE-TO-SURFACE MISSILE
  1 SRBM bde

COMBAT SUPPORT
  1 arty bde
  1 MRL bde
  2 engr bde
  1 EW unit
  1 NBC regt
  1 ptn bridging regt
  2 sigs bde
EQUIPMENT BY TYPE
ARMOURED FIGHTING VEHICLES
  APC • APC (T) 20 MT-LB
NBC VEHICLES BRDM-2RKhB; RKhM-4; RKhM-K
ARTILLERY 112
  SP 152mm 36 2S5 *Giatsint-S*
  TOWED 152mm 36 2A65 *Msta*-B
  MRL 300mm 40: 36 9A52 *Smerch*; 4 *Polonez*
SURFACE-TO-SURFACE MISSILE LAUNCHERS
  SRBM • Conventional 96: 36 9K79 *Tochka* (SS-21 *Scarab*); 60 9K72 *Elbrus* (SS-1C *Scud* B)

Paramilitary 110,000

State Border Troops 12,000
Ministry of Interior

Militia 87,000
Ministry of Interior

Internal Troops 11,000

DEPLOYMENT
LEBANON: UN • UNIFIL 5

Georgia GEO

Georgian Lari		2018	2019	2020
GDP	lari	41.1bn	44.7bn	
	US$	16.2bn	15.9bn	
per capita	US$	4,346	4,289	
Growth	%	4.7	4.6	
Inflation	%	2.6	4.3	
Def bdgt	lari	815m	875m	880m
	US$	321m	311m	
FMA (US)	US$	35.0m	0m	20m
US$1=lari		2.53	2.81	

Real-terms defence budget trend (US$m, constant 2015)

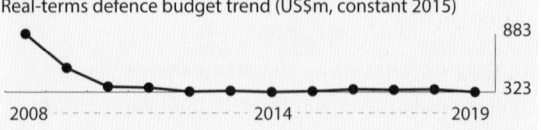

Population	4,927,349					
Age	0–14	15–19	20–24	25–29	30–64	65 plus
Male	9.6%	2.8%	3.2%	4.0%	21.9%	6.5%
Female	8.8%	2.4%	2.8%	3.8%	24.3%	10.0%

Capabilities

Georgia's main security preoccupations concern Russian military deployments and the breakaway regions of Abkhazia and South Ossetia. A Strategic Defence Review 2017–20 was published in April 2017. This aimed at improving personnel structures, training facilities and equipment and stressed a 'total defence' approach involving the armed forces and civil society. The document noted the importance of Georgia's reserve component for this framework. A new defence white paper was published in 2017. Long-standing security cooperation with the US includes the Georgia Defence Readiness Program, designed to boost military capabilities. The armed forces are professional and are working to develop NATO compatibility. Conscription was reinstated with revised terms and increased pay in early 2017. Despite participation in several NATO multinational exercises, readiness differs greatly between units and training levels tend to be variable. Georgia's armed forces have limited expeditionary logistic capability. The backbone of the armed forces' military equipment is legacy Soviet-era systems with varying degrees of obsolescence. The Major Systems Acquisitions Strategy 2019–25 outlines efforts to procure new equipment in several areas, including air defence, anti-tank systems, artillery, intelligence and aviation. The country has only recently begun to develop a defence-industrial base, and this is intended mainly to support the armed forces. The State Military Scientific-Technical Center has demonstrated some maintenance, repair, overhaul and design capabilities for the production of light armoured vehicles.

ACTIVE 20,650 (Army 19,050 National Guard 1,600)
Paramilitary 5,400
Conscript liability 12 months

ORGANISATIONS BY SERVICE

Army 15,000; 4,050 conscript (total 19,050)

FORCES BY ROLE
SPECIAL FORCES
  1 SF bde
MANOEUVRE
  Light
  5 inf bde
  Amphibious
  2 mne bn (1 cadre)
COMBAT SUPPORT
  2 arty bde
  1 engr bde
  1 sigs bn
  1 SIGINT bn
  1 MP bn
COMBAT SERVICE SUPPORT
  1 med bn

EQUIPMENT BY TYPE
ARMOURED FIGHTING VEHICLES
  MBT 123: 23 T-55AM2; 100 T-72B/SIM1
  RECCE 5: 1 BRM-1K; 4+ *Didgori*-2
  IFV 71: 25 BMP-1; 46 BMP-2
  APC 189+
    APC (T) 69+: 3+ *Lazika*; 66 MT-LB
    APC (W) 120+: 25 BTR-70; 19 BTR-80; 8+ *Didgori*-1; 3+ *Didgori*-3; 65 *Ejder*
  AUV 10+: ATF *Dingo*; *Cobra*; 10 *Cougar*

ENGINEERING & MAINTENANCE VEHICLES
  ARV IMR-2
ANTI-TANK/ANTI-INFRASTRUCTURE
  MSL • MANPATS 9K111 *Fagot* (AT-4 *Spigot*); 9K113 *Konkurs* (AT-5 *Spandrel*); FGM-148 *Javelin*
  GUNS • TOWED ε40: **85mm** D-44; **100mm** T-12
ARTILLERY 240
  SP 67: **122mm** 20 2S1 *Gvozdika*; **152mm** 46: 32 M-77 *Dana*; 13 2S3 *Akatsiya*; 1 2S19 *Msta*-S; **203mm** 1 2S7 *Pion*
  TOWED 71: **122mm** 58 D-30; **152mm** 13: 3 2A36 *Giatsint*-B; 10 2A65 *Msta*-B
  MRL 122mm 37: 13 BM-21 *Grad*; 6 GradLAR; 18 RM-70
  MOR 120mm 65: 14 2S12 *Sani*; 33 M-75; 18 M120
AIR DEFENCE • SAM
  Short-range *Spyder*-SR
  Point-defence *Grom*; *Mistral*-2; 9K32 *Strela*-2 (SA-7 *Grail*)‡; 9K35 *Strela*-10 (SA-13 *Gopher*); 9K36 *Strela*-3 (SA-14 *Gremlin*); 9K310 *Igla*-1 (SA-16 *Gimlet*)

Aviation and Air Defence Command 1,300 (incl 300 conscript)

1 avn base, 1 hel air base

EQUIPMENT BY TYPE
AIRCRAFT 3 combat capable
  ATK 3 Su-25KM *Frogfoot* (6 Su-25 *Frogfoot* in store)
  TPT • Light 9: 6 An-2 *Colt*; 1 Tu-134A *Crusty* (VIP); 2 Yak-40 *Codling*
  TRG 9 L-29 *Delfin*
HELICOPTERS
  ATK 6 Mi-24 *Hind*
  TPT 29: **Medium** 17 Mi-8T *Hip*; **Light** 12 Bell 205 (UH-1H *Iroquois*)
UNMANNED AERIAL VEHICLES
  ISR • Medium 1+ *Hermes* 450
AIR DEFENCE • SAM
  Medium-range 9K37 *Buk*-M1 (SA-11 *Gadfly*) (1–2 bn)
  Point-defence 8 9K33 *Osa* AK (SA-8B *Gecko*) (two bty); 9K33 *Osa* AKM (6–10 updated SAM systems)

National Guard 1,600 active reservists opcon Army

FORCES BY ROLE
MANOEUVRE
  Light
  1 inf bde

Paramilitary 5,400

Border Police 5,400

Coast Guard

HQ at Poti. The Navy was merged with the Coast Guard in 2009 under the auspices of the Georgian Border Police, within the Ministry of the Interior

EQUIPMENT BY TYPE
PATROL AND COASTAL COMBATANTS 24
  PCC 2 *Ochamchira* (ex-US Island)
  PBF 7: 4 Ares 43m; 1 *Kaan* 33; 1 *Kaan* 20; 1 Project 205P (*Stenka*)

PB 15: 1 *Akhmeta*; 2 *Dauntless*; 2 *Dilos* (ex-GRC); 1 *Kutaisi* (ex-TUR AB 25); 2 *Point*; 7 *Zhuk* (3 ex-UKR)

DEPLOYMENT

AFGHANISTAN: NATO • *Operation Resolute Support* 871; 1 lt inf bn

CENTRAL AFRICAN REPUBLIC: EU • EUTM RCA 35

MALI: EU • EUTM Mali 1

TERRITORY WHERE THE GOVERNMENT DOES NOT EXERCISE EFFECTIVE CONTROL

Following the August 2008 war between Russia and Georgia, the areas of Abkhazia and South Ossetia declared themselves independent. Data presented here represents the de facto situation and does not imply international recognition as sovereign states.

FOREIGN FORCES

Russia 7,000; 1 mil base at Gudauta (Abkhazia) with (1 MR bde; 40 T-90A; 120 BTR-82A; 18 2S3; 12 2S12; 18 BM-21; some S-300 SAM; some atk hel); 1 mil base at Djava/Tskhinvali (S. Ossetia) with (1 MR bde; 40 T-72; 120 BMP-2; 36 2S3; 12 2S12)

Kazakhstan KAZ

Kazakhstani Tenge t		2018	2019	2020
GDP	t	59.6tr	65.4tr	
	US$	173bn	170bn	
per capita	US$	9,401	9,139	
Growth	%	4.1	3.8	
Inflation	%	6.0	5.3	
Def bdgt	t	517bn	610bn	
	US$	1.50bn	1.59bn	
US$1=t		344.71	384.20	

Real-terms defence budget trend (US$bn, constant 2015)

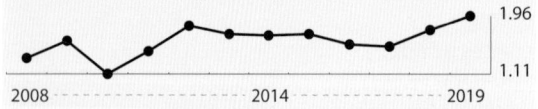

Population 18,923,073

Ethnic groups: Kazakk 63.3%; Russian 23.7%; Uzbek 2.8%; Ukraninans 2.1%; Tatars 1.3%; German 1.1%; other or unspecified 5.7%

Age	0–14	15–19	20–24	25–29	30–64	65 plus
Male	12.8%	3.3%	3.5%	4.2%	21.0%	2.9%
Female	13.3%	3.1%	3.3%	4.2%	23.1%	5.3%

Capabilities

The October 2017 military doctrine indicates a change in focus from countering violent extremism towards a wider concern for border security and hybrid threats to national security. In the army, air-mobile units are held at the highest level of readiness. Kazakhstan entered a bilateral military agreement with Uzbekistan in September 2017 to cooperate on training and education, countering violent extremism and reducing militant movements in their region. Kazakhstan has a close defence relationship with Russia, reinforced by CSTO and SCO membership, and Moscow operates a radar station at Balkash. Kazakhstan takes part in regional and CSTO exercises, including anti-terror drills. In October 2019, in Saint Petersburg, Kazakhstan and four other Caspian littoral states signed a memorandum of understanding on military cooperation, among other discussions including on maritime security. By regional standards, the armed forces are both relatively sizeable and well equipped, following the acquisition of significant amounts of new and upgraded materiel in recent years, primarily from Russia. Orders were placed for fighter/ground-attack aircraft in 2018, though airworthiness across the fleet remains problematic. Russia has also supplied Kazakhstan with S-300PS self-propelled surface-to-air missile systems as part of a Joint Air-Defence Agreement, boosting its long-range air-defence capability. Kazakhstan is growing its indigenous defence industry, and joint ventures and the production of rotary-wing and medium-lift fixed-wing aircraft are envisaged in cooperation with European companies.

ACTIVE 39,000 (Army 20,000 Navy 3,000 Air 12,000 MoD 4,000) **Paramilitary 31,500**

Conscript liability 12 months (due to be abolished)

ORGANISATIONS BY SERVICE

Army 20,000

4 regional comd: Astana, East, West and Southern

FORCES BY ROLE
MANOEUVRE
  Armoured
  1 tk bde
  Mechanised
  3 mech bde
  Air Manoeuvre
  4 air aslt bde
COMBAT SUPPORT
  3 arty bde
  1 SSM unit
  3 cbt engr bde
EQUIPMENT BY TYPE
ARMOURED FIGHTING VEHICLES
  MBT 300 T-72BA
  RECCE 100: 40 BRDM-2; 60 BRM-1
  IFV 607: 500 BMP-2; 107 BTR-80A
  APC 352+ • **APC (T)** 150 MT-LB • **APC (W)** 192: 2 BTR-3E; 190 BTR-80 • **PPV** 10+ *Arlan*
  AUV 17+: 17 *Cobra*; *SandCat*
ENGINEERING & MAINTENANCE VEHICLES
  AEV MT-LB
ANTI-TANK/ANTI-INFRASTRUCTURE
  MSL
    SP 3+: 3 BMP-T; HMMWV with 9K111-1 *Konkurs* (AT-5 *Spandrel*); 9P149 *Shturm* (MT-LB with AT-6 *Spiral*)
    MANPATS 9K111 *Fagot* (AT-4 *Spigot*); 9K111-1 *Konkurs* (AT-5 *Spandrel*); 9K115 *Metis* (AT-7 *Saxhorn*)
  GUNS 100mm 68 MT-12/T-12
ARTILLERY 611
  SP 246: **122mm** 126: 120 2S1 *Gvozdika*; 6 *Semser*; **152mm** 120 2S3 *Akatsiya*

TOWED 150: **122mm** 100 D-30; **152mm** 50 2A65 *Msta*-B (**122mm** up to 300 D-30 in store)
GUN/MOR **120mm** 25 2S9 NONA-S
MRL 127: **122mm** 100 BM-21 *Grad*; **220mm** 3 TOS-1A; **300mm** 24: 6 BM-30 *Smerch*; 18 IMI *Lynx* (with 50 msl) (**122mm** 100 BM-21 *Grad*; **220mm** 180 9P140 *Uragan* all in store)
MOR 63 **SP 120mm** 18 *Cardom*; **120mm** 45 2B11 *Sani/M120*
SURFACE-TO-SURFACE MISSILE LAUNCHERS
SRBM • **Conventional** 12 9K79 *Tochka* (SS-21 *Scarab*)

Navy 3,000
EQUIPMENT BY TYPE
PATROL AND COASTAL COMBATANTS 13
PCGM 3 *Kazakhstan* with 1 4-cell lnchr with 4 *Barrier*-VK SSM, 1 *Arbalet*-K lnchr with 4 9K38 *Igla* (SA-18 *Grouse*)
PCC 1 *Kazakhstan* with 1 122mm MRL
PBF 3 *Sea Dolphin*
PB 6: 3 *Archangel*; 1 *Dauntless*; 1 *Turk* (AB 25); 1 Other
MINE WARFARE • MINE COUNTERMEASURES 1
MCC 1 *Alatau* (Project 10750E)
LOGISTICS AND SUPPORT • AGS 1 *Zhaik*

Coastal Defence
FORCES BY ROLE
MANOEUVRE
Mechanised
1 naval inf bde
EQUIPMENT BY TYPE
ARMOURED FIGHTING VEHICLES
IFV 70 BTR-82A

Air Force 12,000 (incl Air Defence)
FORCES BY ROLE
FIGHTER
1 sqn with MiG-29/MiG-29UB *Fulcrum*
2 sqn with MiG-31B/MiG-31BM *Foxhound*
FIGHTER/GROUND ATTACK
1 sqn with MiG-27 *Flogger* D; MiG-23UB *Flogger* C
1 sqn with Su-27/Su-27UB *Flanker*
1 sqn with Su-27/Su-30SM *Flanker*
GROUND ATTACK
1 sqn with Su-25 *Frogfoot*
TRANSPORT
1 unit with Tu-134 *Crusty*; Tu-154 *Careless*
1 sqn with An-12 *Cub*, An-26 *Curl*, An-30 *Clank*, An-72 *Coaler*, C295M
TRAINING
1 sqn with L-39 *Albatros*
ATTACK HELICOPTER
5 sqn with Mi-24V *Hind*
TRANSPORT HELICOPTER
Some sqn with Bell 205 (UH-1H *Iroquois*); H145; Mi-8 *Hip*; Mi-17V-5 *Hip*; Mi-171Sh *Hip*; Mi-26 *Halo*
AIR DEFENCE
Some regt with S-75M *Volkhov* (SA-2 *Guideline*); S-125 *Neva* (SA-3 *Goa*); S-300/S-300PS (SA-10/10B *Grumble*); 2K11 *Krug* (SA-4 *Ganef*); S-200 *Angara* (SA-5 *Gammon*); 2K12 *Kub* (SA-6 *Gainful*)

EQUIPMENT BY TYPE
AIRCRAFT 110 combat capable
FTR 46: 12 MiG-29 *Fulcrum*; 2 MiG-29UB *Fulcrum*; 32 MiG-31/MiG-31BM *Foxhound*
FGA 50: 12 MiG-27 *Flogger* D; 2 MiG-23UB *Flogger* C; 20 Su-27 *Flanker*; 4 Su-27UB *Flanker*; 12 Su-30SM *Flanker* H
ATK 14: 12 Su-25 *Frogfoot*; 2 Su-25UB *Frogfoot*
ISR 1 An-30 *Clank*
TPT 21: **Medium** 2 An-12 *Cub*; **Light** 18: 6 An-26 *Curl*, 2 An-72 *Coaler*; 8 C295; 2 Tu-134 *Crusty*; **PAX** 1 Tu-154 *Careless*
TRG 18: 17 L-39 *Albatros*; 1 Z-242L
HELICOPTERS
ATK 24: 20 Mi-24V *Hind* (some upgraded); 4 Mi-35M *Hind*
MRH 26: 20 Mi-17V-5 *Hip*; 6 Mi-171Sh *Hip*
TPT 16: **Heavy** 4 Mi-26 *Halo*; **Light** 12: 4 Bell 205 (UH-1H *Iroquois*); 8 H145
UNMANNED AERIAL VEHICLES
CISR • **Heavy** 2 *Wing Loong* (GJ-1)
AIR DEFENCE • SAM
Long-range S-200 *Angara* (SA-5 *Gammon*); S-300 (SA-10 *Grumble*); 40+ S-300PS (SA-10 *Grumble*)
Medium-range 2K11 *Krug* (SA-4 *Ganef*); S-75M *Volkhov* (SA-2 *Guideline*)
Short-range 2K12 *Kub* (SA-6 *Gainful*); S-125 *Neva* (SA-3 *Goa*)
Point-defence 9K35 *Strela*-10 (SA-13 *Gopher*)
AIR-LAUNCHED MISSILES
AAM • **IR** R-60 (AA-8 *Aphid*); R-73 (AA-11A *Archer*); **IR/SARH** R-27 (AA-10 *Alamo*); **SARH** R-33 (AA-9A *Amos*); **ARH** R-77 (AA-12A *Adder* – on MiG-31BM)
ASM Kh-23 (AS-7 *Kerry*)‡; Kh-25 (AS-10 *Karen*); Kh-29 (AS-14 *Kedge*)
ARM Kh-27 (AS-12 *Kegler*); Kh-58 (AS-11 *Kilter*)

Paramilitary 31,500

National Guard ε20,000
Ministry of Interior
AIRCRAFT
TPT • **Medium** 1 Y-8F-200WA

State Security Service 2,500

Border Service ε9,000
Ministry of Interior
EQUIPMENT BY TYPE
AIRCRAFT 7: **Light** 6: 4 An-26 *Curl*; 1 An-74T; 1 An-74TK **PAX** 1 SSJ-100
HELICOPTERS • TPT • **Medium** 15: 1 Mi-171; 14 Mi-171Sh

Coast Guard
EQUIPMENT BY TYPE
PATROL AND COASTAL COMBATANTS 22
PBF 11: 1 *Aibar* (Project 0210); 8 FC-19; 2 *Saygak*
PB 11: 4 *Almaty*; 5 *Sardar*; 2 *Zhuk* (of which 1 may be operational)

DEPLOYMENT

LEBANON: UN • UNIFIL 123; 1 inf coy
WESTERN SAHARA: UN • MINURSO 6

Kyrgyzstan KGZ

Kyrgyzstani Som s		2018	2019	2020
GDP	s	557bn	586bn	
	US$	8.09bn	8.26bn	
per capita	US$	1,293	1,293	
Growth	%	3.5	3.8	
Inflation	%	1.5	1.3	
Def bdgt	s	n.k	n.k	
	US$	n.k	n.k	
US$1=s		68.84	70.89	

Population 5,907,966

Ethnic groups: Kyrgyz 71.7%; Uzbek 14.3%; Russian 7.2%; Dungan 1.1%; Uygur 0.9%; other or unspecified 4.8%

Age	0–14	15–19	20–24	25–29	30–64	65 plus
Male	15.6%	3.9%	4.2%	4.6%	18.6%	2.1%
Female	14.8%	3.8%	4.0%	4.5%	20.4%	3.5%

Capabilities

Kyrgyzstan has started to expand its ties with regional countries on issues such as defence-industrial cooperation, though it remains generally dependent on Russian assistance for its defence requirements. As part of counter-terrorism efforts, the government ordered the creation of an inter-agency working group to devise an anti-extremism and anti-terrorism programme. Kyrgyzstan is a member of both the CSTO and the SCO. Moscow maintains a military presence, including a squadron of Su-25SM ground-attack aircraft at Kant air base, which it has leased since 2003. Talks are ongoing over a possible second Russian base. In 2018, bilateral cooperation agreements were signed with Kazakhstan and Uzbekistan. Joint training is held with regional countries, including on anti-terror drills, but combat readiness remains an issue. Kyrgyzstan has a limited capability to deploy externally, and personnel are deployed to OSCE and UN missions in Ukraine, Serbia and South Sudan. The armed forces possess ageing land equipment and limited air capabilities, relying instead on Russian support, training and deployments. There is little local defence industry, although in 2018 Kazakhstan and Kyrgyzstan discussed defence-industrial cooperation. Defence ties with India have increased and a joint working group has been formed on defence cooperation. Reports in 2019 indicated that India might provide a credit line to enable purchases related to Kyrgyzstan's defence-modernisation plans.

ACTIVE 10,900 (Army 8,500 Air 2,400) **Paramilitary 9,500**

Conscript liability 18 months

ORGANISATIONS BY SERVICE

Army 8,500

FORCES BY ROLE
SPECIAL FORCES
 1 SF bde
MANOEUVRE
 Mechanised
 2 MR bde
 1 (mtn) MR bde
COMBAT SUPPORT
 1 arty bde
 1 AD bde
EQUIPMENT BY TYPE
ARMOURED FIGHTING VEHICLES
 MBT 150 T-72
 RECCE 39: 30 BRDM-2; 9 BRDM-2M
 IFV 320: 230 BMP-1; 90 BMP-2
 APC • APC (W) 55: 25 BTR-70; 20 BTR-70M; 10 BTR-80
ANTI-TANK/ANTI-INFRASTRUCTURE
 MSL • MANPATS 9K11 *Malyutka* (AT-3 *Sagger*); 9K111 *Fagot* (AT-4 *Spigot*); 9K111-1 *Konkurs* (AT-5 *Spandrel*)
 RCL 73mm SPG-9
 GUNS 100mm 36: 18 MT-12/T-12; 18 M-1944
ARTILLERY 228
 SP 122mm 18 2S1 *Gvozdika*
 TOWED 123: **122mm** 107: 72 D-30; 35 M-30 (M-1938); **152mm** 16 D-1
 GUN/MOR 120mm 12 2S9 NONA-S
 MRL 21: **122mm** 15 BM-21; **220mm** 6 9P140 *Uragan*
 MOR 120mm 54: 6 2S12; 48 M-120
AIR DEFENCE
 SAM • Point-defence 9K32 *Strela*-2 (SA-7 *Grail*)‡
 GUNS 48
  SP 23mm 24 ZSU-23-4
  TOWED 57mm 24 S-60

Air Force 2,400

FORCES BY ROLE
FIGHTER
 1 regt with L-39 *Albatros**
TRANSPORT
 1 regt with An-2 *Colt*; An-26 *Curl*
ATTACK/TRANSPORT HELICOPTER
 1 regt with Mi-24 *Hind*; Mi-8 *Hip*
AIR DEFENCE
 Some regt with S-125 *Pechora* (SA-3 *Goa*); S-75 *Dvina* (SA-2 *Guideline*); 2K11 *Krug* (SA-4 *Ganef*)
EQUIPMENT BY TYPE
AIRCRAFT 4 combat capable
 TPT • Light 6: 4 An-2 *Colt*; 2 An-26 *Curl*
 TRG 4 L-39 *Albatros**
HELICOPTERS
 ATK 2 Mi-24 *Hind*
 TPT • Medium 8 Mi-8 *Hip*
AIR DEFENCE • SAM
 Medium-range 2K11 *Krug* (SA-4 *Ganef*); S-75 *Dvina* (SA-2 *Guideline*)
 Short-range S-125 *Pechora* (SA-3 *Goa*)

Paramilitary 9,500

Border Guards 5,000 (KGZ conscript, RUS officers)

Internal Troops 3,500

National Guard 1,000

DEPLOYMENT

SOUTH SUDAN: UN • UNMISS 2
SUDAN: UN • UNAMID 1

FOREIGN FORCES

Russia ε500 Military Air Forces: 13 Su-25SM *Frogfoot*; 2 Mi-8 *Hip*

Moldova MDA

Moldovan Leu L		2018	2019	2020
GDP	L	190bn	207bn	
	US$	11.3bn	11.7bn	
per capita	US$	3,191	3,300	
Growth	%	4.0	3.5	
Inflation	%	3.1	4.9	
Def bdgt	L	639m	747m	
	US$	38.1m	42.1m	
FMA (US)	US$	12.8m	0.0m	0m
US$1=L		16.80	17.74	

Real-terms defence budget trend (US$m, constant 2015)

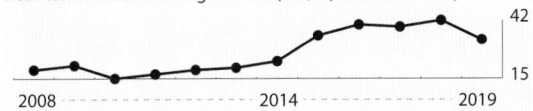

Population 3,401,197

Age	0–14	15–19	20–24	25–29	30–64	65 plus
Male	9.4%	2.8%	3.1%	3.8%	24.3%	5.3%
Female	8.9%	2.6%	2.9%	3.6%	25.0%	8.2%

Capabilities

The primary role of Moldova's armed forces is to maintain territorial integrity, though their size means they would be unable to offer more than token resistance to a determined adversary. The forces are constitutionally neutral. A National Defence Strategy for 2017–21 includes plans to strengthen border defence and airspace control and protection, and improve the military-training system. Moldova continues to build relations with both European states and NATO. The country signed up to the NATO Defence Capacity Building Initiative in September 2014. Moldova is aiming to end mandatory conscription and develop professional armed forces. The Professional Army 2018–2021 programme was approved in June 2018. A draft government action plan (2019–20) circulated in August 2019 reportedly included closer ties with NATO and a continuing emphasis on professionalisation. A long-term Military Capabilities Development Plan is being developed. The services exercise regularly with NATO states. Moldova has no requirement or capability to independently deploy and support its forces overseas. However, service members have deployed as part of KFOR. The country has no defence-industrial capabilities beyond the basic maintenance of front-line equipment.

ACTIVE 5,150 (Army 3,250 Air 600 Logistic Support 1,300) Paramilitary 900

Conscript liability 12 months (3 months for university graduates)

RESERVE 58,000 (Joint 58,000)

ORGANISATIONS BY SERVICE

Army 1,300; 1,950 conscript (total 3,250)
FORCES BY ROLE
SPECIAL FORCES
  1 SF bn
MANOEUVRE
  Light
  3 mot inf bde
  1 lt inf bn
  Other
  1 gd bn
COMBAT SUPPORT
  1 arty bn
  1 engr bn
  1 NBC coy
  1 sigs bn
EQUIPMENT BY TYPE
ARMOURED FIGHTING VEHICLES
  APC 163
    APC (T) 69: 9 BTR-D; 60 MT-LB (variants)
    APC (W) 94: 13 BTR-80; 81 TAB-71
  ABCV 44 BMD-1
ANTI-TANK/ANTI-INFRASTRUCTURE
  MSL • **MANPATS** 9K111 *Fagot* (AT-4 *Spigot*); 9K111-1 *Konkurs* (AT-5 *Spandrel*)
  RCL 73mm SPG-9
  GUNS 100mm 37 MT-12
ARTILLERY 221
  TOWED 69: **122mm** 17 (M-30) M-1938; **152mm** 52: 21 2A36 *Giatsint*-B; 31 D-20
  GUN/MOR • **SP 120mm** 9 2S9 NONA-S
  MRL 220mm 11 9P140 *Uragan*
  MOR 132: **82mm** 75 BM-37; **120mm** 57: 50 M-1989; 7 PM-38
AIR DEFENCE • **GUNS** • **TOWED** 39: **23mm** 28 ZU-23; **57mm** 11 S-60

Air Force 600 (incl 250 conscripts)
FORCES BY ROLE
TRANSPORT
  1 sqn with An-2 *Colt*; Mi-8MTV-1/PS *Hip*; Yak-18
AIR DEFENCE
  1 regt with S-125 *Neva* (SA-3 *Goa*)
EQUIPMENT BY TYPE
AIRCRAFT
  TPT • **Light** 3: 2 An-2 *Colt*; 1 Yak-18
HELICOPTERS
  TPT • **Medium** 6: 2 Mi-8PS *Hip*; 4 Mi-8MTV-1 *Hip*
AIR DEFENCE • **SAM** • **Short-range** 3 S-125 *Neva* (SA-3 *Goa*)

Paramilitary 900

OPON 900 (riot police)
  Ministry of Interior

DEPLOYMENT

CENTRAL AFRICAN REPUBLIC: UN • MINUSCA 5
MALI: EU • EUTM Mali 2
SERBIA: NATO • KFOR 41; UN • UNMIK 1
SOUTH SUDAN: UN • UNMISS 4

FOREIGN FORCES

Russia ε1,500 (including 400 peacekeepers) 7 Mi-24 *Hind*/Mi-8 *Hip*
Ukraine 10 mil obs (Joint Peacekeeping Force)

Russia RUS

Russian Rouble r		2018	2019	2020
GDP	r	104tr	109tr	
	US$	1.66tr	1.64tr	
per capita	US$	11,289	11,163	
Growth	%	2.3	1.1	
Inflation	%	2.9	4.7	
Def exp [a]	r	3.93tr	4.11tr	
	US$	62.7bn	61.6bn	
Def bdgt	r	2.83tr	3.21tr	3.06tr
	US$	45.2bn	48.2bn	
US$1=r		62.68	66.61	

[a] Total defence expenditure, including National Guard, Federal Border Service and military pensions

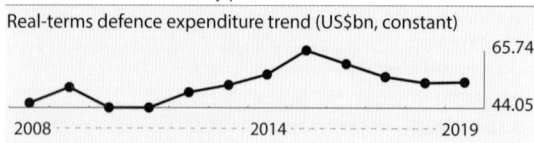

Real-terms defence expenditure trend (US$bn, constant)

Population	141,944,641

Ethnic groups: Tatar 3.71%; Armenian 0.8%; Bashkir 1.1%; Chechen 1%; Chuvash 1%

Age	0–14	15–19	20–24	25–29	30–64	65 plus
Male	8.9%	2.5%	2.4%	3.2%	24.6%	4.8%
Female	8.4%	2.3%	2.3%	3.1%	27.4%	10.3%

Capabilities

Russia supports capable conventional military forces and retains the world's second-largest nuclear arsenal. The armed forces underpin an assertive foreign policy. Military aims are guaranteeing sovereignty and territorial integrity and maintaining and increasing Russia's influence in its near abroad and further afield. Russia is a leading member of both the CSTO and the SCO. The armed forces comprise a mix of volunteers and conscripts. Defence reforms launched in 2008 emphasised the shift from a conscript-based mass-mobilisation army to smaller, more professional ground forces. Morale has improved because of better pay, terms and conditions, and greater prestige associated with military service. The armed forces can independently deploy and sustain forces on a global scale, although likely only in modest size at extended distances. Its air-led intervention in Syria shows Russia can deploy, sustain and maintain a high operational tempo for a fixed- and rotary-wing air force, along with the required force-protection package for the main operating base. Russia continues to modernise its nuclear and conventional weapons. The 2020 State Armament Programme (SAP) has been broadly successful, although several of the more ambitious procurement goals were not met. The follow-on programme, SAP 2027, continues the emphasis on modernisation, though some aims are more modest. Russia can design, develop and manufacture advanced nuclear and conventional weaponry. Its defence-industrial base suffered from a lack of investment in the 1990s, and more recently from the loss of access to Ukrainian components. The defence-aerospace sector has been notably successful in terms of exports, particularly of combat aircraft and surface-to-air missile systems.

ACTIVE 900,000 (Army 280,000 Navy 150,000 Air 165,000 Strategic Rocket Force 50,000 Airborne 45,000 Special Operations Forces 1,000 Railway Forces 29,000 Command and Support 180,000) **Paramilitary 554,000**

Conscript liability 12 months (conscripts now can opt for contract service immediately, which entails a 24-month contract)

RESERVE 2,000,000 (all arms)

Some 2,000,000 with service within last 5 years; reserve obligation to age 50

ORGANISATIONS BY SERVICE

Strategic Deterrent Forces ε80,000 (incl personnel assigned from the Navy and Aerospace Forces)

Navy
EQUIPMENT BY TYPE
SUBMARINES • STRATEGIC • SSBN 10:
  1 *Kalmar* (*Delta* III) with 16 R-29RKU-02 *Stantsia*-02 (SS-N-18 *Stingray*) nuclear SLBM, 2 single 400mm TT with SET-72 LWT, 4 single 533mm TT with 53-65K HWT/SET-65K HWT/USET-80K *Keramika* HWT
  6 *Delfin* (*Delta* IV) with 16 R-29RMU2 *Sineva*/R-29RMU2.1 *Layner* (SS-N-23 *Skiff*) nuclear SLBM, 4 single 533mm TT with 53-65K HWT/SET-65K HWT/USET-80K *Keramika* HWT
  3 *Borey* (*Dolgorukiy*) with 16 *Bulava* (SS-N-32) nuclear SLBM, 6 single 533mm TT with USET-80K *Keramika* HWT/UGST *Fizikov* HWT
  (1 *Akula* (*Typhoon*)† in reserve for training with capacity for 20 *Bulava* (SS-N-32) nuclear SLBM, 6 single 533mm TT with 53-65K HWT/SET-65K HWT/USET-80K *Keramika* HWT)

Strategic Rocket Forces 50,000
3 Rocket Armies operating silo and mobile launchers organised in 12 divs. Regt normally with 10 silos (6 for RS-20/SS-18), or 9 mobile lnchr, and one control centre
FORCES BY ROLE
SURFACE-TO-SURFACE MISSILE
  4 ICBM regt with RS-12M *Topol* (SS-25 *Sickle*)
  8 ICBM regt with RS-12M2 *Topol*-M (SS-27 mod 1)
  3 ICBM regt with RS-18 (SS-19 *Stiletto*)
  9 ICBM regt with RS-20 (SS-18 *Satan*)
  15 ICBM regt with RS-24 *Yars* (SS-27 mod 2)

EQUIPMENT BY TYPE
SURFACE-TO-SURFACE MISSILE LAUNCHERS
ICBM • **Nuclear** 340: ε36 RS-12M *Topol* (SS-25 *Sickle*) (mobile single warhead); 60 RS-12M2 *Topol-M* (SS-27 mod 1) silo-based (single warhead); 18 RS-12M2 *Topol-M* (SS-27 mod 1) road mobile (single warhead); 30 RS-18 (SS-19 *Stiletto*) (mostly mod 3, 6 MIRV per msl) (being withdrawn); 46 RS-20 (SS-18 *Satan*) (mostly mod 5, 10 MIRV per msl); ε136 RS-24 *Yars* (SS-27 mod 2; ε3 MIRV per msl) road mobile; ε14 RS-24 *Yars* (SS-27 mod 2; ε3 MIRV per msl) silo-based

Long-Range Aviation Command
FORCES BY ROLE
BOMBER
1 sqn with Tu-160/Tu-160M1 *Blackjack*
3 sqn with Tu-95MS/MS mod *Bear*
EQUIPMENT BY TYPE
AIRCRAFT
BBR 76: 10 Tu-160 *Blackjack* with Kh-55SM (AS-15B *Kent*) nuclear LACM; 6 Tu-160M1 *Blackjack* with Kh-55SM (AS-15B *Kent*)/Kh-102 (AS-23B *Kodiak*) nuclear LACM; 44 Tu-95MS *Bear* H with Kh-55SM (AS-15B *Kent*) nuclear LACM; 16 Tu-95MS mod *Bear* H with Kh-55SM (AS-15B *Kent*)/Kh-102 (AS-23B *Kodiak*) nuclear LACM

Space Command
EQUIPMENT BY TYPE
SATELLITES 106
  COMMUNICATIONS 61: 2 *Blagovest*; 2 *Garpun*; 15 *Gonets*-D/M (dual-use); 3 Mod *Globus* (*Raduga*-1M); 5 *Meridian*; 2 *Parus*; 3 *Raduga*; 21 *Rodnik* (*Strela*-3M); 8 *Strela*-3
  EARLY WARNING 3 *Tundra*
  NAVIGATION/POSITIONING/TIMING 26 GLONASS
  ISR 11: 2 *Bars*-M; 3 GEO-IK-2; 1 *Kondor*; 1 *Kosmos*-2519; 2 *Persona*; 3 *Resurs*-P
  ELINT/SIGINT 5: 4 *Liana* (*Lotos*-S); 1 *Tselina*-2
RADAR 12; Russia leases ground-based radar stations in Baranovichi (Belarus) and Balkhash (Kazakhstan). It also has radars on its own territory at Lekhtusi (St Petersburg); Armavir (Krasnodar); Olenegorsk (Murmansk); Mishelevka (Irkutsk); Kaliningrad; Pechora (Komi); Yeniseysk (Krasnoyarsk); Baranul (Altayskiy); Orsk (Orenburg) and Gorodets/Kovylkino (OTH)

Aerospace Defence Command
FORCES BY ROLE
AIR DEFENCE
2 AD div HQ
4 SAM regt with S-300PM1/PM2 (SA-20 *Gargoyle*)
5 SAM regt with S-400 (SA-21 *Growler*); 96K6 *Pantsir*-S1 (SA-22 *Greyhound*)
EQUIPMENT BY TYPE
AIR DEFENCE • SAM 222
  Long-range 186: 90 S-300PM1/PM2 (SA-20 *Gargoyle*); 96 S-400 (SA-21 *Growler*)
  Short-range 36 96K6 *Pantsir*-S1 (SA-22 *Greyhound*)

MISSILE DEFENCE 68 53T6 (ABM-3 *Gazelle*)
RADAR 1 ABM engagement system located at Sofrino (Moscow)

Army ε280,000 (incl conscripts)
4 military districts (West (HQ St Petersburg), Centre (HQ Yekaterinburg), South (HQ Rostov-on-Don) & East (HQ Khabarovsk)), each with a unified Joint Strategic Command
FORCES BY ROLE
COMMAND
12 army HQ
1 corps HQ
SPECIAL FORCES
8 (Spetsnaz) SF bde
1 (Spetsnaz) SF regt
MANOEUVRE
  Reconnaissance
  2 recce bde
  Armoured
  1 (4th) tk div (1 armd recce bn, 2 tk regt, 1 MR regt, 1 arty regt, 1 AD regt)
  1 (90th) tk div (1 armd recce bn, 2 tk regt, 1 MR regt, 1 arty regt)
  2 tk bde (1 armd recce bn, 3 tk bn, 1 MR bn, 1 arty bn, 1 MRL bn, 2 AD bn, 1 engr bn, 1 EW coy, 1 NBC coy)
  2 (3rd & 144th) MR div (1 armd recce bn, 1 tk regt, 2 MR regt, 1 arty regt)
  1 (127th) MR div (1 tk bn, 2 MR regt)
  1 (150th) MR div (1 armd recce bn, 2 tk regt, 1 MR regt; 1 arty regt, 1 AD regt)
  13 (BMP) MR bde (1 armd recce bn, 1 tk bn, 3 armd inf bn, 2 arty bn, 1 MRL bn, 1 AT bn, 2 AD bn, 1 engr bn, 1 EW coy, 1 NBC coy)
  Mechanised
  1 (2nd) MR div (1 armd recce bn, 1 tk regt, 2 MR regt, 1 arty regt, 1 AD regt)
  1 (42nd) MR div (1 armd recce bn, 3 MR regt, 1 arty regt)
  8 (BTR/MT-LB) MR bde (1 recce bn; 1 tk bn; 3 mech inf bn; 2 arty bn; 1 MRL bn; 1 AT bn; 2 AD bn; 1 engr bn; 1 EW coy; 1 NBC coy)
  2 MR bde (4–5 mech inf bn; 1 arty bn; 1 AD bn; 1 engr bn)
  3 (lt/mtn) MR bde (1 recce bn; 2 mech inf bn; 1 arty bn)
  1 (18th) MGA div (2 MGA regt; 1 arty regt; 1 tk bn; 2 AD bn)
SURFACE-TO-SURFACE MISSILE
11 SRBM/GLCM bde with 9K720 *Iskander*-M (SS-26 *Stone*/SSC-7 *Southpaw*) (multiple brigades also with 9M729 (SSC-8 *Screwdriver*))
COMBAT SUPPORT
9 arty bde
1 hy arty bde
4 MRL bde
4 engr bde
7 engr regt
1 MP bde
5 NBC bde
10 NBC regt
COMBAT SERVICE SUPPORT
10 log bde
AIR DEFENCE
15 AD bde

EQUIPMENT BY TYPE
ARMOURED FIGHTING VEHICLES
MBT 2,800: 650 T-72B/BA; 850 T-72B3; 500 T-72B3 mod; 330 T-80BV/U; 120 T-80BVM; 350 T-90/T-90A (10,200 in store: 7,000 T-72/T-72A/B; 3,000 T-80B/BV/U; 200 T-90)
RECCE 1,700: 1,000 BRDM-2/2A (1,000+ BRDM-2 in store); 700 BRM-1K (CP)
IFV 5,160: 500 BMP-1; 3,000 BMP-2; 540 BMP-3; 20+ BMP-3M; 100 BTR-80A; 1,000 BTR-82A/AM (8,500 in store: 7,000 BMP-1; 1,500 BMP-2)
APC 6,100+
  APC (T) 3,500+: some BMO-T; 3,500 MT-LB (2,000 MT-LB in store)
  APC (W) 2,600: 800 BTR-60 (all variants); 200 BTR-70 (all variants); 1,500 BTR-80; 100+ BPM-97 *Dozor* (4,000 BTR-60/70 in store)
  PPV *Typhoon*-K
AUV 100+: 100+ GAZ *Tigr*; some IVECO LMV

ENGINEERING & MAINTENANCE VEHICLES
AEV BAT-2; IMR; IMR-2; IMR-3; IRM; MT-LB
ARV BMP-1; BREM-1/64/K/L; BTR-50PK(B); M1977; MTP-LB; RM-G; T-54/55; VT-72A
VLB KMM; MT-55A; MTU; MTU-20; MTU-72; PMM-2
MW BMR-3M; GMX-3; MCV-2 (reported); MTK; MTK-2; UR-77

ANTI-TANK/ANTI-INFRASTRUCTURE
MSL
  SP BMP-T with 9K120 *Ataka* (AT-9 *Spiral* 2); 9P149 with 9K114 *Shturm* (AT-6 *Spiral*); 9P149M with 9K132 *Shturm*-SM (AT-9 *Spiral*-2); 9P157-2 with 9K123 *Khrizantema* (AT-15 *Springer*); 9P163-3 with 9M133 *Kornet* (AT-14 *Spriggan*); 9K128-1 *Kornet*-T (AT-14 *Spriggan*)
  MANPATS 9K111M *Fagot* (AT-4 *Spigot*); 9K111-1 *Konkurs* (AT-5 *Spandrel*); 9K115 *Metis* (AT-7 *Saxhorn*); 9K115-1 *Metis*-M (AT-13 *Saxhorn* 2); 9K115-2 *Metis*-M1 (AT-13 *Saxhorn* 2); 9K135 *Kornet* (AT-14 *Spriggan*)
RCL 73mm SPG-9
GUNS • TOWED 100mm 526 MT-12 (**100mm** 2,000 T-12/MT-12 in store)
ARTILLERY 4,342+
  SP 1,610: **122mm** 150 2S1 *Gvozdika*; **152mm** 1,400: 800 2S3 *Akatsiya*; 100 2S5 *Giatsint*-S; 500 2S19/2S19M1/2S19M2 *Msta*-S/SM; **203mm** 60 2S7M *Malka* (4,260 in store: **122mm** 2,000 2S1 *Gvozdika*; **152mm** 2,000: 1,000 2S3 *Akatsiya*; 850 2S5 *Giatsint*-S; 150 2S19 *Msta*-S; **203mm** 260 2S7 *Pion*)
  TOWED 150: **152mm** 150 2A65 *Msta*-B (12,415 in store: **122mm** 8,150: 4,400 D-30; 3,750 M-30 (M-1938); **130mm** 650 M-46; **152mm** 3,575: 1,100 2A36 *Giatsint*-B; 600 2A65 *Msta*-B; 1,075 D-20; 700 D-1 (M-1943); 100 M-1937 (ML-20); **203mm** 40 B-4M)
  GUN/MOR 180+
    SP 120mm 80+: 30 2S23 NONA-SVK; 50+ 2S34
    TOWED 120mm 100 2B16 NONA-K
  MRL 862+ **122mm** 550 BM-21 *Grad*/*Tornado*-G; **220mm** 200 9P140 *Uragan*; some 9K512 *Uragan*-1M; some TOS-1A; **300mm** 112: 100 9A52 *Smerch*; 12 9A54 *Tornado*-S (3,220 in store: **122mm** 2,420: 2,000 BM-21 *Grad*; 420 9P138; **132mm** 100 BM-13; **220mm** 700 9P140 *Uragan*)
  MOR 1,540+: **82mm** 800+ 2B14; **120mm** 700 2S12 *Sani*; **240mm** 40 2S4 *Tulpan* (2,590 in store: **120mm** 1,900: 1,000 2S12 *Sani*; 900 M-1938 (PM-38); **160mm** 300 M-160; **SP 240mm** 390 2S4 *Tulpan*)

SURFACE-TO-SURFACE MISSILE LAUNCHERS
SRBM 140:
  Dual-capable 140 9K720 *Iskander*-M (SS-26 *Stone*)
GLCM • Dual-capable Some 9M728 (SSC-7 *Southpaw*); some 9M729 (SSC-8 *Screwdriver*)

UNMANNED AERIAL VEHICLES
ISR • Heavy Tu-243 *Reys*/Tu-243 *Reys* D (service status unclear); **Light** BLA-07; *Pchela*-1; *Pchela*-2

AIR DEFENCE
SAM 1,520+
  Long-range S-300V (SA-12 *Gladiator/Giant*); S-300V4 (SA-23)
  Medium-range 350: ε200 9K37M *Buk*-M1-2 (SA-11 *Gadfly*); ε90 9K317 *Buk*-M2 (SA-17 *Grizzly*); ε60 9K317M *Buk*-M3 (SA-27)
  Short-range 120+ 9K331/9K332 *Tor*-M/M1/M2/M2U (SA-15 *Gauntlet*) (9M338 msl entering service)
  Point-defence 1,050+: 250+ 2K22M *Tunguska* (SA-19 *Grison*); 400 9K33M3 *Osa*-AKM (SA-8B *Gecko*); 400 9K35M3 *Strela*-10 (SA-13 *Gopher*); 9K310 *Igla*-1 (SA-16 *Gimlet*); 9K34 *Strela*-3 (SA-14 *Gremlin*); 9K38 *Igla* (SA-18 *Grouse*); 9K333 *Verba* (SA-29); 9K338 *Igla*-S (SA-24 *Grinch*)
GUNS
  SP 23mm ZSU-23-4
  TOWED 23mm ZU-23-2; **57mm** S-60

Reserves
Cadre formations
FORCES BY ROLE
MANOEUVRE
  Mechanised
  13 MR bde

Navy ε150,000 (incl conscripts)
4 major fleet organisations (Northern Fleet, Pacific Fleet, Baltic Fleet, Black Sea Fleet) and Caspian Sea Flotilla
EQUIPMENT BY TYPE
SUBMARINES 49
  STRATEGIC • SSBN 10:
    1 *Kalmar* (Delta III) with 16 R-29RKU-02 *Stantsia*-02 (SS-N-18 *Stingray*) nuclear SLBM, 2 single 400mm TT with SET-72 LWT, 4 single 533mm TT with 53-65K HWT/SET-65K HWT/USET-80K *Keramika* HWT
    6 *Delfin* (Delta IV) with 16 R-29RMU2 *Sineva*/R-29RMU2.1 *Layner* (SS-N-23 *Skiff*) nuclear SLBM, 4 single 533mm TT with 53-65K HWT/SET-65K HWT/ USET-80K *Keramika* HWT
    3 *Borey* (*Dolgorukiy*) with 16 *Bulava* (SS-N-32) nuclear SLBM, 6 single 533mm TT with USET-80K *Keramika* HWT/UGST *Fizikov* HWT
    (1 *Akula* (*Typhoon*)† in reserve for training with capacity for 20 *Bulava* (SS-N-32) nuclear SLBM, 6 single 533mm TT with 53-65K HWT/SET-65K HWT/ USET-80K *Keramika* HWT)
  TACTICAL 39
    SSGN 7:
      6 *Antey* (*Oscar* II) (2 more non-operational, in long-term refit) with 24 single SM-225A lnchr with 3M45 *Granit* (SS-N-19 *Shipwreck*) AShM, 2 single

650mm TT each with T-65 HWT/RPK-7 (SS-N-16 *Stallion*) ASW msl, 4 single 553mm TT with 53-65K HWT/SET-65K HWT/USET-80K *Keramika* HWT

1 *Yasen* (*Severodvinsk*) with 8 4-cell SM-346 VLS with 3M14K (SS-N-30) dual-capable LACM/3M54K1 (SS-N-27) AShM/3M54K (SS-N-27B *Sizzler*) AShM/3M55 *Onyx* (SS-N-26 *Strobile*) AShM; 10 single 533mm TT with USET-80K *Keramika* HWT/UGST *Fizikov* HWT

SSN 10:

3 *Schuka*-B (*Akula* I) (6 more non-operational, in long-term refit) with 4 single 533mm TT with 53-65K HWT/TEST-71M HWT/USET-80K *Keramika* HWT (3M10 *Granat* (SS-N-21 *Sampson*) nuclear LACM in store), 4 single 650mm TT with 65-73 HWT/RPK-7 (SS-N-16 *Stallion*) ASW msl

2 *Schuka*-B (*Akula* II) (of which 1 in refit) with 4 single 533mm TT with 53-65K HWT/TEST-71M HWT/USET-80K *Keramika* HWT (3M10 *Granat* (SS-N-21 *Sampson*) nuclear LACM in store), 4 single 650mm TT with 65-73 HWT/RPK-7 (SS-N-16 *Stallion*) ASW msl

2 *Kondor* (*Sierra* II) with 4 single 533mm TT with TEST-71M HWT/USET-80K *Keramika* HWT (3M10 *Granat* (SS-N-21 *Sampson*) nuclear LACM in store), 4 single 650mm TT with 65-73 HWT

3 *Schuka* (*Victor* III) with 4 single 533mm TT with 53-65K HWT/SET-65K HWT/USET-80K *Keramika* HWT/3M10 *Granat* (SS-N-21 *Sampson*) nuclear LACM (weapons in store), 2 single 650mm TT with 65-73 HWT

(1 *Barracuda* (*Sierra* I) (in reserve) with 6 single 533mm TT with TEST-71M HWT/USET-80K *Keramika* HWT (3M10 *Granat* (SS-N-21 *Sampson*) nuclear LACM in store))

SSK 22:

15 *Paltus* (*Kilo*) (of which 2 in refit) with 6 single 533mm TT with 53-65K HWT/TEST-71M HWT/USET-80K *Keramika* HWT

6 *Varshavyanka* (Improved *Kilo*) with 6 single 533mm TT with 3M14K *Kalibr*-PL (SS-N-30A) dual-capable LACM/3M54K (SS-N-27B *Sizzler*) AShM/3M54K1 (SS-N-27) AShM/53-65K HWT/TEST-71M HWT/USET-80K *Keramika* HWT

1 *Lada* (*Petersburg*) (in test) with 6 single 533mm TT with 3M14K *Kalibr*-PL (SS-N-30A) dual-capable LACM/3M54K (SS-N-27B *Sizzler*) AShM/3M54K1 (SS-N-27) AShM/USET-80K *Keramika* HWT

PRINCIPAL SURFACE COMBATANTS 33

AIRCRAFT CARRIERS • CV 1 *Admiral Kuznetsov* (in extended refit) with 12 single SM-233A lnchr with 3M45 *Granit* (SS-N-19 *Shipwreck*) AShM, 24 8-cell 3S95 VLS with 3K95 *Kinzhal* (SA-N-9 *Gauntlet*) SAM, 2 RBU 12000 *Udav* 1 A/S mor, 8 3M87 *Kortik* CIWS with 9M311 SAM (CADS-N-1), 6 AK630M CIWS (capacity 18–24 Su-33 *Flanker* D Ftr ac; MiG-29KR/KUBR FGA ac; 15 Ka-27 *Helix* ASW hel, 2 Ka-31R *Helix* AEW hel)

CRUISERS 4

CGHMN 1:

1 *Orlan* (*Kirov*) (1 other non-operational; undergoing extensive refit and planned to return to service in 2021) with 20 single SM-233 lnchr with 3M45 *Granit* (SS-N-19 *Shipwreck*) AShM, 6 6-cell B-203A VLS with S-300F *Fort* (SA-N-6 *Grumble*) SAM, 6 6-cell B-203A VLS with S-300FM *Fort*-M (SA-N-20 *Gargoyle*) SAM, 16 8-cell 3S95 VLS with 3K95 *Kinzhal* (SA-N-9 *Gauntlet*) SAM, 2 quintuple 533mm TT with RPK-6M *Vodopad*-NK (SS-N-16 *Stallion*) A/S msl, 1 RBU 6000 *Smerch* 2 A/S mor, 2 RBU 1000 *Smerch* 3 A/S mor, 6 3M87 *Kortik* CIWS with 9M311 SAM (CADS-N-1), 1 twin 130mm gun (capacity 3 Ka-27 *Helix* ASW hel)

CGHM 3:

3 *Atlant* (*Slava*) with 8 twin SM-248 lnchr with 3M70 *Vulkan* (SS-N-12 mod 2 *Sandbox*) AShM, 8 octuple VLS with S-300F *Fort* (SA-N-6 *Grumble*) SAM/S-300FM *Fort* M (SA-N-20 *Gargoyle*) SAM, 2 twin ZIF-122 lnchr with 4K33 *Osa*-M (SA-N-4 *Gecko*) SAM, 2 quintuple PTA-53-1164 533mm ASTT with SET-65K HWT, 2 RBU 6000 *Smerch* 2 A/S mor, 6 AK630 CIWS, 1 twin 130mm gun (capacity 1 Ka-27 *Helix* ASW hel)

DESTROYERS 13

DDGHM 12:

3 *Sarych* (*Sovremenny*) with 2 quad lnchr with 3M80 *Moskit* (SS-N-22 *Sunburn*) AShM, 2 twin 3S90 lnchr with 9M317 *Yezh* (SA-N-7B) SAM, 2 twin DTA-53-956 533mm TT with 53-65K HWT/SET-65K HWT, 2 RBU 1000 *Smerch* 3 A/S mor, 4 AK630 CIWS, 2 twin 130mm guns (capacity 1 Ka-27 *Helix* ASW hel)

7 *Fregat* (*Udaloy* I) (of which 1 in refit) with 2 quad lnchr with URK-5 *Rastrub*-B (SS-N-14 *Silex*) AShM/ASW, 8 8-cell 3S95 VLS with 3K95 *Kinzhal* (SA-N-9 *Gauntlet*) SAM, 2 quad ChTA-53-1155 533mm ASTT with 53-65K HWT/SET-65K HWT, 2 RBU 6000 *Smerch* 2 A/S mor, 4 AK630 CIWS, 2 100mm guns (capacity 2 Ka-27 *Helix* ASW hel)

(1 *Fregat* (*Udaloy* I) (in reserve) with 2 quad lnchr with URK-5 *Rastrub*-B (SS-N-14 *Silex*) AShM/ASW, 8 8-cell 3S95 VLS with 3K95 *Kinzhal* (SA-N-9 *Gauntlet*) SAM, 2 quad ChTA-53-1155 533mm ASTT with 53-65K HWT/SET-65K HWT, 2 RBU 6000 *Smerch* 2 A/S mor, 4 AK630 CIWS, 2 100mm guns (capacity 2 Ka-27 *Helix* ASW hel))

1 *Fregat* (*Udaloy* II) with 2 quad lnchr with 3M80 *Moskit* (SS-N-22 *Sunburn*) AShM, 8 8-cell 3S95 VLS with 3K95 *Kinzhal* (SA-N-9 *Gauntlet*) SAM, 2 3M87 *Kortik* CIWS with 9M311 SAM (CADS-N-1), 2 quintuple 533mm ASTT with 53-65K HWT/SET-65K HWT, 2 RBU 6000 *Smerch* 2 A/S mor, 1 twin 130mm gun (capacity 2 Ka-27 *Helix* ASW hel)

1 *Admiral Gorshkov* (Project 22350) with 2 8-cell 3S14 UKSK VLS with 3M14T *Kalibr*-NK (SS-N-30A) dual-capable LACM/3M54T (SS-N-27B *Sizzler*) AShM/3M54T1 (SS-N-27) AShM/3M55 *Oniks* (SS-N-26 *Strobile*) AShM/91RT2 A/S msl, 4 8-cell 3S97 VLS with 3K96-2 *Poliment*-*Redut* (SA-N-28) SAM, 2 quad 324mm TT with MTT LWT, 2 3M89 *Palash* CIWS (CADS-N-2), 1 130mm gun (capacity 1 Ka-27 *Helix* ASW hel)

DDGM 1:

1 *Komsomolets Ukrainy* (*Kashin* mod) with 2 quad lnchr with 3M24 *Uran* (SS-N-25 *Switchblade*) AShM, 2 twin ZIF-101 lnchr with M-1 *Volnya* (SA-N-1 *Goa*) SAM, 5 single PTA-53-61 533mm ASTT with 53-65K HWT/SET-65K HWT, 2 RBU 6000 *Smerch* 2 A/S mor, 1 twin 76mm gun

FRIGATES 15

FFGHM 11:

3 *Admiral Grigorovich* (*Krivak* V) with 1 8-cell 3S14 UKSK VLS with 3M14T *Kalibr*-NK (SS-N-30A) dual-capable LACM/3M54T (SS-N-27B *Sizzler*) AShM/3M54T1 (SS-N-27) AShM/3M55 *Oniks* (SS-N-26 *Strobile*) AShM/91RT2 A/S msl, 2 12-cell 3S90.1 VLS with 9M317 *Yezh* (SA-N-7B) SAM/9M317M *Yezh* (SA-N-7C) SAM, 2 twin DTA-53-11356 533mm TT with 53-65K HWT/SET-65K HWT, 1 RBU 6000 A/S mor, 2 AK630 CIWS, 1 100mm gun (capacity 1 Ka-27 *Helix* ASW hel)

2 *Jastreb* (*Neustrashimy*) (of which 1 in refit) with 2 quad lnchr with 3M24 *Uran* (SS-N-25 *Switchblade*) AShM, 4 8-cell 3S95 VLS with 3K95 *Kinzhal* (SA-N-9 *Gauntlet*), 6 single 533mm ASTT with RPK-6M *Vodopad*-NK (SS-N-16 *Stallion*) A/S msl, 1 RBU 6000 *Smerch* 2 A/S mor, 2 3M87 *Kortik* CIWS with 9M311 SAM (CADS-N-1), 1 100mm gun (capacity 1 Ka-27 *Helix* ASW hel)

1 *Steregushchiy* (Project 20380) with 2 quad lnchr with 3M24 *Uran* (SS-N-25 *Switchblade*) AShM, 2 quad SM-588 324mm ASTT with MTT LWT, 1 3M87 *Kortik*-M CIWS with 9M311 SAM (CADS-N-1), 2 AK630 CIWS, 1 100mm gun (capacity 1 Ka-27 *Helix* ASW hel)

5 *Steregushchiy* (Project 20380) with 2 quad lnchr with 3M24 *Uran* (SS-N-25 *Switchblade*) AShM, 3 4-cell 3S97 VLS with 3K96-3 *Redut* (SA-N-28) SAM, 2 quad SM-588 324mm ASTT with MTT LWT, 2 AK630 CIWS, 1 100mm gun (capacity 1 Ka-27 *Helix* ASW hel)

FFGM 4:

1 *Gepard* with 2 quad lnchr with 3M24 *Uran* (SS-N-25 *Switchblade*) AShM, 1 twin ZIF-122 lnchr with 4K33 *Osa*-M (SA-N-4 *Gecko*) SAM, 2 AK630 CIWS, 1 76mm gun

1 *Gepard* with 1 8-cell VLS with 3M14T *Kalibr*-NK (SS-N-30A) dual-capable LACM/3M54T (SS-N-27B *Sizzler*) AShM/3M54T1 (SS-N-27) AShM/3M5S *Oniks* (SS-N-26 *Strobile*) AShM/91RT2 A/S msl, 1 3M89 *Palash* CIWS with 9M337 *Sosna*-R SAM (CADS-N-2), 1 76mm gun

1 *Burevestnik* (*Krivak* I mod)† with 1 quad lnchr with URK-5 *Rastrub*-B (SS-N-14 *Silex*) AShM/ASW, 1 twin ZIF-122 lnchr with *Osa*-M (SA-N-4 *Gecko*) SAM, 2 quad ChTA-53-1135 533mm ASTT with 53-65K HWT/SET-65K HWT, 2 RBU 6000 *Smerch* 2 A/S mor, 2 twin 76mm guns

1 *Burevestnik* M (*Krivak* II) with 1 quad lnchr with URK-5 *Rastrub*-B (SS-N-14 *Silex*) AShM/ASW, 2 twin ZIF-122 lnchr with 4K33 *Osa*-M (SA-N-4 *Gecko* SAM), 2 quad ChTA-53-1135 533mm ASTT with 53-65K HWT/SET-65K HWT, 2 RBU 6000 *Smerch* 2 A/S mor, 2 100mm guns

PATROL AND COASTAL COMBATANTS 118

CORVETTES 50

FSGM 20

7 *Buyan*-M (*Sviyazhsk*) with 1 8-cell 3S14 UKSK VLS with 3M14T *Kalibr*-NK (SS-N-30A) dual-capable LACM/3M54T (SS-N-27B *Sizzler*) AShM/3M54T1 (SS-N-27) AShM/3M5S *Oniks* (SS-N-26 *Strobile*) AShM, 2 sextuple 3M47 *Gibka* lnchr with *Igla*-1M (SA-N-10 *Grouse*) SAM, 1 AK630M-2 CIWS, 1 100mm gun

2 *Sivuch* (*Dergach*) with 2 quad lnchr with 3M80 *Moskit* (SS-N-22 *Sunburn*) AShM, 1 twin ZIF-122 lnchr with 4K33AM *Osa*-MA2 (SA-N-4 *Gecko*) SAM, 2 AK630M CIWS, 1 76mm gun

10 *Ovod* (*Nanuchka* III) with 2 triple lnchr with P-120 *Malakhit* (SS-N-9 *Siren*) AShM, 1 twin ZIF-122 lnchr with 4K33 *Osa*-M (SA-N-4 *Gecko*) SAM, 1 AK630 CIWS, 1 76mm gun

1 *Ovod* (*Nanuchka* III) with 4 quad lnchr with 3M24 *Uran* (SS-N-25 *Switchblade*) AShM, 1 twin lnchr with 4K33 *Osa*-M (SA-N-4 *Gecko*) SAM, 1 AK630 CIWS, 1 76mm gun

FSG 1 *Karakurt* (Project 22800) with 1 8-cell 3S14 VLS with 3M14T *Kalibr*-NK (SS-N-30A) dual-capable LACM/3M54T (SS-N-27B *Sizzler*) AShM/3M54T1 (SS-N-27) AShM/3M5S *Oniks* (SS-N-26 *Strobile*) AShM, 2 AK630M CIWS, 1 76mm gun

FSM 29:

2 *Albatros* (*Grisha* III) with 1 twin ZIF-122 lnchr with 4K33 *Osa*-M (SA-N-4 *Gecko*) SAM, 2 twin DTA-53-1124 533mm ASTT, 2 RBU 6000 *Smerch* 2 A/S mor, 1 twin 57mm gun

18 *Albatros* (*Grisha* V) with 1 twin ZIF-122 lnchr with 4K33 *Osa*-M (SA-N-4 *Gecko*) SAM, 2 twin DTA-53-1124 533mm ASTT, 1 RBU 6000 *Smerch* 2 A/S mor, 1 76mm gun

3 *Buyan* (*Astrakhan*) with 1 sextuple lnchr with 3M47 *Gibka* lnchr with *Igla*-1M (SA-N-10 *Grouse*) SAM, 1 A-215 *Grad*-M 122mm MRL, 1 100mm gun

6 *Parchim* II with 2 quad lnchr with 9K32 *Strela*-2 (SA-N-5 *Grail*) SAM, 2 twin 533mm ASTT, 2 RBU 6000 *Smerch* 2 A/S mor, 1 AK630 CIWS, 1 76mm gun

PSOH 2 *Vasily Bykov* (Project 22160) with 1 76mm gun (capacity 1 Ka-27 *Helix* ASW hel)

PCFG 23:

5 *Molnya* (*Tarantul* II) with 2 twin lnchr with P-22 *Termit*-R (SS-N-2D *Styx*) AShM, 2 AK630M CIWS, 1 76mm gun

17 *Molnya* (*Tarantul* III) with 2 twin lnchr with 3M80 *Moskit* (SS-N-22 *Sunburn*) AShM, 2 AK630M CIWS, 1 76mm gun

1 *Molnya* (*Tarantul* III) with 2 twin lnchr with 3M80 *Moskit* (SS-N-22 *Sunburn*) AShM, 1 3K89 *Palash* (CADS-N-2) CIWS, 1 76mm gun

PCF 1 *Molnya* (*Tarantul* III) with 2 AK630M CIWS, 1 76mm gun

PBF 16: 14 *Raptor* (capacity 20 troops); 2 *Mangust*

PBR 4 *Shmel* with 1 17-cell BM-14 MRL, 1 76mm gun
PB 22 *Grachonok*

MINE WARFARE • MINE COUNTERMEASURES 43
MCC 2 *Alexandrit* (Project 12700)
MHI 8: 7 *Sapfir* (*Lida*) with 1 AK630 CIWS; 1 *Malakhit* (*Olya*)
MHO 2 *Rubin* (*Gorya*) with 2 quad lnchr with 9K32 *Strela-2* (SA-N-5 *Grail*) SAM, 1 AK630 CIWS, 1 76mm gun
MSC 22: 20 *Yakhont* (*Sonya*) with 4 AK630 CIWS (some with 2 quad lnchr with 9K32 *Strela-2* (SA-N-5 *Grail*) SAM; 2 *Korund-E* (*Yevgenya*) (Project 1258E)
MSO 9: 8 *Akvamaren* (*Natya*); 1 *Agat* (*Natya* II) (all with 2 quad lnchr (manual aiming) with 9K32 *Strela-2* (SA-N-5 *Grail*) SAM, 2 RBU 1200 *Uragan* A/S mor, 2 twin AK230 CIWS

AMPHIBIOUS
LANDING SHIPS • LST 20:
12 Project 775 (*Ropucha* I/II) with 2 twin 57mm guns (capacity either 10 MBT and 190 troops or 24 APC (T) and 170 troops)
3 Project 775M (*Ropucha* III) with 2 AK630 CIWS, 1 76mm gun (capacity either 10 MBT and 190 troops or 24 APC (T) and 170 troops)
4 *Tapir* (*Alligator*) with at least 2 twin lnchr with 9K32 *Strela-2* (SA-N-5 *Grail*) SAM, 2 twin 57mm guns (capacity 20 tanks; 300 troops)
1 *Ivan Gren* (Project 11711) with 1 AK630M-2 CIWS, 2 AK630M CIWS (capacity 1 Ka-29 *Helix* B hel; 13 MBT/36 AFV; 300 troops)

LANDING CRAFT 28
LCM 26: 9 *Akula* (*Ondatra*) (capacity 1 MBT); 5 *Dyugon* (capacity 5 APC or 100 troops); 12 *Serna* (Project 11770 (capacity 2 APC or 100 troops)
LCAC 2 *Pomornik* (*Zubr*) with 2 22-cell 140mm MS-227 *Ogon'* MRL, 2 AK630 CIWS (capacity 230 troops; either 3 MBT or 10 APC(T))

LOGISTICS AND SUPPORT 269
SSAN 9: 1 *Orenburg* (*Delta* III Stretch); 1 *Losharik* (reportedly damaged by fire in 2019); 1 *Nelma* (X-Ray) (Project 1851); 2 *Halibut* (*Paltus*) (Project 18511); 3 *Kashalot* (*Uniform*); 1 *Podmoskovye* (Project 09787)
SSA 1 *Sarov* (Project 20120)
ABU 12: 8 *Kashtan*; 4 Project 419 (*Sura*)
AE 8: 6 *Muna*, 1 *Dubnyak*, *Akademik Kovalev* (Project 20181) with 1 hel landing platform
AEM 2: 1 *Kalma-3* (Project 1791R); 1 *Lama*
AFS 1 *Longvinik* (Project 23120)
AG 1 *Potok*
AGB 5: 1 *Dobrynya Mikitich*; 1 *Ilya Muromets*; 2 *Ivan Susanin*; 1 *Vladimir Kavraisky*
AGE 1 *Tchusovoy*
AGHS 2 Project 23040G
AGI 14: 2 *Alpinist*; 2 *Dubridium* (Project 1826); 1 *Moma*; 7 *Vishnya*; 2 *Yuri Ivanov*
AGM 1 *Marshal Nedelin*
AGOR 8: 1 *Akademik Krylov*; 1 *Igor Belousov*; 1 *Seliger*; 2 *Sibiriyakov*; 2 *Vinograd*; 1 *Yantar*
AGS 69: 8 *Biya*; 18 *Finik*; 7 *Kamenka*; 5 *Moma*; 9 *Onega*; 5 *Baklan* (Project 19920); 4 *Baklan* (Project 19920B); 3 *Vaygach*; 10 *Yug*
AGSH 1 *Samara*
AH 3 *Ob†*
AK 3: 2 *Irgiz*; 1 *Pevek*
AOL 9: 2 *Dubna*; 3 *Uda*; 4 *Altay* (mod)
AOR 3 *Boris Chilikin*
AORL 2: 1 *Kaliningradneft*; 1 *Olekma*
AOS 1 *Luza*
AR ε7 *Amur*
ARC 4: 3 *Emba*; 1 Improved *Klasma*
ARS 29: 1 *Kommuna*; 5 *Goryn*; 4 *Mikhail Rudnitsky*; 18 Project 23040; 1 *Zvezdochka* (Project 20180)
AS 3 Project 2020 (*Malina*)
ASR 1 *Elbrus*
ATF 53: 1 *Okhotsk*; 1 *Baklan*; ε3 *Katun*; 3 *Ingul*; 2 *Neftegaz*; 11 *Okhtensky*; 13 *Prometey*; 1 *Prut*; 4 *Sliva*; 14 *Sorum*
ATS 5 Project 22870
AWT 1 *Manych*
AXL 10: 8 *Petrushka*; 2 *Smolny* with 2 RBU 2500 *Smerch* 1 A/S mor, 2 twin 76mm guns

Naval Aviation ε31,000
FORCES BY ROLE
FIGHTER
1 regt with MiG-31B/BS/BM *Foxhound*
1 regt with Su-27/Su-27UB *Flanker*
1 regt with Su-33 *Flanker* D; Su-25UTG *Frogfoot*
FIGHTER/GROUND ATTACK
1 regt with MiG-29KR/KUBR *Fulcrum*
1 regt with MiG-31BM *Foxhound*; Su-24M/M2/MR *Fencer*
ANTI-SURFACE WARFARE/ISR
2 regt with Su-24M/MR *Fencer*; Su-30SM
ANTI-SUBMARINE WARFARE
3 sqn with Il-38/Il-38N *May**; Il-18D; Il-20RT *Coot* A; Il-22 *Coot* B
8 sqn with Ka-27/Ka-29 *Helix*
1 sqn with Mi-14 *Haze* A
2 sqn with Tu-142MK/MZ/MR *Bear* F/J*
1 unit with Ka-31R *Helix*
MARITIME PATROL/TRANSPORT
1 sqn with An-26 *Curl*; Be-12 *Mail**; Mi-8 *Hip*
SEARCH & RESCUE/TRANSPORT
1 sqn with An-12PS *Cub*; An-26 *Curl*; Tu-134
TRANSPORT
1 sqn with An-12BK *Cub*; An-24RV *Coke*; An-26 *Curl*; An-72 *Coaler*; An-140
2 sqn with An-26 *Curl*; Tu-134
TRAINING
1 sqn with L-39 *Albatros*; Su-25UTG *Frogfoot*
1 sqn with An-140; Tu-134; Tu-154, Il-38 *May*
ATTACK/TRANSPORT HELICOPTER
1 sqn with Mi-24P *Hind*; Mi-8 *Hip*
TRANSPORT HELICOPTER
1 sqn with Mi-8 *Hip*
AIR DEFENCE
1 SAM regt with S-300PM1 (SA-20 *Gargoyle*)
1 SAM regt with S-300PM1 (SA-20 *Gargoyle*); S-300PS (SA-10 *Grumble*)
1 SAM regt with S-300PM1 (SA-20 *Gargoyle*); S-400 (SA-21 *Growler*); 96K6 *Pantsir*-S1 (SA-22 *Greyhound*)
1 SAM regt with S-300PS (SA-10B *Grumble*); S-400 (SA-21 *Growler*); 96K6 *Pantsir*-S1 (SA-22 *Greyhound*)

EQUIPMENT BY TYPE
AIRCRAFT 217 combat capable
  FTR 67: 10 MiG-31B/BS *Foxhound*; 22 MiG-31BM *Foxhound*; 17 Su-33 *Flanker* D; 18 Su-27/Su-27UB *Flanker*
  FGA 44: 19 MiG-29KR *Fulcrum*; 3 MiG-29KUBR *Fulcrum*; 22 Su-30SM
  ATK 46: 41 Su-24M *Fencer*; 5 Su-25UTG *Frogfoot* (trg role)
  ASW 44: 12 Tu-142MK/MZ *Bear* F; 10 Tu-142MR *Bear* J (comms); 15 Il-38 *May*; 7 Il-38N *May*
  MP 5: 4 Be-12PS *Mail**; 1 Il-18D
  ISR 12 Su-24MR *Fencer* E*
  SAR 3 An-12PS *Cub*
  ELINT 4: 2 Il-20RT *Coot* A; 2 Il-22 *Coot* B
  TPT 49: **Medium** 2 An-12BK *Cub*; **Light** 45: 1 An-24RV *Coke*; 24 An-26 *Curl*; 6 An-72 *Coaler*; 4 An-140; 9 Tu-134; 1 Tu-134UBL; **PAX** 2 Tu-154M *Careless*
  TRG 4 L-39 *Albatros*
HELICOPTERS
  ATK 8 Mi-24P *Hind*
  ASW 83: 41 Ka-27PL *Helix*; 22 Ka-27M *Helix*; 20 Mi-14 *Haze* A
  EW 8 Mi-8 *Hip* J
  AEW 2 Ka-31R *Helix*
  SAR 56: 16 Ka-27PS *Helix* D; 40 Mi-14PS *Haze* C
  TPT 41: **Medium** 35: 27 Ka-29 *Helix*; 4 Mi-8T *Hip*; 4 Mi-8MT *Hip*; **Light** 6 Ka-226T
AIR DEFENCE • SAM
  Long-range 120: 56 S-300PM1 (SA-20 *Gargoyle*); 40 S-300PS (SA-10 *Grumble*); 24 S-400 (SA-21 *Growler*)
  Short-range 12 96K6 *Pantsir*-S1 (SA-22 *Greyhound*)
AIR-LAUNCHED MISSILES
  AAM • **IR** R-27T/ET (AA-10B/D *Alamo*); R-60 (AA-8 *Aphid*); R-73 (AA-11A *Archer*); **ARH** R-77-1 (AA-12B *Adder*); **SARH** R-27R/ER (AA-10A/C *Alamo*); R-33 (AA-9A *Amos*)
  ARM Kh-25MP (AS-12A *Kegler*); Kh-31P (AS-17A *Krypton*); Kh-58 (AS-11 *Kilter*)
  ASM Kh-59 (AS-13 *Kingbolt*); Kh-29T (AS-14 *Kedge*)
  AShM Kh-31A (AS-17B *Krypton*)

Naval Infantry (Marines) ε35,000
FORCES BY ROLE
COMMAND
  3 corps HQ
SPECIAL FORCES
  4 (OMRP) SF unit
  11 (PDSS) cbt diver unit
MANOEUVRE
  Reconnaissance
  1 recce bde
  Mechanised
  3 MR bde
  1 MR regt
  6 naval inf bde
  1 naval inf regt
SURFACE-TO-SURFACE MISSILE
  1 SRBM/GLCM bde with 9K720 *Iskander*-M (SS-26 *Stone*/SSC-7 *Southpaw*)
COMBAT SUPPORT
  2 arty bde

AIR DEFENCE
  2 SAM regt with 9K33 *Osa* (SA-8 *Gecko*); *Strela*-1/ *Strela*-10 (SA-9 *Gaskin*/SA-13 *Gopher*)
  2 SAM regt with S-400 (SA-21 *Growler*); 96K6 *Pantsir*-S1 (SA-22 *Greyhound*)
  1 SAM regt with S-300V4 (SA-23)
EQUIPMENT BY TYPE
ARMOURED FIGHTING VEHICLES
  MBT 300: 50 T-72B; 150 T-72B3; 50 T-80BV; 50 T-80BVM
  IFV 1,061: 400 BMP-2; 661 BTR-82A
  APC 400
    APC (T) 300 MT-LB
    APC (W) 100 BTR-80
ANTI-TANK/ANTI-INFRASTRUCTURE
  MSL
    SP 60 9P148 with 9K111-1 *Konkurs* (AT-5 *Spandrel*); 9P149 with 9K114 *Shturm* (AT-6 *Spiral*); 9P157-2 with 9K123 *Khrisantema* (AT-15 *Springer*)
    MANPATS 9K111-1 *Konkurs* (AT-5 *Spandrel*); 9K135 *Kornet* (AT-14 *Spriggan*)
  GUNS 100mm T-12
ARTILLERY 383
  SP 163: **122mm** 95 2S1 *Gvozdika*; **152mm** 68: 50 2S3 *Akatsiya*; 18 2S19 *Msta*-S
  TOWED 152mm 100: 50 2A36 *Giatsint*-B; 50 2A65 *Msta*-B
  GUN/MOR 66
    SP 120mm 42: 12 2S23 NONA-SVK; 30 2S9 NONA-S
    TOWED 120mm 24 2B16 NONA-K
  MRL 54: **122mm** 36 BM-21 *Grad/Tornado*-G; **220mm** 18 9P140 *Uragan*
SURFACE-TO-SURFACE MISSILE LAUNCHER
  SRBM • **Dual-capable** 12 9K720 *Iskander*-M (SS-26 *Stone*)
  GLCM • **Dual-capable** Some 9M728 (SSC-7 *Southpaw*)
AIR DEFENCE
  SAM
    Long-range 48+: 48 S-400 (SA-21 *Growler*); S-300V4 (SA-23)
    Short-range 30: 18 96K6 *Pantsir*-S1 (SA-22 *Greyhound*); 12+ *Tor*-M2DT
    Point-defence 70+: 20 9K33 *Osa* (SA-8 *Gecko*); 50 9K31 *Strela*-1/9K35 *Strela*-10 (SA-9 *Gaskin*/SA-13 *Gopher*); 9K338 *Igla*-S (SA-24 *Grinch*)
  GUNS 23mm 60 ZSU-23-4

Coastal Missile and Artillery Forces 2,000
FORCES BY ROLE
COASTAL DEFENCE
  5 AShM bde
  1 AShM regt
EQUIPMENT BY TYPE
COASTAL DEFENCE
  ARTY • **SP 130mm** ε36 A-222 *Bereg*
  AShM 92+: 40 3K60 *Bal* (SSC-6 *Sennight*); 52 3K55 *Bastion* (SSC-5 *Stooge*); some 4K44 *Redut* (SSC-1 *Sepal*); some 4K51 *Rubezh* (SSC-3 *Styx*)

Aerospace Forces ε165,000 (incl conscripts)
A joint CIS Unified Air Defence System covers RUS, ARM, BLR, KAZ, KGZ, TJK, TKM and UZB

FORCES BY ROLE
BOMBER
- 3 regt with Tu-22M3 *Backfire* C
- 3 sqn with Tu-95MS/MS mod *Bear*
- 1 sqn with Tu-160/Tu-160M1 *Blackjack*

FIGHTER
- 1 sqn with MiG-29/MiG-29UB *Fulcrum* (Armenia)
- 2 regt with MiG-31BM *Foxhound*
- 1 regt with MiG-31BM *Foxhound*; Su-35S *Flanker*
- 1 regt with Su-27/Su-27SM/Su-27UB *Flanker*; Su-30M2
- 2 regt with Su-30SM

FIGHTER/GROUND ATTACK
- 1 regt with MiG-31BM *Foxhound*; Su-27SM *Flanker*; Su-30M2; Su-30SM; Su-35S *Flanker*
- 1 regt with Su-27SM *Flanker*; Su-35S *Flanker*
- 1 regt with Su-35S *Flanker*; Su-30SM
- 1 regt with Su-27SM3 *Flanker*; Su-30M2
- 1 regt with Su-25 *Frogfoot*; Su-30SM

GROUND ATTACK
- 1 regt with Su-24M/M2 *Fencer*; Su-34 *Fullback*
- 1 regt with Su-24M *Fencer*; Su-25SM *Frogfoot*
- 3 regt with Su-25SM/SM3 *Frogfoot*
- 1 sqn with Su-25SM *Frogfoot* (Kyrgyzstan)
- 3 regt with Su-34 *Fullback*

ISR
- 2 regt with Su-24MR *Fencer**
- 2 sqn with Su-24MR *Fencer**
- 1 flt with An-30 *Clank*

AIRBORNE EARLY WARNING & CONTROL
- 1 sqn with A-50/A-50U *Mainstay*

TANKER
- 1 sqn with Il-78/Il-78M *Midas*

TRANSPORT
- 6 regt/sqn with An-12BK *Cub*; An-148-100E; An-26 *Curl*; Tu-134 *Crusty*; Tu-154 *Careless*; Mi-8 *Hip*
- 1 regt with An-124 *Condor*; Il-76MD *Candid*
- 1 regt with An-124 *Condor*; Il-76MD *Candid*; Il-76MD-90A *Candid*
- 1 regt with An-12BK *Cub*; Il-76MD *Candid*
- 1 sqn with An-22 *Cock*
- 3 regt with Il-76MD *Candid*

ATTACK/TRANSPORT HELICOPTER
- 1 bde with Ka-52A *Hokum* B; Mi-28N *Havoc* B; Mi-35 *Hind*; Mi-26 *Halo*; Mi-8MTV-5 *Hip*
- 1 bde with Ka-52A *Hokum* B; Mi-26 *Halo*; Mi-8 *Hip*
- 1 bde with Mi-28N *Havoc* B; Mi-35 *Hind*; Mi-26 *Halo*; Mi-8 *Hip*
- 2 regt with Ka-52A *Hokum* B; Mi-28N *Havoc* B; Mi-35 *Hind*; Mi-8 *Hip*
- 1 regt with Ka-52A *Hokum* B; Mi-24P *Hind*; Mi-8PPA *Hip*; Mi-8 *Hip*
- 1 regt with Ka-52A *Hokum* B; Mi-8 *Hip*
- 1 regt with Mi-28N *Havoc* B; Mi-35 *Hind*; Mi-8 *Hip*
- 1 regt with Mi-28N *Havoc* B; Mi-24P *Hind*; Mi-35 *Hind*; Mi-8 *Hip*
- 2 regt with Mi-24P *Hind*; Mi-8 *Hip*
- 2 sqn with Mi-24P *Hind*; Mi-8 *Hip*

AIR DEFENCE
- 9 AD div HQ
- 4 regt with 9K37M *Buk*-M1-2 (SA-11 *Gadfly*); 9K317 *Buk*-M2 (SA-17 *Grizzly*); S-300V (SA-12 *Gladiator/Giant*)
- 1 bde with S-300PS (SA-10 *Grumble*)
- 4 regt with S-300PS (SA-10 *Grumble*)
- 7 regt with S-300PM1/PM2 (SA-20 *Gargoyle*)
- 9 regt with S-400 (SA-21 *Growler*); 96K6 *Pantsir*-S1 (SA-22 *Greyhound*)

EQUIPMENT BY TYPE
AIRCRAFT 1,183 combat capable
- **BBR** 138: 60 Tu-22M3 *Backfire* C; 1 Tu-22M3M *Backfire*; 1 Tu-22MR *Backfire*† (1 in overhaul); 44 Tu-95MS *Bear*; 16 Tu-95MS mod *Bear*; 10 Tu-160 *Blackjack*; 6 Tu-160M1 *Blackjack*
- **FTR** 180: 70 MiG-29/MiG-29UB *Fulcrum*; 80 MiG-31BM *Foxhound*; 20 Su-27 *Flanker*; 10 Su-27UB *Flanker*
- **FGA** 444: 44 MiG-29SMT *Fulcrum*; 6 MiG-29UBT *Fulcrum*; 47 Su-27SM *Flanker*; 24 Su-27SM3 *Flanker*; 20 Su-30M2; 91 Su-30SM; 122 Su-34 *Fullback*; 90 Su-35S *Flanker* M
- **ATK** 264: 70 Su-24M/M2 *Fencer*; 40 Su-25 *Frogfoot*; 139 Su-25SM/SM3 *Frogfoot*; 15 Su-25UB *Frogfoot*
- **ISR** 58: 4 An-30 *Clank*; up to 50 Su-24MR *Fencer**; 2 Tu-214ON; 2 Tu-214R
- **EW** 3 Il-22PP
- **ELINT** 31: 14 Il-20M *Coot* A; 5 Il-22 *Coot* B; 12 Il-22M *Coot* B
- **AEW&C** 9: 5 A-50 *Mainstay*; 4 A-50U *Mainstay*
- **C2** 11: 4 Il-80 *Maxdome*; 2 Il-82; 4 Tu-214SR; 1 Tu-214PU-SBUS
- **TKR** 15: 5 Il-78 *Midas*; 10 Il-78M *Midas*
- **TPT** 439: **Heavy** 120: 11 An-124 *Condor*; 4 An-22 *Cock*; 99 Il-76MD *Candid*; 3 Il-76MD-M *Candid*; 3 Il-76MD-90A *Candid* **Medium** 65 An-12BK *Cub*; **Light** 225: 114 An-26 *Curl*; 25 An-72 *Coaler*; 5 An-140; 27 L-410; 54 Tu-134 *Crusty*; **PAX** 32: 15 An-148-100E; 17 Tu-154 *Careless*
- **TRG** 227: 120 L-39 *Albatros*; 107 Yak-130 *Mitten**

HELICOPTERS
- **ATK** 393+: 127 Ka-52A *Hokum* B; 100 Mi-24D/V/P *Hind*; 90+ Mi-28N *Havoc* B; 12 Mi-28UB *Havoc*; 64+ Mi-35 *Hind*
- **EW** 27: 20 Mi-8PPA *Hip*; 7 Mi-8MTRP-1 *Hip*
- **TPT** 333: **Heavy** 33 Mi-26/Mi-26T *Halo*; **Medium** 300: 100 Mi-8/Mi-8MT *Hip*; 60 Mi-8AMTSh *Hip*; 5 Mi-8AMTSh-VA *Hip*; 135 Mi-8MTV-5-1 *Hip*
- **TRG** 69: 19 Ka-226U; 50 Ansat-U

UNMANNED AERIAL VEHICLES
- **ISR • Medium** *Forpost* (*Searcher* II)

AIR DEFENCE
- **SAM** 620:
  - **Long-range** 490: 160 S-300PS (SA-10 *Grumble*); 150 S-300PM1/PM2 (SA-20 *Gargoyle*); 20 S-300V (SA-12 *Gladiator/Giant*); 160 S-400 (SA-21 *Growler*)
  - **Medium-range** 80 9K37M *Buk*-M1-2/9K317 *Buk*-M2 (SA-11 *Gadfly*/SA-17 *Grizzly*)
  - **Short-range** 50 96K6 *Pantsir*-S1/S2 (SA-22 *Greyhound*)
- **DE • Laser** *Peresvet*

AIR-LAUNCHED MISSILES
- **AAM • IR** R-27T/ET (AA-10B/D *Alamo*); R-73 (AA-11 *Archer*); R-74M (AA-11B *Archer*); R-60T (AA-8 *Aphid*); **SARH** R-27R/ER (AA-10A/C *Alamo*); R-33 (AA-9A

Amos); **ARH** R-77-1 (AA-12B *Adder*); R-37M (AA-13A *Axehead*); **PRH** R-27P/EP (AA-10E/F *Alamo*)
ARM Kh-25MP (AS-12A *Kegler*); Kh-25M (AS-12B *Kegler*); Kh-31P/PM (AS-17A/C *Krypton*); Kh-58 (AS-11 *Kilter*)
ASM Kh-29 (AS-14 *Kedge*); Kh-38; Kh-59/Kh-59M (AS-13 *Kingbolt*/AS-18 *Kazoo*); *Kinzhal*; 9M114 *Kokon* (AT-6 *Spiral*); 9M120 *Ataka* (AT-9 *Spiral 2*); 9M120-1 *Vikhr* (AT-16 *Scallion*)
AShM Kh-22 (AS-4 *Kitchen*); Kh-31A/AM (AS-17B/D *Krypton*); Kh-32 (AS-4A mod); Kh-35U (AS-20 *Kayak*)
LACM
  Nuclear Kh-55SM (AS-15B *Kent*); Kh-102 (AS-23B *Kodiak*)
  Conventional Kh-101 (AS-23A *Kodiak*); Kh-555 (AS-22 *Kluge*)
BOMBS
  Laser-guided KAB-500; KAB-1500L
  TV-guided KAB-500KR; KAB-1500KR; KAB-500OD; UPAB 1500
  INS/GLONASS-guided KAB-500S

Airborne Forces ε45,000
FORCES BY ROLE
SPECIAL FORCES
  1 (AB Recce) SF bde
MANOEUVRE
  Air Manoeuvre
  1 AB div (1 tk bn, 3 para/air aslt regt, 1 arty regt, 1 AD regt)
  1 AB div (1 tk bn, 2 para/air aslt regt, 1 para/air aslt bn, 1 arty regt, 1 AD regt)
  2 AB div (2 para/air aslt regt, 1 arty regt, 1 AD regt)
  1 indep AB bde
  3 air aslt bde
EQUIPMENT BY TYPE
ARMOURED FIGHTING VEHICLES
  MBT 150 T-72B3
  IFV 20 BTR-82AM
  APC • APC (T) 784: 700 BTR-D; 84 BTR-MDM
  AUV GAZ *Tigr*; UAMZ *Toros*
  ABCV 1,336: 100 BMD-1; 1,000 BMD-2; 10 BMD-3; 30 BMD-4; 196 BMD-4M
ENGINEERING & MAINTENANCE VEHICLES
  ARV BREM-D; BREhM-D
ANTI-TANK/ANTI-INFRASTRUCTURE
  MSL
    SP 100 BTR-RD
    MANPATS 9K111 *Fagot* (AT-4 *Spigot*); 9K113 *Konkurs* (AT-5 *Spandrel*); 9K115 *Metis* (AT-7 *Saxhorn*); 9K115-1 *Metis-M* (AT-13 *Saxhorn 2*); 9K135 *Kornet* (AT-14 *Spriggan*)
  RCL 73mm SPG-9
  GUNS • SP 125mm 36+ 2S25 *Sprut*-SD
ARTILLERY 600+
  TOWED 122mm 150 D-30
  GUN/MOR • SP 120mm 250: 220 2S9 NONA-S; 30 2S9 NONA-SM; (500 2S9 NONA-S in store)
  MOR • TOWED 200+ **82mm** 150 2B14; **120mm** 50+ 2B23 NONA-M1

AIR DEFENCE
  SAM • Point-defence 30+: 30 *Strela*-10MN; 9K310 *Igla*-1 (SA-16 *Gimlet*); 9K38 *Igla* (SA-18 *Grouse*); 9K333 *Verba* (SA-29); 9K338 *Igla*-S (SA-24 *Grinch*); 9K34 *Strela*-3 (SA-14 *Gremlin*)
  GUNS • SP 23mm 150 BTR-ZD

Special Operations Forces ε1,000
FORCES BY ROLE
SPECIAL FORCES
  2 SF unit

Railway Forces ε29,000
4 regional commands
FORCES BY ROLE
COMBAT SERVICE SUPPORT
  10 (railway) tpt bde

Russian Military Districts

Western Military District
HQ at St Petersburg

Army
FORCES BY ROLE
COMMAND
  3 army HQ
SPECIAL FORCES
  2 (Spetsnaz) SF bde
MANOEUVRE
  Reconnaissance
  1 recce bde
  Armoured
  1 tk div
  1 tk bde
  2 MR div
  Mechanised
  1 MR div
  3 MR bde
SURFACE-TO-SURFACE MISSILE
  3 SRBM/GLCM bde with *Iskander*-M
COMBAT SUPPORT
  2 arty bde
  1 (hy) arty bde
  1 MRL bde
  1 engr bde
  1 MP bde
  1 NBC bde
  2 NBC regt
COMBAT SERVICE SUPPORT
  2 log bde
AIR DEFENCE
  3 AD bde

Reserves
FORCES BY ROLE
  MANOEUVRE
    Mechanised
    2 MR bde

Northern Fleet

EQUIPMENT BY TYPE
SUBMARINES 25
  STRATEGIC 7 **SSBN** (of which 1 in refit, 1 more in reserve)
  TACTICAL 18: 4 **SSGN**; 8 **SSN**; 6 **SSK** (of which 1 in refit)
PRINCIPAL SURFACE COMBATANTS 8: 1 **CV**; 1 **CGHMN**; 1 **CGHM**; 5 **DDGHM** (1 more in reserve)
PATROL AND COASTAL COMBATANTS 16: 2 **FSGM**; 6 **FSM**; 8 **PB**
MINE WARFARE • MINE COUNTERMEASURES 10: 1 **MHO**; 2 **MSO**; 7 **MSC**
AMPHIBIOUS 7: 5 **LST**; 2 **LCM**

Naval Aviation

FORCES BY ROLE
FIGHTER
  1 regt with Su-33 *Flanker* D; Su-25UTG *Frogfoot*
FIGHTER/GROUND ATTACK
  1 regt with MiG-29KR/KUBR *Fulcrum*
FIGHTER/GROUND ATTACK/ISR
  1 regt with MiG-31BM *Foxhound*; Su-24M/M2/MR *Fencer*
ANTI-SUBMARINE WARFARE
  1 sqn with Il-38 *May*; Il-20RT *Coot A*; Tu-134
  3 sqn with Ka-27/Ka-29 *Helix*
  1 sqn with Tu-142MK/MZ/MR *Bear* F/J
AIR DEFENCE
  3 SAM regt with S-300PS (SA-10 *Grumble*); S-300PM1 (SA-20 *Gargoyle*); S-400 (SA-21 *Growler*); 96K6 *Pantsir*-S1 (SA-22 *Greyhound*)

EQUIPMENT BY TYPE
AIRCRAFT
  FTR 38: 20 MiG-31BM *Foxhound*; 18 Su-33 *Flanker* D
  FGA 25: 19 MiG-29KR *Fulcrum*; 4 MiG-29KUBR *Fulcrum*; 2 Su-30SM
  ATK 18: 13 Su-24M *Fencer*; 5 Su-25UTG *Frogfoot* (trg role)
  ASW 21: 10 Il-38 *May*; 11 Tu-142MK/MZ/MR *Bear* F/J
  ISR 4 Su-24MR *Fencer**
  ELINT 3: 2 Il-20RT *Coot A*; 1 Il-22 *Coot B*
  TPT 9: 8 An-26 *Curl*; 1 Tu-134
HELICOPTERS
  ASW Ka-27 *Helix* A
  TPT • Medium Ka-29 *Helix* B; Mi-8 *Hip*
AIR DEFENCE • SAM
  Long-range S-300PS (SA-10 *Grumble*); S-300PM1 (SA-20 *Gargoyle*); S-400 (SA-21 *Growler*)
  Short-range 96K6 *Pantsir*-S1 (SA-22 *Greyhound*)

Naval Infantry

FORCES BY ROLE
COMMAND
  1 corps HQ
MANOEUVRE
  Mechanised
  2 MR bde
  1 naval inf bde

Coastal Artillery and Missile Forces

FORCES BY ROLE
COASTAL DEFENCE
  1 AShM bde

Baltic Fleet

EQUIPMENT BY TYPE
SUBMARINES • TACTICAL • **SSK** 1
PRINCIPAL SURFACE COMBATANTS 7: 1 **DDGHM**; 6 **FFGHM** (of which 1 in refit)
PATROL AND COASTAL COMBATANTS 29: 6 **FSGM**; 1 **FSG**; 7 **FSM**; 7 **PCFG**; 7 **PBF**; 1 **PB**
MINE WARFARE • MINE COUNTERMEASURES 12: 1 **MCC**; 5 **MSC**; 6 **MHI**
AMPHIBIOUS 13: 4 **LST**; 7 **LCM**; 2 **LCAC**

Naval Aviation

FORCES BY ROLE
FIGHTER
  1 sqn with Su-27 *Flanker*
ANTI-SURFACE WARFARE/ISR
  1 sqn with Su-24M/MR *Fencer*; Su-30SM
ANTI-SUBMARINE WARFARE
  1 sqn with Ka-27/Ka-29 *Helix*
TRANSPORT
  1 sqn with An-26 *Curl*; Tu-134 *Crusty*
ATTACK/TRANSPORT HELICOPTER
  1 sqn with Mi-24P *Hind*; Mi-8 *Hip*
TRANSPORT HELICOPTER
  1 sqn with Mi-8 *Hip*

EQUIPMENT BY TYPE
AIRCRAFT
  FTR 18 Su-27/Su-27UB *Flanker*
  FGA 8 Su-30SM
  ATK 10 Su-24M *Fencer*
  ISR 4 Su-24MR *Fencer**
  TPT 8: 6 An-26 *Curl*; 2 Tu-134 *Crusty*
HELICOPTERS
  ATK Mi-24P *Hind*
  ASW Ka-27 *Helix*
  TPT • Medium Ka-29 *Helix*; Mi-8 *Hip*

Naval Infantry

FORCES BY ROLE
COMMAND
  1 corps HQ
MANOEUVRE
  Mechanised
  1 MR bde
  1 MR regt
  1 naval inf bde
SURFACE-TO-SURFACE MISSILE
  1 SRBM/GLCM bde with *Iskander*-M
  COMBAT SUPPORT
  1 arty bde
AIR DEFENCE
  3 SAM regt

Coastal Artillery and Missile Forces
FORCES BY ROLE
COASTAL DEFENCE
1 AShM regt

Military Air Force

6th Air Force & Air Defence Army
FORCES BY ROLE
FIGHTER
1 regt with Su-30SM
1 regt with MiG-31BM *Foxhound*; Su-35S *Flanker*
1 regt with Su-27SM *Flanker*; Su-35S *Flanker*
GROUND ATTACK
1 regt with Su-34 *Fullback*
ISR
1 sqn with Su-24MR *Fencer*
1 flt with A-30 *Clank*
TRANSPORT
1 regt with An-12 *Cub*; An-26 *Curl*; Tu-134 *Crusty*
ATTACK HELICOPTER
1 bde with Ka-52A *Hokum* B; Mi-28N *Havoc* B; Mi-35 *Hind*; Mi-26 *Halo*; Mi-8MTV-5 *Hip*
1 regt with Mi-24P/Mi-35 *Hind*; Mi-28N *Havoc* B; Mi-8 *Hip*
1 regt with Mi-24P *Hind*; Ka-52A *Hokum* B; Mi-8 *Hip*; Mi-8PPA *Hip*
AIR DEFENCE
1 SAM regt with 9K37M *Buk*-M1-2 (SA-11 *Gadfly*); S-300V (SA-12 *Gladiator/Giant*)
5 SAM regt with S-300PM1 (SA-20 *Gargoyle*)
1 SAM regt with S-400 (SA-21 *Growler*); 96K6 Pantsir-S1 (SA-22 *Greyhound*)
EQUIPMENT BY TYPE
AIRCRAFT
FTR 30 MiG-31BM *Foxhound*
FGA 98: 12 Su-27SM *Flanker*; 24 Su-30SM; 24 Su-34 *Fullback*; 38 Su-35S *Flanker*
ISR 19: 4 An-30 *Clank*; 15 Su-24MR *Fencer**
TPT 12 An-12/An-26/Tu-134
HELICOPTERS
ATK 76+: 24 Ka-52A *Hokum* B; 16 Mi-24P *Hind*; 24 Mi-28N *Havoc* B; 12+ Mi-35 *Hind*
EW 10 Mi-8PPA *Hip*
TPT • **Medium** 50 Mi-8 *Hip*
AIR DEFENCE
SAM
Long-range S-300PM1 (SA-20 *Gargoyle*); S-300V (SA-12 *Gladiator/Giant*); S-400 (SA-21 *Growler*)
Medium-range 9K37M *Buk*-M1-2 (SA-11 *Gadfly*)
Short-range 96K6 Pantsir-S1 (SA-22 *Greyhound*)

Airborne Forces
FORCES BY ROLE
SPECIAL FORCES
1 (AB Recce) SF bde
MANOEUVRE
Air Manoeuvre
3 AB div

Central Military District
HQ at Yekaterinburg

Army
FORCES BY ROLE
COMMAND
2 army HQ
SPECIAL FORCES
2 (Spetsnaz) SF bde
MANOEUVRE
Armoured
1 tk div
3 MR bde
Mechanised
2 MR bde
2 (lt/mtn) MR bde
SURFACE-TO-SURFACE MISSILE
2 SRBM/GLCM bde with *Iskander*-M
COMBAT SUPPORT
2 arty bde
1 MRL bde
1 engr bde
2 NBC bde
2 NBC regt
COMBAT SERVICE SUPPORT
2 log bde
AIR DEFENCE
3 AD bde

Reserves
FORCES BY ROLE
MANOEUVRE
Mechanised
3 MR bde

Military Air Force

14th Air Force & Air Defence Army
FORCES BY ROLE
FIGHTER
2 regt with MiG-31BM *Foxhound*
GROUND ATTACK
1 regt with Su-34 *Fullback*
1 sqn with Su-25SM *Frogfoot* (Kyrgyzstan)
ISR
1 sqn with Su-24MR *Fencer* E
TRANSPORT
1 regt with An-12 *Cub*; An-26 *Curl*; Tu-134 *Crusty*; Tu-154; Mi-8 *Hip*
ATTACK/TRANSPORT HELICOPTER
1 regt with Mi-24P *Hind*; Mi-8 *Hip*
1 sqn with Mi-24P *Hind*; Mi-8 *Hip* (Tajikistan)
AIR DEFENCE
3 regt with S-300PS (SA-10 *Grumble*)
1 bde with S-300PS (SA-10 *Grumble*)
1 regt with S-300PM1 (SA-20 *Gargoyle*)
2 regt with S-400 (SA-21 *Growler*); 96K6 Pantsir-S1 (SA-22 *Greyhound*)
EQUIPMENT BY TYPE
AIRCRAFT
FTR 40 MiG-31BM *Foxhound*
FGA 24 Su-34 *Fullback*

ATK 13 Su-25SM *Frogfoot*
ISR 9 Su-24MR *Fencer* E
TPT 36 An-12 *Cub*/An-26 *Curl*/Tu-134 *Crusty*/Tu-154 *Careless*
HELICOPTERS
ATK 24 Mi-24 *Hind*
TPT 46: 6 Mi-26 *Halo*; 40 Mi-8 *Hip*
AIR DEFENCE
SAM
Long-range S-300PS (SA-10 *Grumble*); S-300PM1 (SA-20 *Gargoyle*); S-400 (SA-21 *Growler*)
Short-range 96K6 *Pantsir*-S1 (SA-22 *Greyhound*)

Airborne Troops
FORCES BY ROLE
MANOEUVRE
Air Manoeuvre
1 AB bde

Southern Military District
HQ located at Rostov-on-Don

Army
FORCES BY ROLE
COMMAND
3 army HQ
SPECIAL FORCES
3 (Spetsnaz) SF bde
1 (Spetsnaz) SF regt
MANOEUVRE
Reconnaissance
1 recce bde
Armoured
1 MR div
3 MR bde
1 MR bde (Armenia)
1 MR bde (South Ossetia)
Mechanised
1 MR div
1 MR bde
1 MR bde (Abkhazia)
1 (lt/mtn) MR bde
SURFACE-TO-SURFACE MISSILE
2 SRBM/GLCM bde with *Iskander* M
COMBAT SUPPORT
2 arty bde
1 MRL bde
1 engr bde
1 NBC bde
2 NBC regt
COMBAT SERVICE SUPPORT
2 log bde
AIR DEFENCE
4 AD bde

Black Sea Fleet
The Black Sea Fleet is primarily based in Crimea, at Sevastopol, Karantinnaya Bay and Streletskaya Bay
EQUIPMENT BY TYPE
SUBMARINES • TACTICAL 7 SSK (of which 1 in refit)
PRINCIPAL SURFACE COMBATANTS 7: 1 CGHM; 1 DDGM; 3 FFGHM; 2 FFGM
PATROL AND COASTAL COMBATANTS 37: 7 FSGM; 6 FSM; 2 PSOH; 5 PCFG; 6 PB; 9 PBF; 2 PBR
MINE WARFARE • MINE COUNTERMEASURES 10: 1 MCC; 1 MHO; 6 MSO; 1 MSC; 1 MHI
AMPHIBIOUS 10: 7 LST; 3 LCM

Naval Aviation
FORCES BY ROLE
FIGHTER
ANTI-SURFACE WARFARE/ISR
1 regt with Su-24M/MR *Fencer*; Su-30SM
ANTI-SUBMARINE WARFARE
1 sqn with Ka-27 *Helix*
1 sqn with Mi-14 *Haze*
MARITIME PATROL/TRANSPORT
1 sqn with An-26 *Curl*; Be-12PS *Mail**; Mi-8
EQUIPMENT BY TYPE
AIRCRAFT
FGA 12 Su-30SM
ATK 13 Su-24M *Fencer*
ISR 4 Su-24MR *Fencer* E
MP 3 Be-12PS *Mail**
TPT 6 An-26
HELICOPTERS
ASW Ka-27 *Helix*
TPT • Medium Mi-8 *Hip* (MP/EW/Tpt)

Naval Infantry
FORCES BY ROLE
COMMAND
1 corps HQ
MANOEUVRE
Mechanised
2 naval inf bde
COMBAT SUPPORT
1 arty bde
AIR DEFENCE
1 SAM regt

Coastal Artillery and Missile Forces
FORCES BY ROLE
COASTAL DEFENCE
2 AShM bde

Caspian Sea Flotilla
EQUIPMENT BY TYPE
PRINCIPAL SURFACE COMBATANTS 2 FFGM
PATROL AND COASTAL COMBATANTS 9: 1 FSGM; 3 FSM; 1 PCFG; 1 PB; 1 PBF; 2 PBR
MINE WARFARE • MINE COUNTERMEASURES 3: 2 MSC; 1 MHI
AMPHIBIOUS 9 LCM

Naval Infantry
FORCES BY ROLE
MANOEUVRE
Mechanised
1 naval inf regt

Military Air Force

4th Air Force & Air Defence Army
FORCES BY ROLE
FIGHTER
  1 regt with Su-30SM
  1 sqn with MiG-29 *Fulcrum* (Armenia)
FIGHTER/GROUND ATTACK
  1 regt with Su-27/Su-27SM *Flanker*; Su-30M2
  1 regt with Su-27SM3 *Flanker*; Su-30M2
GROUND ATTACK
  1 regt with Su-24M *Fencer*; Su-25SM *Frogfoot*
  2 regt with Su-25SM/SM3 *Frogfoot*
  1 regt with Su-34 *Fullback*
ISR
  1 regt with Su-24MR *Fencer* E
TRANSPORT
  1 regt with An-12 *Cub*/Mi-8 *Hip*
ATTACK/TRANSPORT HELICOPTER
  1 bde with Mi-28N *Havoc* B; Mi-35 *Hind*; Mi-8 *Hip*; Mi-26 *Halo*
  1 regt with Mi-28N *Havoc* B; Mi-35 *Hind*; Mi-8 *Hip*
  2 regt with Ka-52A *Hokum* B; Mi-28N *Havoc* B; Mi-35 *Hind*; Mi-8AMTSh *Hip*
  1 sqn with Mi-24P *Hind*; Mi-8 *Hip* (Armenia)
AIR DEFENCE
  1 regt with 9K317 *Buk*-M2 (SA-17 *Grizzly*)
  1 regt with S-300PM1 (SA-20 *Gargoyle*)
  3 regt with S-400 (SA-21 *Growler*); 96K6 *Pantsir*-S1 (SA-22 *Greyhound*)

EQUIPMENT BY TYPE
AIRCRAFT
  FTR 26: 12 MiG-29 *Fulcrum*; 14 Su-27 *Flanker*
  FGA 95: 12 Su-27SM *Flanker*; 24 Su-27SM3 *Flanker*; 14 Su-30M2; 21 Su-30SM; 24 Su-34 *Fullback*
  ATK 97: 12 Su-24M *Fencer*; 85 Su-25SM/SM3 *Frogfoot*
  ISR 24 Su-24MR *Fencer**
  TPT 12 An-12 *Cub*
HELICOPTERS
  ATK 117: 25 Ka-52A *Hokum* B; 44 Mi-28N *Havoc* B; 8 Mi-24P *Hind*; 40 Mi-35 *Hind*
  TPT 72: **Heavy** 10 Mi-26 *Halo*; **Medium** 62 Mi-8 *Hip*
AIR DEFENCE • SAM
  Long-range S-300PM1 (SA-20 *Gargoyle*); S-400 (SA-21 *Growler*)
  Medium-range 9K317 *Buk*-M2 (SA-17 *Grizzly*)
  Short-range 96K6 *Pantsir*-S1 (SA-22 *Greyhound*)

Airborne Forces
FORCES BY ROLE
MANOEUVRE
  Air Manoeuvre
  1 AB div
  1 air aslt bde

Eastern Military District
HQ located at Khabarovsk

Army
FORCES BY ROLE
COMMAND
  4 army HQ
SPECIAL FORCES
  1 (Spetsnaz) SF bde
MANOEUVRE
  Armoured
  1 tk bde
  1 MR div
  5 MR bde
  Mechanised
  3 MR bde
  1 MGA div
SURFACE-TO-SURFACE MISSILE
  4 SRBM/GLCM bde with *Iskander*-M
COMBAT SUPPORT
  3 arty bde
  1 MRL bde
  1 engr bde
  1 NBC bde
  4 NBC regt
COMBAT SERVICE SUPPORT
  4 log bde
AIR DEFENCE
  5 AD bde

Reserves
FORCES BY ROLE
MANOEUVRE
  Mechanised
  8 MR bde

Pacific Fleet
EQUIPMENT BY TYPE
SUBMARINES 19
  STRATEGIC 4 SSBN
  TACTICAL 15: 3 SSGN (2 more non-operational, in long-term refit); 5 SSN (of which 4 in refit); 7 SSK
PRINCIPAL SURFACE COMBATANTS 8: 1 **CGHM**; 5 **DDGHM** (of which 1 in refit); 2 **FFGHM**
PATROL AND COASTAL COMBATANTS 27: 4 **FSGM**; 8 **FSM**; 10 **PCFG**; 5 **PB**
MINE WARFARE 8: 2 **MSO**; 6 **MSC**
AMPHIBIOUS 9: 4 **LST**; 5 **LCM**

Naval Aviation
FORCES BY ROLE
FIGHTER
  1 sqn with MiG-31B/BS *Foxhound*
ANTI-SUBMARINE WARFARE
  3 sqn with Ka-27/Ka-29 *Helix*
  2 sqn with Il-38 *May**; Il-18D; Il-22 *Coot* B
  1 sqn with Tu-142MK/MZ/MR *Bear* F/J*
TRANSPORT
  2 sqn with An-12BK *Cub*; An-26 *Curl*; Tu-134

EQUIPMENT BY TYPE
AIRCRAFT
FTR 12 MiG-31B/BS *Foxhound*
ASW 23: 11 Tu-142MK/MZ/MR *Bear* F/J; 12 Il-38 *May*
EW • ELINT 1 Il-22 *Coot* B
TPT 6: 2 An-12BK *Cub*; 3 An-26 *Curl*; 1 Tu-134
HELICOPTERS
ASW Ka-27 *Helix*
TPT • Medium Ka-29 *Helix*; Mi-8 *Hip*

Naval Infantry
FORCES BY ROLE
MANOEUVRE
Mechanised
2 naval inf bde
AIR DEFENCE
1 SAM regt

Coastal Artillery and Missile Forces
FORCES BY ROLE
COASTAL DEFENCE
2 AShM bde

Military Air Force

11th Air Force & Air Defence Army
FORCES BY ROLE
FIGHTER/GROUND ATTACK
1 regt with MiG-31BM *Foxhound*; Su-27SM *Flanker*; Su-30M2; Su-30SM; Su-35S *Flanker*
1 regt with Su-35S *Flanker*; Su-30SM
1 regt with Su-25 *Frogfoot*; Su-30SM
GROUND ATTACK
1 regt with Su-24M/M2 *Fencer*; Su-34 *Fullback*
1 regt with Su-25SM *Frogfoot*
ISR
1 regt with Su-24MR *Fencer* E
TRANSPORT
2 sqn with An-12 *Cub*/An-26 *Curl*/Tu-134 *Crusty*/Tu-154 *Careless*
ATTACK/TRANSPORT HELICOPTER
1 bde with Ka-52A *Hokum* B; Mi-8 *Hip*; Mi-26 *Halo*
1 regt with Ka-52A *Hokum* B; Mi-8 *Hip*; Mi-26 *Halo*
1 regt with Mi-24P *Hind*; Mi-8 *Hip*
AIR DEFENCE
2 regt with 9K37M *Buk*-M1-2 (SA-11 *Gadfly*); 9K317 *Buk*-M2 (SA-17 *Grizzly*); S-300V (SA-12 *Gladiator/Giant*)
1 regt with S-300PS (SA-10 *Grumble*)
3 regt with S-400 (SA-21 *Growler*); 96K6 *Pantsir*-S1 (SA-22 *Greyhound*)
EQUIPMENT BY TYPE
AIRCRAFT
FTR 20 MiG-31BM *Foxhound*
FGA 120: 23 Su-27SM *Flanker*; 6 Su-30M2; 31 Su-30SM; 26 Su-34 *Fullback*; 34 Su-35S *Flanker*
ATK 102: 20 Su-24M *Fencer*; 10 Su-24M2 *Fencer*; 72 Su-25/Su-25SM *Frogfoot*
ISR 28 Su-24MR *Fencer* E

TPT 24: 22 An-12 *Cub*/An-26 *Curl*; 1 Tu-134 *Crusty*; 1 Tu-154 *Careless*
HELICOPTERS
ATK 36: 24 Ka-52A *Hokum* B; 12 Mi-24P *Hind*
TPT 60: **Heavy** 4 Mi-26 *Halo*; **Medium** 56 Mi-8 *Hip*
AIR DEFENCE • SAM
Long-range S-300PS (SA-10 *Grumble*); S-300V (SA-12 *Gladiator/Giant*); S-400 (SA-21 *Growler*)
Medium-range 9K317 *Buk*-M1-2 (SA-11 *Gadfly*); 9K317 *Buk*-M2 (SA-17 *Grizzly*)
Short-range 96K6 *Pantsir*-S1 (SA-22 *Greyhound*)

Airborne Forces
FORCES BY ROLE
MANOEUVRE
Air Manoeuvre
2 air aslt bde

Paramilitary 554,000

Border Guard Service ε160,000
Subordinate to Federal Security Service
FORCES BY ROLE
10 regional directorates
MANOEUVRE
Other
7 frontier gp
EQUIPMENT BY TYPE
ARMOURED FIGHTING VEHICLES
IFV/APC (W) 1,000 BMP/BTR
ARTILLERY 90:
SP 122mm 2S1 *Gvozdika*
GUN/MOR • SP 120mm 2S9 NONA-S
MOR 120mm 2S12 *Sani*
PRINCIPAL SURFACE COMBATANTS
FRIGATES • FFHM 3 *Nerey* (Krivak III) with 1 twin ZIF-122 lnchr with 4K33 *Osa*-M (SA-N-4 *Gecko*) SAM, 2 quad PTA-53-1135 533mm TT lnchr, 2 RBU 6000 *Smerch* 2 A/S mor, 1 100mm gun (capacity 1 Ka-27 *Helix* A ASW hel)
PATROL AND COASTAL COMBATANTS 195
PSO 5: 4 *Komandor*; 1 *Okean* (Project 22100) with 1 76mm gun, 1 hel landing platform
PCO 25: 8 *Alpinist* (Project 503); 1 *Sprut*; 12 *Okhotnik* (Project 22460) with 1 AK630M CIWS, 1 hel landing platform; 4 *Purga* with 1 hel landing platform
PCC 35: 4 *Molnya* II (*Pauk* II); 3 *Svetlyak* (Project 10410); 18 *Svetlyak* (Project 10410) with 1 AK630M CIWS, 1 76mm gun; 8 *Svetlyak* (Project 10410) with 2 AK630M CIWS; 1 *Svetlyak* (Project 10410) with 1 AK630M CIWS; 1 *Yakhont*
PCR 1 *Slepen* (*Yaz*) with 1 AK630 CIWS, 2 100mm guns
PBF 87: 57 *Mangust*; 3 *Mirazh* (Project 14310); 4 *Mustang*-2 (Project 18623); 21 *Sobol*; 2 *Sokzhoi*
PBR 27: 4 *Ogonek*; 8 *Piyavka* with 1 AK630 CIWS; 15 *Moskit* (*Vosh*) with 1 AK630 CIWS, 1 100mm gun
PB 15: 3 *Gyuys* (Project 03050); 2 *Morzh* (Project 1496M; 10 *Lamantin* (Project 1496M1)

LOGISTICS AND SUPPORT 34
  AE 1 *Muna*
  AGB 2 *Ivan Susanin* (primarily used as patrol ships) with 2 AK630 CIWS, 1 76mm gun, 1 hel landing platform
  AK 8 *Pevek*
  AKSL 5 *Kanin*
  AO 3: 1 *Ishim* (Project 15010); 2 *Envoron*
  ATF 15: 14 *Sorum* (primarily used as patrol ships) with 2 AK230M CIWS; 1 *Sorum* (primarily used as patrol ship)
  AIRCRAFT • TPT ε86: 70 An-24 *Coke*/An-26 *Curl*/An-72 *Coaler*/Il-76 *Candid*/Tu-134 *Crusty*/Yak-40 *Codling*; 16 SM-92
  HELICOPTERS: ε200 Ka-28 (Ka-27) *Helix* ASW/Mi-24 *Hind* Atk/Mi-26 *Halo* Spt/Mi-8 *Hip* Spt

Federal Guard Service ε40,000–50,000

Org include elm of ground forces (mech inf bde and AB regt)

FORCES BY ROLE
MANOEUVRE
  Mechanised
  1 mech inf regt
  Air Manoeuvre
  1 AB regt
  Other
  1 (Presidential) gd regt

Federal Security Service Special Purpose Centre ε4,000

FORCES BY ROLE
SPECIAL FORCES
  2 SF unit (Alfa and Vympel units)

National Guard ε340,000

FORCES BY ROLE
MANOEUVRE
  Other
  10 paramilitary div (2–5 paramilitary regt)
  17 paramilitary bde (3 mech bn, 1 mor bn)
  36 indep paramilitary rgt
  90 paramilitary bn (incl special motorised units)
  Aviation
  8 sqn
COMBAT SUPPORT
  1 arty regt
EQUIPMENT BY TYPE
ARMOURED FIGHTING VEHICLES
  RECCE some BRDM-2A
  IFV/APC (W) 1,650 BMP-2/BTR-70M/BTR-80/BTR-82A/BTR-82AM
ARTILLERY 35
  TOWED 122mm 20 D-30
  MOR 120mm 15 M-1938 (PM-38)
PATROL AND COASTAL COMBATANTS 1
  PB 1 *Grachonok*
AIRCRAFT
  TPT 29: **Heavy** 9 Il-76 *Candid*; **Medium** 2 An-12 *Cub*; **Light** 18: 12 An-26 *Curl*; 6 An-72 *Coaler*

HELICOPTERS
  TPT 71: **Heavy** 10 Mi-26 *Halo*; **Medium** 60+: 60 Mi-8 *Hip*; some Mi-8AMTSh *Hip*; **Light** 1 Ka-226T

DEPLOYMENT

ARMENIA: 3,300: 1 mil base with (1 MR bde; 74 T-72; 80 BMP-1; 80 BMP-2; 12 2S1; 12 BM-21); 1 sqn with 18 MiG-29 *Fulcrum*; 1 sqn with 8 Mi-24P *Hind*; 4 Mi-8MT *Hip*; 2 AD bty with S-300V (SA-12 *Gladiator/Giant*); 1 AD bty with 2K12 *Kub* (SA-6 *Gainful*)

BELARUS: 1 radar station at Baranovichi (*Volga* system; leased); 1 naval comms site

CENTRAL AFRICAN REPUBLIC: UN • MINUSCA 4

DEMOCRATIC REPUBLIC OF THE CONGO: UN • MONUSCO 8

GEORGIA: 7,000; Abkhazia 1 mil base with (1 MR bde; 40 T-90A; 120 BTR-82A; 18 2S3; 12 2S12; 18 BM-21; some S-300 SAM; some atk hel); South Ossetia 1 mil base with (1 MR bde; 40 T-72; 120 BMP-2; 36 2S3; 12 2S12)

KAZAKHSTAN: 1 radar station at Balkash (*Dnepr* system; leased)

KYRGYZSTAN: ε500; 13 Su-25SM *Frogfoot*; 2 Mi-8 *Hip* spt hel

MEDITERRANEAN SEA: 2 SSK; 1 FFGHM; 1 FFGM; 1 AGI

MIDDLE EAST: UN • UNTSO 4

MOLDOVA/TRANSDNIESTR: ε1,500 (including 441 peacekeepers); 2 MR bn; 100 MBT/AIFV/APC; 7 Mi-24 *Hind*; some Mi-8 *Hip*

SOUTH SUDAN: UN • UNMISS 6

SUDAN: UN • UNISFA 2

SYRIA: 5,000: 1 inf BG; 3 MP bn; 1 engr unit; ε10 T-72B3/T-90; ε20 BTR-82A; *Typhoon*-K; *Tigr*; 12 2A65; 4 9A52 *Smerch*; TOS-1A; 9K720 *Iskander*-M; 10 Su-24M *Fencer*; 6 Su-34; 4 Su-35S; 1 A-50 *Mainstay*; 1 Il-20M; 12 Mi-24P/Mi-35M *Hind*; 4 Mi-8AMTSh *Hip*; 1 AShM bty with 3K55 *Bastion*; 1 SAM bty with S-400; 1 SAM bty with *Pantsir*-S1/S2; air base at Latakia; naval facility at Tartus

TAJIKISTAN: 5,000; 1 (201st) mil base with (40 T-72B1; 60 BMP-2; 80 BTR-82A; 40 MT-LB; 18 2S1; 36 2S3; 6 2S12; 12 9P140 *Uragan*); 4 Mi-24P *Hind*; 4 Mi-8MTV *Hip*

UKRAINE: Crimea: 28,000; 1 recce bde, 2 naval inf bde; 1 arty bde; 1 NBC regt; 40 T-72B3 MBT; 80 BMP-2 AIFV; 200 BTR-82A; 20 BTR-80 APC: 150 MT-LB; 18 2S1 arty; 18 2S19 arty; 12 BM-21 MRL; 1 AShM bde with 3K60 *Bal*; 3K55 *Bastion*; 1 FGA regt with Su-24M/MR; Su-30SM; 1 FGA regt with Su-27SM/SM3; Su-30M2; 1 FGA regt with Su-24M/Su-25SM; 1 atk/tpt hel regt; 1 ASW hel regt; 2 AD regt with S-400, *Pantsir*-S1; 1 Fleet HQ located at Sevastopol; 2 radar stations located at Sevastopol (*Dnepr* system) and Mukachevo (*Dnepr* system); Donetsk/Luhansk: 3,000 (reported)

WESTERN SAHARA: UN • MINURSO 14

Tajikistan TJK

Tajikistani Somoni Tr		2018	2019	2020
GDP	Tr	68.8bn	77.7bn	
	US$	7.52bn	8.15bn	
per capita	US$	826	877	
Growth	%	7.3	5.0	
Inflation	%	3.8	7.4	
Def bdgt	Tr	ε1.65bn	ε1.78bn	
	US$	ε180m	ε187m	
US$1=Tr			9.16	9.53

Real-terms defence budget trend (US$m, constant 2015)

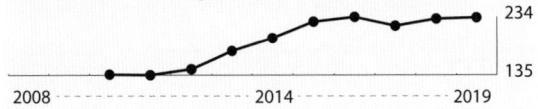

Population 8,740,073

Ethnic groups: Tajik 84.2%; Uzbek 12.2%; Kyrgyz 0.8%; Russian 0.5%; other or unspecified 2.3%

Age	0–14	15–19	20–24	25–29	30–64	65 plus
Male	16.2%	4.7%	4.5%	4.7%	18.2%	1.5%
Female	15.6%	4.5%	4.4%	4.6%	19.1%	2.1%

Capabilities

The Tajik armed forces have little capacity to deploy other than token forces and almost all equipment is of Soviet-era origin. Regional security and terrorism are concerns, due to the possibility that violence could spill over from Afghanistan. Tajikistan has been building its capability in this area by hosting a CSTO counter-terrorism exercise, and by taking part in stability and counter-terror exercises organised by US CENTCOM, hosting the 2017 iteration. Tajikistan is a member of the CSTO and there is a large Russian military presence at the 201st military base. Reports in early 2019 indicated that there may be a Chinese military facility in eastern Tajikistan housing Chinese troops wearing People's Armed Police uniforms, though this remains unconfirmed by either Beijing or Dushanbe. In 2018, India and Tajikistan agreed to strengthen defence cooperation, in particular on counter-terrorism. Border deployments have been stepped up recently in response to regional security and terrorism concerns. In late 2016, a Military Cooperation Plan was signed with Russia. Moscow has indicated that Tajikistan is to receive military equipment, including aircraft. Some donations of personal equipment have been received from the US. Barring maintenance facilities, Tajikistan only has minimal defence-industrial capacity.

ACTIVE 8,800 (Army 7,300 Air Force/Air Defence 1,500) **Paramilitary 7,500**

Conscript liability 24 months

ORGANISATIONS BY SERVICE

Army 7,300
FORCES BY ROLE
MANOEUVRE
  Mechanised
    3 MR bde
  Air Manoeuvre
    1 air aslt bde
COMBAT SUPPORT
  1 arty bde
AIR DEFENCE
  1 SAM regt
EQUIPMENT BY TYPE
ARMOURED FIGHTING VEHICLES
  MBT 37: 30 T-72; 7 T-62
  RECCE 10 BRDM-2M
  IFV 23: 8 BMP-1; 15 BMP-2
  APC • APC (W) 23 BTR-60/BTR-70/BTR-80
ARTILLERY 23
  TOWED 122mm 10 D-30
  MRL 122mm 3 BM-21 *Grad*
  MOR 120mm 10
AIR DEFENCE • SAM
  Medium-range S-75 *Dvina* (SA-2 *Guideline*); S-125 *Pechora*-2M (SA-26)
  Point-defence 9K32 *Strela*-2 (SA-7 *Grail*)‡

Air Force/Air Defence 1,500
FORCES BY ROLE
TRANSPORT
  1 sqn with Tu-134A *Crusty*
ATTACK/TRANSPORT HELICOPTER
  1 sqn with Mi-24 *Hind*; Mi-8 *Hip*; Mi-17TM *Hip H*
EQUIPMENT BY TYPE
AIRCRAFT
  TPT • Light 1 Tu-134A *Crusty*
  TRG 4+: 4 L-39 *Albatros*; some Yak-52
HELICOPTERS
  ATK 4 Mi-24 *Hind*
  TPT • Medium 11 Mi-8 *Hip*/Mi-17TM *Hip H*

Paramilitary 7,500

Internal Troops 3,800

National Guard 1,200

Emergencies Ministry 2,500

Border Guards

FOREIGN FORCES
China ε300 (trg)
Russia 5,000; 1 (201st) mil base with (40 T-72B1; 60 BMP-2; 80 BTR-82A; 40 MT-LB; 18 2S1; 36 2S3; 6 2S12; 12 9P140 *Uragan*); 4 Mi-24P *Hind*; 4 Mi-8MTV *Hip*

Turkmenistan TKM

Turkmen New Manat TMM		2018	2019	2020
GDP	TMM	143bn	163bn	
	US$	40.8bn	46.7bn	
per capita	US$	7,065	7,816	
Growth	%	6.2	6.3	
Inflation	%	13.2	13.4	
Def exp	TMM	n.k	n.k	
	US$	n.k	n.k	
US$1=TMM			3.50	3.50

Population 5,470,233

Ethnic groups: Turkmen 77%; Uzbek 9%; Russian 7%; Kazak 2%

Age	0–14	15–19	20–24	25–29	30–64	65 plus
Male	13.0%	4.1%	4.5%	4.9%	20.9%	2.2%
Female	12.6%	4.0%	4.5%	4.9%	21.6%	2.9%

Capabilities

Turkmenistan has concerns over potential regional spillover from the security situation in Afghanistan, but its armed forces lack significant capabilities and equipment. Ashgabat has maintained a policy of neutrality since 1995 and confirmed this commitment in its 2016 military doctrine. This aimed to increase the armed forces' defensive capability in order to safeguard national interests and territorial integrity. Turkmenistan is not a member of the CSTO. While the ground forces are shifting from a Soviet-era divisional structure to a brigade system, progress is slow. The armed forces are largely conscript-based and reliant on Soviet-era equipment and doctrine, and the government has stated a requirement to improve conditions of service. Turkmenistan has participated in multinational exercises, and is reported to have restarted joint exercises with Russia and Uzbekistan, but has limited capacity to deploy externally and maintains no international deployments. In October 2019, in Saint Petersburg, Turkmenistan and four other Caspian littoral states signed a memorandum of understanding on military cooperation, among other discussions including on maritime security. Most military aircraft are of Soviet-era origin and have either been stored or scrapped, and no significant new procurement has occurred. The 2016 military doctrine was intended to partly redress these issues. There are plans to strengthen the border guard with new equipment and facilities. Plans to bolster the naval forces have resulted in some procurements, leading to a modest improvement in the naval presence in the Caspian Sea. Barring maintenance facilities, Turkmenistan has little domestic defence industry, but is building a number of patrol vessels of Turkish design under licence.

ACTIVE 36,500 (Army 33,000 Navy 500 Air 3,000)
Paramilitary 5,000
Conscript liability 24 months

ORGANISATIONS BY SERVICE

Army 33,000
5 Mil Districts

FORCES BY ROLE
SPECIAL FORCES
  1 spec ops regt
MANOEUVRE
  Armoured
  1 tk bde
  Mechanised
  1 (3rd) MR div (1 tk regt; 3 MR regt, 1 arty regt)
  1 (22nd) MR div (1 tk regt; 1 MR regt, 1 arty regt)
  4 MR bde
  1 naval inf bde
  Other
  1 MR trg div
SURFACE-TO-SURFACE MISSILE
  1 SRBM bde with SS-1 *Scud*
COMBAT SUPPORT
  1 arty bde
  1 (mixed) arty/AT regt
  1 MRL bde
  1 AT regt
  1 engr regt
AIR DEFENCE
  2 SAM bde

EQUIPMENT BY TYPE†
ARMOURED FIGHTING VEHICLES
  MBT 654: 4 T-90S; 650 T-72/T-72UMG
  RECCE 260+: 200 BRDM-2; 60 BRM-1; Nimr *Ajban*
  IFV 1,038: 600 BMP-1/BMP-1M; 430 BMP-2; 4 BMP-3; 4 BTR-80A
  APC 898+
    APC (W) 870+: 120 BTR-60 (all variants); 300 BTR-70; 450 BTR-80
    PPV 28+ *Kirpi*
  AUV 12+: 8 Nimr *Ajban* 440A; 4+ *Cobra*
  ABCV 8 BMD-1
ANTI-TANK/ANTI-INFRASTRUCTURE
  MSL
    SP 58+: 8 9P122 *Malyutka*-M (AT-3 *Sagger* on BRDM-2); 8 9P133 *Malyutka*-P (AT-3 *Sagger* on BRDM-2); 2 9P148 *Konkurs* (AT-5 *Spandrel* on BRDM-2); 36 9P149 *Shturm* (AT-6 *Spiral* on MT-LB); 4+ *Baryer* (on *Karakal*)
    MANPATS 9K11 *Malyutka* (AT-3 *Sagger*); 9K111 *Fagot* (AT-4 *Spigot*); 9K111-1 *Konkurs* (AT-5 *Spandrel*); 9K115 *Metis* (AT-7 *Saxhorn*)
  GUNS 100mm 60 MT-12/T-12
ARTILLERY 765
  SP 122mm 40 2S1
  TOWED 457: 122mm 350 D-30; 130mm 6 M-46; 152mm 101: 17 D-1; 72 D-20; 6 2A36 *Giatsint*-B; 6 2A65 *Msta*-B
  GUN/MOR 120mm 17 2S9 NONA-S
  MRL 154+: 122mm 88: 18 9P138; 70 BM-21 *Grad*; RM-70; 220mm 60 9P140 *Uragan*; 300mm 6 9A52 *Smerch*
  MOR 97: 82mm 31; 120mm 66 M-1938 (PM-38)
SURFACE-TO-SURFACE MISSILE LAUNCHERS
  SRBM • Conventional 16 SS-1 *Scud*
UNMANNED AERIAL VEHICLES
  CISR • Heavy CH-3A; WJ-600
  ISR • Medium *Falco*
AIR DEFENCE
  SAM
    Short-range: FM-90; 2K12 *Kub* (SA-6 *Gainful*)
    Point-defence 53+: 40 9K33 *Osa* (SA-8 *Gecko*); 13 9K35 *Strela*-10 mod (SA-13 *Gopher*); 9K38 *Igla* (SA-18 *Grouse*);

9K32M *Strela*-2M (SA-7 *Grail*)‡; 9K34 *Strela*-3 (SA-14 *Gremlin*); *Mistral* (reported); QW-2
GUNS 70
  SP 23mm 48 ZSU-23-4
  TOWED 22+: **23mm** ZU-23-2; **57mm** 22 S-60
AIR-LAUNCHED MISSILES
  ASM CM-502KG; AR-1

Navy 500
EQUIPMENT BY TYPE
PATROL AND COASTAL COMBATANTS 4
  PCFG 2 *Edermen* (RUS *Molnya*) with 4 quad lnchr with 3M24E *Uran*-E (SS-N-25 *Switchblade*) AShM, 2 AK630 CIWS, 1 76mm gun
  PCGM 2 *Arkadag* (TUR *Tuzla*) with 2 twin lnchr with *Otomat* AShM, 2 twin *Simbad*-RC lnchr with *Mistral* SAM, 1 Roketsan ASW Rocket Launcher System A/S mor
LOGISTICS AND SUPPORT• AGHS 1 (Dearsan 41m)

Air Force 3,000
FORCES BY ROLE
FIGHTER
  2 sqn with MiG-29 *Fulcrum*; MiG-29UB *Fulcrum*;
GROUND ATTACK
  1 sqn with Su-25 *Frogfoot*
  1 sqn with Su-25MK *Frogfoot*
TRANSPORT
  1 sqn with An-26 *Curl*; Mi-8 *Hip*; Mi-24 *Hind*
TRAINING
  1 unit with L-39 *Albatros*
AIR DEFENCE
  Some sqn with S-75 *Dvina* (SA-2 *Guideline*); S-125 *Pechora* (SA-3 *Goa*); S-125 *Pechora*-2M (SA-26); S-200 *Angara* (SA-5 *Gammon*); FD-2000 (HQ-9); KS-1A (HQ-12)
EQUIPMENT BY TYPE
AIRCRAFT 55 combat capable
  FTR 24: 22 MiG-29A/S *Fulcrum*; 2 MiG-29UB *Fulcrum*
  ATK 31: 19 Su-25 *Frogfoot*; 12 Su-25MK *Frogfoot*
  TPT • Light 3: 1 An-26 *Curl*; 2 An-74TK *Coaler*
  TRG 2 L-39 *Albatros*
HELICOPTERS
  ATK 10 Mi-24P *Hind* F
  MRH 2+ AW139
  TPT 11+: **Medium** 8: 6 Mi-8 *Hip*; 2 Mi-17V-V *Hip*; **Light** 3+ AW109
AIR-LAUNCHED MISSILES
  AAM • IR R-60 (AA-8 *Aphid*); R-73 (AA-11A *Archer*)
AIR DEFENCE • SAM
  Long-range S-200 *Angara* (SA-5 *Gammon*); FD-2000 (HQ-9)
  Medium-range S-75 *Dvina* (SA-2 *Guideline*); S-125 *Pechora*-2M (SA-26); KS-1A (HQ-12)
  Short-range S-125 *Pechora* (SA-3 *Goa*); S-125-2BM *Pechora*

Paramilitary 5,000

Federal Border Guard Service ε5,000
EQUIPMENT BY TYPE
PATROL AND COASTAL COMBATANTS 33
  PCGM 8 *Arkadag* (TUR *Tuzla*) with 2 twin lnchr with *Otomat* AShM, 2 twin *Simbad*-RC lnchr with *Mistral* SAM, 1 Roketsan ASW Rocket Launcher System A/S mor
  PBFG 6 *Nazya* (Dearsan 33) with 2 single lnchr with *Marte* Mk2/N AShM
  PBF 18: 10 *Bars*-12; 5 *Grif*-T; 3 *Sobol*
  PB 1 *Point*
AMPHIBIOUS • LCM 1 Dearsan LCM-1
HELICOPTERS
  MRH 2 AW139
  TPT 3+: **Medium** some Mi-8 *Hip*; **Light** 3 AW109

Ukraine UKR

Ukrainian Hryvnia h		2018	2019	2020
GDP	h	3.56tr	4.02tr	
	US$	131bn	150bn	
per capita	US$	3,113	3,592	
Growth	%	3.3	3.0	
Inflation	%	10.9	8.7	
Def bdgt [a]	h	88.6bn	102bn	103bn
	US$	3.26bn	3.83bn	
FMA (US)	US$	95.0m	20.0m	20.0m
US$1=h		27.20	26.75	

[a] Including military pensions

Real-terms defence budget trend (US$bn, constant 2015)

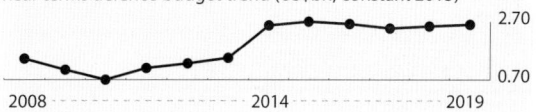

Population	43,964,969					
Age	0–14	15–19	20–24	25–29	30–64	65 plus
Male	8.3%	2.2%	2.6%	3.4%	24.2%	5.6%
Female	7.8%	2.1%	2.5%	3.2%	26.9%	11.1%

Capabilities

Ukraine's overriding security concern is Russia's support for separatists in the east of the country. Sporadic exchanges of fire continued in 2019, though by late year front-line troops were withdrawing under the terms of an agreement signed on 1 October. Defence policy is centred on maintaining sovereignty and territorial integrity. Ukraine adopted a revised doctrine in 2015 that identified Moscow as a 'military adversary', called for 'comprehensive reform' of the security sector and revoked the country's 'nonbloc status'. In 2017, parliament identified NATO membership as a strategic goal, with the 'State Program for the Development of the Armed Forces. Until 2020' intended to support this goal. There are two conscript intakes per year, though professionalisation is a long-term ambition. The defence ministry's development programme aims to improve training, eventually aligning to NATO standards. The armed forces are working towards reforming joint-command structures to NATO standards, and in late 2019 introduced a new NCO rank structure. The armed forces participate in bilateral and multinational exercises. The equipment inventory still consists predominantly of Soviet-era weaponry. Sustaining and in some cases upgrading these systems is a near-term concern, and equipment replacements will be required over the coming decade in order to forestall potential problems with obsolescence. The country has a broad defence industry, though its capabilities remain shaped, and limited, by its Soviet heritage. Ukraine was a key provider of guided-weapons technologies in the Soviet Union. It retains the capability to build Soviet-era land systems and can maintain and modestly upgrade Soviet-era tactical combat aircraft.

ACTIVE 209,000 (Army 145,000 Navy 11,000 Air Force 45,000 Airborne 8,000 Special Operations Forces n.k.) Paramilitary 88,000

Conscript liability Army, Air Force 18 months, Navy 2 years. Minimum age for conscription raised from 18 to 20 in 2015

RESERVE 900,000 (Joint 900,000)
Military service within 5 years

ORGANISATIONS BY SERVICE

Army 145,000
4 regional HQ
FORCES BY ROLE
MANOEUVRE
  Reconnaissance
  5 recce bn
  Armoured
  3 tk bde
  Mechanised
  9 mech bde
  2 mtn bde
  Light
  5 mot inf bde
SURFACE-TO-SURFACE MISSILES
  1 SSM bde
COMBAT SUPPORT
  5 arty bde
  1 MRL bde
  2 MRL regt
  1 engr regt
  1 EW regt
  1 EW bn
  2 EW coy
  1 CBRN regt
  4 sigs regt
COMBAT SERVICE SUPPORT
  3 maint regt
  1 maint coy
HELICOPTERS
  4 avn bde
AIR DEFENCE
  4 AD regt

Reserves
FORCES BY ROLE
MANOEUVRE
  Armoured
  3 tk bde
  Mechanised
  2 mech bde
COMBAT SUPPORT
  1 arty bde

EQUIPMENT BY TYPE
ARMOURED FIGHTING VEHICLES
  MBT 854: 720 T-64/T-64BV/BM; 100 T-72AV/B1; 28 T-80BV; 6 T-84 *Oplot*; (94 T-80; 530 T-72; 578 T-64; 20 T-55 all in store)
  RECCE 548: 433 BRDM-2; 115 BRM-1K (CP)
  IFV 1,137: 193 BMP-1/BMP-1AK; 890 BMP-2; 4 BMP-3; 50+ BTR-3DA; some BTR-3E1; some BTR-4E *Bucephalus*
  APC 338
    APC (T) 15+: 15 BTR-D; some MT-LB
    APC (W) 313: 5 BTR-60; 215 BTR-70; 93 BTR-80
    PPV 10 *Kozak*-2
  ABCV 30: 15 BMD-1, 15 BMD-2
ENGINEERING & MAINTENANCE VEHICLES
  AEV 53 BAT-2; MT-LB
  ARV BREM-1; BREM-2; BREM-64; T-54/T-55
  VLB MTU-20
ANTI-TANK/ANTI-INFRASTRUCTURE
  MSL
    SP 9P149 with 9K114 *Shturm* (AT-6 *Spiral*)
    MANPATS 9K111 *Fagot* (AT-4 *Spigot*); 9K113 *Konkurs* (AT-5 *Spandrel*); FGM-148 *Javelin*; Stugna-P; Corsar
  GUNS 100mm ε500 MT-12/T-12
ARTILLERY 1,770
  SP 565+: **122mm** 271 2S1 *Gvozdika*; **152mm** 288: 235 2S3 *Akatsiya*; 18 2S5 *Giatsint*-S; 35 2S19 *Msta*-S; **203mm** 6+ 2S7 *Pion* (up to 90 2S7 *Pion* in store)
  TOWED 515+: **122mm** 75 D-30; **152mm** 440: 180 2A36 *Giatsint*-B; 130 2A65 *Msta*-B; 130+ D-20
  GUN/MOR • 120mm • TOWED 2 2B16 NONA-K
  MRL 348: **122mm** 203: 18 9P138; 185 BM-21 *Grad*; **220mm** 70 9P140 *Uragan*; **300mm** 75 9A52 *Smerch*
  MOR 120mm 340: 190 2S12 *Sani*; 30 M-1938 (PM-38); 120 M120-15
SURFACE-TO-SURFACE MISSILE LAUNCHERS
  SRBM • Conventional 90 9K79 *Tochka* (SS-21 *Scarab*)
HELICOPTERS
  ATK ε35 Mi-24 *Hind*
  MRH 1 *Lev*-1
  TPT • Medium ε23 Mi-8 *Hip*
AIR DEFENCE
  SAM
    Long-range Some S-300V (SA-12 *Gladiator*)
    Short-range 6 9K330 *Tor*-M
    Point-defence 9K35 *Strela*-10 (SA-13 *Gopher*); 9K33 *Osa*-AKM (SA-8 *Gecko*)
  GUNS
    SP 30mm 70 2S6
    TOWED 23mm ZU-23-2; **57mm** S-60
AIR-LAUNCHED MISSILES • ASM Barrier-V

Navy 11,000 (incl Naval Aviation and Naval Infantry)
After Russia's annexation of Crimea, HQ shifted to Odessa. Several additional vessels remain in Russian possession in Crimea

2 Regional HQ

EQUIPMENT BY TYPE
PRINCIPAL SURFACE COMBATANTS 1

FRIGATES • FFHM 1 *Hetman Sagaidachny* (RUS *Krivak* III) with 1 twin lnchr with 4K33 *Osa*-M (SA-N-4 *Gecko*) SAM, 2 quad 533mm ASTT with SET-65 HWT/53-65K HWT, 2 RBU 6000 *Smerch* 2 A/S mor, 2 AK630M CIWS, 1 100mm gun (capacity 1 Ka-27 *Helix* ASW hel)

PATROL AND COASTAL COMBATANTS 9
CORVETTES • FS 1 *Grisha* (II) with 2 twin 533mm ASTT with SAET-60 HWT, 2 RBU 6000 *Smerch* 2 A/S mor, 2 57mm guns
PCC 2 *Slavyansk* (ex-US *Island*)
PHG 1 *Matka* (FSU *Vekhr*) with 2 single lnchr with P-15M/R *Termit*-M/R (SS-N-2C/D *Styx*) AShM, 1 AK630M CIWS, 1 76mm gun
PBG 4 *Gyurza*-M (Project 51855) with 2 *Katran*-M RWS with *Barrier* SSM
PB 1 *Zhuk* (FSU *Grif*)

MINE WARFARE • MINE COUNTERMEASURES 1
MHI 1 *Korund* (*Yevgenya*) (Project 1258)

AMPHIBIOUS
LANDING SHIPS • LSM 1 *Polnochny* C (capacity 6 MBT; 180 troops)
LANDING CRAFT • LCM 1 *Akula* (*Ondatra*)

LOGISTICS AND SUPPORT 10
ABU 1 Project 419 (*Sura*)
AG 1 *Bereza*
AGI 1 *Muna*
AKL 1
AO 2 *Toplivo*
AWT 1 *Sudak*
AXL 3 *Petrushka*

Naval Aviation ε1,000

EQUIPMENT BY TYPE
FIXED-WING AIRCRAFT
ASW (2 Be-12 *Mail* non-operational)
TPT • Light (2 An-26 *Curl* in store)
HELICOPTERS
ASW 7+: 4+ Ka-27 *Helix* A; 3 Mi-14PS/PL *Haze* A/C
TPT • Medium 1 Ka-29 *Helix*-B

Naval Infantry ε2,000

FORCES BY ROLE
MANOEUVRE
Light
2 nav inf bde
EQUIPMENT BY TYPE
ARMOURED FIGHTING VEHICLES
MBT 31 T-80BV
IFV some BMP-1
APC • APC (W) some BTR-60; some BTR-80
ARTILLERY
SP 122mm 2S1 *Gvozdika*
TOWED 152mm some 2A36 *Giatsint*-B

Air Forces 45,000

3 Regional HQ
FORCES BY ROLE
FIGHTER
4 bde with MiG-29 *Fulcrum*; Su-27 *Flanker*; L-39 *Albatros*

FIGHTER/GROUND ATTACK
2 bde with Su-24M *Fencer*; Su-25 *Frogfoot*
ISR
2 sqn with Su-24MR *Fencer* E*
TRANSPORT
3 bde with An-24; An-26; An-30; Il-76 *Candid*; Tu-134 *Crusty*
TRAINING
Some sqn with L-39 *Albatros*
TRANSPORT HELICOPTER
Some sqn with Mi-8; Mi-9; PZL Mi-2 *Hoplite*
AIR DEFENCE
6 bde with 9K37M *Buk*-M1 (SA-11 *Gadfly*); S-300P/PS/PT (SA-10 *Grumble*)
4 regt with 9K37M *Buk*-M1 (SA-11); S-300P/PS/PT (SA-10)

EQUIPMENT BY TYPE
AIRCRAFT ε125 combat capable
FTR 71: ε37 MiG-29 *Fulcrum*; ε34 Su-27 *Flanker*
FGA ε14 Su-24M *Fencer*
ATK ε31 Su-25 *Frogfoot*
ISR 12: 3 An-30 *Clank*; ε9 Su-24MR *Fencer* E*
TPT 30: **Heavy** 5 Il-76 *Candid*; **Medium** 1 An-70; **Light** ε24: 3 An-24 *Coke*; ε20 An-26 *Curl*; 1 Tu-134 *Crusty*
TRG ε31 L-39 *Albatros*
HELICOPTERS
C2 ε14 Mi-9
TPT 32: **Medium** ε30 Mi-8 *Hip*; **Light** 2 PZL Mi-2 *Hoplite*
UNMANNED AERIAL VEHICLES
CISR • Medium 6 Bayraktar TB2
AIR DEFENCE • SAM 322:
Long-range 250 S-300P/PS/PT (SA-10 *Grumble*)
Medium-range 72 9K37M *Buk*-M1 (SA-11 *Gadfly*)
AIR-LAUNCHED MISSILES
AAM • IR R-60 (AA-8 *Aphid*); R-73 (AA-11A *Archer*)
SARH R-27 (AA-10A *Alamo*)
ASM Kh-25 (AS-10 *Karen*); Kh-29 (AS-14 *Kedge*); MAM-L
ARM Kh-25MP (AS-12A *Kegler*); Kh-58 (AS-11 *Kilter*); Kh-28 (AS-9 *Kyle*) (likely WFU)

High-Mobility Airborne Troops ε8,000

FORCES BY ROLE
MANOEUVRE
Air Manoeuvre
1 AB bde
4 air mob bde
EQUIPMENT BY TYPE
ARMOURED FIGHTING VEHICLES
IFV some BTR-3E1; some BTR-4 *Bucephalus*
APC 180+
APC (T) 25 BTR-D
APC (W) 155+: 1 BTR-60; 2 BTR-70; 122 BTR-80; 30+ *Dozor*-B
ABCV 75: 30 BMD-1; 45 BMD-2
ANTI-TANK/ANTI-INFRASTRUCTURE
MSL • MANPATS 9K111 *Fagot* (AT-4 *Spigot*); 9K111-1 *Konkurs* (AT-5 *Spandrel*)
ARTILLERY 118
TOWED • 122mm 54 D-30

GUN/MOR • SP • **120mm** 40 2S9 *NONA-S*
MOR **120mm** 24 2S12 *Sani*
AIR DEFENCE • GUNS • SP **23mm** some ZU-23-2 (truck mounted)

Special Operations Forces n.k.
SPECIAL FORCES
2 SF regt

Paramilitary 88,000

National Guard ε46,000
Ministry of Internal Affairs; 5 territorial comd
FORCES BY ROLE
MANOEUVRE
  Armoured
    Some tk bn
  Mechanised
    Some mech bn
  Light
    Some lt inf bn
EQUIPMENT BY TYPE
ARMOURED FIGHTING VEHICLES
  MBT T-64; T-64BV; T-64BM; T-72
  IFV 83: BTR-3; 32+ BTR-3E1; ε50 BTR-4 *Bucephalus*; 1 BMP-2
  APC 22+
    APC (W) BTR-70; BTR-80
    PPV 22+: Streit *Cougar*; Streit *Spartan*; 22 *Kozak*-2
ANTI-TANK/ANTI-INFRASTRUCTURE
  RCL **73mm** some SPG-9
ARTILLERY
  TOWED **122mm** some D-30
  MOR **120mm** some
AIRCRAFT
  TPT • **Light** 24: 20 An-26 *Curl*; 2 An-72 *Coaler*; 2 Tu-134 *Crusty*
HELICOPTERS • TPT 8: **Medium** 7 Mi-8 *Hip*; **Light** 1 Mi-2MSB
AIR DEFENCE
  SAM • Point-defence 9K38 *Igla* (SA-18 *Grouse*)
  GUNS • SP **23mm** some ZU-23-2 (truck mounted)

Border Guard ε42,000
FORCES BY ROLE
MANOEUVRE
  Light
    some mot inf gp
EQUIPMENT BY TYPE
ARMOURED FIGHTING VEHICLES
  APC • PPV 17 *Kozak*-2

Maritime Border Guard
The Maritime Border Guard is an independent subdivision of the State Commission for Border Guards and is not part of the navy
EQUIPMENT BY TYPE
PATROL AND COASTAL COMBATANTS 21
  PCT 1 *Pauk* I with 4 single 406mm TT, 2 RBU 1200 *Uragan* A/S mor, 1 76mm gun
  PCC 4 *Stenka*
  PB 12: 11 *Zhuk*; 1 *Orlan*
  PBR 4 *Shmel* with 1 76mm gun
LOGISTICS AND SUPPORT • AGF 1
  AIRCRAFT • TPT **Medium** An-8 *Camp*; **Light** An-24 *Coke*; An-26 *Curl*; An-72 *Coaler*
  HELICOPTERS • ASW: Ka-27 *Helix* A

DEPLOYMENT

AFGHANISTAN: NATO • *Operation Resolute Support* 21
CYPRUS: UN • UNFICYP 1
DEMOCRATIC REPUBLIC OF THE CONGO: UN • MONUSCO 259; 1 atk hel sqn
MALI: UN • MINUSMA 2
MOLDOVA: 10 obs
SERBIA: NATO • KFOR 40; **UN** • UNMIK 2
SOUTH SUDAN: UN • UNMISS 4
SUDAN: UN • UNISFA 6

FOREIGN FORCES

Canada *Operation Unifier* 200
Lithuania JMTG-U 26
Poland JMTG-U 40
United Kingdom *Operation Orbital* 53
United States JMTG-U 220

TERRITORY WHERE THE GOVERNMENT DOES NOT EXERCISE EFFECTIVE CONTROL

In late February 2014, Russian forces occupied Crimea. The region then requested to join the Russian Federation after a referendum in March, regarded as unconstitutional by the government in Kiev. Months after Russia's annexation of Crimea, fighting began in Ukraine's Donetsk and Luhansk oblasts, with separatist forces there allegedly operating with Russian support. Conflict in the east has persisted since that date. The information displayed for these forces reflects equipment that has been observed as employed in support of the separatist cause in eastern Ukraine. Data presented here represents the de facto situation and does not imply international recognition.

EASTERN UKRAINE SEPARATIST FORCES

ORGANISATIONS BY SERVICE

Donetsk People's Republic ε20,000
FORCES BY ROLE
SPECIAL FORCES
  2 (Spetsnaz) SF bn
MANOEUVRE
  Reconnaissance
    1 recce bn
  Armoured
    1 tk bn
  Light
    6 mot inf bde

COMBAT SUPPORT
1 arty bde
1 engr coy
1 EW coy
COMBAT SERVICE SUPPORT
1 log bn
AIR DEFENCE
1 AD bn

Luhansk People's Republic ε14,000
FORCES BY ROLE
MANOEUVRE
Reconnaissance
1 recce bn
Armoured
1 tk bn
Light
4 mot inf bde
COMBAT SUPPORT
1 arty bde
1 engr coy
1 EW coy
COMBAT SERVICE SUPPORT
1 log bn
AIR DEFENCE
1 AD bn
EQUIPMENT BY TYPE
ARMOURED FIGHTING VEHICLES
 MBT T-64BV; T-64B; T-64BM†; T-72B1; T-72BA
 RECCE BDRM-2
 IFV BMP-1; BMP-2; BTR-4
 APC
  APC (T) BTR-D; MT-LB; GT-MU
  APC (W) BTR-60; BTR-70; BTR-80
 ABCV BMD-1, BMD-2
ANTI-TANK/ANTI-INFRASTRUCTURE
 MSL 9K115 *Metis* (AT-7 *Saxhorn*); 9K135 *Kornet* (AT-14 *Spriggan*)
 RCL 73mm SPG-9
 GUNS 100mm MT-12
ARTILLERY
 SP 122mm 2S1 *Gvozdika*; 152mm 2S3 *Akatsiya*; 2S19 *Msta-S*†; 203mm 2S7 *Pion*
 TOWED 122mm D-30; 152mm 2A65 *Msta-B*
 GUN/MOR
  SP 120mm 2S9 NONA-S
  TOWED 120mm 2B16 NONA-K
 MRL 122mm BM-21 *Grad*
 MOR 82mm 2B14; 120mm 2B11 *Sani*
AIR DEFENCE
 SAM
  Short-range 9K332 *Tor*-M2 (SA-15 *Gauntlet*)
  Point-defence 2K22 *Tunguska* (SA-19 *Grison*); 9K32M *Strela*-2M (SA-7B *Grail*); 9K33 *Osa* (SA-8 *Gecko*); 9K35 *Strela*-10 (SA-13 *Gopher*); 9K38 *Igla* (SA-18 *Grouse*); GROM
 GUNS
  SP 23mm ZU-23-2 (tch/on MT-LB)
  TOWED 14.5mm ZPU-2; 57mm S-60

FOREIGN FORCES
Russia Crimea: 28,000; 1 recce bde, 2 naval inf bde; 1 arty bde; 1 NBC bde; 40 T-72B3 MBT; 80 BMP-2 AIFV; 200 BTR-82A; 20 BTR-80 APC: 150 MT-LB; 18 2S1 arty; 18 2S19 arty; 12 BM-21 MRL; 1 AShM bde with 3K60 Bal; 3K55 *Bastion*; 1 FGA regt with Su-24M/MR; Su-30SM; 1 FGA regt with Su-27SM/SM3; Su-30M2; 1 FGA regt with Su-24M/Su-25SM; 1 atk/tpt hel regt; 1 ASW hel regt; 1 AD regt with S-300PM; 1 AD regt with S-400; 1 Fleet HQ located at Sevastopol; 2 radar stations located at Sevastopol (*Dnepr* system) and Mukachevo (*Dnepr* system) • Donetsk/Luhansk: 3,000 (reported)

Uzbekistan UZB

Uzbekistani Som s		2018	2019	2020
GDP	s	408tr	523tr	
	US$	50.5bn	60.5bn	
per capita	US$	1,550	1,832	
Growth	%	5.1	5.5	
Inflation	%	17.5	14.7	
Def exp	s	n.k	n.k	
	US$	n.k	n.k	
US$1=s		8071.99	8652.22	

Population 30,296,157

Ethnic groups: Uzbek 73%; Russian 6%; Tajik 5%; Kazakh 4%; Karakalpak 2%; Tatar 2%; Korean <1%; Ukrainian <1%

Age	0–14	15–19	20–24	25–29	30–64	65 plus
Male	12.0%	4.1%	4.7%	5.1%	21.4%	2.4%
Female	11.4%	3.9%	4.5%	5.1%	22.1%	3.2%

Capabilities

Uzbekistan enacted a new military doctrine in early 2018, which highlighted increased concern over terrorism and the potential impact of conflicts including Afghanistan. It also noted a requirement for military modernisation. The doctrine also focuses on border security and hybrid-warfare concerns. Uzbekistan is a member of the SCO, but suspended its CSTO membership in 2012. It maintains bilateral defence ties with Moscow and in late 2018 a defence-cooperation agreement was reported with India. The armed forces are army-dominated and conscript-based. Uzbekistan has a limited capacity to deploy its forces externally and does not have any international deployments. The armed forces use mainly Soviet-era equipment. A sizeable air fleet was inherited from the Soviet Union, but minimal recapitalisation in the intervening period has substantially reduced the active inventory. Logistical and maintenance shortcomings hinder aircraft availability. Uzbekistan is reliant on foreign suppliers for advanced military equipment, and procured equipment including military helicopters and armoured personnel carriers from Russia in 2019. A State Committee for the Defence Industry was established in late 2017 to organise domestic industry and defence orders. The 2018 defence doctrine calls for improvements to the domestic defence industry.

ACTIVE 48,000 (Army 24,500 Air 7,500 Joint 16,000)
Paramilitary 20,000
Conscript liability 12 months

ORGANISATIONS BY SERVICE

Army 24,500
4 Mil Districts; 2 op comd; 1 Tashkent Comd

FORCES BY ROLE
SPECIAL FORCES
  1 SF bde
MANOEUVRE
  Armoured
  1 tk bde
  Mechanised
  11 MR bde
  Air Manoeuvre
  1 air aslt bde
  1 AB bde
  Mountain
  1 lt mtn inf bde
COMBAT SUPPORT
  3 arty bde
  1 MRL bde

EQUIPMENT BY TYPE
ARMOURED FIGHTING VEHICLES
  MBT 340: 70 T-72; 100 T-64; 170 T-62
  RECCE 19: 13 BRDM-2; 6 BRM-1
  IFV 270 BMP-2
  APC 388
    APC (T) 50 BTR-D
    APC (W) 259: 24 BTR-60; 25 BTR-70; 210 BTR-80
    PPV 79: 50 *Maxxpro+*; 24 *Ejder Yalcin*; 5 *Typhoon*-K
  ABCV 129: 120 BMD-1; 9 BMD-2
  AUV 11+: 7 *Cougar*; 4+ M-ATV; some *Tigr*-M
ENGINEERING & MAINTENANCE VEHICLES
  ARV 20 *Maxxpro* ARV
ANTI-TANK/ANTI-INFRASTRUCTURE
  MSL • MANPATS 9K11 *Malyutka* (AT-3 *Sagger*); 9K111 *Fagot* (AT-4 *Spigot*)
  GUNS 100mm 36 MT-12/T-12
ARTILLERY 487+
  SP 83+: **122mm** 18 2S1 *Gvozdika*; **152mm** 17+: 17 2S3 *Akatsiya*; 2S5 *Giatsint*-S (reported); **203mm** 48 2S7 *Pion*
  TOWED 200: **122mm** 60 D-30; **152mm** 140 2A36 *Giatsint*-B
  GUN/MOR 120mm 54 2S9 NONA-S
  MRL 108: **122mm** 60: 36 BM-21 *Grad*; 24 9P138; **220mm** 48 9P140 *Uragan*
  MOR 120mm 42: 5 2B11 *Sani*; 19 2S12 *Sani*; 18 M-120
AIR DEFENCE • SAM
  Point-defence QW-18 (CH-SA-11)

Air Force 7,500
FORCES BY ROLE
FIGHTER
  1 sqn with MiG-29/MiG-29UB *Fulcrum*;
  1 sqn with Su-27/Su-27UB *Flanker*
GROUND ATTACK
  1 sqn with Su-24 *Fencer*
  1 sqn with Su-25/Su-25BM *Frogfoot*
ELINT/TRANSPORT
  1 regt with An-12/An-12PP *Cub*; An-26/An-26RKR *Curl*
TRANSPORT
  Some sqn with An-24 *Coke*; C295W; Tu-134 *Crusty*
TRAINING
  1 sqn with L-39 *Albatros*
ATTACK/TRANSPORT HELICOPTER
  1 regt with Mi-24 *Hind*; Mi-26 *Halo*; Mi-8 *Hip*;
  1 regt with Mi-6 *Hook*; Mi-6AYa *Hook* C

EQUIPMENT BY TYPE
AIRCRAFT 41 combat capable
  FTR 12 MiG-29/MiG-29UB *Fulcrum* (18 more in store)
  FGA 13 Su-27/Su-27UB *Flanker* (11 more in store) (26 Su-17M (Su-17MZ)/Su-17UM-3 (Su-17UMZ) *Fitter* C/G non-operational)
  ATK 16: 12 Su-25/Su-25BM *Frogfoot*; 4 Su-24 *Fencer*
  EW/Tpt 26 An-12 *Cub* (med tpt)/An-12PP *Cub* (EW) **ELINT/Tpt** 13 An-26 *Curl* (lt tpt)/An-26RKR *Curl* (ELINT)
  TPT 7: **Heavy** 1 Il-76 *Candid*; **Light** 6: 1 An-24 *Coke*; 4 C295W; 1 Tu-134 *Crusty*
  TRG 14 L-39 *Albatros*
HELICOPTERS
  ATK 29 Mi-24 *Hind*
  TPT 69: **Heavy** 9: 8 H225M *Caracal*; 1 Mi-26 *Halo*; **Medium** 52 Mi-8 *Hip*; **Light** 8 AS350 *Ecureuil*
AIR DEFENCE • SAM 45
  Long-range S-200 *Angara* (SA-5 *Gammon*); FD-2000 (HQ-9)
  Medium-range S-75 *Dvina* (SA-2 *Guideline*)
  Short-range S-125 *Pechora* (SA-3 *Goa*)
AIR-LAUNCHED MISSILES
  AAM • IR R-60 (AA-8 *Aphid*); R-73 (AA-11A *Archer*); **IR/SARH** R-27 (AA-10 *Alamo*)
  ASM Kh-23 (AS-7 *Kerry*); Kh-25 (AS-10 *Karen*)
  ARM Kh-25P (AS-12 *Kegler*); Kh-28 (AS-9 *Kyle*); Kh-58 (AS-11 *Kilter*)

Paramilitary up to 20,000

Internal Security Troops up to 19,000
Ministry of Interior

National Guard 1,000
Ministry of Defence

Arms procurements and deliveries – Russia and Eurasia

Significant events in 2019

FEBRUARY
ROSTEC ACQUISITION

Russian conglomerate Rostec acquired 74.5% of KurganMashZavod (KMZ) from its other company, Concern Tractor Plants (KTZ). KMZ is currently developing the *Kurganets* tracked armoured vehicle and manufactures the BMP-3 infantry fighting vehicle, among other products. Rostec took over operational management of KTZ in 2017 due to the firm's poor financial results. Rostec acquired KMZ shares as a means of investing capital in the firm. KMZ had posted losses in recent years and had proven unable to fulfil its planned schedule of vehicle deliveries.

JUNE
S-500 *PROMETEY*

Rostec Chief Executive Officer Sergey Chemezov announced that production has begun of the S-500 *Prometey*, Russia's next-generation air- and missile-defence system. A designer at manufacturer Almaz-Antey had previously stated that the S-500 will be capable of the exo-atmospheric interception of targets, and that it will augment existing S-300 and S-400 systems.

JUNE
SU-57 CONTRACT

Russia awarded Sukhoi a contract for the series production of 76 Su-57 combat aircraft. The first delivery is planned for 2021. However, these aircraft will not be fitted with the new *Izdeliye*-30 engine, which is still in development. To date, prototype Su-57s have been fitted with the AL-41F-1 engine that powers the Su-35S (*Flanker* M). It is possible that aircraft delivered before the new engine is ready will have it retrofitted, adding to the programme's overall cost.

AUGUST
UAV CO-DEVELOPMENT

Ukraine's Ukrspecexport, representing the UkrOboronProm conglomerate, and Turkey's Baykar Makina established a joint venture to develop aerospace and precision-weapon technologies. Since 2011, Baykar Makina has supplied more than 90 *Bayraktar* TB2 uninhabited aerial vehicles (UAV) to the Turkish military and gendarmerie and in 2019 delivered a system, consisting of six *Bayraktar* TB2 UAVs, to Ukraine. The new joint venture aims to develop a new armed UAV fitted with Ukrainian-made engines. This is not the only example of Ukrainian-Turkish defence-industrial cooperation. In October 2019, Aselsan opened a production line in Kiev to supply the Ukrainian military with very high frequency communications systems and negotiations are also ongoing to co-produce transport aircraft and active protection systems and remote weapon stations for armoured vehicles. In recent years, Ukraine has sought to increase foreign investment in its defence industry as part of a modernisation drive necessitated by ongoing conflict in the east of the country and Russia's annexation of the Crimean peninsula in 2014.

SEPTEMBER
HELICOPTER CARRIERS

Russia's deputy minister for industry and trade, Oleg Ryazantsev, said that the next State Armament Programme will include the acquisition of the first of two planned helicopter carriers for the navy. Russia had previously ordered two *Mistral*-class ships from France in 2011 for €1.2 billion (US$1.67bn), though this deal was cancelled in 2015 following Russia's annexation of Crimea. Russia's capacity to still build naval vessels of this size has been questioned. For instance, although the first Project 11711 *Ivan Gren* landing ship tank was commissioned in 2018, construction of the vessel – which is roughly one-third the size of the planned helicopter carrier – had started in 2004.

Table 13 Kazakhstan: aerospace and air-defence procurement, 2010–19

Contract date	Equipment	Type	Quantity	Value	Prime contractor	Deliveries
2010	UH-1H *Huey* II	Light transport helicopter	4	US$0	US government surplus	2016–17
2011	EC145	Light transport helicopter	45 (at least 8 to air force)	n.k.	Eurocopter / Kazakhstan Engineering	2011–16
2012	Mi-171Sh *Terminator*	Medium transport helicopter	At least 14	n.k.	Russian Helicopters	2013–18
2014	Su-30SM *Flanker* H	Fighter/ground-attack aircraft	4	est. R5bn (US$130.28m)	United Aircraft Corporation	2015
c. 2014	S-300PS (SA-10B *Grumble*)	Long-range surface-to-air missile	5 battalions-worth	n.k.	Russian government surplus	2015
c. 2014	Mi-171Sh *Terminator*	Medium transport helicopter	6	n.k.	Russian Helicopters	2015–16
2015	Mi-35M *Hind*	Attack helicopter	4 (batch 1)	n.k.	Russian Helicopters	2016
Dec 2015	Su-30SM *Flanker* H	Fighter/ground-attack aircraft	8	est. R10bn (US$164.1m)	United Aircraft Corporation	2016–18
c. 2015	C295M	Light transport aircraft	2 (batch 3)	n.k.	Airbus Defence & Space	2016
2016	*Wing Loong*	Heavy CISR UAV	n.k.	n.k.	Chengdu Aircraft Industrial Corporation	2017
c. 2016	Z-242L	Training aircraft	n.k.	n.k.	Zlin Aviation	2017–ongoing
c. 2017	C295M	Light transport aircraft	2 (batch 4)	n.k.	Airbus Defence & Space	2018
c. 2017	Y-8F-200W	Medium transport aircraft	4	US$148m	Shaanxi Aircraft Industrial Corporation	2018
May 2018	Mi-35M *Hind*	Attack helicopter	4 (Batch 2)	n.k.	Russian Helicopters	n.k.
May 2018	Su-30SM *Flanker* H	Fighter/ground-attack aircraft	8	est. R10bn (US$159.57m)	United Aircraft Corporation	n.k.
Jan 2019	Mi-8AMT/171	Medium transport helicopter	n.k. (licence-assembly agreement)	n.k.	Kazakhstan Engineering / Russian Helicopters	n.k.
Mar 2019	C295	Light transport aircraft	1 (Border Guard)	n.k.	Airbus Defence & Space	n.k.
Aug 2019	n.k.	UAV	n.k. (licence-assembly agreement)	n.k.	Kazakhstan Aviation Industry / Elbit Systems	n.k.

Table 14 Turkmenistan: aerospace and air-defence procurement, 2010–19

Contract date	Equipment	Type	Quantity	Value	Prime contractor	Deliveries
2010	*Falco*	Medium ISR UAV	At least 2	€8.7m (US$11.54m)	Selex ES (now Leonardo)	2011
2011	An-74TK-200 *Coaler*	Light transport aircraft	2	n.k.	Kharkiv State Aircraft Manufacturing Company	2011–12
2011	AW109EP	Multi-role helicopter	At least 3	n.k.	AgustaWestland (now Leonardo)	2016–17
2011	AW139	Multi-role helicopter	5	€64m (US$89.05m)	AgustaWestland (now Leonardo)	2011–12
c. 2014	Mi-17V-5 *Hip*	Multi-role helicopter	2	n.k.	Russian Helicopters	2015
c. 2015	CH-3	Heavy CISR UAV	n.k.	n.k.	CASC	2016
c. 2015	WJ-600	Heavy CISR UAV	n.k.	n.k.	CASC	2016
c. 2015	FD-2000 (HQ-9)	Long-range surface-to-air missile	n.k.	n.k.	CASIC	2016
	KS-1A (HQ-12)	Medium-range surface-to-air missile				

Figure 12 Russian Navy: surface-combatant acquisition

Russian naval-shipbuilding output reduced significantly in the 1990s and early 2000s, in line with a broader economic downturn. Although defence spending rose after the late 2000s, and shipbuilding output rose once more, the vessels subsequently built have typically been smaller frigates, corvettes and missile boats instead of vessels like the 7,000+ tonne *Fregat* (*Udaloy* I/II) of the late Soviet era. It is possible that many of the staff with experience in building larger vessels have retired and that in future large Russian shipyards may have to relearn associated skills; indeed, this influenced the decision to order *Mistral* amphibious-assault ships from France in 2011. At the same time, some delays have been caused by the loss of access to Ukrainian gas turbines in 2014, as well as to diesel engines from other European states, after Russia's 2014 annexation of Crimea. Import-substitution initiatives have shown some results, with the first UEC-Saturn M90FR gas turbines delivered in 2019 for the *Gorshkov*-class destroyer. However, in some instances, Russia has had to source Chinese diesel engines, though these were reported to have suffered from reliability problems. While Russia maintains the ambition to build ships of the size of cruisers and aircraft carriers, as things stand its shipbuilding sector would likely struggle to achieve this.

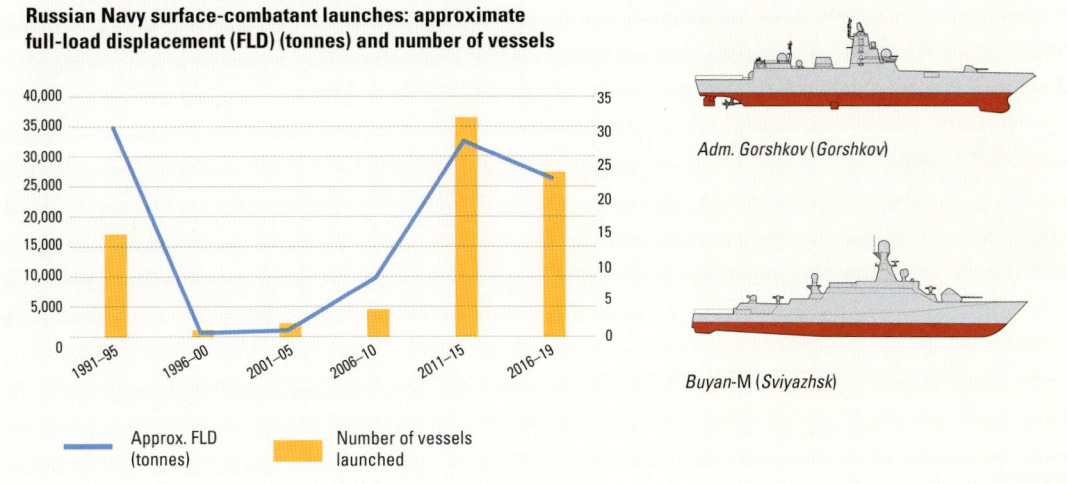

Adm. Gorshkov (*Gorshkov*)

Buyan-M (*Sviyazhsk*)

© IISS

Table 15 Russian Navy: selected ongoing surface-combatant programmes

Project number (name)	NATO designation	Type	Quantity ordered	Number in service	Approximate FLD (tonnes)	Shipyard/s	Part of United Shipbuilding Corporation?
22350	*Gorshkov*	DDGHM	6	1	5,400	Severnaya Verf	Y
11356	*Grigorovich*	FFGHM	6	3	3,900	Yantar Shipyard	Y
20380	*Steregushchiy*	FFGHM	10	6	2,100	Severnaya Verf	Y
						Amur Shipyard	Y
20385	*Gremyashchiy*	FFGHM	2	0	2,100	Severnaya Verf	Y
20386	*Improved Steregushchiy*	FFGHM	1	0	2,300	Severnaya Verf	Y
22160	*Bykov*	PSOH	6	2	1,700	Zelenodolsk Shipyard	N
21631 (*Buyan-M*)	*Sviyazhsk*	FSGM	12	7	950	Zelenodolsk Shipyard	N
22800 (*Karakurt*)	n.k.	FSGM	18	1	800	Pella Shipyard	N
						Zelenodolsk Shipyard	N
						Vostochnaya Verf	N
						Amur Shipyard	Y

Chapter Six
Asia

- As China's navy has expanded in capability and now deploys more frequently beyond the first island chain, maritime surveillance and situational awareness has become a key priority for a number of regional states, with ageing maritime-patrol aircraft fleets giving way to a mix of new fixed-wing and uninhabited platforms.
- In the run-up to the 2020 Taiwanese presidential election, the current government signed a number of foreign military sales agreements with the United States for new platforms and weapon systems in an attempt to keep up with the modernisation efforts of the People's Liberation Army. Most notable were deals for F-16V combat aircraft and M1A2 *Abrams* main battle tanks, both long sought by the Taiwanese military.
- North Korea resumed its short-range-missile testing programme, unveiling several new designs.
- Meanwhile South Korea continues to remodel its armed forces, particularly the army, with a reduction in the size of its mechanised forces.
- Budgetary issues still complicate many Southeast Asian states' plans to both recapitalise their ageing defence inventories with foreign systems and develop domestic defence-industrial bases. Singapore remains a notable exception, as the city state continues to pursue an ambitious programme of renewal for all of its services.
- The de facto border between India and Pakistan in Kashmir remains tense, underscored by continuing terrorist activities, an exchange of airstrikes in February and the Indian government's imposition of direct rule. Both India and Pakistan claimed success in the brief February campaign and are now looking to improve the capabilities of their respective air forces.

Asia defence spending, 2019 – top 5

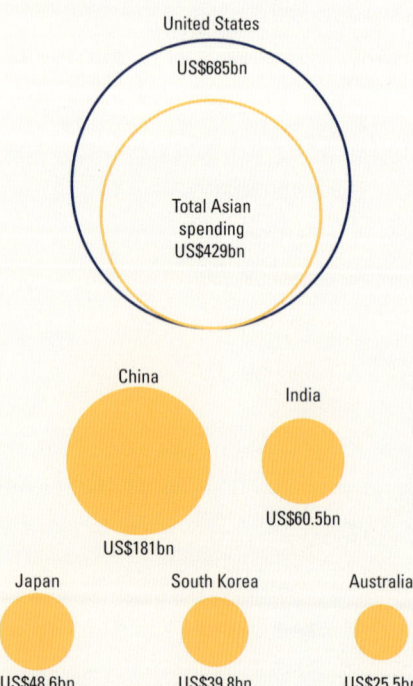

United States US$685bn
Total Asian spending US$429bn
China US$181bn
India US$60.5bn
Japan US$48.6bn
South Korea US$39.8bn
Australia US$25.5bn

Active military personnel – top 10
(15,000 per unit)

Country	Personnel
China	2,035,000
India	1,455,550
North Korea	1,280,000
Pakistan	653,800
South Korea	599,000
Vietnam	482,000
Myanmar	406,000
Indonesia	395,500
Thailand	360,850
Sri Lanka	255,000

Global total 19,719,000
Regional total 9,326,000

Regional defence policy and economics 222 ▶
Armed forces data section 250 ▶
Arms procurements and deliveries 321 ▶

India and Pakistan: fighter and ground-attack aircraft

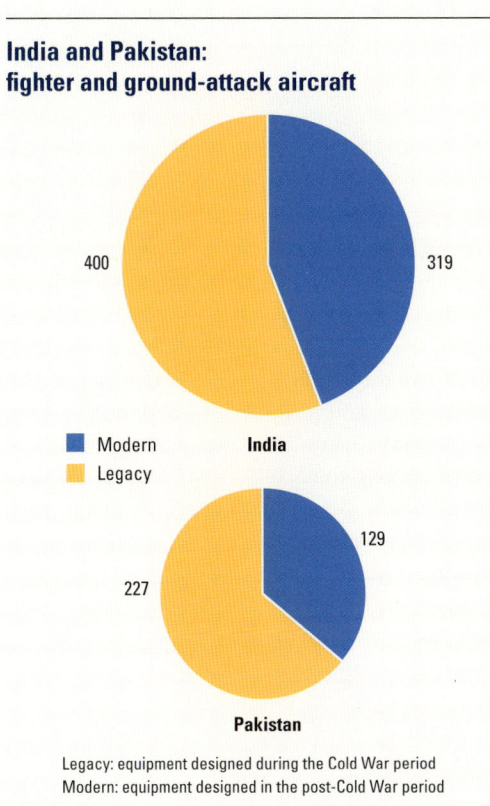

Legacy: equipment designed during the Cold War period
Modern: equipment designed in the post-Cold War period

Republic of Korea: restructuring mechanised forces

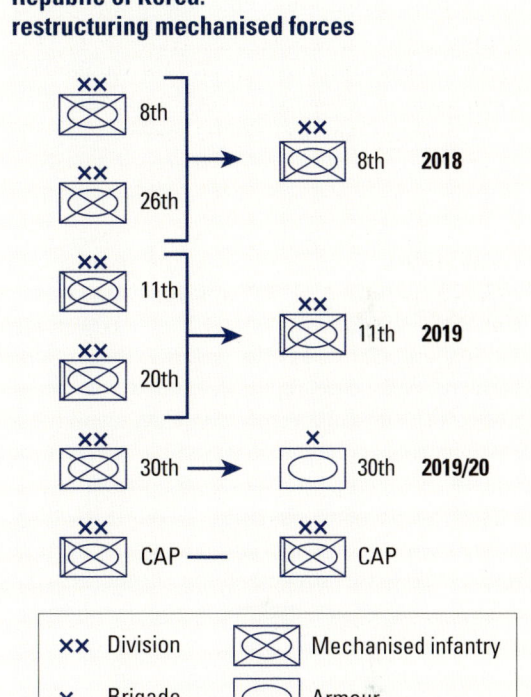

Selected regional maritime-patrol aircraft and uninhabited aerial vehicles

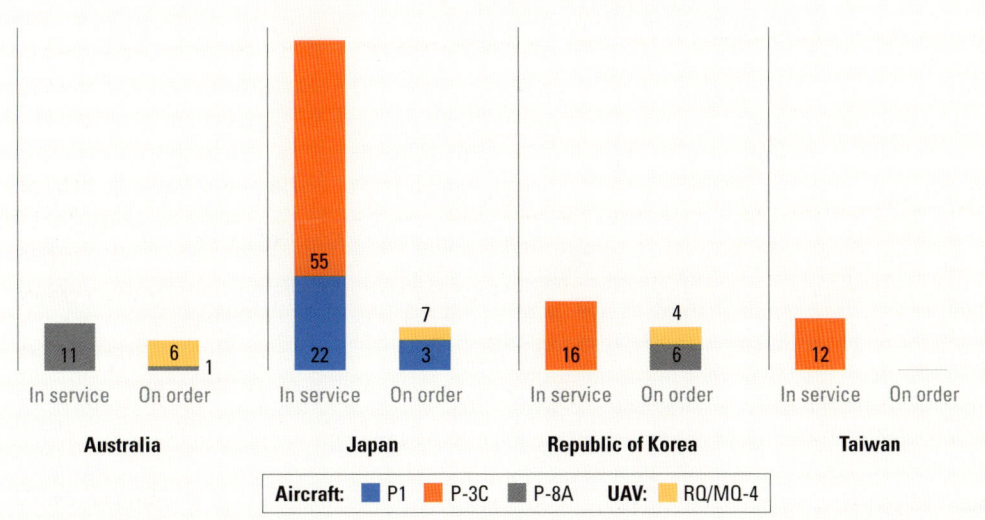

Asia

In 2019, the region's major military powers continued efforts to enhance the capabilities of their armed forces. At the same time, the United States maintained its focus on strengthening its regional military posture, in response to the continuing challenges from China's military modernisation, North Korea's missile and nuclear-weapons programmes, and Russia's re-emergence as a security challenge.

United States

The US Department of Defense's (DoD's) Indo-Pacific Strategy Report, released in early June, identified the region as the 'priority theater' for its armed forces. The report reiterated the intent of the 2018 National Defense Strategy, saying the US would bolster the 'combat-credible' posture of US forces and 'enhance Joint Force preparedness for the most pressing scenarios'. While providing concrete examples of important new platforms and systems intended to strengthen the US Indo-Pacific Command's order of battle, the report emphasised that the DoD was developing a 'more dynamic and distributed presence', including 'flexible and resilient' logistic support, across the region. It also noted the importance of defence and security cooperation for the United States' military posture in the Indo-Pacific. One potentially important example was US support for future work by Australia to rebuild the naval base at Lombrum on Papua New Guinea's Manus Island.

However, regional allies were not always prepared automatically to accommodate US strategic interests. This was evident in August 2019 when, following Washington's withdrawal from the Intermediate-range Nuclear Forces Treaty, Secretary of Defense Mark Esper said that to counter China's own expanding missile force he was in favour of stationing US land-based intermediate-range conventional missiles in the region within months. The response to this from key allies Australia, Japan and South Korea was unenthusiastic. Nevertheless, their own defence programmes all indicate these countries' intent to boost their own security in the face of intensifying regional challenges.

South Korea

South Korea's 2018 defence white paper, released in January 2019, included well-funded defence plans for the period 2019–23. It reiterated Seoul's prioritisation of the Defense Reform 2.0 initiative, which is intended to create by 2022 smaller but more technologically advanced and operationally effective armed forces. The reform and modernisation programme is intended to help the Republic of Korea to realise the long-established plan (agreed with the US in 2007) of assuming wartime operational control of its own forces. An important step towards this objective was the amalgamation in January of the ROK Army's 1st and 3rd Army Commands to form a new Ground Operations Command, which will unify control over the army's seven regional corps, an expeditionary corps, a logistics command, and artillery and intelligence formations. In August 2019, Seoul's Mid-Term Defense Plan for 2020–24 revealed a projected increase in procurement funding for new weapons platforms and systems, including a 30,000-ton LPX-II large amphibious-assault ship capable of carrying F-35B combat aircraft (yet to be ordered) and a 'combined fires' ship (probably based on the KDD-II destroyer) armed with land-attack cruise missiles, as well as additional KDD-III cruisers and KSS-III submarines. Also in the plan are new missile-defence systems, surveillance satellites, uninhabited aerial vehicles (UAVs), anti-submarine-warfare (ASW) helicopters and electromagnetic-pulse strike weapons.

While Defense Reform 2.0 and the Mid-Term Defense Plan indicated that the ROK's defence modernisation was broadly following a well-established trajectory, the thinking behind Seoul's defence policy has undergone important changes under the administration of President Moon Jae-in, who took office in 2017. Crucially, Moon and his administration embarked in 2018 on a path of diplomatic reconciliation as a means of managing the threat posed by North Korea. Moon's diplomacy facilitated the tentative peace process involving Pyongyang and the US administration (which saw a second summit between US President Donald Trump and North Korean leader Kim Jong-un in Hanoi in

February 2019, and then a meeting at the Korean Demilitarized Zone in June), and is linked to domestic politics in South Korea, where public opinion broadly favours detente with the North. Reflecting this approach, although the 2018 South Korean defence white paper described Pyongyang's nuclear-weapons programme as a threat to peace and stability on the Korean Peninsula, it no longer referred to North Korea itself as an 'enemy', instead emphasising the potential for military confidence-building and arms control and noting other transnational threats.

However, by September 2019, the signs from Pyongyang were no longer encouraging. In early August 2019, and apparently in protest at the US–ROK command-post training drill (which, according to reports, was originally intended to be called the *19-2 Dong Maeng* exercise), the North Korean regime launched what were thought to be two short-range ballistic missiles into the Sea of Japan and dismissed Moon's call for further inter-Korean talks. The missile launches were the latest in a series that has also included multiple-rocket-launcher tests since May 2019. Further launches followed in September. Although North Korea tested no additional nuclear weapons, photographs in July showing Kim inspecting a large submarine potentially able to carry intercontinental-range missiles suggested that Pyongyang was continuing nuclear-weapons and missile programmes that potentially threaten the US, as well as other neighbouring states.

Meanwhile, Seoul's relations with Japan have been affected by a bilateral dispute triggered in October 2018 when a South Korean court ruled that the Japanese company Nippon Steel could be held liable for using Korean slave workers during the 1930s and 1940s. In early August 2019, bilateral tensions escalated into a trade dispute, and later that month directly affected security relations when Seoul said it would withdraw from the General Security of Military Information Agreement – an important arrangement for directly sharing intelligence on North Korea with Japan. Within days, Seoul staged a two-day naval exercise – delayed since earlier in the year in order to avoid exacerbating the bilateral dispute – around the disputed Dokdo/Takeshima islets, which are occupied by South Korea but claimed by Japan. While Seoul suspended its withdrawal from the agreement in late November, following discussions with Japan and also with the US, the risk remained that competition with Japan could influence South Korea's defence strategy and policy more overtly in the future.

Taiwan

China's continuing military modernisation spurred reciprocal efforts not only by the US and Japan but also Taiwan, where since 2016 the government led by President Tsai Ing-wen has been trying to find ways of mitigating the continuing shift in the military balance across the Taiwan Strait in China's favour. Taipei's latest biennial National Defense Report, released in September 2019, emphasised Taiwan's support for the US Indo-Pacific Strategy, as well as its own security cooperation with US allies in the region. The report also itemised arms sales agreed with the US over the previous two years, including M1A2T *Abrams* main battle tanks, BGM-71 TOW and FGM-148 *Javelin* anti-tank missiles, and FIM-92 *Stinger* surface-to-air missiles. More strategically important, though, was the US administration's August 2019 agreement (subject to congressional approval) to sell Taiwan 66 F-16C/D Block 70 combat aircraft. These aircraft will be equipped with conformal fuel tanks, allowing them significantly extended operational range compared to Taiwan's F-16A/Bs (in service since 1996), which are due to be locally upgraded to F-16V Block 70 standard by 2022. Another important defence-procurement programme involves the local construction by the Taiwanese shipbuilder CSBC, with major foreign support, of six to eight diesel-electric submarines; the US is unable to supply these and no other government is willing to provide them. Taiwan's defence minister, Yen De-fa, said in March 2019 that the first submarine should be completed by the mid-2020s, though reports that a Gibraltar-based company won a design contract in 2018 were subsequently cast into doubt. Taiwan's defence strategy is not entirely focused on the cross-Strait challenge: it also has concerns over tensions in the South China Sea, where it occupies the largest feature, Taiping Island (also known as Itu Aba). A planned class of amphibious-assault vessels may be intended in part for South China Sea operations. Construction of the first vessel began in May 2019.

Southeast Asia

Among Southeast Asian states, Singapore and Vietnam continued to make the most successful efforts to enhance their military capabilities to deter and, if necessary, defend against external threats. During 2019, Vietnam faced renewed maritime pressure from Beijing in the South China Sea: a major Chinese survey vessel began surveying the seabed within Hanoi's exclusive economic zone

(EEZ). Meanwhile, the clash in April 2019 between a Vietnamese Fisheries Resources Surveillance vessel and an Indonesian navy corvette – reportedly inside Indonesia's EEZ – showed that China was not the only maritime challenge for Vietnam. Evidently intent on complicating China's military options through its own anti-access/area-denial strategy, Vietnam's capability-development efforts focused particularly on the navy and air force. Although there remains a requirement for a relatively light combat aircraft, many of the platforms that will allow the Vietnam People's Army (VPA) to realise this strategy, including Russian-built *Varshavyanka* (Improved *Kilo*) submarines, *Gepard*-class frigates and Su-30MK2 fighters, have entered service. Vietnam's defence establishment is now particularly emphasising the upgrading of the VPA's C5ISR (command, control, communications, computers, combat systems, intelligence, surveillance and reconnaissance) capabilities. In May 2019, the US DoD announced that Hanoi had ordered six *Scan Eagle* UAVs. In the same month, the Viettel Military Industry and Telecoms Group (which is owned by Vietnam's Ministry of National Defence) established a new defence-focused subsidiary, Viettel High Technology Industries Corporation, which will apply advances in artificial intelligence and big-data analysis to developing defence technology in areas such as communications, electronic warfare, radars and command-and-control systems.

The Philippines, like Vietnam, faced direct Chinese pressure on its claims and interests in the South China Sea in 2019. Under the Duterte administration, Manila's policy towards China's role there remained ambiguous. In November 2018, the Philippines and China agreed a range of cooperative initiatives, including on joint oil and gas development in the South China Sea, as well as the development of infrastructure in the Philippines. Simultaneously, the Philippines continued efforts to develop its maritime-defence capabilities. In September 2019, the armed forces staged their first-ever exercise involving all service branches, DAGIT-PA 03-19, including amphibious-assault, urban-warfare and 'airfield-retake' components. Before this exercise, the Philippine Navy and Marine Corps engaged in an 'expert exchange activity' with the US Marine Corps, focusing on amphibious-landing operations using Korean-supplied Armoured Amphibious Vehicles launched from one of the navy's two *Tarlac*-class Strategic Sealift Vessels. However, plans to order a frigate, corvettes, patrol vessels, ASW helicopters, maritime-patrol aircraft and armoured amphibious vehicles seem unlikely to be realised in full by the target date of 2022 because of the country's limited defence budget and the need to fund a large army still involved extensively in counter-insurgency operations. While stated as a requirement, procuring submarines is an even more distant prospect. Nevertheless, the South Korean government's offer to provide financial support for the Corvette Acquisition Project, which would see two ships built by Hyundai Heavy Industries, may provide a means of significantly enhancing the navy's presently limited combat capabilities in the medium term.

In May 2018, Malaysia's opposition Pakatan Harapan coalition displaced the Barisan Nasional administration (which had been in power in one form or another since 1957). Within weeks of taking office, the new government initiated a defence white-paper process involving independent experts as well as officials. According to Deputy Defence Minister Senator Liew Chin Tong, one major outcome of the white-paper process will be a major change in the country's defence-procurement system, with the aim of ensuring that it is driven by strategic interests and military requirements rather than by equipment suppliers. The white paper will reportedly also seek to identify ways of overcoming shortfalls in military capacity, despite pressure on the defence budget as the government attempts to control the overall budget deficit and reduce sovereign debt. However, one issue is that, while the country's most important security challenges are essentially maritime, the Malaysian Army has remained disproportionately large, despite the end of the main internal security threat from communist insurgents three decades ago. One partial solution, suggested by analysts, may be to move some army units into an amphibious-assault role.

South Asia

In South Asia, the major military confrontation between India and Pakistan in late February 2019 saw the first air attack across the Line of Control (between the Indian- and Pakistani-administered zones of Kashmir) since the 1971 Indo-Pakistani War. There were also heavy exchanges of fire between the Indian and Pakistani armies along the Line of Control. Pakistan's air force carried out its own attack against multiple targets in Jammu and Kashmir.

India claimed to have shot down a Pakistani aircraft; Pakistan claimed to have shot down two

Indian aircraft, and one Indian MiG-21 *Bison* pilot was captured after ejecting. While the two countries retreated from the brink of a major conflict, the clashes were significant in that – following India's rejection of some previous self-imposed constraints – they were the first occasion in which any two nuclear-armed states had mounted airstrikes against each other.

Efforts by India and Pakistan to develop their military capabilities have for decades mirrored and reacted to each other, but New Delhi's concerns over China have exerted an increasingly important influence over the development of the strategic elements of India's armed forces. However, India's defence spending remains insufficient to meet military-equipment requirements, particularly those of the navy and air force. Following the 1 February budget announcement for the 2019–20 fiscal year, the chiefs of these two services complained over major shortfalls in funding that left no money for new procurement or upgrade programmes.

Australia and New Zealand

There is a stark contrast between Canberra's determined efforts to enhance its military capabilities and Wellington's relatively relaxed attitude towards the defence of New Zealand against external threats. Nevertheless, New Zealand's Strategic Defence Policy Statement 2018 highlighted 'complex transnational threats' in the country's neighbourhood and disruptive behaviour on the part of China and Russia, as well as uncertainty over the United States' future international role. To a limited extent, these concerns fed into the Defence Capability Plan 2019, released in June, which set out planned investments (NZ$20 billion until 2030, or US$13.4bn) in the New Zealand Defence Force for the next decade. Defence Minister Ron Mark emphasised that this was 'a humanitarian plan' that would allow New Zealand to take the lead in assisting neighbouring countries and to contribute 'to the security of our friends in the Pacific'. The Defence Capability Plan revealed that, in addition to acquisition of four P-8A maritime-patrol aircraft announced in July 2018, New Zealand's air force would bring C-130J-30 transport aircraft into service from 2023, replacing its current 'H' variants. These will support operations in the South Pacific and Antarctica, as well as coalition operations further from home. Other planned procurement will involve new training aircraft, long-range UAVs, maritime helicopters, an 'enhanced sealift vessel', offshore-patrol vessels and protected mobility vehicles. The plan also indicated that the army's personnel strength would grow to 6,000 by 2035, allowing it 'to respond to multiple events concurrently'. However, replacement of the navy's two ANZAC-class frigates – which are being upgraded with new combat-management systems – was deferred until after 2030.

DEFENCE ECONOMICS

Macroeconomics

In 2019, Asia's economies once more propelled global growth, though economic dynamism faded somewhat in comparison with the preceding two years. Notably, the slowdown in global trade affected Asian GDP growth, as exports and investments weakened.

The electronics sector is experiencing a downward cycle because of market saturation, as consumers replace electronic products more slowly and the deployment of 5G networks continues to be delayed. This is significant for Asian economies, given the key role the semiconductor and electronics industries play in the region. A September 2019 study by the Asian Development Bank (ADB) revealed that the electronics sector constitutes 3.8% of China's GDP and 6–16% of GDP in Malaysia, South Korea, Singapore and Taiwan.

The pace of China's economic growth slowed from 6.8% GDP in 2017 to 6.6% in 2018 and 6.1% in 2019, according to the International Monetary Fund (IMF). In the first half of 2019, China's exports to the United

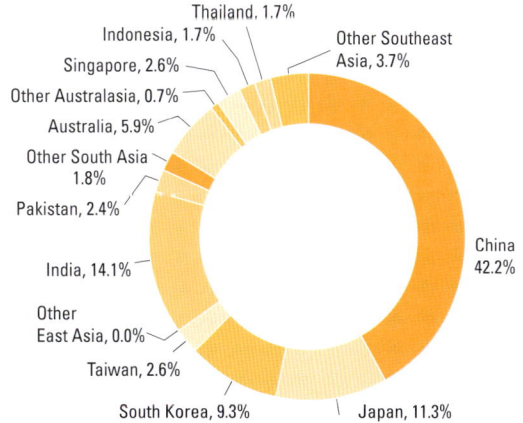

▼ Figure 13 **Asia defence spending by country and sub-region, 2019**

Thailand, 1.7%
Indonesia, 1.7%
Singapore, 2.6%
Other Southeast Asia, 3.7%
Other Australasia, 0.7%
Australia, 5.9%
Other South Asia, 1.8%
Pakistan, 2.4%
India, 14.1%
Other East Asia, 0.0%
Taiwan, 2.6%
South Korea, 9.3%
Japan, 11.3%
China, 42.2%

Note: analysis excludes North Korea and Laos due to insufficient data.

© IISS

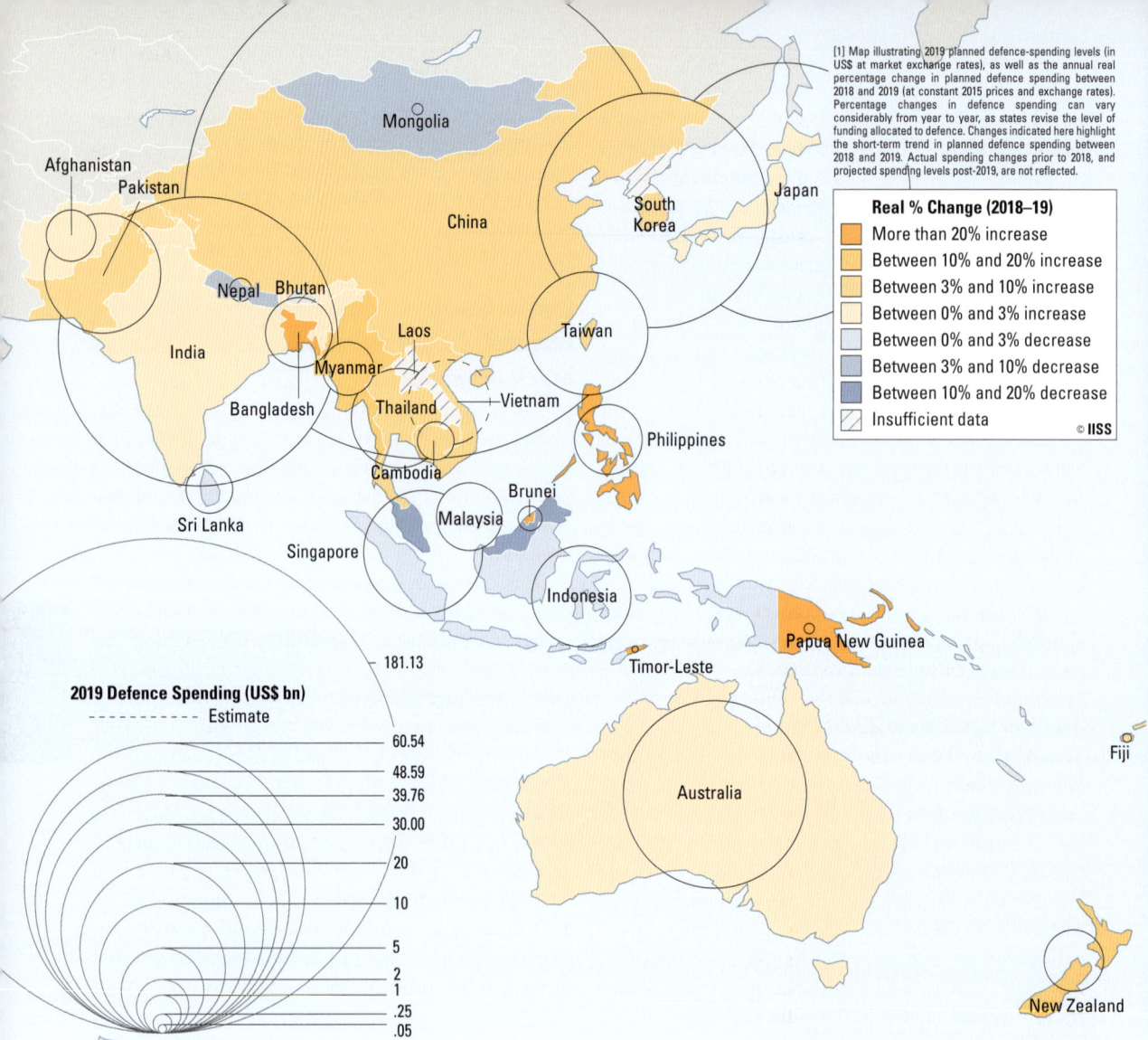

▲ Map 8 **Asia regional defence spending**[1]

States contracted by 12% compared to the same period in 2018. In response, the Chinese authorities lowered bank-reserve ratios (the minimum amount of capital commercial banks should hold) to support bank lending and introduced subsidies and tax cuts in 2019. While these measures were intended to sustain domestic demand, mounting private and public debt are a risk to China's economic stability.

Meanwhile, 2019 saw Australia experience its slowest rate of GDP growth (1.7%) in a decade. The main causes for this were increased uncertainty over the global trade environment, the end of a real-estate bubble and a severe drought. The central bank reacted by lowering its interest rate to 1%, a record low, while the government has introduced tax cuts.

Australia and China were not the only countries in the region to implement supportive monetary policies. India, Indonesia, Malaysia, the Philippines, South Korea, Thailand and New Zealand also reduced their policy interest rates (set by central banks) in 2019, reflecting a search for responses to weaker external demand and the global economic slowdown.

That said, in a region which remains highly dependent on exports, the consequences of the ongoing trade disputes were not all negative. These disputes, between China and the US but also between the US and other Asian countries including India, Japan and South Korea, have seen rising tariffs and uncertainty reduce global trade. According to the ADB, if all the announced tariffs were implemented,

99.3% of US imports from China and 77.7% of Chinese imports from the US could be affected by higher tariffs by the end of 2019. The resulting higher costs for firms have led some to restructure global supply chains, with some manufacturers based in China looking to move production to countries not so affected by US import tariffs. For instance, Taiwanese, South Korean and Japanese manufacturers of electronics or advanced machinery are moving home. Southeast Asia too may benefit from this trend. For instance, according to the ADB, Chinese and Hong Kong foreign direct investments in Vietnam were greater by 200% between January and July 2019 than they were in the same time frame in 2018. And in the first five months of 2019, Vietnam's exports to the US grew by 28%.

Defence spending and procurement

Overall, Asia's defence spending grew by 5.2% in 2019. With total defence spending in the region standing at more than US$423 billion in real terms (constant 2015 dollars), this represents an increase of more than 50% in a decade (from US$275bn in 2010). However, the 2019 increase was driven by East Asia. Spending also increased in Australasia, South Asia and Southeast Asia, but in each case fell below the overall growth rate (see Figure 14). This repeated the pattern seen in 2018 when East Asian states also grew faster than the region as a whole.

To some extent, these differences reflect differing national-security concerns. In Southeast Asia, threat perceptions did not outweigh other economic policy priorities, and over the past five years Malaysia and Indonesia in particular have seen a consistent decline in both actual defence spending and defence spending as a share of GDP (see Figure 15).

As a result, both countries have experienced difficulties in funding defence procurements. In late 2018, for example, Jakarta asked to renegotiate the deal with South Korea over the development of the KAI KF-X fighter aircraft. Jakarta had committed to contribute 20% of the development costs. Payments restarted in early 2019, but by September Indonesia had again defaulted. To remedy the situation, Jakarta was considering contributions through counter-trade instead of cash, either by proposing its licence-produced CN235 transport aircraft or other goods such as palm oil or rubber. Similarly, the Malaysian government reportedly began discussions with some of its foreign suppliers of defence equipment regarding potential payment with palm oil. Malaysia is also looking to renegotiate the terms of some existing contracts in order to reduce costs, such as that for LG1 howitzers produced by Nexter and its local partner Advanced Defence Systems.

There were also defence-spending and procurement difficulties in South Asia during 2019, albeit for different reasons. In India, defence spending increased by 2.9% in real terms between 2018 and 2019. However, the share of defence investments (procurement and research-and-development (R&D) spending) in India's total defence budget has declined from a third in 2012 to just above a quarter in 2019. Additionally, the Indian authorities have not yet found a way to tackle dysfunctional arms-procurement processes. Although the Ministry of Defence has been working on a draft 'defence production policy' and a revised offset policy, these are yet to be implemented.

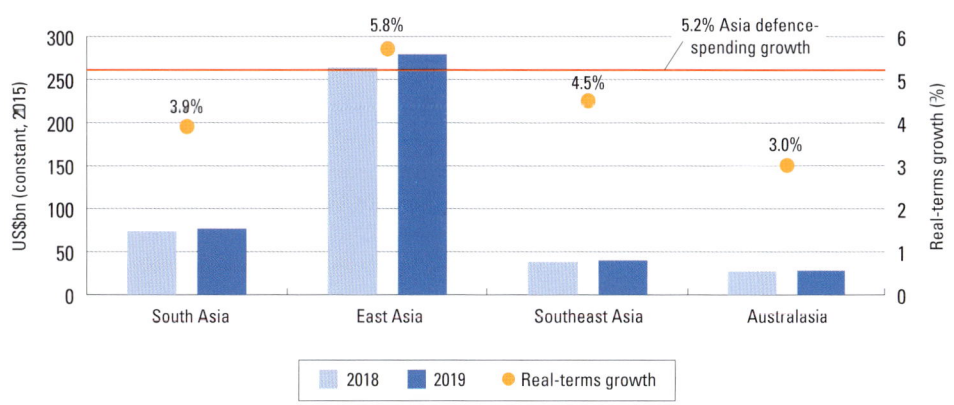

▼ Figure 14 **Asia: sub-regional real-terms defence-spending growth, 2018–19 (US$bn, constant 2015)**

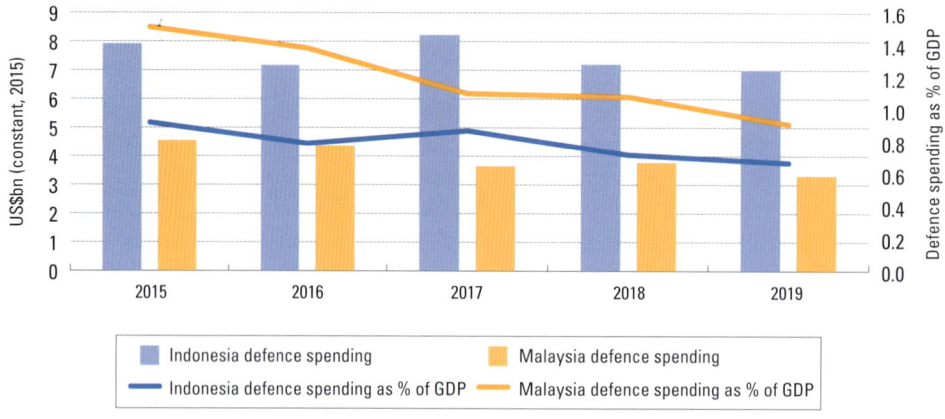

▲ Figure 15 **Indonesia and Malaysia: real-terms defence spending, 2015–19 (US$bn)**

Pakistan's defence spending increased by 4.0% in real terms in 2019 compared to 2018. However, this was because the 2018 budget had been revised and reduced significantly. Although the amount dedicated to military pensions remained unchanged in the 2018 budget (at US$2.4bn), the public-sector development programme for defence, part of which contributes to arms acquisitions, declined by almost 50% compared to the original 2018 allocation (falling from US$314 million to US$164m). Another challenge facing Islamabad was the decline in US foreign military financing (FMF) since the start of the Trump presidency. FMF funding for Pakistan fell from US$242m in 2017 to US$80m in 2019.

Meanwhile, security challenges in East Asia pushed defence spending upwards. China's defence budget rose by 6.6% in real terms between 2018 and 2019. (The IISS now includes in its assessment the funding of local militias.) Altogether, China's defence budget amounted to US$181bn in 2019. By way of comparison, in 2010 the figure was US$78.8bn – a real-terms increase of 86% in ten years. South Korean outlays have also risen, by 9.2% in real terms between 2018 and 2019, taking the budget almost to the US$40bn mark. However, part of this additional spending will go towards the costs of the US military presence in the country. Seoul has agreed to increase its contribution from just under W960bn (US$872m) in 2018 to W1,040bn (US$886m) in 2019.

Taiwan's defence-spending increase is in line with the regional trend, rising by 3.4% in real terms between 2018 and 2019. However, Taipei has projected a more than 20% real-terms increase between 2019 and 2020, from NT$340.5bn (US$10.9bn) to NT$411.3bn (US$13.3bn), due largely to a NT$53bn (US$1.7bn) injection of 'special funds' likely to be dedicated to arms imports from the US. Concerns over China's military expansion are central to Taiwan's defence spending and procurement. The special funds will probably underwrite the procurement of 66 F-16C/D Block 70 combat aircraft from the US, and the upgrading of its current fleet of F-16s. In mid-2019, Taiwan received approval for the purchase from the US of 100 M1A2 *Abrams* main battle tanks. These procurements not only reinforce Taiwan's deterrence posture in relation to China but also signal continued US support for Taipei.

Japan is also concerned by China's military modernisation and increased its defence outlays to US$48.6bn in 2019 (up from US$47.0bn in 2018). It continued strengthening its defence capabilities with a commitment to buy 105 F-35 combat aircraft, in

▼ Figure 16 **Asia regional defence expenditure** as % of GDP

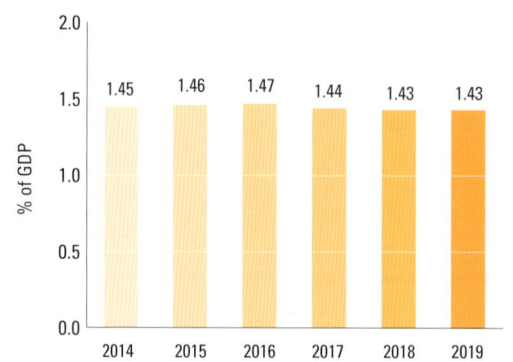

addition to the 42 aircraft originally planned, and to reconfigure its two *Izumo*-class helicopter carriers so that they can carry F-35Bs.

Defence industry

Most governments in the region now consider defence-industrial policy to be a key component of their overall defence strategies. For example, in August 2019, Australia's Department of Defence published the Science, Technology, Engineering and Mathematics (STEM) Workforce Strategic Vision 2019–2030, designed to support the development of defence-relevant industrial skills. That same month, it signed a first 'defence export facility' loan, intended to help small and medium enterprises (SMEs) expand their business and exports.

The Indian government, for its part, set up two 'defence industrial corridors' in Tamil Nadu and Uttar Pradesh. This policy aims to create clusters where companies engaged in defence production can improve collaboration. The defence ministry and large state-owned defence entities such as the Ordnance Factory Board pledged financial support to help set up these corridors. The defence ministry also developed a '5-points plan' for the defence industry to raise total turnover to US$25bn annually by 2025. India is also seeking to support defence exports by simplifying its licensing system and developing credit mechanisms.

South Korea's Defense Acquisition Program Administration has worked to improve the regulatory environment for the country's defence-industrial base, in order to boost innovation and reduce dependence on foreign suppliers. Seoul updated its offset policy in December 2018, expanded its import-substitution programme in 2019 to improve its security of supply in the defence sector and has launched a plan to support military R&D development in SMEs. It has also launched a 'defence business council' to improve coordination between defence-industry stakeholders.

Taiwan introduced the National Defense Industry Development Act in June 2019, also aiming to promote domestic armaments production. It includes the creation of an intergovernmental budget mechanism to direct funding to non-sensitive defence R&D.

There were also developments in the region's defence firms in 2019. In May, Vietnam's principal state-owned defence entity, Viettel Military Industry and Telecoms Group, set up a subsidiary, Viettel High Technology Industries Corporation, to focus on defence electronics and communications products.

Meanwhile, under pressure due to the downturn in the commercial shipbuilding sector, naval shipyards were forced to restructure. In China, the merger of the state-owned conglomerates China Shipbuilding Industry Corporation and China State Shipbuilding Corporation was announced in summer 2019. The two groups were separated 20 years ago from the China National Shipbuilding Corporation, but Beijing is now looking to improve coordination and reduce competition in the defence-industrial base. Once completed, the new joint entity could appear in the top-ten list of the world's largest defence firms, based on its combined defence-related revenue.

Another important merger was announced in South Korea, where Hyundai Heavy Industries is set to take a majority share in Daewoo Shipbuilding & Marine Engineering. The two companies are the dominant naval shipbuilders in South Korea. However, continued challenges in the global shipbuilding sector still had an impact. Another South Korean shipbuilding group, Hanjin Heavy Industries and Construction, saw its Philippines-based shipyard file for bankruptcy. The yard is located in Subic Bay – 100 nautical miles from Scarborough Shoal, an area in the South China Sea contested by China and the Philippines. It was reported that while Chinese companies considered buying the shipyard, Manila resisted the move.

AUSTRALIA'S MODERNISING ARMED FORCES

The Australian Defence Force (ADF) is now well into a process of renewing its major equipment platforms and supporting systems. The modernisation process was instigated by the 2000 Defence White Paper, written in the wake of lessons learned after Australia led the INTERFET mission to Timor-Leste.

The INTERFET operation highlighted, according to the white paper, 'that a mismatch had developed between our strategic objectives, our defence capabilities and our levels of defence funding'. The most significant shortcomings were found to be in sealift and the army's ability to sustain a large deployed force, but contingency planning for a possible escalation to hostilities with the Indonesian armed forces also revealed problems with the capability and especially the capacity of air and maritime combat forces. The result was a significant modernisation programme, initially set out in the white paper and subsequently modified in light of lessons from the ADF's involvement in the wars in Afghanistan and Iraq, as well as a number of large-scale natural disasters in Australia's local region. Of the latter, the 2004 Indian Ocean tsunami was the most demanding because of its scale, and led to the addition of two large *Canberra*-class landing helicopter docks (LHDs) to the modernisation plan.

More recently, China's growing military and geostrategic power, as well as increasing competition between China and the United States, has led to ADF interoperability with US forces being given greater emphasis in the most recent defence white paper than before. There has also been recognition that Australia needs to spend more on its own defence and do more to encourage continued US engagement in the Asia-Pacific.

Navy

The Royal Australian Navy (RAN) has recently taken delivery of two *Aegis* combat-system-equipped *Hobart*-class destroyers, an acquisition first promulgated in the 2000 white paper. HMAS *Hobart* was commissioned in 2017 and HMAS *Brisbane* in 2018. A third ship, *Sydney*, was on sea trials in late 2019 and will likely be accepted by the RAN in early 2020. In order to reduce project risk, the initial delivery did not include the most recent version of the *Aegis* combat system. An upgrade is scheduled for the first half of the 2020s, which might include the addition of ballistic-missile-defence capability. Meanwhile, the RAN's eight *Anzac*-class frigates have in recent years undergone a significant upgrade to boost their capability to defeat anti-ship missiles, being fitted with a bespoke Australian-designed phased-array radar and a combat system developed by Saab Australia.

There are also extensive plans for future domestic naval shipbuilding, including nine *Hunter*-class frigates based on the UK's Type-26 (but with an *Aegis* combat system and an evolved and larger version of the Australian-developed phased-array radar fitted to the *Anzac* class) and 12 *Attack*-class submarines designed by France's Naval Group. But those programmes will only deliver new frigates from the late 2020s and submarines in the 2030s. Anti-submarine-warfare (ASW) capability has also been boosted with the arrival of 24 MH-60R combat helicopters, the last of which was delivered in 2016, though the helicopter-to-ship networking required for integrated ASW operations does not yet exist across the fleet.

Army

The Australian Army has invested significant effort and resources into reorganising itself for amphibious operations, enabled by its LHDs and, under *Plan Beersheba*, to be capable of sustaining a brigade-sized deployment indefinitely. *Beersheba* configures the land forces as three brigades, similar in structure, allowing for one to be deployed, one resetting and one 'resting'. However, there is currently only one specialised amphibious battalion in the service, and some force elements – including armour – are not numerous enough to populate all three brigades.

The army is also networking and hardening its forces. Its deployment to Afghanistan illustrated the importance of advanced situational awareness and of the threat that even low-tech adversaries can present to lightly protected vehicles. Progress has been made in networking land elements together, though issues relating to legacy systems and the sourcing of materiel from diverse suppliers have complicated and slowed the development of a single integrated battle-management system. Full integration with the rest of the ADF is perhaps proving more challenging, as air and maritime C4ISR (command, control, communications, computers, intelligence, surveillance and reconnaissance) systems are more closely aligned with US standards than those fielded by the army. However, the requirement to develop an amphibious capability, working closely with the navy, is prompting the development of joint C4ISR capabilities and doctrine. The army will also be occupied over the next decade with the acquisition of major systems, including combat reconnaissance and infantry fighting vehicles, ground-based air defence, self-propelled artillery and new attack helicopters.

Air force

In contrast, the Royal Australian Air Force (RAAF) has already renewed much of its fleet, with most of its combat platforms and enablers being less than a decade old, including the F-35A combat aircraft, EA-7A *Wedgetail* airborne early-warning and control (AEW&C) aircraft, P-8 *Poseidon* maritime-patrol aircraft, EA-18G *Growler* and (in the future) MQ-4C *Triton* uninhabited aerial vehicles. Much of the RAAF's future effort will therefore be devoted to combining the effects of its new key platforms into a fully integrated fifth-generation force under its *Plan Jericho*. The RAAF also has a head start on the other two services when it comes to intra-service connectivity; much of this will already be 'baked-in' to its mainly US-sourced platforms.

Driving integration
However, the overall picture for the ADF is uneven. Observers of Australia's force-development efforts have sometimes remarked that a fully 'joined-up' ADF will resemble a smaller version of the US Marine Corps. But the ADF is currently short of the level of integration of that force, and in some respects remains a federated three-service structure coordinated through a joint headquarters.

A significant risk to ADF integration is that the air force will end up ahead of the other services, although the presence of many US platforms in the RAAF's inventory and the selection of the *Aegis* combat system for the navy's surface combatants will nonetheless provide a good basis for integration. One step likely to be taken early in the next decade is the development of a cooperative-engagement capability between the *Hobart*-class destroyers and air platforms via the *Wedgetail* AEW&C aircraft.

While integrating the army with the other services may be challenging, the ADF's emerging amphibious capability will lead to improved ship-to-shore connectivity. In addition, the acquisition of land-based anti-ship missiles 'to support operations to protect deployed forces and vital offshore assets such as oil and natural gas platforms' announced in the 2016 defence white paper will necessitate closer coordination with the rest of the ADF.

At the same time, cyber and space capabilities are also driving greater ADF integration. After some early single-service initiatives, Australia's cyber-operations capability has been centralised and co-located with the Australian Signals Directorate (ASD). The Joint Capabilities Group, which houses the ADF's Information Warfare Division, is a three-star appointment; so too are the service chiefs and the deputy director of ASD. Space capabilities are also centrally managed and, after being a consumer of foreign space systems for many years, Australia has recently stood up its own national space agency. There is now, for the first time, a major defence project designed to provide Australia with an indigenous space-based ISR capability from the late 2020s. That is planned to augment existing arrangements that allow the ADF to access commercial and US military systems.

CHINA

In 2019, China's Central Military Commission and People's Liberation Army (PLA) remained focused on reaching the goal of achieving mechanisation of the PLA's ground forces by 2020, improving 'informatisation', and working towards achieving the 2035 goal of armed-forces modernisation and dominant regional power-projection capabilities. The 1 October 2019 parade marking the 70th anniversary of the founding of the People's Republic reflected the breadth of China's defence modernisation, with particular attention paid to new additions to China's missile, uninhabited-aerial-vehicle (UAV) and hypersonic capabilities. Apart from hardware, the parade also seemed to reflect the organisational and doctrinal shifts in the PLA. The inclusion of personnel from all branches in the Strategic Support Force (SSF) and Joint Logistics Support Force sections of the parade, for example, sought to highlight China's progress towards joint operational capability across services. Meanwhile, the presence of officers and scientists from the National Defense University, University of Defense Technology and Academy of Military Sciences highlighted China's focus on civil–military integration.

The PLA continues its efforts to improve combat capabilities under realistic training conditions. The navy and air force were particularly active in 2019, though the PLA Rocket Force and SSF also conducted drills. The PLA Army conducted the *Firepower*-2019 exercise in Inner Mongolia, while the PLA Navy (PLAN) conducted multiple exercises in the East and South China seas, as well as near Taiwan. The PLA Rocket Force practised its ability to withstand an attack and launch a counter-strike. The SSF remains little discussed publicly, though reports point to it having also participated in joint-operations exercises and drills. The navy has been active in joint exercises in the East China Sea and around Taiwan through 2019, timing these 'routine drills' with political developments in the region. On 15 April, the day before Taiwan and the United States marked the 40th anniversary of the Taiwan Relations Act with a high-level forum in Taipei, the PLA held 'necessary drills' with warships, bombers and reconnaissance aircraft around the island. The PLA Air Force (PLAAF) has focused on continuing to develop offensive and defensive air and space integration. Chinese media reports points to the PLAAF's 'circle of friends' growing larger, with joint exercises with the air forces of Brazil and Russia in 2019. In 2019, Beijing also acknowledged for the first time the existence of theatre-level joint exercises, code-named North, East, South and West. A possible example is the July 2019 exercise involving all five service branches off China's southeast coast, although there was no official confirmation of this.

China's latest defence white paper, released in July 2019, constituted a progress report on PLA reforms, with attention given to the specific strengths and weaknesses of each service branch. Though the PLA is making progress across the board, the white paper notes that mechanisation and informatisation were behind schedule – in contrast to President Xi Jinping's statement in 2017 at the Army Day Parade when he announced that the PLA had already achieved mechanisation and made rapid progress towards informatisation. The 2019 white paper is likely to be more accurate in its description, and it signals that the 2020 goal of achieving mechanisation and making significant progress towards informatisation may not be met. Beijing's definition of these two goals remains unclear.

However, a breakdown of defence expenditure was provided for the first time since the 2010 white paper. The new detail, and the framing of China's defence modernisation and military spending as

PLA Eastern Theatre Command

The Eastern Theatre Command is almost entirely based on units and assets from the old Nanjing Military Region, although one or two units were exchanged with other theatre commands, and it retains the same geographic areas of responsibility and missions.

Army

The Eastern Theatre Army comprises three Group Armies: the 71st, 72nd and 73rd.

The 71st is based in Anhui and Northern Jiangsu provinces and is primarily an armoured formation; four of its six combined-arms brigades are 'heavy' formations, with tracked armoured fighting vehicles and artillery, with the remainder comprising one medium and one light brigade. It still has a relatively high proportion of older armoured vehicles and artillery pieces in its brigades (vehicles that entered service before 2000), but the medium-weight brigade has been re-equipped with the latest ZBL-08 family of armoured vehicles.

The 72nd and 73rd Group Armies have a common structure aimed at cross-strait amphibious taskings, each with two amphibious-assault brigades and two light, one medium and one heavy combined-arms brigade. The 72nd is based in Shanghai, Zhejiang and southern Jiangsu provinces, with the 73rd stationed opposite Taiwan in Fujian province. These two armies are earmarked to comprise the initial waves in any Taiwan contingency operations and have a higher proportion of modern equipment compared to the 71st Group Army, although much of it nonetheless predates the latest PLA re-organisation, which began in 2015.

The 74th Group Army, the PLA's third amphibious army, remains assigned to the Southern Theatre Command, although it can be presumed that in the event of an amphibious operation against Taiwan, it would come under the control of the Eastern Theatre Army headquarters.

Navy

The Eastern Theatre Navy is mostly home-ported around Shanghai and the estuaries of the Qiantang and Yangtze rivers in Hangzhou Bay. Of the two assigned diesel-electric submarine flotillas, one (the 22nd) is completely equipped with the latest indigenous Type-039A design (*Yuan* class), while the other (the 42nd) is equipped with the *Kilo*-/Improved *Kilo*-class submarines acquired from Russia in the 1990s. Like the *Kilo*s, the Russian-origin *Sovremenny*-class destroyers assigned to the 3rd Destroyer Flotilla were once considered the most advanced platforms in the PLA Navy, but are now undergoing refits with modern Chinese anti-ship and surface-to-air missiles to bring them up to the standard of the indigenous modern Type-052C/D (*Luyang* II/III-class) destroyers and Type-054A (*Jiangkai* II-class) frigates that now equip the rest of the 3rd and 6th destroyer flotillas based at Dinghai.

These formations are supported by four littoral frigate flotillas, equipped with a mix of legacy frigates and new Type-056/056A (*Jiangdao* I/II-class) corvettes, two mine-warfare flotillas, two fast-attack squadrons with Type-022 (*Houbei*-class) missile boats, an amphibious-landing-ship flotilla based at Shanghai and a large support flotilla at Dinghai.

The 4th and 6th naval-aviation divisions that existed in the Eastern Theatre Command before 2017 have both been disbanded and their assigned regiments consolidated into two new large brigades: one with Su-30MK2 and J-10A fighter aircraft and the other with JH-7 maritime-attack aircraft. A new division (the 1st) has been activated to command the KQ-200 anti-submarine

'reasonable and appropriate', signals an attempt by the Chinese Communist Party to quell external criticism of China's military build-up. While the 2019 white paper compares China's defence spending to that of other countries, to highlight that it represents a relatively small percentage of GDP, it is also presented in a domestic context alongside the budgets of the other government ministries with which the PLA competes for resources.

The white paper emphasises increasing instability in various geographical regions. It portrays China as the architect of, contributor to and mediator within the 'community with a shared future for mankind' in the 'new era'. The US-led alliance structure in the Asia-Pacific is considered outdated and ill-suited. Although the white paper considers the regional security situation 'generally stable', it suggests that Asia-Pacific states have become 'increasingly aware' that they are part of this regional community of shared destiny. Bilateral negotiations between the Association of Southeast Asian Nations and China over a code of conduct for the South China Sea would likely be Beijing's preferred model for any such 'regional' security architecture.

Nevertheless, for the moment the regional security architecture is unlikely to expand to include new aircraft that had been delivered to the navy by 2018. It is not yet clear whether the existing independent bomber and helicopter regiments have also been reassigned to this division or have retained their independent status.

The two newly reassigned brigades of the Eastern Theatre Command Marine Corps – the 3rd and 4th – appear to still be working up and continue to lack significant amphibious-assault equipment. Previously they were both Coastal Defence units in the PLA Army.

Air Force
The Eastern Theatre Command Air Force (TCAF) can now muster 13 fighter/ground-attack brigades, organisationally split on geographical lines between two deputy-corps-leader grade organisations designated Shanghai and Fuzhou Bases. Each now also has responsibility for two long-range surface-to-air missile brigades, mostly equipped with Russian-origin S-300PMU1/PMU2 systems. These are supported by the 10th Bomber Division, with three regiments operating multiple variants of the H-6 bomber and the airborne early-warning aircraft of the 26th Special Mission Division, all based to the west of Shanghai. There are also independent tactical reconnaissance and search-and-rescue formations attached to the TCAF HQ.

The majority of these units are based in the north of the Eastern Theatre Command; opposite Taiwan, the People's Liberation Army Air Force (PLAAF) maintains a number of forward-operating bases, ordinarily occupied by units temporarily deployed on rotation. This allows the PLAAF to maintain regular air operations over the Taiwan Strait and East China Sea while minimising its exposure to Taiwan's counter-force capabilities, including long-range ground- and air-launched cruise missiles, in the event of hostilities.

Already relatively well equipped prior to the latest reorganisation, the Eastern TCAF has recently been given higher priority in receiving the PLAAF's most advanced tactical aircraft. Two brigades, the 7th and 40th, have now received the advanced Shenyang J-16 multi-role aircraft, the PLAAF's latest iteration of the Russian *Flanker* airframe, while in 2019 the 9th Brigade at Wuhu was the first front-line combat brigade to take delivery of the new low-observable Chengdu J-20A design. This reflects the PLA's belief that airpower will be a key factor in maritime or amphibious operations across the Taiwan Strait and elsewhere in the South China Sea.

Rocket Force
The PLA Rocket Force is not officially part of the Theatre Command structure. Nonetheless, the Rocket Force's 61 Base is almost entirely located within the Eastern Theatre Command's geographical area of responsibility and, given that it commands the majority of the PLA's conventional short- and medium-range ballistic-missile forces, is assessed to have a close working relationship, at the very least, with the Theatre Command HQ. Of the seven missile brigades under the command of 61 Base, two are equipped with road-mobile nuclear DF-21A (CH-SS-5 mod 2) medium-range ballistic missiles and may be in the process of receiving an upgraded version of the same missile (CH-SS-5 mod 6). Three brigades still operate a mix of road-mobile DF-11A (CH-SS-7 mod 2), DF-15B (CH-SS-6 mod 3) and DF-16 (CH-SS-11 mod 1 and 2) shorter-range conventional missiles, while the final two are now believed to have converted to the new DF-17 conventional medium-range ballistic-missile/hypersonic glide vehicle system first displayed publicly in 2019. In the event of military conflict with Taiwan, these forces would be supplemented by additional theatre ballistic and cruise missiles drawn from the Rocket Force's adjoining 62 Base and 63 Base missile brigades, which are mostly deployed in the Southern Theatre Command, to the south and west of 61 Base.

arms-control regimes. Following the dissolution of the Intermediate-range Nuclear Forces (INF) Treaty between Russia and the United States, the US indicated any new arms-control treaty could usefully expand beyond the original two signatories and include China as well. However, Beijing has made it clear that INF and post-INF Treaty arms-control issues should be resolved first between Russia and the US. While China is concerned about the consequences of potential US deployment of intermediate-range missiles in the Asia-Pacific, in the wake of the INF Treaty, China's missile development has generally been in line with 'China's national defense policies' (for instance, a large number of its missile systems are based within range of Taiwan) and Beijing has stated that it will 'in no way agree to making the INF Treaty multilateral'.

While mentioning a range of challenges, the 2019 white paper reaffirms that the status of Taiwan remains one of China's main national-security concerns. In his New Year address for 2019, President Xi emphasised that resolving the Taiwan question and completing reunification was a historic task and could not be stopped. 'One country, two systems' and peaceful reunification were the best paths to China's national reunification, Xi said, though he made 'no promise to renounce the use of force' and reserved 'the option of taking all necessary means'. This sentiment was echoed in Defense Minister Wei Fenghe's speech at the 2019 IISS Shangri-La Dialogue. Despite numerous military exercises and live-fire drills in the Taiwan Strait and off Taiwan's east coast throughout 2019, Beijing faces a difficult choice. As President Tsai Ing-wen gears up for the 2020 presidential election in Taiwan, China's military drills and political unrest in Hong Kong are reinforcing narratives that reunification is not in Taiwan's interest. Indeed, in response to Xi's speech on Taiwan, both the Democratic Progressive Party and Kuomintang have stated that one country, two systems is no longer a viable option.

PLA Army

The process of re-equipping the PLA Army continues, with a focus on the objectives of completing basic mechanisation and improving informatisation by 2020. Legacy equipment, such as the ZTZ-59 tank and PL-59 howitzer, is now being cycled out of front-line units, although it is unlikely that all of it will be replaced by the 2020 target date. Additional heavy combined-arms brigades in the Central and Northern theatre commands are now finally receiving the long-awaited ZTZ-99A main battle tank. However, the Eastern and Southern theatre commands will likely continue to operate lighter tank designs – primarily the ZTZ-96A and ZTQ-15 – because of the terrain in those areas. The Central Theatre Command's 161st Air Assault Brigade has begun taking delivery of the Z-20 medium transport helicopter – an indigenous version of the US *Black Hawk* design.

The army's *Stride* series of exercises for its combined-arms brigades continues, albeit not at a fast pace, with only one exercise at Zhurihe (for heavy brigades) and two at Queshan (for medium and light brigades) completed by September 2019; these all involved Central Theatre Command formations as the 'Red Force' (friendly) under evaluation. Following the PLA's participation in Russia's *Vostok*-2018 exercise, China once again sent a relatively small contingent of 1,600 personnel to participate in Russia's *Tsentr*-2019 exercise in September, primarily drawing on a heavy combined-arms battlegroup and aviation detachment from the Western Theatre Command's 76th Group Army.

PLA Rocket Force

New missile systems were publicly unveiled in October at the parade marking the 70th anniversary of the People's Republic of China. This underscored the PLA Rocket Force's continuing expansion and highlighted priority areas of capability development. The DF-41 (CH-SS-20) road-mobile intercontinental ballistic missile (ICBM), like the existing DF-5B and DF-31A(G) ICBM variants, is believed to have the capacity to carry either multiple warheads or a single warhead and multiple jammers, penetration aids and decoys. The parade also featured two new high-speed conventional systems: the DF-17 medium-range ballistic missile and hypersonic glide vehicle, and the CJ-100 cruise missile. This emphasis on additional capacity and higher speed for nuclear and conventional systems respectively reflects the Rocket Force's approach to retaining credible capabilities in light of the improving missile defences of potential adversaries.

While the DF-17 was described at the parade as a purely conventional system, media reports in 2019 quoting unnamed officials at the China Aerospace and Industry Corporation suggested that in future the system may have both nuclear and conventional payload variants, much like the DF-26 intermediate-range ballistic missile before it.

The DF-41, DF-17 and CJ-100 are all now believed to have officially entered PLA service with Rocket Force brigades. However, there is traditionally a lag between a system's official entry into PLA service and the declaration of initial operating capability, and it is unclear if any of these new systems have reached that stage.

PLA Navy

The PLAN continues to make significant strides in filling the gaps in its capabilities in order to operate as a blue-water navy. In 2019, these included the public debut of the first Type-055 (*Renhai*-class) cruiser at the navy's 70th-anniversary fleet review in April. In September, China launched the fifth of eight Type-055s that are either currently under construction or already complete.

Another important milestone in the development of the PLAN's power-projection capability was the launch in September of the first Type-075 landing helicopter dock (LHD) large amphibious-assault ship. Another Type-075 is under construction and it is thought that at least one more is planned; the ships are estimated at around 30,000 tonnes full-load displacement. Meanwhile, the sixth Type-071 (*Yuzhao*-class) landing platform dock entered service in January, with at least two more under construction.

Beyond the Type-055, China's output of surface combatants remains striking, with the 19th and 20th Type-052D (*Luyang* III-class) destroyers launched in May and a 63rd Type-056/056A (*Jiangdao* I/II-class) corvette later in August. Meanwhile, the PLAN also retired a number of older destroyers and frigates. The PLAN's focus so far seems to have been more on raising the capability levels of its platforms rather than just boosting inventory numbers.

In this context, speculation continues regarding China's aircraft-carrier ambitions. In some respects, progress remains cautious – for example, in the relatively modest operations so far of the first carrier, the *Liaoning* (RUS *Kuznetsov* class), and the extended initial sea trials of the second, as-yet unnamed ship (RUS *Kuznetsov* mod). A third, larger vessel is under construction. China may still be struggling with the challenge of creating an effective carrier capability, and so there is uncertainty over when the PLAN might be able to achieve a step change in capability, particularly in terms of long-range carrier deployments or integrated task-group operations. Similarly, bringing the complex Type-075 LHD into full operational service may take some time. A second Type-901 (*Fuyu*-class) fast large under way replenishment vessel, perhaps intended to accompany the carriers, entered service in February. However, the PLAN will need more such vessels if China maintains ambitions to deploy a truly global multi-carrier capability in the future.

While China's defence minister gave a forthright speech at the IISS Shangri-La Dialogue in June 2019, blaming tensions in the South China Sea on 'foreign' naval deployments, China's own naval activities in the region appeared more assertive and in July it reportedly carried out a drill that included what appeared to be a first salvo-launch of anti-ship ballistic missiles in the South China Sea.

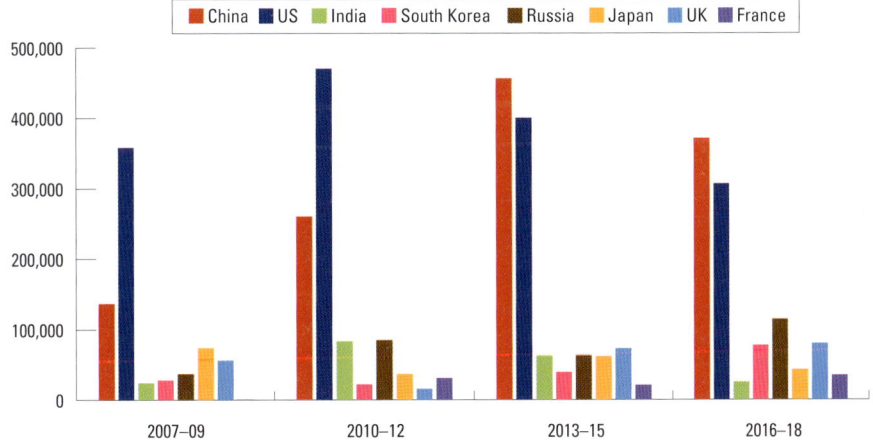

▼ Figure 17 **China and selected states: domestically built naval vessels launched between 2007–18**

Figure 18 PLAN Type-055 *Renhai*-class cruiser

Filling a major gap in People's Liberation Army Navy (PLAN) capabilities, the Type-055 may be the most capable multi-role surface combatant currently at sea. At least eight have been completed or are under construction, with the first accepted into PLAN service in 2019. Although in some ways little more than a significantly enlarged development of the Type-052D destroyer, it will, assuming the PLAN is able to realise the potential capability it offers, represent a step change in PLAN abilities to mount independent long-range deployments or task-group operations, with the additional space needed for flagship facilities and the ability to operate as a command ship for air-defence or strike missions. The design also has the size and space needed to accept new weapons systems and the power generation needed to support them. The Type-055 has few direct equivalents, with the closest rivals in the cruiser class operating in the Japanese, South Korean, Russian and United States navies.

- Capacity for up to two Z-18 anti-submarine-warfare helicopters
- Equipped with bow, variable-depth and towed-array sonars
- All gas-turbine propulsion, plus significant electrical-generator capacity
- Later versions are likely to have an integrated electrical power system for higher/more flexible output to power future systems
- Twenty-four-cell HHQ-10 missile launcher for close-in defence
- Possible future replacement by directed-energy system
- Further development of the Type-346 *Dragon Eye* phased-array radar
- Integrated mast with additional sensors for improved radar coverage
- H/PJ-38 130 mm main gun
- Possibly to be replaced in later ships with a rail gun for significantly enhanced capability

Type-055 missile fit

The Type-055 cruiser will share many of the same missile systems as the Type-052D destroyer. The principal difference is that it will have a magazine of 112 vertical-launch-system (VLS) cells – 64 forward and 48 aft, as opposed to 64 on the Type-052D. The Chinese VLS system is larger and potentially more flexible than the United States' standard Mk.41 launchers. Weapons may include the HHQ-9 extended-range missile for area air and missile defence, the YJ-18A long-range anti-ship cruise missile and the Yu-8 anti-submarine missile. Potential or future capabilities also include ballistic-missile defence and land-attack cruise missiles. The US Department of Defense has also speculated about whether the type could carry a ship-launched anti-ship ballistic missile, possibly including a hypersonic glide vehicle. For short-range air defence, the Type-055 is equipped with a 24-cell launcher for HHQ-10 missiles, with a maximum range of approximately 10 kilometres.

HHQ-9 extended-range air-defence missile
150km

YJ-18A anti-ship missile
540km

Type-055 and selected US Navy platforms

US Arleigh Burke-class Flight III destroyer (in production)
9,800 tonnes FLD; length 156 metres; 96 VLS cells
Possible interim *Ticonderoga* successor

US Zumwalt class (first of class commissioned in 2016)
16,000 tonnes FLD; length 190 metres; 80 VLS cells
More radical stealth design than the Type-055 but with a different role. May provide the basis for a future Type-055 rival

PLAN Type-055 *Renhai*-class cruiser
Approx. 13,000 tonnes FLD; length c.180 metres; 112 VLS cells

US *Ticonderoga*-class cruiser (in service since 1983)
10,100 tonnes FLD; length 173 metres; 122 VLS cells
This benchmark high-capability cruiser has received multiple updates but is now ageing and in need of replacement

Cruiser inventories, 2019: Japan, Russia and South Korea

Country	Class	Number in service	Number planned	First of class in service	*Full-load displacement (tonnes)	Length overall (metres)	Vertical-launch cells
Japan	Atago	2	2	2007	10,160	165	96
	Maya	0	2	2020	10,250	170	96
Russia	Orlan	2	2	1980	26,300	250	116
	Atlant	3	3	1982	11,200	186	64
South Korea	Sejong	3	6	2008	10,600	166	80 (+48)

Meanwhile, two tests were reported of the navy's new JL-3 submarine-launched ballistic missile, which is intended for its next-generation ballistic-missile submarines – these may be the Type-096. This combination has the potential to provide Beijing with significantly longer-range submarine-based ballistic-missile capability sometime in the next decade.

At the same time, there continues to be increased focus on Chinese 'hybrid' or 'grey zone' activities, highlighted by the tensions raised by Beijing's deployment into Vietnam's exclusive economic zone of a survey vessel with coastguard escort. Increasing attention has been paid to the maritime militia, which is based chiefly on large numbers of supposed fishing vessels. The latest US Defense Intelligence Agency (DIA) 'China Military Power' report stated that the PLAN, the coastguard and the maritime militia are increasingly visible throughout the region.

PLA Air Force

It is known that China has been developing a next-generation 'strategic' bomber, but the US DIA in 2019 also suggested that a 'tactical bomber' in the same class was part of the PLAAF's acquisition programme. The 'China Military Power' report characterised the latter project as a 'fighter-bomber', capable of carrying long-range air-to-air missiles (AAMs).

New air systems displayed during China's 70th-anniversary parade included the WZ-8 high-speed reconnaissance UAV and the GJ-11 uninhabited combat air vehicle. A new variant of the Xian H-6 bomber, the H-6N, was shown for the first time. This airframe was observed with a large under-belly recess, although the anti-ship ballistic missile that some analysts contend may be associated with this new variant was not displayed.

Meanwhile, the successor to the H-6 series, likely to be designated the H-20, is anticipated by the US Department of Defense to enter PLAAF service around the middle of the next decade. Some reports suggest the H-20 is a low-observable flying-wing design. While senior Chinese officials have confirmed that a new bomber is in development, at the time of writing there has been no similar comment regarding a tactical bomber.

The tactical bomber's association with a long-range AAM may be an allusion to the PLAAF's PL-17 very-long-range dual-mode AAM, now in development. This missile is likely fitted with an active electronically scanned-array radar and an imaging-infrared adjunct seeker. The PL-17 appears to be aimed at countering high-value low-density targets, such as tankers, but also airborne early-warning and control, as well as intelligence, surveillance and reconnaissance, aircraft. The PL-17, and a rocket-ramjet-powered AAM possibly known as the PL-21, could enter service in the early years of the next decade.

The first operational Chengdu J-20A fighter/ground-attack aircraft PLAAF unit was formed in 2019, and production of the type is likely to increase over the next few years as more units are re-equipped with it. At the same time, the Shenyang J-31 multi-role combat-aircraft project continues, but at a slower pace than that of the J-20A.

DEFENCE ECONOMICS

The year 2020 is an important milestone in the development of China's defence economy and military system. It should mark the end of the first stage of the three-step long-term military-development strategy that President Xi Jinping outlined at the 19th Party Congress in 2017, and which is central to his efforts to turn China into a world-class military power. The primary goal in this initial phase is to achieve 'mechanisation' and advance significantly towards 'informatisation' and greatly improved strategic capabilities'.

This objective was made clear at the 70th National Day military parade in October 2019 with the unveiling of platforms including the DF-41 intercontinental ballistic missile, the DF-17 hypersonic glide vehicle, the WZ-8 high-speed-reconnaissance uninhabited aerial vehicle and the HSU001 uninhabited underwater vehicle.

The 2019 defence white paper suggested that as well as preparing for 'informatised' wars, the era of 'intelligentised' warfare (the military application of artificial intelligence (AI)/machine learning to warfighting) is now 'on the horizon'. Both the People's Liberation Army and non-military government agencies are investing heavily in the development of AI and machine-learning capabilities.

Five-Year Plan

Meanwhile, a host of critical programmes that relate to military modernisation, technological development and the structural reform of China's defence industry are now due for renewal. Many of them fall under the rubric of the 2016–20 13th Five-Year Plan (FYP).

One of the most important is the 13th Five-Year Defense Science-and-Technology (S&T) Plan. Its key priorities include the promotion of civil–military integration (also termed civil–military fusion); major structural reforms of the defence-industrial base, especially consolidating state-owned monopoly firms; bringing into production new generations of advanced weaponry; increasing arms exports and international cooperation; and upgrading the defence-industrial engineering and manufacturing system. The 2019 defence white paper highlighted several key weapons programmes that have been commissioned so far during this current five-year plan, including Type-15 main battle tanks, Type-052D destroyers, J-20 combat aircraft and DF-26 intermediate-range ballistic missiles.

China's military authorities are pushing the defence-industrial base and PLA to meet defence-related targets for the 13th FYP and provide added momentum going into the 14th FYP, which starts in 2021. At the annual meeting of the National People's Congress in March 2019, Xi noted this was 'a crucial year for implementing the development and construction of our military's 13th FYP to achieve the 2020 targets for national defence and army building'.

The 13th Five-Year Special Plan for Science and Technology Military–Civil Fusion is another important defence-related programme. This plan is overseen by the Science and Technology Commission under the Central Military Commission and the Ministry of Science and Technology. Though it only began in 2017, civil–military integration is one of Xi's highest priorities. The plan's main goals include creating an integrated research and development system to undertake advanced work in AI, bio-engineering, quantum technology, advanced manufacturing, new composite materials and other newly emerging areas in order to 'capture the commanding heights of international competition'. Beijing has said that by 2020 a transitional development phase in civil–military integration will be 'basically' complete; a phase of 'deep integration' will then begin.

The 2006–20 Medium and Long-Term Defense Science and Technology Development Plan is a longer-term mechanism intended to address the reform and development of the defence-innovation ecosystem. This includes building a more robust system for basic and applied research and establishing a more sophisticated governance system in order to create incentives for domestic high-end innovation. There is a parallel national medium- and long-term S&T development plan, which will be replaced with a new version for 2021–35. There are no indications as to whether there will be a replacement long-range defence S&T plan.

Financial resources

Securing access to adequate funding is one of the biggest challenges for China's defence S&T system as it looks to maintain its momentum and promote indigenisation across a growing range of technological domains. State allocations for defence S&T spending continue to increase robustly, although growth rates have gradually decreased as economic growth has slowed. The official 2019 defence budget, including funding for local militias, is RMB1.22 trillion (US$181 billion), an 8.4% increase in local currency in comparison with 2018, and accounts for 1.28% of GDP. The 2019 central S&T budget is RMB354.3bn (US$52.5bn), a 13.4% increase in local currency compared with 2018 (RMB312.5bn, or US$47.2bn).

Beijing's ability to ensure sufficient funding for the defence sector will be increasingly challenged if economic growth continues to decelerate. To mitigate this trend, the defence-industrial base is being encouraged to make more use of the capital markets. A key initiative is the use of asset-securitisation deals, in which funds are raised by defence firms to support weapons projects through special-purpose vehicles. This initiative began in 2013 and the average asset-securitisation rate among the country's major defence-industrial conglomerates reached 33% in 2018, although Aviation Industry Corporation of China leads the way with a 60% ratio.

Great-power competition and cooperation

Intensifying US efforts to clamp down on economic, technological and knowledge flows to China – based on a widening interpretation of US national-security considerations – are another obstacle to the long-term development of China's defence and strategic capabilities. This was underscored in 2019 by US efforts to isolate Huawei by excluding the firm from access to US markets or technology. US export-, investment-, and academic-exchange controls have also been significantly tightened. In response, Chinese leaders have urged the country's S&T establishment to step up their efforts to develop indigenous technological capabilities, particularly in emerging core areas such as AI, semiconductors and 5G.

The defence white paper makes clear that China is in long-term military-technological competition with the US and that 'the PLA still lags far behind the world's leading militaries'. The white paper warns that the Chinese armed forces need to make 'greater efforts to invest in military modernization to meet national demands' and are at risk of being surprised by technological developments elsewhere and a widening generational gap in technologies.

As Sino-US military-technological competition intensifies, Beijing and Moscow are forging closer defence-technological cooperation. China is reportedly examining whether to purchase another 24 Su-35 combat aircraft to complement those it has already received. Russian arms-export officials have also been keen to market the export version of the Su-57 fifth-generation combat aircraft to the PLA Air Force, although there are no indications that a deal is close.

China's defence-industrial base

The restructuring of China's defence-industrial apparatus made steady progress in 2019. The main development was the consolidation of the shipbuilding sector, which had been adversely affected by the downturn in the global shipbuilding market. China State Shipbuilding Corporation and China Shipbuilding Industry Corporation (CSIC) announced their merger in July 2019. CSIC had been China's only loss-making defence-industrial firm, showing that a flourishing naval shipbuilding programme could not offset weaknesses in its commercial operations. Only the ordnance, space and missile sectors have not yet been consolidated.

Despite problems in the shipbuilding sector, China's defence industry is in good health overall. Revenue for the ten leading defence corporations totalled RMB2.39trn (US$362bn) in 2018, compared to RMB2.31trn (US$342bn) in 2017.

However, there are emerging signs that China's defence industry, especially its commercial operations, is also being affected by the country's economic slowdown. One of the firms hardest hit is China South Industries Group, which saw its revenue almost halve between 2016 (US$71.2bn) and 2018 (US$38.5bn) because of weaknesses in its vehicle and power-transmission operations.

JAPAN

On 18 December 2018, Prime Minister Shinzo Abe's cabinet approved the revised National Defense Program Guidelines (NDPG) and Medium-Term Defense Program (MTDP) for 2019–23. Previously revised under Abe in 2013, these documents outline Japan's defence doctrine and the necessary force structure of the Japan Self-Defense Forces (JSDF).

The latest revision of the NDPG took place against the background of North Korea's ongoing development of its nuclear and missile programmes, China's continuing military modernisation and Sino-Japanese tensions in the East China Sea. Moreover, in the face of the Trump administration's approach to alliance relations, Japan has felt obliged to demonstrate yet greater commitment to supporting the United States' military presence in the region. There have also been more purchases of US defence equipment.

The NDPG is notable for its emphasis on the development of a 'multidimensional joint defence force'. Previous iterations had designated the JSDF as first a 'dynamic' and then a 'joint dynamic' force. The latest NDPG stresses the need for 'cross-domain' JSDF operations not only in the land, sea and air domains but also in space and in the electromagnetic spectrum, including cyber operations and electronic warfare.

Equipment developments

The MTDP highlighted Japan's decision to procure from the US an additional 63 F-35A combat aircraft for the Japan Air Self-Defense Force (JASDF) and, for the first time, 42 F-35Bs for the Japan Maritime Self-Defense Force (JMSDF). Tokyo is looking to acquire 147 F-35s in total, making it the second-largest operator of the aircraft after the US. The MTDP also provides for the JASDF's procurement of long-range air-to-surface stand-off missiles to assist in defending offshore islands.

The MTDP emphasised Japan's determination to defend its airspace, with plans to replace its Mitsubishi F-2s with a new fighter that would 'play a central role' in future networked warfare. Japan has been developing the X-2 *Shinshin* Advanced Technology Demonstrator, an experimental fighter with signature management characteristics. Analysts understand that Japan will transfer lessons from the X-2 project into the development an F-3 sixth-generation twin-engine stealth fighter, with significant international technological and cost sharing. The F-3 may utilise the XF-9 engine developed by IHI, reported to be capable of generating sufficient power for directed-energy weapons. Tokyo has reportedly been in discussions with Lockheed Martin about a possible sixth-generation fighter design and with BAE Systems about collaboration in the United Kingdom's

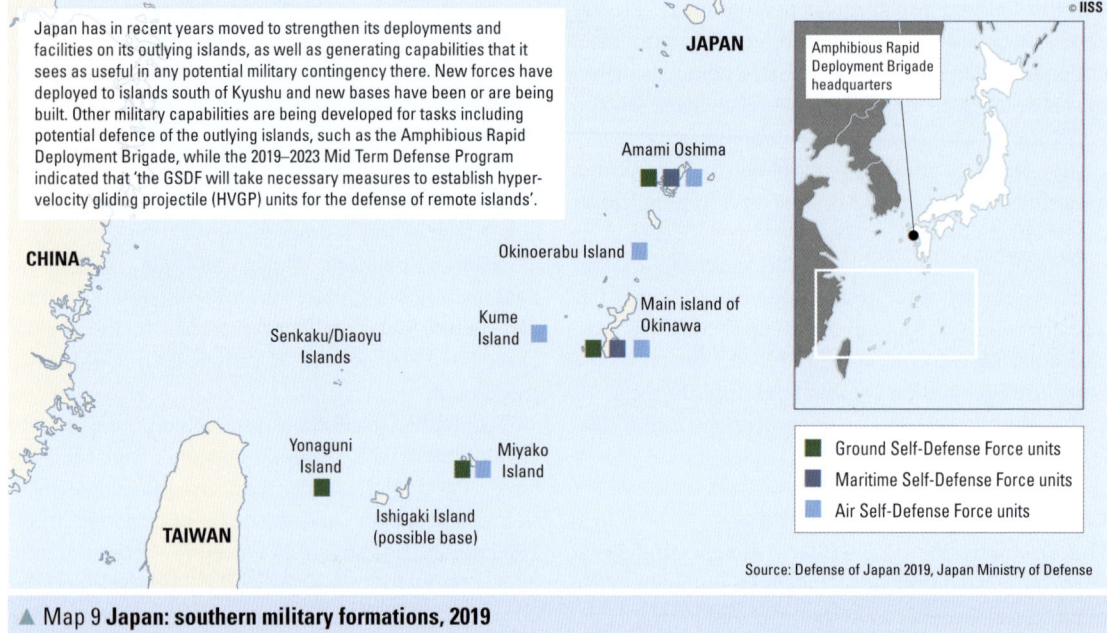

▲ Map 9 **Japan: southern military formations, 2019**

Tempest future-fighter project. In its FY2019 budget the defence ministry also included funds for research into scramjets for a hypersonic cruise missile, along with funds for research on a 'hyper-velocity gliding projectile'.

Meanwhile, the JMSDF is proceeding with plans to modify its two *Izumo*-class helicopter carriers to enable them to operate F-35B aircraft. These 'multi-functional destroyers', as they are termed by the JMSDF, will allow considerable power-projection capabilities.

The JSDF plans to improve cross-domain operations by constructing an integrated air- and missile-defence system that will bring together the JMSDF's and JASDF's respective sea-based *Aegis* and land-based *Patriot* ballistic-missile-defence systems, as well as satellites and early-warning systems and the *Aegis* Ashore system due to be procured from the US by 2023.

Force developments

Under the NDPG and MTDP, the Japan Ground Self-Defense Force is continuing to develop its Amphibious Rapid Deployment Brigade (ARDB). The ARDB conducted exercises with the US Marine Corps in northern Australia in July 2019.

By 2022 the defence ministry also plans to establish a Space Domain Mission Unit to improve space situational awareness. The new unit is intended to monitor satellites and space debris in order to ensure that JSDF communications, intelligence and navigation – and thereby joint operability – are not jeopardised. The revised 2015 US–Japan Defense Guidelines include the pledge that Japan will assist the US in preserving the continuity of its space operations. The Japanese Ministry of Defense's Cyber Defence Unit will continue its work on defending against distributed-denial-of-service attacks and is to examine how possible retaliatory attacks may fit within Japan's 'exclusively defence-oriented posture'.

Defence economics and regional diplomacy

In order to implement its MTDP plans, Tokyo would have to increase its defence budget to around ¥27 trillion (US$250 billion) for the current MTDP period, up from ¥25trn (US$231bn). The defence ministry hopes to control costs through improved equipment-procurement processes. However, Japan's defence-budget planning may be challenged in the coming year by Washington's demands for increased host-nation support, despite Tokyo already providing around three-quarters of the costs of US bases in Japan.

In addition to building up the JSDF's own defence capabilities, the NDPG seeks to improve Japan's security environment through cooperation with neighbouring states. In line with its 2016 Vientiane

▼ Figure 19 **Type-16 Mobile Combat Vehicle**

The Type-16 Mobile Combat Vehicle (MCV) is an 8×8 armoured vehicle intended to provide direct fire support for the Japan Ground Self-Defense Force's (JGSDF's) new rapid-reaction units. It is broadly similar to the United States' M1128 *Stryker* Mobile Gun System and the Chinese ZTL-11, as well as older European designs such as the French AMX-10RC and Italian *Centauro*. The Type-16 is replacing the ageing Type-74 main battle tanks as part of the Dynamic Joint Defense Force concept, as the JGSDF restructures to become more mobile and responsive. It is sized to be air-portable in the Japan Air Self-Defense Force's new Kawasaki C-2 heavy transport aircraft, allowing equipped units to be quickly redeployed around Japan, including to outlying islands. Development work on the design began in 2007, and the first unit deliveries occurred in 2017.

Design: Technical Research and Development Institute
Prime contractor: Mitsubishi Heavy Industries

Crew:	4 (commander, driver, gunner, loader)
Length:	8.45 m
Width:	2.98 m
Height:	2.87 m
Combat Weight:	<26 tonnes
Armament:	52-calibre 105 mm low-recoil main gun and co-axial 7.62 mm machine gun; 12.7 mm machine gun on cupola
Top speed:	100 km/h (on road)

Procurement

- Orders / Deliveries
- 2016: 36 / 0
- 2017: 33 / 33
- 2018: 18 / 36
- 2019: 29 / 15+

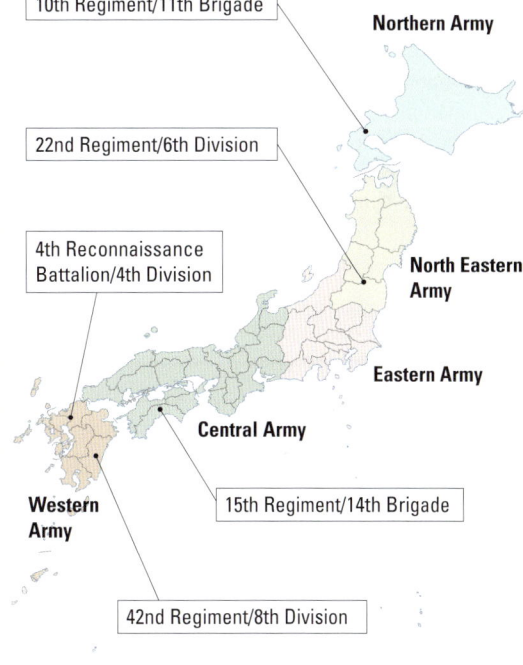

Type-16 MCV unit deployments

- 10th Regiment/11th Brigade — Northern Army
- 22nd Regiment/6th Division — North Eastern Army
- 4th Reconnaissance Battalion/4th Division — Eastern Army
- 15th Regiment/14th Brigade — Central Army
- 42nd Regiment/8th Division — Western Army

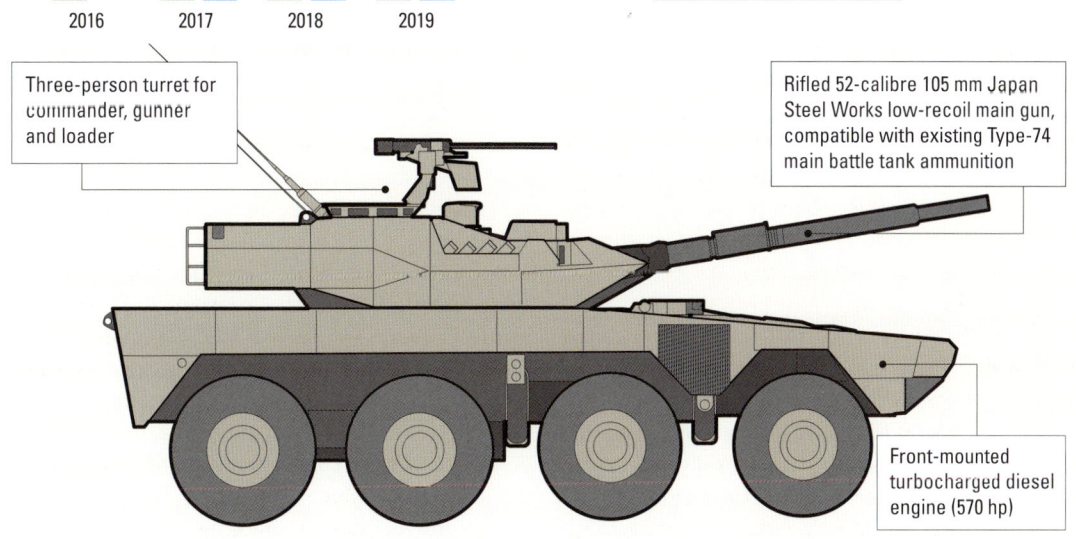

- Three-person turret for commander, gunner and loader
- Rifled 52-calibre 105 mm Japan Steel Works low-recoil main gun, compatible with existing Type-74 main battle tank ammunition
- Front-mounted turbocharged diesel engine (570 hp)

© IISS

Japan: ground-force modernisation

The 2013 Dynamic Joint Defense Force concept aims to restructure the Japan Ground Self-Defense Force (JGSDF) from a relatively static and regionally based territorial-defence force into an integrated and mobile force more suited to the country's evolving defence requirements. In addition to establishing a dedicated amphibious force within the JGSDF, the plan called for the conversion of existing infantry divisions and brigades into new 'mobile' formations.

These mobile units would reduce their artillery holdings and replace their ageing Type-74 main battle tanks with new Type-16 8×8 mobile combat vehicles. The latter combines a locally manufactured 105 mm low-recoil main gun with a new wheeled chassis, suitable for rapid mobility on roads and also sized for transport in the Japan Air Self-Defense Force's new Kawasaki C2 heavy transport aircraft and by amphibious shipping. The Type-16 is intended to allow JGSDF units to redeploy faster than before, both within Japan's main islands and in response to threats to remote or outlying territory.

The 2014 Medium-Term Defense Plan (MTDP) funded the initial conversion of two divisions and two brigades. Initial series production of the Type-16 began in 2016, and in 2018 the 8th Division (Western Army) and 14th Brigade (Central Army) both converted one of their infantry regiments into new mechanised 'quick reaction' regiments. Each of these battalion-sized organisations combine a single company equipped with the new Type-16 and mechanised infantry companies equipped with the existing Type-96 wheeled armoured personnel carrier. In 2019, the 6th Division (Northwestern Army) and 11th Brigade (Northern Army) both underwent a similar conversion process.

Under the 2019 MTDP, three more formations are also scheduled to convert to a similar formation within the next five years: the 2nd Division and 5th Brigade (Northern Army), and the 12th Brigade (Eastern Army). This will bring the total number of mobile formations to seven – three divisions and four brigades.

Vision, Japan has continued to transfer military equipment to Association of Southeast Asian Nations (ASEAN) states, donating TC-90 maritime-patrol aircraft to the Philippines and in March 2019 concluding an agreement to supply spare parts for the Philippines' UH-1H helicopters. Moreover, as part of its Official Development Assistance policy, Japan has continued to transfer coastguard cutters to ASEAN members including Indonesia, Malaysia, the Philippines and Vietnam. In contrast, Japan's defence exchanges with South Korea declined in 2019. Diplomatic ties have deteriorated due to historical and territorial issues, with trade disputes also arising. Their effect on security was apparent in late August when Seoul said it would terminate the General Security of Military Information Agreement. The US feared that this would jeopardise trilateral US–Japan–South Korea cooperation in areas such as missile defence.

NORTH KOREA: MISSILE TESTING IN 2019

In May 2019, North Korea once again started testing ballistic missiles. Prior to this, Pyongyang's early 2018 moratorium on nuclear- and long-range-missile tests had seemingly been extended to all ballistic-missile tests, irrespective of range. The moratorium took shape in April 2018 when Kim Jong-un reportedly said to the central committee of the Workers' Party of Korea that the North would stop nuclear tests and launches of intercontinental ballistic missiles.

At the time of writing, the moratorium technically remains in place. Until the October 2019 test of a submarine-launched ballistic missile, Pyongyang's testing had focused on short-range systems and emphasised – at least in state media – their tactical (conventional) credentials, although a dual-use capability cannot be discounted.

The two short-range ballistic-missile (SRBM) types tested in 2019 are, at the time of writing, still without publicly available official designations. While their lineage also remains unclear, they have reportedly demonstrated at least some performance characteristics that are similar to the Russian 9K720 *Iskander* and the United States' MGM-140 ATACMS systems, which they visually resemble. These include utilising depressed aeroballistic trajectories, which have the potential to complicate the task of missile-defence systems. Moreover, analysis of the tests of the *Iskander* lookalike – which may have received the US designation 'KN-23' – suggested that the weapon had the capacity to alter its trajectory mid-flight, which could present further challenges to a defending force. In addition, North Korea also conducted four

Table 16 **North Korea: missile testing as of October 2019**

Date (local)	Type	Classification	Outcome[1]	Maximum altitude (km)	Distance flown (km)
02 Oct 2019	n.k.	SLBM (MRBM)	Success	910[2]	450
16 Aug 2019	ATACMS lookalike	SRBM	Success	30	230
	ATACMS lookalike	SRBM	Success		
10 Aug 2019	ATACMS lookalike	SRBM	Success	48	400
	ATACMS lookalike	SRBM	Success		
06 Aug 2019	*Iskander* lookalike (KN-23?)	SRBM	Success	37	450
	Iskander lookalike (KN-23?)	SRBM	Success		
25 Jul 2019	*Iskander* lookalike (KN-23?)	SRBM	Success	50	690
	Iskander lookalike (KN-23?)	SRBM	Success		430
09 May 2019	*Iskander* lookalike (KN-23?)	SRBM	Success	50	≤420
	Iskander lookalike (KN-23?)	SRBM	Success		
04 May 2019	*Iskander* lookalike (KN-23?)	SRBM	Success	n.k.	≤240
	Iskander lookalike (KN-23?)	SRBM	Success		

[1] Test objectives are unknown; published reports relate only to claimed successes. Outcomes are therefore an assessment of information released by, or reported from, DPRK, ROK and US officials
[2] Lofted trajectory

salvo tests of a new large-calibre – possibly 600 mm – multiple-rocket-launch system with long-range guided projectiles; the systems in these tests also flew with depressed trajectories.

The emergence of *Iskander-* and ATACMs-like missiles suggests that North Korea is placing a higher premium on the accuracy of conventionally armed systems that have military utility against tactical targets.

The test in October 2019 of a submarine-launched ballistic missile – launched from a submerged platform – represented a significant escalation in Pyongyang's renewed testing regime. The missile flew on a lofted trajectory and fell within Japan's exclusive economic zone. Analysts have posited a theoretical range of up to 2,000 kilometres for this system, which would make it a medium-range missile and so outside the scope of the moratorium. However, the most significant aspect of the test is that Pyongyang once again used a nuclear-capable delivery system. Even though North Korea maintained its moratorium for 522 days, it is clear that during this time the country has been actively developing new missile capabilities. This raises the possibility that, even if the moratorium continues, North Korea might again test existing or new missiles in a way that would fall outside the definition of an intercontinental system (taken to mean a missile with an assessed range of over 5,000 km).

SOUTH KOREA

South Korea's military posture has changed significantly following the first inter-Korean summit and the first United States–North Korea summit, both of which took place in 2018. Large-scale South Korea–US combined exercises were significantly scaled back after the US–North Korea summit. The 9/19 military agreement, signed during the September 2018 inter-Korean summit held in Pyongyang – the last of the three inter-Korean leaders' summits held that year – resulted in a number of other measures.

The 9/19 agreement

Under the 9/19 agreement, the armed forces of South and North Korea agreed to cease all hostile activities directed against each other, demilitarise the Joint Security Area (JSA) at Panmunjom, jointly withdraw guard posts from the Demilitarised Zone (DMZ) on a trial basis, remove mines and construct roads in areas designated for the joint recovery of human remains from the Korean War, and conduct a joint study of the waterways in the Han river estuary. It stipulated that North and South Korea should halt artillery fire and manoeuvre training above regimental level inside a buffer zone stretching five kilometres either side of the Military Demarcation Line (MDL). According to South Korea's Ministry of National Defense (MND), North Korea has not conducted these activities since the agreement. South Korea's armed forces now conduct artillery training at replacement bases and using targets outside the buffer zone. Both countries have also placed covers on coastal batteries and naval gun barrels and have closed the doors of artillery positions in the buffer zone, though there have been allegations by both sides of violations.

No-fly zones have been established along the DMZ and flights within them only take place with prior notification. The no-fly zones, ranging from 10 to 40 km, have been established on either side of the MDL with differing limits for uninhabited aerial vehicles (UAVs), rotary-wing aircraft and fixed-wing aircraft. The MND says that this has stopped North Korean reconnaissance balloons and the infiltration into South Korean airspace of small UAVs on reconnaissance missions.

However, the South Korean and US armed forces have an advantage in terms of reconnaissance assets (UAVs, fixed-wing and rotary-wing) close to the DMZ. For this reason, some South Korean defence commentators have argued that the no-fly zone risks blunting the South Korean armed forces' intelligence, surveillance and reconnaissance (ISR) advantage. In response, the defence ministry has said it has taken steps to prevent surveillance gaps by using its Hawker 800SIG signals-intelligence and Hawker 800RA ISR aircraft, as well as other surveillance assets. Nonetheless, South Korea's Joint Chiefs of Staff (JCS) reported to the National Assembly (likely in September) that the capability of forward-deployed UAVs to detect North Korean targets has reduced, with UAVs operated by South Korea's forward-deployed Army Corps now able to identify only 399 potential targets, including North Korea's long-range artillery pieces, compared to 713 before the no-fly zone came into effect. The effect of this varies from unit to unit, but according to the JCS report, the target-identification rate in some forward-deployed corps' area of operations has fallen by up to 83%.

In December 2018, both the North and South Korean armed forces completed the trial withdrawal from and destruction of 22 guard posts that were located close to each other (it is understood that these posts were within around 1 km proximity). The MND has announced that it will continue to discuss the complete withdrawal of all such posts in the DMZ according to the 9/19 military agreement, based on the results of the trial withdrawal process. Before the agreement took effect, North Korea was reported to have 160 guard posts and South Korea 60.

A trilateral consultative body has been established to discuss the demilitarisation of the JSA at Panmunjom. This first met in October 2018 and consists of personnel from North and South Korea and the United Nations Command. A number of tasks were reported as complete by the end of October 2019, including mine clearance, the withdrawal of guard posts and weapons, and joint site verification. However, other points are still outstanding, including the plan that North and South Korean forces mount guard duty 'side by side' at two new guard posts at Panmunjom.

South Korea's MND said on 18 September that 'North Korea has not once undertaken local provocations or violated the agreement since the 9.19 military agreement was signed', and that the agreement is contributing to peace and stability on the Korean Peninsula. However, in May the North started to once again test certain ballistic missiles and rockets, though technically not in contravention of its moratorium on testing. Pyongyang has also continued to protest against Seoul's military training and defence acquisitions, saying these are violations of the 9/19 agreement. North Korea cites Article 1 Paragraph 1 of the agreement, which states: 'The two sides agreed to have consultations on matters including large-scale military exercises and military buildup aimed at each other … through the "Inter-Korean Joint Military Committee".' Some South Korean analysts have said that the ambiguity of the term 'military buildup' (which can also be translated as 'armament augmentations') gives the North scope to criticise South Korean defence acquisitions.

Military training

Following the June 2018 Singapore summit, the US announced that it would temporarily suspend large-scale combined exercises. Subsequently, the three principal combined South Korea–US exercises, *Key Resolve*, *Foal Eagle* and *Ulchi Freedom Guardian*, have been replaced by combined exercises conducted on a different scale and with different names and characteristics.

Key Resolve and *Foal Eagle*, which had taken place annually in March and April, were replaced in March 2019 by the *Dong Maeng* (*Alliance*) exercise. While *Key Resolve* was a large-scale command-post exercise (CPX) and *Foal Eagle* was a large-scale field training exercise, the first (19-1) *Alliance* exercise was a scaled-back CPX. Meanwhile, *Ulchi Freedom Guardian*, which had been held each August, was separated into two separate exercises. (It had been a combination of the Korean *Ulchi* drill and the combined South Korea–US *Freedom Guardian* exercise.) However, in 2019, the *Ulchi* exercise was combined with the South Korean *Taeguk* exercise: the *Ulchi Taeguk* exercise ran from 27 to 30 May. The *Freedom Guardian* exercise, meanwhile, transformed into the early August 'ROK–US command post training' drill (it is understood that this was initially billed as the second of the year's *Dong Maeng* exercises), focused initially on verifying the South Korean armed forces' capabilities for assuming wartime operational control.

The large *Max Thunder* and *Vigilant Ace* joint air exercises have also been suspended, though training continues at squadron level. This overall reduction in joint training, as well as the cancellation of some exercises and the lower level at which training is now conducted (it was reported that no joint drills above regimental level took place in 2019), has attracted some negative comment in South Korea. However, the MND, the Pentagon and US Forces Korea have emphasised that the effect of these changes has been offset by other forms of training.

Defence modernisation

In August 2019, the MND announced a Mid-Term Defense Plan for 2020–24, detailing defence plans and procurements for the next five years. The MND has allocated a total budget of W290.5 trillion (US$247.4 billion) for the plan. Of this, W103.8trn (US$88.4bn) has been allocated to force improvement (including research and development and acquisition), an annual increase of 10.3%. Force maintenance (including construction) has been allocated W186.7trn (US$159bn), an annual increase of 5.3%.

There was some media focus in 2019 on the plan for a large multipurpose amphibious-assault vessel capable of operating the F-35B combat aircraft. Reportedly to be based on the existing *Dokdo* class, it is as yet unclear if it will – like the two *Dokdo* vessels – also have a well deck. Reports indicate the design may displace 30,000 tonnes, contrasting with the *Dokdo*, which displaces around 19,000 tonnes. The plan also includes a 'combined fires naval vessel', based on the US 'arsenal ship' concept and capable of engaging ground targets with a range of missiles.

The air force's F-15K fighters are due to be upgraded in the next five years, with active electronically scanned-array (AESA) radars replacing their current mechanical radars, and the air force is also now beginning to receive its order of F-35A combat aircraft. The acquisition of a large transport aircraft is also being discussed, with the A-400M and C-130J understood to be under consideration.

The defence ministry plans to boost by 2023 its space-based capabilities by acquiring five reconnaissance satellites. This project (including synthetic aperture radar, electro-optical and infrared satellites) is planned to cost W1.22trn (US$1.0bn) and is seen as key to strengthening ISR capabilities in preparation for the transfer of wartime operational control. A satellite-tracking and -monitoring system is also planned. The 2018 defence-budget documentation contained references to a 'blackout bomb', while there are also reports of interest in electromagnetic-pulse systems.

Other modernisation plans continue, amid an overall reduction in personnel numbers. The army intends to field the new counter-battery radar-II, the *Chunmoo* multiple-rocket launcher (MRL) and the KTSSM tactical surface-to-surface missile in order to reinforce counter-battery capabilities against North Korea's long-range artillery and MRLs. Reorganisation has also continued under the 'Defense Reform 2.0' initiative. In 2018, the army's 8th and 26th Mechanised Infantry Divisions merged into a new 8th Division. Other changes, due to take place by the end of 2020, include the merger of the 11th and 20th Mechanised Infantry Divisions. Meanwhile, the 2nd Infantry Division was due to deactivate in late 2019, to be replaced by a division-sized Rapid Reaction Force. Two of the existing 2nd Infantry Division's three regiments were due to be reassigned to the neighbouring 12th and 21st Divisions at the same time. Two corps are also due to be deactivated by 2025, though their identity is as yet unclear. Other changes include the navy's expansion and reorganisation of its 6th Air Wing as Naval Air Command, the air force expanding the Air Intelligence Group into the Air Intelligence Wing and the marine corps expanding its Air Squadron into an Air Wing, partly to boost reconnaissance capabilities.

Kill Chain, KAMD, KMPR; changes to the 'three-axis' system

In January 2019, one month after it was first discussed by Defense Minister Jeong Kyeong-doo as part of his report on defence planning in 2019, the MND announced that the previous 'three-axis system', comprising the Kill Chain, Korean Air and Missile Defense (KAMD) and Korean Massive Punishment and Retaliation (KMPR) strategies, would be renamed as a 'Nuclear–WMD response system'. The 'three-axis' strategy dates back to the administration of Park Gyun-hye.

Kill Chain refers to a strategy and associated systems capable of the real-time detection and engagement of enemy launchers and missiles. This strategy is understood by South Korean defence analysts to include the concept of pre-emptive strikes, despite legal debate in South Korea over this. KAMD is a missile-defence system intended to be capable of intercepting North Korean ballistic missiles. The concept consists of lower-tier missile-defence capabilities, including variants of *Patriot* missiles and the indigenously developed *Cheongung* (M-SAM derivative) interceptor missile. KMPR refers to actions that would take place if North Korea were to launch a nuclear attack, including South Korean assaults on strategic and leadership targets by capabilities including *Hyunmoo*-II and -III missiles and special mission brigades of the army's Special Warfare Command.

The concepts underpinning this have now been renamed. 'Kill Chain' has been changed to 'strategic strike system', KAMD to 'Korean missile defense' and KMPR to 'overwhelming response capabilities'. Some South Korean analysts have speculated that these names may have been changed because of sensitivities over inter-Korean relations and the diplomatic reconciliation that the Moon administration has followed in order to alleviate the North Korean threat. Despite the change in terminology, the MND has said that it will not alter the basic force package envisaged under the three-axis system. Indeed, the MND said – around the time it launched the Defense Mid-Term Report – that it needed capabilities able to tackle not just North Korea's legacy systems but also its short-range ballistic missile shown after May 2019. For instance, there are plans to boost radar coverage with the acquisition of additional *Green Pine* early-warning radars and US *Aegis* ship-based battle-management systems and associated radars. South Korean analysts understand that the extra *Green Pine* systems may be intended to address potential submarine-launched ballistic-missile launches. Meanwhile, the development phase for the indigenous long-range air-defence system (L-SAM) is due to end by 2024. Its intercept altitude is understood to be in the range of 50–90 km. The plan is that, when L-SAM development is complete, South Korea has a multilayered missile-defence structure. As well as enhancements to its *Patriot* missiles, it was reported in late 2018 that South Korea's defence-acquisition administration was looking to buy Standard Missiles for future *Aegis*-equipped vessels.

SINGAPORE

The city state of Singapore is one of the world's most densely defended territories, belying its relatively small size of 721.5 square kilometres and population of only 5.7 million. Since the late 1960s, its People's Action Party government has devoted substantial resources to developing armed forces capable of deterring and, if necessary, defending the island against external threats. Singapore has always been concerned about potential adversaries within its immediate neighbourhood. However, over time, the Singapore Armed Forces (SAF) have developed capabilities with longer range and more operational flexibility, as well as greater firepower, aimed at deterring challenges from further afield and potentially facilitating involvement in coalition operations. While the SAF's orientation has always been overwhelmingly external and geared towards potential conventional warfare, since the early 2000s the armed forces have also developed a capacity to engage in counter-terrorist operations, on home territory if necessary.

Defence policy and defence relations

Singapore's defence strategy, doctrine and force structure have been shaped by its geographical and demographic constraints. Since the country's foundation, a central objective for its political and military leaders has been to develop forces that are technologically superior in the immediate region. The resources that Singapore devotes to defence – and the capabilities it seeks to acquire – reflect this goal. On 1 March 2019, Minister for Defence Dr Ng Eng Hen revealed elements of the SAF's 'capability transformation roadmap' during the post-budget Committee of Supply debate in parliament. A key aspect of Singapore's defence philosophy has always been that it must be prepared to defend itself using its own resources. The government sometimes cites the British military collapse in 1941–42, which left the island at the mercy of invading Japanese forces, as evidence of the dangers of relying on others for defence.

Nevertheless, despite this philosophy of self-reliance and Singapore's formal diplomatic posture of non-alignment, the defence ministry and the SAF have cultivated a wide range of bilateral partnerships. There are important arrangements with Australia, Brunei, Germany, New Zealand, Taiwan, Thailand and the United States, and army units regularly train and exercise in these countries.

Republic of Singapore Air Force (RSAF) operational training squadrons for F-15SG and F-16C/D combat aircraft and AH-64 attack helicopters are based in the US under long-term arrangements, and it can be expected that an F-35 training unit will also be located there. RSAF flying-training units (fixed-wing basic training and rotary-wing) are located in Australia, and the advanced jet-training squadron is based in France. Defence relations with the US deepened in 2015 with the signing of an enhanced Defence Cooperation Arrangement. US forces are stationed in Singapore under a bilateral arrangement that was extended for a further 15 years in September 2019. These include US Indo-Pacific Command's Western Pacific logistics command, a littoral combat ship, maritime-patrol aircraft and US Air Force fighter detachments.

Singapore has frequently reaffirmed the value of its engagement in the Five Power Defence Arrangements alongside Australia, Malaysia, New Zealand and the United Kingdom. The SAF also engages in multilateral defence cooperation through the 18-member Association of Southeast Asian Nations (ASEAN) Defence Ministers' Meeting (ADMM)-Plus, which involves the armed forces of all ten member states and eight ASEAN dialogue partners, including China. In October 2018, Singapore's navy joined the first ASEAN–China naval exercise, and in May 2019 the city state's defence ministry agreed to negotiate a revised bilateral Agreement on Defence Exchanges and Security Cooperation (ADESC) with Beijing, which was signed on 20 October 2019. However, the bilateral exercises conducted since the original ADESC was signed in 2008 have been small in scale and seem likely to remain so.

Personnel and training

Singapore relies on conscription ('National Service', or 'NS') to supply the majority of its military personnel. This gives it something in common with other countries that have small populations and seek to develop convincing defence postures, such as Israel and Switzerland. NS is mandatory for all medically fit 18-year-old males who are citizens or permanent residents, providing an annual cohort of approximately 15,000. Some of these serve in the police or civil-defence force rather than the SAF, but NS is a particularly useful source of army personnel. Following full-time conscript service of up to two years, 'NS Men' then remain in the reserves for a ten-year training cycle, which includes seven 'high-key' and three 'low-key' annual call-up periods, each of more than seven or up to six days respectively. Guards, infantry, armoured, artillery and combat-engineer battalions comprising conscript personnel pass into the reserves as whole, fully trained units – a system that has allowed Singapore's army to develop a large order of battle, which if fully mobilised would include five divisions (three combined arms, one rapid deployment and one home defence) and more than 200,000 personnel. Conversely, Singapore's air force and navy are relatively small in terms of personnel numbers. However, a high proportion of their active personnel are regulars (probably around 50% in the air force and 75% in the navy) and they have increasingly fielded advanced platforms and systems providing considerable long-range striking power.

Nonetheless, adverse demographic trends pose a major challenge for the SAF. Despite decades of governmental efforts, by 2018 the city state's total fertility rate (the average number of live births per woman) had fallen to 1.14, the lowest in the world. This has already had serious implications for the size of the annual NS cohort, which declined from 21,000 in 2011 to 15,000 in 2019 and is expected to contract further over the next decade. Reservist numbers will also decline over time.

The defence ministry and SAF response to this has taken several forms. Army units have become smaller and there have been efforts to increase their firepower. At the same time, there has been emphasis on developing and acquiring military equipment with reduced personnel requirements. This includes uninhabited systems – and not just aerial vehicles (UAVs). The SAF has also brought into service the *Protector* uninhabited surface vessel (USV), used by the navy for surveillance and force protection. Specialised variants of the larger *Venus* 16 USV are likely to be integrated with new Multi-Role Combat Vessels (MRCVs), with which the navy plans to replace its *Victory*-class missile corvettes. These MRCVs are expected to play a major role in future mine-countermeasures (MCM) operations and will probably also replace the navy's current Swedish-built *Bedok*-class MCM vessels. Important further steps may see the army using uninhabited ground vehicles in conjunction with the *Hunter* armoured fighting vehicle (AFV), and air force F-35s controlling 'loyal wingman' UAVs.

Another effort to mitigate the effects of the personnel deficit has involved attempts to increase the recruitment of women as SAF regular personnel. Despite this – and the fact that most military vocations, including those for infantry officers and specialists, are now open to women – the number of female regulars has remained stubbornly low at around 1,500 or 8% of the SAF's total regular strength. Another measure has involved re-establishing the Singapore Volunteer Corps as an SAF element providing part-time voluntary military service opportunities for women and others, including older permanent residents ineligible for NS. Some in Singapore have suggested that conscripting women as well as men would resolve the personnel problem, but the government has so far ruled this out.

The government is also looking to improve the provision of training. During the March 2019 Committee of Supply debate in parliament, Dr Ng also said that the SAF would enhance its training infrastructure. In June 2019, he announced that from 2023 the army would establish a major new urban-warfare complex for homeland-security, counter-terrorism, and humanitarian assistance and disaster relief (HADR) training. The initial phase of the new facility, to be known as SAFTI City, will comprise more than 70 buildings, including 12-storey blocks, a bus interchange and an underground railway station, and will be equipped with interactive targets able to 'shoot' back at personnel under training. The Ministry of Defence, through its Defence Cyber Organisation, has also placed an increased emphasis on cyber-warfare training, opening a new Cyber Defence School in February 2019 and creating new cyber vocations for military and non-uniformed defence-ministry personnel.

Defence economics

Singapore's economy emerged relatively unscathed from the Asian financial crisis of 1997–98. Since then, it has had the largest defence budget in Southeast Asia. Its northern neighbour Malaysia has not prioritised defence spending since the financial crisis, and though Indonesia's defence budget has recovered in parallel with its economic growth, its defence disbursements do not match Singapore's. In the meantime, Singapore has been able to afford to develop capabilities that put the SAF on a par with Western armed forces in some areas, particularly in terms of airpower. Developments during 2019 have highlighted the intent of Singapore's government to ensure that the SAF retains superior capabilities in its immediate region and, at the same time, the capacity to exercise with and, if necessary, fight alongside the forces of its security partners, whether regional or Western. On 18 February, the government's 2019 budget announcement revealed that defence spending would increase by 4.8% in local currency terms compared with the previous year, to SGD15.5 billion (US$11.3bn), equating to 19% of government spending and 3.11% of GDP. Defence Minister Ng's March 2019 speech on the SAF's capability-transformation road map identified the major military-procurement programmes over the next decade. According to the minister, these programmes will be supported by defence spending equivalent to 3–4% of GDP.

Building the future force

Perhaps the single-most important acquisition announced by Dr Ng was an initial four F-35 combat aircraft, with an option to buy an additional eight. The order had been long anticipated, but Dr Ng had emphasised previously that Singapore was not in a 'hurry' to commit itself to the F-35 programme, despite having been a 'security cooperative participant' in the F-35 development programme as far back as 2003. Singapore's incremental approach to F-35 acquisition was probably intended partly to mitigate the concerns of other regional states, while at the same time bringing benefits in terms of a lower unit price and the platform's technological maturity. The defence minister explained the small number of aircraft to be purchased initially on the grounds that these would be used for evaluation purposes 'before deciding on the acquisition of a full fleet'. The F-35s will eventually replace the 60 F-16C/D Block 52/52+ fighters currently flown by the RSAF, though not necessarily on a one-for-one basis. Whether Singapore will buy F-35As or F-35Bs (suitable for off-base and shipborne operations) remained unclear at the time of writing; an eventual mixed fleet of both types might be a possibility. In the Committee of Supply debate, Dr Ng also confirmed that from 2020 the air force will replace its AS332M and CH-47D/SD transport helicopters with H225Ms and CH-47Fs. He also said that new UAVs would replace the service's current *Heron* 1 and *Hermes* 450 platforms over the next several years. There was no mention, though, of any replacements in the short or medium term for

Defence industry and research and development

Singapore's defence industry actively contributes to the continual modernisation of the Singapore Armed Forces' (SAF's) equipment inventory. ST Engineering, in which government investment arm Temasek Holdings is a majority shareholder, dominates the local defence-industrial sector through its aerospace, electronics, land-systems and marine divisions. The company supplies the SAF not only with most of its surface warships, but also a large proportion of its armoured vehicles, artillery and other army equipment.

With 5,000 personnel, Singapore's Defence Technology Community (DTC) comprises SAF engineers and several entities within the Ministry of Defence (MINDEF), as well as two MINDEF statutory boards, the DSTA and DSO National Laboratories. The DSTA implements defence-technology plans, develops defence infrastructure and manages defence procurement, while DSO is Singapore's main defence research-and-development organisation and is 'charged with the critical mission of developing technological solutions to sharpen the cutting edge of Singapore's national security'. Niche systems developed by the DTC include an integrated 'island air defence system', a battlefield-management system for the *Terrex* armoured vehicle, lightweight ceramic armour and autonomous underwater vehicles.

the ageing C-130 transport and Fokker 50 maritime-patrol aircraft.

Major new naval equipment will include not just the four German-built Type-218SG *Invincible*-class submarines being built to replace the present *Archer*- (refurbished former Swedish *Västergötland*-) and *Challenger*- (former *Sjöormen*-) class boats in Singaporean service by 2025. The first Type-218SG boat was launched in February 2019. The new class of MRCVs will replace the *Victory*-class missile corvettes between 2025 and 2030. The latter will by then have been in service for around 35 years. Highlighting the fact that the MRCVs will be 'custom-built for lean manning', Dr Ng said they will require only about half the personnel complement of modern frigates. However, these ships promise to deliver considerable new capability by acting as what the minister called 'motherships' for uninhabited air, surface and underwater vehicles. The Joint Multi Mission Ship (JMMS) will replace the navy's *Endurance*-class landing platform docks. While no details have been released, it seems likely that the JMMS will be larger than its predecessor class and could be a through-deck ship similar to ST Engineering Marine's proposed *Endurance* 160/170 landing helicopter dock vessels, which were first revealed in 2014 and 2017 respectively. If so, the JMMS vessels would be able to operate as amphibious-assault ships carrying H225M, CH-47F and AH-64D helicopters, and possibly even as platforms for F-35Bs, thereby providing Singapore with enhanced capacity for expeditionary as well as HADR operations.

The most important new army equipment mentioned by Dr Ng is the Next Generation Armoured Fighting Vehicle (NGAFV), developed collaboratively by the army and Singapore's Defence Science and Technology Agency (DSTA), and manufactured by Singapore Technologies Engineering. It will replace the upgraded M113A1 *Ultra* armoured personnel carriers that in their current and earlier forms have provided the backbone of SAF mechanised units since the early 1970s. In June 2019, the NGAFV was renamed *Hunter* and commissioned into service during a ceremony to mark the 50th anniversary of the Singapore Armoured Regiment. The *Hunter* represents a major improvement over the *Ultra* and has been designed for 'closed-hatch' operations. It features an all-round surveillance system that will feed data into ARTEMIS, a new command-and-control system intended to manage the vehicle's critical functions and enable mission planning while exchanging intelligence with other SAF vehicles and units. Reports indicate that *Hunter* will be the first Singaporean AFV equipped with anti-tank guided missiles (ATGMs), its remote-weapon system being armed with up to two *Spike* ATGMs as well as a 30 mm cannon and 7.62 mm machine gun. There are five planned variants of the vehicle: bridge, combat, command, engineer and recovery. Once regular instructors and NS commanders have been trained, the first unit to operate the AFV will be the 42nd Battalion SAR during 2020. Other important new army equipment will include the Next Generation Howitzer (possibly based on the ST Engineering 8x8 Advanced Mobile Gun System), which will provide a better rate of fire while requiring fewer gun crew than the army's present towed howitzer, the FH2000. There will also be a new armoured all-terrain tracked carrier vehicle and a range of small UAVs.

Afghanistan AFG

New Afghan Afghani Afs		2018	2019	2020
GDP	Afs	1.42tr	1.50tr	
	US$	19.6bn	18.7bn	
per capita	US$	545	513	
Growth	%	2.7	3.0	
Inflation	%	0.6	2.6	
Def bdgt [a]	Afs	147bn	153bn	
	US$	2.03bn	1.91bn	
US$1=Afs		72.41	80.20	

[a] Security expenditure. Includes expenditure on Ministry of Defence, Ministry of Interior, Ministry of Foreign Affairs, National Security Council and the General Directorate of National Security. Also includes donor funding

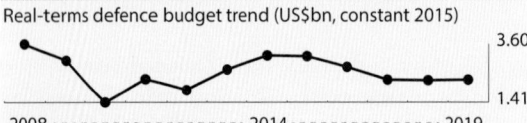
Real-terms defence budget trend (US$bn, constant 2015)

Population 35,780,458

Ethnic groups: Pashtun 38%; Tajik 25%; Hazara 19%; Uzbek 12%; Aimaq 4%; Baluchi 0.5%

Age	0–14	15–19	20–24	25–29	30–64	65 plus
Male	20.7%	5.6%	5.4%	4.4%	13.4%	1.2%
Female	20.1%	5.4%	5.2%	4.2%	13.1%	1.4%

Capabilities

The Afghan National Defence and Security Forces (ANDSF) are optimised for counter-insurgency and counter-terrorist operations against the Taliban and other groups. Although ANDSF casualties are no longer reported by the US and NATO, reports suggested that already high losses and high levels of desertion further increased in 2019. The ANDSF has difficulty in sustaining personnel levels, with a reported 22% shortage in mid-2019, and there are problems in retaining key specialists including pilots, aircraft mechanics and special-operations troops. Army and police special forces are well regarded by NATO and bear the brunt of offensive operations and intelligence-led strike operations against insurgent networks, while regular forces are held in a defensive posture, mainly restricted to bases and outposts and at risk from Taliban attack. NATO advisers remain embedded in the defence and interior ministries, although the ANDSF are now responsible for the majority of training, albeit with NATO support. The Trump administration has expressed an intention to withdraw US forces from Afghanistan and US troop levels declined in 2019. Efforts are under way to improve leadership, intelligence, logistics and coordination between different service arms. The ANDSF Road Map contains ambitious plans to improve capability but depends on continued international support. Air-force modernisation continues, but maintenance difficulties have reduced aircraft availability. Afghan forces' logistics are optimised for internal deployments, but remain of limited effectiveness. The ANDSF depends on imported military equipment.

ACTIVE 180,900 (Army 173,600 Air Force 7,300)
Paramilitary 91,600

ORGANISATIONS BY SERVICE

Afghan National Army (ANA) 173,600
5 regional comd
FORCES BY ROLE
SPECIAL FORCES
1 spec ops div (1 (National Mission) SF bde (1 SF gp; 1 mech inf bn (2 mech inf coy)); 2 cdo bde (1 mech inf coy, 4 cdo bn); 1 (1st MSF) mech bde (2 mech inf bn))
MANOEUVRE
Mechanised
1 (2nd MSF) mech bde (3 mech inf bn)
Light
1 (201st) corps (3 inf bde (4 inf bn, 1 sy coy, 1 cbt spt bn, 1 CSS bn), 1 inf bde (3 inf bn, 1 sy coy, 1 cbt spt bn, 1 CSS bn), 1 engr bn, 1 int bn, 2 MP coy, 1 sigs bn)
1 (203rd) corps (2 inf bde (5 inf bn, 1 sy coy, 1 cbt spt bn, 1 CSS bn), 2 inf bde (4 inf bn, 1 sy coy, 1 cbt spt bn, 1 CSS bn), 1 engr bn, 1 int bn, 2 MP coy, 1 sigs bn)
1 (205th) corps (4 inf bde (4 inf bn, 1 sy coy, 1 cbt spt bn, 1 CSS bn), 1 engr bn, 1 int bn, 2 MP coy, 1 sigs bn)
1 (207th) corps (3 inf bde (4 inf bn, 1 sy coy, 1 cbt spt bn, 1 CSS bn), 1 engr bn, 1 int bn, 2 MP coy, 1 sigs bn)
1 (209th) corps (2 inf bde (4 inf bn, 1 sy coy, 1 cbt spt bn, 1 CSS bn), 1 engr bn, 1 int bn, 2 MP coy, 1 sigs bn)
1 (215th) corps (3 inf bde (4 inf bn, 1 sy coy, 1 cbt spt bn, 1 CSS bn), 1 inf bde (2 inf bn, 1 cbt spt bn, 1 CSS bn), 1 engr bn, 1 int bn, 2 MP coy, 1 sigs bn)
1 (217th) corps (2 inf bde (4 inf bn, 1 sy coy, 1 cbt spt bn, 1 CSS bn))
1 (111st Capital) div (1 inf bde (1 tk bn, 1 mech inf bn, 2 inf bn, 1 sy coy, 1 cbt spt bn, 1 CSS bn), 1 inf bde (4 inf bn, 1 sy coy, 1 cbt spt bn, 1 CSS bn), 1 int bn)
Other
6 (border) sy bde

EQUIPMENT BY TYPE
ARMOURED FIGHTING VEHICLES
  MBT 20 T-55/T-62 (24 more in store†)
  APC 1,013
    APC (T) 173 M113A2†
    APC (W) ε640 MSFV (inc variants)
    PPV 200 Maxxpro
ENGINEERING & MAINTENANCE VEHICLES
  ARV 20 Maxxpro ARV
  MW Bozena
ARTILLERY 775
  TOWED 109: 122mm 85 D-30†; 155mm 24 M114A1†
  MOR 82mm 666: 521 2B14†; 105 M-69†; 40 M252†

Afghan Air Force (AAF) 7,300
Including Special Mission Wing
EQUIPMENT BY TYPE
AIRCRAFT 27 combat capable
  ISR 5 Cessna AC-208 Combat Caravan*
  TPT 47: Medium 4 C-130H Hercules; Light 42: 24 Cessna 208B; 18 PC-12 (Special Mission Wing); PAX 1 B-727 (2 more in store)
  TRG 22 EMB-314 Super Tucano* (of which 7 in the US for trg)

HELICOPTERS
ATK 6 Mi-35 *Hind*
MRH 120: 3 *Cheetal*; 41 MD-530F (11 armed); 76 Mi-17 *Hip* H (incl 30 Special Mission Wing hel)
TPT • **Medium** 35 UH-60A+ *Black Hawk*
BOMBS
Laser-guided GBU-58 *Paveway* II

Paramilitary 91,600

Afghan National Police 91,600
Under control of Interior Ministry. Includes Afghan Uniformed Police (AUP), Afghan National Civil Order Police (ANCOP), Police Special Forces (GDPSU) and Afghan Anti-Crime Police (AACP)

FOREIGN FORCES
All *Operation Resolute Support* unless otherwise specified
Albania 135
Armenia 121
Australia 300; 1 SF unit; 1 sy unit; 1 sigs unit
Austria 16
Azerbaijan 120
Belgium 83
Bosnia-Herzegovina 68
Bulgaria 159
Croatia 110
Czech Republic 334; 1 sy coy; 1 MP unit
Denmark 155
Estonia 42
Finland 67
Georgia 871; 1 lt inf bn
Germany 1,300; 1 bde HQ; 1 recce bn; 1 hel flt with CH-53G *Stallion*; 1 ISR UAV flt with *Heron* UAV
Greece 11
Hungary 93
India Indo-Tibetan Border Police 335 (facilities protection)
Italy 895; 1 mech inf bde HQ; 1 mech inf regt(-); 1 hel regt(-) with AW129 *Mangusta*; NH90; RQ-7
Latvia 40
Lithuania 50
Luxembourg 2
Macedonia, North 47
Mongolia 233
Montenegro 27
Netherlands 160
New Zealand 13
Norway 54
Poland 354 • UNAMA 1
Portugal 214
Romania 797; 1 inf bn
Slovakia 33
Slovenia 8
Spain 66
Sweden 25
Turkey 579; 1 mot inf bn(-)
Ukraine 21
United Kingdom 1,100; 1 inf bn(+); 1 hel flt with 3 SA330 *Puma* HC2
United States 8,475; 1 div HQ; 2 div HQ (fwd); 1 spec ops bn; 2 inf bde(-); 2 ARNG inf bn; 1 arty bty with M777A2; 1 ARNG MRL bty with M142 HIMARS; 1 EOD bn; 1 cbt avn bde with AH-64D *Apache*; CH-47F *Chinook*; UH-60M *Black Hawk*; 1 FGA sqn with F-16C *Fighting Falcon*; 1 atk sqn with 12 A-10C *Thunderbolt* II; 1 ISR unit with RC-12X *Guardrail*; 1 EW sqn with EC-130H *Compass Call*, 1 tpt sqn with C-130J-30 *Hercules*, 1 CSAR sqn with HH-60G *Pave Hawk*; 1 CISR UAV sqn with MQ-9A *Reaper*; 1 ISR UAV unit with RQ-21A *Blackjack* • *Operation Freedom's Sentinel* 5,500

Australia AUS

Australian Dollar A$		2018	2019	2020
GDP	A$	1.90tr	1.98tr	
	US$	1.42tr	1.38tr	
per capita	US$	56,420	53,825	
Growth	%	2.7	1.7	
Inflation	%	2.0	1.6	
Def bdgt	A$	35.2bn	36.7bn	37.8bn
	US$	26.3bn	25.5bn	
US$1=A$		1.34	1.44	

Real-terms defence budget trend (US$bn, constant 2015)

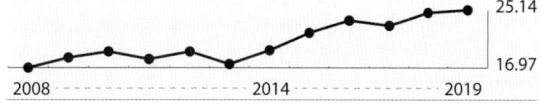

25.14
16.97
2008 - - - - - - - - - - 2014 - - - - - - - - - - 2019

Population	23,705,630					
Age	0–14	15–19	20–24	25–29	30–64	65 plus
Male	9.1%	3.0%	3.4%	3.7%	23.2%	7.7%
Female	8.6%	2.9%	3.2%	3.5%	22.7%	9.0%

Capabilities

The Australian Defence Force (ADF) is capable, well trained and well equipped, with strong doctrine, logistic support and C4ISR. It also has considerable recent operational experience. In March 2016, the government published Australia's third defence white paper in seven years. This identified China's growing regional role, regional military modernisation and inter-state rivalry as among the influences shaping defence policy. The defence of Australia, securing maritime Southeast Asia and the Pacific, and contributing to stability and the 'rules-based order' across the wider Indo-Pacific region are the country's three main 'defence objectives'. The country's primary ally is the US, but it is also forging closer defence ties with India, Japan and South Korea, while remaining committed to the Five Power Defence Arrangements and close defence relations with New Zealand. The armed forces have considerable operational experience and have played an active part in operations in Afghanistan as well as in the coalition fighting ISIS in Iraq and Syria. Strategic air- and sealift platforms give the ADF considerable capability to move and sustain deployments overseas. Australia is significantly modernising its navy and locally building submarines, destroyers and frigates based on European designs. Combat-air, maritime-patrol and armoured-vehicle capabilities are also being boosted, and more closely integrating Australia's armed forces – and its modern platforms – is becoming a priority. Australia imports most of its significant defence equipment but possesses a growing defence industry. Its largest naval shipbuilders are ASC Shipbuilding and Austal, whose US subsidiary, Austal USA, builds vessels for the US Navy.

ACTIVE 57,200 (Army 29,000 Navy 13,800 Air 14,400)

RESERVE 21,050 (Army 13,200 Navy 2,800 Air 5,050)

Integrated units are formed from a mix of reserve and regular personnel. All ADF operations are now controlled by Headquarters Joint Operations Command (HQJOC)

ORGANISATIONS BY SERVICE

Space
EQUIPMENT BY TYPE
SATELLITES • COMMUNICATIONS 1 *Optus* C1 (dual use for civil/mil comms)

Army 29,000
FORCES BY ROLE
COMMAND
  1 (1st) div HQ (1 sigs regt)
MANOEUVRE
  Mechanised
  1 (1st) mech inf bde (1 armd cav regt, 1 mech inf bn, 1 lt mech inf bn, 1 arty regt, 1 cbt engr regt, 1 sigs regt, 1 CSS bn)
  2 (3rd & 7th) mech inf bde (1 armd cav regt, 2 mech inf bn, 1 arty regt, 1 cbt engr regt, 1 sigs regt, 1 CSS bn)
  Amphibious
  1 (2nd RAR) amph bn
  Aviation
  1 (16th) avn bde (1 regt (2 ISR hel sqn), 1 regt (3 tpt hel sqn), 1 regt (2 spec ops hel sqn, 1 avn sqn))
COMBAT SUPPORT
  1 (6th) cbt spt bde (1 STA regt (1 STA bty, 1 UAV bty, 1 CSS bty), 1 AD/FAC regt (integrated), 1 engr regt (2 construction sqn, 1 EOD sqn), 1 EW regt, 1 int bn)
COMBAT SERVICE SUPPORT
  1 (17th) CSS bde (3 log bn, 3 med bn, 1 MP bn)

Special Operations Command
FORCES BY ROLE
SPECIAL FORCES
  1 (SAS) SF regt
  1 (SF Engr) SF regt
  2 cdo regt
COMBAT SUPPORT
  3 sigs sqn (incl 1 reserve sqn)
COMBAT SERVICE SUPPORT
  1 CSS sqn

Reserve Organisations 13,200 reservists
FORCES BY ROLE
COMMAND
  1 (2nd) div HQ
MANOEUVRE
  Reconnaissance
  3 (regional force) surv unit (integrated)
  Light
  1 (4th) inf bde (1 recce regt, 2 inf bn, 1 engr regt, 1 spt bn)
  1 (5th) inf bde (1 recce bn, 4 inf bn, 1 engr regt, 2 spt bn)
  1 (9th) inf bde (1 recce sqn, 2 inf bn, 1 spt bn)
  1 (11th) inf bde (1 recce regt, 3 inf bn, 1 engr regt, 1 spt bn)
  1 (13th) inf bde (1 recce sqn, 2 inf bn, 1 spt bn)
COMBAT SUPPORT
  1 arty regt
  1 sigs regt
COMBAT SERVICE SUPPORT
  1 trg bde

EQUIPMENT BY TYPE
ARMOURED FIGHTING VEHICLES
  MBT 59 M1A1 *Abrams*
  RECCE 1 *Boxer* CRV (in test)
  IFV 253 ASLAV-25 (all variants)
  APC • APC (T) 431 M113AS4
  AUV 1,120: 1,020 *Bushmaster* IMV; 100 *Hawkei*
ENGINEERING & MAINTENANCE VEHICLES
  ARV 51: 15 ASLAV-F; 17 ASLAV-R; 19 M88A2
  VLB 5 *Biber*
  MW 20: 12 *Husky*; 8 MV-10
ANTI-TANK/ANTI-INFRASTRUCTURE
  MSL • MANPATS FGM-148 *Javelin*
  RCL • 84mm *Carl Gustav*
ARTILLERY 239
  TOWED 155mm 54 M777A2
  MOR 81mm 185
AIR DEFENCE • SAM • Point-defence RBS-70
AMPHIBIOUS 15 LCM-8 (capacity either 1 MBT or 200 troops)
HELICOPTERS
  ATK 22 *Tiger*
  TPT 85: **Heavy** 10 CH-47F *Chinook*; **Medium** 75: 41 NH90 TTH (MRH90 TTH); 34 S-70A *Black Hawk*
UNMANNED AERIAL VEHICLES
  ISR • **Medium** 15 RQ-7B *Shadow* 200
AIR-LAUNCHED MISSILES
  ASM AGM-114M *Hellfire*

Navy 13,800
Fleet Comd HQ located at Sydney. Naval Strategic Comd HQ located at Canberra

EQUIPMENT BY TYPE
SUBMARINES • TACTICAL • SSK 6 *Collins* with 6 single 533mm TT with Mk 48 ADCAP mod 7 HWT/UGM-84C *Harpoon* Block 1B AShM
PRINCIPAL SURFACE COMBATANTS 10
  DESTROYERS • DDGHM 2 *Hobart* with *Aegis* Baseline 7.1 C2, 2 quad lnchr with RGM-84L *Harpoon* Block II AShM, 6 8-cell Mk 41 VLS with SM-2 Block IIIB SAM/RIM-162A ESSM SAM, 2 twin SVTT Mk 32 mod 9 324mm ASTT with MU90 LWT/Mk 54 LWT, 1 MK 15 *Phalanx* Block 1B CIWS, 1 127mm gun (capacity 1 MH-60R *Seahawk*)
  FRIGATES • FFGHM 8 *Anzac* (GER MEKO 200) with 2 quad lnchr with RGM-84L *Harpoon* Block II AShM, 1

8-cell Mk 41 VLS with RIM-162B ESSM SAM, 2 triple SVTT Mk 32 mod 5 324mm ASTT with MU90 LWT, 1 127mm gun (capacity 1 MH-60R *Seahawk* ASW hel)

PATROL AND COASTAL COMBATANTS 15
  PCO 15: 13 *Armidale* (*Bay* mod); 2 *Cape* (leased)
MINE WARFARE • MINE COUNTERMEASURES •
MHC 4 *Huon*
AMPHIBIOUS
  PRINCIPAL AMPHIBIOUS SHIPS 3
    LHD 2 *Canberra* (capacity 18 hel; 4 LCM-1E; 110 veh; 12 M1 *Abrams* MBT; 1,000 troops)
    LSD 1 *Choules* (ex-UK *Bay*) (capacity 1 med hel; 2 LCVP; 24 MBT; 350 troops)
  LANDING CRAFT 17
    LCM 12 LCM-1E
    LCVP 5
LOGISTICS AND SUPPORT 12
  AGHS 2 *Leeuwin* with 1 hel landing platform
  AGS 4 *Paluma*
  AOR 1 *Sirius*
  AX 1 *Sycamore* (capacity 1 med hel) (operated by private company, Teekay Shipping; multi-role aviation training vessel)
  AXS 1 *Young Endeavour*
  The following vessels are operated by a private company, DMS Maritime:
  ASR 2: 1 *Besant*; 1 *Stoker*
  AXL 1 *Seahorse Mercator*

Naval Aviation 1,350

FORCES BY ROLE
ANTI SUBMARINE WARFARE
  1 sqn with NH90 (MRH90)
  1 sqn with MH-60R *Seahawk*
TRAINING
  1 OCU sqn with MH-60R *Seahawk*
  1 sqn with H135
EQUIPMENT BY TYPE
HELICOPTERS
  ASW 24 MH-60R *Seahawk*
  TPT 21: **Medium** 6 NH90 (MRH90); **Light** 15 H135
AIR-LAUNCHED MISSILES
  ASM AGM-114M *Hellfire*

Clearance Diving Branch

FORCES BY ROLE
SPECIAL FORCES
  2 diving unit

Air Force 14,400

FORCES BY ROLE
FIGHTER/GROUND ATTACK
  2 sqn with F/A-18A/B *Hornet*
  1 sqn with F/A-18F *Super Hornet*
  1 sqn (forming) with F-35A *Lightning* II
ANTI SUBMARINE WARFARE
  1 sqn with P-8A *Poseidon*
ELECTRONIC WARFARE
  1 sqn with EA-18G *Growler*

ISR
  1 (FAC) sqn with PC-9/A(F); PC-21
  1 sqn with AP-3C *Orion*
AIRBORNE EARLY WARNING & CONTROL
  1 sqn with B-737-700 *Wedgetail* (E-7A)
TANKER/TRANSPORT
  1 sqn with A330 MRTT (KC-30A)
TRANSPORT
  1 VIP sqn with B-737BBJ; CL-604 *Challenger*; *Falcon* 7X
  1 sqn with C-17A *Globemaster* III
  1 sqn with C-27J *Spartan*
  1 sqn with C-130J-30 *Hercules*
TRAINING
  1 OCU with F/A-18A/B *Hornet*
  1 sqn with Beech 350 *King Air*
  2 sqn with PC-9/A; PC-21
  2 (LIFT) sqn with *Hawk* MK127*

EQUIPMENT BY TYPE
AIRCRAFT 164 combat capable
  FGA 109: 53 F/A-18A *Hornet*; 16 F/A-18B *Hornet*; 24 F/A-18F *Super Hornet*; 16 F-35A *Lightning* II (in test)
  ASW 11 P-8A *Poseidon*
  EW 13: 2 AP-3C *Orion* mod; 11 EA-18G *Growler**
  AEW&C 6 B-737-700 *Wedgetail* (E-7A)
  TKR/TPT 7 A330 MRTT (KC-30A)
  TPT 54: **Heavy** 8 C-17A *Globemaster* III; **Medium** 22: 10 C-27J *Spartan*; 12 C-130J-30 *Hercules*; **Light** 16 Beech 350 *King Air*; **PAX** 8: 2 B-737BBJ (VIP); 3 CL-604 *Challenger* (VIP); 3 *Falcon* 7X (VIP)
  TRG 141: 33 *Hawk* Mk127*; 62 PC-9/A (being withdrawn by end 2019); 46 PC-21
AIR-LAUNCHED MISSILES
  AAM • **IIR** AIM-9X *Sidewinder* II; ASRAAM; **ARH** AIM-120B/C-5/C-7 AMRAAM
  AShM AGM-84A *Harpoon*
  LACM Conventional AGM-158A JASSM
BOMBS
  Laser-guided *Paveway* II/IV; Laser JDAM
  INS/GPS-guided AGM-154C JSOW; JDAM; JDAM-ER

DEPLOYMENT

AFGHANISTAN: NATO • ISAF *Operation Resolute Support* (*Operation Highroad*) 300; 1 SF unit; 1 sy unit; 1 sigs unit

CYPRUS: UN • UNFICYP 3

EGYPT: MFO (*Operation Mazurka*) 27

IRAQ: *Operation Inherent Resolve* (*Okra*) 380; 1 SF gp; 1 trg unit; **NATO** • NATO Mission Iraq 2

MALAYSIA: 120; 1 inf coy (on 3-month rotational tours); 1 P-8A *Poseidon* (on rotation)

MIDDLE EAST: UN • UNTSO (*Operation Paladin*) 13

PHILIPPINES: *Operation Augury* 100 (trg team)

SOUTH SUDAN: UN • UNMISS (*Operation Aslan*) 19

SYRIA/ISRAEL: UN • UNDOF 1

UNITED ARAB EMIRATES: *Operation Accordion* 500: 1 tpt det with 2 C-130J-30 *Hercules*; 1 P-8A *Poseidon*; *Operation*

Inherent Resolve (Okra) 150; 1 B-737-700 *Wedgetail* (E-7A); 1 A330 MRTT (KC-30A)

FOREIGN FORCES

New Zealand 9 (air navigation trg)
Singapore 230: 1 trg sqn at Pearce with PC-21 trg ac; 1 trg sqn at Oakey with 12 AS332 *Super Puma*; AS532 *Cougar*
United States US Pacific Command: 1,500; 1 SEWS at Pine Gap; 1 comms facility at NW Cape; 1 SIGINT stn at Pine Gap • US Strategic Command: 1 detection and tracking radar at Naval Communication Station Harold E. Holt

Bangladesh BGD

Bangladeshi Taka Tk		2018	2019	2020
GDP	Tk	24.1tr	27.4tr	
	US$	288bn	317bn	
per capita	US$	1,749	1,906	
Growth	%	7.9	7.8	
Inflation	%	5.6	5.5	
Def bdgt	Tk	211bn	307bn	321bn
	US$	2.53bn	3.55bn	
FMA (US)	US$	1.5m	0m	0m
US$1=Tk		83.54	86.46	

Real-terms defence budget trend (US$bn, constant 2015)

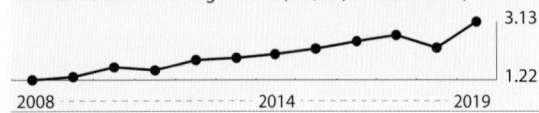

Population 161,062,905
Religious groups: Muslim 90%; Hindu 9%; Buddhist 1%

Age	0–14	15–19	20–24	25–29	30–64	65 plus
Male	13.7%	4.8%	4.7%	4.1%	18.8%	3.1%
Female	13.2%	4.6%	4.8%	4.4%	20.3%	3.5%

Capabilities

Bangladesh has limited military capability that is optimised for border and domestic security. A wide-ranging defence-modernisation plan is under way, called Forces 2030. Bangladesh has relied on Chinese and Russian aid and credit to overcome its limited procurement funding. It has increased defence collaboration with India. The country has a long record of UN peacekeeping deployments, with UN payments reportedly providing an important income source. A major naval-recapitalisation and -expansion programme, including the procurement of Chinese corvettes, is under way to better protect the country's large EEZ. Airlift capability will improve with the addition of ex-UK C-130Js, with UK firm Marshall Aerospace also due to provide maintenance and logistics support for this fleet under a 2019 agreement. Substantial efforts have also been made to strengthen the nascent shipbuilding industry and work has begun on a new submarine-support facility. The armed forces reportedly retain extensive business interests, in real estate, banks and other businesses.

ACTIVE 163,050 (Army 132,150 Navy 16,900 Air 14,000) **Paramilitary 63,900**

ORGANISATIONS BY SERVICE

Army 132,150
FORCES BY ROLE
COMMAND
  10 inf div HQ
SPECIAL FORCES
  1 cdo bde (2 cdo bn)
MANOEUVRE
  Armoured
  1 armd bde
  3 indep armd regt
  Light
  25 inf bde
  2 (composite) bde
COMBAT SUPPORT
  10 arty bde
  1 engr bde
  1 sigs bde
AVIATION
  1 avn regt (1 avn sqn; 1 hel sqn)
AIR DEFENCE
  1 AD bde
EQUIPMENT BY TYPE
ARMOURED FIGHTING VEHICLES
  MBT 276: 174 Type-59/-59G(BD); 58 Type-69/-69G; 44 Type-90-II (MBT-2000)
  LT TK 8 Type-62
  RECCE 8+ BOV M11
  APC 464
    APC (T) 134 MT-LB
    APC (W) 330 BTR-80
  AUV 17 *Cobra*
ENGINEERING & MAINTENANCE VEHICLES
  AEV MT-LB
  ARV 3+: T-54/T-55; Type-84; 3 Type-654
  VLB MTU
ANTI-TANK/ANTI-INFRASTRUCTURE
  MSL • MANPATS 9K115-2 *Metis* M1 (AT-13 *Saxhorn*-2)
  RCL 106mm 238 M40A1
ARTILLERY 889+
  SP 155mm 18 NORA B-52
  TOWED 363+: **105mm** 170 Model 56 pack howitzer; **122mm** 131: 57 Type-54/54-1 (M-30); 20 Type-83; 54 Type-96 (D-30), **130mm** 62 Type-59-1 (M-46)
  MRL 122mm 36+ WS-22
  MOR 472: **81mm** 11 M29A1; **82mm** 366 Type-53/type-87/M-31 (M-1937); **120mm** 95 AM-50/UBM 52
AMPHIBIOUS • LANDING CRAFT 3: 1 **LCT**; 2 **LCVP**
AIRCRAFT • TPT • Light 7: 1 C295; 5 Cessna 152; 1 PA-31T *Cheyenne*
HELICOPTERS
  MRH 2 AS365N3 *Dauphin*
  TPT 6: **Medium** 3 Mi-171Sh **Light** 3 Bell 206L-4
AIR DEFENCE
  SAM
    Short-range FM-90
    Point-defence FN-16 (CH-SA-14); QW-2
  GUNS • TOWED 174: **35mm** 8 GDF-009 (with *Skyguard*-3); **37mm** 132 Type-65/74; **57mm** 34 Type-59 (S-60)

Navy 16,900
EQUIPMENT BY TYPE
SUBMARINES • TACTICAL • SSK 2 *Nabajatra* (ex-PRC *Ming* Type-035G) with 8 single 533mm TT
PRINCIPAL SURFACE COMBATANTS • FRIGATES 4
  FFGHM 1 *Bangabandhu* (ROK modified *Ulsan*) with 2 twin lnchr with *Otomat* Mk2 AShM, 1 octuple FM-90N (CH-SA-N-4) SAM, 2 triple ILAS-3 (B-515) 324mm TT with A244/S LWT, 1 76mm gun (capacity: 1 AW109E hel)
  FFG 3:
    2 *Abu Bakr* (ex-PRC *Jianghu* III) with 2 twin lnchr with C-802A AShM, 2 RBU 1200 *Uragan* A/S mor, 2 twin 100mm gun
    1 *Osman* (ex-PRC *Jianghu* I) with 2 quad lnchr with C-802 (CH-SS-N-6) AShM, 2 RBU 1200 *Uragan* A/S mor, 2 twin 100mm gun
PATROL AND COASTAL COMBATANTS 50
  CORVETTES 10
  FSGM 4 *Shadhinota* (PRC C13B) with 2 twin lnchr with C-802 (CH-SS-N-6) AShM, 1 octuple lnchr with FL-3000N (HHQ-10) (CH-SA-N-17) SAM, 1 76mm gun, 1 hel landing platform
  FSG 4:
    2 *Durjoy* with 2 twin lnchr with C-704 AShM, 1 76mm gun
    2 *Bijoy* (ex-UK *Castle*) with 2 twin lnchr with C-704 AShM, 1 76mm gun, 1 hel landing platform
  FS 2 *Durjoy* with 2 triple 324mm ASTT, 1 76mm gun
  PSOH 2 *Somudra Joy* (ex-USCG *Hero*) with 1 76mm gun, hel landing platform
  PCFG 4 *Durdarsha* (ex-PRC *Huangfeng*) with 4 single lnchr with HY-2 (CH-SS-N-2 *Safflower*) AShM
  PCO 6: 1 *Madhumati* (*Sea Dragon*) with 1 57mm gun; 5 *Kapatakhaya* (ex-UK *Island*)
  PCC 8:
    2 *Meghna* with 1 57mm gun (fishery protection)
    1 *Nirbhoy* (ex-PRC *Hainan*) with 4 RBU 1200 *Uragan* A/S mor; 2 twin 57mm gun
    5 *Padma*
  PBFG 5 *Durbar* (PRC *Hegu*) with 2 single lnchr with SY-1 (CH-SS-N-1 *Scrubbrush*) AShM
  PBF 4 *Titas* (ROK *Sea Dolphin*)
  PB 11: 1 *Barkat* (ex-PRC *Shanghai* III); 2 *Karnaphuli*; 1 *Salam* (ex PRC *Huangfen*), 7 *Shaheed Daulat* (PRC *Shanghai* II)
MINE WARFARE • MINE COUNTERMEASURES 5
  MSO 5: 1 *Sagar*; 4 *Shapla* (ex-UK *River*)
AMPHIBIOUS
  LANDING SHIPS • LSL 1
  LANDING CRAFT 14
    LCT 2
    LCU 4 (of which 2†)
    LCM 5 *Darshak* (*Yuchin*)
    LCVP 3†
LOGISTICS AND SUPPORT 9
  AG 1
  AGHS 2: 1 *Agradoot*; 1 *Anushandhan*
  AOR 2 (coastal)
  AOT 1 *Khan Jahangir Ali*
  AR 1†
  ATF 1†
  AX 1 *Shaheed Ruhul Amin*

Naval Aviation
EQUIPMENT BY TYPE
AIRCRAFT • TPT • Light 2 Do-228NG (MP)
HELICOPTERS • TPT • Light 2 AW109E *Power*

Special Warfare and Diving Command 300

Air Force 14,000
FORCES BY ROLE
FIGHTER
  1 sqn with MiG-29/MiG-29UB *Fulcrum*
FIGHTER/GROUND ATTACK
  1 sqn with F-7MB/FT-7B *Airguard*
  1 sqn with F-7BG/FT-7BG *Airguard*
  1 sqn with F-7BGI/FT-7BGI *Airguard*
GROUND ATTACK
  1 sqn with Yak-130 *Mitten**
TRANSPORT
  1 sqn with An-32 *Cline*
  1 sqn with C-130B *Hercules*
  1 sqn with L-410UVP
TRAINING
  1 sqn with K-8W *Karakorum**; L-39ZA *Albatros**
  1 sqn with PT-6
TRANSPORT HELICOPTER
  1 sqn with AW139; Mi-17 *Hip* H; Mi-17-1V *Hip* H; Mi-171Sh
  1 sqn with Mi-17 *Hip* H; Mi-17-1V *Hip* H; Mi-171Sh
  1 sqn with Bell 212
  1 trg sqn with Bell 206L *Long Ranger*; AW119 *Koala*
EQUIPMENT BY TYPE
AIRCRAFT 81 combat capable
  FTR 53: 9 F-7MB *Airguard*; 11 F-7BG *Airguard*; 12 F-7BGI *Airguard*; 5 FT-7B *Airguard*; 4 FT-7BG *Airguard*; 4 FT-7BGI *Airguard*; 6 MiG-29 *Fulcrum*; 2 MiG-29UB *Fulcrum*
  TPT 11: **Medium** 4 C-130B *Hercules*; **Light** 7: 3 An-32 *Cline*†; 3 L-410UVP; 1 C295W
  TRG 42: 8 K-8W *Karakorum**; 7 L-39ZA *Albatros**; 14 PT-6; 13 Yak-130 *Mitten**
HELICOPTERS
  MRH 16: 2 AW139 (SAR); 12 Mi-17 *Hip* H; 2 Mi-17-1V *Hip* H (VIP)
  TPT 19: **Medium** 11 Mi-171Sh; **Light** 8: 2 Bell 206L *Long Ranger*; 4 Bell 212; 2 AW119 *Koala*
AIR-LAUNCHED MISSILES
  AAM • IR R-73 (AA-11A *Archer*); PL-5; PL-7; **SARH** R-27R (AA-10A *Alamo*)

Paramilitary 63,900

Ansars 20,000+
Security Guards

Rapid Action Battalions 5,000
Ministry of Home Affairs
FORCES BY ROLE
MANOEUVRE
  Other
    14 paramilitary bn

Border Guard Bangladesh 38,000

FORCES BY ROLE
MANOEUVRE
Amphibious
  1 rvn coy
Other
  54 paramilitary bn

Coast Guard 900

EQUIPMENT BY TYPE
PATROL AND COASTAL COMBATANTS 13
  PSO 4 *Syed Nazrul* (ex-ITA *Minerva*) with 1 hel landing platform
  PB 4: 1 *Ruposhi Bangla*; 1 *Shaheed Daulat*; 2 *Shetgang*
  PBR 5 *Pabna*

DEPLOYMENT

CENTRAL AFRICAN REPUBLIC: UN • MINUSCA 1,028; 1 cdo coy; 1 inf bn; 1 med coy

DEMOCRATIC REPUBLIC OF THE CONGO: UN • MONUSCO 1,672; 1 inf bn; 1 engr coy; 1 avn coy; 1 hel coy

LEBANON: UN • UNIFIL 117; 1 FSG

MALI: UN • MINUSMA 1,295; 1 inf bn; 1 engr coy; 2 sigs coy; 1 tpt coy

SOUTH SUDAN: UN • UNMISS 1,619; 1 inf bn; 2 rvn coy; 2 engr coy

SUDAN: UN • UNISFA 2

WESTERN SAHARA: UN • MINURSO 27; 1 fd hospital

Brunei BRN

Brunei Dollar B$		2018	2019	2020
GDP	B$	18.3bn	16.9bn	
	US$	13.6bn	12.5bn	
per capita	US$	30,668	27,871	
Growth	%	0.1	1.8	
Inflation	%	0.1	0.1	
Def bdgt	B$	493m	590m	
	US$	365m	435m	
US$1=B$		1.35	1.36	

Real-terms defence budget trend (US$m, constant 2015)

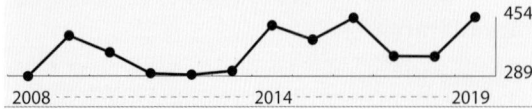

Population 457,533

Ethnic groups: Malay 65.7%; Chinese 10.3%; Indigenous 3.4%; other or unspecified 23.6%

Age	0–14	15–19	20–24	25–29	30–64	65 plus
Male	11.6%	3.9%	4.3%	4.5%	22.1%	2.7%
Female	11.0%	3.8%	4.5%	4.8%	24.1%	2.8%

Capabilities

The Royal Brunei Armed Forces are professional and well trained. The 2011 defence white paper set out missions such as ensuring territorial integrity and upholding the constitution. C4ISR capabilities are being improved to offset the forces' relatively small size, and the white paper advocates pursuing procurement to strengthen airspace control, hardening C4 systems against cyber attack and protecting national communications infrastructure. Brunei plans to develop a fully mechanised battalion and stated in the white paper that it would examine potential replacements for its Scorpion light tanks. There is a long-established relationship with the UK, for whom Brunei has hosted a garrison since 1962 and a jungle-warfare school since 1972. Brunei is a member of ASEAN and has a close relationship with Singapore, for whom it hosts a permanent training base. The white paper advocates participation in regional exercises, with an emphasis on command and control, humanitarian assistance and disaster response, and maritime patrol. Brunei does not have the ability to deploy abroad without assistance, but has maintained a small deployment to UNIFIL in Lebanon since 2008. Brunei has no domestic defence industry and imports its military equipment. In 2010, the Centre of Science and Technology Research and Development was established to lead on defence-technology research, manage defence procurements, and provide engineering and support services to the armed forces.

ACTIVE 7,200 (Army 4,900 Navy 1,200 Air 1,100)
Paramilitary 400–500

RESERVE 700 (Army 700)

ORGANISATIONS BY SERVICE

Army 4,900

FORCES BY ROLE
MANOEUVRE
Light
  3 inf bn
COMBAT SUPPORT
  1 cbt spt bn (1 armd recce sqn, 1 engr sqn)

Reserves 700

FORCES BY ROLE
MANOEUVRE
Light
  1 inf bn

EQUIPMENT BY TYPE
ARMOURED FIGHTING VEHICLES
  LT TK 20 FV101 *Scorpion* (incl FV105 *Sultan* CP)
  APC • APC (W) 45 VAB
ENGINEERING & MAINTENANCE VEHICLES
  ARV 2 *Samson*
ARTILLERY • MOR 81mm 24

Navy 1,200

FORCES BY ROLE
SPECIAL FORCES
  1 SF sqn

EQUIPMENT BY TYPE
PATROL AND COASTAL COMBATANTS 9
  CORVETTES • FSG 4 *Darussalam* with 2 twin lnchr with MM40 *Exocet* Block 2 AShM, 1 57mm gun, 1 hel landing platform

PCC 4 *Ijtihad*
PBF 1 *Mustaed*
AMPHIBIOUS • LANDING CRAFT • LCM 4: 2 *Teraban*;
2 *Cheverton Loadmaster*

Air Force 1,100

FORCES BY ROLE
MARITIME PATROL
1 sqn with CN235M
TRAINING
1 sqn with PC-7; Bell 206B *Jet Ranger* II
TRANSPORT HELICOPTER
1 sqn with Bell 214 (SAR)
1 sqn with Bo-105
1 sqn with S-70i *Black Hawk*
AIR DEFENCE
1 sqn with *Rapier*
1 sqn with *Mistral*
EQUIPMENT BY TYPE
AIRCRAFT
MP 1 CN235M
TRG 4 PC-7
HELICOPTERS
TPT 21: **Medium** 13: 1 Bell 214 (SAR); 12 S-70i *Black Hawk*; **Light** 8: 2 Bell 206B *Jet Ranger* II; 6 Bo-105 (armed, 81mm rockets)
AIR DEFENCE • SAM • Point-defence *Rapier*; *Mistral*

Paramilitary 400–500

Gurkha Reserve Unit 400–500
FORCES BY ROLE
MANOEUVRE
Light
2 inf bn(-)

DEPLOYMENT

LEBANON: UN • UNIFIL 29
PHILIPPINES: IMT 8

FOREIGN FORCES

Singapore 1 trg camp with infantry units on rotation; 1 trg school; 1 hel det with AS332 *Super Puma*
United Kingdom 1,000; 1 Gurkha bn; 1 jungle trg centre; 1 hel flt with 3 Bell 212

Cambodia CAM

Cambodian Riel r		2018	2019	2020
GDP	r	98.9tr	108tr	
	US$	24.4bn	26.7bn	
per capita	US$	1,504	1,621	
Growth	%	7.5	7.0	
Inflation	%	2.4	2.2	
Def bdgt [a]	r	ε3.90tr	4.24tr	
	US$	ε964m	1.0bn	
US$1=r		4046.75	4055.25	

[a] Defence and security budget

Real-terms defence budget trend (US$m, constant 2015)

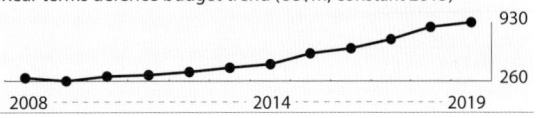

| Population | 16,690,861 |

Ethnic groups: Khmer 90%; Vietnamese 5%; Chinese 1%

Age	0–14	15–19	20–24	25–29	30–64	65 plus
Male	15.4%	4.4%	4.3%	4.9%	18.0%	1.7%
Female	15.1%	4.4%	4.4%	5.1%	19.6%	2.8%

Capabilities

Despite their name, which reflects Cambodia's formal status as a constitutional monarchy, the Royal Cambodian Armed Forces (RCAF) are essentially the modern manifestation of the armed forces of the former People's Republic of Kampuchea, established in 1979 following Vietnam's invasion. Cambodia faces no direct external military threats, besides border clashes with Thailand. Security concerns regard mainly transnational threats generating instability, such as drug trafficking. Cambodia's most important international links are with the Chinese and Vietnamese armed forces. China and Cambodia have developed training ties in recent years, and exercises have grown in scale. Skirmishes on the border with Thailand since 2008 provided little indication of capacity for high-intensity combat. Cambodia lacks significant resources for personnel training, which is partly financed by Chinese military assistance. The RCAF has an excessive number of senior officers, while many formations and units appear to be of only nominal status. Cambodia has contributed personnel to UN peacekeeping missions, including MINUSCA and MINUSMA. Despite increased defence spending in recent years, the armed forces rely largely on equipment donations and second-hand procurements, including from China and South Korea. Cambodia has no domestic defence industry, with no ability to design and manufacture modern equipment for its armed forces.

ACTIVE 124,300 (Army 75,000 Navy 2,800 Air 1,500 Provincial Forces 45,000) **Paramilitary 67,000**

Conscript liability 18 months service authorised but not implemented since 1993

ORGANISATIONS BY SERVICE

Army ε75,000

6 Military Regions (incl 1 special zone for capital)

FORCES BY ROLE
SPECIAL FORCES
  1 (911th) AB/SF Bde
MANOEUVRE
  Light
    2 (2nd & 3rd Intervention) inf div (3 inf bde)
    5 (Intervention) indep inf bde
    8 indep inf bde
  Other
    1 (70th) sy bde (4 sy bn)
    17 (border) sy bn
COMBAT SUPPORT
  2 arty bn
  4 fd engr regt
COMBAT SERVICE SUPPORT
  1 (construction) engr regt
  2 tpt bde
AIR DEFENCE
  1 AD bn

EQUIPMENT BY TYPE
ARMOURED FIGHTING VEHICLES
  MBT 200+: 50 Type-59; 150+ T-54/T-55
  LT TK 20+: Type-62; 20 Type-63
  RECCE 4+ BRDM-2
  IFV 70 BMP-1
  APC 230+
    APC (T) M113
    APC (W) 230: 200 BTR-60/BTR-152; 30 OT-64
ENGINEERING & MAINTENANCE VEHICLES
  ARV T-54/T-55
  MW *Bozena*; RA-140 DS
ANTI-TANK/ANTI-INFRASTRUCTURE
  RCL 82mm B-10; **107mm** B-11
ARTILLERY 433+
  TOWED 400+: **76mm** ZIS-3 (M-1942)/**122mm** D-30/**122mm** M-30 (M-1938)/**130mm** Type-59-I
  MRL 33+: **107mm** Type-63; **122mm** 13: 8 BM-21; 5 RM-70; **132mm** BM-13-16 (BM-13); **140mm** 20 BM-14-16 (BM-14)
  MOR 82mm M-37; **120mm** M-43; **160mm** M-160
AIR DEFENCE
  SAM • Point-defence FN-6; FN-16 (reported)
  GUNS • TOWED 14.5mm ZPU-1/ZPU-2/ZPU-4; **37mm** M-1939; **57mm** S-60

Navy ε2,800 (incl 1,500 Naval Infantry)
EQUIPMENT BY TYPE
PATROL AND COASTAL COMBATANTS 14
  PBF 3 *Stenka*
  PB 9: 4 (PRC 46m); 3 (PRC 20m); 2 *Shershen*
  PBR 2 *Kaoh Chhlam*
AMPHIBIOUS • LANDING CRAFT
  LCU 1
LOGISTICS AND SUPPORT • AFDL 1

Naval Infantry 1,500
FORCES BY ROLE
MANOEUVRE
  Light
    1 (31st) nav inf bde

COMBAT SUPPORT
  1 arty bn

Air Force 1,500
FORCES BY ROLE
ISR/TRAINING
  1 sqn with P-92 *Echo* (L-39 *Albatros** in store)
TRANSPORT
  1 VIP sqn (reporting to Council of Ministers) with An-24RV *Coke*; AS350 *Ecureuil*; AS355F2 *Ecureuil* II
  1 sqn with BN-2 *Islander*; Y-12 (II)
TRANSPORT HELICOPTER
  1 sqn with Mi-17 *Hip* H; Mi-8 *Hip*; Z-9; (Mi-26 *Halo* in store)

EQUIPMENT BY TYPE
AIRCRAFT
  TPT • Light 9: 2 MA60; 5 P-92 *Echo* (pilot trg/recce); 2 Y-12 (II) (2 An-24RV *Coke*; 1 BN-2 *Islander* in store)
  TRG (5 L-39 *Albatros** in store)
HELICOPTERS
  MRH 14: 3 Mi-17 *Hip* H; 11 Z-9
  TPT 4: **Heavy** (2 Mi-26 *Halo* in store); **Light** 4: 2 AS350 *Ecureuil*; 2 AS355F2 *Ecureuil* II

Provincial Forces 45,000+
Reports of at least 1 inf regt per province, with varying numbers of inf bn (with lt wpn)

Paramilitary
Police 67,000 (including gendarmerie)

DEPLOYMENT
CENTRAL AFRICAN REPUBLIC: UN • MINUSCA 212; 1 engr coy

LEBANON: UN • UNIFIL 184; 1 EOD coy

MALI: UN • MINUSMA 292: 2 engr coy; 1 EOD coy

SOUTH SUDAN: UN • UNMISS 83; 1 MP unit

China, People's Republic of PRC

Chinese Yuan Renminbi	Y	2018	2019	2020
GDP	Y	88.4tr	95.5tr	
	US$	13.4tr	14.1tr	
per capita	US$	9,580	10,099	
Growth	%	6.6	6.1	
Inflation	%	2.1	2.3	
Def exp	Y	1.49tr	n.k	
	US$	225bn	n.k	
Def bdgt [a]	Y	1.13tr	1.22tr	
	US$	171bn	181bn	
US$1=Y		6.62	6.75	

[a] Central Expenditure budget

Real-terms defence budget trend (US$bn, constant 2015)

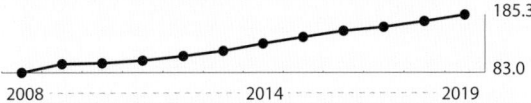

Population 1,397,462,098

Ethnic groups: Han 91.5%; Zhuang 1.3%; Hui 0.8%; Manchu 0.8%; Uighur 0.7%; Tibetan 0.5%; other or unspecified 4.4%

Age	0–14	15–19	20–24	25–29	30–64	65 plus
Male	9.3%	2.9%	3.4%	4.2%	25.9%	5.6%
Female	8.0%	2.5%	3.0%	3.8%	25.1%	6.2%

Capabilities

China's People's Liberation Army (PLA) is the world's largest armed force, with an increasingly modern, advanced equipment inventory. Its operational effectiveness, however, remains hampered by training and doctrine issues. China's 2019 defence white paper did not significantly alter the strategic direction laid out in the 2015 edition, focusing more on updating the progress of PLA modernisation efforts. A major restructuring process is now mostly in effect and the Strategic Support Force continues to develop China's cyber, space and information-dominance capabilities. China does not maintain any formal alliances, but it does have a number of key defence relationships with regional states and through its membership of the SCO. It has also worked to develop defence ties with several African states. Improving readiness for combat operations is a key objective of the current reforms; the PLA currently lacks any significant recent combat experience and its training has traditionally suffered from over-scripted and unrealistic exercises. Though these weaknesses are acknowledged and possibly being addressed, it is unclear how effective the newly established structures will be at generating and controlling high-intensity combined-arms capabilities. In the short term, changes to roles and requirements for officers may have had a detrimental effect on morale within the PLA, as well as on its overall level of readiness. The requirement for out-of-area operations is relatively new for the PLA; the navy is the only service to have experience in extended deployments, assisted by its support base in Djibouti. Major platform inventories in all the services comprise a heterogeneous mix of modern, older and obsolescent designs. The reduction in overall force size as part of the restructuring process has seen some older equipment designs finally withdrawn from service. China has an extensive defence-industrial base, capable of indigenously producing advanced equipment across all domains, although questions persist over quality and reliability.

ACTIVE 2,035,000 (Ground Forces 975,000 Navy 250,000 Air Force 395,000 Strategic Missile Forces 120,000 Strategic Support Force 145,000 Other 150,000) **Paramilitary 660,000**

Conscript liability Selective conscription; all services 24 months

RESERVE ε510,000

ORGANISATIONS BY SERVICE

Strategic Missile Forces 120,000+

People's Liberation Army Rocket Force

The People's Liberation Army Rocket Force (formerly the Second Artillery Force) organises and commands its own troops to launch nuclear counter-attacks with strategic missiles and to conduct operations with conventional missiles. Organised as launch bdes subordinate to 6 army-level msl bases. Org varies by msl type

FORCES BY ROLE
SURFACE-TO-SURFACE MISSILE
 1 ICBM bde with DF-4
 2 ICBM bde with DF-5A
 1 ICBM bde with DF-5B
 1 ICBM bde with DF-31
 2 ICBM bde with DF-31A
 2 ICBM bde with DF-31A(G)
 2 ICBM bde with DF-41
 4 IRBM bde with DF-26
 2 MRBM bde with DF-16
 2 MRBM bde with DF-17 with HGV
 6 MRBM bde with DF-21A/E
 2 MRBM bde with DF-21C
 2 MRBM bde with DF-21D
 3 SRBM bde with DF-11A/DF-15B
 2 GLCM bde with CJ-10/CJ-10A/CJ-100
 2+ SSM bde (forming)

EQUIPMENT BY TYPE
SURFACE-TO-SURFACE MISSILE LAUNCHERS
 ICBM • Nuclear 98: ε10 DF-4 (CH-SS-3); ε20 DF-5A/B (CH-SS-4 Mod 2/3); ε8 DF-31 (CH-SS-10 Mod 1); ε24 DF-31A (CH-SS-10 Mod 2); ε18 DF-31A(G) (CH-SS-10 Mod 3); ε18 DF-41 (CH-SS-20) (entering service)
 IRBM • Dual-capable ε72 DF-26
 MRBM 174: **Nuclear** ε80 DF-21A/DF-21E (CH-SS-5 Mod 2/6); **Conventional** 94: ε24 DF-16 (CH-SS-11 Mod 1/2); ε16 DF-17 with HGV (entering service); ε24 DF-21C (CH-SS-5 Mod 4); ε30 DF-21D (CH-SS-5 Mod 5 - ASBM)
 SRBM • Conventional 189: ε108 DF-11A (CH-SS-7 Mod 2); ε81 DF-15B (CH-SS-6 Mod 3)
 GLCM • Conventional 70: ε54 CJ-10/CJ-10A; ε16 CJ-100 (entering service)

Navy

EQUIPMENT BY TYPE
SUBMARINES • STRATEGIC • SSBN 4:
 4 *Jin* (Type-094) with up to 12 JL-2 (CH-SS-N-14) strategic SLBM, 6 single 533mm TT with Yu-6 HWT

Defensive
EQUIPMENT BY TYPE
RADAR • STRATEGIC: 4+ large phased array radars; some detection and tracking radars

Space
EQUIPMENT BY TYPE
SATELLITES 117
  COMMUNICATIONS 9: 2 *Shen Tong*-1; 3 *Shen Tong*-2; 2 *Feng Huo*-1; 2 *Feng Huo*-2
  NAVIGATION/POSITIONING/TIMING 34: 3 *Beidou*-2(M); 5 *Beidou*-2(G); 7 *Beidou*-2(IGSO); 18 *Beidou*-3(M); 1 *Beidou*-3(ISGO)
  METEOROLOGY/OCEANOGAPHY 8: 2 *Yunhai*-1; 6 *Yunhai*-2
  ISR 25: 2 *Jianbing*-5; 4 *Jianbing*-6; 2 *Jianbing*-7; 5 *Jianbing*-9; 2 *Jianbing*-10; 3 *Jianbing*-11/-12; 4 LKW; 2 *Tianhui*-2; 1 ZY-1
  ELINT/SIGINT 41: 9 *Jianbing*-8; 8 *Shijian* 6 (4 pairs – reported ELINT/SIGINT role); 7 *Shijian* 11 (reported ELINT/SIGINT role); 15 *Yaogan*-30; 2 *Yaogan*-32
COUNTERSPACE • MSL SC-19 (reported)

Ground Forces ε975,000
FORCES BY ROLE
COMMAND
  13 (Group) army HQ
SPECIAL FORCES
  15 spec ops bde
MANOEUVRE
  Armoured
  27 (cbd arms) armd bde
  1 hy mech inf div (1 armd regt, 2 mech inf regt, 1 arty regt, 1 AD regt)
  Mechanised
  1 (high alt) mech inf div (1 armd regt, 2 mech inf regt, 1 arty regt, 1 AD regt)
  23 (cbd arms) mech inf bde
  1 indep mech inf regt
  Light
  3 (high alt) mot inf div (1 armd regt, 2 mot inf regt, 1 arty regt, 1 AD regt)
  24 (cbd arms) inf bde
  Air Manoeuvre
  2 air aslt bde
  Amphibious
  6 amph aslt bde
  Other
  1 (OPFOR) armd bde
  1 mech gd div (1 armd regt, 2 mech inf regt, 1 arty regt, 1 AD regt)
  1 sy gd div (4 sy regt)
  16 (border) sy bde
  15 (border) sy regt
  1 (border) sy gp
COMBAT SUPPORT
  15 arty bde
  14 engr/NBC bde
  1 engr regt
COMBAT SERVICE SUPPORT
  13 spt bde

COASTAL DEFENCE
  19 coastal arty/AShM bde
AVIATION
  1 mixed avn bde
HELICOPTER
  12 hel bde
TRAINING
  4 hel trg regt
AIR DEFENCE
  15 AD bde

Reserves
The People's Liberation Army Reserve Force is being restructured, and the army component reduced. As a result some of the units below may have been re-roled or disbanded
FORCES BY ROLE
MANOEUVRE
  Armoured
  2 armd regt
  Light
  18 inf div
  4 inf bde
  3 indep inf regt
COMBAT SUPPORT
  3 arty div
  7 arty bde
  15 engr regt
  1 ptn br bde
  3 ptn br regt
  10 chem regt
  10 sigs regt
COMBAT SERVICE SUPPORT
  9 log bde
  1 log regt
AIR DEFENCE
  17 AD div
  8 AD bde
  8 AD regt
EQUIPMENT BY TYPE
ARMOURED FIGHTING VEHICLES
  MBT 5,850: 300 ZTZ-59; 650 ZTZ-59-II; 600 ZTZ-59D; 200 ZTZ-79; 300 ZTZ-88A/B; 1,000 ZTZ-96; 1,500 ZTZ-96A; 600 ZTZ-99; 500 ZTZ-99A; 200 ZTQ-15
  LT TK 350: 250 ZTD-05; 100 ZTS-63A
  ASLT 800 ZTL-11
  IFV 5,800: 400 ZBD-04; 1,500 ZBD-04A; 1,500 ZBL-08; 600 ZBD-86; 650 ZBD-86A; 550 ZSL-92; 600 ZSL-92B
  APC 3,950
    APC (T) 2,700: 750 ZSD-63; 200 ZSD-63C; 1,750 ZSD-89
    APC (W) 1,250: 700 ZSL-92A; 500 ZSL-10; 50 ZSL-93
  AAV 600 ZBD-05
  AUV Dongfeng Mengshi; *Tiger* 4×4
ENGINEERING & MAINTENANCE VEHICLES
  ARV Type-73; Type-84; Type-85; Type-97; Type-654
  VLB KMM; MTU; TMM; Type-84A
  MW Type-74; Type-79; Type-81-II; Type-84

ANTI-TANK/ANTI-INFRASTRUCTURE
MSL
SP 1,000: 450 HJ-8 (veh mounted); 100 HJ-10; 450 ZSL-02B
MANPATS HJ-73D; HJ-8A/C/E; HJ-11
RCL 3,966: **75mm** PF-56; **82mm** PF-65 (B-10); PF-78; **105mm** PF-75; **120mm** PF-98
GUNS 1,788
SP 480: **100mm** 250 PTL-02; **120mm** 230 PTZ-89
TOWED • **100mm** 1,308 PT-73 (T-12)/PT-86
ARTILLERY 8,994+
SP 2,140: **122mm** 1,650: 500 PLZ-89; 350 PLZ-07A; 150 PLZ-07B; 300 PCL-09; 350 PLL-09; **152mm** 150 PLZ-83A/B; **155mm** 340: 320 PLZ-05; 20+ PCL-18; (400 in store: **122mm** 200 PLZ-89; **152mm** 200 PLZ-83A)
TOWED 1,234: **122mm** 500 PL-96 (D-30); **130mm** 234 PL-59 (M-46)/PL-59-I; **152mm** 500 PL-66 (D-20); (4,400 in store: **122mm** 2,800 PL-54-1 (M-1938)/PL-83/PL-60 (D-74)/PL-96 (D-30); **152mm** 1,600 PL-54 (D-1)/PL-66 (D-20))
GUN/MOR 120mm 1,250: 450 PLL-05; 800 PPZ-10
MRL 1,570+ **107mm** PH-63; **122mm** 1,375: 550 PHL-81/PHL-90; 350 PHL-11; 375 PHZ-89; 100 PHZ-11; **300mm** 175 PHL-03; **370mm** 20+ PHL-19; (700 in store: **122mm** 700 PHL-81)
MOR 2,800: **82mm** PP-53 (M-37)/PP-67/PP-82/PP-87; **SP 82mm** PCP-001; **100mm** PP-89
COASTAL DEFENCE
AShM HY-1 (CH-SSC-2 *Silkworm*); HY-2 (CH-SSC-3 *Seersucker*); HY-4 (CH-SSC-7 *Sadsack*); YJ-62
PATROL AND COASTAL COMBATANTS 25
PB 25: 9 *Huzong*; 16 *Shenyang*
AMPHIBIOUS • **LANDING CRAFT** • **LCM** 205: 3+ *Yugong*; 50+ *Yunnan* II; 100+ *Yupen*; 2+ *Yutu*; 50 *Yuwei*
LOGISTICS AND SUPPORT 22
AK 6+ *Leizhuang*
AKR 1 *Yunsong* (capacity 1 MBT; 1 med hel)
ARC 1
AOT 11: 1 *Fuzhong*; 8 *Fubing*; 2 *Fulei*
ATF 2 *Huntao*
AX 1 *Haixun* III
AIRCRAFT • **TPT** 10: **Medium** 6: 4 Y-8; 2 Y-9; **Light** 4 Y-7
HELICOPTERS
ATK 270+: 150 WZ-10; 120+ WZ-19
MRH 351: 22 Mi-17 *Hip* H; 3 Mi-17-1V *Hip* H; 38 Mi-17V-5 *Hip* H; 25 Mi-17V-7 *Hip* H; 8 SA342L *Gazelle*; 21 Z-9A; 31 Z-9W; 10 Z-9WA; 193 Z-9WZ
TPT 394: **Heavy** 105: 9 Z-8A; 96 Z-8B; **Medium** 221: 50 Mi-8T *Hip*; 140 Mi-171; 19 S-70C2 (S-70C) *Black Hawk*; 12+ Z-20; **Light** 68: 53 AS350 *Ecureuil*; 15 H120 *Colibri*
UNMANNED AERIAL VEHICLES
ISR • **Heavy** BZK-005; BZK-009 (reported); **Medium** BZK-006 (incl variants); BZK-007; BZK-008; **Light** *Harpy* (anti-radiation)
AIR DEFENCE
SAM
Medium-range 270+: 150+ HQ-16A/B (CH-SA-16); 120 HQ-17 (CH-SA-15)
Short-range 254: 24 9K331 *Tor*-M1 (SA-15 *Gauntlet*); 30 HQ-6D (CH-SA-6); 200 HQ-7A/B (CH-SA-4)
Point-defence HN-5A/B (CH-SA-3); FN-6 (CH-SA-10); QW-1 (CH-SA-7); QW-2

GUNS 7,396+
SP 396: **25mm** 270 PGZ-04A; **35mm** 120 PGZ-07; **37mm** 6 PGZ-88
TOWED 7,000+: **25mm** PG-87; **35mm** PG-99 (GDF-002); **37mm** PG-55 (M-1939)/PG-65/PG-74; **57mm** PG-59 (S-60); **100mm** PG-59 (KS-19)
AIR-LAUNCHED MISSILES
AAM • **IR** TY-90
ASM AKD-8; AKD-9; AKD-10

Navy ε250,000

The PLA Navy is organised into five service arms: submarine, surface, naval aviation, coastal defence and marine corps, as well as other specialised units. There are three fleets, one each in the Eastern, Southern and Northern theatre commands

EQUIPMENT BY TYPE
SUBMARINES 59
STRATEGIC • **SSBN** 4:
    4 *Jin* (Type-094) with up to 12 JL-2 (CH-SS-N-14) strategic SLBM, 6 single 533mm TT with Yu-6 HWT (2 more in test)
TACTICAL 55
SSN 6:
    2 *Shang* I (Type-093) with 6 single 533mm TT with YJ-82 (CH-SS-N-7) AShM or YJ-18 (CH-SS-N-13) AShM/Yu-3 HWT/Yu-6 HWT
    4 *Shang* II (Type-093A) with 6 single 533mm TT with YJ-82 (CH-SS-N-7) AShM or YJ-18 (CH-SS-N-13) AShM/Yu-3 HWT/Yu-6 HWT
    (3 *Han* (Type-091) in reserve with 6 single 533mm TT with YJ-82 (CH-SS-N-7) AShM/Yu-3 HWT)
SSK 48:
    2 *Kilo* (Project 877) with 6 single 533mm TT with TEST-71ME HWT/53-65KE HWT
    2 Improved *Kilo* (Project 636) with 6 single 533mm TT with TEST-71ME HWT/53-65KE HWT
    8 Improved *Kilo* (Project 636M) with 6 single 533mm TT with TEST-71ME HWT/53-65KE HWT/3M54E Klub-S (SS-N-27B *Sizzler*) AShM
    6 *Ming* (2 Type-035(G), 4 Type-035B) with 8 single 533mm TT with Yu-3 HWT/Yu-4 HWT
    12 *Song* (Type-039(G)) with 6 single 533mm TT with YJ-82 (CH-SS-N-7) AShM or YJ-18 (CH-SS-N-13) AShM/Yu-3 HWT/Yu-6 HWT
    4 *Yuan* (Type-039A) with 6 533mm TT with YJ-82 (CH-SS-N-7) AShM or YJ-18 (CH-SS-N-13) AShM/Yu-3 HWT/Yu-6 HWT
    14 *Yuan* II (Type-039B) with 6 533mm TT with YJ-82 (CH-SS-N-7) AShM or YJ-18 (CH-SS-N-13) AShM/Yu-3 HWT/Yu-6 HWT
    (8 *Ming* (Type-035(G)) in reserve with 8 single 533mm TT with Yu-3 HWT/Yu-4 HWT)
SSB 1 *Qing* (Type-032) (SLBM trials)
PRINCIPAL SURFACE COMBATANTS 82
    AIRCRAFT CARRIERS • **CV** 1
    1 *Liaoning* (RUS *Kuznetsov*) with 4 18-cell GMLS with HHQ-10 (CH-SA-N-17) SAM, 2 RBU 6000 *Smerch* 2 A/S mor, 3 H/PJ-11 CIWS (capacity 18–24 J-15 ac; 17 Ka-28/Ka-31/Z-8S/Z-8JH/Z-8AEW hel)

CRUISERS • CGHM 1 *Renhai* (Type-055) with 14 8-cell VLS (8 fore, 6 aft) with YJ-18A (CH-SS-N-13) AShM/HHQ-9B (CH-SA-N-21) SAM/Yu-8 A/S msl, 1 24-cell GMLS with HHQ-10 (CH-SA-N-17) SAM, 2 triple 324mm TT with Yu-7 LWT, 1 H/PJ-11 CIWS, 1 130mm gun (capacity 2 med hel) (in trials)

DESTROYERS 28
DDGHM 26:
- 1 *Hangzhou* (RUS *Sovremenny* I (Project 956E)) with 2 quad lnchr with 3M80E *Moskit*-E (SS-N-22A *Sunburn*) AShM, 2 single 3S90E lnchr with 9M38E M-22E *Shtil* (SA-N-7 *Gadfly*) SAM, 2 twin DTA-53-956 533mm ASTT with SET-65KE HWT/53-65KE HWT, 2 RBU 1000 *Smerch* 3 A/S mor, 4 AK630 CIWS, 2 twin 130mm gun (capacity 1 Z-9C/Ka-28 *Helix* A hel)
- 2 *Hangzhou* (RUS *Sovremenny* II (Project 956EM)) with 2 quad lnchr with 3M80MVE *Moskit*-E (SS-N-22B *Sunburn*) AShM, 2 single 3S90E lnchr with 9M38E M-22E *Shtil* (SA-N-7 *Gadfly*) SAM, 2 twin DTA-53-956 533mm ASTT with SET-65KE HWT/53-65KE HWT, 2 RBU 1000 *Smerch* 3 A/S mor, 2 *Kashtan* (CADS-N-1) CIWS, 1 twin 130mm gun (capacity 1 Z-9C/Ka-28 *Helix* A hel)
- 1 *Hangzhou* (RUS *Sovremenny* III (Project 956E)) with 2 quad lnchr with YJ-12A AShM, 4 8-cell H/AJK-16 VLS with HHQ-16 (CH-SA-N-16) SAM/Yu-8 A/S msl, 2 triple 324mm ASTT with Yu-7 LWT, 4 AK630M CIWS, 2 twin 130mm gun (capacity 1 Z-9C/Ka-28 *Helix* A hel)
- 1 *Luhai* (Type-051B) with 2 quad lnchr with YJ-12A AShM, 4 8-cell H/AJK-16 VLS with HHQ-16 (CH-SA-N-16) SAM/Yu-8 A/S msl, 2 triple 324mm ASTT with Yu-7 LWT, 2 H/PJ-11 CIWS, 1 twin 100mm gun (capacity 2 Z-9C/Ka-28 *Helix* A hel)
- 2 *Luhu* (Type-052) with 4 quad lnchr with YJ-83 AShM, 1 octuple lnchr with HHQ-7 (CH-SA-N-4) SAM, 2 triple 324mm ASTT with Yu-7 LWT, 2 FQF 2500 A/S mor, 2 H/PJ-12 CIWS, 1 twin 100mm gun (capacity 2 Z-9C hel)
- 2 *Luyang* (Type-052B) with 4 quad lnchr with YJ-83 AShM, 2 single 3S90E lnchr with 9M317E *Shtil*-1 (SA-N-7B) SAM, 2 triple 324mm ASTT with Yu-7 LWT, 2 H/PJ-12 CIWS, 1 100mm gun (capacity 1 Ka-28 *Helix* A hel)
- 6 *Luyang* II (Type-052C) with 2 quad lnchr with YJ-62 AShM, 8 8-cell VLS with HHQ-9 (CH-SA-N-9) SAM (CH-SA-N-9), 2 triple 324mm TT with Yu-7 LWT, 2 H/PJ-12 CIWS, 1 100mm gun (capacity 2 Ka-28 *Helix* A hel)
- 9 *Luyang* III (Type-052D) with 8 octuple VLS with YJ-18A (CH-SS-N-13) AShM/HHQ-9B (CH-SA-N-21) SAM/Yu-8 A/S msl, 1 24-cell GMLS with HHQ-10 (CH-SA-N-17) SAM, 2 triple 324mm TT with Yu-7 LWT, 1 H/PJ-12 CIWS, 1 130mm gun (capacity 2 Ka-28 *Helix* A hel)
- 2 *Luyang* III (Type-052D) with 8 octuple VLS with YJ-18A (CH-SS-N-13) AShM/HHQ-9B (CH-SA-N-21) SAM/Yu-8 A/S msl, 1 24-cell GMLS with HHQ-10 (CH-SA-N-17) SAM, 2 triple 324mm TT with Yu-7 LWT, 1 H/PJ-11 CIWS, 1 130mm gun (capacity 2 Ka-28 *Helix* A hel)

DDGM 2:
- 2 *Luzhou* (Type-051C) with 2 quad lnchr with YJ-83 AShM; 6 6-cell B-204 VLS with S-300FM *Rif*-M (SA-N-20 *Gargoyle*) SAM, 2 H/PJ-12 CIWS, 1 100mm gun, 1 hel landing platform

FRIGATES 52
FFGHM 40:
- 2 *Jiangkai* (Type-054) with 2 quad lnchr with YJ-83 AShM, 1 octuple lnchr with HHQ-7 (CH-SA-N-4) SAM, 2 triple 324mm TT with Yu-7 LWT, 2 RBU 1200 A/S mor, 4 AK630 CIWS, 1 100mm gun (capacity 1 Ka-28 *Helix* A/Z-9C hel)
- 16 *Jiangkai* II (Type-054A) with 2 quad lnchr with YJ-83 AShM, 4 8-cell VLS with Yu-8 A/S msl/HHQ-16 (CH-SA-N-16) SAM, 2 triple 324mm TT with Yu-7 LWT, 2 FQF 2300 A/S mor, 2 H/PJ-12 CIWS, 1 76mm gun (capacity 1 Ka-28 *Helix* A/Z-9C hel)
- 14 *Jiangkai* II (Type-054A) with 2 quad lnchr with YJ-83 AShM, 4 8-cell VLS with Yu-8 A/S msl/HHQ-16 (CH-SA-N-16) SAM, 2 triple 324mm TT with Yu-7 LWT, 2 FQF 2300 A/S mor, 2 H/PJ-11 CIWS, 1 76mm gun (capacity 1 Ka-28 *Helix* A/Z-9C hel)
- 5 *Jiangwei* II (Type-053H3) with 2 quad lnchr with YJ-83 AShM, 1 octuple lnchr with HHQ-7 (CH-SA-N-4) SAM, 2 RBU 1200 A/S mor, 1 twin 100mm gun (capacity 2 Z-9C hel)
- 3 *Jiangwei* II (Type-053H3) with 2 quad lnchr with YJ-83 AShM, 1 8-cell GMLS with HHQ-10 (CH-SA-N-17) SAM, 2 RBU 1200 A/S mor, 1 twin 100mm gun (capacity 2 Z-9C hel)

FFGM 2 *Luda* IV (Type-051G) with 4 quad lnchr with YJ-83 AShM, 1 octuple lnchr with HHQ-7 (CH-SA-N-4) SAM, 2 FQF 2500 A/S mor, 2 triple 324mm ASTT, 2 twin 100mm gun

FFG 10:
- 3 *Jianghu* I (Type-053H1) with 2 twin lnchr with HY-2 (CH-SS-N-2 *Sunflower*) AShM, 2 RBU 1200 *Uragan* A/S mor, 1 twin 100mm gun (capacity 1 Z-9C hel)
- 1 *Jianghu* III (Type-053H2) with 2 quad lnchr with YJ-83 AShM, 2 RBU 1200 *Uragan* A/S mor, 2 twin 100mm gun
- 6 *Jianghu* I Upgrade (Type-053H1G) with 2 quad lnchr with YJ-83 AShM, 2 RBU 1200 *Uragan* A/S mor, 2 twin 100mm gun

PATROL AND COASTAL COMBATANTS ε209
CORVETTES • FSGM 43:
- 21 *Jiangdao* I (Type-056) with 2 twin lnchr with YJ-83 AShM, 1 8-cell GMLS with HHQ-10 (CH-SA-N-17) SAM, 2 triple 324mm ASTT with Yu-7 LWT, 1 76mm gun, 1 hel landing platform
- 22 *Jiangdao* II (Type-056A) with 2 twin lnchr with YJ-83 AShM, 1 8-cell GMLS with HHQ-10 (CH-SA-N-17) SAM, 2 triple 324mm ASTT with Yu-7 LWT, 1 76mm gun, 1 hel landing platform

PCFG ε60 *Houbei* (Type-022) with 2 quad lnchr with YJ-83 AShM, 1 H/PJ-13 CIWS

PCG 26
- 6 *Houjian* (Type-037-II) with 2 triple lnchr with YJ-8 (CH-SS-N-4) AShM
- 20 *Houxin* (Type-037-IG) with 2 twin lnchr with YJ-8 (CH-SS-N-4) AShM

PCC 48
    2 *Haijiu* (Type-037-I) with 4 RBU 1200 *Uragan* A/S mor, 1 twin 57mm gun
    30 *Hainan* (Type-037) with ε4 RBU 1200 *Uragan* A/S mor, 2 twin 57mm gun
    16 *Haiqing* (Type-037-IS) with 2 FQF-3200 A/S mor
PB ε32 *Shanghai* III (Type-062-1)

MINE WARFARE
  MINE COUNTERMEASURES 54
    MCO 17: 4 *Wochi* (Type-081); 6 *Wochi* mod (Type-081A); 7 *Wozang* (Type-082II)
    MSC 16: 4 *Wosao* I (Type-082); 12 *Wosao* II (Type-082-II)
    MSD 21 *Wonang* (Type-529) (operated by *Wozang* MCO)

AMPHIBIOUS
  PRINCIPAL AMPHIBIOUS SHIPS • LPD 6 *Yuzhao* (Type-071) with 4 AK630 CIWS, 1 76mm gun (capacity 4 *Yuyi* LCAC plus supporting vehicles; 800 troops; 60 armoured vehs; 4 hel)
  LANDING SHIPS 49
    LSM 21:
      1 *Yudeng* (Type-073-II) with 1 twin 57mm gun (capacity 5 tk or 500 troops)
      7 *Yuhai* (Type-074) (capacity 2 tk; 250 troops)
      10 *Yunshu* (Type-073A) (capacity 6 tk)
      3 Type-074 (mod)
    LST 28:
      4 *Yukan* (Type-072-IIG) (capacity 2 LCVP; 10 tk; 200 troops)
      9 *Yuting* I (Type-072-II/III) (capacity 10 tk; 250 troops; 2 hel)
      9 *Yuting* II (Type-072A) (capacity 4 LCVP; 10 tk; 250 troops)
      6 *Yuting* II (Type-072B) (capacity 4 LCVP; 10 tk; 250 troops)
  LANDING CRAFT 67
    LCM ε30 *Yunnan*
    LCU 11 *Yubei* (Type-074A) (capacity 10 tanks or 150 troops)
    LCAC 14: 10 *Yuyi*; 4 *Zubr*
    UCAC 12 *Payi* (Type-724)

LOGISTICS AND SUPPORT 148
  ABU 1 Type-744A
  AFS 2: 1 *Dayun* (Type-904); 1 *Danyao* I (Type-904A)
  AFSH 2 *Danyao* II (Type 904B)
  AG 7: 6 *Kanhai*; 1 *Kanwu*
  AGB 2 *Yanrao* (Type-272) with 1 hel landing platform
  AGE 8: 2 *Dahua* (Type-909) with 1 hel landing platform (weapons test platform); 1 *Kantan*; 3 *Shupang* (Type-636); 1 *Yanqian* (Type-904I); 1 *Yuting* I (naval rail gun test ship)
  AGI 17: 1 *Dadie*; 1 *Dongdiao* (Type-815) with 1 hel landing platform; 7 *Dongdiao* (Type-815A) with 1 hel landing platform; 8 FT-14
  AGM 4 *Yuan Wang* (Type-718) (space and missile tracking)
  AGOR 2 *Dahua*
  AGS 8 *Shupang* (Type-636A) with 1 hel landing platform
  AH 8: 5 *Ankang*; 1 *Anwei* (Type-920); 2 *Qiongsha* (hospital conversion)
  AOEH 2 *Fuyu* (Type-901) with 2 H/PJ-13 CIWS
  AOR 1 *Fuqing* (Type-905) with 1 hel landing platform
  AORH 9: 2 *Fuchi* (Type-903); 6 *Fuchi* mod (Type-903A); 1 *Fusu*
  AOT 22: 4 *Fubai*; 16 *Fujian* (Type-632); 2 *Fuxiao*
  AP 4: 2 *Daguan*; 2 *Darong*
  ARC 2 *Youlan*
  ARS 14: 1 *Dadao*; 1 *Dadong*; 1 *Dalang* II (Type-922III); 3 *Dalang* III (Type-922IIIA); 3 *Dasan*; 2 *Dazhou*; 3 *Hai Jiu* 101 with 1 hel landing platform
  ASR 6: 3 *Dalao* (Type-926); 3 *Dajiang* (Type-925) (capacity 2 Z-8)
  ATF 14: ε11 *Hujiu*; 3 *Tuqiang*
  AWT 8: 4 *Fujian*; 3 *Fushi*; 1 *Jinyou*
  AX 4:
    1 *Dashi* (Type-0891A) with 2 hel landing platforms
    1 *Daxin* with 2 FQF 1200 A/S mor, 1 57mm gun, 1 hel landing platform
    1 *Qi Ji Guang* (Type-927) with 1 76mm gun, 1 hel landing platform
    1 *Yudao*
  ESD 1 *Donghaidao*

COASTAL DEFENCE • AShM 72 YJ-12/YJ-62 (3 regt)

Naval Aviation 26,000

FORCES BY ROLE
Naval aviation fighter/ground-attack units adopted brigade structure in 2017

BOMBER
  2 regt with H-6DU/G/J

FIGHTER/GROUND ATTACK
  1 bde with J-10A/S *Firebird*; Su-30MK2 *Flanker* G
  1 bde with J-11B/BS *Flanker* L
  1 bde with J-11B/BS *Flanker* L; JH-7A *Flounder*
  1 bde with J-8F *Finback*; JH-7A *Flounder*
  1 regt with J-15 *Flanker*

GROUND ATTACK
  1 bde with JH-7 *Flounder*

ANTI-SUBMARINE WARFARE
  2 regt with KQ-200

ELINT/ISR/ASW
  1 regt with Y-8JB/X; Y-9JZ; KQ-200

AIRBORNE EARLY WARNING & CONTROL
  3 regt with Y-8J; KJ-200; KJ-500

TRANSPORT
  1 regt with Y-7H; Y-8C; CRJ-200/700

TRAINING
  1 regt with CJ-6A
  1 regt with HY-7
  2 regt with JL-8
  1 regt with JL-9G
  1 regt with JL-9
  1 regt with JL-10
  1 regt with Z-9C

HELICOPTER
  1 regt with Ka-27PS; Ka-28; Ka-31
  1 regt with SH-5; AS365N; Z-9C/D; Z-8J/JH
  1 regt with Y-7G; Z-8; Z-8J; Z-8S; Z-9C/D

AIR DEFENCE
  2 SAM bde with HQ-9 (CH-SA-9)

EQUIPMENT BY TYPE
AIRCRAFT 404 combat capable
  BBR 35: 27 H-6G; 8 H-6J

FTR 24 J-8F *Finback*
FGA 139: 16 J-10A *Firebird*; 7 J-10S *Firebird*; 72 J-11B/BS *Flanker* L; 20 J-15 *Flanker*; 24 Su-30MK2 *Flanker* G
ATK 120: 48 JH-7; 72 JH-7A *Flounder*
ASW 18+: 3 SH-5; 15+ KQ-200
ELINT 13: 4 Y-8JB *High New* 2; 3 Y-8X; 6 Y-9JZ
AEW&C 16: 6 KJ-200 *Moth*; 6 KJ-500; 4 Y-8J *Mask*
TKR 5 H-6DU
TPT 38: **Medium** 6 Y-8C; **Light** 28: 20 Y-5; 2 Y-7G; 6 Y-7H; **PAX** 4: 2 CRJ-200; 2 CRJ-700
TRG 118: 38 CJ-6; 12 HY-7; 16 JL-8*; 28 JL-9*; 12 JL-9G*; 12 JL-10*
HELICOPTERS
ASW 28: 14 Ka-28 *Helix* A; 14 Z-9C
AEW 10+: 9 Ka-31; 1+ Z-18 AEW
MRH 18: 7 AS365N; 11 Z-9D
SAR 11: 3 Ka-27PS; 4 Z-8JH; 2 Z-8S; 2 Z-9S
TPT 38: **Heavy** 30: 8 SA321 *Super Frelon*; 9 Z-8; 13 Z-8J; **Medium** 8 Mi-8 *Hip*
UNMANNED AERIAL VEHICLES
ISR **Heavy** BZK-005; **Medium** BZK-007
AIR DEFENCE
SAM • **Long-range** 32 HQ-9 (CH-SA-9)
AIR-LAUNCHED MISSILES
AAM • **IR** PL-5; PL-8; PL-9; R-73 (AA-11A *Archer*); **IR/SARH** R-27 (AA-10 *Alamo*); **SARH** PL-11; **ARH** R-77 (AA-12A *Adder*); PL-12
ASM KD-88
AShM Kh-31A (AS-17B *Krypton*); YJ-12; YJ-61; YJ-8K; YJ-83K; YJ-9
ARM Kh-31P (AS-17A *Krypton*); YJ-91
BOMBS
Laser-guided: LS-500J
TV-guided: KAB-500KR; KAB-1500KR

Marines ε25,000
FORCES BY ROLE
SPECIAL FORCES
 1 spec ops bde
MANOEUVRE
 Mechanised
  1 mne bde
 Light
  3 mne bde
 Amphibious
  2 mne bde
EQUIPMENT BY TYPE
ARMOURED FIGHTING VEHICLES
 MBT some ZTQ-15
 LT TK 73 ZTD-05
 ASLT 2+ ZTL-11
 IFV 10+ ZBL-08
 AAV 152 ZBD-05
ANTI-TANK/ANTI-INFRASTRUCTURE
 MSL • **MANPATS** HJ-73; HJ-8
 RCL **120mm** Type-98
ARTILLERY 40+
 SP **122mm** 40+: 20+ PLZ-07; 20+ PLZ-89
 MRL **107mm** PH-63
 MOR **82mm**
AIR DEFENCE • SAM • **Point-defence** HN-5 (CH-SA-3)

Air Force 395,000
FORCES BY ROLE
BOMBER
 1 regt with H-6M
 2 regt with H-6H
 5 regt with H-6K
 1 bde with H-6N (forming)
FIGHTER
 5 bde with J-7 *Fishcan*
 5 bde with J-7E *Fishcan*
 3 bde with J-7G *Fishcan*
 4 bde with J-8F/H *Finback*
 2 bde with J-11A/Su-27SK/Su-27UBK *Flanker*
 4 bde with J-11A/J-11B/Su-27UBK *Flanker*
 3 bde with J-11B/BS *Flanker* L
FIGHTER/GROUND ATTACK
 7 bde with J-10A/S *Firebird*
 1 bde with J-10A/C/S *Firebird*
 2 bde with J-10B/S *Firebird*
 1 bde with J-10B/C/S *Firebird*
 2 bde with J-10C/S *Firebird*
 1 bde with Su-35 *Flanker* M; Su-30MKK *Flanker* G
 3 bde with J-16 *Flanker*
 2 bde with Su-30MKK *Flanker* G
 1 bde with J-20A (forming)
GROUND ATTACK
 6 bde with JH-7A *Flounder*
ELECTRONIC WARFARE
 2 regt with Y-8CB/G/XZ
ISR
 1 regt with JZ-8F *Finback**
 1 bde with JZ-8F *Finback**
 1 regt with Y-8H1
AIRBORNE EARLY WARNING & CONTROL
 1 regt with KJ-200 *Moth*; KJ-500; KJ-2000; Y-8T
SEARCH & RESCUE
 4 bde with Y-5; Mi-171E; Z-8
 1 regt with Y-5; Mi-171E; Z-8
TANKER
 1 bde with H-6U
TRANSPORT
 1 (VIP) regt with B-737; CRJ-200/700
 1 (VIP) regt with B-737; Tu-154M; Tu-154M/D
 1 regt with Il-76MD/TD *Candid*
 1 regt with Il-76MD *Candid*; Il-78 *Midas*
 1 regt with Mi-17V-5; Y-7
 1 regt with Y-5/Y-7/Z-9
 1 regt with Y-5/Y-7
 3 regt with Y-7
 1 regt with Y-8
 1 regt with Y-8; Y-9
TRAINING
 5 bde with CJ-6/6A/6B; Y-5
 8 bde with J-7; JJ-7A
 13 bde with JL-8; JL-9; JL-10
TRANSPORT HELICOPTER
 1 regt with AS332 *Super Puma*; H225 (VIP)
ISR UAV
 2 bde with GJ-1; GJ-2

AIR DEFENCE
1 SAM div
23 SAM bde
EQUIPMENT BY TYPE
AIRCRAFT 2,517 combat capable
  BBR 176: ε12 H-6A (trg role); ε60 H-6H/M; ε100 H-6K; 4+ H-6N
  FTR 759: 200 J-7 *Fishcan*; 192 J-7E *Fishcan*; 120 J-7G *Fishcan*; 50 J-8F *Finback*; 50 J-8H *Finback*; 95 J-11; 20 Su-27SK *Flanker*; 32 Su-27UBK *Flanker*
  FGA 794+: 220 J-10A *Firebird*; 55+ J-10B *Firebird*; 100+ J-10C *Firebird*; 70 J-10S *Firebird*; 130 J-11B/BS *Flanker L*; 100+ J-16 *Flanker*; 22+ J-20A (entering service); 73 Su-30MKK *Flanker G*; 24 Su-35 *Flanker M*
  ATK 140 JH-7A *Flounder*
  EW 14: 4 Y-8CB *High New* 1; 6 Y-8G *High New* 3; 2 Y-8XZ *High New* 7; 2 Y-9XZ
  ELINT 4 Tu-154M/D *Careless*
  ISR 51: 24 JZ-8 *Finback**; 24 JZ-8F *Finback**; 3 Y-8H1
  AEW&C 13: 4 KJ-200 *Moth*; 5 KJ-500; 4 KJ-2000
  C2 5: 2 B-737; 3 Y-8T *High New* 4
  TKR 13: 10 H-6U; 3 Il-78 *Midas*
  TPT 336+ **Heavy** 28+: 20 Il-76MD/TD *Candid*; 8+ Y-20; **Medium** 42+: 30 Y-8C; 12+ Y-9; **Light** 239: 170 Y-5; 41 Y-7/Y-7H; 20 Y-11; 8 Y-12; **PAX** 27: 9 B-737 (VIP); 5 CRJ-200; 5 CRJ-700; 8 Tu-154M *Careless*
  TRG 1,012+: 400 CJ-6/-6A/-6B; 12+ HY-7; 50 JJ-7*; 150 JJ-7A*; 350 JL-8*; 30 JL-9*; 20+ JL-10*
HELICOPTERS
  MRH 22: 20 Z-9; 2 Mi-17V-5 *Hip* H
  TPT 31+: **Heavy** 18+ Z-8; **Medium** 13+: 6+ AS332 *Super Puma* (VIP); 3 H225 (VIP); 4+ Mi-171
UNMANNED AERIAL VEHICLES
  CISR • Heavy 12+ GJ-1; GJ-2; GJ-11 (in test)
  ISR • Heavy 14+: 12+ EA-03; 2+ WZ-8
AIR DEFENCE
  SAM 850+
    Long-range 516+: 180 HQ-9 (CH-SA-9); 60 HQ-9B (CH-SA-21); 100+ HQ-22; 32 S-300PMU (SA-10 *Grumble*); 64 S-300PMU1 (SA-20 *Gargoyle*); 64 S-300PMU2 (SA-20 *Gargoyle*); 16 S-400 (SA-21B *Growler*)
    Medium-range 230: ε80 HQ-2/-2A/-2B (CH-SA-1); 150 HQ-12 (CH-SA-12)
    Short-range 104+: 50+ HQ-6A (CH-SA-6); 24 HQ-6D (CH-SA-6); ε30 HQ-7 (CH-SA-4)
  GUNS 16,000 **100mm/85mm**
AIR-LAUNCHED MISSILES
  AAM • IR PL-5B/C; PL-8; R-73 (AA-11A *Archer*); **IIR** PL-10; **IR/SARH** R-27 (AA-10 *Alamo*); **SARH** PL-11; **ARH** PL-12; PL-15 (entering service); R-77 (AA-12A *Adder*); R-77-1 (RVV-SD) (AA-12B *Adder*)
  ASM AKD-9; AKD-10; KD-88; Kh-29 (AS-14 *Kedge*); Kh-59M (AS-18 *Kazoo*)
  AShM Kh-31A (AS-17B *Krypton*)
  ARM Kh-31P (AS-17A *Krypton*); YJ-91 (Domestically produced Kh-31P variant)
  ALCM • Conventional CJ-20; YJ(KD)-63
BOMBS
  Laser-guided: LS-500J; LT-2
  TV-guided: KAB-500KR; KAB-1500KR

Airborne Corps
FORCES BY ROLE
SPECIAL FORCES
1 spec ops bde
MANOEUVRE
  Air Manoeuvre
  6 AB bde
  Aviation
  1 hel regt
COMBAT SERVICE SUPPORT
1 spt bde
TRANSPORT
1 bde with Y-7; Y-8
EQUIPMENT BY TYPE
ARMOURED FIGHTING VEHICLES
  ABCV 180 ZBD-03
  APC • APC (T) 4 ZZZ-03 (CP)
ANTI-TANK/ANTI-INFRASTRUCTURE
  SP some HJ-9
ARTILLERY 162+
  TOWED 122mm ε54 PL-96 (D-30)
  MRL 107mm ε54 PH-63
  MOR 54+: **82mm** some; **100mm** 54
AIRCRAFT • TPT 20: **Medium** 6 Y-8; **Light** 14: 2 Y-7; 12 Y-12D
HELICOPTERS
  ATK 8 WZ-10K
  CSAR 8 Z-8KA
  MRH 12 Z-9WZ
AIR DEFENCE
  SAM • Point-defence QW-1 (CH-SA-7)
  GUNS • TOWED 25mm 54 PG-87

Strategic Support Force ε175,000

At the end of 2015, a new Strategic Support Force was established by drawing upon capabilities previously exercised by the PLA's 3rd and 4th departments and other central functions. It reports to the Central Military Commission and is responsible for the PLA's space and cyber capabilities

Theatre Commands

In early 2016, the previous seven military regions were consolidated into five new theatre commands

Eastern Theatre Command

Eastern Theatre Ground Forces
71st Group Army
(1 spec ops bde, 4 armd bde, 1 mech inf bde, 1 inf bde, 1 arty bde, 1 engr/NBC bde bde, 1 spt bde, 1 hel bde, 1 AD bde)
72nd Group Army
(1 spec ops bde, 1 armd bde, 1 mech inf bde, 2 inf bde, 2 amph bde, 1 arty bde, 1 engr/NBC bde, 1 spt bde, 1 hel bde, 1 AD bde)
73rd Group Army
(1 spec ops bde, 1 armd bde, 1 mech inf bde, 2 inf bde, 2 amph bde, 1 arty bde, 1 engr/NBC bde, 1 spt bde, 1 hel bde, 1 AD bde)

Eastern Theatre Navy

Coastal defence from south of Lianyungang to Dongshan (approx. 35°10′N to 23°30′N), and to seaward; HQ at Ningbo; support bases at Fujian, Zhoushan, Ningbo

17 **SSK**; 11 **DDGHM**; 17 **FFGHM**; 6 **FFG**; 19 **FSGM**; ε30 **PCFG/PCG**; ε22 **MCMV**; 2 **LPD**; ε22 **LST/M**

Eastern Theatre Navy Aviation
1st Naval Aviation Division
(1 AEW&C regt with KJ-500; 1 ASW regt with KQ-200)
Other Forces
(1 bbr regt with H-6DU/G; 1 FGA bde with JH-7; 1 FGA bde with Su-30MK2; J-10A; 1 hel regt with Ka-27PS; Ka-28; Ka-31)

Eastern Theatre Air Force
10th Bomber Division
(1 bbr regt with H-6H; 1 bbr regt with H-6K; 1 bbr regt with H-6M)
26th Special Mission Division
(1 AEW&C regt with KJ-200/KJ-500/Y-8T; 1 AEW&C regt with KJ-2000/Y-8T)
Fuzhou Base
(1 ftr bde with J-7E; 1 ftr bde with J-11A/B; 1 FGA bde with J-16; 1 FGA bde with Su-30MKK; 2 SAM bde)
Shanghai Base
(1 ftr bde with J-7E; 1 ftr bde with J-8F; 1 ftr bde with J-11B; 1 FGA bde with J-10A; 1 FGA bde with J-16; 1 FGA bde with J-20A; 2 atk bde with JH-7A; 1 trg bde with J-7/JJ-7A; 2 SAM bde)
Other Forces
(1 ISR bde with JZ-8F; 1 SAR bde; 1 Flight Instructor Training Base with CJ-6; JL-8; JL-9; JL-10)

Other Forces
Marines
(2 mne bde)

Southern Theatre Command

Southern Theatre Ground Forces
74th Group Army
(1 spec ops bde, 1 armd bde, 1 mech inf bde, 2 inf bde, 2 amph bde, 1 arty bde, 1 engr/NBC bde, 1 spt bde, 1 hel bde, 1 AD bde)
75th Group Army
(1 spec ops bde, 4 armd bde, 1 mech inf bde, 1 inf bde, 1 air aslt bde, 1 arty bde, 1 engr/NBC bde, 1 spt bde, 1 AD bde)
Other Forces
(1 (composite) inf bde (Hong Kong); 1 hel sqn (Hong Kong), 1 AD bn (Hong Kong))

Southern Theatre Navy
Coastal defence from Dongshan (approx. 23°30′N) to VNM border, and to seaward (including Paracel and Spratly islands); HQ at Zhanjiang; support bases at Yulin, Guangzhou

4 **SSBN**; 2 **SSN**; 16 **SSK**; 10 **DDGHM**; 12 **FFGHM**; 2 **FFGM**; 4 **FFG**; 15 **FSGM**; ε38 **PCFG/PCG**; ε16 **MCMV**; 4 **LPD**; ε21 **LST/M**

Southern Theatre Navy Aviation
3rd Naval Aviation Division
(1 ASW regt with KQ-200; 1 AEW&C regt with KJ-500)
Other Forces
(1 FGA bde with J-11B; 1 FGA bde with J-11B; JH-7A; 1 bbr regt with H-6DU/G/J; 1 tpt/hel regt with Y-7G; Z-8; Z-8J; Z-8S; Z-9C/D; 1 SAM bde)

Southern Theatre Air Force
8th Bomber Division
(2 bbr regt with H-6K)
20th Special Mission Division
(3 EW regt with Y-8CB/G/XZ)
Kunming Base
(1 FGA bde with J-10A; 1 FGA bde with J-10C; 1 trg bde with JJ-7A; 1 SAM bde)
Nanning Base
(1 ftr bde with J-11A; 2 FGA bde with J-10A; 1 FGA bde with J-10B/C; 1 FGA bde with Su-35; 1 FGA bde with Su-30MKK; 1 atk bde with JH-7A; 2 trg bde with J-7/JJ-7A; 1 SAM bde)
Other Forces
(1 tkr bde with H-6U; 1 SAR bde)

Other Forces
Marines
(1 spec ops bde; 2 mne bde)

Western Theatre Command

Western Theatre Ground Forces
76th Group Army
(1 spec ops bde, 3 armd bde, 1 mech inf bde, 2 inf bde, 1 arty bde, 1 engr/NBC bde, 1 spt bde, 1 hel bde, 1 AD bde)
77th Group Army
(1 spec ops bde, 1 armd bde, 2 mech inf bde; 3 inf bde, 1 arty bde, 1 engr/NBC bde, 1 spt bde, 1 hel bde, 1 AD bde)
Xinjiang Military District
(1 spec ops bde, 1 (high alt) mech div, 3 (high alt) mot div, 1 mech inf regt, 1 arty bde, 1 AD bde, 1 engr regt, 1 hel bde)
Xizang Military District
(1 spec ops bde; 1 mech inf bde; 2 inf bde; 1 arty bde, 1 AD bde, 1 engr/NBC bde, 1 hel bde)

Western Theatre Air Force
4th Transport Division
(1 tpt regt with Y-8/Y-9; 1 tpt regt with Y-7; 1 tpt regt with Mi-17V-5/Y-7/Y-20)
Lanzhou Base
(1 ftr bde with J-11AB; 1 ftr bde with J-7; 1 ftr bde with J-7E; 1 FGA bde with J-16; 1 SAM bde)
Urumqi Base
(1 ftr bde with J-8H; 1 ftr bde with J-11A/B; 1 atk bde with JH-7A; 2 SAM bde)
Lhasa Base
(1 SAM bde)
Xi'an Flying Academy
(1 trg bde with JJ-7A; 1 trg bde with JL-9; 2 trg bde with JL-8; 1 trg bde with Y-7; Y-8)

Other Forces
(1 SAR regt)

Northern Theatre Command
Northern Theatre Ground Forces
78th Group Army
(1 spec ops bde, 4 armd bde, 1 mech inf bde, 1 inf bde, 1 arty bde, 1 engr/NBC bde, 1 spt bde, 1 hel bde, 1 AD bde)
79th Group Army
(1 spec ops bde, 2 armd bde, 3 mech inf bde, 1 inf bde, 1 arty bde, 1 engr/NBC bde, 1 spt bde, 1 hel bde, 1 AD bde)
80th Group Army
(1 spec ops bde, 1 armd bde; 1 mech inf bde, 4 inf bde, 1 arty bde, 1 engr/NBC bde, 1 spt bde, 1 hel bde, 1 AD bde)

Northern Theatre Navy
Coastal defence from the DPRK border (Yalu River) to south of Lianyungang (approx 35°10′N), and to seaward; HQ at Qingdao; support bases at Lushun, Qingdao.
4 **SSN**; 16 **SSK**; 1 **CV**; 1 **CGHM**; 5 **DDGHM**; 2 **DDGM**; 11 **FFGHM**; 9 **FSGM**; ε18 **PCFG/PCG**; ε16 **MCMV**; ε7 **LST/M**

Northern Theatre Navy Aviation
2nd Naval Air Division
(1 EW/ISR/ASW regt with KQ-200; Y-8JB/X; Y-9JZ; 1 AEW&C regt with Y-8J; KJ-200; KJ-500; 1 MP/hel regt with SH-5; AS365N; Z-8J/JH; Z-9C/D)
Other Forces
(1 FGA regt with J-15; 1 FGA bde with JH-7A; J-8F; 1 tpt regt with Y-7H/Y-8C/CRJ-200/CRJ-700; 1 trg regt with CJ-6A; 2 trg regt with JL-8; 1 trg regt with HY-7; 1 trg regt with JL-9G; 1 trg regt with JL-9; 1 trg regt with JL-10)

Northern Theatre Air Force
16th Special Mission Division
(1 EW regt with Y-8/Y-8CB/Y-8G; 1 ISR regt with JZ-8F)
Dalian Base
(2 ftr bde with J-7E; 2 ftr bde with J-7H; 1 ftr bde with J-8F; 2 ftr bde with J-11B; 1 FGA bde with J-10A/C; 1 FGA bde with J-10B; 1 atk bde with JH-7A; 1 trg bde with JJ-7A; 3 SAM bde)
Jinan Base
(1 ftr bde with J-7G; 1 ftr bde with J-8F/H; 1 FGA bde with J-10A; 1 atk bde with JH-7A; 2 SAM bde)
Harbin Flying Academy
(1 trg bde with CJ-6; Y-5; 1 trg bde with H-6; HY-7; 2 trg bde with JL-8; 1 trg bde with JL-9)
Other Forces
(1 SAR bde)

Other Forces
Marines
(2 mne bde)

Central Theatre Command
Central Theatre Ground Forces
81st Group Army
(1 spec ops bde, 2 armd bde, 1 (OPFOR) armd bde, 2 mech inf bde, 1 inf bde, 1 arty bde, 1 engr/NBC bde, 1 spt bde, 1 avn bde, 1 AD bde)
82nd Group Army
(1 spec ops bde, 2 armd bde, 2 mech inf bde, 2 inf bde, 1 arty bde, 1 engr/NBC bde, 1 spt bde, 1 hel bde, 1 AD bde)
83rd Group Army
(1 spec ops bde, 1 armd bde, 5 mech inf bde, 1 air aslt bde, 1 arty bde, 1 engr/NBC bde, 1 spt bde, 1 AD bde)
Other Forces
(1 hy mech inf div, 2 (Beijing) gd div)

Central Theatre Air Force
13th Transport Division
(1 tpt regt with Y-8C; 1 tpt regt with Il-76MD/TD; 1 tpt regt with Il-76MD; Il-78)
34th VIP Transport Division
(1 tpt regt with B-737; CRJ200/700; 1 tpt regt with B-737; Tu-154M; Tu-154M/D; 1 tpt regt with Y-7; 1 hel regt with AS332; H225)
36th Bomber Division
(2 bbr regt with H-6K; 1 bbr regt with H-6H)
Datong Base
(1 ftr bde with J-7; 2 ftr bde with J-7E/G; 1 ftr bde with J-11A/B; 2 FGA bde with J-10A; 1 FGA bde with J-10C; 1 SAM div; 4 SAM bde)
Wuhan Base
(2 ftr bde with J-7; 1 ftr bde with Su-27SK/J-11A; 1 FGA bde with J-10B; 1 trg bde with J-7/JJ-7A; 2 SAM bde)
Shijiazhuang Flying Academy
(3 trg bde with JL-8; 1 trg bde with JL-8; JL-10)
Airborne Corps
(6 AB bde)
Other Forces
(1 bbr bde with H-6N; 1 surv regt with Y-8H1; 1 SAR bde)

Paramilitary 660,000+ active

People's Armed Police ε660,000
In 2018 the People's Armed Police (PAP) divested its border defence, firefighting, gold, forest, hydropower and security-guard units. In addition to the forces listed below, PAP also has 32 regional commands, each with one or more mobile units

FORCES BY ROLE
MANOEUVRE
Other
1 (1st Mobile) paramilitary corps (3 SF regt; 9 (mobile) paramilitary units; 1 engr/CBRN unit; 1 hel unit)
1 (2nd Mobile) paramilitary corps (2 SF unit; 9 (mobile) paramilitary units; 1 engr/CBRN unit; 1 hel unit)

China Coast Guard (CCG)
In 2018 the CCG was moved from the authority of the SOA to that of the People's Armed Police

EQUIPMENT BY TYPE
PATROL AND COASTAL COMBATANTS 523
  PSOH 42:
    2 *Zhaotou* with 1 76mm gun (capacity 2 med hel)
    7 *Zhaoduan* (Type-054 mod) with 1 76mm gun (capacity 1 med hel)
    3 *Jiangwei* I (Type-053H2G) (capacity 1 med hel) (ex-PLAN)
    4 *Shuoshi* II (capacity 1 med hel)
    2 *Shucha* I (capacity 1 med hel)
    10 *Shucha* II (capacity 1 med hel)
    12 *Zhaoyu* (capacity 1 med hel)
    1 *Zhoachang* (capacity 1 med hel)
    1 *Zhongyang* (capacity 1 med hel)
  PSO 45:
    9 *Zhaojun* (Type-718B) with 1 76mm gun, 1 hel landing platform
    1 *Dalang* I (Type-922) (ex-PLAN) 1 *Haixun* II with 1 hel landing platform
    1 *Hai Yang* (Type-625C) (ex-PLAN)
    1 *Jianghu* I (Type-053H) (ex-PLAN)
    1 *Kanjie* (Type-636A) with 1 hel landing platform (ex-PLAN)
    6 *Shusheng* with 1 hel landing platform
    3 *Shuwu*
    3 *Tuzhong* (ex-PLAN)
    1 *Wolei* (Type-918) (ex-PLAN)
    1 *Xiang Yang Hong* 9 (ex-PLAN)
    4 *Zhaolai* with 1 hel landing platform
    14 *Zhaotim*
  PCO 33: 4 *Zhaogao* (Type-056 mod) with 1 hel landing platform; 1 *Shuke* I; 4 *Shuke* II; 14 *Shuke* III; 3 *Shuyou*; 4 *Zhaodai*; 3 *Zhaoming*
  PCC 103: 25+ Type-618B-II; 45 *Hailin* I/II; 1 *Shuzao* II; 14 *Shuzao* III; 9 *Zhongeng*; 2 *Zhongmel*; 7 *Zhongsui*
  PB/PBF 300+
AMPHIBIOUS • **LST** 2 *Yuting* I (Type-072-II) (Ex-PLAN; used as hospital vessels and island supply)
LOGISTICS AND SUPPORT 27
  AG 6: 5+ *Kaobo*; 1 *Shutu*
  AGB 1 *Yanbing* (Type-071) (ex-PLAN)
  AGOR 9: 4 *Haijian*; 3 *Shuguang* 04 (ex-PLAN); 2 *Xiang Yang Hong* 9
  ATF 11
AIRCRAFT
  MP 1+ MA60H
  TPT • **Light** Y-12 (MP role)
HELICOPTERS
  TPT • **Light** Z-9

Maritime Militia

Made up of full- and part-time personnel. Reports to PLA command and trains to assist PLAN and CCG in a variety of military roles. These include ISR, maritime law enforcement, island supply, troop transport and supporting sovereignty claims. The Maritime Militia operates a variety of civilian vessels including fishing boats and oil tankers.

DEPLOYMENT

DEMOCRATIC REPUBLIC OF THE CONGO: UN • MONUSCO 232; 1 engr coy; 1 fd hospital

DJIBOUTI: 240; 1 mne coy(-); 1 med unit; 2 ZTL-11; 8 ZBL-08; 1 LPD; 1 ESD

GULF OF ADEN: 1 DDGHM; 1 FFGHM; 1 AORH

LEBANON: UN • UNIFIL 419; 2 engr coy; 1 med coy

MALI: UN • MINUSMA 421; 1 sy coy; 1 engr coy; 1 fd hospital

MIDDLE EAST: UN • UNTSO 5

SOUTH SUDAN: UN • UNMISS 1,057; 1 inf bn; 1 engr coy; 1 fd hospital

SUDAN: UN • UNAMID 6

TAJIKISTAN: ε300 (trg)

WESTERN SAHARA: UN • MINURSO 12

Fiji FJI

Fijian Dollar F$		2018	2019	2020
GDP	F$	11.6bn	12.2bn	
	US$	5.52bn	5.71bn	
per capita	US$	6,208	6,380	
Growth	%	3.5	2.7	
Inflation	%	4.1	3.5	
Def bdgt	F$	107m	121m	112m
	US$	51.3m	56.4m	
US$1=F$		2.09	2.14	

Real-terms defence budget trend (US$m, constant 2015)

Population 931,295

Ethnic groups: Fijian 51%; Indian 44%; European/other 5%

Age	0–14	15–19	20–24	25–29	30–64	65 plus
Male	13.9%	4.0%	4.0%	4.0%	21.6%	3.2%
Female	13.3%	3.8%	3.9%	3.8%	20.7%	3.8%

Capabilities

The Republic of Fiji Military Forces (RFMF) are an infantry-dominated defence force with a small naval element. The RFMF has intervened heavily in Fiji's domestic politics, and between a third coup in 2006 and 2014, democracy was effectively suspended. Guidelines issued in 2018 emphasised the need to confront non-traditional threats such as climate change, terrorism and transnational crime. The RFMF is constructing a deployable force headquarters, funded by Australia, which will administer and train all peacekeeping and HADR forces. International peacekeeping operations are an important revenue source for the government. Fiji's principal allies are Australia and New Zealand, with whom the RFMF regularly conducts training and maritime patrols. Defence relations with China, South Korea and the US are growing, with all three countries providing training or donating equipment. The RFMF has instituted a Regimental Sergeant Major's course to improve the quality of senior NCOs and to raise standards across the rest of the force. Previously, personnel were sent overseas to receive this level of training. Fiji has no significant defence industry and is only able to carry out basic equipment maintenance domestically. Significant upgrade and maintenance work is usually conducted in Australia.

ACTIVE 4,040 (Army 3,700 Navy 340)

RESERVE ε6,000
(to age 45)

ORGANISATIONS BY SERVICE

Army 3,700 (incl 300 recalled reserves)
FORCES BY ROLE
SPECIAL FORCES
 1 spec ops coy
MANOEUVRE
 Light
 3 inf bn
COMBAT SUPPORT
 1 arty bty
 1 engr bn
COMBAT SUPPORT
 1 log bn

Reserves 6,000
FORCES BY ROLE
MANOEUVRE
 Light
 3 inf bn
EQUIPMENT BY TYPE
ARMOURED FIGHTING VEHICLES
 AUV 10 *Bushmaster* IMV
ARTILLERY 16
 TOWED 85mm 4 25-pdr (ceremonial)
 MOR 81mm 12

Navy 340
EQUIPMENT BY TYPE
PATROL AND COASTAL COMBATANTS • PB 4: 2 *Kula* (AUS *Pacific*); 2 *Levuka*
LOGISTICS AND SUPPORT • AGHS 1 *Kacau*

DEPLOYMENT

EGYPT: MFO 170; elm 1 inf bn
IRAQ: UN • UNAMI 165; 2 sy unit
LEBANON: UN • UNIFIL 1
MIDDLE EAST: UN • UNTSO 2
SOUTH SUDAN: UN • UNMISS 5
SYRIA/ISRAEL: UN • UNDOF 290; 1 inf bn(-); elm 1 log bn

India IND

Indian Rupee Rs		2018	2019	2020
GDP	Rs	190tr	209tr	
	US$	2.72tr	2.94tr	
per capita	US$	2,038	2,172	
Growth	%	6.8	6.1	
Inflation	%	3.4	3.4	
Def bdgt [a]	Rs	4.04tr	4.31tr	
	US$	57.8bn	60.5bn	
US$1=Rs		69.9	71.2	

[a] Includes defence civil estimates, which include military pensions

Real-terms defence budget trend (US$bn, constant 2015)

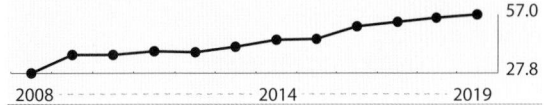

Population 1,311,559,204

Religious groups: Hindu 80%; Muslim 14%; Christian 2%; Sikh 2%

Age	0–14	15–19	20–24	25–29	30–64	65 plus
Male	14.1%	4.7%	4.6%	4.3%	20.9%	3.1%
Female	12.5%	4.2%	4.1%	3.9%	20.0%	3.5%

Capabilities

India continues its military modernisation, though progress in some areas remains slow. The armed forces are orientated against both China and Pakistan. Large numbers of paramilitary forces remain employed in the internal-security role. Army doctrine issued in late 2018 identified requirements including for 'integrated battle groups' and improved cyber, information-warfare and electronic-warfare capabilities. Earlier, a Joint Armed Forces Doctrine was issued in 2017, much of which was consistent with similar US and NATO doctrines. It set out joint doctrine for Indian nuclear command and control, and envisaged an 'emerging triad' of space, cyber and special-operations capabilities complementing conventional land, sea and air capabilities. Joint space, cyber and special-forces commands are being formed. Defence cooperation with the US continues to grow, with an increasing level of exercising and sales of US equipment, though India is also showing interest in Russian equipment, including an order for the S-400 missile-defence system. Indian personnel participate in numerous bilateral and multilateral exercises, and the country is one of the top troop contributors to UN peacekeeping operations. However, the overall capability of the conventional forces is limited by inadequate logistics, maintenance and shortages of ammunition and spare parts. India continues to modernise its conventional military capabilities and its nuclear forces, particularly its delivery systems, but many equipment projects have experienced significant delays and cost overruns, particularly indigenous systems. The government's 'Make in India' policy aims to strengthen the defence-industrial base. Apart from nuclear weapons and missiles, its indigenous defence industry is often slower to field new capabilities than foreign suppliers.

ACTIVE 1,455,550 (Army 1,237,000 Navy 66,100 Air 139,850 Coast Guard 12,600) **Paramilitary 1,585,950**

RESERVE 1,155,000 (Army 960,000 Navy 55,000 Air 140,000) **Paramilitary 941,000**
Army first-line reserves (300,000) within 5 years of full-time service, further 500,000 have commitment to age 50

ORGANISATIONS BY SERVICE

Strategic Forces Command
Strategic Forces Command (SFC) is a tri-service command established in 2003. The commander-in-chief of SFC, a senior three-star military officer, manages and administers all strategic forces through separate army and air-force chains of command

FORCES BY ROLE
SURFACE-TO-SURFACE MISSILE
  1 SRBM gp with *Agni* I
  1 MRBM gp with *Agni* II
  1 IRBM gp (reported forming) with *Agni* III
  2 SRBM gp with SS-250 *Prithvi* II

EQUIPMENT BY TYPE
SURFACE-TO-SURFACE MISSILE LAUNCHERS 54
  ICBM • Nuclear *Agni* V (in test)
  IRBM • Nuclear *Agni* III (entering service); *Agni* IV (in test)
  MRBM • Nuclear ε12 *Agni* II
  SRBM • Nuclear 42: ε12 *Agni* I; ε30 SS-250 *Prithvi* II; some SS-350 *Dhanush* (naval testbed)
SUBMARINES • STRATEGIC • SSBN 1 *Arihant* with 4 1-cell VLS with K-15 *Sagarika* SLBM, 6 533mm TT
AIR-LAUNCHED MISSILES
  ALCM • Nuclear *Nirbhay* (likely nuclear capable; in development)
Some Indian Air Force assets (such as *Mirage* 2000H or Su-30MKI) may be tasked with a strategic role

Space
EQUIPMENT BY TYPE
SATELLITES 21
  NAVIGATION, POSITIONING, TIMING: 7 IRNSS
  COMMUNICATIONS: 2 GSAT-7/-7A
  ISR 11: 8 *Cartosat*; 3 RISAT
  ELINT/SIGINT 1 EMISAT

Army 1,237,000
6 Regional Comd HQ (Northern, Western, Central, Southern, Eastern, Southwestern), 1 Training Comd (ARTRAC)

FORCES BY ROLE
COMMAND
  4 (strike) corps HQ
  10 (holding) corps HQ
SPECIAL FORCES
  8 SF bn
MANOEUVRE
  Armoured
  3 armd div (2–3 armd bde, 1 arty bde (2 arty regt))
  8 indep armd bde
  Mechanised
  6 (RAPID) mech inf div (1 armd bde, 2 mech inf bde, 1 arty bde)
  2 indep mech bde
  Light
  15 inf div (2–5 inf bde, 1 arty bde)
  1 inf div (forming)
  7 indep inf bde
  12 mtn div (3-4 mtn inf bde, 3–4 arty regt)
  2 indep mtn bde
  Air Manoeuvre
  1 para bde
SURFACE-TO-SURFACE MISSILE
  1 SRBM gp with *Agni* I
  1 MRBM gp with *Agni* II
  1 IRBM gp (reported forming) with *Agni* III
  2 SRBM gp with SS-250 *Prithvi* II
  3 GLCM regt with PJ-10 *Brahmos*
COMBAT SUPPORT
  3 arty div (2 arty bde, 1 MRL bde)
  2 indep arty bde
  4 engr bde
HELICOPTER
  23 hel sqn
AIR DEFENCE
  8 AD bde

Reserve Organisations

Reserves 300,000 reservists (first-line reserve within 5 years full-time service); **500,000 reservists** (commitment until age 50) (total 800,000)

Territorial Army 160,000 reservists (only 40,000 regular establishment)

FORCES BY ROLE
MANOEUVRE
  Light
  42 inf bn
COMBAT SUPPORT
  6 (Railway) engr regt
  2 engr regt
  1 sigs regt
COMBAT SERVICE SUPPORT
  6 ecological bn
EQUIPMENT BY TYPE
ARMOURED FIGHTING VEHICLES
  MBT 3,565+: 122 *Arjun*; 2,418 T-72M1; 1,025+ T-90S (ε1,100 various models in store)
  RECCE *Ferret* (used for internal-security duties along with some indigenously built armd cars)
  IFV 3,100: 700 BMP-1; 2,400 BMP-2 *Sarath* (incl some BMP-2K CP)
  APC 336+
    APC (W) 157+ OT-64
    PPV 179: 165 *Casspir*; 14+ *Yukthirath* MPV
ENGINEERING & MAINTENANCE VEHICLES
  AEV BMP-2; FV180
  ARV 730+: T-54/T-55; 156 VT-72B; 222 WZT-2; 352 WZT-3

VLB AM-50; BLG-60; BLG T-72; *Kartik*; MTU-20; MT-55; *Sarvatra*
MW 24 910 MCV-2
ANTI-TANK/ANTI-INFRASTRUCTURE
MSL
SP 110 9P148 *Konkurs* (AT-5 *Spandrel*)
MANPATS 9K113 *Konkurs* (AT-5 *Spandrel*); *Milan* 2
RCL 3,000+: **84mm** *Carl Gustav*; **106mm** 3,000+ M40A1 (10 per inf bn)
ARTILLERY 9,719+
SP 155mm 10 K9 *Vajra*-T
TOWED 2,975+: **105mm** 1,350+: 600+ IFG Mk1/Mk2/Mk3; up to 700 LFG; 50 M-56; **122mm** 520 D-30; **130mm** ε600 M-46 (500 in store) **155mm** 505: ε300 FH-77B; ε200 M-46 (mod); 5 M777A2
MRL 214: **122mm** ε150 BM-21/LRAR **214mm** 36 *Pinaka*; **300mm** 28 9A52 *Smerch*
MOR 6,520+: **81mm** 5,000+ E1; **120mm** ε1,500 AM-50/E1; **SP 120mm** E1; **160mm** 20 M-58 Tampella
SURFACE-TO-SURFACE MISSILE LAUNCHERS
IRBM • Nuclear some *Agni*-III (entering service)
MRBM • Nuclear ε12 *Agni*-II
SRBM • Nuclear 42: ε12 *Agni*-I; ε30 250 *Prithvi* II
GLCM • Conventional 15 PJ-10 *Brahmos*
AMPHIBIOUS 2 LCVP
HELICOPTERS
MRH 320+: 79 *Dhruv*; 12 *Lancer*; 50+ *Rudra*; 119 SA315B *Lama* (*Cheetah*); 60 SA316B *Alouette* III (*Chetak*)
UNMANNED AERIAL VEHICLES
ISR • Medium 25: 13 *Nishant*; 12 *Searcher* Mk I/II
AIR DEFENCE
SAM
Medium-range *Akash*
Short-range 180 2K12 *Kub* (SA-6 *Gainful*)
Point-defence 500+: 50+ 9K33 *Osa* (SA-8B *Gecko*); 200 9K31 *Strela*-1 (SA-9 *Gaskin*); 250 9K35 *Strela*-10 (SA-13 *Gopher*); 9K310 *Igla*-1 (SA-16 *Gimlet*); 9K38 *Igla* (SA-18 *Grouse*)
GUNS 2,395+
SP 155+: **23mm** 75 ZSU-23-4; ZU-23-2 (truck-mounted); **30mm** 20-80 2S6 *Tunguska*
TOWED 2,240+: **20mm** Oerlikon (reported); **23mm** 320 ZU-23-2; **40mm** 1,920 L40/70

Navy 66,100 (incl 7,000 Naval Avn and 1,200 Marines)

Fleet HQ New Delhi. Commands located at Mumbai, Vishakhapatnam, Kochi & Port Blair
EQUIPMENT BY TYPE
SUBMARINES 17
STRATEGIC • SSBN 1 *Arihant* with 4 1-cell VLS with K-15 *Sagarika* SLBM, 6 533mm TT
TACTICAL 16
SSN 1 *Chakra* (ex-RUS *Akula* II) with 4 single 533mm TT with 3M14E *Klub-S* (SS-N-30B) LACM/3M54E1/E *Klub-S* (SS-N-27A/B) (*Klub-S* AShM variant unclear) AShM, 4 single 650mm TT with 65-73 HWT (RUS lease agreement; damaged in 2017, awaiting repair)
SSK 15:
4 *Shishumar* (GER T-209/1500) with 8 single 533mm TT with SUT mod 1 HWT

2 *Sindhughosh* (FSU *Kilo*) with 6 single 533mm TT with 53-65KE HWT/TEST-71ME HWT/SET-65E HWT
7 *Sindhughosh* (FSU *Kilo*) with 6 single 533mm TT with 3M54E1/E *Klub-S* (SS-N-27A/B) (*Klub-S* AShM variant unclear) AShM/53-65KE HWT/TEST-71ME HWT/SET-65E HWT
2 *Kalvari* (FRA *Scorpène*) with 6 533mm TT with SM39 *Exocet* Block 2 AShM

PRINCIPAL SURFACE COMBATANTS 27
AIRCRAFT CARRIERS 1
CV 1 *Vikramaditya* (ex-FSU *Kiev* mod) with 3 8-cell VLS with *Barak*-1 SAM, 4 AK630M CIWS (capacity: 12 MiG-29K/KUB *Fulcrum* FGA ac; 6 Ka-28 *Helix* A ASW hel/Ka-31 *Helix* B AEW hel)

DESTROYERS 13
DDGHM 9:
2 *Delhi* with 4 quad lnchr with 3M24E *Uran*-E (SS-N-25 *Switchblade*) AShM, 2 single 3S90E lnchr with 9M38E M-22E *Shtil* (SA-N-7 *Gadfly*) SAM, 4 8-cell VLS with *Barak*-1 SAM, 5 single 533mm ASTT with SET-65E HWT/*Varunastra* HWT, 2 RBU 6000 *Smerch* 2 A/S mor; 2 AK630 CIWS, 1 100mm gun (capacity either 2 *Dhruv* hel/*Sea King* Mk42A ASW hel)
1 *Delhi* with 4 quad lnchr with 3M24E *Uran*-E (SS-N-25 *Switchblade*) AShM, 2 single 3S90E lnchr with 9M38E M-22E *Shtil* (SA-N-7 *Gadfly*) SAM, 5 single 533mm ASTT with SET-65E HWT/*Varunastra* HWT, 2 RBU 6000 *Smerch* 2 A/S mor; 2 AK630 CIWS, 1 100mm gun (capacity either 2 *Dhruv* hel/*Sea King* Mk42A ASW hel)
3 *Kolkata* with 2 8-cell UVLM VLS with *Brahmos* AShM, 4 8-cell VLS with *Barak*-8 SAM; 2 twin 533mm TT with SET-65E HWT/*Varanustra* HWT, 2 RBU 6000 *Smerch* 2 A/S mor, 4 AK630M CIWS, 1 76mm gun (capacity 2 *Dhruv*/*Sea King* Mk42B hel)
3 *Shivalik* with 1 8-cell 3S14E VLS with 3M54TE *Klub*-N (SS-N-27B *Sizzler*) AShM/*Brahmos* AShM, 4 8-cell VLS with *Barak*-1 SAM, 1 single 3S90E lnchr with 9M317E *Shtil*-1 (SA-N-7B) SAM, 2 triple ILAS-3 (B-515) 324mm ASTT, 2 RBU 6000 *Smerch* 2 A/S mor, 2 AK630M CIWS, 1 76mm gun (capacity 1 *Sea King* Mk42B ASW hel)

DDGM 4:
1 *Rajput* (FSU *Kashin*) with 2 twin lnchr with P-27 *Termit*-R (SS-N-2D *Styx*) AShM, 2 twin ZIF-101 lnchr with 4K91 M-1 *Volnya* (SA-N-1 *Goa*) SAM, 5 single PTA-51-61ME 533mm ASTT with SET-65E HWT/*Varanustra* HWT, 2 RBU 6000 *Smerch* 2 A/S mor, 2 AK630M CIWS, 1 76mm gun (capacity Ka-28 *Helix* A hel)
1 *Rajput* (FSU *Kashin*) with 2 twin lnchr with *Brahmos* AShM, 2 single lnchr with P-27 *Termit*-R (SS-N-2D *Styx*) AShM, 2 twin ZIF-101 lnchr with 4K91 M-1 *Volnya* (SA-N-1 *Goa*) SAM, 5 single 533mm ASTT with SET-65E HWT/*Varanustra* HWT, 2 RBU 6000 *Smerch* 2 A/S mor, 4 AK630M CIWS, 1 76mm gun (capacity 1 Ka-28 *Helix* A hel)
2 *Rajput* (FSU *Kashin*) with 1 8-cell UVLM VLS with *Brahmos* AShM, 2 twin lnchr with P-27 *Termit*-R

(SS-N-2D *Styx*) AShM, 2 8-cell VLS with *Barak*-1 SAM, 1 twin ZIF-101 lnchr with 4K91 M-1 *Volnya* (SA-N-1 *Goa*) SAM, 5 single 533mm ASTT with SET-65E HWT/*Varanustra* HWT, 2 RBU 6000 *Smerch* 2 A/S mor, 4 AK630M CIWS, 1 76mm gun (capacity 1 Ka-28 *Helix* A hel)

FRIGATES 13
  FFGHM 10:
    3 *Brahmaputra* with 4 quad lnchr with 3M24E *Uran*-E (SS-N-25 *Switchblade*) AShM, 3 8-cell VLS with *Barak*-1 SAM, 2 triple ILAS-3 (B-515) 324mm ASTT with A244 LWT, 4 AK630M CIWS, 1 76mm gun (capacity 2 SA316B *Alouette* III (*Chetak*)/*Sea King* Mk42 ASW hel) (of which 1 non-operational)
    1 *Godavari* with 4 single lnchr with P-27 *Termit*-R (SS-N-2D *Styx*) AShM, 1 8-cell VLS with *Barak*-1 SAM, 2 triple ILAS-3 (B-515) 324mm ASTT with A244 LWT, 4 AK630 CIWS, 1 76mm gun (capacity 2 SA316B *Alouette* III (*Chetak*)/*Sea King* Mk42 ASW hel)
    3 *Talwar* I with 1 8-cell 3S14E VLS with 3M54TE *Klub*-N (SS-N-27B *Sizzler*) AShM, 1 single 3S90E lnchr with 9M317E *Shtil*-1 (SA-N-7B) SAM, 2 twin DTA-53-11356 533mm ASTT with SET-65E HWT/*Varunastra* HWT, 2 RBU 6000 *Smerch* 2 A/S mor, 2 *Kashtan* (CADS-N-1) CIWS, 1 100mm gun (capacity 1 *Dhruv*/Ka-28 *Helix* A ASW hel)
    3 *Talwar* II with 1 8-cell UVLM VLS with *Brahmos* AShM, 1 single 3S90E lnchr with 9M317E *Shtil*-1 (SA-N-7B) SAM, 2 twin DTA-53-11356 533mm ASTT with SET-65E HWT/*Varunastra* HWT, 2 RBU 6000 *Smerch* 2 A/S mor, 2 AK630M CIWS, 1 100mm gun (capacity 1 *Dhruv*/Ka-28 *Helix* A ASW hel)
  FFH 3:
    3 *Kamorta* with 2 twin ITTL 533mm ASTT with *Varunastra* HWT, 2 RBU 6000 *Smerch* 2 A/S mor, 2 AK630 CIWS, 1 76mm gun (capacity 1 *Dhruv*/Ka-28 *Helix* A ASW hel)

PATROL AND COASTAL COMBATANTS 170
  CORVETTES • FSGM 8:
    4 *Khukri* with 2 twin lnchr with P-27 *Termit*-R (SS-N-2D *Styx*) AShM, 2 twin lnchr (manual aiming) with 9K32M *Strela*-2M (SA-N-5 *Grail*) SAM, 2 AK630M CIWS, 1 76mm gun, 1 hel landing platform (for *Dhruv*/SA316 *Alouette* III (*Chetak*))
    4 *Kora* with 4 quad lnchr with 3M24E *Uran*-E (SS-N-25 *Switchblade*) AShM, 1 quad lnchr (manual aiming) with 9K32M *Strela*-2M (SA-N-5 *Grail*) SAM, 2 AK630M CIWS, 1 76mm gun, 1 hel landing platform (for *Dhruv*/SA316 *Alouette* III (*Chetak*))
  PSOH 10: 4 *Saryu* with 2 AK630M CIWS, 1 76mm gun (capacity 1 *Dhruv*); 6 *Sukanya* with 4 RBU 2500 A/S mor (capacity 1 SA316 *Alouette* III (*Chetak*))
  PCFGM 8:
    6 *Veer* (FSU *Tarantul*) with 4 single lnchr with P-27 *Termit*-R (SS-N-2D *Styx*) AShM, 2 quad lnchr (manual aiming) with 9K32M *Strela*-2M (SA-N-5 *Grail*), 2 AK630M CIWS, 1 76mm gun
    2 *Prabal* (mod *Veer*) each with 4 quad lnchr with 3M24E *Uran*-E (SS-N-25 *Switchblade*) AShM, 1 quad lnchr (manual aiming) with 9K32M *Strela*-2M (SA-N-5 *Grail*) SAM, 2 AK630M CIWS, 1 76mm gun
  PCMT 3 *Abhay* (FSU *Pauk* II) with 1 quad lnchr (manual aiming) with 9K32M *Strela*-2M (SA-N-5 *Grail*) SAM, 2 twin DTA-53 533mm ASTT with SET-65E, 2 RBU 1200 *Uragan* A/S mor, 1 AK630M CIWS, 1 76mm gun
  PCC 15: 4 *Bangaram*; 10 *Car Nicobar*; 1 *Trinkat* (SDB Mk5)
  PCF 4 *Tarmugli* (*Car Nicobar* mod)
  PBF 122: 9 Immediate Support Vessel (Rodman 78); 13 Immediate Support Vessel (Craftway); 15 Plascoa 1300 (SPB); 5 *Super Dvora*; 79 Solas Marine Interceptor

AMPHIBIOUS
  PRINCIPAL AMPHIBIOUS VESSELS 1
    LPD 1 *Jalashwa* (ex-US *Austin*) with 1 Mk 15 *Phalanx* CIWS (capacity up to 6 med spt hel; either 9 LCM or 4 LCM and 2 LCAC; 4 LCVP; 930 troops)
  LANDING SHIPS 8
    LSM 3 *Kumbhir* (FSU *Polnocny* C) (capacity 5 MBT or 5 APC; 160 troops)
    LST 5:
      2 *Magar* (capacity 15 MBT or 8 APC or 10 trucks; 500 troops)
      3 *Magar* mod (capacity 11 MBT or 8 APC or 10 trucks; 500 troops)
  LANDING CRAFT 10
    LCM 4 LCM 8 (for use in *Jalashwa*)
    LCT 6 LCU Mk-IV (capacity 1 *Arjun* MBT/2 T-90 MBT/4 IFV/160 troops)

LOGISTICS AND SUPPORT 40
  AFD 2: 1 FDN-1; 1 FDN-2
  AGOR 1 *Sagardhwani* with 1 hel landing platform
  AGHS 8: 1 *Makar*; 7 *Sandhayak*
  AO 2 GSL 1,000T Fuel Barge
  AOL 10: 1 *Ambika*; 2 *Poshak* II; 7 *Purak*
  AOR 1 *Jyoti* with 1 hel landing platform
  AORH 3: 1 *Aditya* (based on *Deepak* (1967) Bremer Vulkan design); 2 *Deepak* with 4 AK630 CIWS
  AP 3 *Nicobar* with 1 hel landing platform
  ASR 1
  ATF 1
  AWT 3 *Ambuda* II
  AX 1 *Tir*
  AXS 4: 2 *Mhadei*; 2 *Tarangini*

Naval Aviation 7,000
FORCES BY ROLE
FIGHTER/GROUND ATTACK
  2 sqn with MiG-29K/KUB *Fulcrum*
ANTI-SUBMARINE WARFARE
  1 sqn with Ka-28 *Helix* A
  1 sqn with *Sea King* Mk42B
MARITIME PATROL
  3 sqn with BN-2 *Islander*; Do-228-101
  1 sqn with Do-228
  1 sqn with Il-38SD *May*
  1 sqn with P-8I *Neptune*
AIRBORNE EARLY WARNING & CONTROL
  1 sqn with Ka-31 *Helix* B
SEARCH & RESCUE
  1 sqn with SA316B *Alouette* III (*Chetak*); *Sea King* Mk42C
  1 sqn with *Dhruv*

TRANSPORT
  1 sqn with HS-748M (HAL-748M)
TRAINING
  1 sqn with Do-228
  1 sqn with HJT-16 *Kiran* MkI/II, *Hawk* Mk132
  1 hel sqn with *Sea King* Mk42B
TRANSPORT HELICOPTER
  1 sqn with UH-3H *Sea King*
ISR UAV
  3 sqn with *Heron*; *Searcher* MkII

EQUIPMENT BY TYPE
AIRCRAFT 74 combat capable
  FTR 44 MiG-29K/KUB *Fulcrum*
  ASW 13: 5 Il-38SD *May*; 8 P-8I *Neptune*
  MP 13+ Do-228-101
  TPT 37:
    Light 27: 17 BN-2 *Islander*; 10 Do-228
    PAX 10 HS-748M (HAL-748M)
  TRG 29: 6 HJT-16 *Kiran* MkI; 6 HJT-16 *Kiran* MkII; 17 *Hawk* Mk132*
HELICOPTERS
  ASW 30: 12 Ka-28 *Helix* A; 18 *Sea King* Mk42B
  MRH 57: 10 *Dhruv*; 24 SA316B *Alouette* III (*Chetak*); 23 SA319 *Alouette* III
  AEW 11 Ka-31 *Helix* B
  TPT • Medium 11: 5 *Sea King* Mk42C; up to 6 UH-3H *Sea King*
UNMANNED AERIAL VEHICLES
  ISR 10: Heavy 4 *Heron*; Medium 6 *Searcher* Mk II
AIR-LAUNCHED MISSILES
  AAM • IR R-550 *Magic*/*Magic* 2; R-73 (AA-11A *Archer*) IR/SARH R-27 (AA-10 *Alamo*); ARH: R-77 (AA-12A *Adder*)
  AShM AGM-84 *Harpoon* (on P-8I ac); Kh-35 (AS-20 *Kayak*; on *May* ac); *Sea Eagle* (service status unclear)

Marines ε1,200 (Additional 1,000 for SPB duties)
After the Mumbai attacks, the Sagar Prahari Bal (SPB), with 80 PBF, was established to protect critical maritime infrastructure
FORCES BY ROLE
SPECIAL FORCES
  1 (marine) cdo force
MANOEUVRE
  Amphibious
  1 amph bde

Air Force 139,850
5 regional air comds: Western (New Delhi), Southwestern (Gandhinagar), Eastern (Shillong), Central (Allahabad), Southern (Trivandrum). 2 support comds: Maintenance (Nagpur) and Training (Bangalore)
FORCES BY ROLE
FIGHTER
  3 sqn with MiG-29 *Fulcrum*; MiG-29UB *Fulcrum*
FIGHTER/GROUND ATTACK
  4 sqn with *Jaguar* IB/IS
  6 sqn with MiG-21 *Bison*
  1 sqn with MiG-27ML/MiG-23UB *Flogger*
  3 sqn with *Mirage* 2000E/ED/I/IT (2000H/TH – secondary ECM role)
  1 sqn with *Rafale* (forming)
  10 sqn with Su-30MKI *Flanker*
  1 sqn with *Tejas*
ANTI SURFACE WARFARE
  1 sqn with *Jaguar* IM
ISR
  1 unit with Gulfstream IV SRA-4
AIRBORNE EARLY WARNING & CONTROL
  1 sqn with Il-76TD *Phalcon*
TANKER
  1 sqn with Il-78 *Midas*
TRANSPORT
  1 sqn with C-130J-30 *Hercules*
  1 sqn with C-17A *Globemaster* III
  5 sqn with An-32/An-32RE *Cline*
  1 (comms) sqn with B-737; B-737BBJ; EMB-135BJ
  4 sqn with Do-228; HS-748
  1 sqn with Il-76MD *Candid*
  1 flt with HS-748
TRAINING
  1 OCU sqn with Su-30MKI *Flanker*
ATTACK HELICOPTER
  1 sqn with Mi-25 *Hind*; Mi-35 *Hind*
  1 sqn with Mi-25 *Hind*; Mi-35 *Hind*; AH-64E *Apache Guardian*
TRANSPORT HELICOPTER
  5 sqn with *Dhruv*
  7 sqn with Mi-17/Mi-17-1V *Hip* H
  12 sqn with Mi-17V-5 *Hip* H
  2 sqn with SA316B *Alouette* III (*Chetak*)
  1 flt with Mi-26 *Halo*
  2 flt with SA315B *Lama* (*Cheetah*)
  2 flt with SA316B *Alouette* III (*Chetak*)
ISR UAV
  5 sqn with *Heron*; *Searcher* MkII
AIR DEFENCE
  25 sqn with S-125 *Pechora* (SA-3B *Goa*)
  6 sqn with 9K33 *Osa*-AK (SA-8B *Gecko*)
  2 sqn with *Akash*
  10 flt with 9K38 *Igla*-1 (SA-18 *Grouse*)

EQUIPMENT BY TYPE
AIRCRAFT 776 combat capable
  FTR 62: 55 MiG-29 *Fulcrum* (incl 12+ MiG-29UPG); 7 MiG-29UB *Fulcrum*
  FGA 498: 112 MiG-21 *Bison*; 38 MiG-21U/UM *Mongol*; 20 MiG-27ML *Flogger* (all UPG - to be withdrawn end 2019); 4 MiG-23UB *Flogger*; 39 *Mirage* 2000E/I (2000H); 10 *Mirage* 2000ED/IT (2000TH); 4 *Rafale*; 255 Su-30MKI *Flanker*; 16 *Tejas*
  ATK 115: 28 *Jaguar* IB; 79 *Jaguar* IS; 8 *Jaguar* IM
  ISR 3 Gulfstream IV SRA-4
  AEW&C 5: 2 EMB-145AEW *Netra* (1 more in test); 3 Il-76TD *Phalcon*
  TKR 6 Il-78 *Midas*
  TPT 243: Heavy 28: 11 C-17A *Globemaster* III; 17 Il-76MD *Candid*; Medium 10 C-130J-30 *Hercules*; Light 141: 57 An-32; 45 An-32RE *Cline*; 35 Do-228; 4 EMB-135BJ; PAX 64: 1 B-707; 4 B-737; 3 B-737BBJ; 56 HS-748

TRG 308: 101 *Hawk* Mk132*; 90 HJT-16 *Kiran* MkI/IA; 42 HJT-16 *Kiran* MkII; 75 PC-7 *Turbo Trainer* MkII
HELICOPTERS
ATK 25: 8 AH-64E *Apache Guardian*; 17 Mi-25/Mi-35 *Hind*
MRH 389: 60 *Dhruv*; 35 Mi-17 *Hip* H; 45 Mi-17-1V *Hip* H; 148 Mi-17V-5 *Hip* H; 59 SA315B *Lama* (*Cheetah*); 39 SA316B *Alouette* III (*Chetak*); 3+ *Rudra*
TPT • **Heavy** 5: 4 CH-47F *Chinook*; 1+ Mi-26 *Halo*
UNMANNED AERIAL VEHICLES
ISR • **Heavy** 9 *Heron*; **Medium** some *Searcher* MkII
AIR DEFENCE • SAM
Medium-range *Akash*
Short-range S-125 *Pechora* (SA-3B *Goa*); *Spyder*-SR
Point-defence 9K33 *Osa*-AK (SA-8B *Gecko*); 9K38 *Igla* (SA-18 *Grouse*)
AIR-LAUNCHED MISSILES
AAM • **IR** R-60 (AA-8 *Aphid*); R-73 (AA-11A *Archer*) R-550 *Magic*; **IIR** *Mica* IR; **IR/SARH** R-27 (AA-10 *Alamo*); **SARH** Super 530D **ARH** R-77 (AA-12A *Adder*); *Mica* RF
AShM AGM-84 *Harpoon*; AM39 *Exocet*; Kh-31A (AS-17B *Krypton*); *Sea Eagle*†
ASM AGM-114L/R *Hellfire*; Kh-29 (AS-14 *Kedge*); Kh-59 (AS-13 *Kingbolt*); Kh-59M (AS-18 *Kazoo*); AS-30; Kh-23 (AS-7 *Kerry*)‡; *Popeye* II (*Crystal Maze*)
ARM Kh-25MP (AS-12A *Kegler*); Kh-31P (AS-17A *Krypton*)
ALCM • **Nuclear** *Nirbhay* (likely nuclear capable; in development)
BOMBS
INS/SAT guided *Spice*
Laser-guided *Paveway* II

Coast Guard 12,600
EQUIPMENT BY TYPE
PATROL AND COASTAL COMBATANTS 125
PSOH 19: 2 *Sankalp* (capacity 1 *Chetak*/*Dhruv* hel); 4 *Samar* with 1 76mm gun (capacity 1 *Chetak*/*Dhruv* hel); 6 *Samarth*; 4 *Vikram* (capacity 1 *Dhruv* hel); 3 *Vishwast* (capacity 1 *Dhruv* hel)
PSO 3 *Samudra Prahari* with 1 hel landing platform
PCC 41: 20 *Aadesh*; 8 *Rajshree* (Flight I); 1 *Rajshree* (Flight II) 5 *Rani Abbakka*; 7 *Sarojini Naidu*
PBF 61: 6 C-154; 2 C-141; 11 C-143; 42 C-401
PB 1 *Priyadarshini*
AMPHIBIOUS
UCAC 18: 6 H-181 (*Griffon* 8000TD); 12 H-187 (*Griffon* 8000TD)
AIRCRAFT • MP 23 Do-228-101
HELICOPTERS • MRH 21: 4 *Dhruv*; 17 SA316B *Alouette* III (*Chetak*)

Paramilitary 1,585,950

Rashtriya Rifles 65,000
Ministry of Defence. 15 sector HQ
FORCES BY ROLE
MANOEUVRE
Other
65 paramilitary bn

Assam Rifles 63,750
Ministry of Home Affairs. Security within northeastern states, mainly army-officered; better trained than BSF
FORCES BY ROLE
Equipped to roughly same standard as an army inf bn
COMMAND
7 HQ
MANOEUVRE
Other
46 paramilitary bn
EQUIPMENT BY TYPE
ARTILLERY • MOR 81mm 252

Border Security Force 257,350
Ministry of Home Affairs
FORCES BY ROLE
MANOEUVRE
Other
186 paramilitary bn
EQUIPMENT BY TYPE
Small arms, lt arty, some anti-tank weapons
ARTILLERY • MOR 81mm 942+
AIRCRAFT • TPT some (air spt)
HELICOPTERS • MRH 2 Mi-17V-5 *Hip*

Central Industrial Security Force 144,400 (lightly armed security guards)
Ministry of Home Affairs. Guards public-sector locations

Central Reserve Police Force 313,650
Ministry of Home Affairs. Internal-security duties, only lightly armed, deployable throughout the country
FORCES BY ROLE
MANOEUVRE
Other
236 paramilitary bn
10 (rapid action force) paramilitary bn
10 (CoBRA) paramilitary bn
6 (Mahila) paramilitary bn (female)
2 sy gp
COMBAT SUPPORT
5 sigs bn

Defence Security Corps 31,000
Provides security at Defence Ministry sites

Indo-Tibetan Border Police 89,450
Ministry of Home Affairs. Tibetan border security SF/ guerrilla-warfare and high-altitude-warfare specialists
FORCES BY ROLE
MANOEUVRE
Other
56 paramilitary bn

National Security Guards 12,000
Anti-terrorism contingency deployment force, comprising elements of the armed forces, CRPF and Border Security Force

Railway Protection Forces 70,000

Sashastra Seema Bal 76,350
Guards the borders with Nepal and Bhutan

Special Frontier Force 10,000
Mainly ethnic Tibetans

Special Protection Group 3,000
Protection of ministers and senior officials

State Armed Police 450,000
For duty primarily in home state only, but can be moved to other states. Some bn with GPMG and army-standard infantry weapons and equipment

FORCES BY ROLE
MANOEUVRE
  Other
    144 (India Reserve Police) paramilitary bn

Reserve Organisations

Civil Defence 500,000 reservists
Operate in 225 categorised towns in 32 states. Some units for NBC defence

Home Guard 441,000 reservists (547,000 authorised str)
In all states except Arunachal Pradesh and Kerala; men on reserve lists, no trg. Not armed in peacetime. Used for civil defence, rescue and firefighting provision in wartime; 6 bn (created to protect tea plantations in Assam)

DEPLOYMENT

AFGHANISTAN: 335 (Indo-Tibetan Border Police paramilitary: facilities protection)

CYPRUS: UN • UNFICYP 1

DEMOCRATIC REPUBLIC OF THE CONGO: UN • MONUSCO 3,036; 3 inf bn; 1 fd hospital

LEBANON: UN • UNIFIL 781; 1 inf bn; 1 med coy

MIDDLE EAST: UN • UNTSO 3

SOUTH SUDAN: UN • UNMISS 2,396; 2 inf bn; 1 engr coy; 1 sigs coy; 2 fd hospital

SUDAN: UN • UNISFA 5

SYRIA/ISRAEL: UN • UNDOF 194; 1 log bn(-)

WESTERN SAHARA: UN • MINURSO 3

FOREIGN FORCES
Total numbers for UNMOGIP mission in India and Pakistan
Chile 2
Croatia 9
Italy 2
Korea, Republic of 7
Philippines 7
Romania 2
Sweden 5
Switzerland 3
Thailand 4
Uruguay 3

Indonesia IDN

Indonesian Rupiah Rp		2018	2019	2020
GDP	Rp	14826tr	16076tr	
	US$	1.02tr	1.11tr	
per capita	US$	3,871	4,164	
Growth	%	5.2	5.0	
Inflation	%	3.2	3.2	
Def bdgt	Rp	107tr	107tr	127tr
	US$	7.37bn	7.43bn	
FMA (US)	US$	14.0m	0m	0m
US$1=Rp		14500.41	14460.38	

Real-terms defence budget trend (US$bn, constant 2015)
8.23
3.30
2008 — 2014 — 2019

Population 264,935,824

Ethnic groups: Jawa 40.2%; Sunda, Priangan 15.5%; Banjar, Melayu Banjar 4%; other or unspecified 40.5%

Age	0–14	15–19	20–24	25–29	30–64	65 plus
Male	12.4%	4.3%	4.3%	3.9%	21.9%	3.3%
Female	11.9%	4.2%	4.1%	3.7%	21.8%	4.2%

Capabilities

Indonesia's TNI is the largest armed force in Southeast Asia. It has traditionally been concerned primarily with internal security and counter-insurgency. All three services are based on regional commands. The army remains the dominant service and is deployed operationally in West Papua, central Sulawesi and elsewhere. A modernisation plan adopted in 2010 called for the establishment by 2024 of a 'Minimum Essential Force' including strengthened naval and air capabilities. The 2015 defence white paper outlined Indonesia's 'Global Maritime Fulcrum' policy and advocated building up maritime, satellite and UAV capabilities. In 2018, Indonesia expanded its forces in the eastern areas of the country and stood up a long-expected third naval fleet command and a third air-force command to organise existing units in that area. Indonesia also created a new army reserve division and a third marines group, both to be stationed in the east. An ASEAN member, Indonesia has no formal defence alliances but there are defence-cooperation agreements with other states. It also maintains good relations with China, which has supplied some military equipment, including UAVs. The armed forces have contributed to UN and other international peacekeeping operations. Indonesia regularly exercises with Australian and US armed forces and those of Southeast Asian states. Indonesia's inventory comprises equipment from diverse international sources, and the country uses technology-transfer agreements to develop its national defence industry. Defence-industrial policy priorities for 2020–24, outlined in July 2019, focus on emerging technologies with a military application. Indonesia has a number of public and private defence companies that provide services and equipment across the domains.

ACTIVE 395,500 (Army 300,400 Navy 65,000 Air 30,100) **Paramilitary 280,000**
Conscription liability 24 months selective conscription authorised (not required by law)

RESERVE 400,000
Army cadre units; numerical str n.k., obligation to age 45 for officers

ORGANISATIONS BY SERVICE

Army ε300,400

Mil Area Commands (KODAM)
14 comd (I, II, III, IV, V, VI, VII, IX, XII, XVI, XVII, XVIII, Jaya & Iskandar Muda)
FORCES BY ROLE
MANOEUVRE
  Mechanised
  3 armd cav bn
  5 cav bn
  1 mech inf bde (1 cav bn, 3 mech inf bn)
  1 mech inf bde (3 mech inf bn)
  Light
  4 inf bde (2 cdo bn, 1 inf bn)
  3 inf bde (3 inf bn)
  26 indep inf bn
  21 indep cdo bn
COMBAT SUPPORT
  12 fd arty bn
  7 cbt engr bn
COMBAT SERVICE SUPPORT
  4 construction bn
AVIATION
  1 composite avn sqn
HELICOPTER
  1 hel sqn with Bo-105; Bell 205A; Bell 412; AH-64E *Apache Guardian*
  1 hel sqn Mi-35P *Hind*; Mi-17V-5 *Hip H*
AIR DEFENCE
  1 AD regt (2 ADA bn, 1 SAM unit)
  6 ADA bn
  3 SAM unit

Special Forces Command (KOPASSUS)
FORCES BY ROLE
SPECIAL FORCES
  3 SF gp (total: 2 cdo/para unit, 1 CT unit, 1 int unit)

Strategic Reserve Command (KOSTRAD)
FORCES BY ROLE
COMMAND
  3 div HQ
MANOEUVRE
  Armoured
  2 tk bn
  Mechanised
  1 mech inf bde (3 mech inf bn)
  Light
  1 inf bde (3 cdo bn)
  1 inf bde (2 cdo bn)
  1 inf bde (2 inf bn)
  Air Manoeuvre
  3 AB bde (3 AB bn)
COMBAT SUPPORT
  2 arty regt (1 SP arty bn; 1 MRL bn; 1 fd arty bn)
  1 fd arty bn
  2 cbt engr bn
AIR DEFENCE
  2 AD bn

EQUIPMENT BY TYPE
ARMOURED FIGHTING VEHICLES
  MBT 103: 42 *Leopard* 2A4; 61 *Leopard* 2RI
  LT TK 350: 275 AMX-13 (partially upgraded); 15 PT-76; 60 FV101 *Scorpion*-90
  RECCE 142: 55 *Ferret* (13 upgraded); 69 *Saladin* (16 upgraded); 18 VBL
  IFV 64: 22 *Black Fox*; 42 *Marder* 1A3
  APC 834+
    APC (T) 267: 75 AMX-VCI; 34 BTR-50PK; 15 FV4333 *Stormer*; 143 M113A1-B
    APC (W) 567+: 350 *Anoa*; some *Barracuda*; 40 BTR-40; 45 FV603 *Saracen* (14 upgraded); 100 LAV-150 *Commando*; 32 VAB-VTT
    PPV some *Casspir*
  AUV 39: 14 APR-1; 3 *Bushmaster*; 22 *Commando Ranger*
ENGINEERING & MAINTENANCE VEHICLES
  AEV 4: 3 *Leopard* 2; 1 M113A1-B-GN
  ARV 15+: 2 AMX-13; 6 AMX-VCI; 3 BREM-2; 4 BPz-3 *Buffel*; *Stormer*; T-54/T-55
  VLB 16: 10 AMX-13; 4 *Leguan*; 2 *Stormer*
ANTI-TANK/ANTI-INFRASTRUCTURE
  MSL • MANPATS FGM-148 *Javelin*; SS.11; *Milan*; 9K11 *Malyutka* (AT-3 *Sagger*)
  RCL 90mm M67; **106mm** M40A1
  RL 89mm LRAC
ARTILLERY 1,198+
  SP 74: **105mm** 20 AMX Mk61; **155mm** 54: 36 CAESAR; 18 M109A4
  TOWED 133+: **105mm** 110+: some KH-178; 60 M101; 50 M-56; **155mm** 23: 5 FH-88; 18 KH-179
  MRL 127mm 36 ASTROS II Mk6
  MOR 955: **81mm** 800; **120mm** 155: 75 Brandt; 80 UBM 52
AMPHIBIOUS • LCU 17: 1 ADRI XXXII; 4 ADRI XXXIII; 1 ADRI XXXIX; 1 ADRI XL; 3 ADRI XLI; 2 ADRI XLIV; 2 ADRI XLVI; 2 ADRI XLVIII; 1 ADRI L
AIRCRAFT • TPT • Light 9: 1 BN-2A *Islander*; 6 C-212 *Aviocar* (NC-212); 2 *Turbo Commander* 680
HELICOPTERS
  ATK 14: 6 Mi-35P *Hind*; 8 AH-64E *Apache Guardian*
  MRH 40: 6 H125M *Fennec*; 17 Bell 412 *Twin Huey* (NB-412); 17 Mi-17V-5 *Hip H*
  TPT • Light 29: 7 Bell 205A; 20 Bo-105 (NBo-105); 2 H120 *Colibri*
  TRG up to 19 Hughes 300C
AIR DEFENCE
  SAM • Point-defence 95+: 2 *Kobra* (with 125 GROM-2 msl); TD-2000B (*Giant Bow* II); 51 *Rapier*; 42 RBS-70; QW-3
  GUNS • TOWED 411: **20mm** 121 Rh 202; **23mm** *Giant Bow*; **40mm** 90 L/70; **57mm** 200 S-60

AIR-LAUNCHED MISSILES
ASM AGM-114 *Hellfire*

Navy ε65,000 (including Marines and Aviation)

Three fleets: East (Sorong), Central (Surabaya) and West (Jakarta). Two Forward Operating Bases at Kupang (West Timor) and Tahuna (North Sulawesi)

EQUIPMENT BY TYPE
SUBMARINES • TACTICAL • SSK 4:
  2 *Cakra* (Type-209/1300) with 8 single 533mm TT with SUT HWT
  2 *Nagapasa* (Type-209/1400) with 8 single 533mm TT with *Black Shark* HWT

PRINCIPAL SURFACE COMBATANTS 11
  FRIGATES 11
    FFGHM 3:
      1 *Ahmad Yani* (ex-NLD *Van Speijk*) with 2 twin-cell VLS with 3M55E *Yakhont* (SS-N-26 *Strobile*) AShM; 2 twin *Simbad* lnchr (manual) with *Mistral* SAM, 2 triple SVTT Mk 32 324mm ASTT with Mk 46 LWT, 1 76mm gun (capacity 1 Bo-105 (NBo-105) hel)
      2 *Ahmad Yani* (ex-NLD *Van Speijk*) with 2 twin lnchr with C-802 (CH-SS-N-6) AShM, 2 twin *Simbad* lnchr (manual) with *Mistral* SAM, 2 triple SVTT Mk 32 324mm ASTT with Mk 46 LWT, 1 76mm gun (capacity 1 Bo-105 (NBo-105) hel)
    FFGM 4:
      4 *Diponegoro* (SIGMA 9113) with 2 twin lnchr with MM40 *Exocet* Block 2 AShM, 2 quad *Tetral* lnchr with *Mistral* SAM, 2 triple ILAS-3 (B-515) 324mm ASTT with MU90 LWT, 1 76mm gun, 1 hel landing platform
    FFHM 2:
      2 *Ahmad Yani* (ex-NLD *Van Speijk*) with 2 twin *Simbad* lnchr (manual) with *Mistral* SAM, 2 triple 324mm ASTT with Mk 46 LWT, 1 76mm gun (capacity 1 Bo-105 (NBo-105) hel)
    FFH 2:
      2 *R.E. Martadinata* (SIGMA 10514) with 1 76mm gun (capacity 1 med hel) (being fitted with VL-MICA SAM and *Millennium* CIWS)

PATROL AND COASTAL COMBATANTS 116
  CORVETTES 20
    FSGM 3 *Bung Tomo* with 2 quad lnchr with MM40 *Exocet* Block 2 AShM, 1 18-cell VLS with *Sea Wolf* SAM, 2 triple 324mm ASTT, 1 76mm gun (capacity: 1 Bo-105 hel)
    FSGH 1 *Nala* with 2 twin lnchr with MM38 *Exocet* AShM, 1 twin Bofors ASW Rocket Launcher System 375mm A/S mor, 1 120mm gun (capacity 1 lt hel)
    FSG 2:
      1 *Fatahillah* with 2 twin lnchr with MM38 *Exocet* AShM, 2 triple SVTT Mk 32 324mm ASTT with Mk 46 LWT, 1 twin 375mm A/S mor, 1 120mm gun
      1 *Fatahillah* with 2 twin lnchr with MM40 *Exocet* Block 3 AShM, 2 triple SVTT Mk 32 324mm ASTT with Mk 46 LWT, 1 twin 375mm A/S mor, 1 120mm gun
    FS 14 *Kapitan Pattimura* (GDR *Parchim* I) with 4 single 400mm ASTT, 2 RBU 6000 *Smerch* 2 A/S mor, 1 twin 57mm gun
  PCFG 3 *Mandau* with 4 single lnchr with MM38 *Exocet* AShM, 1 57mm gun
  PCG 4:
    2 *Sampari* (KCR-60M) with 2 twin lnchr for C-705 AShM
    2 *Todak* with 2 single lnchr with C-802 (CH-SS-N-6), 1 57mm gun
  PCT 2 *Andau* with 2 single 533mm TT with SUT, 1 57mm gun
  PCC 13: 4 *Kakap* with 1 hel landing platform; 2 *Pandrong*; 3 *Pari*; 2 *Sampari* (KCR-60M) with 1 NG-18 CIWS; 2 *Todak* with 1 57mm gun
  PBG 8:
    2 *Clurit* with 2 single lnchr with C-705 AShM, 1 AK630 CIWS
    6 *Clurit* with 2 single lnchr with C-705 AShM
  PBF 4 Combat Boat AL D-18
  PB 62: 2 *Badau* (ex-BRN *Waspada*); 9 *Boa*; 1 *Cucut* (ex-SGP *Jupiter*); 4 *Kobra*; 1 *Krait*; 8 *Sibarau*; 22 *Sinabang* (KAL 28); 4 *Tarihu*; 7 *Tatihu* (PC-40); 4 *Viper*

MINE WARFARE • MINE COUNTERMEASURES 8
  MCO 2 *Pulau Rengat*
  MSC 6 *Pulau Rote* (ex-GDR *Wolgast*)

AMPHIBIOUS
  PRINCIPAL AMPHIBIOUS VESSELS • LPD 6:
    1 *Dr Soeharso* (ex-*Tanjung Dalpele*; capacity 2 LCU/LCVP; 13 tanks; 500 troops; 2 AS332L *Super Puma*) (used in AH role)
    4 *Makassar* (capacity 2 LCU or 4 LCVP; 13 tanks; 500 troops; 2 AS332L *Super Puma*)
    1 *Semarang* (IDN *Makassar* mod) (capacity 2 LCM; 3 hels; 28 vehs; 650 troops) (used in AH role)
  LANDING SHIPS • LST 17
    1 *Teluk Amboina* (capacity 16 tanks; 800 troops)
    1 *Teluk Bintuni* (capacity 10 MBT)
    10 *Teluk Gilimanuk* (ex-GDR *Frosch*)
    1 *Teluk Lada* with 1 hel landing platform (capacity 4 LCVP; 470 troops; 15 APC; 10 MBT)
    4 *Teluk Semangka* (capacity 17 tanks; 200 troops)
  LANDING CRAFT 54
    LCM 20
    LCU 4
    LCVP 30

LOGISTICS AND SUPPORT 22
  AGF 1 *Multatuli* with 1 hel landing platform
  AGOR 2 *Rigel*
  AGOS 1 *Leuser*
  AGHS 1
  AGS 2 *Pulau Rote* (ex-GDR *Wolgast*)
  AKSL 3
  AORLH 1 *Arun* (ex-UK *Rover*) (damaged at sea 2018, in repair)
  AOR 1 *Tarakan* with 1 hel landing platform
  AOT 2: 1 *Khobi*; 1 *Sorong*
  AP 4: 1 *Tanjung Kambani* (troop transport) with 1 hel landing platform; 1 *Tanjung Nusanive* (troop transport); 2 *Karang Pilang* (troop transport)
  ATF 1
  AXS 3

Naval Aviation ε1,000
EQUIPMENT BY TYPE
AIRCRAFT
  MP 28: 3 C212-200; 5 CN235-220 (MPA); 14 N-22B *Searchmaster* B; 6 N-22SL *Searchmaster* L
  TPT • Light 33: 1 Beech 350i *King Air* (VIP transport); 8 Beech G36 *Bonanza*; 2 Beech G38 *Baron*; 17 C-212-200 *Aviocar*; 3 TB-9 *Tampico*; 2 TB-10
HELICOPTERS
  ASW 10 AS565MBe *Panther*
  MRH 4 Bell 412 (NB-412) *Twin Huey*
  CSAR 4 H225M *Caracal*
  TPT 15: **Medium** 3 AS332L *Super Puma* (NAS322L); **Light** 12: 3 H120 *Colibri*; 9 Bo-105 (NBo-105)

Marines ε20,000
FORCES BY ROLE
SPECIAL FORCES
  1 SF bn
MANOEUVRE
  Amphibious
  2 mne gp (1 cav regt, 3 mne bn, 1 arty regt, 1 cbt spt regt, 1 CSS regt)
  1 mne gp (forming)
  1 mne bde (3 mne bn)
EQUIPMENT BY TYPE
ARMOURED FIGHTING VEHICLES
  LT TK 65: 10 AMX-10 PAC 90; 55 PT-76†
  RECCE 21 BRDM-2
  IFV 114: 24 AMX-10P; 22 BMP-2; 54 BMP-3F; 2 BTR-4; 12 BTR-80A
  APC 103: • **APC (T)** 100 BTR-50P; **APC (W)** 3 BTR-4M
  AAV 15: 10 LVTP-7A1; 5 M113 *Arisgator*
ARTILLERY 71+
  TOWED 50: **105mm** 22 LG1 MK II; **122mm** 28 M-38
  MRL 122mm 21: 4 PHL-90B; 9 RM-70; 8 RM-70 *Vampir*
  MOR 81mm
  AIR DEFENCE • GUNS • 40mm 5 L/60/L/70; **57mm** S-60

Air Force 30,100
3 operational comd (East, Central and West) plus trg comd
FORCES BY ROLE
FIGHTER
  1 sqn with F-5E/F *Tiger* II 1 sqn with F-16A/B/C/D *Fighting Falcon*
FIGHTER/GROUND ATTACK
  1 sqn with F-16C/D *Fighting Falcon*
  1 sqn with Su-27SK/SKM *Flanker*; Su-30MK/MK2 *Flanker*
  2 sqn with *Hawk* Mk109*/Mk209*
  1 sqn with T-50i *Golden Eagle**
GROUND ATTACK
  1 sqn with EMB-314 (A-29) *Super Tucano**
MARITIME PATROL
  1 sqn with B-737-200; CN235M-220 MPA
TANKER/TRANSPORT
  1 sqn with C-130B/KC-130B *Hercules*
TRANSPORT
  1 VIP sqn with B-737-200; C-130H/H-30 *Hercules*; L-100-30; F-27-400M *Troopship*; F-28-1000/3000
  1 sqn with C-130H/H-30 *Hercules*; L-100-30
  1 sqn with C-130H *Hercules*
  1 sqn with C-212 *Aviocar* (NC-212)
  1 sqn with CN235M-110; C295M
TRAINING
  1 sqn with Grob 120TP
  1 sqn with KT-1B
TRANSPORT HELICOPTER
  2 sqn with H225M; AS332L *Super Puma* (NAS332L); SA330J/L *Puma* (NAS330J/L)
  1 VIP sqn with AS332L *Super Puma* (NAS332L); SA330SM *Puma* (NAS300SM)
  1 sqn with H120 *Colibri*
ISR UAV
  1 sqn with *Aerostar*
EQUIPMENT BY TYPE
Only 45% of ac op
AIRCRAFT 109 combat capable
  FTR 9: 7 F-16A *Fighting Falcon*; 2 F-16B *Fighting Falcon* (8 F-5E *Tiger* II; 4 F-5F *Tiger* II non-operational)
  FGA 40: 19 F-16C *Fighting Falcon*; 5 F-16D *Fighting Falcon*; 2 Su-27SK; 3 Su-27SKM; 2 Su-30MK; 9 Su-30MK2
  MP 6: 3 B-737-200; 3 CN235M-220 MPA
  C2 1 C295
  TKR 1 KC-130B *Hercules*
  TPT 48: **Medium** 16: 4 C-130B *Hercules*; 4 C-130H *Hercules*; 6 C-130H-30 *Hercules*; 2 L-100-30; **Light** 23: 9 C295; 9 C-212 *Aviocar* (NC-212); 5 CN235-110; **PAX** 9: 1 B-737-200; 3 B-737-400; 1 B-737-500; 1 B-737-800BBJ; 1 F-28-1000; 2 F-28-3000
  TRG 104: 15 EMB-314 (A-29) *Super Tucano**; 30 Grob 120TP; 7 *Hawk* Mk109*; 23 *Hawk* Mk209*; 14 KT-1B; 15 T-50i *Golden Eagle**
HELICOPTERS
  TPT 36: **Heavy** 6 H225M (CSAR); **Medium** 18: 9 AS332 *Super Puma* (NAS332L) (VIP/CSAR); 1 SA330SM *Puma* (NAS330SM) (VIP); 4 SA330J *Puma* (NAS330J); 4 SA330L *Puma* (NAS330L); **Light** 12 H120 *Colibri*
UNMANNED AERIAL VEHICLES
  ISR • Medium *Aerostar*
AIR-LAUNCHED MISSILES
  AAM • IR AIM-9P *Sidewinder*; R-73 (AA-11A *Archer*); **IR/SARH** R-27 (AA-10 *Alamo*)
  ARH R-77 (AA-12A *Adder*)
  ASM AGM-65G *Maverick*
  ARM Kh-31P (AS-17A *Krypton*)

Special Forces (Paskhasau)
FORCES BY ROLE
SPECIAL FORCES
  3 (PASKHASAU) SF wg (total: 6 spec ops sqn)
  4 indep SF coy
EQUIPMENT BY TYPE
AIR DEFENCE
  SAM • Point *Chiron*; QW-3
  GUNS • TOWED 35mm 6 Oerlikon *Skyshield*

Paramilitary 280,000+

Police ε280,000 (including 14,000 police 'mobile bde' (BRIMOB) org in 56 coy, incl CT unit (Gegana))

EQUIPMENT BY TYPE
ARMOURED FIGHTING VEHICLES
  APC (W) 34 *Tactica*
AIRCRAFT • TPT • Light 6: 2 Beech 18; 2 C-212 *Aviocar* (NC-212); 1 C295; 1 *Turbo Commander* 680
HELICOPTERS • TPT • Light 22: 3 Bell 206 *Jet Ranger*; 19 Bo-105 (NBo-105)

KPLP (Coast and Seaward Defence Command)

Responsible to Military Sea Communications Agency
EQUIPMENT BY TYPE
PATROL AND COASTAL COMBATANTS 31
  PCO 4: 2 *Arda Dedali*; 2 *Trisula*
  PB 27: 4 *Golok* (SAR); 5 *Kujang*; 3 *Rantos*; 15 (various)
LOGISTICS AND SUPPORT • ABU 1 *Jadayat*

Bakamla (Maritime Security Agency)
EQUIPMENT BY TYPE
PATROL AND COASTAL COMBATANTS 10
  PSO 4: 3 *Pulau Nipah* with 1 hel landing platform; 1 *Tanjung Datu* with 1 hel landing platform
  PB 6 *Bintang Laut* (KCR-40 mod)

Reserve Organisations

Kamra People's Security ε40,000

Report for 3 weeks' basic training each year; part-time police auxiliary

DEPLOYMENT

CENTRAL AFRICAN REPUBLIC: UN • MINUSCA 214; 1 engr coy

DEMOCRATIC REPUBLIC OF THE CONGO: UN • MONUSCO 1,038; 1 inf bn; 3 engr coy

LEBANON: UN • UNIFIL 1,309; 1 inf bn; 1 MP coy; 1 FFGM

MALI: UN • MINUSMA 9

PHILIPPINES: IMT 9

SOUTH SUDAN: UN • UNMISS 4

SUDAN: UN • UNISFA 4

WESTERN SAHARA: UN • MINURSO 4

Japan JPN

Japanese Yen ¥		2018	2019	2020
GDP	¥	549tr	558tr	
	US$	4.97tr	5.15tr	
per capita	US$	39,304	40,847	
Growth	%	0.8	0.9	
Inflation	%	1.0	1.0	
Def bdgt	¥	5.19tr	5.26tr	5.32tr
	US$	47.0bn	48.6bn	
US$1=¥		110.42	108.20	

Real-terms defence budget trend (US$bn, constant 2015)

43.2

38.5

2008 — 2014 — 2019

Population   125,853,035
Ethnic groups: Korean <1%

Age	0–14	15–19	20–24	25–29	30–64	65 plus
Male	6.5%	2.4%	2.6%	2.5%	21.9%	12.6%
Female	6.1%	2.2%	2.3%	2.4%	22.3%	16.2%

Capabilities

Japan's concerns over its regional security environment have heightened, as evidenced in its 2019–23 Medium-Term Defense Program. These principally relate to an emerging security challenge from China and an established concern over North Korea. This has stimulated defence-budget increases and defence-policy and legislative reforms to enable Japan to play a more active international security role and strengthen the Japan Self-Defense Force (JSDF). While the JSDF's offensive capacity remains weak, the navy has strengths in anti-submarine warfare and air defence. In 2018, a Ground Component Command was created to oversee the Ground Self-Defense Force, previously organised into five regional commands. An Amphibious Rapid Deployment Brigade was also created, tasked mainly with the defence of remote islands. There are now plans to convert the *Izumo* helicopter carriers into aircraft carriers. The 2018 National Defense Program Guidelines plan to strengthen Japan's capabilities in non-traditional domains, including space, cyberspace and the electromagnetic spectrum. Japan's alliance with the US remains the cornerstone of its defence policy, reflected by the continued US basing, the widespread use of US equipment across all three services and regular training with US forces. The JSDF trains regularly, including in US-led international exercises. However, personnel recruitment and retention are an issue in the context of an ageing population. Due to their defensive mandate, JSDF deployments are mostly for peacekeeping purposes. The ongoing military-procurement drive has focused for the first time on power projection, mobility and ISR. Japan has expressed a desire to boost its ballistic-missile-defence capability by purchasing the *Aegis* Ashore system. Budget documents also note research on a hypersonic glide body and new anti-ship missiles. Japan has an advanced defence-industrial base, which produces modern equipment for the JSDF.

ACTIVE 247,150 (Ground Self-Defense Force 150,850 Maritime Self-Defense Force 45,350 Air Self-Defense Force 46,950 Central Staff 4,000)
Paramilitary 14,200

RESERVE 56,000 (General Reserve Army (GSDF) 46,000 Ready Reserve Army (GSDF) 8,100 Navy 1,100 Air 800)

ORGANISATIONS BY SERVICE

Space
EQUIPMENT BY TYPE
SATELLITES 11
  COMMUNICATIONS 2: 1 *Kirameki*-1; 1 *Kirameki*-2
  ISR 9 IGS

Ground Self-Defense Force 150,850
FORCES BY ROLE
COMMAND
  5 army HQ (regional comd)
SPECIAL FORCES
  1 spec ops unit (bn)
MANOEUVRE
  Armoured
  1 (7th) armd div (1 armd recce sqn, 3 tk regt, 1 armd inf regt, 1 hel sqn, 1 SP arty regt, 1 AD regt, 1 cbt engr bn, 1 sigs bn, 1 NBC bn, 1 log regt)
  1 indep tk bn
  Mechanised
  1 (2nd) inf div (1 armd recce sqn, 1 tk regt, 3 inf regt, 1 hel sqn, 1 SP arty regt, 1 AT coy, 1 ADA bn, 1 cbt engr bn, 1 sigs bn, 1 NBC bn, 1 log regt)
  1 (4th) inf div (1 armd recce bn, 3 inf regt, 1 inf coy, 1 hel sqn, 1 AT coy, 1 SAM bn, 1 cbt engr bn, 1 sigs bn, 1 NBC bn, 1 log regt)
  1 (6th) inf div (1 recce sqn, 1 mech inf regt; 3 inf regt, 1 hel sqn, 1 fd arty regt, 1 SAM bn, 1 cbt engr bn, 1 sigs bn, 1 NBC bn, 1 log regt)
  1 (9th) inf div (1 armd recce sqn, 1 tk bn, 3 inf regt, 1 hel sqn, 1 fd arty regt, 1 SAM bn, 1 cbt engr bn, 1 sigs bn, 1 NBC bn, 1 log regt)
  1 (5th) inf bde (1 armd recce sqn, 1 tk bn, 3 inf regt, 1 hel sqn, 1 SP arty bn, 1 SAM coy, 1 cbt engr coy, 1 sigs coy, 1 NBC coy, 1 log bn)
  1 (11th) inf bde (1 armd recce sqn, 1 tk sqn, 3 inf regt, 1 hel sqn, 1 SP arty bn, 1 SAM coy, 1 cbt engr coy, 1 sigs coy, 1 NBC coy, 1 log bn)
  Light
  2 (1st & 3rd) inf div (1 recce sqn, 1 tk bn, 3 inf regt, 1 hel sqn, 1 fd arty bn, 1 SAM bn, 1 cbt engr bn, 1 sigs bn, 1 NBC bn, 1 log regt)
  1 (10th) inf div (1 recce sqn, 1 tk bn, 3 inf regt, 1 hel sqn, 1 fd arty regt, 1 SAM bn, 1 cbt engr bn, 1 sigs bn, 1 NBC bn, 1 log regt)
  1 (8th) inf div (1 recce sqn, 3 inf regt, 1 hel sqn, 1 SAM bn, 1 cbt engr bn, 1 sigs bn, 1 NBC bn, 1 log regt)
  1 (13th) inf bde (1 recce sqn, 1 tk coy, 3 inf regt, 1 hel sqn, 1 fd arty bn, 1 SAM coy, 1 cbt engr coy, 1 NBC coy, 1 sigs coy, 1 log bn)
  1 (14th) inf bde (1 recce sqn, 2 inf regt, 1 hel sqn, 1 SAM coy, 1 cbt engr coy, 1 NBC coy, 1 sigs coy, 1 log bn)
  1 (15th) inf bde (1 recce sqn, 1 inf regt, 1 avn sqn, 1 AD regt, 1 cbt engr coy, 1 NBC coy, 1 sigs coy, 1 log bn)

  Air Manoeuvre
  1 (1st) AB bde (3 AB bn, 1 fd arty bn, 1 cbt engr coy, 1 sigs coy, 1 log bn)
  1 (12th) air mob inf bde (1 recce sqn, 3 inf regt, 1 avn sqn, 1 fd arty bn, 1 SAM coy, 1 cbt engr coy, 1 NBC coy, 1 sigs coy, 1 log bn)
  Amphibious
  1 amph bde(-) (1 amph regt)
COMBAT SUPPORT
  1 arty bde (2 SP arty regt; 3 AShM regt)
  1 (Western Army) fd arty regt
  2 arty unit (1 MRL bn; 1 AShM regt)
  1 (Central Army) fd arty bn
  4 engr bde
  1 engr unit
  1 EW bn
  5 int bn
  1 MP bde
  1 sigs bde
COMBAT SERVICE SUPPORT
  5 log unit (bde)
  5 trg bde
HELICOPTER
  1 hel bde (5 tpt hel sqn; 1 VIP tpt hel bn)
  5 hel gp (1 atk hel bn, 1 hel bn)
AIR DEFENCE
  2 SAM bde (2 SAM gp)
  2 SAM gp
EQUIPMENT BY TYPE
ARMOURED FIGHTING VEHICLES
  MBT 617: 76 Type-10; 200 Type-74; 341 Type-90
  ASLT 87 Type-16 MCV
  RECCE 111 Type-87
  IFV 68 Type-89
  APC 795
    APC (T) 226 Type-73
    APC (W) 569: 204 Type-82; 365 Type-96
  AAV 4 AAV-7
  AUV 8 *Bushmaster*
ENGINEERING & MAINTENANCE VEHICLES
  ARV 70: 4 Type-11; 36 Type-78; 30 Type-90
  VLB 22 Type-91
NBC VEHICLES 57: 41 Chemical Reconnaissance Vehicle; 16 NBC Reconnaissance Vehicle
ANTI-TANK/ANTI-INFRASTRUCTURE
  MSL
    SP 37 Type-96 MPMS
    MANPATS Type-79 *Jyu-MAT*; Type-87 *Chu-MAT*; Type-01 LMAT
  RCL • **84mm** *Carl Gustav*
ARTILLERY 1,716
  SP 172: **155mm** 105 Type-99; **203mm** 67 M110A2
  TOWED 155mm 340 FH-70
  MRL 227mm 99 M270 MLRS
  MOR 1,105: **81mm** 652 L16 **120mm** 429; **SP 120mm** 24 Type-96
COASTAL DEFENCE • **AShM** 104: 22 Type-12; 82 Type-88
AIRCRAFT • **TPT** • **Light** 7 Beech 350 *King Air* (LR-2)
HELICOPTERS
  ATK 104: 55 AH-1S *Cobra*; 12 AH-64D *Apache*; 37 OH-1

ISR 26 OH-6D
TPT 255: **Heavy** 55: 20 CH-47D *Chinook* (CH-47J); 35 CH-47JA *Chinook*; **Medium** 43: 3 H225 *Super Puma* MkII+ (VIP); 40 UH-60L *Black Hawk* (UH-60JA); **Light** 157: 127 Bell 205 (UH-1J); 30 Enstrom 480B (TH-480B)
AIR DEFENCE
SAM
Medium-range 163: 43 Type-03 *Chu*-SAM; 120 MIM-23B I-*Hawk*
Short-range 5 Type-11 *Tan*-SAM
Point-defence 159+: 46 Type-81 *Tan*-SAM; 113 Type-93 *Kin*-SAM; Type-91 *Kei*-SAM
GUNS • **SP 35mm** 52 Type-87

Maritime Self-Defense Force 45,350

Surface units organised into 4 Escort Flotillas with a mix of 8 warships each. Bases at Yokosuka, Kure, Sasebo, Maizuru, Ominato. SSK organised into two flotillas with bases at Kure and Yokosuka

EQUIPMENT BY TYPE
SUBMARINES • TACTICAL • SSK 21:
  2 *Oyashio* (trg role) with 6 single 533mm TT with UGM-84C *Harpoon* Block 1B AShM/Type-89 HWT
  9 *Oyashio* with 6 single 533mm TT with UGM-84C *Harpoon* Block 1B AShM/Type-89 HWT
  10 *Soryu* (AIP fitted) with 6 single 533mm TT with UGM-84C *Harpoon* Block 1B AShM/Type-89 HWT
PRINCIPAL SURFACE COMBATANTS 51
AIRCRAFT CARRIERS • CVH 4:
  2 *Hyuga* with 2 8-cell Mk 41 VLS with ASROC/RIM-162B ESSM SAM, 2 triple HOS-303 324mm ASTT with Mk 46/Type-97 LWT, 2 Mk 15 *Phalanx* Block 1B CIWS (normal ac capacity 3 SH-60 *Seahawk* ASW hel; plus additional ac embarkation up to 7 SH-60 *Seahawk* or 7 MCH-101)
  2 *Izumo* with 2 11-cell Mk 15 SeaRAM lnchr with RIM-116 SAM, 2 Mk 15 *Phalanx* Block 1A CIWS (normal ac capacity 7 SH-60 *Seahawk* ASW hel; plus additional ac embarkation up to 5 SH-60 *Seahawk*/MCH-101 hel)
CRUISERS • CGHM 2:
  1 *Atago* with *Aegis* Baseline 7 C2, 2 quad lnchr with SSM-1B (Type-90) AShM, 12 8-cell Mk 41 VLS (8 fore, 4 aft) with ASROC A/S msl/SM-2 Block IIIA/B SAM/SM-3 Block IA SAM, 2 triple HOS-302 324mm ASTT with Mk 46 LWT, 2 Mk 15 *Phalanx* Block 1B CIWS, 1 127mm gun (capacity 1 SH-60 *Seahawk* ASW hel)
  1 *Atago* with *Aegis* Baseline 9 C2, 2 quad lnchr with SSM-1B (Type-90) AShM, 12 8-cell Mk 41 VLS (8 fore, 4 aft) with ASROC A/S msl/SM-2 Block IIIA/B SAM/SM-3 Block IA/IB SAM, 2 triple HOS-302 324mm ASTT with Mk 46 LWT, 2 Mk 15 *Phalanx* Block 1B CIWS, 1 127mm gun (capacity 1 SH-60 *Seahawk* ASW hel)
DESTROYERS 34
  DDGHM 28:
    8 *Asagiri* with 2 quad lnchr with RGM-84C *Harpoon* Block 1B AShM, 1 octuple Mk 29 lnchr with RIM-7M *Sea Sparrow* SAM, 2 triple SVTT Mk 32 324mm ASTT with Mk 46 LWT, 1 octuple Mk 112 lnchr with ASROC, 2 Mk 15 *Phalanx* CIWS, 1 76mm gun (capacity 1 SH-60 *Seahawk* ASW hel)
    4 *Akizuki* with 2 quad lnchr with SSM-1B (Type-90) AShM, 4 8-cell Mk 41 VLS with ASROC/RIM-162B ESSM SAM, 2 triple HOS-303 324mm ASTT with Type-97 LWT, 2 Mk 15 *Phalanx* Block 1B CIWS, 1 127mm gun (capacity 1 SH-60 *Seahawk* ASW hel)
    2 *Asahi* (*Akizuki* mod) with 2 quad lnchr with SSM-1B (Type-90) AShM, 4 8-cell Mk 41 VLS with RIM-162B ESSM SAM/Type-07 A/S msl, 2 triple HOS-303 324mm ASTT with Type-12 LWT, 2 Mk 15 *Phalanx* Block 1B CIWS, 1 127mm gun (capacity 1 SH-60 *Seahawk* ASW hel)
    9 *Murasame* with 2 quad lnchr with SSM-1B (Type-90) AShM, 1 16-cell Mk 48 mod 0 VLS with RIM-162C ESSM SAM, 2 triple HOS-302 324mm TT with Mk 46 LWT, 2 8-cell Mk 41 VLS with ASROC, 2 Mk 15 *Phalanx* CIWS, 2 76mm gun (capacity 1 SH-60 *Seahawk* ASW hel)
    5 *Takanami* (improved *Murasame*) with 2 quad lnchr with SSM-1B (Type-90) AShM, 4 8-cell Mk 41 VLS with RIM-162B ESSM SAM/ASROC A/S msl, 2 triple HOS-302 324mm TT with Mk 46 LWT, 2 Mk 15 *Phalanx* Block 1B CIWS, 1 127mm gun (capacity 1 SH-60 *Seahawk* ASW hel)
  DDGM 6:
    2 *Hatakaze* with 2 quad lnchr with RGM-84C *Harpoon* Block 1B AShM, 1 Mk 13 GMLS with SM-1MR Block VI SAM, 2 triple HOS-301 324mm ASTT with Mk 46 LWT, 1 octuple Mk 112 lnchr with ASROC, 2 Mk 15 *Phalanx* CIWS, 2 127mm gun, 1 hel landing platform
    4 *Kongou* with *Aegis* Baseline 4/5 C2, 2 quad lnchr with RGM-84C *Harpoon* Block 1B AShM, 10 8-cell Mk 41 VLS (3 fore, 7 aft) with SM-2 Block IIIA/B SAM/SM-3 Block IA SAM/ASROC A/S msl, 2 5-cell Mk 41 VLS (1 fore, 1 aft; with at-sea reload crane) with SM-2 Block IIIA/B SAM/SM-3 Block IA SAM/ASROC A/S msl, 2 triple HOS-302 324mm ASTT with Mk 46 LWT, 2 Mk 15 *Phalanx* Block 1B CIWS, 1 127mm gun
FRIGATES 11
  FFGHM 5 *Hatsuyuki* with 2 quad lnchr with RGM-84C *Harpoon* Block 1B AShM, 1 octuple Mk 29 lnchr with RIM-7F/M *Sea Sparrow* SAM, 2 triple HOS-301 ASTT with Mk 46 LWT, 1 octuple Mk 112 lnchr with ASROC A/S msl, 2 Mk 15 *Phalanx* CIWS, 1 76mm gun (capacity 1 SH-60 *Seahawk* ASW hel) (of which 3 in trg role)
  FFG 6 *Abukuma* with 2 quad lnchr with RGM-84C *Harpoon* Block 1B AShM, 2 triple HOS-301 ASTT with Mk 46 LWT, 1 octuple Mk 112 lnchr with ASROC A/S msl, 1 Mk 15 *Phalanx* CIWS, 1 76mm gun
PATROL AND COASTAL COMBATANTS 6
  PBFG 6 *Hayabusa* with 4 SSM-1B (Type-90) AShM, 1 76mm gun
MINE WARFARE • MINE COUNTERMEASURES 25
  MCCS 4:
    1 *Ieshima*
    1 *Uraga* with 1 76mm gun, 1 hel landing platform (for MCH-101 hel)

1 *Uraga* with 1 hel landing platform (for MCH-101)
1 *Uwajima*
MSC 19: 3 *Hirashima*; 12 *Sugashima*; 1 *Uwajima*; 3 *Enoshima*
MSO 2 *Awaji*
AMPHIBIOUS
PRINCIPAL AMPHIBIOUS SHIPS • LHD 3 *Osumi* with 2 Mk 15 *Phalanx* CIWS (capacity for 2 CH-47 hel) (capacity 10 Type-90 MBT; 2 LCAC(L) ACV; 330 troops)
LANDING CRAFT 8
LCM 2 LCU-2001
LCAC 6 LCAC(L) (capacity either 1 MBT or 60 troops)
LOGISTICS AND SUPPORT 18
AGBH 1 *Shirase* (capacity 2 AW101 *Merlin* hel)
AGEH 1 *Asuka* with 1 8-cell Mk 41 VLS (wpn trials) (capacity 1 SH-60 *Seahawk* hel)
AGOS 2 *Hibiki* with 1 hel landing platform
AGS 3: 1 *Futami*; 1 *Nichinan*; 1 *Shonan*
AOE 5: 2 *Mashu* (capacity 1 med hel); 3 *Towada* with 1 hel landing platform
ARC 1 *Muroto*
ASR 2: 1 *Chihaya* with 1 hel landing platform; 1 *Chiyoda II* with 1 hel landing platform
AX 3:
1 *Kashima* with 2 triple HOS-301 324mm ASTT, 1 76mm gun, 1 hel landing platform
1 *Kurobe* with 1 76mm gun (trg spt ship)
1 *Tenryu* (trg spt ship); with 1 76mm gun (capacity: 1 med hel)

Naval Aviation ε9,800

7 Air Groups
FORCES BY ROLE
ANTI SUBMARINE/SURFACE WARFARE
5 sqn with SH-60B (SH-60J)/SH-60K *Seahawk*
MARITIME PATROL
1 sqn with P-1; P-3C *Orion*
3 sqn with P-3C *Orion*
ELECTRONIC WARFARE
1 sqn with EP-3 *Orion*
MINE COUNTERMEASURES
1 sqn with MCH-101
SEARCH & RESCUE
1 sqn with *Shin Meiwa* US-1A/US-2
2 sqn with UH-60J *Black Hawk*
TRANSPORT
1 sqn with AW101 *Merlin* (CH-101); Beech 90 *King Air* (LC-90); KC-130R *Hercules*
TRAINING
1 sqn with Beech 90 *King Air* (TC-90)
1 sqn with P-3C *Orion*
1 sqn with T-5J
1 hel sqn with H135 (TH-135); OH-6DA; SH-60B (SH-60J) *Seahawk*
EQUIPMENT BY TYPE
AIRCRAFT 77 combat capable
ASW 77: 22 P-1; 55 P-3C *Orion*
ELINT 5 EP-3C *Orion*
SAR 5: 1 *Shin Meiwa* US-1A; 4 *Shin Meiwa* US-2
TPT 24: **Medium** 6 C-130R *Hercules*; **Light** 18: 5 Beech 90 *King Air* (LC-90); 13 Beech 90 *King Air* (TC-90)
TRG 30 T-5J
HELICOPTERS
ASW 82: 24 SH-60B *Seahawk* (SH-60J); 58 SH-60K *Seahawk*
MCM 10 MCH-101
SAR 12 UH-60J *Black Hawk*
TPT 18: **Medium** 3 AW101 *Merlin* (CH-101); **Light** 15 H135 (TH-135)
AIR-LAUNCHED MISSILES
AShM ASM-1C (Type-90)

Air Self-Defense Force 46,950

7 cbt wg
FORCES BY ROLE
FIGHTER
7 sqn with F-15J *Eagle*
1 sqn with F-4EJ (F-4E) *Phantom* II
3 sqn with Mitsubishi F-2
1 sqn with F-35A *Lightning* II
ELECTRONIC WARFARE
2 sqn with Kawasaki EC-1; YS-11E
ISR
1 sqn with RF-4EJ (RF-4E) *Phantom* II*
AIRBORNE EARLY WARNING & CONTROL
2 sqn with E-2C *Hawkeye*
1 sqn with E-767
SEARCH & RESCUE
1 wg with U-125A *Peace Krypton*; UH-60J *Black Hawk*
TANKER
1 sqn with KC-767J
TRANSPORT
1 (VIP) sqn with B-747-400
1 sqn with C-1; Gulfstream IV (U-4)
1 sqn with C-2
1 sqn with C-130H *Hercules*
Some (liaison) sqn with Gulfstream IV (U-4); T-4*
TRAINING
1 (aggressor) sqn with F-15J *Eagle*
TEST
1 wg with F-15J *Eagle*; T-4*
TRANSPORT HELICOPTER
4 flt with CH-47JA *Chinook*
EQUIPMENT BY TYPE
AIRCRAFT 546 combat capable
FTR 201: 156 F-15J *Eagle*; 45 F-15DJ *Eagle*
FGA 137: 64 F-2A; 27 F-2B; 34 F-4E *Phantom* II (F-4EJ); 12 F-35A *Lightning* II
EW 3: 1 Kawasaki EC-1; 2 YS-11EA
ISR 14: 10 RF-4E *Phantom* II* (RF-4J); 4 YS-11EB
AEW&C 18: 13 E-2C *Hawkeye*; 1 E-2D *Hawkeye*; 4 E-767
SAR 26 U-125A *Peace Krypton*
TKR 6: 2 KC-130H *Hercules*; 4 KC-767J
TPT 57: **Medium** 37: 14 C-130H *Hercules*; 13 C-1; 10 C-2; **PAX** 20: 2 B-777-300ER (VIP); 13 Beech T-400; 5 Gulfstream IV (U-4)
TRG 247: 198 T-4*; 49 T-7
HELICOPTERS
SAR 39 UH-60J *Black Hawk*

TPT • **Heavy** 15 CH-47JA *Chinook*
AIR-LAUNCHED MISSILES
AAM • IR AAM-3 (Type-90); AIM-9L *Sidewinder*; **IIR** AAM-5 (Type-04); **SARH** AIM-7 *Sparrow*; **ARH** AAM-4 (Type-99); AIM-120C5/C7 AMRAAM (limited numbers) **AShM** ASM-1 (Type-80); ASM-2 (Type-93)
BOMBS
INS/SAT guided GBU-38 JDAM; GBU-54 Laser JDAM

Air Defence

Ac control and warning. 4 wg; 28 radar sites
FORCES BY ROLE
AIR DEFENCE
6 SAM gp (total: 24 SAM bty with MIM-104D/F *Patriot* PAC-2/3)
1 AD gp with Type-81 *Tan-SAM*; M167 *Vulcan*
EQUIPMENT BY TYPE
AIR DEFENCE
  SAM
    Long-range 120 MIM-104D/F *Patriot* PAC-2 GEM/PAC-3
    Point-defence Type-81 *Tan-SAM*
  GUNS • TOWED 20mm M167 *Vulcan*

Paramilitary 14,200

Coast Guard 14,200

Ministry of Land, Transport, Infrastructure and Tourism (no cbt role)
EQUIPMENT BY TYPE
PATROL AND COASTAL COMBATANTS 373
  PSOH 14: 2 *Mizuho* (capacity 2 hels); 2 *Shikishima* (capacity 2 hels); 1 *Soya* (capacity 1 hel) (icebreaking capability); 9 *Tsugaru* (*Soya* mod) (capacity 1 hel)
  PSO 43:
    3 *Hida* with 1 hel landing platform
    1 *Izu* with 1 hel landing platform
    9 *Hateruma* with 1 hel landing platform
    6 *Iwami*
    1 *Kojima* (trg) with 1 hel landing platform
    2 *Kunigami* with 1 hel landing platform
    1 *Miura* with 1 hel landing platform
    6 *Ojika* with 1 hel landing platform
    14 *Taketomi* with 1 hel landing platform
  PCO 16: 3 *Aso*; 8 *Katori*; 5 *Teshio*
  PCC 26: 4 *Amami*; 22 *Tokara*
  PBF 49: 22 *Hayagumo*; 4 *Mihashi*; 15 *Raizan*; 2 *Takatsuki*; 6 *Tsuruugi*
  PB 58: 4 *Asogiri*; 4 *Hamagumo*; 11 *Hayanami*; 15 *Katonami*; 1 *Matsunami*; 2 *Murakumo*; 2 *Natsugiri*; 9 *Shimoji*; 10 *Yodo*
  PBI 167: 2 *Hakubai*; 1 *Hayagiku*; 164 *Himegiku*
LOGISTICS AND SUPPORT 16
  ABU 1 *Teshio*
  AGS 12: 6 *Hamashio*; 1 *Jinbei*; 2 *Meiyo*; 1 *Shoyo*; 1 *Takuyo*; 1 *Tenyo*
  AX 3
AIRCRAFT
  MP 2 *Falcon* 900 MPAT
  SAR 4 Saab 340B

TPT 25: **Light** 23: 5 Cessna 172; 9 Beech 350 *King Air* (LR-2); 9 DHC *Dash-7* (Bombardier 300) (MP); **PAX** 2 Gulfstream V (MP)
HELICOPTERS
MRH 5 Bell 412 *Twin Huey*
SAR 11 S-76D
TPT 33: **Medium** 8: 2 AS332 *Super Puma*; 6 H225 *Super Puma*; **Light** 25: 18 AW139; 4 Bell 505 *Jet Ranger X*; 3 S-76C

DEPLOYMENT

ARABIAN SEA & GULF OF ADEN: Combined Maritime Forces • CTF-151: 2 DDGHM
DJIBOUTI: 170; 2 P-3C *Orion*
SOUTH SUDAN: UN • UNMISS 4

FOREIGN FORCES

United States
US Pacific Command: 55,600
  Army 2,650; 1 corps HQ (fwd); 1 SF gp; 1 avn bn; 1 SAM bn
  Navy 20,950; 1 CVN; 3 CGHM; 2 DDGHM; 8 DDGM (2 non-op); 1 LCC; 4 MCO; 1 LHD; 1 LPD; 2 LSD; 3 FGA sqn with 10 F/A-18E *Super Hornet*; 1 FGA sqn with 10 F/A-18F *Super Hornet*; 2 ASW sqn with 6 P-8A *Poseidon*; 1 ASW flt with 2 P-3C *Orion*; 2 EW sqn with 5 EA-18G *Growler*; 1 AEW&C sqn with 5 E-2D *Hawkeye*; 2 ASW hel sqn with 12 MH-60R *Seahawk*; 1 tpt hel sqn with MH-60S *Knight Hawk*; 1 base at Sasebo; 1 base at Yokosuka
  USAF: 12,550; 1 HQ (5th Air Force) at Okinawa–Kadena AB; 1 ftr wg at Misawa AB (2 ftr sqn with 22 F-16C/D *Fighting Falcon*); 1 ftr wg at Okinawa–Kadena AB (2 ftr sqn with 27 F-15C/D *Eagle*; 1 FGA sqn with 14 F-22A *Raptor*; 1 tkr sqn with 15 KC-135R *Stratotanker*; 1 AEW sqn with 2 E-3B *Sentry*; 1 CSAR sqn with 10 HH-60G *Pave Hawk*); 1 tpt wg at Yokota AB with 10 C-130J-30 *Hercules*; 2 Beech 1900C (C-12J); 1 spec ops gp at Okinawa–Kadena AB with (1 sqn with 5 MC-130H *Combat Talon*; 1 sqn with 5 MC-130J *Commando* II; 1 unit with 5 CV-22A *Osprey*); 1 ISR sqn with RC-135 *Rivet Joint*; 1 ISR UAV flt with 5 RQ-4A *Global Hawk*
  USMC 19,450; 1 mne div; 1 mne regt HQ; 1 arty regt HQ; 1 recce bn; 1 mne bn; 1 amph aslt bn; 1 arty bn; 2 FGA sqn at Iwakuni with 12 F/A-18D *Hornet*; 1 FGA sqn at Iwakuni with 12 F-35B *Lightning* II; 1 tkr sqn at Iwakuni with 15 KC-130J *Hercules*; 2 tpt sqn at Futenma with 12 MV-22B *Osprey*
US Strategic Command: 1 AN/TPY-2 X-band radar at Shariki; 1 AN/TPY-2 X-band radar at Kyogamisaki

Korea, Democratic People's Republic of DPRK

North Korean Won		2018	2019	2020
GDP	US$			
per capita	US$			
Def exp	won			
	US$			

US$1=won
*definitive economic data not available

Population	25,513,061					
Age	0–14	15–19	20–24	25–29	30–64	65 plus
Male	10.5%	3.8%	4.0%	4.1%	23.0%	3.3%
Female	10.1%	3.7%	3.9%	3.9%	23.5%	6.2%

Capabilities

Renewed diplomacy has reduced tensions on the Korean Peninsula since 2018, though the prospect of limiting Pyongyang's nuclear ambitions remains uncertain. Aware of the qualitative inferiority of its conventional forces, North Korea has invested in asymmetric capabilities, particularly the development of nuclear weapons and ballistic-missile delivery systems. The 2018 moratorium covering nuclear- and long-range-missile tests remains in place, despite a resumption of shorter-range-missile tests in May 2019. A number of new tactical missiles and guided rockets have since been successfully demonstrated, and Pyongyang's ambition to develop a nuclear-capable submarine-launched ballistic missile has resurfaced. North Korea remains diplomatically isolated. While foreign defence cooperation is restricted by international pressure and sanctions, Pyongyang has nonetheless often found ways to develop military ties. Official conscription for both men and women is often extended, sometimes indefinitely. Training is focused on fighting a short intensive war on the peninsula, but the armed forces' overall effectiveness in a modern conflict against technologically superior opposition is unclear. Internal exercises are conducted regularly, but those shown are staged and are not necessarily representative of wider operational capability. North Korea's conventional forces remain reliant on increasingly obsolete equipment, with older Soviet-era and Chinese-origin equipment supplemented by a number of indigenous designs and upgrades. Overall effectiveness and serviceability of some equipment remains in doubt but there is local maintenance, repair and overhaul capacity. Local defence-industrial capacity includes the manufacture of light arms, armoured vehicles, artillery and missile systems. North Korea has exported arms in the past. It is unclear whether the country would have had the capability to indigenously develop some of the technical advances it has demonstrated, including in rocket propulsion.

ACTIVE 1,280,000 (Army 1,100,000 Navy 60,000 Air 110,000 Strategic Forces 10,000) **Paramilitary 189,000**

Conscript liability Army 5–12 years, Navy 5–10 years, Air Force 3–4 years, followed by compulsory part-time service to age 40. Thereafter service in the Worker/Peasant Red Guard to age 60

RESERVE ε600,000 (Armed Forces ε600,000), **Paramilitary 5,700,000**

Reservists are assigned to units (see also Paramilitary)

ORGANISATIONS BY SERVICE

Strategic Forces ε10,000

North Korea's ballistic missiles and obsolete H-5 (Il-28) bombers could be used to deliver nuclear warheads or bombs. At present, however, there is no conclusive evidence to verify that North Korea has successfully produced a warhead or bomb capable of being delivered by these systems

EQUIPMENT BY TYPE (ε)
SURFACE-TO-SURFACE MISSILE LAUNCHERS
  ICBM 6+: *Hwasong-13/Hwasong-13* mod/*Hwasong-14* (in test); *Hwasong-15* (in test)
  IRBM *Hwasong-12* (in test)
  MRBM ε10 *Nodong* mod 1/mod 2 (ε90+ msl); some *Scud-ER*; *Pukgusong-2* (in test); *Hwasong-10* (*Musudan*) (in test)
  SBRM 30+ *Hwasong-5* (SS-1C *Scud*-B)/*Hwasong*-6 (SS-1D *Scud*-C) (ε200+ msl); some *Scud* (mod) (in test)

Army ε1,100,000
FORCES BY ROLE
COMMAND
  2 mech corps HQ
  10 inf corps HQ
  1 (Capital Defence) corps HQ
MANOEUVRE
  Armoured
  1 armd div
  15 armd bde
  Mechanised
  4 mech div
  Light
  27 inf div
  14 inf bde
COMBAT SUPPORT
  1 arty div
  21 arty bde
  9 MRL bde
  5–8 engr river crossing/amphibious regt
  1 engr river crossing bde

Special Purpose Forces Command 88,000
FORCES BY ROLE
SPECIAL FORCES
  8 (Reconnaissance General Bureau) SF bn
MANOEUVRE
  Reconnaissance
  17 recce bn
  Light
  9 lt inf bde
  6 sniper bde
  Air Manoeuvre
  3 AB bde
  1 AB bn
  2 sniper bde
  Amphibious
  2 sniper bde

Reserves 600,000
FORCES BY ROLE
MANOEUVRE
Light
40 inf div
18 inf bde
EQUIPMENT BY TYPE (ε)
ARMOURED FIGHTING VEHICLES
MBT 3,500+ T-34/T-54/T-55/T-62/Type-59/*Chonma/ Pokpoong*
LT TK 560+: 560 PT-76; M-1985
IFV 32 BTR-80A
APC 2,500+
APC (T) BTR-50; Type-531 (Type-63); VTT-323
APC (W) 2,500 BTR-40/BTR-60/M-1992/1/BTR-152/M-2010 (6×6)/M-2010 (8×8)
ANTI-TANK/ANTI-INFRASTRUCTURE
MSL
SP 9K11 *Malyutka* (AT-3 *Sagger*); M-2010 ATGM
MANPATS 2K15 *Shmel* (AT-1 *Snapper*); 9K111 *Fagot* (AT-4 *Spigot*); 9K113 *Konkurs* (AT-5 *Spandrel*)
RCL 82mm 1,700 B-10
ARTILLERY 21,600+
SP/TOWED 8,600:
SP 122mm M-1977; M-1981; M-1985; M-1991; 130mm M-1975; M-1981; M-1991; 152mm M-1974; M-1977; M-2018; 170mm M-1978; M-1989
TOWED 122mm D-30; D-74; M-1931/37; 130mm M-46; 152mm M-1937; M-1938; M-1943
GUN/MOR 120mm (reported)
MRL 5,500: 107mm Type-63; VTT-323 107mm; 122mm BM-11; M-1977 (BM-21); M-1985; M-1992; M-1993; VTT-323 122mm; 200mm BMD-20; 240mm BM-24; M-1985; M-1989; M-1991; 300mm some
MOR 7,500: 82mm M-37; 120mm M-43; 160mm M-43
SURFACE-TO-SURFACE MISSILE LAUNCHERS
SBRM 24 FROG-3/5/7; some *Toksa* (SS-21B *Scarab* mod); some (*Iskander* lookalike); some (ATACMS lookalike)
AIR DEFENCE
SAM
Point-defence 9K35 *Strela*-10 (SA-13 *Gopher*); 9K310 *Igla*-1 (SA-16 *Gimlet*); 9K32 *Strela*-2 (SA-7 *Grail*)‡
GUNS 11,000
SP 14.5mm M-1984, 23mm M-1992; 37mm M-1992; 57mm M-1985
TOWED 11,000: 14.5mm ZPU-1/ZPU-2/ZPU-4; 23mm ZU-23; 37mm M-1939; 57mm S-60; 85mm M-1939 KS-12; 100mm KS-19

Navy ε60,000
EQUIPMENT BY TYPE
SUBMARINES • TACTICAL 73
SSB 1 *Gorae* with 1 *Pukguksong*-1 SLBM (SLBM trials)
SSK 20 PRC Type-033/FSU *Romeo*† with 8 single 533mm TT with SAET-60 HWT
SSC 32+:
ε30 *Sang-O* some with 2 single 533mm TT with 53–65E HWT
2+ *Sang-O* II with 4 single 533mm TT with 53–65E HWT
SSW ε20† (some *Yugo* some with 2 single 406mm TT; some *Yeono* some with 2 single 533mm TT)

PRINCIPAL SURFACE COMBATANTS 2
FRIGATES • FFG 2:
1 *Najin* with 2 single lnchr with P-20 (SS-N-2A *Styx*) AShM, 2 RBU 1200 *Uragan* A/S mor, 2 100mm gun, 2 twin 57mm gun
1 *Najin* with 2 twin lnchr with *Kumsong*-3 (KN-SS-N-2 *Stormpetrel*) AShM, 2 RBU 1200 *Uragan* A/S mor, 2 100mm gun, 2 twin 57mm gun (operational status unclear)
PATROL AND COASTAL COMBATANTS 383+
CORVETTES • FS 5
4 *Sariwon* with 2 twin 57mm gun
1 *Tral* with 1 85mm gun
PCG 10:
10 *Soju* (FSU *Osa* I (Project 205) mod) with 4 single lnchr with P-20 (SS-N-2A *Styx*) AShM
PCC 18:
6 *Hainan* with 4 RBU 1200 A/S mor, 2 twin 57mm gun
7 *Taechong* I with 2 RBU 1200 *Uragan* A/S mor, 1 85mm gun, 1 twin 57mm gun
5 *Taechong* II with 2 RBU 1200 *Uragan* A/S mor, 1 100mm gun, 1 twin 57mm gun
PBFG 25+:
4 *Huangfeng* (Type-021) with 4 single lnchr with P-15 *Termit* (SS-N-2) AShM, 2 twin AK230 CIWS
6 *Komar* with 2 single lnchr with P-20 (SS-N-2A *Styx*) AShM
8 *Osa* I with 4 single lnchr with P-20 (SS-N-2A *Styx*) AShM, 2 twin AK230 CIWS
6 *Sohung* (Komard mod) with 2 single lnchr with P-20 (SS-N-2A *Styx*) AShM
1+ *Nongo* with 2 twin lnchr with *Kumsong*-3 (KN-SS-N-2 *Stormpetrel*) AShM, 2 30mm CIWS (operational status unknown)
PBF 229:
54 *Chong-Jin* with 1 85mm gun
142 *Ku Song/Sin Hung/Sin Hung* (mod)
33 *Sinpo*
PB 96:
59 *Chaho*
6 *Chong-Ju* with 2 RBU 1200 *Uragan* A/S mor, 1 85mm gun
13 *Shanghai* II
18 SO-1 with 4 RBU 1200 *Uragan* A/S mor, 2 twin 57mm gun
MINE WARFARE • MINE COUNTERMEASURES 24
MSC 24: 19 *Yukto* I; 5 *Yukto* II
AMPHIBIOUS
LANDING SHIPS • LSM 10 *Hantae* (capacity 3 tanks; 350 troops)
LANDING CRAFT 257
LCPL 96 *Nampo* (capacity 35 troops)
LCM 25
UCAC 136 *Kongbang* (capacity 50 troops)
LOGISTICS AND SUPPORT 23:
AGI 14 (converted fishing vessels)
AS 8 (converted cargo ships)
ASR 1 *Kowan*

Coastal Defence

FORCES BY ROLE
COASTAL DEFENCE
2 AShM regt with HY-1/*Kumsong*-3 (6 sites, some mobile launchers)
EQUIPMENT BY TYPE
COASTAL DEFENCE
ARTY 130mm M-1992; SM-4-1
AShM HY-1; *Kumsong*-3
ARTILLERY • TOWED 122mm M-1931/37; **152mm** M-1937

Air Force 110,000

4 air divs. 1st, 2nd and 3rd Air Divs (cbt) responsible for N, E and S air-defence sectors respectively; 8th Air Div (trg) responsible for NE sector. The AF controls the national airline

FORCES BY ROLE
BOMBER
3 lt regt with H-5; Il-28 *Beagle*
FIGHTER
1 regt with MiG-15 *Fagot*
6 regt with J-5; MiG-17 *Fresco*
4 regt with J-6; MiG-19 *Farmer*
5 regt with J-7; MiG-21F-13/PFM *Fishbed*
1 regt with MiG-21bis *Fishbed*
1 regt with MiG-23ML/P *Flogger*
1 regt with MiG-29A/S/UB *Fulcrum*
GROUND ATTACK
1 regt with Su-25K/UBK *Frogfoot*
TRANSPORT
Some regt with An-2 *Colt*/Y-5 (to infiltrate 2 air-force sniper brigades deep into ROK rear areas); An-24 *Coke*; Il-18 *Coot*; Il-62M *Classic*; Tu-134 *Crusty*; Tu-154 *Careless*
TRAINING
Some regt with CJ-6; FT-2; MiG-21U/UM
TRANSPORT HELICOPTER
Some regt with Hughes 500D/E; Mi-8 *Hip*; Mi-17 *Hip* H; Mil-26 *Halo*; PZL Mi-2 *Hoplite*; Z-5
AIR DEFENCE
19 bde with S-125 *Pechora* (SA-3 *Goa*); S-75 *Dvina* (SA-2 *Guideline*); S-200 *Angara* (SA-5 *Gammon*); 9K36 Strela-3 (SA-14 *Gremlin*); 9K310 Igla-1 (SA-16 *Gimlet*); 9K32 Strela-2 (SA-7 *Grail*)‡; Pongae-5
EQUIPMENT BY TYPE
AIRCRAFT 545 combat capable
BBR 80 Il-28 *Beagle*/H-5†
FTR 401+: MiG-15 *Fagot*; 107 MiG-17 *Fresco*/J-5; 100 MiG-19 *Farmer*/J-6; 120 MiG-21F-13 *Fishbed*/J-7; MiG-21PFM *Fishbed*; 46 MiG-23ML *Flogger*; 10 MiG-23P *Flogger*; 18+ MiG-29A/S/UB *Fulcrum*
FGA 30 MiG-21bis *Fishbed* (18 Su-7 *Fitter* in store)
ATK 34 Su-25K/UBK *Frogfoot*
TPT 217+: **Heavy** some Il-76 (operated by state airline); **Light** 208: 6 An-24 *Coke*; 2 Tu-134 *Crusty*; ε200 An-2 *Colt*/Y-5; **PAX** 9: 2 Il-18 *Coot*; 2 Il-62M *Classic*; 4 Tu-154 *Careless*; 1 Tu-204-300
TRG 215+: 180 CJ-6; 35 FT-2; some MiG-21U/UM
HELICOPTERS
MRH 80 Hughes 500D/E†
TPT 206: **Heavy** 4 Mi-26 *Halo*; **Medium** 63: 15 Mi-8 *Hip*/Mi-17 *Hip* H; 48 Mi-4 *Hound*/Z-5; **Light** 139 PZL Mi-2 *Hoplite*
UNMANNED AERIAL VEHICLES
ISR • Medium some (unidentified indigenous type); **Light** Pchela-1 (*Shmel*) (reported)
AIR DEFENCE • SAM
Long-range 38 S-200 *Angara* (SA-5 *Gammon*)
Medium-range 179+: some Pongae-5 (status unknown); 179+ S-75 *Dvina* (SA-2 *Guideline*)
Short-range 133 S-125 *Pechora* (SA-3 *Goa*)
Point-defence 9K32 Strela-2 (SA-7 *Grail*)‡; 9K36 Strela-3 (SA-14 *Gremlin*); 9K310 Igla-1 (SA-16 *Gimlet*)
AIR-LAUNCHED MISSILES
AAM • IR R-3 (AA-2 *Atoll*)‡; R-60 (AA-8 *Aphid*); R-73 (AA-11A *Archer*); PL-5; PL-7; **SARH** R-23/24 (AA-7 *Apex*); R-27R/ER (AA-10 A/C *Alamo*)
ASM Kh-23 (AS-7 *Kerry*)‡; Kh-25 (AS-10 *Karen*)

Paramilitary 189,000 active

Security Troops 189,000 (incl border guards, public-safety personnel)
Ministry of Public Security

Worker/Peasant Red Guard ε5,700,000 reservists
Org on a province/town/village basis; comd structure is bde–bn–coy–pl; small arms with some mor and AD guns (but many units unarmed)

Korea, Republic of ROK

South Korean Won		2018	2019	2020
GDP	won	1893tr	1914tr	
	US$	1.72tr	1.63tr	
per capita	US$	33,320	31,431	
Growth	%	2.7	2.0	
Inflation	%	1.5	0.5	
Def bdgt	won	43.2tr	46.7tr	50.2tr
	US$	39.2bn	39.8bn	
US$1=won		1100.56	1174.35	

Real-terms defence budget trend (US$bn, constant 2015)

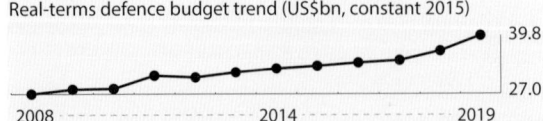

Population 51,635,813

Age	0–14	15–19	20–24	25–29	30–64	65 plus
Male	6.6%	2.7%	3.5%	3.7%	27.1%	6.5%
Female	6.3%	2.5%	3.1%	3.2%	26.3%	8.6%

Capabilities

South Korea's defence policy remains focused on its difficult relationship with North Korea, notwithstanding recent diplomatic re-engagement. Seoul has looked to recapitalise conventional military capabilities to ensure a qualitative edge over Pyongyang.

It continues to prioritise acquiring new capabilities to respond to the neighbouring nuclear threat; formerly known as 'Kill Chain', 'Korea Air and Missile Defense' and 'Korea Massive Punishment and Retaliation', the three-axis approach was reported rebranded in early 2019. The Defense Reform 2.0 project announced in 2018 sets out ambitions to modernise and restructure the armed forces, placing emphasis on new technologies. The established alliance with the US is a major element of defence strategy, though the planned transfer of wartime operational control of forces to Seoul is now 'conditions based' with no firm date set. A large number of US military personnel and equipment remained stationed in South Korea including the THAAD missile-defence system. South Korea's forces remain some of the best equipped and trained in the region. South Korea has demonstrated the capacity to support small international deployments, including contributions to UN missions and counter-piracy operations in the Arabian Sea. The inventory increasingly comprises modern systems. South Korea has developed a broad range of domestic defence industries, which are capable of supplying the majority of military requirements. However, there is still reliance on the US in areas such as front-line combat aircraft. Local defence industries are finding growing export success, particularly with the T-50 jet trainer and K-9 self-propelled howitzer.

ACTIVE 599,000 (Army 464,000 Navy 70,000 Air 65,000) **Paramilitary 9,000**

Conscript liability Service period reducing from Oct 2018, by three months for the army and marines (now 18 months), and the navy (now 20 months); and by two months for the air force (now 22 months).

RESERVE 3,100,000

Reserve obligation of three days per year. First Combat Forces (Mobilisation Reserve Forces) or Regional Combat Forces (Homeland Defence Forces) to age 33

Reserve Paramilitary 3,000,000

Being reorganised

ORGANISATIONS BY SERVICE

Army 464,000
FORCES BY ROLE
COMMAND
  8 corps HQ
  1 (Capital Defence) comd HQ
SPECIAL FORCES
  1 (Special Warfare) SF comd
  6 SF bde
  1 indep SF bn
  2 cdo bde
  6 cdo regt
  2 indep cdo bn
MANOEUVRE
  Armoured
  5 armd bde
  1 mech inf div (1 recce bn, 1 armd bde, 2 armd inf bde, 1 arty bde, 1 engr bn)
  2 mech inf div (1 recce bn, 1 armd bde, 1 armd inf bde; 1 mech inf bde, 1 arty bde, 1 engr bn)
  1 mech inf div (1 recce bn, 2 armd inf bde, 1 arty bde, 1 engr bn)
  Mechanised
  1 mech inf div (1 recce bn, 2 mech inf bde, 1 arty bde, 1 engr bn)
  Light
  16 inf div (1 recce bn, 1 tk bn, 3 inf regt, 1 arty regt (4 arty bn), 1 engr bn)
  2 indep inf bde
  Air Manoeuvre
  1 air aslt bde
  Other
  5 sy regt
SURFACE-TO-SURFACE MISSILE
  3 SSM bn
COMBAT SUPPORT
  6 engr bde
  5 engr gp
  1 CBRN defence bde
  8 sigs bde
COMBAT SERVICE SUPPORT
  4 log spt comd
HELICOPTER
  1 (army avn) comd
AIR DEFENCE
  1 ADA bde
  5 ADA bn

Reserves
FORCES BY ROLE
COMMAND
  1 army HQ
MANOEUVRE
  Light
  24 inf div
EQUIPMENT BY TYPE
ARMOURED FIGHTING VEHICLES
  MBT 2,221: 1,000 K1/K1E1; 484 K1A1/K1A2; 100 K2; 597 M48A5; 40 T-80U
  IFV 540: ε500 K21; 40 BMP-3
  APC 2,490
    APC (T) 2,260: 300 Bv 206; 1,700 KIFV; 420 M113; 140 M577 (CP)
    APC (W) 220; 20 BTR-80; 200 KM-900/-901 (Fiat 6614)
  PPV 10 *MaxxPro*
ENGINEERING & MAINTENANCE VEHICLES
  AEV 207 M9
  ARV 238+: 200 K1; K21 ARV; K288A1; M47; 38 M88A1
  VLB 56 K1
ANTI-TANK/ANTI-INFRASTRUCTURE
  MSL
    SP *Hyeongung*
    MANPATS 9K115 *Metis* (AT-7 *Saxhorn*); *Hyeongung*; TOW-2A
  RCL 75mm; 90mm M67; **106mm** M40A2
  GUNS 58
    SP 90mm 50 M36
    TOWED 76mm 8 M18 *Hellcat* (AT gun)
ARTILLERY 11,067+
  SP 1,353+: **155mm** 1,340: ε300 K9/K9A1 *Thunder*; 1,040 M109A2 (K55/K55A1); **175mm** some M107; **203mm** 13 M110

TOWED 3,500+: **105mm** 1,700 M101/KH-178; **155mm/203mm** 1,800+ KH-179/M114/M115
MRL 214+: **130mm** 156 K136 *Kooryong*; **227mm** 58: 48 M270 MLRS; 10 M270A1 MLRS; **239mm** some *Chunmoo*
MOR 6,000: **81mm** KM29 (M29); **107mm** M30
SURFACE-TO-SURFACE MISSILE LAUNCHERS
SRBM • **Conventional** 30 *Hyonmu* IIA/IIB; MGM-140A/B ATACMS (launched from M270/M270A1 MLRS)
GLCM • **Conventional** *Hyonmu* III
HELICOPTERS
ATK 96: 60 AH-1F/J *Cobra*; 36 AH-64E *Apache*
MRH 175: 130 Hughes 500D; 45 MD-500
TPT 336+: **Heavy** 37: 31 CH-47D *Chinook*; 6 MH-47E *Chinook*; **Medium** 187+: 100+ KUH-1 *Surion*; 87 UH-60P *Black Hawk*; **Light** 112: ε100 Bell 205 (UH-1H *Iroquois*); 12 Bo-105
AIR DEFENCE
SAM • **Point-defence** *Chiron*; *Chun Ma* (*Pegasus*); FIM-92 *Stinger*; *Javelin*; *Mistral*; 9K310 *Igla*-1 (SA-16 *Gimlet*)
GUNS 330+
SP 170: **20mm** ε150 KIFV *Vulcan* SPAAG; **30mm** 20 BIHO *Flying Tiger*
TOWED 160: **20mm** 60 M167 *Vulcan*; **35mm** 20 GDF-003; **40mm** 80 L/60/L/70; M1
AIR-LAUNCHED MISSILES
ASM AGM-114R1 *Hellfire*

Navy 70,000 (incl marines)

Three separate fleet elements: 1st Fleet Donghae (East Sea/Sea of Japan); 2nd Fleet Pyeongtaek (West Sea/Yellow Sea); 3rd Fleet Busan (South Sea/Korea Strait); independent submarine command; three additional flotillas (incl SF, mine warfare, amphibious and spt elements) and 1 Naval Air Wing (3 gp plus spt gp)

EQUIPMENT BY TYPE
SUBMARINES • TACTICAL 22
SSK 16:
6 *Chang Bogo* I (GER Type-209/1200; KSS-1) with 8 single 533mm TT with SUT HWT/K731 *White Shark* HWT
3 *Chang Bogo* I (GER Type-209/1200; KSS-1) with 8 single 533mm TT with UGM-84 *Harpoon* AShM/SUT HWT/K731 *White Shark* HWT
7 *Chang Bogo* II (GER Type-214; KSS-2; AIP fitted) with 8 single 533mm TT with *Hae Sung* III LACM/*Hae Sung* I AShM/SUT HWT/K731 *White Shark* HWT
SSC 6 *Cosmos*
PRINCIPAL SURFACE COMBATANTS 26
CRUISERS • CGHM 3:
3 *Sejong* (KDD-III) with *Aegis* Baseline 7 C2, 6 8-cell K-VLS with *Hae Sung* II LACM/*Red Shark* A/S msl, 4 quad lnchr with *Hae Sung* I AShM, 10 8-cell Mk 41 VLS (6 fore, 4 aft) with SM-2 Block IIIA/B SAM, 1 21-cell Mk 49 GMLS with RIM-116 RAM SAM, 2 triple SVTT Mk 32 324mm ASTT with K745 *Blue Shark* LWT, 1 *Goalkeeper* CIWS, 1 127mm gun (capacity 2 *Lynx* Mk99/AW159 *Wildcat* hels)
DESTROYERS • DDGHM 6:
6 *Chungmugong Yi Sun-Sin* (KDD-II) with 2 8-cell K-VLS with *Hae Sung* II LACM/*Red Shark* A/S msl, 2 quad lnchr with RGM-84 *Harpoon* AShM/*Hae Sung* I AShM, 4 8-cell Mk 41 VLS with SM-2 Block IIIA/B SAM, 1 21-cell Mk 49 GMLS with RIM-116 RAM SAM, 2 triple SVTT Mk 32 324mm ASTT with Mk 46 LWT, 1 *Goalkeeper* CIWS, 1 127mm gun (capacity 1 *Lynx* Mk99/AW159 *Wildcat* hel)
FRIGATES 17
FFGHM 10:
3 *Gwanggaeto Daewang* (KDD-I) with 2 quad lnchr with RGM-84 *Harpoon* AShM, 2 8-cell Mk 48 mod 2 VLS with RIM-7P *Sea Sparrow* SAM, 2 triple SVTT Mk 32 324mm ASTT with Mk 46 LWT, 2 *Goalkeeper* CIWS, 1 127mm gun (capacity 1 *Lynx* Mk99/AW159 *Wildcat* hel)
6 *Incheon* with 2 quad lnchr with TSLM LACM/*Hae Sung* I AShM, 1 21-cell Mk 49 lnchr with RIM-116 SAM, 2 triple KMk. 32 324mm ASTT with K745 *Blue Shark* LWT, 1 Mk 15 *Phalanx* Block 1B CIWS, 1 127 mm gun (capacity 1 *Lynx* Mk99/AW159 *Wildcat* hel)
1 *Daegu* (*Incheon* Batch II) with 2 8-cell K-VLS with *Hae Sung* II LACM/TSLM LACM/*Haegung* (K-SAAM) SAM/*Red Shark* A/S msl, 2 quad lnchr with TSLM LACM/*Hae Sung* I AShM, 2 KMk. 32 triple 324mm ASTT with K745 *Blue Shark* LWT, 1 Mk 15 *Phalanx* Block 1B CIWS, 1 127mm gun (capacity 1 *Lynx* Mk99/AW159 *Wildcat* hel)
FFG 7 *Ulsan* with 2 quad lnchr with RGM-84 *Harpoon* AShM, 2 triple SVTT Mk 32 324mm ASTT with Mk 46 LWT, 2 76mm gun
PATROL AND COASTAL COMBATANTS ε101
CORVETTES • FSG 32:
18 *Gumdoksuri* with 2 twin lnchr with *Hae Sung* I AShM, 1 76mm gun
8 *Po Hang* (Flight IV) with 2 twin lnchr with RGM-84 *Harpoon* AShM, 2 triple 324mm ASTT with Mk 46 LWT, 2 76mm gun
6 *Po Hang* (Flight V) with 2 twin lnchr with *Hae Sung* I AShM, 2 KMk. 32 triple 324mm ASTT with K745 *Blue Shark* LWT, 2 76mm gun
PCFG 1 *Chamsuri* II with 1 12-cell 130mm MRL, 1 76mm gun
PBF ε68 *Sea Dolphin*
MINE WARFARE 11
MINE COUNTERMEASURES 9
MHO 6 *Kan Kyeong*
MSO 3 *Yang Yang*
MINELAYERS • ML 2
1 *Won San* with 2 triple SVTT Mk 32 324mm ASTT with Mk 46 LWT/K745 *Blue Shark* LWT, 1 76mm gun, 1 hel landing platform
1 *Nampo* (MLS-II) with 1 4-cell K-VLS VLS with *Haegung* (K-SAAM) SAM, 2 triple KMk. 32 triple 324mm ASTT with K745 *Blue Shark* LWT, 1 76mm gun (capacity 1 med hel)
AMPHIBIOUS
PRINCIPAL AMPHIBIOUS SHIPS 5
LHD
1 *Dokdo* with 1 Mk 49 GMLS with RIM-116 SAM, 2 *Goalkeeper* CIWS (capacity 2 LCAC; 10 tanks; 700 troops; 10 UH-60 hel)

LPD 4:
  4 *Cheonwangbong* (LST-II) (capacity 3 LCM; 2 MBT; 8 AFV; 300 troops; 2 med hel)
LANDING SHIPS • LST 4 *Go Jun Bong* with 1 hel landing platform (capacity 20 tanks; 300 troops)
LANDING CRAFT 22
  LCAC 5: 3 *Tsaplya* (capacity 1 MBT; 130 troops); 2 LSF-II (capacity 150 troops or 1 MBT & 24 troops)
  LCM 10 LCM-8
  LCT 3 *Mulgae* II
  LCU 4 *Mulgae* I
LOGISTICS AND SUPPORT 9
  AG 1 *Sunjin* (trials spt)
  AOEH 1 *Soyangham* (AOE-II) with 1 Mk 15 *Phalanx* Block 1B CIWS (capacity 1 med hel)
  AORH 3 *Chun Jee*
  ARS 1 *Cheong Hae Jin*
  ATS 2 *Tongyeong*
  AX 1 MTB

Naval Aviation
EQUIPMENT BY TYPE
AIRCRAFT 16 combat capable
  ASW 16: 8 P-3C *Orion*; 8 P-3CK *Orion*
  TPT • Light 5 Cessna F406 *Caravan* II
HELICOPTERS
  ASW 31: 11 *Lynx* Mk99; 12 *Lynx* Mk99A; 8 AW159 *Wildcat*
  MRH 3 SA319B *Alouette* III
  TPT 15: **Medium** 8 UH-60P *Black Hawk* **Light** 7 Bell 205 (UH-1H *Iroquois*)

Marines 29,000
FORCES BY ROLE
SPECIAL FORCES
  1 SF regt
MANOEUVRE
  Amphibious
  2 mne div (1 recce bn, 1 tk bn, 3 mne regt, 1 amph bn, 1 arty regt, 1 engr bn)
  1 mne bde
COMBAT SUPPORT
  Some cbt spt unit
EQUIPMENT BY TYPE
ARMOURED FIGHTING VEHICLES
  MBT 100: 50 K1A1; 50 M48
  AAV 166 AAV-7A1
ANTI-TANK/ANTI-INFRASTRUCTURE • MSL
  SP *Spike* NLOS
  MANPATS *Hyeongung*
ARTILLERY
  SP 155mm K9/K9A1 *Thunder*
  TOWED 105mm KH-178; 155mm KH-179
  MRL 130mm K136 *Kooryong*
  MOR 81mm KM29 (M29)
COASTAL DEFENCE • AShM RGM-84A *Harpoon* (truck mounted)
HELICOPTERS • TPT • Medium 5+ MUH-1 *Surion*
AIR DEFENCE
  GUNS • Towed • 20mm M167 *Vulcan* (direct fire role)

Naval Special Warfare Flotilla

Air Force 65,000
4 Comd (Ops, Southern Combat, Logs, Trg)
FORCES BY ROLE
FIGHTER/GROUND ATTACK
  1 sqn with F-4E *Phantom* II
  6 sqn with F-5E/F *Tiger* II
  3 sqn with F-15K *Eagle*
  10 sqn with F-16C/D *Fighting Falcon* (KF-16C/D)
  2 sqn with FA-50 *Fighting Eagle*
ISR
  1 wg with KO-1
SIGINT
  1 sqn with Hawker 800RA/XP
SEARCH & RESCUE
  2 sqn with AS332L *Super Puma*; Bell 412EP; HH-47D *Chinook*; HH-60P *Black Hawk*; Ka-32 *Helix* C
TRANSPORT
  1 VIP sqn with B-737-300; B-747; CN235-220; S-92A *Superhawk*; VH-60P *Black Hawk* (VIP)
  3 sqn (incl 1 Spec Ops) with C-130H/H-30/J-30 *Hercules*
  2 sqn with CN235M-100/220
TRAINING
  2 sqn with F-5E/F *Tiger* II
  1 sqn with F-16C/D *Fighting Falcon*
  4 sqn with KT-1
  1 sqn with Il-103
  3 sqn with T-50/TA-50 *Golden Eagle**
TRANSPORT HELICOPTER
  1 sqn with UH-60P *Black Hawk* (Spec Ops)
AIR DEFENCE
  3 AD bde (total: 3 SAM bn with MIM-23B I-*Hawk*/*Cheongung*; 2 SAM bn with MIM-104E *Patriot* PAC-2 GEM-T)
EQUIPMENT BY TYPE
AIRCRAFT 563 combat capable
  FTR 174: 142 F-5E *Tiger* II; 32 F-5F *Tiger* II
  FGA 309: 30 F-4E *Phantom* II; 59 F-15K *Eagle*; 118 F-16C *Fighting Falcon* (KF-16C); 44 F-16D *Fighting Falcon* (KF-16D); 8 F-35A *Lightning* II; 50 FA-50 *Fighting Eagle*
  AEW&C 4 B-737 AEW
  ISR 24: 4 Hawker 800RA; 20 KO-1
  SIGINT 6. 4 Hawker 800SIG; 2 *Falcon* 2000 (COMINT/SIGINT)
  TKR/TPT 2 A330 MRTT
  TPT 38: **Medium** 16: 8 C-130H *Hercules*; 4 C-130H-30 *Hercules*; 4 C-130J-30 *Hercules*; **Light** 20: 12 CN235M-100; 8 CN235M-220 (incl 2 VIP); **PAX** 2: 1 B-737-300; 1 B-747-400
  TRG 183: 83 KT-1; 49 T-50 *Golden Eagle**; 9 T-50B *Black Eagle** (aerobatics); 22 TA-50 *Golden Eagle**; ε20 KT-100
HELICOPTERS
  SAR 16: 5 HH-47D *Chinook*; 11 HH-60P *Black Hawk*
  MRH 3 Bell 412EP
  TPT • **Medium** 30: 2 AS332L *Super Puma*; 8 Ka-32 *Helix* C; 3 S-92A *Super Hawk*; 7 UH-60P *Black Hawk*; 10 VH-60P *Black Hawk* (VIP)
UNMANNED AERIAL VEHICLES • ISR 103+: **Medium** 3+: some *Night Intruder*; 3 *Searcher* **Light** 100 *Harpy* (anti-radiation)

AIR DEFENCE • SAM 206
  Long-range 48 MIM-104 *Patriot* PAC-2 GEM-T/PAC-3 CRI
  Medium-range *Cheongung* (KM-SAM); 158 MIM 23B I-*Hawk*
AIR-LAUNCHED MISSILES
  AAM • IR AIM-9 *Sidewinder*; **IIR** AIM-9X *Sidewinder* II; **SARH** AIM-7 *Sparrow*; **ARH** AIM-120B/C-5/7 AMRAAM
  ASM AGM-65A *Maverick*; AGM-130
  AShM AGM-84L *Harpoon* Block II; AGM-142 *Popeye*
  ARM AGM-88 HARM
  ALCM AGM-84H SLAM-ER; KEPD-350 *Taurus*
BOMBS • Laser-guided *Paveway* II

Paramilitary 9,000 active

Civilian Defence Corps 3,000,000 reservists (to age 50)

Coast Guard 9,000
Part of the Ministry of Maritime Affairs and Fisheries. Five regional headquarters with 19 coastguard stations and one guard unit
EQUIPMENT BY TYPE
PATROL AND COASTAL COMBATANTS 82
  PSOH 15: 1 *Lee Cheong-ho* with 1 76mm gun; 1 *Sambongho*; 13 *Tae Pung Yang* with 1 med hel
  PSO 21: 3 *Han Kang* with 1 76mm gun, 1 hel landing platform; 5 *Han Kang* II with 1 76mm gun, 1 hel landing pllatform; 12 *Jaemin* with 1 hel landing platform; 1 *Sumjinkang*
  PCO 16 *Tae Geuk*
  PCC 26: 4 *Bukhansan*; 6 (430 tonne); 14 *Hae Uri*; 2 *Hae Uri* II
  PB ε4 (various)
AMPHIBIOUS
  LANDING CRAFT • UCAC 8: 1 BHT-150; 4 *Griffon* 470TD; 3 *Griffon* 8000TD
AIRCRAFT
  MP 5: 1 C-212-400 MP; 4 CN235-110 MPA
  TPT • PAX 1 CL-604
HELICOPTERS
  MRH 7: 5 AS565MB *Panther*; 1 AW139; 1 Bell 412SP
  SAR 2 S-92
  TPT • Medium 8 Ka-32 *Helix* C

DEPLOYMENT

ARABIAN SEA & GULF OF ADEN: Combined Maritime Forces • CTF-151: 1 DDGHM

INDIA/PAKISTAN: UN • UNMOGIP 7

LEBANON: UN • UNIFIL 331; 1 mech inf coy; 1 engr coy; 1 sigs coy; 1 maint coy

SOUTH SUDAN: UN • UNMISS 275; 1 engr coy

UNITED ARAB EMIRATES: 139 (trg activities at UAE Spec Ops School)

FOREIGN FORCES
Sweden NNSC: 5 obs
Switzerland NNSC: 5 obs
United States US Pacific Command: 28,500
  Army 19,200; 1 HQ (8th Army) at Yongsan; 1 div HQ at Ujieongbu; 1 armd bde with M1A2 SEPv2 *Abrams*; M2A2/M3A3 *Bradley*; M109A6; 1 (cbt avn) hel bde with AH-64 *Apache*; CH-47 *Chinook*; UH-60 *Black Hawk*; 1 MRL bde with M270A1 MLRS; 1 AD bde with MIM-104 *Patriot*/FIM-92A *Avenger*; 1 SAM bty with THAAD; 1 (APS) armd bde eqpt set
  Navy 250
  USAF 8,800; 1 HQ (7th Air Force) at Osan AB; 1 ftr wg at Kunsan AB (2 ftr sqn with 20 F-16C/D *Fighting Falcon*); 1 ftr wg at Osan AB (1 ftr sqn with 20 F-16C/D *Fighting Falcon*, 1 atk sqn with 24 A-10C *Thunderbolt* II); 1 ISR sqn at Osan AB with U-2S
  USMC 250

Laos LAO

New Lao Kip		2018	2019	2020
GDP	kip	152tr	164tr	
	US$	18.1bn	19.1bn	
per capita	US$	2,566	2,670	
Growth	%	6.3	6.4	
Inflation	%	2.0	3.1	
Def exp	kip	n.k.	n.k.	
	US$	n.k.	n.k.	
US$1=kip		8411.37	8581.95	

Population 7,341,182
Ethnic groups: Lao 55%; Khmou 11%; Hmong 8%

Age	0–14	15–19	20–24	25–29	30–64	65 plus
Male	16.0%	5.4%	4.9%	4.6%	16.8%	1.8%
Female	15.7%	5.4%	5.0%	4.7%	17.4%	2.2%

Capabilities

The Lao People's Armed Forces (LPAF) have considerable military experience from the Second Indo-China War and the 1988 border war with Thailand. They are closely linked to the ruling Communist Party and their primary role is internal security. A lack of financial resources has limited defence spending and military procurement for two decades. Contacts continue with the Chinese and Vietnamese armed forces, while there is strong defence cooperation with Russia. Laos also participates in ADMM-Plus military exercises, and in 2014–15 was co-chair with Japan of the ADMM-Plus expert working group on humanitarian assistance and disaster relief. Training support is provided by friendly countries such as Russia and Vietnam. The LPAF have participated in regional exercises with neighbouring countries but have made no international deployments and have little capacity for sustained operations. Laos still operates Soviet-era military equipment, and relies on Russian supplies, as illustrated by ongoing deliveries of training aircraft and main battle tanks. The country lacks a traditional defence-industrial base and maintenance capacity is limited, reflected in a support contract for a Russian firm to maintain the air force's Mi-17 helicopters.

ACTIVE 29,100 (Army 25,600 Air 3,500) **Paramilitary 100,000**

Conscript liability 18 months minimum

ORGANISATIONS BY SERVICE

Space
EQUIPMENT BY TYPE
SATELLITES • ISR 1 LaoSat-1

Army 25,600
FORCES BY ROLE
4 mil regions
MANOEUVRE
  Armoured
    1 armd bn
  Light
    5 inf div
    7 indep inf regt
    65 indep inf coy
COMBAT SUPPORT
  5 arty bn
  1 engr regt
  2 (construction) engr regt
AIR DEFENCE
  9 ADA bn
EQUIPMENT BY TYPE
ARMOURED FIGHTING VEHICLES
  MBT 25: 15 T-54/T-55; 10 T-72B1
  LT TK 10 PT-76
  RECCE BRDM-2M
  IFV 10+ BMP-1
  APC • **APC (W)** 50: 30 BTR-40/BTR-60; 20 BTR-152
  AUV Dongfeng Mengshi 4×4; ZYZ-8002 (CS/VN3)
ENGINEERING & MAINTENANCE VEHICLES
  ARV T-54/T-55
  VLB MTU
ANTI-TANK/ANTI-INFRASTRUCTURE • **RCL** 57mm M18/A1; **75mm** M20; **106mm** M40; **107mm** B-11
ARTILLERY 62+
  TOWED 62: **105mm** 20 M101; **122mm** 20 D-30/M-30 M-1938; **130mm** 10 M-46; **155mm** 12 M114
  MOR **81mm**; **82mm**; **107mm** M-1938/M2A1; **120mm** M-43
AIR DEFENCE
  SAM
    Short-range S-125 *Pechora* (SA-3 *Goa*); Yitian (CH-SA-13)
    Point-defence 9K32M *Strela*-2M (SA-7 *Grail*)‡; 9K35 *Strela*-10 (SA-13 *Gopher*); 9K310 *Igla*-1 (SA-16 *Gimlet*)
  GUNS
    SP **23mm** ZSU-23-4
    TOWED **14.5mm** ZPU-1/ZPU-4; **23mm** ZU-23; **37mm** M-1939; **57mm** S-60

Army Marine Section ε600
EQUIPMENT BY TYPE
PATROL AND COASTAL COMBATANTS • PBR some
AMPHIBIOUS • LCM some

Air Force 3,500
FORCES BY ROLE
TRANSPORT
  1 regt with MA60; MA600; Mi-17 *Hip* H
EQUIPMENT BY TYPE
AIRCRAFT 4 combat capable
  TPT • **Light** 5: 1 An-74TK *Coaler*; 2 MA60; 2 MA600
  TRG 4 Yak-130 *Mitten**
HELICOPTERS
  MRH 15: 6 Mi-17 *Hip* H; 5 Mi-17V-5 *Hip*; 4 Z-9A
  TPT 4: **Medium** 1 Ka-32T *Helix* C; **Light** 3 SA360 *Dauphin*

Paramilitary

Militia Self-Defence Forces 100,000+
Village 'home guard' or local defence

Malaysia MYS

Malaysian Ringgit RM		2018	2019	2020
GDP	RM	1.45tr	1.53tr	
	US$	359bn	365bn	
per capita	US$	11,072	11,137	
Growth	%	4.7	4.5	
Inflation	%	1.0	1.0	
Def bdgt	RM	15.7bn	13.9bn	15.6bn
	US$	3.89bn	3.33bn	
US$1=RM		4.04	4.18	

Real-terms defence budget trend (US$bn, constant 2015)

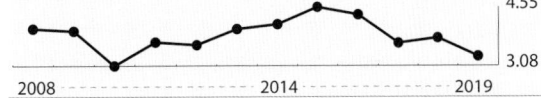

Population 32,233,022

Ethnic groups: Malay 50.1%; Chinese 22.5%; Indian 6.5%; other or unspecified 20.9%

Age	0–14	15–19	20–24	25–29	30–64	65 plus
Male	14.0%	4.4%	4.1%	3.9%	21.2%	3.1%
Female	13.2%	4.2%	4.0%	3.8%	20.7%	3.5%

Capabilities

Substantial modernisation programmes over the past 30 years have developed the Malaysian armed forces' capacity for external defence. However, the 2013 armed intrusion at Lahad Datu in Sabah state, the aftermath of the March 2014 disappearance of Malaysia Airlines flight MH370 and Chinese naval intrusions into Malaysia's EEZ in 2015–16 revealed capability shortcomings, particularly in air and maritime surveillance. Addressing these capability gaps is a high priority, and the government put forward its first-ever defence white paper in late 2019, which emphasises Malaysia's maritime-security interests. However, budgetary constraints have slowed equipment procurement and infrastructural improvements. Malaysian forces regularly participate in ADMM-Plus, Five Power Defence Arrangements and other exercises with regional and international partners, including the US. Malaysia has invested in synthetic military training aids. In 2017, Malaysia began trilateral joint maritime patrols and joint Sulu Sea air patrols with Indonesia and the Philippines. The majority of Malaysia's military equipment is ageing and in several cases non-operational. However, some modest investments in new equipment have been made. For example, 22 Squadron was established in 2015 to operate Malaysia's new A400M transport aircraft. In recent decades, Malaysia has maintained a small defence industry providing maintenance, repair and overhaul services. Several companies now licence-build several major equipment types, such as *Gowind*-class frigates.

ACTIVE 113,000 (Army 80,000 Navy 18,000 Air 15,000) Paramilitary 22,500

RESERVE 51,600 (Army 50,000, Navy 1,000 Air Force 600) Paramilitary 244,700

ORGANISATIONS BY SERVICE

Army 80,000
2 mil region, 4 area comd (div)
FORCES BY ROLE
SPECIAL FORCES
  1 SF bde (3 SF bn)
MANOEUVRE
  Armoured
  1 tk regt
  Mechanised
  4 armd regt
  1 mech inf bde (4 mech bn, 1 cbt engr sqn)
  Light
  5 inf bde (3 inf bn, 1 arty regt)
  2 inf bde (3 inf bn)
  1 inf bde (2 inf bn, 1 arty regt)
  1 inf bde (2 inf bn)
  Air Manoeuvre
  1 (Rapid Deployment Force) AB bde (1 lt tk sqn, 4 AB bn, 1 lt arty regt, 1 engr sqn)
  Other
  1 (border) sy bde (5 bn)
  1 (border) sy bde (forming)
COMBAT SUPPORT
  9 arty regt
  1 STA regt
  1 MRL regt
  1 cbt engr sqn
  3 fd engr regt (total: 7 cbt engr sqn, 3 engr spt sqn)
  1 construction regt
  1 int unit
  4 MP regt
  1 sigs regt
HELICOPTER
  1 hel sqn
  1 tpt sqn with S-61A-4 *Nuri* (forming)
AIR DEFENCE
  3 ADA regt
EQUIPMENT BY TYPE
ARMOURED FIGHTING VEHICLES
  MBT 48 PT-91M *Twardy*
  LT TK 21 *Scorpion*-90
  RECCE 74 SIBMAS (some†)
  IFV 136: 31 ACV300 *Adnan* (25mm *Bushmaster*); 13 ACV300 *Adnan* AGL; 46 AV8 *Gempita* IFV25; 46 AV8 *Gempita* IFV30 (incl 10 with *Ingwe* ATGM)
  APC 591
    APC (T) 265: 149 ACV300 *Adnan* (incl 69 variants); 13 FV4333 *Stormer* (upgraded); 63 K200A; 40 K200A1
    APC (W) 326: 26 AV8 *Gempita* APC (incl 13 CP; 3 sigs); 300 *Condor* (incl variants)
  PPV 29: 9 IAG *Guardian*; 20 *Lipanbara*
ENGINEERING & MAINTENANCE VEHICLES
  AEV 3 MID-M
  ARV 47+: *Condor*; 15 ACV300; 4 K288A1; 22 SIBMAS; 6 WZT-4
  VLB 5+: *Leguan*; 5 PMCz-90
NBC VEHICLES K216A1
ANTI-TANK/ANTI-INFRASTRUCTURE • MSL
  SP 8 ACV300 *Baktar Shikan*
  MANPATS 9K115 *Metis* (AT-7 *Saxhorn*); 9K115-2 *Metis-M* (AT-13 *Saxhorn* 2); *Eryx*; *Baktar Shihan* (HJ-8); SS.11
RCL 84mm *Carl Gustav*;
ARTILLERY 412
  TOWED 122: **105mm** 100 Model 56 pack howitzer; **155mm** 22 G-5
  MRL 36 ASTROS II (equipped with 127mm SS-30)
  MOR 254: **81mm** 232; **SP 81mm** 14: 4 K281A1; 10 ACV300-S; **SP 120mm** 8 ACV-S
AMPHIBIOUS • LANDING CRAFT
  LCA 165 Damen Assault Craft 540 (capacity 10 troops)
HELICOPTERS • TPT 12: **Medium** 2 S-61A-4 *Nuri*; **Light** 10 AW109
AIR DEFENCE
  SAM • Point-defence 15+: 15 *Jernas* (*Rapier* 2000); *Anza*-II; HY-6 (FN-6); 9K38 *Igla* (SA-18 *Grouse*); *Starstreak*
  GUNS 52+
    SP 20mm K263
    TOWED 52: **35mm** 16 GDF-005; **40mm** 36 L40/70

Reserves

Territorial Army
Some paramilitary forces to be incorporated into a re-organised territorial organisation
FORCES BY ROLE
MANOEUVRE
  Mechanised
  4 armd sqn
  Light
  16 inf regt (3 inf bn)
  Other
  5 (highway) sy bn
COMBAT SUPPORT
  5 arty bty
  2 fd engr regt
  1 int unit
  3 sigs sqn
COMBAT SUPPORT
  4 med coy
  5 tpt coy

Navy 18,000

3 Regional Commands: MAWILLA 1 (Kuantan), MAWILLA 2 (Sabah) and MAWILLA 3 (Langkawi). A fourth is being formed (Bintulu)

EQUIPMENT BY TYPE
SUBMARINES • TACTICAL • SSK 2 *Tunku Abdul Rahman* (FRA *Scorpène*) with 6 single 533mm TT with SM39 *Exocet* AShM/*Black Shark* HWT

PRINCIPAL SURFACE COMBATANTS 10
  FRIGATES 10
    FFGHM 2:
      2 *Lekiu* with 2 quad lnchr with MM40 *Exocet* Block 2 AShM, 1 16-cell VLS with *Sea Wolf* SAM, 2 triple ILAS-3 (B-515) 324mm ASTT with A244/S LWT, 1 57mm gun (capacity 1 *Super Lynx* hel)
    FFG 2:
      2 *Kasturi* with 2 quad lnchr with MM40 *Exocet* Block 2 AShM, 2 triple ILAS-3 (B-515) 324mm ASTT with A244/S LWT, 1 57mm gun, 1 hel landing platform
    FFH 6:
      6 *Kedah* (GER MEKO) with 1 76mm gun, 1 hel landing platform (fitted for but not with MM40 *Exocet* AShM & RAM SAM)

PATROL AND COASTAL COMBATANTS 37
  CORVETTES • FSM 4 *Laksamana* with 1 *Albatros* quad lnchr with *Aspide* SAM, 1 76mm gun
  PCF 4 *Perdana* (FRA *Combattante* II) with 1 57mm gun
  PB 4 *Handalan* (SWE *Spica*-M) with 1 57mm gun
  PBF 17 *Tempur* (SWE CB90)
  PB 8: 6 *Jerong* (Lurssen 45) with 1 57mm gun; 2 *Sri Perlis*

MINE WARFARE • MINE COUNTERMEASURES 4
  MCO 4 *Mahamiru* (ITA *Lerici*)

LOGISTICS AND SUPPORT 12
  AFS 2: 1 *Mahawangsa* with 2 57mm guns, 1 hel landing platform; 1 *Sri Indera Sakti* with 1 57mm gun, 1 hel landing platform
  AG 2 *Bunga Mas Lima* with 1 hel landing platform
  AGS 1 *Perantau*
  AP 2 *Sri Gaya*
  ASR 1 *Mega Bakti*
  ATF 1
  AX 2 *Gagah Samudera* with 1 hel landing platform
  AXS 1

Naval Aviation 160

EQUIPMENT BY TYPE
HELICOPTERS
  ASW 6 *Super Lynx* 300
  MRH 6 AS555 *Fennec*
AIR-LAUNCHED MISSILES • AShM *Sea Skua*

Special Forces

FORCES BY ROLE
SPECIAL FORCES
  1 (mne cdo) SF unit

Air Force 15,000

1 air op HQ, 2 air div, 1 trg and log comd, 1 Intergrated Area Def Systems HQ

FORCES BY ROLE
FIGHTER/GROUND ATTACK
  1 sqn with F/A-18D *Hornet*
  1 sqn with Su-30MKM *Flanker*
  2 sqn with *Hawk* Mk108*/Mk208*
MARITIME PATROL
  1 sqn with Beech 200T
TANKER/TRANSPORT
  2 sqn with KC-130H *Hercules*; C-130H *Hercules*; C-130H-30 *Hercules*; Cessna 402B
TRANSPORT
  1 sqn with A400M *Atlas*
  1 (VIP) sqn with A319CT; AW109; B-737-700 BBJ; BD700 *Global Express*; F-28 *Fellowship*; *Falcon* 900
  1 sqn with CN235
TRAINING
  1 unit with PC-7; SA316 *Alouette* III
TRANSPORT HELICOPTER
  4 (tpt/SAR) sqn with H225M *Super Cougar*; S-61A-4 *Nuri*; S-61N; S-70A *Black Hawk*
AIR DEFENCE
  1 sqn with *Starburst*
SPECIAL FORCES
  1 (Air Force Commando) unit (airfield defence/SAR)

EQUIPMENT BY TYPE
AIRCRAFT 43 combat capable
  FTR (8 F-5E *Tiger* II; 3 F-5F *Tiger* II; 8 MiG-29 *Fulcrum* (MiG-29N); 2 MiG-29UB *Fulcrum* (MIG-29NUB) in store)
  FGA 26: 8 F/A-18D *Hornet* (some serviceability in doubt); 18 Su-30MKM (some serviceability in doubt)
  ISR 3 Beech 200T (2 RF-5E *Tigereye** in store)
  TKR 4 KC-130H *Hercules*
  TKR/TPT 4 A400M *Atlas*
  TPT 30: **Medium** 10: 2 C-130H *Hercules*; 8 C-130H-30 *Hercules*; **Light** 16: 7 CN235M-220 (incl 1 VIP); 9 Cessna 402B (2 modified for aerial survey); **PAX** 4: 1 A319CT; 1 BD700 *Global Express*; 1 F-28 *Fellowship*; 1 *Falcon* 900
  TRG 71: 5 *Hawk* Mk108*; 12 *Hawk* Mk208*; 7 MB-339C; 30 PC-7; 17 PC-7 Mk II *Turbo Trainer*
HELICOPTERS
  TPT 41: **Heavy** 12 H225M *Super Cougar*; **Medium** 28: 24 S-61A-4 *Nuri*; 2 S-61N; 2 S-70A *Black Hawk*; **Light** 1 AW109
AIR DEFENCE • SAM • Point-defence *Starstreak*
AIR-LAUNCHED MISSILES
  AAM • IR AIM 9 *Sidewinder*; R-73 (AA-11A *Archer*); **IIR** AIM-9X *Sidewinder* II; **IR/SARH** R-27 (AA-10 *Alamo*); **SARH** AIM-7 *Sparrow*; **ARH** AIM-120C AMRAAM; R-77 (AA-12A *Adder*)
  ASM AGM-65 *Maverick*; Kh-29T (AS-14B *Kedge*); Kh-29L (AS-14A *Kedge*); Kh-31P (AS-17A *Krypton*); Kh-59M (AS-18 *Kazoo*)
  ARM Kh-31P (AS-17A *Krypton*);
  AShM AGM-84D *Harpoon*; Kh-31A (AS-17B *Krypton*)
BOMBS
  Electro-optical guided KAB-500KR; KAB-500OD
  Laser-guided *Paveway* II

Paramilitary ε22,500

Police–General Ops Force 18,000
FORCES BY ROLE
COMMAND
  5 bde HQ
SPECIAL FORCES
  1 spec ops bn
MANOEUVRE
  Other
   19 paramilitary bn
   2 (Aboriginal) paramilitary bn
   4 indep paramilitary coy
EQUIPMENT BY TYPE
ARMOURED FIGHTING VEHICLES
  APC • APC (W) AT105 *Saxon*
  AUV ε30 SB-301

Malaysian Maritime Enforcement Agency (MMEA) ε4,500
Controls 5 Maritime Regions (Northern Peninsula; Southern Peninsula; Eastern Peninsula; Sarawak; Sabah), subdivided into a further 18 Maritime Districts. Supported by one provisional MMEA Air Unit
EQUIPMENT BY TYPE
PATROL AND COASTAL COMBATANTS 127
  PSO 4: 1 *Arau* (ex-JPN *Nojima*) with 1 hel landing platform; 2 *Langkawi* with 1 57mm gun, 1 hel landing platform; 1 *Pekan* (ex-JPN *Ojika*) with 1 hel landing platform
  PCC 3 *Bagan Datuk*
  PBF 57: 18 *Penggalang* 17 (TUR MRTP 16); 2 *Penggalang 18*; 6 *Penyelamat 20*; 16 *Penggalang 16*; 15 *Tugau*
  PB 63: 15 *Gagah*; 4 *Malawali*; 2 *Nusa*; 3 *Nusa 28*; 1 *Peninjau*; 7 *Ramunia*; 2 *Rhu*; 4 *Semilang*; 8 *Icarus 1650*; 10 *Pengawal*; 4 *Penyelamat*; 2 *Perwira*; 1 *Sugut*
  LOGISTICS AND SUPPORT • AX 1 *Marlin*
  AIRCRAFT • MP 2 Bombardier 415MP
  HELICOPTERS
   SAR 3 AW139
   MRH 3 AS365 *Dauphin*

Area Security Units 3,500 reservists
(Auxiliary General Ops Force)
FORCES BY ROLE
MANOEUVRE
  Other
   89 paramilitary unit

Border Scouts 1,200 reservists
in Sabah, Sarawak

People's Volunteer Corps 240,000 reservists (some 17,500 armed)
RELA

DEPLOYMENT

DEMOCRATIC REPUBLIC OF THE CONGO: UN • MONUSCO 6

LEBANON: UN • UNIFIL 813; 1 mech inf bn
PHILIPPINES: IMT 11
SUDAN: UN • UNAMID 2; UN • UNISFA 2
WESTERN SAHARA: UN • MINURSO 10

FOREIGN FORCES
Australia 130; 1 inf coy (on 3-month rotational tours); 1 P-8A *Poseidon* (rotational)

Mongolia MNG

Mongolian Tugrik t		2018	2019	2020
GDP	t	32.1tr	37.1tr	
	US$	13.0bn	13.6bn	
per capita	US$	4,017	4,133	
Growth	%	6.9	6.5	
Inflation	%	7.7	9.0	
Def bdgt	t	257bn	261bn	295bn
	US$	104m	96.0m	
FMA (US)	US$	2.6m	0m	0m
US$1=t		2467.03	2722.660	

Real-terms defence budget trend (US$m, constant 2015)

Population 3,136,737

Ethnic groups: Khalkh 81.9%; Kazak 3.8%; Dorvod 2.7%; other or unspecified 11.6%

Age	0–14	15–19	20–24	25–29	30–64	65 plus
Male	13.8%	3.7%	4.1%	4.6%	20.9%	1.8%
Female	13.2%	3.6%	4.0%	4.6%	23.0%	2.7%

Capabilities

Mongolia's latest defence-policy document, from 2015, stresses the importance of peacekeeping and anti-terrorist capabilities. The country has no formal military alliances, but pursues defence ties and bilateral training with multiple regional powers and others including India, Turkey and the US. Mongolia is also seeking to develop its security relationship with China. Mongolia hosts the annual *Khaan Quest* multinational peacekeeping-training exercises. The country's main exercise partners are India and Russia, with each country running regular bilateral exercises. Mongolia's most significant deployments are to the UN peacekeeping missions in South Sudan and Afghanistan. The armed forces remain reliant on Soviet-era equipment, although this has been supplemented by deliveries of second-hand Russian weapons. Barring maintenance facilities, there is no significant defence-industrial base, and Mongolia relies on imports from Russia to equip its armed forces.

ACTIVE 9,700 (Army 8,900 Air 800) **Paramilitary 7,500**

Conscript liability 12 months for males aged 18–25

RESERVE 137,000 (Army 137,000)

ORGANISATIONS BY SERVICE

Army 5,600; 3,300 conscript (total 8,900)

FORCES BY ROLE
MANOEUVRE
Mechanised
  1 MR bde
Light
  1 (rapid deployment) lt inf bn (2nd bn to form)
Air Manoeuvre
  1 AB bn
COMBAT SUPPORT
  1 arty regt

EQUIPMENT BY TYPE
ARMOURED FIGHTING VEHICLES
  MBT 420: 370 T-54/T-55; 50 T-72A
  RECCE 120 BRDM-2
  IFV 310 BMP-1
  APC • APC (W) 210: 150 BTR-60; 40 BTR-70M; 20 BTR-80
ENGINEERING & MAINTENANCE VEHICLES
  ARV T-54/T-55
ANTI-TANK/ANTI-INFRASTRUCTURE
  GUNS • TOWED 200: **85mm** D-44/D-48; **100mm** M-1944/MT-12
ARTILLERY 570
  TOWED ε300: **122mm** D-30/M-30 (M-1938); **130mm** M-46; **152mm** ML-20 (M-1937)
  MRL **122mm** 130 BM-21
  MOR 140: **120mm**; **160mm**; **82mm**
AIR DEFENCE
  SAM Medium-range 2+ S-125 *Pechora*-2M (SA-26)
  GUNS • TOWED **23mm** ZU-23-2

Air Force 800

FORCES BY ROLE
TRANSPORT
  1 sqn with An-24 *Coke*; An-26 *Curl*
ATTACK/TRANSPORT HELICOPTER
  1 sqn with Mi-8 *Hip*; Mi-171
AIR DEFENCE
  2 regt with S-60/ZPU-4/ZU-23

EQUIPMENT BY TYPE
AIRCRAFT • TPT • Light 3: 2 An-24 *Coke*; 1 An-26 *Curl*
HELICOPTERS
  TPT • Medium 12: 10 Mi-8 *Hip*; 2 Mi-171
AIR DEFENCE • GUNS • TOWED 150: **14.5mm** ZPU-4; **23mm** ZU-23; **57mm** S-60

Paramilitary 7,500 active

Border Guard 1,300; 4,700 conscript (total 6,000)

Internal Security Troops 400; 800 conscript (total 1,200)

FORCES BY ROLE
MANOEUVRE
Other
  4 gd unit

Construction Troops 300

DEPLOYMENT

AFGHANISTAN: NATO • *Operation Resolute Support* 233
DEMOCRATIC REPUBLIC OF THE CONGO: UN • MONUSCO 2
SOUTH SUDAN: UN • UNMISS 872; 1 inf bn
SUDAN: UN • UNISFA 3
WESTERN SAHARA: UN • MINURSO 4

Myanmar MMR

Myanmar Kyat K		2018	2019	2020
GDP	K	94.9tr	104tr	
	US$	68.7bn	66.0bn	
per capita	US$	1,300	1,245	
Growth	%	6.8	6.2	
Inflation	%	5.9	7.8	
Def bdgt	K	2.66tr	3.26tr	3.39tr
	US$	1.93bn	2.06bn	
US$1=K		1381.92	1582.84	

Real-terms defence budget trend (US$bn, constant 2015)

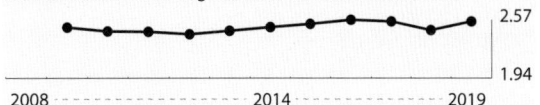

Population 56,111,671

Ethnic groups: Burman 68%; Shan 9%; Karen 7%; Rakhine 4%; Chinese 3+%; other Chin, Kachin, Kayan, Lahu, Mon, Palaung, Pao, Wa 9%

Age	0–14	15–19	20–24	25–29	30–64	65 plus
Male	13.4%	4.3%	4.3%	4.1%	20.5%	2.5%
Female	12.8%	4.2%	4.3%	4.2%	21.8%	3.3%

Capabilities

Since the country's independence struggle in the 1940s, Myanmar's large, army-dominated Tatmadaw (armed forces) has been intimately involved in domestic politics. Even though the National League for Democracy (NLD) won the November 2015 election, the armed forces remain politically powerful. A defence white paper published in 2016 placed as a key priority ending conflicts with domestic armed groups. It also gives a 'state-building' role to the Tatmadaw, legitimising continued intervention in the country's politics. In its counter-insurgency operations, the Tatmadaw has been accused by international organisations of human-rights abuses, and concerns have increased after military actions against the Rohingya minority in 2017. China and Russia are key defence-cooperation partners, including bilateral military exercises and the provision of weapons. In 2016, Myanmar and Russia signed a broad cooperation agreement including military training. Due to long-running domestic conflicts, the Tatmadaw has experience with counter-insurgency operations and jungle warfare. Although there have been small deployments to UN missions, the Tatmadaw remains essentially an internally focused force. Since the 1990s, the armed forces have attempted to develop limited conventional-warfare capabilities, and have brought into service new armoured vehicles, air-defence weapons, artillery, combat aircraft and ships procured mainly from China and Russia. There is limited defence-industrial capacity. The Aircraft Production and Maintenance Base has assembled Chinese K-8 trainer aircraft and Myanmar allegedly aims to negotiate license-production for the Chinese JF-17 combat aircraft. Myanmar also has growing shipbuilding capabilities, notably through the Naval Dockyard in Yangon, which launched patrol and utility vessels in 2018.

ACTIVE 406,000 (Army 375,000 Navy 16,000 Air 15,000) **Paramilitary 107,000**
Conscript liability 24–36 months

ORGANISATIONS BY SERVICE

Army ε375,000
14 military regions, 7 regional op comd
FORCES BY ROLE
COMMAND
  20 div HQ (military op comd)
  10 inf div HQ
  34+ bde HQ (tactical op comd)
MANOEUVRE
  Armoured
  10 armd bn
  Light
  100 inf bn (coy)
  337 inf bn (coy) (regional comd)
COMBAT SUPPORT
  7 arty bn
  37 indep arty coy
  6 cbt engr bn
  54 fd engr bn
  40 int coy
  45 sigs bn
AIR DEFENCE
  7 AD bn
EQUIPMENT BY TYPE
ARMOURED FIGHTING VEHICLES
  MBT 185+: 10 T-55; 50 T-72S; 25+ Type-59D; 100 Type-69-II
  LT TK 105 Type-63 (ε60 serviceable)
  ASLT 24 PTL-02 mod
  RECCE 87+: 12+ EE-9 *Cascavel*; 45 *Ferret*; 30 Mazda; MAV-1
  IFV 10+ BTR-3U
  APC 431+
    APC (T) 331: 26 MT-LB; 250 Type-85; 55 Type-90
    APC (W) 90+: 20 Hino; 40 Humber *Pig*; 30+ Type-92
    PPV 10 MPV
ENGINEERING & MAINTENANCE VEHICLES
  ARV Type-72
  VLB MT-55A
ANTI-TANK/ANTI-INFRASTRUCTURE
  RCL 84mm *Carl Gustav*; **106mm** M40A1
  GUNS • TOWED 60: **57mm** 6-pdr; **76mm** 17-pdr
  ARTILLERY 422+
    SP 155mm 42: 30 NORA B-52; 12 SH-1
    TOWED 264+: **105mm** 132: 36 M-56; 96 M101; **122mm** 100 D-30; **130mm** 16 M-46; **140mm** 16 Soltam M-845P
    MRL 36+: **107mm** 30 Type-63; **122mm** BM-21 *Grad* (reported); Type-81; **240mm** 6+ M-1985 mod
    MOR 80+: **82mm** Type-53 (M-37); **120mm** 80+: 80 Soltam; Type-53 (M-1943)

SURFACE-TO-SURFACE MISSILE LAUNCHERS
  SRBM • Conventional some *Hwasong*-6 (reported)
AIR DEFENCE
  SAM
    Medium-range 4+: 4 KS-1A (HQ-12); S-125 *Pechora*-2M (SA-26); 2K12 *Kvadrat*-M (SA-6 *Gainful*)
    Point-defence Some 2K22 *Tunguska* (SA-19 *Grison*); HN-5 *Hong Nu/Red Cherry* (reported); 9K310 *Igla*-1 (SA-16 *Gimlet*)
  GUNS 46
    SP 57mm 12 Type-80
    TOWED 34: **37mm** 24 Type-74; **40mm** 10 M1

Navy ε16,000
EQUIPMENT BY TYPE
PRINCIPAL SURFACE COMBATANTS • FRIGATES 5
  FFGHM 2 *Kyansitthar* with 2 twin lnchr with C-802 (CH-SS-N-6) AShM, 1 sextuple lnchr with MANPAD SAM, 2 RDC-32 A/S mor, 4 AK630 CIWS, 1 76mm gun (capacity 1 med hel)
  FFG 3:
    1 *Aung Zeya* with 2 quad lnchr with DPRK AShM (possibly 3M24 derivative), 4 AK630 CIWS, 1 76mm gun, 1 hel landing platform
    2 *Mahar Bandoola* (PRC Type-053H1) with 2 quad lnchr with C-802 (CH-SS-N-6) AShM, 2 RBU 1200 *Uragan* A/S mor, 2 twin 100mm gun
PATROL AND COASTAL COMBATANTS 77
  CORVETTES 3
    FSGHM 1 *Tabinshwethi* (*Anawrahta* mod) with 2 twin lnchr with C-802 (CH-SS-N-6), 1 sectuple lnchr with unknown MANPADs, 2 RBU 1200 *Uragan* A/S mor, 1 76mm gun (capacity 1 med hel)
    FSG 2 *Anawrahta* with 2 twin lnchr with C-802 (CH-SS-N-6) AShM, 2 RDC-32 A/S mor, 1 76mm gun, 1 hel landing platform
  PSOH 1 *Inlay* with 1 twin 57mm gun
  PCG 7: 6 *Houxin* with 2 twin lnchr with C-801 (CH-SS-N-4) AShM; 1 FAC(M) mod with 2 twin lnchr with C-802 (CH-SS-N-6) AShM, 1 AK630 CIWS
  PCO 2 *Indaw*
  PCC 11: 2 *Admirable* (ex-US); 9 *Hainan* with 4 RBU 1200 *Uragan* A/S mor, 2 twin 57mm gun
  PBG 4 *Myanmar* with 2 single lnchr with C-801 (CH-SS-N-4) AShM
  PBF 3: 1 Type-201; 2 *Super Dvora* Mk III
  PB 32: 3 PB-90; 6 PGM 401; 6 PGM 412; 14 *Myanmar*; 3 *Swift*
  PBR 14: 4 *Sagu*; 9 Y-301†; 1 Y-301 (Imp)
AMPHIBIOUS
  PRINCIPAL AMPHIBIOUS VESSELS • LPD 1:
    1 *Moattama* (ROK *Makassar*) (capacity 2 LCVP; 2 hels; 13 tanks; 500 troops)
  LANDING CRAFT 15: **LCU** 5; **LCM** 10
LOGISTICS AND SUPPORT 13
  ABU 1
  AGHS 2: 1 *Innya*; 1 (near shore)
  AGS 1
  AH 2
  AK 1

AKSL 5
AP 1 *Chindwin*

Naval Infantry 800
FORCES BY ROLE
MANOEUVRE
Light
1 inf bn

Air Force ε15,000
FORCES BY ROLE
FIGHTER
4 sqn with F-7 *Airguard*; FT-7; JF-17 *Thunder*; MiG-29B *Fulcrum*; MiG-29SM *Fulcrum*; MiG-29UB *Fulcrum*
GROUND ATTACK
2 sqn with A-5C *Fantan*
TRANSPORT
1 sqn with An-12 *Cub*; F-27 *Friendship*; FH-227; PC-6A/B *Turbo Porter*
TRAINING
2 sqn with G-4 *Super Galeb**; PC-7 *Turbo Trainer**; PC-9*
1 (trg/liaison) sqn with Cessna 550 *Citation* II; Cessna 180 *Skywagon*; K-8 *Karakorum**
TRANSPORT HELICOPTER
4 sqn with Bell 205; Bell 206 *Jet Ranger*; Mi-17 *Hip* H; Mi-35P *Hind*; PZL Mi-2 *Hoplite*; PZL W-3 *Sokol*; SA316 *Alouette* III
EQUIPMENT BY TYPE
AIRCRAFT 158 combat capable
FTR 63: 21 F-7 *Airguard*; 10 FT-7; 11 MiG-29 *Fulcrum*; 6 MiG-29SE *Fulcrum*; 10 MiG-29SM *Fulcrum*; 5 MiG-29UB *Fulcrum*
FGA 5: 4 JF-17 *Thunder* (FC-1 Block 2); 1 JF-17B *Thunder* (FC-1 Block 2)
ATK 22 A-5C *Fantan*
TPT 20: **Medium** 5: 4 Y-8D; 1 Y-8F-200W **Light** 16: 3 Beech 1900D; 4 Cessna 180 *Skywagon*; 1 Cessna 550 *Citation* II; 3 F-27 *Friendship*; 5 PC-6A/B *Turbo Porter*; **PAX** 1+ FH-227
TRG 88: 11 G-4 *Super Galeb**; 20 Grob G120; 24+ K-8 *Karakorum**; 12 PC-7 *Turbo Trainer**; 9 PC-9*; 12 Yak-130 *Mitten**
HELICOPTERS
ATK 10 Mi-35P *Hind*
MRH 23: 3 AS365; 11 Mi-17 *Hip* H; 9 SA316 *Alouette* III
TPT 45: **Medium** 10 PZL W-3 *Sokol*; **Light** 35: 12 Bell 205; 6 Bell 206 *Jet Ranger*; 17 PZL Mi-2 *Hoplite*
UNMANNED AERIAL VEHICLES
CISR • **Heavy** 4 CH-3
AIR-LAUNCHED MISSILES
AAM • **IR** PL-5; R-73 (AA-11A *Archer*); PL-5E-II; **IR/SARH** R-27 (AA-10 *Alamo*); **ARH** PL-12
AShM C-802A

Paramilitary 107,000

People's Police Force 72,000

People's Militia 35,000

Nepal NPL

Nepalese Rupee NR		2018	2019	2020
GDP	NR	3.03tr	3.46tr	
	US$	29.0bn	29.8bn	
per capita	US$	1,034	1,048	
Growth	%	6.7	7.1	
Inflation	%	4.2	4.5	
Def bdgt	NR	45.0bn	44.9bn	50.1bn
	US$	431m	387m	
FMA (US)	US$	1.7m	0m	0m
US$1=NR		104.37	116.20	

Real-terms defence budget trend (US$m, constant 2015)

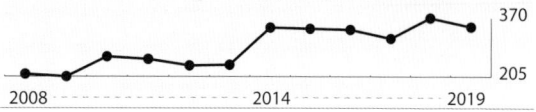

Population 30,032,493
Religious groups: Hindu 90%; Buddhist 5%; Muslim 3%

Age	0–14	15–19	20–24	25–29	30–64	65 plus
Male	15.2%	5.5%	5.4%	4.4%	15.8%	2.7%
Female	13.8%	5.1%	5.3%	4.9%	19.2%	2.8%

Capabilities

The principal role of Nepal's armed forces is maintaining territorial integrity, but they have also traditionally focused on internal security and humanitarian relief. Nepal has a policy of providing contingents to UN peacekeeping operations in the Middle East and Africa. Training support is provided by several countries, including China, India and the US. Following a 2006 peace accord with the Maoist People's Liberation Army, Maoist personnel underwent a process of demobilisation or integration into the armed forces. Gurkhas continue to be recruited by the British and Indian armed forces and the Singaporean police. The small air wing provides a limited transport and support capacity but mobility remains a challenge, in part because of the country's topography. This deficit was highlighted by Nepal's dependence on foreign-military logistical and medical assistance following the earthquake in April 2015. This dependence remains. Nepal's logistic capability appears to be sufficient for internal-security operations, including countering IEDs, however its contingents on UN peacekeeping operations appear to largely depend on contracted logistic support. Modernisation plans include a very limited increase in the size of its air force. Barring maintenance capacities there is no defence-industrial base, and Nepal is dependent on foreign suppliers for modern equipment.

ACTIVE 96,600 (Army 96,600) Paramilitary 15,000

ORGANISATIONS BY SERVICE

Army 96,600
FORCES BY ROLE
COMMAND
6 inf div HQ
1 (valley) comd
SPECIAL FORCES
1 bde (1 SF bn, 1 AB bn, 1 cdo bn, 1 ranger bn, 1 mech inf bn)

MANOEUVRE
Light
 16 inf bde (total: 62 inf bn; 32 indep inf coy)
COMBAT SUPPORT
 4 arty regt
 5 engr bn
AIR DEFENCE
 2 AD regt
 4 indep AD coy
EQUIPMENT BY TYPE
ARMOURED FIGHTING VEHICLES
 RECCE 40 *Ferret*
 APC 253
  APC (W) 13: 8 OT-64C; 5 WZ-551
  PPV 240: 90 *Casspir*; 150 MPV
 ARTILLERY 92+
  TOWED 105mm 22: 8 L118 Light Gun; 14 pack howitzer (6 non-operational)
  MOR 70+: **81mm**; **120mm** 70 M-43 (est 12 op)
 AIR DEFENCE • GUNS • TOWED 32+: **14.5mm** 30 Type-56 (ZPU-4); **37mm** (PRC); **40mm** 2 L/60

Air Wing 320
EQUIPMENT BY TYPE†
 AIRCRAFT • TPT • **Light** 3: 1 BN-2T *Islander*; 1 CN235M-220; 1 M-28 *Skytruck*
 HELICOPTERS
  MRH 12: 2 *Dhruv*; 2 *Lancer*; 3 Mi-17-1V *Hip* H; 2 Mi-17V-5 *Hip*; 1 SA315B *Lama (Cheetah)*; 2 SA316B *Alouette III*
  TPT 3: **Medium** 1 SA330J *Puma*; **Light** 2 AS350B2 *Ecureuil*

Paramilitary 15,000

Armed Police Force 15,000
Ministry of Home Affairs

DEPLOYMENT
CENTRAL AFRICAN REPUBLIC: UN • MINUSCA 737; 1 inf bn

DEMOCRATIC REPUBLIC OF THE CONGO: UN • MONUSCO 895; 1 inf bn; 1 engr coy

IRAQ: UN • UNAMI 77; 1 sy unit

LEBANON: UN • UNIFIL 873; 1 mech inf bn

LIBYA: UN • UNISMIL 230; 2 sy coy

MALI: UN • MINUSMA 157; 1 EOD coy

MIDDLE EAST: UN • UNTSO 3

SOUTH SUDAN: UN • UNMISS 1,744; 2 inf bn

SUDAN: UN • UNISFA 8

SYRIA/ISRAEL: UN • UNDOF 333; 2 mech inf coy

WESTERN SAHARA: UN • MINURSO 7

FOREIGN FORCES
United Kingdom 60 (Gurkha trg org)

New Zealand NZL

New Zealand Dollar NZ$		2018	2019	2020
GDP	NZ$	293bn	305bn	
	US$	203bn	205bn	
per capita	US$	41,205	40,634	
Growth	%	2.8	2.5	
Inflation	%	1.6	1.4	
Def bdgt	NZ$	3.40bn	4.05bn	5.06bn
	US$	2.35bn	2.72bn	
US$1=NZ$		1.44	1.49	

Real-terms defence budget trend (US$bn, constant 2015)
2.63 / 1.93
2008 – 2014 – 2019

Population	4,545,627					
Age	0–14	15–19	20–24	25–29	30–64	65 plus
Male	10.0%	3.3%	3.4%	3.4%	22.3%	7.3%
Female	9.5%	3.2%	3.2%	3.4%	22.5%	8.5%

Capabilities
New Zealand has a strong military tradition. The New Zealand Defence Force (NZDF) is well trained and has operational experience. The June 2016 defence white paper foresaw a range of challenges likely to affect the country's security in the period to 2040, including rising tension in the South and East China seas. The white paper indicated investment in improved maritime air-surveillance capability, new cyber-support capability for deployed operations and additional intelligence personnel, but said that until 2030 defence spending was expected to remain pegged at around 1% of GDP. New Zealand's closest defence partner is Australia but the country has revived defence relations with the US. The 2016 Defence Capability Plan outlined plans including deliveries of new frigates in the late 2020s and P-8A *Poseidon* maritime-patrol aircraft in the 2020s. The decommissioning of HMNZS *Endeavour* in 2017 meant New Zealand lost its at-sea-replenishment capability, which will not return until HMNZS *Aotearoa* enters service in 2020. A new 2019 Defence Capability Plan detailed plans to expand the army to 6,000 personnel by 2035, as well as to acquire a sealift vessel in the late 2020s to complement the navy's single cargo ship. Replacement of the ANZAC frigates, both of which are being upgraded, has now been postponed until the 2030s. New Zealand has a small defence industry consisting of numerous private companies and subsidiaries of larger North American and European companies. These companies are able to provide some maintenance, repair and overhaul capability but significant work, such as the frigate upgrade, is contracted to foreign companies.

ACTIVE 9,400 (Army 4,750 Navy 2,150 Air 2,500)
RESERVE 2,650 (Army 1,800 Navy 550 Air Force 300)

ORGANISATIONS BY SERVICE

Army 4,500
FORCES BY ROLE
SPECIAL FORCES
 1 SF regt

MANOEUVRE
  Light
    1 inf bde (1 armd recce regt, 2 lt inf bn, 1 arty regt (2 arty bty), 1 engr regt(-), 1 MP coy, 1 sigs regt, 2 log bn)
EQUIPMENT BY TYPE
ARMOURED FIGHTING VEHICLES
  IFV 93 NZLAV-25
ENGINEERING & MAINTENANCE VEHICLES
  AEV 7 NZLAV
  ARV 3 LAV-R
ANTI-TANK/ANTI-INFRASTRUCTURE
  MSL • MANPATS FGM-148 *Javelin*
  RCL **84mm** *Carl Gustav*
ARTILLERY 60
  TOWED **105mm** 24 L118 Light Gun
  MOR **81mm** 36

Reserves

Territorial Force 1,650 reservists
Responsible for providing trained individuals for augmenting deployed forces
FORCES BY ROLE
COMBAT SERVICE SUPPORT
  3 (Territorial Force Regional) trg regt

Navy 2,150

Fleet based in Auckland. Fleet HQ at Wellington
EQUIPMENT BY TYPE
PRINCIPAL SURFACE COMBATANTS • FRIGATES • FFHM 2:
  2 *Anzac* (GER MEKO 200) with 1 8-cell Mk 41 VLS with RIM-7M *Sea Sparrow* SAM, 2 triple SVTT Mk 32 324mm TT with Mk 46 mod 5 LWT, 1 Mk 15 *Phalanx* Block 1B CIWS, 1 127mm gun (capacity 1 SH-2G(I) *Super Seasprite* ASW hel) (both vessels in refit in Canada since 2018)
PATROL AND COASTAL COMBATANTS 4
  PSOH 2 *Otago* (capacity 1 SH-2G(I) *Super Seasprite* ASW hel) (ice-strengthened hull)
  PCC 2 *Lake*
AMPHIBIOUS • LANDING CRAFT • LCM 2 (operated off HMNZS *Canterbury*)
LOGISTICS AND SUPPORT • 2
  AGHS 1 *Manawanui* with 1 hel landing platform
  AKRH 1 *Canterbury* (capacity 4 NH90 tpt hel; 1 SH-2G(I) *Super Seasprite* ASW hel; 2 LCM; 16 NZLAV; 14 NZLAV; 20 trucks; 250 troops)

Air Force 2,500

FORCES BY ROLE
MARITIME PATROL
  1 sqn with P-3K2 *Orion*
TRANSPORT
  1 sqn with B-757-200 (upgraded); C-130H *Hercules* (upgraded)
ANTI-SUBMARINE/SURFACE WARFARE
  1 (RNZAF/RNZN) sqn with SH-2G(I) *Super Seasprite*
TRAINING
  1 sqn with T-6C *Texan* II
  1 sqn with Beech 350 *King Air* (leased)

TRANSPORT HELICOPTER
  1 sqn with AW109LUH; NH90
EQUIPMENT BY TYPE
AIRCRAFT 6 combat capable
  ASW 6 P-3K2 *Orion*
  TPT 11: **Medium** 5 C-130H *Hercules* (upgraded); **Light** 4 Beech 350 *King Air* (leased); **PAX** 2 B-757-200 (upgraded)
  TRG 11 T-6C *Texan* II
HELICOPTERS
  ASW 8 SH-2G(I) *Super Seasprite*
  TPT 13: **Medium** 8 NH90; **Light** 5 AW109LUH
AIR-LAUNCHED MISSILES • AShM AGM-119 *Penguin* Mk2 mod7

DEPLOYMENT

AFGHANISTAN: NATO • *Operation Resolute Support* 13
EGYPT: MFO 26; 1 trg unit; 1 tpt unit
IRAQ: *Operation Inherent Resolve* 100; 1 trg unit
MIDDLE EAST: UN • UNTSO 8
SOUTH SUDAN: UN • UNMISS 4

Pakistan PAK

Pakistani Rupee Rs		2018	2019	2020
GDP	Rs	34.6tr	38.6tr	
	US$	315bn	284bn	
per capita	US$	1,565	1,388	
Growth	%	5.5	3.3	
Inflation	%	3.9	7.3	
Def bdgt [a]	Rs	1.26tr	1.40tr	1.48tr
	US$	11.4bn	10.3bn	
FMA (US)	US$	0m	80.0m	0m
US$1=Rs		110.04	135.67	

[a] Includes defence allocations to the Public Sector Development Programme (PSDP), including funding to the Defence Division and the Defence Production Division

Real-terms defence budget trend (US$bn, constant 2015)

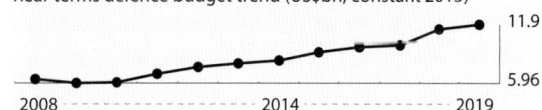

Population 210,797,836
Religious groups: Hindu less than 3%

Age	0–14	15–19	20–24	25–29	30–64	65 plus
Male	15.5%	5.4%	5.3%	4.9%	18.1%	2.2%
Female	14.7%	5.1%	5.0%	4.6%	16.9%	2.5%

Capabilities

The armed forces have considerable domestic political influence, including a strong voice on security policy. Pakistan's nuclear and conventional forces have traditionally been oriented and structured against a prospective threat from India. Since 2008, however, counter-insurgency and counter-terrorism have been of increasing importance and have been the forces' main effort. Although an army-led counter-terrorism operation has improved domestic security, terrorist attacks continue. The armed forces have a major role in disaster relief and are well practised in such operations. China is Pakistan's main defence partner, with all three services employing a large amount of Chinese equipment. Military cooperation with the US is limited by sanctions aiming to improve cooperation on counter-terrorism. Recruitment is good, retention is high and the forces are well trained. The army and air force have considerable operational experience from a decade of counter-insurgency operations in Pakistan's tribal areas. Major investment is being made in security on the border with Afghanistan, including increasing the size of the paramilitary Frontier Corps. Major investment in military nuclear programmes continues, including the testing of a nuclear-capable sea-launched cruise missile. The air force is modernising its inventory while improving its precision-strike and ISR capabilities. Recent and likely future naval investment in Chinese-supplied frigates, missile craft and submarines would improve sea-denial capabilities. The indigenous defence industry exports defence equipment, weapons and ammunition. There is considerable defence-industrial collaboration with China, notably through the co-development of the JF-17 combat aircraft.

ACTIVE 653,800 (Army 560,000 Navy 23,800 Air 70,000) Paramilitary 282,000

ORGANISATIONS BY SERVICE

Strategic Forces

Operational control rests with the National Command Authority. The Strategic Plans Directorate (SPD) manages and commands all of Pakistan's military nuclear capability. The SPD also commands a reportedly 25,000-strong military security force responsible for guarding military nuclear infrastructure

Army Strategic Forces Command 12,000–15,000

Commands all land-based strategic nuclear forces

EQUIPMENT BY TYPE
SURFACE-TO-SURFACE MISSILE LAUNCHERS 60+
  MRBM • Nuclear ε30 *Ghauri/Ghauri* II (*Hatf*-5)/ *Shaheen*-2 (*Hatf*-6 – in test); *Shaheen*-3 (in test)
  SRBM • Nuclear 30+: ε30 *Ghaznavi* (*Hatf*-3 – PRC M-11)/*Shaheen*-1 (*Hatf*-4); some *Abdali* (*Hatf*-2); some *Nasr* (*Hatf*-9)
  GLCM • Nuclear *Babur* (*Hatf*-7); *Ra'ad* (*Hatf*-8 – in test)

Air Force

1–2 sqn of F-16A/B or *Mirage* 5 may be assigned a nuclear-strike role

Army 560,000
FORCES BY ROLE
COMMAND
  9 corps HQ
  1 (area) comd
SPECIAL FORCES
  2 SF gp (total: 4 SF bn)
MANOEUVRE
  Armoured
  2 armd div
  7 indep armd bde
  Mechanised
  2 mech inf div
  1 indep mech bde
  Light
  18 inf div
  5 indep inf bde
  Other
  1 sy div (1 more div forming)
COMBAT SUPPORT
  1 arty div
  14 arty bde
  7 engr bde
AVIATION
  1 VIP avn sqn
  4 avn sqn
HELICOPTER
  3 atk hel sqn
  2 ISR hel sqn
  2 SAR hel sqn
  2 tpt hel sqn
  1 spec ops hel sqn
AIR DEFENCE
  1 AD comd (3 AD gp (total: 8 AD bn))
EQUIPMENT BY TYPE
ARMOURED FIGHTING VEHICLES
  MBT 2,433: 300 *Al-Khalid* (MBT 2000); ε50 *Al-Khalid* I; 315 T-80UD; ε500 *Al-Zarrar*; 400 Type-69; 268 Type-85-IIAP; ε600 ZTZ-59
  APC 3,545
    APC (T) 3,200: 2,300 M113A1/A2/P; ε200 *Talha*; 600 VCC-1/VCC-2; ε100 ZSD-63
    APC (W) 120 BTR-70/BTR-80
  PPV 225 *Maxxpro*
  AUV 10 *Dingo* 2
ENGINEERING & MAINTENANCE VEHICLES
  ARV 262+: 175 Type-70/Type-84 (W653/W653A); *Al-Hadeed*; 52 M88A1; 35 *Maxxpro* ARV; T-54/T-55
  VLB M47M; M48/60
  MW *Aardvark* Mk II
ANTI-TANK/ANTI-INFRASTRUCTURE
  MSL
    SP M901 TOW; ε30 *Maaz* (HJ-8 on *Talha* chassis)
    MANPATS HJ-8; TOW
  RCL 75mm Type-52; **106mm** M40A1 **RL 89mm** M20
  GUNS 85mm 200 Type-56 (D-44)
ARTILLERY 4,595+
  SP 498: **155mm** 438: 200 M109A2; ε115 M109A5; 123 M109L; **203mm** 60 M110/M110A2
  TOWED 1,659: **105mm** 329: 216 M101; 113 M-56; **122mm** 570: 80 D-30 (PRC); 490 Type-54 (M-1938); **130mm** 410 Type-59-I; **155mm** 322: 144 M114; 148 M198; ε30 *Panter*; **203mm** 28 M115
  MRL 88+: **107mm** Type-81; **122mm** 52+: 52 *Azar* (Type-83); some KRL-122; **300mm** 36 A100
  MOR 2,350+: **81mm**; **120mm** AM-50
SURFACE-TO-SURFACE MISSILE LAUNCHERS
  MRBM • Nuclear ε30 *Ghauri/Ghauri* II (*Hatf*-5); some *Shaheen*-2 (*Hatf*-6 – in test); *Shaheen*-3 (in test)
  SRBM 135+: **Nuclear** 30+: ε30 *Ghaznavi* (*Hatf*-3 – PRC M-11)/*Shaheen*-1 (*Hatf*-4); some *Abdali* (*Hatf*-2); some *Nasr* (*Hatf*-9); **Conventional** 105 *Hatf*-1

GLCM • **Nuclear** some *Babur* (Hatf-7)
AIRCRAFT
TPT • Light 13: 1 Beech 350 *King Air*; 3 Cessna 208B; 1 Cessna 421; 1 Cessna 550 *Citation*; 1 Cessna 560 *Citation*; 2 Turbo Commander 690; 4 Y-12(II)
TRG 87 MFI-17B *Mushshak*
HELICOPTERS
ATK 42: 38 AH-1F/S *Cobra* with TOW; 4 Mi-35M *Hind* (1 Mi-24 *Hind* in store)
MRH 115+: 10 H125M *Fennec*; 7 AW139; 26 Bell 412EP *Twin Huey*; 38+ Mi-17 *Hip* H; 2 Mi-171E *Hip*; 12 SA315B *Lama*; 20 SA319 *Alouette* III
TPT 76: **Medium** 36: 31 SA330 *Puma*; 4 Mi-171; 1 Mi-172; **Light** 40: 17 H125 *Ecureuil* (SAR); 5 Bell 205 (UH-1H *Iroquois*); 5 Bell 205A-1 (AB-205A-1); 13 Bell 206B *Jet Ranger* II
TRG 10 Hughes 300C
UNMANNED AERIAL VEHICLES
ISR • Light *Bravo*; *Jasoos*; *Vector*
AIR DEFENCE
SAM
Medium-range LY-80 (CH-SA-16)
Short-range FM-90 (CH-SA-4)
Point-defence M113 with RBS-70; *Anza-II*; *Mistral*; QW-18 (CH-SA-11); RBS-70
GUNS • TOWED 1,933: **14.5mm** 981; **35mm** 248 GDF-002/GDF-005 (with 134 *Skyguard* radar units); **37mm** 310 Type-55 (M-1939)/Type-65; **40mm** 50 L/60; **57mm** 144 Type-59 (S-60); **85mm** 200 Type-72 (M-1939) KS-12

Navy 23,800 (incl ε3,200 Marines and ε2,000 Maritime Security Agency (see Paramilitary))
EQUIPMENT BY TYPE
SUBMARINES • TACTICAL 8
SSK 5:
2 *Hashmat* (FRA *Agosta* 70) with 4 single 533mm ASTT with UGM-84 *Harpoon* AShM/F-17P HWT
3 *Khalid* (FRA *Agosta* 90B – 2 with AIP) with 4 single 533mm ASTT with SM39 *Exocet* AShM/*SeaHake* mod 4 (DM2A4) HWT
SSI 3 MG110 (SF delivery) each with 2 single 533mm TT with F-17P HWT
PRINCIPAL SURFACE COMBATANTS • FRIGATES 9
FFGHM 4 *Sword* (F-22P) with 2 quad lnchr with C-802A AShM, 1 octuple lnchr with FM-90N (CH-SA-N-4) SAM, 2 triple 324mm ASTT with ET-52C (A244/S) LWT, 2 RDC-32 A/S mor, 1 Type 730B (H/PJ-12) CIWS, 1 76mm gun (capacity 1 Z-9C *Haitun* hel)
FFGH 3:
1 *Alamgir* (ex-US *Oliver Hazard Perry*) with 2 quad lnchr with RGM-84 *Harpoon* AShM, 2 triple 324mm ASTT with Mk 46 LWT, 1 Mk 15 *Phalanx* CIWS, 1 76mm gun
1 *Tariq* (ex-UK *Amazon*) with 2 quad lnchr with RGM-84 *Harpoon* AShM, 2 triple 324mm ASTT with Mk 46 LWT, 1 Mk 15 *Phalanx* Block 1B CIWS, 1 114mm gun (capacity 1 hel)
1 *Tariq* (ex-UK *Amazon*) with 2 quad lnchr with RGM-84 *Harpoon* AShM, 1 Mk 15 *Phalanx* Block 1B CIWS, 1 114mm gun (capacity 1 hel)
FFHM 2 *Tariq* (ex-UK *Amazon*) with 1 sextuple lnchr with LY-60N SAM, 2 triple 324mm ASTT with Mk 46 LWT, 1 Mk 15 *Phalanx* Block 1B CIWS, 1 114mm gun (capacity 1 hel)
PATROL AND COASTAL COMBATANTS 17
PCG 3:
2 *Azmat* (FAC(M)) with 2 quad lnchr with C-802A AShM, 1 AK630 CIWS
1 *Azmat* (FAC(M)) with 2 triple lnchr with C-602 AShM, 1 AK630 CIWS
PBG 4:
2 *Jalalat* with 2 twin lnchr with C-802 (CH-SS-N-6) AShM
2 *Jurrat* with 2 twin lnchr with C-802 (CH-SS-N-6) AShM
PBF 4: 2 *Kaan* 15; 2 *Zarrar* (33)
PB 6: 1 *Larkana*; 1 *Rajshahi*; 4 M16 Fast Assault Boat
MINE WARFARE • MINE COUNTERMEASURES
MCC 3 *Munsif* (FRA *Eridan*)
AMPHIBIOUS • LANDING CRAFT 8
LCM 2
LCAC 2 *Griffon* 8100TD
UCAC 4 *Griffon* 2000
LOGISTICS AND SUPPORT 9
AGS 2: 1 *Behr Masa*; 1 *Behr Paima*
AOL 2 *Madagar*
AOR 1 *Moawin* II (Fleet Tanker) with 1 hel landing platform
AORH 1 *Fuqing* with 1 Mk 15 *Phalanx* CIWS (capacity 1 SA319 *Alouette* III hel)
AOT 2 *Gwadar*
AXS 1

Marines ε3,200
FORCES BY ROLE
SPECIAL FORCES
1 cdo gp
MANOEUVRE
Amphibious
3 mne bn
AIR DEFENCE
1 AD bn

Naval Aviation
EQUIPMENT BY TYPE
AIRCRAFT 9 combat capable
ASW 9: 7 P-3B/C *Orion*; 2 ATR-72-500
MP 6 F-27-200 MPA
TPT 3: **Light** 2 ATR-72-500; **PAX** 1 Hawker 850XP
HELICOPTERS
ASW 11: 4 *Sea King* Mk45; 7 Z 9C *Haitun*
MRH 6 SA319B *Alouette* III
SAR 1 *Sea King* (ex-HAR3A)
TPT • Medium 1 *Sea King* (ex-HC4)
AIR-LAUNCHED MISSILES • AShM AM39 *Exocet*

Coastal Defence
FORCES BY ROLE
COASTAL Defence
1 AShM regt with *Zarb* (YJ-62)
EQUIPMENT BY TYPE
COASTAL DEFENCE • AShM *Zarb* (YJ-62)

Air Force 70,000

3 regional comds: Northern (Peshawar), Central (Sargodha), Southern (Masroor). The Composite Air Tpt Wg, Combat Cadres School and PAF Academy are Direct Reporting Units

FORCES BY ROLE
FIGHTER
  3 sqn with F-7PG/FT-7PG *Airguard*
  1 sqn with F-16A/B MLU *Fighting Falcon*
  1 sqn with F-16A/B ADF *Fighting Falcon*
  1 sqn with *Mirage* IIID/E (IIIOD/EP)
FIGHTER/GROUND ATTACK
  2 sqn with JF-17 *Thunder*
  3 sqn with JF-17 *Thunder* Block II
  1 sqn with F-16C/D Block 52 *Fighting Falcon*
  3 sqn with *Mirage* 5 (5PA)
ANTI-SURFACE WARFARE
  1 sqn with *Mirage* 5PA2/5PA3 with AM-39 *Exocet* AShM
ELECTRONIC WARFARE/ELINT
  1 sqn with *Falcon* 20F
AIRBORNE EARLY WARNING & CONTROL
  1 sqn with Saab 2000; Saab 2000 *Erieye*
  1 sqn with ZDK-03 **SEARCH & RESCUE**
  1 sqn with Mi-171Sh (SAR/liaison)
  6 sqn with SA316 *Alouette* III
  1 sqn with AW139
TANKER
  1 sqn with Il-78 *Midas*
TRANSPORT
  1 sqn with C-130B/E *Hercules*; CN235M-220; L-100-20
  1 VIP sqn with B-707; Cessna 560XL *Citation Excel*; CN235M-220; F-27-200 *Friendship*; *Falcon* 20E; Gulfstream IVSP
  1 (comms) sqn with EMB-500 *Phenom* 100; Y-12 (II)
TRAINING
  1 OCU sqn with F-7P/FT-7P *Skybolt*
  1 OCU sqn with *Mirage* III/*Mirage* 5
  1 OCU sqn with F-16A/B MLU *Fighting Falcon*
  2 sqn with K-8 *Karakorum**
  2 sqn with MFI-17
  2 sqn with T-37C *Tweet*
AIR DEFENCE
  1 bty with HQ-2 (SA-2 *Guideline*); 9K310 *Igla*-1 (SA-16 *Gimlet*)
  6 bty with *Crotale*
  10 bty with SPADA 2000
EQUIPMENT BY TYPE
AIRCRAFT 404 combat capable
  FTR 153: 46 F-7PG *Airguard*; 20 F-7P *Skybolt*; 24 F-16A MLU *Fighting Falcon*; 21 F-16B MLU *Fighting Falcon*; 9 F-16A ADF *Fighting Falcon*; 4 F-16B ADF *Fighting Falcon*; 21 FT-7; 6 FT-7PG; 2 *Mirage* IIIB
  FGA 203: 12 F-16C Block 52 *Fighting Falcon*; 6 F-16D Block 52 *Fighting Falcon*; 49 JF-17 *Thunder* (FC-1 Block 1); 62 JF-17 *Thunder* (FC-1 Block 2); 7 *Mirage* IIID (*Mirage* IIIOD); 30 *Mirage* IIIE (IIIEP); 25 *Mirage* 5 (5PA)/5PA2; 2 *Mirage* 5D (5DPA)/5DPA2; 10 *Mirage* 5PA3 (ASuW)
  ISR 10 *Mirage* IIIR* (*Mirage* IIIRP)
  ELINT 2 *Falcon* 20F
  AEW&C 10: 6 Saab 2000 *Erieye*; 4 ZDK-03
  TKR 4 Il-78 *Midas*
  TPT 35: **Medium** 16: 5 C-130B *Hercules*; 10 C-130E *Hercules*; 1 L-100-20; **Light** 14: 2 Cessna 208B; 1 Cessna 560XL *Citation Excel*; 4 CN235M-220; 4 EMB-500 *Phenom* 100; 1 F-27-200 *Friendship*; 2 Y-12 (II); **PAX** 5: 1 B-707; 1 *Falcon* 20E; 2 Gulfstream IVSP; 1 Saab 2000
  TRG 142: 38 K-8 *Karakorum**; 80 MFI-17B *Mushshak*; 24 T-37C *Tweet*
HELICOPTERS
  MRH 19: 15 SA316 *Alouette* III; 4 AW139
  TPT • Medium 4 Mi-171Sh
UNMANNED AERIAL VEHICLES
  CISR • Heavy CH-3 (*Burraq*); CH-4 (reported)
  ISR • Medium *Falco*
AIR DEFENCE • SAM 190+
  Medium-range 6 HQ-2 (CH-SA-1)
  Short-range 184: 144 *Crotale*; ε40 SPADA 2000
  Point-defence 9K310 *Igla*-1 (SA-16 *Gimlet*)
AIR-LAUNCHED MISSILES
  AAM • IR AIM-9L/P *Sidewinder*; U-Darter; PL-5; PL-5E-II; **SARH** Super 530; **ARH** PL-12; AIM-120C AMRAAM
  ASM AGM-65 *Maverick*; *Raptor* II
  AShM AM39 *Exocet*
  ARM MAR-1
  ALCM • Nuclear *Ra'ad*
BOMBS
  INS/SAT-guided FT-6 (REK)
  Laser-guided *Paveway* II

Paramilitary 291,000 active

Airport Security Force 9,000
Government Aviation Division

Pakistan Coast Guards
Ministry of Interior
EQUIPMENT BY TYPE
PATROL AND COASTAL COMBATANTS 5
  PBF 4
  PB 1

Frontier Corps 70,000
Ministry of Interior
FORCES BY ROLE
MANOEUVRE
  Reconnaissance
    1 armd recce sqn
  Other
    11 paramilitary regt (total: 40 paramilitary bn)
EQUIPMENT BY TYPE
ARMOURED FIGHTING VEHICLES
  APC (W) 45 UR-416

Maritime Security Agency ε2,000
FORCES BY ROLE
MARITIME PATROL
  1 sqn with BN-2T *Defender*
EQUIPMENT BY TYPE
PATROL AND COASTAL COMBATANTS 19
  PSO 1 *Kashmir*

PCC 10: 4 *Barkat*; 4 *Hingol*; 2 *Sabqat* (ex-US *Island*)
PBF 5
PB 3 *Guns*
AIRCRAFT • TPT • Light 3 BN-2T *Defender*

National Guard 185,000
Incl Janbaz Force; Mujahid Force; National Cadet Corps; Women Guards

Pakistan Rangers 25,000
Ministry of Interior

DEPLOYMENT

CENTRAL AFRICAN REPUBLIC: UN • MINUSCA 1,253; 1 inf bn; 2 engr coy; 1 hel sqn

CYPRUS: UN • UNFICYP 1

DEMOCRATIC REPUBLIC OF THE CONGO: UN • MONUSCO 2,722; 4 inf bn; 1 hel sqn

MALI: UN • MINUSMA 14

SOMALIA: UN • UNSOS 1

SOUTH SUDAN: UN • UNMISS 11

SUDAN: UN • UNAMID 906; 1 inf bn; **UN** • UNISFA 1

WESTERN SAHARA: UN • MINURSO 13

FOREIGN FORCES
Figures represent total numbers for UNMOGIP mission in India and Pakistan
Chile 2
Croatia 9
Italy 2
Korea, Republic of 7
Philippines 7
Romania 2
Sweden 5
Switzerland 3
Thailand 4
Uruguay 3

Papua New Guinea PNG

Papua New Guinea Kina K		2018	2019	2020
GDP	K	76.0bn	80.2bn	
	US$	23.2bn	23.6bn	
per capita	US$	2,752	2,742	
Growth	%	-1.1	5.0	
Inflation	%	5.2	3.9	
Def bdgt	K	209m	267m	
	US$	63.6m	78.5m	
US$1=K		3.28	3.40	

Real-terms defence budget trend (US$m, constant 2015)

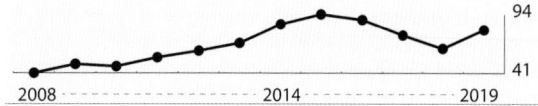

Population	7,143,996					
Age	0–14	15–19	20–24	25–29	30–64	65 plus
Male	16.5%	5.3%	4.8%	4.2%	17.9%	2.2%
Female	15.9%	5.1%	4.7%	4.1%	16.9%	2.3%

Capabilities

Since independence in 1975, the Papua New Guinea Defence Force (PNGDF) has suffered from underfunding and lack of capacity to perform its core roles. A reform programme reduced personnel strength from around 4,000 to 2,100 between 2002 and 2007. However, during the current decade, the government has made efforts to revive defence capability. A 2013 defence white paper identified the PNGDF's core roles, including defending the state and civil-emergency assistance, but noted that 'defence capabilities have deteriorated to the extent that we have alarming gaps in our land, air and maritime borders'. The white paper called for strengthening defence capability on an ambitious scale, with long-term plans calling for a 'division-sized force' of 10,000 personnel by 2030. The PNGDF continues to receive substantial external military assistance from Australia but also from China, which has donated equipment. In late 2018, plans to build a joint US–Australia–Papua New Guinea naval base at Lombrum were announced. The PNGDF is not able to deploy outside of the country without outside assistance and there have only been small PNGDF deployments to UN peacekeeping missions. The PNGDF will receive four of the *Guardian*-class patrol boats that Australia is donating to small Pacific Ocean nations, which will replace the four *Pacific*-class boats Australia donated in the 1980s. Papua New Guinea has no significant defence industry, though there is some local maintenance capacity.

ACTIVE 3,600 (Army 3,300 Maritime Element 200 Air 100)

ORGANISATIONS BY SERVICE

Army ε3,300
FORCES BY ROLE
SPECIAL FORCES
  1 spec ops unit
MANOEUVRE
  Light
  2 inf bn

COMBAT SUPPORT
1 engr bn
1 EOD unit
1 sigs sqn

EQUIPMENT BY TYPE
ARTILLERY • MOR 3+: 81mm Some; 120mm 3

Maritime Element ε200
1 HQ located at Port Moresby

EQUIPMENT BY TYPE
PATROL AND COASTAL COMBATANTS 4
　PCO 1 *Guardian* (AUS *Bay* mod)
　PB 3 *Rabaul* (*Pacific*)
AMPHIBIOUS • LANDING SHIPS • LCT 3 *Salamaua* (ex-AUS *Balikpapan*) (of which 1 in trg role)

Air Force ε100
FORCES BY ROLE
TRANSPORT
　1 sqn with CN235M-100; IAI-201 *Arava*
TRANSPORT HELICOPTER
　1 sqn with Bell 205 (UH-1H *Iroquois*)†

EQUIPMENT BY TYPE
AIRCRAFT • TPT • Light 3: 1 CN235M-100 (1 more in store); 2 IAI-201 *Arava*
HELICOPTERS • TPT • Light 3: 2 Bell 412 (leased); 1 Bell 212 (leased) (2 Bell 205 (UH-1H *Iroquois*) non-operational)

Philippines PHL

Philippine Peso P		2018	2019	2020
GDP	P	17.4tr	18.7tr	
	US$	331bn	357bn	
per capita	US$	3,104	3,294	
Growth	%	6.2	5.7	
Inflation	%	5.2	2.5	
Def bdgt [a]	P	137bn	183bn	189bn
	US$	2.59bn	3.49bn	
FMA (US)	US$	40.0m	30.0m	45.9m
US$1=P		52.66	52.50	

[a] Excludes military pensions

Real-terms defence budget trend (US$bn, constant 2015)

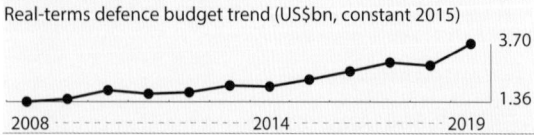

Population	107,535,277					
Age	0–14	15–19	20–24	25–29	30–64	65 plus
Male	16.7%	5.1%	4.7%	4.2%	17.5%	1.9%
Female	16.0%	4.9%	4.5%	4.0%	17.6%	2.8%

Capabilities

Despite modest increases in defence funding in recent years, mainly in response to rising tensions in the South China Sea, the capabilities and procurement plans of the Armed Forces of the Philippines (AFP) remain limited. The Philippines would still struggle to provide more than a token national capability to defend its maritime claims. Organisational changes include the establishment in 2018 of an AFP Special Operations Command to command all special-forces units. Lessons learned after the Marawi siege in 2017 will also likely lead to renewed focus on the capabilities and tactics needed for urban operations. The army in 2019 expanded its aviation component to regimental size and is forming new rocket and missile units. There are also plans to upgrade anti-submarine-warfare capabilities and create a space agency with a national-security mandate. Although President Duterte announced in 2016 a 'separation' from the US and the pursuit of closer relations with China, he described the US as an important security ally, especially in support of counter-terrorism, in September 2017. The Philippines is an ASEAN member. In 2017 it began trilateral joint maritime patrols and joint Sulu Sea patrols with Indonesia and Malaysia to counter regional terrorist activity. The armed forces continue to be deployed on internal-security duties in the south, where Manila faces continuing challenges from insurgent groups. The second phase (2018–22) of the 'second horizon' AFP modernisation programme was approved in 2018. Plans include new artillery systems, multi-role fighters, radars, transport aircraft and frigates. Feasibility studies are under way for the creation of a defence-industry zone in Limay, Bataan, to better enable technology transfer. The Philippine Aerospace Development Corporation has assembled a variety of small helicopters and aircraft for the AFP, as well as providing maintenance, repair and overhaul services for military aircraft.

ACTIVE 142,350 (Army 101,000 Navy 23,750 Air 17,600) **Paramilitary 11,100**

RESERVE 131,000 (Army 100,000 Navy 15,000 Air 16,000) **Paramilitary 50,000** (to age 49)

ORGANISATIONS BY SERVICE

Army 101,000

5 Area Unified Comd (joint service), 1 National Capital Region Comd

FORCES BY ROLE
SPECIAL FORCES
　1 spec ops comd (1 ranger regt, 1 SF regt, 1 CT regt)
MANOEUVRE
　Mechanised
　　1 mech inf div (2 mech bde (total: 3 lt armd sqn; 7 armd cav tp; 4 mech inf bn; 1 cbt engr coy; 1 avn regt; 1 cbt engr coy, 1 sigs coy))
　Light
　　1 div (4 inf bde; 1 arty bn, 1 int bn, 1 sigs bn)
　　9 div (3 inf bde; 1 arty bn, 1 int bn, 1 sigs bn)
　　1 bde (1 mech inf bn; 2 inf bn, 1 arty bn)
　Other
　　1 (Presidential) gd gp
COMBAT SUPPORT
　1 arty regt HQ
　1 MRL bty (forming)
　5 engr bde
SURFACE-TO-SURFACE MISSILE
　1 SSM bty (forming)
AIR DEFENCE
　1 AD bty

EQUIPMENT BY TYPE
ARMOURED FIGHTING VEHICLES
　LT TK 7 FV101 *Scorpion*

IFV 54: 2 YPR-765; 34 M113A1 FSV; 18 M113A2 FSV
APC 387
   APC (T) 168: 6 ACV300; 42 M113A1; 120 M113A2 (some with *Dragon* RWS)
   APC (W) 219: 73 LAV-150 *Commando*; 146 *Simba*
ENGINEERING & MAINTENANCE VEHICLES
   ARV ACV-300; *Samson*; M578; 4 M113 ARV
ANTI-TANK-ANTI-INFRASTRUCTURE • RCL 75mm M20; 90mm M67; 106mm M40A1
ARTILLERY 260+
   TOWED 220: 105mm 204 M101/M102/Model 56 pack howitzer; 155mm 16: 10 M114/M-68; 6 Soltam M-71
   MOR 40+: 81mm M29; 107mm 40 M30
AIRCRAFT
   TPT • Light 4: 1 Beech 80 *Queen Air*; 1 Cessna 170; 1 Cessna 172; 1 Cessna P206A
UNMANNED AERIAL VEHICLES • ISR • Medium *Blue Horizon*

Navy 23,750
EQUIPMENT BY TYPE
PATROL AND COASTAL COMBATANTS 65
   CORVETTES • FS 1 *Conrado Yap* (ex-ROK *Po Hang* (Flight III)) with 2 SVTT Mk 32 ASTT, 2 76mm gun
   PSOH 3 *Del Pilar* (ex-US *Hamilton*) with 1 76mm gun (capacity 1 Bo 105)
   PCF 1 *General Mariano Alvares* (ex-US *Cyclone*)
   PCO 8:
      3 *Emilio Jacinto* (ex-UK *Peacock*) with 1 76mm gun
      3 *Miguel Malvar* (ex-US) with 1 76mm gun
      2 *Rizal* (ex-US *Auk*) with 2 76mm gun
   PBFG 3 MPAC Mk3 with 1 *Typhoon* MLS-ER quad lnchr with *Spike*-ER SSM
   PBF 13: 4 *Tomas Batilo* (ex-ROK *Chamsuri*); 6 MPAC Mk1/2; 3 MPAC Mk3 (to be fitted with *Spike*-ER SSM)
   PB 30: 22 *Jose Andrada*; 2 *Kagitingan*; 2 *Point* (ex-US); 4 *Swift* Mk3 (ex-US)
   PBR 6 Silver Ships
AMPHIBIOUS
   PRINCIPAL AMPHIBIOUS SHIPS 2
      LPD 2 *Tarlac* (IDN *Makassar*) (capacity 2 LCVP; 2 hels; 13 tanks; 500 troops)
   LANDING SHIPS • LST 4:
      2 *Bacolod City* (US *Besson*) with 1 hel landing platform (capacity 32 tanks; 150 troops)
      2 LST-1/542 (ex US) (capacity 16 tanks; 200 troops)
   LANDING CRAFT 11
      LCM 2: 1 *Manobo*; 1 *Tagbanua* (capacity 100 tons; 200 troops)
      LCT 5 *Ivatan* (ex-AUS *Balikpapan*)
      LCU 4: 3 LCU Mk 6 (ex-US); 1 *Mulgae* I (ex-RoK)
LOGISTICS AND SUPPORT 6
   AGOR 1 *Gregorio Velasquez* (ex-US *Melville*)
   AOL 1
   AO 1 *Lake Caliraya*
   AP 1
   AWT 2

Naval Aviation
EQUIPMENT BY TYPE
AIRCRAFT • TPT • Light 11: 4 BN-2A *Defender*; 2 Cessna 177 *Cardinal*; 5 Beech 90 *King Air* (TC-90)
HELICOPTERS
   ASW 2 AW159 *Wildcat*
   TPT 13: Medium 4 Mi-171Sh; Light 9: 3 AW109; 2 AW109E; 4 Bo-105

Marines 8,300
FORCES BY ROLE
SPECIAL FORCES
   1 (force recon) spec ops bn
MANOEUVRE
   Amphibious
   4 mne bde (total: 12 mne bn)
COMBAT SUPPORT
   1 CSS bde (6 CSS bn)
EQUIPMENT BY TYPE
ARMOURED FIGHTING VEHICLES
   APC • APC (W) 42: 19 LAV-150 *Commando*; 23 LAV-300
   AAV 67: 8 AAV-7A1; 4 LVTH-6†; 55 LVTP-7
ARTILLERY 37+
   TOWED 37: 105mm 31: 23 M101; 8 M-26; 155mm 6 Soltam M-71
   MOR 107mm M30

Naval Special Operations Group
FORCES BY ROLE
SPECIAL FORCES
   1 SEAL unit
   1 diving unit
   10 naval spec ops unit
   1 special boat unit
COMBAT SUPPORT
   1 EOD unit

Air Force 17,600
FORCES BY ROLE
FIGHTER
   1 sqn with FA-50PH *Fighting Eagle*¤
GROUND ATTACK
   1 sqn with OV-10A/C *Bronco**
ISR
   1 sqn with *Turbo Commander* 690A
SEARCH & RESCUE
   4 (SAR/Comms) sqn with Bell 205 (UH-1M *Iroquois*); AUH-76
TRANSPORT
   1 sqn with C-130B/H/T *Hercules*
   1 sqn with N-22B *Nomad*; N-22SL *Searchmaster*; C-212 *Aviocar* (NC-212i)
   1 sqn with F-27-200 MPA; F-27-500 *Friendship*
   1 VIP sqn with F-28 *Fellowship*
TRAINING
   1 sqn with SF-260F/TP
   1 sqn with T-41B/D/K *Mescalero*
   1 sqn with S-211*

ATTACK HELICOPTER
1 sqn with MD-520MG
TRANSPORT HELICOPTER
1 sqn with AUH 76
1 sqn with W-3 *Sokol*
4 sqn with Bell 205 (UH-1H *Iroquois*)
1 (VIP) sqn with Bell 412EP *Twin Huey*; S-70A *Black Hawk* (S-70A-5)

EQUIPMENT BY TYPE
AIRCRAFT 33 combat capable
  FGA 12 FA-50PH *Fighting Eagle*
  MP 3: 1 C-130T MP mod; 1 F-27-200 MPA; 1 N-22SL *Searchmaster*
  ISR 11: 2 Cessna 208B *Grand Caravan*; 9 OV-10A/C *Bronco**
  TPT 14: **Medium** 4: 1 C-130B *Hercules*; 2 C-130H *Hercules*; 1 C-130T *Hercules* **Light** 9: 3 C295; 1 C295M; 1 F-27-500 *Friendship*; 1 N-22B *Nomad*; 1 *Turbo Commander* 690A; 2 C-212 *Aviocar* (NC-212i); **PAX** 1 F-28 *Fellowship* (VIP)
  TRG 39: 12 S-211*; 7 SF-260F; 10 SF-260TP; 10 T-41B/D/K *Mescalero*
HELICOPTERS
  MRH 40: 8 W-3 *Sokol*; 3 AUH-76; 8 AW109E; 8 Bell 412EP *Twin Huey*; 2 Bell 412HP *Twin Huey*; 11 MD-520MG
  TPT 32: **Medium** 1 S-70A *Black Hawk* (S-70A-5); **Light** 31: 11 Bell 205 (UH-1D); 20 Bell 205 (UH-1H *Iroquois*) (25 more non-operational)
UNMANNED AERIAL VEHICLES
  ISR • **Medium** 5: 2 *Blue Horizon* II; 3 *Hermes* 900
AIR-LAUNCHED MISSILES
  AAM • **IR** AIM-9L *Sidewinder*
  ASM AGM-65D *Maverick*; AGM-65G2 *Maverick*

Paramilitary 11,100

Coast Guard 11,100
EQUIPMENT BY TYPE
Rodman 38 and Rodman 101 owned by Bureau of Fisheries and Aquatic Resources
PATROL AND COASTAL COMBATANTS 86
  PCO 5: 4 *San Juan* with 1 hel landing platform; 1 *Balsam*
  PCC 2 *Tirad*
  PB 68: 4 *Boracay* (FPB 72 Mk II); 3 *De Haviland*; 4 *Ilocos Norte*; 1 *Palawan*; 12 PCF 50 (US *Swift* Mk1/2); 10 PCF 46; 10 PCF 65 (US *Swift* Mk3); 4 Rodman 38; 10 Rodman 101; 10 *Parola* (MRRV)
  PBR 11
LOGISTICS AND SUPPORT • **ABU** 1 *Corregidor*
AIRCRAFT • **TPT** • **Light** 2 BN-2 *Islander*
HELICOPTERS • **TPT** • **Light** 2 Bo-105

Citizen Armed Force Geographical Units
50,000 reservists
FORCES BY ROLE
MANOEUVRE
  Other 56 militia bn (part-time units which can be called up for extended periods)

DEPLOYMENT

CENTRAL AFRICAN REPUBLIC: UN • MINUSCA 2
INDIA/PAKISTAN: UN • UNMOGIP 7
SOUTH SUDAN: UN • UNMISS 2

FOREIGN FORCES

Australia Operation Augury 100
Brunei IMT 8
Indonesia IMT 9
Malaysia IMT 11
United States US Pacific Command: Operation Pacific Eagle - Philippines 200

Singapore SGP

Singapore Dollar S$		2018	2019	2020
GDP	S$	491bn	498bn	
	US$	364bn	363bn	
per capita	US$	64,579	63,987	
Growth	%	3.1	0.5	
Inflation	%	0.4	0.7	
Def bdgt	S$	14.8bn	15.5bn	
	US$	10.9bn	11.3bn	
US$1=S$		1.35	1.37	

Real-terms defence budget trend (US$bn, constant 2015)

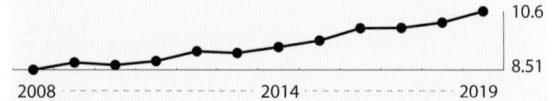

Population 6,102,937

Ethnic groups: Chinese 74.1%; Malay 13.4%; Indian 9.2%; other or unspecified 3.3%

Age	0–14	15–19	20–24	25–29	30–64	65 plus
Male	6.5%	3.1%	4.5%	5.2%	24.7%	4.8%
Female	6.2%	3.1%	4.8%	5.5%	25.8%	5.7%

Capabilities

The Singapore Armed Forces (SAF) are the best equipped in Southeast Asia. They are organised essentially along Israeli lines, with the air force and navy staffed mainly by professional personnel while, apart from a small core of regulars, the much larger army is based on conscripts and reservists. Although there are no publicly available defence-policy documents, it is widely presumed that the SAF's primary role is to deter attacks on the city state or interference with its vital interests – particularly its sea lines of communication – by potential regional adversaries. There is now an additional focus on counter-terrorist operations. With an ageing population and declining conscript cohort, there is a significant personnel challenge, which the defence ministry is looking to address by lean staffing and increased use of technology. There is routine overseas training, and plans have been announced to further improve domestic training areas. The SAF also engages extensively in bilateral and multilateral exercises with regional and international partners. Singaporean forces have gradually become more involved in multinational operations, including the US-led air offensive against ISIS. While such deployments have provided some operational experience, and training standards and operational readiness are high, the army's reliance on conscripts and reservists limits its capacity for sustained operations abroad.

Equipment modernisation continues, with plans to acquire F-35 combat aircraft, new domestically produced armoured fighting vehicles, multi-role combat vessels and multi-mission ships, with a view to retaining Singapore's military edge over other Southeast Asian powers. There is a small but sophisticated defence industry. ST Engineering group manufactures several types of armoured vehicles and corvettes for the SAF.

ACTIVE 51,000 (Army 41,000 Navy 4,000 Air 6,000)
Paramilitary 8,400
Conscription liability 22–24 months

RESERVE 252,500 (Army 240,000 Navy 5,000 Air 7,500)
Annual trg to age 40 for army other ranks, 50 for officers

ORGANISATIONS BY SERVICE

Army 41,000 (including 26,000 conscripts)
FORCES BY ROLE
COMMAND
  3 (combined arms) div HQ
  1 (rapid reaction) div HQ
  4 armd bde HQ
  9 inf bde HQ
  1 air mob bde HQ
  1 amph bde HQ
SPECIAL FORCES
  1 cdo bn
MANOEUVRE
  Reconnaissance
  3 lt armd/recce bn
  Armoured
  1 armd bn
  Mechanised
  6 mech inf bn
  Light
  2 (gds) inf bn
  Other
  2 sy bn
COMBAT SUPPORT
  2 arty bn
  1 STA bn
  2 engr bn
  1 EOD bn
  1 ptn br bn
  1 int bn
  2 ISR bn
  1 CBRN bn
  3 sigs bn
COMBAT SERVICE SUPPORT
  3 med bn
  2 tpt bn
  3 spt bn

Reserves
Activated units form part of divisions and brigades listed above; 1 op reserve div with additional armd & inf bde; People's Defence Force Comd (homeland defence) with 12 inf bn

FORCES BY ROLE
SPECIAL FORCES
  1 cdo bn
MANOEUVRE
  Reconnaissance
  6 lt armd/recce bn
  Mechanised
  6 mech inf bn
  Light
  ε56 inf bn
COMBAT SUPPORT
  ε12 arty bn
  ε8 engr bn
EQUIPMENT BY TYPE
ARMOURED FIGHTING VEHICLES
  MBT 96+ *Leopard* 2SG
  LT TK 372: 22 AMX-10 PAC 90; ε350 AMX-13 SM1
  IFV 572+: 22 AMX-10P; 250 *Bionix* IFV-25; 250 *Bionix* IFV-40/50; 50+ M113A1/A2 (some with 40mm AGL, some with 25mm gun)
  APC 1,655+
    APC (T) 1,100+: 700+ M113A1/A2; 400+ ATTC *Bronco*
    APC (W) 415: 250 LAV-150 *Commando*/V-200 *Commando*; 135 *Terrex* ICV; 30 V-100 *Commando*
    PPV 140: 74 *Belrex*; 15 *MaxxPro Dash*; 51 *Peacekeeper*
ENGINEERING & MAINTENANCE VEHICLES
  AEV 94: 18 CET; 54 FV180; 14 *Kodiak*; 8 M728
  ARV *Bionix*; *Büffel*; LAV-150; LAV-300
  VLB 72+: *Bionix*; LAB 30; *Leguan*; M2; 60 M3; 12 M60
  MW 910-MCV-2; *Trailblazer*
ANTI-TANK/ANTI-INFRASTRUCTURE
  MSL • MANPATS *Milan*; *Spike*-SR; *Spike*-MR
  RCL 90+: **84mm** *Carl Gustav*; **106mm** 90 M40A1
ARTILLERY 798+
  SP 155mm 54 SSPH-1 *Primus*
  TOWED 88: **105mm** (37 LG1 in store); **155mm** 88: 18 FH-2000; ε18 *Pegasus*; 52 FH-88
  MRL 227mm 18 M142 HIMARS
  MOR 638+
    SP 90+: **81mm**; **120mm** 90: 40 on *Bronco*; 50 on M113
    TOWED 548: **81mm** 500 **120mm** 36 M-65; **160mm** 12 M-58 Tampella
UNMANNED AERIAL VEHICLES • ISR • Light *Skylark*

Navy 4,000 (incl 1,000 conscripts)
EQUIPMENT BY TYPE
SUBMARINES • TACTICAL • SSK 4:
  2 *Challenger* (ex-SWE *Sjoormen*) with 2 single 400mm TT with Torped 431, 4 single 533mm TT with Torped 613
  2 *Archer* (ex-SWE *Västergötland*) (AIP fitted) with 3 single 400mm TT with Torped 431, 6 single 533mm TT with *Black Shark* HWT
PRINCIPAL SURFACE COMBATANTS 6:
  FRIGATES • FFGHM 6 *Formidable* with 2 quad lnchr with RGM-84 *Harpoon* AShM, 4 8-cell *Sylver* A43 VLS with *Aster* 15 SAM, 2 triple ILAS-3 (B-515) 324mm ASTT with A244/S LWT, 1 76mm gun (capacity 1 S-70B *Sea Hawk* hel)

PATROL AND COASTAL COMBATANTS 21
  CORVETTES 11
    FSGM 6 *Victory* with 2 quad lnchr with RGM-84 *Harpoon* AShM, 2 8-cell VLS with *Barak*-1 SAM, 2 triple ILAS-3 (B-515) 324mm ASTT with A244/S LWT, 1 76mm gun
    FSM 5 *Independence* (Littoral Mission Vessel) with 1 12-cell CLA VLS with VL-MICA, 1 76mm gun, 1 hel landing platform
  PCO 2 *Fearless* with 1 76mm gun (can be fitted with 2 sextuple *Sadral* lnchr with *Mistral* SAM)
  PBF 8: 2 SMC Type 1; 6 SMC Type 2
MINE WARFARE • MINE COUNTERMEASURES
  MCC 4 *Bedok*
AMPHIBIOUS
  PRINCIPAL AMPHIBIOUS SHIPS • LPD 4 *Endurance* with 2 twin *Simbad* lnchr with *Mistral* SAM, 1 76mm gun (capacity 2 hel; 4 LCVP; 18 MBT; 350 troops)
  LANDING CRAFT • LCVP 23: ε17 FCEP; 6 FCU
LOGISTICS AND SUPPORT 2
  ASR 1 *Swift Rescue*
  AX 1

Naval Diving Unit
FORCES BY ROLE
SPECIAL FORCES
  1 SF gp
  1 (diving) SF gp
COMBAT SUPPORT
  1 EOD gp

Air Force 6,000 (incl 3,000 conscripts)
5 comds
FORCES BY ROLE
FIGHTER/GROUND ATTACK
  2 sqn with F-15SG *Eagle*
  3 sqn with F-16C/D *Fighting Falcon* (some used for ISR with pods)
ANTI-SUBMARINE WARFARE
  1 sqn with S-70B *Seahawk*
MARITIME PATROL/TRANSPORT
  1 sqn with F-50
AIRBORNE EARLY WARNING & CONTROL
  1 sqn with G550-AEW
TANKER
  1 sqn with A330 MRTT
TANKER/TRANSPORT
  1 sqn with KC-130B/H *Hercules*; C-130H *Hercules*
TRAINING
  1 (FRA-based) sqn with M-346 *Master*
  4 (US-based) units with AH-64D *Apache*; CH-47D *Chinook*; F-15SG: F-16C/D
  1 (AUS-based) sqn with PC-21
  1 hel sqn with H120 *Colibri*
ATTACK HELICOPTER
  1 sqn with AH-64D *Apache*
TRANSPORT HELICOPTER
  1 sqn with CH-47SD *Super D Chinook*
  2 sqn with AS332M *Super Puma*; AS532UL *Cougar*
ISR UAV
  1 sqn with *Hermes* 450

  2 sqn with *Heron* 1
AIR DEFENCE
  1 AD bn with *Mistral* (opcon Army)
  3 AD bn with RBS-70; 9K38 *Igla* (SA-18 *Grouse*); Mechanised *Igla* (opcon Army)
  1 ADA sqn with Oerlikon
  1 AD sqn with SAMP/T
  1 AD sqn with *Spyder*-SR
  1 radar sqn with radar (mobile)
  1 radar sqn with LORADS
MANOEUVRE
  Other
  4 (field def) sy sqn
EQUIPMENT BY TYPE
AIRCRAFT 105 combat capable
  FGA 100: 40 F-15SG *Eagle*; 20 F-16C Block 52 *Fighting Falcon*; 20 F-16D Block 52 *Fighting Falcon*; 20 F-16D Block 52+ *Fighting Falcon* (incl reserves)
  MP 5 F-50 *Maritime Enforcer**
  AEW&C 4 G550-AEW
  TKR 1 KC-130H *Hercules*
  TKR/TPT 7: 3 A330 MRTT; 4 KC-130B *Hercules*
  TPT 9: **Medium** 5 C-130H *Hercules* (2 ELINT); **PAX** 4 F-50
  TRG 31: 12 M-346 *Master*; 19 PC-21
HELICOPTERS
  ATK 19 AH-64D *Apache*
  ASW 8 S-70B *Seahawk*
  TPT 51: **Heavy** 16: 6 CH-47D *Chinook*; 10 CH-47SD *Super D Chinook*; **Medium** 30: 18 AS332M *Super Puma* (incl 5 SAR); 12 AS532UL *Cougar*; **Light** 5 H120 *Colibri* (leased)
UNMANNED AERIAL VEHICLES
  ISR 17+: **Heavy** 8+ *Heron* 1; **Medium** 9+ *Hermes* 450
AIR DEFENCE
  SAM
    Long-range 4+ SAMP/T
    Short-range *Spyder*-SR
    Point-defence 9K38 *Igla* (SA-18 *Grouse*); Mechanised *Igla*; *Mistral*; RBS-70
  GUNS 34
    SP 20mm GAI-C01
    TOWED 34 **20mm** GAI-C01; **35mm** 34 GDF (with 25 *Super-Fledermaus* fire-control radar)
AIR-LAUNCHED MISSILES
  AAM • IR AIM-9P/S *Sidewinder*; *Python* 4 (reported); **IIR** AIM-9X *Sidewinder* II; **SARH** AIM-7P *Sparrow*; **ARH** (AIM-120C5/7 AMRAAM in store in US)
  ASM: AGM-65B/G *Maverick*; AGM-114K/L *Hellfire*; AGM-154A/C JSOW
  AShM AGM-84 *Harpoon*; AM39 *Exocet*
BOMBS
  INS/GPS guided GBU-31 JDAM
  Laser-guided *Paveway* II

Paramilitary 8,400 active

Civil Defence Force 5,600 (incl conscripts); 500 auxiliaries (total 6,100)

Singapore Police Coast Guard 1,000
EQUIPMENT BY TYPE
PATROL AND COASTAL COMBATANTS 102
  PBF 81: 25 *Angler Ray*; 2 *Atlantic Ray*; 1 *Marlin*; 11 *Sailfish*; 10 *Shark*; 32 other
  PB 21: 19 *Amberjack*; 2 *Manta Ray*

Singapore Gurkha Contingent 1,800
Under the Police
FORCES BY ROLE
MANOEUVRE
  Other
    6 paramilitary coy

DEPLOYMENT

AUSTRALIA: 2 trg schools – 1 with 12 AS332 *Super Puma*/AS532 *Cougar* (flying trg) located at Oakey; 1 with PC-21 (flying trg) located at Pearce. Army: prepositioned AFVs and heavy equipment at Shoalwater Bay training area

BRUNEI: 1 trg camp with inf units on rotation; 1 hel det with AS332 *Super Puma*

FRANCE: 200: 1 trg sqn with 12 M-346 *Master*

KUWAIT: *Operation Inherent Resolve* 11

TAIWAN: 3 trg camp (incl inf and arty)

THAILAND: 1 trg camp (arty, cbt engr)

UNITED STATES: Trg units with F-16C/D; 12 F-15SG; AH-64D *Apache*; 6+ CH-47D *Chinook*

FOREIGN FORCES

United States US Pacific Command: 200; 1 naval spt facility at Changi naval base; 1 USAF log spt sqn at Paya Lebar air base

Sri Lanka LKA

Sri Lankan Rupee Rs		2018	2019	2020
GDP	Rs	14.5tr	15.5tr	
	US$	88.9bn	86.6bn	
per capita	US$	4,099	3,947	
Growth	%	3.2	2.7	
Inflation	%	4.3	4.1	
Def bdgt	Rs	292bn	298bn	
	US$	1.80bn	1.67bn	
FMA (US)	US$	0.5m	0m	0m
US$1=Rs		162.54	178.49	

Real-terms defence budget trend (US$bn, constant 2015)

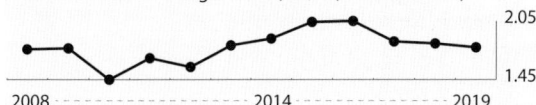

Population	22,736,505				
Age	0–14	15–19	20–24	25–29	30–64	65 plus
Male	11.9%	3.9%	3.5%	3.6%	21.5%	4.3%
Female	11.5%	3.7%	3.4%	3.6%	23.0%	6.0%

Capabilities

Since the defeat of the Tamil Tigers, the armed forces have reoriented to a peacetime internal-security role. Support has been provided by China, in an indication of a growing military-to-military relationship. The US has eased its long-standing military trade restrictions and Japan has stated an intention to increase maritime cooperation with the country. Sri Lanka has little capacity for force projection beyond its national territory but has sent small numbers of troops on UN missions. The navy's littoral capability, based on fast-attack and patrol boats, has been strengthened with the acquisition of offshore patrol vessels, while the US has gifted a former US coastguard cutter and China has gifted a frigate. The army is reducing in size and there appears to have been little spending on new equipment since the end of the civil war, although Sri Lanka is looking to begin a series of procurements to fill key capability gaps. Beyond maintenance facilities and limited fabrication, such as at Sri Lanka's shipyards, there is no defence-industrial base.

ACTIVE 255,000 (Army 177,000 Navy 50,000 Air 28,000) Paramilitary 62,200

RESERVE 5,500 (Army 1,100 Navy 2,400 Air Force 2,000) Paramilitary 30,400

ORGANISATIONS BY SERVICE

Army 113,000; 64,00 active reservists (recalled) (total 177,000)

Regt are bn sized
FORCES BY ROLE
COMMAND
  7 region HQ
  21 div HQ
SPECIAL FORCES
  1 indep SF bde
MANOEUVRE
  Reconnaissance
    3 armd recce regt
  Armoured
    1 armd bde(-)
  Mechanised
    1 mech inf bde
  Light
    60 inf bde
    1 cdo bde
  Air Manoeuvre
    1 air mob bde
COMBAT SUPPORT
  7 arty regt
  1 MRL regt
  8 engr regt
  6 sigs regt
EQUIPMENT BY TYPE
ARMOURED FIGHTING VEHICLES
  MBT 62 T-55A/T-55AM2
  RECCE 15 *Saladin*
  IFV 62+: 13 BMP-1; 49 BMP-2; WZ-551 20mm
  APC 211+
    APC (T) 30+: some Type-63; 30 Type-85; some Type-89

APC (W) 181: 25 BTR-80/BTR-80A; 31 *Buffel*; 20 WZ-551; 105 *Unicorn*

ENGINEERING & MAINTENANCE VEHICLES
ARV 16 VT-55
VLB 2 MT-55

ANTI-TANK/ANTI-INFRASTRUCTURE
MANPATS HJ-8
RCL 40: **105mm** ε10 M-65; **106mm** ε30 M40
GUNS **85mm** 8 Type-56 (D-44)

ARTILLERY 908
TOWED 96: **122mm** 20; **130mm** 30 Type-59-I; **152mm** 46 Type-66 (D-20)
MRL **122mm** 28: 6 KRL-122; 22 RM-70
MOR 784: **81mm** 520; **82mm** 209; **120mm** 55 M-43

UNMANNED AERIAL VEHICLES
ISR • **Medium** 1 *Seeker*

Navy ε37,000; ε13,000 active reserves (total 50,000)

Seven naval areas

EQUIPMENT BY TYPE
PATROL AND COASTAL COMBATANTS 130
PSOH 5: 1 *Gajabahu* (ex-US *Hamilton*) with 1 76mm gun (capacity 1 med hel); 1 *Parakramabahu* (*Jiangwei* I (ex-PRC Type-053H2G) with 1 twin 100mm gun (capacity 1 med hel); 1 *Sayura* (IND *Vigraha*); 2 *Sayurala* (IND *Samarth*)
PCG 2 *Nandimithra* (ISR *Sa'ar* 4) with 3 single lnchr with *Gabriel* II AShM, 1 76mm gun
PCO 2: 1 *Samudura* (ex-US *Reliance*); 1 *Sagara* (IND *Vikram*) with 1 hel landing platform
PCC 1 *Jayasagara*
PBF 74: 26 *Colombo*; 6 *Shaldag*; 4 *Super Dvora* Mk II; 6 *Super Dvora* Mk III; 5 *Trinity Marine*; 27 *Wave Rider*
PB 20: 4 *Cheverton*; 2 *Mihikatha* (ex-AUS *Bay*); 2 *Prathapa* (PRC mod *Haizhui*); 3 *Ranajaya* (PRC *Haizhui*); 1 *Ranarisi* (PRC mod *Shanghai* II); 5 *Weeraya* (PRC *Shanghai* II); 3 (various)
PBR 26

AMPHIBIOUS
LANDING SHIPS • LSM 1 *Shakthi* (PRC *Yuhai*) (capacity 2 tanks; 250 troops)
LANDING CRAFT 8
LCM 2
LCP 3 *Hansaya*
LCU 2 *Yunnan*
UCAC 1 M 10 (capacity 56 troops)
LOGISTICS AND SUPPORT 3: 2 AP; 1 AX

Marines ε500
FORCES BY ROLE
MANOEUVRE
Amphibious
1 mne bn

Special Boat Service ε100

Reserve Organisations

Sri Lanka Volunteer Naval Force (SLVNF) 13,000 active reservists

Air Force 28,000 (incl SLAF Regt)

FORCES BY ROLE
FIGHTER
1 sqn with F-7BS/G; FT-7
FIGHTER/GROUND ATTACK
1 sqn with *Kfir* C-2
1 sqn with K-8 *Karakorum**
TRANSPORT
1 sqn with An-32B *Cline*; C-130K *Hercules*; Cessna 421C *Golden Eagle*
1 sqn with Beech B200 *King Air*; Y-12 (II)
TRAINING
1 wg with PT-6, Cessna 150L
ATTACK HELICOPTER
1 sqn with Mi-24V *Hind* E; Mi-35P *Hind*
TRANSPORT HELICOPTER
1 sqn with Mi-17 *Hip* H; Mi-171Sh
1 sqn with Bell 206A/B (incl basic trg), Bell 212
1 (VIP) sqn with Bell 212; Bell 412 *Twin Huey*
ISR UAV
1 sqn with *Blue Horizon* II
1 sqn with *Searcher* MkII
MANOEUVRE
Other
1 (SLAF) sy regt

EQUIPMENT BY TYPE
AIRCRAFT 13 combat capable
FTR 5: 3 F-7GS; 2 FT-7 (3 F-7BS; 1 F-7GS non-operational)
FGA 1 *Kfir* C-2 (2 *Kfir* C-2; 1 *Kfir* C-7; 2 *Kfir* TC-2; 6 MiG-27M *Flogger* J; 1 MiG-23UB *Flogger* C non-operational)
TPT 21: **Medium** 2 C-130K *Hercules*; **Light** 19: 3 An-32B *Cline*; 6 Cessna 150L; 1 Cessna 421C *Golden Eagle*; 7 Y-12 (II); 2 Y-12 (IV)
TRG 13: 7 K-8 *Karakorum**; 6 PT-6
HELICOPTERS
ATK 11: 6 Mi-24P *Hind*; 3 Mi-24V *Hind* E; 2 Mi-35V *Hind*
MRH 18: 6 Bell 412 *Twin Huey* (VIP); 2 Bell 412EP (VIP); 10 Mi-17 *Hip* H
TPT 16: **Medium** 4 Mi-171Sh; **Light** 12: 2 Bell 206A *Jet Ranger*; 2 Bell 206B *Jet Ranger*; 8 Bell 212
UNMANNED AERIAL VEHICLES
ISR • **Medium** 2+: some *Blue Horizon* II; 2 *Searcher* MkII
AIR DEFENCE • **GUNS** • **TOWED** 27: **40mm** 24 L/40; **94mm** 3 (3.7in)
AIR-LAUNCHED MISSILES
AAM • **IR** PL-5E

Paramilitary ε62,200

Home Guard 13,000

National Guard ε15,000

Police Force 30,200; 1,000 (women) (total 31,200) 30,400 reservists

Ministry of Defence Special Task Force 3,000
Anti-guerrilla unit

Coast Guard n/k
Ministry of Defence

EQUIPMENT BY TYPE
PATROL AND COASTAL COMBATANTS 17
  PCO 1 *Suraksha* (ex-IND *Vikram*) with 1 hel landing platform
  PBF 11: 2 *Dvora*; 4 *Super Dvora* Mk I; 3 *Killer* (ROK); 2 (Inshore Patrol Craft)
  PB 4: 2 Simonneau Type-508; 2 *Samudra Raksha*
  PBR 1

DEPLOYMENT

CENTRAL AFRICAN REPUBLIC: UN • MINUSCA 116; 1 hel sqn

LEBANON: UN • UNIFIL 149; 1 inf coy

MALI: UN • MINUSMA 203; 1 sy coy

SOUTH SUDAN: UN • UNMISS 173; 1 fd hospital; 1 hel sqn

SUDAN: UN • UNISFA 7

WESTERN SAHARA: UN • MINURSO 4

Taiwan (Republic of China) ROC

New Taiwan Dollar NT$		2018	2019	2020
GDP	NT$	17.8tr	18.2tr	
	US$	590bn	586bn	
per capita	US$	25,008	24,828	
Growth	%	2.6	2.0	
Inflation	%	1.5	0.8	
Def bdgt	NT$	328bn	341bn	411bn
	US$	10.9bn	10.9bn	
US$1=NT$		30.16	31.12	

Real-terms defence budget trend (US$bn, constant 2015)

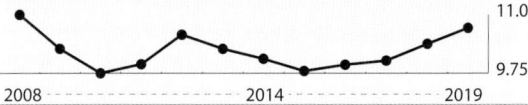

Population 23,577,456

Ethnic groups: Taiwanese 84%; mainland Chinese 14%

Age	0–14	15–19	20–24	25–29	30–64	65 plus
Male	6.4%	2.8%	3.4%	3.5%	26.5%	6.8%
Female	6.1%	2.7%	3.2%	3.4%	27.1%	8.2%

Capabilities

Taiwan's relationship with China and its attempts to sustain a credible military capability dominate its security policy. Taiwan's current focus is therefore on air defence and deterrence in coastal areas, on both sides of the island. The 2019 National Defence report, published in August, also highlighted the importance of coastal defence. The armed forces are well trained and exercise regularly. Demographic pressure has influenced plans for force reductions and a shift towards an all-volunteer force. Taiwan's main alliance partnership is with the US. The Taiwan Relations Act from 1979 states that 'the United States shall provide Taiwan with arms of a defensive character'. In 2019, the United States approved the transfer of new F-16C/D Block 70 combat aircraft to Taiwan, which had previously obtained US assistance to modernise its current fleet of F-16s to F-16V standard. Nevertheless, Taipei maintains an interest in the F-35. Due to the lack of potential foreign equipment suppliers, Taiwan is modernising its existing holdings and developing its domestic defence-industry capabilities through increased funding and the development of new weapons programmes. The government launched a new defence-industrial policy in 2019, aimed at further strengthening independent defence-manufacturing capacities. Taiwan's defence-industrial base has strengths in aerospace, shipbuilding and missiles.

ACTIVE 163,000 (Army 88,000 Navy 40,000 Air 35,000) **Paramilitary 11,450**

Conscript liability
(19–40 years) 12 months for those born before 1993; four months for those born after 1994 (alternative service available).

RESERVE 1,657,000 (Army 1,500,000 Navy 67,000 Air Force 90,000)
Some obligation to age 30

ORGANISATIONS BY SERVICE

Space
EQUIPMENT BY TYPE
SATELLITES • ISR 1 *Formosat*-5

Army 88,000 (incl ε5,000 MP)
FORCES BY ROLE
COMMAND
  3 corps HQ
  5 defence comd HQ
SPECIAL FORCES/HELICOPTER
  1 SF/hel comd (2 spec ops gp, 2 hel bde)
MANOEUVRE
  Armoured
  4 armd bde
  Mechanised
  3 mech inf bde
  Light
  6 inf bde
COMBAT SUPPORT
  3 arty gp
  3 engr gp
  3 CBRN gp
  3 sigs gp
COASTAL DEFENCE
  1 AShM bn

Reserves
FORCES BY ROLE
MANOEUVRE
  Light
  21 inf bde
EQUIPMENT BY TYPE
ARMOURED FIGHTING VEHICLES
  MBT 565: 200 M60A3; 100 M48A5; 265 M48H *Brave Tiger*
  LT TK ε100 M41A3/D
  IFV 225 CM-25 (M113 with 20–30mm cannon)
  APC 1,318
    APC (T) 650 M113

APC (W) 668: 368 CM-32 *Yunpao*; 300 LAV-150 *Commando*

ENGINEERING & MAINTENANCE VEHICLES
AEV 18 M9
ARV CM-27/A1; 37 M88A1
VLB 22 M3; M48A5

NBC VEHICLES 48+: BIDS; 48 K216A1; KM453

ANTI-TANK/ANTI-INFRASTRUCTURE
MSL
SP TOW
MANPATS FGM-148 *Javelin*; TOW
RCL 500+: **90mm** M67; **106mm** 500+: 500 M40A1; Type-51

ARTILLERY 2,093
SP 488: **105mm** 100 M108; **155mm** 318: 225 M109A2/A5; 48 M44T; 45 T-69; **203mm** 70 M110
TOWED 1,060+: **105mm** 650 T-64 (M101); **155mm** 340+: 90 M59; 250 T-65 (M114); M44; XT-69; **203mm** 70 M115
MRL 223: **117mm** 120 *Kung Feng* VI; **126mm** 103: 60 *Kung Feng* III/*Kung Feng* IV; 43 RT 2000 *Thunder*
MOR 322+:
SP 162+: **81mm** 72+: M29; 72 M125; **107mm** 90 M106A2
TOWED 81mm 160 M29; T-75; **107mm** M30; **120mm** K5; XT-86

COASTAL DEFENCE
ARTY 54: **127mm** ε50 US Mk32 (reported); **240mm** 4 M1
AShM *Ching Feng*

HELICOPTERS
ATK 96: 67 AH-1W *Cobra*; 29 AH-64E *Apache*
MRH 38 OH-58D *Kiowa Warrior*
TPT 38: **Heavy** 8 CH-47SD *Super D Chinook*; **Medium** 30 UH-60M *Black Hawk*
TRG 29 TH-67 *Creek*

UNMANNED AERIAL VEHICLES
ISR • Light *Mastiff* III

AIR DEFENCE
SAM • Point-defence 76: 74 M1097 *Avenger*; 2 M48 *Chaparral*; FIM-92 *Stinger*
GUNS
SP 40mm M42
TOWED 40mm L/70

Navy 40,000

EQUIPMENT BY TYPE
SUBMARINES • TACTICAL • SSK 4:
2 *Hai Lung* with 6 single 533mm TT with UGM-84L *Harpoon* Block II AShM/SUT HWT
2 *Hai Shih*† (ex-US *Guppy* II – trg role) with 10 single 533mm TT (6 fwd, 4 aft) with SUT HWT

PRINCIPAL SURFACE COMBATANTS 26
CRUISERS • CGHM 4 *Keelung* (ex-US *Kidd*) with 2 quad lnchr with RGM-84L *Harpoon* Block II AShM, 2 twin Mk 26 GMLS with SM-2 Block IIIA SAM, 2 triple SVTT Mk 32 324mm ASTT with Mk 46 LWT, 2 Mk 15 *Phalanx* Block 1B CIWS, 2 127mm gun (capacity 1 S-70 ASW hel)
FRIGATES 22
FFGHM 21:
8 *Cheng Kung* (US *Oliver Hazard Perry* mod) with 2 quad lnchr with *Hsiung Feng* II/III AShM, 1 Mk 13 GMLS with SM-1MR Block VI SAM, 2 triple SVTT Mk 32 324mm ASTT with Mk 46 LWT, 1 Mk 15 *Phalanx* Block 1B CIWS, 1 76mm gun (capacity 2 S-70C ASW hel)
2 *Meng Chuan* (ex-US *Oliver Hazard Perry*) with 1 Mk13 GMLS with RGM-84 *Harpoon* AShM/SM-1MR Block VI SAM, 2 triple SVTT Mk 32 324mm ASTT with Mk 46 LWT, 1 Mk 15 *Phalanx* Block 1B CIWS, 1 76mm gun (capacity 2 S-70C ASW hel)
5 *Chin Yang* (ex-US *Knox*) with 1 octuple Mk 16 lnchr with RGM-84C *Harpoon* Block 1B AShM/ASROC A/S msl, 2 triple lnchr with SM-1MR Block VI SAM, 2 twin lnchr with SM-1MR Block VI SAM, 2 twin SVTT Mk 32 324mm ASTT with Mk 46 LWT, 1 Mk 15 *Phalanx* Block 1B CIWS, 1 127mm gun (capacity 1 MD-500 hel)
6 *Kang Ding* with 2 quad lnchr with *Hsiung Feng* II AShM, 1 quad lnchr with *Sea Chaparral* SAM, 2 SVTT Mk 32 triple 324mm ASTT with Mk 46 LWT, 1 Mk 15 *Phalanx* Block 1B CIWS, 1 76mm gun (capacity 1 S-70C ASW hel)
FFGH 1 *Chin Yang* (ex-US *Knox*) with 1 octuple Mk 112 lnchr with RGM-84C *Harpoon* Block 1B AShM, 2 twin SVTT Mk 32 324mm ASTT with Mk 46 LWT, 1 Mk 15 *Phalanx* Block 1B CIWS, 1 127mm gun (capacity 1 MD-500 hel)

PATROL AND COASTAL COMBATANTS 44
CORVETTES • FSG 1 *Tuo Jiang* (*Hsun Hai*) with 4 twin lnchr with *Hsiung Feng* II AShM, 4 twin lnchr with *Hisung Feng* III AShM, 2 triple SVTT Mk 32 324mm ASTT, 1 Mk 15 *Phalanx* Block 1B CIWS; 1 76mm gun
PCG 11:
1 *Jin Chiang* with 1 twin lnchr with *Hsiung Feng* II AShM
4 *Jin Chiang* with 2 twin lnchr with *Hsiung Feng* II AShM, 1 76mm gun
6 *Jin Chiang* with 1 twin lnchr with *Hsiung Feng* III AShM, 1 76mm gun
PCC 1 *Jin Chiang* (test platform)
PBG 31 *Kwang Hua* with 2 twin lnchr with *Hsiung Feng* II AShM

MINE WARFARE • MINE COUNTERMEASURES 9
MHC 6: 4 *Yung Feng*; 2 *Yung Jin* (ex-US *Osprey*)
MSO 3 *Yung Yang* (ex-US *Aggressive*)

COMMAND SHIPS • LCC 1 *Kao Hsiung*

AMPHIBIOUS
PRINCIPAL AMPHIBIOUS SHIPS • LSD 1 *Shiu Hai* (ex-US *Anchorage*) with 2 Mk 15 *Phalanx* CIWS, 1 hel landing platform (capacity either 2 LCU or 18 LCM; 360 troops)
LANDING SHIPS
LST 8:
6 *Chung Hai* (capacity 16 tanks; 200 troops)
2 *Chung Ho* (ex-US *Newport*) with 1 Mk 15 *Phalanx* CIWS, 1 hel landing platform (capacity 3 LCVP, 23 AFVs, 400 troops)
LANDING CRAFT 47
LCM ε35 (various)
LCU 12 LCU 1610 (capacity 2 M60A3 or 400 troops) (minelaying capability)

LOGISTICS AND SUPPORT 12
AGOR 1 *Ta Kuan*

AOEH 1 *Panshih* with 1 quad lnchr with *Sea Chaparral* SAM, 2 Mk 15 *Phalanx* CIWS (capacity 3 med hel)
AOE 1 *Wu Yi* with 1 quad lnchr with *Sea Chaparral* SAM, 1 hel landing platform
ARS 2: 1 *Da Hu* (ex-US *Diver*); 1 *Da Juen* (ex-US *Bolster*)
ATF 7 *Ta Tung* (ex-US *Cherokee*)

Marines 10,000
FORCES BY ROLE
MANOEUVRE
  Amphibious
  3 mne bde
COMBAT SUPPORT
  Some cbt spt unit
EQUIPMENT BY TYPE
ARMOURED FIGHTING VEHICLES
  AAV 202: 52 AAV-7A1; 150 LVTP-5A1
ENGINEERING & MAINTENANCE VEHICLES
  ARV 2 AAVR-7
ANIT-TANK/ANTI-INFRASTRUCTURE
  RCL 106mm
ARTILLERY • **TOWED** 105mm; 155mm

Naval Aviation
FORCES BY ROLE
ANTI SUBMARINE WARFARE
  2 sqn with S-70C *Seahawk* (S-70C *Defender*)
  1 sqn with MD-500 *Defender*
ISR UAV
  1 bn with *Chung Shyang* II
EQUIPMENT BY TYPE
HELICOPTERS
  ASW 20 S-70C *Seahawk* (S-70C *Defender*)
  MRH 10 MD-500 *Defender*
UNMANNED AERIAL VEHICLES • **ISR** • **Medium** ε28 *Chung Shyang* II

Air Force 35,000
FORCES BY ROLE
FIGHTER
  3 sqn with *Mirage* 2000-5E/D (2000-5EI/DI)
FIGHTER/GROUND ATTACK
  3 sqn with F-5E/F *Tiger* II
  6 sqn with F-16A/B *Fighting Falcon*
  5 sqn with F-CK-1A/B/C/D *Ching Kuo*
ANTI-SUBMARINE WARFARE
  1 sqn with P-3C *Orion*
ELECTRONIC WARFARE
  1 sqn with C-130HE *Tien Gian*
ISR
  1 sqn with RF-5E *Tigereye*
AIRBORNE EARLY WARNING & CONTROL
  1 sqn with E-2T *Hawkeye*
SEARCH & RESCUE
  1 sqn with H225; UH-60M *Black Hawk*
TRANSPORT
  2 sqn with C-130H *Hercules*
  1 (VIP) sqn with B-727-100; B-737-800; Beech 1900; F-50; S-70C *Black Hawk*

TRAINING
  1 sqn with AT-3A/B *Tzu-Chung**
  1 sqn with Beech 1900
  1 (basic) sqn with T-34C *Turbo Mentor*
EQUIPMENT BY TYPE
AIRCRAFT 479 combat capable
  FTR 285: 87 F-5E/F *Tiger* II (some in store); up to 139 F-16A/B *Fighting Falcon*; 4 F-16V *Fighting Falcon*; 9 *Mirage* 2000-5D (2000-5DI); 46 *Mirage* 2000-5E (2000-5EI)
  FGA 127 F-CK-1C/D *Ching Kuo*
  ASW 12 P-3C *Orion*
  EW 1 C-130HE *Tien Gian*
  ISR 7 RF-5E *Tigereye*
  AEW&C 6 E-2T *Hawkeye*
  TPT 33: **Medium** 19 C-130H *Hercules*; **Light** 10 Beech 1900; **PAX** 4: 1 B-737-800; 3 F-50
  TRG 97: 55 AT-3A/B *Tzu-Chung**; 42 T-34C *Turbo Mentor*
HELICOPTERS
  TPT • **Medium** 18: 3 H225; 15 UH-60M *Black Hawk*
AIR-LAUNCHED MISSILES
  AAM • **IR** AIM-9J/P *Sidewinder*; R-550 *Magic* 2; *Shafrir*; *Sky Sword* I; **IIR** AIM-9X *Sidewinder* II; **IR/ARH** *Mica*; **ARH** AIM-120C AMRAAM; *Sky Sword* II
  ASM AGM-65A *Maverick*
  AShM AGM-84 *Harpoon*
  ARM *Sky Sword* IIA
  LACM Conventional *Wan Chien*
BOMBS • **Laser-guided** *Paveway* II

Air Defence and Missile Command
FORCES BY ROLE
SURFACE-TO-SURFACE MISSILE
  1 GLCM bde (2 GLCM bn with *Hsiung Feng* IIE)
AIR DEFENCE
  1 (792) SAM bde (1 SAM bn with *Tien Kung* III; 2 ADA bn)
  2 (793 & 794) SAM bde (1 SAM bn with Tien Kung II; 1 SAM bn with MIM-104F *Patriot* PAC-3; 1 SAM bn with MIM-23 *Hawk*)
  1 (795) SAM bde (1 SAM bn with MIM-104F *Patriot* PAC-3; 2 ADA bn)
EQUIPMENT BY TYPE
SURFACE-TO-SURFACE MISSILE LAUNCHERS
  GLCM • **Conventional** ε12 *Hsiung Feng* IIE
AIR DEFENCE
  SAM
    Long-range 122+: 72+ MIM-104F *Patriot* PAC-3; ε50 *Tien Kung* II
    Medium-range 50 MIM-23 *Hawk*
    Short-range 30 RIM-7M *Sparrow* with *Skyguard*
    Point-defence *Antelope*
  GUNS • **20mm** some T-82; **35mm** 20+ GDF-006 with *Skyguard*
  MISSILE DEFENCE *Tien Kung* III

Paramilitary 11,450

Coast Guard 11,450
EQUIPMENT BY TYPE
PATROL AND COASTAL COMBATANTS 161
  PSOH 4: 2 *Tainan*; 2 *Yilan*

PSO 6: 4 *Miaoli* with 1 hel landing platform; 2 *Ho Hsing*
PCO 13: 2 *Kinmen*; 2 *Mou Hsing*; 3 *Shun Hu 7*; 4 *Taichung*; 2 *Taipei*
PBF ε56 (various)
PB 82: 1 *Shun Hu 6*; ε81 (various)

FOREIGN FORCES
Singapore 3 trg camp (incl inf and arty)

Thailand THA

Thai Baht b		2018	2019	2020
GDP	b	16.3tr	16.9tr	
	US$	505bn	529bn	
per capita	US$	7,448	7,792	
Growth	%	4.1	2.9	
Inflation	%	1.1	0.9	
Def bdgt	b	217bn	227bn	233bn
	US$	6.72bn	7.10bn	
US$1=b		32.32	31.98	

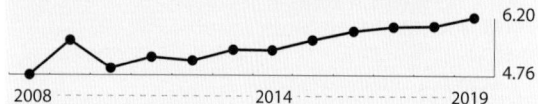
Real-terms defence budget trend (US$bn, constant 2015)

Population 68,804,427

Ethnic and religious groups: Thai 75%; Chinese 14%; Muslim 4%

Age	0–14	15–19	20–24	25–29	30–64	65 plus
Male	8.5%	3.2%	3.7%	3.8%	24.9%	5.0%
Female	8.1%	3.0%	3.6%	3.7%	26.2%	6.4%

Capabilities

Thailand has large, well-funded armed forces and its air force is one of the best equipped and trained in Southeast Asia. The Vision 2026 defence-modernisation plan, approved by the defence council in October 2017, outlines the armed forces' capability improvements over the next decade. Thailand is considered a major non-NATO ally by the US, while the country has developed deeper defence ties with China since the military coup in 2014. The armed forces regularly take part in international military exercises. A small number of personnel remain deployed on the UNAMID mission to Darfur, Sudan. The military-modernisation effort includes the development of submarines, anti-submarine-warfare capabilities and a surface-ship procurement programme. The armoured vehicle fleet has been recapitalised with deliveries from China and Ukraine. The arrival of Saab 340 AEW aircraft, *Gripen* combat aircraft and a command-and-control system has provided a step change in air capability. The armed forces are looking to create a space-operations centre. Under its Defence Industry Masterplan, the government indicates that expanding Thailand's presently limited defence sector can be an important way of developing military capability. The government is making efforts to reform defence procurement and offsets by expanding the role of its Defence Technology Institute.

ACTIVE 360,850 (Army 245,000 Navy 69,850 Air 46,000) **Paramilitary 93,700**
Conscription liability 24 months

RESERVE 200,000 Paramilitary 45,000

ORGANISATIONS BY SERVICE

Army 130,000; ε115,000 conscript (total 245,000)

FORCES BY ROLE
COMMAND
 4 (regional) army HQ
 3 corps HQ
SPECIAL FORCES
 1 SF div
 1 SF regt
MANOEUVRE
 Armoured
 3 cav div (1 recce bn; 3 tk regt (3 tk bn); 1 indep tk bn; 1 sigs bn; 1 maint bn; 1 hel sqn)
 Mechanised
 1 mech inf div (1 recce coy; 1 recce sqn; 1 tk bn; 1 inf regt (4 inf bn); 3 inf regt; 1 engr bn; 1 sigs bn)
 Light
 8 inf div (1 recce sqn; 3 inf regt (3 inf bn); 1 engr bn; 1 sigs bn)
COMBAT SUPPORT
 1 arty div
 1 engr div
COMBAT SERVICE SUPPORT
 4 economic development div
HELICOPTER
 Some hel flt
ISR UAV
 1 UAV bn with *Hermes* 450; *Searcher* II
AIR DEFENCE
 1 ADA div (6 bn)

EQUIPMENT BY TYPE
ARMOURED FIGHTING VEHICLES
 MBT 360: 53 M60A1; 125 M60A3; 105 M48A5; 49 T-84 *Oplot*; 28 VT-4; (50 Type-69 in store)
 LT TK 194: 24 M41; 104 *Scorpion* (50 in store); 66 *Stingray*
 RECCE 32 S52 *Shorland*
 IFV 168 BTR-3E1
 APC 1,150
  APC (T) 880: *Bronco*; 430 M113A1/A3; 450 Type-85
  APC (W) 170: 9 BTR-3K (CP); 6 BTR-3C (amb); 18 *Condor*; 142 LAV-150 *Commando*; 10 M1126 *Stryker* ICV
 PPV 100 REVA
ENGINEERING & MAINTENANCE VEHICLES
 ARV 58: 2 BREM-84 *Atlet*; 13 BTR-3BR; 22 M88A1; 6 M88A2; 10 M113; 5 Type-653; WZT-4
 VLB Type-84
 MW *Bozena*; *Giant Viper*
ANTI-TANK/ANTI-INFRASTRUCTURE
 MSL
  SP 30+: 18+ M901A5 (TOW); 12 BTR-3RK
  MANPATS M47 *Dragon*
 RCL 180: 75mm 30 M20; 106mm 150 M40
ARTILLERY 2,643
 SP 155mm 32: 6 ATMOS-2000; 6 CAESAR; 20 M109A5
 TOWED 617: 105mm 340: 24 LG1 MkII; 12 M-56; 200 M101/M425; 12 M102; 32 M618A2; 60 L119 Light Gun; 155mm 277: 90 GHN-45 A1; 48 M114; 118 M198; 21 M-71

MRL 68: **122mm** 4 SR-4; **130mm** 60 PHZ-85; **302mm** 4: 1 DTI-1 (WS-1B); 3 DTI-1G (WS-32)
MOR 1,926+: SP **81mm** 39: 18 BTR-3M1; 21 M125A3; SP **107mm** M106A3; **SP 120mm** 20: 8 BTR-3M2; 12 M1064A3; 1,867 **81mm/107mm/120mm**

AIRCRAFT
TPT • **Light** 19: 2 Beech 200 *King Air*; 2 Beech 1900C; 1 C-212 *Aviocar*; 1 C295W; 9 Cessna A185E (U-17B); 2 ERJ-135LR; 2 *Jetstream* 41
TRG 33: 11 MX-7-235 *Star Rocket*; 22 T-41B *Mescalero*

HELICOPTERS
ATK 7 AH-1F *Cobra*
MRH 17: 8 AS550 *Fennec*; 2 AW139; 7 Mi-17V-5 *Hip* H
TPT 216: **Heavy** 5 CH-47D *Chinook*; **Medium** 12: 9 UH-60L *Black Hawk*; 3 UH-60M *Black Hawk*; **Light** 199: 93 Bell 205 (UH-1H *Iroquois*); 27 Bell 206 *Jet Ranger*; 52 Bell 212 (AB-212); 16 Enstrom 480B; 6 H145M (VIP tpt); 5 UH-72A *Lakota*
TRG 53 Hughes 300C

UNMANNED AERIAL VEHICLES
ISR • **Medium** 4+: 4 *Hermes* 450; *Searcher*; *Searcher* II

AIR DEFENCE
SAM
  Short-range *Aspide*
  Point-defence 8+: 8 *Starstreak*; 9K338 *Igla-S* (SA-24 *Grinch*)
GUNS 184
  SP 54: **20mm** 24 M163 *Vulcan*; **40mm** 30 M1/M42 SP
  TOWED 138: **20mm** 24 M167 *Vulcan*; **35mm** 8 GDF-007 with *Skyguard* 3; **37mm** 52 Type-74; **40mm** 48 L/70; **57mm** ε6 Type-59 (S-60) (18+ more non-operational)

Reserves
FORCES BY ROLE
COMMAND
1 inf div HQ

Navy 44,000 (incl Naval Aviation, Marines, Coastal Defence); 25,850 conscript (total 69,850)

EQUIPMENT BY TYPE
PRINCIPAL SURFACE COMBATANTS 10
  AIRCRAFT CARRIERS • **CVH** 1 *Chakri Naruebet* with 3 sextuple *Sadral* lnchr with *Mistral* SAM (capacity 6 S-70B *Seahawk* ASW hel)
  FRIGATES 9
    FFGHM 3:
      2 *Naresuan* with 2 quad lnchr with RGM-84 *Harpoon* AShM, 1 8 cell Mk 41 VLS with RIM-162B ESSM SAM, 2 triple SVTT Mk 32 324mm TT with Mk 46 LWT, 1 127mm gun (capacity 1 *Super Lynx* 300 hel)
      1 *Bhumibol Adulyadej* (DW3000F) with 2 quad lnchr with RGM-84L *Harpoon* Block II AShM, 1 8-cell Mk 41 VLS with RIM-162B ESSM SAM, 2 triple SEA TLS 324mm ASTT with Mk 54 LWT, 1 Mk 15 *Phalanx* Block 1B CIWS, 1 76mm gun (capacity 1 med hel)
    FFG 4:
      2 *Chao Phraya* (trg role) with 4 twin lnchr with C-802A AShM, 2 RBU 1200 *Uragan* A/S mor, 2 twin 100mm gun
      2 *Chao Phraya* with 4 twin lnchr with C-802A AShM, 2 RBU 1200 *Uragan* A/S mor, 1 twin 100mm gun, 1 hel landing platform
    FF 2:
      1 *Makut Rajakumarn* with 2 triple 324mm ASTT, 2 114mm gun
      1 *Pin Klao* (ex-US *Cannon*) (trg role) with 6 single SVTT Mk 32 324mm ASTT, 3 76mm gun

PATROL AND COASTAL COMBATANTS 83
  CORVETTES 8
    FSGM 2 *Rattanakosin* with 2 twin lnchr with RGM-84 *Harpoon* AShM, 1 octuple *Albatros* lnchr with *Aspide* SAM, 2 triple SVTT Mk 32 324mm ASTT with *Stingray* LWT, 1 76mm gun
    FSG 1 *Krabi* (UK *River* mod) with 2 twin lnchr with RGM-84L *Harpoon* Block II AShM, 1 76mm gun
    FS 5:
      3 *Khamronsin* with 2 triple 324mm ASTT with *Stingray* LWT, 1 76mm gun
      2 *Tapi* with 2 triple SVTT Mk 32 324mm ASTT with Mk 46 LWT, 1 76mm gun
  PSO 1 *Krabi* (UK *River* mod) with 1 76mm gun
  PCFG 4:
    3 *Prabparapak* with 2 single lnchr with *Gabriel* I AShM, 1 triple lnchr with *Gabriel* I AShM, 1 57mm gun
    1 *Ratcharit* with 2 twin lnchr with MM38 *Exocet* AShM, 1 76mm gun
  PCOH 2 *Pattani* (1 in trg role) with 1 76mm gun
  PCO 4: 3 *Hua Hin* with 1 76mm gun; 1 M58 Patrol Gun Boat with 1 76mm gun
  PCC 9: 3 *Chon Buri* with 2 76mm gun; 6 *Sattahip* with 1 76mm gun
  PBF 4 M18 Fast Assault Craft (capacity 18 troops)
  PB 51: 1 T-11 (US PGM-71); 3 T-81; 6 T-91; 3 M36 Patrol Boat; 13 T-213; 1 T-227; 18 M21 Patrol Boat; 3 T-991; 3 T-994

MINE WARFARE • MINE COUNTERMEASURES 17
  MCCS 1 *Thalang*
  MCO 2 *Lat Ya*
  MCC 2 *Bang Rachan*
  MSR 12: 7 T1; 5 T6

AMPHIBIOUS
  PRINCIPAL AMPHIBIOUS SHIPS 1
    LPD 1 *Angthong* (SGP *Endurance*) with 1 76mm gun (capacity 2 hel; 19 MBT; 500 troops)
  LANDING SHIPS 2
    LST 2 *Sichang* with 2 hel landing platform (capacity 14 MBT; 300 troops)
  LANDING CRAFT 14
    LCU 9: 3 *Man Nok*; 2 *Mataphun* (capacity either 3–4 MBT or 250 troops); 4 *Thong Kaeo*
    LCM 2
    UCAC 3 *Griffon* 1000TD

LOGISTICS AND SUPPORT 13
  ABU 1 *Suriya*
  AGOR 1 *Sok*
  AGS 2
  AOL 6: 1 *Matra* with 1 hel landing platform; 3 *Proet*; 1 *Prong*; 1 *Samui*
  AOR 1 *Chula*

AORH 1 *Similan* (capacity 1 hel)
AWT 1

Naval Aviation 1,200
EQUIPMENT BY TYPE
AIRCRAFT 3 combat capable
  ASW 2 P-3A *Orion* (P-3T)
  ISR 9 *Sentry* O-2-337
  MP 1 F-27-200 MPA*
  TPT • Light 15: 7 Do-228-212; 2 ERJ-135LR; 2 F-27-400M *Troopship*; 3 N-24A *Searchmaster*; 1 UP-3A *Orion* (UP-3T)
HELICOPTERS
  ASW 8: 6 S-70B *Seahawk*; 2 *Super Lynx* 300
  MRH 2 MH-60S *Knight Hawk*
  TPT 18: **Medium** 2 Bell 214ST (AB-214ST); **Light** 16: 6 Bell 212 (AB-212); 5 H145M; 5 S-76B
AIR-LAUNCHED MISSILES • AShM AGM-84 *Harpoon*

Marines 23,000
FORCES BY ROLE
COMMAND
  1 mne div HQ
MANOEUVRE
  Reconnaissance
  1 recce bn
  Light
  2 inf regt (total: 6 bn)
  Amphibious
  1 amph aslt bn
COMBAT SUPPORT
  1 arty regt (3 fd arty bn, 1 ADA bn)
EQUIPMENT BY TYPE
ARMOURED FIGHTING VEHICLES
  IFV 14 BTR-3E1
  APC (W) 24 LAV-150 *Commando*
  AAV 33 LVTP-7
ENGINEERING & MAINTENANCE VEHICLES
  ARV 1 AAVR-7
ANTI-TANK/ANTI-INFRASTRUCTURE • MSL
  SP 10 M1045A2 HMMWV with TOW
  MANPATS M47 *Dragon*; TOW
ARTILLERY • TOWED 48: **105mm** 36 (reported); **155mm** 12 GC-45
AIR DEFENCE
  SAM Point-defence QW-18
  GUNS 12.7mm 14

Naval Special Warfare Command

Air Force ε46,000
4 air divs, one flying trg school
FORCES BY ROLE
FIGHTER
  2 sqn with F-5E/5F *Tiger* II
  3 sqn with F-16A/B *Fighting Falcon*
FIGHTER/GROUND ATTACK
  1 sqn with *Gripen* C/D
GROUND ATTACK
  1 sqn with *Alpha Jet**
  1 sqn with AU-23A *Peacemaker*
  1 sqn with L-39ZA *Albatros**; T-50TH *Golden Eagle**
ELINT/ISR
  1 sqn with DA42 MPP *Guardian*
AIRBORNE EARLY WARNING & CONTROL
  1 sqn with Saab 340B; Saab 340 *Erieye*
TRANSPORT
  1 (Royal Flight) sqn with A319CJ; A340-500; B-737-800
  1 sqn with ATR-72; BAe-748
  1 sqn with BT-67
  1 sqn with C-130H/H-30 *Hercules*
TRAINING
  1 sqn with L-39ZA *Albatros**
  1 sqn with CT-4A/B *Airtrainer*; T-41D *Mescalero*
  1 sqn with CT-4E *Airtrainer*
  1 sqn with PC-9
TRANSPORT HELICOPTER
  1 sqn with Bell 205 (UH-1H *Iroquois*)
  1 sqn with Bell 412 *Twin Huey*; S-92A
EQUIPMENT BY TYPE
AIRCRAFT 151 combat capable
  FTR 78: 1 F-5B *Freedom Fighter*; 20 F-5E *Tiger* II; 2 F-5F *Tiger* II (F-5E/F being upgraded); 1 F-5TH(E) *Tiger* II; 1 F-5TH(F) *Tiger* II; 38 F-16A *Fighting Falcon*; 15 F-16B *Fighting Falcon*
  FGA 11: 7 *Gripen* C; 4 *Gripen* D
  ATK 16 AU-23A *Peacemaker*
  ISR 5 DA42 MPP *Guardian*
  AEW&C 2 Saab 340 *Erieye*
  ELINT 2 Saab 340 *Erieye* (COMINT/ELINT)
  TPT 42: **Medium** 14: 6 C-130H *Hercules*; 6 C-130H-30 *Hercules*; 2 Saab 340B; **Light** 21: 3 ATR-72; 3 Beech 200 *King Air*; 8 BT-67; 1 *Commander* 690; 6 DA42M; **PAX** 7: 1 A319CJ; 1 A320CJ; 1 A340-500; 1 B-737-800; 3 SSJ-100-95LR (1 A310-324 in store)
  TRG 113: 16 *Alpha Jet**; 13 CT-4A *Airtrainer*; 6 CT-4B *Airtrainer*; 20 CT-4E *Airtrainer*; 26 L-39ZA *Albatros**; 21 PC-9; 7 T-41D *Mescalero*; 4 T-50TH *Golden Eagle**
HELICOPTERS
  MRH 11: 2 Bell 412 *Twin Huey*; 2 Bell 412SP *Twin Huey*; 1 Bell 412HP *Twin Huey*; 6 Bell 412EP *Twin Huey*
  CSAR 8 H225M *Super Cougar*
  TPT 20: **Medium** 3 S-92A *Super Hawk*; **Light** 17 Bell 205 (UH-1H *Iroquois*)
UNMANNED AERIAL VEHICLES • ISR • Light U-1
AIR-LAUNCHED MISSILES
  AAM • IR AIM-9P/S *Sidewinder*; *Python* 3; **IIR** IRIS-T; **ARH** AIM-120 AMRAAM
  ASM AGM-65 *Maverick*
  AShM RBS15F
BOMBS
  Laser-guided *Paveway* II
  INS/GPS-guided GBU-38 JDAM

Paramilitary ε93,700

Border Patrol Police 20,000

Marine Police 2,200
EQUIPMENT BY TYPE
PATROL AND COASTAL COMBATANTS 98

PCO 1 *Srinakrin*
PCC 2 *Hameln*
PB 49: 2 *Chasanyabadee*; 3 *Cutlass*; 2 *Ratayapibanbancha* (*Reef Ranger*); 1 *Sriyanont*; 41 (various)
PBR 46

National Security Volunteer Corps 45,000 – Reserves

Police Aviation 500
EQUIPMENT BY TYPE
AIRCRAFT 6 combat capable
ATK 6 AU-23A *Peacemaker*
TPT 16: **Light** 15: 2 CN235; 8 PC-6 *Turbo-Porter*; 3 SC-7 3M *Skyvan*; 2 Short 330UTT; **PAX** 1 F-50
HELICOPTERS
MRH 12: 6 Bell 412 *Twin Huey*; 6 Bell 429
TPT • **Light** 61: 27 Bell 205A; 14 Bell 206 *Jet Ranger*; 20 Bell 212 (AB-212)

Provincial Police 50,000 (incl ε500 Special Action Force)

Thahan Phran (Hunter Soldiers) 21,000
Volunteer irregular force
FORCES BY ROLE
MANOEUVRE
Other
22 paramilitary regt (total: 275 paramilitary coy)

DEPLOYMENT
INDIA/PAKISTAN: UN • UNMOGIP 4
SOUTH SUDAN: UN • UNMISS 278; 1 engr coy

FOREIGN FORCES
United States US Pacific Command: 300

Timor-Leste TLS

US$		2018	2019	2020
GDP	US$	2.75bn	2.94bn	
per capita	US$	2,164	2,263	
Growth	%	-0.2	4.5	
Inflation	%	2.3	2.5	
Def bdgt	US$	20.6m	31.3m	

Real-terms defence budget trend (US$m, constant 2015)

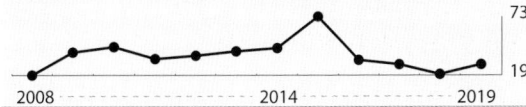

Population	1,352,718				
Age	0–14	15–19	20–24	25–29	30–64	65 plus
Male	20.6%	5.8%	4.6%	3.8%	13.2%	1.9%
Female	19.5%	5.6%	4.5%	4.0%	14.3%	2.1%

Capabilities

The small Timor-Leste Defence Force (F-FDTL) has been afflicted by funding, personnel and morale challenges since it was established in 2001. The F-FDTL has been reconstituted but is still a long way from meeting the ambitious force-structure goals set out in the Force 2020 plan published in 2007. In 2016, the government published a Strategic Defence and Security Concept (SDSC). This outlined the roles of the F-FDTL as including the protection of the country from external threats and combating violent crime. However, this parallel internal-security role has sometimes brought it into conflict with the national police force. The SDSC also stated that the F-FDTL needs to improve its naval capabilities, owing to the size of Timor-Leste's exclusive economic zone. The origins of the F-FDTL in the Falintil national resistance force, and continuing training and doctrinal emphasis on low-intensity infantry tactics, mean that the force provides a deterrent to invasion. In 2017, Portugal and Timor-Leste signed a defence-cooperation agreement up to 2022. The F-FDTL sometimes receives training from Australian and US personnel. Australia is also donating two *Guardian*-class patrol vessels as part of its Pacific Patrol Boat Replacement programme, which are due to arrive in 2023. Maintenance capacity is unclear and the country has no traditional defence industry.

ACTIVE 2,280 (Army 2,200 Naval Element 80)

ORGANISATIONS BY SERVICE

Army 2,200
Training began in January 2001 with the aim of deploying 1,500 full-time personnel and 1,500 reservists. Authorities are engaged in developing security structures with international assistance
FORCES BY ROLE
MANOEUVRE
Light
2 inf bn
COMBAT SUPPORT
1 MP pl
COMBAT SERVICE SUPPORT
1 log spt coy

Naval Element 80
EQUIPMENT BY TYPE
PATROL AND COASTAL COMBATANTS 7
PB 7: 2 *Albatros*; 2 *Dili* (ex-ROK); 2 *Shanghai* II; 1 *Kamenassa* (ex-ROK *Chamsuri*)

Air Component
EQUIPMENT BY TYPE
AIRCRAFT • TPT • **Light** 1 Cessna 172

Vietnam VNM

Vietnamese Dong d		2018	2019	2020
GDP	d	5535tr	6085tr	
	US$	241bn	262bn	
per capita	US$	2,551	2,740	
Growth	%	7.1	6.5	
Inflation	%	3.5	3.6	
Def bdgt	d	ε110tr	ε121tr	
	US$	ε4.80bn	ε5.21bn	
FMA (US)	US$	12.0m	12.0m	45m
US$1=d		22942.02	23257.65	

Real-terms defence budget trend (US$bn, constant 2015)

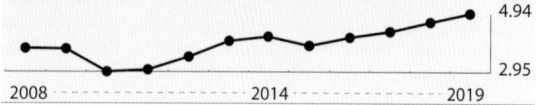

Population	97,894,734

Ethnic groups: Kinh 85.7%; Tay 1.9%; Thai 1.8%; Khome 1.4%; Hmong 1.3%; other or unspecified 7.1%

Age	0–14	15–19	20–24	25–29	30–64	65 plus
Male	12.1%	4.0%	4.1%	4.6%	22.8%	2.6%
Female	10.9%	3.6%	3.8%	4.4%	23.2%	4.0%

Capabilities

Vietnam has a stronger military tradition and its armed forces have more operational experience than any of its neighbours. Its defence efforts and armed forces also benefit from broad popular support, particularly in the context of tensions with China over conflicting claims in the South China Sea. Vietnam released its new defence white paper in late 2019, which reiterated the country's non-aligned policy. Hanoi nonetheless looks to diversify its security partnerships. Vietnam adopted a new Law on National Defence in 2018 that focused, among other areas, on information warfare. Hanoi is also looking to diversify its security partnerships. Washington lifted its arms embargo on Vietnam in 2016, while New Delhi and Seoul are understood to be seeking inroads into Vietnam's defence market. The forces are conscript-based, and there is a plan to reduce their numbers in the armed forces and other institutions, such as military colleges and hospitals, by 2022. Recapitalisation efforts have focused on the navy and air force, mainly with a view to disputes in the Spratly Islands. While Hanoi cannot hope to balance China's power on its own, the recent development of a submarine capability and the procurement of additional Su-30MK2 combat aircraft and new air-defence capabilities would complicate Beijing's military options. Vietnam may also be looking to procure assets that would increase its surveillance capacities in the South China Sea, such as UAVs. In addition, the coastguard's capabilities are being enhanced. Vietnam is developing its limited defence-industrial capacities, with the launch of a defence-focused subsidiary to state-owned Viettel Military Industry and Telecoms Group. Called Viettel High Technology Industries Corporation, it will focus on defence electronics and communications.

ACTIVE 482,000 (Army 412,000 Navy 40,000 Air 30,000) Paramilitary 40,000

Conscript liability 2 years army and air defence, 3 years air force and navy, specialists 3 years, some ethnic minorities 2 years

RESERVES Paramilitary 5,000,000

ORGANISATIONS BY SERVICE

Space
EQUIPMENT BY TYPE
SATELLITES • ISR 1 VNREDSat

Army ε412,000
8 Mil Regions (incl capital)
FORCES BY ROLE
COMMAND
  4 corps HQ
SPECIAL FORCES
  1 SF bde (1 AB bde, 1 demolition engr regt)
MANOEUVRE
  Armoured
  9 armd bde
  Mechanised
  2 mech inf div
  Light
  23 inf div
SURFACE-TO-SURFACE MISSILE
  1 SRBM bde
COMBAT SUPPORT
  13 arty bde
  1 arty regt
  11 engr bde
  1 engr regt
  1 EW unit
  3 sigs bde
  2 sigs regt
COMBAT SERVICE SUPPORT
  9 economic construction div
  1 log regt
  1 med unit
  1 trg regt
AIR DEFENCE
  11 AD bde

Reserve
FORCES BY ROLE
MANOEUVRE
  Light
  9 inf div
EQUIPMENT BY TYPE
ARMOURED FIGHTING VEHICLES
  MBT 1,379: 45 T-34; 850 T-54/T-55; 70 T-62; 64 T-90S; 350 Type-59;
  LT TK 620: 300 PT-76; 320 Type-62/Type-63
  RECCE 100 BRDM-1/BRDM-2
  IFV 300 BMP-1/BMP-2
  APC 1,380+
    APC (T) 280+: Some BTR-50; 200 M113 (to be upgraded); 80 Type-63
    APC (W) 1,100 BTR-40/BTR-60/BTR-152
ENGINEERING & MAINTENANCE VEHICLES
  AEV IMR-2
  ARV BREM-1M
  VLB TMM-3

ANTI-TANK/ANTI-INFRASTRUCTURE
MSL • MANPATS 9K11 *Malyutka* (AT-3 *Sagger*)
RCL **75mm** Type-56; **82mm** Type-65 (B-10); **87mm** Type-51
GUNS
SP **100mm** SU-100; **122mm** SU-122
TOWED **100mm** T-12 (arty); M-1944
ARTILLERY 3,040+
SP 30+: **122mm** 2S1 *Gvozdika*; **152mm** 30 2S3 *Akatsiya*; **175mm** M107
TOWED 2,300: **105mm** M101/M102; **122mm** D-30/Type-54 (M-1938)/Type-60 (D-74); **130mm** M-46; **152mm** D-20; **155mm** M114
MRL 710+: **107mm** 360 Type-63; **122mm** 350 BM-21 *Grad*; **140mm** BM-14
MOR **82mm**; **120mm** M-1943; **160mm** M-1943
SURFACE-TO-SURFACE MISSILE LAUNCHERS
SRBM • Coventional *Scud*-B/C
AIR DEFENCE
SAM • Point-defence 9K32 *Strela*-2 (SA-7 *Grail*)‡; 9K310 *Igla*-1 (SA-16 *Gimlet*); 9K38 *Igla* (SA-18 *Grouse*)
GUNS 12,000
SP **23mm** ZSU-23-4
TOWED **14.5mm/30mm/37mm/57mm/85mm/100mm**

Navy ε40,000 (incl ε27,000 Naval Infantry)
EQUIPMENT BY TYPE
SUBMARINES • TACTICAL 8
SSK 6 *Hanoi* (RUS *Varshavyanka*) with 6 533mm TT with 3M14E *Klub*-S (SS-N-30B) LACM/3M54E1/E *Klub*-S (SS-N-27A/B) AShM (*Klub*-S AShM variant unclear)/53-65KE HWT/TEST-71ME HWT
SSI 2 *Yugo* (DPRK)
PRINCIPAL SURFACE COMBATANTS 4
FRIGATES • FFGM 4
2 *Dinh Tien Hoang* (RUS *Gepard* 3.9 (Project 11661E)) with 2 quad lnchr with 3M24E *Uran*-E (SS-N-25 *Switchblade*) AShM, 1 3M89E *Palma* (*Palash*) CIWS with *Sosna*-R SAM (CADS-N-2), 2 AK630M CIWS, 1 76mm gun, 1 hel landing platform
2 *Tran Hung Dao* (RUS *Gepard* 3.9 (Project 11661E)) with 2 quad lnchr with 3M24E *Uran*-E (SS-N-25 *Switchblade*), 1 3M89E *Palma* (*Palash*) CIWS with *Sosna*-R SAM (CADS-N-2), 2 twin 533mm TT with SET-53M HWT, 2 AK630M CIWS, 1 76mm gun, 1 hel landing platform
PATROL AND COASTAL COMBATANTS 72
CORVETTES 8:
FSGM 1 BPS-500 with 2 quad lnchr with 3M24E *Uran*-E (SS-N-25 *Switchblade*) AShM, 1 9K32 *Strela*-2M (SA-N-5 *Grail*) SAM (manually operated), 2 twin 533mm TT, 1 RBU 1600 A/S mor, 1 AK630 CIWS, 1 76mm gun
FSG 1 *Po Hang* (Flight III) (ex-ROK) with 2 quad lnchr with 3M24E *Uran*-E (SS-N-25 *Switchblade*) AShM, 2 76mm guns
FS 6:
3 *Petya* II (FSU) with 1 quintuple 406mm ASTT, 4 RBU 6000 *Smerch* 2 A/S mor, 2 twin 76mm gun

2 *Petya* III (FSU) with 1 triple 533mm ASTT with SET-53ME HWT, 4 RBU 2500 *Smerch* 1 A/S mor, 2 twin 76mm gun
1 *Po Hang* (Flight III) (ex-ROK) with 2 76mm guns
PCFGM 12:
4 *Tarantul* (FSU) with 2 twin lnchr with P-15 *Termit*-R (SS-N-2D *Styx*) AShM, 1 quad lnchr with 9K32 *Strela*-2M (SA-N-5 *Grail*) SAM (manually operated), 2 AK630M CIWS, 1 76mm gun
8 *Tarantul* V with 4 quad lnchr with 3M24E *Uran*-E (SS-N-25 *Switchblade*) AShM, 1 quad lnchr with 9K32 *Strela*-2M (SA-N-5 *Grail*) SAM (manually operated), 2 AK630M CIWS, 1 76mm gun
PCO 7: 1 Project FC264; 6 TT-400TP with 2 AK630M CIWS, 1 76mm gun
PCC 6 *Svetlyak* with 1 AK630M CIWS, 1 76mm gun
PBFG 8 *Osa* II with 4 single lnchr with P-20U (SS-N-2B *Styx*) AShM
PBFT 2 *Shershen*† (FSU) with 4 single 533mm TT
PH 2 *Turya*† with 1 twin 57mm gun
PHT 3 *Turya*† with 4 single 533mm TT, 1 twin 57mm gun
PB 20: 14 *Zhuk*†; 4 *Zhuk* (mod); 2 TP-01
PBR 4 *Stolkraft*
MINE WARFARE • MINE COUNTERMEASURES 13
MSO 2 *Yurka*
MSC 4 *Sonya*
MHI 2 *Korund* (*Yevgenya*) (Project 1258)
MSR 5 K-8
AMPHIBIOUS
LANDING SHIPS 7
LSM 5:
1 *Polnochny* A (capacity 6 Lt Tk/APC; 200 troops)
2 *Polnochny* B (capacity 6 Lt Tk/APC; 200 troops)
2 *Nau Dinh*
LST 2 *Tran Khanh Du* (ex-US LST 542) with 1 hel landing platform (capacity 16 Lt Tk/APC; 140 troops)
LANDING CRAFT • LCM 12
8 LCM 6 (capacity 1 Lt Tk or 80 troops)
4 LCM 8 (capacity 1 MBT or 200 troops)
LOGISTICS AND SUPPORT 27
AFD 2
AGS 1 *Tran Dai Nia* (Damen Research Vessel 6613)
AGSH 1
AKSL 18
AP 1 *Truong Sa*
AT 2
AWT 1
AXS 1 *Le Quy Don*

Naval Infantry ε27,000
EQUIPMENT BY TYPE
ARMOURED FIGHTING VEHICLES
LT TK PT-76; Type-63
APC • APC (W) BTR-60

Coastal Defence
FORCES BY ROLE
COASTAL DEFENCE
3 AShM bde
1 coastal arty bde

EQUIPMENT BY TYPE
COASTAL DEFENCE • AShM 4K44 *Redut* (SSC-1B *Sepal*); 4K51 *Rubezh* (SSC-3 *Styx*); K-300P *Bastion*-P (SSC-5 *Stooge*)
ARTILLERY • MRL 160mm AccuLAR-160; **306mm** EXTRA

Navy Air Wing
FORCES BY ROLE
ASW/SAR
  1 regt with H225; Ka-28 (Ka-27PL) *Helix* A; Ka-32 *Helix* C
EQUIPMENT BY TYPE
AIRCRAFT • TPT • Light 6 DHC-6-400 *Twin Otter*
HELICOPTERS
  ASW 10 Ka-28 *Helix* A
  TPT • Medium 4: 2 H225; 2 Ka-32 *Helix* C

Air Force 30,000
3 air div, 1 tpt bde
FORCES BY ROLE
FIGHTER/GROUND ATTACK
  3 regt with Su-22M3/M4/UM *Fitter* (some ISR)
  1 regt with Su-27SK/Su-27UBK *Flanker*
  1 regt with Su-27SK/Su-27UBK *Flanker*; Su-30MK2 *Flanker*
  2 regt with Su-30MK2 *Flanker*
TRANSPORT
  2 regt with An-2 *Colt*; An-26 *Curl*; Bell 205 (UH-1H *Iroquois*); Mi-8 *Hip*; Mi-17 *Hip* H; M-28 *Bryza*
TRAINING
  1 regt with L-39 *Albatros*
  1 regt with Yak-52
ATTACK/TRANSPORT HELICOPTER
  2 regt with Mi-8 *Hip*; Mi-17 *Hip* H; Mi-171; Mi-24 *Hind*
AIR DEFENCE
  6 AD div HQ
  2 SAM regt with S-300PMU1 (SA-20 *Gargoyle*)
  2 SAM regt with *Spyder*-MR
  3 SAM regt with S-75 *Dvina* (SA-2 *Guideline*)
  4 SAM regt with S-135-2TM *Pechora* (SA-26)
  5 ADA regt
EQUIPMENT BY TYPE
AIRCRAFT 72 combat capable
  FGA 72: 26 Su-22M3/M4/UM *Fitter* (some ISR); 6 Su-27SK *Flanker*; 5 Su-27UBK *Flanker*; 35 Su-30MK2 *Flanker*
  TPT • Light 24: 6 An-2 *Colt*; 12 An-26 *Curl*; 3 C295M; 1 M-28 *Bryza*; 2 C-212 *Aviocar* (NC-212i)
  TRG 47: 17 L-39 *Albatros*; 30 Yak-52
HELICOPTERS
  MRH 6 Mi-17 *Hip* H
  TPT 28: **Medium** 17: 14 Mi-8 *Hip*; 3 Mi-171; **Light** 11 Bell 205 (UH-1H *Iroquois*)
AIR DEFENCE
  SAM 12+:
    Long-range 12 S-300PMU1 (SA-20 *Gargoyle*)
    Medium-range S-75 *Dvina* (SA-2 *Guideline*); S-125-2TM *Pechora* (SA-26), *Spyder*-MR
    Short-range 2K12 *Kub* (SA-6 *Gainful*);
    Point-defence 9K32 *Strela*-2 (SA-7 *Grail*)‡; 9K310 *Igla*-1 (SA-16 *Gimlet*)
  GUNS 37mm; 57mm; 85mm; 100mm; 130mm
AIR-LAUNCHED MISSILES
  AAM • IR R-60 (AA-8 *Aphid*); R-73 (AA-11A *Archer*); **IR/SARH** R-27 (AA-10 *Alamo*); **ARH** R-77 (AA-12A *Adder*)
  ASM Kh-29L/T (AS-14 *Kedge*); Kh-59M (AS-18 *Kazoo*)
  AShM Kh-31A (AS-17B *Krypton*)
  ARM Kh-28 (AS-9 *Kyle*); Kh-31P (AS-17A *Krypton*)

Paramilitary 40,000+ active

Border Defence Corps ε40,000

Coast Guard
EQUIPMENT BY TYPE
PATROL AND COASTAL COMBATANTS 69+
  PSO 4 DN2000 (Damen 9014)
  PCO 13+: 1 *Mazinger* (ex-ROK); 9 TT-400; 3+ other
  PCC 2 *Hae Uri* (ex-ROK)
  PBF 24: 22 MS-50S; 2 *Shershen*
  PB 26: 1 MS-50; 12 TT-200; 13 TT-120
LOGISTICS AND SUPPORT 5
  AFS 1
  ATF 4 Damen Salvage Tug
AIRCRAFT • MP 3 C-212-400 MPA

Local Forces ε5,000,000 reservists
Incl People's Self-Defence Force (urban units) and People's Militia (rural units); comprises static and mobile cbt units, log spt and village protection pl; some arty, mor and AD guns; acts as reserve

DEPLOYMENT
CENTRAL AFRICAN REPUBLIC: UN • MINUSCA 5
SOUTH SUDAN: UN • UNMISS 68; 1 fd hospital

Arms procurements and deliveries – Asia

Significant events in 2019

MARCH — HHI ACQUIRES DSME

Shipbuilding firm Hyundai Heavy Industries (HHI) announced an agreement to acquire Daewoo Shipbuilding & Marine Engineering (DSME). As well as manufacturing commercial vessels, HHI and DSME have in recent years constructed most of the South Korean Navy's new ships and submarines. While this will partially consolidate South Korea's shipbuilding sector, which has suffered from a downturn in recent years, it leaves only STX Offshore & Shipbuilding and Hanjin Heavy Industries as competitors to HHI for future naval contracts.

APRIL — DEFENCE R&D

The Republic of Korea Defense Acquisition Program Administration (DAPA) announced plans to encourage private companies to invest more in defence research and development (R&D). Until now, DAPA completed most defence R&D and then contracted manufacturing out to private firms. Legislation is also being drafted to allow the government and private companies to share intellectual property. South Korea wants to reduce its reliance on imports and to grow its own defence industry.

MAY — DEFENCE PARTNERSHIPS

Taiwan passed the National Defense Industry Development Act. This is intended to promote public–private partnerships on defence development and production. The Ministry of National Defense (MND) will classify companies based on their technical capability and track record and then match them to procurement programmes. The MND will also assist companies in exporting. Taiwan wants to reduce its reliance on defence imports, as states are often reluctant to supply equipment to Taipei because of the potential impact on relations with China.

SEPTEMBER — TAX EXEMPTIONS

India's Ministry of Finance announced that imports of certain defence equipment would for five years be exempt from the Goods and Services Tax. India is modernising its armed forces, and is looking to foreign suppliers for some requirements, at the same time as developing its domestic defence industry and improving procurement processes.

NOVEMBER — SHIPBUILDING MERGER

China's two state-owned shipbuilding conglomerates, China State Shipbuilding Corporation (CSSC) and China Shipbuilding Industry Corporation (CSIC), merged again under the former. They were separated in 1999 so that CSSC could focus on military shipbuilding and CSIC on the civilian market. The global shipbuilding sector has suffered a downturn since the financial crisis and the merger aims to make Chinese shipbuilding more competitive in the commercial sector, as well as in naval shipbuilding; this may be achieved by closing some shipyards, as well as merging some administrative and design departments.

Table 17 Royal Malaysian Navy: '15 To 5' transformation programme

The Royal Malaysian Navy (RMN) is in the middle of an upgrade programme. Many of its platforms are approximately 30 years old, which results in high operating costs and related wear and tear. In the mid-2010s the navy launched the '15 to 5' programme, aiming to replace 15 ship classes with five. This programme incorporated existing procurements such as the Submarine and New Generation Patrol Vessel acquisitions. The RMN aims to reduce training, maintenance and operating costs. It also wants to develop the local naval-shipbuilding sector, for example through the Littoral Combat Ship programme. However, the Littoral Mission Ship contract was recently modified. All four ships will now be built in China, in order to save money, although there are plans to build future vessels locally. Older classes due for retirement include logistics and mine-countermeasures vessels. It is unclear whether these capabilities will be replaced under the '15 to 5' programme.

© IISS

Programme	Equipment	Type	Quantity ordered as of Nov 2019 (total planned)	Contract date	Value	Prime contractor	Shipyard/s	In-service date	Notes
Submarine	*Tunku Abdul Rahman* (FRA *Scorpène*)	Attack submarine (SSK)	2 (4)	Jun 2002	€1bn (US$944m)	Armaris	DCN; IZAR	2009	Deal includes the sale of a second-hand *Agosta*-class SSK for training.
Littoral Combat Ship	*Maharaja Lela* (FRA *Gowind*)	Guided-missile frigate with a hangar and surface-to-air missiles	6 (12)	Dec 2011	MYR9bn (US$2.94bn)	Boustead Naval Shipyard	Boustead Naval Shipyard; Naval Group	2019*–24*	Design supplied by Naval Group; programme two years behind schedule
New Generation Patrol Vessel	*Kedah* (GER MEKO 100)	Frigate	6 (18)	Sep 1998	MYR5.35bn (US$1.36bn)	German Naval Group	Blohm + Voss; Boustead Naval Shipyard	2006–10	Remaining 12 vessels likely to be built to modified design developed by Boustead Naval Shipyard
Littoral Mission Ship	*Keris*	Coastal patrol craft	4 (18)	Mar 2017	MYR1.05bn (US$255.67m)	Boustead Naval Shipyard	Wuchang Shipbuilding Industry Co., Ltd.	2019*–20*	First two were to be built in China and the second pair in Malaysia; contract amended in Mar 2019 for all four vessels to be built in China
Multi Role Support Ship	TBD	Landing platform dock/ landing helicopter dock	0 (3)	–	–	TBD	TBD	–	Negotiations ongoing between the RMN and the Malaysian defence ministry

* Planned

Figure 20 Republic of Korea: FA-50 *Fighting Eagle*/T-50 *Golden Eagle*

The Korean Trainer eXperimental (KTX) project began in the late 1980s. One of several programmes intended to develop South Korea's defence industry, it ultimately produced for the Korean Air Force (ROKAF) the turboprop KT-1 (KTX-1) and the jet-powered T-50 (KTX-2).

The T-50 can trace its lineage to the early 1990s, when Seoul contracted Samsung Aerospace to supply 120 General Dynamics KF-16 fighter aircraft as part of the Peace Bridge II programme. The contract included agreements on technology transfer and licenced assembly or production of most of the KF-16s in South Korea. Seoul financed most of the KTX-2 programme. However, the project was suspended for financial reasons in the mid-1990s and resumed in 1997. Korea Aerospace Industries (KAI) took over as the prime contractor for the programme in 1999, when it was founded as a joint venture between Samsung Aerospace, Daewoo Heavy Industries and Hyundai Space and Aircraft Company. The prototype T-50 was first flown in 2002 and a year later KAI was awarded a production contract. Over 180 aircraft based on the T-50 design have since been delivered and the aircraft is the country's most successful defence export, worth over US$3 billion in overseas contracts as of 2019. Although it

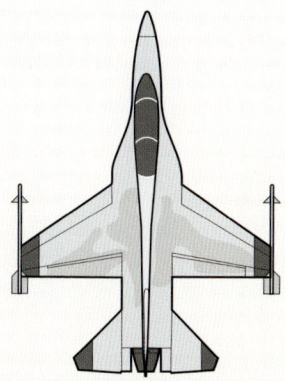

was not selected for the US Air Force's T-X trainer programme, the T-50 is illustrative of what may become a common sight: South Korean companies proving competitive against well-established Western firms. This has already begun in the maritime sector, where South Korean shipyards have won some contracts in Asia; they have in recent years also won contracts to supply Norway and the United Kingdom with fleet-replenishment ships.

© IISS

Table 18 T-50/FA-50 production contracts

Order date	Aircraft	Type	Quantity	Customer	Contract value	Deliveries
Dec 2003	T-50	Training	25	ROK	KRW1.02trn (US$854.42m)	2005–08
Oct 2006	T-50 TA-50	Training	25 22	ROK	KRW1.5trn (US$1.57bn)	2008–10
Mar 2008	T-50B	Training (Aerobatic display use)	10	ROK	KRW220bn (US$199.63m)	2010–11
May 2011	T-50I	Training	16	IDN	US$400m	2013–14
Dec 2011	FA-50	Fighter/ground attack	20	ROK	KRW710bn (US$630.29m)	2013–16
May 2013	FA-50	Fighter/ground attack	40	ROK	KRW1.1trn (US$1bn)	2013–16
Dec 2013	T-50IQ	Training	24	IRQ	US$1.1bn	2017–19
Mar 2014	FA-50PH	Fighter/ground attack	12	PHL	PHP18.9bn (US$425.72m)	2015–17
May 2014	T-50B	Training (Aerobatic display use)	2	ROK	KRW49.24bn (US$46.77m)	2015
Sep 2015	T-50TH	Training	4	THA	US$110m	2018
Jul 2017	T-50TH	Training	8	THA	US$258m	2019–20*
TOTAL:			**208**		**US$6.59bn**	

* Planned

Chapter Seven
Middle East and North Africa

- Egypt, Oman, Qatar and Saudi Arabia are all recapitalising elements of their combat-aircraft fleets. Egypt and Qatar are introducing the Dassault *Rafale* into service, Oman has bought the Eurofighter *Typhoon* and Saudi Arabia continues to take delivery of its Boeing F-15SA. Qatar and Kuwait are also Eurofighter customers, although deliveries have yet to begin, while the former country is also purchasing the F-15.
- Iranian aggression in the Strait of Hormuz and elsewhere prompted the US in July to try to build a coalition under the banner of the International Maritime Security Construct (IMSC).
- US forces in Syria have withdrawn from positions in the north of the country, but some remain in the east to ensure the security of oilfields in the region. A Turkish incursion into northern Syria in November 2019 led to coordinated patrols in the region between Russian and Turkish personnel.
- Many countries in the region continue to operate highly mixed fleets of armoured vehicles and aircraft. Examples include Egypt and Saudi Arabia.
- Turkey has found success in recent years in exporting several systems to regional customers, particularly in the land domain. These orders and deliveries have included wheeled armoured personnel carriers to Tunisia, the United Arab Emirates, Oman, Bahrain and Qatar.
- While Egypt has the largest fleet of heavy armour in the region, only around half is modern, with a third of its total inventory in storage. Similarly, while Iran has the second-largest inventory in the region, most are outclassed by modern main battle tanks. Algeria, meanwhile, with the third-largest total, has an inventory comprising a range of Soviet and Russian designs.

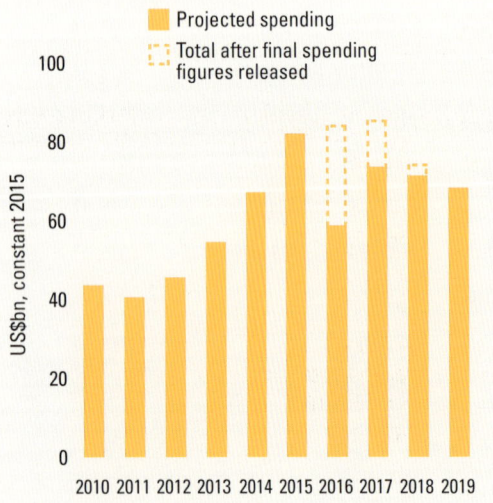

Saudi Arabia, real-terms defence spending, 2010–19 (US$bn, constant 2015)*

*Note: Saudi authorities in recent years have later revised defence-spending totals upwards when the government releases its actual spending figures. As such, it is possible that the US$68.2bn announced for 2019 might be an underestimate.

Active military personnel – top 10
(25,000 per unit)

Country	Personnel
Iran	610,000
Egypt	439,000
Saudi Arabia	227,000
Morocco	196,000
Iraq	193,000
Israel	170,000
Syria	169,000
Algeria	130,000
Jordan	101,000
United Arab Emirates	63,000

Global total 19,852,000
Regional total 2,533,000

Regional defence policy and economics 326 ▶
Armed forces data section 340 ▶
Arms procurements and deliveries 385 ▶

Egypt and Saudi Arabia: mixed armoured-vehicle and tactical-aviation-aircraft fleets, by origin

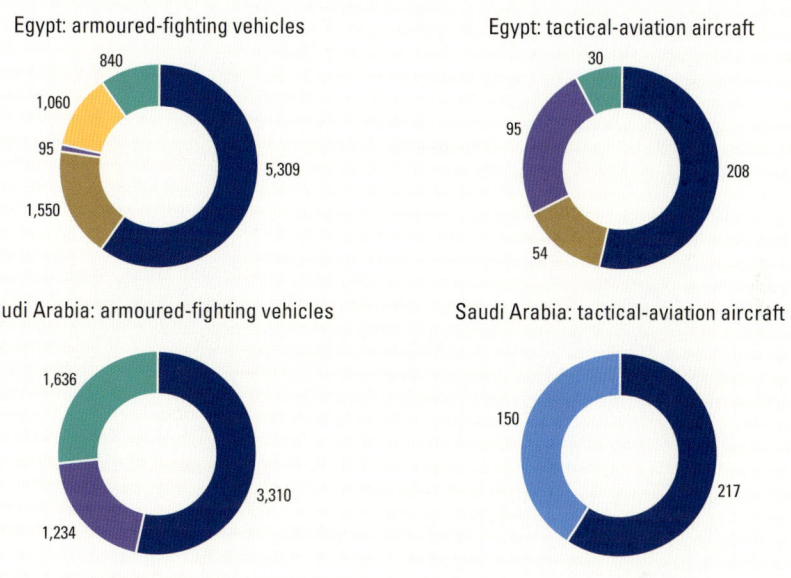

Egypt: armoured-fighting vehicles
- 5,309
- 840
- 1,060
- 95
- 1,550

Egypt: tactical-aviation aircraft
- 208
- 30
- 95
- 54

Saudi Arabia: armoured-fighting vehicles
- 3,310
- 1,636
- 1,234

Saudi Arabia: tactical-aviation aircraft
- 217
- 150

■ US ■ Russia ■ France ■ UK ■ Domestic ■ Other

Main battle tanks, 2019
(250 per unit) Oldest type shown in brackets (incl in store)

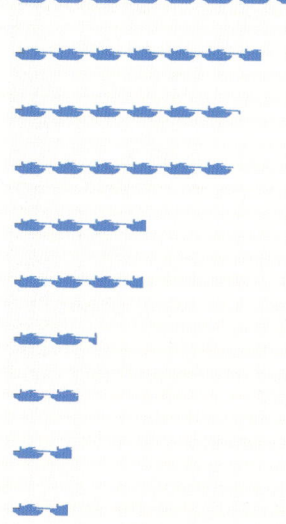

Egypt 3,620
(includes 840 T-54/T-55)

Israel 1,650
(includes 370 *Merkava* Mk II)

Iran 1,513
(includes T-54/55)

Algeria 1,467
(includes 270 T-55)

Saudi Arabia 880
(includes est. 370 M60A3 *Patton*)

Morocco 862
(includes 200 M48 A5 *Patton*)

Jordan 556
(includes 274 FV4030/2 *Khalid*)

UAE 433
(includes 45 AMX-30)

Iraq 391
(includes est. 50 T-55)

Kuwait 368
(includes 150 M-84)

Selected regional holdings of Turkish-manufactured defence equipment

Country	Product	Number delivered
Bahrain	APC (W) ARMA	n.k.
Oman	APC (W) *Pars* III 8x8	20 of 145
	RECCE *Pars* III 6x6	6 of 27
Qatar	PPV *Kirpi*	n.k. of 50
	PPV *Yalcin*	est. 100 of 342
	AUV NMS	n.k. of 214
	Medium CISR UAV *Bayraktar* TB2	0 of 6
	PBF MRTP	n.k. of 4
Tunisia	PPV *Yalcin*	71 of 71
	PPV *Kirpi*	At least 100 delivered of n.k.
United Arab Emirates	IFV/APC (W) ARMA (*Rabdan*)	n.k. of 400

Middle East and North Africa

The prospects for conflict in the Gulf region seemed to increase in 2019. Tensions rose after the United States decided, in 2018, to leave the 2015 nuclear deal (the Joint Comprehensive Plan of Action) and apply 'maximum pressure' on Iran. US sanctions affected Iranian oil exports, and the head of Iran's Islamic Revolutionary Guard Corps (IRGC), when speaking in July 2019, said that Washington's strategy amounted to economic warfare. The sanctions were tightened further in early 2019, with the US in April 2019 designating the IRGC as a 'foreign terrorist organization'.

In the spring, Tehran began challenging its rivals in the region using asymmetric methods. Despite Iran's reliance on a network of militia partners across the region, its campaign primarily took the form of attacks on tankers in the United Arab Emirates' port of Fujairah, the use of limpet mines against tankers in the Arabian Sea and uninhabited aerial vehicle (UAV) attacks on Saudi Arabia's oil infrastructure. In each of these incidents, Iran maintained plausible deniability and harvested political capital by avoiding direct retaliation and signalling that it was ready to disrupt maritime traffic and oil exports.

In June 2019, Iran shot down a US Navy MQ-4C Broad Area Maritime Surveillance (BAMS-D) UAV. This prompted perhaps the most significant military escalation of the year. Iran alleged afterwards that the UAV had violated its airspace. In response, US forces planned strikes that were then cancelled at the last minute by President Donald Trump – reportedly when aircraft were airborne – ostensibly over concerns about the proportionality of the response, potential casualties and unwanted escalation.

In September, two major oil facilities in Saudi Arabia were targeted by a combination of UAVs and cruise missiles, reportedly reducing Saudi oil exports by 50% and global oil supplies by 5% for several weeks. The attack was widely blamed on Iran, which denied responsibility, but there was no immediate retaliation. Indeed, a seeming reluctance to engage in military action against Iran appeared to be widely shared. President Trump had concerns over domestic politics and feared becoming enmeshed in a new conflict in the Middle East; European states were uncertain about US policy; Middle Eastern countries such as Iraq were wary about the risk of a new conflict; and Saudi Arabia and the UAE were aware of their vulnerability to Iranian asymmetric capabilities.

This string of attacks and their aftermath illustrated changing military dynamics in the Gulf region. The increasing use of low-cost UAVs and cruise missiles, and the deniability employed by states like Iran, generated a new sense of insecurity. Maritime security was imperilled and oil exports were directly compromised, yet there was no cohesive response and US policy proved incoherent and ambivalent. For Riyadh, meanwhile, its significant investment in air and missile defences failed to intercept an attack against its most important oil facility – though the means chosen to conduct the attack complicated the task for the air-defence radars and interceptors then in the region – while its main ally, Washington, did not initiate automatic retaliation. Instead, the US increased its military presence in the region, deploying to Saudi Arabia troops and equipment, including additional air-defence systems (*Patriot* and THAAD), radars, fighter aircraft and an Expeditionary Air Wing, and maintaining an aircraft-carrier group in the region. The US announced in October that, since May, it had boosted its forces in the Central Command (CENTCOM) area of responsibility by 14,000 personnel.

Syria

In 2019, conflict in Syria once again intensified, notably when a long-expected regime campaign to capture Idlib, the last rebel holdout, began in the spring. The ground offensive mobilised Syrian government forces, allied militias and Russian advisers in combination with Syrian and Russian airpower. Also deployed were the Russian-backed Tiger Force, commanded by Syrian Brigadier-General Suhail al-Hassan, and the Syrian 5th Corps, a Russian-organised unit comprising former rebels.

The goal was to advance along the main highways connecting regime-held territory to the city of Aleppo. For the first three months of the operation

Map 10 US Central Command (CENTCOM) area of responsibility: force dispositions, 2019

US Army

Afghanistan	3rd Brigade Combat Team, 82nd Airborne Division 2nd Security Force Assistance Brigade 10th Combat Aviation Brigade
Iraq	1st Stryker Brigade Combat Team, 25th Infantry Division
Qatar	12th Missile Defence Battery
Saudi Arabia	3/4th Air Defense Artillery Battalion*
Bahrain; Kuwait	1/7th Air Defense Artillery Battalion
Iraq; Kuwait	244th Army Reserve Expeditionary Combat Aviation Brigade
Kuwait; Syria	30th ARNG Armored Brigade Combat Team
Qatar; UAE	4/3rd Air Defense Artillery Battalion

US Marine Corps

Bahrain	VMA-311 fighter/ground-attack squadron with AV-8B
Afghanistan; Iraq; Kuwait; Syria	1 & 2/7th Marine Regiment

US Air Force

Afghanistan	79th Expeditionary Fighter Squadron with F-16C 354th Expeditionary Fighter Squadron with A-10C 62nd Expeditionary Attack Squadron with MQ-9A
Jordan	389th Expeditionary Fighter Squadron with F-15E 46th Expeditionary Attack Squadron with MQ-9A
Kuwait	361st Expeditionary Attack Squadron with MQ-9A
Qatar	340th Expeditionary Air Refueling Squadron with KC-135 7th Expeditionary Airborne Command and Control Squadron with E-8C
	763rd Expeditionary Reconnaissance Squadron with RC-135
Saudi Arabia	27th Expeditionary Fighter Squadron with F-22A*
United Arab Emirates	4th Expeditionary Fighter Squadron with F-35A 159th Expeditionary Fighter Squadron with F-15C 494th Expeditionary Fighter Squadron with F-15E* 908th Expeditionary Air Refueling Squadron with KC-10A 968th Expeditionary Airborne Air Control Squadron with E-3 99th Expeditionary Reconnaissance Squadron with U-28/RQ-4 Reconnaissance Unit with RQ-170/RQ-180

US Navy

Arabian Sea; Persian Gulf	1 *Ohio*-class submarine 2–3 *Los Angeles-/Virginia*-class submarines USS *Abraham Lincoln* aircraft carrier<ul><li>Strike Fighter Squadron 25 with F/A-18E</li><li>Strike Fighter Squadron 86 with F/A-18E</li><li>Strike Fighter Squadron 103 with F/A-18F</li><li>Strike Fighter Squadron 143 with F/A-18E</li><li>Electronic Attack Squadron 140 with EA-18G</li><li>Airborne Early Warning Squadron 121 with E-2D</li></ul>USS *Leyte Gulf* cruiser USS *Normandy* cruiser USS *Farragut* destroyer USS *Forrest Sherman* destroyer USS *Lassen* destroyer
Bahrain	Patrol Squadron 45 with P-8A
Saudi Arabia	Electronic Attack Squadron 134 with EA-18G

the campaign achieved little, despite significant air support. The readiness of opposition forces – a combination of jihadi groups and Turkey-backed rebels – frustrated the regime's strategy, exposing the Syrian Army's long-standing structural and personnel weaknesses. However, artillery and logistics support, together with the mobilisation of Iranian-backed forces, led to significant regime advances in the late summer, although the army took heavy casualties.

A crucial question was how the regime would eventually look to exert control over the northern strip of the country that had been occupied by the Kurdish Syrian Democratic Forces (SDF) after they defeated the Islamic State, also known as ISIS or ISIL, jihadists. In late 2019, however, the regime was unexpectedly presented with an opportunity to advance in this area in a way that contrasted with operations around Idlib, where they had made gains but only at significant cost.

Small numbers of US forces operated across the area, providing de facto cover for the SDF and frustrating the interests of the regime, Iran and Russia. However, US support for the SDF led to tensions with Turkey, which viewed the Kurdish forces as aligned with the Kurdistan Workers' Party (PKK), which led a multi-decade insurgency inside Turkey. The US sought to mediate these tensions, including by positioning troops as a buffer between the Kurdish forces and the Turkish border.

President Trump's decision in October 2019 to withdraw US personnel from positions in northern Syria in the face of an impending Turkish incursion led directly to the unravelling of a fragile equilibrium there. (Trump had earlier, in December 2018, said he would withdraw US troops.) In some places SDF forces resisted the Turkish advance, and in others retreated under US advice. ISIS prisoners, meanwhile, escaped from SDF-run jails. The precipitous nature of the US move redrew relationships: Turkey and Russia began to coordinate, agreeing on joint patrols; the SDF opened negotiations with the Assad regime; Russian and Syrian forces settled in abandoned US bases; and ISIS saw an opportunity for a comeback, despite the killing of leader Abu Bakr al-Baghdadi in Idlib. US allies, notably NATO members and Kurdish forces, sought to salvage their positions and maintain pressure on ISIS. (At the time of writing, some US forces remained in northern Syria, ostensibly to deny ISIS and Iran access to oilfields.)

Yemen

The complex war in Yemen remains intense and destructive. The first half of 2019 saw a United Nations-led effort to avoid fighting between the Houthi militia and the Saudi-led coalition over the city of Hodeidah, the main port of entry for humanitarian assistance and food. UN mediation was moderately successful, compelling the two sides to redeploy away from critical civilian infrastructure. However, fighting continued elsewhere in Yemen, not only between the Houthis and their opponents, but also within the anti-Houthi coalition, between the Saudi-backed Yemeni government and the UAE-backed southern secessionist movement. This fracturing threatened the coalition's already halting military campaign.

A significant development was the UAE's decision in the summer to immediately draw down and redeploy troops, an announcement that some analysts perceived as an admission that the political, reputational and military costs of involvement in Yemen had become prohibitive. The UAE had become a relatively successful military player in Yemen, deploying special forces alongside local militia partners that it had carefully nurtured and organised, as well as conventional military power. The risk was that the UAE's drawdown might create a void in certain parts of the country that could be filled by competing militias.

The Houthi movement continues to display striking resilience. It is still able to deploy a wide array of weapons both to defend its territory and to inflict significant damage on its better-equipped adversaries. The group has used UAVs, and missiles of increasing range, for signalling purposes and as an irritant to Saudi Arabia. While a UN panel found that Iranian technology had increased the Houthis' rocket and missile capabilities, Houthi attacks have exposed limitations in Saudi Arabia's defences.

Gulf region ground forces

When the Saudi-led coalition began its operations in Yemen, in March 2015, the campaign design was to apply airpower to compel Houthi forces to relinquish control of Aden and to drive them from Sana'a. The resilience of the adversary forces (which included troops from the regular forces loyal to former president Ali Abdullah Saleh) proved surprising, but their decision to fight in the northern part of the country should perhaps have been less of a surprise. The rugged terrain overlooking the regions of Asir, Jizan and Najran favoured local forces who had withstood not only an earlier Saudi military campaign in 2009, but also long-running operations by the Yemeni armed forces. The Royal Saudi Land Forces, National Guard and Border Guard were soon tested on operations. In August 2015, a Saudi brigadier was killed in Houthi cross-border attacks and uniformed casualties were estimated by then to be around one hundred. On 4 September 2015, five Bahraini and up to 50 Emirati troops were killed in a missile strike on their position in Ma'rib. According to regional sources, Bahrain's casualties would have been higher had the major commanding the Royal Guard contingent not insisted on erecting blast protection for the Bahraini sleeping quarters. The same officer reportedly took command when the Emirati brigadier commanding the site was wounded.

There is a regional tradition of ground-force officers dominating the top military ranks. Within the Gulf Cooperation Council (GCC) states, the current chiefs of defence are all from the ground forces, with the exception of Qatar and Saudi Arabia. However, in comparison to other services, the ground forces perhaps have the least exposure to the contemporary operating environment. One reason for this is that operating advanced aircraft and naval vessels requires a high degree of technical ability, while the same applies to the engineering and logistics officers who maintain complex platforms. Moreover, English is the international language of air and maritime forces and career officers in these services tend to require a high degree of language proficiency. The region's air forces train with outside partners and achieve high levels of interoperability. Since 9/11 and the siting of the US Air Force's Combined Air Operations Center at Al Udeid Air Base in Qatar, regional air forces have been integrated into US-led air operations and take part in bilateral and multilateral exercises. The United Kingdom and Omani air forces train regularly in the *Magic Carpet* series of exercises, and Qatari air-force officers and ground crew were scheduled in 2019 to begin integration into the Royal Air Force's 12 Squadron, the UK–Qatar Joint Typhoon Squadron. The same level of international collaboration is true of the GCC navies. All are involved in Combined Task Force 152, which lies within the Combined Maritime Forces (CMF), itself commanded by a US Navy vice-admiral who is also the commander of the US 5th Fleet and US Naval Forces Central Command. Bilateral exercises are also commonplace as extra-regional naval units enter the Gulf to operate as part of the CMF.

Nonetheless, such factors do not necessarily always lead to greater military efficiency. For instance, the extent to which national exercises reflect the same elements of unpredictability and surprise as may be found in Western exercises is unclear. And while regional air forces, such as those of Saudi Arabia and the United Arab Emirates, may operate advanced Western combat aircraft and associated weapons, they still lack operational experience, particularly in challenging tasks like air-to-ground missions in urban environments and in generating associated support, including for the targeting process.

Yet the region's ground forces lack even these advantages. Foreign-language and technical proficiency is reportedly lower in the ground forces than in the other services. Additionally, few regional ground forces have recent operational experience. The former Qatari minister of state for defence affairs was a mid-ranking tank officer during the recapture of Khafji in the First Gulf War in 1991. Since then, aside from Bahrain, Saudi Arabia and the UAE, none of the other GCC states have had to face a determined enemy and adapt during military conflict. Moreover, there are questions over leadership quality. For instance, challenge for young commanders is reported as often lacking and there is little evidence of a feedback loop from unit experimentation and operations that would lead to a 'lessons-learned' process. Western reports continue to point to a tendency towards rote learning in some military institutions.

Furthermore, bilateral exercises sometimes constitute little more than security-force assistance training by the visiting force. While such exercises are useful for both the visiting force and the indigenous units, they are not genuine examples of coalition collaboration. All too often, the most important part of any exercise is the culminating firepower demonstration. Heavily scripted and rehearsed, these can resemble mechanised ballet rather than the disciplined and concentrated application of lethal force. For instance, Qatar's exercise *Nasr*, held in October 2015, was a two-week exercise involving Qatari land forces and a Turkish infantry company complete with 30 infantry fighting vehicles. Some observers reported that it constituted two weeks of training for a 'distinguished visitors' day' and involved no more than an hour of scripted live-fire manoeuvres. Exercise *Northern Thunder*, held in northern Saudi Arabia in February and March 2016, was presented as an ambitious multinational Arab and Islamic nations' exercise. Though its specific purpose was unclear, the deployment to the exercise area, management of the exercise area and the level of interoperability training was reportedly haphazard. 'Distinguished visitors' day' firepower exhibitions are also seen in Oman, though its 2018 exercise *Saif Sareea III* with the UK was based on a sophisticated scenario involving a multi-agency response (reportedly involving more than 80,000 Omani civil servants in addition to local and British forces) to unrest and a territorial threat.

Looking to the future

While it would be misleading to view the region's armed forces simply through the prism of Western experience, or to assume that armed forces in the Gulf are necessarily intended for tasks analogous to those of Western military forces, some regional governments are looking to try to derive improved performance from their armed forces, including their ground components. Developing an ethos of military professionalism is recognised as important, and there has been progress towards this in the UAE under the scrutiny of the deputy supreme commander. The UAE has also sought operational exposure from the Balkans to Afghanistan and Yemen. The main focus seems to be on the Presidential Guard, but there is a spillover effect into the land forces. Analysts consider that on operations in Yemen there has been significant cross-fertilisation between these two services, presumably so that the latter can gain experience. For instance, many of the task-force commanders were from land forces, which provided much of the support to the Yemeni and Sudanese infantry. By doing this, the UAE has changed the previously held judgement of some international observers that the Presidential Guard was expeditionary while the land forces were designed for territorial defence. Moreover, some observers have judged that the UAE has demonstrated adaptability in its operations during the campaign. In Yemen's southern regions, the UAE often used special forces working with and through local forces often more familiar with the local topography and population.

Meanwhile, where indigenous experience and talent is lacking, the UAE has brought in outside help. Major-General Mike Hindmarsh, a former Australian SAS officer, commands the Presidential Guard while Major-General Stephen Toumajan, a former US armed-forces pilot, commands the Joint Aviation Command. There is also a corps of foreign advisers who work alongside Emirati commanders. Bahrain has taken a slightly different direction, most evidently in its Royal Guard. The commander of this special-operations force is understood to set high standards of entry and continuation training. Bilateral training is pursued with the clear intention that Bahrain's ground forces should be comparatively as proficient as the visiting force. Like the UAE, Bahrain has sought opportunities to acquire operational experience, be it in Afghanistan, where it deployed troops in Helmand province, or more recently in Yemen. Bahrain also employs foreign advisers, but it would appear that their efforts are concentrated in tactics and training. Kuwait, meanwhile, acknowledges that its land forces need external support to improve and there appears, according to outside observers, to be a determination among senior land-forces officers to raise standards.

While there does not appear to be general recognition of these challenges to regional states' ground forces, elements of the Bahraini, Emirati and Kuwaiti examples illustrate areas where capability might be improved, although these factors – derived from Western experience – would in each case be influenced by local circumstances. Options to consider could include raising the standards for officer entry, so that there is approaching parity with the educational potential of the air and maritime domains. And attempting to instil a professional ethos that strives for joint or combined military effectiveness, rather than scripted firepower displays, might help create a lessons-learned feedback loop in training activities. At the same time, seeking opportunities to test capabilities, either in bilateral exercises or on operations, could help challenge military leaders and soldiers and expose them to other nations' operational methods. Where indigenous capability is lacking, hiring experience – either in select but empowered command appointments or as well-placed advisers – might help compensate for otherwise sparse contact with the contemporary operating environment. Additionally, broader military reforms, like those being pursued by Saudi Arabia, are designed to improve the efficiency of defence organisations and supporting infrastructure at home.

There have been in recent years significant developments towards the creation in some states of what might be called an emerging military – or at the very least a 'national security' – culture. For instance, the UAE introduced national military service in 2014 and in subsequent years introduced a range of benefits for service. It also holds a 'Commemoration Day' in November each year and homecoming ceremonies have been observed for troops returning from missions, or even from troop rotations, while repatriation ceremonies have taken place in some regional states for those killed on operations. These are designed, perhaps, to generate *esprit de corps* by honouring those who died and demonstrating to other serving troops that neither they nor their families would be forgotten. Such activities also serve to reflect a greater acceptance of military risk by the state, as well as a desire by the authorities to demonstrate to the population that, while military service is not without risk, it is sometimes necessary for the state to defend its interests by projecting power.

Israel: defence-policy developments

Domestic politics dominated debate in Israel in 2019. At the time of writing, following inconclusive elections in April and September and serious legal problems, Benjamin Netanyahu was faced with a chance of losing the premiership. However, neither he nor rival Benny Gantz, former chief of the general staff of the Israel Defense Forces (IDF), was able to form an administration. Although retaining a strategy of containment regarding the Palestinians, Netanyahu continued to present a tough line on Iran. Since 2018, Israel has significantly increased its number of attacks on Iranian and Hizbullah targets in Syria and, more recently, in Iraq. There was also at least one Israeli attack in Lebanon. Israeli security analysts understand that in some cases Israel had direct military contact with Iran's expeditionary Quds Force in Syria. In December 2018, Israel exposed and destroyed six tunnels dug by Hizbullah under the Lebanese border into Israeli territory.

Netanyahu still considers Iran to be the most serious strategic threat to Israel. He has defined the IDF's priorities as, firstly, preventing Iran from becoming a nuclear force; secondly, blocking Iranian efforts to improve the accuracy of Hizbullah's rocket arsenal; and thirdly, blocking Iran's attempts to entrench itself militarily in Syria and western Iraq. Netanyahu has actively supported President Trump's policy of 'maximum pressure' on Tehran. However, Washington's decision in mid-2019 not to launch military action against Iran has led some Israeli analysts to consider that Netanyahu may be concerned that Trump might look to sign an 'improved' nuclear deal with Iran. In summer 2019, Netanyahu tried to persuade Trump to sign a US–Israel defence treaty, which elicited a favourable tweet from the White House, but also an indication that the US would wait for Israel's election results.

Although security cooperation with the Palestinian Authority (PA) in the West Bank has been maintained, the Israeli government still suspects the PA of providing financial assistance to Palestinian prisoners serving sentences in Israeli jails. Meanwhile, sanctions imposed on the PA by Israel and the United States have contributed to increased economic problems in the West Bank, while the number of violent incidents in the area has also risen.

After the latest Israeli military campaign in August 2014, the Gazan border had been relatively calm. Then, in March 2018, prompted by the territory's financial problems, demonstrations were mounted along the border. Demonstrators were also pressing for the right to return. Hamas was, Israeli analysts maintain, looking to force Egypt and Israel to lift their joint blockade on Gaza. Protests continued through 2018 and the UN reported that nearly 200 people were killed there between March and December 2018. Incidents of rocket fire from Gaza into Israel have been followed by diplomatic initiatives designed to reduce tensions. Though Netanyahu was consistently criticised by his political opponents for being 'soft' on Hamas, he persisted in this approach. Analysts judged that Netanyahu saw little advantage in another military operation in Gaza, fearing that it would not end in a clear Israeli victory.

This approach changed only once, a week before the second elections in September 2019. After rockets from Gaza forced Netanyahu to stop a political speech in the southern city of Ashdod, he attempted to force a decision in favour of a wide military response. His security chiefs resisted and, with the attorney general warning Netanyahu that he would have to bring the decision to the security cabinet, the prime minister abandoned his attempt. (Israeli forces later killed a senior leader of Palestinian Islamic Jihad, and his wife, in a November 2019 attack in Gaza.)

Plan Gideon – the next phase

In January 2019, Lieutenant-General Aviv Kochavi became the IDF's new chief of staff. Kochavi had prepared an ambitious five-year plan, called *Tnufa* ('momentum' or 'drive'), for the army, meant to replace his predecessor Gadi Eizenkot's current five-year plan, *Gideon*. Kochavi even asked that *Gideon* be concluded a year early, in January 2020. However, Israel's political crisis has postponed all budget discussions until spring 2020. Furthermore, amid Israel's budgetary deficit, a significant increase in military funding, as hoped for by Kochavi, is unlikely to come to pass.

Kochavi is understood to consider that regional instability will persist for at least the next decade. He also reportedly believes that the threat to Israel's civilian population, on the home front, will increase through the use of more accurate and longer-range rockets and missiles by organisations such as Hamas and Hizbullah, which will begin to acquire capabilities that the new chief of staff says will turn them into 'terrorist armies'. According to Kochavi, the IDF should prepare for more serious technological developments, in which its opponents (not just states, but organisations) learn to operate sophisticated cyber tools and navigation systems. He is also understood to believe that the army should also consider the potential impact of unpredictable events, perhaps including an Iran close to nuclear-power status or unexpected regime change in relatively friendly neighbours such as Egypt and Jordan.

Kochavi's initial plans as chief of staff are understood to include an emphasis on airpower, technology and intelligence-gathering, and an improved combination of the three. He is also recommending significant improvements to the ground forces. However, there are barriers to boosting ground-force capabilities, including budgets and politics, and whether Israel's politicians and public view the use of ground forces in large numbers as being decisive in future operations. According to Israeli specialists, when Netanyahu presented his '2030 Vision' for the IDF to senior commanders in early 2019, the ground forces were not even among the top five priorities noted for investment. These were cyber capabilities, border protection, precision weapons for the air force, improved infrastructure protection (civilian, military and strategic locations) and increased stocks of interceptors for air and missile defence. Improvements to ground forces were reportedly added later, though detail remains scant.

Saudi Arabia: reforming the defence establishment

Saudi Arabia has in recent years consistently ranked near the top of the global rankings for both the total amount of defence spending and the amount spent on importing armaments. Riyadh has long had a close defence relationship with the United States, and among its range of foreign defence equipment it operates advanced fighter aircraft from the United Kingdom and the US.

Despite high levels of defence funding and an advanced equipment inventory, Saudi Arabia continues to face challenges in securing its borders, projecting power and delivering a successful outcome in its fight against adversaries in Yemen. Analysts have posited reasons for the country's military underperformance, including inefficiency and poor organisation. Some have argued that Saudi security organisations have been designed to duplicate each other's roles. Coordination between the various services reportedly remains problematic, while progress is required in other areas, such as the standardisation of weapons and training. In addition, the equipment-acquisition process is opaque and – at least in public – lacks a defined road map. To address these long-standing concerns, Riyadh has embarked on a comprehensive defence-reform programme and looked to enact broader measures across government, including an anti-corruption drive. These reforms are intended to give Saudi Arabia a modern ministerial framework for mission-based joint planning and acquisition decisions.

Saudi Arabia's defence-reform programme has four main pillars: ministerial reform; the establishment of a General Authority for Military Industries (GAMI); the establishment of Saudi Arabia Military Industries (SAMI); and the reform/expansion of professional military education.

Traditionally, the Ministry of Defence tended to be more of a ceremonial than a functional office: it did not coordinate plans or military operations and procurement decisions were made by individual services, which then petitioned the Royal Court for money. With assistance from the UK and the US, Riyadh intends to establish an organisation that is more capable of defining the country's military requirements, matching resources to these requirements, and developing and executing plans and policy guidance. There are also plans to establish a standing military headquarters, similar to the Permanent Joint Headquarters in the UK, to be formed and staffed for contingency operations, replacing the current ad hoc system of designating commanders for each operation. Both Washington and London are planning to provide on-site advisers for this effort.

GAMI was established in 2017. It is charged with evaluating proposed equipment acquisitions and ensuring greater alignment in requirements across the armed services. Since GAMI is not tied to any one service and is intended to minimise parochialism, corruption and inefficiency, the authority will be roughly analogous to the acquisition, technology and procurement division of a Western defence ministry. Once a requirement is defined and vetted by GAMI, it will then look for suppliers. In theory, this should ensure that objective decisions are made on procurement matters.

SAMI, also launched in 2017, is intended to become Saudi Arabia's 'national champion' in the defence sector and is the principal medium through which Riyadh looks to meet the target of spending 50% of defence-procurement funds locally by 2030, as laid out in Saudi Arabia's Vision 2030 programme. The agency is tasked with establishing factories to produce equipment in the Kingdom, not just assembling kits from overseas. SAMI's leadership has been clear in its desire to import (and ultimately export) technology and defence processes. While some of its operations will require foreign partners, the goal is to foster a completely indigenous defence-industrial sector. One near-term risk is that SAMI's focus on national sovereignty and domestic production may run counter to the country's overall goals of generating greater military and fiscal efficiency.

In addition, Riyadh is seeking assistance from the UK and US in reforming professional military education. Starting with the War College and working through the Staff College to the military academies, the plan is that the Saudi armed forces overhaul their curriculum, develop their own instructors and replace rote learning with critical thinking. However, the timescale for this significant task is unclear. The armed forces are also seeking UK and US assistance in developing a professional non-commissioned-officer system.

Sustained support from senior leaders will be vital to the success of these plans, while obvious difficulties in securing a clear military success in the Yemen war will likely continue to remind military leaders of the requirement to improve the defence establishment. Significant challenges remain to Riyadh's ambitions, and the results of some of the changes being made will likely be felt earlier than others. That said, while there is no guarantee that the defence-reform plan will succeed, those engaged in the process now have a road map to guide these efforts.

DEFENCE ECONOMICS

The region's economic prospects dimmed somewhat in 2019, largely due to unstable global oil prices and continuing regional security challenges, principally those between Iran and the United States and Gulf Cooperation Council (GCC) member states, as well as continued conflict in Libya, Syria and Yemen. Regional GDP growth continued to slow and was estimated by the International Monetary Fund (IMF) to be around 0.5% in 2019. (The IMF definition of the Middle East and North Africa includes Afghanistan and Pakistan, as well as Djibouti and Sudan.) However, the IMF projects a modest recovery in 2020, with growth estimated at around 3%, mostly due to improving economic prospects for non-GCC oil exporters, especially Iraq.

Oil prices fell slightly in 2019, partly due to weaker global growth and increased production in the US. In October 2019, US oil production hit a record 12.6 million barrels per day. This reflects Washington's move in 2015 to maximise the production of shale oil and alternative fuels. As a result of US output and low levels of demand from other key importers (particularly China and European states), Brent oil prices fell from an average of US$71.1 per barrel in 2018 to around US$60 per barrel in 2019. However, following the attacks on Saudi oil facilities and continued tensions in the Gulf, oil prices remain volatile.

GCC states' economies have experienced low growth for the second year in a row, at about 0.7% in 2019, but they are projected to rise to around 2.5% in 2020. These states recovered slowly from the oil-price collapse in 2014 and associated budget deficits, though Qatar and the United Arab Emirates have been relative exceptions. GDP growth in these two countries is increasingly linked not just to oil exports but also to infrastructure investments, in preparation for Expo 2020 in the UAE and the 2022 FIFA World Cup in Qatar and also to the longer-term Vision 2030 project in Saudi Arabia.

The economies of non-GCC oil exporters are expected to contract, with this trend largely driven by Libya and Iran. In the latter, the economy continues to suffer because of tightening US sanctions, declining from -4.8% in 2018 to an expected -9.5% in 2019.

Regional economic growth is led by developing oil-importing states, which were estimated to grow by 3.6% in 2019. Of these countries, Egypt – which accounts for more than 8% of the region's GDP – is expected to show strong growth at 5.5%, followed by Morocco with about 2.7%.

Defence spending: still prioritised

Despite the overall economic slowdown in the region, defence spending has remained high, particularly in GCC states. This stems from concerns over regional security and the costs associated with operational deployments, including to Libya and Yemen. It also owes something to the role weapons procurements have played in these states' foreign and security policies. Saudi Arabia, which is in its fourth year of military operations in Yemen, saw its defence budget rise from an average of 8% of GDP in 2009–13 to an average of 12% of GDP in 2015–19, though this contracted from US$86.4 billion in 2018 to US$78.4bn in 2019. This last number is subject to change, however, as in previous years Saudi Arabia has issued revised figures later in the year, indicating higher defence spending. Oman has broadly mirrored this trend, increasing its defence allocations from an average of 8% to an average of 13% of overall GDP in the same time periods, reaching US$8.9bn in 2018.

In October 2018, the UAE's prime minister and defence minister reportedly announced that the country would increase its defence spending by 41% in

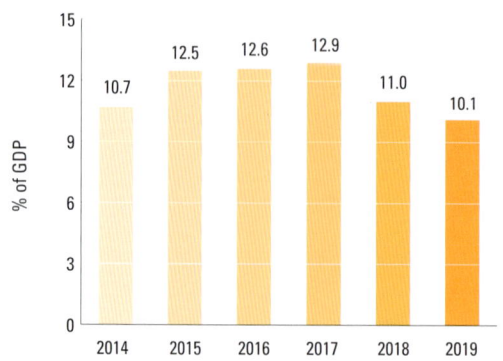

▲ Figure 21 **Saudi Arabia defence expenditure** as % of GDP

the 2019 federal budget. However, this announcement likely did not cover the UAE's total defence outlays, as it would amount to only 0.6% of the country's GDP in 2019. The official announcement indicated that defence spending amounted to US$2.3bn for 2019, which, though it is a significant increase from the US$1.66bn approved for 2018, does not include procurement costs. Analysts also consider that Qatar has possibly increased its defence spending not just to

▼ Map 11 **Middle East and North Africa regional defence spending**[1]

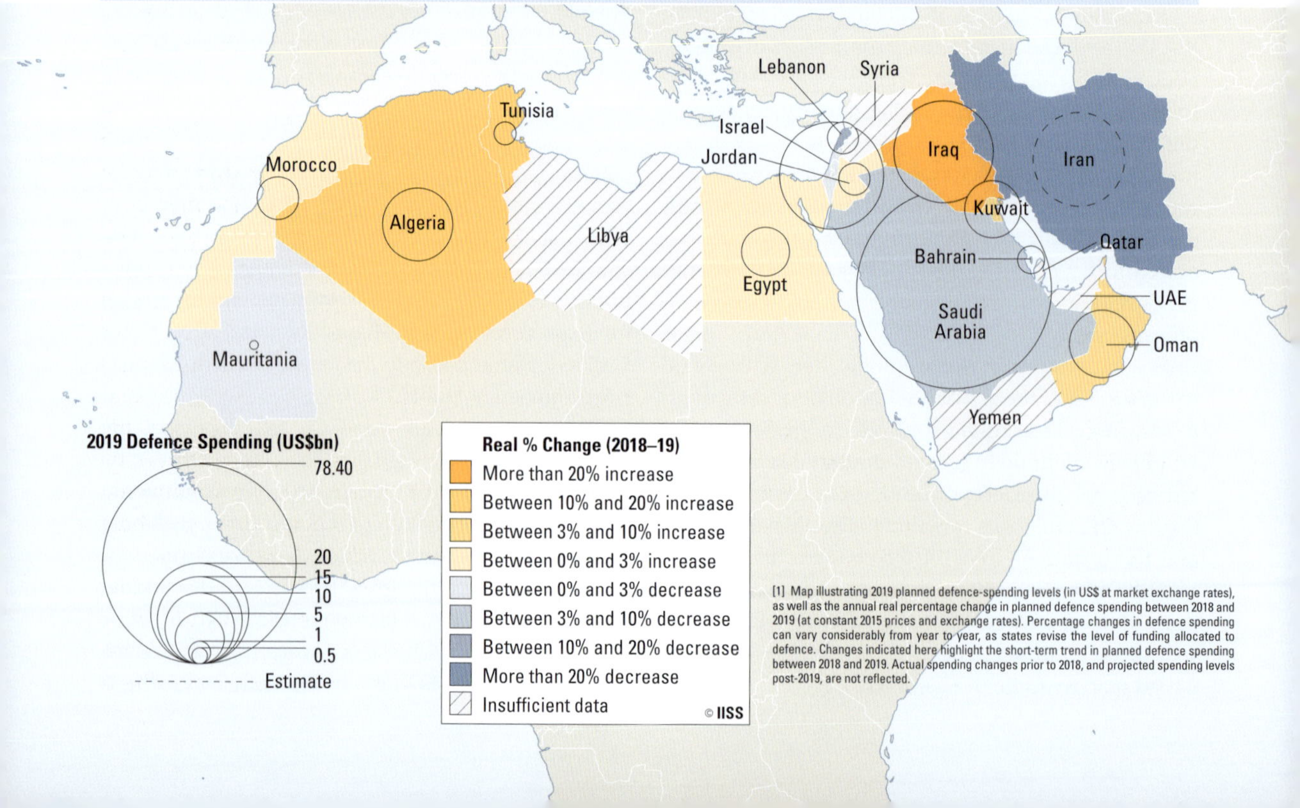

[1] Map illustrating 2019 planned defence-spending levels (in US$ at market exchange rates), as well as the annual real percentage change in planned defence spending between 2018 and 2019 (at constant 2015 prices and exchange rates). Percentage changes in defence spending can vary considerably from year to year, as states revise the level of funding allocated to defence. Changes indicated here highlight the short-term trend in planned defence spending between 2018 and 2019. Actual spending changes prior to 2018, and projected spending levels post-2019, are not reflected.

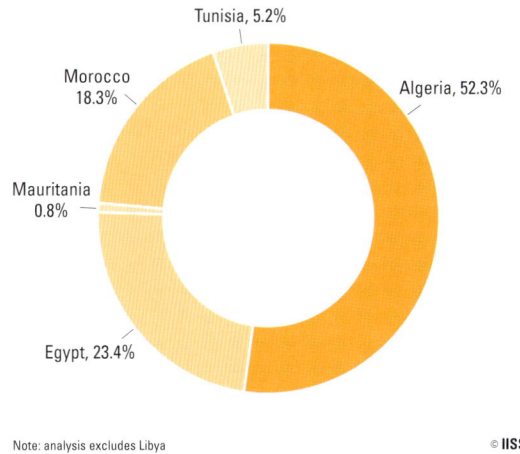

▲ Figure 22 **North Africa defence expenditure 2019: sub-regional breakdown**

Defence procurement and industry

The Middle East and North Africa is only beaten by Asia when considering the volume of arms imports, and the gap is closing. Given regional security concerns, it is possible that procurement spending might continue its current upward trajectory. The GCC states and Egypt (where analysts assert that procurement is largely enabled by economic assistance from Saudi Arabia and the UAE) are also likely to continue diversifying their sources of supply while further investing in local industries.

Gulf states are continuing efforts to modernise their combat-aircraft fleets, as evidenced in Saudi Arabia by the continued delivery of F-15SA fighter aircraft (since 2016) and the launch of the first locally assembled *Hawk* trainer in April 2019, and in the UAE by the ongoing *Project Dolphin*, in which a pair of Bombardier Global 6000 business jets are being adapted for an unspecified special-mission role (likely related to electronic and signals intelligence-gathering tasks). This focus on airpower is seen also in Egypt and Qatar, which both bought the French *Rafale*. The first batch was delivered to Doha in early June 2019. Doha has also made further progress in its deal with the UK for *Typhoon* and *Hawk* aircraft, with the first batch of Qatari personnel reported in 2019 as arriving in the UK for training.

GCC states have also looked to procure more maritime assets. The UAE has signed contracts for blue-water surface combatants and expeditionary naval platforms, including a US$842m deal with France's Naval Group for two *Gowind* frigates in June 2019. Saudi Arabia agreed a US$6bn deal with Lockheed Martin in 2018 for four Multi-Mission Surface Combatant ships and Egypt exercised the option for a second pair of Type-209/1400 mod class submarines in 2014, with Germany's TKMS launching the third boat in May 2019.

Air-defence systems remain procurement targets for some states. Algeria, Egypt, Iran and Syria either operate or are receiving various versions of Russia's S-300 system, while Gulf states Kuwait, Qatar and Saudi Arabia either operate or are receiving the US *Patriot* system. The UAE has also received the THAAD system – the second battery was delivered in 2018 – after a 2011 order. Although these procurements reflect traditional regional defence trade partnerships, future orders might not follow this pattern. For instance, trade restrictions have been put in place by some Western countries in light of the war in Yemen. Previously, when Western states have

account for security requirements associated with the 2022 World Cup, but also against the background of regional security challenges, perhaps even including the diplomatic crisis with its GCC neighbours.

However, these countries' budget breakdowns and defence-spending data overall remain opaque. This includes not only the UAE and Qatar but also Syria since 2011 and Libya and Yemen since 2014. In February 2019 alone, US$5.45bn in defence contracts were announced at the biennial UAE-hosted International Defence Exhibition and Conference (IDEX). The UAE's defence spending was estimated by the IISS to be about US$14.4bn (and Qatar US$5.1bn) in 2014, the last year when data and reliable estimates were available.

Meanwhile, Bahrain's annual defence budget has been relatively consistent, at about US$1.5bn for the past five years (around 4% of GDP), while Kuwait's budget, at US$6.4bn in 2019, is closer to 5% of GDP. Across the Gulf, Iran's nominal defence spending is expected to have contracted in 2019, from about US$21.9bn in 2018 to US$17.4bn in 2019, in part due to exchange-rate deterioration.

Defence now seems to be a lower priority for some oil importers. Egypt's defence budget has decreased but appears to have stabilised at around 1.5% of GDP (US$4.7bn, including US$1.3bn of US foreign military financing, in 2019). Tunisia and Morocco devote relatively modest sums to defence, in 2019 respectively around 2.7% and 3.1% of GDP and, when including US foreign military financing, amounting to US$1.03bn and US$3.6bn respectively.

proven unable or unwilling to sell defence equipment (such as uninhabited aerial vehicles, UAVs), other suppliers have been sought. Chinese armed UAVs, for instance, have been observed in the inventories of Saudi Arabia and the UAE. Russia has been keen to expand on its traditional set of regional relationships, perhaps for political as much as economic reasons. In the wake of the attack on Saudi oil facilities on 14 September 2019, Russia's President Vladimir Putin was reported as saying that Riyadh should purchase Russian air-defence equipment. Putin apparently followed up on this offer when he visited Riyadh in mid-October.

While most defence equipment purchased in the region comes from external suppliers, indigenous arms production continues to expand. Most local defence-industrial companies are to be found in Israel and Turkey, but there has been growth in recent years in the defence sectors in Saudi Arabia and the UAE. As a result, engaging with local firms is becoming an increasingly important part of military contracts signed with these countries. Developments currently under way in these countries' defence industries indicate that this trend will only continue.

Saudi Arabia, through Vision 2030 and its broader defence-reform initiatives, continues to look to develop its local defence industries, while in February 2019, the UAE's Tawazun Economic Council announced the launch of a US$680m Defence and Security Development Fund aimed at stimulating national economic development through local defence industries. The UAE's creation of the Emirates Defence Industries Company (EDIC) in 2014 is a prime example of regional states' desire not just to 'bring onshore' more defence production and improve the range of high-technology jobs available to citizens but also to realise greater domestic benefit from their own defence investments. In late 2019, the UAE looked to further invigorate its local defence sector through consolidation and a bid to more closely integrate commercial-sector developments into the defence industry. A new conglomerate named 'Edge' will reportedly consolidate around 25 subsidiaries from EDIC, Emirates Advanced Investments and Tawazun, also rolling in these groups. A key reason underpinning this move is to boost local defence research and development. Edge said that it will organise firms into five clusters: platforms and systems, missiles and weapons, cyber defence, electronic warfare and intelligence, and mission support.

MOROCCO

Morocco's armed forces are engaged in a period of significant modernisation and transformation. This has involved structural changes to the armed forces, made evident with the reintroduction of conscription in 2019, and the continued introduction of modern military equipment. As a result, defence funding is increasing. At the same time, Rabat remains considered in its approach to foreign military relations and military deployments. The United States is the leading supplier of military equipment to Morocco. There are also defence relations with a number of European and Middle Eastern states, and Morocco was until early 2019 a participant in the Saudi-led coalition in Yemen. Meanwhile, tensions with Algeria continue and the border between the two countries remains closed.

Defence-policy priorities

Morocco's military forces are postured principally against potential challenges from the Popular Front for the Liberation of Saguia el-Hamra and Río de Oro (POLISARIO Front) in Western Sahara and the Algerian Army on the southern and eastern border. Moroccan forces were engaged in operations against POLISARIO from 1975 until the United Nations-brokered ceasefire took effect in 1991. (Both sides intermittently allege ceasefire violations in reports to the UN.) In Western Sahara, the UN maintains its MINURSO mission, which according to the UN in 2019 conducted both political and military activities, the latter in terms of de-mining and monitoring the sand berm that currently separates the two parties. This barrier, completed in 1987, runs for over 2,500 kilometres from Morocco to Mauritania along the Algerian border. Moroccan troops staff guard posts at intervals along the berm, with POLISARIO forces on the other side. The UN secretary-general's October 2019 report on MINURSO said that he remained 'convinced that a solution to the question of Western Sahara is possible'. UN-brokered talks in March 2019 saw representatives from Algeria, Mauritania, Morocco and POLISARIO convene in Geneva. The UN passed Security Council Resolution (SCR) 2440 in October 2018, which urges parties to continue dialogue and 'to demonstrate further political will towards a solution including by expanding upon their discussion of each other's proposals'. The UN noted (in SCR 2440 and 2494) that proposals were presented by both Morocco and POLISARIO in 2007.

In 2019, Morocco reiterated its autonomy initiative as Rabat's proposed solution.

Meanwhile, tensions with Algeria are long-standing. The border between the two countries has been closed since the 1990s, and it was reported in 2018 that Morocco would establish further towers there. Across the border, Algeria maintains the 8th Armoured Division at Ras el Ma, the 40th Mechanised Division at Béchar and the 38th Motorised Brigade at Tindouf. However, both Algeria and Morocco are also pursuing border-security measures in order to restrict the smuggling of goods (such as narcotics or weapons) and illicit population flows, which could potentially be exploited by terrorists. Morocco's armed forces are expected to periodically provide counter-terrorist capabilities and also likely monitor the two Spanish enclaves at Ceuta and Melilla in the north, for border-security purposes, as well as monitoring population movements and potential risks to international shipping lanes in the strait of Gibraltar.

Morocco has a wide range of international defence relationships with Western and Arab states. Some are prompted by Morocco's geographical position and its importance in relation to Mediterranean and broader security dynamics in North Africa and the Middle East. Others will likely be prompted by Morocco's relative political stability; in North Africa it is the only state not to have undergone regime change after 2011. Morocco too looks to benefit from its range of foreign defence ties. It maintains significant relations with France and each year the two nations conduct the CHEBEC maritime exercise. Meanwhile, military relations are developing with the United Kingdom. A Strategic Dialogue was signed by London and Rabat in 2018 (a second meeting took place in 2019) and joint exercises have been organised.

Morocco dispatched forces in 2015 to take part in the Saudi-led coalition in Yemen. It lost an F-16 on operations there the same year. However, in early 2019 it announced that it would no longer participate in the military action. Reports suggest that this withdrawal indicated a strain in ties between Rabat and Riyadh, but this remains unclear. Nonetheless, there were reports in recent years of significant Saudi Arabian investment in Morocco's defence sector.

The armed forces are also engaged on UN peacekeeping operations in Côte d'Ivoire and the Democratic Republic of the Congo. Morocco's position as a major non-NATO ally has also fostered international cooperation. In 1999, Morocco sent forces to Kosovo, and its contingent only withdrew in 2014. During this time, according to NATO, Morocco had dispatched some 11,000 troops to the mission. But perhaps the most important defence relationship is with the US. Morocco and the US organise a major joint exercise, *African Lion*, each year amid a range of other smaller unit-training activities.

Personnel

The return of conscription, and its extension to women, has been a significant recent development. Compulsory military service was originally enacted in 1966 and was abolished in 2006, with the forces then turning fully professional. National service now involves a one-year term of service for men between the ages of 20 and 35 but is on a voluntary basis for women aged 20 to 27 years. A range of supporting activities are now under way, including census initiatives in order to inform the draft process. Conscripts are due to receive four months of basic training, followed by trade training during the remaining eight months. Reasons for reinstating the draft reportedly included strengthening social cohesion, but analysts also highlighted its potential role in reducing youth unemployment as another driver.

Officer training takes place at the Royal Military Academy in Meknes, which includes a high school that ensures new potential cadets are educated to baccalaureate level. The Royal College of Higher Military Education at Kenitra serves as the higher staff college. It trains around 100–150 officers from the three armed services and gendarmerie, as well as students from sub-Saharan African countries. Training is focused on operational planning and joint national and multinational operations.

Armed forces

The air force has received significant investment in recent years. Its principal modern capability revolves around the F-16 Block 50/52, with envisaged tasks including air defence, precision strike, long-range strike and the suppression of enemy air defences (SEAD). Moroccan pilots have been dispatched on air-to-air refuelling and SEAD training courses in the US and Middle Eastern states. The air force has requested from the US 25 new F-16Vs and upgrades of the entire fleet of 23 F-16Cs and Ds to V format. The air force's other main combat aircraft, the F-5, has been in service since the 1970s and, analysts understand, is intended to be phased out from the mid-2020s. The

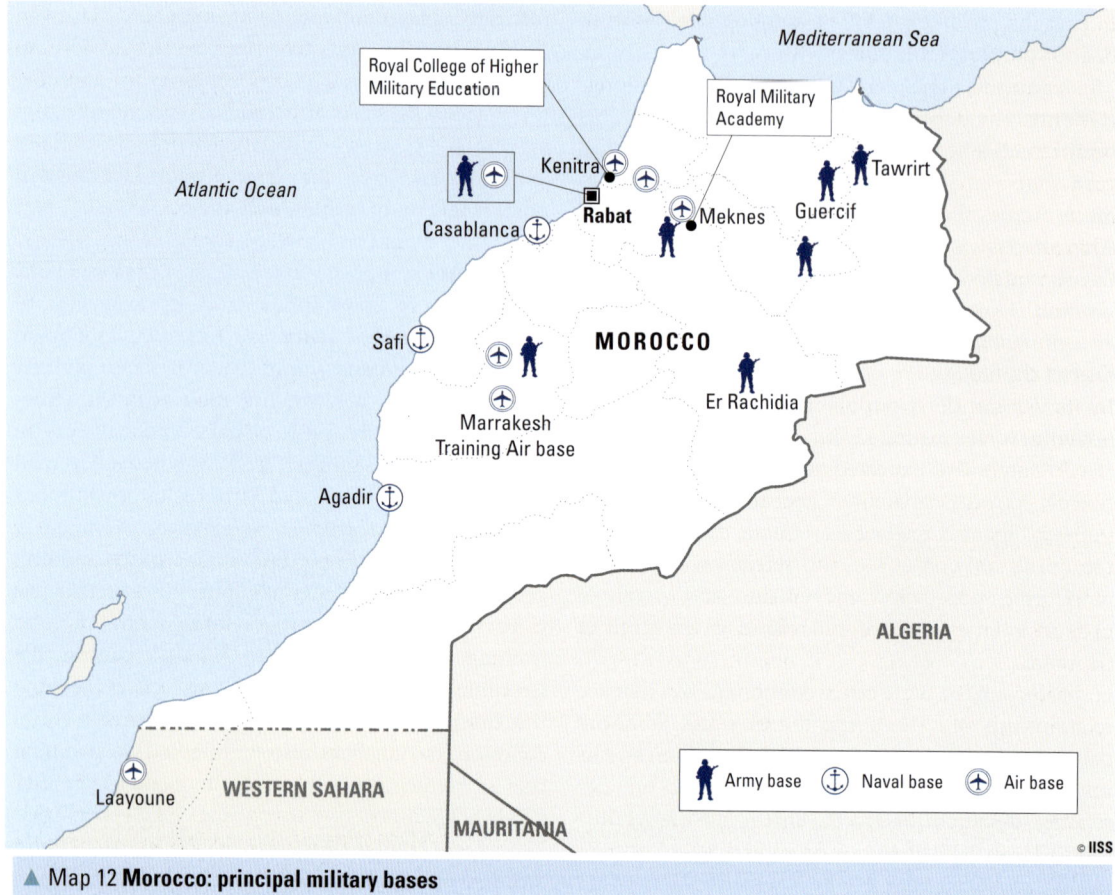

▲ Map 12 **Morocco: principal military bases**

attack-helicopter fleet, composed of *Gazelle*s with the HOT anti-tank missile, is planned to be strengthened by 2022 with the adoption of the AH-1Z *Viper* or AH-64E *Apache Guardian*. This possible sale, under US Foreign Military Sales arrangements, was approved by the US State Department in November 2019. The army is also looking to improve its long-range air-defence systems, and it is understood that the US *Patriot* PAC-2 or Chinese HQ-9 systems may be under consideration. The armed forces have already acquired the Chinese-manufactured DK-9 system, which is believed to comprise a *Skyguard*-type gun/missile combination with land-based PL-9 missiles and PG-99 35 mm guns, for short-range air defence.

The navy operates one French-manufactured FREMM destroyer and three SIGMA-class frigates. The acquisition of these vessels will have boosted the navy's anti-submarine-warfare capabilities. Some analysts understand that the navy may also be considering a submarine capability. Indeed, in 2013, Russian sources reported that Rosoboronexport would offer its *Amur* 1600 submarine to Morocco, if Rabat announced a tender (the *Amur* is likely an export version of Russia's *Lada*-class boat). In 2019, meanwhile, Portuguese media sources indicated that the two nations' navies may be developing cooperation related to submarine capability. Portuguese shipyards have in recent years conducted refit work on a number of Moroccan naval vessels. Possible Moroccan interest in Germany's Type-209/1400 or Type-214 boats has also been reported.

Meanwhile, the army has benefited from a major acquisition programme based on the US Excess Defense Articles mechanism. Morocco received 222 M1A1SA *Abrams* main battle tanks between 2016 and 2018. According to the US Defense Security Cooperation Agency, there is a plan to upgrade 162 of these tanks to one of three variants: the M1A1 situational-awareness (baseline) version, the M1A2M (with the commander's independent thermal viewer) or the M1A1 US Marine Corps version, which includes 'slew to cue'. This reportedly enables the turret to move to align with the commander's view at the push of a button. The Moroccan tank fleet consists also of US M60A1 and A3 *Patton*s and Russian T-72Bs. However, it is understood that Chinese-origin MBT-2000s were returned. The army's principal armoured personnel carrier is the French VAB. Moroccan artillery includes around 200 US M109 self-propelled howitzers and Chinese multiple-rocket launcher systems (possibly the 302 mm WS-1, while the 300 mm+ PHL-03 has been reported in-country).

Defence economics and industry

In its Article IV consultation report on Morocco, issued in July 2019, the International Monetary Fund (IMF) highlighted that economic activity in Morocco had weakened in 2018, partly due to reduced growth in the heavily weather-dependent agricultural sector, though the IMF projected that overall growth would reach 4.5% by 2024. This outlook depends on a range of factors, including internal reforms and the effect of international oil prices. Significant revenues are accrued from the automobile and phosphate sectors. Unemployment reduced slightly to a rate of 8.5% in August 2019, though it is reported that unemployment rates are significantly higher for younger Moroccans.

The Moroccan defence budget has been steadily increasing in local currency in recent years and rose from D34.3 billion (US$3.65bn) in 2018 to D35.1bn (US$3.63bn) in 2019 and is projected to rise to D45.4bn (US$4.69bn) in 2020. The amount allocated to personnel costs is projected to rise significantly in the 2020 budget, to D33.47bn (US$3.45bn), from D24.33bn (US$2.51bn) in 2019. In 2020, this sum will amount to 73.7% of the defence budget; in percentage terms, this is a modest increase. Analysts have posited that this rise may owe much to the costs associated with the return to conscription.

The defence industry is currently limited in scope, with experience only in maintenance and the manufacture of small-arms ammunition. However, since 2010, Morocco has attracted investments in the civil-aviation sector, and it is understood that around 140 companies are active in the sector. The Moroccan authorities are also understood to have been increasing international contacts in order to establish an industrial strategy. The visits in April 2019 by Spanish Minister of Defense Angel Olivares Ramirez and in July 2019 by then UK minister of state for the armed forces Mark Lancaster reportedly led to discussions on this subject. Meanwhile, French firm Arquus (formerly Renault Truck Defense) is working with Morocco on vehicle-modernisation projects, while Belgian firm Mecar has reportedly constructed a munitions-manufacturing plant in Morocco.

Algeria ALG

Algerian Dinar D		2018	2019	2020
GDP	D	20.3tr	20.4tr	
	US$	174bn	173bn	
per capita	US$	4,081	3,980	
Growth	%	1.4	2.6	
Inflation	%	4.3	2.0	
Def bdgt	D	1.12tr	1.23tr	
	US$	9.59bn	10.4bn	
US$1=D		116.59	118.34	

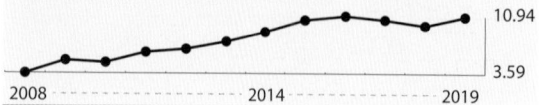

Real-terms defence budget trend (US$bn, constant 2015)

Population   42,325,923

Age	0–14	15–19	20–24	25–29	30–64	65 plus
Male	15.1%	3.6%	3.7%	4.3%	21.1%	2.8%
Female	14.4%	3.4%	3.6%	4.1%	20.7%	3.2%

Capabilities

The armed forces are among the most capable and best equipped in North Africa. Their primary roles are territorial integrity, internal security and regional stability. In April 2019, the army was instrumental in ending President Bouteflika's two decades in power, after widespread demonstrations, and it retains a key political role. Algeria is part of the African Union's North African Regional Capability Standby Force, hosting the force's logistics base in Algiers. Algeria discusses with its neighbours regional security challenges like counter-terrorism, and has particularly close security cooperation with Tunisia. The conscript-based force exercises regularly, with training appearing to be of a relatively good standard. There is an ongoing attempt to make the armed forces more professional, which was reflected in the reduction of conscription liability from 18 to 12 months in 2014. The armed forces' logistics capabilities appear sufficient to support internal deployments. The army's and air force's inventories consist of a core of modern, primarily Russian-sourced equipment, though China has also supplied equipment, including self-propelled artillery. Algiers has continued investing in fixed-wing combat-aircraft recapitalisation and the navy has invested in its submarine and frigate fleet. Local industry, and the services, are capable of equipment maintenance. However, while Algeria is largely dependent on foreign suppliers for new equipment, it has in recent years made significant investments towards developing a domestic defence industry. This has led to a number of joint ventures with foreign partners, such as with Italy's Leonardo and Germany's Rheinmetall over the licensed production of helicopters.

ACTIVE 130,000 (Army 110,000 Navy 6,000 Air 14,000) **Paramilitary 187,200**
Conscript liability 12 months

RESERVE 150,000 (Army 150,000) to age 50

ORGANISATIONS BY SERVICE

Army 35,000; 75,000 conscript (total 110,000)

FORCES BY ROLE
6 Mil Regions
MANOEUVRE
  Armoured
    2 (1st & 8th) armd div (3 tk regt; 1 mech regt, 1 arty gp)
    1 indep armd bde
  Mechanised
    2 (12th & 40th) mech div (1 tk regt; 3 mech regt, 1 arty gp)
    3 indep mech bde
  Light
    2 indep mot bde
  Air Manoeuvre
    1 AB div (4 para regt; 1 SF regt)
COMBAT SUPPORT
  2 arty bn
  1 AT regt
  4 engr bn
AIR DEFENCE
  7 AD bn

EQUIPMENT BY TYPE
ARMOURED FIGHTING VEHICLES
  MBT 1,467: 270 T-55AMV; 300 T-62; 325 T-72M1/M1M; 572 T-90SA
  RECCE 134: 44 AML-60; 26 BRDM-2; 64 BRDM-2M with 9M133 *Kornet* (AT-14 *Spriggan*)
  IFV 1,089: 285 BMP-1; 304 BMP-2; 400 BMP-2M with 9M133 *Kornet* (AT-14 *Spriggan*); 100 BMP-3
  APC 1,007+
    APC (T) VP-6
    APC (W) 1,005: 250 BTR-60; 150 BTR-80; 150 OT-64; 55 M3 Panhard; ε300 *Fuchs* 2; 100 *Fahd*
  PPV 2 *Marauder*
  AUV Nimr *Ajban*; Nimr *Ajban* LRSOV
ENGINEERING & MAINTENANCE VEHICLES
  AEV IMR-2
  ARV BREM-1
  MW M58 MICLIC
ANTI-TANK/ANTI-INFRASTRUCTURE
  SP 28 9P163-3 *Kornet*-EM (AT-14 *Spriggan*)
  MSL • MANPATS 9K11 *Malyutka* (AT-3 *Sagger*); 9K111 *Fagot* (AT-4 *Spigot*); 9K111-1 *Konkurs* (AT-5 *Spandrel*); 9K115-2 *Metis*-M1 (AT-13 *Saxhorn*-2); 9K135 *Kornet*-E (AT-14 *Spriggan*); Luch *Skif*; Milan
  RCL 180: **82mm** 120 B-10; **107mm** 60 B-11
  GUNS 100mm 10 T-12
ARTILLERY 1,106
  SP 224: **122mm** 140 2S1 *Gvozdika*; **152mm** 30 2S3 *Akatsiya*; **155mm** ε54 PLZ-45
  TOWED 393: **122mm** 345: 160 D-30; 25 D-74; 100 M-1931/37; 60 M-30; **130mm** 10 M-46; **152mm** 20 M-1937 (ML-20); **155mm** 18 Type-88 (PLL-01)
  MRL 151: **122mm** 51: 48 BM-21 *Grad*; 3+ SR5; **140mm** 48 BM-14; **220mm** 4 TOS-1A; **240mm** 30 BM-24; **300mm** 18 9A52 *Smerch*
  MOR 338: **82mm** 150 M-37; **120mm** 120 M-1943; W86; **SP 120mm** 8 SM4; W86 (SP); **160mm** 60 M-1943
SURFACE-TO-SURFACE MISSILE LAUNCHERS
  SRBM 4 *Iskander*-E
AIR DEFENCE
  SAM 106+

Short-range 38 96K6 *Pantsir*-S1 (SA-22 *Greyhound*); *Pantsir*-SM
Point-defence 68+: ε48 9K33M *Osa* (SA-8B *Gecko*); ε20 9K31 *Strela*-1 (SA-9 *Gaskin*); 9K32 *Strela*-2 (SA-7A/B *Grail*)‡; QW-2
GUNS ε425
SP 23mm ε225 ZSU-23-4
TOWED 200: **14.5mm** 100: 60 ZPU-2; 40 ZPU-4; **23mm** 100 ZU-23-2

Navy ε6,000
EQUIPMENT BY TYPE
SUBMARINES • TACTICAL • SSK 6:
 2 *Paltus* (FSU *Kilo*) with 6 single 533mm TT with Test-71ME HWT
 4 *Varshavyanka* (RUS Improved *Kilo*) with 6 single 533mm TT with 3M14E *Klub*-S (SS-N-30B) LACM/3M54E1/E *Klub*-S (SS-N-27A/B) AShM (*Klub*-S AShM variant unclear)/TEST-71ME HWT
PRINCIPAL SURFACE COMBATANTS • FRIGATES 8
 FFGHM 5:
  3 *Adhafer* (C28A) with 2 quad lnchr with C-802A AShM, 1 octuple lnchr with FM-90 (CH-SA-N-4) SAM, 2 triple 324mm ASTT, 2 Type-730B (H/PJ-12) CIWS, 1 76mm gun (capacity 1 hel)
  2 *Erradii* (MEKO 200AN) with 2 octuple lnchrs with RBS15 Mk3 AShM, 4 8-cell VLS with *Umkhonto*-IR SAM, 2 twin 324mm TT with MU90 LWT, 1 127mm gun (capacity 1 *Super Lynx* 300)
 FF 3 *Mourad Rais* (FSU *Koni*) with 2 twin 533mm TT, 2 RBU 6000 *Smerch* 2 A/S mor, 2 twin 76mm gun
PATROL AND COASTAL COMBATANTS 25
 CORVETTES 7
  FSGM 3 *Rais Hamidou* (FSU *Nanuchka* II) with 4 twin lnchr with 3M24E *Uran*-E (SS-N-25 *Switchblade*) AShM, 1 twin lnchr with 4K33 *Osa*-M (SA-N-4 *Gecko*) SAM, 1 AK630 CIWS, 1 twin 57mm gun
  FSG 4:
   3 *Djebel Chenoua* with 2 twin lnchr with C-802 (CH-SS-N-6) AShM, 1 AK630 CIWS, 1 76mm gun
   1 *Rais Hassen Barhiar* (*Djebel Chenoua* mod) with 2 twin lnchr with C-802 (CH-SS-N-6) AShM, 1 Type-730 (H/PJ-12) CIWS, 1 76mm gun
 PBFG 9 *Osa* II (3†) with 4 single lnchr with P-20U (SS-N-2B *Styx*) AShM
 PB 9 *Kebir* with 1 76mm gun
MINE WARFARE • MINE COUNTERMEASURES 1
 MCC 1 *El-Kasseh* (ITA *Gaeta* mod)
AMPHIBIOUS 7
 PRINCIPAL AMPHIBIOUS SHIPS • LHD 1 *Kalaat Beni Abbes* with 1 8-cell *Sylver* A50 VLS with *Aster* 15 SAM, 1 76mm gun (capacity 5 med hel; 3 LCVP; 15 MBT; 350 troops)
 LANDING SHIPS 3:
  LSM 1 *Polnochny* B with 1 twin AK230 CIWS (capacity 6 MBT; 180 troops)
  LST 2 *Kalaat beni Hammad* (capacity 7 MBT; 240 troops) with 1 med hel landing platform
 LANDING CRAFT • LCVP 3

LOGISTICS AND SUPPORT 3
 AGS 1 *El Idrissi*
 AX 1 *Daxin* with 2 AK230 CIWS, 1 76mm gun, 1 hel landing platform
 AXS 1 *El Mellah*

Naval Infantry
FORCES BY ROLE
MANOEUVRE
 Amphibious
 1 naval inf bn

Naval Aviation
EQUIPMENT BY TYPE
HELICOPTERS
 MRH 9: 3 AW139 (SAR); 6 *Super Lynx* 300
 SAR 9: 5 AW101 SAR; 4 *Super Lynx* Mk130

Coastal Defence
EQUIPMENT BY TYPE
COASTAL DEFENCE
 AShM 4K51 *Rubezh* (SSC-3 *Styx*)

Coast Guard ε500
EQUIPMENT BY TYPE
PATROL AND COASTAL COMBATANTS 55
 PBF 6 *Baglietto* 20
 PB 49: 6 *Baglietto Mangusta*; 12 *Jebel Antar*; 21 *Deneb*; 4 *El Mounkid*; 6 *Kebir* with 1 76mm gun
LOGISTICS AND SUPPORT 9
 AR 1 *El Mourafek*
 ARS 3 *El Moundjid*
 AXL 5 *El Mouderrib* (PRC *Chui-E*) (2 more in reserve†)

Air Force 14,000
FORCES BY ROLE
FIGHTER
 1 sqn with MiG-25PDS/RU *Foxbat*
 4 sqn with MiG-29S/UB *Fulcrum*
FIGHTER/GROUND ATTACK
 3 sqn with Su-30MKA *Flanker*
GROUND ATTACK
 2 sqn with Su-24M/MK *Fencer* D
ELINT
 1 sqn with Beech 1900D
MARITIME PATROL
 2 sqn with Beech 200T/300 *King Air*
ISR
 1 sqn with Su-24MR *Fencer* E*; MiG-25RBSh *Foxbat* D*
TANKER
 1 sqn with Il-78 *Midas*
TRANSPORT
 1 sqn with C-130H/H-30 *Hercules*; L-100-30
 1 sqn with C295M
 1 sqn with Gulfstream IV-SP; Gulfstream V
 1 sqn with Il-76MD/TD *Candid*
TRAINING
 2 sqn with Z-142

1 sqn with Yak-130 *Mitten**
2 sqn with L-39C/ZA *Albatros*
1 hel sqn with PZL Mi-2 *Hoplite*
ATTACK HELICOPTER
3 sqn with Mi-24 *Hind* (one re-equipping with Mi-28NE *Havoc*)
TRANSPORT HELICOPTER
1 sqn with AS355 *Ecureuil*
5 sqn with Mi-8 *Hip*; Mi-17 *Hip* H
1 sqn with Ka-27PS *Helix* D; Ka-32T *Helix*
ISR UAV
1 sqn with *Seeker* II
AIR DEFENCE
3 ADA bde
3 SAM regt with S-125 *Neva* (SA-3 *Goa*); 2K12 *Kub* (SA-6 *Gainful*); S-300PMU2 (SA-20 *Gargoyle*)
EQUIPMENT BY TYPE
AIRCRAFT 134 combat capable
 FTR 34: 11 MiG-25PDS/RU *Foxbat*; 23 MiG-29S/UB *Fulcrum*
 FGA 44 Su-30MKA
 ATK 33 Su-24M/MK *Fencer* D
 ISR 7: 4 MiG-25RBSh *Foxbat* D*; 3 Su-24MR *Fencer* E*
 TKR 6 Il-78 *Midas*
 TPT 65: **Heavy** 11: 3 Il-76MD *Candid* B; 8 Il-76TD *Candid*; **Medium** 16: 8 C-130H *Hercules*; 6 C-130H-30 *Hercules*; 2 L-100-30; **Light** 32: 3 Beech C90B *King Air*; 5 Beech 200T *King Air*; 6 Beech 300 *King Air*; 12 Beech 1900D (electronic surv); 5 C295M; 1 F-27 *Friendship*; **PAX** 6: 1 A340; 4 Gulfstream IV-SP; 1 Gulfstream V
 TRG 99: 36 L-39ZA *Albatros*; 7 L-39C *Albatros*; 16 Yak-130 *Mitten**; 40 Z-142
HELICOPTERS
 ATK 44: 30 Mi-24 *Hind*; 14+ Mi-28NE/UB *Havoc*
 SAR 3 Ka-27PS *Helix* D
 MRH 85: 8 AW139 (SAR); 3 Bell 412EP; 74 Mi-8 *Hip* (med tpt)/Mi-17 *Hip* H
 TPT 62: **Heavy** 14 Mi-26T2 *Halo*; **Medium** 4 Ka-32T *Helix*; **Light** 44: 8 AW119KE *Koala*; 8 AS355 *Ecureuil*; 28 PZL Mi-2 *Hoplite*
UNMANNED AERIAL VEHICLES
 CISR • Heavy CH-3; CH-4; *Yabhon United*-30
 ISR • Medium *Seeker* II; *Yabhon Flash*-20
AIR DEFENCE
 Long-range S-300PMU2 (SA-20 *Gargoyle*)
 Medium-range 9K317 *Buk*-M2E (SA-17 *Grizzly*); S-125 *Pechora*-M (SA-3 *Goa*)
 Short-range 2K12 *Kvadrat* (SA-6 *Gainful*)
AIR-LAUNCHED MISSILES
 AAM • IR R-60 (AA-8 *Aphid*); R-73 (AA-11A *Archer*); **IR/SARH** R-40/46 (AA-6 *Acrid*); R-23/24 (AA-7 *Apex*); R-27 (AA-10 *Alamo*); **ARH** R-77 (AA-12A *Adder*);
 ASM Kh-25 (AS-10 *Karen*); Kh-29 (AS-14 *Kedge*); Kh-59ME (AS-18 *Kazoo*); ZT-35 *Ingwe*; 9M120 *Ataka* (AT-9 *Spiral-2*)
 AShM Kh-31A (AS-17B *Krypton*)
 ARM Kh-25MP (AS-12A *Kegler*); Kh-31P (AS-17A *Krypton*)

Paramilitary ε187,200

Gendarmerie 20,000
Ministry of Defence control; 6 regions
EQUIPMENT BY TYPE
ARMOURED FIGHTING VEHICLES
 RECCE AML-60
 APC • APC (W) 210: 100 TH-390 *Fahd*; 110 Panhard M3
HELICOPTERS • TPT • Light 12+: 12 AW109; Some PZL Mi-2 *Hoplite*

National Security Forces 16,000
Directorate of National Security. Small arms

Republican Guard 1,200
EQUIPMENT BY TYPE
ARMOURED FIGHTING VEHICLES
 RECCE AML-60
 APC • APC (T) M3 half-track

Legitimate Defence Groups ε150,000
Self-defence militia, communal guards (60,000)

DEPLOYMENT
DEMOCRATIC REPUBLIC OF THE CONGO: UN • MONUSCO 1

Bahrain BHR

Bahraini Dinar D		2018	2019	2020
GDP	D	14.2bn	14.4bn	
	US$	37.7bn	38.2bn	
per capita	US$	25,483	25,273	
Growth	%	1.8	2.0	
Inflation	%	2.1	1.4	
Def bdgt [a]	D	557m	564m	564m
	US$	1.48bn	1.50bn	
FMA (US)	US$	0m	0m	0m
US$1=D		0.38	0.38	

[a] Excludes funds allocated to the Ministry of the Interior

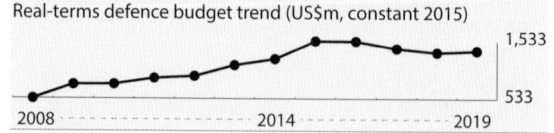
Real-terms defence budget trend (US$m, constant 2015)

Population 1,474,016

Ethnic groups: Nationals 46%; Asian 45.5%; African 1.5%; other or unspecified 7%

Age	0–14	15–19	20–24	25–29	30–64	65 plus
Male	9.5%	3.7%	5.0%	6.3%	34.5%	1.6%
Female	9.2%	3.1%	3.5%	3.9%	18.1%	1.6%

Capabilities
Bahrain's armed forces are capable and well equipped. The country occupies a critical and challenging strategic position between

regional rivals Iran and Saudi Arabia. The principal roles of the armed forces are territorial defence and internal-security support. Bahrain is a member of the GCC. Its most critical security relationship is with Saudi Arabia, but it also has a strong defence relationship with the US. The US 5th Fleet is headquartered in Bahrain, as is the combined-maritime-forces headquarters. In 2018, the UK reopened a permanent naval facility in Bahrain. Military service is voluntary and personnel are relatively well trained. Despite their small size, the armed forces have carried out a number of limited expeditionary deployments to support coalition operations, including in support of the Saudi-led intervention in Yemen. For a period in 2017–18, Bahrain commanded Combined Task Force 151, focused on countering piracy and other armed criminality at sea – the first time a GCC nation had assumed command of a CTF outside the Arabian Gulf. In a major enhancement to Bahrain's air mobility, it has bought ex-UK C-130J transport aircraft. As part of a major air-force modernisation, Bahrain intends to buy F-16V fighters and to upgrade its existing F-16C/Ds to that configuration. It has also signed a letter of offer and acceptance with the US to procure the *Patriot* air- and missile-defence system. The armed forces have their own maintenance support, but Bahrain has little in the way of a defence-industrial base beyond the limited naval-ship maintenance support provided by the Arab Shipbuilding and Repair Yard.

ACTIVE 8,200 (Army 6,000 Navy 700 Air 1,500)
Paramilitary 11,260

ORGANISATIONS BY SERVICE

Army 6,000
FORCES BY ROLE
SPECIAL FORCES
  1 SF bn
MANOEUVRE
  Armoured
  1 armd bde(-) (1 recce bn, 2 armd bn)
  Mechanised
  1 inf bde (2 mech bn, 1 mot bn)
  Light
  1 (Amiri) gd bn
COMBAT SUPPORT
  1 arty bde (1 hvy arty bty, 2 med arty bty, 1 lt arty bty, 1 MRL bty)
  1 engr coy
COMBAT SERVICE SUPPORT
  1 log coy
  1 tpt coy
  1 med coy
AIR DEFENCE
  1 AD bn (1 ADA bty, 2 SAM bty)
EQUIPMENT BY TYPE
ARMOURED FIGHTING VEHICLES
  MBT 180 M60A3
  RECCE 22 AML-90
  IFV 67: 25 YPR-765 PRI; 42 AIFV-B-C25
  APC 303+
    APC (T) 303: 300 M113A2; 3 AIFV-B
    APC (W) *Arma* 6×6
  AUV M-ATV
ENGINEERING & MAINTENANCE VEHICLES
  ARV 53 *Fahd* 240

ANTI-TANK/ANTI-INFRASTRUCTURE
  MSL
    SP 5 AIFV-B-*Milan*; HMMWV with BGM-71A TOW
    MANPATS BGM-71A TOW; *Kornet*-EM
  RCL 31: **106mm** 25 M40A1; **120mm** 6 MOBAT
ARTILLERY 175
  SP 82: **155mm** 20 M109A5; **203mm** 62 M110A2
  TOWED 36: **105mm** 8 L118 Light Gun; **155mm** 28 M198
  MRL 13: **220mm** 4 SR5; **227mm** 9 M270 MLRS
  MOR 44: **81mm** 32: 12 L16; 20 EIMOS; **SP 120mm** 12 M113A2
SURFACE-TO-SURFACE MISSILE LAUNCHERS
  SRBM • Conventional MGM-140A ATACMS (launched from M270 MLRS)
AIR DEFENCE
  SAM
    Medium-range 6 MIM-23B I-*Hawk*
    Short-range 7 *Crotale*
    Point-defence 9K338 *Igla*-S (SA-24 *Grinch*) (reported); FIM-92 *Stinger*; RBS-70
  GUNS 24: **35mm** 12 GDF-003/-005; **40mm** 12 L/70

Navy 700
EQUIPMENT BY TYPE
PRINCIPAL SURFACE COMBATANTS 1
  FRIGATES • FFGHM 1 *Sabha* (ex-US *Oliver Hazard Perry*) with 1 Mk 13 GMLS with SM-1MR Block VI SAM/RGM-84C *Harpoon* Block 1B AShM, 2 triple 324mm SVTT Mk 32 ASTT with Mk 46 LWT, 1 Mk 15 *Phalanx* Block 1B CIWS, 1 76mm gun (capacity 1 Bo-105 hel)
PATROL AND COASTAL COMBATANTS 12
  CORVETTES • FSG 2 *Al Manama* (GER Lurssen 62m) with 2 twin lnchr with MM40 *Exocet* AShM, 2 76mm guns, 1 hel landing platform
  PCFG 4 *Ahmed el Fateh* (GER Lurssen 45m) with 2 twin lnchr with MM40 *Exocet* AShM, 1 76mm gun
  PB 4: 2 *Al Jarim* (US *Swift* FPB-20); 2 *Al Riffa* (GER Lurssen 38m)
  PBF 2 Mk V SOC
AMPHIBIOUS • LANDING CRAFT 9
  LCM 7: 1 *Loadmaster*; 4 *Mashtan*; 2 *Dinar* (ADSB 42m)
  LCVP 2 *Sea Keeper*

Naval Aviation
EQUIPMENT BY TYPE
HELICOPTERS • TPT • Light 2 Bo-105

Air Force 1,500
FORCES BY ROLE
FIGHTER
  2 sqn with F-16C/D *Fighting Falcon*
FIGHTER/GROUND ATTACK
  1 sqn with F-5E/F *Tiger* II
TRANSPORT
  1 (Royal) flt with B-727; B-747; BAe-146; Gulfstream II; Gulfstream IV; Gulfstream 450; Gulfstream 550; S-92A
TRAINING
  1 sqn with *Hawk* Mk129*
  1 sqn with T-67M *Firefly*

ATTACK HELICOPTER
2 sqn with AH-1E/F *Cobra*; TAH-1P *Cobra*
TRANSPORT HELICOPTER
1 sqn with Bell 212 (AB-212)
1 sqn with UH-60M *Black Hawk*
1 (VIP) sqn with Bo-105; S-70A *Black Hawk*; UH-60L *Black Hawk*

EQUIPMENT BY TYPE
AIRCRAFT 38 combat capable
FTR 12: 8 F-5E *Tiger* II; 4 F-5F *Tiger* II
FGA 20: 16 F-16C Block 40 *Fighting Falcon*; 4 F-16D Block 40 *Fighting Falcon*
TPT 12: **Medium** 2 C-130J *Hercules*; **PAX** 10: 1 B-727; 2 B-747; 1 Gulfstream II; 1 Gulfstream IV; 1 Gulfstream 450; 1 Gulfstream 550; 3 BAe-146
TRG 9: 6 *Hawk* Mk129*; 3 T-67M *Firefly*
HELICOPTERS
ATK 28: 16 AH-1E *Cobra*; 12 AH-1F *Cobra*
TPT 27: **Medium** 13: 3 S-70A *Black Hawk*; 1 S-92A (VIP); 1 UH-60L *Black Hawk*; 8 UH-60M *Black Hawk*; **Light** 14: 11 Bell 212 (AB-212); 3 Bo-105
TRG 6 TAH-1P *Cobra*
AIR-LAUNCHED MISSILES
AAM • **IR** AIM-9P *Sidewinder*; **SARH** AIM-7 *Sparrow*; **ARH** AIM-120B/C AMRAAM
ASM AGM-65D/G *Maverick*; some TOW
BOMBS
Laser-guided GBU-10/12 *Paveway* II

Paramilitary ε11,260

Police 9,000
Ministry of Interior
EQUIPMENT BY TYPE
ARMOURED FIGHTING VEHICLES
RECCE 8 S52 *Shorland*
APC • **APC (W)** Otokar ISV; *Cobra*
HELICOPTERS
MRH 2 Bell 412 *Twin Huey*
ISR 2 Hughes 500
TPT • **Light** 1 Bo-105

National Guard ε2,000
FORCES BY ROLE
MANOEUVRE
Other
3 paramilitary bn
EQUIPMENT BY TYPE
ARMOURED FIGHTING VEHICLES
APC • **APC (W)** Arma 6×6; *Cobra*

Coast Guard ε260
Ministry of Interior
PATROL AND COASTAL COMBATANTS 55
PBF 26: 2 Ares 18; 3 *Response Boat-Medium* (RB-M); 4 *Jaris*; 6 *Saham*; 6 *Fajr*; 5 *Jarada*
PB 29: 6 *Haris*; 1 *Al Muharraq*; 10 *Deraa* (of which 4 *Halmatic* 20, 2 *Souter* 20, 4 *Rodman* 20); 10 *Saif* (of which 4 *Fairey Sword*, 6 *Halmatic* 160); 2 *Hawar*

AMPHIBIOUS • LANDING CRAFT • LCU 1 *Loadmaster* II

DEPLOYMENT

SAUDI ARABIA: Operation Restoring Hope 250; 1 SF gp; 1 arty gp; 6 F-16C *Fighting Falcon*

FOREIGN FORCES

United Kingdom Air Force 160: 1 naval base
United States US Central Command 5,000; 1 HQ (5th Fleet); 1 FGA sqn(-) with 5 AV-8B *Harrier* II; 1 ASW sqn with 5 P-8A *Poseidon*; 2 AD bty with MIM-104E/F *Patriot* PAC-2/3

Egypt EGY

Egyptian Pound E£		2018	2019	2020
GDP	E£	4.44tr	5.32tr	
	US$	250bn	302bn	
per capita	US$	2,573	3,047	
Growth	%	5.3	5.5	
Inflation	%	20.9	13.9	
Def bdgt	E£	51.6bn	59.0bn	
	US$	2.90bn	3.35bn	
FMA (US)	US$	1.30bn	1.30bn	1.30bn
US$1=E£		17.78	17.62	

Real-terms defence budget trend (US$bn, constant 2015)

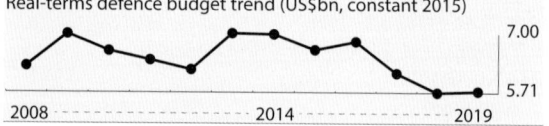

Population	101,776,661					
Age	0–14	15–19	20–24	25–29	30–64	65 plus
Male	17.3%	4.7%	4.8%	4.7%	17.5%	2.1%
Female	16.2%	4.4%	4.5%	4.5%	17.1%	2.3%

Capabilities

Egypt's armed forces are the largest in the region and are principally focused on territorial integrity and internal security, including combating ISIS-affiliated groups in northern Sinai. The armed forces remain deeply involved in the civilian economy and retain a central role in Egyptian politics. Egypt and the US maintain a strong strategic partnership, which has seen significant US equipment deliveries and ongoing foreign military aid payments. Defence relations with Russia have developed, particularly regarding procurements. Operational experience will have been bolstered by counter-insurgency operations in the Sinai since 2011 and contributions to several UN deployments. Training is supplemented by regular involvement in a number of multinational exercises. Egypt has a developing capacity to deploy independently beyond its borders. It contributes to UN missions, has intervened militarily in Libya and sent combat aircraft to support the Saudi-led coalition in Yemen. The navy's two *Mistral*-class amphibious ships will bolster the capacity to deploy regionally. The armed forces' inventory primarily comprises obsolete Soviet-era systems and newer Western equipment. However, the armed forces are undertaking an extensive equipment-recapitalisation programme, which is seeing the delivery of Russian multi-role fighters, attack helicopters and SAM systems. Combat aircraft have also been sourced from France and armed UAVs from China. Naval recapitalisation includes German-built submarines and French-designed frigates. Egypt has an established domestic defence industry, supplying equipment for both the armed forces and export markets, ranging from small arms to armoured vehicles. There is a history of licensed and co-production with foreign companies, including the local assembly of M1A1 main battle tanks from US-supplied kits and the production of frigates with French assistance.

ACTIVE 438,500 (Army 310,000 Navy 18,500 Air 30,000 Air Defence Command 80,000) **Paramilitary 397,000**

Conscription liability 12–36 months (followed by refresher training over a period of up to 9 years)

RESERVE 479,000 (Army 375,000 Navy 14,000 Air 20,000 Air Defence Command 70,000)

ORGANISATIONS BY SERVICE

Space
EQUIPMENT BY TYPE
SATELLITES • ISR 1 *Egyptsat*-A

Army 90,000–120,000; 190,000–220,000 conscript (total 310,000)
FORCES BY ROLE
SPECIAL FORCES
 5 cdo gp
 1 counter-terrorist unit
MANOEUVRE
 Armoured
 4 armd div (2 armd bde, 1 mech bde, 1 arty bde)
 4 indep armd bde
 1 Republican Guard bde
 Mechanised
 8 mech div (1 armd bde, 2 mech bde, 1 arty bde)
 4 indep mech bde
 Light
 1 inf div
 2 indep inf bde
 Air Manoeuvre
 2 air mob bde
 1 para bde
SURFACE-TO-SURFACE MISSILE
 1 SRBM bde with FROG-7
 1 SRBM bde with *Scud*-B
COMBAT SUPPORT
 15 arty bde
 6 engr bde (3 engr bn)
 2 spec ops engr bn
 6 salvage engr bn
 24 MP bn
 18 sigs bn
COMBAT SERVICE SUPPORT
 36 log bn
 27 med bn

EQUIPMENT BY TYPE
ARMOURED FIGHTING VEHICLES
 MBT 2,480: 1,130 M1A1 *Abrams*; 300 M60A1; 850 M60A3; 200 T-62 (840 T-54/T-55; 300 T-62 all in store)
 RECCE 412: 300 BRDM-2; 112 *Commando Scout*
 IFV 690: 390 YPR-765 25mm; 300 BMP-1
 APC 5,177+
  APC (T) 2,700: 2,000 M113A2/YPR-765 (incl variants); 500 BTR-50; 200 OT-62
  APC (W) 1,560: 250 BMR-600P; 250 BTR-60; 410 *Fahd*-30/TH 390 *Fahd*; 650 *Walid*
  PPV 917+: 468 *Caiman*; some REVA III; some REVA V LWB; 360 RG-33L; 89 RG-33 HAGA (amb)
  AUV 95+: *Panthera* T6; 95+ *Sherpa Light Scout*
ENGINEERING & MAINTENANCE VEHICLES
 ARV 367+: *Fahd* 240; BMR 3560.55; 12 *Maxxpro* ARV; 220 M88A1; 90 M88A2; M113 ARV; 45 M578; T-54/55 ARV
 VLB KMM; MTU; MTU-20
 MW *Aardvark* JFSU Mk4
ANTI-TANK/ANTI-INFRASTRUCTURE • MSL
 SP 352+: 52 M901, 300 YPR-765 PRAT; HMMWV with TOW-2
 MANPATS 9K11 *Malyutka* (AT-3 *Sagger*) (incl BRDM-2); HJ-73; Luch *Corsar* (reported); *Milan*; *Stugna*-P (reported); TOW-2
ARTILLERY 4,468
 SP 492+: **122mm** 124+: 124 SP 122; D-30 mod; **130mm** M-46 mod; **155mm** 368: 164 M109A2; 204 M109A5
 TOWED 962: **122mm** 526: 190 D-30M; 36 M-1931/37; 300 M-30; **130mm** 420 M-46; **155mm** 16 GH-52
 MRL 450: **122mm** 356: 96 BM-11; 60 BM-21; 50 *Sakr*-10; 50 *Sakr*-18; 100 *Sakr*-36; **130mm** 36 K136 *Kooryong*; **140mm** 32 BM-14; **227mm** 26 M270 MLRS; **240mm** (48 BM-24 in store)
 MOR 2,564: **81mm** 50 M125A2; **82mm** 500; SP **107mm** 100: 65 M106A1; 35 M106A2; **120mm** 1,848: 1,800 M-1943; 48 Brandt; SP **120mm** 36 M1064A3; **160mm** 30 M-160
SURFACE-TO-SURFACE MISSILE LAUNCHERS
 SRBM • **Conventional** 42+: 9 FROG-7; 24 *Sakr*-80; 9 *Scud*-B
UNMANNED AERIAL VEHICLES
 ISR • **Medium** R4E-50 *Skyeye*; ASN 209
AIR DEFENCE
 SAM
  Point-defence 45 *Sinai*-23 with *Ayn al-Saqr*; *Ayn al-Saqr*; FIM-92 *Stinger*; 9K38 *Igla* (SA-18 *Grouse*)
 GUNS
  SP 160: **23mm** 120 ZSU-23-4; **57mm** 40 ZSU-57-2
  TOWED 700: **14.5mm** 300 ZPU-4; **23mm** 200 ZU-23-2; **57mm** 200 S-60

Navy ε8,500 (incl 2,000 Coast Guard); 10,000 conscript (total 18,500)
EQUIPMENT BY TYPE
SUBMARINES • TACTICAL • SSK 6
 4 *Romeo*† (PRC Type-033) with 8 single 533mm TT with UGM-84C *Harpoon* Block 1B AShM/Mk 37 HWT
 2 Type-209/1400 with 8 single 533mm TT with UGM-84L *Harpoon* Block II AShM/*SeaHake* mod 4 (DM2A4) HWT

PRINCIPAL SURFACE COMBATANTS 10
  DESTROYERS • DDGHM 1 *Tahya Misr* (FRA *Aquitaine*) with 2 quad lnchr with MM40 *Exocet* Block 3 AShM, 2 8-cell *Sylver* A43 VLS with *Aster* 15 SAM, 2 twin B-515 324mm ASTT with MU90 LWT, 1 76mm gun (capacity 1 med hel)
  FRIGATES 9
    FFGHM 5:
      4 *Alexandria* (ex-US *Oliver Hazard Perry*) with 1 Mk 13 GMLS with RGM-84C *Harpoon* Block 1B AShM/ SM-1MR Block VI SAM, 2 triple 324mm ASTT with Mk 46 LWT, 1 Mk 15 *Phalanx* CIWS, 1 76mm gun (capacity 2 SH-2G *Super Seasprite* ASW hel)
      1 *El Fateh* (*Gowind* 2500) with 2 quad lnchrs with MM40 *Exocet* Block 3 AShM, 1 16-cell CLA VLS with VL-MICA SAM, 2 triple 324mm ASTT with MU90 LWT, 1 76mm gun (capacity 1 med hel)
    FFGH 2 *Damyat* (ex-US *Knox*) with 1 octuple Mk 16 GMLS with RGM-84C *Harpoon* Block 1B AShM/ ASROC, 2 twin 324mm SVTT Mk 32 TT with Mk 46 LWT, 1 Mk 15 *Phalanx* CIWS, 1 127mm gun (capacity 1 SH-2G *Super Seasprite* ASW hel)
    FFG 2 *Najim Al Zaffer* (PRC *Jianghu* I) with 2 twin lnchr with HY-2 (CH-SS-N-2 *Safflower*) AShM, 4 RBU 1200 A/S mor, 2 twin 57mm guns
PATROL AND COASTAL COMBATANTS 61
  CORVETTES 7
    FSGM 6:
      2 *Abu Qir* (ESP *Descubierta* – 1†) with 2 quad lnchr with RGM-84C *Harpoon* Block 1B AShM, 1 octuple *Albatros* lnchr with *Aspide* SAM, 2 triple SVTT Mk 32 324mm ASTT with *Sting Ray* LWT, 1 twin 375mm Bofors ASW Rocket Launcher System A/S mor, 1 76mm gun
      4 *Ezzat* (US *Ambassador Fast Missile Craft*) with 2 quad lnchr with RGM-84L *Harpoon* Block II AShM, 1 21-cell Mk49 lnchr with RAM Block 1A SAM, 1 Mk15 Mod 21 Block 1B *Phalanx* CIWS 1 76mm gun
    FS 1 *Shabab Misr* (ex-RoK *Po Hang*) with 2 76mm guns
  PCFG 8:
    1 *Molnya* (RUS *Tarantul* IV) with 2 twin lnchr with 3M80E *Moskit* (SS-N-22A *Sunburn*), 2 AK630 CIWS, 1 76mm gun
    6 *Ramadan* with 4 single lnchr with *Otomat* Mk2 AShM, 1 76mm gun
    1 *Tiger* with 2 twin lnchr with RGM-84 *Harpoon* AShM, 1 76mm gun
  PCF 4 *Tiger* with 1 76mm gun
  PCC 5 *Al-Nour* (ex-PRC *Hainan* – 3 more in reserve†) with 2 triple 324mm TT, 4 RBU 1200 A/S mor, 2 twin 57mm guns
  PBFGM 8 *Osa* I (ex-YUG – 3†) with 4 single lnchr with P-20 (SS-N-2A *Styx*) AShM, 1 9K32 *Strela*-2 (SA-N-5 *Grail*) SAM (manual aiming)
  PBFG 9:
    4 *Hegu* (PRC – *Komar* type) with 2 single lnchr with SY-1 (CH-SS-N-1 *Scrubbrush*) AShM (2 additional vessels in reserve)
    5 *October* (FSU *Komar* – 1†) with 2 single lnchr with *Otomat* Mk2 AShM (1 additional vessel in reserve)
  PBFM 4 *Shershen* (FSU) with 1 9K32 *Strela*-2 (SA-N-5 *Grail*) SAM (manual aiming), 1 12-tube BM-24 MRL
  PBF 10:
    6 *Kaan* 20 (TUR MRTP 20)
    4 *Osa* II (ex-FIN)
  PB 6:
    4 *Shanghai* II (PRC)
    2 *Shershen* (FSU – 1†) with 4 single 533mm TT, 1 8-tube BM-21 MRL
MINE WARFARE • MINE COUNTERMEASURES 14
  MHC 5: 2 *Al Siddiq* (ex-US *Osprey*); 3 *Dat Assawari* (US Swiftships)
  MSI 2 *Safaga* (US Swiftships)
  MSO 7: 3 *Assiout* (FSU T-43 class); 4 *Aswan* (FSU *Yurka*)
AMPHIBIOUS 20
  PRINCIPAL AMPHIBIOUS SHIPS • LHD 2 *Gamal Abdel Nasser* (FRA *Mistral*) (capacity 16 med hel; 2 LCT or 4 LCM; 13 MBTs; 50 AFVs; 450 troops)
  LANDING SHIPS • LSM 3 *Polnochny* A (FSU) (capacity 6 MBT; 180 troops)
  LANDING CRAFT 15:
    LCM 13: 4 CTM NG; 9 *Vydra* (FSU) (capacity either 3 MBT or 200 troops)
    LCT 2 EDA-R
LOGISTICS AND SUPPORT 24
  AOT 7 *Ayeda* (FSU *Toplivo* – 1 additional in reserve)
  AE 1 *Halaib* (ex-GER *Westerwald* class)
  AKR 3 *Al Hurreya*
  AR 1 *Shaledin* (ex-GER *Luneberg* class)
  ARS 2 *Al Areesh*
  ATF 5 *Al Maks*† (FSU *Okhtensky*)
  AX 5: 1 *El Fateh*† (ex-UK 'Z' class); 1 *El Horriya* (also used as the presidential yacht); 1 *Al Kousser*; 1 *Intishat*; 1 other

Coastal Defence

Army tps, Navy control
EQUIPMENT BY TYPE
COASTAL DEFENCE
  ARTY 100mm; **130mm** SM-4-1; **152mm**
  AShM 4K87 (SSC-2B *Samlet*); *Otomat* MkII

Naval Aviation

All aircraft operated by Air Force
AIRCRAFT • TPT • Light 4 Beech 1900C (maritime surveillance)
UNMANNED AERIAL VEHICLES
  ISR • Light 2 S-100 *Camcopter*

Coast Guard 2,000

EQUIPMENT BY TYPE
PATROL AND COASTAL COMBATANTS 89
  PBF 14: 6 *Crestitalia*; 5 *Swift Protector*; 3 *Peterson*
  PB 75: 5 *Nisr*; 12 *Sea Spectre* MkIII; 25 Swiftships; 21 *Timsah*; 3 Type-83; 9 *Peterson*

Air Force 30,000 (incl 10,000 conscript)

FORCES BY ROLE
FIGHTER
  1 sqn with F-16A/B *Fighting Falcon*

8 sqn with F-16C/D *Fighting Falcon*
1 sqn with J-7
3 sqn with MiG-21 *Fishbed*/MiG-21U *Mongol* A
2 sqn with *Mirage* 5D/E
1 sqn with *Mirage* 2000B/C
FIGHTER/GROUND ATTACK
1 sqn with *Mirage* 5E2
1 sqn (forming) with *Rafale* DM/EM
1 sqn (forming) with MiG-29M/M2 *Fulcrum*
ANTI-SUBMARINE WARFARE
1 sqn with SH-2G *Super Seasprite*
MARITIME PATROL
1 sqn with Beech 1900C
ELECTRONIC WARFARE
1 sqn with Beech 1900 (ELINT); *Commando* Mk2E (ECM)
ELECTRONIC WARFARE/TRANSPORT
1 sqn with C-130H/VC-130H *Hercules*
AIRBORNE EARLY WARNING
1 sqn with E-2C *Hawkeye*
SEARCH & RESCUE
1 unit with AW139
TRANSPORT
1 sqn with An-74TK-200A
1 sqn with C-130H/C-130H-30 *Hercules*
1 sqn with C295M
1 sqn with DHC-5D *Buffalo*
1 sqn with B-707-366C; B-737-100; Beech 200 *Super King Air*; *Falcon* 20; Gulfstream III; Gulfstream IV; Gulfstream IV-SP
TRAINING
1 sqn with *Alpha Jet**
1 sqn with DHC-5 *Buffalo*
3 sqn with EMB-312 *Tucano*
1 sqn with Grob 115EG
ε6 sqn with K-8 *Karakorum**
1 sqn with L-39 *Albatros*; L-59E *Albatros**
ATTACK HELICOPTER
2 sqn with AH-64D *Apache*
1 sqn with Ka-52A *Hokum* B
2 sqn with SA-342K *Gazelle* (with HOT)
1 sqn with SA-342L *Gazelle*
TRANSPORT HELICOPTER
1 sqn with CH-47C/D *Chinook* 1 sqn with Mi-8
1 sqn with Mi-8/Mi-17-1V *Hip*
1 sqn with S-70 *Black Hawk*; UH-60A/L *Black Hawk*
UAV
Some sqn with R4E-50 *Skyeye*; *Wing Loong* (GJ-1)
EQUIPMENT BY TYPE
AIRCRAFT 584 combat capable
FTR 62: 26 F-16A *Fighting Falcon*; 6 F-16B *Fighting Falcon*; ε30 J-7
FGA 319: 139 F-16C *Fighting Falcon*; 37 F-16D *Fighting Falcon*; 2 *Mirage* 2000B; 15 *Mirage* 2000C; 36 *Mirage* 5D/E; 12 *Mirage* 5E2; ε40 MiG-21 *Fishbed*/MiG-21U *Mongol* A; ε14 MiG-29M/M2 *Fulcrum*; 16 *Rafale* DM; 8 *Rafale* EM
ELINT 2 VC-130H *Hercules*
ISR 12: ε6 AT-802 *Air Tractor**; 6 *Mirage* 5R (5SDR)*
AEW&C 7 E-2C *Hawkeye*
TPT 82: **Heavy** 2 Il-76MF *Candid*; **Medium** 24: 21 C-130H *Hercules*; 3 C-130H-30 *Hercules*; **Light** 45: 3 An-74TK-200A; 1 Beech 200 *King Air*; 4 Beech 1900 (ELINT); 4 Beech 1900C; 24 C295M; 9 DHC-5D *Buffalo* (being withdrawn) **PAX** 11: 1 B-707-366C; 3 *Falcon* 20; 2 Gulfstream III; 1 Gulfstream IV; 4 Gulfstream IV-SP
TRG 329: 36 *Alpha Jet**; 54 EMB-312 *Tucano*; 74 Grob 115EG; 120 K-8 *Karakorum**; 10 L-39 *Albatros*; 35 L-59E*
HELICOPTERS
ATK 75: 45 AH-64D *Apache*; ε30 Ka-52A *Hokum* B
ASW 10 SH-2G *Super Seasprite* (opcon Navy)
ELINT 4 *Commando* Mk2E (ECM)
MRH 72: 2 AW139 (SAR); 65 SA342K *Gazelle* (some with HOT); 5 SA342L *Gazelle* (opcon Navy)
TPT 96: **Heavy** 19: 3 CH-47C *Chinook*; 16 CH-47D *Chinook*; **Medium** 77: 2 AS-61; 24 *Commando* (of which 3 VIP); 40 Mi-8T *Hip*; 3 Mi-17-1V *Hip*; 4 S-70 *Black Hawk* (VIP); 4 UH-60L *Black Hawk* (VIP)
TRG 17 UH-12E
UNMANNED AERIAL VEHICLES
CISR • Heavy 4+ *Wing Loong* (GJ-1)
ISR • Medium R4E-50 *Skyeye*
AIR LAUNCHED MISSILES
AAM • IR R-3 (AA-2 *Atoll*)‡; AIM-9M/P *Sidewinder*; R-550 *Magic*; 9M39 *Igla*-V; **IIR** *Mica* IR; **ARH** *Mica* RF; **SARH** AIM-7F/M *Sparrow*; R-530
ASM AASM; AGM-65A/D/F/G *Maverick*; AGM-114F/K *Hellfire*; AS-30L; HOT; AKD-10 (LJ-7); 9M120 *Ataka* (AT-9 *Spiral*-2)
AShM AGM-84L *Harpoon* Block II; AM39 *Exocet*;
ARM *Armat*; Kh-25MP (AS-12A *Kegler*)
BOMBS
Laser-guided GBU-10/12 *Paveway* II

Air Defence Command 80,000 conscript; 70,000 reservists (total 150,000)

FORCES BY ROLE
AIR DEFENCE
5 AD div (geographically based) (total: 12 SAM bty with M48 *Chaparral*, 12 radar bn, 12 ADA bde (total: 100 ADA bn), 12 SAM bty with MIM-23B I-*Hawk*, 14 SAM bty with *Crotale*, 18 AD bn with RIM-7M *Sea Sparrow* with *Skyguard*/GDF-003 with *Skyguard*, 110 SAM bn with S-125 *Pechora*-M (SA-3A *Goa*); 2K12 *Kub* (SA-6 *Gainful*); S-75M *Volkhov* (SA-2 *Guideline*))
EQUIPMENT BY TYPE
AIR DEFENCE
  SAM
    Long-range S-300V4 (SA-23)
    Medium-range 612+: 40+ *Buk*-M1-2/M2E (SA-11/SA-17); 78+ MIM-23B I-*Hawk*; 282 S-75M *Volkhov* (SA-2 *Guideline*); 212+ S-125 *Pechora*-M (SA-3A *Goa*)
    Short-range 160+: 56+ 2K12 *Kub* (SA-6 *Gainful*); 10 9K331M *Tor*-M1 (SA-15 *Gauntlet*); 10+ *Tor*-M2E (SA-15 *Gauntlet*); 24+ *Crotale*; 80 RIM-7M *Sea Sparrow* with *Skyguard*
    Point-defence 136+: 50 M1097 *Avenger*; 50+ M48 *Chaparral*; 36+ *Sinai*-23 with *Ayn al-Saqr*
  GUNS 910
    SP • 23mm 230 ZSU-23-4 *Shilka*
    TOWED 680: **35mm** 80 GDF-005 with *Skyguard*; **57mm** 600 S-60

Paramilitary ε397,000 active

Central Security Forces ε325,000
Ministry of Interior; includes conscripts
ARMOURED FIGHTING VEHICLES
  APC • **APC (W)** *Walid*
  AUV *Sherpa Light Scout*

National Guard ε60,000
Lt wpns only
FORCES BY ROLE
MANOEUVRE
  Other
    8 paramilitary bde (cadre) (3 paramilitary bn)
EQUIPMENT BY TYPE
  ARMOURED FIGHTING VEHICLES APC • **APC (W)** 250 *Walid*

Border Guard Forces ε12,000
Ministry of Interior; lt wpns only
FORCES BY ROLE
MANOEUVRE
  Other
    18 Border Guard regt

DEPLOYMENT

CENTRAL AFRICAN REPUBLIC: UN • MINUSCA 993; 1 inf bn; 1 tpt coy
DEMOCRATIC REPUBLIC OF THE CONGO: UN • MONUSCO 18
LIBERIA: UN • UNMIL 2 obs
MALI: UN • MINUSMA 1,103; 1 sy bn; 1 MP coy
SAUDI ARABIA: *Operation Restoring Hope* 6 F-16C *Fighting Falcon*
SOUTH SUDAN: UN • UNMISS 4
SUDAN: UN • UNAMID 11
WESTERN SAHARA: UN • MINURSO 29

FOREIGN FORCES
Australia MFO (*Operation Mazurka*) 27
Canada MFO 68
Colombia MFO 275; 1 inf bn
Czech Republic MFO 18; 1 C295M
Fiji MFO 170; elm 1 inf bn
France MFO 1
Italy MFO 77; 3 PB
New Zealand MFO 26; 1 trg unit; 1 tpt unit
Norway MFO 3
United Kingdom MFO 2
United States MFO 454; elm 1 ARNG recce bn; 1 ARNG spt bn (1 EOD coy, 1 medical coy, 1 hel coy)
Uruguay MFO 41 1 engr/tpt unit

Iran IRN

Iranian Rial r		2018	2019	2020
GDP	r	18690tr	22982tr	
	US$	446bn	459bn	
per capita	US$	5,417	5,506	
Growth	%	-4.8	-9.5	
Inflation	%	30.5	35.7	
Def bdgt	r	918tr	874tr	
	US$	21.9bn	17.4bn	
US$1=r		41894.94	50124.97	

Real-terms defence budget trend (US$bn, constant 2015)

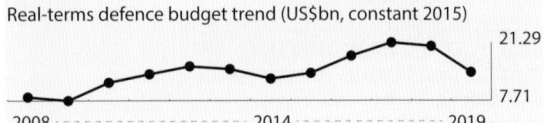

Population 83,993,282

Ethnic groups: Persian 51%; Azeri 24%; Gilaki/Mazandarani 8%; Kurdish 7%; Arab 3%; Lur 2%; Baloch 2%; Turkman 2%

Age	0–14	15–19	20–24	25–29	30–64	65 plus
Male	12.4%	3.5%	3.5%	4.9%	23.8%	2.6%
Female	11.8%	3.3%	3.3%	4.7%	23.1%	3.0%

Capabilities

Iran is a major regional military power, due to a combination of asymmetric and other strategies, despite significant handicaps to its conventional capabilities because of international sanctions and restrictions on arms imports. Iran's armed forces consist of the regular armed forces, with a mix of ageing combat equipment, and the Islamic Revolutionary Guard Corps (IRGC), with a focus on asymmetric capabilities. Chiefly through the IRGC, Iran exerts significant military influence via a range of regional allies and proxies, in effect a form of expeditionary capability. It has also developed a ballistic-missile inventory. Iran has been largely isolated since 1979 though it has a key relationship with Syria and ties with Russia, including for defence sales. It has developed significant influence in weaker regional states like Lebanon, Iraq and Yemen through a network of non-state groups, such as Hizbullah and Houthi forces. The armed forces are numerous by regional standards and their personnel are reasonably well trained, with some benefiting from operational experience. The IRGC's Quds Force is a principal element of Iran's military power abroad, while elements of the Basij militia also play a foreign role. There are suggestions that Iran has developed an enhanced ability to conduct complex strikes utilising land-attack missiles and UAVs. The regular navy has limited power-projection capabilities, while the IRGC navy is responsible for maritime security close to home. The armed forces struggle with an ageing inventory of primary combat equipment that ingenuity and asymmetric-warfare techniques can only partially offset. China and Russia are potentially major suppliers. Tehran procured from Russia what is believed to be the S-300PMU2 (SA-20 *Gargoyle*) long-range SAM system. In regional terms, Iran has a well-developed defence-industrial base, which has displayed the capacity to support and sustain equipment. Key sectors continue to develop, including missiles and guided weapons, but the defence industry is still incapable of meeting the need for modern weapons systems.

ACTIVE 610,000 (Army 350,000 Islamic Revolutionary Guard Corps 190,000 Navy 18,000 Air 37,000 Air Defence 15,000) **Paramilitary 40,000**

Armed Forces General Staff coordinates two parallel organisations: the regular armed forces and the Islamic Revolutionary Guard Corps

Conscript liability 18–21 months (reported, with variations depending on location in which service is performed)

RESERVE 350,000 (Army 350,000, ex-service volunteers)

ORGANISATIONS BY SERVICE

Army 130,000; 220,000 conscript (total 350,000)

FORCES BY ROLE
5 corps-level regional HQ
COMMAND
 1 cdo div HQ
 4 armd div HQ
 2 mech div HQ
 4 inf div HQ
SPECIAL FORCES
 1 cdo div (3 cdo bde)
 6 cdo bde
 1 SF bde
MANOEUVRE
 Armoured
  8 armd bde
 Mechanised
  14 mech bde
 Light
  12 inf bde
 Air Manoeuvre
  1 AB bde
 Aviation
  Some avn gp
COMBAT SUPPORT
 5 arty gp
EQUIPMENT BY TYPE
Totals incl those held by IRGC Ground Forces. Some equipment serviceability in doubt
ARMOURED FIGHTING VEHICLES
 MBT 1,513+: 480 T-72S; 150 M60A1; 75+ T-62; 100 *Chieftain* Mk3/Mk5; 540 T-54/T-55/Type-59/*Safir*-74; 168 M47/M48
 LT TK 80+: 80 *Scorpion*
 RECCE 35 EE-9 *Cascavel*
 IFV 610+: 210 BMP-1; 400 BMP-2 with 9K111 *Fagot* (AT-4 *Spigot*); BMT-2 *Cobra*
 APC 640+
  APC (T) 340: 140 *Boragh* with 9K111 *Fagot* (AT-4 *Spigot*); 200 M113
  APC (W) 300+: 300 BTR-50/BTR-60; *Rakhsh*
ENGINEERING & MAINTENANCE VEHICLES
 ARV 20+: BREM-1 reported; 20 *Chieftain* ARV; M578; T-54/55 ARV reported
 VLB 15: 15 *Chieftain* AVLB
 MW *Taftan* 1

ANTI-TANK/ANTI-INFRASTRUCTURE
 MSL • **MANPATS** 9K11 *Malyutka* (AT-3 *Sagger*/I-*Raad*); 9K111 *Fagot* (AT-4 *Spigot*); 9K111-1 *Konkurs* (AT-5 *Spandrel*/*Towsan*-1); *Dehleavieh* (*Kornet*); *Saeqhe* 1; *Saeqhe* 2; *Toophan*; *Toophan* 2
 RCL 200+: **75mm** M20; **82mm** B-10; **106mm** ε200 M40; **107mm** B-11
ARTILLERY 6,798+
 SP 292+: **122mm** 60+: 60 2S1 *Gvozdika*; *Raad*-1 (*Thunder* 1); **155mm** 150+: 150 M109A1; *Raad*-2 (*Thunder* 2); **170mm** 30 M-1978; **175mm** 22 M107; **203mm** 30 M110
 TOWED 2,030+; **105mm** 150: 130 M101A1; 20 M-56; **122mm** 640: 540 D-30; 100 Type-54 (M-30); **130mm** 985 M-46; **152mm** 30 D-20; **155mm** 205: 120 GHN-45; 70 M114; 15 Type-88 WAC-21; **203mm** 20 M115
 MRL 1,476+: **107mm** 1,300: 700 Type-63; 600 HASEB *Fadjr* 1; **122mm** 157: 7 BM-11; 100 BM-21 *Grad*; 50 *Arash*/*Hadid*/*Noor*; **240mm** 19+: ε10 *Fadjr* 3; 9 M-1985; **330mm** *Fadjr* 5
 MOR 3,000: **81mm**; **82mm**; **107mm** M30; **120mm** M-65
SURFACE-TO-SURFACE MISSILE LAUNCHERS
 SRBM • **Conventional** ε30 CH-SS-8 (175 msl); *Shahin*-1/*Shahin*-2; *Nazeat*; *Oghab*
AIRCRAFT • **TPT** 17 **Light** 16: 10 Cessna 185; 2 F-27 *Friendship*; 4 Turbo Commander 690; **PAX** 1 Falcon 20
HELICOPTERS
 ATK 50 AH-1J *Cobra*
 TPT 167: **Heavy** ε20 CH-47C *Chinook*; **Medium** 69: 49 Bell 214; 20 Mi-171; **Light** 78: 68 Bell 205A (AB-205A); 10 Bell 206 *Jet Ranger* (AB-206)
UNMANNED AERIAL VEHICLES
 CISR • **Medium** *Mohajer* 6
 ISR • **Medium** *Ababil* 2; *Ababil* 3; *Mohajer*; *Mohajer* 4; **Light** *Mohajer* 2
AIR DEFENCE
 SAM
  Short-range FM-80
  Point-defence 9K36 *Strela*-3 (SA-14 *Gremlin*); 9K32 *Strela*-2 (SA-7 *Grail*)‡; *Misaq* 1 (QW-1 *Vanguard*); *Misaq* 2 (QW-18); 9K338 *Igla*-S (SA-24 *Grinch*) (reported); HN-5A
 GUNS 1,122
  SP 180: **23mm** 100 ZSU-23-4; **57mm** 80 ZSU-57-2
  TOWED 942+: **14.5mm** ZPU-2; ZPU-4; **23mm** 300 ZU-23-2; **35mm** 92 GDF-002; **37mm** M-1939; **40mm** 50 L/70; **57mm** 200 S-60; **85mm** 300 M-1939
 BOMBS
  Laser-guided *Qaem*
  Electro-optical guided *Qaem*

Islamic Revolutionary Guard Corps 190,000

Islamic Revolutionary Guard Corps Ground Forces 150,000

Controls Basij paramilitary forces. Lightly manned in peacetime. Primary role: internal security; secondary role: external defence, in conjunction with regular armed forces

FORCES BY ROLE
COMMAND
 31 provincial corps HQ (2 in Tehran)

SPECIAL FORCES
 3 spec ops div
 1 AB bde
MANOEUVRE
 Armoured
  2 armd div
  3 armd bde
 Light
  8+ inf div
  5+ inf bde

Islamic Revolutionary Guard Corps Naval Forces 20,000+ (incl 5,000 Marines)

FORCES BY ROLE
COMBAT SUPPORT
 Some arty bty
 Some AShM bty with HY-2 (CH-SSC-3 *Seersucker*) AShM

EQUIPMENT BY TYPE
In addition to the vessels listed, the IRGC operates a substantial number of patrol boats with a full-load displacement below 10 tonnes, including ε40 *Boghammar*-class vessels and small *Bavar*-class wing-in-ground effect air vehicles

PATROL AND COASTAL COMBATANTS 126
 PBFG 56:
  5 C14 with 2 twin lnchr with C-701 (*Kosar*)/C-704 (*Nasr*) AShM
  10 Mk13 with 2 single lnchr with C-704 (*Nasr*) AShM, 2 single 324mm TT
  10 *Thondor* (PRC *Houdong*) with 2 twin lnchr with C-802A (*Ghader*) AShM, 2 AK230 CIWS
  25 *Peykaap* II (IPS-16 mod) with 2 single lnchr with C-701 (*Kosar*) AShM/C-704 (*Nasr*), 2 single 324mm TT
  6 *Zolfaghar* (*Peykaap* III/IPS-16 mod) with 2 single lnchr with C-701 (*Kosar*)/C-704 (*Nasr*) AShM
 PBFT 15 *Peykaap* I (IPS -16) with 2 single 324mm TT
 PBF 35: 15 *Kashdom* II; 10 *Tir* (IPS-18); ε10 *Pashe* (MIG-G-1900)
 PB ε20 *Ghaem*
AMPHIBIOUS
 LANDING SHIPS • LST 3 *Hormuz* 24 (*Hejaz* design for commercial use)
 LANDING CRAFT • LCT 2 *Hormuz* 21 (minelaying capacity)
LOGISTICS AND SUPPORT • AP 3 *Naser*
COASTAL DEFENCE • AShM C-701 (*Kosar*); C-704 (*Nasr*); C-802; HY-2 (CH-SSC-3 *Seersucker*)
HELICOPTERS
 MRH 5 Mi-171 *Hip*
 TPT • Light some Bell 206 (AB-206) *Jet Ranger*

Islamic Revolutionary Guard Corps Marines 5,000+

FORCES BY ROLE
MANOEUVRE
 Amphibious
  1 mne bde

Islamic Revolutionary Guard Corps Aerospace Force 15,000

Controls Iran's strategic missile force

FORCES BY ROLE
MISSILE
 ε1 bde with *Shahab*-1/-2; *Qiam*-1
 ε1 bn with *Shahab*-3
EQUIPMENT BY TYPE
SURFACE-TO-SURFACE MISSILE LAUNCHERS
 MRBM • Conventional up to 50: *Shahab*-3 (mobile & silo); some *Ghadr*-1 (in test); some *Emad*-1 (in test); some *Sajjil*-2 (in devt); some *Khorramshahr* (in devt)
 SRBM • Conventional up to 100: some *Fateh* 110; Some *Khalij Fars* (*Fateh* 110 mod ASBM); some *Shahab*-1/-2; some *Qiam*-1; some *Zelzal*
 GLCM • Conventional some *Ya'ali* (*Quds*-1)
UNMANNED AERIAL VEHICLES
 CISR • Heavy *Shahed* 129
 ISR • Medium *Ababil* 3; *Mohajer* 4; *Shahed* 123
AIR DEFENCE
 SAM
  Medium-range *Ra'ad*/3rd *Khordad*; *Talash*/15th *Khordad*
  Point-defence *Misaq* 1 (QW-1 *Vanguard*); *Misaq* 2 (QW-18)
BOMBS
 Laser-guided *Sadid*
 Electro-optical guided *Sadid*

Islamic Revolutionary Quds Force 5,000

Navy 18,000

HQ at Bandar Abbas
EQUIPMENT BY TYPE
In addition to the vessels listed, the Iranian Navy operates a substantial number of patrol boats with a full-load displacement below 10 tonnes
SUBMARINES • TACTICAL 19
 SSK 3 *Taregh* (RUS *Paltus* Project 877EKM) with 6 single 533mm TT (of which 1†)
 SSC 1 *Fateh* with 4 single 533mm TT with C-704 (*Nasr*-1) AShM/*Valfajar* HWT
 SSW 15: 14 *Ghadir* with 2 single 533mm TT with *Valfajar* HWT (additional vessels in build); 1 *Nahang*
PATROL AND COASTAL COMBATANTS 68
 CORVETTES 7
  FSGM 2 *Jamaran* (UK Vosper Mk 5 derivative – 1 more undergoing sea trials) with 2 twin lnchr with C-802 (*Noor*) (CH-SS-N-6) AShM, 2 single lnchr with SM-1 SAM, 2 triple 324mm SVTT Mk 32 ASTT, 1 76mm gun, 1 hel landing platform
  FSG 5:
   3 *Alvand* (UK Vosper Mk 5) with 2 twin lnchr with C-802 (CH-SS-N-6) AShM, 2 triple 324mm SVTT Mk 32 ASTT, 1 114mm gun
   2 *Bayandor* (US PF-103) with 2 twin lnchr with C-802 (CH-SS-N-6) AShM, 2 triple 324mm SVTT Mk 32 ASTT, 1 76mm gun
 PCFG 13 *Kaman* (FRA *Combattante* II) with 1 twin lnchr with C-802 (*Noor*) (CH-SS-N-6) AShM, 1 76mm gun

PBG 9:
  3 *Hendijan* with 2 twin lnchr with C-802 (*Noor*) (CH-SS-N-6) AShM
  3 *Kayvan* with 2 single lnchr with C-704 (*Nasr*) AShM
  3 *Parvin* with 2 single lnchr with C-704 (*Nasr*) AShM
PBFT 3 *Kajami* (semi-submersible) with 2 324mm TT
PBF 1 MIL55
PB 34: 9 C14; 9 *Hendijan*; 6 MkII; 10 MkIII
AMPHIBIOUS
  LANDING SHIPS 12
    LSM 3 *Farsi* (ROK) (capacity 9 tanks; 140 troops)
    LST 3 *Hengam* with 1 hel landing platform (capacity 9 tanks; 225 troops)
    LSL 6 *Fouque*
  LANDING CRAFT 11
    LCT 2
    LCU 1 *Liyan* 110
    UCAC 8: 2 *Wellington* Mk 4; 4 *Wellington* Mk 5; 2 *Tondar* (UK *Winchester*)
LOGISTICS AND SUPPORT 18
  AE 2 *Delvar*
  AFD 2 *Dolphin*
  AG 1 *Hamzah* with 2 single lnchr with C-802 (*Noor*) (CH-SS-N-6) AShM
  AK 3 *Delvar*
  AORH 3: 2 *Bandar Abbas*; 1 *Kharg* with 1 76mm gun
  AWT 5: 4 *Kangan*; 1 *Delvar*
  AX 2 *Kialas*
COASTAL DEFENCE • **AShM** C-701 (*Kosar*); C-704 (*Nasr*); C-802 (*Noor*); C-802A (*Ghader*); Ra'ad (reported)

Marines 2,600
FORCES BY ROLE
MANOEUVRE
  Amphibious
    2 mne bde

Naval Aviation 2,600
EQUIPMENT BY TYPE
AIRCRAFT
  TPT 16: **Light** 13: 5 Do-228; 4 F-27 *Friendship*; 4 *Turbo Commander* 680; **PAX** 3 *Falcon* 20 (ELINT)
HELICOPTERS
  ASW ε10 SH-3D *Sea King*
  MCM 3 RH-53D *Sea Stallion* **TPT** • **Light** 17: 5 Bell 205A (AB-205A); 2 Bell 206 *Jet Ranger* (AB-206); 10 Bell 212 (AB-212)

Air Force 18,000
FORCES BY ROLE
Serviceability probably about 60% for US ac types and about 80% for PRC/Russian ac. Includes IRGC AF equipment
FIGHTER
  1 sqn with F-7M *Airguard*; JJ-7*
  2 sqn with F-14 *Tomcat*
  2 sqn with MiG-29A/UB *Fulcrum*
FIGHTER/GROUND ATTACK
  1 sqn with *Mirage* F-1E; F-5E/F *Tiger* II
  5 sqn with F-4D/E *Phantom* II
  3 sqn with F-5E/F *Tiger* II
  1 sqn (forming) with Su-22M4 *Fitter K*; Su-22UM-3K *Fitter G*
GROUND ATTACK
  1 sqn with Su-24MK *Fencer D*
MARITIME PATROL
  1 sqn with P-3F *Orion*
ISR
  1 (det) sqn with RF-4E *Phantom* II*
SEARCH & RESCUE
  Some flt with Bell 214C (AB-214C)
TANKER/TRANSPORT
  1 sqn with B-707; B-747; B-747F
TRANSPORT
  1 sqn with B-707; *Falcon* 50; L-1329 *Jetstar*; Bell 412
  2 sqn with C-130E/H *Hercules*
  1 sqn with F-27 *Friendship*; *Falcon* 20
  1 sqn with Il-76 *Candid*; An-140 (Iran-140 *Faraz*)
TRAINING
  1 sqn with Beech F33A/C *Bonanza*
  1 sqn with F-5B *Freedom Fighter*
  1 sqn with PC-6
  1 sqn with PC-7 *Turbo Trainer*
  Some units with EMB-312 *Tucano*; MFI-17 *Mushshak*; TB-21 *Trinidad*; TB-200 *Tobago*
TRANSPORT HELICOPTER
  1 sqn with CH-47 *Chinook*
  Some units with Bell 206A *Jet Ranger* (AB-206A); *Shabaviz* 2-75; *Shabaviz* 2061

EQUIPMENT BY TYPE
AIRCRAFT 333 combat capable
  FTR 184+: 20 F-5B *Freedom Fighter*; 55+ F-5E/F *Tiger* II 24 F-7M *Airguard*; up to 43 F-14 *Tomcat*; 36 MiG-29A/UB *Fulcrum*; up to 6 *Azarakhsh* (reported)
  FGA 87: 62 F-4D/E *Phantom* II; 10 *Mirage* F-1E; up to 6 *Saegheh* (reported); up to 7 Su-22M4 *Fitter K*; 3+ Su-22UM-3K *Fitter G*
  ATK 39: 29 Su-24MK *Fencer D*; 7 Su-25K *Frogfoot* (status unknown); 3 Su-25UBK *Frogfoot* (status unknown)
  ASW 3 P-3F *Orion*
  ISR: 6+ RF-4E *Phantom* II*
  TKR/TPT 3: ε1 B-707; ε2 B-747
  TPT 116: **Heavy** 12 Il-76 *Candid*; **Medium** ε19 C-130E/H *Hercules*; **Light** 75: 11 An-74TK-200; 5 An-140 (Iran-140 *Faraz*); 10 F-27 *Friendship*; 1 L-1329 *Jetstar*; 10 PC-6B *Turbo Porter*; 8 TB-21 *Trinidad*; 4 TB-200 *Tobago*; 3 *Turbo Commander* 680; 14 Y-7; 9 Y-12; **PAX** 10: ε1 B-707; 1 B-747; 4 B-747F; 1 *Falcon* 20; 3 *Falcon* 50
  TRG 141: 25 Beech F33A/C *Bonanza*; 15 EMB-312 *Tucano*; 14 JJ-7*; 25 MFI-17 *Mushshak*; 12 *Parustu*; 15 PC-6; 35 PC-7 *Turbo Trainer*
HELICOPTERS
  MRH 2 Bell 412
  TPT 34+: **Heavy** 2+ CH-47 *Chinook*; **Medium** 30 Bell 214C (AB-214C); **Light** 2+: 2 Bell 206A *Jet Ranger* (AB-206A); some *Shabaviz* 2-75 (indigenous versions in production); some *Shabaviz* 2061
AIR-LAUNCHED MISSILES
  AAM • **IR** PL-2A‡; PL-7; R-60 (AA-8 *Aphid*); R-73 (AA-11A *Archer*); AIM-9J *Sidewinder*; **IR/SARH** R-27 (AA-10 *Alamo*); **SARH** AIM-7E-2 *Sparrow*; **ARH** AIM-54 *Phoenix*†

ASM AGM-65A *Maverick*; Kh-25 (AS-10 *Karen*); Kh-25ML (AS-10 *Karen*); Kh-29L/T (AS-14A/B *Kedge*)
AShM C-801K
ARM Kh-58 (AS-11 *Kilter*)
BOMBS
Electro-optical guided GBU-87/B *Qassed*

Air Defence Force 12,000
New service branch formed mid-2019
FORCES BY ROLE
AIR DEFENCE
16 bn with MIM-23B I-*Hawk*/*Shahin*
4 bn with S-300PMU2 (SA-20 *Gargoyle*)
5 sqn with FM-80 (*Crotale*); *Rapier*; S-75M *Volkhov* (SA-2 *Guideline*); S-200 *Angara* (SA-5 *Gammon*); 9K331 *Tor*-M1 (SA-15 *Gauntlet*)
EQUIPMENT BY TYPE
AIR DEFENCE
SAM 546+:
  Long-range 42+: 10 S-200 *Angara* (SA-5 *Gammon*); 32 S-300PMU2 (SA-20 *Gargoyle*); *Bavar*-373
  Medium-range 195+: 150+ MIM-23B I-*Hawk*/*Shahin*; 45 S-75 *Dvina* (SA-2 *Guideline*); *Talash*/15th *Khordad*
  Short-range 279: 250 FM-80 (*Crotale*); 29 9K331 *Tor*-M1 (SA-15 *Gauntlet*)
  Point-defence 30+: 30 *Rapier*; *Misaq* 1 (QW-1 *Vanguard*); *Misaq* 2 (QW-18)
GUNS • TOWED 23mm ZU-23-2; 35mm GDF-002

Paramilitary 40,000–60,000

Law-Enforcement Forces 40,000–60,000 (border and security troops); 450,000 on mobilisation (incl conscripts)
Part of armed forces in wartime
EQUIPMENT BY TYPE
PATROL AND COASTAL COMBATANTS • PB ε90
AIRCRAFT • TPT • Light 2+: 2 An-140; some Cessna 185/Cessna 310
HELICOPTERS • TPT • Light ε24 AB-205 (Bell 205)/AB-206 (Bell 206) *Jet Ranger*

Basij Resistance Force ε600,000 on mobilisation
Paramilitary militia with claimed membership of 12.6 million; ε600,000 combat capable
FORCES BY ROLE
MANOEUVRE
  Other
    2,500 militia bn(-) (claimed, limited permanent membership)

DEPLOYMENT

GULF OF ADEN AND SOMALI BASIN: Navy: 1 FSG; 1 AORH
SUDAN: UN • UNAMID 1
SYRIA: 3,000

Iraq IRQ

Iraqi Dinar D		2018	2019	2020
GDP	D	265tr	265tr	
	US$	224bn	224bn	
per capita	US$	5,882	5,738	
Growth	%	-0.6	3.4	
Inflation	%	0.4	-0.3	
Def bdgt [a]	D	20.4tr	24.2tr	
	US$	17.3bn	20.5bn	
FMA (US$)	US$	250m	0m	0m
US$1=D		1182.00	1182.00	

[a] Defence and security budget

Real-terms defence budget trend (US$bn, constant 2015)

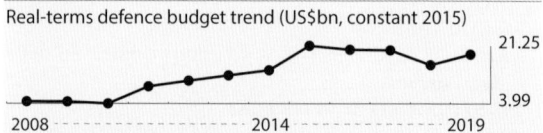

Population 41,204,228
Ethnic and religious groups: Arab 75–80% (of which Shia Muslim 55%, Sunni Muslim 45%); Kurdish 20–25%

Age	0–14	15–19	20–24	25–29	30–64	65 plus
Male	19.7%	5.4%	4.6%	3.8%	15.4%	1.6%
Female	18.9%	5.2%	4.4%	3.7%	15.2%	2.0%

Capabilities

The armed forces' capabilities and morale have improved since the collapse of several divisions in the face of the ISIS advance in the north in 2014. The recapture of Mosul demonstrated incremental growth in capability, in terms of combat power and tactics, as the Iraqi armed forces adapted to fight ISIS in urban areas. The future of the Kurdish Peshmerga forces and the Popular Mobilisation Units militias, particularly questions over their integration into a national-security framework, remains an issue for Baghdad. The government's most critical security relationship is with the US, and other participants in the international counter-ISIS coalition. The level of attrition among Iraqi forces has caused concern, particularly among the well-regarded Counter-Terrorism Service, which is often used as a spearhead force. The US has been engaged in a training effort, not least in regenerating air-force capabilities. In late 2018 NATO established a new training and capacity-building mission. A key focus is adapting Iraqi forces to address a developing ISIS insurgency beyond the urban areas, particularly in northern and western Iraq. Iraqi forces appear to have improved their ability to conduct complex operations, including at range within the country. However, there has been a reliance on US air support and coalition ISR assistance, suggesting continuing capability limitations in this area. Significant logistical shortcomings remain, including logistics support and intelligence integration. Internal political frictions, revived US–Iran tensions and efforts to rein in corruption add to concerns over the cohesion and reliability of the armed forces and associated PMU militias. The inventory comprises Soviet-era and Russian equipment combined with newer European- and US-sourced platforms, the latter including F-16 combat aircraft and attack helicopters. Barring military maintenance facilities, the Iraqi defence industry has only a limited ability to manufacture light weapons and ammunition.

ACTIVE 193,000 (Army 180,000 Navy 3,000 Air 5,000 Air Defence 5,000) **Paramilitary 145,000**

ORGANISATIONS BY SERVICE

Army ε180,000
Includes Counter Terrorism Service
FORCES BY ROLE
SPECIAL FORCES
3 SF bde
1 ranger bde (1 ranger bn)
MANOEUVRE
  Armoured
  1 (9th) armd div (2 armd bde, 2 mech bde, 1 engr bn, 1 sigs regt, 1 log bde)
  Mechanised
  3 (5th, 8th & 10th) mech div (4 mech inf bde, 1 engr bn, 1 sigs regt, 1 log bde)
  1 (7th) mech div (2 mech inf bde, 1 inf bde, 1 engr bn, 1 sigs regt, 1 log bde)
  Light
  1 (6th) mot div (3 mot inf bde, 1 inf bde, 1 engr bn, 1 sigs regt, 1 log bde)
  1 (14th) mot div (2 mot inf bde, 3 inf bde, 1 engr bn, 1 sigs regt, 1 log bde)
  1 (1st) inf div (2 inf bde)
  1 (11th) inf div (3 lt inf bde, 1 engr bn, 1 sigs regt, 1 log bde)
  1 (15th) inf div (5 inf bde)
  1 (16th) inf div (2 inf bde)
  1 (17th Cdo) inf div (4 inf bde, 1 engr bn, 1 sigs regt, 1 log bde)
  1 inf bde
  Other
  1 (PM SF) sy div (3 inf bde)
HELICOPTER
1 atk hel sqn with Mi-28NE *Havoc*
1 atk hel sqn with Mi-35M *Hind*
1 sqn with Bell 205 (UH-1H *Huey* II)
3 atk hel sqn with Bell T407; H135M
3 sqn with Mi-17 *Hip* H; Mi-171Sh
1 ISR sqn with SA342M *Gazelle*
2 trg sqn with Bell 206; OH-58C *Kiowa*
1 trg sqn with Bell 205 (UH-1H *Huey* II)
1 trg sqn with Mi-17 *Hip*
EQUIPMENT BY TYPE
ARMOURED FIGHTING VEHICLES
  MBT 391+: ε100 M1A1 *Abrams*; 168+ T-72M/M1; ε50 T-55; 73 T-90S
  RECCE 453: ε400 *Akrep*; 18 BRDM 2; 35 EE-9 *Cascavel*;
  IFV 300+: ε80 BMP-1; 60+ BMP-3; ε60 BTR-4 (inc variants); 100 BTR-80A
  APC 1,592+
    APC (T) 900: ε500 M113A2/*Talha*; ε400 MT-LB
    PPV 692+: 12 *Barracuda*; 250 *Caiman*; ε400 ILAV *Badger*; *Mamba*; 30 *Maxxpro*
    AUV M-ATV
ENGINEERING & MAINTENANCE VEHICLES
  ARV 222+: 180 BREM; 35+ M88A1/2; 7 *Maxxpro* ARV; T-54/55 ARV; Type-653; VT-55A

NBC VEHICLES 20 *Fuchs* NBC
ANTI-TANK/ANTI-INFRASTRUCTURE
  MSL • MANPATS 9K135 *Kornet* (AT-14 *Spriggan*) (reported)
ARTILLERY 1,061+
  SP 48+: **152mm** 18+ Type-83; **155mm** 30: 6 M109A1; 24 M109A5
  TOWED 60+: **130mm** M-46/Type-59; **152mm** D-20; Type-83; **155mm** ε60 M198
  MRL 3+: **122mm** some BM-21 *Grad*; **220mm** 3+ TOS-1A
  MOR 950+: **81mm** ε500 M252; **120mm** ε450 M120; **240mm** M-240
HELICOPTERS
  ATK 28: 11 Mi-28NE *Havoc*; 4 Mi-28UB *Havoc*; 13 Mi-35M *Hind*
  MRH 63+: 4+ SA342 *Gazelle*; 17 Bell IA407; 23 H135M; ε19 Mi-17 *Hip* H/Mi-171Sh
  ISR 10 OH-58C *Kiowa*
  TPT • Light 44: 16 Bell 205 (UH-1H *Huey* II); 10 Bell 206B3 *Jet Ranger*; ε18 Bell T407
UNMANNED AERIAL VEHICLES • CISR Heavy 10 CH-4†
AIR-LAUNCHED MISSILES • ASM 9K114 *Shturm* (AT-6 *Spiral*); AR-1; *Ingwe*

Navy 3,000
EQUIPMENT BY TYPE
PATROL AND COASTAL COMBATANTS 32
  PCO 2 *Al Basra* (US *River Hawk*)
  PCC 4 *Fateh* (ITA *Diciotti*)
  PB 20: 12 Swiftships 35; 5 *Predator* (PRC 27m); 3 *Al Faw*
  PBR 6: 2 Type-200; 4 Type-2010

Marines 1,000
FORCES BY ROLE
MANOEUVRE
  Amphibious
  2 mne bn

Air Force ε5,000
FORCES BY ROLE
FIGHTER/GROUND ATTACK
  1 sqn with F-16C/D *Fighting Falcon*
GROUND ATTACK
  1 sqn with Su-25/Su-25K/Su-25UBK *Frogfoot*
  1 sqn with L-159A; L-159T1
ISR
  1 sqn with CH 2000 *Sama*; SB7L-360 *Seeker*
  1 sqn with Cessna 208B *Grand Caravan*; Cessna AC-208B *Combat Caravan**
  1 sqn with Beech 350 *King Air*
TRANSPORT
  1 sqn with An-32B *Cline*
  1 sqn with C-130E/J-30 *Hercules*
TRAINING
  1 sqn with Cessna 172, Cessna 208B
  1 sqn with *Lasta*-95
  1 sqn with T-6A
  1 sqn with T-50IQ *Golden Eagle**

EQUIPMENT BY TYPE
AIRCRAFT 90 combat capable
  FGA 36: 26 F-16C *Fighting Falcon*; 8 F-16D *Fighting Falcon*;
  ATK 30: 10 L-159A; 1 L-159T1; ε19 Su-25/Su-25K/Su-25UBK *Frogfoot*
  ISR 10: 2 Cessna AC-208B *Combat Caravan**; 2 SB7L-360 *Seeker*; 6 Beech 350ER *King Air*
  TPT 29: **Medium** 15: 3 C-130E *Hercules*; 6 C-130J-30 *Hercules*; 6 An-32B *Cline* (of which 2 combat capable); **Light** 14: 1 Beech 350 *King Air*; 5 Cessna 208B *Grand Caravan*; 8 Cessna 172
  TRG 55+: 8 CH-2000 *Sama*; 10+ *Lasta*-95; 15 T-6A; 22 T-50IQ *Golden Eagle**
AIR-LAUNCHED MISSILES
  AAM • **IR** AIM-9L *Sidewinder*; AIM-9M *Sidewinder*
  ASM AGM-114 *Hellfire*
BOMBS
  Laser-guided GBU-12 *Paveway* II
  INS/GPS-guided FT-9

Air Defence Command ε5,000
FORCES BY ROLE
AIR DEFENCE
1 bn with 96K6 *Pantsir*-S1 (SA-22 *Greyhound*)
1 bn with M1097 *Avenger*
1 bn with 9K338 *Igla*-S (SA-24 *Grinch*)
1 bn with ZU-23-2; S-60
EQUIPMENT BY TYPE
AIR DEFENCE
  SAM
    Short-range 24 96K6 *Pantsir*-S1 (SA-22 *Greyhound*)
    Point-defence M1097 *Avenger*; 9K338 *Igla*-S (SA-24 *Grinch*)
  GUNS • **TOWED 23mm** ZU-23-2; **57mm** S-60

Paramilitary ε145,000
Iraqi Federal Police ε36,000
Border Enforcement ε9,000
Militias ε100,000
Popular Mobilisation Units include: Badr Organisation; Kataib Hizbullah; Kataib Imam Ali; Kataib Sayyid al-Shuhada

FOREIGN FORCES
Australia Operation Inherent Resolve (*Okra*) 380 • NATO Mission Iraq 2
Belgium Operation Inherent Resolve (*Valiant Phoenix*) 5
Canada Operation Inherent Resolve (*Impact*) 120; 1 SF gp; 1 med unit • NATO Mission Iraq 250; 1 hel flt with 3 Bell 412 (CH-146 *Griffon*)
Czech Republic Operation Inherent Resolve 60
Denmark Operation Inherent Resolve 190; 1 SF gp; 1 trg team
Estonia Operation Inherent Resolve 10 • NATO Mission Iraq 5
Fiji UNAMI 165; 2 sy unit
Finland Operation Inherent Resolve 80; 1 trg unit • NATO Mission Iraq 1
France Operation Inherent Resolve (*Chammal*) 400; 1 SF gp; 1 trg unit
Germany Operation Inherent Resolve 150; some trg units
Greece NATO Mission Iraq 1
Hungary Operation Inherent Resolve 170
Italy Operation Inherent Resolve (*Prima Parthica*) 600; 1 inf regt; 1 trg unit; 1 hel sqn with 4 NH90 • NATO Mission Iraq 12
Latvia Operation Inherent Resolve 10
Lithuania Operation Inherent Resolve 6 • NATO Mission Iraq 9
Nepal UNAMI 77; 1 sy unit
Netherlands Operation Inherent Resolve 60; 2 trg units • NATO Mission Iraq 2
New Zealand Operation Inherent Resolve 100; 1 trg unit
Norway Operation Inherent Resolve 60; 1 trg unit • NATO Mission Iraq 10
Poland Operation Inherent Resolve 150 • NATO Mission Iraq 65
Portugal Operation Inherent Resolve 34
Romania Operation Inherent Resolve 10 • NATO Mission Iraq 4
Slovakia NATO Mission Iraq 42
Slovenia Operation Inherent Resolve 6
Spain Operation Inherent Resolve 500; 2 trg units; 1 hel unit • NATO Mission Iraq 70
Sweden Operation Inherent Resolve 66 • NATO Mission Iraq 1
Turkey Army 1,000; 1 cdo unit • NATO Mission Iraq up to 30
United Kingdom Operation Inherent Resolve (*Shader*) 400; 2 inf bn(-); 1 engr sqn(-)
United States Operation Inherent Resolve 6,000; 1 mech inf bde(-); 1 EOD pl; 1 atk hel sqn with AH-64E *Apache*

Israel ISR

New Israeli Shekel NS		2018	2019	2020
GDP	NS	1.33tr	1.39tr	
	US$	371bn	388bn	
per capita	US$	41,728	42,823	
Growth	%	3.4	3.1	
Inflation	%	0.8	1.0	
Def bdgt	NS	70.4bn	69.1bn	
	US$	19.6bn	19.3bn	
FMA (US)	US$	3.10bn	3.30bn	3.30bn
US$1=NS		3.59	3.59	

Real-terms defence budget trend (US$bn, constant 2015)

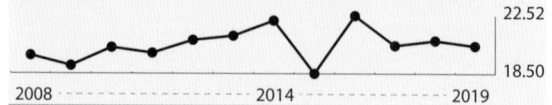

Population	8,550,149					
Age	0–14	15–19	20–24	25–29	30–64	65 plus
Male	13.8%	4.2%	3.8%	3.6%	19.6%	5.3%
Female	13.2%	4.0%	3.7%	3.4%	19.0%	6.5%

Capabilities

The Israel Defense Forces (IDF) are organised for territorial defence, short-term interventions in neighbouring states and limited regional power projection. Israel is widely believed to possess a nuclear-weapons capability. The 2015 Plan *Gideon* focused efforts on front-line combat formations, and plans for a new combined arms brigade concept are in their early stages. There are plans for a new multi-year plan as a successor to Plan *Gideon*, though progress will likely depend on resolving political and budgetary challenges. The US remains Israel's key defence partner, as well as a significant source of funding, and is instrumental in several of the IDF's equipment programmes, particularly in missile defence and combat aviation. Israel also maintains discreet ties with a number of Arab states. Personnel quality and training are generally high, despite the IDF's continuing reliance on national service. Ground-forces training is being overhauled, with new training centres under construction. The IDF has no requirement for out-of-area deployments and its logistics capabilities are limited to sustaining operations within Israel itself or in immediate neighbouring territories. The largely asymmetric nature of the threats faced by the IDF in recent years has focused modernisation efforts on force-protection, missile-defence and precision-strike capabilities. Israel maintains a broad defence-industrial base, with world-class capabilities in several areas, notably armoured vehicles, uninhabited systems, guided weapons and cyber security.

ACTIVE 169,500 (Army 126,000 Navy 9,500 Air 34,000) **Paramilitary 8,000**

Conscript liability Officers 48 months, other ranks 32 months, women 24 months (Jews and Druze only; Christians, Circassians and Muslims may volunteer)

RESERVE 465,000 (Army 400,000 Navy 10,000 Air 55,000)

Annual trg as cbt reservists to age 40 (some specialists to age 54) for male other ranks, 38 (or marriage/pregnancy) for women

ORGANISATIONS BY SERVICE

Strategic Forces

Israel is widely believed to have a nuclear capability – delivery means include F-15I and F-16I ac, *Jericho* 2 IRBM and, reportedly, *Dolphin/Tanin*-class SSKs with LACM

FORCES BY ROLE
SURFACE-TO-SURFACE MISSILE
  3 IRBM sqn with *Jericho* 2

EQUIPMENT BY TYPE
SURFACE-TO-SURFACE MISSILE LAUNCHERS
  IRBM • Nuclear: ε24 *Jericho* 2

Strategic Defences

FORCES BY ROLE
AIR DEFENCE
  3 bty with *Arrow* 2 ATBM with *Green Pine*/*Super Green Pine* radar and *Citrus Tree* command post
  10 bty with *Iron Dome* (incl reserve bty)
  6 bty with MIM-104C *Patriot* PAC-2
  2 bty with *David's Sling*

Space

EQUIPMENT BY TYPE
SATELLITES 9
COMMUNICATIONS 3 *Amos*
ISR 6: 1 EROS; 4 *Ofeq* (7, 9, 10 & 11); 1 TecSAR-1 (*Polaris*)

Army 26,000; 100,000 conscript (total 126,000)

Organisation and structure of formations may vary according to op situations. Equipment includes that required for reserve forces on mobilisation

FORCES BY ROLE
COMMAND
  3 (regional comd) corps HQ
  2 armd div HQ
  5 (territorial) inf div HQ
  1 (home defence) comd HQ
SPECIAL FORCES
  3 SF bn
  1 spec ops bde (4 spec ops unit)
MANOEUVRE
  Reconnaissance
  1 indep recce bn
  Armoured
  3 armd bde (1 armd recce coy, 3 armd bn, 1 AT coy, 1 cbt engr bn)
  Mechanised
  3 mech inf bde (1 recce bn, 3 mech inf bn, 1 sigs coy)
  1 mech inf bde (1 recce bn, 4 mech inf bn)
  1 indep mech inf bn
  Light
  2 indep inf bn
  Air Manoeuvre
  1 para bde (3 para bn, 1 cbt spt bn, 1 sigs coy)
  Other
  1 armd trg bde (3 armd bn)
COMBAT SUPPORT
  3 arty bde
  3 engr bn
  1 EOD coy
  1 CBRN bn
  1 int bde (3 int bn)
  1 SIGINT unit
  2 MP bn

Reserves 400,000+ on mobilisation

FORCES BY ROLE
COMMAND
  3 armd div HQ
  1 AB div HQ
MANOEUVRE
  Armoured
  9 armd bde
  Mechanised
  8 mech inf bde
  Light
  16 (territorial/regional) inf bde
  Air Manoeuvre
  4 para bde
  Mountain
  1 mtn inf bn
COMBAT SUPPORT
  5 arty bde

COMBAT SERVICE SUPPORT
  6 log unit

EQUIPMENT BY TYPE
ARMOURED FIGHTING VEHICLES
  MBT 490: ε160 *Merkava* MkIII; ε330 *Merkava* MkIV (ε370 *Merkava* MkII; ε570 *Merkava* MkIII; ε220 *Merkava* MkIV all in store)
  APC • APC (T) 1,330: ε230 *Namer*; ε200 *Achzarit* (modified T-55 chassis); 500 M113A2; ε400 *Nagmachon* (*Centurion* chassis); *Nakpadon* (5,000 M113A1/A2 in store)
  AUV 100 *Ze'ev*

ENGINEERING & MAINTENANCE VEHICLES
  AEV D9R; *Namer*; *Puma*
  ARV *Centurion* Mk2; *Nemmera*; M88A1; M113 ARV
  VLB *Alligator* MAB; M48/60; MTU

NBC VEHICLES ε8 TPz-1 *Fuchs* NBC

ANTI-TANK/ANTI-INFRASTRUCTURE • MSL
  SP M113 with *Spike*; *Tamuz* (*Spike* NLOS)
  MANPATS IMI MAPATS; *Spike* SR/MR/LR/ER

ARTILLERY 530
  SP 250: **155mm** 250 M109A5 (**155mm** 30 M109A2; **175mm** 36 M107; **203mm** 36 M110 all in store)
  TOWED (**155mm** 171: 40 M-46 mod; 50 M-68/M-71; 81 M-839P/M-845P all in store)
  MRL 30: **227mm** 30 M270 MLRS; **306mm** IMI *Lynx* (**160mm** 50 LAR-160; **227mm** 18 M270 MLRS; **290mm** 20 LAR-290 all in store)
  MOR 250: **81mm** 250 (**81mm** 1,100; **120mm** 650; **160mm** 18 Soltam M-66 all in store)

SURFACE-TO-SURFACE MISSILE LAUNCHERS
  IRBM • Nuclear ε24 *Jericho* 2
  SRBM • Dual-capable (7 *Lance* in store)

AIR DEFENCE • SAM • Point-defence 20 *Machbet*; FIM-92 *Stinger*

Navy 7,000; 2,500 conscript (total 9,500)

EQUIPMENT BY TYPE
SUBMARINES • TACTICAL
  SSK 5:
    3 *Dolphin* (GER HDW design) with 6 single 533mm TT with UGM-84C *Harpoon* Block 1B AShM/*SeaHake* (DM2A3) HWT/*SeaHake* mod 4 (DM2A4) HWT/*Kaved* HWT, 4 single 650mm TT
    2 *Tanin* (GER HDW design with AIP) with 6 single 533mm TT with UGM-84C *Harpoon* Block 1B AShM/*SeaHake* (DM2A3) HWT/*SeaHake* mod 4 (DM2A4) HWT/*Kaved* HWT, 4 single 650mm TT

PATROL AND COASTAL COMBATANTS 45
  CORVETTES • FSGHM 3:
    2 *Eilat* (*Sa'ar* 5) with 2 quad lnchr with RGM-84 *Harpoon* AShM/*Gabriel* V AShM, 4 8-cell VLS with *Barak*-1 SAM (being upgraded to *Barak*-8), 2 triple 324mm TT with Mk 46 LWT, 1 Mk 15 *Phalanx* CIWS (capacity 1 AS565SA *Panther* ASW hel)
    1 *Eilat* (*Sa'ar* 5) with 2 quad lnchr with RGM-84 *Harpoon* AShM/*Gabriel* V AShM, 4 8-cell VLS with *Barak*-8 SAM, 2 triple 324mm TT with Mk 46 LWT, 1 Mk 15 *Phalanx* CIWS (capacity 1 AS565SA *Panther* ASW hel)
  PCGM 8 *Hetz* (*Sa'ar* 4.5) with 2 quad lnchr with RGM-84 *Harpoon* AShM (can also be fitted with up to 6 single lnchr with *Gabriel* II AShM), 2 8-cell VLS with *Barak*-1 SAM, (can be fitted with 2 triple 324mm Mk32 TT with Mk46 LWT), 1 Mk 15 *Phalanx* CWIS, 1 76mm gun
  PBF 34: 5 *Shaldag*; 3 *Stingray*; 9 *Super Dvora* Mk I (SSM & TT may be fitted); 4 *Super Dvora* Mk II (SSM & TT may be fitted); 6 *Super Dvora* Mk II-I (SSM & TT may be fitted); 4 *Super Dvora* Mk III (SSM & TT may be fitted); 3 *Super Dvora* Mk III (SSM may be fitted)

AMPHIBIOUS • LANDING CRAFT • LCVP 3 *Manta*
LOGISTICS AND SUPPORT • AG 1 *Bat Yam* (ex-GER Type-745)

Naval Commandos ε300
FORCES BY ROLE
SPECIAL FORCES
  1 cdo unit

Air Force 34,000

Responsible for Air and Space Coordination

FORCES BY ROLE
FIGHTER & FIGHTER/GROUND ATTACK
  1 sqn with F-15A/B/D *Eagle*
  1 sqn with F-15B/C/D *Eagle*
  1 sqn with F-15I *Ra'am*
  6 sqn with F-16C/D *Fighting Falcon*
  4 sqn with F-16I *Sufa*
  1 sqn with F-35I *Adir*
ANTI-SUBMARINE WARFARE
  1 sqn with AS565SA *Panther* (missions flown by IAF but with non-rated aircrew)
ELECTRONIC WARFARE
  2 sqn with RC-12D *Guardrail*; Beech A36 *Bonanza* (*Hofit*); Beech 200 *King Air*; Beech 200T *King Air*; Beech 200CT *King Air*
AIRBORNE EARLY WARNING & CONTROL
  1 sqn with Gulfstream G550 *Eitam*; Gulfstream G550 *Shavit*
TANKER/TRANSPORT
  1 sqn with C-130E/H *Hercules*; KC-130H *Hercules*
  1 sqn with C-130J-30 *Hercules*
  1 sqn with KC-707
TRAINING
  1 OPFOR sqn with F-16C/D *Fighting Falcon*
  1 sqn with M-346 *Master* (*Lavi*)
ATTACK HELICOPTER
  1 sqn with AH-64A *Apache*
  1 sqn with AH-64D *Apache*
TRANSPORT HELICOPTER
  2 sqn with CH-53D *Sea Stallion*
  2 sqn with S-70A *Black Hawk*; UH-60A *Black Hawk*
  1 medevac unit with CH-53D *Sea Stallion*
UAV
  1 ISR sqn with *Hermes* 450
  1 ISR sqn with *Heron* (*Shoval*); *Heron* TP (*Eitan*)
  1 ISR sqn with *Heron* (*Shoval*) (MP role)
AIR DEFENCE
  3 bty with *Arrow* 2/3
  10 bty with *Iron Dome*
  6 bty with MIM-104C *Patriot* PAC-2
  2 bty with *David's Sling*

SPECIAL FORCES
1 SF unit
1 spec ops unit

EQUIPMENT BY TYPE
AIRCRAFT 354 combat capable
  FTR 58: 16 F-15A *Eagle*; 6 F-15B *Eagle*; 17 F-15C *Eagle*; 19 F-15D *Eagle*
  FGA 266: 25 F-15I *Ra'am*; 78 F-16C *Fighting Falcon*; 49 F-16D *Fighting Falcon*; 98 F-16I *Sufa*; 16 F-35I *Adir*
  ISR 6 RC-12D *Guardrail*
  ELINT 4: 1 EC-707; 3 Gulfstream G550 *Shavit*
  AEW 4: 2 B-707 *Phalcon*; 2 Gulfstream G550 *Eitam* (1 more on order)
  TKR/TPT 10: 4 KC-130H *Hercules*; 6 KC-707
  TPT 65: **Medium** 18: 5 C-130E *Hercules*; 6 C-130H *Hercules*; 7 C-130J-30 *Hercules*; **Light** 47: 3 AT-802 *Air Tractor*; 9 Beech 200 *King Air*; 8 Beech 200T *King Air*; 5 Beech 200CT *King Air*; 22 Beech A36 *Bonanza* (*Hofit*)
  TRG 67: 17 Grob G-120; 30 M-346 *Master* (*Lavi*)*; 20 T-6A
HELICOPTERS
  ATK 43: 26 AH-64A *Apache*; 17 AH-64D *Apache* (*Sarat*)
  ASW 7 AS565SA *Panther* (missions flown by IAF but with non-rated aircrew)
  ISR 12 OH-58B *Kiowa*
  TPT 81: **Heavy** 26 CH-53D *Sea Stallion*; **Medium** 49: 39 S-70A *Black Hawk*; 10 UH-60A *Black Hawk*; **Light** 6 Bell 206 *Jet Ranger*
UNMANNED AERIAL VEHICLES
  ISR 3+: **Heavy** 3+: *Heron* (*Shoval*); 3 Heron TP (*Eitan*); RQ-5A *Hunter*; **Medium** *Hermes* 450; *Hermes* 900 (22+ *Searcher* MkII in store); **Light** *Harpy* (anti-radiation UAV)
AIR DEFENCE
  SAM 64+:
    Long-range MIM-104C *Patriot* PAC-2
    Medium-range some *David's Sling*
    Short-range up to 40 *Iron Dome*
    Point-defence *Machbet*
  GUNS • TOWED 20mm M167 *Vulcan*
MISSILE DEFENCE • SAM 24 *Arrow 2*/*Arrow 3*;
AIR-LAUNCHED MISSILES
  AAM • IR AIM-9 *Sidewinder*; *Python* 4; **IIR** *Python* 5; **ARH** AIM-120C AMRAAM
  ASM AGM-114 *Hellfire*; AGM-62B *Walleye*; AGM-65 *Maverick*; *Delilah* AL; *Popeye* I/*Popeye* II; *Spike* NLOS
BOMBS
  IIR guided *Opher*
  Laser-guided *Griffin*; *Lizard*; *Paveway* II
  INS/GPS guided GBU-31 JDAM; GBU-39 Small Diameter Bomb (*Barad Had*); *Spice*

Airfield Defence 3,000 active (15,000 reservists)

Paramilitary ε8,000

  Border Police ε8,000

FOREIGN FORCES
UNTSO unless specified. UNTSO figures represent total numbers for mission

Argentina 3
Australia 13 • UNDOF 1
Austria 5
Belgium 1
Bhutan 4 • UNDOF 3
Canada 4
Chile 3
China 5
Czech Republic UNDOF 3
Denmark 11
Estonia 3
Fiji 2 • UNDOF 290; 1 inf bn(-); elm 1 log bn
Finland 15
Ghana UNDOF 12
India 3 • UNDOF 194; 1 log bn(-)
Ireland 12 • UNDOF 126; 1 inf coy
Nepal 3 • UNDOF 333; 2 mech inf coy
Netherlands 12 • UNDOF 2
New Zealand 8
Norway 13
Russia 4
Serbia 2
Slovakia 2
Slovenia 3
Sweden 5
Switzerland 12
United States 2 • US Strategic Command; 1 AN/TPY-2 X-band radar at Mount Keren

Jordan JOR

Jordanian Dinar D		2018	2019	2020
GDP	D	30.0bn	31.3bn	
	US$	42.3bn	44.2bn	
per capita	US$	4,270	4,387	
Growth	%	1.9	2.2	
Inflation	%	4.5	2.0	
Def bdgt [a]	D	1.16bn	1.20bn	
	US$	1.63bn	1.69bn	
FMA (US)	US$	425m	350m	350m
US$1=D		0.71	0.71	

[a] Excludes expenditure on public order and safety

Real-terms defence budget trend (US$bn, constant 2015)
2.15
1.58
2008   2014   2019

Population   10,669,786
Ethnic groups: Palestinian ε50–60%

Age	0–14	15–19	20–24	25–29	30–64	65 plus
Male	17.3%	5.4%	5.1%	4.7%	18.4%	1.8%
Female	16.3%	4.9%	4.4%	3.9%	15.8%	1.8%

Capabilities

The Jordanian armed forces are structured to provide border security and an armoured response to conventional threats. Their well-regarded operational capability belies their moderate size and ageing equipment inventory. There is no recent public statement of defence policy, although the ongoing civil war in Syria is a clear concern. Jordan is a major non-NATO ally of the US with whom it maintains a close defence relationship. The country has developed a bespoke special-forces training centre and has hosted training for numerous state and non-state military forces. Personnel are well trained, particularly aircrew and special forces, who are highly regarded internationally. Jordanian forces are able to independently deploy regionally and have participated in ISAF operations in Afghanistan and in coalition air operations over Syria and Yemen. In contrast to the GCC states, the Jordanian inventory largely comprises older systems. Although the state-owned King Abdullah II Design and Development Bureau (KADDB) has demonstrated a vehicle-upgrade capacity, the army has largely recapitalised its armoured-vehicle fleet with second-hand armour from European countries. KADDB produces some light armoured vehicles for domestic use, but the company currently has little export profile.

ACTIVE 100,500 (Army 86,000 Navy 500 Air 14,000) Paramilitary 15,000

RESERVE 65,000 (Army 60,000 Joint 5,000)

ORGANISATIONS BY SERVICE

Army 86,000
FORCES BY ROLE
SPECIAL FORCES
  1 (Royal Guard) SF gp (1 SF regt, 1 SF bn, 1 CT bn)
  1 (AB) SF bde (3 SF bn)
MANOEUVRE
  Armoured
  3 armd bde
  1 armd inf bn
  Mechanised
  5 mech bde
  Light
  3 lt inf bde
  Air Manoeuvre
  1 (QRF) AB bde (1 SF bn, 2 AB bn)
COMBAT SUPPORT
  4 arty bde
  4 AD bde
  1 MRL bn
  1 engr bn
COMBAT SERVICE SUPPORT
  1 log bn
EQUIPMENT BY TYPE
ARMOURED FIGHTING VEHICLES
  MBT 282: ε100 FV4034 *Challenger* 1 (*Al Hussein*) (being withdrawn); 182 M60A3 (274 FV4030/2 *Khalid* in store)
  LT TK (19 FV101 *Scorpion* in store)
  ASLT 141 B1 *Centauro*
  IFV 720: 13 AIFV-B-C25; 50 *Marder* 1A3; 321 *Ratel*-20; 336 YPR-765 PRI
  APC 879+
   APC (T) 729: 370 M113A1/A2 Mk1J; 269 M577A2 (CP); 87 YPR-765 PRCO (CP); 3 AIFV-B
   PPV 150: 25 *Marauder*; 25 *Matador*; 100 *MaxxPro*
  AUV 35 *Cougar*
ENGINEERING & MAINTENANCE VEHICLES
  ARV 155+: *Al Monjed*; 55 *Chieftain* ARV; *Centurion* Mk2; 20 M47; 32 M88A1; 30 M578; 18 YPR-806
  MW 12 *Aardvark* Mk2
ANTI-TANK/ANTI-INFRASTRUCTURE • MSL
  SP 115: 70 M901; 45 AIFV-B-*Milan*
  MANPATS FGM-148 *Javelin*; TOW/TOW-2A; 9K135 *Kornet* (AT-14 *Spriggan*); Luch *Corsar*; *Stugna*-P
ARTILLERY 1,393+
  SP 506: **155mm** 358 M109A1/A2; **203mm** 148 M110A2
  TOWED 94: **105mm** 66: 54 M102; 12 M119A2; **155mm** 28: 10 M1/M59; 18 M114; **203mm** (4 M115 in store)
  MRL 16+: **227mm** 12 M142 HIMARS; **273mm** 4+ WM-80
  MOR 777: **81mm** 359; **SP 81mm** 50; **107mm** 50 M30; **120mm** 300 Brandt **SP 120mm** 18 *Agrab* Mk2
AIR DEFENCE
  SAM • **Point-defence** 140+: 92 9K35 *Strela*-10 (SA-13 *Gopher*); 48 9K33 *Osa*-M (SA-8 *Gecko*); 9K36 *Strela*-3 (SA-14 *Gremlin*); 9K310 *Igla*-1 (SA-16 *Gimlet*); 9K38 *Igla* (SA-18 *Grouse*)
  GUNS • **SP 35mm** 60 *Gepard*

Navy ε500
EQUIPMENT BY TYPE
PATROL AND COASTAL COMBATANTS 9
  PBF 2 *Response Boat-Medium* (RB-M)
  PB 7: 3 *Al Hussein* (UK Vosper 30m); 4 *Abdullah* (US *Dauntless*)

Marines
FORCES BY ROLE
MANOEUVRE
  Amphibious
  1 mne unit

Air Force 14,000
FORCES BY ROLE
FIGHTER/GROUND ATTACK
  2 sqn with F-16AM/BM *Fighting Falcon*
GROUND ATTACK
  1 sqn with AC-235
ISR
  1 sqn with AT-802U *Air Tractor*; Cessna 208B
TRANSPORT
  1 sqn with C-130E *Hercules*
TRAINING
  1 OCU with F-16AM/BM *Fighting Falcon*
  1 OCU with *Hawk* Mk63
  1 sqn with PC-21
  1 sqn with Grob 120TP
  1 hel sqn with R-44 *Raven* II
ATTACK HELICOPTER
  2 sqn with AH-1F *Cobra* (with TOW)
TRANSPORT HELICOPTER
  1 sqn with AS332M *Super Puma*
  1 sqn with UH-60A *Black Hawk*

1 sqn with H135M (Tpt/SAR)
1 sqn with MD-530F
1 sqn with UH-60L *Black Hawk*
1 sqn with Mi-26T2 *Halo* (forming)
1 (Royal) flt with S-70A *Black Hawk*; UH-60L/M *Black Hawk*; AW139

ISR UAV
1 sqn with S-100 *Camcopter*

AIR DEFENCE
2 bde with MIM-104C *Patriot* PAC-2; MIM-23B Phase III I-*Hawk*

EQUIPMENT BY TYPE
AIRCRAFT 57 combat capable
 FGA 47: 33 F-16AM *Fighting Falcon*; 14 F-16BM *Fighting Falcon*
 ATK (2 AC235 in store, offered for sale)
 ISR 10 AT-802U *Air Tractor**
 TPT 10 **Medium** 3 C-130E *Hercules* (1 C-130B *Hercules*; 4 C-130H *Hercules* in store); **Light** 7: 5 Cessna 208B; 2 M-28 *Skytruck* (2 C295M in store, offered for sale)
 TRG 24: up to 16 Grob 120TP; 8 PC-21 (12 *Hawk* Mk63* in store, offered for sale)
HELICOPTERS
 ATK 12 AH-1F *Cobra* (17 more in store, offered for sale)
 MRH 14: 3 AW139; 11 H135M (Tpt/SAR) (6 MD-530F in store, offered for sale)
 TPT 49: **Heavy** 2 Mi-26T2 *Halo*; **Medium** 35: 10 AS332M *Super Puma* (being WFU); 25 S-70A/UH-60A/UH-60L/VH-60M *Black Hawk*; **Light** 12 R-44 *Raven* II (13 Bell 205 (UH-1H *Iroquois*) in store, offered for sale)
UNMANNED AERIAL VEHICLES
 CISR • **Heavy** (some CH-4B in store, offered for sale)
 ISR • **Light** up to 10 S-100 *Camcopter*
AIR DEFENCE • SAM 64:
 Long-range 40 MIM-104C *Patriot* PAC-2
 Medium-range 24 MIM-23B Phase III I-*Hawk*
AIR-LAUNCHED MISSILES
 AAM • IR AIM-9J/N/P *Sidewinder*; SARH AIM-7 *Sparrow*; ARH AIM-120C AMRAAM
 ASM AGM-65D/G *Maverick*; BGM-71 TOW
BOMBS
 Laser-guided GBU-10/12 *Paveway* II

Paramilitary ε15,000 active

Gendarmerie ε15,000 active
3 regional comd

FORCES BY ROLE
SPECIAL FORCES
 2 SF unit
MANOEUVRE
 Other
 10 sy bn

EQUIPMENT BY TYPE
ARMOURED FIGHTING VEHICLES
 APC • APC (W) 25+: AT105 *Saxon* (reported); 25+ EE-11 *Urutu*
 AUV AB2 *Al-Jawad*

DEPLOYMENT
CENTRAL AFRICAN REPUBLIC: UN • MINUSCA 10
DEMOCRATIC REPUBLIC OF THE CONGO: UN • MONUSCO 8
MALI: UN • MINUSMA 66
SAUDI ARABIA: *Operation Restoring Hope* 6 F-16C *Fighting Falcon*
SOUTH SUDAN: UN • UNMISS 5
WESTERN SAHARA: UN • MINURSO 4

FOREIGN FORCES
France *Operation Inherent Resolve* (*Chammal*) 8 *Rafale* F3; 1 *Atlantique* 2
Germany *Operation Inherent Resolve* 280; 4 *Tornado* ECR; 1 A310 MRTT
Norway *Operation Inherent Resolve* 20
United States Central Command: *Operation Inherent Resolve* 2,300; 1 FGA sqn with 12 F-15E *Strike Eagle*; 1 CISR sqn with 12 MQ-9A *Reaper*

Kuwait KWT

Kuwaiti Dinar D		2018	2019	2020
GDP	D	42.8bn	41.5bn	
	US$	142bn	138bn	
per capita	US$	30,969	29,267	
Growth	%	1.2	0.6	
Inflation	%	0.6	1.5	
Def bdgt	D	1.87bn	1.93bn	
	US$	6.18bn	6.40bn	
US$1=D		0.30	0.30	

Real-terms defence budget trend (US$bn, constant 2015)

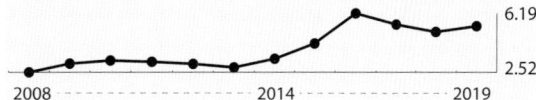

Population 2,955,097

Ethnic groups: Nationals 35.5%; other non-Arab Asian countries 37.7%; other Arab countries 17.5%; other or unspecified 9.3%

Age	0–14	15–19	20–24	25–29	30–64	65 plus
Male	12.8%	3.2%	5.0%	7.2%	28.7%	1.2%
Female	11.8%	3.0%	3.8%	4.3%	17.5%	1.5%

Capabilities

Kuwait's small but capable armed forces have benefited considerably from the significant presence on Kuwaiti territory of sizeable US forces. The primary responsibility is territorial defence, through a strategy of sufficient readiness to provide a holding force until the mobilisation of friendly forces. The National Guard, under its Strategic Vision 2020 plan, intends to boost readiness and equipment capability. Kuwait is a member of the GCC and has a bilateral defence-cooperation agreement with the US, which provides for a range of joint activities and mentoring, and the stationing and pre-positioning of significant numbers of US personnel and supplies of equipment. Since 2004, Kuwait has been designated a US major non-NATO ally. Kuwait operates a system of voluntary military service but suffers from a limited population pool. Contributions of air and ground assets have been made to the Saudi-led coalition in Yemen, but otherwise the country has limited deployment ambitions. There is limited logistic-support capacity, although heavy-airlift and airborne-tanking assets grant a limited airborne-expeditionary capability. The equipment inventory includes a range of modern European- and US-sourced platforms, including advanced air-defence-missile batteries. Kuwait is recapitalising its combat-aircraft fleet with the F/A-18E/F *Super Hornet* and Eurofighter *Typhoon*, which together will significantly enhance its air-combat capabilities. There are also indications that it wants to upgrade its fleet of main battle tanks and seek additional attack helicopters, and possibly new missile-armed multi-mission fast attack craft for the navy. Kuwait lacks a domestic defence-industrial base and is reliant on imports, albeit with offset requirements to help stimulate the country's wider industrial sector.

ACTIVE 17,500 (Army 13,000 Navy 2,000 Air 2,500)
Paramilitary 7,100
Conscript liability 12 months

RESERVE 23,700 (Joint 23,700)
Reserve obligation to age 40; 1 month annual trg

ORGANISATIONS BY SERVICE

Army 13,000
FORCES BY ROLE
SPECIAL FORCES
  1 SF unit
MANOEUVRE
  Reconnaissance
  1 mech/recce bde
  Armoured
  3 armd bde
  Mechanised
  2 mech inf bde
  Light
  1 cdo bn
  Other
  1 (Amiri) gd bde
COMBAT SUPPORT
  1 arty bde
  1 engr bde
  1 MP bn
COMBAT SERVICE SUPPORT
  1 log gp
  1 fd hospital

Reserve
FORCES BY ROLE
MANOEUVRE
  Mechanised
  1 bde
EQUIPMENT BY TYPE
ARMOURED FIGHTING VEHICLES
  MBT 293: 218 M1A2 *Abrams*; 75 M-84 (75 more in store)
  IFV 492: 76 BMP-2; 180 BMP-3; 236 *Desert Warrior*† (incl variants)
  APC 260

  APC (T) 260: 230 M113A2; 30 M577 (CP)
  APC (W) (40 TH 390 *Fahd* in store)
ENGINEERING & MAINTENANCE VEHICLES
  ARV 24+: 24 M88A1/2; Type-653A; *Warrior*
  MW *Aardvark* Mk2
NBC VEHICLES 11 TPz-1 *Fuchs* NBC
ARTY 211
  SP 155mm 106: 37 M109A3; 18 Mk F3; 51 PLZ-45 (18 AU-F-1 in store)
  MRL 300mm 27 9A52 *Smerch*
  MOR 78: **81mm** 60; **107mm** 6 M30; **120mm** ε12 RT-F1
ANTI-TANK/ANTI-INFRASTRUCTURE
  MSL
    SP 74: 66 HMMWV TOW; 8 M901
    MANPATS TOW-2; M47 *Dragon*
  RCL 84mm *Carl Gustav*
AIR DEFENCE
  SAM • Point-defence *Starburst*; FIM-92 *Stinger*
  GUNS • TOWED 35mm 12+ Oerlikon

Navy ε2,000 (incl 500 Coast Guard)
EQUIPMENT BY TYPE
PATROL AND COASTAL COMBATANTS 20
  PCFG 2:
    1 *Al Sanbouk* (GER Lurssen TNC-45) with 2 twin lnchr with MM40 *Exocet* AShM, 1 76mm gun
    1 *Istiqlal* (GER Lurssen FPB-57) with 2 twin lnchr with MM40 *Exocet* AShM, 1 76mm gun
  PBF 10 *Al Nokatha* (US Mk V *Pegasus*)
  PBG 8 *Um Almaradim* (FRA P-37 BRL) with 2 twin lnchr with *Sea Skua* AShM
AMPHIBIOUS LANDING CRAFT 6
  LCM 1 *Abhan* (ADSB 42m)
  LCVP 5 ADSB 16m
LOGISTICS AND SUPPORT • AG 1 *Sawahil* with 1 hel landing platform

Air Force 2,500
FORCES BY ROLE
FIGHTER/GROUND ATTACK
  2 sqn with F/A-18C/D *Hornet*
TRANSPORT
  1 sqn with C-17A *Globemaster* III; KC-130J *Hercules*; L-100-30
TRAINING
  1 unit with EMB-312 *Tucano**; *Hawk* Mk64*
ATTACK HELICOPTER
  1 sqn with AH-64D *Apache*
  1 atk/trg sqn with SA342 *Gazelle* with HOT
TRANSPORT HELICOPTER
  1 sqn with AS532 *Cougar*; SA330 *Puma*; S-92
EQUIPMENT BY TYPE
AIRCRAFT 66 combat capable
  FGA 39: 31 F/A-18C *Hornet*; 8 F/A-18D *Hornet*
  TKR 3 KC-130J *Hercules*
  TPT 5: **Heavy** 2 C-17A *Globemaster* III; **Medium** 3 L-100-30
  TRG 27: 11 *Hawk* Mk64*; 16 EMB-312 *Tucano**
HELICOPTERS
  ATK 16 AH-64D *Apache*
  MRH 13 SA342 *Gazelle* with HOT

TPT • **Medium** 13: 3 AS532 *Cougar*; 7 SA330 *Puma*; 3 S-92
AIR-LAUNCHED MISSILES
AAM • **IR** AIM-9L *Sidewinder*; R-550 *Magic*; **SARH** AIM-7F *Sparrow*; **ARH** AIM-120C7 AMRAAM
ASM AGM-65G *Maverick*; AGM-114K *Hellfire*; HOT
AShM AGM-84D *Harpoon* Block IC

Air Defence Command

FORCES BY ROLE
AIR DEFENCE
  1 SAM bde (7 SAM bty with MIM-104D *Patriot* PAC-2 GEM)
  1 SAM bde (6 SAM bty with *Skyguard/Aspide*)
EQUIPMENT BY TYPE
AIR DEFENCE • SAM 52:
  Long-range 40 MIM-104D *Patriot* PAC-2 GEM
  Short-range 12 *Aspide* with *Skyguard*

Paramilitary ε7,100 active

National Guard ε6,600 active
FORCES BY ROLE
SPECIAL FORCES
  1 SF bn
MANOEUVRE
  Reconnaissance
  1 armd car bn
  Other
  3 security bn
COMBAT SUPPORT
  1 MP bn
EQUIPMENT BY TYPE
ARMOURED FIGHTING VEHICLES
  RECCE 20 VBL
  IFV 70 *Pandur* (incl variants)
  APC • APC (W) 27+: 5+ *Desert Chameleon*; 22 S600 (incl variants)
ENGINEERING & MAINTENANCE VEHICLES
  ARV *Pandur*

Coast Guard 500
EQUIPMENT BY TYPE
PATROL AND COASTAL COMBATANTS 32
  PBF 12 *Manta*
  PB 20: 3 *Al Shaheed*; 4 *Inttisar* (Austal 31.5m); 3 *Kassir* (Austal 22m); 10 *Subahi*
  AMPHIBIOUS • LANDING CRAFT • LCU 4: 2 *Al Tahaddy*; 1 *Saffar*; 1 other
  LOGISTICS AND SUPPORT • AG 1 *Sawahil*

DEPLOYMENT
SAUDI ARABIA: *Operation Restoring Hope* 4 F/A-18A *Hornet*

FOREIGN FORCES
Canada *Operation Inherent Resolve* (*Impact*) 1 A310 MRTT (C-150T); 2 C-130J-30 *Hercules* (CC-130J)
Denmark *Operation Inherent Resolve* 20
Italy *Operation Inherent Resolve* (*Prima Parthica*) 250; 4 Eurofighter *Typhoon*; 2 MQ-9A *Reaper*; 1 KC-767A
Singapore *Operation Inherent Resolve* 11
United Kingdom *Operation Inherent Resolve* (*Shader*) 50; 1 CISR UAV sqn with 8 MQ-9A *Reaper*
United States Central Command: 13,500; 1 ARNG armd bde(-); 1 USAR (cbt avn) hel bde; 1 spt bde; 3 AD bty with MIM-104E/F *Patriot* PAC-2/3; 1 CISR UAV sqn with MQ-9A *Reaper*; 1 (APS) armd bde eqpt set; 1 (APS) inf bde eqpt set

Lebanon LBN

Lebanese Pound LP		2018	2019	2020
GDP	LP	85.0tr	88.3tr	
	US$	56.4bn	58.6bn	
per capita	US$	9,251	9,655	
Growth	%	0.3	0.2	
Inflation	%	6.1	3.1	
Def bdgt	LP	3.20tr	2.91tr	
	US$	2.12bn	1.93bn	
FMA (US)	US$	105.0m	50.0m	50.0m
US$1=LP		1507.51	1507.51	

Real-terms defence budget trend (US$bn, constant 2015)

Population 6,100,075

Ethnic and religious groups: Christian 30%; Druze 6%; Armenian 4%; excl ε300,000 Syrians and ε350,000 Palestinian refugees

Age	0–14	15–19	20–24	25–29	30–64	65 plus
Male	11.4%	4.0%	4.0%	4.2%	23.3%	3.2%
Female	10.9%	3.8%	3.8%	4.1%	23.2%	4.2%

Capabilities

The Lebanese Armed Forces (LAF) are focused on internal and border security. However, the LAF's ability to fulfil its missions remains under strain from Hizbullah's position in national politics and from the spillover effects of the Syrian conflict. Publication of a new National Defence Strategy continues to be delayed by political divisions. Training and material support are received from the US, as well as from France, Italy and the UK. Previous material support from Saudi Arabia was curtailed for political reasons. Personnel quality and capability is relatively high for the region and US special-operations personnel continue to provide operational advice and assistance. LAF operations against ISIS have demonstrated improved capability. The LAF has no requirement for extra-territorial deployment and minimal capability to do so. It remains dependent on foreign support to replace and modernise its ageing equipment inventory. Barring some light maintenance facilities in the services, Lebanon has no significant domestic defence industry.

ACTIVE 60,000 (Army 56,600 Navy 1,800 Air 1,600)
Paramilitary 20,000

ORGANISATIONS BY SERVICE

Army 56,600

FORCES BY ROLE
5 regional comd (Beirut, Bekaa Valley, Mount Lebanon, North, South)
SPECIAL FORCES
 1 cdo regt
MANOEUVRE
 Armoured
 1 armd regt
 Mechanised
 11 mech inf bde
 Air Manoeuvre
 1 AB regt
 Amphibious
 1 mne cdo regt
 Other
 1 Presidential Guard bde
 6 intervention regt 4 border sy regt
COMBAT SUPPORT
 2 arty regt
 1 cbt spt bde (1 engr regt, 1 AT regt, 1 sigs regt; 1 log bn)
 1 MP gp
COMBAT SERVICE SUPPORT
 1 log bde
 1 med gp
 1 construction regt
EQUIPMENT BY TYPE
MBT 334: 92 M48A1/A5; 10 M60A2; 185 T-54; 47 T-55
RECCE 55 AML
IFV 48: 16 AIFV-B-C25; 32 M2A2 *Bradley*
APC 1,378
 APC (T) 1,274 M113A1/A2 (incl variants)
 APC (W) 96: 86 VAB VCT; 10 VBPT-MR *Guarani*
 PPV 8 *Maxxpro*
ENGINEERING & MAINTENANCE VEHICLES
 ARV 3 M88A1; M113 ARV; T-54/55 ARV (reported)
 VLB MTU-72 reported
 MW *Bozena*
ARTILLERY 641
 SP 155mm 12 M109A2
 TOWED 313: **105mm** 13 M101A1; **122mm** 35: 9 D-30; 26 M-30; **130mm** 15 M-46; **155mm** 250: 18 M114A1; 218 M198; 14 Model-50
 MRL 122mm 11 BM-21
 MOR 305: **81mm** 134; **82mm** 112; **120mm** 59: 29 Brandt; 30 M120
ANTI-TANK/ANTI-INFRASTRUCTURE
 MSL
  SP 35 VAB with HOT
  MANPATS *Milan*; TOW
 RCL 106mm 113 M40A1
UNMANNED AERIAL VEHICLES
 ISR • Medium 8 *Mohajer* 4
AIR DEFENCE
 SAM • Point-defence 9K32 *Strela*-2M (SA-7B *Grail*)‡
 GUNS • TOWED 77: **20mm** 20; **23mm** 57 ZU-23-2

Navy 1,800

EQUIPMENT BY TYPE
PATROL AND COASTAL COMBATANTS 13
 PCC 1 *Trablous*
 PB 11: 1 *Aamchit* (ex-GER *Bremen*); 1 *Al Kalamoun* (ex-FRA *Avel Gwarlarn*); 7 *Tripoli* (ex-UK *Attacker/Tracker* Mk 2); 1 *Naquora* (ex-GER *Bremen*); 1 *Tabarja* (ex-GER *Bergen*)
 PBF 1
AMPHIBIOUS
 LANDING CRAFT • LCT 2 *Sour* (ex-FRA EDIC – capacity 8 APC; 96 troops)

Air Force 1,600

4 air bases
FORCES BY ROLE
GROUND ATTACK
 1 sqn with Cessna AC-208 *Combat Caravan**
 1 sqn with EMB-314 *Super Tucano**
ATTACK HELICOPTER
 1 sqn with SA342L *Gazelle*
TRANSPORT HELICOPTER
 4 sqn with Bell 205 (UH-1H)
 1 sqn with SA330/IAR330SM *Puma*
 1 trg sqn with R-44 *Raven* II
EQUIPMENT BY TYPE
AIRCRAFT 9 combat capable
 ISR 3 Cessna AC-208 *Combat Caravan**
 TRG 9: 3 *Bulldog*; 6 EMB-314 *Super Tucano**
HELICOPTERS
 MRH 9: 1 AW139; 8 SA342L *Gazelle* (5 SA342L *Gazelle*; 5 SA316 *Alouette* III; 1 SA318 *Alouette* II all non-operational)
 TPT 38: **Medium** 13: 3 S-61N (fire fighting); 10 SA330/IAR330 *Puma*; **Light** 25: 18 Bell 205 (UH-1H *Huey*); 3 Bell 205 (UH-1H *Huey* II); 4 R-44 *Raven* II (basic trg) (11 Bell 205; 7 Bell 212 all non-operational)
AIR LAUNCHED MISSILES
 ASM AGM-114 *Hellfire*

Paramilitary ε20,000 active

Internal Security Force ε20,000

Ministry of Interior
FORCES BY ROLE
Other Combat Forces
 1 (police) judicial unit
 1 regional sy coy
 1 (Beirut Gendarmerie) sy coy
EQUIPMENT BY TYPE
ARMOURED FIGHTING VEHICLES
 APC • APC (W) 60 V-200 *Chaimite*

Customs

EQUIPMENT BY TYPE
PATROL AND COASTAL COMBATANTS 7
 PB 7: 5 *Aztec*; 2 *Tracker*

FOREIGN FORCES

Unless specified, figures refer to UNTSO and represent total numbers for the mission
Argentina 3
Armenia UNIFIL 33
Australia 13
Austria 5 • UNIFIL 185: 1 log coy

Bangladesh UNIFIL 117: 1 FSG
Belarus UNIFIL 5
Belgium 1
Bhutan 4
Brazil UNIFIL 198: 1 FFGHM
Brunei UNIFIL 29
Cambodia UNIFIL 184: 1 EOD coy
Canada 4 (*Operation Jade*)
Chile 3
China, People's Republic of 5 • UNIFIL 419: 2 engr coy; 1 med coy
Colombia UNIFIL 1
Croatia UNIFIL 1
Cyprus UNIFIL 2
Denmark 11
El Salvador UNIFIL 52: 1 inf pl
Estonia 3 • UNIFIL 1
Fiji 2 • UNIFIL 1
Finland 15 • UNIFIL 198; 1 maint coy
France UNIFIL 670: 1 mech inf bn(-); VBL; VBCI; VAB; *Mistral*
Germany UNIFIL 182: 1 FFGM
Ghana UNIFIL 870: 1 mech inf bn
Greece UNIFIL 146: 1 FFGHM
Guatemala UNIFIL 1
Hungary UNIFIL 2
India 3 • UNIFIL 781: 1 inf bn; 1 med coy
Indonesia UNIFIL 1,309: 1 inf bn; 1 MP coy; 1 FFGM
Ireland 12 • UNIFIL 461: 1 mech inf bn(-)
Italy UNIFIL 1,066: 1 mech bde HQ; 1 mech inf bn; 1 engr coy; 1 sigs coy; 1 hel bn
Kazakhstan UNIFIL 123; 1 inf coy
Kenya UNIFIL 2
Korea, Republic of UNIFIL 331: 1 mech inf coy; 1 engr coy; 1 sigs coy; 1 maint coy
Macedonia, North UNIFIL 2
Malaysia UNIFIL 813: 1 mech inf bn
Malta UNIFIL 11
Nepal 3 • UNIFIL 873: 1 mech inf bn
Netherlands 12 • UNIFIL 1
New Zealand 8
Nigeria UNIFIL 1
Norway 13
Peru UNIFIL 1
Qatar UNIFIL 2
Russia 4
Serbia 2 • UNIFIL 177; 1 mech inf coy
Sierra Leone UNIFIL 3
Slovakia 2
Slovenia 3 • UNIFIL 15
Spain UNIFIL 635: 1 mech bde HQ; 1 mech inf bn(-); 1 engr coy; 1 sigs coy
Sri Lanka UNIFIL 149: 1 inf coy
Sweden 5
Switzerland 12
Tanzania UNIFIL 159: 1 MP coy
Turkey UNIFIL 85: 1 PCFG
United States 2
Uruguay UNIFIL 1

Libya LBY

Libyan Dinar D		2018	2019	2020
GDP	D	56.7bn	45.7bn	
	US$	41.0bn	33.0bn	
per capita	US$	6,288	5,020	
Growth	%	17.9	-19.1	
Inflation	%	9.3	4.2	
Def exp	D	n.k.	n.k.	
	US$	n.k.	n.k.	
US$1=D		1.39	1.39	

Population	6,850,229					
Age	0–14	15–19	20–24	25–29	30–64	65 plus
Male	13.0%	4.2%	4.3%	4.5%	23.6%	2.2%
Female	12.3%	4.0%	4.0%	4.1%	21.5%	2.3%

Capabilities

Armed groups in Libya are composed of a mix of semi-regular military units, tribal militias and armed civilians based around General Haftar's Libyan National Army (LNA) in the eastern part of the country and Prime Minister Fayez al-Sarraj's internationally recognised Government of National Accord (GNA) in the west. Both the GNA's and LNA's affiliated forces have relatively low levels of training. The presence in these formations of units from the former Gadhafi-era army has bolstered their military capability. Meanwhile, the GNA-affiliated forces have since 2016 benefited from several military advisory and training programmes, including EUNAVFOR–MED maritime-security training for the Libyan Navy and Coast Guard. LNA troops have combat experience from fighting ISIS in the eastern coastal region and they have allegedly received training and combat support from external actors in the region. Both organisations' equipment is mainly of Russian or Soviet origin, including items from the former Libyan armed forces, and suffers from varying degrees of obsolescence. However, the lack of high-technology platforms has allowed both forces to maintain minimum operational standards. Since the beginning of the LNA campaign to take Tripoli, launched in early 2019, both sides have suffered significant equipment losses. The country has no domestic defence-industrial capability.

Forces loyal to the Government of National Accord (Tripoli-based)

ACTIVE n.k.

ORGANISATIONS BY SERVICE

Ground Forces n.k.
EQUIPMENT BY TYPE
ARMOURED FIGHTING VEHICLES
 MBT T-55; T-72
 IFV BMP-2
 APC • APC (T) 4K-7FA *Steyr*
 AUV Nimr *Ajban*

ENGINEERING & MAINTENANCE VEHICLES
ARV Centurion 105 AVRE
ANTI-TANK/ANTI-INFRASTRUCTURE
MSL • SP 9P157-2 Khrizantema-S (AT-15 Springer)
ARTILLERY
SP 155mm Palmaria
TOWED 122mm D-30
AIR DEFENCE
GUNS • SP 14.5mm ZPU-2 (on tch); 23mm ZU-23-2 (on tch)

Navy n.k.
A number of intact naval vessels remain in Tripoli, although serviceability is questionable
EQUIPMENT BY TYPE
PRINCIPAL SURFACE COMBATANTS 1
FRIGATES • FFGM 1 Al Hani (FSU Koni) (in Malta for refit since 2013) with 2 twin lnchr with P-22 (SS-N-2C Styx) AShM, 1 twin lnchr with 4K33 Osa-M (SA-N-4 Gecko) SAM, 2 twin 406mm ASTT, 1 RBU 6000 Smerch 2 A/S mor, 2 AK230 CIWS, 2 twin 76mm gun
PATROL AND COASTAL COMBATANTS 3+
PBFG 1 Sharaba (FRA Combattante II) with 4 single lnchr with Otomat Mk2 AShM, 1 76mm gun†
PB 2+ PV30
AMPHIBIOUS
LANDING SHIPS • LST 1 Ibn Harissa (capacity 1 hel; 11 MBT; 240 troops)
LOGISTICS AND SUPPORT 2
AFD 1
ARS 1 Al Munjed (YUG Spasilac)†

Air Force n.k.
EQUIPMENT BY TYPE
AIRCRAFT 13+ combat capable
FGA 2 MiG-23BN
ATK 1 J-21 Jastreb†
TRG 10+: 3 G-2 Galeb*; up to 7 L-39ZO*; some SF-260
HELICOPTERS
ATK Mi-24 Hind
TPT • Medium Mi-17 Hip
AIR-LAUNCHED MISSILES • AAM • IR R-3 (AA-2 Atoll)‡; R-60 (AA-8 Aphid); R-24 (AA-7 Apex)

Paramilitary n.k.

Coast Guard n.k.
EQUIPMENT BY TYPE
PATROL AND COASTAL COMBATANTS 9
PCC 1 Damen Stan 2909 with 1 sextuple 122mm MRL
PBF 5: 4 Bigliani; 1 Fezzan (ex-ITA Corrubia)
PB 3: 1 Burdi (Damen Stan 1605); 1 Hamelin; 1 Ikrimah (FRA RPB 20)

TERRITORY WHERE THE RECOGNISED AUTHORITY DOES NOT EXERCISE EFFECTIVE CONTROL
Data here represents the de facto situation. This does not imply international recognition

ACTIVE n.k.

ORGANISATIONS BY SERVICE

Libyan National Army n.k.
EQUIPMENT BY TYPE
ARMOURED FIGHTING VEHICLES
MBT T-55; T-62; T-72
RECCE BRDM-2; EE-9 Cascavel
IFV BMP-1; Ratel-20
APC
APC (T) M113
APC (W) Al-Mared; BTR-60PB; Mbombe-6; Nimr Jais; Puma
PPV Al-Wahsh; Caiman; Streit Spartan; Streit Typhoon
AUV Panthera T6; Panthera F9
ANTI-TANK/ANTI-INFRASTRUCTURE
MSL
SP 10 9P157-2 Khryzantema-S (status unknown)
MANPATS 9K11 Malyutka (AT-3 Sagger); 9K111 Fagot (AT-4 Spigot); 9K111-1 Konkurs (AT-5 Spandrel); Milan
RCL some: 106mm M40A1; 84mm Carl Gustav
ARTILLERY
SP 122mm 2S1 Gvodzika
TOWED 122mm D-30
MRL 107mm Type-63; 122mm BM-21 Grad
MOR M106
AIR DEFENCE
SAM
Short-range 2K12 Kvadrat (SA-6 Gainful)
Point-defence 9K338 Igla-S (SA-24 Grinch)
GUNS • SP 14.5mm ZPU-2 (on tch); 23mm ZSU-23-4 Shilka; ZU-23-2 (on tch)

Navy n.k.
EQUIPMENT BY TYPE
PATROL AND COASTAL COMBATANTS 7+
PB: 7+: 2 Burdi (Damen Stan 1605); 1 Burdi (Damen Stan 1605) with 1 73mm gun; 2 Ikrimah (FRA RPB20); 1 Hamelin; 1+ PV30
LOGISTICS AND SUPPORT 1
AFD 1

Air Force n.k.
EQUIPMENT BY TYPE
AIRCRAFT 5+ combat capable
FTR MiG-23 Flogger
FGA 5+: 3+ MiG-21bis/MF Fishbed; 1 Mirage F-1ED; 1 Su-22UM-3K Fitter
TRG 1+ MiG-21UM Mongol B
HELICOPTERS
ATK Mi-24/35 Hind
TPT Medium Mi-8/Mi-17 Hip
AIR-LAUNCHED MISSILES • AAM • IR R-3 (AA-2 Atoll)‡; R-60 (AA-8 Aphid)

FOREIGN FORCES
Germany UNSMIL 2
Italy MIASIT 300
Nepal UNSMIL 230; 2 sy coy

United Arab Emirates 6 AT-802; 2 UH-60M; *Wing Loong* I UAV; *Wing Loong* II UAV; *Pantsir*-S1
United Kingdom UNSMIL 1
United States UNSMIL 1

Mauritania MRT

Mauritanian Ouguiya OM		2018	2019	2020
GDP	OM	187bn	209bn	
	US$	5.24bn	5.65bn	
per capita	US$	1,319	1,392	
Growth	%	3.6	6.6	
Inflation	%	3.1	3.0	
Def bdgt	OM	5.68bn	5.91bn	
	US$	159m	160m	
US$1=OM			35.69	37.02

Real-terms defence budget trend (US$m, constant 2015)

Population	3,922,758				
Age	0–14	15–19	20–24	25–29	30–64	65 plus
Male	19.0%	5.2%	4.5%	3.9%	13.9%	1.6%
Female	18.9%	5.3%	4.8%	4.3%	16.4%	2.2%

Capabilities

The country's small and modestly equipped armed forces are tasked with maintaining territorial integrity and internal security. In light of the regional threat from extremist Islamist groups, border security is also a key role for the armed forces, which are accustomed to counter-insurgency operations in the desert. The country is a member of the G5 Sahel group. Mauritania's armed forces take part in the US-led special-operations *Flintlock* training exercise. The country also benefits from training with French armed forces. Deployment capabilities are limited to neighbouring countries without external support, but the armed forces have demonstrated mobility and sustainability in desert regions. Mauritania has a limited and ageing equipment inventory, which hampers operational capability. Despite some recent acquisitions, including small ISR aircraft, aviation resources are insufficient considering the size of the country. Naval equipment is geared toward coastal-surveillance missions and China's donation of a landing ship has helped establish a basic sealift capability. There is no domestic defence industry.

ACTIVE 15,850 (Army 15,000 Navy 600 Air 250)
Paramilitary 5,000
Conscript liability 24 months

ORGANISATIONS BY SERVICE

Army 15,000
FORCES BY ROLE
6 mil regions
MANOEUVRE
  Reconnaissance
  1 armd recce bn
  Armoured
  1 armd bn
  Light
  7 mot inf bn
  8 (garrison) inf bn
  Air Manoeuvre
  1 cdo/para bn
  Other
  2 (camel corps) bn
  1 gd bn
COMBAT SUPPORT
  3 arty bn
  4 ADA bty
  1 engr coy
EQUIPMENT BY TYPE
ARMOURED FIGHTING VEHICLES
  MBT 35 T-54/T-55
  RECCE 70: 20 AML-60; 40 AML-90; 10 *Saladin*
  APC • APC (W) 25: 5 FV603 *Saracen*; ε20 Panhard M3
  AUV 12 *Cobra*
ENGINEERING & MAINTENANCE VEHICLES
  ARV T-54/55 ARV reported
ANTI-TANK/ANTI-INFRASTRUCTURE
  MSL • MANPATS *Milan*
  RCL • **106mm** ε90 M40A1
ARTILLERY 180
  TOWED 80: **105mm** 36 HM-2/M101A1; **122mm** 44: 20 D-30; 24 D-74
  MRL 10: **107mm** 4 Type-63; **122mm** 6 Type-81
  MOR 90: **81mm** 60; **120mm** 30 Brandt
AIR DEFENCE
  SAM • Point-defence ε4 SA-9 *Gaskin* (reported); 9K32 *Strela*-2 (SA-7 *Grail*)‡
  GUNS • TOWED 82: **14.5mm** 28: 16 ZPU-2; 12 ZPU-4; **23mm** 20 ZU-23-2; **37mm** 10 M-1939; **57mm** 12 S-60; **100mm** 12 KS-19

Navy ε600
EQUIPMENT BY TYPE
PATROL AND COASTAL COMBATANTS 17
  PCO 1 *Voum-Legleita*
  PCC 7: 1 *Abourbekr Ben Amer* (FRA OPV 54); 1 *Arguin*; 2 *Conejera*; 1 *Limam El Hidrami* (PRC); 2 *Timbédra* (PRC *Huangpu* Mod)
  PB 9: 1 *El Nasr*† (FRA *Patra*); 4 *Mandovi*; 2 *Saeta*-12; 2 *Megsem Bakkar* (FRA RPB20 – for SAR duties)
AMPHIBIOUS • LANDING SHIPS 1 *Nimlane* (PRC)

Fusiliers Marins
FORCES BY ROLE
MANOEUVRE
  Amphibious
  1 mne unit

Air Force 250
EQUIPMENT BY TYPE
AIRCRAFT 2 combat capable
  ISR 2 Cessna 208B *Grand Caravan*
  TPT 9: **Light** 8: 2 BN-2 *Defender*; 1 C-212; 1 CN235; 2 PA-31T *Cheyenne* II; 2 Y-12(II); **PAX** 1 BT-67 (with sensor turret)

TRG 11: 3 EMB-312 *Tucano*; 2 EMB-314 *Super Tucano**; 4 SF-260E
HELICOPTERS • MRH 3: 1 SA313B *Alouette* II; 2 Z-9

Paramilitary ε5,000 active

Gendarmerie ε3,000
Ministry of Interior
FORCES BY ROLE
MANOEUVRE
  Other
    6 regional sy coy
EQUIPMENT BY TYPE
ARMOURED FIGHTING VEHICLES
  AUV 12 *Cobra*
PATROL AND COASTAL COMBATANTS • 2 Rodman 55M

National Guard 2,000
Ministry of Interior

Customs
EQUIPMENT BY TYPE
PATROL AND COASTAL COMBATANTS • PB 2: 1 *Dah Ould Bah* (FRA *Amgram* 14); 1 *Yaboub Ould Rajel* (FRA RPB18)

DEPLOYMENT

CENTRAL AFRICAN REPUBLIC: UN • MINUSCA 565; 1 inf bn(-)
MALI: UN • MINUSMA 6
SOMALIA: UN • UNSOS 1

Morocco MOR

Moroccan Dirham D		2018	2019	2020
GDP	D	1.11tr	1.15tr	
	US$	119bn	119bn	
per capita	US$	3,366	3,345	
Growth	%	3.0	2.7	
Inflation	%	1.9	0.7	
Def bdgt	D	34.3bn	35.2bn	45.4bn
	US$	3.65bn	3.63bn	
FMA (US)	US$	10.0m	0.0m	0.0m
US$1=D		9.39	9.68	

Real-terms defence budget trend (US$bn, constant 2015)

Population 34,637,293

Age	0–14	15–19	20–24	25–29	30–64	65 plus
Male	12.8%	4.2%	4.1%	4.0%	20.8%	3.3%
Female	12.4%	4.2%	4.2%	4.1%	22.2%	3.9%

Capabilities

Regional security challenges rank highly for Morocco's armed forces, who have gained experience in operations in Western Sahara. Despite the UN-brokered 1991 ceasefire between Morocco and the Polisario Front, the conflict in Western Sahara remains unresolved. Morocco maintains long-standing defence ties with France and the US, receiving military training and equipment from both. There is also close cooperation with NATO, and in 2016 Morocco was granted access to the Alliance's Interoperability Platform in order to strengthen the defence and security sectors and bring the armed forces to NATO standards. In 2017, Morocco rejoined the African Union. The armed forces have also gained experience from UN peacekeeping deployments and a number of multinational exercises. Conscription was reintroduced in early 2019. The armed forces have some capacity to deploy independently within the region and on UN peacekeeping missions in sub-Saharan Africa, although they lack heavy sealift and airlift capabilities. Morocco has also recently deployed overseas in a combat role, contributing F-16 aircraft to the Saudi-led coalition intervention in Yemen from 2015 to early 2019. The inventory primarily comprises ageing French and US equipment. However, there are plans to re-equip all the services and to invest significantly in the navy. Morocco has also launched two Earth-observation satellites, aboard European rockets, which can meet some surveillance requirements. Morocco does not yet have an established domestic defence industry and relies on imports and donations for major defence equipment. However, its relative stability has attracted Western defence companies, such as Airbus, Safran and Thales, to establish aerospace manufacturing and servicing facilities in the country.

ACTIVE 195,800 (Army 175,000 Navy 7,800 Air 13,000) **Paramilitary 50,000**
Conscript liability 12 months for men and women aged 19–25 (agreed in late 2018)

RESERVE 150,000 (Army 150,000)
Reserve obligation to age 50

ORGANISATIONS BY SERVICE

Space
EQUIPMENT BY TYPE
SATELLITES 2
  ISR 2 *Mohammed* VI

Army 175,000
FORCES BY ROLE
2 comd (Northern Zone, Southern Zone)
MANOEUVRE
  Armoured
    1 armd bde
    11 armd bn
  Mechanised
    3 mech inf bde
  Mechanised/Light
    8 mech/mot inf regt (2–3 bn)
  Light
    1 lt sy bde
    3 (camel corps) mot inf bn
    35 lt inf bn
    4 cdo unit

Air Manoeuvre
2 para bde
2 AB bn
Mountain
1 mtn inf bn
COMBAT SUPPORT
11 arty bn
7 engr bn
AIR DEFENCE
1 AD bn

Royal Guard 1,500

FORCES BY ROLE
MANOEUVRE
  Other
  1 gd bn
  2 cav sqn
EQUIPMENT BY TYPE
ARMOURED FIGHTING VEHICLES
  MBT 602: 222 M1A1SA *Abrams*; 220 M60A1 *Patton*; 120 M60A3 *Patton*; 40 T-72B (ε200 M48A5 *Patton* & ε60 T-72B in store)
  LT TK 116: 5 AMX-13; 111 SK-105 *Kuerassier*
  ASLT 80 AMX-10RC
  RECCE 284: 38 AML-60-7; 190 AML-90; 40 EBR-75; 16 *Eland*
  IFV 238: 10 AMX-10P; 30 *Ratel* Mk3-20; 30 *Ratel* Mk3-90; 45 VAB VCI; 123 YPR-765
  APC 1,225
    APC (T) 905: 400 M113A1/A2; 419 M113A3; 86 M577A2 (CP)
    APC (W) 320 VAB VTT
ENGINEERING & MAINTENANCE VEHICLES
  ARV 48+: 10 *Greif*; 18 M88A1; M578; 20 VAB-ECH
ANTI-TANK/ANTI-INFRASTRUCTURE
  MSL
    SP 80 M901
    MANPATS 9K11 *Malyutka* (AT-3 *Sagger*); HJ-8L; M47 *Dragon*; *Milan*; TOW
  RCL 106mm 350 M40A1
  GUNS • SP 36: 90mm 28 M56; 100mm 8 SU-100
  ARTILLERY 2,319
  SP 357: 105mm 5 AMX Mk 61; 155mm 292: 84 M109A1/A1B; 43 M109A2; 4 M109A3; 1 M109A4; 70 M109A5; 90 Mk F3; 203mm 60 M110
  TOWED 118: 105mm 50: 30 L118 Light Gun; 20 M101; 130mm 18 M-46; 155mm 50: 30 FH-70; 20 M114
  MRL 47: 122mm 35 BM-21 *Grad*; 300mm 12+ PHL-03
  MOR 1,797: 81mm 1,100 Expal model LN; SP 107mm 36 M106A2; 120mm 550 Brandt; SP 120mm 110: 20 (VAB APC); 91 M1064A3
UNMANNED AERIAL VEHICLES
  ISR • Medium R4E-50 *Skyeye*
AIR DEFENCE
  SAM
    Short-range DK-9 (CH-SA-5)
    Point-defence 49+: 12 2K22M *Tunguska*-M (SA-19 *Grison*); 37 M48 *Chaparral*; 9K38 *Igla* (SA-18 *Grouse*)
  GUNS 390
    SP 20mm 60 M163 *Vulcan*

TOWED 330: 14.5mm 200: 150–180 ZPU-2; 20 ZPU-4; 20mm 40 M167 *Vulcan*; 23mm 75–90 ZU-23-2; 35mm some PG-99

Navy 7,800 (incl 1,500 Marines)

EQUIPMENT BY TYPE
PRINCIPAL SURFACE COMBATANTS 6
  DESTROYERS 1
    DDGHM 1 *Mohammed VI*-class (FRA FREMM) with 2 quad lnchr with MM40 *Exocet* Block 3 AShM, 2 8-cell *Sylver* A43 VLS with *Aster* 15 SAM, 2 triple ILAS-3 (B-515) 324mm ASTT with MU90 LWT, 1 76mm gun (capacity 1 AS565SA *Panther*)
  FRIGATES 5
    FFGHM 3 *Tarik ben Ziyad* (NLD SIGMA 9813/10513) with 4 single lnchr with MM40 *Exocet* Block 2/3 AShM, 2 6-cell CLA VLS with VL-MICA SAM, 2 triple ILAS-3 (B-515) 324mm ASTT with MU90 LWT, 1 76mm gun (capacity 1 AS565SA *Panther*)
    FFGH 2 *Mohammed V* (FRA *Floreal*) with 2 single lnchr with MM38 *Exocet* AShM, 1 76mm gun (can be fitted with *Simbad* SAM) (capacity 1 AS565SA *Panther*)
PATROL AND COASTAL COMBATANTS 50
  CORVETTES • FSGM 1
    1 *Lt Col Errhamani* (ESP *Descubierto*) with 2 twin lnchr with MM38 *Exocet* AShM, 1 octuple *Albatros* lnchr with *Aspide* SAM, 2 triple 324mm ASTT with Mk46 LWT, 1 76mm gun
  PSO 1 *Bin an Zaran* (OPV 70) with 1 76mm gun
  PCG 4 *Cdt El Khattabi* (ESP *Lazaga* 58m) with 4 single lnchr with MM38 *Exocet* AShM, 1 76mm gun
  PCO 5 *Rais Bargach* (under control of fisheries dept)
  PCC 12:
    4 *El Hahiq* (DNK *Osprey* 55, incl 2 with customs)
    6 *LV Rabhi* (ESP 58m B-200D)
    2 *Okba* (FRA PR-72) each with 1 76mm gun
  PB 27: 6 *El Wacil* (FRA P-32); 10 VCSM (RPB 20); 10 Rodman 101; 1 other (UK *Bird*)
AMPHIBIOUS 5
  LANDING SHIPS 4:
    LSM 3 *Ben Aicha* (FRA *Champlain* BATRAL) with 1 hel landing platform (capacity 7 tanks; 140 troops)
    LST 1 *Sidi Mohammed Ben Abdallah* (US *Newport*) (capacity 3 LCVP; 400 troops)
  LANDING CRAFT 2:
    LCM 1 CTM (FRA CTM-5)
    LCT 1 *Sidi Ifni*
LOGISTICS AND SUPPORT 9
  AG 1 Damen 3011
  AGHS 1 *Dar Al Beida* (FRA BHO2M)
  AGOR 1 *Abou Barakat Albarbari*† (ex-US *Robert D. Conrad*)
  AGS 1 Stan 1504
  AK 2
  AX 1 *Essaouira*
  AXS 2

Marines 1,500

FORCES BY ROLE
MANOEUVRE
  Amphibious
  2 naval inf bn

Naval Aviation
EQUIPMENT BY TYPE
HELICOPTERS • ASW/ASUW 3 AS565SA *Panther*

Air Force 13,000
FORCES BY ROLE
FIGHTER/GROUND ATTACK
  2 sqn with F-5E/F-5F *Tiger* II
  3 sqn with F-16C/D *Fighting Falcon*
  1 sqn with *Mirage* F-1C (F-1CH)
  1 sqn with *Mirage* F-1E (F-1EH)
ELECTRONIC WARFARE
  1 sqn with EC-130H *Hercules*; *Falcon* 20 (ELINT)
MARITIME PATROL
  1 flt with Do-28
TANKER/TRANSPORT
  1 sqn with C-130/KC-130H *Hercules*
TRANSPORT
  1 sqn with CN235
  1 VIP sqn with B-737BBJ; Beech 200/300 *King Air*; *Falcon* 50; Gulfstream II/III/V-SP/G550
TRAINING
  1 sqn with *Alpha Jet**
  1 sqn T-6C
ATTACK HELICOPTER
  1 sqn with SA342L *Gazelle* (some with HOT)
TRANSPORT HELICOPTER
  1 sqn with Bell 205A (AB-205A); Bell 206 *Jet Ranger* (AB-206); Bell 212 (AB-212)
  1 sqn with CH-47D *Chinook*
  1 sqn with SA330 *Puma*

EQUIPMENT BY TYPE
AIRCRAFT 90 combat capable
  FTR 22: 19 F-5E *Tiger* II; 3 F-5F *Tiger* II
  FGA 49: 15 F-16C *Fighting Falcon*; 8 F-16D *Fighting Falcon*; 15 *Mirage* F-1C (F-1CH); 11 *Mirage* F-1E (F-1EH)
  ELINT 1 EC-130H *Hercules*
  TKR/TPT 2 KC-130H *Hercules*
  TPT 47: **Medium** 17: 4 C-27J *Spartan*; 13 C-130H *Hercules*; **Light** 19: 4 Beech 100 *King Air*; 2 Beech 200 *King Air*; 1 Beech 200C *King Air*; 2 Beech 300 *King Air*; 3 Beech 350 *King Air*; 5 CN235; 2 Do-28; **PAX** 11: 1 B-737BBJ; 2 *Falcon* 20; 2 *Falcon* 20 (ELINT); 1 *Falcon* 50 (VIP); 1 Gulfstream II (VIP); 1 Gulfstream III; 1 Gulfstream V-SP; 2 Gulfstream G550
  TRG 80: 12 AS-202 *Bravo*; 19 *Alpha Jet**; 2 CAP-10; 24 T-6C *Texan*; 9 T-34C *Turbo Mentor*; 14 T-37B *Tweet*
HELICOPTERS
  MRH 19 SA342L *Gazelle* (7 with HOT, 12 with cannon)
  TPT 76: **Heavy** 10 CH-47D *Chinook*; **Medium** 24 SA330 *Puma*; **Light** 42: 24 Bell 205A (AB-205A); 11 Bell 206 *Jet Ranger* (AB-206); 3 Bell 212 (AB-212); 4 Bell 429
AIR-LAUNCHED MISSILES
  AAM • **IR** AIM-9J *Sidewinder*; R-550 *Magic*; Mica IR; **IIR** AIM-9X *Sidewinder* II; **ARH** AIM-120C7 AMRAAM; Mica RF
  ASM AASM; AGM-65 *Maverick*; HOT
  ARM AGM-88B HARM
BOMBS
  Laser-guided *Paveway* II; GBU-54 Laser JDAM
  INS/GPS-guided GBU-31 JDAM

Paramilitary 50,000 active

Gendarmerie Royale 20,000
FORCES BY ROLE
MANOEUVRE
  Air Manoeuvre
    1 para sqn
  Other
    1 paramilitary bde
    4 (mobile) paramilitary gp
    1 coast guard unit
TRANSPORT HELICOPTER
  1 sqn
EQUIPMENT BY TYPE
PATROL AND COASTAL COMBATANTS • PB 15 Arcor 53
AIRCRAFT • TRG 2 R-235 *Guerrier*
HELICOPTERS
  MRH 14: 3 SA315B *Lama*; 2 SA316 *Alouette* III; 3 SA318 *Alouette* II; 6 SA342K *Gazelle*
  TPT 8: **Medium** 6 SA330 *Puma*; **Light** 2 SA360 *Dauphin*

Force Auxiliaire 30,000 (incl 5,000 Mobile Intervention Corps)

Customs/Coast Guard
EQUIPMENT BY TYPE
PATROL AND COASTAL COMBATANTS • PB 36: 4 *Erraid*; 18 *Arcor* 46; 14 (other SAR craft)

DEPLOYMENT

CENTRAL AFRICAN REPUBLIC: UN • MINUSCA 764; 1 inf bn

DEMOCRATIC REPUBLIC OF THE CONGO: UN • MONUSCO 1,373; 2 inf bn; 1 fd hospital

Oman OMN

Omani Rial R		2018	2019	2020
GDP	R	30.5bn	29.5bn	
	US$	79.3bn	76.6bn	
per capita	US$	18,970	17,791	
Growth	%	1.8	0.0	
Inflation	%	0.9	0.8	
Def bdgt	R	3.44bn	3.45bn	
	US$	8.95bn	8.97bn	
US$1=R		0.38	0.38	

Real-terms defence budget trend (US$bn, constant 2015)

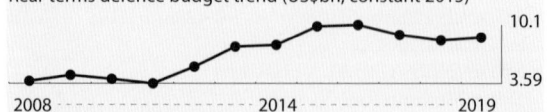

Population	3,564,276

Expatriates: 27%

Age	0–14	15–19	20–24	25–29	30–64	65 plus
Male	15.4%	4.3%	5.0%	5.8%	21.8%	1.7%
Female	14.7%	4.1%	4.4%	4.6%	16.3%	1.9%

Capabilities

Oman maintains small but capable armed forces, with a particular emphasis on personnel quality and training. Their principal task is ensuring territorial integrity. Oman is uniquely placed with a long coastline outside the Gulf, so it has a particular focus on maritime security. With relatively limited resources, it maintains modern but modest equipment. Oman is a member of the GCC but has not contributed any forces to the Saudi-led intervention in Yemen. It has close defence and security ties with the UK and the US, for whom it hosts forward-deployed forces. There is a particular emphasis on training, especially with the UK. In late 2018, the two countries announced the establishment of a new joint training base in Oman, and a new joint defence agreement was signed in February 2019. Recent deployment experience beyond Oman has been limited, but the country maintains modest logistics assets, particularly in the naval domain. The country is developing the port of Duqm into a major potential logistics hub for partners. Oman is in the process of recapitalising its core inventory with the procurement of air and naval systems, including combat aircraft and patrol and high-speed support vessels. Oman has very limited indigenous defence-industrial capacity, but it has begun local production of various types of ammunition.

ACTIVE 42,600 (Army 25,000 Navy 4,200 Air 5,000 Foreign Forces 2,000 Royal Household 6,400) Paramilitary 4,400

ORGANISATIONS BY SERVICE

Army 25,000
FORCES BY ROLE
(Regt are bn size)
MANOEUVRE
  Armoured
  1 armd bde (2 armd regt, 1 recce regt)
  Light
  1 inf bde (5 inf regt, 1 arty regt, 1 fd engr regt, 1 engr regt, 1 sigs regt)
  1 inf bde (3 inf regt, 2 arty regt)
  1 indep inf coy (Musandam Security Force)
  Air Manoeuvre
  1 AB regt
COMBAT SERVICE SUPPORT
  1 tpt regt
AIR DEFENCE
  1 ADA regt (2 ADA bty)
EQUIPMENT BY TYPE
ARMOURED FIGHTING VEHICLES
  MBT 117: 38 *Challenger* 2; 6 M60A1 *Patton*; 73 M60A3 *Patton*
  LT TK 37 FV101 *Scorpion*
  RECCE 143: 13 FV105 *Sultan* (CP); 6 Pars III 6×6; 124 VBL
  IFV 20 Pars III 8×8
  APC 200
    APC (T) 10 FV4333 *Stormer*
    APC (W) 190: 175 *Piranha* (incl variants); 15 AT-105 *Saxon*
  AUV 6 FV103 *Spartan*
ENGINEERING & MAINTENANCE VEHICLES
  ARV 11: 4 *Challenger*; 2 M88A1; 2 *Piranha*; 3 *Samson*

ARTILLERY 233
  SP 155mm 24 G-6
  TOWED 108: **105mm** 42 L118 Light Gun; **122mm** 30 D-30; **130mm** 24: 12 M-46; 12 Type-59-I; **155mm** 12 FH-70
  MOR 101: **81mm** 69; **107mm** 20 M30; **120mm** 12 Brandt
ANTI-TANK/ANTI-INFRASTRUCTURE • MSL
  SP 8 VBL with TOW
  MANPATS FGM-148 *Javelin*; Milan; TOW/TOW-2A
AIR DEFENCE
  SAM • Point-defence 8 Mistral 2; *Javelin*; 9K32 *Strela*-2 (SA-7 *Grail*)‡
  GUNS 26: **23mm** 4 ZU-23-2; **35mm** 10 GDF-005 (with *Skyguard*); **40mm** 12 L/60 (Towed)

Navy 4,200
EQUIPMENT BY TYPE
PRINCIPAL SURFACE COMBATANTS 3
  FFGHM 3 *Al-Shamikh* with 2 twin lnchr with MM40 *Exocet* Block 3 AShM, 2 6-cell CLA VLS with VL-MICA SAM, 1 76mm gun
PATROL AND COASTAL COMBATANTS 10
  CORVETTES • FSGM 2:
    2 *Qahir Al Amwaj* with 2 quad lnchr with MM40 *Exocet* AShM, 1 octuple lnchr with *Crotale* SAM, 1 76mm gun, 1 hel landing platform
  PCFG 1 *Dhofar* with 2 quad lnchr with MM40 *Exocet* AShM, 1 76mm gun
  PCO 4 *Al Ofouq* with 1 76mm gun, 1 hel landing platform
  PCC 3 *Al Bushra* (FRA P-400) with 1 76mm gun
AMPHIBIOUS 6
  LANDING SHIPS • LST 1 *Nasr el Bahr*† with 1 hel landing platform (capacity 7 tanks; 240 troops) (in refit since 2017)
  LANDING CRAFT 5: 1 LCU; 3 LCM; 1 LCT
LOGISTICS AND SUPPORT 8
  AGS 1 *Al Makhirah*
  AK 1 *Al Sultana*
  AP 2 *Shinas* (commercial tpt – auxiliary military role only) (capacity 56 veh; 200 tps)
  AX 1 *Al-Mabrukah*
  AXS 1 *Shabab Oman* II
  EPF 2 *Al Mubshir* (High Speed Support Vessel 72) with 1 hel landing platform (capacity 260 troops)

Air Force 5,000
FORCES BY ROLE
FIGHTER/GROUND ATTACK
  2 sqn with F-16C/D Block 50 *Fighting Falcon*
  1 sqn with *Hawk* Mk103; *Hawk* Mk203; *Hawk* Mk166
  1 sqn with *Typhoon*
MARITIME PATROL
  1 sqn with C295MPA; SC.7 3M *Skyvan*
TRANSPORT
  1 sqn with C-130H/J/J-30 *Hercules*
  1 sqn with C295M
TRAINING
  1 sqn with MFI-17B *Mushshak*; PC-9*; Bell 206 (AB-206) *Jet Ranger*
TRANSPORT HELICOPTER
  4 (med) sqn; Bell 212 (AB-212); NH-90; *Super Lynx* Mk300 (maritime/SAR)

AIR DEFENCE
2 sqn with *Rapier*; *Blindfire*; S713 *Martello*

EQUIPMENT BY TYPE
AIRCRAFT 63 combat capable
  FGA 35: 17 F-16C Block 50 *Fighting Falcon*; 6 F-16D Block 50 *Fighting Falcon*; 12 *Typhoon*
  MP 4 C295MPA
  TPT 19: **Medium** 6: 3 C-130H *Hercules*; 2 C-130J *Hercules*; 1 C-130J-30 *Hercules* (VIP); **Light** 11: 4 C295M; 7 SC.7 3M *Skyvan* (radar-equipped, for MP); **PAX** 2 A320-300
  TRG 43: 4 *Hawk* Mk103*; 7 *Hawk* Mk166; 12 *Hawk* Mk203*; 8 MFI-17B *Mushshak*; 12 PC-9*
HELICOPTERS
  MRH 15 *Super Lynx* Mk300 (maritime/SAR)
  TPT 26+ **Medium** 20 NH90 TTH; **Light** 6: 3 Bell 206 (AB-206) *Jet Ranger*; 3 Bell 212 (AB-212)
AIR DEFENCE • SAM
  Short-range NASAMS
  Point-defence 40 *Rapier*
MSL
  AAM • IR AIM-9/M/P *Sidewinder*; **IIR** AIM-9X *Sidewinder* II; **ARH** AIM-120C7 AMRAAM
  ASM AGM-65D/G *Maverick*
  AShM AGM-84D *Harpoon*
BOMBS
  Laser-guided EGBU-10 *Paveway* II; EGBU-12 *Paveway* II
  INS/GPS guided GBU-31 JDAM

Royal Household 6,400
(incl HQ staff)

FORCES BY ROLE
SPECIAL FORCES
  2 SF regt

Royal Guard Brigade 5,000

FORCES BY ROLE
MANOEUVRE
  Other
    1 gd bde (1 armd sqn, 2 gd regt, 1 cbt spt bn)
EQUIPMENT BY TYPE
ARMOURED FIGHTING VEHICLES
  ASLT 9 *Centauro* MGS (9 VBC-90 in store)
  IFV 14 VAB VCI
  APC • APC (W) ε50 Type-92
ANTI-TANK/ANTI-INFRASTRUCTURE
  MSL • MANPATS *Milan*
ARTILLERY • MRL 122mm 6 Type-90A
AIR DEFENCE
  SAM • Point-defence *Javelin*
  GUNS • SP 9: **20mm** 9 VAB VDAA

Royal Yacht Squadron 150
EQUIPMENT BY TYPE
LOGISTICS AND SUPPORT 3
  AP 1 *Fulk Al Salamah* (also veh tpt) with up to 2 AS332 *Super Puma* hel

Royal Flight 250
EQUIPMENT BY TYPE
AIRCRAFT • TPT • PAX 5: 2 B-747SP; 1 DC-8-73CF; 2 Gulfstream IV

HELICOPTERS • TPT • Medium 6: 3 SA330 (AS330) *Puma*; 2 AS332F *Super Puma*; 1 AS332L *Super Puma*

Paramilitary 4,400 active

Tribal Home Guard 4,000
org in teams of ε100

Police Coast Guard 400
EQUIPMENT BY TYPE
PATROL AND COASTAL COMBATANTS 32
  PCO 2 *Haras*
  PBF 3 *Haras* (US Mk V *Pegasus*)
  PB 27: 3 Rodman 101; 1 *Haras* (SWE CG27); 3 *Haras* (SWE CG29); 14 Rodman 58; 1 D59116; 5 *Zahra*

Police Air Wing
EQUIPMENT BY TYPE
AIRCRAFT • TPT • Light 4: 1 BN-2T *Turbine Islander*; 2 CN235M; 1 Do-228
HELICOPTERS • TPT • Light 5: 2 Bell 205A; 3 Bell 214ST (AB-214ST)

FOREIGN FORCES
United Kingdom 90

Palestinian Territories PT

New Israeli Shekel NS		2018	2019	2020
GDP	US$			
per capita	US$			
Growth	%			
Inflation	%			

US$1=NS					
Population	4,726,998				

Age	0–14	15–19	20–24	25–29	30–64	65 plus
Male	19.9%	5.7%	5.1%	4.4%	14.1%	1.5%
Female	18.9%	5.5%	4.9%	4.4%	14.0%	1.7%

Capabilities

The Palestinian Territories remain effectively divided between the Palestinian Authority-run West Bank and Hamas-run Gaza. Each organisation controls their own security forces, principally the National Security Forces (NSF) in the West Bank and the Izz al-Din al-Qassam Brigades in Gaza. Both have generally proved effective at maintaining internal security in their respective territories. The Palestinian Authority has received support from the EU, Jordan and the US. NSF battalions, as well as the Presidential Guard and Civil Police, conduct US-funded internal-security training at the Jordanian International Police Training Center. A small number of Izz al-Din al-Qassam Brigades personnel are claimed by Israel to have received military training in Iran and Syria; the brigades have substantial experience in conducting asymmetric military action against Israel. None of the Palestinian security organisations conduct external military deployments, and they lack a formal military-logistics structure. Both Hamas and the Palestinian Authority lack heavy military equipment, although the former have retained a substantial arsenal of improvised rocket and mortar capabilities, as well as some man-portable guided weapons. No formal defence industry exists, although Hamas is able to acquire light or improvised weapons, either smuggled into Gaza or of local construction.

ACTIVE 0 Paramilitary n.k.
Precise personnel-strength figures for the various Palestinian groups are not known

ORGANISATIONS BY SERVICE
There is little available data on the status of the organisations mentioned below. Following internal fighting in June 2007, Gaza has been under the de facto control of Hamas, while the West Bank is controlled by the Palestinian Authority. In October 2017, both sides agreed a preliminary reconciliation deal on control of Gaza.

Paramilitary

Palestinian Authority n.k.
Presidential Security ε3,000
Special Forces ε1,200
Police ε9,000
National Security Force ε10,000
FORCES BY ROLE
MANOEUVRE
  Other
    9 paramilitary bn
Preventative Security ε4,000
Civil Defence ε1,000
The al-Aqsa Brigades n.k.
Profess loyalty to the Fatah group that dominates the Palestinian Authority

Hamas n.k.
Izz al-Din al-Qassam Brigades ε15,000–20,000
FORCES BY ROLE
COMMAND
  6 bde HQ (regional)
MANOEUVRE
  Other
    1 cdo unit (Nukhba)
    27 paramilitary bn
    100 paramilitary coy
COMBAT SUPPORT Some engr units
COMBAT SERVICE SUPPORT
  Some log units
EQUIPMENT BY TYPE
ANTI-TANK/ANTI-INFRASTRUCTURE • MSL •
MANPATS 9K11 *Malyutka* (AT-3 *Sagger*) (reported); *Dehlavieh* (*Kornet*) (reported)
ARTILLERY
  MRL • *Qassam* rockets (multiple calibres); **122mm** *Grad*
  MOR some (multiple calibres)

Martime Police ε600

Qatar QTR

Qatari Riyal R		2018	2019	2020
GDP	R	697bn	698bn	
	US$	191bn	192bn	
per capita	US$	70,379	69,688	
Growth	%	1.5	2.0	
Inflation	%	0.2	-0.4	
Def exp	R	n.k.	n.k.	
	US$	n.k.	n.k.	
US$1=R			3.64	3.64

Population 2,406,676

Ethnic groups: Nationals 25%; expatriates 75% of which Indian 18%; Iranian 10%; Pakistani 18%

Age	0–14	15–19	20–24	25–29	30–64	65 plus
Male	6.5%	2.4%	6.1%	10.8%	50.8%	0.7%
Female	6.3%	1.6%	1.9%	2.7%	9.9%	0.4%

Capabilities

Qatar is attempting to transform its military capabilities and regional defence standing based on significant equipment acquisitions, with the aim of creating one of the most well-equipped forces in the region. The diplomatic crisis with several of its GCC neighbours has brought Qatar and Turkey closer together in their limited but significant defence cooperation, which includes a small Turkish military presence in-country. The crisis appears not to have affected the significant Qatar–US military relationship, including the presence of forces from the US and other Western states at Al-Udeid air base, and the key US-run coalition air-operations centre. The pressure on personnel requirements is increasing significantly due to Qatar's acquisition programme. Changes were reported to national-service liabilities in 2018, increasing terms of service and making national service voluntary for women. The speed and scale of the equipment plan suggests that Qatar will need significant foreign help to integrate and operate its new capabilities. The Italian Navy is supporting training for new Italian-built vessels and a joint Eurofighter *Typhoon* squadron is being stood up with the UK. The Qatari armed forces initially sent air and ground elements to support the Saudi-led intervention in Yemen. The country is also acquiring platforms with potentially significant power-projection capability. Qatar's ambitious across the board re-equipment programme includes significant purchases of combat aircraft. These procurements will, when combined, dramatically increase the size of the air force, and it is in terms of air capabilities that there are the most questions about Qatar's ability to procure the necessary infrastructure, maintenance and personnel. Coastal-defence missiles are being acquired, while an AN/FPS-132 early-warning radar is being installed. Qatar currently has a limited indigenous defence-industrial capability, including in ship repair.

ACTIVE 16,500 (Army 12,000 Navy 2,500 Air 2,000)
Paramilitary up to 5,000
Conscript liability 12 months for all men, regardless of education; voluntary conscription for women

ORGANISATIONS BY SERVICE

Space
EQUIPMENT BY TYPE
SATELLITES • COMMUNICATIONS 1 *Es'hail-2*

Army 12,000 (including Emiri Guard)

FORCES BY ROLE
SPECIAL FORCES
  1 SF coy
MANOEUVRE
  Armoured
  1 armd bde (1 tk bn, 1 mech inf bn, 1 mor sqn, 1 AT bn)
  Mechanised
  3 mech inf bn
  1 (Emiri Guard) bde (3 mech regt)
COMBAT SUPPORT
  1 SP arty bn
  1 fd arty bn
EQUIPMENT BY TYPE
ARMOURED FIGHTING VEHICLES
  MBT 62 *Leopard* 2A7+
  ASLT 48: 12 AMX-10RC; 36 *Piranha* II 90mm
  RECCE 50: 26 *Fennek*; 8 V-150 *Chaimite*; 16 VBL
  IFV 40 AMX-10P
  APC 290
    APC (T) 30 AMX-VCI
    APC (W) 160 VAB
    PPV 100 *Ejder Yalcin*
    AUV 14 *Dingo* 2
ENGINEERING & MAINTENANCE VEHICLES
  AEV 6 *Wisent* 2
  ARV 3: 1 AMX-30D; 2 *Piranha*
ANTI-TANK/ANTI-INFRASTRUCTURE
  MSL
    SP 24 VAB VCAC HOT; NMS with *Kornet*
    MANPATS FGM-148 *Javelin*; *Kornet*-EM
  RCL 84mm *Carl Gustav*
ARTILLERY 87+
  SP 155mm 24 PzH 2000
  TOWED 155mm 12 G-5
  MRL 6+: **122mm** 2+ (30-tube); **127mm** 4 ASTROS II Mk3
  MOR 45: **81mm** 26 L16; **SP 81mm** 4 VAB VPM 81; **120mm** 15 Brandt
SURFACE-TO-SURFACE MISSILE LAUNCHERS
  SRBM • Conventional 2 BP-12A (CH-SS-14 mod 2)

Navy 2,500 (incl Coast Guard)

EQUIPMENT BY TYPE
PATROL AND COASTAL COMBATANTS 11
  PCFG 4 *Barzan* (UK *Vita*) with 2 quad lnchr with MM40 *Exocet* Block 3 AShM, 1 sextuple *Sadral* lnchr with *Mistral* SAM, 1 *Goalkeeper* CIWS, 1 76mm gun
  PCFG 3 *Damsah* (FRA *Combattante* III) with 2 quad lnchr with MM40 *Exocet* AShM, 1 76mm gun
  PBF 3 MRTP 16
  PB 1 MRTP 34

Coast Guard
EQUIPMENT BY TYPE
PATROL AND COASTAL COMBATANTS 12
  PBF 4 DV 15
  PB 8: 4 *Crestitalia* MV-45; 3 *Halmatic* M160; 1 other

Coastal Defence

FORCES BY ROLE
COASTAL DEFENCE
  1 bty with 3 quad lnchr with MM40 *Exocet* AShM
EQUIPMENT BY TYPE
COASTAL DEFENCE • AShM 12 MM40 *Exocet* AShM

Air Force 2,000

FORCES BY ROLE
FIGHTER/GROUND ATTACK
  1 sqn with *Alpha Jet**
  1 sqn with *Mirage* 2000ED; *Mirage* 2000D
  1 sqn with *Rafale* DQ/EQ
TRANSPORT
  1 sqn with C-17A *Globemaster* III; C-130J-30 *Hercules*
  1 sqn with A340; B-707; B-727; *Falcon* 900
ATTACK HELICOPTER
  1 ASuW sqn with *Commando* Mk3 with *Exocet*
  1 sqn with SA341 *Gazelle*; SA342L *Gazelle* with HOT
TRANSPORT HELICOPTER
  1 sqn with *Commando* Mk2A; *Commando* Mk2C
  1 sqn with AW139
EQUIPMENT BY TYPE
AIRCRAFT 33 combat capable
  FGA 27: 9 *Mirage* 2000ED; 3 *Mirage* 2000D; 3 *Rafale* DQ; 12 *Rafale* EQ
  TPT 18: **Heavy** 8 C-17A *Globemaster* III; **Medium** 4 C-130J-30 *Hercules*; **PAX** 6: 1 A340; 2 B-707; 1 B-727; 2 *Falcon* 900
  TRG 27: 6 *Alpha Jet**; 21 PC-21
HELICOPTERS
  ATK 2+ AH-64E *Apache*
  ASuW 8 *Commando* Mk3
  MRH 34: 21 AW139 (incl 3 for medevac); 2 SA341 *Gazelle*; 11 SA342L *Gazelle*
  TPT 5: **Medium** 4: 3 *Commando* Mk2A; 1 *Commando* Mk2C; **Light** 1 H125 *Ecureuil* (trg config)
AIR DEFENCE • SAM
  Long-range MIM-104E/F *Patriot* PAC-2 GEM-T/PAC-3
  Point-defence FIM-92 *Stinger*; FN-6 (CH-SA-10); *Mistral*
AIR-LAUNCHED MISSILES
  AAM • IR R-550 *Magic* 2; **ARH** *Mica* RF
  ASM *Apache*; HOT
  AShM AM39 *Exocet*

Paramilitary up to 5,000 active

Internal Security Force up to 5,000

DEPLOYMENT

LEBANON: UN • UNIFIL 2

FOREIGN FORCES

Turkey 300 (trg team); 1 mech coy; 1 arty unit
United States US Central Command: 10,000; CAOC; 1 ISR sqn with 4 RC-135 *Rivet Joint*; 1 ISR sqn with 4 E-8C JSTARS; 1 tkr sqn with 24 KC-135R/T *Stratotanker*; 1 tpt

sqn with 4 C-17A *Globemaster*; 4 C-130H/J-30 *Hercules*; 2 AD bty with MIM-104E/F *Patriot* PAC-2/3 • US Strategic Command: 1 AN/TPY-2 X-band radar

Saudi Arabia SAU

Saudi Riyal R		2018	2019	2020
GDP	R	2.95tr	2.92tr	
	US$	787bn	779bn	
per capita	US$	23,539	22,865	
Growth	%	2.4	0.2	
Inflation	%	2.5	-1.1	
Def exp	R	324bn	294bn	
	US$	86.4bn	78.4bn	
US$1=R		3.75	3.75	

Real-terms defence budget trend (US$bn, constant 2015)

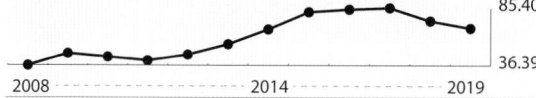

Population 33,631,439

Ethnic groups: Nationals 73%, of which Bedouin up to 10%, Shi'a 6%; expatriates 27%, of which Asians 20%, Arabs 6%, Africans 1%, Europeans <1%

Age	0–14	15–19	20–24	25–29	30–64	65 plus
Male	12.9%	4.1%	3.9%	4.7%	29.1%	1.8%
Female	12.4%	3.9%	3.5%	3.9%	18.1%	1.6%

Capabilities

The armed forces are one of the best equipped in the region, and the kingdom has displayed an increasing willingness to use them as part of a more assertive foreign policy. Principal roles are securing territorial integrity, internal security and regional stability. Saudi Arabia's defence posture continues to emphasise the deployment of airpower. Saudi Arabia is the leading member of the GCC. However, its most critical defence relationship is with the US, which is the ultimate external guarantor of its security. In 2017, the two countries agreed to establish a Strategic Joint Consultative Group, and furthered existing defence and security cooperation. Riyadh also has significant security relationships with France and the UK, though recently there has been diversification of defence relationships, including with China. Significant training support is supplied by the US and, to a lesser extent, the UK. The armed forces continue to gain combat experience from their involvement in the conflict in Yemen. However, the operation has exposed areas of comparative weakness and capability gaps, especially in the application of precision airpower, air–ground coordination and in logistics support, such as aerial refuelling, while the cruise missile and UAV attacks on Saudi oil infrastructure in September 2019 exposed further capability weaknesses. The US remains the country's main source of advanced weaponry, followed by the UK, with whom it signed a new Military and Security Cooperation Agreement in September 2017, although a number of European countries continue to review their arms-export policies regarding Saudi Arabia. Saudi Arabia continues its equipment recapitalisation, with orders for combat aircraft, corvettes and multi-mission surface combatants. There is a modest domestic defence-industrial base, mainly in the assembly and overhaul of land systems. Riyadh has declared an intention to spend 50% of its defence outlays locally as part of its Vision 2030 initiative and established the state-owned Saudi Arabian Military Industries to oversee local defence production.

ACTIVE 227,000 (Army 75,000 Navy 13,500 Air 20,000 Air Defence 16,000 Strategic Missile Forces 2,500 National Guard 100,000) **Paramilitary 24,500**

ORGANISATIONS BY SERVICE

Army 75,000
FORCES BY ROLE
MANOEUVRE
  Armoured
    4 armd bde (1 recce coy, 3 tk bn, 1 mech bn, 1 fd arty bn, 1 AD bn, 1 AT bn, 1 engr coy, 1 log bn, 1 maint coy, 1 med coy)
  Mechanised
    5 mech bde (1 recce coy, 1 tk bn, 3 mech bn, 1 fd arty bn, 1 AD bn, 1 AT bn, 1 engr coy, 1 log bn, 1 maint coy, 1 med coy)
  Light
    2 lt inf bde
  Other
    1 (Al-Saif Al-Ajrab) gd bde
    1 (Royal Guard) gd regt (3 lt inf bn)
  Air Manoeuvre
    1 AB bde (2 AB bn, 3 SF coy)
  Aviation
    1 comd (3 hel gp)
COMBAT SUPPORT
  3 arty bde
EQUIPMENT BY TYPE
  MBT 880: 140 AMX-30; 370 M1A2/A2S *Abrams*; ε370 M60A3 *Patton*
  RECCE 300 AML-60/AML-90
  IFV 760: 380 AMX-10P; 380 M2A2 *Bradley*
  APC 1,340
    APC (T) 1,190 M113A4 (incl variants)
    APC (W) 150 Panhard M3 (ε40 AF-40-8-1 *Al-Fahd* in store)
  AUV 1,100+: 100 *Didgori* (amb); 1,000+ M-ATV; *Al-Shibl* 2; Sherpa *Light Scout*; Terradyne *Gurkha*;
  ENGINEERING & MAINTENANCE VEHICLES
    AEV 15 M728
    ARV 275+: 8 ACV ARV; AMX-10EHC; 55 AMX-30D; *Leclerc* ARV; 122 M88A1; 90 M578
    VLB 10 AMX-30
    MW *Aardvark* Mk2
  NBC VEHICLES 10 TPz-1 *Fuchs* NBC
  ANTI-TANK/ANTI-INFRASTRUCTURE
    MSL
      SP 290+: 90+ AMX-10P (HOT); 200 VCC-1 ITOW; M-ATV with *Milan*
      MANPATS *Hyeongung*; Luch *Corsar* (reported); Luch *Skif* (reported); *Stugna*-P (reported); TOW-2A
    RCL 84mm *Carl Gustav*; **90mm** M67; **106mm** M40A1
  ARTILLERY 764
    SP 155mm 224: 60 AU-F-1; 110 M109A1B/A2; 54 PLZ-45
    TOWED 110: **105mm** some LG1; (100 M101/M102 in store); **155mm** 110: 50 M114; 60 M198; **203mm** (8 M115 in store)
    MRL 63: **127mm** 60 ASTROS II Mk3; **220mm** 3+ TOS-1A

MOR 367: **SP 81mm** 70; **SP 107mm** 150 M30; **120mm** 147: 110 Brandt; 37 M12-1535; **SP 120mm** 2R2M
HELICOPTERS
ATK 35: 11 AH-64D *Apache*; 24 AH-64E *Apache*
MRH 21: 6 AS365N *Dauphin* 2 (medevac); 15 Bell 406CS *Combat Scout*
TPT • **Medium** 58: 12 S-70A1 *Desert Hawk*; 22 UH-60A *Black Hawk* (4 medevac); 24 UH-60L *Black Hawk*
AIR DEFENCE • SAM
Short-range *Crotale*
Point-defence FIM-92 *Stinger*

Navy 13,500

Navy HQ at Riyadh; Eastern Fleet HQ at Jubail; Western Fleet HQ at Jeddah
EQUIPMENT BY TYPE
PRINCIPAL SURFACE COMBATANTS 7
DESTROYERS • DDGHM 3 *Al Riyadh* (FRA *La Fayette* mod) with 2 quad lnchr with MM40 *Exocet* Block 2 AShM, 2 8-cell *Sylver* A43 VLS with *Aster* 15 SAM, 4 single 533mm TT with F17P HWT, 1 76mm gun (capacity 1 AS365N *Dauphin* 2 hel)
FRIGATES • FFGHM 4 *Madina* (FRA F-2000) with 2 quad lnchr with *Otomat* Mk2 AShM, 1 octuple lnchr with *Crotale* SAM, 4 single 533mm TT with F17P HWT, 1 100mm gun (capacity 1 AS365N *Dauphin* 2 hel)
PATROL AND COASTAL COMBATANTS 32
CORVETTES • FSG 4 *Badr* (US *Tacoma*) with 2 quad Mk140 lnchr with RGM-84C *Harpoon* Block 1B AShM, 2 triple 324mm ASTT with Mk 46 LWT, 1 Mk 15 *Phalanx* CIWS, 1 76mm gun
PCFG 9 *Al Siddiq* (US 58m) with 2 twin lnchr with RGM-84C *Harpoon* Block 1B AShM, 1 Mk 15 *Phalanx* CIWS, 1 76mm gun
PB 19: 17 (US) *Halter Marine* 24m; 2 *Plascoa* 2200
MINE WARFARE • MINE COUNTERMEASURES 3
MHC 3 *Al Jawf* (UK *Sandown*)
AMPHIBIOUS • LANDING CRAFT 5
LCM 3 LCM 6 (capacity 80 troops)
LCU ε2 *Al Qiaq* (US LCU 1610) (capacity 120 troops)
LOGISTICS AND SUPPORT 2
AORH 2 *Boraida* (mod FRA *Durance*) (capacity either 2 AS365F *Dauphin* 2 hel or 1 AS332C *Super Puma*)

Naval Aviation
EQUIPMENT BY TYPE
HELICOPTERS
MRH 34: 6 AS365N *Dauphin* 2; 15 AS565; 13 Bell 406CS *Combat Scout*
TPT • **Medium** 12 AS332B/F *Super Puma*
AIR-LAUNCHED MISSILES
AShM AM39 *Exocet*; AS-15TT

Marines 3,000
FORCES BY ROLE
SPECIAL FORCES
1 spec ops regt with (2 spec ops bn)
EQUIPMENT BY TYPE
ARMOURED FIGHTING VEHICLES
RECCE *Bastion Patsas*
APC • **APC (W)** 135 BMR-600P

Air Force 20,000
FORCES BY ROLE
FIGHTER
4 sqn with F-15C/D *Eagle*
FIGHTER/GROUND ATTACK
3 sqn with F-15S/SA *Eagle*
3 sqn with *Typhoon*
GROUND ATTACK
3 sqn with *Tornado* IDS; *Tornado* GR1A
AIRBORNE EARLY WARNING & CONTROL
1 sqn with E-3A *Sentry*
1 sqn with Saab 2000 *Erieye*
ELINT
1 sqn with RE-3A/B; Beech 350ER *King Air*
TANKER
1 sqn with KE-3A
TANKER/TRANSPORT
1 sqn with KC-130H/J *Hercules*
1 sqn with A330 MRTT
TRANSPORT
3 sqn with C-130H *Hercules*; C-130H-30 *Hercules*; CN-235; L-100-30HS (hospital ac)
2 sqn with Beech 350 *King Air* (forming)
TRAINING
1 OCU sqn with F-15SA *Eagle*
3 sqn with *Hawk* Mk65*; *Hawk* Mk65A*; *Hawk* Mk165*
1 sqn with *Jetstream* Mk31
1 sqn with MFI-17 *Mushshak*; SR22T
2 sqn with PC-9; PC-21
TRANSPORT HELICOPTER
4 sqn with AS532 *Cougar* (CSAR); Bell 212 (AB-212); Bell 412 (AB-412) *Twin Huey* (SAR)
EQUIPMENT BY TYPE
AIRCRAFT 429 combat capable
FTR 81: 56 F-15C *Eagle*; 25 F-15D *Eagle*
FGA 207: up to 67 F-15S *Eagle* (being upgraded to F-15SA configuration); 69 F-15SA *Eagle*; 71 *Typhoon*
ATK 67 *Tornado* IDS
ISR 14+: 12 *Tornado* GR1A*; 2+ Beech 350ER *King Air*
AEW&C 7: 5 E-3A *Sentry*; 2 Saab 2000 *Erieye*
ELINT 2: 1 RE-3A; 1 RE-3B
TKR/TPT 15: 6 A330 MRTT; 7 KC-130H *Hercules*; 2 KC-130J *Hercules*
TKR 7 KE-3A
TPT 47+: **Medium** 36: 30 C-130H *Hercules*; 3 C-130H-30 *Hercules*; 3 L-100-30; **Light** 11+: 10+ Beech 350 *King Air*; 1 *Jetstream* Mk31
TRG 181: 24 *Hawk* Mk65* (incl aerobatic team); 16 *Hawk* Mk65A*; 22 *Hawk* Mk165*; 20 MFI-17 *Mushshak*; 20 PC-9; 55 PC-21; 24 SR22T
HELICOPTERS
MRH 15 Bell 412 (AB-412) *Twin Huey* (SAR)
TPT 30: **Medium** 10 AS532 *Cougar* (CSAR); **Light** 20 Bell 212 (AB-212)
UNMANNED AERIAL VEHICLES
CISR • **Heavy** some *Wing Loong* 1 (GJ-1) (reported); some CH-4
ISR • **Medium** some *Falco*

AIR-LAUNCHED MISSILES
AAM • IR AIM-9P/L *Sidewinder*; IIR AIM-9X *Sidewinder* II; IRIS-T; SARH AIM-7 *Sparrow*; AIM-7M *Sparrow*; ARH AIM-120C AMRAAM
ASM AGM-65 *Maverick*; AR-1
AShM AGM-84L *Harpoon* Block II
ARM ALARM
ALCM *Storm Shadow*
BOMBS
Laser-guided GBU-10/12 *Paveway* II; *Paveway* IV
INS/GPS-guided GBU-31 JDAM; FT-9

Royal Flt
EQUIPMENT BY TYPE
AIRCRAFT • TPT 24: **Medium** 8: 5 C-130H *Hercules*; 3 L-100-30; **Light** 3: 1 Cessna 310; 2 Learjet 35; PAX 13: 1 A340; 1 B-737-200; 2 B-737BBJ; 2 B-747SP; 4 BAe-125-800; 2 Gulfstream III; 1 Gulfstream IV
HELICOPTERS • TPT 3+: **Medium** 3: 2 AS-61; 1 S-70 *Black Hawk*; **Light** some Bell 212 (AB-212)

Air Defence Forces 16,000
FORCES BY ROLE
AIR DEFENCE
6 bn with MIM-104D/F *Patriot* PAC-2 GEM/PAC-3
17 bty with *Shahine*/AMX-30SA
16 bty with MIM-23B I-*Hawk*
EQUIPMENT BY TYPE
AIR DEFENCE
SAM
Long-range 108 MIM-104D/F *Patriot* PAC-2 GEM/PAC-3
Medium-range 128 MIM-23B I-*Hawk*
Short-range 181: 40 *Crotale*; 141 *Shahine*
Point-defence 400+: 400 M1097 *Avenger*; *Mistral*
GUNS 268
SP 140: **20mm** 90 M163 *Vulcan*; **30mm** 50 AMX-30SA
TOWED 128: **35mm** 128 GDF Oerlikon; **40mm** (150 L/70 in store)

Strategic Missile Forces 2,500
EQUIPMENT BY TYPE
MSL • TACTICAL
IRBM 10+ DF-3 (CH-SS-2) (service status unclear)
MRBM Some DF-21 (CH-SS-5 – variant unclear) (reported)

National Guard 73,000 active; 27,000 (tribal levies) (total 100,000)
FORCES BY ROLE
MANOEUVRE
Mechanised
5 mech bde (1 recce coy, 3 mech inf bn, 1 SP arty bn, 1 cbt engr coy, 1 sigs coy, 1 log bn)
Light
5 inf bde (3 combined arms bn, 1 arty bn, 1 log bn)
3 indep lt inf bn
Other
1 (Special Security) sy bde (3 sy bn)
1 (ceremonial) cav sqn

COMBAT SUPPORT
1 MP bn
EQUIPMENT BY TYPE
ARMOURED FIGHTING VEHICLES
ASLT 204 LAV-AG (90mm)
IFV 683: ε635 LAV-25; ε48 LAV 6.0
APC 778
APC (W) 514: 116 LAV-A (amb); 30 LAV-AC (ammo carrier); 296 LAV-CC (CP); 72 LAV-PC
PPV 264 *Aravis*; some *Arive*
ENGINEERING & MAINTENANCE VEHICLES
AEV 58 LAV-E
ARV 111 LAV-R; V-150 ARV
ANTI-TANK/ANTI-INFRASTRUCTURE
MSL
SP 182 LAV-AT
MANPATS TOW-2A; M47 *Dragon*
RCL • **106mm** M40A1
ARTILLERY 363+
SP **155mm** up to 136 CAESAR
TOWED 108: **105mm** 50 M102; **155mm** 58 M198
MOR 119+: **81mm** some; **120mm** 119 LAV-M
HELICOPTERS
ATK 12 AH-64E *Apache*
MRH 35: 23 AH-6i *Little Bird*; 12 MD530F (trg role)
TPT • **Medium** 23 UH-60M *Black Hawk*
AIR DEFENCE
SAM
Short-range 5 VL MICA
Point-defence 68 MPCV
GUNS • TOWED • **20mm** 30 M167 *Vulcan*
AIR-LAUNCHED MISSILES
ASM AGM-114R *Hellfire* II

Paramilitary 24,500+ active

Border Guard 15,000
FORCES BY ROLE
Subordinate to Ministry of Interior. HQ in Riyadh. 9 subordinate regional commands
MANOEUVRE
Other
Some mobile def (long-range patrol/spt) units
2 border def (patrol) units
12 infrastructure def units
18 harbour def units
Some coastal def units
COMBAT SUPPORT
Some MP units
EQUIPMENT BY TYPE
ARMOURED FIGHTING VEHICLES
APC • PPV *Caprivi* Mk1/Mk3
PATROL AND COASTAL COMBATANTS 106
PCC 13 CSB 40
PBF 85: 4 *Al Jouf*; 2 *Sea Guard*; 79 *Plascoa* FIC 1650
PB 8: 6 Damen Stan Patrol 2606; 2 *Al Jubatel*
AMPHIBIOUS • LANDING CRAFT 8: 5 UCAC *Griffon* 8000; 3 other
LOGISTICS AND SUPPORT 4: 1 AXL; 3 AO

Facilities Security Force 9,000+
Subordinate to Ministry of Interior

General Civil Defence Administration Units
EQUIPMENT BY TYPE
HELICOPTERS • TPT • **Medium** 10 Boeing *Vertol* 107

Special Security Force 500
EQUIPMENT BY TYPE
ARMOURED FIGHTING VEHICLES
  APC • **APC (W)** UR-416
  AUV *Gurkha* LAPV

DEPLOYMENT
YEMEN: *Operation Restoring Hope* 2,500; 2 armd BG; M60A3; M2A2 Bradley; M113A4; M-ATV; 2+ MIM-104D/F *Patriot* PAC-2/3

FOREIGN FORCES
Bahrain *Operation Restoring Hope* 250; 1 SF gp; 1 arty gp; 6 F-16C *Fighting Falcon*
Egypt *Operation Restoring Hope* 6 F-16C *Fighting Falcon*
Jordan *Operation Restoring Hope* 6 F-16AM *Fighting Falcon*
Kuwait *Operation Restoring Hope* 4 F/A-18A *Hornet*
Sudan *Operation Restoring Hope* 3 Su-24 *Fencer*
United Arab Emirates *Operation Restoring Hope* 12 F-16E *Fighting Falcon*
United States US Central Command: 2,000; 1 ftr sqn with 12 F-22A *Raptor*; 1 EW sqn with 5 EA-18G *Growler*; 2 SAM bty with MIM-104 *Patriot* PAC-2/-3

Syria SYR

Syrian Pound S£		2018	2019	2020
GDP	S£			
	US$			
per capita	US$			
Growth	%			
Inflation	%			
Def exp	S£			
	US$			
US$1=S£				

Population	20,893,752					
Age	0–14	15–19	20–24	25–29	30–64	65 plus
Male	16.0%	5.1%	4.8%	4.3%	18.1%	2.0%
Female	15.2%	4.9%	4.7%	4.3%	18.2%	2.4%

Capabilities
The civil war has significantly depleted the combat capabilities of the Syrian armed forces and transformed them into an irregularly structured militia-style organisation focused on internal security. There is no published defence doctrine or white paper, the ongoing war instead dictating de facto requirements and priorities. Most formal pre-war structures and formations exist in name only, as resources have been channelled into an irregular network of military organisations that form the regime's most effective military capabilities. Russia is the regime's dominant ally and has provided essential direct combat support and assistance to Syrian military activities, as well as significant amounts of replacement equipment. Russia is also involved in efforts to reconstitute the army's pre-war divisions. Iran and Hizbullah also continue to assist in the provision and training of militias and other ground forces. Overall levels of training remain poor, but select regular and irregular military formations have gained a reasonable degree of proficiency through combat experience. The armed forces lack the requisite capabilities for external deployment, although they remain able to redeploy moderate numbers of formations and capabilities within the country. Logistics support for major internal operations away from established bases remains a challenge. The large pre-war equipment inventory has long suffered from indifferent maintenance, a situation that has deteriorated further. Before the civil war, Syria did not have a major domestic defence industry, although it possessed facilities for the overhaul and maintenance of its existing systems. It did, however, possess some capacity in focused areas, such as ballistic missiles and chemical weapons.

ACTIVE 169,000 (Army 130,000 Navy 4,000 Air 15,000 Air Defence 20,000) **Paramilitary 100,000**
Conscript liability 30 months (there is widespread avoidance of military service)

ORGANISATIONS BY SERVICE

Army ε130,000
FORCES BY ROLE
The Syrian Arab Army combines conventional formations, special forces and auxiliary militias. The main fighting units are the 4th Armoured Division, the Republican Guard, the Special Forces (including Tiger Forces) and the brigades assigned to the 5th Assault Corps; they receive the most attention and training. Most other formations are under-strength, at an estimated 500–1,000 personnel in brigades and regiments, but Russia has been assisting in the reconstruction and re-equipment of some divisions.
COMMAND
  4 corps HQ
  1 (5th Assault) corps HQ
SPECIAL FORCES
  2 SF div (total: 11 SF regt; 1 tk regt)
MANOEUVRE
  Armoured
  1 (4th) armd div (1 SF regt, 2 armd bde, 2 mech bde, 1 arty regt, 1 SSM bde (3 SSM bn with *Scud*-B/C))
  3 armd div (being reconstituted)
  2 armd div(-)
  Mechanised
  1 (Republican Guard) mech div (3 mech bde, 2 sy regt, 1 arty regt)
  1 mech div (being reconstituted)
  2 mech div(-)
  8 mech bde (assigned to 5th Assault Corps)
  2 indep inf bde(-)
  Amphibious
  1 mne unit
COMBAT SUPPORT
  2 arty bde
  2 AT bde

1 SSM bde (3 SSM bn with FROG-7)
1 SSM bde (3 SSM bn with SS-21)

EQUIPMENT BY TYPE
Attrition during the civil war has severely reduced equipment numbers for almost all types. It is unclear how much remains available for operations

ARMOURED FIGHTING VEHICLES
MBT T-55A; T-55AM; T-55AMV; T-62; T-62M; T-72; T-72AV; T-72B; T-72B3; T-72M1; T-90
RECCE BRDM-2
IFV BMP-1; BMP-2; BTR-82A
APC
  APC (T) BTR-50
  APC (W) BTR-152; BTR-60; BTR-70; BTR-80
  APC IVECO LMV
ENGINEERING & MAINTENANCE VEHICLES
ARV BREM-1 reported; T-54/55
VLB MTU; MTU-20
MW UR-77
ANTI-TANK/ANTI-INFRASTRUCTURE • MSL
SP 9P133 *Malyutka*-P (BRDM-2 with AT-3C *Sagger*); 9P148 *Konkurs* (BRDM-2 with AT-5 *Spandrel*)
MANPATS 9K111 *Fagot* (AT-4 *Spigot*); 9K111-1 *Konkurs* (AT-5 *Spandrel*); 9K115 *Metis* (AT-7 *Saxhorn*); 9K115-2 *Metis*-M (AT-13 *Saxhorn* 2); 9K135 *Kornet* (AT-14 *Spriggan*); Milan
ARTILLERY
SP 122mm 2S1 *Gvozdika*; D-30 (mounted on T-34/85 chassis); 130mm M-46 (truck–mounted); 152mm 2S3 *Akatsiya*
TOWED 122mm D-30; M-30 (M1938); 130mm M-46; 152mm D-20; ML-20 (M-1937); 180mm S-23
GUN/MOR 120mm 2S9 NONA-S
MRL 107mm Type-63; 122mm BM-21 *Grad*; 140mm BM-14; 220mm 9P140 *Uragan*; 300mm 9A52 *Smerch*; 330mm some (also improvised systems of various calibres)
MOR 82mm some; 120mm M-1943; 160mm M-160; 240mm M-240
SURFACE-TO-SURFACE MISSILE LAUNCHERS
SRBM • **Conventional** *Scud*-B/C/D; *Scud* look-a-like; 9K79 *Tochka* (SS-21 *Scarab*); *Fateh*-110/M-600
UNMANNED AERIAL VEHICLES
ISR • **Medium** *Mohajer* 3/4; **Light** *Ababil*
AIR DEFENCE
SAM
  Medium-range 9K37 *Buk* (SA-11 *Gadfly*); 9K317 *Buk*-M2 (SA-17 *Grizzly*)
  Short-range 96K6 *Pantsir*-S1 (SA-22 *Greyhound*)
  Point-defence 9K31 *Strela*-1 (SA-9 *Gaskin*); 9K33 *Osa* (SA-8 *Gecko*); 9K35 *Strela*-10 (SA-13 *Gopher*); 9K32 *Strela*-2 (SA-7 *Grail*)‡; 9K38 *Igla* (SA-18 *Grouse*); 9K36 *Strela*-3 (SA-14 *Gremlin*); 9K338 *Igla*-S (SA-24 *Grinch*)
GUNS
  SP 23mm ZSU-23-4; 57mm ZSU-57-2; S-60 (on 2K12 chassis)
  TOWED 23mm ZU-23-2; 37mm M-1939; 57mm S-60; 100mm KS-19

Navy ε4,000
Some personnel are likely to have been drafted into other services

EQUIPMENT BY TYPE
PATROL AND COASTAL COMBATANTS 31:
  CORVETTES • FS 1 *Petya* III† with 1 triple 533mm ASTT with SAET-60 HWT, 4 RBU 2500 *Smerch* 1 A/S mor, 2 twin 76mm gun
  PBFG 22:
    16 *Osa* I/II† with 4 single lnchr with P-22 (SS-N-2C *Styx*) AShM
    6 *Tir* with 2 single lnchr with C-802 (CH-SS-N-6) AShM
  PB 8 *Zhuk*†
MINE WARFARE • MINE COUNTERMEASURES 7
  MHC 1 *Sonya* with 2 quad lnchr with 9K32 *Strela*-2 (SA-N-5 *Grail*)‡ SAM, 2 AK630 CIWS
  MSO 1 *Natya* with 2 quad lnchr with 9K32 *Strela*-2 (SA-N-5 *Grail*)‡ SAM
  MSI 5 *Korund* (*Yevgenya*) (Project 1258)
AMPHIBIOUS • LANDING SHIPS • LSM 3 *Polnochny* B (capacity 6 MBT; 180 troops)
LOGISTICS AND SUPPORT • AX 1 *Al Assad*

Coastal Defence
FORCES BY ROLE
COASTAL DEFENCE
  1 AShM bde with P-35 (SSC-1B *Sepal*); P-15M *Termit*-R (SSC-3 *Styx*); C-802; K-300P *Bastion* (SSC-5 *Stooge*)
EQUIPMENT BY TYPE
COASTAL DEFENCE • AShM P-35 (SSC-1B *Sepal*); P-15M *Termit*-R (SSC-3 *Styx*); C-802; K-300P *Bastion* (SSC-5 *Stooge*)

Naval Aviation
All possibly non-operational after vacating base for Russian deployment
EQUIPMENT BY TYPE
HELICOPTERS • ASW 10: 4 Ka-28 *Helix* A; 6 Mi-14 *Haze*

Air Force ε15,000(-)
FORCES BY ROLE
FIGHTER
2 sqn with MiG-23 MF/ML/UM *Flogger*
2 sqn with MiG-29A/UB/SM *Fulcrum*
FIGHTER/GROUND ATTACK
4 sqn with MiG-21MF/bis *Fishbed*; MiG-21U *Mongol* A
2 sqn with MiG-23BN/UB *Flogger*
GROUND ATTACK
4 sqn with Su-22 *Fitter* D
1 sqn with Su-24 *Fencer*
1 sqn with L-39 *Albatros**
TRANSPORT
1 sqn with An-24 *Coke*; An-26 *Curl*; Il-76 *Candid*
1 sqn with *Falcon* 20; *Falcon* 900
1 sqn with Tu-134B-3
1 sqn with Yak-40 *Codling*
ATTACK HELICOPTER
3 sqn with Mi-25 *Hind* D
2 sqn with SA342L *Gazelle*

TRANSPORT HELICOPTER
6 sqn with Mi-8 *Hip*/Mi-17 *Hip* H

EQUIPMENT BY TYPE
Heavy use of both fixed- and rotary-wing assets has likely reduced readiness and availability to very low levels. It is estimated that no more than 30–40% of the inventory is operational

AIRCRAFT 236 combat capable
　FTR 64: 34 MiG-23MF/ML/UM *Flogger*; 30 MiG-29A/SM/UB *Fulcrum*
　FGA 118: 68 MiG-21MF/bis *Fishbed*; 9 MiG-21U *Mongol* A; 41 MiG-23BN/UB *Flogger*;
　ATK 39: 28 Su-22 *Fitter* D; 11 Su-24 *Fencer*
　TPT 23: **Heavy** 3 Il-76 *Candid*; **Light** 13: 1 An-24 *Coke*; 6 An-26 *Curl*; 2 PA-31 *Navajo*; 4 Yak-40 *Codling*; **PAX** 7: 2 *Falcon* 20; 1 *Falcon* 900; 4 Tu-134B-3
　TRG 15 L-39 *Albatros**
HELICOPTERS
　ATK 24 Mi-25 *Hind* D
　MRH 54: 26 Mi-17 *Hip* H; 28 SA342L *Gazelle*
　TPT • Medium 27 Mi-8 *Hip*
AIR-LAUNCHED MISSILES
　AAM • IR R-60 (AA-8 *Aphid*); R-73 (AA-11 *Archer*); **IR/SARH**; R-23/24 (AA-7 *Apex*); R-27 (AA-10 *Alamo*); **ARH** R-77 (AA-12A *Adder*)
　ASM Kh-25 (AS-10 *Karen*); Kh-29T/L (AS-14 *Kedge*); HOT
　ARM Kh-31P (AS-17A *Krypton*)

Air Defence Command ε20,000(-)
FORCES BY ROLE
AIR DEFENCE
　4 AD div with S-125 *Pechora* (SA-3 *Goa*); 2K12 *Kub* (SA-6 *Gainful*); S-75 *Dvina* (SA-2 *Guideline*)
　3 AD regt with S-200 *Angara* (SA-5 *Gammon*); S-300PMU2 (SA-20 *Gargoyle*)
EQUIPMENT BY TYPE
AIR DEFENCE • SAM
　Long-range S-200 *Angara* (SA-5 *Gammon*); 24 S-300PMU2 (SA-20 *Gargoyle*)
　Medium-range S-75 *Dvina* (SA-2 *Guideline*)
　Short-range 2K12 *Kub* (SA-6 *Gainful*); S-125 *Pechora* (SA-3 *Goa*)
　Point-defence 9K32 *Strela*-2/2M (SA-7A/B *Grail*)‡

Paramilitary ε100,000

National Defence Force ε50,000
An umbrella of disparate regime militias performing a variety of roles, including territorial control

Other Militias ε50,000
Numerous military groups fighting for the Assad regime, including Afghan, Iraqi, Pakistani and sectarian organisations. Some receive significant Iranian support

FOREIGN FORCES
Hizbullah 7,000–8,000
Iran 3,000
Russia 5,000: 1 inf BG; 3 MP bn; 1 engr unit; ε10 T-72B3/T-90; ε20 BTR-82A; 12 2A65; 4 9A52 *Smerch*; TOS-1A; 9K720 *Iskander*-M; 10 Su-24M *Fencer*; 6 Su-34; 4 Su-35S; 1 Il-20M; 12 Mi-24P/Mi-35M *Hind*; 4 Mi-8AMTSh *Hip*; 1 AShM bty with 3K55 *Bastion* (SSC-5 *Stooge*); 1 SAM bty with S-400 (SA-21 *Growler*); 1 SAM bty with S-300V4 (SA-23); 1 SAM bty with *Pantsir*-S1/S2; air base at Latakia; naval facility at Tartus

TERRITORY WHERE THE GOVERNMENT DOES NOT EXERCISE EFFECTIVE CONTROL
Data here represents the de facto situation for selected armed opposition groups and their observed equipment

National Front for Liberation ε50,000
A coalition of surviving Islamist and nationalist rebel factions formed in 2018, reportedly backed by Turkey, and operating in northwestern Syria; particularly in and around Idlib.

EQUIPMENT BY TYPE
ANTI-TANK/ANTI-INFRASTRUCTURE
　MSL • MANPATS 9K11 *Malyutka* (AT-3 *Sagger*); 9K111 *Fagot* (AT-4 *Spigot*); 9K113 *Konkurs* (AT-5 *Spandrel*); 9K115-2 *Metis*-M (AT-13 *Saxhorn* 2); 9K135 *Kornet* (AT-14 *Spriggan*); BGM-71 TOW; *Milan*
ARTILLERY
　TOWED 122mm D-30
　MRL 107mm Type-63; **122mm** BM-21 *Grad*; *Grad* (6-tube tech)
　MOR 82mm some
AIR DEFENCE
　SAM
　　Point-defence MANPADS some
　GUNS
　　SP 14.5mm ZPU-1; ZPU-2 **23mm** ZU-23-2; ZSU-23-4 *Shilka*

Syrian Democratic Forces ε50,000
A coalition of predominantly Kurdish rebel groups in de facto control of much of northeastern Syria. Kurdish forces from the YPG/J (People's Protection Units/Women's Protection Units) provide military leadership and main combat power, supplemented by Arab militias and tribal groups. The SDF has benefited from considerable US and coalition air support, embedded special-operations forces and weaponry.

EQUIPMENT BY TYPE
ARMOURED FIGHTING VEHICLES
　MBT T-55; T-72 (reported)
　IFV BMP-1
　APC • PPV *Guardian*
　AUV M-ATV
ANTI-TANK/ANTI-INFRASTRUCTURE
　MSL • MANPATS 9K111-1 *Konkurs*
　RCL 73mm SPG-9; **90mm** M-79 *Osa*
ARTILLERY
　MRL 122mm BM-21 *Grad*; 9K132 *Grad*-P
　MOR 82mm 82-BM-37; M-1938; **120mm** M-1943; improvised mortars of varying calibre

AIR DEFENCE • GUNS
SP **14.5mm** ZPU-4 (tch); ZPU-2 (tch); ZPU-1 (tch); 1 ZPU-2 (tch/on T-55); **23mm** ZSU-23-4 *Shilka*; ZU-23-2 (tch); **57mm** S-60
TOWED **14.5mm** ZPU-2; ZPU-1; **23mm** ZU-23-2

Syrian National Army ε20,000
Formed in late 2017 from Syrian Arab and Turkmen rebel factions operating under Turkish command in the Aleppo governate and northwestern Syria, including Afrin province.

EQUIPMENT BY TYPE
ARMOURED FIGHTING VEHICLES
  MBT T-54; T-55; T-62
  IFV BMP-1
ANTI-TANK/ANTI-INFRASTRUCTURE
  MSL • MANPATS BGM-71 TOW; 9K115 *Metis* (AT-7 *Saxhorn*)
  RCL **73mm** SPG-9; **82mm** B-10
ARTILLERY
  MRL **107mm** Type-63; **122mm** 9K132 *Grad*-P
  MOR **82mm** 2B9 *Vasilek*; improvised mortars of varying calibre
AIR DEFENCE • GUNS
  SP **14.5mm** ZPU-4 (tch); ZPU-2 (tch); ZPU-1 (tch); **23mm** ZU-23-2 (tch); **57mm** AZP S-60
  TOWED **14.5mm** ZPU-1; ZPU-2; ZPU-4; **23mm** ZU-23-2

Hayat Tahrir al-Sham (HTS) ε20,000
HTS was formed by Jabhat Fateh al-Sham (formerly known as Jabhat al-Nusra) in January 2017 by absorbing other hardline groups. It is designated a terrorist organisation by the US for its links to al-Qaeda.

EQUIPMENT BY TYPE
ANTI-TANK/ANTI-INFRASTRUCTURE
  MSL • MANPATS 9K11 *Malyutka* (AT-3 *Sagger*); 9K113 *Konkurs* (AT-5 *Spandrel*); 9K115-2 *Metis*-M (AT-13 *Saxhorn 2*); 9K135 *Kornet* (AT-14 *Spriggan*)
  RCL **73mm** SPG-9; **106mm** M-40
ARTILLERY
  MRL **107mm** Type-63
  MOR **120mm** some; improvised mortars of varying calibres
AIR DEFENCE
  SAM
    Point-defence 9K32M *Strela*-2M (SA-7B *Grail*)‡
  GUNS
    SP **14.5mm** ZPU-1; ZPU-2; **23mm** ZU-23-2; **57mm** S-60

FOREIGN FORCES
France Operation Inherent Resolve (*Chammal*) 1 SF unit
Turkey ε1,000; some cdo units; 1 gendarmerie unit
United States Operation Inherent Resolve 1,500; 1 ARNG armd BG; 1 mne bn

Tunisia TUN

Tunisian Dinar D		2018	2019	2020
GDP	D	106bn	114bn	
	US$	39.9bn	38.7bn	
per capita	US$	3,422	3,287	
Growth	%	2.5	1.5	
Inflation	%	7.3	6.6	
Def bgt	D	2.33bn	2.93bn	
	US$	881m	993m	
FMA (US)	US$	65.0m	40.0m	40.0m
US$1=D		2.65	2.95	

Real-terms defence budget trend (US$m, constant 2015)

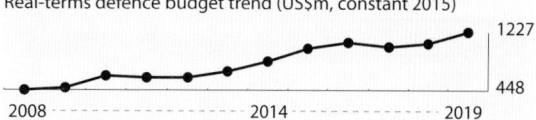

Population	11,622,134					
Age	0–14	15–19	20–24	25–29	30–64	65 plus
Male	13.1%	3.3%	3.3%	3.8%	22.1%	4.0%
Female	12.2%	3.2%	3.3%	4.0%	23.1%	4.5%

Capabilities
Ensuring territorial sovereignty and internal security are the main tasks of the armed forces, which have limited capacities but are undergoing a modernisation process. The civil war in Libya and Islamist terrorist groups operating from there continue to pose a security concern. In the light of terrorist attacks, the armed forces are engaged in counter-terrorism operations, and have been tasked with securing sensitive industrial sites. Designated a major non-NATO ally by the US in 2015, Tunisia also benefits from defence and security cooperation with US AFRICOM and with France. In 2019, Tunisia sent a transport aircraft to support the UN's MINUSMA peacekeeping mission in Mali and reportedly plans to deploy an infantry battalion and military police to the mission. The country has received training from Algeria and is a member of the Saudi-led Islamic Military Counter Terrorism Coalition. The armed forces are involved in multinational exercises, notably those led by the US. The country is also strengthening its intelligence capabilities. Overall military capability is limited by the ageing equipment inventory, although Tunisia has been the recipient of surplus US systems, including armed utility helicopters. The country has limited defence-industrial capabilities.

ACTIVE 35,800 (Army 27,000 Navy 4,800 Air 4,000)
Paramilitary 12,000
Conscript liability 12 months selective

ORGANISATIONS BY SERVICE

Army 5,000; 22,000 conscript (total 27,000)
FORCES BY ROLE
SPECIAL FORCES
  1 SF bde
  1 (Sahara) SF bde

MANOEUVRE
  Reconnaissance
  1 recce regt
  Mechanised
  3 mech bde (1 armd regt, 2 mech inf regt, 1 arty regt, 1 AD regt, 1 engr regt, 1 sigs regt, 1 log gp)
COMBAT SUPPORT
  1 engr regt
EQUIPMENT BY TYPE
ARMOURED FIGHTING VEHICLES
  MBT 84: 30 M60A1; 54 M60A3
  LT TK 48 SK-105 *Kuerassier*
  RECCE 60: 40 AML-90; 20 FV601 *Saladin*
  APC 425+
    APC (T) 140 M113A1/A2
    APC (W) 110 Fiat 6614
    PPV 175+: 4 Bastion APC: 71 *Ejder Yalcin*; 100+ *Kirpi*
ENGINEERING & MAINTENANCE VEHICLES
  AEV 2 *Greif*
  ARV 9: 3 *Greif*; 6 M88A1
ANTI-TANK/ANTI-INFRASTRUCTURE • MSL
  SP 35 M901 ITV TOW
  MANPATS *Milan*; TOW
ARTILLERY 276
  TOWED 115: **105mm** 48 M101A1/A2; **155mm** 67: 12 M114A1; 55 M198
  MOR 161: **81mm** 95; **SP 107mm** 48 M106; **120mm** 18 Brandt
AIR DEFENCE
  SAM • Point-defence 26 M48 *Chaparral*; RBS-70
  GUNS 127
    SP 40mm 12 M42
    TOWED 115: **20mm** 100 M-55; **37mm** 15 Type-55 (M-1939)/Type-65

Navy ε4,800

EQUIPMENT BY TYPE
PATROL AND COASTAL COMBATANTS 33
  PSO 2 *Jugurtha* (Damen Stan MSOPV 1400) with 1 hel landing platform
  PCFG 3 *La Galite* (FRA *Combattante* III) with 2 quad lnchr with MM40 *Exocet* AShM, 1 76mm gun
  PCC 3 *Bizerte* (FRA P-48)
  PCFT 6 *Albatros* (GER Type-143B) with 2 single 533mm TT, 2 76mm guns
  PBF 2 20m Fast Patrol Boat
  PB 17: 3 *Istiklal*; 3 *Utique* (mod PRC *Haizhui* II); 5 *Joumhouria*; 6 V Series
LOGISTICS AND SUPPORT 7:
  ABU 3: 2 *Tabarka* (ex-US *White Sumac*); 1 *Sisi Bou Said*
  AGE 1 *Hannibal*
  AGS 1 *Khaireddine* (ex-US *Wilkes*)
  AWT 1 *Ain Zaghouan* (ex-ITA *Simeto*)
  AX 1 *Salambo* (ex-US *Conrad*, survey)

Air Force 4,000

FORCES BY ROLE
FIGHTER/GROUND ATTACK
  1 sqn with F-5E/F-5F *Tiger* II
TRANSPORT
  1 sqn with C-130B/H/J-30 *Hercules*; G.222; L-410 *Turbolet*
  1 liaison unit with S-208A
TRAINING
  2 sqn with L-59 *Albatros**; MB-326B; SF-260
  1 sqn with MB-326K; MB-326L
TRANSPORT HELICOPTER
  2 sqn with AS350B *Ecureuil*; AS365 *Dauphin* 2; AB-205 (Bell 205); SA313; SA316 *Alouette* III; UH-1H *Iroquois*; UH-1N *Iroquois*
  1 sqn with HH-3E
EQUIPMENT BY TYPE
AIRCRAFT 23 combat capable
  FTR 11: 9 F-5E *Tiger* II; 2 F-5F *Tiger* II
  ATK 3 MB-326K
  ISR 12 *Maule* MX-7-180B
  TPT 18: **Medium** 13: 5 C-130B *Hercules*; 1 C-130H *Hercules*; 2 C-130J-30 *Hercules*; 5 G.222; **Light** 5: 3 L-410 *Turbolet*; 2 S-208A
  TRG 30: 9 L-59 *Albatros**; 4 MB-326B; 3 MB-326L; 14 SF-260
HELICOPTERS
  MRH 34: 1 AS365 *Dauphin* 2; 6 SA313; 3 SA316 *Alouette* III; 24 OH-58D *Kiowa Warrior*
  SAR 11 HH-3E
  TPT 39: **Medium** 8 UH-60M *Black Hawk*; **Light** 31: 6 AS350B *Ecureuil*; 15 Bell 205 (AB-205); 8 Bell 205 (UH-1H *Iroquois*); 2 Bell 212 (UH-1N *Iroquois*)
AIR-LAUNCHED MISSILES
  AAM • IR AIM-9P *Sidewinder*
  ASM AGM-114R *Hellfire*

Paramilitary 12,000

National Guard 12,000
Ministry of Interior
EQUIPMENT BY TYPE
ARMOURED FIGHTING VEHICLES
  ASLT 2 EE-11 *Urutu* FSV
  APC 29+
    APC (W) 16 EE-11 *Urutu* (anti-riot); VAB Mk3
    PPV 13 Streit *Typhoon*
  AUV IVECO LMV
PATROL AND COASTAL COMBATANTS 24
  PCC 6 *Rais el Blais* (ex-GDR *Kondor* I)
  PBF 7: 4 *Gabes*; 3 *Patrouiller*
  PB 11: 5 *Breitla* (ex-GDR *Bremse*); 4 Rodman 38; 2 *Socomena*
HELICOPTERS
  MRH 8 SA318 *Alouette* II/SA319 *Alouette* III
  TPT • Light 3 Bell 429

DEPLOYMENT

CENTRAL AFRICAN REPUBLIC: UN • MINUSCA 2
DEMOCRATIC REPUBLIC OF THE CONGO: UN • MONUSCO 9
MALI: UN • MINUSMA 82; 1 tpt flt with C-130J-30
SOUTH SUDAN: UN • UNMISS 3

United Arab Emirates UAE

Emirati Dirham D		2018	2019	2020
GDP	D	1.52tr	1.49tr	
	US$	414bn	406bn	
per capita	US$	39,709	37,750	
Growth	%	1.7	1.6	
Inflation	%	3.1	-1.5	
Def exp	D	n.k	n.k	
	US$	n.k	n.k	
US$1=D		3.67	3.67	

Population 9,843,829

Ethnic groups: Nationals 24%; expatriates 76%, of which Indian 30%, Pakistani 20%; other Arab 12%; other Asian 10%; UK 2%; other European 1%

Age	0–14	15–19	20–24	25–29	30–64	65 plus
Male	7.5%	2.0%	2.3%	4.2%	55.0%	1.3%
Female	7.0%	1.7%	1.8%	2.6%	14.3%	0.4%

Capabilities

The UAE's armed forces are arguably the best trained and most capable among the GCC states. In recent years, there has been a growing willingness to take part in operations, including sending an F-16 detachment to Afghanistan, participating in the air campaign in Libya and joining the Saudi-led intervention in Yemen. However, a drawdown of deployed forces in 2019 may suggest a reprioritisation of security concerns closer to home, following attacks on tankers off the UAE coast and on oil infrastructure. A new defence agreement with the US, signed in May 2017 and designed to deepen military cooperation, came into force in May 2019. The UAE hosts a French base and is diversifying its security relationships, including with China, India and Japan. A significant part of the UAE approach to regional security, particularly around the Horn of Africa, has been engaging in capacity-building and training. The UAE's involvement in the Yemen campaign has offered combat lessons, not least of all in limited amphibious operations. This operation also demonstrates the country's developing approach to the use of force and there are signs of an acceptance of military risk. In the case of Yemen, the UAE has committed air and ground forces, particularly but not exclusively the presidential guard, deployed armour and demonstrated the use of a range of air munitions, including precision-guidance kits. The country is developing regional staging posts to support the Yemen operation. The UAE has an advanced inventory of modern equipment across the domains and is taking steps to upgrade its airborne ISR capabilities. In 2016, the UAE began to receive US-manufactured THAAD ballistic-missile-defence batteries. The country continues to develop its defence-industrial base and in 2019 announced a new state-owned defence group, EDGE, that will include some of the UAE's leading defence firms and also absorb the existing defence-industry groupings EAIG, EDIC and Tawazun Holdings. The UAE remains reliant on external providers for major weapons systems.

ACTIVE 63,000 (Army 44,000 Navy 2,500 Air 4,500 Presidential Guard 12,000)

Conscript liability 24 months for those with no secondary-school certificate, 16 months for secondary-school graduates. Women – 9 months regardless of education

ORGANISATIONS BY SERVICE

Space
EQUIPMENT BY TYPE
SATELLITES • COMMUNICATIONS 3 *Yahsat*

Army 44,000
FORCES BY ROLE
MANOEUVRE
  Armoured
  2 armd bde
  Mechanised
  2 mech bde
  Light
  1 inf bde
COMBAT SUPPORT
  1 arty bde (3 SP arty regt)
  1 engr gp
EQUIPMENT BY TYPE
ARMOURED FIGHTING VEHICLES
  MBT 383: 45 AMX-30; 338 *Leclerc*
  LT TK 76 FV101 *Scorpion*
  RECCE 73: 49 AML-90; 24 VBL
  IFV 405: 15 AMX-10P; 390 BMP-3; some *Rabdan*
  APC 1,161
    APC (T) 136 AAPC (incl 53 engr plus other variants)
    APC (W) 185: 45 AMV 8×8 (one with BMP-3 turret); 120 EE-11 *Urutu*; 20 VAB
    PPV 840: 465 *Caiman*; 180 *Maxxpro* LWB; 150 Nimr *Hafeet* 630A (CP); 45 Nimr *Hafeet* (Amb)
  AUV 650 M-ATV; Nimr *Adjban*; Nimr *Jais*
ENGINEERING & MAINTENANCE VEHICLES
  AEV 53 ACV-AESV; *Wisent-2*
  ARV 158: 8 ACV-AESV Recovery; 4 AMX-30D; 85 BREM-L; 46 *Leclerc* ARV; 15 *Maxxpro* ARV
NBC VEHICLES 32 TPz-1 *Fuchs* NBC
ANTI-TANK/ANTI-INFRASTRUCTURE
  MSL
    SP 135: 20 HOT; 115 Nimr *Ajban* 440A with *Kornet*-E
    MANPATS FGM-148 *Javelin*; *Milan*; TOW
  RCL 84mm *Carl Gustav*
ARTILLERY 613+
  SP 155mm 181: 78 G-6; 85 M109A3; 18 Mk F3
  TOWED 93: 105mm 73 L118 Light Gun; 130mm 20 Type-59-I; 155mm 6 AH-4
  MRL 88+: 122mm 50+: 48 Firos-25 (est 24 op); 2 *Jobaria*; Type-90 (reported); 227mm 32 M142 HIMARS; 300mm 6 9A52 *Smerch*
  MOR 251: 81mm 134: 20 Brandt; 114 L16; 120mm 21 Brandt; SP 120mm 96 RG-31 MMP *Agrab* Mk2
SURFACE-TO-SURFACE MISSILE LAUNCHERS
  SRBM • Conventional 6 *Scud*-B (up to 20 msl); MGM-140A/B ATACMS (launched from M142 HIMARS)
UNMANNED AERIAL VEHICLES
  ISR • Medium *Seeker* II
AIR DEFENCE
  SAM • Point-defence *Mistral*

Navy 2,500

EQUIPMENT BY TYPE
PRINCIPAL SURFACE COMBATANTS 1
  FRIGATES • FFGH 1
    1 *Abu Dhabi* with 2 twin lnchr with MM40 *Exocet* Block 3 AShM, 1 76mm gun
PATROL AND COASTAL COMBATANTS 42
  CORVETTES 10
    FSGHM 6:
      6 *Baynunah* with 2 quad lnchr with MM40 *Exocet* Block 3 AShM, 1 8-cell Mk 56 VLS with RIM-162 ESSM SAM, 1 21-cell Mk 49 GMLS with RIM-116C RAM Block 2 SAM, 1 76mm gun
    FSGM 4:
      2 *Muray Jib* (GER Lurssen 62m) with 2 quad lnchr with MM40 *Exocet* Block 2 AShM, 1 octuple lnchr with *Crotale* SAM, 1 *Goalkeeper* CIWS, 1 76mm gun, 1 hel landing platform
      2 *Ganthoot* with 2 twin lnchr with MM40 *Exocet* Block 3 AShM, 2 3-cell VLS with VL-*MICA* SAM, 1 76mm gun, 1 hel landing platform
  PCFGM 2 *Mubarraz* (GER Lurssen 45m) with 2 twin lnchr with MM40 *Exocet* AShM, 1 sextuple *Sadral* lnchr with *Mistral* SAM, 1 76mm gun
  PCFG 6 *Ban Yas* (GER Lurssen TNC-45) with 2 twin lnchr with MM40 *Exocet* Block 3 AShM, 1 76mm gun
  PBFG 12 *Butinah* (*Ghannatha* mod) with 4 single lncher with *Marte* Mk2/N AShM
  PBF 12: 6 *Ghannatha* with 1 120mm NEMO mor (capacity 42 troops); 6 *Ghannatha* (capacity 42 troops)
MINE WARFARE • MINE COUNTERMEASURES 2
  MHO 2 *Al Murjan* (ex-GER Frankenthal-class Type-332)
AMPHIBIOUS 19
  LANDING SHIPS • LST 2 *Alquwaisat* with 1 hel landing platform
  LANDING CRAFT 17
    LCM 5: 3 *Al Feyi* (capacity 56 troops); 2 (capacity 40 troops and additional vehicles)
    LCP 4 Fast Supply Vessel (multipurpose)
    LCT 8: 1 *Al Shareeah* (LSV 75m) with 1 hel landing platform; 7 (various)
LOGISTICS AND SUPPORT 3:
  AFS 2 *Rmah* with 4 single 533mm TT
  AX 1 *Al Semeih* with 1 hel landing platform

Air Force 4,500

FORCES BY ROLE
FIGHTER/GROUND ATTACK
  3 sqn with F-16E/F Block 60 *Fighting Falcon*
  3 sqn with *Mirage* 2000-9DAD/EAD/RAD
AIRBORNE EARLY WARNING AND CONTROL
  1 flt with Saab 340 *Erieye*
SEARCH & RESCUE
  2 flt with AW109K2; AW139
TANKER
  1 flt with A330 MRTT
TRANSPORT
  1 sqn with C-17A *Globemaster*
  1 sqn with C-130H/H-30 *Hercules*; L-100-30
  1 sqn with CN235M-100

TRAINING
  1 sqn with Grob 115TA
  1 sqn with *Hawk* Mk102*
  1 sqn with PC-7 *Turbo Trainer*
  1 sqn with PC-21
TRANSPORT HELICOPTER
  1 sqn with Bell 412 *Twin Huey*

EQUIPMENT BY TYPE
AIRCRAFT 156 combat capable
  FGA 137: 54 F-16E Block 60 *Fighting Falcon* (*Desert Eagle*); 24 F-16F Block 60 *Fighting Falcon* (13 to remain in US for trg); 15 *Mirage* 2000-9DAD; 44 *Mirage* 2000-9EAD
  ISR 7 *Mirage* 2000 RAD*
  SIGINT 1 Global 6000
  AEW&C 2 Saab 340 *Erieye*
  TPT/TKR 3 A330 MRTT
  TPT 24: **Heavy** 7 C-17 *Globemaster* III; **Medium** 6: 3 C-130H *Hercules*; 1 C-130H-30 *Hercules*; 2 L-100-30; **Light** 11: 2 C295W; 5 CN235; 4 DHC-8 *Dash* 8 (MP)
  TRG 79: 12 Grob 115TA; 12 *Hawk* Mk102*; 30 PC-7 *Turbo Trainer*; 25 PC-21
HELICOPTERS
  MRH 21: 12 AW139; 9 Bell 412 *Twin Huey*
  TPT • Light 4: 3 AW109K2; 1 Bell 407
UNMANNED AERIAL VEHICLES
  CISR • Heavy *Wing Loong* I; *Wing Loong* II
  ISR • Heavy RQ-1E *Predator* XP
AIR-LAUNCHED MISSILES
  AAM • IR AIM-9L *Sidewinder*; R-550 *Magic*; **IIR** AIM-9X *Sidewinder* II; **IIR/ARH** *Mica*; **ARH** AIM-120B/C AMRAAM
  ASM AGM-65G *Maverick*; *Hakeem* 1/2/3 (A/B)
  ARM AGM-88C HARM
  ALCM *Black Shaheen* (*Storm Shadow*/SCALP EG variant)
BOMBS
  INS/SAT guided *Al Tariq*
  Laser-guided GBU-12/58 *Paveway* II

Air Defence

FORCES BY ROLE
AIR DEFENCE
  2 AD bde (3 bn with MIM-23B I-*Hawk*; MIM-104F *Patriot* PAC-3)
  3 (short range) AD bn with *Crotale*; *Mistral*; *Rapier*; RB-70; *Javelin*; 9K38 *Igla* (SA-18 *Grouse*); 96K6 *Pantsir*-S1
  2 SAM bty with THAAD
EQUIPMENT BY TYPE
AIR DEFENCE •
  SAM
    Medium-range MIM-23B I-*Hawk*; MIM-104F *Patriot* PAC-3
    Short-range *Crotale*; 50 96K6 *Pantsir*-S1
    Point-defence 9K38 *Igla* (SA-18 *Grouse*); RBS-70; *Rapier*; *Mistral*
  GUNS • Towed 35mm GDF-005
MISSILE DEFENCE 12 THAAD

Presidential Guard Command 12,000
FORCES BY ROLE
SPECIAL FORCES
1 SF bn
1 spec ops bn
MANOEUVRE
Reconaissance
1 recce sqn
Mechanised
1 mech bde (1 tk bn, 4 mech inf bn, 1 AT coy, 1 cbt engr coy, 1 CSS bn)
Amphibious
1 mne bn
EQUIPMENT BY TYPE
ARMOURED FIGHTING VEHICLES
MBT 50 *Leclerc*
IFV 290: 200 BMP-3; 90 BTR-3U *Guardian*
ANTI-TANK/ANTI-INFRASTRUCTURE
MSL • SP HMMWV with 9M133 *Kornet*

Joint Aviation Command
FORCES BY ROLE
GROUND ATTACK
1 sqn with *Archangel*; AT802 *Air Tractor*
ANTI-SURFACE/ANTI-SUBMARINE WARFARE
1 sqn with AS332F *Super Puma*; AS565 *Panther*
TRANSPORT
1 (Spec Ops) gp with AS365F *Dauphin* 2; H125M *Fennec*; AW139; Bell 407MRH; Cessna 208B *Grand Caravan*; CH-47C/F *Chinook*; DHC-6-300/400 *Twin Otter*; UH-60L/M *Black Hawk*
ATTACK HELICOPTER
1 gp with AH-64D *Apache*
EQUIPMENT BY TYPE
AIRCRAFT 37 combat capable
ATK 23 *Archangel*
ISR ε6 AT802 *Air Tractor**
TPT • Light 15: 2 Beech 350 *King Air*; 8 Cessna 208B *Grand Caravan**; 1 DHC-6-300 *Twin Otter*; 4 DHC-6-400 *Twin Otter*
HELICOPTERS
ATK 28 AH-64D *Apache*
ASW 7 AS332F *Super Puma* (5 in ASuW role)
MRH 47: 4 AS365F *Dauphin* 2 (VIP); 9 H125M *Fennec*; 7 AS565 *Panther*; 3 AW139 (VIP); 20 Bell 407MRH; 4 SA316 *Alouette* III
TPT 62+: **Heavy** 22 CH-47F *Chinook*; **Medium** 40+: 11 UH-60L *Black Hawk*; 29+ UH-60M *Black Hawk*
AIR-LAUNCHED MISSILES
ASM AGM-114 *Hellfire*; *Cirit*; *Hydra*-70; HOT
AShM AS-15TT; AM39 *Exocet*

Paramilitary
Critical Infrastructure and Coastal Protection Agency (CICPA)
Ministry of Interior
EQUIPMENT BY TYPE
PATROL AND COASTAL COMBATANTS 113
PSO 1 *Al Wtaid*
PCM 1 *Arialah* (Damen Sea Axe 6711) with 1 11-cell Mk 15 SeaRAM GMLS with RIM-116C RAM Block 2 SAM, 1 57mm gun, 1 hel landing platform
PBF 58: 6 *Baglietto* GC23; 3 *Baglietto* 59; 15 DV-15; 34 MRTP 16
PB 53: 2 *Protector*; 16 (US Camcraft 65); 5 (US Camcraft 77); 6 Watercraft 45; 12 *Halmatic Work*; 12 *Al Saber*

DEPLOYMENT
ERITREA: *Operation Restoring Hope* 1,000; 1 armd BG; *Leclerc*; BMP-3; G-6; *Agrab* Mk2; 2 FSGHM; 2 LST; 6 LCT; 4 *Archangel*; 3 AH-64D *Apache*; 2 CH-47F *Chinook*; 4 UH-60M *Black Hawk*; *Wing Loong* 1 (GJ-1) UAV; 4 MIM-104F *Patriot* PAC-3

LIBYA: 6 AT-802; 2 UH-60M; *Wing Loong* I UAV; *Wing Loong* II UAV

SAUDI ARABIA: *Operation Restoring Hope* 12 F-16E *Fighting Falcon*

FOREIGN FORCES
Australia 650; 1 tpt det with 1 B-737-700 *Wedgetail* (E-7A); 1 A330 MRTT (KC-30A); 2 C-130J-30 *Hercules*; 1 P-8A *Poseidon*
Denmark *Operation Inherent Resolve* 20
France 650: 1 armd BG (1 tk coy, 1 armd inf coy; 1 aty bty); *Leclerc*; VBCI; CAESAR; 6 *Rafale*
Italy 113; 1 tpt flt with 2 C-130J *Hercules*
Korea, Republic of 139 (trg activities at UAE Spec Ops School)
United Kingdom 200; 1 tkr/tpt flt with C-17A *Globemaster*; C-130J *Hercules*; A330 MRTT *Voyager*
United States 5,500; 1 ftr sqn with 12 F-15C *Eagle*; 1 FGA sqn with 18 F-15E *Strike Eagle*; 1 FGA sqn with 12 F-35A *Lightning* II; 1 ISR sqn with 4 U-2S; 1 AEW&C sqn with 4 E-3 *Sentry*; 1 tkr sqn with 12 KC-10A; 1 ISR UAV sqn with RQ-4 *Global Hawk*; 2 AD bty with MIM-104E/F *Patriot* PAC-2/3

Yemen, Republic of YEM

Yemeni Rial R		2018	2019	2020
GDP	R	13.6tr	16.9tr	
	US$	27.6bn	29.9bn	
per capita	US$	895	943	
Growth	%	0.8	2.1	
Inflation	%	27.6	14.7	
Def bdgt	R	n.k	n.k	
	US$	n.k	n.k	
US$1=R		493.00	566.01	

Population 29,282,399

Ethnic groups: Majority Arab, some African and South Asian

Age	0–14	15–19	20–24	25–29	30–64	65 plus
Male	19.6%	5.8%	5.0%	4.4%	14.5%	1.3%
Female	18.9%	5.6%	4.9%	4.3%	14.2%	1.6%

Capabilities

Yemen continues to be wracked by a conflict that is, according to the UN, the world's worst humanitarian crisis. There appears to be little apparent prospect that any of the competing forces will be able to gain a decisive upper hand. The government of President Hadi appears to exercise limited control over the forces nominally loyal to it, while the proxy forces supposedly allied to the government and supported by the members of the Saudi-led coalition answer to those member states rather than Yemeni military authorities. The rebel Houthi forces, who are assumed to receive material support from Iran, are largely tribal-based militias, along with some elements of the Yemeni armed forces who were loyal to the late former president Saleh. Al-Qaeda affiliates also appear active in the country. Government forces tend to be underequipped and poorly paid compared to the proxy groups supported by the Saudi-led coalition. The Houthi rebel forces gained from the training and capabilities of the former Yemeni armed forces previously loyal to former president Saleh. The Houthi rebels appear to retain most of the more capable heavy armour and armoured fighting vehicles. Opposition forces have maintained their ability to launch surface-to-surface missiles at Saudi Arabia. The Saudi-led coalition continues to provide ground and air support for the Hadi government, although the UAE is drawing down its forces. The conflict appears to have been sustained by a combination of large existing stockpiles of weapons and ammunition and external supplies, despite UN embargoes. There is no domestic defence industry, barring some limited maintenance and workshop facilities.

ACTIVE 40,000 (Goverment forces 40,000)

ORGANISATIONS BY SERVICE

Government forces ε40,000 (incl militia)

President Hadi's government is nominally supported by parts of the Yemeni armed forces, as well as a number of militia organisations in southern and eastern Yemen. The government's ability to exercise direct control over most of these forces is extremely limited, with local leaders and state sponsors, such as Saudi Arabia and the UAE, exercising stronger influence. While the theoretical strength of the Yemeni armed forces is reported at almost 140,000 personnel, very few of these are actually available for tasking by Hadi's government.

FORCES BY ROLE
MANOEUVRE
  Mechanised
  up to 20 bde(-)
EQUIPMENT BY TYPE
ARMOURED FIGHTING VEHICLES
  MBT Some M60A1; T-34†; T-54/55; T-62; T-72
  RECCE some BRDM-2
  IFV BMP-2; BTR-80A; Ratel-20
  APC
    APC (W) BTR-60
    PPV Streit *Cougar*; Streit *Spartan*
  AUV M-ATV
ANTI-TANK/ANTI-INFRASTRUCTURE
  MSL • MANPATS 9K11 *Malyutka* (AT-3 *Sagger*); M47 *Dragon*; TOW
  GUNS • SP 100mm SU-100†
ARTILLERY • SP 122mm 2S1 *Gvozdika*
AIRCRAFT • ISR 6 AT-802 *Air Tractor**

AIR DEFENCE • GUNS • TOWED 14.5mm ZPU-4; 23mm ZU-23-2

DEPLOYMENT

MALI: UN • MINUSMA 2

FOREIGN FORCES

All *Operation Restoring Hope* unless stated
Saudi Arabia 2,500: 2 armd BG; M60A3; M2A2 *Bradley*; M113A4; M-ATV; AH-64 *Apache*; 2+ MIM-104D/F *Patriot* PAC-2/3
Sudan 950; 1 mech BG; T-72AV; BTR-70M *Kobra* 2

TERRITORY WHERE THE GOVERNMENT DOES NOT EXERCISE EFFECTIVE CONTROL

Insurgent forces 20,000 (incl Houthi and tribes)

The Houthi-run de facto administration has controlled northern Yemen since 2015 and is supported by a combination of Houthi tribal militias and elements of the Yemeni armed forces loyal to former president Ali Abdullah Saleh. Following a break between the Houthis and Saleh in late 2017 that resulted in the latter's death, his former forces have become further split between those that remained affiliated with the Houthis and those who have joined Saleh's son and nephew to fight against them.

FORCES BY ROLE
MANOEUVRE
  Mechanised
  up to 20 bde(-)
EQUIPMENT BY TYPE
ARMOURED FIGHTING VEHICLES
  MBT T-55; T-72
  IFV BMP-2; BTR-80A
  APC • APC (W) Some BTR-40; BTR-60
  AUV M-ATV
ANTI-TANK/ANTI-INFRASTRUCTURE
  MSL • MANPATS M47 *Dragon*; 9K111-1 *Konkurs* (AT-5B *Spandrel/Towsan*-1); 9K115 *Metis* (AT-7 *Saxhorn*); *Dehlavieh* (*Kornet*)
  RCL 82mm B-10
SURFACE-TO-SURFACE MISSILE LAUNCHERS
  SRBM • Conventional 9K79 *Tochka* (SS-21 *Scarab*); 9K72 *Elbrus* (SS-1C *Scud-B*); *Hwasong*-5 (SS-1C *Scud-B*); *Hwasong*-6 (SS-1D *Scud-C*); *Borkan*-1 (extended-range *Scud* derivative); *Borkan*-2H (*Qiam*-1); *Qaher*-1 (converted S-75 SAM)
  GLCM • Conventional *Quds*-1
COASTAL DEFENCE • AShM C-801; C-802
UNMANNED AERIAL VEHICLES
  ISR • Medium *Qasef*-1; *Qasef*-2K; *Sammad*-1; *Sammad*-2; *Sammad*-3 (many of these systems have been fitted with a warhead payload to function as a form of improvised missile)
AIR DEFENCE • GUNS • TOWED 20mm M167 *Vulcan*; 23mm ZU-23-2

Arms procurements and deliveries – Middle East and North Africa

Significant events in 2019

FEBRUARY — QATAR: NAVAL PLANS

Italian shipbuilder Fincantieri began to build the first Offshore Patrol Vessel for Qatar's navy. This is part of a €5 billion (US$5.64bn) deal agreed in 2017 for seven vessels. It includes several frigates and a landing helicopter dock vessel fitted with an active electronically scanned array radar intended to be capable of tracking short-range ballistic missiles. It is planned that all seven vessels are delivered by the end of 2024.

AUGUST — ALGERIA'S EDST

Algeria authorised the establishment of a Technical System Development Establishment (EDST) to develop complex weapons and ammunition for the Algerian armed forces. In recent years, Algeria has partnered with several Western companies, such as Leonardo and Rheinmetall, to licence-produce equipment. It is possible that Algeria hopes licence-production agreements will boost domestic industrial capability, as well as provide employment.

SEPTEMBER — SAMI-NAVANTIA TIE-UP

Saudi Arabian Military Industries (SAMI) signed a €900 million (US$1.03bn) contract with Spanish firm Navantia to create a joint venture called SAMI Navantia Naval Industries. The joint venture will develop a version of the *Catiz* combat-management system for Saudi Arabia's *Avante* 2200 corvettes, being built by Navantia. This development takes place within the context of Riyadh's ambitious Vision 2030 project, which includes the aspiration for 50% of Saudi Arabia's defence-procurement spending to go to local companies by 2030.

NOVEMBER — MOROCCO: F-16 AND APACHE

The US government approved the sale of 36 new *Apache* attack helicopters to Morocco with an estimated cost of US$4.25bn. Earlier, in March, the US State Department approved the sale of 25 new Block 72 F-16 fighter aircraft (US$3.79bn) and upgrades to the existing fleet of 23 F-16s (US$985.2m). If these sales proceed, they will enhance Morocco's military modernisation, particularly in terms of attack helicopters, and boost the defence relationship with Washington.

NOVEMBER — NEW DEFENCE CONCERN

The United Arab Emirates brought together 25 defence and security companies under a new parent company called Edge. This new company has a combined revenue of US$5bn, and 12,000 employees. The UAE wants to field equipment more quickly and will also invest more money in R&D.

Table 19 Italy–Israel: defence-equipment procurement agreement

In 2012, Israel and Italy agreed to acquire approximately US$1 billion of defence equipment from each others' companies. Deliveries under the initial announcement were completed in 2017. In early 2019, Israel announced a contract to acquire seven AW119 training helicopters. This is reportedly the second part of the 2012 agreement, although as of late 2019 Italy had yet to announce a reciprocal order.

© IISS

Contract date	Recipient country	Equipment	Type	Quantity	Value	Prime contractor	Deliveries
Jul 2012	Israel	M-346 *Lavi*	Training aircraft	30	US$1bn	🇮🇹 Alenia Aermacchi	2014–16
	Italy	OPTSAT-3000	ISR satellite	1	US$200m	🇮🇹 Telespazio (satellite built by IAI)	2017
		G550-AEW	Airborne early-warning and control aircraft	2	US$750m	🇮🇱 IAI Elta	2016–17
Feb 2019	Israel	AW119	Training helicopter	7	n.k.	🇮🇹 Leonardo	n.k.

Table 20 Oman: defence-equipment procurement, 2010–19

Contract date	Equipment	Type	Quantity	Value	Prime contractor	Deliveries
Aug 2010	C-130J *Hercules*	Medium transport aircraft	2	n.k.	🇺🇸 Lockheed Martin	2014
Dec 2011	F-16C/D (Block 50) *Fighting Falcon*	Fighter/ground-attack aircraft	12 (batch 2)	US$600m	🇺🇸 Lockheed Martin	2014
May 2012	C295MPA	Maritime-patrol aircraft	4	n.k.	M Airbus Military	2013–16
	C295M	Transport aircraft	4			
Apr 2012	*Al-Ofouq* (SGP *Fearless*)	Offshore-patrol craft	4	SGD880m (US$704.18m)	🇸🇬 ST Marine	2015–16
Dec 2012	Eurofighter *Typhoon*	Fighter/ground-attack aircraft	12	£2.5bn (US$3.96bn)	🇬🇧 BAE Systems	2017–18
	Hawk Mk166	Training aircraft	8			
2013	NASAMS II	Short-range surface-to-air missile	n.k.	US$1.28bn	🇺🇸 Raytheon	n.k.
Mar 2014	*Al Mubshir* (HSSV 72)	Expeditionary fast transport vessel	2	US$124.9m	🇦🇺 Austal	2016
Feb 2016	*Pars* III	Infantry fighting vehicle	172	n.k.	🇹🇷 FNSS	2017–ongoing

M - multinational

Table 21 **Egypt: naval procurement, 2008–19**

Equipment	Contract date	Type	Quantity	Value	Prime contractor	Weapons fit	Deliveries
Ezzat (Ambassador Fast Missile Craft)	Sep 2008	Corvette with anti-ship and surface-to-air missiles	4	US$807m	🇺🇸 VT Halter Marine	■ RGM-84L *Harpoon* Block II AShM ■ RIM-116B RAM Block 1A SAM ■ Mk 15 *Phalanx* Block 1B CIWS ■ Oto Melara 76/62 *Super Rapid* naval gun	2013–15
Type-209/1400	2011	Attack submarine	2	€920m (US$1.28bn)	🇩🇪 Howaldtswerke-Deutsche Werft	■ UGM-84L *Harpoon* Block II AShM ■ *SeaHAKE* mod 4 HWT	2017
Type-209/1400	Feb 2014	Attack submarine	2	est. €920m (est. US$1.28bn)	🇩🇪 Howaldtswerke-Deutsche Werft	■ UGM-84L *Harpoon* Block II AShM ■ *SeaHAKE* mod 4 HWT	
El Fateh (FRA Gowind 2500)	Mar 2014	Guided-missile frigate with a hangar and surface-to-air missiles	4	€1bn (US$1.33bn)	🇫🇷 DCNS (Three being built in EGY)	■ MM40 *Exocet* Block 3 AShM ■ VL MICA SAM ■ MU90 LWT ■ Oto Melara 76/62 *Super Rapid* naval gun	2017–ongoing
Tahya Misr (FRA FREMM)	Feb 2015	Guided-missile frigate with a hangar and surface-to-air missiles	1	€1bn (US$1.1bn)	🇫🇷 DCNS	■ MM40 *Exocet* Block 3 AShM ■ *Aster* 15 SAM ■ MU90 LWT ■ Oto Melara 76/62 *Super Rapid* naval gun	2015
Molnya (RUS *Tarantul* IV)	2015	Fast guided-missile patrol craft	1	n.k.	🇷🇺 RUS government surplus	■ 3M80E *Moskit* (SS-N-22A *Sunburn*) AShM ■ AK630 CIWS ■ AK-176 naval gun	2016
Gamal Abdel Nasser (FRA *Mistral*)	Oct 2015	Landing helicopter dock	2	€950m (US$1.05bn)	🇫🇷 DCNS	–	2016
Shabab Misr (Ex-ROK *Po Hang*)	Sep 2017	Corvette	1	US$0 (donation)	🇰🇷 ROK government surplus	■ Oto Melara 76/62 *Compact* naval gun	2017

Chapter Eight
Latin America and the Caribbean

- Limited and increasingly ageing equipment inventories, together with economic constraints, continue to affect regional military capability development.
- Tensions have risen between Venezuela and Colombia, with Colombia's leaders alleging the presence in Venezuela of armed groups like the ELN. In response to Venezuela's military exercises across the border, Colombia in September alerted its armed forces.
- Key defence-industry projects in Brazil saw progress. Embraer delivered to the Brazilian Air Force the first KC-390 transport aircraft built in partnership with Boeing, Saab successfully conducted the first test flight with the first Brazilian-built *Gripen* E fighter aircraft, and sea trials began for Brazil's first submarine built under the PROSUB project, the *Scorpène*-class boat *Riachuelo*.
- The Mexican government set up a National Guard in response to the still-fragile security situation. The force began operations in mid-year and is planned to have a total establishment strength of 58,000, drawn from the army's military-police units, naval police and the federal police.
- The lack of funding has hampered the replacement of the ageing fleets of fighter aircraft in Chile, Colombia and Peru. The latter has recently decided to extend the life of its fleet of F-16 Block 50s beyond 2040.

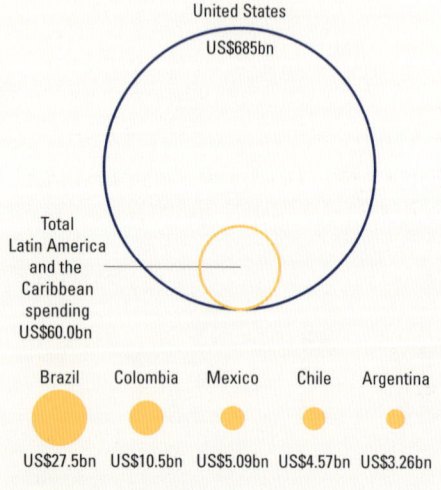

Latin America and the Caribbean defence spending, 2019 – top 5, including US foreign military financing

United States US$685bn
Total Latin America and the Caribbean spending US$60.0bn

Brazil US$27.5bn
Colombia US$10.5bn
Mexico US$5.09bn
Chile US$4.57bn
Argentina US$3.26bn

Active military personnel – top 10
(15,000 per unit)

Brazil 367,000
Colombia 293,200
Mexico 236,450
Venezuela 123,000
Peru 81,000
Chile 77,200
Argentina 74,200
Dominican Republic 56,050
Cuba 49,000
Ecuador 40,250

Global total 19,852,000
Regional total 1,523,000

Regional submarine inventories, 2019
(1 per unit)

Peru 6
Brazil 5
Chile 4
Colombia 4
Ecuador 2
Venezuela 2

Regional defence policy and economics 390 ▶
Armed forces data section 398 ▶
Arms procurements and deliveries 442 ▶

Venezuela: national military exercises, 2019

Fighter, fighter/ground-attack and attack aircraft fleets, 2009
(20 per unit)

✈✈✈✈✈	Argentina 99
✈	Bolivia 15
✈✈✈✈✈✈✈✈✈✈✈✈✈✈✈✈	Brazil 316
✈✈✈✈	Chile 75
✈✈	Colombia 49
✈✈	Cuba 31
✈✈✈	Ecuador 59
✈	El Salvador 5
✈	Guatemala 2
✈	Honduras 16
✈	Mexico 10
✈✈	Peru 32
✈	Uruguay 16
✈✈✈	Venezuela 55

Fighter, fighter/ground-attack and attack aircraft fleets, 2019
(20 per unit)

✈✈	Argentina 30
	Bolivia 0
✈✈✈✈✈	Brazil 97
✈✈✈✈	Chile 74
✈✈	Colombia 34
✈✈✈	Cuba 44
✈✈	Ecuador 25
✈	El Salvador 14
	Guatemala 1
✈	Honduras 17
	Mexico 0
✈✈✈✈	Peru 67
✈	Uruguay 12
✈✈	Venezuela 40

Latin America and the Caribbean

Security challenges in the region in 2019 were broadly similar to those in previous years, with responses to criminal activity, including narco-trafficking, absorbing significant attention. However, this year there were further instances of armed forces assuming internal-security roles, while governments in some states also had to contend with a range of protest movements.

Regional developments

The effects of the economic and political crisis in **Venezuela** continue to occupy the attention of regional governments and their security forces. This is not only because of the presence in Venezuelan territory of non-state groups – the Lima Group said in May that President Nicolás Maduro was protecting 'terrorist groups' – but also because of the movement of Venezuelan citizens. According to the United Nations, as of November 2019 around 4.5 million Venezuelans had left the country, mostly to neighbouring states – the population movement constituted the 'largest exodus in South American history', according to a UN report. More than one million are living in Colombia. In a speech to the UN in September, Colombia's President Iván Duque alleged that insurgents from the National Liberation Army, a Colombian insurgent group, were being sheltered in Venezuela.

President Maduro, meanwhile, looked by the end of the year to have survived perhaps the most serious threat to his leadership since he took power. This came in January when opposition politician Juan Guaidó, president of Venezuela's National Assembly, declared himself acting president, following protests against Maduro's inauguration after elections in 2018 that were widely alleged to be deeply flawed. Attempts to encourage members of the armed forces to help unseat Maduro led to some defections, but the high command remained loyal.

In **Colombia**, the armed forces continued in 2019 to tackle small groups of remaining dissidents and other forms of criminality, as well as supporting the security forces. After the 2016 peace deal signed in Havana with the Revolutionary Armed Forces of Colombia (FARC), the armed forces had been looking to future roles, structures and capabilities beyond those required for internal-security operations. However, the decision by a FARC splinter group, the FARC-EP, in August 2019 to resume their military campaign led Colombia's armed forces to refocus on the internal-security challenge.

Nonetheless, the outward vision remains. It is designed to grow international ties and allow Colombia's armed forces to become a security provider, as much as it is intended to help them hone military skills and gain greater experience. For instance, for the second year in a row, Colombia sent its sole KC-767 tanker to the US to take part in exercise *Red Flag*. (In 2018 it also sent *Kfir* combat aircraft.) According to US sources, Colombia's tanker was the only one capable of refuelling US EA-18G *Growler* aircraft during the 2019 exercise.

President Jair Bolsonaro assumed office in **Brazil** in January 2019. The armed forces remain engaged on a modernisation and re-equipment drive, with notable capability acquisitions planned. The delayed PROSUB programme, to deliver four conventional and one nuclear-powered submarine, finally saw the first boat enter the water in December 2018, when both Bolsonaro and his predecessor, Michel Temer, attended the launch of the *Riachuelo*, a *Scorpène*-class diesel-electric boat built in Brazil. In September it was announced that Brazil would acquire 28 Embraer KC-390 transport aircraft. Portugal is also buying the aircraft, which is being marketed globally by Embraer in conjunction with Boeing. The KC-390 will assist Brazil's armed forces in internal mobility tasks. In August, Bolsonaro signed a Law and Order Guarantee to enable military deployments to the Amazon region, amid widespread forest fires there. In late 2019, plans were announced to restructure military career, pay and pension provisions.

Chile's armed forces were deployed internally in late 2019 after unrest broke out following protests reportedly sparked by a rise in Metro fares in Santiago. A state of emergency was declared by the government in mid-October and troops deployed in Santiago. Significant infrastructure damage was caused. By mid-November, and amid criticism – some of which the authorities contested – of the security forces' response, the government announced it would hold a constitutional referendum in 2020. As of late November, with unrest persisting, the Senate had approved the use of the armed forces to protect critical infrastructure.

In early 2019, the Piñera administration published changes to military retirement ages, raising the service limit for officers from 38 to 41 years of age and from 35 to 40 years of age for NCOs. This was intended to retain skills within the armed forces and stress progression based on merit and qualification rather than necessarily on seniority. The regulations for pension benefits were also adjusted, raising the age at which a full pension could be claimed from 30 to 35 years and the age at which a minimum pension could be claimed from 20 to 23 years.

It was reported in late 2019 that the army was requesting funds for the procurement of *Piranha* wheeled armoured fighting vehicles, in order to convert some motorised infantry units into mechanised infantry. But perhaps the most noteworthy structural change in Chilean defence in 2019 came with the long-discussed replacement of the Copper Law.

In **Argentina**, a legislative commission reported in mid-year on the loss of the submarine *San Juan* (a German-built Type-TR-1700 boat) and its 44-strong crew in November 2017. It said that organisational failings and low budgets (which have reportedly affected maintenance, weapons, training, structure and operational capacity) were contributory factors in the loss of the submarine, though it reportedly attributed the proximate cause for the loss to a fault in the battery compartment.

In October 2019, Mauricio Macri was defeated by Alberto Fernández in Argentina's presidential election. Former president Cristina Fernández de Kirchner was his running mate. Before leaving office, the Macri administration was likely to publish details on changes to operational concepts proposed in July 2018, reorienting the armed forces away from a focus on external threats and legislation that restricted them to this task. A notable element of these changes was that the armed forces were now able to more easily deploy on internal tasks, as evidenced by deployments in 2019 on *Operation Northern Frontier*. The precise defence-policy direction of the Fernández administration remained unclear at the time of writing, including that relating to foreign defence ties, though it was reported that a review of the just-enacted changes to operational concepts might take place.

Mexico: military developments

Andrés Manuel López Obrador (aka AMLO) assumed office as Mexican president on 1 December 2018, after a landslide election victory in July. His campaign called for Mexico's 'Fourth Transformation' (4T), following three earlier historically significant episodes: independence from Spain in 1810, the civil war that led to the re-establishment of the Republic in 1857 (the Reform War) and the revolution of 1910. This programme reportedly aspires to end corruption, grow the economy, build infrastructure, end violence and tackle poverty.

During the previous two administrations, of presidents Felipe Calderón (2006–12) and Enrique Peña Nieto (2012–18), the armed forces were used to tackle organised crime, while at the same time investing in their conventional military capabilities. Over this period, the air force acquired a range of assets including a new ground-based air-surveillance radar network, a light turbo-prop aircraft (the T-6C *Texan* II), a *King Air* intelligence, surveillance and reconnaissance aircraft, and transport aviation, both fixed- and rotary-wing fleets. The army has also now established the military police, a force which is focused on tackling the threat from the cartels, and procured a range of associated equipment, including protected vehicles. The navy launched a fleet-modernisation programme centred on the local production of a POLA-class frigate, as well as *Oaxaca*-class offshore-patrol vessels (OPVs), coastal-patrol vessels, landing ships and interceptor craft, while the naval-aviation service procured T-6C *Texan* IIs and *King Airs*, as well as light transport and maritime-patrol aircraft.

New roles

AMLO had been a critic of the Mexican armed forces during the three previous presidential campaigns (in 2006, 2012 and 2018). However, his tone softened when he became president-elect and future commander in chief. During the first few months of his administration, AMLO deployed thousands of troops in support of his plan to improve protection for oil and gas pipelines. The army and navy were also tasked with establishing a fuel-transportation programme, using fuel tankers sourced from military and commercial fleets after pipelines were closed due to illicit extraction by criminals, in January and February 2019. In addition, AMLO has tasked the armed forces with a variety of non-traditional missions, including the transformation of the air force's largest air base, Santa Lucia, into Mexico City's new international airport, after he cancelled the construction of a new airport, while the navy has additionally been tasked with removing sargassum seaweed from the Gulf of Mexico coastline.

AMLO has stated that there is no direct conventional threat to Mexico. He has said that the armed forces will therefore still be used to support a variety of internal-security roles and that in the (unlikely) event of aggression by another state, national defence would be undertaken by the 'Mexican people'.

National Guard

Upon assuming office, AMLO directed the Ministry of National Defence (comprising the Secretaría de la Defensa Nacional, SEDENA, the army and the air force), as well as the Ministry of the Navy (Secretaría de Marina, SEMAR) and the new Secretariat of Public Security (Secretaría de Seguridad y Protección Ciudadana, SSPyC), to support the creation of the National Guard. It was established under the SSPyC's civilian political leadership on 26 March 2019. Army Brigadier-General Luis Rodríguez Bucio was selected to form, train and command the force. The National Guard's first mission was to deploy 6,000 personnel on immigration-enforcement duties in June 2019 to curtail the flow of Central American immigrants on Mexico's southern and northern borders.

Defence budget

Mexico's defence budget is expected to remain relatively stable, with any slight increases used to fund niche procurement programmes. Though it is unlikely to be funded in the short term, the army announced as part of its 2019–24 defence plan the requirement for an additional 1,300 HMMWVs, as well as an initial 42 6x6 or 8x8 armoured vehicles and an unknown number of 105 mm artillery pieces. The army also plans to relocate its defence-industrial factories to a new complex in Puebla city. The air force has announced plans for a study on the replacement of its F-5E/F *Tiger* II combat aircraft after 2024. The navy expects to continue its fleet-modernisation programme and has requested funding for a further three POLA-class frigates (based on the Damen SIGMA 10514 design) and four *Oaxaca*-class OPVs, as well as the construction of small auxiliary vessels.

Colombia–Venezuela border crisis

The situation on the Colombia–Venezuela border has in 2018–19 become a key strategic issue in Latin America, because of the humanitarian crisis in Venezuela, the deterioration of the security situation within Colombia, and growing tension between the Maduro regime in Caracas and the administration of President Iván Duque in Bogota. Indeed, some analysts perceive a risk that the border area could become a de facto ungoverned space.

By November 2019, the United Nations estimated that 4.5 million Venezuelans had left the country, fleeing the economic collapse, political repression and criminal violence. There were in 2019 approximately 1.4m living in Colombia alone. The continued movement of Venezuelan migrants into Colombian territory has led to increased challenges around providing for them. There have also been reports of increased security problems, including cross-border criminality. The Colombian government and international agencies have enacted measures to cope, including in education and medical care, but it remains a significant financial challenge for Colombia. The sheer volume of the population flow has perhaps inevitably meant that some of these people remain vulnerable. The challenge for regional governments will likely be in future not just providing for immediate requirements but also planning for the long-term needs of these populations.

Venezuelan exodus

There is little sign that Venezuela's political and economic situation will improve to such a degree as to stem the flow of Venezuelan citizens to Colombia and other Latin American countries. After Colombia, Peru has the greatest number of Venezuelan refugees and migrants, numbering just under 800,000 as of June 2019. Meanwhile, according to OPEC, Venezuelan oil production fell to 687,000 barrels per day in October 2019, down from 735,000 in August 2019 (Venezuelan reporting suggested slightly higher rates), in the wake of continued US sanctions that not only banned the acquisition of Venezuelan oil by US refineries but also extended to third-party actors engaged in business with Caracas.

The strategy of the Venezuelan opposition to alleviate the humanitarian situation and gain legitimacy by introducing international aid into Venezuela failed after the Maduro government closed access routes into the country and partially destroyed aid deliveries in February 2019. Two months later, the opposition suffered another blow when a military rebellion against the regime could not mobilise enough support and was suppressed by Maduro loyalists. These failures have left the regime pursuing a familiar policy direction and an opposition unable to implement an effective strategy to remove Maduro from power. The risk is that the continuation of this situation may lead more Venezuelans to decide that emigration is their only option.

At the same time, however, Colombia is facing security challenges from the criminal and guerrilla groups that operate in the border area with Venezuela. These groups include the National Liberation Army (ELN), the dissident Maoist group commonly known as Pelusos and several groups of former FARC militants who rejected the peace agreement with the Colombian government. These criminal actors compete and cooperate in order to exert control in the border area and profit from drug and human trafficking, smuggling, extortion and other illegal activities.

Colombian armed groups in Venezuela

Support from the Venezuelan regime has been critical in enabling these Colombian guerrilla groups to survive. This has been the case for the ELN, which five years ago was almost defunct. The group can now operate across the country and execute highly visible terrorist attacks in Colombian cities such as Barranquilla and Bogota.

In August, a new FARC dissident group was announced in Venezuela by Luciano Marin (aka Iván Márquez), a former FARC leader. Marin's decision to abandon the peace process was a political blow for President Duque, who had promised to continue implementing the peace agreement with FARC.

Meanwhile, reported connections between Colombian insurgent groups and the Venezuelan regime, analysts contend, may have the effect of transforming them into transnational organisations. At the UN in August, Duque said Venezuela was a 'sanctuary for terrorists and drug smugglers'. The ELN and FARC dissident groups are understood to be recruiting dispossessed Venezuelans in their home country, as well as in Colombia. Both are also running significant illegal money-making schemes in Venezuela, including drug trafficking and illegal mining.

The leaders of both countries have provided support for the other's opponents, raising tensions. President Maduro in July said that FARC leaders Iván Márquez and Jesús Santrich were 'welcome in Venezuela'. Meanwhile, the Duque administration has recognized Juan Guaidó as Venezuela's leader. In 2019, Venezuela conducted the *Venezuela Soberanía y Paz* (*Venezuela Sovereignty and Peace*) military exercise, which, even though the economic collapse has significantly affected military capabilities, was presented as a show of force.

Shortly afterwards, Colombia began a diplomatic offensive and a majority of the members of the Organisation of American States voted to invoke an 'Organ of Consultation' under the Rio treaty, a possible early step towards collective action. United States Secretary of State Mike Pompeo said that Venezuela's troop movements were 'bellicose', while Elliott Abrams, US special envoy for Venezuela, said that if cross-border attacks took place from Venezuela, 'we can expect Colombians to react. And obviously, we would fully support Colombia in that situation.' Amid general diplomatic isolation, the Maduro regime retained close contacts with Russia, which was reported to have provided financial support in 2019. Russian military advisers remain in the country, ostensibly to provide technical support for ongoing military-equipment contracts.

Venezuela: the role of the armed forces

Both President Nicolás Maduro and the Head of National Assembly and self-proclaimed president Juan Guaidó have in 2019 been striving to exert influence over the country's armed forces. However, although there were some defections shortly after Guaidó called on 30 April for the ouster of Maduro, the senior military leadership remained behind Maduro. The armed forces' loyalty will be a determining factor in the continuing survival of the regime.

Chávez era

The armed forces gained greater influence during the presidency of Hugo Chávez, from 1999 to 2013. Chávez, a military officer by profession, enhanced the armed forces' political and economic role, in 1999 amending the constitution to revoke the law preventing military involvement in Venezuela's political life and granting active-duty members of the armed forces the right to vote. He then cemented the support of senior officers by creating several military-run state companies across different sectors, ranging from defence production to mineral extraction, and further consolidated his power by granting the president the right to unilaterally nominate, promote and remove military officers.

In the 2005 Venezuelan Military Doctrine, Chávez officially introduced the concept of 'integral defence', extending responsibility for the protection and safeguarding of the country to the whole of Venezuelan society, while expanding the armed forces' broader role in society and industry. This 'civil–military alliance' was expanded in 2008 with the creation of the Bolivarian National Militia, a civilian armed paramilitary body that is integrated as a branch of the armed forces.

Maduro's approach

The support of the armed forces has been crucial to Chávez's successor, Nicolás Maduro, since he assumed the presidency after Chávez's death. His presidency has been characterised by the progressive collapse of the economy and by a growing authoritarianism that has increased discontent among the population and led over 4.5 million Venezuelans to flee the country.

Maduro has, like Chávez, favoured senior military leaders. Between 2013 and 2017, the defence ministry created 12 new military-run defence companies, including the Military Company of Mining and Oil and Gas Industries Ltd, guaranteeing revenue from the mineral-extraction and petroleum-refining sectors for senior officers. Reportedly, 60 of Venezuela's 567 state-run companies are controlled by the military. In addition, between 2013 and 2016, Maduro consolidated the armed forces' political influence by nominating ten former officers as cabinet ministers. He then reshuffled the entire chiefs of staff committee and nominated new commanders for all eight strategic regions.

As well as the cadre of senior military officers, Maduro can count on the support of paramilitary groups, mainly the Bolivarian National Militia, party militias (the so-called *colectivos*), and several criminal gangs and organisations. Over the past few years, the government has expanded the Bolivarian Militia, which according to the president's social-media channels now has almost two million members. Furthermore, in 2016, a presidential decree started a process giving public-order roles to paramilitary groups and has recently integrated the first Bolivarian Militia contingent into the National Guard. By empowering the internal-security forces and voluntary civilian militias, Maduro has been widening his support base. Indeed, the expanded Bolivarian Militia now outnumbers the comparatively small but better-equipped armed forces, which is currently estimated to comprise about 123,000 personnel.

Growing discontent

However, analysts understand that discontent is increasing among lower- and middle-ranking service personnel, who have felt the effects of Venezuela's economic and social crisis. For instance, salaries have shrunk in actual value because of hyperinflation. This is arguably one of the factors behind the increase in desertions across the Brazilian and Colombian borders, which reached 4,000 troops in 2018 and more than 2,000 in the first months of 2019 alone, according to Bogota and Brasilia.

Opposition leader Guaidó has tried to leverage this discontent to win support from armed-forces personnel. In 2019, he offered amnesty to any member of the armed forces or police who defected from the regime. According to government sources, several coup attempts were foiled in 2019, including one organised by a group of soldiers in the Caracas neighbourhood of Altamira. To prevent such anti-regime activity, the government has systematically infiltrated the military with local intelligence agents, as well as members of the Cuban intelligence services. Some personnel have also been dismissed, and others imprisoned. The international NGO Human Rights Watch reported that several Venezuelan soldiers were detained and tortured by members of the General Directorate of Military Counterintelligence or by the Bolivarian National Intelligence Service.

Military capabilities

Venezuela's economic crisis has not only negatively impacted conditions for military personnel, but has caused a deterioration in military capabilities, affecting maintenance and replacement programmes.

Nevertheless, Russia has continued to provide training and technical support to Caracas, including personnel to carry out maintenance on Russian-origin military hardware. In March and September 2019, Russian Il-62 transport aircraft reportedly disembarked military specialists at Simón Bolívar International Airport in Caracas, though how many may have remained in the country or were instead part of maintenance contracts remained unclear. Russia has also been taking part in joint military exercises with the Venezuelan armed forces, including in areas such as air combat, air defence and logistics.

Military exercises have increased in frequency in recent years, in a bid to boost the readiness of at least some front-line units. One such exercise took place in September 2019 in the Amazonas, Tachira and Zulia regions. Just a few days later, in response to Colombian President Iván Duque's accusation that Caracas is harbouring FARC terrorists in Venezuelan territory, Maduro declared an alert on the border.

The defections and revolts that took place in 2019 have not been significant enough to undermine Maduro's authority, even if they indicate that military morale may be fragile. The government has so far succeeded in containing discontent in the lower ranks through punitive measures and in securing the loyalty of the senior officers through economic inducements. At the same time, despite Venezuela's economic crisis, the government has been trying to increase the readiness of some of its units, perhaps as much for strategic messaging purposes as actual military utility.

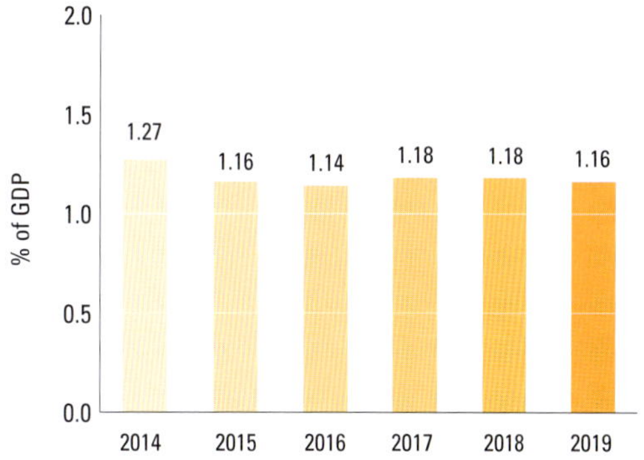

DEFENCE ECONOMICS

Macroeconomics

According to the International Monetary Fund (IMF), regional economies grew by 0.2% between 2018 and 2019. Excluding Venezuela, however, raises this number to 0.9%. The economic crisis in Venezuela continued in 2019 with GDP contracting by 35%, following on from an 18% contraction in 2018. Although the region's overall economic situation has improved compared to 2016, when GDP fell by 0.6%, it nonetheless constitutes a slowdown when compared to growth levels seen in 2017 (1.2%) and 2018 (1.0%).

While forecasts for the coming years are more positive (1.8% in 2020), these are at risk from mounting regional political uncertainty. This is particularly the case in Bolivia and Chile, where unrest broke out at the end of 2019. In Chile, demonstrations were focused on social and economic issues, while in Bolivia protests took place both before and after the ouster of President Evo Morales; the former protests by opponents alleging that Morales had rigged the election, while after his ouster his supporters also took to the streets. Meanwhile, the continuing political crisis in Nicaragua contributed to investors' lack of confidence in Latin America and the Caribbean. These events, when combined with economic difficulties in Argentina and Brazil (the region's largest economies), as well as global trade uncertainties, mean that expectations for robust growth will not necessarily be met in the near future.

For the time being, the effects on the region of the US–China trade dispute remain indirect. According to the World Bank, the volume of regional exports has increased since early 2018, and trade diversion after the hike in tariffs between Beijing and Washington may benefit some Latin American states. Figures from the United Nations Conference on Trade and Development show that as a result of US–China tariffs, Mexico is likely to benefit from a 5.9% boost in exports and Brazil a 3.8% boost. In the first half of 2019, Mexico became the United States' largest trading partner, before China.

Latin American states rely to some extent on commodity prices, including metals exporters (such as Chile and Peru) and agricultural producers (Brazil and Argentina). Of Colombia's exports in 2017, 47.5% were related to minerals and 16.8% to agriculture. However, in the first half of the year, extractive-industry prices remained volatile, while those of coffee, soybean, oil and sugar markedly declined. The

▲ Figure 24 **Latin America and the Caribbean regional defence expenditure** as % of GDP

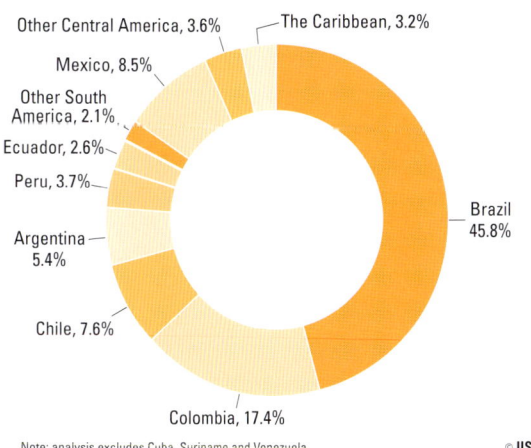

▼ Figure 23 **Latin America and the Caribbean defence spending by country and sub-region, 2019**

Note: analysis excludes Cuba, Suriname and Venezuela © IISS

▲ Map 13 **Latin America and the Caribbean regional defence spending**[1]

end of high oil and gas prices at the turn of 2014–15 precipitated Venezuela's current economic turmoil. The situation has escalated to a humanitarian crisis, with shortages of electricity, water, food and medicine. As a result, over 10% of the country's population has fled, in large part to neighbouring countries, in turn taking a toll on these states' public finances.

Defence economics

The economic and social challenges across the continent mean that defence spending is generally not a public-policy priority, all the more so in the absence of obvious external security threats to any of the major states. Internal-security challenges remain acute, though these do not require the same level of investment as conventional military threats. Altogether, states in Latin America and the Caribbean spent 1.16% of GDP on defence in 2019, meaning that of all regions worldwide, it disbursed the second-lowest proportion of its wealth on defence, with only sub-Saharan Africa spending less (at 0.99%).

Between 2018 and 2019, regional defence spending

fell by 0.9% in real terms. However, spending increased in Brazil and Colombia. Brazil, already possessing the region's largest defence budget, saw spending increase by almost US$450 million, when measured in 2015 constant US dollars. Colombia, with the second-largest defence budget in the region, saw funds increase by almost US$300m. Although these two states accounted for more than 60% of regional defence outlays, it was not enough to offset defence-budget decreases elsewhere, notably in Mexico (down by US$430m) and Argentina (US$760m). Publicly available information suggests that the downturn will be even more pronounced in 2020. Argentina announced that its 2020 defence budget would be P205.13 billion, compared to P158.32bn in 2019. Although this appears to be a significant boost, currency conversion rates mean that it is a decline of 14% (from US$3.26bn to US$2.81bn), when measured in nominal US dollars.

Although Brazil's President Jair Bolsonaro is a former military officer, the armed forces were not insulated in his administration's first budget. Indeed, Brasilia is looking to reduce the defence budget to R68.34bn in 2020, down from R107.03bn in 2019. In current US dollars, this would mean a fall of 38%, from US$27.5bn to US$16.9bn. Within this, the investment budget will reduce by 33%, falling from US$1.61bn to US$1.08bn, which could lead to procurement delays or changes to procurement orders, such as for the Saab *Gripen* combat aircraft or the KC-390 transport aircraft. This follows a budget freeze imposed in 2019 on several ministries, including the defence ministry, in an effort to rein in the public deficit in the face of lower tax revenue.

These cases highlight overall low procurement budgets in the region. In Colombia, investment expenses accounted for only 3.5% of the total defence budget in 2019 (US$10.45bn, excluding the US foreign military financing programme allocation of US$20m). In Chile, where defence procurement had been in large part covered by 'Copper Law' allocations, a dedicated fund for arms acquisitions was instead established. The objective of this reform was to improve transparency on how these funds are spent, as the National Congress did not have oversight of funds resulting from the Copper Law.

Antigua and Barbuda ATG

East Caribbean Dollar EC$		2018	2019	2020
GDP	EC$	4.35bn	4.56bn	
	US$	1.61bn	1.69bn	
per capita	US$	17,464	18,109	
Growth	%	7.4	4.0	
Inflation	%	1.2	1.6	
Def bdgt [a]	EC$	19.2m	19.5m	
	US$	7.1m	7.2m	
US$1=EC$		2.70	2.70	

[a] Budget for the Ministry of Legal Affairs, Public Safety, Immigration & Labour

Real-terms defence budget trend (US$m, constant 2015)

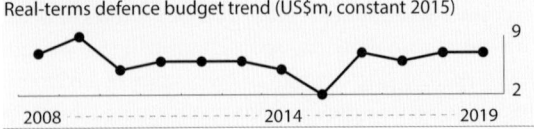

Population   97,031

Age	0–14	15–19	20–24	25–29	30–64	65 plus
Male	11.5%	4.0%	4.1%	3.6%	20.2%	3.7%
Female	11.2%	4.0%	4.2%	3.9%	24.6%	4.9%

Capabilities

The Antigua and Barbuda Defence Force (ABDF) focuses on internal security and disaster relief, and also contributes to regional counter-narcotics efforts. It comprises a light-infantry element, which carries out internal-security duties, and a coastguard, which is tasked with fishery protection and counter-narcotics. Antigua and Barbuda is a member of the Caribbean Community and the Caribbean Regional Security System. The country maintains defence ties with the UK and sends personnel to train in the US. The ABDF participates in US SOUTHCOM's annual *Tradewinds* disaster-relief exercise, though it has no independent capacity to deploy forces other than in its immediate neighbourhood, most recently for disaster-relief efforts in Dominica. The equipment inventory is limited to small arms and light weapons (there is a range of mainly soft-skinned vehicles), while the coastguard maintains ex-US patrol vessels and a number of smaller boats. Aside from limited maintenance facilities, there is no significant indigenous defence industry.

ACTIVE 180 (Army 130 Coast Guard 50)
(all services form combined Antigua and Barbuda Defence Force)

RESERVE 80 (Joint 80)

ORGANISATIONS BY SERVICE

Army 130
FORCES BY ROLE
MANOEUVRE
  Light
  1 inf bn HQ
  1 inf coy
COMBAT SERVICE SUPPORT
  1 spt gp (1 engr unit, 1 med unit)

Coast Guard 50
EQUIPMENT BY TYPE
PATROL AND COASTAL COMBATANTS • PB 2: 1
Dauntless; 1 *Swift*

Argentina ARG

Argentine Peso P		2018	2019	2020
GDP	P	14.6tr	21.6tr	
	US$	519bn	445bn	
per capita	US$	11,658	9,888	
Growth	%	-2.5	-3.1	
Inflation	%	34.3	54.4	
Def bdgt	P	121bn	158bn	205bn
	US$	4.32bn	3.26bn	
US$1=P		28.12	48.50	

Real-terms defence budget trend (US$bn, constant 2015)

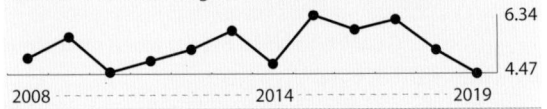

Population   45,089,492

Age	0–14	15–19	20–24	25–29	30–64	65 plus
Male	12.5%	4.0%	3.8%	3.8%	20.4%	5.0%
Female	11.7%	3.8%	3.6%	3.7%	20.8%	6.9%

Capabilities

Argentina's armed forces have sufficient training and equipment to fulfil internal-security tasks, although any power-projection ambition is limited by lack of funding. The armed forces principally focus on border security, surveillance and counter-narcotics operations, in part due to the increase in drug-trafficking activity in and around the country, and cooperate with Bolivia and Paraguay. In 2018, the government approved a decree allowing greater latitude in deploying the armed forces for internal-security purposes, including logistic support in border areas. Military cooperation with the US centres on enhancing readiness, as well as disaster response, border security and peacekeeping. The armed forces participate in multinational exercises and bilateral peacekeeping exercises with neighbour Chile. There are limited deployment capabilities, and the equipment inventory is increasingly obsolete, with modernisation hampered by limited funding. The air force faces significant equipment-availability challenges and the navy has seen its capability decline in areas such as anti-submarine warfare, mine warfare and airborne early warning. Argentina possesses an indigenous defence-manufacturing capacity covering land, sea and air systems, although industry fortunes have dipped in recent years because of lack of investment. State-owned aviation firm FAdeA has aircraft-maintenance capabilities, but is reliant on external assistance for some manufacturing tasks.

ACTIVE 74,200 (Army 42,800 Navy 18,500 Air 12,900) **Paramilitary 31,250**

ORGANISATIONS BY SERVICE

Army 42,800
Regt and gp are usually bn-sized

FORCES BY ROLE
SPECIAL FORCES
1 SF gp
MANOEUVRE
Mechanised
1 (1st) div (1 armd bde (4 tk regt, 1 mech inf regt, 1 SP arty gp, 1 cbt engr bn, 1 int coy, 1 sigs sqn, 1 log coy), 1 (3rd) jungle bde (2 jungle inf regt, 2 jungle inf coy, 1 arty gp, 1 engr bn, 1 int coy, 1 sigs coy, 1 log coy, 1 med coy); 1 (12th) jungle bde (2 jungle inf regt, 1 jungle inf coy, 1 arty gp, 1 engr bn, 1 int coy, 1 sigs coy, 1 log coy, 1 med coy), 2 engr bn, 1 sigs bn, 1 log coy)

1 (3rd) div (1 armd bde (1 armd recce sqn, 3 tk regt, 1 mech inf regt, 1 SP arty gp, 1 cbt engr sqn, 1 int coy, 1 sigs sqn, 1 log coy); 1 mech bde (1 armd recce regt, 1 tk regt, 2 mech inf regt, 1 SP arty gp, 1 cbt engr bn, 1 int coy, 1 sigs coy, 1 log coy); 1 mech bde (1 armd recce sqn, 1 tk regt, 2 mech inf regt, 1 SP arty gp, 1 cbt engr bn, 1 int coy, 1 sigs coy, 1 log coy); 1 int bn, 1 sigs bn, 1 log coy, 1 AD gp (2 AD bn))

1 (Rapid Deployment) force (1 mech bde (1 armd recce regt, 3 mech inf regt, 1 arty gp, 1 cbt engr coy, 1 int coy, 1 sigs coy, 1 log coy); 1 AB bde (1 recce tp, 2 para regt, 1 arty gp, 1 cbt engr coy, 1 sigs coy, 1 log coy))

Light
1 (2nd) mtn inf div (1 mtn inf bde (1 armd recce regt, 3 mtn inf regt, 2 arty gp, 1 cbt engr bn, 1 sigs coy, 1 log coy); 1 mtn inf bde (1 armd recce regt, 3 mtn inf regt, 1 arty gp, 1 cbt engr bn, 1 sigs coy, 1 log coy); 1 mtn inf bde (1 armd recce bn, 2 mtn inf regt, 2 arty gp, 1 cbt engr bn, 1 sigs coy, 1 construction coy, 1 log coy), 1 arty gp, 1 AD gp, 1 sigs bn)

1 mot cav regt (presidential escort)

Air Manoeuvre
1 air aslt regt
COMBAT SUPPORT
1 arty gp (bn)
1 engr bn
1 sigs gp (1 EW bn, 1 sigs bn, 1 maint bn)
1 sigs bn
1 sigs coy
COMBAT SERVICE SUPPORT
5 maint bn
HELICOPTER
1 avn gp (bde) (1 avn bn, 1 hel bn)
EQUIPMENT BY TYPE
ARMOURED FIGHTING VEHICLES
MBT 231: 225 TAM, 6 TAM S21
LT TK 117: 107 SK 105A1 *Kuerassier*; 6 SK-105A2 *Kuerassier*; 4 *Patagón*
RECCE 47 AML-90
IFV 232: 118 VCTP (incl variants); 114 M113A2 (20mm cannon)
APC 278
  APC (T) 274: 70 M113A1-ACAV; 204 M113A2
  APC (W) 4 WZ-551B1
ENGINEERING & MAINTENANCE VEHICLES
ARV *Greif*
ANTI-TANK/ANTI-INFRASTRUCTURE
MSL • **SP** 3 M1025 HMMWV with TOW-2A
RCL 105mm 150 M-1968

ARTILLERY 1,108
SP 155mm 42: 23 AMX F3; 19 VCA 155 *Palmaria*
TOWED 172: **105mm** 64 Model 56 pack howitzer; **155mm** 108: 28 CITEFA M-77/CITEFA M-81; 80 SOFMA L-33
MRL 8: **105mm** 4 SLAM *Pampero*; **127mm** 4 CP-30
MOR 886: **81mm** 492; **SP 107mm** 25 M106A2; **120mm** 330 Brandt; **SP 120mm** 39 TAM-VCTM
AIRCRAFT
TPT • **Light** 14: 1 Beech 80 *Queen Air*; 3 C-212-200 *Aviocar*; 2 Cessna 208EX *Grand Caravan*; 1 Cessna 500 *Citation* (survey); 1 Cessna 550 *Citation Bravo*; 3 DA42 (to be converted to ISR role); 2 DHC-6 *Twin Otter*; 1 Sabreliner 75A (*Gaviao* 75A)
TRG 5 T-41 *Mescalero*
HELICOPTERS
MRH 5: 4 SA315B *Lama*; 1 Z-11
TPT 67: **Medium** 3 AS332B *Super Puma*; **Light** 64: 1 Bell 212; 25 Bell 205 (UH-1H *Iroquois* – 6 armed); 5 Bell 206B3; 13 UH-1H-II *Huey* II; 20 AB206B1
AIR DEFENCE
SAM • **Point-defence** RBS-70
GUNS • **TOWED** 229: **20mm** 200 GAI-B01; **30mm** 21 HS L81; **35mm** 8 GDF Oerlikon (*Skyguard* fire control)

Navy 18,500
Commands: Surface Fleet, Submarines, Naval Avn, Marines
FORCES BY ROLE
SPECIAL FORCES
1 (diver) SF gp
EQUIPMENT BY TYPE
SUBMARINES • TACTICAL • SSK 1:
1 *Santa Cruz* (GER TR-1700) with 6 single 533mm TT with SST-4 HWT (undergoing MLU)
(1 *Salta* (GER T-209/1100) (non-operational since 2013) with 8 single 533mm TT with Mk 37/SST-4 HWT)
PRINCIPAL SURFACE COMBATANTS 11
DESTROYERS • **DDH** 1 *Hercules* (UK Type-42 – utilised as a fast troop-transport ship), with 1 114mm gun (capacity 2 SH-3H *Sea King* hel)
FRIGATES 10
  FFGHM 4 *Almirante Brown* (GER MEKO 360) with 2 quad lnchr with MM40 *Exocet* AShM, 1 octuple *Albatros* lnchr with *Aspide* SAM, 2 triple ILAS-3 (B-515) 324mm TT with A244/S LWT, 1 127mm gun (capacity 1 AS555 *Fennec* hel)
  FFGH 6 *Espora* (GER MEKO 140) with 2 twin lnchr with MM38 *Exocet* AShM, 2 triple ILAS-3 (B-515) 324mm ASTT with A244/S LWT, 1 76mm gun (capacity 1 AS555 *Fennec* hel)
PATROL AND COASTAL COMBATANTS 13
CORVETTES • **FSG** 1 *Drummond* (FRA A-69) (2 laid up in 2019) with 2 twin lnchr with MM38 *Exocet* AShM, 2 triple ILAS-3 (B-515) 324mm ASTT with A244/S LWT, 1 100mm gun
PSO 3:
  2 *Irigoyen* (ex-US *Cherokee*)
  1 *Teniente Olivieri* (ex-US oilfield tug)

PCO 1 *Murature* (ex-US *King* – trg/river-patrol role) with 2 105mm gun
PCGT 1 *Intrepida* (GER Lurssen 45m) with 2 single lnchr with MM38 *Exocet* AShM, 2 single 533mm TT with SST-4 HWT, 1 76mm gun
PCC 1 *Intrepida* (GER Lurssen 45m) with 1 76mm gun
PB 6: 4 *Baradero* (*Dabur*); 2 *Punta Mogotes* (ex-US *Point*)
AMPHIBIOUS 6 LCVP
LOGISTICS AND SUPPORT 17
  ABU 3 *Red*
  AFS 4 *Puerto Argentina* (ex-RUS *Neftegaz*)
  AGB 1 *Almirante Irizar* (damaged by fire in 2007; returned to service in mid-2017)
  AGHS 3: 1 *Austral*; 1 *Cormoran*; 1 *Puerto Deseado* (ice-breaking capability, used for polar research)
  AGOR 1 *Commodoro Rivadavia*
  AK 3 *Costa Sur* (capacity 4 LCVP)
  AOR 1 *Patagonia* (FRA *Durance*) with 1 hel platform
  AXS 1 *Libertad*

Naval Aviation 2,000

EQUIPMENT BY TYPE
AIRCRAFT 25 combat capable
  FGA 7 *Super Etendard* (9 more in store)
  ATK 1 AU-23 *Turbo Porter*
  ASW 7: 3 S-2T *Tracker*‡; 4 P-3B *Orion*‡
  TPT • **Light** 7 Beech 200F/M *King Air*
  TRG 10 T-34C *Turbo Mentor**
HELICOPTERS
  ASW 2 SH-3H (ASH-3H) *Sea King*
  MRH 4 AS555 *Fennec*
  TPT • **Medium** 4 UH-3H *Sea King*
AIR-LAUNCHED MISSILES
  AAM • **IR** R-550 *Magic*
  AShM AM39 *Exocet*

Marines 2,500

FORCES BY ROLE
MANOEUVRE
  Amphibious
  1 (fleet) force (1 cdo gp, 1 (AAV) amph bn, 1 mne bn, 1 arty bn, 1 ADA bn)
  1 (fleet) force (2 mne bn, 2 navy det)
  1 force (1 mne bn)
EQUIPMENT BY TYPE
ARMOURED FIGHTING VEHICLES
  RECCE 12 ERC-90F *Sagaie*
  APC • **APC (W)** 31 VCR
  AAV 11 LVTP-7
ENGINEERING & MAINTENANCE VEHICLES
  ARV AAVR 7
ANTI-TANK/ANTI-INFRASTRUCTURE
  RCL 105mm 30 M-1974 FMK-1
ARTILLERY 89
  TOWED 19: **105mm** 13 Model 56 pack howitzer; **155mm** 6 M114
  MOR 70: **81mm** 58; **120mm** 12
AIR DEFENCE
  SAM • **Point-defence** RBS-70
  GUNS 40mm 4 Bofors 40L

Air Force 12,900

4 Major Comds – Air Operations, Personnel, Air Regions, Logistics, 8 air bde

Air Operations Command
FORCES BY ROLE
GROUND ATTACK
  2 sqn with A-4/OA-4 (A-4AR/OA-4AR) *Skyhawk*
  2 (tac air) sqn with EMB-312 *Tucano* (on loan for border surv/interdiction)
ISR
  1 sqn with Learjet 35A
SEARCH & RESCUE/TRANSPORT HELICOPTER
  2 sqn with Bell 212; Bell 212 (UH-1N); Mi-171, SA-315B *Lama*
TANKER/TRANSPORT
  1 sqn with C-130H *Hercules*; KC-130H *Hercules*; L-100-30
TRANSPORT
  1 sqn with B-707
  1 sqn with DHC-6 *Twin Otter*; Saab 340
  1 sqn with F-27 *Friendship*
  1 sqn with F-28 *Fellowship*; Learjet 60
  1 (Pres) flt with B-757-23ER; S-70A *Black Hawk*, S-76B
TRAINING
  1 sqn with AT-63 *Pampa*
  1 sqn with EMB-312 *Tucano*
  1 sqn with Grob 120TP
  1 hel sqn with Hughes 369; SA-315B *Lama*
TRANSPORT HELICOPTER
  1 sqn with Hughes 369; MD-500; MD500D
EQUIPMENT BY TYPE
AIRCRAFT 42 combat capable
  ATK 22: 20 A-4 (A-4AR) *Skyhawk*‡; 2 OA-4 (OA-4AR) *Skyhawk*‡
  ELINT 1 Cessna 210
  TKR 2 KC-130H *Hercules*
  TPT 22: **Medium** 4: 3 C-130H *Hercules*; 1 L-100-30; **Light** 16: 1 Cessna 310; 6 DHC-6 *Twin Otter*; 4 Learjet 35A (test and calibration); 1 Learjet 60 (VIP); 4 Saab 340; **PAX** 2: 1 B-737; 1 B-757-23ER
  TRG 67: 20 AT-63 *Pampa** (LIFT); 19 EMB-312 *Tucano*; 8 Grob 120TP; 4 IA-63 *Pampa* III; 6 P2002JF *Sierra*; 10 T-6C *Texan* II
HELICOPTERS
  MRH 27: 4 Bell 412EP; 11 Hughes 369; 3 MD-500; 4 MD-500D; 5 SA315B *Lama*
  TPT 12: **Medium** 3: 2 Mi-171E; 1 S-70A *Black Hawk*; **Light** 9: 7 Bell 212; 2 S-76B (VIP)
AIR DEFENCE
  GUNS 88: **20mm**: 86 Oerlikon/Rh-202 with 9 Elta EL/M-2106 radar; **35mm**: 2 Oerlikon GDF-001 with *Skyguard* radar
AIR-LAUNCHED MISSILES
  AAM • **IR** AIM-9L *Sidewinder*; R-550 *Magic*; *Shafrir* 2‡

Paramilitary 31,250

Gendarmerie 18,000
Ministry of Security
FORCES BY ROLE
COMMAND
  7 regional comd

SPECIAL FORCES
1 SF unit
MANOEUVRE
Other
17 paramilitary bn
Aviation
1 (mixed) avn bn
EQUIPMENT BY TYPE
ARMOURED FIGHTING VEHICLES
RECCE S52 *Shorland*
APC (W) 87: 47 *Grenadier*; 40 UR-416
ARTILLERY • MOR 81mm
AIRCRAFT
TPT 13: **Light** 12: 3 Cessna 152; 3 Cessna 206; 1 Cessna 336; 1 PA-28 *Cherokee*; 2 PC-6B *Turbo Porter*; 2 PC-12; PAX 1 Learjet 35
HELICOPTERS
MRH 2 MD-500C
TPT • **Light** 20: 3 AW119 *Koala*; 5 Bell 205 *(*UH-1H *Iroquois)*; 7 AS350 *Ecureuil*; 1 H135; 1 H155; 3 R-44 *Raven* II
TRG 1 S-300C

Prefectura Naval (Coast Guard) 13,250
Ministry of Security
EQUIPMENT BY TYPE
PATROL AND COASTAL COMBATANTS 71
PCO 7: 1 *Correa Falcon*; 1 *Delfin*; 5 *Mantilla* (F30 *Halcón* – undergoing modernisation)
PCC 1 *Mariano Moreno*
PB 58: 1 *Dorado*; 25 *Estrellemar*; 2 *Lynch* (US *Cape*); 18 *Mar del Plata* (Z-28); 1 *Surel*; 8 Damen Stan 2200; 3 Stan Tender 1750
PBF 4 *Shaldag* II
PBR 1 *Tonina*
LOGISTICS & SUPPORT 11
AAR 1 *Tango*
AFS 1 *Prefecto Garcia*
AG 2
ARS 1 *Prefecto Mansilla*
AX 5: 1 *Mandubi*; 4 other
AXS 1 *Dr Bernardo Houssay*
AIRCRAFT
MP 1 Beech 350ER *King Air*
TPT • **Light** 6: 5 C-212 *Aviocar*; 1 Beech 350ER *King Air*
TRG 2 Piper PA-28 *Archer* III
HELICOPTERS
SAR 3 AS565MA *Panther*
MRH 1 AS365 *Dauphin* 2
TPT 5: **Medium** 3: 1 H225 *Puma*; 2 SA330L (AS330L) *Puma*; **Light** 2 AS355 *Ecureuil* II
TRG 4 S-300C

DEPLOYMENT
CENTRAL AFRICAN REPUBLIC: UN • MINUSCA 2
CYPRUS: UN • UNFICYP 243; 2 inf coy; 1 hel flt with 2 Bell 212
MIDDLE EAST: UN • UNTSO 3
WESTERN SAHARA: UN • MINURSO 3

Bahamas BHS

Bahamian Dollar B$		2018	2019	2020
GDP	B$	12.4bn	12.7bn	
	US$	12.4bn	12.7bn	
per capita	US$	32,997	33,261	
Growth	%	1.6	0.9	
Inflation	%	2.2	1.8	
Def bdgt	B$	84.7m	92.3m	85.8m
	US$	84.7m	92.3m	
US$1=B$		1.00	1.00	

Real-terms defence budget trend (US$m, constant 2015)

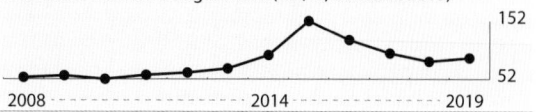

Population 335,210

Age	0–14	15–19	20–24	25–29	30–64	65 plus
Male	11.3%	3.8%	4.2%	4.3%	22.3%	3.2%
Female	10.9%	3.7%	4.1%	4.1%	23.0%	5.1%

Capabilities

The Royal Bahamas Defence Force (RBDF) is an entirely naval force primarily tasked with disaster relief, maritime security and countering narcotics trafficking. Its single commando squadron is tasked with base and internal security. The Bahamas is a member of the Caribbean Community, and the RBDF maintains training relationships with the UK and US. The RBDF participates in US SOUTHCOM's multinational annual *Tradewinds* disaster-response exercise. There is very little independent capacity to deploy abroad, aside from recent regional disaster-relief efforts. The RBDF's Sandy Bottom Project, the largest-ever capital investment in the service, includes the acquisition of patrol craft, harbour dredging, and the development of bases and port facilities. A new permanent naval base on Grand Bahama is under discussion to bolster the RBDF's counter-narcotics work. The maritime wing is focused around patrol vessels and smaller patrol boats, while the air wing has a small inventory of light aircraft. Apart from limited maintenance facilities, the Bahamas has no indigenous defence industry.

ACTIVE 1,300

ORGANISATIONS BY SERVICE

Royal Bahamian Defence Force 1,300
FORCES BY ROLE
MANOEUVRE
Amphibious
1 mne coy (incl marines with internal- and base-security duties)
EQUIPMENT BY TYPE
PATROL AND COASTAL COMBATANTS 21
PCC 2 *Bahamas*
PBF 6 Nor-Tech
PB 13: 4 *Arthur Dion Hanna*; 2 *Dauntless*; 3 *Lignum Vitae* (Damen 3007); 2 Sea Ark 12m; 2 Sea Ark 15m

LOGISTICS & SUPPORT 1
  AKR 1 *Lawrence Major* (Damen 5612)
  AIRCRAFT • TPT • Light 3: 1 Beech A350 *King Air*; 1 Cessna 208 *Caravan*; 1 P-68 *Observer*

FOREIGN FORCES
Guyana Navy: Base located at New Providence Island

Barbados BRB

Barbados Dollar B$		2018	2019	2020
GDP	B$	10.2bn	10.4bn	
	US$	5.09bn	5.19bn	
per capita	US$	17,758	18,069	
Growth	%	-0.6	-0.1	
Inflation	%	3.7	1.9	
Def bdgt [a]	B$	80.8m	76.7m	
	US$	40.4m	38.4m	
US$1=B$		2.00	2.00	

[a] Defence & security expenditure

Real-terms defence budget trend (US$m, constant 2015)

Population	293,874					
Age	0–14	15–19	20–24	25–29	30–64	65 plus
Male	8.8%	3.1%	3.1%	3.6%	24.5%	5.3%
Female	8.8%	3.1%	3.1%	3.6%	25.3%	7.7%

Capabilities
Maritime security and resource protection are the main tasks of the Barbados Defence Force (BDF), but it has a secondary public-safety role in support of the police force. The BDF has been active in counter-narcotics work in recent years, and troops have also been tasked with supporting law-enforcement patrols. The BDF has been taking steps to improve its disaster-relief capacity. The Caribbean Regional Security System is headquartered in Barbados, and it is also a member of the Caribbean Community. The BDF participates in US SOUTHCOM's multinational annual *Tradewinds* disaster-response exercise. There is limited capacity to independently deploy within the region, most recently on hurricane-relief duties. The inventory consists principally of a small number of patrol vessels. Apart from limited maintenance facilities, Barbados has no indigenous defence industry.

ACTIVE 610 (Army 500 Coast Guard 110)

RESERVE 430 (Joint 430)

ORGANISATIONS BY SERVICE

Army 500
FORCES BY ROLE
MANOEUVRE
  Light
    1 inf bn (cadre)

Coast Guard 110
HQ located at HMBS Pelican, Spring Garden
EQUIPMENT BY TYPE
PATROL AND COASTAL COMBATANTS • PB 6:
1 *Dauntless*; 2 *Enterprise* (Damen Stan 1204); 3 *Trident* (Damen Stan Patrol 4207)

Belize BLZ

Belize Dollar BZ$		2018	2019	2020
GDP	BZ$	3.85bn	4.00bn	
	US$	1.93bn	2.00bn	
per capita	US$	4,862	4,925	
Growth	%	3.0	2.7	
Inflation	%	0.3	1.2	
Def bdgt [a]	BZ$	46.4m	46.7m	
	US$	23.2m	23.4m	
FMA (US)	US$	1m	0m	0m
US$1=BZ$		2.00	2.00	

[a] Excludes funds allocated to Coast Guard and Police Service

Real-terms defence budget trend (US$m, constant 2015)

Population	392,771					
Age	0–14	15–19	20–24	25–29	30–64	65 plus
Male	16.9%	5.5%	4.3%	4.5%	16.8%	2.2%
Female	16.2%	5.1%	4.0%	4.5%	17.9%	2.3%

Capabilities
Belize maintains a small Defence Force (BDF) and coastguard to provide national security, particularly control of the borders with Guatemala and Mexico. The National Security and Defence Strategy (2017–20) identifies territorial defence and combating transnational crime as key objectives. The UK has a long-standing security relationship with Belize and maintains a small training unit there, and the BDF also trains with US SOUTHCOM. Overall training levels are limited but generally sufficient for the BDF's tasks. Belize is a member of the Caribbean Community. The BDF does not deploy internationally and logistics support is adequate for border-security missions. The conventional equipment inventory is limited and there is no significant domestic defence industry.

ACTIVE 1,500 (Army 1,500) **Paramilitary** 150

RESERVE 700 (Joint 700)

ORGANISATIONS BY SERVICE

Army ε1,500
FORCES BY ROLE
MANOEUVRE
  Light
    2 inf bn (3 inf coy)
COMBAT SERVICE SUPPORT
  1 spt gp

EQUIPMENT BY TYPE
ANTI-TANK/ANTI-INFRASTRUCTURE • RCL 84mm
Carl Gustav
ARTILLERY • MOR 81mm 6

Air Wing
EQUIPMENT BY TYPE
AIRCRAFT
  TPT • **Light** 2: 1 BN-2B *Defender*†; 1 Cessna 182 *Skylane*†
  TRG 1 T-67M-200 *Firefly*
HELICOPTERS
  TPT • **Light** 3: 2 Bell 205 (UH-1H *Iroquois*); 1 Bell 407

Reserve
FORCES BY ROLE
MANOEUVRE
  Light
    1 inf bn (3 inf coy)

Paramilitary 150

Coast Guard 150
EQUIPMENT BY TYPE
All operational patrol vessels under 10t FLD

FOREIGN FORCES
United Kingdom BATSUB 12

Bolivia BOL

Bolivian Boliviano B		2018	2019	2020
GDP	B	278.4bn	290.9bn	
	US$	40.6bn	42.4bn	
per capita	US$	3,566	3,671	
Growth	%	4.2	3.9	
Inflation	%	2.3	1.7	
Def bdgt	B	3.45bn	3.29bn	
	US$	502.8m	479.4m	
US$1=B		6.86	6.86	

Real-terms defence budget trend (US$m, constant 2015)

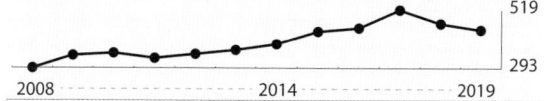

Population	11,473,676				
Age	0–14	15–19	20–24	25–29	30–64	65 plus
Male	15.7%	5.1%	4.7%	4.4%	17.1%	2.4%
Female	15.1%	4.9%	4.6%	4.4%	18.4%	3.1%

Capabilities
The armed forces are constitutionally tasked with maintaining sovereignty and territorial defence, but counter-narcotics and internal and border security are in practical terms the main tasks of the armed forces. Joint task forces have been formed and dispatched to border regions to combat smuggling activities, and a series of border posts are being established. Modest procurement programmes are intended to improve the services' ability to undertake these roles. Airspace control is an emerging strategic priority, and a system of civilian and military radars has recently been built to help address this requirement. There is defence-technology cooperation with Russia, but China remains a significant supplier of military materiel and delivered logistics vehicles in late 2018. Bolivia cooperates with Peru on countering illicit trafficking and disaster relief. Amid greater internal deployments to border areas on counter-trafficking tasks, the armed forces have stressed the need to improve conditions for personnel. An Aerospace Research and Development Centre was created in 2018 in the military-engineering school with the objective of developing munitions and ISR UAVs. There is some local maintenance, repair and overhaul capacity for the services.

ACTIVE 34,100 (Army 22,800 Navy 4,800 Air 6,500)
Paramilitary 37,100
Conscript liability 12 months voluntary conscription for both males and females

ORGANISATIONS BY SERVICE

Army 9,800; 13,000 conscript (total 22,800)
FORCES BY ROLE
COMMAND
  6 mil region HQ
  10 div HQ
SPECIAL FORCES
  3 SF regt
MANOEUVRE
  Reconnaissance
    1 mot cav gp
  Armoured
    1 armd bn
  Mechanised
    1 mech cav regt
    2 mech inf regt
  Light
    1 (aslt) cav gp
    5 (horsed) cav gp
    3 mot inf regt
    21 inf regt
  Air Manoeuvre
    2 AB regt (bn)
  Other
    1 (Presidential Guard) inf regt
COMBAT SUPPORT
  6 arty regt (bn)
  6 engr bn
  1 int coy
  1 MP bn
  1 sigs bn
COMBAT SERVICE SUPPORT
  2 log bn
AVIATION
  2 avn coy
AIR DEFENCE
  1 ADA regt

EQUIPMENT BY TYPE
ARMOURED FIGHTING VEHICLES
  LT TK 54: 36 SK-105A1 *Kuerassier*; 18 SK-105A2 *Kuerassier*
  RECCE 24 EE-9 *Cascavel*
  APC 148+
    APC (T) 87+: 50+ M113, 37 M9 half-track
    APC (W) 61: 24 EE-11 *Urutu*; 22 MOWAG *Roland*; 15 V-100 *Commando*
  AUV 19 *Tiger* 4×4
ENGINEERING & MAINTENANCE VEHICLES
  ARV 4 *Greif*; M578 LARV
ANTI-TANK/ANTI-INFRASTRUCTURE
  MSL
    SP 2 *Koyak* with HJ-8
    MANPATS HJ-8
  RCL 90mm M67; **106mm** M40A1
ARTILLERY 311+
  TOWED 61: **105mm** 25 M101A1; **122mm** 36 M-30 (M-1938)
  MOR 250+: **81mm** 250 M29; Type-W87; **107mm** M30; **120mm** M120
AIRCRAFT
  TPT • Light 4: 1 Fokker F-27-200; 1 Beech 90 *King Air*; 1 C-212 *Aviocar*; 1 Cessna 210 *Centurion*
HELICOPTERS
  MRH 6 H425
  TRG 1 Robinson R55
AIR DEFENCE • GUNS • TOWED 37mm 18 Type-65

Navy 4,800
Organised into six naval districts with HQ located at Puerto Guayaramerín
EQUIPMENT BY TYPE
PATROL AND COASTAL COMBATANTS • PBR 3: 1 *Santa Cruz*; 2 others
LOGISTICS AND SUPPORT 3
  AG 1
  AH 2

Marines 1,700 (incl 1,000 Naval Military Police)
FORCES BY ROLE
MANOEUVRE
  Mechanised
  1 mech inf bn
  Amphibious
  6 mne bn (1 in each Naval District)
COMBAT SUPPORT
  4 (naval) MP bn

Air Force 6,500 (incl conscripts)
FORCES BY ROLE
GROUND ATTACK
  1 sqn with K-8WB *Karakorum*
ISR
  1 sqn with Cessna 206; Cessna 402; Learjet 25B/25D (secondary VIP role)
SEARCH & RESCUE
  1 sqn with AS332B *Super Puma*; H125 *Ecureuil*; H145
TRANSPORT
  1 (TAM) sqn with B-727; B-737; BAe-146-100; MA60
  1 (TAB) sqn with C-130A *Hercules*; MD-10-30F
  1 sqn with C-130B/H *Hercules*
  1 sqn with F-27-400M *Troopship*
  1 (VIP) sqn with Beech 90 *King Air*; Beech 200 *King Air*; Beech 1900; *Falcon* 900EX; *Sabreliner* 60
  6 sqn with Cessna 152/206; IAI-201 *Arava*; PA-32 *Saratoga*; PA-34 *Seneca*
TRAINING
  1 sqn with DA40; T-25
  1 sqn with Cessna 152/172
  1 sqn with PC-7 *Turbo Trainer*
  1 hel sqn with R-44 *Raven* II
TRANSPORT HELICOPTER
  1 (anti-drug) sqn with Bell 205 (UH-1H *Iroquois*)
AIR DEFENCE
  1 regt with Oerlikon; Type-65
EQUIPMENT BY TYPE
AIRCRAFT 22 combat capable
  TPT 88: **Heavy** 1 MD-10-30F; **Medium** 4: 1 C-130A *Hercules*; 2 C-130B *Hercules*; 1 C-130H *Hercules*; **Light** 72: 1 *Aero Commander* 690; 3 Beech 90 *King Air*; 1 Beech 55 *Baron*; 2 Beech 200 *King Air*; 1 Beech 1900; 3 C-212-100; 10 Cessna 152; 2 Cessna 172; 19 Cessna 206; 3 Cessna 210 *Centurion*; 1 Cessna 402; 9 DA40; 3 F-27-400M *Troopship*; 4 IAI-201 *Arava*; 2 Learjet 25B/D; 2 MA60†; 1 PA-32 *Saratoga*; 4 PA-34 *Seneca*; 1 *Sabreliner* 60; **PAX** 11: 1 B-727; 5 B-737-200; 1 B-737-300; 1 BAe-146-100; 2 BAe-146-200; 1 *Falcon* 900EX (VIP)
  TRG 30: 6 K-8WB *Karakorum**; 6 T-25; 16 PC-7 *Turbo Trainer**; 2 Z-242L
HELICOPTERS
  MRH 1 SA316 *Alouette* III
  TPT 35: **Medium** 6 H215 *Super Puma*; **Light** 29: 2 H125 *Ecureuil*; 19 Bell 205 (UH-1H *Iroquois*); 2 H145; 6 R-44 *Raven* II
AIR DEFENCE • GUNS 18+: **20mm** Oerlikon; **37mm** 18 Type-65

Paramilitary 37,100+
National Police 31,100+
FORCES BY ROLE
MANOEUVRE
  Other
  27 frontier sy unit
  9 paramilitary bde
  2 (rapid action) paramilitary regt

Narcotics Police 6,000+
FOE (700) – Special Operations Forces

DEPLOYMENT
CENTRAL AFRICAN REPUBLIC: UN • MINUSCA 5
DEMOCRATIC REPUBLIC OF THE CONGO: UN • MONUSCO 4
SOUTH SUDAN: UN • UNMISS 1
SUDAN: UN • UNISFA 4

Brazil BRZ

Brazilian Real R		2018	2019	2020
GDP	R	6.82tr	7.20tr	
	US$	1.87tr	1.85tr	
per capita	US$	8,959	8,797	
Growth	%	1.1	0.9	
Inflation	%	3.7	3.8	
Def bdgt [a]	R	100.7bn	107.0bn	68.6bn
	US$	27.6bn	27.5bn	
US$1=R		3.65	3.90	

[a] Includes military pensions

Real-terms defence budget trend (US$bn, constant 2015)

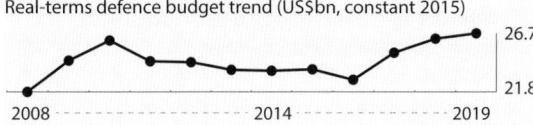

Population 210,301,591

Age	0–14	15–19	20–24	25–29	30–64	65 plus
Male	11.0%	4.2%	4.1%	3.9%	22.4%	3.8%
Female	10.5%	4.0%	4.0%	3.9%	23.3%	5.1%

Capabilities

The armed forces are among the most capable in the region. Brazil seeks to enhance its power-projection capabilities, boost surveillance of the Amazon region and coastal waters, and further develop its defence industry, though economic difficulties continue to affect its ability to develop these ambitions. However, security challenges from organised crime have seen the armed forces deploy on internal-security operations. Brazil maintains military ties with most of its neighbours including personnel exchanges and joint military training with Chile and Colombia. There is also defence cooperation with France, Sweden and the US, centred on procurement, technical advice and personnel training. Brazil's air-transport fleet enables it to independently deploy forces. It contributes small contingents to several UN missions across Europe, the Middle East and sub-Saharan Africa. Despite substantial budgetary constraints, Brazil is attempting to modernise its equipment across all domains. Major platform developments include PROSUB (one nuclear-powered and four diesel-electric submarines) and the acquisition in 2018 of a former UK helicopter carrier. Brazil has a well-developed defence-industrial base, across all domains, with a capability to design and manufacture equipment for its armed forces. There is a significant aerospace sector, with some private companies such as Avibras and Embraer exporting to international customers. Local companies are also involved in the SISFRON border-security programme. There are industrial partnerships, including technology transfers and R&D support, with France's Naval Group (PROSUB) and Sweden's Saab (FX-2 fighter).

ACTIVE 366,500 (Army 214,000 Navy 85,000 Air 67,500) Paramilitary 395,000

Conscript liability 12 months (can go to 18; often waived)

RESERVE 1,340,000

ORGANISATIONS BY SERVICE

Space
EQUIPMENT BY TYPE
SATELLITES • COMMUNICATIONS 1 SGDC-1 (civil–military use)

Army 102,000; 112,000 conscript (total 214,000)
FORCES BY ROLE
COMMAND
 8 mil comd HQ
 12 mil region HQ
 7 div HQ (2 with regional HQ)
SPECIAL FORCES
 1 SF bde (1 SF bn, 1 cdo bn)
 1 SF coy
MANOEUVRE
 Reconnaissance
 3 mech cav regt
 Armoured
 1 (5th) armd bde (1 mech cav sqn, 2 tk regt, 2 mech inf bn, 1 SP arty bn, 1 engr bn, 1 sigs coy, 1 log bn)
 1 (6th) armd bde (1 mech cav sqn, 2 tk regt, 2 mech inf bn, 1 SP arty bn, 1 AD bty, 1 engr bn, 1 sigs coy, 1 log bn)
 Mechanised
 4 (1st, 3rd & 4th) mech cav bde (1 armd cav regt, 3 mech cav regt, 1 arty bn, 1 engr coy, 1 sigs coy, 1 log bn)
 1 (2nd) mech cav bde (1 armd cav regt, 2 mech cav regt, 1 SP arty bn, 1 engr coy, 1 sigs coy, 1 log bn)
 1 (15th) mech inf bde (3 mech inf bn, 1 arty bn, 1 engr coy, 1 log bn)
 Light
 1 (3rd) mot inf bde (1 mech cav sqn, 1 mech inf bn, 1 mot inf bn, 1 inf bn, 1 arty bn, 1 engr coy, 1 sigs coy, 1 log bn)
 1 (4th) mot inf bde (1 mech cav sqn, 1 mot inf bn, 1 inf bn, 1 mtn inf bn, 1 arty bn, 1 sigs coy, 1 log bn)
 1 (7th) mot inf bde (3 mot inf bn, 1 arty bn)
 1 (8th) mot inf bde (1 mech cav sqn, 3 mot inf bn, 1 arty bn, 1 log bn)
 1 (10th) mot inf bde (1 mech cav sqn, 4 mot inf bn, 1 inf coy, 1 arty bn, 1 engr coy, 1 sigs coy)
 1 (13th) mot inf bde (1 mot inf bn, 2 inf bn, 1 inf coy, 1 arty bn)
 1 (14th) mot inf bde (1 mech cav sqn, 3 inf bn, 1 arty bn)
 1 (11th) lt inf bde (1 mech cav regt, 3 inf bn, 1 arty bn, 1 engr coy, 1 sigs coy, 1 MP coy, 1 log bn)
 10 inf bn
 1 (1st) jungle inf bde (1 mech cav sqn, 2 jungle inf bn, 1 arty bn)
 4 (2nd, 16th, 17th & 22nd) jungle inf bde (3 jungle inf bn)
 1 (23rd) jungle inf bde (1 cav sqn, 4 jungle inf bn, 1 arty bn, 1 sigs coy, 1 log bn)
 Air Manoeuvre
 1 AB bde (1 cav sqn, 3 AB bn, 1 arty bn, 1 engr coy, 1 sigs coy, 1 log bn)

1 (12th) air mob bde (1 cav sqn, 3 air mob bn, 1 arty bn, 1 engr coy, 1 sigs coy, 1 log bn)
Other
1 (9th) mot trg bde (3 mot inf bn, 1 arty bn, 1 log bn)
1 (18th) sy bde (2 sy bn, 2 sy coy)
1 sy bn
7 sy coy
3 gd cav regt
1 gd inf bn
COMBAT SUPPORT
3 SP arty bn
6 fd arty bn
1 MRL bn
1 STA bty
6 engr bn
1 engr gp (1 engr bn, 4 construction bn)
1 engr gp (4 construction bn, 1 construction coy)
2 construction bn
1 CBRN bn
1 EW coy
1 int coy
8 MP bn
2 MP coy
4 sigs bn
2 sigs coy
COMBAT SERVICE SUPPORT
5 log bn
1 tpt bn
4 spt bn
HELICOPTER
1 avn bde (3 hel bn, 1 maint bn)
1 hel bn
AIR DEFENCE
1 ADA bde (5 ADA bn)
EQUIPMENT BY TYPE
ARMOURED FIGHTING VEHICLES
MBT 393: 128 *Leopard* 1A1BE; 220 *Leopard* 1A5BR; 45 M60A3/TTS
LT TK 50 M41C
RECCE 408 EE-9 *Cascavel*
IFV 6 VBTP-MR *Guarani* 30mm
APC 1,253
  APC (T) 630: 184 M113A1; 400 M113BR; 12 M113A2; 34 M577A2
  APC (W) 623: 223 EE-11 *Urutu*; 400 VBTP-MR *Guarani* 6×6
ENGINEERING & MAINTENANCE VEHICLES
AEV 6+: *Greif*; 2 Sabiex HART; 4+ Pioneerpanzer 2 *Dachs*
ARV 4+: BPz-2; 4 M88A1; M578 LARV
VLB 4+: XLP-10; 4 *Leopard* 1 with *Biber*
ANTI-TANK/ANTI-INFRASTRUCTURE
MSL • MANPATS *Eryx*; *Milan*; MSS-1.2 AC
RCL 194+: **84mm** *Carl Gustav*; **106mm** 194 M40A1
ARTILLERY 1,953
SP 241: **105mm** 72 M108; **155mm** 169: 37 M109A3; 100 M109A5; 32 M109A5+
TOWED 431
  105mm 336: 233 M101/M102; 40 L118 Light Gun; 63 Model 56 pack howitzer
  155mm 95 M114

MRL 127mm 36: 18 ASTROS II Mk3M; 18 ASTROS II Mk6
MOR 1,245: **81mm** 1,168: 453 L16, 715 M936 AGR; **120mm** 77 M2
HELICOPTERS
MRH 51: 29 AS565 *Panther* (HM-1); 5 AS565 K2 *Panther* (HM-1); 17 AS550U2 *Fennec* (HA-1 – armed)
TPT 38: **Heavy** 11 H225M *Caracal* (HM-4); **Medium** 12: 8 AS532 *Cougar* (HM-3); 4 S-70A-36 *Black Hawk* (HM-2); **Light** 15 AS350L1 *Ecureuil* (HA-1)
AIR DEFENCE
SAM • Point-defence RBS-70; 9K38 *Igla* (SA-18 *Grouse*); 9K338 *Igla*-S (SA-24 *Grinch*)
GUNS 100:
  SP 35mm 34 *Gepard* 1A2
  TOWED 66: **35mm** 39 GDF-001 towed (some with *Super Fledermaus* radar); **40mm** 27 L/70 (some with BOFI)

Navy 85,000

Organised into 9 districts with HQ I Rio de Janeiro, HQ II Salvador, HQ III Natal, HQ IV Belém, HQ V Rio Grande, HQ VI Ladario, HQ VII Brasilia, HQ VIII Sao Paulo, HQ IX Manaus
FORCES BY ROLE
SPECIAL FORCES
1 (diver) SF gp
EQUIPMENT BY TYPE
SUBMARINES • TACTICAL • SSK 5:
  2 *Tupi* (GER T-209/1400) with 8 single 533mm TT with Mk 24 *Tigerfish* HWT (of which 1 in refit)
  2 *Tupi* (GER T-209/1400) with 8 single 533mm TT with Mk 48 HWT
  1 *Tikuna* (GER T-209/1450) with 8 single 533mm TT with Mk 24 *Tigerfish* HWT (in refit)
PRINCIPAL SURFACE COMBATANTS 10
DESTROYERS • DDGHM 2:
  1 *Greenhalgh* (ex-UK *Broadsword*) with 4 single lnchr with MM38 *Exocet* AShM, 2 sextuple lnchr with *Sea Wolf* SAM, 6 single STWS Mk.2 324mm ASTT with Mk 46 LWT (capacity 2 *Super Lynx* Mk21A hel)
  1 *Greenhalgh* (ex-UK *Broadsword*) with 4 single lnchr with MM40 *Exocet* Block 2 AShM, 2 sextuple lnchr with *Sea Wolf* SAM, 6 single STWS Mk.2 324mm ASTT with Mk 46 LWT (capacity 2 *Super Lynx* Mk21A hel)
FRIGATES 8
FFGHM 5 *Niterói* with 2 twin lnchr with MM40 *Exocet* Block 2 AShM, 1 octuple *Albatros* lnchr with *Aspide* SAM, 2 triple SVTT Mk 32 324mm ASTT with Mk 46 LWT, 1 twin 375mm Bofors ASW Rocket Launcher System A/S mor, 1 115mm gun (capacity 1 *Super Lynx* Mk21A hel)
FFGH 3:
  2 *Inhaúma* with 2 twin lnchr with MM40 *Exocet* Block 2 AShM, 2 triple SVTT Mk 32 324mm ASTT with Mk 46 LWT, 1 115mm gun (1 *Super Lynx* Mk21A hel)
  1 *Barroso* with 2 twin lnchr with MM40 *Exocet* Block 2 AShM, 2 triple SVTT Mk 32 324mm ASTT with

Mk 46 LWT, 1 115mm gun (capacity 1 *Super Lynx* Mk21A hel)

PATROL AND COASTAL COMBATANTS 44
  PSO 3 *Amazonas* with 1 hel landing platform
  PCO 6: 4 *Bracui* (ex-UK *River*); 1 *Imperial Marinheiro* with 1 76mm gun; 1 *Parnaiba* with 1 hel landing platform
  PCC 2 *Macaé*
  PCR 5: 2 *Pedro Teixeira* with 1 hel landing platform; 3 *Roraima*
  PB 24: 12 *Grajau*; 6 *Marlim*; 6 *Piratini* (US PGM)
  PBR 4 LPR-40

MINE WARFARE • MINE COUNTERMEASURES •
MSC 4 *Aratu* (GER *Schutze*)

AMPHIBIOUS
  PRINCIPAL AMPHIBIOUS SHIPS 2
    LPD 1 *Bahia* (ex-FRA *Foudre*) (capacity 4 hels; 8 LCM, 450 troops)
    LPH 1 *Atlantico* (ex-UK *Ocean*) (capacity 18 hels; 4 LCVP; 40 vehs; 800 troops)
  LANDING SHIPS 3
    LST 1 *Mattoso Maia* (ex-US *Newport*) with 1 Mk 15 *Phalanx* CIWS (capacity 3 LCVP; 1 LCPL; 400 troops)
    LSLH 2: 1 *Garcia D'Avila* (ex-UK *Sir Galahad*) (capacity 1 hel; 16 MBT; 340 troops); 1 *Almirante Saboia* (ex-UK *Sir Bedivere*) (capacity 1 med hel; 18 MBT; 340 troops)
  LANDING CRAFT 16:
    LCM 12: 10 EDVM-25; 2 *Icarai* (ex-FRA CTM)
    LCT 1 *Marambaia* (ex-FRA CDIC)
    LCU 3 *Guarapari* (LCU 1610)

LOGISTICS AND SUPPORT 44
  ABU 5: 4 *Comandante Varella*; 1 *Faroleiro Mario Seixas*
  ABUH 1 *Almirante Graca Aranah* (lighthouse tender)
  AFS 1 *Potengi*
  AGHS 5: 1 *Caravelas* (riverine); 4 *Rio Tocantin*
  AGOS 2: 1 *Ary Rongel* with 1 hel landing platform; 1 *Almirante Maximiano* (capacity 2 AS350/AS355 *Ecureuil* hel)
  AGS 8: 1 *Aspirante Moura*; 1 *Cruzeiro do Sul*; 1 *Antares*; 3 *Amorim do Valle* (ex-UK *Rover*); 1 *Rio Branco*; 1 *Vital de Oliveira*
  AGSH 1 *Sirius*
  AH 5: 2 *Oswaldo Cruz* with 1 hel landing platform; 1 *Dr Montenegro*; 1 *Tenente Maximianol* with 1 hel landing platform; 1 *Soares de Meirelles*
  AOR 2: 1 *Almirante Gastão Motta*; 1 *Marajó*
  AP 3: 1 *Almirante Leverger*; 1 *Paraguassu*; 1 *Pará* (all river transports)
  ASR 1 *Felinto Perry* (NOR *Wildrake*) with 1 hel landing platform
  ATF 5: 3 *Triunfo*; 2 *Almirante Guihem*
  AX 1 *Brasil* (*Niterói* mod) with 1 hel landing platform
  AXL 3 *Nascimento*
  AXS 1 *Cisne Barco*

Naval Aviation 2,100

FORCES BY ROLE
GROUND ATTACK
  1 sqn with A-4M (AF-1B) *Skyhawk*; TA-4M (AF-1C) *Skyhawk*
ANTI SURFACE WARFARE
  1 sqn with *Super Lynx* Mk21A

ANTI SUBMARINE WARFARE
  1 sqn with S-70B *Seahawk* (MH-16)
TRAINING
  1 sqn with Bell 206B3 *Jet Ranger* III
TRANSPORT HELICOPTER
  1 sqn with AS332 *Super Puma*; AS532 *Cougar*
  1 sqn with AS350 *Ecureuil* (armed); AS355 *Ecureuil* II (armed); H225M *Caracal* (UH-15A)
  3 sqn with AS350 *Ecureuil* (armed); AS355 *Ecureuil* II (armed)

EQUIPMENT BY TYPE
AIRCRAFT 3 combat capable
  ATK 3: 2 A-4M (AF-1B) *Skyhawk*; 1 TA-4M (AF-1C) *Skyhawk* (15 A-4 (AF-1) *Skyhawk*; 2 TA-4 (AF-1A) *Skyhawk* in store)
HELICOPTERS
  ASW 18: 4 *Super Lynx* Mk21A; 8 *Super Lynx* Mk21B; 6 S-70B *Seahawk* (MH-16)
  CSAR 3 H225M *Caracal* (UH-15A)
  TPT 52: **Heavy** 7 H225M *Caracal* (UH-15); **Medium** 7: 5 AS332 *Super Puma*; 2 AS532 *Cougar* (UH-14); **Light** 38: 15 AS350 *Ecureuil* (armed); 8 AS355 *Ecureuil* II (armed); 15 Bell 206B3 *Jet Ranger* III (IH-6B)
AIR-LAUNCHED MISSILES • AShM: AM39 *Exocet*; *Sea Skua*; AGM-119 *Penguin*

Marines 16,000

FORCES BY ROLE
SPECIAL FORCES
  1 SF bn
MANOEUVRE
  Amphibious
  1 amph div (1 lt armd bn, 3 mne bn, 1 arty bn)
  1 amph aslt bn
  7 (regional) mne gp
  1 rvn bn
COMBAT SUPPORT
  1 engr bn
COMBAT SERVICE SUPPORT
  1 log bn

EQUIPMENT BY TYPE
ARMOURED FIGHTING VEHICLES
  LT TK 18 SK-105 *Kuerassier*
  APC 60
    APC (T) 30 M113A1 (incl variants)
    APC (W) 30 *Piranha* IIIC
  AAV 47: 13 AAV-7A1; 20 AAVP-7A1 RAM/RS; 2 AAVC-7A1 RAM/RS (CP); 12 LVTP-7
ENGINEERING VEHICLES • ARV 2: 1 AAVR-7; 1 AAVR-7A1 RAM/RS
ANTI-TANK/ANTI-INFRASTRUCTURE
  MSL• MANPATS RB-56 *Bill*; MSS-1.2 AC
ARTILLERY 65
  TOWED 41: **105mm** 33: 18 L118 *Light Gun*; 15 M101; **155mm** 8 M114
  MRL 127mm 6 ASTROS II Mk6
  MOR 81mm 18 M29
AIR DEFENCE • GUNS 40mm 6 L/70 (with BOFI)

Air Force 67,500

Brazilian airspace is divided into 7 air regions, each of which is responsible for its designated air bases. Air assets are divided among 4 designated air forces (I, II, III & V) for operations (IV Air Force temporarily deactivated)

FORCES BY ROLE
FIGHTER
 4 sqn with F-5EM/FM *Tiger* II
FIGHTER/GROUND ATTACK
 2 sqn with AMX (A-1A/B)
GROUND ATTACK/ISR
 4 sqn with EMB-314 *Super Tucano* (A-29A/B)*
MARITIME PATROL
 1 sqn with P-3AM *Orion*
 2 sqn with EMB-111 (P-95A/B/M)
ISR
 1 sqn with AMX-R (RA-1)*
 1 sqn with Learjet 35 (R-35A); EMB-110B (R-95)
AIRBORNE EARLY WARNING & CONTROL
 1 sqn with EMB-145RS (R-99); EMB-145SA (E-99)
TANKER/TRANSPORT
 1 sqn with C-130H/KC-130H *Hercules*
TRANSPORT
 1 VIP sqn with A319 (VC-1A); EMB-190 (VC-2); AS355 *Ecureuil* II (VH-55); H135M (VH-35); H225M *Caracal* (VH-36)
 1 VIP sqn with EMB-135BJ (VC-99B); ERJ-135LR (VC-99C); ERJ-145LR (VC-99A); Learjet 35A (VU-35); Learjet 55C (VU-55C)
 2 sqn with C-130E/H *Hercules*
 2 sqn with C295M (C-105A)
 7 (regional) sqn with Cessna 208/208B (C-98); Cessna 208-G1000 (C-98A); EMB-110 (C-95); EMB-120 (C-97)
 1 sqn with ERJ-145 (C-99A)
 1 sqn with EMB-120RT (VC-97), EMB-121 (VU-9)
TRAINING
 1 sqn with EMB-110 (C-95)
 2 sqn with EMB-312 *Tucano* (T-27) (incl 1 air show sqn)
 1 sqn with T-25A/C
ATTACK HELICOPTER
 1 sqn with Mi-35M *Hind* (AH-2)
TRANSPORT HELICOPTER
 1 sqn with H225M *Caracal* (H-36)
 1 sqn with AS350B *Ecureuil* (H-50); AS355 *Ecureuil* II (H-55)
 1 sqn with Bell 205 (H-1H); H225M *Caracal* (H-36)
 2 sqn with UH-60L *Black Hawk* (H-60L)
ISR UAV
 1 sqn with *Hermes* 450/900

EQUIPMENT BY TYPE
AIRCRAFT 209 combat capable
 FTR 46: 43 F-5EM *Tiger* II; 3 F-5FM *Tiger* II
 FGA 48: 38 AMX (A-1); 10 AMX-T (A-1B)
 ASW 9 P-3AM *Orion*
 MP 19: 10 EMB-111 (P-95A *Bandeirulha*)*; 9 EMB-111 (P-95BM *Bandeirulha*)*
 ISR 8: 4 AMX-R (RA-1)*; 4 EMB-110B (R-95)
 ELINT 6: 3 EMB-145RS (R-99); 3 Learjet 35A (R-35A)
 AEW&C 5 EMB-145SA (E-99)
 SAR 6: 1 C295M *Amazonas* (SC-105); 4 EMB-110 (SC-95B), 1 SC-130E *Hercules*
 TKR/TPT 2 KC-130H
 TPT 199: **Heavy** 1 KC-390; **Medium** 20: 4 C-130E *Hercules*; 16 C-130H *Hercules*; **Light** 170: 11 C295M (C-105A); 7 Cessna 208 (C-98); 9 Cessna 208B (C-98); 13 Cessna 208-G1000 (C-98A); 52 EMB-110 (C-95A/B/C/M); 16 EMB-120 (C-97); 4 EMB-120RT (VC-97); 5 EMB-121 (VU-9); 7 EMB-135BJ (VC-99B); 3 EMB-201R *Ipanema* (G-19); 2 EMB-202A *Ipanema* (G-19A); 2 ERJ-135LR (VC-99C); 7 ERJ-145 (C-99A); 1 ERJ-145LR (VC-99A); 9 Learjet 35A (VU-35); 1 Learjet 55C (VU-55); 9 PA-34 *Seneca* (U-7); 12 U-42 *Regente*; **PAX** 8: 1 A319 (VC-1A); 3 EMB-190 (VC-2); 4 Hawker 800XP (EU-93A – calibration)
 TRG 264: 100 EMB-312 *Tucano* (T-27); 39 EMB-314 *Super Tucano* (A-29A)*; 44 EMB-314 *Super Tucano* (A-29B)*; 81 T-25A/C
HELICOPTERS
 ATK 12 Mi-35M *Hind* (AH-2)
 MRH 2 H135M (VH-35)
 TPT 59: **Heavy** 13 H225M *Caracal* (11 H-36 & 2 VH-36); **Medium** 16 UH-60L *Black Hawk* (H-60L); **Light** 30+: 24 AS350B *Ecureuil* (H-50); 4 AS355 *Ecureuil* II (H-55/VH-55); 2+ Bell 205 (H-1H)
UNMANNED AERIAL VEHICLES
 ISR • Medium 5: 4 *Hermes* 450; 1 *Hermes* 900
AIR-LAUNCHED MISSILES
 AAM • IR MAA-1 *Piranha*; R-550 *Magic* 2; *Python* 3; **IIR** *Python* 4; **SARH** Super 530F; **ARH** *Derby*
 AShM AM39 *Exocet*
 ARM MAR-1 (in development)

Paramilitary 395,000 opcon Army

Public Security Forces 395,000

State police organisation technically under army control. However, military control is reducing, with authority reverting to individual states

EQUIPMENT BY TYPE
UNMANNED AERIAL VEHICLES
 ISR • Heavy 3 *Heron* (deployed by Federal Police for Amazon and border patrols)

DEPLOYMENT

CENTRAL AFRICAN REPUBLIC: UN • MINUSCA 10

CYPRUS: UN • UNFICYP 2

DEMOCRATIC REPUBLIC OF THE CONGO: UN • MONUSCO 21

LEBANON: UN • UNIFIL 198; 1 FFGH

SOUTH SUDAN: UN • UNMISS 13

SUDAN: UN • UNISFA 3

WESTERN SAHARA: UN • MINURSO 9

Chile CHL

Chilean Peso pCh		2018	2019	2020
GDP	pCh	191tr	200tr	
	US$	298bn	294bn	
per capita	US$	15,902	15,399	
Growth	%	4.0	2.5	
Inflation	%	2.3	2.2	
Def bdgt [a]	pCh	3.01tr	3.11tr	
	US$	4.70bn	4.57bn	
US$1=pCh		641.22	680.09	

[a] Includes military pensions

Real-terms defence budget trend (US$bn, constant 2015)

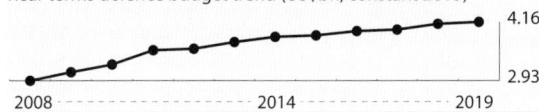

Population	18,057,855				
Age	0–14	15–19	20–24	25–29	30–64	65 plus
Male	10.1%	3.4%	3.8%	4.1%	22.8%	4.8%
Female	9.7%	3.3%	3.7%	4.0%	23.5%	6.6%

Capabilities

Chile's 2017 defence white paper noted core roles of assuring sovereignty and territorial integrity, but also indicated an increasing shift towards non-traditional military roles such as disaster relief, humanitarian assistance and peacekeeping. Chile maintains military ties with most of it neighbours. Personnel-exchange programmes and R&D cooperation are under way with Brazil and Colombia. Defence cooperation with the US is centred on procurement, technical advisory and personnel training. Training takes place regularly on a national basis, and the armed forces routinely participate in international exercises. Chile has a limited capacity to deploy independently beyond its borders. Without upgrades, some equipment might begin to face serviceability issues. However, in mid-2019 an upgrade plan started for Chile's F-16s; some of these are reaching the end of their operational life. Due to a reduced risk of conventional conflict and border crises, priorities have changed to reflect a new focus on littoral and blue-water surveillance and rotary-wing capabilities. Chile has a developed defence-industrial base, with ENAER conducting aircraft maintenance. ASMAR and FAMAE are key maritime and land firms respectively, with the former building a new icebreaker that will enhance Chile's ability to support operations in Antarctica.

ACTIVE 77,200 (Army 46,350 Navy 19,800 Air 11,050) **Paramilitary 44,700**

Conscript liability Army 12 months; Navy 18 months; Air Force 12 months. Legally, conscription can last for 2 years

RESERVE 40,000 (Army 40,000)

ORGANISATIONS BY SERVICE

Space
EQUIPMENT BY TYPE
SATELLITES
 ISR 1 SSOT (Sistema Satelital de Observación de la Tierra)

Army 46,350
6 military administrative regions
FORCES BY ROLE
Currently being reorganised into 1 SF bde, 4 armd bde, 1 armd det, 4 mot bde, 2 mot det, 4 mtn det and 1 avn bde
COMMAND
 6 div HQ
SPECIAL FORCES
 1 SF bde (1 SF bn, 1 (mtn) SF gp, 1 para bn, 3 cdo coy, 1 log coy)
MANOEUVRE
 Reconnaissance
 4 cav sqn
 2 recce sqn
 2 recce pl
 Armoured
 1 (1st) armd bde (1 armd recce pl, 1 armd cav gp, 1 mech inf bn, 2 arty gp, 1 AT coy, 1 engr coy, 1 sigs coy)
 2 (2nd & 3rd) armd bde (1 armd recce pl, 1 armd cav gp, 1 mech inf bn, 1 arty gp, 1 AT coy, 1 engr coy, 1 sigs coy)
 1 (4th) armd bde (1 armd recce pl, 1 armd cav gp, 1 mech inf bn, 1 arty gp, 1 engr coy)
 1 (5th) armd det (1 armd cav gp, 1 mech inf coy, 1 arty gp)
 Mechanised
 1 (1st) mech inf regt
 Light
 1 (1st) mot inf bde (1 recce coy, 1 mot inf bn, 1 arty gp, 3 AT coy, 1 engr bn)
 1 (4th) mot inf bde (1 mot inf bn, 1 MRL gp, 2 AT coy, 1 engr bn)
 1 (24th) mot inf bde (1 mot inf bn, 1 arty gp, 1 AT coy)
 1 (Maipo) mot inf bde (3 mot inf regt, 1 arty regt)
 1 (6th) reinforced regt (1 mot inf bn, 1 arty gp, 1 sigs coy)
 1 (10th) reinforced regt (1 mot inf bn, 2 AT coy, 1 engr bn)
 1 (11th) mot inf det (1 inf bn, 1 arty gp)
 1 (14th) mot inf det (1 mot inf bn, 1 arty gp, 1 sigs coy, 1 AT coy)
 4 mot inf regt
 1 (3rd) mtn det (1 mtn inf bn, 1 arty gp, 1 engr coy)
 1 (9th) mtn det (1 mtn inf bn, 1 engr coy, 1 construction bn)
 2 (8th & 17th) mtn det (1 mtn inf bn, 1 arty coy)
COMBAT SUPPORT
 1 engr regt
 4 sigs bn
 1 sigs coy
 2 int regt
 1 MP regt
COMBAT SERVICE SUPPORT
 1 log div (2 log regt)
 4 log regt
 6 log coy
 1 maint div (1 maint regt)
AVIATION
 1 avn bde (1 tpt avn bn, 1 hel bn, 1 spt bn)

EQUIPMENT BY TYPE
ARMOURED FIGHTING VEHICLES
  MBT 246: 115 *Leopard 1*; 131 *Leopard 2A4*
  IFV 191: 173 *Marder* 1A3; 18 YPR-765 PRI
  APC 548
    APC (T) 369 M113A1/A2
    APC (W) 179 *Piranha*
ENGINEERING & MAINTENANCE VEHICLES
  AEV 9 Pioneerpanzer 2 *Dachs*
  ARV 35 BPz-2
  VLB 16 *Biber*
  MW 3+: *Bozena* 5; 3 *Leopard* 1
ANTI-TANK/ANTI-INFRASTRUCTURE
  MSL • MANPATS *Spike*-LR; *Spike*-ER
  RCL 84mm *Carl Gustav*; **106mm** 213 M40A1
ARTILLERY 1,407
  SP 155mm 48: 24 M109A3; 24 M109A5+
  TOWED 240: **105mm** 192: 88 M101; 104 Model 56 pack howitzer; **155mm** 48 M-68
  MRL 160mm 12 LAR-160
  MOR 1,107: **81mm** 743: 303 ECIA L65/81; 175 FAMAE; 265 Soltam; **120mm** 293: 173 ECIA L65/120; 17 FAMAE; 93 M-65; **SP 120mm** 71: 35 FAMAE (on *Piranha* 6x6); 36 Soltam (on M113A2)
AIRCRAFT
  TPT • Light 8: 2 C-212-300 *Aviocar*; 3 Cessna 208 *Caravan*; 3 CN235
HELICOPTERS
  ISR 9 MD-530F *Lifter* (armed)
  TPT 17: **Medium** 12: 8 AS532AL *Cougar*; 2 AS532ALe *Cougar*; 2 SA330 *Puma*; **Light** 5: 4 H125 *Ecureuil*; 1 AS355F *Ecureuil* II
AIR DEFENCE
  SAM • Point-defence *Mistral*
  GUNS 41:
    SP 20mm 17 *Piranha*/TCM-20
    TOWED 20mm 24 TCM-20

Navy 19,800

5 Naval Zones; 1st Naval Zone and main HQ at Valparaiso; 2nd Naval Zone at Talcahuano; 3rd Naval Zone at Punta Arenas; 4th Naval Zone at Iquique; 5th Naval Zone at Puerto Montt

FORCES BY ROLE
SPECIAL FORCES
  1 (diver) SF comd
EQUIPMENT BY TYPE
SUBMARINES • TACTICAL • SSK 4:
  2 *O'Higgins* (*Scorpène*) with 6 single 533mm TT with SM39 *Exocet* Block 2 AShM/*Black Shark* HWT
  2 *Thomson* (GER T-209/1400) with 8 single 533mm TT with SM39 *Exocet* Block 2 AShM/*Black Shark* HWT/SUT HWT (of which 1 in refit)
PRINCIPAL SURFACE COMBATANTS 8
  DESTROYERS • DDGHM 1 *Almirante Williams* (ex-UK *Broadsword* Type-22) with 2 quad lnchr with RGM-84 *Harpoon* AShM, 2 8-cell VLS with *Barak*-1 SAM; 2 triple 324mm ASTT with Mk 46 LWT, 1 76mm gun (capacity 1 AS532SC *Cougar*)
  FRIGATES 7:
  FFGHM 5:
    3 *Almirante Cochrane* (ex-UK *Norfolk* Type-23) with 2 quad lnchr with RGM-84C *Harpoon* Block 1B AShM, 1 32-cell VLS with *Sea Wolf* SAM, 2 twin 324mm ASTT with Mk 46 mod 2 LWT, 1 114mm gun (capacity 1 AS-532SC *Cougar*) (MLU begun 2018)
    2 *Almirante Riveros* (ex-NLD *Karel Doorman*) with 2 quad lnchr with MM40 *Exocet* Block 3 AShM, 1 8-cell Mk 48 VLS with RIM-7P *Sea Sparrow* SAM, 4 single SVTT Mk 32 mod 9 324mm ASTT with Mk 46 mod 5 HWT, 1 76mm gun (capacity 1 AS532SC *Cougar*)
  FFGM 2:
    2 *Almirante Lattore* (ex-NLD *Jacob Van Heemskerck*) with 2 quad lnchr with RGM-84 *Harpoon* AShM, 1 Mk 13 GMLS with SM-1MR SAM, 1 octuple Mk 29 lnchr with RIM-7P *Sea Sparrow* SAM, 2 twin SVTT Mk32 324mm ASTT with Mk 46 LWT, 1 *Goalkeeper* CIWS
PATROL AND COASTAL COMBATANTS 12
  PSOH 4: 2 *Piloto Pardo*; 2 *Piloto Pardo* with 1 76mm gun (ice-strengthened hull)
  PCG 3:
    2 *Casma* (ISR *Sa'ar* 4) with 6 single lnchr with *Gabriel* I AShM, 2 76mm guns
    1 *Casma* (ISR *Sa'ar* 4) with 4 single lnchr with *Gabriel* I AShM, 2 twin lnchr with MM40 *Exocet* AShM, 2 76mm guns
  PCO 5 *Micalvi*
AMPHIBIOUS
  PRINCIPAL AMPHIBIOUS SHIPS
    LPD 1 *Sargento Aldea* (ex-FRA *Foudre*) with 3 twin *Simbad* lnchr with *Mistral* SAM (capacity 4 med hel; 1 LCT; 2 LCM; 22 tanks; 470 troops)
  LANDING SHIPS 3
    LSM 1 *Elicura*
    LST 2 *Maipo* (FRA *Batral*) with 1 hel landing platform (capacity 7 tanks; 140 troops)
  LANDING CRAFT 3
    LCT 1 CDIC (for use in *Sargento Aldea*)
    LCM 2 (for use in *Sargento Aldea*)
LOGISTICS AND SUPPORT 12
  ABU 1 *George Slight Marshall* with 1 hel landing platform
  AFD 3
  AGOR 1 *Cabo de Hornos*
  AGHS 1 *Micalvi*
  AOR 2: 1 *Almirante Montt* with 1 hel landing platform; 1 *Araucano*
  AP 1 *Aguiles* (1 hel landing platform)
  ATF 2 *Veritas*
  AXS 1 *Esmeralda*

Naval Aviation 600

EQUIPMENT BY TYPE
AIRCRAFT 14 combat capable
  ASW 4: 2 C295ASW *Persuader*; 2 P-3ACH *Orion*
  MP 4: 1 C295MPA *Persuader*; 3 EMB-111 *Bandeirante**
  ISR 7 P-68
  TRG 7 PC-7 *Turbo Trainer**

HELICOPTERS
ASW 5 AS532SC *Cougar*
MRH 8 AS365 *Dauphin*
TPT • **Light** 6: 2 Bell 206 *Jet Ranger*; 4 Bo-105S
AIR-LAUNCHED MISSILES • **AShM** AM39 *Exocet*

Marines 3,600
FORCES BY ROLE
MANOEUVRE
Amphibious
1 amph bde (2 mne bn, 1 cbt spt bn, 1 log bn)
2 coastal def unit
EQUIPMENT BY TYPE
ARMOURED FIGHTING VEHICLES
 LT TK 15 FV101 *Scorpion*
 APC • **APC (W)** 25 MOWAG *Roland*
 AAV 12 AAV-7
ARTILLERY 39
 TOWED 23: **105mm** 7 KH-178; **155mm** 16 M-71
 MOR **81mm** 16
COASTAL DEFENCE • **AShM** MM38 *Exocet*
AIR DEFENCE • **SAM** • **Point-defence** 14: 4 M998 *Avenger*; 10 M1097 *Avenger*

Coast Guard
Integral part of the Navy
EQUIPMENT BY TYPE
PATROL AND COASTAL COMBATANTS 55
 PBF 26 *Archangel*
 PB 29: 18 *Alacalufe* (*Protector*-class); 4 *Grumete Diaz* (*Dabor*-class); 6 *Pelluhue*; 1 *Ona*

Air Force 11,050
FORCES BY ROLE
FIGHTER
 1 sqn with F-5E/F *Tiger* III+
 2 sqn with F-16AM/BM *Fighting Falcon*
FIGHTER/GROUND ATTACK
 1 sqn with F-16C/D Block 50 *Fighting Falcon* (*Puma*)
ISR
 1 (photo) flt with; DHC-6-300 *Twin Otter*; Learjet 35A
AIRBORNE EARLY WARNING
 1 flt with B-707 *Phalcon*
TANKER/TRANSPORT
 1 sqn with B-737-300; C-130B/H *Hercules*; KC-130R *Hercules*; KC-135 *Stratotanker*
TRANSPORT
 3 sqn with Bell 205 (UH-1H *Iroquois*); C-212-200/300 *Aviocar*; Cessna O-2A; Cessna 525 *Citation* CJ1; DHC-6-100/300 *Twin Otter*; PA-28-236 *Dakota*; Bell 205 (UH-1H *Iroquois*)
 1 VIP flt with B-737-500 (VIP); Gulfstream IV
TRAINING
 1 sqn with EMB-314 *Super Tucano**
 1 sqn with PA-28-236 *Dakota*; T-35A/B *Pillan*
TRANSPORT HELICOPTER
 1 sqn with Bell 205 (UH-1H *Iroquois*); Bell 206B (trg); Bell 412 *Twin Huey*; Bo-105CBS-4; S-70A *Black Hawk*
AIR DEFENCE
 1 AD regt (5 AD sqn) with *Crotale*; NASAMS; *Mistral*; M163/M167 *Vulcan*; Oerlikon GDF-005

EQUIPMENT BY TYPE
AIRCRAFT 90 combat capable
 FTR 48: 10 F-5E *Tigre* III+; 2 F-5F *Tigre* III+; 29 F-16AM *Fighting Falcon*; 7 F-16BM *Fighting Falcon*
 FGA 10: 6 F-16C Block 50 *Fighting Falcon*; 4 F-16D Block 50 *Fighting Falcon*
 ATK 16 C-101CC *Aviojet* (A-36 *Halcón*)
 ISR 3 Cessna O-2A
 AEW&C 1 B-707 *Phalcon*
 TKR 5: 2 KC-130R *Hercules*: 3 KC-135 *Stratotanker*
 TPT 37: **Medium** 3: 1 C-130B *Hercules*; 2 C-130H *Hercules*; **Light** 29: 2 C-212-200 *Aviocar*; 1 C-212-300 *Aviocar*; 4 Cessna 525 *Citation* CJ1; 3 DHC-6-100 *Twin Otter*; 7 DHC-6-300 *Twin Otter*; 2 Learjet 35A; 10 PA-28-236 *Dakota*; **PAX** 5: 1 B-737-300; 1 B-737-500; 1 B-767-300ER; 2 Gulfstream IV
 TRG 47: 4 Cirrus SR-22T; 16 EMB-314 *Super Tucano**; 27 T-35A/B *Pillan*
HELICOPTERS
 MRH 12 Bell 412EP *Twin Huey*
 TPT 28: **Medium** 7: 1 S-70A *Black Hawk*; 6 S-70i (MH-60M) *Black Hawk*; **Light** 21: 13 Bell 205 (UH-1H *Iroquois*); 5 Bell 206B (trg); 2 BK-117; 1 Bo-105CBS-4
UNMANNED AERIAL VEHICLES
 ISR • **Medium** 3 *Hermes* 900
AIR DEFENCE
 SAM
  Short-range 17: 5 *Crotale*; 12 NASAMS
  Point-defence Mistral (including some *Mygale*/*Aspic*)
 GUNS • **TOWED 20mm** M163/M167 *Vulcan*; **35mm** Oerlikon GDF-005
AIR-LAUNCHED MISSILES
 AAM • **IR** AIM-9J/M *Sidewinder*; Python 3; *Shafrir*‡; **IIR** Python 4; **ARH** AIM-120C AMRAAM; *Derby*
 ASM AGM-65G *Maverick*
BOMBS
 Laser-guided *Paveway* II
 INS/GPS guided JDAM

Paramilitary 44,700

Carabineros 44,700
Ministry of Interior; 15 zones, 36 districts, 179 *comisaria*
EQUIPMENT BY TYPE
ARMOURED FIGHTING VEHICLES
 APC • **APC (W)** 20 MOWAG *Roland*
ARTILLERY • **MOR 81mm**
AIRCRAFT
 TPT • **Light** 4: 1 Beech 200 *King Air*; 1 Cessna 208; 1 Cessna 550 *Citation* V; 1 PA-31T *Cheyenne* II
HELICOPTERS • **TPT** • **Light** 16: 5 AW109E *Power*; 1 AW139; 1 Bell 206 *Jet Ranger*; 2 BK-117; 5 Bo-105; 2 H135

DEPLOYMENT

BOSNIA-HERZEGOVINA: EU • EUFOR • *Operation Althea* 15

CYPRUS: UN • UNFICYP 12

INDIA/PAKISTAN: UN • UNMOGIP 2

MIDDLE EAST: UN • UNTSO 3

Colombia COL

Colombian Peso pC		2018	2019	2020
GDP	pC	978tr	1052tr	
	US$	331bn	328bn	
per capita	US$	6,642	6,508	
Growth	%	2.6	3.4	
Inflation	%	3.2	3.6	
Def bdgt [a]	pC	31.3tr	33.5tr	35.8tr
	US$	10.6bn	10.5bn	
FMA (US)	US$	38.5m	20.0m	20.0m
US$1=pC		2,956.36	3,207.65	

[a] Includes Defence and Security

Real-terms defence budget trend (US$bn, constant 2015)

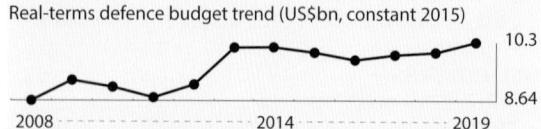

Population	48,631,464					
Age	0–14	15–19	20–24	25–29	30–64	65 plus
Male	12.1%	4.2%	4.3%	4.3%	21.2%	3.4%
Female	11.5%	4.0%	4.2%	4.2%	22.1%	4.7%

Capabilities

Colombia's armed forces have over recent decades significantly improved their level of training and their overall capabilities. Internal security remains a priority, and the armed forces are focused on fulfilling counter-insurgency and counter-narcotics operations. While the armed forces are looking towards new security roles and organisations for the post-FARC era, the emergence of a FARC splinter group in mid-2019 will mean continued focus on internal-security tasks. In response to the humanitarian and security challenge from Venezuela, Colombia is strengthening cooperation with Brazil on border controls, while also housing a large number of Venezuelan refugees. There are good military ties with Argentina, Chile and Peru. The US is Colombia's closest international military partner, with cooperation involving equipment procurement, technical advice and personnel training. In May 2018, Colombia joined NATO as a global partner. The forces train regularly, including multilateral drills such as the US *Red Flag* exercise, to which Colombia sent *Kfir* combat aircraft and its KC-767 tanker in 2018 and 2019. Although the equipment inventory mainly comprises legacy systems, Colombia has the capability to independently deploy its forces beyond national borders. The army is planning to modernise its oldest APCs, while the navy may look to replace both its submarine and frigate fleets in the medium term. The air force's ground-attack capabilities remain limited, though a substantial number of multi-role and transport helicopters have been procured. Colombia's defence industry is active in all domains. CIAC is developing its first indigenous UAVs, while CODALTEC is developing an air-defence system for regional export. COTECMAR has supplied patrol boats and amphibious ships for national and export markets.

ACTIVE 293,200 (Army 223,150, Navy 56,400 Air 13,650) **Paramilitary 187,900**

Conscript liability 18-months duration with upper age limit of 24, males only

RESERVE 34,950 (Army 25,050 Navy 6,500 Air 3,400)

ORGANISATIONS BY SERVICE

Army 223,150

FORCES BY ROLE
SPECIAL FORCES
 1 SF div (3 SF regt)
 1 (anti-terrorist) SF bn
MANOEUVRE
 Mechanised
 1 (1st) mech div (1 (2nd) mech bde (2 mech inf bn, 1 mtn inf bn, 1 engr bn, 1 MP bn, 1 spt bn, 2 Gaula anti-kidnap gp); 1 (10th) mech bde (1 armd recce bn, 1 mech cav bn, 1 mech inf bn, 1 mtn inf bn, 3 sy bn, 2 arty bn, 1 engr bn, 1 spt bn, 2 Gaula anti-kidnap gp); 1 (urban) spec ops bn)
 Light
 1 (2nd) inf div (1 (1st) inf bde (1 mech cav bn, 2 inf bn, 1 mtn inf bn, 1 sy bn, 1 arty bn, 1 spt bn, 1 Gaula anti-kidnap gp); 1 (5th) inf bde (3 inf bn, 1 jungle inf bn, 1 sy bn, 1 arty bn, 1 engr bn, 1 spt bn, 1 Gaula anti-kidnap gp); 1 (30th) inf bde (1 mech cav bn, 2 inf bn, 1 sy bn, 1 arty bn, 1 engr bn, 1 spt bn); 1 AD bn; 1 rapid reaction force (1 (urban) spec ops bn, 4 COIN bn, 3 sy bn))
 1 (3rd) inf div (1 (3rd) inf bde (2 inf bn, 1 mtn inf bn, 1 COIN bn, 1 arty bn, 1 engr bn, 1 cbt spt bn, 1 MP bn, 1 log bn, 1 Gaula anti-kidnap gp); 1 (23rd) inf bde (1 cav gp, 1 lt inf bn, 1 jungle inf bn, 1 spt bn, 1 log bn); 1 (29th) mtn bde (1 mtn inf bn, 1 inf bn, 2 COIN bn, 1 spt bn, 1 log bn); 1 mtn inf bn)
 1 (4th) inf div (1 (7th) air mob bde (2 air mob inf bn, 1 lt inf bn, 1 COIN bn, 1 engr bn, 1 spt bn, 1 log bn, 1 Gaula anti-kidnap gp); 1 (22nd) jungle bde (1 air mob inf bn, 1 lt inf bn, 1 jungle inf bn, 1 COIN bn, 1 spt bn, 1 log bn); 1 (31st) jungle bde (1 lt inf bn, 1 jungle inf bn))
 1 (5th) inf div (1 (6th) lt inf bde (2 lt inf bn, 1 mtn inf bn, 3 COIN bn, 1 EOD bn, 2 spt bn, 1 Gaula anti-kidnap gp); 1 (8th) inf bde (1 inf bn, 1 mtn inf bn, 1 arty bn, 1 engr bn, 1 spt bn, 1 Gaula anti-kidnap gp); 1 (9th) inf bde (2 inf bn, 1 arty bn, 1 COIN bn, 1 sy bn, 1 spt bn, 1 Gaula anti-kidnap gp); 1 (13th) inf bde (1 (urban) spec ops bn, 1 recce bn, 3 inf bn, 1 mtn inf bn, 1 air mob bn, 1 COIN bn, 1 arty bn, 1 engr bn, 2 MP bn, 1 spt bn, 1 Gaula anti-kidnap gp))
 1 (6th) inf div (1 (12th) inf bde (1 inf bn, 1 jungle inf bn, 1 mtn inf bn, 1 COIN bn, 1 engr bn, 1 spt bn, 1 Gaula anti-kidnap gp); 1 (26th) jungle bde (1 jungle inf bn, 1 spt bn); 1 (27th) jungle inf bde (1 inf bn, 1 jungle inf bn, 1 sy bn, 1 arty bn, 1 engr bn, 1 spt bn); 1 (13th) mobile sy bde; 2 COIN bn)
 1 (7th) inf div (1 (4th) inf bde (1 (urban) spec ops bn; 1 mech cav gp, 3 inf bn, 1 sy bn, 1 arty bn, 1 engr bn, 1 MP bn, 1 spt bn, 2 Gaula anti-kidnap gp); 1 (11th) inf bde (1 inf bn, 1 air mob bn, 1 sy bn, 1 spt bn, 2 Gaula anti-kidnap gp); 1 (14th) inf bde (2 inf bn, 1 sy bn, 1 engr bn, 1 spt bn); 1 (15th) jungle bde (1 inf bn, 2 COIN bn, 1 engr bn); 1 (17th) inf bde (2 inf bn, 1 engr bn, 1 spt bn))

1 (8th) inf div (1 (16th) lt inf bde (1 recce bn, 1 inf bn, 1 spt bn, 1 Gaula anti-kidnap gp); 1 (18th) inf bde (1 air mob gp, 2 sy bn, 1 arty bn, 1 engr bn, 1 spt bn); 1 (28th) jungle bde (2 inf, 2 COIN, 1 spt bn); 3 COIN bn) 3 COIN mobile bde (each: 4 COIN bn, 1 spt bn)

Other
1 indep rapid reaction force (1 SF bde, 3 mobile sy bde)

COMBAT SUPPORT
1 cbt engr bde (1 SF engr bn, 1 (emergency response) engr bn, 1 EOD bn, 1 construction bn, 1 demining bn, 1 maint bn)
1 int bde (2 SIGINT bn, 1 log bn, 1 maint bn)

COMBAT SERVICE SUPPORT
2 spt/log bde (each: 1 spt bn, 1 maint bn, 1 supply bn, 1 tpt bn, 1 medical bn, 1 log bn)

AVIATION
1 air aslt div (1 counter-narcotics bde (4 counter-narcotics bn, 1 spt bn); 1 (25th) avn bde (4 hel bn; 5 avn bn; 1 avn log bn); 1 (32nd) avn bde (1 avn bn, 2 maint bn, 1 trg bn, 1 spt bn); 1 SF avn bn)

EQUIPMENT BY TYPE
ARMOURED FIGHTING VEHICLES
  RECCE 121 EE-9 *Cascavel*
  IFV 60: 28 *Commando Advanced*; 32 LAV III
  APC 114
    APC (T) 54: 28 M113A1 (TPM-113A1); 26 M113A2 (TPM-113A2)
    APC (W) 56 EE-11 *Urutu*
  PPV 4 RG-31 *Nyala*
  AUV 38 M1117 *Guardian*
ANTI-TANK/ANTI-INFRASTRUCTURE
  MSL
    SP 77 *Nimrod*
    MANPATS TOW; *Spike*-ER
  RCL 106mm 73 M40A1
ARTILLERY 1,796
  TOWED 120: **105mm** 107: 22 LG1 MkIII; 85 M101; **155mm** 13 155/52 APU SBT-1
  MOR 1,676: **81mm** 1,507; **120mm** 169
AIRCRAFT
  ELINT 3: 2 Beech B200 *King Air*; 1 Beech 350 *King Air*
  TPT • Light 23: 2 An-32B; 2 Beech B200 *King Air*; 3 Beech 350 *King Air*; 1 Beech C90 *King Air*; 2 C-212 *Aviocar* (Medevac); 8 Cessna 208B *Grand Caravan*; 1 Cessna 208B-EX *Grand Caravan*; 4 *Turbo Commander* 695A
HELICOPTERS
  MRH 19: 8 Mi-17-1V *Hip*; 6 Mi-17MD; 5 Mi-17V-5 *Hip*
  TPT 93: **Medium** 54: 47 UH-60L *Black Hawk*; 7 S-70i *Black Hawk*; **Light** 39: 24 Bell 205 (UH-1H *Iroquois*); 15 Bell 212 (UH-1N *Twin Huey*)
AIR DEFENCE • GUNS • TOWED 40mm 4 M1A1

Navy 56,400 (incl 12,100 conscript)

HQ located at Puerto Carreño

EQUIPMENT BY TYPE
SUBMARINES • TACTICAL • SSK 4:
  2 *Pijao* (GER T-209/1200) each with 8 single 533mm TT each with *SeaHake* (DM2A3) HWT
  2 *Intrepido* (GER T-206A) each with 8 single 533mm TT each with *SeaHake* (DM2A3) HWT

PRINCIPAL SURFACE COMBATANTS 4
  FRIGATES • FFGHM 4 *Almirante Padilla* with 2 quad lnchr with *Hae Sung* I AShM, 2 twin *Simbad* lnchr with *Mistral* SAM, 2 triple ILAS-3 (B-515) 324mm ASTT each with A244/S LWT, 1 76mm gun (capacity 1 Bo-105/AS555SN *Fennec* hel)
PATROL AND COASTAL COMBATANTS 61
  CORVETTES • FS 1 *Narino* (ex-ROK *Dong Hae*) with 2 triple SVTT Mk 32 324mm ASTT with Mk 46 LWT
  PSOH 3 *20 de Julio*
  PCO 2: 1 *Valle del Cauca Durable* (ex-US *Reliance*) with 1 hel landing platform; 1 *San Andres* (ex-US *Balsam*)
  PCC 3 *Punta Espada* (CPV-46)
  PCR 10: 2 *Arauca* with 1 76mm guns; 8 *Nodriza* (PAF-II) with hel landing platform
  PB 12: 1 *11 de Noviembre* (CPV-40) with 1 *Typhoon* CIWS; 2 *Castillo y Rada* (Swiftships 105); 2 *Jaime Gomez*; 1 *José Maria Palas* (Swiftships 110); 4 *Point*; 2 *Toledo*
  PBR 30: 5 *Diligente*; 7 LPR-40; 3 Swiftships; 9 *Tenerife*; 2 PAF-L; 4 others
AMPHIBIOUS 21
  LCM 3 LCM-8
  LCT 5 *Golfo de Tribuga*
  LCU 5 *Morrosquillo* (LCU 1466)
  UCAC 8 *Griffon* 2000TD
LOGISTICS AND SUPPORT 8
  ABU 1 *Quindio*
  AG 2: 1 *Inirida*; 1 *Luneburg* (ex-GER, depot ship for patrol vessels)
  AGHS 1 *Roncador*
  AGOR 2 *Providencia*
  AGS 1 *Gorgona*
  AXS 1 *Gloria*

Naval Aviation 150

EQUIPMENT BY TYPE
AIRCRAFT
  MP 3 CN235 MPA *Persuader*
  ISR 1 PA-31 *Navajo* (upgraded for ISR)
  TPT • Light 11: 1 C-212 (Medevac); 4 Cessna 206; 3 Cessna 208 *Caravan*; 1 PA-31 *Navajo*; 1 PA-34 *Seneca*; 1 Beech 350 *King Air*
HELICOPTERS
  SAR 2 AS365 *Dauphin*
  MRH 8: 1 AS555SN *Fennec*; 3 Bell 412 *Twin Huey*; 4 Bell 412EP *Twin Huey*
  TPT • Light 9: 1 Bell 212; 5 Bell 212 (UH-1N); 1 BK-117; 2 Bo-105

Marines 22,250

FORCES BY ROLE
SPECIAL FORCES
  1 SF bde (4 SF bn)
MANOEUVRE
  Amphibious
  1 mne bde (1 SF (Gaula) bn, 5 mne bn, 2 rvn bn, 1 spt bn)
  1 mne bde (1 SF bn, 2 mne bn, 2 rvn bn, 1 spt bn)
  1 rvn bde (1 SF bn, 1 mne bn, 2 rvn bn, 1 spt bn)
  1 rvn bde (4 rvn bn)
  1 rvn bde (3 rvn bn)

COMBAT SERVICE SUPPORT
1 log bde (6 spt bn)
1 trg bde (7 trg bn, 1 spt bn)
EQUIPMENT BY TYPE
ARTILLERY • MOR 82: 81mm 74; 120mm 8
AIR DEFENCE • SAM Point-defence Mistral

Air Force 13,650
FORCES BY ROLE
FIGHTER/GROUND ATTACK
2 sqn with Kfir C-10/C-12/TC-12
GROUND ATTACK/ISR
1 sqn with A-37B/OA-37B Dragonfly
1 sqn with AC-47T
1 sqn with EMB-312 Tucano*
2 sqn with EMB-314 Super Tucano* (A-29)
EW/ELINT
2 sqn with Beech 350 King Air; Cessna 208; Cessna 560; C-26B Metroliner; SA 2-37; 1 Turbo Commander 695
TRANSPORT
1 (Presidential) sqn with B-737BBJ; EMB-600 Legacy; Bell 412EP; F-28 Fellowship; UH-60L Black Hawk
1 sqn with B-727; B-737-400; C-130B/H Hercules; C-212; C295M; CN235M; ; IAI Arava; KC-767
1 sqn with Beech C90 King Air; Beech 350C King Air; Cessna 208B; Cessna 550; EMB-110P1 (C-95)
TRAINING
1 sqn with Lancair Synergy (T-90 Calima)
1 sqn with T-37B
1 hel sqn with Bell 206B3
1 hel sqn with TH-67
HELICOPTER
1 sqn with AH-60L Arpia III
1 sqn with UH-60L Black Hawk (CSAR)
1 sqn with Hughes 500M
1 sqn with Bell 205 (UH-1H)
1 sqn with Bell 206B3 Jet Ranger III
1 sqn with Bell 212
EQUIPMENT BY TYPE
AIRCRAFT 72 combat capable
FGA 22: 10 Kfir C-10; 9 Kfir C-12; 3 Kfir TC-12
ATK 12: 6 A-37B/OA-37B Dragonfly; 6 AC-47T Spooky (Fantasma)
ISR 13: 1 Beech C90 King Air; 1 C-26B Metroliner; 5 Cessna 560 Citation II; 6 SA 2-37
ELINT 13: 4 Beech 350 King Air; 6 Cessna 208 Grand Caravan; 2 Cessna 337G; 1 Turbo Commander 695
TKR/TPT 1 KC-767
TPT 64: Medium 7: 3 C-130B Hercules (3 more in store); 3 C-130H Hercules; 1 B-737F; Light 49: 10 ATR-42; 2 Beech 300 King Air; 2 Beech 350C King Air; 1 Beech 350i King Air (VIP); 4 Beech C90 King Air; 4 C-212; 6 C295M; 1 Cessna 182R; 12 Cessna 208B (medevac); 1 Cessna 550; 2 CN235M; 2 EMB-110P1 (C-95); 1 EMB-170-100LR; 1 IAI-201 Arava; PAX 8: 2 B-727; 1 B-737-400; 1 B-737BBJ; 1 EMB-600 Legacy; 1 F-28-1000 Fellowship; 1 F-28-3000 Fellowship; 1 Learjet 60
TRG 78: 14 EMB-312 Tucano*; 24 EMB-314 Super Tucano (A-29)*; 23 Lancair Synergy (T-90 Calima); 17 T-37B

HELICOPTERS
MRH 17: 6 AH-60L Arpia III; 8 AH-60L Arpia IV; 1 Bell 412EP Twin Huey (VIP); 2 Hughes 500M
TPT 48: Medium 13 UH-60L Black Hawk (incl 1 VIP hel); Light 35: 12 Bell 205 (UH-1H Iroquois); 12 Bell 206B3 Jet Ranger III; 11 Bell 212
TRG 30 TH-67
UNAMMED AERIAL VEHICLES • ISR • Medium 8: 6 Hermes 450; 2 Hermes 900
AIR-LAUNCHED MISSILES
AAM • IR Python 3; IIR Python 4; Python 5; ARH Derby; I-Derby ER (reported)
ASM Spike-ER; Spike-NLOS
BOMBS
Laser-guided Paveway II
INS/GPS guided Spice

Paramilitary 187,900

National Police Force 187,900
EQUIPMENT BY TYPE
AIRCRAFT
ELINT 5 C-26B Metroliner
TPT • Light 42: 5 ATR-42; 3 Beech 200 King Air; 2 Beech 300 King Air; 2 Beech 1900; 1 Beech C99; 4 BT-67; 2 C-26 Metroliner; 3 Cessna 152; 3 Cessna 172; 9 Cessna 206; 2 Cessna 208 Caravan; 2 DHC-6 Twin Otter; 1 DHC-8; 3 PA-31 Navajo
HELICOPTERS
MRH 4: 1 Bell 407GXP; 1 Bell 412EP; 2 MD-500D
TPT 75: Medium 17: 5 UH-60A Black Hawk; 9 UH-60L Black Hawk; 3 S-70i Black Hawk; Light 58: 34 Bell 205 (UH-1H-II Huey II); 6 Bell 206B; 5 Bell 206L/L3/L4 Long Ranger; 8 Bell 212; 5 Bell 407

DEPLOYMENT
CENTRAL AFRICAN REPUBLIC: UN • MINUSCA 2
EGYPT: MFO 275; 1 inf bn
LEBANON: UN • UNIFIL 1

FOREIGN FORCES
United States US Southern Command: 50

Costa Rica CRI

Costa Rican Colon C		2018	2019	2020
GDP	C	34.7tr	36.5tr	
	US$	60.5bn	61.0bn	
per capita	US$	12,039	12014.8	
Growth	%	2.6	2.0	
Inflation	%	2.2	2.7	
Sy Bdgt [a]	C	259bn	259bn	267bn
	US$	451m	433m	
FMA (US)	US$	5m	0m	0m
US$1=C		573.79	597.74	

[a] Paramilitary budget

Real-terms defence budget trend (US$m, constant 2015)

462
223
2008 — — — — — — 2014 — — — — — — 2019

Population 5,043,084

Age	0–14	15–19	20–24	25–29	30–64	65 plus
Male	11.4%	3.8%	4.1%	4.3%	22.6%	3.9%
Female	10.9%	3.7%	4.0%	4.2%	22.7%	4.6%

Capabilities

Costa Rica's armed forces were constitutionally abolished in 1949, and the country relies on paramilitary-type police organisations for internal-security and counter-narcotics tasks, as well as participation in regional peacekeeping operations. A new National Security Strategy was adopted in 2018 in order to help tackle rising crime. Colombia and the US have provided assistance and training, focused on policing and internal-security tasks rather than conventional military operations. The Special Intervention Unit (UEI) has received specialist training from non-regional states, including the US. The Public Force, Coast Guard and Air Surveillance units have little heavy military equipment, and recent modernisation has depended on donations from countries such as China and the US. Apart from limited maintenance facilities, Costa Rica has no domestic defence industry.

Paramilitary 9,800

ORGANISATIONS BY SERVICE

Paramilitary 9,800

Special Intervention Unit
FORCES BY ROLE
SPECIAL FORCES
  1 spec ops unit

Public Force 9,000
11 regional directorates

Coast Guard Unit 400
EQUIPMENT BY TYPE
PATROL AND COASTAL COMBATANTS 10:
  PCC 2 *Libertador Juan Rafael Mora* (ex-US *Island*)
PB 8: 2 *Cabo Blanco* (US *Swift* 65); 1 *Isla del Coco* (US *Swift* 105); 3 *Point*; 1 *Primera Dama* (US *Swift* 42); 1 *Puerto Quebos* (US *Swift* 36)

Air Surveillance Unit 400
EQUIPMENT BY TYPE
AIRCRAFT • TPT • Light 14: 2 Cessna T210 *Centurion*; 4 Cessna U206G *Stationair*; 2 PA-31 *Navajo*; 2 PA-34 *Seneca*; 1 Piper PA-23 *Aztec*; 1 Cessna 182RG; 2 Y-12E
HELICOPTERS
  MRH 3: 1 MD-500E; 2 MD-600N
  TPT • Light 4 Bell 212 (UH-1N)

Cuba CUB

Cuban Peso P		2018	2019	2020
GDP	US$			
per capita	US$			
Growth				
Inflation				
Def exp	P			
	US$			
US$1=P				

Population 11,086,996
*definitive data not available

Age	0–14	15–19	20–24	25–29	30–64	65 plus
Male	8.4%	3.1%	3.1%	3.4%	24.6%	7.1%
Female	7.9%	2.9%	2.9%	3.1%	25.0%	8.4%

Capabilities

Cuba's armed forces are principally focused on protecting territorial integrity, and rely on a mass-mobilisation system. Military capability is limited by equipment obsolescence and a largely conscript-based force. Cuba maintains military ties with China and Russia, and the latter has stepped in to supply oil and fuel following Venezuela's economic collapse. Defence cooperation with Russia is largely centred around technical support for the maintenance of Cuba's ageing Soviet-era equipment. Cooperation with China appears to be on a smaller scale and involves training agreements and personnel exchanges. Training levels are uncertain and flying hours are likely to be low due to the limited availability of serviceable aircraft. The armed forces are no longer designed for expeditionary operations, and have little logistical capability to support deployments abroad. The inventory is almost entirely composed of legacy Soviet-era systems with varying degrees of obsolescence. Serviceability appears a problem, with much equipment at a low level of availability and maintenance demands growing as fleets age. Much of the aviation fleet is reported to be in storage. Russian assistance should improve availability, but is only a short-term solution given the advanced age of much of the inventory. It is unlikely that Havana will be in a position to finance significant equipment recapitalisation in the near term. Cuba has little in the way of domestic defence industry, bar some upgrade and maintenance capacity. Cuba has sent maintainers to South Africa, highlighting not just revenue-raising requirements for the forces but also the potential effect this might have on remaining maintenance capacity in Cuba.

ACTIVE 49,000 (Army 38,000 Navy 3,000 Air 8,000)
Paramilitary 26,500
Conscript liability 2 years

RESERVE 39,000 (Army 39,000) **Paramilitary 1,120,000**
Ready Reserves (serve 45 days per year) to fill out Active and Reserve units; see also Paramilitary

ORGANISATIONS BY SERVICE

Army ε38,000
FORCES BY ROLE
COMMAND
   3 regional comd HQ
   3 army comd HQ
COMMAND
   3 SF regt
MANOEUVRE
  Armoured
   1 tk div (3 tk bde)
  Mechanised
   2 (mixed) mech bde
  Light
   2 (frontier) bde
  Air Manoeuvre
   1 AB bde
AIR DEFENCE
   1 ADA regt
   1 SAM bde

Reserves 39,000
FORCES BY ROLE
MANOEUVRE
  Light
   14 inf bde

EQUIPMENT BY TYPE†
ARMOURED FIGHTING VEHICLES
  MBT ε900 T-34/T-54/T-55/T-62
  LT TK PT-76
  ASLT BTR-60 100mm
  RECCE BRDM-2;
  AIFV ε50 BMP-1/1P
  APC ε500 BTR-152/BTR-50/BTR-60
ANTI-TANK/ANTI-INFRASTRUCTURE
  MSL
    SP 2K16 *Shmel* (AT-1 *Snapper*)
    MANPATS 9K11 *Malyutka* (AT-3 *Sagger*)
  GUNS 600+: **57mm** 600 ZIS-2 (M-1943); **85mm** D-44
ARTILLERY 1,715+
  SP 40+: **100mm** AAPMP-100; CATAP-100; **122mm** 2S1 *Gvozdika*; AAP-T-122; AAP-BMP-122; *Jupiter* III; *Jupiter* IV; **130mm** AAP-T-130; *Jupiter* V; **152mm** 2S3 *Akatsiya*
  TOWED 500: **122mm** D-30; M-30 (M-1938); **130mm** M-46; **152mm** D-1; M-1937 (ML-20)
  MRL • SP 175: **122mm** BM-21 *Grad*; **140mm** BM-14
  MOR 1,000: **82mm** M-41; **82mm** M-43; **120mm** M-43; M-38

AIR DEFENCE
  SAM
    Short-range 2K12 *Kub* (SA-6 *Gainful*)
    Pont-defence 200+: 200 9K35 *Strela*-10 (SA-13 *Gopher*); 9K33 *Osa* (SA-8 *Gecko*); 9K31 *Strela*-1 (SA-9 *Gaskin*); 9K36 *Strela*-3 (SA-14 *Gremlin*); 9K310 *Igla*-1 (SA-16 *Gimlet*); 9K32 *Strela*-2 (SA-7 *Grail*)‡
  GUNS 400
    SP 23mm ZSU-23-4; **30mm** BTR-60P SP; **57mm** ZSU-57-2
    TOWED 100mm KS-19/M-1939/**85mm** KS-12/**57mm** S-60/**37mm** M-1939/**30mm** M-53/**23mm** ZU-23

Navy ε3,000
Western Comd HQ at Cabanas; Eastern Comd HQ at Holquin
EQUIPMENT BY TYPE
PATROL AND COASTAL COMBATANTS 9
  PCG 2 *Rio Damuji* with two single P-22 (SS-N-2C *Styx*) AShM, 2 57mm guns, 1 hel landing platform
  PCM 1 *Pauk* II (FSU) with 1 quad lnchr (manual aiming) with 9K32 *Strela*-2 (SA-N-5 *Grail*) SAM, 2 RBU 1200 A/S mor, 1 76mm gun
  PBF 6 *Osa* II† (FSU) each with 4 single lnchr (for P-20U (SS-N-2B *Styx*) AShM – missiles removed to coastal-defence units)
MINE WARFARE AND MINE COUNTERMEASURES 5
  MHI 3 *Korund* (*Yevgenya*) (Project 1258)†
  MSC 2 *Sonya*† (FSU)
LOGISTICS AND SUPPORT 2
  ABU 1
  AX 1

Coastal Defence
ARTILLERY • TOWED 122mm M-1931/37; **130mm** M-46; **152mm** M-1937
COASTAL DEFENCE • AShM 4+: *Bandera* IV (reported); 4 4K51 *Rubezh* (SSC-3 *Styx*)

Naval Infantry 550+
FORCES BY ROLE
MANOEUVRE
  Amphibious
   2 amph aslt bn

Anti-aircraft Defence and Revolutionary Air Force ε8,000 (incl conscripts)
Air assets divided between Western Air Zone and Eastern Air Zone
FORCES BY ROLE
FIGHTER/GROUND ATTACK
   3 sqn with MiG-21ML *Fishbed*; MiG-23ML/MF/UM *Flogger*; MiG-29A/UB *Fulcrum*
TRANSPORT
   1 (VIP) tpt sqn with An-24 *Coke*; Mi-8P *Hip*; Yak-40
ATTACK HELICOPTER
   2 sqn with Mi-17 *Hip* H; Mi-35 *Hind*
TRAINING
   2 (tac trg) sqn with L-39C *Albatros* (basic); Z-142 (primary)

EQUIPMENT BY TYPE
AIRCRAFT 44 combat capable
  FTR 33: 16 MiG-23ML *Flogger*; 4 MiG-23MF *Flogger*;
  4 MiG-23U *Flogger*; 4 MiG-23UM *Flogger*; 2 MiG-29A
  Fulcrum; 3 MiG-29UB *Fulcrum* (6 MiG-15UTI *Midget*;
  4+ MiG-17 *Fresco*; 4 MiG-23MF *Flogger*; 6 MiG-23ML
  Flogger; 2 MiG-23UM *Flogger*; 2 MiG-29 *Fulcrum* in store)
  FGA 11: 3 MiG-21MF *Fishbed* J; 8 MiG-21U *Mongol* A
  (up to 70 MiG-21bis *Fishbed*; 30 MiG-21F *Fishbed*; 28
  MiG-21PFM *Fishbed*; 7 MiG-21UM *Fishbed*; 20 MiG-23BN
  Flogger in store)
  ISR 1 An-30 *Clank*
  TPT 11: **Heavy** 2 Il-76 *Candid*; **Light** 9: 1 An-2 *Colt*; 3 An-24 *Coke*; 2 An-32 *Cline*; 3 Yak-40 (8 An-2 *Colt*; 17 An-26 *Curl* in store)
  TRG 45: 25 L-39 *Albatros*; 20 Z-326 *Trener Master*
HELICOPTERS
  ATK 4 Mi-35 *Hind* (8 more in store)
  ASW (5 Mi-14 in store)
  MRH 8 Mi-17 *Hip* H (12 more in store)
  TPT • **Medium** 2 Mi-8P *Hip*
AIR DEFENCE • SAM
  Medium-range S-75 *Dvina* (SA-2 *Guideline*); S-75 *Dvina* mod (SA-2 *Guideline* – on T-55 chassis)
  Short-range S-125 *Pechora* (SA-3 *Goa*); S-125 *Pechora* mod (SA-3 *Goa* – on T-55 chassis)
AIR-LAUNCHED MISSILES
  AAM • **IR** R-3‡ (AA-2 *Atoll*); R-60 (AA-8 *Aphid*); R-73 (AA-11A *Archer*); **IR/SARH** R-23/24‡ (AA-7 *Apex*); R-27 (AA-10 *Alamo*)
  ASM Kh-23‡ (AS-7 *Kerry*)

Paramilitary 26,500 active

State Security 20,000
Ministry of Interior

Border Guards 6,500
Ministry of Interior
PATROL AND COASTAL COMBATANTS 20
  PCC 2 *Stenka*
  PB 18 *Zhuk*

Youth Labour Army 70,000 reservists

Civil Defence Force 50,000 reservists

Territorial Militia ε1,000,000 reservists

FOREIGN FORCES
United States US Southern Command: 1,000 (JTF-GTMO) at Guantanamo Bay

Dominican Republic DOM

Dominican Peso pRD		2018	2019	2020
GDP	pRD	4.24tr	4.55tr	
	US$	85.6bn	89.5bn	
per capita	US$	8,341	8,629	
Growth	%	7.0	5.0	
Inflation	%	3.6	1.8	
Def bdgt	pRD	29.8bn	31.6bn	33.3bn
	US$	603m	621m	
US$1=pRD		49.47	50.85	

Real-terms defence budget trend (US$m, constant 2015)

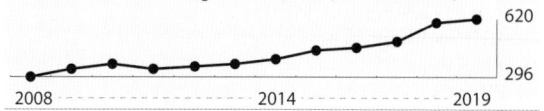

Population	10,400,027					
Age	0–14	15–19	20–24	25–29	30–64	65 plus
Male	13.8%	4.7%	4.6%	4.3%	20.3%	2.9%
Female	13.4%	4.6%	4.4%	4.2%	19.6%	3.2%

Capabilities

The principal tasks for the Dominican armed forces include internal- and border-security missions, as well as disaster relief. Training and operations increasingly focus on counter-narcotics and include collaboration with the police in an inter-agency task force. The US sends training teams to the country under the terms of a 2015 military-partnership agreement, and the navy has trained with French forces. The Dominican Republic is a regular participant in the US SOUTHCOM's annual *Tradewinds* disaster-response exercise. The army has strengthened its presence along the border with Haiti, establishing new surveillance posts. There is little capacity to deploy and sustain forces abroad. The army's equipment inventory is small and outdated, and the small number of armoured vehicles are obsolete and likely increasingly difficult to maintain. The air force operates a modest number of light fixed- and rotary-wing assets, and the navy a small fleet of mainly ex-US patrol craft of varying size. Aside from maintenance facilities, the country does not have a domestic defence industry.

ACTIVE 56,050 (Army 28,750 Navy 11,200 Air 16,100) **Paramilitary 15,000**

ORGANISATIONS BY SERVICE

Army 28,750
5 Defence Zones
FORCES BY ROLE
SPECIAL FORCES
  3 SF bn
MANOEUVRE
  Light
  4 (1st, 2nd, 3rd & 4th) inf bde (3 inf bn)
  2 (5th & 6th) inf bde (2 inf bn)
  Air Manoeuvre
  1 air cav bde (1 cdo bn, 1 (6th) mtn bn, 1 hel sqn with Bell 205 (op by Air Force); OH-58 *Kiowa*; R-22; R-44 *Raven* II)

Other
1 (Presidential Guard) gd regt
1 (MoD) sy bn
COMBAT SUPPORT
1 cbt spt bde (1 lt armd bn; 1 arty bn; 1 engr bn; 1 sigs bn)
EQUIPMENT BY TYPE
ARMOURED FIGHTING VEHICLES
LT TK 12 M41B (76mm)
APC • APC (W) 8 LAV-150 Commando
ANTI-TANK/ANTI-INFRASTRUCTURE
RCL 106mm 20 M40A1
GUNS 37mm 20 M3
ARTILLERY 104
TOWED 105mm 16: 4 M101; 12 Reinosa 105/26
MOR 88: 81mm 60 M1; 107mm 4 M30; 120mm 24 Expal Model L
HELICOPTERS
ISR 8: 4 OH-58A Kiowa; 4 OH-58C Kiowa
TPT • Light 6: 4 R-22; 2 R-44 Raven II

Navy 11,200

HQ located at Santo Domingo
FORCES BY ROLE
SPECIAL FORCES
1 (SEAL) SF unit
MANOEUVRE
Amphibious
1 mne sy unit
EQUIPMENT BY TYPE
PATROL AND COASTAL COMBATANTS 17
PCO 1 Almirante Didiez Burgos (ex-US Balsam)
PCC 2 Tortuguero (ex-US White Sumac)
PB 14: 2 Altair (Swiftships 35m); 4 Bellatrix (US Sewart Seacraft); 2 Canopus (Swiftships 101); 3 Hamal (Damen Stan 1505); 3 Point
AMPHIBIOUS • LCU 1 Neyba (ex-US LCU 1675)
LOGISTICS AND SUPPORT 8
AG 8

Air Force 16,100

FORCES BY ROLE
GROUND ATTACK
1 sqn with EMB-314 Super Tucano*
SEARCH & RESCUE
1 sqn with Bell 205 (UH-1H Huey II); Bell 205 (UH-1H Iroquois); Bell 430 (VIP); OH-58 Kiowa (CH-136); S-333
TRANSPORT
1 sqn with C-212-400 Aviocar; PA-31 Navajo
TRAINING
1 sqn with T-35B Pillan
AIR DEFENCE
1 ADA bn with 20mm guns
EQUIPMENT BY TYPE
AIRCRAFT 8 combat capable
ISR 1 AMT-200 Super Ximango
TPT • Light 13: 3 C-212-400 Aviocar; 1 Cessna 172; 1 Cessna 182; 1 Cessna 206; 1 Cessna 207; 1 Commander 690; 3 EA-100; 1 PA-31 Navajo; 1 P2006T
TRG 12: 8 EMB-314 Super Tucano*; 4 T-35B Pillan

HELICOPTERS
ISR 9 OH-58 Kiowa (CH-136)
TPT • Light 16: 8 Bell 205 (UH-1H Huey II); 5 Bell 205 (UH-1H Iroquois); 1 H155 (VIP); 2 S-333
AIR DEFENCE • GUNS 20mm 4

Paramilitary 15,000

National Police 15,000

Ecuador ECU

United States Dollar $		2018	2019	2020
GDP	US$	108bn	108bn	
per capita	US$	6,368	6,249	
Growth	%	1.4	-0.5	
Inflation	%	-0.2	0.4	
Def bdgt	US$	1.70bn	1.59bn	

Real-terms defence budget trend (US$bn, constant 2015)

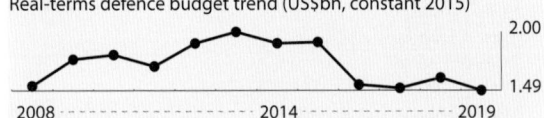

Population 16,703,254

Age	0–14	15–19	20–24	25–29	30–64	65 plus
Male	13.4%	4.6%	4.6%	4.2%	19.2%	3.7%
Female	12.8%	4.4%	4.4%	4.2%	20.3%	4.2%

Capabilities

Ecuador's armed forces are able to fulfil internal-security tasks, although the crisis in Venezuela and resulting refugee flows transiting Colombia have added to existing security challenges in the northern border area. Due to the security conditions along the northern border area, the armed forces created a joint task force for counter-insurgency and counter-narcotics operations. Greater defence cooperation with Peru is focused on demining efforts on the border. Military ties with Washington have been revived, representing a turning point in bilateral relations after defence ties were curtailed in 2009 and US troops left Manta air base. The armed forces train regularly and have participated in large regional and international military exercises. There is limited capability to independently deploy beyond its borders. The equipment inventory is derived from a variety of sources and suffers from a general state of obsolescence and low availability. Modernisation plans will target the small fleet of fighter aircraft, transport and training aircraft, and the army's personnel carriers. Ecuador's defence industries are centred on the army's Office of Industries (DINE), which produces military equipment through army-run enterprises. The state-owned shipyard ASTINAVE has some construction, maintenance and repair capabilities; however, the navy's submarines are being modernised in Chile.

ACTIVE 40,250 (Army 24,750 Navy 9,100 Air 6,400)
Paramilitary 500
Conscript liability Voluntary conscription

RESERVE 118,000 (Joint 118,000)
Ages 18–55

ORGANISATIONS BY SERVICE

Army 24,750
FORCES BY ROLE
gp are bn sized
COMMAND
4 div HQ
SPECIAL FORCES
1 (9th) SF bde (3 SF gp, 1 SF sqn, 1 para bn, 1 sigs sqn, 1 log comd)
MANOEUVRE
Mechanised
1 (11th) armd cav bde (3 armd cav gp, 1 mech inf bn, 1 SP arty gp, 1 engr gp)
1 (5th) inf bde (1 SF sqn, 2 mech cav gp, 2 inf bn, 1 cbt engr coy, 1 sigs coy, 1 log coy)
Light
1 (1st) inf bde (1 SF sqn, 1 armd cav gp, 1 armd recce sqn, 3 inf bn, 1 med coy)
1 (3rd) inf bde (1 SF gp, 1 mech cav gp, 1 inf bn, 1 arty gp, 1 hvy mor coy, 1 cbt engr coy, 1 sigs coy, 1 log coy)
1 (7th) inf bde (1 SF sqn, 1 armd recce sqn, 1 mech cav gp, 3 inf bn, 1 jungle bn, 1 arty gp, 1 cbt engr coy, 1 sigs coy, 1 log coy, 1 med coy)
1 (13th) inf bde (1 SF sqn, 1 armd recce sqn, 1 mot cav gp, 3 inf bn, 1 arty gp, 1 hvy mor coy, 1 cbt engr coy, 1sigs coy, 1 log coy)
2 (17th & 21st) jungle bde (3 jungle bn, 1 cbt engr coy, 1 sigs coy, 1 log coy)
1 (19th) jungle bde (3 jungle bn, 1 jungle trg bn, 1 cbt engr coy, 1 sigs coy, 1 log coy)
COMBAT SUPPORT
1 (27th) arty bde (1 SP arty gp, 1 MRL gp, 1 ADA gp, 1 cbt engr coy, 1 sigs coy, 1 log coy)
1 (23rd) engr bde (3 engr bn)
2 indep MP coy
1 indep sigs coy
COMBAT SERVICE SUPPORT
1 (25th) log bde
2 log bn
2 indep med coy
AVIATION
1 (15th) avn bde (2 tpt avn gp, 2 hel gp, 1 mixed avn gp)
AIR DEFENCE
1 ADA gp
EQUIPMENT BY TYPE
ARMOURED FIGHTING VEHICLES
LT TK 24 AMX-13
RECCE 67: 25 AML-90; 10 EE-3 *Jararaca*; 32 EE-9 *Cascavel*
APC 122
APC (T) 95: 80 AMX-VCI; 15 M113
APC (W) 27: 17 EE-11 *Urutu*; 10 UR-416
ANTI-TANK/ANTI-INFRASTRUCTURE
RCL 404: **90mm** 380 M67; **106mm** 24 M40A1
ARTILLERY 541+
SP **155mm** 5 Mk F3
TOWED 100: **105mm** 78: 30 M101; 24 M2A2; 24 Model 56 pack howitzer; **155mm** 22: 12 M114; 10 M198
MRL **122mm** 24: 18 BM-21 *Grad*; 6 RM-70
MOR 412+: **81mm** 400 M29; **107mm** M30; **160mm** 12 M-66
AIRCRAFT
TPT • **Light** 14: 1 Beech 200 *King Air*; 2 C-212; 1 CN235; 4 Cessna 172; 2 Cessna 206; 1 Cessna 500 *Citation* I; 3 IAI-201 *Arava*
TRG 6: 2 MX-7-235 *Star Rocket*; 2 T-41D *Mescalero*; 2 CJ-6A
HELICOPTERS
MRH 33: 7 H125M (AS550C3) *Fennec*; 6 Mi-17-1V *Hip*; 2 SA315B *Lama*; 18 SA342L *Gazelle* (13 with HOT for anti-armour role)
TPT 11: **Medium** 7: 5 AS332B *Super Puma*; 2 Mi-171E; (3 SA330 *Puma* in store); **Light** 4: 2 H125 (AS350B2) *Ecureuil*; 2 H125 (AS350B3) *Ecureuil*
AIR DEFENCE
SAM • **Point-defence** *Blowpipe*; 9K32 *Strela*-2 (SA-7 *Grail*)‡; 9K38 *Igla* (SA-18 *Grouse*)
GUNS 240
SP **20mm** 44 M163 *Vulcan*
TOWED 196: **14.5mm** 128 ZPU-1/-2; **20mm** 38: 28 M-1935, 10 M167 *Vulcan*; **40mm** 30 L/70/M1A1
AIR-LAUNCHED MISSILES • ASM HOT

Navy 9,100 (incl Naval Aviation, Marines and Coast Guard)
EQUIPMENT BY TYPE
SUBMARINES • TACTICAL • SSK 2:
2 *Shyri* (GER T-209/1300) with 8 single 533mm TT each with A184 mod 3 HWT
PRINCIPAL SURFACE COMBATANTS • FRIGATES 2
FFGHM 2 *Moran Valverde* (ex-UK *Leander* batch II) with 1 quad lnchr with MM40 *Exocet* AShM, 3 twin *Simbad* lnchr with *Mistral* SAM, 2 triple ILAS-3 (B-515) 324mm ASTT with A244 LWT, 1 Mk 15 *Phalanx* CIWS, 1 twin 114mm gun (capacity 1 Bell 206B *Jet Ranger* II hel)
PATROL AND COASTAL COMBATANTS 9
CORVETTES • FSGM 6
4 *Esmeraldas* with 2 triple lnchr with MM40 *Exocet* AShM, 1 quad *Albatros* lnchr with *Aspide* SAM, 2 triple ILAS-3 (B-515) 324mm ASTT with A244 LWT, 1 76mm gun, 1 hel landing platform
2 *Esmeraldas* with 2 triple lnchr with MM40 *Exocet* AShM, 1 quad *Albatros* lnchr with *Aspide* SAM, 1 76mm gun, 1 hel landing platform
PCFG 3 *Quito* (GER Lurssen TNC-45 45m) with 4 single lnchr with MM38 *Exocet* AShM, 1 76mm gun (upgrade programme ongoing)
LOGISTICS AND SUPPORT 8
AE 1 *Calicuchima*
AGOS 1 *Orion* with 1 hel landing platform
AGS 1 *Sirius*
AK 1 *Galapagos*
ATF 1
AWT 2: 1 *Quisquis*; 1 *Atahualpa*
AXS 1 *Guayas*

Naval Aviation 380
EQUIPMENT BY TYPE
AIRCRAFT
  MP 1 CN235-300M
  ISR 3: 2 Beech 200T *King Air*; 1 Beech 300 *Catpass King Air*
  TPT • Light 3: 1 Beech 200 *King Air*; 1 Beech 300 *King Air*; 1 CN235-100
  TRG 6: 2 T-34C *Turbo Mentor*; 4 T-35B *Pillan*
HELICOPTERS
  TPT • Light 9: 3 Bell 206A; 3 Bell 206B; 1 Bell 230; 2 Bell 430
UNMANNED AERIAL VEHICLES
  ISR 5: **Heavy** 2 *Heron*; **Medium** 3 *Searcher* Mk.II

Marines 2,150
FORCES BY ROLE
SPECIAL FORCES
  1 cdo unit
MANOEUVRE
  Amphibious
  5 mne bn (on garrison duties)
EQUIPMENT BY TYPE
ARTILLERY • MOR 32+ 81mm/120mm
AIR DEFENCE • SAM • Point-defence *Mistral*; 9K38 *Igla* (SA-18 *Grouse*)

Air Force 6,400

Operational Command
FORCES BY ROLE
FIGHTER
  1 sqn with *Cheetah* C/D
FIGHTER/GROUND ATTACK
  2 sqn with EMB-314 *Super Tucano**
  1 sqn with *Kfir* C-10 (CE); *Kfir* C-2; *Kfir* TC-2

Military Air Transport Group
FORCES BY ROLE
SEARCH & RESCUE/TRANSPORT HELICOPTER
  1 sqn with Bell 206B *Jet Ranger* II
  1 sqn with PA-34 *Seneca*
TRANSPORT
  1 sqn with C-130/H *Hercules*; L-100-30
  1 sqn with HS-748
  1 sqn with DHC-6-300 *Twin Otter*
  1 sqn with B-727; EMB-135BJ *Legacy* 600; *Sabreliner* 40
TRAINING
  1 sqn with Cessna 206; DA20-C1; MXP-650; T-34C *Turbo Mentor*
EQUIPMENT BY TYPE
AIRCRAFT 42 combat capable
  FGA 25: 10 *Cheetah* C; 2 *Cheetah* D; 4 *Kfir* C-2; 7 *Kfir* C-10 (CE); 2 *Kfir* TC-2
  TPT 31: **Medium** 4: 2 C-130B *Hercules*; 1 C-130H *Hercules*; 1 L-100-30; **Light** 16: 1 Beech E90 *King Air*; 3 C295M; 1 Cessna 206; 3 DHC-6 *Twin Otter*; 1 EMB-135BJ *Legacy* 600; 2 EMB-170; 2 EMB-190; 1 M-28 *Skytruck*; 1 MXP-650; 1 PA-34 *Seneca*; **PAX** 11: 2 A320; 2 B-727; 1 *Falcon 7X*; 1 *Gulfstream* G-1159; 5 HS-748
  TRG 39: 11 DA20-C1; 17 EMB-314 *Super Tucano**; 11 T-34C *Turbo Mentor*
HELICOPTERS • TPT • Light 11: 4 AW119 *Koala*; 7 Bell 206B *Jet Ranger* II
AIR-LAUNCHED MISSILES • AAM • IR *Python* 3; R-550 *Magic*; *Shafrir*‡; **IIR** *Python* 4; **SARH** *Super* 530
AIR DEFENCE
  SAM • Point-defence 13+: 6 9K33 *Osa* (SA-8 *Gecko*); 7 M48 *Chaparral*; *Blowpipe*; 9K32 *Strela-2* (SA-7 *Grail*)‡; 9K310 *Igla-1* (SA-16 *Gimlet*); 9K38 *Igla* (SA-18 *Grouse*)
  GUNS
    SP 20mm 28 M35
    TOWED 64: **23mm** 34 ZU-23; **35mm** 30 GDF-002 (twin)

Paramilitary 500

Coast Guard 500
EQUIPMENT BY TYPE
PATROL AND COASTAL COMBATANTS 21
  PCC 4: 3 *Isla Fernandina* (*Vigilante*); 1 *Isla San Cristóbal* (Damen Stan Patrol 5009)
  PB 14: 1 *10 de Agosto*; 2 *Espada*; 2 *Manta* (GER Lurssen 36m); 1 *Point*; 4 *Rio Coca*; 4 *Isla Santa Cruz* (Damen Stan 2606)
  PBR 3: 2 *Río Esmeraldas*; 1 *Rio Puyango*

DEPLOYMENT
SOUTH SUDAN: UN • UNMISS 2
SUDAN: UN • UNISFA 3
WESTERN SAHARA: UN • MIUNRSO 4

El Salvador SLV

United States Dollar $		2018	2019	2020
GDP	US$	26.1bn	26.9bn	
per capita	US$	3,922	4,008	
Growth	%	2.5	2.5	
Inflation	%	1.1	0.9	
Def bdgt	US$	141m	145m	172m
FMA (US)	US$	1.9m	0m	0m

Real-terms defence budget trend (US$m, constant 2015)

Population	6,187,271					
Age	0–14	15–19	20–24	25–29	30–64	65 plus
Male	12.7%	4.9%	4.9%	4.4%	17.6%	3.5%
Female	12.1%	4.7%	4.9%	4.6%	21.2%	4.5%

Capabilities
El Salvador's armed forces' primary challenge is tackling organised crime and narcotics trafficking in support of the National Civil Police. A new Territorial Control Plan implemented in 2019 has seen mixed military and police patrols deployed to areas with high crime rates. El Salvador switched diplomatic recognition

from Taiwan to China in 2018, a move which has halted planned equipment donations from Taiwan. El Salvador participates in a tri-national border task force with Guatemala and Honduras. The armed forces have long-standing training programmes, including with regional states and with the US, focused on internal security, disaster relief and support to civilian authorities. El Salvador has deployed on UN peacekeeping missions up to company strength but lacks the logistical support to sustain independent international deployments. The armed forces have received little new heavy military equipment in recent years and are dependent on an inventory of Cold War-era platforms; the majority of these are operational, indicating adequate support and maintenance. El Salvador lacks a substantive defence industry but has successfully produced light armoured vehicles based upon commercial vehicles.

ACTIVE 24,500 (Army 20,500 Navy 2,000 Air 2,000)
Paramilitary 17,000
Conscript liability 12 months (selective); 11 months for officers and NCOs

RESERVE 9,900 (Joint 9,900)

ORGANISATIONS BY SERVICE

Army 20,500
FORCES BY ROLE
SPECIAL FORCES
    1 spec ops gp (1 SF coy, 1 para bn, 1 (naval inf) coy)
MANOEUVRE
    Reconnaissance
    1 armd cav regt (2 armd cav bn)
    Light
    6 inf bde (3 inf bn)
    Other
    1 (special) sy bde (2 border gd bn, 2 MP bn)
COMBAT SUPPORT
    1 arty bde (2 fd arty bn, 1 AD bn)
    1 engr comd (2 engr bn)
EQUIPMENT BY TYPE
ARMOURED FIGHTING VEHICLES
    RECCE 5 AML-90 (4 more in store)
    APC • **APC (W)** 38: 30 VAL *Cashuat* (mod); 8 UR-416
ANTI-TANK/ANTI-INFRASTRUCTURE
    RCL 399: **106mm** 20 M40A1 (incl 16 SP); **90mm** 379 M67
ARTILLERY 217+
    TOWED **105mm** 54: 36 M102; 18 M-56 (FRY)
    MOR 163+: **81mm** 151 M29; **120mm** 12+: 12 UBM 52; (some M-74 in store)
AIR DEFENCE • GUNS 35: **20mm** 31 M-55; 4 TCM-20

Navy 2,000
EQUIPMENT BY TYPE
PATROL AND COASTAL COMBATANTS 10
    PB 10: 3 Camcraft (30m); 1 *Point*; 1 Swiftships 77; 1 Swiftships 65; 4 Type-44 (ex-USCG)
AMPHIBIOUS • LANDING CRAFT • LCM 4

Naval Inf (SF Commandos) 90
FORCES BY ROLE
SPECIAL FORCES
    1 SF coy

Air Force 2,000
FORCES BY ROLE
FIGHTER/GROUND ATTACK/ISR
    1 sqn with A-37B/OA-37B *Dragonfly*; O-2A/B *Skymaster**
TRANSPORT
    1 sqn with BT-67; Cessna 210 *Centurion*; Cessna 337G; Commander 114; IAI-202 *Arava*; SA-226T *Merlin* IIIB
TRAINING
    1 sqn with R-235GT *Guerrier*; T-35 *Pillan*; T-41D *Mescalero*; TH-300
TRANSPORT HELICOPTER
    1 sqn with Bell 205 (UH-1H *Iroquois*); Bell 407; Bell 412EP *Twin Huey*; MD-500E; UH-1M *Iroquois*
EQUIPMENT BY TYPE
AIRCRAFT 25 combat capable
    ATK 14 A-37B *Dragonfly*
    ISR 11: 6 O-2A/B *Skymaster**; 5 OA-37B *Dragonfly**
    TPT • **Light** 10: 2 BT-67; 2 Cessna 210 *Centurion*; 1 Cessna 337G *Skymaster*; 1 Commander 114; 3 IAI-201 *Arava*; 1 SA-226T *Merlin* IIIB
    TRG 11: 5 R-235GT *Guerrier*; 5 T-35 *Pillan*; 1 T-41D *Mescalero*
HELICOPTERS
    MRH 14: 4 Bell 412EP *Twin Huey*; 8 MD-500E; 2 UH-1M *Iroquois*
    TPT• **Light** 9: 8 Bell 205 (UH-1H *Iroquois*); 1 Bell 407 (VIP tpt, govt owned)
    TRG 5 TH-300
AIR-LAUNCHED MISSILES • AAM • IR *Shafrir*‡

Paramilitary 17,000

National Civilian Police 17,000
Ministry of Public Security
AIRCRAFT
    ISR 1 O-2A *Skymaster*
    TPT • **Light** 1 Cessna 310
HELICOPTERS
    MRH 2 MD-520N
    TPT • **Light** 3: 1 Bell 205 (UH-1H *Iroquois*); 2 R-44 *Raven* II

DEPLOYMENT

LEBANON: UN • UNIFIL 52; 1 inf pl
MALI: UN • MINUSMA 211; 1 hel sqn with 3 MD-500E
SOUTH SUDAN: UN • UNMISS 3
SUDAN: UN • UNISFA 1
WESTERN SAHARA: UN • MINURSO 3

FOREIGN FORCES

United States US Southern Command: 1 Forward Operating Location (Military, DEA, USCG and Customs personnel)

Guatemala GUA

Guatemalan Quetzal q		2018	2019	2020
GDP	q	590bn	634bn	
	US$	78.5bn	81.3bn	
per capita	US$	4,545	4,617	
Growth	%	3.1	3.4	
Inflation	%	3.8	4.2	
Def bdgt	q	1.91bn	2.63bn	2.83bn
	US$	255m	337m	
FMA (US)	US$	1.74m	0m	0m
US$1=q		7.52	7.79	

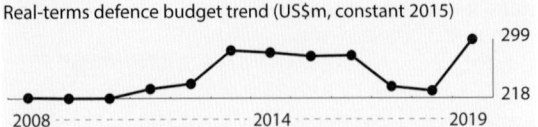

Real-terms defence budget trend (US$m, constant 2015)

Population	16,867,133					
Age	0–14	15–19	20–24	25–29	30–64	65 plus
Male	17.4%	5.1%	4.9%	4.4%	15.7%	2.1%
Female	16.7%	5.0%	4.9%	4.4%	16.8%	2.5%

Capabilities

The armed forces are refocusing on border security, having drawn down their decade-long direct support for the National Civil Police in 2018 as part of the inter-agency Plan Fortaleza. Guatemala maintains an inter-agency task force with neighbouring El Salvador and Honduras. The army has trained with US SOUTHCOM, as well as with regional partners such as Brazil and Colombia. Training for conventional military operations is limited by budget constraints and the long focus on providing internal security. Guatemala maintains a company-sized contingent as part of the UN mission to the DRC, but otherwise lacks the capability for significant international deployments. The equipment inventory is small and ageing. The US has provided several soft-skinned vehicles to the army, while the air force has undertaken some modest recapitalisation of its fixed-wing transport and surveillance capacity. Funding is being sought for additional maritime- and air-patrol capabilities. Aside from limited maintenance facilities, the country has no domestic defence industry.

ACTIVE 18,050 (Army 15,550 Navy 1,500 Air 1,000)
Paramilitary 25,000

RESERVE 63,850 (Navy 650 Air 900 Armed Forces 62,300)
(National Armed Forces are combined; the army provides log spt for navy and air force)

ORGANISATIONS BY SERVICE

Army 15,550
15 Military Zones
FORCES BY ROLE
SPECIAL FORCES
  1 SF bde (1 SF bn, 1 trg bn)
  1 SF bde (1 SF coy, 1 ranger bn)
  1 SF mtn bde
MANOEUVRE
  Light
  1 (strategic reserve) mech bde (1 inf bn, 1 cav regt, 1 log coy)
  6 inf bde (1 inf bn)
  Air Manoeuvre
  1 AB bde with (2 AB bn)
  Amphibious
  1 mne bde
  Other
  1 (Presidential) gd bde (1 gd bn, 1 MP bn, 1 CSS coy)
COMBAT SUPPORT
  1 engr comd (1 engr bn, 1 construction bn)
  2 MP bde with (1 MP bn)

Reserves
FORCES BY ROLE
MANOEUVRE
  Light
  ε19 inf bn
EQUIPMENT BY TYPE
ARMOURED FIGHTING VEHICLES
  RECCE (7 M8 in store)
  APC 47
    APC (T) 10 M113 (5 more in store)
    APC (W) 37: 30 *Armadillo*; 7 V-100 *Commando*
ANTI-TANK/ANTI-INFRASTRUCTURE
  RCL 120+: **75mm** M20; **105mm** 64 M-1974 FMK-1 (ARG); **106mm** 56 M40A1
ARTILLERY 149
  TOWED **105mm** 76: 12 M101; 8 M102; 56 M-56
  MOR 73: **81mm** 55 M1; **107mm** (12 M30 in store); **120mm** 18 ECIA
AIR DEFENCE • GUNS • TOWED 32: **20mm** 16 GAI-D01; 16 M-55

Navy 1,500
EQUIPMENT BY TYPE
PATROL AND COASTAL COMBATANTS 10
  PB 10: 6 *Cutlass*; 1 *Dauntless*; 1 *Kukulkan* (US *Broadsword* 32m); 2 *Utatlan* (US *Sewart*)
AMPHIBIOUS • LANDING CRAFT • LCP 2 *Machete*
LOGISTICS AND SUPPORT • AXS 3

Marines 650 reservists
FORCES BY ROLE
MANOEUVRE
  Amphibious
  2 mne bn(-)

Air Force 1,000
2 air comd
FORCES BY ROLE
FIGHTER/GROUND ATTACK/ISR
  1 sqn with A-37B *Dragonfly*
TRANSPORT
  1 sqn with BT-67; Beech 90/200 *King Air*
  1 (tactical support) sqn with Cessna 206
TRAINING
  1 sqn with T-35B *Pillan*

TRANSPORT HELICOPTER
1 sqn with Bell 212 (armed); Bell 407GX; Bell 412 *Twin Huey* (armed); UH-1H *Iroquois*

EQUIPMENT BY TYPE
Serviceability of ac is less than 50%
AIRCRAFT 1 combat capable
ATK 1 A-37B *Dragonfly*
TPT • Light 15: 1 Beech 90 *King Air*; 2 Beech 200 *King Air*; 2 Cessna 206; 3 Cessna 208B *Grand Caravan*; 3 Cessna 210 *Centurion*; 2 Piper PA-28 *Archer* III; 2 PA-34 *Seneca* (5 Cessna R172K *Hawk* XP in store)
TRG 1 SR22; (4 T-35B *Pillan* in store)
HELICOPTERS
MRH 4: 2 Bell 412 *Twin Huey* (armed); 2 Bell 407GX
TPT • Light 9: 2 Bell 205 (UH-1H *Iroquois*); 3 Bell 206B *Jet Ranger*; 2 Bell 212 (armed); 2 Bell 407GX

Tactical Security Group
Air Military Police

Paramilitary 25,000

National Civil Police 25,000
FORCES BY ROLE
SPECIAL FORCES
1 SF bn
MANOEUVRE
Other
1 (integrated task force) paramilitary unit (incl mil and treasury police)

DEPLOYMENT

CENTRAL AFRICAN REPUBLIC: UN • MINUSCA 4
DEMOCRATIC REPUBLIC OF THE CONGO: UN • MONUSCO 154; 1 SF coy
LEBANON: UN • UNIFIL 1
MALI: UN • MINUSMA 2
SOUTH SUDAN: UN • UNMISS 6
SUDAN: UN • UNISFA 3

Guyana GUY

Guyanese Dollar G$		2018	2019	2020
GDP	G$	806bn	852bn	
	US$	3.90bn	4.12bn	
per capita	US$	4,984	5,252	
Growth	%	4.1	4.4	
Inflation	%	1.3	2.1	
Def bdgt	G$	12.5bn	14.0bn	
	US$	60.7m	67.8m	
US$1=G$		206.63	206.84	

Real-terms defence budget trend (US$m, constant 2015)

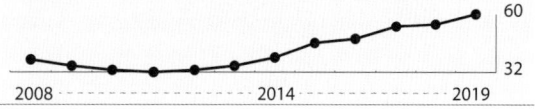

Population	744,845					
Age	0–14	15–19	20–24	25–29	30–64	65 plus
Male	12.5%	5.5%	5.4%	4.6%	19.6%	2.7%
Female	12.1%	5.3%	5.2%	4.2%	18.8%	4.0%

Capabilities

The Guyana Defence Force (GDF) has minimal conventional military capability, and its activities are focused on border control and support for law-enforcement operations and assistance to the civil power. The government is planning to restructure the GDF to improve its flexibility. Guyana is part of the Caribbean Basin Security Initiative. It has close military ties with Brazil, with whom it cooperates on border security via annual military regional exchange meetings. The country also has bilateral agreements with France, China and the US, who provide military training and equipment. The GDF trains regularly and takes part in bilateral and multinational exercises. A training initiative with China helped two Guyanese pilots to acquire air-combat certification although Guyana has no combat aircraft in its inventory. There is no expeditionary or associated logistics capability. Equipment is mostly composed of second-hand platforms, mainly of Brazilian and North American manufacture. The air force has expanded its modest air-transport capabilities with some second-hand utility aircraft. Apart from maintenance facilities, there is no defence-industrial sector.

ACTIVE 3,400 (Army 3,000 Navy 200 Air 200)
Active numbers combined Guyana Defence Force

RESERVE 670 (Army 500 Navy 170)

ORGANISATIONS BY SERVICE

Army 3,000
FORCES BY ROLE
SPECIAL FORCES
1 SF coy
MANOEUVRE
Light
1 inf bn
Other
1 (Presidential) gd bn

COMBAT SUPPORT
1 arty coy
1 (spt wpn) cbt spt coy
1 engr coy

EQUIPMENT BY TYPE
ARMOURED FIGHTING VEHICLES
RECCE 9: 6 EE-9 *Cascavel* (reported); 3 S52 *Shorland*
ARTILLERY 54
TOWED 130mm 6 M-46†
MOR 48: 81mm 12 L16A1; 82mm 18 M-43; 120mm 18 M-43

Navy 200
EQUIPMENT BY TYPE
PATROL AND COASTAL COMBATANTS 5
PCO 1 *Essequibo* (ex-UK *River*)
PB 4 *Barracuda* (ex-US Type-44)

Air Force 200
FORCES BY ROLE
TRANSPORT
1 unit with Bell 206; Cessna 206; Y-12 (II)

EQUIPMENT BY TYPE
AIRCRAFT • TPT • Light 6: 2 BN-2 *Islander*; 1 Cessna 206; 2 SC.7 3M *Skyvan*; 1 Y-12 (II)
HELICOPTERS
MRH 1 Bell 412 *Twin Huey*†
TPT • Light 2 Bell 206

Haiti HTI

Haitian Gourde G		2018	2019	2020
GDP	G	632bn	744bn	
	US$	9.66bn	8.82bn	
per capita	US$	869	784	
Growth	%	1.5	0.1	
Inflation	%	12.9	17.6	
Def bdgt	G	514m	1.09bn	
	US$	7.9m	13.0m	
FMA (US)	US$	5m	0m	0m
US$1=G		65.42	84.32	

Real-terms defence budget trend (US$m, constant 2015)

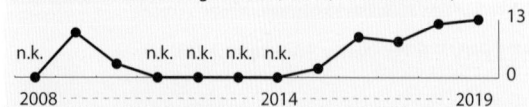

Population   10,928,926

Age	0–14	15–19	20–24	25–29	30–64	65 plus
Male	15.8%	5.3%	5.2%	4.6%	16.7%	1.9%
Female	15.9%	5.3%	5.2%	4.6%	17.2%	2.4%

Capabilities
Haiti possesses almost no military capability. A small coastguard is tasked with maritime security and law enforcement and, while the country's embryonic army is hoped to eventually number around 5,000 personnel, it is still in the very early stages of development.

Plans for military expansion were outlined in the 2015 White Paper on Security and Defence. A road map for the re-establishment of the Haitian armed forces was distributed to ministers in early 2017 and in March 2018 an army high command was established. Ecuador and Brazil have both pledged to assist with training the new army. The army's primary missions will reportedly be disaster relief and border security. The initial 500 troops are focused on engineering and medical capability for disaster-relief tasks. However, it is unclear whether the current budgetary provision is sufficient to fund the level of capability required. Haiti is a member of the Caribbean Community and participates in US Southern Command's annual *Tradewinds* disaster-response exercise. There is no heavy military equipment, and no defence industry.

ACTIVE 500 (Army 500) **Paramilitary** 50

ORGANISATIONS BY SERVICE

Army 500
FORCES BY ROLE
MANOEUVRE
1 inf bn (forming)

Paramilitary 50

Coast Guard ε50
EQUIPMENT BY TYPE
PATROL AND COASTAL COMBATANTS • PB 8: 5 *Dauntless*; 3 3812-VCF

Honduras HND

Honduran Lempira L		2018	2019	2020
GDP	L	573bn	611bn	
	US$	23.8bn	24.4bn	
per capita	US$	2,524	2,548	
Growth	%	3.7	3.36	
Inflation	%	4.3	4.412	
Def bdgt [a]	L	7.96bn	8.53bn	8.48bn
	US$	331m	341m	
FMA (US)	US$	4m	0m	0m
US$1=L		24.07	24.99	

[a] Defence & national security budget

Real-terms defence budget trend (US$m, constant 2015)

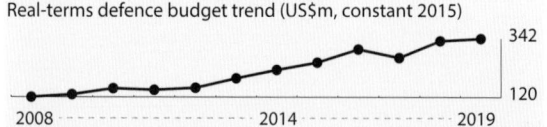

Population   9,325,005

Age	0–14	15–19	20–24	25–29	30–64	65 plus
Male	16.3%	5.4%	5.1%	4.6%	17.0%	2.0%
Female	15.6%	5.2%	4.9%	4.5%	16.9%	2.6%

Capabilities
The armed forces have been deployed in support of the police to combat organised crime and narcotics trafficking since 2011; this mission remains their prime focus. Honduras maintains diplomatic

relations with Taiwan, which has supplied surplus military equipment, and also receives US security assistance, though this has been reduced in recent years. Honduras hosts a US base at the Soto Cano airfield. Honduras is also part of a tri-national border-security task force with neighbouring El Salvador and Guatemala, and a separate border-security force with Nicaragua. Training remains focused on internal- and border-security requirements, and training for conventional military action is limited. Honduras does not have the capability to maintain substantial overseas deployments. Most equipment is ageing, with serviceability in doubt. The air force and Public Order Military Police are working with Israel to modernise their inventories. Apart from limited maintenance facilities, the country has no domestic defence industry.

ACTIVE 14,950 (Army 7,300 Navy 1,350 Air 2,300 Military Police 4,000) **Paramilitary 8,000**

RESERVE 60,000 (Joint 60,000; Ex-servicemen registered)

ORGANISATIONS BY SERVICE

Army 7,300
FORCES BY ROLE
SPECIAL FORCES
  1 (special tac) spec ops gp (2 spec ops bn, 1 inf bn; 1 AB bn; 1 arty bn)
MANOEUVRE
  Mechanised
  1 inf bde (1 mech cav regt, 1 inf bn, 1 arty bn)
  Light
  1 inf bde (3 inf bn, 1 arty bn)
  3 inf bde (2 inf bn)
  1 indep inf bn
  Other
  1 (Presidential) gd coy
COMBAT SUPPORT
  1 engr bn
  1 sigs bn
EQUIPMENT BY TYPE
ARMOURED FIGHTING VEHICLES
  LT TK 12 FV101 *Scorpion*
  RECCE 57: 1 FV105 *Sultan* (CP); 3 FV107 *Scimitar*; 40 FV601 *Saladin*; 13 RBY-1
ANTI-TANK/ANTI-INFRASTRUCTURE
  RCL 50+: **84mm** *Carl Gustav*; **106mm** 50 M40A1
ARTILLERY 118+
  TOWED 28: **105mm**: 24 M102; **155mm**: 4 M198
  MOR 90+: **81mm**; **120mm** 60 FMK-2; **160mm** 30 M-66

Navy 1,350
EQUIPMENT BY TYPE
PATROL AND COASTAL COMBATANTS 17
  PB 17: 2 *Lempira* (Damen Stan Patrol 4207 – leased); 1 *Chamelecon* (Swiftships 85); 1 *Tegucilgalpa* (US *Guardian* 32m); 4 *Guanaja* (ex-US Type-44); 3 *Guaymuras* (Swiftships 105); 5 *Nacaome* (Swiftships 65); 1 *Rio Coco* (US PB Mk III)
AMPHIBIOUS • LANDING CRAFT 4
  LCT 2: 1 *Gracias a Dios* (COL *Golfo de Tribuga*); 1 *Punta Caxinas*
  LCM 2 LCM 8

Marines 1,000
FORCES BY ROLE
MANOEUVRE
  Amphibious
  2 mne bn

Air Force 2,300
FORCES BY ROLE
FIGHTER/GROUND ATTACK
  1 sqn with A-37B *Dragonfly*
  1 sqn with F-5E/F *Tiger* II
GROUND ATTACK/ISR/TRAINING
  1 unit with Cessna 182 *Skylane*; EMB-312 *Tucano*; MXT-7-180 *Star Rocket*
TRANSPORT
  1 sqn with Beech 200 *King Air*; C-130A *Hercules*; Cessna 185/210; IAI-201 *Arava*; PA-42 *Cheyenne*; Turbo Commander 690
  1 VIP flt with PA-31 *Navajo*; Bell 412EP/SP *Twin Huey*
TRANSPORT HELICOPTER
  1 sqn with Bell 205 (UH-1H *Iroquois*); Bell 412SP *Twin Huey*
AIR DEFENCE
  1 ADA bn
EQUIPMENT BY TYPE
AIRCRAFT 17 combat capable
  FTR 11: 9 F-5E *Tiger* II†; 2 F-5F *Tiger* II†
  ATK 6 A-37B *Dragonfly*
  TPT 17: **Medium** 1 C-130A *Hercules*; **Light** 16: 1 Beech 200 *King Air*; 2 Cessna 172 *Skyhawk*; 2 Cessna 182 *Skylane*; 1 Cessna 185; 3 Cessna 208B *Grand Caravan*; 1 Cessna 210; 1 EMB-135 *Legacy* 600; 1 IAI-201 *Arava*; 1 L-410 (leased); 1 PA-31 *Navajo*; 1 PA-42 *Cheyenne*; 1 Turbo Commander 690
  TRG 16: 9 EMB-312 *Tucano*; 7 MXT-7-180 *Star Rocket*
HELICOPTERS
  MRH 8: 1 Bell 412EP *Twin Huey* (VIP); 5 Bell 412SP *Twin Huey*; 2 Hughes 500
  TPT • **Light** 7: 6 Bell 205 (UH-1H *Iroquois*); 1 H125 *Ecureuil*
AIR DEFENCE • GUNS 20mm 48: 24 M-55A2; 24 TCM-20
AIR-LAUNCHED MISSILES • AAM • IR *Shafrir*‡

Military Police 4,000
FORCES BY ROLE
MANOEUVRE
  Other
  8 sy bn

Paramilitary 8,000

Public Security Forces 8,000
Ministry of Public Security and Defence; 11 regional comd

DEPLOYMENT

WESTERN SAHARA: UN • MINURSO 12

FOREIGN FORCES

United States US Southern Command: 450; 1 avn bn with CH-47F *Chinook*; UH-60 *Black Hawk*

Jamaica JAM

Jamaican Dollar J$		2018	2019	2020
GDP	J$	2.00tr	2.10tr	
	US$	15.5bn	15.7bn	
per capita	US$	5,406	5,461	
Growth	%	1.6	1.1	
Inflation	%	3.7	3.6	
Def bdgt	J$	29.8bn	34.9bn	
	US$	230m	262m	
US$1=J$		129.54	133.56	

Real-terms defence budget trend (US$m, constant 2015)

Population	2,810,520					
Age	0–14	15–19	20–24	25–29	30–64	65 plus
Male	13.0%	4.7%	4.5%	3.8%	19.2%	4.2%
Female	12.6%	4.5%	4.4%	3.9%	20.4%	4.7%

Capabilities

The Jamaica Defence Force (JDF) is focused principally on maritime and internal security, including support to police operations. Jamaica maintains military ties, including for training purposes, with Canada, the UK and the US and is a member of the Caribbean Community. The defence force participates in US SOUTHCOM's annual *Tradewinds* disaster-response exercise. Jamaica is host to the Caribbean Special Tactics Centre, which trains special-forces units from Jamaica and other Caribbean nations. The JDF does not have any capacity to support independent deployment abroad. Funds have been allocated to procure new vehicles and helicopters. Other than limited maintenance facilities, Jamaica has no domestic defence industry.

ACTIVE 5,950 (Army 5,400 Coast Guard 300 Air 250)
(combined Jamaican Defence Force)

RESERVE 2,580 (Army 2,500 Coast Guard 60 Air 20)

ORGANISATIONS BY SERVICE

Army 5,400
FORCES BY ROLE
MANOEUVRE
  Mechanised
    1 (PMV) lt mech inf coy
  Light
    4 inf bn

COMBAT SUPPORT
  1 engr regt (4 engr sqn)
  1 MP bn
  1 cbt spt bn
COMBAT SERVICE SUPPORT
  1 spt bn (1 med coy, 1 log coy, 1 tpt coy)
EQUIPMENT BY TYPE
ARMOURED FIGHTING VEHICLES
  AUV 12 *Bushmaster*
ARTILLERY • **MOR 81mm** 12 L16A1

Reserves
FORCES BY ROLE
MANOEUVRE
  Light
    3 inf bn
COMBAT SERVICE SUPPORT
  1 spt bn

Coast Guard 300
EQUIPMENT BY TYPE
PATROL AND COASTAL COMBATANTS 10
  PBF 3
  PB 7: 2 *County* (Damen Stan Patrol 4207); 4 *Dauntless*; 1 *Paul Bogle* (US 31m)

Air Wing 250
Plus National Reserve
FORCES BY ROLE
MARITIME PATROL/TRANSPORT
  1 flt with Beech 350ER *King Air*; BN-2A *Defender*; Cessna 210M *Centurion*
SEARCH & RESCUE/TRANSPORT HELICOPTER
  1 flt with Bell 407
  1 flt with Bell 412EP
TRAINING
  1 unit with Bell 206B3; DA40-180FP *Diamond Star*
EQUIPMENT BY TYPE
AIRCRAFT
  MP 1 Beech 350ER *King Air*
  TPT • **Light** 4: 1 BN-2A *Defender*; 1 Cessna 210M *Centurion*; 2 DA40-180FP *Diamond Star*
HELICOPTERS
  MRH 2 Bell 412EP
  TPT • **Light** 6: 1 Bell 206B3 *Jet Ranger*; 3 Bell 407; 2 Bell 429

Mexico MEX

Mexican Peso NP		2018	2019	2020
GDP	NP	23.5tr	24.5tr	
	US$	1.22tr	1.27tr	
per capita	US$	9,797	10,118	
Growth	%	2.0	0.4	
Inflation	%	4.9	3.8	
Def bdgt [a]	NP	102.3bn	97.6bn	115bn
	US$	5.31bn	5.09bn	
FMA (US)	US$	3.75m	0m	0m
US$1=NP		19.24	19.19	

[a] National security expenditure

Real-terms defence budget trend (US$bn, constant 2015)

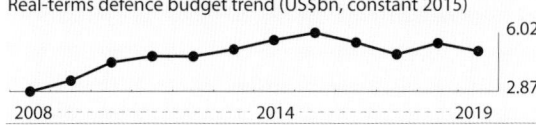

Population 127,318,112

Age	0–14	15–19	20–24	25–29	30–64	65 plus
Male	13.5%	4.4%	4.3%	4.1%	19.4%	3.3%
Female	12.9%	4.2%	4.2%	4.1%	21.4%	4.1%

Capabilities

Mexico has the most capable armed forces in Central America. They have been committed to providing internal-security support within Mexico for nearly a decade. Under the National Plan for Peace and Security 2018–24, the armed forces are now to hand over lead responsibility for tackling drugs cartels and other organised crime to a newly created National Guard gendarmerie. The Military Police Corps, which has expanded in recent years, has been used to form the basis of this new organisation alongside the naval police and elements of the Federal Police. Mexico has a close defence relationship with the US, which has provided equipment and training to Mexican forces under the Mérida Initiative, as well as via bilateral programmes via the Pentagon. The armed forces have a moderate capability to deploy independently, but do not do so in significant numbers. There are plans to recapitalise diverse and ageing conventional combat platforms across all three services. State-owned shipyards have produced patrol craft for the navy and will produce modules for the frigates currently under construction. Army factories have produced light armoured utility vehicles for domestic use. Airbus Helicopters operates a manufacturing plant in Querétaro.

ACTIVE 236,450 (Army 173,650 Navy 54,800 Air 8,000) **Paramilitary 132,400**

Conscript liability 12 months (partial, selection by ballot) from age 18, serving on Saturdays; voluntary for women; conscripts allocated to reserves.

RESERVE 81,500 (National Military Service)

ORGANISATIONS BY SERVICE

Space
EQUIPMENT BY TYPE
SATELLITES • COMMUNICATIONS 2 Mexsat

Army 173,650
12 regions (total: 46 army zones)

FORCES BY ROLE
SPECIAL FORCES
  1 (1st) SF bde (5 SF bn)
  1 (2nd) SF bde (7 SF bn)
  1 (3rd) SF bde (4 SF bn)
MANOEUVRE
  Reconnaissance
  3 (2nd, 3rd & 4th Armd) mech bde (2 armd recce bn, 2 lt mech bn, 1 arty bn, 1 (Canon) AT gp)
  25 mot recce regt
  Light
  1 (1st) inf corps (1 (1st Armd) mech bde (2 armd recce bn, 2 lt mech bn, 1 arty bn, 1 (Canon) AT gp), 3 (2nd, 3rd & 6th) inf bde (each: 3 inf bn, 1 arty regt, 1 (Canon) AT gp), 1 cbt engr bde (3 engr bn))
  3 (1st, 4th & 5th) indep lt inf bde (2 lt inf bn, 1 (Canon) AT gp)
  92 indep inf bn
  25 indep inf coy
  Air Manoeuvre
  1 para bde with (1 (GAFE) SF gp, 3 bn, 1 (Canon) AT gp)
COMBAT SUPPORT
  1 indep arty regt

EQUIPMENT BY TYPE
ARMOURED FIGHTING VEHICLES
  RECCE 255: 19 DN-5 *Toro*; 127 ERC-90F1 *Lynx* (7 trg); 40 M8; 37 MAC-1; 32 VBL
  IFV 390 DNC-1 (mod AMX-VCI)
  APC 309
    APC (T) 73: 40 HWK-11; 33 M5A1 half-track
    APC (W) 236: 95 BDX; 16 DN-4; 2 DN-6; 28 LAV-100 (*Pantera*); 26 LAV-150 ST; 25 MOWAG *Roland*; 44 VCR (3 amb; 5 cmd post)
  AUV 347: 100 DN-XI; 247 *Sandcat*
ENGINEERING & MAINTENANCE VEHICLES
  ARV 7: 3 M32 *Recovery Sherman*; 4 VCR ARV
ANTI-TANK/ANTI-INFRASTRUCTURE
  MSL • SP 8 VBL with *Milan*
  RCL • 106mm 1,187+ M40A1 (incl some SP)
  GUNS 37mm 30 M3
ARTILLERY 1,390
  TOWED 123: **105mm** 123: 40 M101; 40 M-56; 16 M2A1, 14 M3; 13 NORINCO M90
  MOR 1,267: **81mm** 1,100: 400 M1; 400 Brandt; 300 SB
  120mm 167: 75 Brandt; 60 M-65; 32 RT-61
AIR DEFENCE • GUNS • TOWED 80: **12.7mm** 40 M55; **20mm** 40 GAI-B01

Navy 54,800
Two Fleet Commands: Gulf (6 zones), Pacific (11 zones)

EQUIPMENT BY TYPE
PATROL AND COASTAL COMBATANTS 128
  PSOH 7:
    4 *Oaxaca* with 1 76mm gun (capacity 1 AS565MB *Panther* hel)
    3 *Oaxaca* (mod) with 1 57mm gun (capacity 1 AS565MB *Panther* hel)

PCOH 16:
 4 *Durango* with 1 57mm gun (capacity 1 Bo-105 hel)
 4 *Holzinger* (capacity 1 MD-902 *Explorer*)
 3 *Sierra* with 1 57mm gun (capacity 1 MD-902 *Explorer*)
 5 *Uribe* (ESP *Halcon*) (capacity 1 Bo-105 hel)
PCO 9: 6 *Valle* (US *Auk* MSF) with 1 76mm gun; 3 *Valle* (US *Auk* MSF) with 1 76mm gun, 1 hel landing platform
PCGH 1 *Huracan* (ISR *Aliya*) with 4 single lnchr with *Gabriel* II AShM, 1 Mk 15 *Phalanx* CIWS
PCC 2 *Democrata*
PBF 73: 6 *Acuario*; 2 *Acuario B*; 48 *Polaris* (SWE CB90); 17 *Polaris* II (SWE IC 16M)
PB 20: 3 *Azteca*; 3 *Cabo* (US *Cape Higgon*); 2 *Lago*; 2 *Punta* (US *Point*); 10 *Tenochtitlan* (Damen Stan Patrol 4207)
AMPHIBIOUS • LS • LST 4: 2 *Monte Azule*s with 1 hel landing platform; 1 *Papaloapan* (ex-US *Newport*) with 2 twin 76mm guns, 1 hel landing platform; 1 *Papaloapan* (ex-US *Newport*) with 1 hel landing platform
LOGISTICS AND SUPPORT 24
 AGOR 3 *Altair* (ex-US *Robert D. Conrad*)
 AGS 6: 3 *Arrecife*; 1 *Onjuku*; 1 *Rio Hondo*; 1 *Rio Tuxpan*
 AK 1 *Rio Suchiate*
 AOTL 2 *Aguascalientes*
 AP 2: 1 *Isla Maria Madre* (Damen Fast Crew Supplier 5009); 1 *Nautla*
 ATF 4 *Otomi* with 1 76mm gun
 ATS 4 *Kukulkan*
 AX 2 *Huasteco* (also serve as troop transport, supply and hospital ships)
 AXS 1 *Cuauhtemoc*

Naval Aviation 1,250
FORCES BY ROLE
MARITIME PATROL
 5 sqn with Cessna 404 *Titan*; MX-7 *Star Rocket*; Lancair IV-P; T-6C+ *Texan* II
 1 sqn with Beech 350ER *King Air*; C-212PM *Aviocar*; CN235-300 MPA *Persuader*
 1 sqn with L-90 *Redigo*
TRANSPORT
 1 sqn with An-32B *Cline*
 1 (VIP) sqn with DHC-8 *Dash 8*; Learjet 24; *Turbo Commander* 1000
TRANSPORT HELICOPTER
 2 sqn with AS555 *Fennec*; AS565MB/AS565MBe *Panther*; MD-902
 2 sqn with Bo-105 CBS-5
 5 sqn with Mi-17-1V/V-5 *Hip*
TRAINING
 1 sqn with Z-242L; Z-143Lsi
EQUIPMENT BY TYPE
AIRCRAFT 3 combat capable
 MP 6 CN235-300 MPA *Persuader*
 ISR 4: 2 C-212PM *Aviocar*; 2 Z-143Lsi
 TPT 32: **Light** 30: 5 Beech 350ER *King Air* (4 used for ISR); 3 Beech 350i *King Air*; 4 C295M; 2 C295W; 1 Cessna 404 *Titan*; 1 DHC-8 *Dash 8*; 6 Lancair IV-P; 2 Learjet 31A; 1 Learjet 60; 5 *Turbo Commander* 1000; **PAX** 2: 1 CL-605 *Challenger*; 1 Gulfstream 550
 TRG 47: 3 L-90TP *Redigo**; 4 MX-7 *Star Rocket*; 13 T-6C+ *Texan* II; 27 Z-242L

HELICOPTERS
 MRH 27: 2 AS555 *Fennec*; 4 MD-500E; 17 Mi-17-1V *Hip*; 4 Mi-17V-5 *Hip*
 SAR 14: 4 AS565MB *Panther*; 10 AS565MBe *Panther*
 TPT 27: **Heavy** 3 H225M *Caracal*; **Medium** 10 UH-60M *Black Hawk*; **Light** 14: 1 AW109SP; 5 MD-902 (SAR role); 8 S-333
 TRG 4 Schweizer 300C

Marines 21,500 (Expanding to 26,560)
FORCES BY ROLE
SPECIAL FORCES
 3 SF unit
MANOEUVRE
 Light
 32 inf bn(-)
 Air Manoeuvre
 1 AB bn
 Amphibious
 1 amph bde (4 inf bn, 1 amph bn, 1 arty gp)
 Other
 1 (Presidential) gd bn (included in army above)
COMBAT SERVICE SUPPORT
 2 spt bn
EQUIPMENT BY TYPE
ARMOURED FIGHTING VEHICLES
 APC • APC (W) 29: 3 BTR-60 (APC-60); 26 BTR-70 (APC-70)
ANTI-TANK/ANTI-INFRASTRUCTURE
 RCL 106mm M40A1
ARTILLERY 22+
 TOWED 105mm 16 M-56
 MRL 122mm 6 *Firos*-25
 MOR 81mm some
AIR DEFENCE • SAM • Point-defence 9K38 *Igla* (SA-18 *Grouse*)

Air Force 8,000
FORCES BY ROLE
GROUND ATTACK/ISR
 4 sqn with T-6C+ *Texan* II
 1 sqn with PC-7/PC-9M
ISR/AEW
 1 sqn with Beech 350ER *King Air*; EMB-145AEW *Erieye*; EMB-145RS; SA-2-37B; SA-227-BC *Metro* III (C-26B)
TRANSPORT
 1 sqn with C295M; PC-6B
 1 sqn with B-737; Beech 90
 1 sqn with C-27J *Spartan*; C-130E/K-30 *Hercules*; L-100-30
 5 (liaison) sqn with Cessna 182/206
 1 (anti-narcotic spraying) sqn with Bell 206; Cessna T206H;
 1 (Presidential) gp with AS332L *Super Puma*; AW109SP; B-737; B-757; B-787; Gulfstream 150/450/550; H225; Learjet 35A; Learjet 36; *Turbo Commander* 680
 1 (VIP) gp with B-737; Beech 200 *King Air*; Beech 350i *King Air*; Cessna 501/680 *Citation*; CL-605 *Challenger*; Gulfstream 550; Learjet 35A; Learjet 45; S-70A-24
TRAINING
 1 sqn with Cessna 182

1 sqn with PC-7; T-6C+ *Texan* II
1 sqn with Beech F33C *Bonanza*; Grob G120TP; SF-260EU

TRANSPORT HELICOPTER
4 sqn with Bell 206B; Bell 212; Bell 407GX
1 sqn with MD-530MF/MG
1 sqn with Mi-17 *Hip*
1 sqn with H225M *Caracal*; Bell 412EP *Twin Huey*; S-70A-24 *Black Hawk*
1 sqn with UH-60M *Black Hawk*

ISR UAV
1 unit with *Hermes* 450; S4 *Ehécatl*

EQUIPMENT BY TYPE
AIRCRAFT 76 combat capable
ISR 8: 2 Cessna 501 *Citation*; 2 SA-2-37A; 4 SA-227-BC *Metro* III (C-26B)
ELINT 8: 6 Beech 350ER *King Air*; 2 EMB-145RS
AEW&C 1 EMB-145AEW *Erieye*
TPT 114: **Medium** 9: 4 C-27J *Spartan*; 2 C-130E *Hercules*; 2 C-130K-30 *Hercules*; 1 L-100-30; **Light** 92: 2 Beech 90 *King Air*; 1 Beech 200 *King Air*; 1 Beech 350i *King Air*; 6 C295M; 2 C295W; 59 Cessna 182; 3 Cessna 206; 8 Cessna T206H; 1 Cessna 501 *Citation*; 1 Cessna 680 *Citation*; 2 Learjet 35A; 1 Learjet 36; 1 Learjet 45XP; 3 PC-6B; 1 Turbo Commander 680; **PAX** 13: 6 B-737; 1 B-757; 1 B-787; 1 CL-605 *Challenger*; 2 Gulfstream 150; 1 Gulfstream 450; 1 Gulfstream 550
TRG 134: 4 Beech F33C *Bonanza*; 25 Grob G120TP; 20 PC-7* (30 more possibly in store); 1 PC-9M*; 4 PT-17; 25 SF-260EU; 55 T-6C+ *Texan* II*

HELICOPTERS
MRH 44: 15 Bell 407GXP; 11 Bell 412EP *Twin Huey*; 18 Mi-17 *Hip* H
ISR 13: 4 MD-530MF; 9 MD-530MG
TPT 125: **Heavy** 12 H225M *Caracal*; **Medium** 31: 3 AS332L *Super Puma* (VIP); 2 H225 (VIP); 2 Mi-8T *Hip*; 6 S-70A-24 *Black Hawk*; 18 UH-60M *Black Hawk* **Light** 82: 5 AW109SP; 45 Bell 206; 13 Bell 206B *Jet Ranger* II; 6 Bell 206L; 13 Bell 212

UNMANNED AERIAL VEHICLES • ISR 8: **Medium** 3 *Hermes* 450; **Light** 5 S4 *Ehécatl*

Paramilitary 132,400

Federal Police 30,500
Public Security Secretariat

EQUIPMENT BY TYPE
AIRCRAFT
TPT 13: **Light** 7: 2 CN235M; 2 Cessna 182 *Skylane*; 1 Cessna 500 *Citation*; 2 Turbo Commander 695; **PAX** 6: 4 B-727; 1 *Falcon* 20; 1 Gulfstream II

HELICOPTERS
MRH 3 Mi-17 *Hip* H
TPT 27: **Medium** 13: 1 SA330J *Puma*; 6 UH-60L *Black Hawk*; 6 UH-60M *Black Hawk*; **Light** 14: 2 AS350B *Ecureuil*; 1 AS355 *Ecureuil* II; 6 Bell 206B; 5 H120 *Colibri*

UNMANNED AERIAL VEHICLES
ISR 12: **Medium** 2 *Hermes* 900; **Light** 10 S4 *Ehécatl*

Federal Ministerial Police 4,500
EQUIPMENT BY TYPE
HELICOPTERS
TPT • **Light** 25: 18 Bell 205 (UH-1H); 7 Bell 212
UNMANNED AERIAL VEHICLES
ISR • **Heavy** 2 *Dominator* XP

National Guard 80,000
Public Security Secretariat. Gendarmerie created in 2019 from elements of the Army, Navy, Air Force and Federal Police

FORCES BY ROLE
MANOEUVRE
Other
12 sy bde (3 sy bn)

Rural Defense Militia 17,400
FORCES BY ROLE
MANOEUVRE
Light
13 inf unit
13 (horsed) cav unit

DEPLOYMENT
CENTRAL AFRICAN REPUBLIC: UN • MINUSCA 1
MALI: UN • MINUSMA 3
WESTERN SAHARA: UN • MINURSO 4

Nicaragua NIC

Nicaraguan Gold Cordoba Co		2018	2019	2020
GDP	Co	414bn	415bn	
	US$	13.1bn	12.5bn	
per capita	US$	2,031	1,919	
Growth	%	-3.8	-5.0	
Inflation	%	5.0	5.6	
Def bdgt	Co	2.58bn	2.60bn	
	US$	81.7m	78.4m	
US$1=Co		31.55	33.14	

Real-terms defence budget trend (US$m, constant 2015)

Population 6,144,442

Age	0–14	15–19	20–24	25–29	30–64	65 plus
Male	13.3%	5.0%	5.1%	5.1%	17.7%	2.5%
Female	12.8%	4.8%	5.1%	5.2%	20.2%	3.1%

Capabilities
Nicaragua's armed forces are primarily a territorial light-infantry force, with a vestigial coastal-patrol capability. They are tasked with border and internal security, as well as with support for disaster-relief efforts and ecological protection. Nicaragua has training relationships with Russia and the US, as well as with neighbouring and

regional states, including Cuba and Venezuela. Training is largely focused on key internal- and border-security tasks, although the mechanised brigade has received Russian training in conventional military operations. The armed forces do not undertake significant international deployments and lack the logistical support for large-scale military operations, although the strategic-reserve mechanised brigade can deploy internally. Equipment primarily consists of ageing Cold War-era platforms. Russia has supplied some second-hand tanks and armoured vehicles to help re-equip the mechanised brigade and has supported the establishment of a repair workshop to maintain the vehicles in-country. Barring maintenance facilities there is no domestic defence industry.

ACTIVE 12,000 (Army 10,000 Navy 800 Air 1,200)

ORGANISATIONS BY SERVICE

Army ε10,000
FORCES BY ROLE
SPECIAL FORCES
  1 SF bde (2 SF bn)
MANOEUVRE
  Mechanised
  1 mech inf bde (1 armd recce bn, 1 tk bn, 1 mech inf bn, 1 arty bn, 1 MRL bn, 1 AT coy) **Light**
  1 regional comd (3 lt inf bn)
  1 regional comd (2 lt inf bn; 1 arty bn)
  3 regional comd (2 lt inf bn)
  2 indep lt inf bn
  Other
  1 comd regt (1 inf bn, 1 sy bn, 1 int unit, 1 sigs bn)
  1 (ecological) sy bn
COMBAT SUPPORT
  1 engr bn
COMBAT SERVICE SUPPORT
  1 med bn
  1 tpt regt
EQUIPMENT BY TYPE
ARMOURED FIGHTING VEHICLES
  MBT 82: 62 T-55 (65 more in store); 20 T-72B1
  LT TK (10 PT-76 in store)
  RECCE 20 BRDM-2
  IFV 17+ BMP-1
  APC • APC (W) 90+: 41 BTR-152 (61 more in store); 45 BTR-60 (15 more in store); 4+ BTR-70M
ENGINEERING & MAINTENANCE VEHICLES
  AEV T-54/T-55 AEV
  VLB TMM-3
ANTI-TANK/ANTI-INFRASTRUCTURE
  MSL
    SP 12 9P133 *Malyutka* (AT-3 *Sagger*)
    MANPATS 9K11 *Malyutka* (AT-3 *Sagger*)
  RCL 82mm B-10
  GUNS 281: **57mm** 174 ZIS-2; (90 more in store); **76mm** 83 ZIS-3; **100mm** 24 M-1944
ARTILLERY 766
  TOWED 12: **122mm** 12 D-30; (**152mm** 30 D-20 in store)
  MRL 151: **107mm** 33 Type-63: **122mm** 118: 18 BM-21 *Grad*; 100 *Grad* 1P (BM-21P) (single-tube rocket launcher, man portable)

  MOR 603: **82mm** 579; **120mm** 24 M-43; (**160mm** 4 M-160 in store)
AIR DEFENCE • SAM • Point-defence 9K36 *Strela*-3 (SA-14 *Gremlin*); 9K310 *Igla*-1 (SA-16 *Gimlet*); 9K32 *Strela*-2 (SA-7 *Grail*)‡

Navy ε800
EQUIPMENT BY TYPE
PATROL AND COASTAL COMBATANTS • PB 9: 3 *Dabur*; 4 Rodman 101; 2 *Soberania* (ex-JAM Damen Stan Patrol 4207)

Marines
FORCES BY ROLE
MANOEUVRE
  Amphibious
  1 mne bn

Air Force 1,200
FORCES BY ROLE
TRANSPORT
  1 sqn with An-26 *Curl*; Beech 90 *King Air*; Cessna U206; Cessna 404 *Titan* (VIP)
TRAINING
  1 unit with Cessna 172; PA-18 *Super Cub*; PA-28 *Cherokee*
TRANSPORT HELICOPTER
  1 sqn with Mi-17 *Hip* H (armed)
AIR DEFENCE
  1 gp with ZU-23
EQUIPMENT BY TYPE
AIRCRAFT
  TPT • Light 9: 3 An-26 *Curl*; 1 Beech 90 *King Air*; 1 Cessna 172; 1 Cessna U206; 1 Cessna 404 *Titan* (VIP); 2 PA-28 *Cherokee*
  TRG 2 PA-18 *Super Cub*
HELICOPTERS
  MRH 7 Mi-17 *Hip* H (armed)†
  TPT • Medium 2 Mi-171E
AIR DEFENCE • GUNS 23mm 18 ZU-23
AIR-LAUNCHED MISSILES • ASM 9M17 *Skorpion* (AT-2 *Swatter*)

Panama PAN

Panamanian Balboa B		2018	2019	2020
GDP	B	65.1bn	68.5bn	
	US$	65.1bn	68.5bn	
per capita	US$	15,643	16,245	
Growth	%	3.7	4.3	
Inflation	%	0.8	-0.0	
Def bdgt [a]	B	738m	805m	
	US$	738m	805m	
FMA (US)	US$	2m	0m	0m
US$1=B		1.00	1.00	

[a] Public security expenditure

Real-terms defence budget trend (US$m, constant 2015)

Population 3,847,647

Age	0–14	15–19	20–24	25–29	30–64	65 plus
Male	13.2%	4.3%	4.2%	3.9%	20.6%	4.0%
Female	12.7%	4.1%	4.1%	3.8%	20.3%	4.8%

Capabilities

Panama abolished its armed forces in 1990, but has a border service, a police force and an air/maritime service for low-level security tasks. The primary security focus is on the southern border with Colombia, and the majority of the border service is deployed there. Both Colombia and the US have provided training and support. Training is focused on internal and border security rather than conventional military operations and there is no capability to mount significant external deployments. None of Panama's security services maintain heavy military equipment, focusing instead on light transport, patrol and surveillance capabilities. Aside from limited maintenance facilities, the country has no domestic defence industry.

Paramilitary 26,000

ORGANISATIONS BY SERVICE

Paramilitary 26,000

National Border Service 4,000
FORCES BY ROLE
SPECIAL FORCES
 1 SF gp
MANOEUVRE
Other
 1 sy bde (5 sy bn(-))
 1 indep sy bn

National Police Force 20,000
No hvy mil eqpt, small arms only
FORCES BY ROLE
SPECIAL FORCES
 1 SF unit

MANOEUVRE
Other
 1 (presidential) gd bn(-)

National Aeronaval Service 2,000
FORCES BY ROLE
TRANSPORT
 1 sqn with C-212M *Aviocar*; Cessna 210; PA-31 *Navajo*; PA-34 *Seneca*
 1 (Presidential) flt with ERJ-135BJ; S-76C
TRAINING
 1 unit with Cessna 152; Cessna 172; T-35D *Pillan*
TRANSPORT HELICOPTER
 1 sqn with AW139; Bell 205; Bell 205 (UH-1H *Iroquois*); Bell 212; Bell 407; Bell 412EP; H145; MD-500E

EQUIPMENT BY TYPE
PATROL AND COASTAL COMBATANTS 17
 PCO 1 *Independencia* (ex-US *Balsam*)
 PCC 2 *Saettia*
 PB 14: 1 *Cocle*; 1 *Chiriqui* (ex-US PB MkIV); 2 *Panquiaco* (UK Vosper 31.5m); 5 *3 De Noviembre* (ex-US *Point*), 1 *Taboga*; 4 Type-200
AMPHIBIOUS • LANDING CRAFT • LCU 1 *General Estaban Huertas*
LOGISTICS AND SUPPORT • AG 2
AIRCRAFT
 TPT • **Light** 11: 1 DHC-6-400 *Twin Otter*; 3 C-212M *Aviocar*; 1 Cessna 152, 1 Cessna 172; 1 Cessna 210; 1 ERJ-135BJ; 1 PA-31 *Navajo*; 2 PA-34 *Seneca*
 TRG 6 T-35D *Pillan*
HELICOPTERS
 MRH 10: 8 AW139; 1 Bell 412EP; 1 MD-500E
 TPT • **Light** 21: 2 Bell 205; 13 Bell 205 (UH-1H *Iroquois*); 2 Bell 212; 2 Bell 407; 1 H145; 1 S-76C

Paraguay PRY

Paraguayan Guarani Pg		2018	2019	2020
GDP	Pg	240tr	251tr	
	US$	41.9bn	40.7bn	
per capita	US$	5,934	5,692	
Growth	%	3.7	1.0	
Inflation	%	4.0	3.5	
Def bdgt	Pg	1.78tr	1.77tr	1.88tr
	US$	311m	288m	
US$1=Pg		5,732.06	6,162.78	

Real-terms defence budget trend (US$m, constant 2015)

Population 7,108,524

Age	0–14	15–19	20–24	25–29	30–64	65 plus
Male	12.1%	4.3%	4.8%	4.7%	20.6%	3.6%
Female	11.7%	4.3%	4.8%	4.7%	20.4%	4.0%

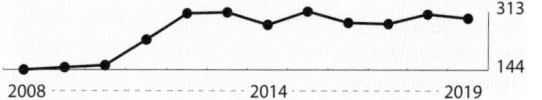

Capabilities

The armed forces are small by regional standards and the equipment inventory for all services is ageing and largely obsolete. The country faces internal challenges from insurgency and transnational organised crime, chiefly drug trafficking. Conscript numbers have reduced in recent years, and there are a significant number of higher ranks in the force structure. Key formations have long been under-strength. There has been some training support by the US, and the MOD reported in 2018 a training cooperation agreement with Germany. Paraguay has had a consistent if limited tradition of contributing to UN peacekeeping operations since 2001. There is only limited ability to self-sustain forces abroad, and no effective power-projection capacity. There is a small force of river-patrol craft, though some of the older of these have finally been retired. Armoured capability is very limited. While there are plans to acquire more modern equipment, including tanks, naval equipment and aircraft of all types for the air force, recent acquisitions of heavier materiel have been confined to small quantities of engineering and transport equipment. There is some local maintenance capacity but the effectiveness of systems is limited by age and while there is some R&D and manufacturing cooperation with local research institutes, there is no traditional defence-industrial base.

ACTIVE 13,950 (Army 7,400 Navy 3,800 Air 2,750)
Paramilitary 14,800
Conscript liability 12 months

RESERVE 164,500 (Joint 164,500)

ORGANISATIONS BY SERVICE

Army 7,400

Much of the Paraguayan army is maintained in a cadre state during peacetime; the nominal inf and cav divs are effectively only at coy strength. Active gp/regt are usually coy sized

FORCES BY ROLE
MANOEUVRE
  Light
  3 inf corps (total: 6 inf div(-), 3 cav div(-), 6 arty bty)
  Other
  1 (Presidential) gd regt (1 SF bn, 1 inf bn, 1 sy bn, 1 log gp)
COMBAT SUPPORT
  1 arty bde with (2 arty gp, 1 ADA gp)
  1 engr bde with (1 engr regt, 3 construction regt)
  1 sigs bn

Reserves
FORCES BY ROLE
MANOEUVRE
  Light
  14 inf regt (cadre)
  4 cav regt (cadre)
EQUIPMENT BY TYPE
ARMOURED FIGHTING VEHICLES
  RECCE 28 EE-9 *Cascavel*
  APC • APC (W) 12 EE-11 *Urutu*
ARTILLERY 99
  TOWED 105mm 19 M101
  MOR 81mm 80

AIR DEFENCE • GUNS 22:
  SP 20mm 3 M9 half track
  TOWED 19: 40mm 13 M1A1, 6 L/60

Navy 3,800
EQUIPMENT BY TYPE
PATROL AND COASTAL COMBATANTS 20
  PCR 1 *Itaipú*
  PBR 19: 1 *Capitan Cabral*; 2 *Capitan Ortiz* (ROC *Hai Ou*); 2 *Novatec*; 6 Type-701; 3 *Croq* 15; 5 others
AMPHIBIOUS • LANDING CRAFT • LCVP 3

Naval Aviation 100
FORCES BY ROLE
TRANSPORT
  1 (liaison) sqn with Cessna 150; Cessna 210 *Centurion*; Cessna 310; Cessna 401
TRANSPORT HELICOPTER
  1 sqn with AS350 *Ecureuil* (HB350 *Esquilo*)
EQUIPMENT BY TYPE
AIRCRAFT • TPT • Light 6: 2 Cessna 150; 1 Cessna 210 *Centurion*; 2 Cessna 310; 1 Cessna 401
HELICOPTERS • TPT • Light 2 AS350 *Ecureuil* (HB350 *Esquilo*)

Marines 700; 200 conscript (total 900)
FORCES BY ROLE
MANOEUVRE
  Amphibious
  3 mne bn(-)
ARTILLERY • TOWED 105mm 2 M101

Air Force 2,750
FORCES BY ROLE
GROUND ATTACK/ISR
  1 sqn with EMB-312 *Tucano**
TRANSPORT
  1 gp with C-212-200/400 *Aviocar*; DHC-6 *Twin Otter*
  1 VIP gp with Beech 58 *Baron*; Bell 427; Cessna U206 *Stationair*; Cessna 208B *Grand Caravan*; Cessna 210 *Centurion*; Cessna 402B; PA-32R *Saratoga* (EMB-721C *Sertanejo*); PZL-104 *Wilga* 80
TRAINING
  1 sqn with T-25 *Universal*; T-35A/B *Pillan*
TRANSPORT HELICOPTER
  1 gp with AS350 *Ecureuil* (HB350 *Esquilo*); Bell 205 (UH-1H *Iroquois*)
MANOEUVRE
  Air Manoeuvre
  1 AB bde
EQUIPMENT BY TYPE
AIRCRAFT 6 combat capable
  TPT • Light 18: 1 Beech 58 *Baron*; 4 C-212-200 *Aviocar*; 1 C-212-400 *Aviocar*; 2 Cessna 208B *Grand Caravan*; 1 Cessna 210 *Centurion*; 1 Cessna 310; 2 Cessna 402B; 1 Cessna U206 *Stationair*; 1 DHC-6 *Twin Otter*; 1 PA-32R *Saratoga* (EMB-721C *Sertanejo*); 2 PZL-104 *Wilga* 80
  TRG 21: 6 EMB-312 *Tucano**; 6 T-25 *Universal*; 6 T-35A *Pillan*; 3 T-35B *Pillan*

HELICOPTERS • TPT • **Light** 12: 3 AS350 *Ecureuil* (HB350 *Esquilo*); 7 Bell 205 (UH-1H *Iroquois*); 1 Bell 407; 1 Bell 427 (VIP)

Paramilitary 14,800

Special Police Service 10,800; 4,000 conscript (total 14,800)

DEPLOYMENT

CENTRAL AFRICAN REPUBLIC: UN • MINUSCA 3
CYPRUS: UN • UNFICYP 12
DEMOCRATIC REPUBLIC OF THE CONGO: UN • MONUSCO 6
SOUTH SUDAN: UN • UNMISS 3

Peru PER

Peruvian Nuevo Sol NS		2018	2019	2020
GDP	NS	741bn	775bn	
	US$	225bn	229bn	
per capita	US$	7,007	7,047	
Growth	%	4.0	2.6	
Inflation	%	1.3	2.2	
Def bdgt	NS	7.51bn	7.47bn	7.45bn
	US$	2.29bn	2.21bn	
FMA (US)	US$	3.05m	0m	0m
US$1=NS		3.29	3.39	

Real-terms defence budget trend (US$bn, constant 2015)

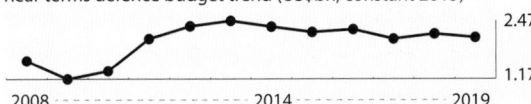

Population   31,624,207

Age	0–14	15–19	20–24	25–29	30–64	65 plus
Male	13.1%	4.3%	4.5%	4.4%	19.1%	3.7%
Female	12.6%	4.2%	4.5%	4.5%	20.9%	4.1%

Capabilities

Peru's armed forces have sufficient training and capabilities to fulfil domestic-security tasks, although they are limited by an increasingly ageing equipment inventory and economic constraints. The armed forces are primarily orientated towards preserving territorial integrity and security, focusing on counter-insurgency and counter-narcotics operations, while strengthening their disaster-relief capabilities. Peru maintains close military ties with Colombia. The two countries signed a cooperation agreement on air control, humanitarian assistance and counter-narcotics. The armed forces train regularly and take part in national and multilateral exercises. The armed forces are capable of independently deploying externally and contribute to UN missions abroad. There has been some aviation modernisation, though not across the whole fleet. The navy is looking to acquire new corvettes and modernise its ageing submarines. The state-owned shipyard SIMA and aviation firm SEMAN are key players in Peru's defence industry, both in terms of manufacturing and maintenance. SEMAN completed in 2017 final assembly for the last Korean-designed KT-1 trainer, and the navy in 2018 commissioned the first locally built and South Korean-designed multipurpose vessel.

ACTIVE 81,000 (Army 47,500 Navy 24,000 Air 9,500)
Paramilitary 77,000
Conscript liability 12 months voluntary conscription for both males and females

RESERVE 188,000 (Army 188,000)

ORGANISATIONS BY SERVICE

Space
EQUIPMENT BY TYPE
SATELLITES • ISR PERÚSAT-1

Army 47,500
4 mil region
FORCES BY ROLE
SPECIAL FORCES
  1 (1st) SF bde (2 spec ops bn, 2 cdo bn, 1 cdo coy, 1 CT coy, 1 airmob arty gp, 1 MP coy, 1 cbt spt bn)
  1 (3rd) SF bde (1 spec ops bn, 2 cdo bn, 1 airmob arty gp, 1 MP coy)
  1 (6th) SF bde (2 spec ops bn, 2 cdo bn, 1 cdo coy, 1 MP coy)
MANOEUVRE
Armoured
  1 (3rd) armd bde (2 tk bn, 1 armd inf bn, 1 arty gp, 1 AT coy, 1 AD gp, 1 engr bn, 1 cbt spt bn)
  1 (9th) armd bde (2 tk bn, 1 armd inf bn, 1 SP arty gp, 1 ADA gp)
Mechanised
  1 (3rd) armd cav bde (3 mech cav bn, 1 mot inf bn, 1 arty gp, 1 AD gp, 1 engr bn, 1 cbt spt bn)
  1 (1st) cav bde (4 mech cav bn, 1 MP coy, 1 cbt spt bn)
Light
  2 (2nd & 31st) mot inf bde (4 mot inf bn, 1 arty gp, 1 MP coy, 1 log bn)
  3 (1st, 7th & 32nd) inf bde (3 inf bn, 1 MP coy, 1 cbt spt bn)
  1 (33rd) inf bde (4 inf bn)
  1 (4th) mtn bde (1 armd regt, 3 mot inf bn, 1 arty gp, 1 MP coy, 1 cbt spt bn)
  1 (5th) mtn bde (1 armd regt, 2 mot inf bn, 3 jungle coy, 1 arty gp, 1 MP coy, 1 cbt spt bn)
  1 (6th) jungle inf bde (4 jungle bn, 1 engr bn, 1 MP coy, 1 cbt spt bn)
  1 (35th) jungle inf bde (1 SF gp, 3 jungle bn, 3 jungle coy, 1 jungle arty gp, 1 AT coy, 1 AD gp, 1 jungle engr bn)
COMBAT SUPPORT
  1 arty gp (bde) (4 arty gp, 2 AD gp, 1 sigs gp)
  1 (3rd) arty bde (4 arty gp, 1 AD gp, 1 sigs gp)
  1 (22nd) engr bde (3 engr bn, 1 demining coy)
COMBAT SERVICE SUPPORT
  1 (1st Multipurpose) spt bde
AVIATION
  1 (1st) avn bde (1 atk hel/recce hel bn, 1 avn bn, 2 aslt hel/tpt hel bn)
AIR DEFENCE
  1 AD gp (regional troops)

EQUIPMENT BY TYPE
ARMOURED FIGHTING VEHICLES
  MBT 165 T-55; (75† in store)
  LT TK 96 AMX-13
  RECCE 95: 30 BRDM-2; 15 Fiat 6616; 50 M9A1
  APC 295
    APC (T) 120 M113A1
    APC (W) 175: 150 UR-416; 25 Fiat 6614
ENGINEERING & MAINTENANCE VEHICLES
  ARV M578
  VLB GQL-111
ANTI-TANK-ANTI-INFRASTRUCTURE
  MSL
    SP 22 M1165A2 HMMWV with 9K135 *Kornet* E (AT-14 *Spriggan*)
    MANPATS 9K11 *Malyutka* (AT-3 *Sagger*); HJ-73C; 9K135 *Kornet* E (AT-14 *Spriggan*); Spike-ER
  RCL 106mm M40A1
ARTILLERY 1,011
  SP 155mm 12 M109A2
  TOWED 290: **105mm** 152: 44 M101; 24 M2A1; 60 M-56; 24 Model 56 pack howitzer; **122mm**; 36 D-30; **130mm** 36 M-46; **155mm** 66: 36 M114, 30 Model 50
  MRL 122mm 35: 22 BM-21 *Grad*; 13 Type-90B
  MOR 674+: **81mm/107mm** 350; **SP 107mm** 24 M106A1; **120mm** 300+ Brandt/Expal Model L
AIRCRAFT
  TPT • Light 16: 2 An-28 *Cash*; 3 An-32B *Cline*; 1 Beech 350 *King Air*; 1 Beech 1900D; 4 Cessna 152; 1 Cessna 208 *Caravan* I; 2 Cessna U206 *Stationair*; 1 PA-31T *Cheyenne* II; 1 PA-34 *Seneca*
  TRG 4 IL-103
HELICOPTERS
  MRH 7 Mi-17 *Hip* H
  TPT 35: **Heavy** (3 Mi-26T *Halo* in store); **Medium** 22 Mi-171Sh; **Light** 13: 2 AW109K2; 9 PZL Mi-2 *Hoplite*; 2 R-44
  TRG 4 F-28F
AIR DEFENCE
  SAM • Point-defence 9K36 *Strela*-3 (SA-14 *Gremlin*); 9K310 *Igla*-1 (SA-16 *Gimlet*); 9K32 *Strela*-2 (SA-7 *Grail*)‡
  GUNS 165
    SP 23mm 35 ZSU-23-4
    TOWED 23mm 130: 80 ZU-23-2; 50 ZU-23

Navy 24,000 (incl 1,000 Coast Guard)
Commands: Pacific, Lake Titicaca, Amazon River
EQUIPMENT BY TYPE
SUBMARINES • TACTICAL • SSK 6:
  4 *Angamos* (GER T-209/1200) with 8 single 533mm TT with SST-4 HWT (of which 1 in refit)
  2 *Islay* (GER T-209/1100) with 8 single 533mm TT with SUT 264 HWT
PRINCIPAL SURFACE COMBATANTS 7
  FRIGATES • FFGHM 7:
    2 *Aguirre* (ex-ITA *Lupo*) with 8 single lnchr with *Otomat* Mk2 AShM, 1 octuple Mk 29 lnchr with RIM-7P *Sea Sparrow* SAM, 2 triple 324mm ASTT with A244 LWT, 1 127mm gun (capacity 1 Bell 212 (AB-212)/SH-3D *Sea King*)
    2 *Aguirre* (ex-ITA *Lupo*) with 2 twin lnchr with MM40 *Exocet* Block 3 AShM, 1 octuple Mk 29 lnchr with RIM-7P *Sea Sparrow* SAM, 2 triple 324mm ASTT with A244 LWT, 1 127mm gun (capacity 1 Bell 212 (AB-212)/SH-3D *Sea King*)
    1 *Carvajal* (mod ITA *Lupo*) with 8 single lnchr with *Otomat* Mk2 AShM, 1 octuple *Albatros* lnchr with *Aspide* SAM, 2 triple 324mm ASTT with A244 LWT, 1 127mm gun (capacity 1 Bell 212 (AB-212)/SH-3D *Sea King*)
    2 *Carvajal* (mod ITA *Lupo*) with 8 single lnchr with MM40 *Exocet* Block 3 AShM, 1 octuple *Albatros* lnchr with *Aspide* SAM, 2 triple 324mm ASTT with A244 LWT, 1 127mm gun (capacity 1 Bell 212 (AB-212)/SH-3D *Sea King*)
PATROL AND COASTAL COMBATANTS 12
  CORVETTES • FSG 6 *Velarde* (FRA PR-72 64m) with 4 single lnchr with MM38 *Exocet* AShM, 1 76mm gun
  PCR 6:
    2 *Amazonas* with 1 76mm gun
    2 *Manuel Clavero*
    2 *Marañon* with 2 76mm guns
AMPHIBIOUS
  PRINCIPAL AMPHIBIOUS SHIPS • LPD 1 *Pisco* (IDN *Makassar*) (capacity 2 LCM; 3 hels; 24 IFV; 450 troops)
  LANDING SHIPS • LST 2 *Paita* (capacity 395 troops) (ex-US *Terrebonne Parish*)
  LANDING CRAFT • UCAC 7 *Griffon* 2000TD (capacity 22 troops)
LOGISTICS AND SUPPORT 25
  AG 4 *Rio Napo*
  AGOR 1 *Humboldt*
  AGORH 1 *Carrasco*
  AGS 5: 1 *Carrasco* (ex-NLD *Dokkum*); 2 *Van Straelen*; 1 *La Macha*, 1 *Stiglich* (river survey vessel for the upper Amazon)
  AH 4 (river hospital craft)
  AO 2 *Noguera*
  AOR 1 *Mollendo*
  AORH 1 *Tacna* (ex-NLD *Amsterdam*)
  AOT 2 *Bayovar*
  ATF 1
  AWT 1 *Caloyeras*
  AXS 2: 1 *Marte*; 1 *Union*

Naval Aviation ε800
FORCES BY ROLE
MARITIME PATROL
  1 sqn with Beech 200T; Bell 212 ASW (AB-212 ASW); F-27 *Friendship*; Fokker 60; SH-2G *Super Seasprite*; SH-3D *Sea King*
TRANSPORT
  1 flt with An-32B *Cline*; Cessna 206; Fokker 50
TRAINING
  1 sqn with F-28F; T-34C *Turbo Mentor*
TRANSPORT HELICOPTER
  1 (liaison) sqn with Bell 206B *Jet Ranger* II; Mi-8 *Hip*
EQUIPMENT BY TYPE
AIRCRAFT
  MP 8: 4 Beech 200T; 4 Fokker 60
  ELINT 1 F-27 *Friendship*
  TPT • Light 6: 3 An-32B *Cline*; 1 Cessna 206; 2 Fokker 50
  TRG 5 T-34C *Turbo Mentor*

HELICOPTERS
ASW 6: 2 Bell 212 ASW (AB-212 ASW); 1 SH-2G *Super Seasprite*; 3 SH-3D *Sea King*
MRH 3 Bell 412SP
TPT 11: **Medium** 8: 2 Mi-8 *Hip*; 6 UH-3H *Sea King*; **Light** 3 Bell 206B *Jet Ranger* II
TRG 5 F-28F
MSL • **AShM** AM39 *Exocet*

Marines 4,000
FORCES BY ROLE
SPECIAL FORCES
3 cdo gp
MANOEUVRE
Light
2 inf bn
1 inf gp
Amphibious
1 mne bde (1 SF gp, 1 recce bn, 2 inf bn, 1 amph bn, 1 arty gp)
Jungle
1 jungle inf bn
EQUIPMENT BY TYPE
ARMOURED FIGHTING VEHICLES
APC • **APC (W)** 47+: 32 LAV II; V-100 *Commando*; 15 V-200 *Chaimite*
ANTI-TANK/ANTI-INFRASTRUCTURE
RCL 84mm *Carl Gustav*; **106mm** M40A1
ARTILLERY 18+
TOWED 122mm D-30
MOR 18+: **81mm** some; **120mm** ε18
AIR DEFENCE • **GUNS 20mm** SP (twin)

Air Force 9,500
Divided into five regions – North, Lima, South, Central and Amazon
FORCES BY ROLE
FIGHTER
1 sqn with MiG-29S/SE *Fulcrum* C; MiG-29UB *Fulcrum* B
FIGHTER/GROUND ATTACK
1 sqn with *Mirage* 2000E/ED (2000P/DP)
2 sqn with A-37B *Dragonfly*
1 sqn with Su-25A *Frogfoot* A†; Su-25UB *Frogfoot* B†
ISR
1 (photo-survey) sqn with Learjet 36A; SA-227-BC *Metro* III (C-26B)
TRANSPORT
1 sqn with B-737; An-32 *Cline*
1 sqn with DHC-6 *Twin Otter*; DHC-6-400 *Twin Otter*; PC-6 *Turbo Porter*
1 sqn with L-100-20
TRAINING
2 (drug interdiction) sqn with EMB-312 *Tucano*
1 sqn with MB-339A*
1 sqn with Z-242
1 hel sqn with Schweizer 300C
ATTACK HELICOPTER
1 sqn with Mi-25/Mi-35P *Hind*
TRANSPORT HELICOPTER
1 sqn with Mi-17 *Hip* H

1 sqn with Bell 206 *Jet Ranger*; Bell 212 (AB-212); Bell 412 *Twin Huey*
1 sqn with Bo-105C/LS
AIR DEFENCE
6 bn with S-125 *Pechora* (SA-3 *Goa*)
EQUIPMENT BY TYPE
AIRCRAFT 77 combat capable
FTR 19: 9 MiG-29S *Fulcrum* C; 3 MiG-29SE *Fulcrum* C; 5 MiG-29SMP *Fulcrum*; 2 MiG-29UBM *Fulcrum* B
FGA 12: 2 *Mirage* 2000ED (2000DP); 10 *Mirage* 2000E (2000P) (some†)
ATK 36: 18 A-37B *Dragonfly*; 1 Su-25A *Frogfoot* A; 9 Su-25A *Frogfoot* A†; 8 Su-25UB *Frogfoot* B†
ISR 6: 2 Learjet 36A; 4 SA-227-BC *Metro* III (C-26B)
TPT 37: **Medium** 6: 4 C-27J *Spartan*; 2 L-100-20; **Light** 27: 4 An-32 *Cline*; 7 Cessna 172 *Skyhawk*; 3 DHC-6 *Twin Otter*; 12 DHC-6-400 *Twin Otter*; 1 PC-6 *Turbo-Porter*; **PAX** 4 B-737
TRG 69: 2 CH-2000; 19 EMB-312 *Tucano*; 20 KT-1P; 10 MB-339A*; 6 T-41A/D *Mescalero*; 12 Z-242
HELICOPTERS
ATK 18: 16 Mi-25 *Hind* D; 2 Mi-35P *Hind* E
MRH 20: 2 Bell 412 *Twin Huey*; 18 Mi-17 *Hip* H
TPT 28: **Medium** 7 Mi-171Sh; **Light** 21: 8 Bell 206 *Jet Ranger*; 6 Bell 212 (AB-212); 1 Bo-105C; 6 Bo-105LS
TRG 4 Schweizer 300C
AIR DEFENCE • SAM
Short-range S-125 *Pechora* (SA-3 *Goa*)
Point-defence *Javelin*
AIR-LAUNCHED MISSILES
AAM • **IR** R-3 (AA-2 *Atoll*)‡; R-60 (AA-8 *Aphid*)‡; R-73 (AA-11A *Archer*); R-550 *Magic*; **IR/SARH** R-27 (AA-10 *Alamo*); **ARH** R-77 (AA-12 *Adder*)
ASM AS-30; Kh-29L (AS-14A *Kedge*)
ARM Kh-58 (AS-11 *Kilter*)

Paramilitary 77,000

National Police 77,000 (100,000 reported)
EQUIPMENT BY TYPE
ARMOURED FIGHTING VEHICLES
APC (W) 120: 20 BMR-600; 100 MOWAG *Roland*
AIRCRAFT
TPT • **Light** 1 An-32B *Cline*
HELICOPTERS
MRH 1 Mi-17 *Hip* H

General Police 43,000

Security Police 21,000

Technical Police 13,000

Coast Guard 1,000
Personnel included as part of Navy
EQUIPMENT BY TYPE
PATROL AND COASTAL COMBATANTS 39
PSOH 1 *Carvajal* (mod ITA *Lupo*) with 1 127mm gun (capacity 1 Bell 212 (AB-212)/SH-3D *Sea King*)
PCC 9: 1 *Ferré* (ex-ROK *Po Hang*) with 1 76mm gun; 4 *Río Pativilca* (ROK *Tae Geuk*); 4 *Río Nepena*
PB 10: 6 *Chicama* (US *Dauntless*); 1 *Río Chira*; 3 *Río Santa*
PBR 19: 1 *Río Viru*; 8 *Parachique*; 10 *Zorritos*

LOGISTICS AND SUPPORT • AH 1 *Puno*
AIRCRAFT
  TPT • Light 3: 1 DHC-6 *Twin Otter*; 2 F-27 *Friendship*

Rondas Campesinas
Peasant self-defence force. Perhaps 7,000 rondas 'gp', up to pl strength, some with small arms. Deployed mainly in emergency zone

DEPLOYMENT
CENTRAL AFRICAN REPUBLIC: UN • MINUSCA 220; 1 engr coy
DEMOCRATIC REPUBLIC OF THE CONGO: UN • MONUSCO 3
LEBANON: UN • UNIFIL 1
SOUTH SUDAN: UN • UNMISS 2
SUDAN: UN • UNISFA 4

Suriname SUR

Suriname Dollar srd		2018	2019	2020
GDP	srd	25.6bn	28.5bn	
	US$	3.43bn	3.77bn	
per capita	US$	5,798	6,311	
Growth	%	2.0	2.2	
Inflation	%	6.9	5.5	
Def bdgt	srd	n.k.	n.k.	
	US$	n.k.	n.k.	
US$1=srd		7.46	7.55	
Population	603,823			

Age	0–14	15–19	20–24	25–29	30–64	65 plus
Male	12.1%	4.4%	4.4%	4.1%	22.6%	2.8%
Female	11.6%	4.3%	4.2%	4.0%	22.0%	3.6%

Capabilities
The armed forces are principally tasked with preserving territorial integrity. They also assist the national police in internal- and border-security missions, as well as tackling transnational criminal activity and drug trafficking. They have also been involved in disaster-relief and humanitarian-assistance operations. The country is a member of the Caribbean Disaster Emergency Management Agency and the Caribbean Basin Security Initiative. Ties with Brazil, China, India and the US have been crucial for the supply of equipment, including a limited number of armoured vehicles and helicopters, as well as training activity. The armed forces take part in the multilateral *Tradewinds* disaster-response exercise. The armed forces are not sized or equipped for power projection and are no longer engaged in any international peacekeeping operations. Resource challenges and limited equipment serviceability means the armed forces are constrained in providing sufficient border and coastal control and surveillance. There is no capability to design and manufacture modern military equipment and Suriname has looked to its foreign military cooperation to improve not just trade training but also military maintenance capacity.

ACTIVE 1,840 (Army 1,400 Navy 240 Air 200)
(All services form part of the army)

ORGANISATIONS BY SERVICE

Army 1,400
FORCES BY ROLE
MANOEUVRE
  Mechanised
    1 mech cav sqn
  Light
    1 inf bn (4 coy)
COMBAT SUPPORT
  1 MP bn (coy)
EQUIPMENT BY TYPE
ARMOURED FIGHTING VEHICLES
  RECCE 6 EE-9 *Cascavel*
  APC • APC (W) 15 EE-11 *Urutu*
ANTI-TANK/ANTI-INFRASTRUCTURE
  RCL 106mm M40A1
ARTILLERY • MOR 81mm 6

Navy ε240
EQUIPMENT BY TYPE
PATROL AND COASTAL COMBATANTS 10
  PB 5: 3 Rodman 101†; 2 others
  PBR 5 Rodman 55

Air Force ε200
EQUIPMENT BY TYPE
AIRCRAFT 2 combat capable
  TPT • Light 2: 1 BN-2 *Defender**; 1 Cessna 182
  TRG 1 PC-7 *Turbo Trainer**
HELICOPTERS • MRH 3 SA316B *Alouette* III (*Chetak*)

Trinidad and Tobago TTO

Trinidad and Tobago Dollar TT$		2018	2019	2020
GDP	TT$	153bn	153bn	
	US$	22.5bn	22.6bn	
per capita	US$	16,379	16,366	
Growth	%	0.3	0.0	
Inflation	%	1.0	0.9	
Def bdgt	TT$	6.24bn	6.12bn	6.44bn
	US$	921m	904m	
US$1=TT$		6.77	6.77	

Real-terms defence budget trend (US$m, constant 2015)

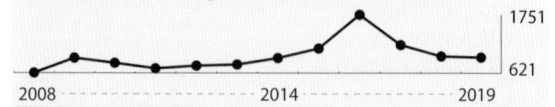

Population	1,212,401					
Age	0–14	15–19	20–24	25–29	30–64	65 plus
Male	9.8%	3.0%	2.9%	3.4%	26.6%	5.1%
Female	9.4%	2.8%	2.6%	3.1%	24.8%	6.5%

Capabilities

The Trinidad and Tobago Defence Force (TTDF) focuses on border protection and maritime security, as well as counter-narcotics tasks. A larger role in law-enforcement support is planned for the army. Trinidad and Tobago is a member of the Caribbean Community, and cooperates with other countries in the region in disaster-relief efforts. It also takes part in US SOUTHCOM's annual *Tradewinds* disaster-response exercise and sends personnel to the US and UK for training. Trinidad and Tobago has no capacity to deploy and maintain troops abroad, and bar limited maintenance facilities has no domestic defence industry.

ACTIVE 4,050 (Army 3,000 Coast Guard 1,050)
(All services form the Trinidad and Tobago Defence Force)

ORGANISATIONS BY SERVICE

Army ε3,000
FORCES BY ROLE
SPECIAL FORCES
1 SF unit
MANOEUVRE
Light
2 inf bn
COMBAT SUPPORT
1 engr bn
COMBAT SERVICE SUPPORT
1 log bn
EQUIPMENT BY TYPE
ANTI-TANK/ANTI-INFRASTRUCTURE
RCL 84mm *Carl Gustav*
ARTILLERY • MOR 81mm 6 L16A1

Coast Guard 1,050
FORCES BY ROLE
COMMAND
1 mne HQ
EQUIPMENT BY TYPE
PATROL AND COASTAL COMBATANTS 26
PCO 1 *Nelson II* (ex-PRC)
PCC 6: 2 *Point Lisas* (Damen Fast Crew Supplier 5009); 4 *Speyside* (Damen Stan Patrol 5009)
PB 19: 2 *Gasper Grande*; 1 *Matelot*; 4 *Plymouth*; 4 *Point*; 6 *Scarlet Ibis* (Austal 30m); 2 *Wasp*; (1 *Cascadura* (SWE *Karlskrona* 40m) non-operational)

Air Wing 50
EQUIPMENT BY TYPE
AIRCRAFT
TPT • Light 2 SA-227 *Metro* III (C-26)
HELICOPTERS
MRH 2 AW139
TPT • Light 1 S-76

Uruguay URY

Uruguayan Peso pU		2018	2019	2020
GDP	pU	1.83tr	2.00tr	
	US$	59.7bn	59.9bn	
per capita	US$	17,014	17,029	
Growth	%	1.6	0.4	
Inflation	%	7.6	7.6	
Def bdgt	pU	14.8bn	14.8bn	
	US$	481m	442m	
US$1=pU		30.70	33.38	

Real-terms defence budget trend (US$m, constant 2015)

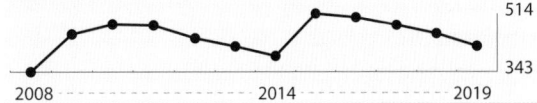

Population 3,378,471

Age	0–14	15–19	20–24	25–29	30–64	65 plus
Male	10.0%	3.8%	4.0%	3.8%	20.9%	5.8%
Female	9.7%	3.7%	3.9%	3.7%	21.9%	8.7%

Capabilities

Principal tasks for the armed forces are assuring sovereignty and territorial integrity, restated in the 2018 draft military law. This also reinforced civilian control over the military. In 2019, parliament approved the new Military Law, which aims, among other measures, to reduce the number of senior officers and address promotion issues across all services. Uruguay and Argentina have a joint peacekeeping unit and take part in joint exercises. In 2018 a defence cooperation agreement was signed with Russia, including training exchanges. The armed forces participate regularly in multinational exercises and deployments, notably on UN missions. The air force is focused on the counter-insurgency role, but ambitions to purchase a light fighter aircraft remain hampered by funding problems. The acquisition of air-defence radars may have improved the military's ability to monitor domestic airspace, but the lack of interdiction capability will continue to limit the capacity to respond to contingencies. Much of the equipment inventory is second-hand, and there is little capacity for independent power projection. Maintenance work is sometimes outsourced to foreign companies, such as Chile's ENAER.

ACTIVE 21,100 (Army 13,500 Navy 5,000 Air 2,600)
Paramilitary 1,400

ORGANISATIONS BY SERVICE

Army 13,500
Uruguayan units are substandard size, mostly around 30%. Div are at most bde size, while bn are of reinforced coy strength. Regts are also coy size, some bn size, with the largest formation being the 2nd armd cav regt
FORCES BY ROLE
COMMAND
4 mil region/div HQ
MANOEUVRE
Mechanised
2 (1st & 2nd Cav) mech bde (1 armd cav regt, 2 mech cav regt)

1 (3rd Cav) mech bde (2 mech cav regt, 1 mech inf bn)
3 (2nd, 3rd & 4th Inf) mech bde (2 mech inf bn; 1 inf bn)
1 (5th Inf) mech bde (1 armd cav regt; 1 armd inf bn; 1 mech inf bn)

Light
1 (1st Inf) inf bde (2 inf bn)

Air Manoeuvre
1 para bn

COMBAT SUPPORT
1 (strategic reserve) arty regt
5 fd arty gp
1 (1st) engr bde (2 engr bn)
4 cbt engr bn

AIR DEFENCE
1 AD gp

EQUIPMENT BY TYPE
ARMOURED FIGHTING VEHICLES
  MBT 15 *Tiran-5*
  LT TK 47: 22 M41A1UR; 25 M41C
  RECCE 15 EE-9 *Cascavel*
  IFV 18 BMP-1
  APC 376
    APC (T) 27: 24 M113A1UR; 3 MT-LB
    APC (W) 349: 54 *Condor*; 48 GAZ-39371 *Vodnik*; 53 OT-64; 47 OT-93; 147 *Piranha*
ENGINEERING & MAINTENANCE VEHICLES
  AEV MT-LB
ANTI-TANK/ANTI-INFRASTRUCTURE
  MSL • MANPATS *Milan*
  RCL 69: **106mm** 69 M40A1
ARTILLERY 185
  SP **122mm** 6 2S1 *Gvozdika*
  TOWED 44: **105mm** 36: 28 M101A1; 8 M102; **155mm** 8 M114A1
  MOR 135: **81mm** 91: 35 M1, 56 Expal Model LN; **120mm** 44 Model SL
UNMANNED AERIAL VEHICLES • ISR • Light 1 *Charrua*
AIR DEFENCE • GUNS • TOWED 14: **20mm** 14: 6 M167 *Vulcan*; 8 TCM-20 (w/Elta M-2106 radar)

Navy 5,000

HQ at Montevideo

EQUIPMENT BY TYPE
PRINCIPAL SURFACE COMBATANTS • FRIGATES 2
  FF 2 *Uruguay* (PRT *Joao Belo*) with 2 triple SVTT Mk 32 324mm ASTT with Mk 46 LWT, 2 100mm gun
PATROL AND COASTAL COMBATANTS 15
  PB 15: 2 *Colonia* (ex-US *Cape*); 1 *Paysandu*; 9 Type-44; 3 PS
MINE WARFARE • MINE COUNTERMEASURES 3
  MSO 3 *Temerario* (*Kondor* II)
AMPHIBIOUS 3: 2 LCVP; 1 LCM
LOGISTICS AND SUPPORT 8
  ABU 1
  AG 2: 1 *Artigas* (GER *Freiburg*, general spt ship with replenishment capabilities); 1 *Maldonado* (also used as patrol craft)
  AGS 2: 1 *Helgoland*; 1 *Trieste*
  ARS 1 *Vanguardia*
  AXS 2: 1 *Capitan Miranda*; 1 *Bonanza*

Naval Aviation 210
FORCES BY ROLE
MARITIME PATROL
  1 flt with Beech 200T*; Cessna O-2A *Skymaster*
SEARCH & RESCUE/TRANSPORT HELICOPTER
  1 sqn with AS350B2 *Ecureuil* (*Esquilo*); Bell 412SP *Twin Huey*
TRANSPORT/TRAINING
  1 flt with T-34C *Turbo Mentor*
EQUIPMENT BY TYPE
AIRCRAFT 2 combat capable
  ISR 4: 2 Beech 200T*; 2 Cessna O-2A *Skymaster*
  TRG 2 T-34C *Turbo Mentor*
HELICOPTERS
  MRH 2 Bell 412SP *Twin Huey*
  TPT • **Light** 1 AS350B2 *Ecureuil* (*Esquilo*)

Naval Infantry 700
FORCES BY ROLE
MANOEUVRE
  Amphibious
  1 mne bn(-)

Air Force 2,600
FORCES BY ROLE
FIGHTER/GROUND ATTACK
  1 sqn with A-37B *Dragonfly*
ISR
  1 flt with EMB-110 *Bandeirante*
TRANSPORT
  1 sqn with C-130B *Hercules*; C-212 *Aviocar*; EMB–110C *Bandeirante*; EMB-120 *Brasilia*
  1 (liaison) sqn with Cessna 206H; T-41D
  1 (liaison) flt with Cessna 206H
TRAINING
  1 sqn with PC-7U *Turbo Trainer*
  1 sqn with Beech 58 *Baron* (UB-58); SF-260EU
TRANSPORT HELICOPTER
  1 sqn with AS365 *Dauphin*; Bell 205 (UH–1H *Iroquois*); Bell 212
EQUIPMENT BY TYPE
AIRCRAFT 13 combat capable
  ATK 12 A-37B *Dragonfly*
  ISR 1 EMB-110 *Bandeirante**
  TPT 23: **Medium** 2 C-130B *Hercules*; **Light** 21: 1 BAe-125-700A; 2 Beech 58 *Baron* (UB-58); 6 C-212 *Aviocar*; 9 Cessna 206H; 1 Cessna 210; 2 EMB-110C *Bandeirante*; 1 EMB-120 *Brasilia*; **PAX** 1 C-29 *Hawker*
  TRG 17: 5 PC-7U *Turbo Trainer*; 12 SF-260EU
HELICOPTERS
  MRH 2 AS365N2 *Dauphin* II
  TPT • **Light** 9: 5 Bell 205 (UH–1H *Iroquois*); 4 Bell 212

Paramilitary 1,400

Guardia Nacional Republicana 1,400

DEPLOYMENT

CENTRAL AFRICAN REPUBLIC: UN • MINUSCA 3
DEMOCRATIC REPUBLIC OF THE CONGO: UN • MONUSCO 941; 1 inf bn; 1 log coy; 1 hel sqn
EGYPT: MFO 41; 1 engr/tpt unit
INDIA/PAKISTAN: UN • UNMOGIP 3
LEBANON: UN • UNIFIL 1

Venezuela VEN

Venezuelan Bolivar Fuerte Bs		2018	2019	2020
GDP	Bs	2.04tr	n.k	
	US$	98.4bn	70.1bn	
per capita	US$	3,411	2,548	
Growth	%	-18.0	-35.0	
Inflation	%	65,374.1	200,000.0	
Def bdgt	Bs	n.k	n.k	
	US$ [a]	n.k	n.k	
US$1=Bs		20.71	n.k	

[a] US dollar figures should be treated with caution due to high levels of currency volatility as well as wide differentials between official and parallel exchange rates

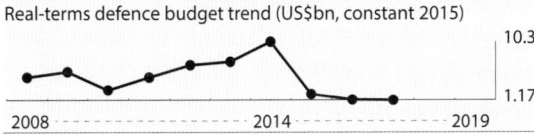

Real-terms defence budget trend (US$bn, constant 2015)

Population 32,068,672

Age	0–14	15–19	20–24	25–29	30–64	65 plus
Male	13.7%	4.3%	4.2%	4.1%	20.1%	3.5%
Female	13.0%	4.1%	4.1%	4.1%	20.6%	4.2%

Capabilities

The armed forces and national guard are tasked with protecting sovereignty, assuring territorial integrity and assisting with internal-security and counter narcotics operations. They have sufficient capabilities and funding to fulfil internal-security tasks and fulfil their regime-protection role, but the economic crisis will impact future equipment availability and training levels. Incidents such as the apparent attempted assassination of President Maduro in 2018 and the attack on the supreme court by a police helicopter pilot in 2017 point to some internal stresses in the armed forces. Venezuela is almost completely isolated regionally, with frictions relating to the humanitarian crisis leading to troop deployments near the Colombia–Venezuela border. There are close ties with China and Russia. Caracas relies on both countries for procurements and technical support. The armed forces train regularly, with a recent increase in large-scale, civil–military cooperation. Venezuela has also taken part in joint combined exercises with China, Cuba and Russia. There is little logistics capability that would support deployment abroad. Equipment is relatively modern and mainly of Chinese and Russian manufacture, with advanced Su-30MKV combat aircraft and S-300VM air-defence systems in the inventory. However, the economic crisis has seriously affected the government's ability to sustain its military expenditure; maintenance and further procurement may suffer as a consequence. Venezuela's defence industry is based on a series of small, state-owned companies, mainly focused on the production of small arms, ammunition and explosives. Venezuela has no capability to design modern defence equipment, and local platform production is limited to small coastal-patrol boats.

ACTIVE 123,000 (Army 63,000 Navy 25,500 Air 11,500 National Guard 23,000) **Paramilitary 220,000**

Conscript liability 30 months selective, varies by region for all services

RESERVE 8,000 (Army 8,000)

ORGANISATIONS BY SERVICE

Space
EQUIPMENT BY TYPE
SATELLITES • COMMUNICATIONS 1 *Venesat-1*

Army ε63,000
FORCES BY ROLE
MANOEUVRE
  Armoured
  1 (4th) armd div (1 armd bde, 1 lt armd bde, 1 AB bde, 1 arty bde)
  Mechanised
  1 (9th) mot cav div (1 mot cav bde, 1 ranger bde, 1 sy bde)
  Light
  1 (1st) inf div (1 SF bn, 1 armd bde, 1 mech inf bde, 1 ranger bde, 1 inf bde, 1 arty unit, 1 spt unit)
  1 (2nd) inf div (1 mech inf bde, 1 inf bde, 1 mtn inf bde)
  1 (3rd) inf div (1 inf bde, 1 ranger bde, 1 sigs bde, 1 MP bde)
  1 (5th) inf div (1 SF bn, 1 cav sqn, 2 jungle inf bde, 1 engr bn)
COMBAT SUPPORT
  1 cbt engr corps (3 engr regt)
COMBAT SERVICE SUPPORT
  1 log comd (2 log regt)
AVIATION
  1 avn comd (1 tpt avn bn, 1 atk hel bn, 1 ISR avn bn)

Reserve Organisations 8,000
FORCES BY ROLE
MANOEUVRE
  Armoured
  1 armd bn
  Light
  4 inf bn
  1 ranger bn
COMBAT SUPPORT
  1 arty bn
  2 engr regt
EQUIPMENT BY TYPE
ARMOURED FIGHTING VEHICLES
  MBT 173: 81 AMX-30V; 92 T-72B1
  LT TK 109: 31 AMX-13; 78 *Scorpion*-90
  RECCE 121: 42 *Dragoon* 300 LFV2; 79 V-100/V-150
  IFV 237: 123 BMP-3 (incl variants); 114 BTR-80A (incl variants)

APC 81
  APC (T) 45: 25 AMX-VCI; 12 AMX-PC (CP); 8 AMX-VCTB (Amb)
  APC (W) 36 Dragoon 300
ENGINEERING & MAINTENANCE VEHICLES
  ARV 5: 3 AMX-30D; BREM-1; 2 Dragoon 300RV; Samson
  VLB Leguan
NBC VEHICLES 10 TPz-1 Fuchs NBC
ANTI-TANK/ANTI-INFRASTRUCTURE
  MSL • MANPATS IMI MAPATS
  RCL 106mm 175 M40A1
  GUNS • SP 76mm 75 M18 Hellcat
ARTILLERY 515+
  SP 60: 152mm 48 2S19 Msta-S (replacing Mk F3s); 155mm 12 Mk F3
  TOWED 92: 105mm 80: 40 M101A1; 40 Model 56 pack howitzer; 155mm 12 M114A1
  MRL 56: 122mm 24 BM-21 Grad; 160mm 20 LAR SP (LAR-160); 300mm 12 9A52 Smerch
  GUN/MOR 120mm 13 2S23 NONA-SVK
  MOR 294+: 81mm 165; SP 81mm 21 Dragoon 300PM; AMX-VTT; 120mm 108: 60 Brandt; 48 2S12
AIRCRAFT
  TPT • Light 28: 1 Beech 90 King Air; 1 Beech 200 King Air; 1 Beech 300 King Air; 1 Cessna 172; 6 Cessna 182 Skylane; 2 Cessna 206; 2 Cessna 207 Stationair; 1 IAI-201 Arava; 2 IAI-202 Arava; 11 M-28 Skytruck
HELICOPTERS
  ATK 9 Mi-35M2 Hind
  MRH 32: 10 Bell 412EP; 2 Bell 412SP; 20 Mi-17V-5 Hip H TPT 9: Heavy 3 Mi-26T2 Halo; Medium 2 AS-61D; Light 4: 3 Bell 206B Jet Ranger, 1 Bell 206L3 Long Ranger II

Navy ε22,300; ε3,200 conscript (total ε25,500)

EQUIPMENT BY TYPE
SUBMARINES • TACTICAL • SSK 2:
  2 Sabalo (GER T-209/1300) with 8 single 533mm TT with SST-4 HWT
PRINCIPAL SURFACE COMBATANTS • FRIGATES 6
  FFGHM 6 Mariscal Sucre (ITA mod Lupo) with 8 single lnchr with Otomat Mk2 AShM, 1 octuple Albatros lnchr with Aspide SAM, 2 triple 324mm ASTT with A244 LWT, 1 127mm gun (capacity 1 Bell 212 (AB-212) hel)
PATROL AND COASTAL COMBATANTS 10
  PSOH 3 Guaiqueri with 1 Millennium CIWS, 1 76mm gun (1 damaged in explosion in 2016)
  PBG 3 Federación (UK Vosper 37m) with 2 single lnchr with Otomat Mk2 AShM
  PB 4: 3 Constitucion (UK Vosper 37m) with 1 76mm gun; 1 Fernando Gomez de Saa (Damen 4207)
AMPHIBIOUS
  LANDING SHIPS • LST 4 Capana (capacity 12 tanks; 200 troops) (FSU Alligator)
  LANDING CRAFT 3:
    LCU 2 Margarita (river comd)
    UCAC 1 Griffon 2000TD
LOGISTICS AND SUPPORT 10
  AGOR 1 Punta Brava
  AGS 2
  AKL 4 Los Frailes
  AORH 1 Ciudad Bolivar
  ATF 1
  AXS 1 Simon Bolivar

Naval Aviation 500

FORCES BY ROLE
ANTI-SUBMARINE WARFARE
  1 sqn with Bell 212 (AB-212)
MARITIME PATROL
  1 flt with C-212-200 MPA
TRANSPORT
  1 sqn with Beech 200 King Air; C-212 Aviocar; Turbo Commander 980C
TRAINING
  1 hel sqn with Bell 206B Jet Ranger II; TH-57A Sea Ranger
TRANSPORT HELICOPTER
  1 sqn with Bell 412EP Twin Huey; Mi-17V-5 Hip H
EQUIPMENT BY TYPE
AIRCRAFT 2 combat capable
  MP 2 C-212-200 MPA*
  TPT • Light 7: 1 Beech C90 King Air; 1 Beech 200 King Air; 4 C-212 Aviocar; 1 Turbo Commander 980C
HELICOPTERS
  ASW 4 Bell 212 ASW (AB-212 ASW)
  MRH 12: 6 Bell 412EP Twin Huey; 6 Mi-17V-5 Hip
  TPT • Light 1 Bell 206B Jet Ranger II (trg)
  TRG 1 TH-57A Sea Ranger

Marines ε15,000

FORCES BY ROLE
COMMAND
  1 div HQ
SPECIAL FORCES
  1 spec ops bde
MANOEUVRE
  Amphibious
  1 amph aslt bde
  3 mne bde
  3 (rvn) mne bde
COMBAT SUPPORT
  1 cbt engr bn
  1 MP bde
  1 sigs bn
COMBAT SERVICE SUPPORT
  1 log bn
EQUIPMENT BY TYPE
ARMOURED FIGHTING VEHICLES
  LT TK 10 VN-16
  IFV 21: 11 VN-1; 10 VN-18
  APC • APC (W) 37 EE-11 Urutu
  AAV 11 LVTP-7
ENGINEERING & MAINTENANCE VEHICLES
  ARV 1 VN-16 ARV
  AEV 1 AAVR7
ANTI-TANK/ANTI-INFRASTRUCTURE
  RCL 84mm Carl Gustav; 106mm M40A1
ARTILLERY 30
  TOWED 105mm 18 M-56
  MOR 120mm 12 Brandt

PATROL AND COASTAL COMBATANTS • PBR 23:
18 *Constancia*; 2 *Manaure*; 3 *Terepaima* (*Cougar*)
AMPHIBIOUS • LANDING CRAFT • 1 LCM; 1 LCU;
12 LCVP

Coast Guard 1,000
EQUIPMENT BY TYPE
PATROL AND COASTAL COMBATANTS 22
  PSO 3 *Guaicamacuto* with 1 *Millennium* CIWS, 1 76mm gun (capacity 1 Bell 212 (AB-212) hel) (1 additional vessel in build)
  PB 19: 12 *Gavion*; 1 *Pagalo* (Damen Stan 2606); 4 *Petrel* (US *Point*); 2 *Protector*
LOGISTICS AND SUPPORT 5
  AG 2 *Los Tanques* (salvage ship)
  AKSL 1
  AP 2

Air Force 11,500
FORCES BY ROLE
FIGHTER/GROUND ATTACK
  1 sqn with F-5 *Freedom Fighter* (VF-5)
  2 sqn with F-16A/B *Fighting Falcon*
  4 sqn with Su-30MKV
  2 sqn with K-8W *Karakorum**
GROUND ATTACK/ISR
  1 sqn with EMB-312 *Tucano**
ELECTRONIC WARFARE
  1 sqn with *Falcon* 20DC; SA-227 *Metro* III (C-26B)
TRANSPORT
  1 sqn with Y-8; C-130H *Hercules*; KC-137
  1 sqn with A319CJ; B-737
  4 sqn with Cessna T206H; Cessna 750
  1 sqn with Cessna 500/550/551; *Falcon* 20F; *Falcon* 900
  1 sqn with G-222; Short 360 *Sherpa*
TRAINING
  1 sqn with Cessna 182N; SF-260E
  2 sqn with DA40NG; DA42VI
  1 sqn with EMB-312 *Tucano**
TRANSPORT HELICOPTER
  1 VIP sqn with AS532UL *Cougar*; Mi-172
  3 sqn with AS332B *Super Puma*, AS532 *Cougar*
  2 sqn with Mi-17 *Hip* H
EQUIPMENT BY TYPE
AIRCRAFT 82 combat capable
  FTR 18: 15 F-16A *Fighting Falcon*†; 3 F-16B *Fighting Falcon*†
  FGA 22 Su-30MKV
  EW 4: 2 *Falcon* 20DC; 2 SA-227 *Metro* III (C-26B)
  TKR 1 KC-137
  TPT 75: **Medium** 14: 5 C-130H *Hercules* (some in store); 1 G-222; 8 Y-8; **Light** 56: 6 Beech 200 *King Air*; 2 Beech 350 *King Air*; 10 Cessna 182N *Skylane*; 12 Cessna 206 *Stationair*; 4 Cessna 208B *Caravan*; 1 Cessna 500 *Citation* I; 3 Cessna 550 *Citation* II; 1 Cessna 551; 1 Cessna 750 *Citation* X; 2 Do-228-212; 1 Do-228-212NG; 11 Quad City *Challenger* II; 2 Short 360 *Sherpa*; **PAX** 5: 1 A319CJ; 1 B-737; 1 *Falcon* 20F; 2 *Falcon* 900
  TRG 84: 24 DA40NG; 6 DA42VI; 18 EMB-312 *Tucano**; 24 K-8W *Karakorum**; 12 SF-260E

HELICOPTERS
  MRH 8 Mi-17 (Mi-17VS) *Hip* H
  TPT 22: **Medium** 14: 3 AS332B *Super Puma*; 7 AS532 *Cougar*; 2 AS532UL *Cougar*; 2 Mi-172 (VIP); **Light** 8+ Enstrom 480B
AIR-LAUNCHED MISSILES
  AAM • IR AIM-9L/P *Sidewinder*; R-73 (AA-11A *Archer*); PL-5E; R-27T/ET (AA-10B/D *Alamo*); IIR *Python* 4; SARH R-27R/ER (AA-10A/C *Alamo*); ARH R-77 (AA-12 *Adder*)
  ASM Kh-29L/T (AS-14A/B *Kedge*); Kh-59M (AS-18 *Kazoo*)
  AShM Kh-31A (AS-17B *Krypton*); AM39 *Exocet*
  ARM Kh-31P (AS-17A *Krypton*)

Air Defence Command (CODAI)
Joint service command with personnel drawn from other services
FORCES BY ROLE
AIR DEFENCE
  5 AD bde
COMBAT SERVICE SUPPORT
  1 log bde (5 log gp)
EQUIPMENT BY TYPE
AIR DEFENCE
  SAM
    Long-range S-300VM
    Medium-range 9K317M2 *Buk*-M2E (SA-17 *Grizzly*); S-125 *Pechora*-2M (SA-26)
    Point-defence 9K338 *Igla*-S (SA-24 *Grinch*); ADAMS; *Mistral*; RBS-70
  GUNS 440+
    SP 40mm 12+: 6+ AMX-13 *Rafaga*; 6 M42
    TOWED 428+: **20mm**: 114 TCM-20; **23mm** ε200 ZU-23-2; **35mm**; **40mm** 114+: 114+ L/70; Some M1

National Guard (Fuerzas Armadas de Cooperacion) 23,000
(Internal sy, customs) 9 regional comd
EQUIPMENT BY TYPE
ARMOURED FIGHTING VEHICLES
  APC • APC (W) 44: 24 Fiat 6614; 20 UR-416
ARTILLERY • MOR 50 81mm
PATROL AND COASTAL COMBATANTS • PB 34: 12 *Protector*; 12 *Punta*; 10 *Rio Orinoco* II
AIRCRAFT
  TPT • **Light** 34: 1 Beech 55 *Baron*; 1 Beech 80 *Queen Air*; 1 Beech 90 *King Air*; 1 Beech 200C *King Air*; 3 Cessna 152 *Aerobat*; 2 Cessna 172; 2 Cessna 402C; 4 Cessna U206 *Stationair*; 6 DA42 MPP; 1 IAI-201 *Arava*; 12 M-28 *Skytruck*
  TRG 3: 1 PZL 106 *Kruk*; 2 PLZ M2-6 *Isquierka*
HELICOPTERS
  MRH 13: 8 Bell 412EP; 5 Mi-17V-5 *Hip* H
  TPT • **Light** 19: 9 AS355F *Ecureuil* II; 4 AW109; 5 Bell 206B/L *Jet Ranger/Long Ranger*; 1 Bell 212 (AB 212);
  TRG 5 F-280C

Paramilitary ε220,000

Bolivarian National Militia ε220,000

Arms procurements and deliveries – Latin America and the Caribbean

Significant events in 2019

JULY — COTECMAR

Colombia's state-owned shipbuilder COTECMAR set out five strategic projects it plans to complete by 2022. The first will see shipyard capacity expand so that it can accept vessels of up to 18,000 tonnes. COTECMAR's two yards near Cartagena can currently handle vessels up to 1,200 and 3,600 tonnes. Secondly, an oceanographic and hydrographic survey vessel will be built for the Colombian Navy by the end of 2021. Thirdly, COTECMAR will complete the design of the OPV-93C, a modification of the three patrol ships it built under licence, between 2008 and 2017, to a Fassmer OPV-80 design. Fourthly, it will develop a design, with another as yet unnamed firm, for the Strategic Surface Platform project to replace the navy's four *Almirante Padilla*-class frigates. Finally, COTECMAR will look to complete the preliminary design for the navy's Multipurpose Vessel (MPP) programme. The MPP will replace the ARC *Buenaventura* that was bought second-hand from Germany in the late 1990s.

SEPTEMBER — PROSUB

The Brazilian Navy began sea trials of its first *Scorpène*-class submarine, *Riachuelo* (S-40). This is the first of four diesel-powered boats being built as part of the Submarine Development Programme (PROSUB), which also aims to build a nuclear-powered submarine. PROSUB began in 2008 when contracts were signed with the French government and shipbuilder DCNS. However, the project has since suffered from funding problems and also corruption allegations. *Riachuelo* is expected to enter service in 2020, five years behind schedule.

SEPTEMBER — KC-390

Brazil took delivery of the first of 28 KC-390 transport aircraft ordered in 2014 from Embraer. A month earlier, the firm secured its first export customer, when Portugal signed a contract for five aircraft worth €827 million (US$948.48m). Several Portuguese companies are involved in the KC-390 supply chain. Development of the aircraft began in the late 2000s and Embraer has partnered with Boeing to market the aircraft globally.

NOVEMBER — CHILEAN F-16S

Chile's defence minister confirmed that the country intends to upgrade and extend the service life of its F-16 fighter aircraft out to beyond 2040. There is also a plan to standardise maintenance and training across the fleet. Chile currently operates ten Block 50 aircraft and 36 ex-Netherlands F-16s at Block 20 mid-life-upgrade standard; these were all acquired between 2006 and 2011. Israeli firms Elbit Systems, IAI and Rafael have all presented solutions for the programme in recent years; they may compete for the work with F-16 manufacturer Lockheed Martin.

Figure 25 Embraer: EMB-314 (A-29) *Super Tucano* light-attack/training aircraft

In 1992, Embraer teamed up with Northrop to offer an improved version of its EMB-312 *Tucano* for the US Air Force's (USAF's) Joint Primary Aircraft Training System (JPATS) competition to replace the T-37B trainer. At the same time, several Brazilian Air Force (FAB) junior officers began designing a variant of the *Tucano* optimised for ground-attack and air-interdiction missions. Embraer lost out to Beechcraft's T-6A *Texan* II in the JPATS competition. However, in 1995 the development work by then completed – combined with the requirements generated by the junior FAB officers – saw Embraer awarded a contract to develop a light aircraft capable of patrolling airspace over the Amazon, as well as fulfilling a training role. In 2001, Brazil signed a production contract for 76, with an option for a further 23, and deliveries began in 2003. Since entering service with the FAB that year, the *Super Tucano* has been ordered by 15 other countries, mostly in Latin America and Africa. With an average unit cost of US$10–20 million, depending on configuration and weapons package, the *Super Tucano* is affordable for many countries that cannot meet the expense of fourth-generation fighter aircraft or even small Western jet-fighter or training aircraft. The requirements addressed by the EMB-314 tend to be focused on aerial surveillance and ground-attack missions, which the smaller turbo-prop can perform at a relatively low cost per flight hour. Embraer's success with this product has in part contributed to several other companies developing similar systems. Although Embraer lost out in the JPATS competition, the *Super Tucano* was selected for the Light Air Support programme, intended to provide the Afghan Air Force with a light-attack capability. With production for those orders transferred to Embraer's US partner, the Sierra Nevada Corporation, the *Super Tucano* is also one of two shortlisted aircraft for the USAF's OA-X Light Attack Aircraft programme. However, with the origins of the OA-X requirement dating back to 2009, it is unclear whether the USAF wants to commit to buying an aircraft of this type, despite support in the US Congress for the idea.

© IISS

Table 22 *Super Tucano* production contracts

Order date	Country	Quantity	Value	Production line	Deliveries
Aug 2001	Brazil	99	est. US$800m	Embraer	2003–12
Dec 2005	Colombia	25	US$235m	Embraer	2005–07
Aug 2008	Chile	12	US$120m	Embraer	2009–10
May 2008	Ecuador	18 (originally 24)	US$270m	Embraer	2010–11
Dec 2008	Dominican Republic	8	US$92m	Embraer	2009–10
Mar 2011	Burkina Faso	3	n.k.	Embraer	2012
Jun 2011	Indonesia	8	n.k.	Embraer	2012
Mar 2012	Angola	6	US$94m	Embraer	2012–13
Jul 2012	Indonesia	8	n.k.	Embraer	2014
2012	Mauritania	2	n.k.	Embraer	2012
Feb 2013	Afghanistan	20	US$427.5m (paid by US)	Sierra Nevada Corp.	2016–18
Apr 2013	Senegal	3	n.k.	Embraer	n.k.
Jun 2015	Ghana	5	US$88m	Embraer	n.k.
Jun 2015	Mali	6	n.k.	Embraer	2018–ongoing
Oct 2015	Lebanon	6	US$172.5m (paid by US)	Sierra Nevada Corp.	2017–18
Oct 2017	Chile	6	n.k.	Embraer	2018–ongoing
Oct 2017	Afghanistan	6	n.k. (paid by US)	Sierra Nevada Corp.	2019–20*
Nov 2017	Philippines	6	US$98.5m	Embraer	2020*
Nov 2018	Nigeria	12	US$329.08m	Sierra Nevada Corp.	n.k.

* Planned

Chapter Nine
Sub-Saharan Africa

- With few exceptions, a combination of ageing inventories and a lack coherent and consistent procurement investment is limiting the region's ability to generate efficient combat capabilities.

- The African Union continues to work towards harmonising its African Standby Force concept with the range of ad hoc groupings that have developed, such as the G-5 Sahel and the Multi-National Joint Task Force combating Boko Haram.

- Despite increasing international commitment, and amid persistent military operations, the security situation in West Africa and the Sahel region continues to deteriorate.

- Russia has renewed and deepened its defence partnerships in the region. Russian contractors are reported operating in different sub-Saharan African countries and Moscow has signed a range of defence and security cooperation agreements in recent years.

Sub-Saharan Africa defence spending, 2019 – top 5

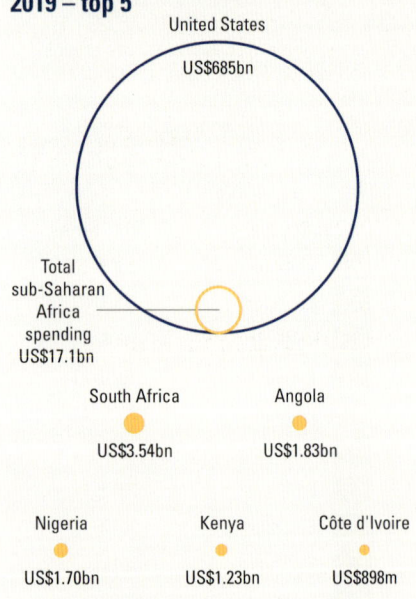

United States US$685bn
Total sub-Saharan Africa spending US$17.1bn
South Africa US$3.54bn
Angola US$1.83bn
Nigeria US$1.70bn
Kenya US$1.23bn
Côte d'Ivoire US$898m

Active military personnel – top 10
(10,000 per unit)

Eritrea 202,000
South Sudan 185,000
Nigeria 143,000
Ethiopia 138,000
Democratic Republic of the Congo 134,250
Angola 107,000
Sudan 104,300
South Africa 75,000
Uganda 45,000
Rwanda 33,000

Global total 19,852,000
Regional total 1,594,000

Patrol and coastal combatants
(10 per unit)

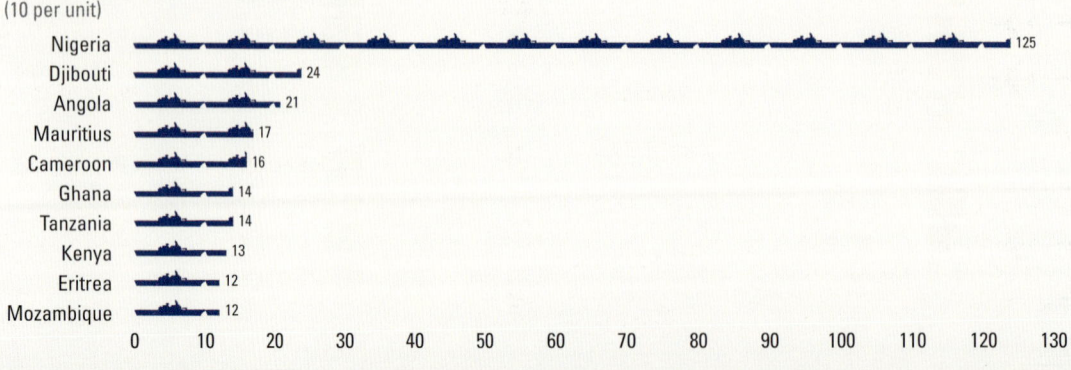

Nigeria 125
Djibouti 24
Angola 21
Mauritius 17
Cameroon 16
Ghana 14
Tanzania 14
Kenya 13
Eritrea 12
Mozambique 12

Regional defence policy and economics 446 ▶
Armed forces data section 460 ▶
Arms procurements and deliveries 513 ▶

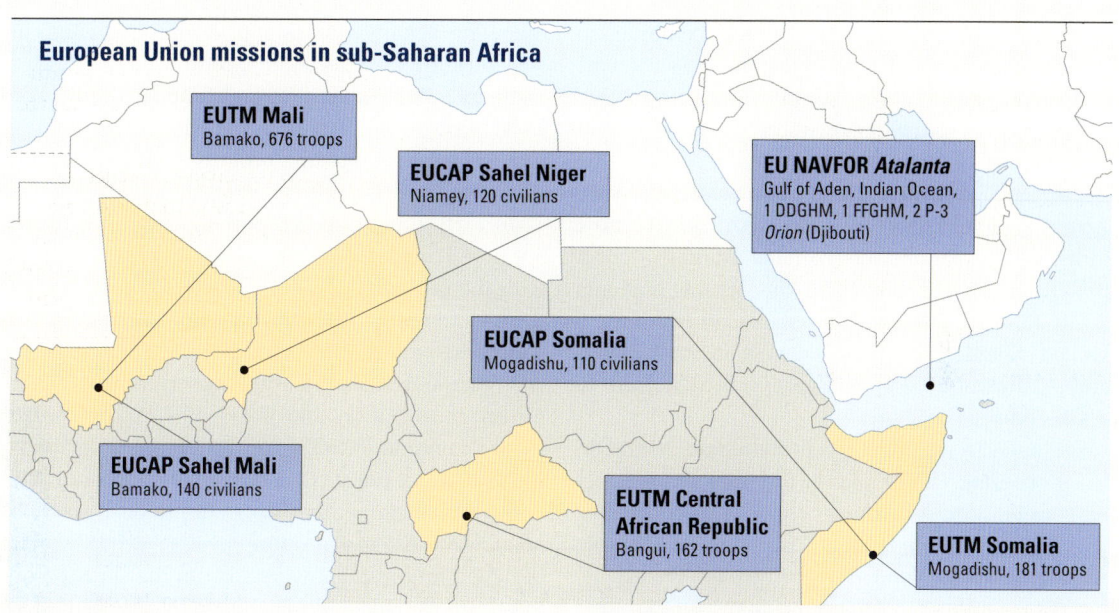

European Union missions in sub-Saharan Africa

EUTM Mali — Bamako, 676 troops
EUCAP Sahel Niger — Niamey, 120 civilians
EU NAVFOR *Atalanta* — Gulf of Aden, Indian Ocean, 1 DDGHM, 1 FFGHM, 2 P-3 *Orion* (Djibouti)
EUCAP Somalia — Mogadishu, 110 civilians
EUCAP Sahel Mali — Bamako, 140 civilians
EUTM Central African Republic — Bangui, 162 troops
EUTM Somalia — Mogadishu, 181 troops

Crewed ELINT and ISR aircraft
(1 per unit)

Angola	1
Niger	6
Botswana	5
Namibia	5
Cameroon	2
Chad	2
Mozambique	2
Sudan	2
Zimbabwe	2
Burkina Faso	1
Mali	3
Nigeria	3
Tanzania	1

Protected patrol vehicles
(100 per unit)

South Africa	810
Kenya	130
Nigeria	112
Uganda	92
Senegal	89
Mali	64
Burkina Faso	61
Congo, Republic of	55
Ghana	50
Namibia	48

Sub-Saharan Africa

Complex security crises in Africa continue to dominate the attention of both regional governments and international actors. Conflict and instability persist from the Sahel region and some West African states across to Somalia in the east. In Somalia, the deployment of African Union (AU) personnel to the African Union Mission to Somalia (AMISOM) is now in its twelfth year and international training support to bolster the capabilities of the Somali National Army (SNA) continues. For instance, in late 2019, a United Kingdom-supported course in intelligence, surveillance and reconnaissance was delivered to AMISOM and the SNA.

In line with the Somali Transition Plan, AMISOM is proceeding with plans to transfer security responsibility to local forces by 2021. Nonetheless, and despite military action targeting al-Shabaab, including by the United States armed forces, the group continues to mount regular attacks and demonstrate its operational capability. Media reports indicate that al-Shabaab may have changed its modus operandi (for example, now moving in the open in smaller groups) in order to minimise risk.

Coup attempts were thwarted in Gabon and in Ethiopia (targeting a regional government) in 2019, though the Ethiopian Army's chief of staff was killed. Conflict once again flared in the eastern Democratic Republic of the Congo (DRC) late in the year, particularly in North Kivu and Ituri provinces, where its effects were complicated by another outbreak of the Ebola virus. The long-running United Nations presence in the country continued, with operations by the UN's Stabilisation Mission in the DR Congo (MONUSCO) sometimes undertaken in coordination with local troops, and others conducted by the UN's Force Intervention Brigade.

Change in Sudan, but how much?

The power-sharing deal signed in August by Sudan's Transitional Military Council (TMC) and the opposition Forces of Freedom and Change seemed to mark a key point in a tumultuous year in Sudan. The 30-year reign of military leader Omar al-Bashir had ended in early April with his ouster by the army, following demonstrations after a sharp reduction in subsidies after the economy contracted. GDP had fallen by a third since 2010, in US dollar values. The TMC, which took power in the wake of al-Bashir's removal, faced continuing protests amid intermittent dialogue.

In early June, troops reportedly from the Rapid Support Forces (RSF) – a group closely associated with the Janjaweed militia – opened fire on civilian demonstrators in Khartoum. Scores were killed. Sudan was subsequently suspended from the AU, with the AU Peace and Security Commission chairman calling for an investigation into the deaths. Accompanied by a communiqué calling on Khartoum to facilitate the transfer of power to a civilian-led authority, the suspension was perhaps an example of a sanction open to the AU in the future. It was reportedly also designed to forestall a worsening of the situation on the ground, amid concern that the TMC had cancelled talks with the opposition and that the security forces might fracture.

The Sudanese armed forces retain key political positions. The Sovereign Council (which is in power as part of the three-year transition agreement, signed in August) is chaired by army chief Lieutenant-General Abdel Fattah Abdelrahman Burhan, and the armed forces will retain this post possibly for 21 months. Meanwhile, RSF commander Mohamad Hamdan Dagolo (aka Hemeti) is a key figure on the Council; he had been the TMC's deputy leader.

There remains concern over the role of the RSF in Darfur and on the Sovereign Council, as well as its future position and role, relative to regular troops and the intelligence services, as Sudan's security and defence structures evolve. For instance, it was reported that some regular troops had moved to protect protesters during the 2019 demonstrations.

Sudan's armed forces have in recent years deployed troops in Yemen as part of the Saudi-led campaign, while Sudanese personnel were also reported in 2019 in Libya, operating with the Libyan National Army opposing the internationally recognised administration in Tripoli. In both cases, reports point to the deployment of RSF troops, as well as suggesting financial assistance for the deployment, at least relating to missions in Yemen, by Saudi Arabia and the United Arab Emirates. The RSF's origins in Darfur were highlighted in June, when the UN Security Council extended the mandate of the AU–UN Hybrid Mission in Darfur (UNAMID), which had been due to draw down its forces prior to closing the mission in mid-2020, following renewed violence in the region. According to the UN, protests there were 'violently repressed by the security forces, including Rapid Support Forces'.

Meanwhile, in South Sudan a peace agreement was signed in 2018 between President Salva Kiir and opposition leader (and former vice-president) Riek Machar. However, while ceasefires have broadly held, there has been little improvement yet for the local population in terms of hastening resettlement and economic improvement. The UN Mission in South Sudan (UNMISS) was, according to the UN secretary-general's special representative, in at least one location (Bor, greater Upper Nile) looking to rebalance the peacekeeping units there 'from a static presence ... to a more mobile posture', in order to generate an environment more conducive to the return of displaced persons in this area. However, in late 2019 the UN Commission on Human Rights in South Sudan said that 'important provisions of the accord are not being implemented, including the disengagement of rival forces in preparation for the creation of a unified military force for South Sudan'. Nevertheless, talks continued, Kiir and Machar had met and, according to the special representative, while 'the peace process remains precarious ... progress is being made'.

China and Russia

While Western states have long maintained security and defence ties with African states, Russia is in some ways revitalising its military relations on the continent. During the Cold War, Russia developed strong defence links with a number of African states and, while these ties faded after the end of the Cold War, Russian- (or Soviet-) origin defence equipment remains a common sight in Africa.

In 2017, Russia received an exemption to the Central African Republic UN arms embargo for weapons transfers and the supply of a training team. Furthermore, though the presence in the CAR of personnel from a Russian private military company has been alleged, and denied by Moscow, Russia has made no secret of the presence of Russian military instructors in the country, training troops, the gendarmerie and police. According to Moscow, these instructors trained more than 3,000 CAR troops between early 2018 and September 2019. At the same time, the post of national security adviser to the president is filled by a Russian national.

The European Union is also engaged in training the CAR armed forces, as are forces from the UN Multidimensional Integrated Stabilization Mission in the CAR (MINUSCA). In 2018, the UN Panel of Experts on the CAR said that 'with the support of MINUSCA and sometimes accompanied by Russian instructors, trained [CAR] personnel have gradually been redeployed'. However, the report also highlighted continuing challenges for local armed forces in that the CAR military 'currently has insufficient capacity or lacks logistical support for conducting operations without the substantive and constant support of MINUSCA and/or the Russian instructors'. In 2019, the UN reported that the redeployment of CAR troops was still hindered by logistical and operational issues.

Russia is stepping up its training assistance more broadly, such as the announcement (by Foreign Minister Sergei Lavrov at the UN) that the Russian interior ministry was starting a training programme for female African police officers. In 2018, it was reported that Russia had signed at least 19 military-cooperation programmes with sub-Saharan African states since 2014.

China too is engaged in expanding its defence ties in Africa. *Military Balance* analysis in the past has highlighted how Chinese defence exports to Africa have been shifting from copies of Soviet-era equipment to that of Chinese-designed equipment. This is exemplified by Chinese armoured vehicles and uninhabited aerial vehicles now in service with some African states, as well as a People's Liberation Army (PLA) base in Djibouti. Russia was organising the first Russia–Africa Summit in late 2019, while in mid-2018 China organised the first China–Africa Defence and Security Forum.

In recent years, Beijing has looked to boost its regional network of defence attachés and deepen its involvement in UN peacekeeping missions on the continent. Such missions are one way of familiarising troops with operations in austere environments, and PLA peacekeeping units have progressed from medical units to engineering and then combat contingents. Peacekeeping missions are also useful as a means of learning from operating alongside other nations' forces.

China – like Western states and Russia – is also looking to deepen its training offering to African nations, doing so as part of continent-wide economic-assistance programmes. EU support comes through vehicles such as the Africa Peace Fund and a range of economic measures such as its 'connectivity strategy', while the US Congress in 2018 passed the Better Utilization of Investments Leading to Development Act. China, meanwhile, was reported to have announced US$60 billion in loans and investments at the 2018 iteration of the Forum on China–Africa Cooperation. Beijing earlier financed the construction of the AU headquarters in Addis Ababa, Ethiopia, and in 2015, President Xi Jinping pledged at the UN to support the AU to the tune of US$100 million in military assistance, in order to help develop the African Standby Force and the African Capacity for Immediate Response to Crisis. In July 2019, China

Developments in the African Standby Force

Since its inception in 2003, the African Union's (AU's) Africa Standby Force (ASF) has not been deployed. This is despite the declaration that it was 'fully operational' following exercise *Amani Africa* II in 2016 and the inauguration of the ASF's Continental Logistics Base (CLB) in Douala, Cameroon, on 5 January 2018.

The AU Commission, the Regional Economic Communities and AU members have debated the gap between being declared operationally ready or fully operational and attaining 'full operational capability'. They have also discussed the need for continental command, control, communications and information systems, as well as logistics and sustainment sufficient to match the declared military, police and civilian components; and an agreed method of holding forces in readiness for rapid deployment.

The ASF now places regional forces on standby on a six-month roster; the East Africa Standby Force (EASF) is the first of the second set of rotations to be declared ready. There are approximately 5,000 troops, police and civilians trained and on standby in each region, including the Rapid Deployment Capability (RDC), which is on shorter notice. However, both the ability to project standby forces from home bases to an operational area and to sustain the force during a mission are not yet in place.

Although a number of AU member states on paper have impressive force-projection assets, which might be capable of moving ASF elements over continental distances – including navies in Algeria, Morocco and South Africa and air forces in Algeria, Egypt, Ethiopia, Nigeria and South Africa – these assets have not been directly assigned to the ASF. Projecting force on this scale in a reasonably quick time frame (such as for Scenario Five multi-dimensional Peace Support Operations (PSOs) and Scenario Six AU interventions in, for example, cases of genocide) is a function of both the necessary military capabilities and coordination. However, both are currently lacking.

Neither the financial resources to fund PSOs nor the logistics capabilities required to sustain them have yet been allocated directly to the ASF. The CLB facility is in place and functioning in Douala, though it is not yet fully operational. Despite completing exercise IMDAD AFRICA I in September 2018, the AU and its member states have neither fully resourced the CLB nor the five regional logistic bases in Botswana (Gaborone), Ethiopia (Addis Ababa) and Sierra Leone (Freetown), and for the North African region, either Algeria or Tunisia (the location is still to be finalised).

Nevertheless, in organisational terms, long-standing confusion over the function of the African Capacity for Immediate Response to Crises (ACIRC) and the RDC may be ending. The ACIRC was intended to plug the operational gap while the RDCs were being established in each region. ACIRC-contributing states are expected to meet in the margins of the January 2021 AU summit to decide the future of the ACIRC. Analysts consider the most likely outcome to be the dissolution of the ACIRC, though without its assets being pledged to the RDCs. In the meantime, discussions continue over the potential mandated strength of the RDCs – whether the size of an enhanced battle group of around 1,250 personnel or a small brigade of 5,000.

Meanwhile, cooperation between the AU and NATO is slowly maturing. NATO first supported the AU in 2005, when the latter requested NATO assistance in deploying the African Union Mission in Sudan to Darfur. NATO provided planners in Addis Ababa and deployment flights for AU troop-contributing countries to the operational area.

However, NATO's intervention in Libya in 2011 caused a rift between the AU and NATO, which had only partly healed by 2015, when NATO reopened a liaison office in Addis Ababa. In April 2019, in a meeting between the AU and NATO in Addis Ababa, the AU acknowledged the importance of advancing AU–NATO cooperation on issues related to 'political connectivity, capacity building and continental collaboration'. It remains to be seen how far and how successfully this cooperation will extend.

and the Economic Community of West African States (ECOWAS) signed the implementation agreement for the construction of a new ECOWAS headquarters building in Abuja.

France's *Operation Barkhane*

France launched *Operation Barkhane* in August 2014. With more than 4,500 troops deployed, it is currently France's most important external military operation. *Barkhane* was designed to overcome the limitations exposed by its predecessor, *Operation Serval*. Limited to Mali, *Serval* had proven unable to effectively address the growing regional challenge posed by Islamist insurgents and terrorists. *Barkhane*'s area of operations, in contrast, extends across those states comprising the G5 Sahel security grouping: Burkina Faso, Chad, Mali, Mauritania and Niger. The operation is intended to support the G5 in its fight against terrorist armed groups in the Sahel region. The objective is to reduce these groups' ability to control territory and populations, and in turn improve the capacity of the region's armed forces, thereby lowering the threat to a level such that it can be tackled effectively by local forces and, in turn, permit a possible French disengagement.

Barkhane utilises three main bases, at N'djamena, Gao and Niamey, but also draws on France's long-established regional logistics bases in Abidjan, Dakar and Douala. The operation is supported by a larger network of temporary forward operating bases (FOBs). However, the risk of overstretch has led Paris to consider ways of flexibly managing its basing. For instance, in order to support the main effort in the Liptako Gourma region straddling Burkina Faso, Mali and Niger, French commanders reduced their presence at a FOB in Madama, in northern Niger,

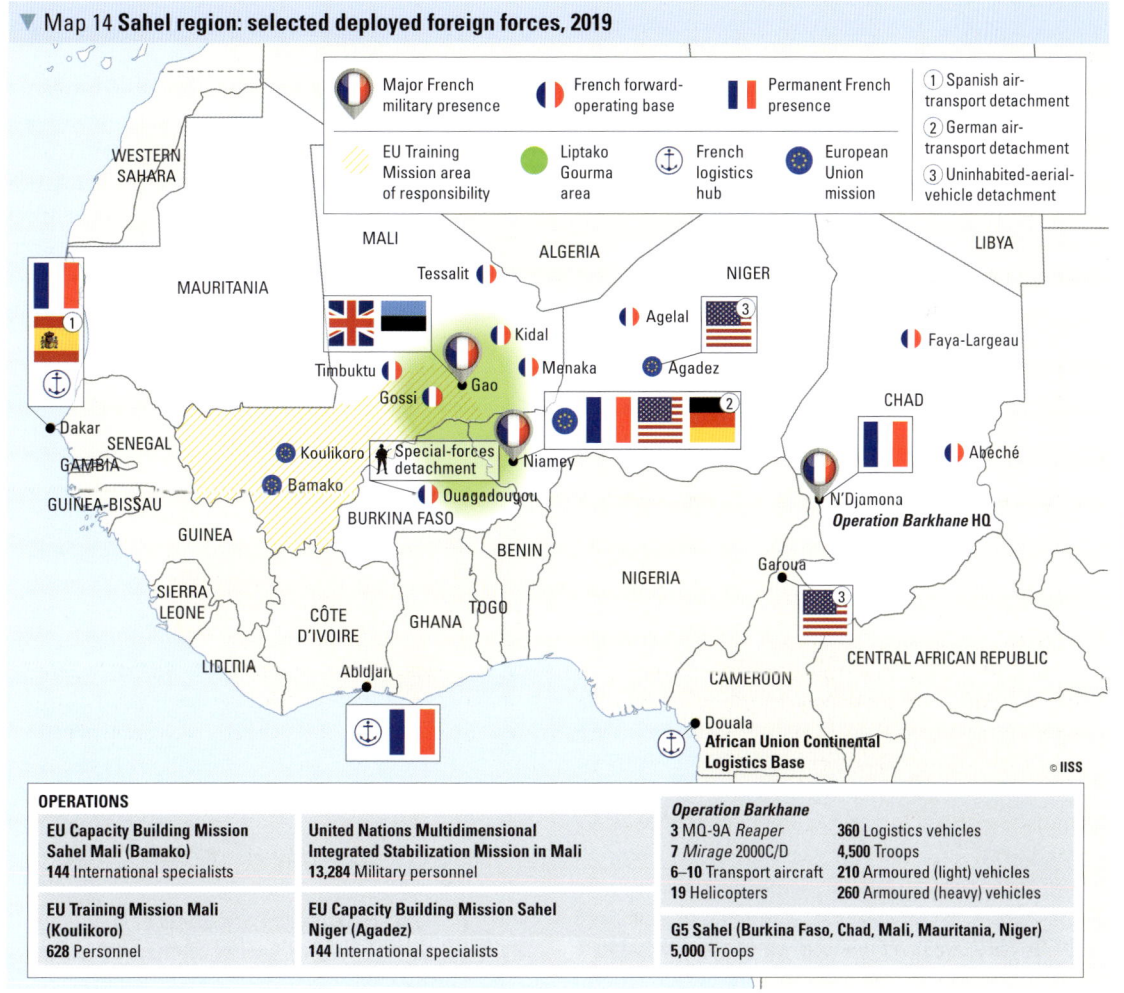

in order to reallocate the resources to a new FOB in Gossi. The Madama base was transferred to Niger's armed forces.

In addition, *Barkhane* aims to support local troops – often with air assets – by acting as a Quick Reaction Force in areas where France has less presence on the ground. At the same time, two *Groupements Tactiques Désert* (battalion-size joint tactical groups) are intended to mount long-range ground missions to deny territory to and create a more unpredictable environment for non-state armed groups. Special forces also conduct long-range patrols, using four-wheel-drive vehicles. Though this may improve mobility, better enabling rapid pursuit, there is a reduction in protection when compared to France's heavier VAB or VBCI armoured vehicles.

The risk of overextension posed by geographically dispersed operations in austere environments threatens to exacerbate existing equipment challenges. For example, according to the French Senate, during *Serval* the 1970s-era VAB wheeled armoured personnel carrier was likely to travel a distance six to seven times greater than in operations in Afghanistan and 200 times greater than in metropolitan France, thereby placing a premium on the armed forces' maintenance capabilities. Meanwhile, *Barkhane* is also being used as a way to test new equipment in harsh environments, including the VHM all-terrain vehicle (BvS10) and, possibly, the armed *Reaper* uninhabited aerial vehicle. The Estonian Army has also tested the THeMIS uninhabited ground vehicle during its *Barkhane* deployment.

Barkhane has particularly highlighted strategic and tactical airlift. France's medium airlift fleet is ageing (the C-160 *Transall* was first introduced in the 1960s) and according to a parliamentary report, aircraft availability has suffered. As of November 2019, France's heavy airlift fleet consists of 15 A400Ms in service of a planned fleet of 50. It was reported in 2019 that four of these were at 'tactical standard', enabling increased ability to operate in austere environments. France also still uses contracted strategic airlift support.

France's allies have also provided airlift support. The United Kingdom's Royal Air Force, for instance, deployed its *Sentinel* intelligence, surveillance and reconnaissance aircraft and C-17s (alongside US Air Force C-17s) to *Serval* for strategic airlift support when the rapid movement of heavy supplies was required. UK C-17 support was also in evidence early in 2019, delivering supplies to the UK's HC-5 *Chinook* detachment at Gao. *Chinook*s are useful because they have higher load-carrying capacity than other helicopters in-theatre, and, according to the commander of the initial British *Chinook* deployment, because they grant French helicopters greater freedom to concentrate on combat operations. Denmark announced in 2019 that it will deploy two *Merlin* transport helicopters to *Barkhane*, while also increasing its contribution to the United Nations Multidimensional Integrated Stabilisation Mission in Mali. This will bring to seven the number of nations engaged in or supporting the *Barkhane* mission, in addition to France, Germany, Estonia and the UK.

DEFENCE ECONOMICS

Macroeconomics

Economic growth in sub-Saharan Africa was expected to reach 3.2% in 2019, similar to 2018. However, this is below the International Monetary Fund (IMF) estimate for growth in the global emerging market and in developing economies. The Fund said this should be 3.9% in 2019.

The region's economic performance was hindered by its largest economies: GDP in Angola contracted by 0.3% in 2019, and South Africa registered GDP growth of only 0.7%. Slow growth in South Africa is explained, according to the IMF, by political uncertainty – with a transition of power from Jacob Zuma to Cyril Ramaphosa in February 2018 and then elections in May 2019 – as well as industrial unrest,

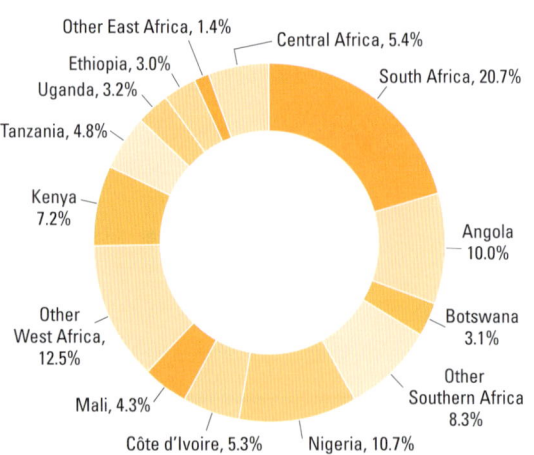

▼ Figure 26 **Sub-Saharan Africa defence spending by country and sub-region, 2019**

Note: Analysis excludes Djibouti, Equatorial Guinea, Eritrea, Gambia, Guinea Bissau, Seychelles, Somalia, Sudan

energy-supply issues and weak agricultural output. Angola, meanwhile, has been affected by three years of recession, and according to the World Bank, still needs to diversify its economy in order to reduce its reliance on oil exports. To compensate for the loss of oil-export revenues resulting from lower prices after the 2014 energy-price crash, Angola's government cut public spending and planned to introduce a new value-added tax in 2019. The authorities introduced a floating exchange-rate regime in 2018 to make up for a reduction in foreign-exchange reserves.

By comparison, those smaller sub-Saharan African economies less reliant on commodity prices as a growth engine performed better than their neighbours in 2019. For example, Benin achieved 6.6% GDP growth in 2019, Burkina Faso 6.0%, Côte d'Ivoire 7.5%, Ethiopia 7.4% and Senegal 6.0%. In these countries, private consumption and public spending were the principal drivers of growth. In Ethiopia, a privatisation plan and tax reforms improved the business environment for investors.

This contrasting picture illustrates that since energy prices fell in 2014, sub-Saharan Africa's economies have been divided into resource-intensive and non-resource-intensive countries. Even though energy prices were higher in 2019 (around US$60 per barrel (bbl) on average for Brent crude oil between January and October 2019) than in 2015 (US$52.4/bbl), the impact of the fiscal consolidation that took place after 2015–16, when governments started to implement tax reforms and improve tax collection, is still felt today.

Regional economies could also suffer from the initial effects of the trade dispute between China and the United States. China accounts for 50% of the world's metals demand; a persistent slowdown in the

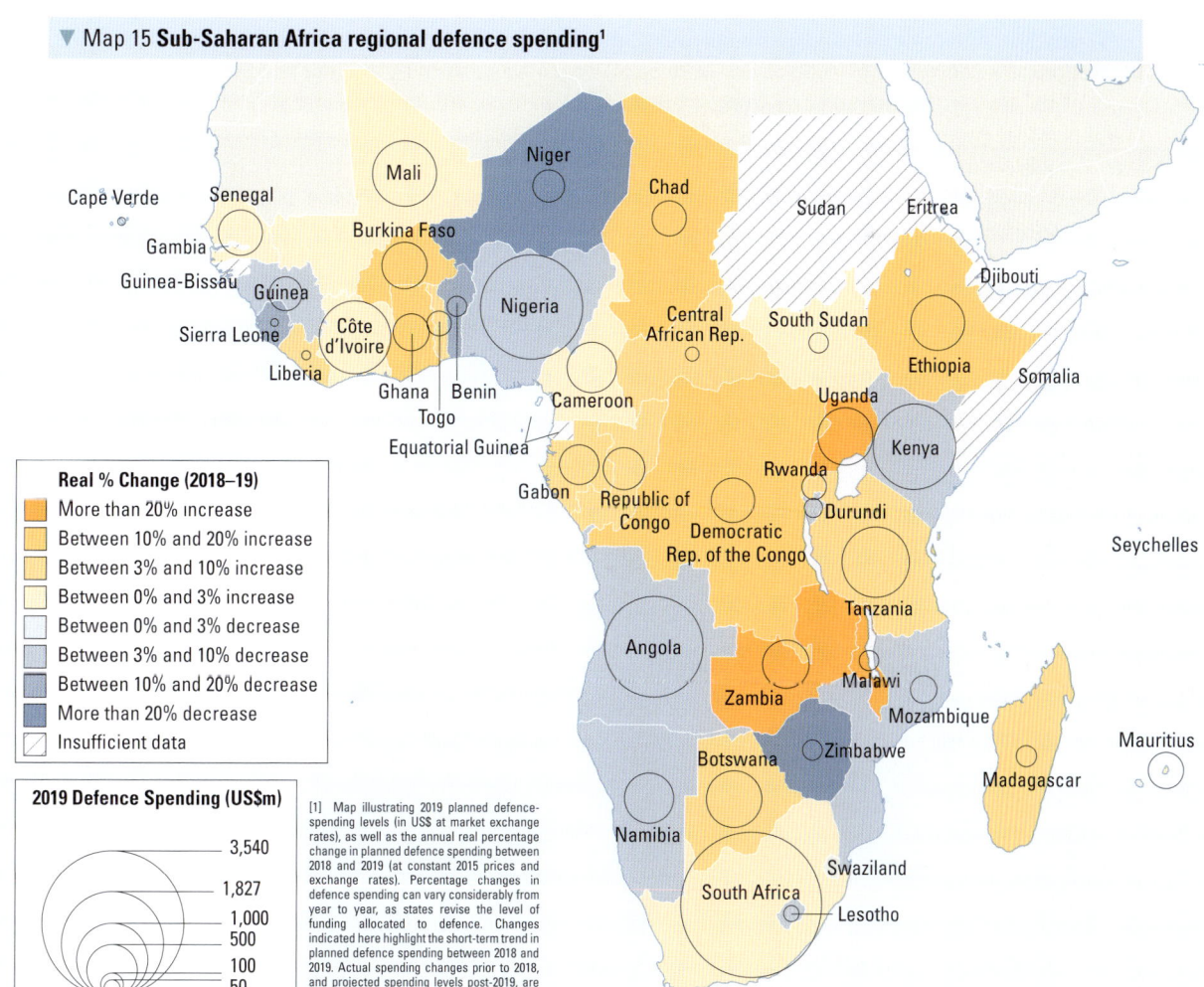

Map 15 **Sub-Saharan Africa regional defence spending**[1]

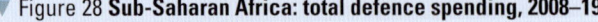

Note: Analysis excludes Djibouti, Equatorial Guinea, Eritrea, Gambia, Guinea Bissau, Seychelles, Somalia, Sudan

▲ Figure 27 **Sub-Saharan Africa regional defence expenditure** as % of GDP

spending has fallen every year since 2014: by 2.2% in 2015, 6.9% in 2016, 4.8% in 2017 and 4.3% in 2018. In 2019, defence spending effectively stagnated. It fell to US$16.82 billion from US$16.83bn in 2018 – a decline, but only by 0.05%. To put it in perspective, this sum is US$1.3bn less than Canada's 2019 defence budget. At the same time, defence spending as a proportion of sub-Saharan African countries' total GDP has also declined since 2014 (see Figure 27).

A combination of economic and security challenges means that defence spending in the continent's sub-regions has followed differing trajectories (see Figure 29). West Africa is the only sub-region to have seen defence spending increase over the past five years. The region is confronted by persistent security challenges such as terrorism, and defence-budget increases in Burkina Faso, Cameroon, Chad and Mali have partially offset the real-terms cuts seen in Nigeria's defence budget.

Southern Africa, meanwhile, has seen spending fall by 30%, in real terms, over the past five years. This was driven by Angola and South Africa, which in 2019 constituted 24% and 50% of the sub-region's total defence spending respectively. South Africa's defence budget grew by 0.9% between 2018 and 2019. This slight increase is likely insufficient to overcome the effects of years of real-terms cuts (see Table 23), all the more so given that procurement spending (the 'special defence account' in South Africa's budget document) is expected to fall from 10.5% of the defence budget in 2019 to 1.6% in 2021 (from US$371 million to approximately US$54m), while personnel costs are projected to rise from 57.8% in 2019 to 63.9% in 2021 (from US$2.05bn to US$2.21bn).

Chinese economy could affect prices and therefore the revenues of metal exporters in sub-Saharan Africa.

Meanwhile, international and regional financial institutions are concerned by high levels of debt in parts of the region. The Republic of Congo, Eritrea, Gambia, Mozambique, South Sudan and Zimbabwe are considered to be in debt distress, while other countries, such as Cameroon and Ethiopia, are at 'high risk' of debt distress. High levels of public debt tend to mean that governments dedicate significant proportions of revenue to debt servicing rather than public investment.

Defence-budget constraints

Defence spending in sub-Saharan Africa remains low due to economic constraints, despite pressing security demands in parts of the region. Total regional defence

▼ Figure 28 **Sub-Saharan Africa: total defence spending, 2008–19**

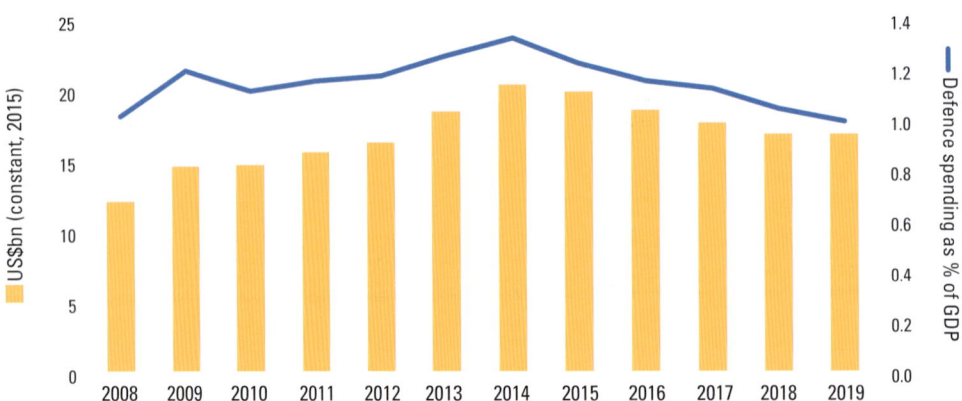

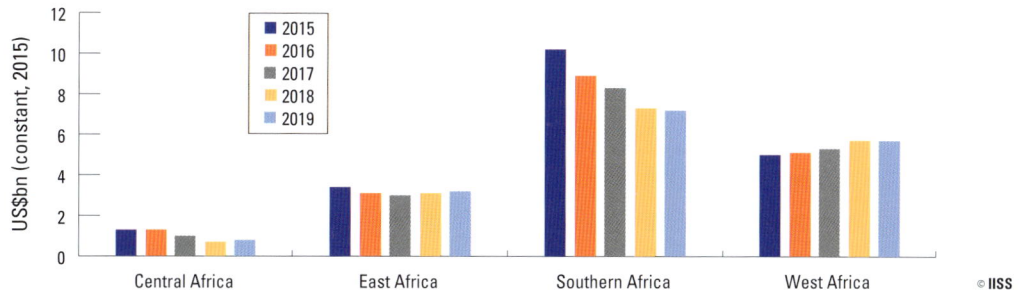

▲ Figure 29 **Sub-Saharan Africa: total defence spending by sub-region, 2015–19** (US$bn, constant 2015)

Table 23 **South Africa: real-terms defence spending, 2015–19**

	2015	2016	2017	2018	2019
US$bn (constant 2015)	3.53	3.46	3.38	3.21	3.24
Year-on-year % change	0.0%	-2.2%	-2.2%	-5.1%	0.92%

Challenging times for the region's main defence-industrial power

The constraints placed on South Africa's defence budget have been exacerbated by a crisis in the country's defence industry. State-owned Denel is experiencing a range of challenges and has faced liquidity problems. It was reported that the company had difficulty in paying its employees and suppliers in 2018 and 2019. In the *Defense News* annual list of the top 100 defence companies worldwide, Denel has slipped from 84th position in 2017 to 95th in 2018 (falling by US$243m, in revenue terms).

Denel's predicament does not stem primarily from a lack of domestic orders, even though it relies on South Africa for 49% of its revenue (see Figure 30), but reportedly from issues including poor governance. Nonetheless, the planned reduction in the South African National Defence Forces' acquisition spending will not help the business's recovery.

To tackle these problems, Denel changed its leadership and launched a restructuring plan. It withdrew from the Airbus A400M transport-aircraft supply chain and is expected to divest itself of subsidiary companies, including sensor, radar, armoured-vehicle and ammunition firms. The company has also secured R1.8bn (US$126m) from the government for recapitalisation, through a special appropriations bill that will also support other state-owned enterprises. However, this will in turn further burden South Africa's already strained public finances.

NIGERIA

Nigeria's armed forces contend with a complex security environment dominated by the decade-long Boko Haram insurgency in the northeast, as well as long-running instability in the southern delta area, rising banditry in the northwest and conflict between pastoralists and farmers mainly in the central and northern states (Nigeria's 'Middle Belt'). Against these and other challenges, the armed forces – though the largest in sub-Saharan Africa in terms of their personnel strength – have struggled, not just in the face of adaptable and resilient adversaries but also due to their own institutional weakness.

Efforts made in 2015–17 to rejuvenate the armed forces, after a period of stagnation aggravated

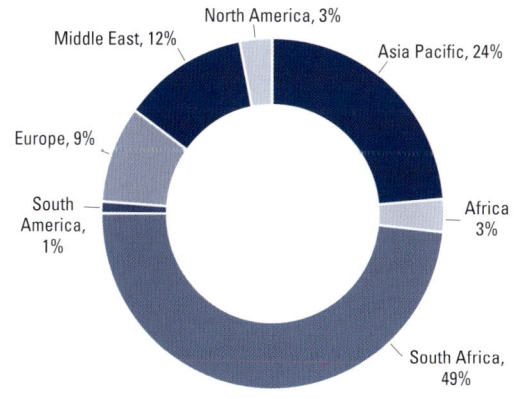

▼ Figure 30 **Denel Group: sales by destination, 2018**

Source: Denel Annual Report 2019 (p.21), http://www.denel.co.za/financials

by military setbacks in the northeast, resulted in some successes against Boko Haram. However, this situation, at least in the northeast, also owed much to the cumulative effect of military action by neighbouring countries (such as the members of the Multi-National Joint Task Force, MNJTF) and to internal rifts within Boko Haram. The jihadist group pledged allegiance to the Islamic State, also known as ISIS or ISIL, in 2015 and rebranded itself as the Islamic State West Africa Province (ISWAP). In 2016, the group split into two principal factions – one loyal to former Boko Haram leader Aboubakr Shekau, who commands the majority of Boko Haram, and another that retained the ISWAP title and is led by Abu Abdullah Ibn Umar al-Barnawi.

Looking ahead, a key challenge for Nigeria's armed forces will be building on operational successes against such non-state groups, such that readiness, training and tactics improve, as well as equipment availability and quality, in addition to enhancing the efficiency, accountability and modernisation of the country's defence institutions. As important to ensuring durable improvements to security will be action taken by local and federal authorities to deliver improvements to the economy and in governance, as well as across the broader security sector.

Defence policy and strategy

Muhammadu Buhari, who had been Nigeria's military ruler for a year in the 1980s, was first elected to the post of president in 2015 and was re-elected in February 2019. The start of Buhari's first term was marked by pledges to improve the country's economy and security, tackle the Boko Haram challenge and

Financing African peace-support operations:

The African Union (AU) has argued since 2003 for African Peace Support Operations (PSOs) to be funded, or part funded, by United Nations assessed contributions (contributions by states to UN peacekeeping operations). This is based on the view that PSOs are undertaken by the AU on behalf of the UN under Chapter 8 of the UN Charter. The AU's request has been resisted by the UN, and in particular by the UN Security Council (UNSC), recognising the primacy of the UNSC in the maintenance of international peace and security. As a result, the AU's PSOs have been largely funded by ad hoc groups of supporters and underpinned by the European Union, whose African Peace Facility has committed nearly €2.4 billion (US$2.7bn) to the AU's Peace and Security Architecture and PSOs since 2004.

In discussions between the UN Secretariat and the AU Commission (AUC) there now appears to be broad consensus, and agreement in principle, on an arrangement that would see the UN funding 75% of the costs of AU PSOs mandated by the AUC and authorised by the UNSC. The remaining 25% of the costs would be provided from the AU's Peace Fund. Although this 75/25% split has not been agreed by the UNSC (the United States' position is that it wishes the UNSC to continue overseeing UN funding), the AU has in the past three years made some progress in finding its projected 25% contribution.

The 2015 Kaberuka Report established a new mechanism to generate funds for African PSOs by imposing a 0.2% tariff on goods entering Africa from other continents. The revitalised Peace Fund (which was established in 2003 but received little support from African states) was launched in November 2018 with the objective of raising US$400 million by the end of 2021. In November 2018 the fund stood at US$56m and had risen to US$89m by February 2019. As of November 2019, it stood at around US$200m and was expected to reach US$290m by the end of 2019. The AU is therefore well on its way to achieving its goal of US$400m by 2021.

The key task for the AU now is to build political support among member states and ensure that all contribute to the fund. To this end, it was agreed in November 2018 at the AU's extraordinary summit that payment to the Peace Fund would be obligatory and that member states that failed to pay would face sanctions.

The Peace Fund is organised around three 'thematic windows': mediation and preventive diplomacy; institutional capacity; and PSOs. The fund is overseen by a board of trustees comprising five African members, one from each of the five regions in the Africa Standby Force, with the EU and UN present as international partners. This structure goes some way to allaying both African and international concerns over the management of such a large fund, but there are still concerns among some AU member states over the possible generation of surpluses.

There has not yet been any detailed consideration of what would be covered by the AU's 25% and the UN's 75% contribution. Proposals have included pooling the funds to cover all expenditures and earmarking some for certain activities, such as AU funding for political engagement, mediation and observers, and UN funding for troop, equipment and logistics costs. It has also been proposed that operations costing up to US$10m should be fully

eliminate institutional corruption. For the armed forces, he pledged to improve the living standards of military personnel and their families, bolster establishment strength and equipment numbers, and enhance training. Nevertheless, although some territory held by Boko Haram has been recaptured, the insurgency still poses a persistent and deadly challenge to the armed forces and wider population, while other promised changes are yet to materialise and, importantly, the economy largely remains moribund.

A Nigerian counter-insurgency doctrine was issued in 2011 (there is also a document focused on counter-terrorism), which according to analysts was developed in field operations. However, the extent to which such activities are coordinated with broader security-stabilisation work in conflict-afflicted areas is unclear. So too is the extent to which improvements in human rights have been institutionalised, in light of persistent allegations of violations by the armed forces. These were noted by Buhari in his 2015 inauguration speech, and an army special board of enquiry and a presidential commission were established in 2017. The Presidential Investigation Panel to Review Compliance of the Armed Forces with Human Rights Obligations and Rules of Engagement is understood to have reported in early 2018. Though reporting in early 2019 indicated that some allegations of abuse had been corroborated, the United Nations special rapporteur stated in late 2019 that the report had yet to be publicly released. The rapporteur said that 'there have been more than 20 commissions of inquiry, panels, fact-finding exercises established by the Federal government, State

funded by the AU and those over US$30m co-funded on a 25/75% basis by the AU and the UN. Operations between the two would be decided on a case-by-case basis. Other ideas include a gradual increase in AU funding from 25% to 50% then to 70% over an unspecified time frame, as the Peace Fund grows.

A proposed resolution that would formalise UN support to AU PSOs has been circulating since November 2018. While acknowledging the AU's need for predictable, dependable and sustainable funding, the drafts have all emphasised the primacy of the UNSC in being responsible for maintaining international peace and security. They have also noted a requirement for oversight by, and accountability to, the UNSC for any African PSO receiving support from UN-assessed costs. The drafts have also emphasised the need for a clear chain of UN authorisation, and perhaps mandating, as well as strict compliance with international humanitarian, refugee and human-rights laws, as well as civil protection and zero tolerance of sexual abuse. The drafts also talk of presenting pre-deployment and operational budgets to the UNSC and of external audits and evaluations. These audit and evaluation requirements are not new to the AU; they are also a requirement for all EU funding to AU PSOs.

However, if agreement in principle might appear to be closer than before, the UN peacekeeping budget that would support African PSOs is currently short by US$2bn, of which US arrears amount to US$750m. While this situation persists, it is unlikely that any significant support could be given to an AU PSO. The US has long been opposed to any watering down of the UNSC's responsibilities for directing and overseeing international peace and security efforts. It seems unlikely, therefore, that a resolution concerning UN support to AU PSOs will pass in the short term. The current US position is that it would be premature to move towards UN financing of AU PSOs while the AU itself is still working on internal reforms, and while there are still unanswered questions about the UN's authority to support the type of robust offensive mandates that are seen on many AU PSOs.

In the medium term, therefore, it seems likely that the AU will continue to develop its own Peace Fund, while continuing to rely on the support of the EU and the more limited support currently provided by the UN and other traditional bilateral partners. The concern for the international community might be that the AU develops its ability to mandate, conduct and finance limited PSOs before the international community develops the will to provide UN funding. Without this, the UN would have less oversight over, and less control of, AU operations. That said, the presence of both the EU and the UN as international partners on the African Peace Fund board of trustees will go some way to alleviating concern in this area.

Continuing its support to the AU, the EU approved a further €800m (US$898m) on 22 July 2019 to bolster its support for African peace and security. This additional funding will provide continuing support to PSOs such as the Multi-National Joint Task Force tackling Boko Haram, the African Union Mission to Somalia and the G5 Sahel Joint Force. It will also contribute to strengthening the African Peace and Security Architecture, funding preventive diplomacy, mediation and fact-finding through the Early Response Mechanism, and developing a human-rights and humanitarian-law compliance framework with the AU.

governments, the military and even the [National Human Rights Commission]'.

Continuing allegations of human-rights violations complicate the armed forces' cooperation with foreign partners, and hinder attempts to create trust between them and local communities. This risks undermining attempts to improve control over forces such as the Civilian Joint Task Force (CJTF), which was formed in 2013 with the aim of protecting local communities and tackling Boko Haram and has itself been the subject of concerns over the recruitment and use of child soldiers (an action plan to tackle this was launched in 2017). The allegations may also make it more difficult to recruit and retain human-intelligence sources among the local population. Consequently, it is understood that the armed forces are making significant use of technical intelligence-collection assets, such as intelligence, surveillance and reconnaissance (ISR) aircraft and uninhabited aerial vehicles (UAVs), though these are limited in quantity.

Military leaders have stressed the need to improve leadership training, as was apparent from comments attributed to the army chief of staff when opening a workshop on the subject in June 2019, while effective military cooperation has reportedly been hindered

Nigeria's foreign defence relations

There is continuing military cooperation with neighbouring states. The Multi-National Joint Task Force (MNJTF) – which was established in the 1990s and consists of forces from Benin, Cameroon, Chad, Niger and Nigeria – is now focused on growing concern over Boko Haram's regional impact. The MNJTF has increased its activity in recent years, though most actions against Boko Haram and its Islamic State West Africa Province offshoot are conducted on a bilateral basis. The grouping has been supported by international actors such as France, the United Kingdom and the United States, as well as the European Union (through its African Peace Facility).

Nigeria's armed forces, meanwhile, are benefiting from other sources of military assistance, including from the US. According to the 2019 AFRICOM Posture Statement, this includes support in expanding Nigerian intelligence, surveillance and reconnaissance; intelligence; counter-IED and air–ground-integration capabilities. Weapons sales are another aspect, including the often-mentioned procurement from the US of 12 A-29 *Super Tucano* light attack aircraft.

President Buhari's reform plans were well received in Washington, but continuing concern over allegations of abuses by Nigeria's armed forces led the Obama administration to act cautiously with regard to military assistance. The contract for *Super Tucanos* was blocked, as was an earlier plan for the sale of *Cobra* attack helicopters, reportedly from Israel. However, the Trump administration amended this position and in 2018 finally allowed the *Super Tucano* sale to proceed.

Abuja remains a partner in the US Trans-Sahara Counterterrorism Partnership and the International Military Education & Training programme. These provided Nigeria with US$1.1 million in 2018, more than was given to any other African state (just beating Senegal); but funding levels for 2019 and 2020 were unclear at the time of writing. Cooperation with the US Navy takes place in the framework of the African Partnership Station programme, while US troops have trained Nigerian personnel, including at the Nigerian Army Infantry School in late 2018. According to the US Department of Defense, more than US$16m was planned for train-and-equip programmes in 2018 and 2019. US military assistance for other countries engaged in the MNJTF has also been forthcoming.

The UK has had a long-standing role in training elements of Nigeria's armed forces. Recent training programmes have been delivered by elements of all three UK armed forces, managed by the permanent British Military Advisory and Training Team in Abuja, while courses have also been delivered by a number of Short Term Training Teams. The UK said in August 2018 that it had trained 30,000 Nigerian troops since 2015. However, despite the longevity of the UK–Nigeria relationship, the two countries only signed their first formal defence and security partnership that same month. As part of this agreement, the UK offered, for the first time, to train complete army units before their deployment to Nigeria's northeast in a bid to 'give Nigerian forces a shared understanding and experience that will make them better able to defeat the enemy'.

Nigerian military personnel, notably from elite units or special forces, are reported to have also trained in Pakistan and Russia. Abuja and Moscow signed a military-cooperation agreement in 2017, while a five-year military-cooperation agreement was signed with Turkey in 2018. Defence cooperation is also deepening with China. Nigeria operates the Chinese CH-3 uninhabited aerial vehicle and there were reports of a broader military-cooperation agreement being signed in 2018 following a presidential visit to China.

by inter-service rivalry. Moreover, the armed forces are hampered by weaknesses in the broader security sector that have led to them being called on by the authorities to operate in a law-enforcement role. For instance, in late 2017, it was reported that the air force had been employed to suppress disturbances in Adamawa State, an incident that saw an air-force spokesman reportedly claim that it had 'opened fire to dissuade looters and vandals'. Amnesty International said at least 35 people died as a direct result of that incident, and that the use of air raids was not 'a legitimate law enforcement method'.

Nigerian troops are deployed in 30 out of the country's 36 states, and it is understood that Abuja envisages eventually having combat, combat-support and combat service-support brigades in each state. In the meantime, the armed forces' plan to create in the north what have been termed 'super camps' continues. It was reported that army chiefs had announced in September 2019 a plan to do so in more than 20 locations. In the northeast, the armed forces are also introducing 'garrison towns', where, according to UN special rapporteur Agnes Callamard, suspects can be 'screened' and 'detained', while others are housed in the consolidated 'super camps'. Callamard said that this strategy constituted an effort to 'break up Boko Haram's supply routes and [make] it impossible for the group to rely on local communities for their food and fighters'. While the armed forces assert that these 'super camps' will enable them to rapidly mount operations from better-defended locations, there are concerns that anxiety over force protection might have the unintended consequence of allowing militants greater freedom of movement.

The armed forces

Nigeria's order of battle has evolved considerably in recent years, principally due to operational requirements. Units operating in the northeast are formed in Task Force Brigades and Task Force Battalions, comprising front line units with dedicated combat support and combat service support. Specialist formations have also been created to tackle insurgents, including units equipped with motorcycles, a military working-dog unit within the 7th Division (headquartered in Maiduguri in the northeast) and Mobile Strike Teams. According to the army, these strike teams – established in 2017 – are intended to 'conduct long range patrols and ambushes'.

It was expected that an army light-aviation unit would be established in 2019, though the status of this plan is currently unclear and it may have stalled due to funding constraints. The air force, meanwhile, has reportedly created a special-operations unit and a force-protection contingent, with the latter principally intended to defend fixed and advanced bases. All of Nigeria's military or paramilitary forces now have a special-forces unit, although their levels of training and specialist skills are currently unclear.

Military capability on the ground has eroded somewhat following a period of force generation between 2015 and 2017. This decline has been ascribed to factors including personnel challenges, with reports of psychological and physical exhaustion caused by persistent deployments. In theory, after six months of operations, personnel should rotate back to quieter zones, but it is understood that this does not always happen in practice. Reports have also emerged of issues concerning pay and poor morale, the latter notably in units that have experienced significant combat and suffered from attrition. Recruitment and training have also come under scrutiny, with some analysts pointing to limited training time (reportedly six months) for recruits and potential challenges in meeting personnel targets. Moreover, it is unclear whether an effective process is in place to learn lessons from tactical successes and failures.

There are persistent reports of poor equipment and availability. Not all units use armoured vehicles, and there are only limited numbers of these to support units operating light tactical or 4x4 vehicles. Military activity is also complicated by logistical problems and by the lack of equipment standardisation. There are limited spare parts for maintenance, repair and overhaul, and a plethora of armoured vehicle types and a range of calibres of light and heavy weapons.

In addition, ground–air coordination is limited, and while there are small numbers of suitable ground-attack assets (President Buhari reportedly criticised availability and maintenance not long after taking office), their effective use can be hampered by a lack of real-time information. That said, a large proportion of the air force's tasks are ISR-related, utilising assets including ATR-42 turboprop transports, Dornier Do-228 light transports and Bell 412ep utility helicopters. The air force is also engaged in logistical tasks, including for units deployed in the northeast.

Equipment: requirements and availability
Land
Age and operational use have led to wear and tear on some of the land forces' weapons systems.

The acquisition of a new main battle tank, or at least obtaining additional T-72s, is understood to have been mooted. Although modernisation of the armoured-vehicle fleet has been increasingly undertaken by local industry, some mine-resistant ambush-protected vehicles (MRAPs) have been imported (notably the CS/VP3, for police service). However, the range of armoured vehicles and artillery types (calibres as well as systems) provides a logistical challenge.

Air

The air force is the priority for equipment modernisation, though for the time being it will have to use current equipment in tackling the country's security challenges.

For example, the US$329.08m contract for 12 A-29 *Super Tucano*s, which has been criticised locally on account of the price and procurement procedure, will not be complete until 2024, though the first platform is planned to enter service in 2021. Meanwhile, discussions are continuing about the procurement of JF-17 *Thunder* combat aircraft from Pakistan Aeronautical Complex, though no in-service date is publicly available. Talks began in 2014, and funds have only been allocated to purchase at least three platforms out of an expected dozen.

The air force currently operates F-7NI (Chengdu J-7) light fighters and the FT-7NI trainer variant, as well as, in a number of its air-to-ground engagements, ageing Dassault/Dornier *Alpha Jet* light fighter/trainers. Czech-designed L-39ZA *Albatros* jet trainers have been recently overhauled and reconfigured for light-attack/counter-insurgency tasks, while Chinese-manufactured CH-3 UAVs also provide some strike capability. A domestically produced UAV, the *Tsaigumi*, has also entered service.

The air-force chief noted in August 2019 that some ten helicopter pilots are to be trained in the UK, while other pilots are to receive tactical training in order to enhance air-to-ground capabilities. Deliveries of Mi-35M attack helicopters are in progress from Russian Helicopters (though one crashed on 2 January 2019). In early 2019, more AW109 multi-role helicopters arrived to fulfil the air force's transport and assault helicopter role. AW109s already in service in Nigeria are fitted with a 12.7 mm door gun. According to the chief of the air force, 44 new aircraft and helicopters are due to have entered service by 2021, despite budgetary constraints.

Maritime

French company Ocea has delivered two FPB 110 and seven FPB 72 patrol boats to the Nigerian Navy since 2012 and is building an offshore-support vessel (OSV 190) for hydrographic tasks. Meanwhile, two Chinese-built *Centenary*-class offshore-patrol vessels entered service in 2015 and 2016. In common with the army and air force, the navy is requesting funds to support the purchase of helicopters and UAVs, in addition to offshore-patrol vessels, perhaps with a view to operations in the Gulf of Guinea where the navy undertakes counter-piracy tasks.

Defence economics and industry

Despite a regionally significant defence budget of around US$1.75 billion in 2018 and about US$1.83bn in 2019, allocated funds are insufficient to meet the Nigerian armed forces' requirements. In April 2018, President Buhari promised an extra US$1bn, but by December that year the funds had yet to be delivered. It is unlikely that Nigeria's economic situation will enable a significant increase in the defence budget in the near term. Although Abuja in 2019 increased its defence budget in local currency, which translated into an increase when converted into US current dollar terms, this still resulted in a decrease in real terms. Meanwhile, 64% of Nigeria's total 2019 defence budget was dedicated to personnel expenses, while the service breakdown saw 39% of funds allocated to the army, 17% to the navy and 20% to the air force (see Figure 31). However, in 2018 the non-governmental organisation Transparency International (TI) highlighted that spending on defence and security in Nigeria also includes 'security votes', an opaque mechanism that constitutes a discretionary line item in various ministerial budgets. In 2019, the Nigerian federal government spent N20.3bn (US$62.5 million) on such security votes, according to TI, of which 74% went to defence-ministry departments and agencies.

Paradoxically, budgetary constraints have led to innovation and autonomy in military-equipment production in Nigeria's defence industry, which contains both public and private firms. Armoured vehicles are produced by local firm Proforce, whose products, notably MRAPs, equip both the Nigerian security and armed forces. In March 2019, the army received its first Proforce *Ara* 2 MRAP, and a contract was reportedly signed in June 2019 for the export of 20 *Ara* 2s, with the specialist trade press suggesting Chad as the potential customer.

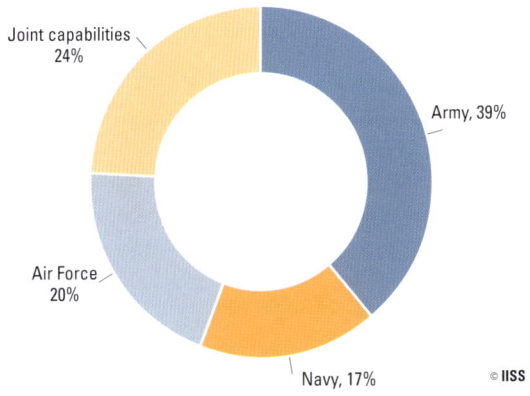

▲ Figure 31 **Nigeria: defence budget 2019, breakdown by service**

Nigeria has an ambition to export armoured vehicles more broadly in Africa by 2030. However, the sector has long been plagued by allegations of corruption. There have been attempts to eliminate graft by changing procurement processes, including by increasing government oversight and ending the use of intermediaries, but in practice, efforts to tackle corruption remain embryonic.

In the aerospace sector, the *Tsaigumi* is the first domestically produced UAV to enter operational service in Nigeria. The development of a mini-UAV, the *Star* tilt-rotor, is under consideration, and it is understood that this system has the capacity to carry at least one weapon.

Several air-force platforms have been overhauled by local industry, including L-39ZAs (three of which were reactivated in-country with the support of Czech industry and handed over in mid-2019) and G.222 medium transport aircraft. A Eurocopter EC-135 light utility helicopter was reactivated after an overhaul with external support in August 2019, while ATR-42s and other aircraft have been overhauled abroad. Nigeria's defence sector is capable of producing some of the munitions for these and other platforms. The air force supports research and development in varying areas. For example, the domestic production of a fighter/bomber was mentioned in August 2019 by the air-force chief, while a project for a domestically designed multi-role aircraft (likely suitable for ISR tasks) began in 2017 in partnership with US companies.

Nigeria also has an active maritime defence sector. The Naval Dockyard Limited (NDL) and Proforce, in partnership with Epenal Group, are progressing with the construction of a number of small vessels intended for riverine and coastal patrols. The sector also envisages more ambitious projects, with the construction of at least three Seaward Defence Boats. It is understood that NDL envisages potential orders for up to ten of these vessels.

Angola ANG

New Angolan Kwanza AOA		2018	2019	2020
GDP	AOA	26.8tr	31.5tr	
	US$	106bn	91.5bn	
per capita	US$	3,621	3,038	
Growth	%	-1.2	-0.3	
Inflation	%	19.6	17.2	
Def bdgt	AOA	546bn	586bn	
	US$	2.16bn	1.70bn	
USD1=AOA		252.86	343.88	

Real-terms defence budget trend (US$bn, constant 2015)

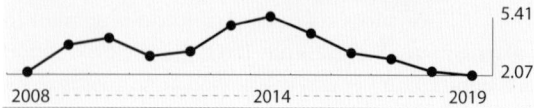

Population 31,427,266

Ethnic groups: Ovimbundu 37%; Kimbundu 25%; Bakongo 13%

Age	0–14	15–19	20–24	25–29	30–64	65 plus
Male	24.0%	5.0%	4.0%	3.3%	11.6%	1.0%
Female	24.1%	5.2%	4.2%	3.7%	12.7%	1.3%

Capabilities

Though numerically one of the region's largest and best-equipped armed forces, Angola's available inventory faces maintenance and readiness challenges. The armed forces are constitutionally tasked with ensuring sovereignty and territorial integrity, and there is growing attention on maritime security and the protection of offshore resources. Defence ties persist with Russia, in the form of equipment deliveries and plans to boost defence-industrial cooperation. There are increasing military ties with China, and Luanda is looking to Beijing for help in military modernisation and defence-industrial development. Angola retains conscription and, in recent years, force health and education have been investment priorities. The armed forces train regularly and have participated in multinational exercises. Angola is the only regional state with a strategic-airlift capacity, though availability remains an issue. Improving the military-logistics system has been identified as a key requirement, but progress is unclear. Modernisation plans have been curtailed by the fall in oil prices though there have nonetheless been some orders and acquisitions. Defence industry is limited to in-service maintenance facilities, but Angola has ambitions to develop greater capacity by partnering with countries such as China, Brazil, Russia and Portugal.

ACTIVE 107,000 (Army 100,000 Navy 1,000 Air 6,000) **Paramilitary 10,000**
Conscript liability 2 years

ORGANISATIONS BY SERVICE

Army 100,000
FORCES BY ROLE
MANOEUVRE
  Armoured
    1 tk bde
  Light
    1 SF bde
    1 (1st) div (1 mot inf bde, 2 inf bde)
    1 (2nd) div (3 mot inf bde, 3 inf bde, 1 arty regt)
    1 (3rd) div (2 mot inf bde, 3 inf bde)
    1 (4th) div (1 tk regt, 5 mot inf bde, 2 inf bde, 1 engr bde)
    1 (5th) div (2 inf bde)
    1 (6th) div (1 mot inf bde, 2 inf bde, 1 engr bde)
COMBAT SUPPORT
  Some engr units
COMBAT SERVICE SUPPORT
  Some log units
EQUIPMENT BY TYPE†
ARMOURED FIGHTING VEHICLES
  MBT 300: ε200 T-55AM2; 50 T-62; 50 T-72
  LT TK 10 PT-76
  ASLT 9 PTL-02 *Assaulter*
  RECCE 600 BRDM-2
  IFV 250 BMP-1/BMP-2
  APC 246
    APC (T) 31 MT-LB
    APC (W) 170+: ε170 BTR-152/BTR-60/BTR-80; WZ-551 (CP)
    PPV 45 *Casspir* NG2000
ENGINEERING & MAINTENANCE VEHICLES
  ARV T-54/T-55
  MW *Bozena*
ARTILLERY 1,439+
  SP 16+: **122mm** 2S1 *Gvozdika*; **152mm** 4 2S3 *Akatsiya*; **203mm** 12 2S7 *Pion*
  TOWED 575: **122mm** 523 D-30; **130mm** 48 M-46; **152mm** 4 D-20
  MRL 98+: **122mm** 98: 58 BM-21 *Grad*; 40 RM-70; **240mm** BM-24
  MOR 750: **82mm** 250; **120mm** 500
ANTI-TANK/ANTI-INFRASTRUCTURE
  MSL • MANPATS 9K11 (AT-3 *Sagger*)
  RCL 500: 400 **82mm** B-10/**107mm** B-11†; 100 M40†
  GUNS • SP 100mm SU-100†
AIR DEFENCE
  SAM • Point-defence 9K32 *Strela*-2 (SA-7 *Grail*)‡; 9K36 *Strela*-3 (SA-14 *Gremlin*); 9K310 *Igla*-1 (SA-16 *Gimlet*)
  GUNS
    SP 23mm ZSU-23-4
    TOWED 450+: **14.5mm** ZPU-4; **23mm** ZU-23-2; **37mm** M-1939; **57mm** S-60

Navy ε1,000
EQUIPMENT BY TYPE
PATROL AND COASTAL COMBATANTS 21
  PCO 2 *Ngola Kiluange* with 1 hel landing platform (Ministry of Fisheries)
  PCC 5 *Rei Bula Matadi* (Ministry of Fisheries)
  PBF 5 PVC-170
  PB 9: 4 *Mandume*; 5 *Comandante Imperial Santana* (Ministry of Fisheries)

Coastal Defence
EQUIPMENT BY TYPE
COASTAL DEFENCE • AShM 4K44 *Utyos* (SS-C-1B *Sepal* – at Luanda)

Air Force/Air Defence 6,000
FORCES BY ROLE
FIGHTER
1 sqn with MiG-21bis/MF *Fishbed*
1 sqn with Su-27/Su-27UB/Su-30K *Flanker*
FIGHTER/GROUND ATTACK
1 sqn with MiG-23BN/ML/UB *Flogger*
1 sqn with Su-22 *Fitter D*
1 sqn with Su-25 *Frogfoot*
MARITIME PATROL
1 sqn with F-27-200 MPA; C-212 *Aviocar*
TRANSPORT
3 sqn with An-12 *Cub*; An-26 *Curl*; An-32 *Cline*; An-72 *Coaler*; BN-2A *Islander*; C-212 *Aviocar*; Do-28D *Skyservant*; EMB-135BJ *Legacy* 600 (VIP); Il-76TD *Candid*
TRAINING
1 sqn with Cessna 172K/R
1 sqn with EMB-312 *Tucano*
1 sqn with L-29 *Delfin*; L-39 *Albatros*
1 sqn with PC-7 *Turbo Trainer*; PC-9*
1 sqn with Z-142
ATTACK HELICOPTER
2 sqn with Mi-24/Mi-35 *Hind*; SA342M *Gazelle* (with HOT)
TRANSPORT HELICOPTER
2 sqn with AS565; SA316 *Alouette* III (IAR-316) (trg)
1 sqn with Bell 212
1 sqn with Mi-8 *Hip*; Mi-17 *Hip H*
1 sqn with Mi-171Sh
AIR DEFENCE
5 bn/10 bty with S-125 *Pechora* (SA-3 *Goa*); 9K35 *Strela*-10 (SA-13 *Gopher*)†; 2K12 *Kub* (SA-6 *Gainful*); 9K33 *Osa* (SA-8 *Gecko*); 9K31 *Strela*-1 (SA-9 *Gaskin*); S-75M *Volkhov* (SA-2 *Guideline*)

EQUIPMENT BY TYPE†
AIRCRAFT 98 combat capable
  FTR 36: 6 Su-27/Su-27UB *Flanker*; 12 Su-30K *Flanker*; 18 MiG-23ML *Flogger*
  FGA 42+: 20 MiG-21bis/MF *Fishbed*; 8 MiG-23BN/UB *Flogger*; 13 Su-22 *Fitter D*; 1+ Su-24 *Fencer*
  ATK 10: 8 Su-25 *Frogfoot*; 2 Su-25UB *Frogfoot*
  ELINT 1 B-707
  TPT 58: **Heavy** 4 Il-76TD *Candid*; **Medium** 6 An-12 *Cub*; **Light** 48: 12 An-26 *Curl*; 2 An-32 *Cline*; 8 An-72 *Coaler*; 8 BN-2A *Islander*; 2 C-212; 5 Cessna 172K; 6 Cessna 172R; 1 Do-28D *Skyservant*; 1 EMB-135BJ *Legacy* 600 (VIP); 2 MA60; 1 Yak-40
  TRG 42: 13 EMB-312 *Tucano*; 6 EMB-314 *Super Tucano**; 6 L-29 *Delfin*; 2 L-39C *Albatros*; 5 PC-7 *Turbo Trainer*; 4 PC-9*; 6 Z-142
HELICOPTERS
  ATK 56: 34 Mi-24 *Hind*; 22 Mi-35 *Hind*
  MRH 64: 8 AS565 *Panther*; 4 AW139; 9 SA316 *Alouette* III (IAR-316) (incl trg); 8 SA342M *Gazelle*; 27 Mi-8 *Hip*/Mi-17 *Hip H*; 8 Mi-171Sh *Terminator*
  TPT • Light 10: 2+ AW109E; 8 Bell 212

AIR DEFENCE • SAM 113
  Medium-range 40 S-75M *Volkhov* (SA-2 *Guideline*)‡
  Short-range 28: 16 2K12 *Kub* (SA-6 *Gainful*) (upgraded to 2K12-ML standard); 12 S-125 *Pechora* (SA-3 *Goa*)
  Point-defence 45: 10 9K35 *Strela*-10 (SA-13 *Gopher*)†; 15 9K33 *Osa* (SA-8 *Gecko*); 20 9K31 *Strela*-1 (SA-9 *Gaskin*)
AIR-LAUNCHED MISSILES
  AAM
    IR R-3 (AA-2 *Atoll*)‡; R-60 (AA-8 *Aphid*); R-73 (AA-11A *Archer*)
    IR/SARH R-23/24 (AA-7 *Apex*)‡; R-27 (AA-10 *Alamo*)
  ASM AT-2 *Swatter*; HOT
  ARM Kh-28 (AS-9 *Kyle*)

Paramilitary 10,000

Rapid-Reaction Police 10,000

Benin BEN

CFA Franc BCEAO fr		2018	2019	2020
GDP	fr	7.92tr	8.40tr	
	US$	14.3bn	14.4bn	
per capita	US$	1,242	1,217	
Growth	%	6.7	6.6	
Inflation	%	0.8	-0.3	
Def bdgt	fr	50.1bn	39.9bn	
	US$	90.3m	68.3m	
US$1=fr		555.19	584.05	

Real-terms defence budget trend (US$m, constant 2015)

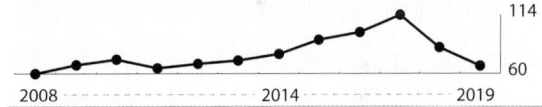

Population	11,646,392				
Age	0–14	15–19	20–24	25–29	30–64	65 plus
Male	21.4%	5.7%	4.8%	4.0%	13.4%	1.1%
Female	20.5%	5.5%	4.6%	3.9%	13.4%	1.8%

Capabilities

The armed forces focus on border- and internal-security issues, as well as combating illicit trafficking. Border patrols increased and security was tightened in light of concern over the regional threat from Islamist groups. Maritime security is a priority in light of continuing piracy in the Gulf of Guinea. There is a military-cooperation agreement with France, whose Senegal-based forces have delivered training to boost Benin's border-surveillance capacity. The US has provided similar training to the army and national police. US forces have also delivered pre-deployment training to the armed forces and training in professional ethics, anti-corruption and accountability to the Republican Police. Benin contributes personnel to the Multi-National Joint Task Force fighting Boko Haram. There is a limited capacity to deploy beyond neighbouring states without external support. There is limited maintenance capability but no defence manufacturing sector.

ACTIVE 7,250 (Army 6,500 Navy 500 Air 250)
Paramilitary 4,800
Conscript liability 18 months (selective)

ORGANISATIONS BY SERVICE

Army 6,500
FORCES BY ROLE
MANOEUVRE
  Armoured
    2 armd sqn
  Light
    1 (rapid reaction) mot inf bn
    8 inf bn
  Air Manoeuvre
    1 AB bn
COMBAT SUPPORT
  2 arty bn
  1 engr bn
  1 sigs bn
COMBAT SERVICE SUPPORT
  1 log bn
  1 spt bn
EQUIPMENT BY TYPE
ARMOURED FIGHTING VEHICLES
  LT TK 18 PT-76†
  RECCE 34: 3 AML-90; 14 BRDM-2; 7 M8; 10 VBL
  APC 34 • APC (T) 22 M113; APC (W) 2 *Bastion* APC;
    PPV 10 *Casspir* NG
ARTILLERY 16+
  TOWED 105mm 16: 12 L118 Light Gun; 4 M101
  MOR 81mm some; 120mm some

Navy ε500
EQUIPMENT BY TYPE
PATROL AND COASTAL COMBATANTS
  PB 6: 2 *Matelot Brice Kpomasse* (ex-PRC); 3 FPB 98; 1 27m (PRC)

Air Force 250
EQUIPMENT BY TYPE
AIRCRAFT
  TPT 3: Light 1 DHC-6 *Twin Otter*†; PAX 2: 1 B-727; 1 HS-748†
  TRG 2 LH-10 *Ellipse*
HELICOPTERS
  TPT • Light 5: 4 AW109BA; 1 AS350B *Ecureuil*†

Paramilitary 4,800

Police Republicaine 4,800
EQUIPMENT BY TYPE
ARMOURED FIGHTING VEHICLES
  APC • PPV *Casspir* NG

DEPLOYMENT

CENTRAL AFRICAN REPUBLIC: UN • MINUSCA 8
CHAD: Lake Chad Basin Commission • MNJTF 150
DEMOCRATIC REPUBLIC OF THE CONGO: UN • MONUSCO 8
MALI: UN • MINUSMA 260; 1 mech inf coy(+)
SOUTH SUDAN: UN • UNMISS 4
SUDAN: UN • UNISFA 2

Botswana BWA

Botswana Pula P		2018	2019	2020
GDP	P	190bn	200bn	
	US$	18.6bn	18.7bn	
per capita	US$	7,973	7,859	
Growth	%	4.5	3.5	
Inflation	%	3.2	3.0	
Def bdgt [a]	P	5.29bn	5.75bn	
	US$	518m	537m	
US$1=P		10.20	10.71	

[a] Defence, Justice and Security Budget

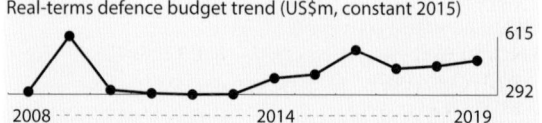
Real-terms defence budget trend (US$m, constant 2015)

Population 2,283,255

Age	0–14	15–19	20–24	25–29	30–64	65 plus
Male	15.6%	4.7%	4.4%	4.3%	16.7%	2.3%
Female	15.4%	4.8%	4.6%	4.5%	19.6%	3.1%

Capabilities

The Botswana Defence Force (BDF) mainly comprises ground forces and a small, but comparatively well-equipped, air wing. The major task for the BDF is to ensure territorial integrity, coupled with domestic missions such as tackling poachers. In 2019 concerns were raised over the alleged politicisation of the intelligence services. There is a history of involvement in peacekeeping operations. The BDF has reportedly been working on a defence doctrine that is believed to be influenced by US concepts and practices. Botswana has a good relationship with the US and regularly sends its officers to train there. The armed forces also train with other African nations, including Namibia, with whom it holds biannual exercises. The operations centre for the Southern African Development Community Standby Force is located in Gaborone. Recent personnel priorities include improving conditions of service, overhauling retirement ages and boosting capability. Growing relations with Beijing have seen some military personnel travel to China for training. The air force has a modest airlift capacity and the BDF is able to deploy a small force by air if required. There is an ongoing effort to identify a successor for the air arm's primary combat aircraft, the F-5, while, in recent years, ground-based air defence has been improved. Local reports suggest a limited capacity in armoured-vehicle maintenance; beyond this, the country has no defence-industrial base.

ACTIVE 9,000 (Army 8,500 Air 500)

ORGANISATIONS BY SERVICE

Army 8,500
FORCES BY ROLE
MANOEUVRE
  Armoured
    1 armd bde(-)

Light
2 inf bde (1 armd recce regt, 4 inf bn, 1 cdo unit, 1 engr regt, 1 log bn, 2 ADA regt)

COMBAT SUPPORT
1 arty bde
1 engr coy
1 sigs coy

COMBAT SERVICE SUPPORT
1 log gp

AIR DEFENCE
1 AD bde(-)

EQUIPMENT BY TYPE
ARMOURED FIGHTING VEHICLES
LT TK 45: ε20 SK-105 *Kurassier*; 25 FV101 *Scorpion*
RECCE 72+: RAM-V-1; ε8 RAM-V-2; 64 VBL
APC 157: **APC (W)** 145: 50 BTR-60; 50 LAV-150 *Commando* (some with 90mm gun); 45 MOWAG *Piranha* III; **PPV** 12 *Casspir*
AUV 6 FV103 *Spartan*

ENGINEERING & MAINTENANCE VEHICLES
ARV *Greif*; M578
MW *Aardvark* Mk2

ANTI-TANK/ANTI-INFRASTRUCTURE
MSL
  SP V-150 TOW
  MANPATS TOW
RCL **84mm** *Carl Gustav*

ARTILLERY 78
TOWED 30: **105mm** 18: 12 L118 Light Gun; 6 Model 56 pack howitzer; **155mm** 12 Soltam
MRL **122mm** 20 APRA-40
MOR 28: **81mm** 22; **120mm** 6 M-43

AIR DEFENCE
SAM • **Point-defence** *Javelin*; 9K310 *Igla*-1 (SA-16 *Gimlet*); 9K32 *Strela*-2 (SA-7 *Grail*)‡
GUNS • **TOWED 20mm** 7 M167 *Vulcan*

Air Wing 500

FORCES BY ROLE
FIGHTER/GROUND ATTACK
1 sqn with F-5A *Freedom Fighter*; F-5D *Tiger* II

ISR
1 sqn with O-2 *Skymaster*

TRANSPORT
2 sqn with BD-700 *Global Express*; BN-2A/B *Defender**; Beech 200 *Super King Air* (VIP); C-130B *Hercules*; C-212-300 *Aviocar*; CN-235M-100; Do-328-110 (VIP)

TRAINING
1 sqn with PC-7 MkII *Turbo Trainer**

TRANSPORT HELICOPTER
1 sqn with AS350B *Ecureuil*; Bell 412EP/SP *Twin Huey*; EC225LP *Super Puma*

EQUIPMENT BY TYPE
AIRCRAFT 28 combat capable
FTR 13: 8 F-5A *Freedom Fighter*; 5 F-5D *Tiger* II
ISR 5 O-2 *Skymaster*
TPT 20: **Medium** 3 C-130B *Hercules*; **Light** 16: 4 BN-2 *Defender**; 6 BN-2B *Defender**; 1 Beech 200 *King Air* (VIP); 1 C-212-300 *Aviocar*; 1 C-212-400 *Aviocar*; 2 CN-235M-100; 1 Do-328-110 (VIP); **PAX** 1 BD700 *Global Express*
TRG 5 PC-7 MkII *Turbo Trainer**

HELICOPTERS
MRH 7: 2 Bell 412EP *Twin Huey*; 5 Bell 412SP *Twin Huey*
TPT 9: **Medium** 1 EC225LP *Super Puma*; **Light** 8 AS350B *Ecureuil*

Burkina Faso BFA

CFA Franc BCEAO fr		2018	2019	2020
GDP	fr	7.85tr	8.48tr	
	US$	14.1bn	14.6bn	
per capita	US$	716	718	
Growth	%	6.8	6.0	
Inflation	%	2.0	1.1	
Def bdgt	fr	174bn	210bn	
	US$	313m	361m	
US$1=fr		555.18	581.36	

Real-terms defence budget trend (US$m, constant 2015)

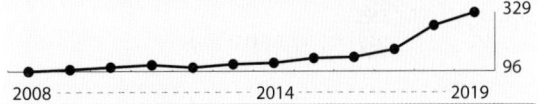

Population	20,288,052					
Age	0–14	15–19	20–24	25–29	30–64	65 plus
Male	22.3%	5.8%	4.3%	3.7%	11.4%	1.4%
Female	21.7%	5.6%	4.6%	4.1%	13.5%	1.8%

Capabilities

Burkina Faso's security forces have in recent years been challenged by an increased terrorist threat. The country is part of the G5 Sahel grouping and, as part of its support for this, France has supplied armed pick-up trucks. The terrorist threat has led Ouagadougou to refocus its military efforts to the north. There is cooperation with France and Mali, particularly on border security. Aviation capacities are slowly improving with the arrival of more helicopters. However, financial challenges hinder broader military-capability developments. Deployment capabilities are limited to neighbouring countries without external support. While there are maintenance facilities there is no defence manufacturing sector.

ACTIVE 11,200 (Army 6,400 Air 600 Gendarmerie 4,200) **Paramilitary 250**

ORGANISATIONS BY SERVICE

Army 6,400

Three military regions. In 2011, several regiments were disbanded and merged into other formations, including the new 24th and 34th *régiments interarmes*

FORCES BY ROLE
MANOEUVRE
  Mechanised
  1 cbd arms regt
  Light
  1 cbd arms regt
  6 inf regt

Air Manoeuvre
1 AB regt (1 CT coy)
COMBAT SUPPORT
1 arty bn (2 arty tp)
1 engr bn
EQUIPMENT BY TYPE
ARMOURED FIGHTING VEHICLES
RECCE 91+: 19 AML-60/AML-90; 8+ *Bastion Patsas*; 24 EE-9 *Cascavel*; 30 *Ferret*; 2 M20; 8 M8
APC 83
  APC (W) 22: 13 Panhard M3; 9 *Bastion* APC
  PPV 61: 6 *Gila*; 31 *Puma* M26-15; 24 Stark Motors *Storm*
  AUV 4 *Cobra*
ENGINEERING & MAINTENANCE VEHICLES
MW 3 *Shrek*-M
ANTI-TANK/ANTI-INFRASTRUCTURE
RCL 75mm Type-52 (M20); 84mm *Carl Gustav*
ARTILLERY 50+
TOWED 14: 105mm 8 M101; 122mm 6
MRL 9: 107mm ε4 Type-63; 122mm 5 APR-40
MOR 27+: 81mm Brandt; 82mm 15; 120mm 12
AIR DEFENCE
SAM • **Point-defence** 9K32 *Strela*-2 (SA-7 *Grail*)‡
GUNS • **TOWED** 42: 14.5mm 30 ZPU; 20mm 12 TCM-20

Air Force 600

FORCES BY ROLE
GROUND ATTACK/TRAINING
  1 sqn with SF-260WL *Warrior**; Embraer EMB-314 *Super Tucano**
TRANSPORT
  1 sqn with AT-802 *Air Tractor*; B-727 (VIP); Beech 200 *King Air*; CN235-220; PA-34 *Seneca*
ATTACK/TRANSPORT HELICOPTER
  1 sqn with AS350 *Ecureuil*; Mi-8 *Hip*; Mi-17 *Hip* H; Mi-35 *Hind*
EQUIPMENT BY TYPE
AIRCRAFT 5 combat capable
ISR 1 DA42M (reported)
TPT 9: **Light** 8: 1 AT-802 *Air Tractor*; 2 Beech 200 *King Air*; 1 CN235-220; 1 PA-34 *Seneca*; 3 *Tetras*; **PAX** 1 B-727 (VIP)
TRG 5: 3 EMB-314 *Super Tucano**; 2 SF-260WL *Warrior**
HELICOPTERS
ATK 2 Mi-35 *Hind*
MRH 3: 2 Mi-17 *Hip* H; 1 AW139
TPT 4: **Medium** 1 Mi-8 *Hip*; **Light** 3: 1 AS350 *Ecureuil*; 2 UH-1H *Huey*

Gendarmerie 4,200

FORCES BY ROLE
SPECIAL FORCES
  1 spec ops gp (USIGN)
EQUIPMENT BY TYPE
ARMOURED FIGHTING VEHICLES
  APC • **APC (W)** some *Bastion* APC

Paramilitary 250

People's Militia (R) 45,000 reservists (trained)

Security Company 250

DEPLOYMENT

CENTRAL AFRICAN REPUBLIC: UN • MINUSCA 39
DEMOCRATIC REPUBLIC OF THE CONGO: UN • MONUSCO 5
MALI: UN • MINUSMA 1,704; 2 inf bn
SUDAN: UN • UNISFA 1

FOREIGN FORCES

France Operation Barkhane 250; 1 SF gp; 1 Tiger; 2 AS532UL; 2 H225M; 3 Gazelle

Burundi BDI

Burundi Franc fr		2018	2019	2020
GDP	fr	6.18tr	6.76tr	
	US$	3.44bn	3.57bn	
per capita	US$	307	310	
Growth	%	0.1	0.4	
Inflation	%	1.2	7.3	
Def bdgt	fr	117bn	117bn	119bn
	US$	64.8m	61.7m	
US$1=fr		1799.57	1891.13	

Real-terms defence budget trend (US$m, constant 2015)

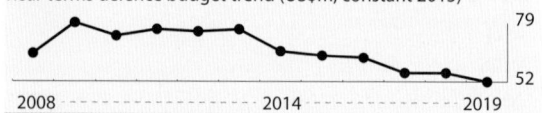

Population   12,232,823
Ethnic groups: Hutu 85%; Tutsi 14%

Age	0–14	15–19	20–24	25–29	30–64	65 plus
Male	22.9%	5.2%	4.4%	3.7%	12.5%	1.2%
Female	22.6%	5.2%	4.4%	3.7%	12.8%	1.6%

Capabilities

The country's political crisis has tested the cohesion of the armed forces. Military-training activity with international partners largely stalled in 2015 as a result. However, Burundi signed a cooperation agreement with Russia in 2018 on counter-terrorism and joint training. The experience accumulated during UN operations, where troops have gained valuable military experience, partly compensates for the otherwise low level of training. The armed forces have a limited capability to deploy externally, though they maintain a deployment to the AMISOM mission in Somalia. Peacekeeping missions help to fund the armed forces, though financial challenges otherwise limit their effectiveness. Apart from limited maintenance facilities, the country has no domestic defence-industrial capability.

ACTIVE 30,050 (Army 30,000 Navy 50) **Paramilitary 21,000**

DDR efforts continue, while activities directed at professionalising the security forces have taken place, some sponsored by United Nations agencies

ORGANISATIONS BY SERVICE

Army 30,000
FORCES BY ROLE
MANOEUVRE
  Mechanised
  2 lt armd bn (sqn)
  Light
  7 inf bn
  Some indep inf coy
COMBAT SUPPORT
  1 arty bn
  1 engr bn
AIR DEFENCE
  1 AD bn
EQUIPMENT BY TYPE
ARMOURED FIGHTING VEHICLES
  RECCE 55: 6 AML-60; 12 AML-90; 30 BRDM-2; 7 S52 *Shorland*
  APC 94
    APC (W) 60: 20 BTR-40; 10 BTR-80; 9 Panhard M3; 15 Type-92; 6 *Walid*
    PPV 34: 12 *Casspir*; 12 RG-31 *Nyala*; 10 RG-33L
  AUV 15 *Cougar* 4×4
ARTILLERY 120
  TOWED 122mm 18 D-30
  MRL 122mm 12 BM-21 *Grad*
  MOR 90: 82mm 15 M-43; 120mm ε75
ANTI-TANK/ANTI-INFRASTRUCTURE
  MSL • MANPATS *Milan* (reported)
  RCL 75mm Type-52 (M20)
AIR DEFENCE
  SAM • Point-defence 9K32 *Strela-2* (SA-7 *Grail*)‡
  GUNS • TOWED 150+: 14.5mm 15 ZPU-4; 135+ 23mm ZU-23/37mm Type-55 (M-1939)

Air Wing 200
EQUIPMENT BY TYPE
AIRCRAFT 1 combat capable
  TPT 2: Light 2 Cessna 150L†
  TRG 1 SF-260W *Warrior**
HELICOPTERS
  ATK 2 Mi-24 *Hind*
  MRH 2 SA342L *Gazelle*
  TPT • Medium (2 Mi-8 *Hip* non-op)

Reserves
FORCES BY ROLE
MANOEUVRE
  Light
  10 inf bn (reported)

Navy 50
EQUIPMENT BY TYPE
PATROL AND COASTAL COMBATANTS • PB 4
AMPHIBIOUS • LCT 2

Paramilitary ε1,000

General Administration of State Security ε1,000

DEPLOYMENT
CENTRAL AFRICAN REPUBLIC: UN • MINUSCA 767; 1 inf bn
MALI: UN • MINUSMA 2
SOMALIA: AU • AMISOM 5,073; 6 inf bn
SUDAN: UN • UNISFA 4

Cameroon CMR

CFA Franc BEAC fr		2018	2019	2020
GDP	fr	21.5tr	22.6tr	
	US$	38.7bn	38.6bn	
per capita	US$	1,556	1,515	
Growth	%	4.1	4.0	
Inflation	%	1.1	2.1	
Def bdgt	fr	239bn	247bn	
	US$	430m	424m	
US$1=fr		555.19	584.07	

Real-terms defence budget trend (US$m, constant 2015)

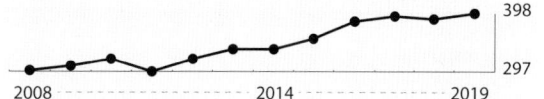

Population 26,299,112

Age	0–14	15–19	20–24	25–29	30–64	65 plus
Male	21.1%	5.3%	4.5%	4.0%	13.7%	1.5%
Female	20.8%	5.3%	4.5%	3.9%	13.6%	1.7%

Capabilities

Internal security has long been a focus for Cameroon's armed forces, and the threats from Boko Haram and separatist movements have generated a significant response, particularly in the north bordering Nigeria. The government continues to boost the size of the armed forces. In 2018, a fifth military region was created in response to security challenges in the west stemming from separatist activity. Cameroon is part of the Multi-National Joint Task Force engaged on operations against Boko Haram. There are long-standing military ties with France, including for support and training. A military assistance agreement was signed with China in 2018. The two countries have cooperated over the new floating dock at Kribi, which it is hoped will improve operational readiness. The African Union's continental logistic base was inaugurated at Douala in early 2018. The armed forces are considered disciplined and well organised, though in 2018 there were allegations of abuses which led the US in February 2019 to halt some military assistance. Deployments continue to UN peacekeeping operations, and additional troops were in 2019 deployed to the CAR. Nonetheless there is only limited organic capability for power projection and deployment capabilities are limited to neighbouring countries without external support. Much of the equipment inventory is ageing, but infantry fighting vehicles and protected patrol vehicles have been acquired from China and South Africa and gifted by the

US. The armed forces are improving their ISR capability with fixed-wing aircraft and small UAVs. Additional patrol vessels, both new and second-hand, have in recent years improved maritime capability. Cameroon has no defence-industrial capacity, bar maintenance facilities.

ACTIVE 25,400 (Army 23,500 Navy 1,500 Air 400)
Paramilitary 9,000

ORGANISATIONS BY SERVICE

Army 23,500
5 Mil Regions
FORCES BY ROLE
MANOEUVRE
  Light
  1 rapid reaction bde (1 armd recce bn, 1 AB bn, 1 amph bn)
  1 mot inf bde (4 mot inf bn, 1 spt bn)
  5 mot inf bde (3 mot inf bn, 1 spt bn)
  6 rapid reaction bn
  4 inf bn
  Air Manoeuvre
  1 cdo/AB bn
  Other
  1 (Presidential Guard) gd bn
COMBAT SUPPORT
  1 arty regt (5 arty bty)
  5 engr regt
AIR DEFENCE
  1 AD regt (6 AD bty)
EQUIPMENT BY TYPE
ARMOURED FIGHTING VEHICLES
  ASLT 18: 6 AMX-10RC; ε12 PTL-02 mod (*Cara* 105)
  RECCE 64: 31 AML-90; 15 *Ferret*; 8 M8; 5 RAM Mk3; 5 VBL
  IFV 42: 8 LAV-150 *Commando* with 20mm gun; 14 LAV-150 *Commando* with 90mm gun; 12 *Ratel*-20 (Engr); ε8 Type-07P
  APC 64
    APC (T) 12 M3 half-track
    APC (W) 36: 15 *Bastion* APC (reported); 21 LAV-150 *Commando*
    PPV 16 Gaia *Thunder*
    AUV 6+: 6 *Cougar* 4×4; *Panthera* T6
ENGINEERING & MAINTENANCE VEHICLES
  ARV WZ-551 ARV
ANTI-TANK/ANTI-INFRASTRUCTURE
  MSL
    SP 24 TOW (on Jeeps)
    MANPATS *Milan*
  RCL 53: **75mm** 13 Type-52 (M20); **106mm** 40 M40A2
ARTILLERY 106+
  SP 155mm 18 ATMOS 2000
  TOWED 52: **105mm** 20 M101; **130mm** 24: 12 M-1982 (reported); 12 Type-59 (M-46); **155mm** 8 M-71
  MRL 122mm 20 BM-21 *Grad*
  MOR 16+: **81mm** (some SP); **120mm** 16 Brandt
AIR DEFENCE • GUNS
  SP 20mm RBY-1 with TCM-20
  TOWED 54: **14.5mm** 18 Type-58 (ZPU-2); **35mm** 18 GDF-002; **37mm** 18 Type-63

Navy ε1,500
HQ located at Douala
EQUIPMENT BY TYPE
PATROL AND COASTAL COMBATANTS 16
  PCC 3: 1 *Dipikar* (ex-FRA *Flamant*); 2 *Le Ntem* (PRC *Limam El Hidrami*)
  PB 11: 2 Aresa 2400; 2 Aresa 3200; 2 Rodman 101; 4 Rodman 46; 1 *Quartier Maître Alfred Motto*
  PBR 2 *Swift*-38
AMPHIBIOUS • LANDING CRAFT 4
  LCM 2: 1 Aresa 2300; 1 *Le Moungo*
  LCU 2 *Yunnan*

Fusiliers Marin
FORCES BY ROLE
MANOEUVRE
  Amphibious
  3 mne bn

Air Force 300–400
FORCES BY ROLE
FIGHTER/GROUND ATTACK
  1 sqn with MB-326K; *Alpha Jet**†
TRANSPORT
  1 sqn with C-130H/H-30 *Hercules*; IAI-201 *Arava*; PA-23 *Aztec*
  1 VIP unit with AS332 *Super Puma*; AS365 *Dauphin* 2; Bell 206B *Jet Ranger*; Gulfstream III
TRAINING
  1 unit with *Tetras*
ATTACK HELICOPTER
  1 sqn with SA342 *Gazelle* (with HOT); Mi-24 *Hind*
TRANSPORT HELICOPTER
  1 sqn with Bell 206L-3; Bell 412; SA319 *Alouette* III
EQUIPMENT BY TYPE
AIRCRAFT 9 combat capable
  ATK 5: 1 MB-326K *Impala* I; 4 MB-326K *Impala* II
  ISR 2 Cessna 208B *Grand Caravan*
  TPT 18: **Medium** 3: 2 C-130H *Hercules*; 1 C-130H-30 *Hercules*; **Light** 14: 1 CN235; 1 IAI-201 *Arava* (in store); 2 J.300 *Joker*; 1 MA60; 2 PA-23 *Aztec*; 7 *Tetras*; **PAX** 1 Gulfstream III
  TRG 4 *Alpha Jet**†
HELICOPTERS
  ATK 2 Mi-24 *Hind*
  MRH 12: 1 AS365 *Dauphin* 2; 1 Bell 412 *Twin Huey*; 2 Mi-17 *Hip* H; 2 SA319 *Alouette* III; 4 SA342 *Gazelle* (with HOT); 2 Z-9
  TPT 7: **Medium** 4: 2 AS332 *Super Puma*; 2 SA330J *Puma*; **Light** 3: 2 Bell 206B *Jet Ranger*; 1 Bell 206L3 *Long Ranger*
AIR-LAUNCHED MISSILES
  ASM HOT

Fusiliers de l'Air
FORCES BY ROLE
MANOEUVRE
  Other
  1 sy bn

Paramilitary 9,000

Gendarmerie 9,000
FORCES BY ROLE
MANOEUVRE
  Reconnaissance
  3 (regional spt) paramilitary gp

DEPLOYMENT

CENTRAL AFRICAN REPUBLIC: UN • MINUSCA 758; 1 inf bn

DEMOCRATIC REPUBLIC OF THE CONGO: UN • MONUSCO 3

MALI: UN • MINUSMA 2

FOREIGN FORCES
United States 300; MQ-1C *Gray Eagle*

Cape Verde CPV

Cape Verde Escudo E		2018	2019	2020
GDP	E	185bn	197bn	
	US$	1.98bn	2.01bn	
per capita	US$	3,579	3,599	
Growth	%	5.1	5.0	
Inflation	%	1.3	1.2	
Def bdgt	E	1.04bn	1.05bn	
	US$	11.1m	10.8m	
US$1=E		93.31	97.74	

Real-terms defence budget trend (US$m, constant 2015)

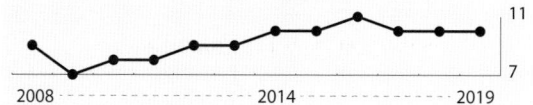

Population	575,839					
Age	0–14	15–19	20–24	25–29	30–64	65 plus
Male	14.2%	4.8%	4.8%	4.7%	18.0%	2.0%
Female	14.1%	4.8%	4.8%	4.8%	19.7%	3.3%

Capabilities

In its legislative programme for 2016–21, the government outlined the priorities for Cape Verde's defence forces, including territorial defence, maritime security, and EEZ and airspace protection. Although the armed forces are small and presently have limited capability, the government has suggested reorganising around marines, engineering and paramilitary national-guard units. The government is interested in greater regional and international defence engagement; international partners provide some maritime-security training support. The armed forces take part in multinational regional exercises and cooperative activities; the 2018 Africa Endeavour senior leaders' symposium was held in Cape Verde. Equipment capabilities remain limited, given the country's geographical position, though the US donated patrol boats in 2018 to bolster its maritime-security capacities. There is no defence industry, beyond limited maintenance facilities.

ACTIVE 1,200 (Army 1,000 Coast Guard 100 Air 100)
Conscript liability Selective conscription (14 months)

ORGANISATIONS BY SERVICE

Army 1,000
FORCES BY ROLE
MANOEUVRE
  Light
  2 inf bn (gp)
COMBAT SUPPORT
  1 engr bn
EQUIPMENT BY TYPE
ARMOURED FIGHTING VEHICLES
  RECCE 10 BRDM-2
ARTILLERY • MOR 18: 82mm 12; 120mm 6 M-1943
AIR DEFENCE
  SAM • Point-defence 9K32 *Strela* (SA-7 *Grail*)‡
  GUNS • TOWED 30: 14.5mm 18 ZPU-1; 23mm 12 ZU-23

Coast Guard ε100
EQUIPMENT BY TYPE
PATROL AND COASTAL COMBATANTS 5
  PCC 2: 1 *Guardião*; 1 *Kondor I*
  PB 2: 1 *Espadarte*; 1 *Tainha* (PRC-27m)
  PBF 1 *Archangel*
AIRCRAFT • TPT • Light 1 Do-228

Air Force up to 100
FORCES BY ROLE
MARITIME PATROL
  1 sqn with An-26 *Curl*
EQUIPMENT BY TYPE
AIRCRAFT • TPT • Light 3 An-26 *Curl*†

Central African Republic CAR

CFA Franc BEAC fr		2018	2019	2020
GDP	fr	1.27tr	1.36tr	
	US$	2.28bn	2.32bn	
per capita	US$	449	448	
Growth	%	3.8	4.5	
Inflation	%	1.6	3.0	
Def bdgt	fr	17.2bn	19.0bn	
	US$	31.0m	32.5m	
US$1=fr		555.25	584.06	

Real-terms defence budget trend (US$m, constant 2015)

Population	5,867,019					
Age	0–14	15–19	20–24	25–29	30–64	65 plus
Male	19.9%	5.3%	4.7%	4.2%	14.2%	1.3%
Female	19.7%	5.3%	4.6%	4.2%	14.4%	2.1%

Capabilities

Effective military and security organisations remain largely absent in the wake of the violence in 2013 and the armed forces are insufficient for the country's internal-security challenges. Instability continues to affect the country and neighbouring states. The May 2015 Bangui Forum on National Reconciliation agreed principles governing DDR. Under the National Recovery and Peacebuilding Plan 2017–21, attempts to improve security focus on DDR and SSR, among others. A National Superior Council on Security will be set up to oversee the overall reform process. However, the UN's MINUSCA mission remains the principal security provider in the country. The CAR benefits from defence partnerships with France and Russia. Moscow has been deepening its military ties in the country and has donated small arms. Russia has sent teams of military instructors to the country. Reports persist that personnel from a Russian private military company are in-country on training tasks. Apart from some equipment deliveries, the country remains under a UN arms embargo, though the terms of this were adjusted in late 2019. The armed forces receive training from UN forces and the European Training Mission. Poor infrastructure and logistics capacity are other factors limiting the ability of the CAR armed forces to provide security across the country. There is no independent capability to deploy troops externally, while the lack of financial resources and defence-industrial capacity makes equipment maintenance problematic.

ACTIVE 9,150 (Army 9,000 Air 150) **Paramilitary 1,000**

Conscript liability Selective conscription 2 years; reserve obligation thereafter, term n.k.

ORGANISATIONS BY SERVICE

Army ε9,000
FORCES BY ROLE
MANOEUVRE
  Light
    1 inf bn
  Amphibious
    1 amph coy
EQUIPMENT BY TYPE
ARMOURED FIGHTING VEHICLES
  MBT 3 T-55†
  RECCE 9: 8 *Ferret*†; 1 BRDM-2
  IFV 18 *Ratel*
  APC • APC (W) 14+: 4 BTR-152†; 10+ VAB†
ARTILLERY • MOR 12+: **81mm**†; **120mm** 12 M-1943†
ANTI-TANK/ANTI-INFRASTRUCTURE
  RCL 106mm 14 M40†
PATROL AND COASTAL COMBATANTS • PBR 9†

Air Force 150
EQUIPMENT BY TYPE
AIRCRAFT • TPT 7: **Medium** 1 C-130A *Hercules*; **Light** 6: 3 BN-2 *Islander*; 1 Cessna 172RJ *Skyhawk*; 2 J.300 *Joker*
HELICOPTERS • TPT • Light 1 AS350 *Ecureuil*

FOREIGN FORCES

MINUSCA unless stated
Argentina 2
Bangladesh 1,028; 1 cdo coy; 1 inf bn; 1 med coy
Benin 8
Bhutan 4
Bolivia 5
Bosnia-Herzegovina EUTM RCA 2
Brazil 10
Burkina Faso 39
Burundi 767; 1 inf bn
Cambodia 212; 1 engr coy
Cameroon 758; 1 inf bn
Colombia 2
Congo 15
Côte d'Ivoire 3
Czech Republic 3
Egypt 993; 1 inf bn; 1 tpt coy
France 9 • EUTM RCA 40 • Army 160
Gabon 408; 1 inf bn(-)
Gambia 6
Georgia EUTM RCA 35
Ghana 16
Guatemala 4
Hungary 1
Indonesia 214; 1 engr coy
Italy EUTM RCA 3
Jordan 10
Kenya 15
Lithuania EUTM RCA 2
Mauritania 565; 1 inf bn
Mexico 1
Moldova 5
Morocco 764; 1 inf bn
Nepal 737; 1 inf bn
Niger 10
Nigeria 2
Pakistan 1,253; 1 inf bn; 2 engr coy; 1 hel sqn
Paraguay 3
Peru 220; 1 engr coy
Philippines 2
Poland EUTM RCA 1
Portugal 188; 1 AB coy • EUTM RCA 45
Romania EUTM RCA 13
Russia 4
Rwanda 1,388; 2 inf bn; 1 fd hospital
Senegal 113; 1 atk hel sqn
Serbia 77; 1 med coy • EUTM RCA 7
Sierra Leone 3
Spain EUTM RCA 5
Sri Lanka 116; 1 avn unit
Sweden EUTM RCA 9
Tanzania 445; 1 inf bn(-)
United States 8
Uruguay 3
Vietnam 5
Zambia 932; 1 inf bn

Chad CHA

CFA Franc BEAC fr		2018	2019	2020
GDP	fr	6.14tr	6.44tr	
	US$	11.1bn	11.0bn	
per capita	US$	885	861	
Growth	%	2.4	2.3	
Inflation	%	4.0	3.0	
Def bdgt	fr	101bn	120bn	
	US$	182m	206m	
US$1=fr		555.21	584.06	

Real-terms defence budget trend (US$m, constant 2015)

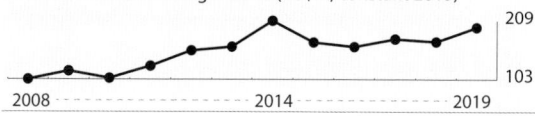

Population 16,349,891

Age	0–14	15–19	20–24	25–29	30–64	65 plus
Male	24.2%	5.6%	4.2%	3.6%	10.9%	1.0%
Female	23.6%	5.5%	4.2%	3.6%	12.2%	1.4%

Capabilities

Chad's principal security concerns relate to instability in West Africa and the Sahel and counter-insurgency operations against Boko Haram in the Lake Chad Basin area. Although the armed forces are combat experienced, some observers judge a requirement for improved strategy and doctrine and command and control. The country is a key contributor to the G5 Sahel and is an important component of the Multi-National Joint Task Force fighting Boko Haram. There is close defence cooperation with France and Operation Barkhane is headquartered in N'Djamena. Chadian military skills are widely recognised by partners, though training levels are not uniform across the force. A lack of logistical capacity has hindered routine rotations for deployed forces. The country's ISR capability has been improved with the arrival of aircraft from the US, following improvements in ground-attack and medium-airlift capability. Barring maintenance facilities, there is no domestic defence-industrial capacity.

ACTIVE 33,250 (Army 27,500 Air 350 State Security Service 5,400) **Paramilitary 4,500**
Conscript liability Conscription authorised

ORGANISATIONS BY SERVICE

Army ε27,500
7 Mil Regions
FORCES BY ROLE
MANOEUVRE
  Armoured
    1 armd bn
  Light
    7 inf bn
COMBAT SUPPORT
  1 arty bn
  1 engr bn
  1 sigs bn
COMBAT SERVICE SUPPORT
  1 log gp

EQUIPMENT BY TYPE
ARMOURED FIGHTING VEHICLES
  MBT 60 T-55
  ASLT 30 PTL-02 Assaulter
  RECCE 309+: 132 AML-60/AML-90; 22 Bastion Patsas; ε100 BRDM-2; 20 EE-9 Cascavel; 4 ERC-90F Sagaie; 31+ RAM Mk3
  IFV 131: 80 BMP-1; 42 BMP-1U; 9 LAV-150 Commando with 90mm gun
  APC • APC (W) 99: 24 BTR-80; 12 BTR-3E; ε20 BTR-60; ε10 Black Scorpion; 25 VAB-VTT; 8 WZ-523
ARTILLERY 26+
  SP 122mm 10 2S1 Gvozdika
  TOWED 105mm 5 M2
  MRL 11+: **107mm** some Type-63; **122mm** 11: 6 BM-21 Grad; 5 Type-81
  MOR 81mm some; **120mm** AM-50
ANTI-TANK/ANTI-INFRASTRUCTURE
  MSL • MANPATS Eryx; Milan
  RCL 106mm M40A1
AIR DEFENCE
  SAM
    Short-range 2K12 Kub (SA-6 Gainful)
    Point-defence 9K310 Igla-1 (SA-16 Gimlet)
  GUNS • TOWED 14.5mm ZPU-1/ZPU-2/ZPU-4; **23mm** ZU-23

Air Force 350
FORCES BY ROLE
GROUND ATTACK
  1 unit with PC-7; PC-9*; SF-260WL Warrior*; Su-25 Frogfoot
TRANSPORT
  1 sqn with An-26 Curl; C-130H-30 Hercules; Mi-17 Hip H; Mi-171
  1 (Presidential) Flt with B-737BBJ; Beech 1900; DC-9-87; Gulfstream II
ATTACK HELICOPTER
  1 sqn with AS550C Fennec; Mi-24V Hind; SA316 Alouette III
EQUIPMENT BY TYPE
AIRCRAFT 14 combat capable
  FTR 1 MiG-29S Fulcrum C†
  ATK 10: 8 Su-25 Frogfoot; 2 Su-25UB Frogfoot B
  ISR 2 Cessna 208B Grand Caravan
  TPT 10: **Medium** 3: 2 C-27J Spartan; 1 C-130H-30 Hercules; **Light** 4: 3 An-26 Curl; 1 Beech 1900; **PAX** 3: 1 B-737BBJ; 1 DC-9-87; 1 Gulfstream II
  TRG 4: 2 PC 7 (only 1*); 1 PC 9 Turbo Trainer*; 1 SF-260WL Warrior*
HELICOPTERS
  ATK 5 Mi-24V Hind
  MRH 8: 3 AS550C Fennec; 3 Mi-17 Hip H; 2 SA316
  TPT • Medium 2 Mi-171

State Security Service General Direction (DGSSIE) 5,400

Paramilitary 4,500 active

Gendarmerie 4,500

DEPLOYMENT

MALI: UN • MINUSMA 1,423; 1 SF coy; 2 inf bn

FOREIGN FORCES

Benin MNJTF 150
France *Operation Barkhane* 1,500; 1 mech inf BG; 1 FGA det with 4 *Mirage* 2000D; 1 tpt det with 1 C-130H; 2 CN235M; 1 UAV det with 1 MQ-9A *Reaper*

Congo, Republic of COG

CFA Franc BEAC fr		2018	2019	2020
GDP	fr	6.48tr	6.76tr	
	US$	11.7bn	11.6bn	
per capita	US$	2,618	2,534	
Growth	%	1.6	4.0	
Inflation	%	1.2	1.5	
Def bdgt	fr	162bn	176bn	179bn
	US$	293m	301m	
US$1=fr		555.20	584.09	

Real-terms defence budget trend (US$m, constant 2015)

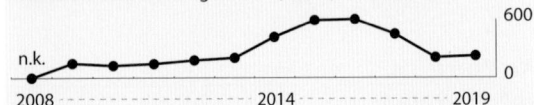

Population 5,174,669

Age	0–14	15–19	20–24	25–29	30–64	65 plus
Male	21.1%	4.6%	4.0%	3.6%	15.6%	1.4%
Female	20.7%	4.5%	4.0%	3.7%	15.3%	1.7%

Capabilities

Congo's small armed forces have low levels of training and limited overall capability, and utilise ageing equipment. They have struggled to recover from the brief but devastating civil war in the late 1990s. France provides advisory assistance and capacity-building support in military administration and military and police capability. A military-cooperation agreement was signed with Russia in 2019. The troop contingent deployed to the CAR was withdrawn by the government in mid-2017, amid allegations of indiscipline. Deployment capability is limited to neighbouring countries without external support. The air force is effectively grounded for lack of spares and serviceable equipment. The navy is largely a riverine force, despite the need for maritime security on the country's small coastline. A modernisation effort is under way and several MRAPs have been bought. Maintenance facilities are limited and the country has no domestic defence-industrial capability.

ACTIVE 10,000 (Army 8,000 Navy 800 Air 1,200)
Paramilitary 2,000

ORGANISATIONS BY SERVICE

Army 8,000
FORCES BY ROLE
MANOEUVRE
  Armoured
    2 armd bn
  Light
    2 inf bn (gp) each with (1 lt tk tp, 1 arty bty)
    1 inf bn
  Air Manoeuvre
    1 cdo/AB bn
COMBAT SUPPORT
  1 arty gp (with MRL)
  1 engr bn
EQUIPMENT BY TYPE†
ARMOURED FIGHTING VEHICLES
  MBT 40: 25 T-54/T-55; 15 Type-59; (some T-34 in store)
  LT TK 13: 3 PT-76; 10 Type-62
  RECCE 25 BRDM-1/BRDM-2
  APC 133+
    APC (W) 78+: 28 AT-105 *Saxon*; 20 BTR-152; 30 BTR-60; Panhard M3
    PPV 55: 18 *Mamba*; 37 *Marauder*
  ARTILLERY 56+
    SP 122mm 3 2S1 *Gvozdika*
    TOWED 15+: **122mm** 10 D-30; **130mm** 5 M-46; **152mm** D-20
    MRL 10+: **122mm** 10 BM-21 *Grad*; **140mm** BM-14; **140mm** BM-16
    MOR 28+: **82mm**; **120mm** 28 M-43
ANTI-TANK/ANTI-INFRASTRUCTURE
  RCL 57mm M18
  GUNS 15: **57mm** 5 ZIS-2 (M-1943); **100mm** 10 M-1944
AIR DEFENCE • GUNS
  SP 23mm ZSU-23-4 *Shilka*
  TOWED 14.5mm ZPU-2/ZPU-4; **37mm** 28 M-1939; **57mm** S-60; **100mm** KS-19

Navy ε800
EQUIPMENT BY TYPE
PATROL AND COASTAL COMBATANTS 8
  PCC 4 *5 Février 1979*
  PBR 4

Air Force 1,200
FORCES BY ROLE
FIGHTER/GROUND ATTACK
  1 sqn with *Mirage* F-1AZ
TRANSPORT
  1 sqn with An-24 *Coke*; An-32 *Cline*; CN235M-100
ATTACK/TRANSPORT HELICOPTER
  1 sqn with Mi-8 *Hip*; Mi-35P *Hind*
EQUIPMENT BY TYPE† 2 combat capable
AIRCRAFT
  FGA 2 *Mirage* F-1AZ
  TPT • Light 4: 1 An-24 *Coke*; 2 An-32 *Cline*; 1 CN235M-100
HELICOPTERS†
  ATK (2 Mi-35P *Hind* in store)
  TPT • Medium (3 Mi-8 *Hip* in store)
AIR-LAUNCHED MISSILES • AAM • IR R-3 (AA-2 *Atoll*)‡

Paramilitary 2,000 active

Gendarmerie 2,000

FORCES BY ROLE
MANOEUVRE
  Other
    20 paramilitary coy

Presidential Guard some
FORCES BY ROLE
MANOEUVRE
  Other
    1 paramilitary bn

DEPLOYMENT

CENTRAL AFRICAN REPUBLIC: UN • MINUSCA 15

Côte d'Ivoire CIV

CFA Franc BCEAO fr		2018	2019	2020
GDP	fr	23.9tr	26.0tr	
	US$	43.0bn	44.4bn	
per capita	US$	1,681	1,691	
Growth	%	7.4	7.5	
Inflation	%	0.4	1.0	
Def bdgt [a]	fr	517bn	525bn	
	US$	931m	898m	
US$1=fr		555.19	584.06	

[a] Defence, order and security expenses

Real-terms defence budget trend (US$m, constant 2015)

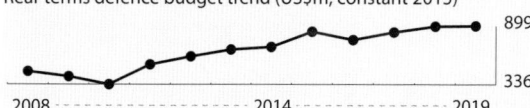

Population 26,867,857

Age	0–14	15–19	20–24	25–29	30–64	65 plus
Male	19.6%	5.4%	4.7%	4.2%	15.1%	1.3%
Female	19.5%	5.4%	4.7%	4.2%	14.6%	1.6%

Capabilities

The armed forces are still regenerating, and SSR initiatives remain in place. A 2015 law on the defence forces' organisation detailed defence zones and military regions as well as the creation of a general staff and general inspectorate for the armed forces. It stressed the armed forces' role in assisting Ivorian society. In 2016 a Military Programme Law for 2016–20 was adopted, planning for an incremental reduction in military strength up to 2020, to enable an increase in the gendarmerie. The end of the UN arms embargo, in 2016, allowed Côte d'Ivoire to start recapitalising its air force, notably with the delivery of Mi-24 helicopters from Russia. As part of the SSR process, an aviation academy was established in Abidjan, with limited rotary-wing-pilot and maintenance training. The ministry has moved to regulate promotion and salary structures to aid professionalisation, and is also looking to improve military infrastructure. There is close defence cooperation with France, which has a significant training mission in the country. Except for limited maintenance facilities, there is no domestic defence-industrial capability.

ACTIVE 27,400 (Army 23,000 Navy 1,000 Air 1,400 Special Forces 2,000) **Paramilitary** n.k.
Moves to restructure and reform the armed forces continue

ORGANISATIONS BY SERVICE

Army ε23,000
FORCES BY ROLE
MANOEUVRE
  Armoured
    1 armd bn
  Light
    7 inf bn
  Air Manoeuvre
    1 cdo/AB bn
COMBAT SUPPORT
    1 arty bn
    1 engr bn
COMBAT SERVICE SUPPORT
    1 log bn
AIR DEFENCE
    1 AD bn
EQUIPMENT BY TYPE
ARMOURED FIGHTING VEHICLES
  MBT 10 T-55†
  RECCE 18: 13 BRDM-2; 5 *Cayman* BRDM
  IFV 10 BMP-1/BMP-2†
  APC 41
    APC (W) 40: 9 *Bastion* APC; 6 BTR-80; 12 Panhard M3; 13 VAB
  PPV 1 *Snake*
ENGINEERING & MAINTENANCE VEHICLES
  VLB MTU
ANTI-TANK/ANTI-INFRASTRUCTURE
  MSL • MANPATS 9K111-1 *Konkurs* (AT-5 *Spandrel*) (reported); 9K135 *Kornet* (AT-14 *Spriggan*) (reported)
  RCL 106mm ε12 M40A1
  ARTILLERY 36+
    TOWED 4+: **105mm** 4 M-1950; **122mm** (reported)
    MRL 122mm 6 BM-21
    MOR 26+: **81mm**; **82mm** 10 M-37; **120mm** 16 AM-50
  AIRCRAFT • TPT • Medium 1 An-12 *Cub*†
AIR DEFENCE
  SAM • Point-defence 9K32 *Strela*-2 (SA-7 *Grail*)‡ (reported)
  GUNS 21+
    SP 20mm 6 M3 VDAA
    TOWED 15+: **20mm** 10; **23mm** ZU-23-2; **40mm** 5 L/60

Navy ε1,000
EQUIPMENT BY TYPE
PATROL AND COASTAL COMBATANTS 4
  PB 4: 3 *L'Emergence*; 1 *Atchan* 2
AMPHIBIOUS • LANDING CRAFT • LCM 1 *Aby*

Air Force ε1,400
EQUIPMENT BY TYPE†
AIRCRAFT
  TPT 3: **Light** 2: 1 An-26 *Curl*; 1 C295W; **PAX** 1 B-727

HELICOPTERS
ATK 4 Mi-24 *Hind*
TPT • Medium 2 SA330L *Puma* (IAR-330L)

Special Forces ε2,000
FORCES BY ROLE
SPECIAL FORCES
1 spec ops bde

Paramilitary n.k.

Republican Guard n.k.

Gendarmerie n.k.
EQUIPMENT BY TYPE†
ARMOURED FIGHTING VEHICLES
RECCE 3 *Cayman* BRDM
APC • APC (W) some VAB
PATROL AND COASTAL COMBATANTS • PB 1 *Bian*

DEPLOYMENT
CENTRAL AFRICAN REPUBLIC: UN • MINUSCA 3
MALI: UN • MINUSMA 161; 1 sy coy
MALI: UN • MINURSO 2

FOREIGN FORCES
France 950; 1 (Marine) inf bn; 2 SA330 *Puma*; 1 *Gazelle*

Democratic Republic of the Congo DRC

Congolese Franc fr		2018	2019	2020
GDP	fr	76.5tr	82.7tr	
	US$	47.1bn	49.0bn	
per capita	US$	496	501	
Growth	%	5.8	4.3	
Inflation	%	29.3	5.5	
Def bdgt	fr	483bn	555bn	
	US$	297m	329m	
US$1=fr		1624.14	1687.53	

Real-terms defence budget trend (US$m, constant 2015)

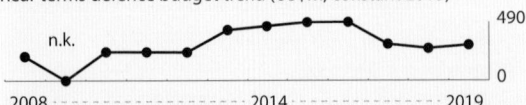

Population 87,265,519

Age	0–14	15–19	20–24	25–29	30–64	65 plus
Male	20.5%	5.7%	5.1%	4.2%	13.2%	1.2%
Female	20.2%	5.6%	5.0%	4.2%	13.4%	1.6%

Capabilities
On paper, the DRC has the largest armed forces in Central Africa. However, given the country's size and the poor levels of training, morale and equipment, they are unable to provide security throughout the country. Kinshasa has pursued several military-modernisation programmes, though plans to re-examine doctrine and organisation have seen little positive impact. When conflict finally abates in the east, significant attention to wide-ranging DDR and SSR will be required, to continue the work intermittently undertaken over the past decade. The mandate of the UN's MONUSCO mission was renewed in March 2019 and the UN's Force Intervention Brigade (FIB) remains active in the east. Training will have improved for units operating with the FIB, and there is also foreign assistance in training and capacity-building. The armed forces, which have incorporated a number of non-state armed groups, struggle with conflicting loyalties. There remains significant scope to improve training, recruitment and retention. Deployment capability is limited and the lack of logistics vehicles significantly reduces transport capacity even within the country. The lack of sufficient tactical airlift and helicopters is a brake on military effectiveness and there is some reliance on MONUSCO capabilities, which are also insufficient given the geographical scale of the country. Much equipment is in poor repair and while new equipment has been acquired, the absence of any defence sector apart from limited maintenance will also hinder military capability.

ACTIVE ε134,250 (Central Staffs ε14,000, Army 103,000 Republican Guard 8,000 Navy 6,700 Air 2,550)

ORGANISATIONS BY SERVICE

Army (Forces du Terre) ε103,000
The DRC has 11 Military Regions. In 2011, all brigades in North and South Kivu provinces were consolidated into 27 new regiments, the latest in a sequence of reorganisations designed to integrate non-state armed groups. The actual combat effectiveness of many formations is doubtful

FORCES BY ROLE
MANOEUVRE
Light
6 (integrated) inf bde
ε3 inf bde (non-integrated)
27+ inf regt
COMBAT SUPPORT
1 arty regt
1 MP bn

EQUIPMENT BY TYPE†
(includes Republican Guard eqpt)
ARMOURED FIGHTING VEHICLES
MBT 174: 12–17 Type-59†; 32 T-55; 25 T-64BV-1; 100 T-72AV
LT TK 40: 10 PT-76; 30 Type-62†
RECCE up to 52: up to 17 AML-60; 14 AML-90; 19 EE-9 *Cascavel*; 2 RAM-V-2
IFV 20 BMP-1
APC 104+:
APC (T) 9: 3 BTR-50; 6 MT-LB
APC (W) 95+: 30–70 BTR-60PB; 58 Panhard M3†; 7 TH 390 *Fahd*
ANTI-TANK/ANTI-INFRASTRUCTURE
RCL 57mm M18; 73mm SPG-9; 75mm M20; 106mm M40A1
GUNS 85mm 10 Type-56 (D-44)
ARTILLERY 726+
SP 16: 122mm 6 2S1 *Gvozdika*; 152mm 10 2S3 *Akatsiya*
TOWED 125: 122mm 77 M-30 (M-1938)/D-30/Type-60; 130mm 42 Type-59 (M-46)/Type-59-I; 152mm 6 D-20 (reported)

MRL 57+: **107mm** 12 Type-63; **122mm** 24+: 24 BM-21 *Grad*; some RM-70; **128mm** 6 M-51; **130mm** 3 Type-82; **132mm** 12
MOR 528+: **81mm** 100; **82mm** 400; **107mm** M30; **120mm** 28: 10 Brandt; 18 other
AIR DEFENCE
SAM • **Point-defence** 9K32 *Strela*-2 (SA-7 *Grail*)‡
GUNS • TOWED 64: **14.5mm** 12 ZPU-4; **37mm** 52 M-1939

Republican Guard 8,000
FORCES BY ROLE
MANOEUVRE
  Armoured
  1 armd regt
  Light
  3 gd bde
COMBAT SUPPORT
  1 arty regt

Navy 6,700 (incl infantry and marines)
EQUIPMENT BY TYPE
PATROL AND COASTAL COMBATANTS 1
  PB 1 *Shanghai* II (Type-062)

Air Force 2,550
EQUIPMENT BY TYPE
AIRCRAFT 4 combat capable
  ATK 4 Su-25 *Frogfoot*
  TPT 4: **Medium** 1 C-130H *Hercules*; **Light** 1 An-26 *Curl*; PAX 2 B-727
HELICOPTERS
  ATK 7: 4 Mi-24 *Hind*; 3 Mi-24V *Hind*
  TPT • **Medium** 3: 1 AS332L *Super Puma*; 2 Mi-8 *Hip*

Paramilitary

National Police Force
Incl Rapid Intervention Police (National and Provincial)

People's Defence Force

FOREIGN FORCES
All part of MONUSCO unless otherwise specified
Algeria 1
Bangladesh 1,672; 1 inf bn; 1 engr coy; 1 avn coy; 1 hel coy
Belgium 2
Benin 8
Bhutan 1
Bolivia 4
Bosnia-Herzegovina 3
Brazil 21
Burkina Faso 5
Cameroon 3
Canada (*Operation Crocodile*) 8
China, People's Republic of 232; 1 engr coy; 1 fd hospital
Czech Republic 2
Egypt 18
France 3
Ghana 482; 1 inf bn
Guatemala 154; 1 SF coy
India 3,036; 3 inf bn; 1 med coy
Indonesia 1,038; 1 inf bn; 3 engr coy
Ireland 3
Jordan 8
Kenya 10
Malawi 864; 1 inf bn
Malaysia 6
Mali 4
Mongolia 2
Morocco 1,373; 2 inf bn; 1 fd hospital
Nepal 895; 1 inf bn; 1 engr coy
Niger 3
Nigeria 9
Pakistan 2,722; 4 inf bn; 1 hel sqn
Paraguay 6
Peru 3
Poland 2
Romania 10
Russia 8
Senegal 7
Serbia 1
South Africa (*Operation Mistral*) 1,131; 1 inf bn; 1 atk hel sqn; 1 hel sqn
Sweden 2
Switzerland 1
Tanzania 961; 1 SF coy; 1 inf bn
Tunisia 9
Ukraine 259; 1 atk hel sqn
United Kingdom 3
United States 3
Uruguay 941; 1 inf bn; 1 log coy; 1 hel sqn
Zambia 8

Djibouti DJB

Djiboutian Franc fr		2018	2019	2020
GDP	fr	520bn	563bn	
	US$	2.92bn	3.17bn	
per capita	US$	2,787	2,936	
Growth	%	5.5	6.0	
Inflation	%	0.1	2.2	
Def exp	fr	n.k	n.k	
	US$	n.k	n.k	
FMA (US)	US$	5m	0m	5m
US$1=fr		177.74	177.74	

Population	902,892

Ethnic groups: Somali 60%; Afar 35%

Age	0–14	15–19	20–24	25–29	30–64	65 plus
Male	15.2%	4.9%	4.8%	4.5%	14.3%	1.7%
Female	15.1%	5.2%	5.7%	5.9%	20.3%	2.2%

Capabilities

Djibouti's strategic location and relative stability have led a number of foreign states to base forces there. The armed forces' main responsibility is internal and border security, and counter-insurgency operations. Ties with Eritrea were normalised in late 2018, ten years after border skirmishes between the two states. The 2017 defence white paper highlighted a requirement to modernise key capabilities, but funds remain limited. Djibouti maintains close defence cooperation with France; Djibouti hosts its largest foreign military base. The US also operates its Combined Joint Task Force–Horn of Africa from Djibouti. Japan has based forces there for regional counter-piracy missions and the EU and NATO have at various times maintained a presence to support their operations. China's first overseas military base, including dock facilities, was officially opened in Djibouti in 2017. France and the US provide training assistance. EU NAVFOR Somalia has delivered maritime-security training to the navy and coastguard. Djibouti participates in a number of regional multinational exercises and contributed to the AMISOM mission in Somalia, but has limited capacity to independently deploy beyond its territory. Army equipment consists predominantly of older French and Soviet-era equipment and while recent acquisitions have focused on mobility and artillery, armoured-warfare capability remains limited. There are some maintenance facilities, but no defence manufacturing sector.

ACTIVE 10,450 (Army 8,000 Navy 200 Air 250 Gendarmerie 2,000) **Paramilitary 2,650**

ORGANISATIONS BY SERVICE

Army ε8,000

FORCES BY ROLE
4 military districts (Tadjourah, Dikhil, Ali-Sabieh and Obock)
MANOEUVRE
  Mechanised
    1 armd regt (1 recce sqn, 3 armd sqn, 1 (anti-smuggling) sy coy)
  Light
    4 inf regt (3-4 inf coy, 1 spt coy)
    1 rapid reaction regt (4 inf coy, 1 spt coy)
  Other
    1 (Republican Guard) gd regt (1 sy sqn, 1 (close protection) sy sqn, 1 cbt spt sqn (1 recce pl, 1 armd pl, 1 arty pl), 1 spt sqn)
COMBAT SUPPORT
  1 arty regt
  1 demining coy
  1 sigs regt
  1 CIS sect
COMBAT SERVICE SUPPORT
  1 log regt
  1 maint coy
EQUIPMENT BY TYPE
ARMOURED FIGHTING VEHICLES
  ASLT 1 PTL-02 *Assaulter*
  RECCE 38: 4 AML-60†; 17 AML-90; 2 BRDM-2; 15 VBL
  IFV 28: 8 BTR-80A; 16-20 *Ratel*
  APC 43
    APC (W) 30+: 12 BTR-60†; 4+ AT-105 *Saxon*; 14 *Puma*
    PPV 13: 3 *Casspir*; 10 RG-33L
  AUV 22: 10 *Cougar* 4×4 (one with 90mm gun); 2 CS/VN3B; 10 PKSV

ANTI-TANK/ANTI-INFRASTRUCTURE
  RCL 106mm 16 M40A1
ARTILLERY 76
  SP 155mm 10 M109L
  TOWED 122mm 9 D-30
  MRL 12: **107mm** 2 PKSV AUV with PH-63; **122mm** 10: 6 (6-tube Toyota Land Cruiser 70 series); 2 (30-tube Iveco 110-16); 2 (30-tube)
  MOR 45: **81mm** 25; **120mm** 20 Brandt
AIR DEFENCE • GUNS 15+
  SP 20mm 5 M693
  TOWED 10: **23mm** 5 ZU-23-2; **40mm** 5 L/70

Navy ε200

EQUIPMENT BY TYPE
PATROL AND COASTAL COMBATANTS 12
  PBF 2 Battalion-17
  PB 10: 1 *Plascoa*†; 2 Sea Ark 1739; 1 *Swari*†; 6 others
AMPHIBIOUS • LCT 1 EDIC 700

Air Force 250

EQUIPMENT BY TYPE
AIRCRAFT
  TPT • Light 6: 1 Cessna U206G *Stationair*; 1 Cessna 208 *Caravan*; 2 Y-12E; 1 L-410UVP *Turbolet*; 1 MA60
HELICOPTERS
  ATK (2 Mi-35 *Hind* in store)
  MRH 5: 1 Mi-17 *Hip* H; 4 AS365 *Dauphin*
  TPT 3: **Medium** 1 Mi-8T *Hip*; **Light** 2 AS355F *Ecureuil* II

Gendarmerie 2,000+

Ministry of Defence
FORCES BY ROLE
MANOEUVRE
  Other
    1 paramilitary bn
EQUIPMENT BY TYPE
  AFV • AUV 2 CS/VN3B
  PATROL AND COASTAL COMBATANTS • 1 PB

Paramilitary ε2,650

National Police Force ε2,500
Ministry of Interior

Coast Guard 150
EQUIPMENT BY TYPE
PATROL AND COASTAL COMBATANTS 11
  PB 11: 2 *Khor Angar*; 9 other

DEPLOYMENT

SOMALIA: AU • AMISOM 1,872; 2 inf bn
WESTERN SAHARA: UN • MINURSO 1

FOREIGN FORCES

China 240: 1 mne coy(-); 1 med unit; 2 ZTL-11; 8 ZBL-08; 1 LPD; 1 ESD

France 1,450: 1 SF unit; 1 (Marine) combined arms regt (2 recce sqn, 2 inf coy, 1 arty bty, 1 engr coy); 1 hel det with 2 SA330 *Puma*; 2 SA342 *Gazelle*; 1 LCM; 1 air sqn with 4 *Mirage* 2000-5; 1 CN235M; 2 SA330 *Puma*

Germany *Operation Atalanta* 1 AP-3C *Orion*
Italy 88
Japan 170; 2 P-3C *Orion*
Spain *Operation Atalanta* 1 P-3M *Orion*
United States US Africa Command: 4,700; 1 tpt sqn with C-130H/J-30 *Hercules*; 1 spec ops sqn with MC-130H; PC-12 (U-28A); 1 CSAR sqn with HH-60G *Pave Hawk*; 1 CISR sqn with MQ-9A *Reaper*; 1 naval air base

Equatorial Guinea EQG

CFA Franc BEAC fr		2018	2019	2020
GDP	fr	7.63tr	7.06tr	
	US$	13.7bn	12.1bn	
per capita	US$	10,453	8,927	
Growth	%	-5.7	-4.6	
Inflation	%	1.3	0.9	
Def exp	fr	n.k	n.k	
	US$	n.k	n.k	
US$1=fr		555.21	581.36	
Population	816,736			

Age	0–14	15–19	20–24	25–29	30–64	65 plus
Male	19.9%	5.4%	4.7%	4.0%	14.3%	1.6%
Female	19.2%	5.2%	4.5%	3.9%	14.9%	2.3%

Capabilities

The army dominates the armed forces, with internal security the principal task. Equatorial Guinea has been trying for several years to modernise its armed forces. France maintains a military-cooperation detachment in Malabo, advising on defence-institutional development issues and providing capacity-building support through the naval-focused regional school at Tica, as well as some training activities with French forces based in Gabon and in the region as part of the Corymbe mission. There is only limited capability for power projection and deployments are limited to neighbouring countries without external support. There has been significant naval investment in recent years, including in both equipment and onshore infrastructure at Bata and Malabo, although naval capabilities remain limited. Maritime-security concerns in the Gulf of Guinea have resulted in an increased emphasis on bolstering the country's maritime-patrol capacity. The air force has received several new transport aircraft. Equatorial Guinea has only limited maintenance capacity and no traditional defence industry.

ACTIVE 1,450 (Army 1,100 Navy 250 Air 100)

ORGANISATIONS BY SERVICE

Army 1,100
FORCES BY ROLE
MANOEUVRE
  Light
    3 inf bn(-)
EQUIPMENT BY TYPE
ARMOURED FIGHTING VEHICLES
  MBT 3 T-55
  RECCE 6 BRDM-2
  IFV 20 BMP-1
  APC 35
    APC (W) 10 BTR-152
  PPV 25 *Reva* (reported)

Navy ε250
EQUIPMENT BY TYPE
PATROL AND COASTAL COMBATANTS 11
  CORVETTES 2
    FSG 1 *Bata* with 2 *Katran*-M RWS with *Barrier* SSM, 2 AK630 CIWS, 1 76mm gun
    FS 1 *Wele Nzas* with 2 MS-227 *Ogon'* 122mm MRL, 2 AK630 CIWS, 2 76mm guns
  PCC 2 OPV 62
  PBF 2 *Shaldag* II
  PB 5: 1 *Daphne*; 2 *Estuario de Muni*; 2 *Zhuk*
LOGISTICS AND SUPPORT
  AKRH 1 *Capitan David Eyama Angue Osa* with 1 76mm gun

Air Force 100
EQUIPMENT BY TYPE
AIRCRAFT 4 combat capable
  ATK 4: 2 Su-25 *Frogfoot*; 2 Su-25UB *Frogfoot* B
  TPT 4: **Light** 3: 1 An-32B *Cline*; 2 An-72 *Coaler*; **PAX** 1 *Falcon* 900 (VIP)
  TRG 2 L-39C *Albatros*
HELICOPTERS
  ATK 5 Mi-24P/V *Hind*
  MRH 1 Mi-17 *Hip* H
  TPT 4: **Heavy** 1 Mi-26 *Halo*; **Medium** 1 Ka-29 *Helix*; **Light** 2 Enstrom 480

Paramilitary

Guardia Civil
FORCES BY ROLE
MANOEUVRE
  Other
    2 paramilitary coy

Coast Guard n.k.

Eritrea ERI

Eritrean Nakfa ERN		2018	2019	2020
GDP	ERN	30.3bn	31.8bn	
	US$	2.01bn	2.11bn	
per capita	US$	332	343	
Growth	%	12.2	3.1	
Inflation	%	-14.4	-27.6	
Def exp	ERN	n.k	n.k	
	US$	n.k	n.k	
USD1=ERN		15.07	15.08	
Population	6,024,854			

Ethnic groups: Tigrinya 50%; Tigre and Kunama 40%; Afar; Saho 3%

Age	0–14	15–19	20–24	25–29	30–64	65 plus
Male	19.6%	5.5%	4.6%	3.7%	14.3%	1.6%
Female	19.3%	5.5%	4.7%	3.8%	15.1%	2.3%

Capabilities

Eritrea has maintained large armed forces largely because of historical military tensions and conflict with Ethiopia, though tensions have reduced after a September 2018 peace agreement. A UN arms embargo was lifted in November 2018. The armed forces have focused on border defence but now may have an opportunity to restructure and recapitalise. Maritime insecurity, including piracy, remains a challenge. The UAE has established a military presence in Eritrea and port and airfield facilities at Assab have been used to support Gulf states participating in the Yemen campaign. Eritrea maintains a large army due to mandatory conscription. For some the term of service is indefinite, and significant numbers of conscripts have chosen to leave the country or otherwise evade service. These factors likely affect overall military cohesion and effectiveness. A UN report alleged that the UAE had trained some air-force and navy personnel. A private European company has allegedly provided pilot training. Eritrea has not demonstrated any capacity to deploy beyond its borders. The armed forces' inventory primarily comprises outdated Soviet-era systems and modernisation was restricted by the UN arms embargo. The embargo will have resulted in serviceability issues, notwithstanding allegations of external support, with some aircraft likely cannibalised for parts and others illicitly overhauled abroad. The navy remains capable of only limited coastal-patrol and interception operations. There are limited maintenance facilities, but no defence manufacturing sector.

ACTIVE 201,750 (Army 200,000 Navy 1,400 Air 350)
Conscript liability 18 months (4 months mil trg) between ages 18 and 40

RESERVE 120,000 (Army ε120,000)

ORGANISATIONS BY SERVICE

Army ε200,000
Heavily cadreised
FORCES BY ROLE
COMMAND
  4 corps HQ
MANOEUVRE
  Mechanised
  1 mech bde
  Light
  19 inf div
  1 cdo div

Reserve ε120,000
FORCES BY ROLE
MANOEUVRE
  Light
  1 inf div

EQUIPMENT BY TYPE
ARMOURED FIGHTING VEHICLES
  MBT 270 T-54/T-55
  RECCE 40 BRDM-1/BRDM-2
  IFV 15 BMP-1
  APC 35
    APC (T) 10 MT-LB†
    APC (W) 25 BTR-152/BTR-60
ENGINEERING & MAINTENANCE VEHICLES
  ARV T-54/T-55 reported
  VLB MTU reported

ANTI-TANK/ANTI-INFRASTRUCTURE
  MSL • MANPATS 9K11 *Malyutka* (AT-3 *Sagger*); 9K111-1 *Konkurs* (AT-5 *Spandrel*) **GUNS 85mm** D-44
ARTILLERY 258
  SP 45: **122mm** 32 2S1 *Gvozdika*; **152mm** 13 2S5 *Giatsint-S*
  TOWED 19+: **122mm** D-30; **130mm** 19 M-46
  MRL 44: **122mm** 35 BM-21 *Grad*; **220mm** 9 9P140 *Uragan*
  MOR 150+: **82mm** 50+; **120mm/160mm** 100+
AIR DEFENCE
  SAM • Point-defence 9K32 *Strela-2* (SA-7 *Grail*)‡
  GUNS 70+
    SP 23mm ZSU-23-4 *Shilka*
    TOWED 23mm ZU-23

Navy 1,400
EQUIPMENT BY TYPE
PATROL AND COASTAL COMBATANTS 12
  PBF 9: 5 Battalion-17; 4 *Super Dvora*
  PB 3 Swiftships
AMPHIBIOUS 3
  LS • LST 2: 1 *Chamo*† (Ministry of Transport); 1 *Ashdod*†
  LC • LCU 1 T-4† (in harbour service)

Air Force ε350
FORCES BY ROLE
FIGHTER/GROUND ATTACK
  1 sqn with MiG-29/MiG-29SE/MiG-29UB *Fulcrum*
  1 sqn with Su-27/Su-27UBK *Flanker*
TRANSPORT
  1 sqn with Y-12(II)
TRAINING
  1 sqn with L-90 *Redigo*
  1 sqn with MB-339CE*
TRANSPORT HELICOPTER
  1 sqn with Bell 412EP *Twin Huey*
  1 sqn with Mi-17 *Hip H*

EQUIPMENT BY TYPE
AIRCRAFT 14 combat capable
  FTR 8: 4 MiG-29 *Fulcrum*; 2 MiG-29UB *Fulcrum*; 1 Su-27 *Flanker*; 1 Su-27UBK *Flanker*
  FGA 2 MiG-29SE *Fulcrum*
  TPT • Light 5: 1 Beech 200 *King Air*; 4 Y-12(II)
  TRG 16+: 8 L-90 *Redigo*; 4 MB-339CE*; 4+ Z-143/Z-242
HELICOPTERS
  MRH 8: 4 Bell 412EP *Twin Huey* (AB-412EP); 4 Mi-17 *Hip H*
AIR-LAUNCHED MISSILES
  AAM • IR R-60 (AA-8 *Aphid*); R-73 (AA-11A *Archer*); **IR/SARH** R-27 (AA-10 *Alamo*)

FOREIGN FORCES

United Arab Emirates *Operation Restoring Hope* 1,000; 1 armd BG; *Leclerc*; BMP-3; G-6; *Agrab* Mk2; 2 FSGHM; 2 LST; 6 LCT; 4 *Archangel*; 3 AH-64D *Apache*; 2 CH-47F *Chinook*; 4 UH-60M *Black Hawk*; *Wing Loong* I (GJ-1) UAV; 4 MIM-104F *Patriot* PAC-3

Ethiopia ETH

Ethiopian Birr EB		2018	2019	2020
GDP	EB	2.20tr	2.64tr	
	US$	80.3bn	91.2bn	
per capita	US$	853	953	
Growth	%	7.7	7.4	
Inflation	%	13.8	14.6	
Def bdgt	EB	12.0bn	15.0bn	
	US$	437m	518m	
US$1=EB		27.43	28.94	

Real-terms defence budget trend (US$m, constant 2015)

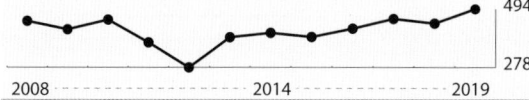

Population   111,483,031

Ethnic groups: Oromo 34.4%; Amhara 27%; Somali 6.2%; Tigray 6.1%; Sidama 4%; Guragie 2.5%; other or unspecified 19.2%

Age	0–14	15–19	20–24	25–29	30–64	65 plus
Male	21.5%	5.5%	4.6%	3.8%	12.9%	1.3%
Female	21.4%	5.5%	4.7%	3.9%	13.2%	1.7%

Capabilities

Ethiopia maintains one of the region's largest and most capable armed forces. It is a significant contributor to regional peacekeeping. The September 2018 peace agreement with Eritrea may affect future military dispositions. Countering al-Shabaab remains an ongoing military commitment. Ethiopia maintains long-standing defence and security ties with the US. Addis Ababa continues to provide military support to the Federal Government of Somalia. The armed forces are experienced by regional standards, following a history of combat operations. Training and experience are also gained through international peacekeeping deployments. Ethiopia has demonstrated the capability to make significant contributions to the UN missions in Darfur and South Sudan. It is the largest overall troop contributor to UN peacekeeping missions and provides significant numbers to the AMISOM mission in Somalia. The country's inventory comprises mostly Soviet-era equipment. Despite engaging in a ten-year (2005–15) modernisation plan, most platform recapitalisation is based on surplus stock from Hungary, Ukraine and the US. Ethiopia has developed a modest local defence-industrial base, primarily centred on small arms, with some licence production of light armoured vehicles. There is adequate maintenance capability but only a limited capacity to support advanced platforms.

ACTIVE 138,000 (Army 135,000 Air 3,000)

ORGANISATIONS BY SERVICE

Army 135,000
4 Mil Regional Commands (Northern, Western, Central and Eastern) each acting as corps HQ
FORCES BY ROLE
MANOEUVRE
  Light
  1 (Agazi Cdo) SF comd
  1 (Northern) corps (1 mech div, 4 inf div)
  1 (Western) corps (1 mech div, 3 inf div)
  1 (Central) corps (1 mech div, 5 inf div)
  1 (Eastern) corps (1 mech div, 5 inf div)
EQUIPMENT BY TYPE
ARMOURED FIGHTING VEHICLES
  MBT 461+: 246+ T-54/T-55/T-62; 215 T-72B
  RECCE ε100 BRDM-1/BRDM-2
  IFV ε20 BMP-1
  APC 300+
    APC (T) some Type-89
    APC (W) 300+: ε300 BTR-60/BTR-152; some Type-92
  AUV some Ze'ev
ENGINEERING & MAINTENANCE VEHICLES
  ARV T-54/T-55 reported; 4 BTS-5B
  VLB MTU reported
  MW Bozena
ANTI-TANK/ANTI-INFRASTRUCTURE
  MSL • MANPATS 9K11 Malyutka (AT-3 Sagger); 9K111 Fagot (AT-4 Spigot); 9K135 Kornet-E (AT-14 Spriggan)
  RCL 82mm B-10; **107mm** B-11
  GUNS 85mm D-44
ARTILLERY 524+
  SP 10+: **122mm** 2S1 Gvozdika; **152mm** 10 2S19 Msta-S
  TOWED 464+: **122mm** 464 D-30/M-30 (M-1938); **130mm** M-46; **155mm** AH2
  MRL 122mm ε50 BM-21 Grad
  MOR 81mm M1/M29; **82mm** M-1937; **120mm** M-1944
AIR DEFENCE
  SAM
    Medium-range S-75 Dvina (SA-2 Guideline)
    Short-range S-125 Pechora (SA-3 Goa)
    Point-defence 9K32 Strela-2 (SA-7 Grail)‡; 96K6 Pantsir-S1 (SA-22 Greyhound)
  GUNS
    SP 23mm ZSU-23-4 Shilka
    TOWED 23mm ZU-23; **37mm** M-1939; **57mm** S-60

Air Force 3,000
FORCES BY ROLE
FIGHTER/GROUND ATTACK
  1 sqn with MiG-23ML Flogger G/MiG-23UB Flogger C
  1 sqn with Su-27/Su-27UB Flanker
TRANSPORT
  1 sqn with An-12 Cub; An-26 Curl; An-32 Cline; C-130B Hercules; DHC-6 Twin Otter; L-100-30; Yak-40 Codling (VIP)
TRAINING
  1 sqn with L-39 Albatros
  1 sqn with SF-260
ATTACK/TRANSPORT HELICOPTER
  2 sqn with Mi-24/Mi-35 Hind; Mi-8 Hip; Mi-17 Hip H; SA316 Alouette III
EQUIPMENT BY TYPE
AIRCRAFT 21 combat capable
  FTR 11: 8 Su-27 Flanker; 3 Su-27UB Flanker
  FGA 8 MiG-23ML/UB Flogger G/C
  ATK 2+ Su-25/UB Frogfoot†

TPT 15: **Medium** 9: 3 An-12 *Cub*; 2 C-130B *Hercules*; 2 C-130E *Hercules*; 2 L-100-30; **Light** 6: 1 An-26 *Curl*; 1 An-32 *Cline*; 3 DHC-6 *Twin Otter*; 1 Yak-40 *Codling* (VIP)
TRG 16: 12 L-39 *Albatros*; 4 SF-260

HELICOPTERS
ATK 18: 15 Mi-24 *Hind*; 3 Mi-35 *Hind*
MRH 19: 1 AW139; 6 SA316 *Alouette* III; 12 Mi-8 *Hip*/Mi-17 *Hip* H

AIR-LAUNCHED MISSILES
AAM • **IR** R-3 (AA-2 *Atoll*)‡; R-60 (AA-8 *Aphid*); R-73 (AA-11A *Archer*); **IR/SARH** R-23/R-24 (AA-7 *Apex*); R-27 (AA-10 *Alamo*)

DEPLOYMENT

MALI: UN • MINUSMA 1

SOMALIA: AU • AMISOM 4,323; 6 inf bn

SOUTH SUDAN: UN • UNMISS 2,138; 3 inf bn

SUDAN: UN • UNAMID 826; 1 inf bn; UN • UNISFA 4,131; 3 inf bn; 2 arty coy; 1 engr coy; 1 sigs coy; 8 fd hospital; 1 hel sqn

Gabon GAB

CFA Franc BEAC fr		2018	2019	2020
GDP	fr	9.37tr	9.81tr	
	US$	16.9bn	16.9bn	
per capita	US$	8,220	8,112	
Growth	%	0.8	2.9	
Inflation	%	4.8	3.0	
Def bdgt [a]	fr	145bn	156bn	
	US$	261m	269m	
US$1=fr		555.19	581.36	

[a] Includes funds allocated to Republican Guard

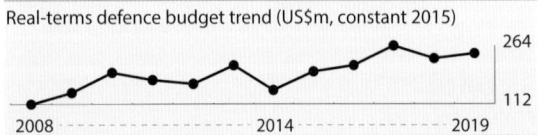
Real-terms defence budget trend (US$m, constant 2015)

Population	2,175,885				
Age	0–14	15–19	20–24	25–29	30–64	65 plus
Male	18.9%	5.9%	5.6%	5.0%	14.7%	2.0%
Female	18.1%	5.5%	5.0%	4.1%	13.3%	2.0%

Capabilities

Oil revenues have allowed the government to support small but regionally capable armed forces, while the country has benefited from the long-term presence of French troops acting as a security guarantor. There is regular training with French forces and with the regionally deployed French navy, as well as with the US and other international partners. Gabonese forces have taken part in the US Navy-led *Obangame Express* exercise. A new maritime-operations centre was built by the US in 2019. Military medicine is well regarded. The armed forces retain sufficient airlift to ensure mobility within the country and even a limited capability to project power by sea and air. Apart from limited maintenance facilities, there is no domestic defence-industrial capacity.

ACTIVE 4,700 (Army 3,200 Navy 500 Air 1,000)
Paramilitary 2,000

ORGANISATIONS BY SERVICE

Army 3,200

Republican Guard under direct presidential control

FORCES BY ROLE
MANOEUVRE
  Light
  1 (Republican Guard) gd gp (bn)
    (1 armd/recce coy, 3 inf coy, 1 arty bty, 1 ADA bty)
  8 inf coy
  Air Manoeuvre
  1 cdo/AB coy
COMBAT SUPPORT
  1 engr coy

EQUIPMENT BY TYPE
ARMOURED FIGHTING VEHICLES
  RECCE 77: 24 AML-60/AML-90; 12 EE-3 *Jararaca*; 14 EE-9 *Cascavel*; 6 ERC-90F4 *Sagaie*; 7 RAM V-2; 14 VBL
  IFV 17: 12 EE-11 *Urutu* (with 20mm gun); 5+ VN-1
  APC 74
    APC (W) 35: 9 LAV-150 *Commando*; 5 *Bastion* APC; 3 WZ-523; 5 VAB; 12 VXB-170; 1 *Pandur*
    PPV 39: 5 *Aravis*; 34 Ashok Leyland MPV
ANTI-TANK/ANTI-INFRASTRUCTURE
  MSL • **MANPATS** *Milan*
  RCL 106mm M40A1
ARTILLERY 67
  TOWED 105mm 4 M101
  MRL 24: **107mm** 16 PH-63; **140mm** 8 *Teruel*
  MOR 39: **81mm** 35; **120mm** 4 Brandt
AIR DEFENCE • **GUNS** 41
  SP 20mm 4 ERC-20
  TOWED 37+: **14.5mm** ZPU-4; **23mm** 24 ZU-23-2; **37mm** 10 M-1939; **40mm** 3 L/70

Navy ε500

HQ located at Port Gentil
EQUIPMENT BY TYPE
PATROL AND COASTAL COMBATANTS 9
  PB 9: 4 *Port Gentil* (FRA VCSM); 4 Rodman 66; 1 *Patra*†
AMPHIBIOUS LANDING CRAFT • **LCM** 1 Mk 9 (ex-UK)

Air Force 1,000

FORCES BY ROLE
FIGHTER/GROUND ATTACK
  1 sqn with *Mirage* F-1AZ
TRANSPORT
  1 (Republican Guard) sqn with AS332 *Super Puma*; ATR-42F; *Falcon* 900; Gulfstream IV-SP/G650ER
  1 sqn with C-130H *Hercules*; CN-235M-100
ATTACK/TRANSPORT HELICOPTER
  1 sqn with Bell 412 *Twin Huey* (AB-412); SA330C/H *Puma*; SA342M *Gazelle*

EQUIPMENT BY TYPE
AIRCRAFT 8 combat capable
  FGA 6 *Mirage* F-1AZ
  ATK 2 MB-326 *Impala* I

MP (1 EMB-111* in store)
TPT 6: **Medium** 1 C-130H *Hercules*; (1 L-100-30 in store); **Light** 2: 1 ATR-42F; 1 CN-235M-100; **PAX** 3: 1 *Falcon* 900; 1 Gulfstream IV-SP; 1 Gulfstream G650ER
TRG (4 CM-170 *Magister* in store)
HELICOPTERS
MRH 2: 1 Bell 412 *Twin Huey* (AB-412); 1 SA342M *Gazelle*; (2 SA342L *Gazelle* in store)
TPT 7: **Medium** 4: 1 AS332 *Super Puma*; 3 SA330C/H *Puma*; **Light** 3: 2 H120 *Colibri*; 1 H135
AIR-LAUNCHED MISSILES • AAM • IR U-*Darter* (reported)

Paramilitary 2,000

Gendarmerie 2,000
FORCES BY ROLE
MANOEUVRE
  Armoured
    2 armd sqn
  Other
    3 paramilitary bde
    11 paramilitary coy
  Aviation
    1 unit with AS350 *Ecureuil*; AS355 *Ecureuil* II
EQUIPMENT BY TYPE
HELICOPTERS • TPT • **Light** 4: 2 AS350 *Ecureuil*; 2 AS355 *Ecureuil* II

DEPLOYMENT

CENTRAL AFRICAN REPUBLIC: UN • MINUSCA 408; 1 inf bn(-)

FOREIGN FORCES

France 450; 1 AB bn
Spain *Operation Barkhane* 45: 1 C295M

Gambia GAM

Gambian Dalasi D		2018	2019	2020
GDP	D	70.6bn	89.2bn	
	US$	1.6bn	1.8bn	
per capita	US$	713	755	
Growth	%	6.5	6.5	
Inflation	%	6.5	6.9	
Def bdgt	D	n.k	n.k	
	US$	n.k	n.k	
US$1=D			48.38	50.30

Population	2,133,640					
Age	0–14	15–19	20–24	25–29	30–64	65 plus
Male	18.3%	5.2%	4.8%	4.4%	15.0%	1.7%
Female	18.2%	5.3%	4.9%	4.6%	15.7%	2.0%

Capabilities

Reform of Gambia's security structure, and the armed forces, has been a key objective of the SSR process that was implemented following political instability in 2016–17. The launch of a National Security Policy in mid-2019 is a key part of this process. Gambia's small forces have traditionally focused on maritime security and countering human trafficking. The armed forces were also, it was said in 2019, looking to diversify roles, potentially into the agricultural sector, with private-sector partners. The SSR process is supported by the AU, EU, ECOWAS, France and the US. France and the US also provide some military assistance and there was in 2019 the first exercise in over a decade with UK forces. There is also cooperation with neighbouring states and with the AU, which maintains a technical-support mission to assist in the SSR process, including on defence reform, military reorganisation and the rule of law. The ECOMIG mission remains in place, with its mandate extended until early 2020. The armed forces participate in some multinational exercises and have deployed in support of UN missions in Africa. The equipment inventory is limited, with serviceability in doubt for some types. Gambia has no significant defence-industrial capabilities.

ACTIVE 4,100 (Army 3,500 Navy 300 National Guard 300)

ORGANISATIONS BY SERVICE

Gambian National Army 3,500
FORCES BY ROLE
MANOEUVRE
  Light
    4 inf bn
COMBAT SUPPORT
  1 engr sqn

Air Wing
EQUIPMENT BY TYPE
AIRCRAFT
  TPT 5: **Light** 2 AT-802A *Air Tractor*; **PAX** 3: 1 B-727; 1 CL-601; 1 Il-62M *Classic* (VIP)

Gambia Navy 300
EQUIPMENT BY TYPE
PATROL AND COASTAL COMBATANTS 8
  PBF 4: 2 Rodman 55; 2 *Fatimah* I
  PB 4: 1 *Bolong Kanta*†; 3 *Taipei* (ROC *Hai Ou*) (one additional damaged and in reserve)

Republican National Guard 300
FORCES BY ROLE
MANOEUVRE
  Other
    1 gd bn (forming)

DEPLOYMENT

CENTRAL AFRICAN REPUBLIC: UN • MINUSCA 6
MALI: UN • MINUSMA 3
SOUTH SUDAN: UN • UNMISS 1
SUDAN: UN • UNAMID 132; 1 inf coy

FOREIGN FORCES

Ghana ECOMIG 50
Nigeria ECOMIG 197
Senegal ECOMIG 250

Ghana GHA

Ghanaian New Cedi C		2018	2019	2020
GDP	C	301bn	348bn	
	US$	65.5bn	67.1bn	
per capita	US$	2,217	2,223	
Growth	%	6.3	7.5	
Inflation	%	9.8	9.3	
Def bdgt	C	991m	1.21bn	
	US$	216m	233m	
US$1=C		4.59	5.19	

Real-terms defence budget trend (US$m, constant 2015)

Population 28,715,894

Age	0–14	15–19	20–24	25–29	30–64	65 plus
Male	18.9%	4.9%	4.3%	3.8%	15.3%	2.0%
Female	18.7%	5.0%	4.4%	3.9%	16.3%	2.4%

Capabilities

Ghana's armed forces are among the most capable in the region, with a long-term development plan covering both the current and the next decade. The ability to control its maritime EEZ is of increasing importance due to piracy and resource exploitation, and this underpins the navy's expansion plans, including the opening of a new forward-operating base. Internal and maritime security are central military tasks, along with participation in peacekeeping missions. The US delivers training and support and there is also significant and long-standing defence engagement with the UK. Air-force training, close-air support and airlift capabilities have developed in recent years. There are plans to organise additional realistic training programmes and exercises, as well as to improve military infrastructure. The army is a regular contributor to UN peacekeeping operations and has pledged to maintain 1,000 personnel in readiness for such missions. Ghana has started to develop forward-operating bases, principally with the objective of protecting oil resources. Plans persist to develop air capabilities. There have been some defence acquisitions from China. Ghana has a limited defence-industrial base, including maintenance facilities and ammunition manufacturing as well as a more recent armoured-vehicle production capability. The Defence Industries Holding Company was formed in order to enable the armed forces to engage in civil–military collaborative projects.

ACTIVE 15,500 (Army 11,500 Navy 2,000 Air 2,000)

ORGANISATIONS BY SERVICE

Army 11,500
FORCES BY ROLE
COMMAND
  2 comd HQ
MANOEUVRE
  Reconnaissance
  1 armd recce regt (3 recce sqn)
  Light
  1 (rapid reaction) mot inf bn
  6 inf bn
  Air Manoeuvre
  2 AB coy
COMBAT SUPPORT
  1 arty regt (1 arty bty, 2 mor bty)
  1 fd engr regt (bn)
  1 sigs regt
  1 sigs sqn
COMBAT SERVICE SUPPORT
  1 log gp
  1 tpt coy
  2 maint coy
  1 med coy
  1 trg bn
EQUIPMENT BY TYPE
ARMOURED FIGHTING VEHICLES
  RECCE 3 EE-9 *Cascavel*
  IFV 48: 24 *Ratel*-90; 15 *Ratel*-20; 4 *Piranha* 25mm; 5+ Type-05P 25mm
  APC 105
    APC (W) 55+: 46 *Piranha*; 9+ Type-05P
    PPV 50 Streit *Typhoon*
ARTILLERY 87+
  TOWED 122mm 6 D-30
  MRL 3+: 107mm Type-63; 122mm 3 Type-81
  MOR 78: 81mm 50; 120mm 28 *Tampella*
ENGINEERING & MAINTENANCE VEHICLES
  AEV 1 Type-05P AEV
  ARV *Piranha* reported
ANTI-TANK/ANTI-INFRASTRUCTURE
  RCL 84mm *Carl Gustav*
AIR DEFENCE
  SAM • Point-defence 9K32 *Strela*-2 (SA-7 *Grail*)‡
  GUNS • TOWED 8+: 14.5mm 4+: 4 ZPU-2; ZPU-4; 23mm 4 ZU-23-2

Navy 2,000
Naval HQ located at Accra; Western HQ located at Sekondi; Eastern HQ located at Tema
EQUIPMENT BY TYPE
PATROL AND COASTAL COMBATANTS 14
  PCO 2 *Anzone* (US)
  PCC 10: 2 *Achimota* (GER Lurssen 57m) with 1 76mm gun; 2 *Dzata* (GER Lurssen 45m); 2 *Yaa Asantewa* (ex-GER *Albatros*); 4 *Snake* (PRC 47m)
  PBF 1 *Stephen Otu* (ROK *Sea Dolphin*)
  PB 1 *David Hansen* (US)

Special Boat Squadron
FORCES BY ROLE
SPECIAL FORCES
  1 SF unit

Air Force 2,000
FORCES BY ROLE
GROUND ATTACK
  1 sqn with K-8 *Karakorum**; L-39ZO*; MB-339A*
ISR
  1 unit with DA-42

TRANSPORT
1 sqn with BN-2 *Defender*; C295; Cessna 172
TRANSPORT HELICOPTER
1 sqn with AW109A; Bell 412SP *Twin Huey*; Mi-17V-5 *Hip* H; SA319 *Alouette* III; Z-9EH

EQUIPMENT BY TYPE†
AIRCRAFT 8 combat capable
 ATK (3 MB-326K in store)
 TPT 10: **Light** 10: 1 BN-2 *Defender*; 3 C295; 3 Cessna 172; 3 DA42; (**PAX** 1 F-28 *Fellowship* (VIP) in store)
 TRG 8: 4 K-8 *Karakorum**; 2 L-39ZO*; 2 MB-339A*
HELICOPTERS
 MRH 10: 1 Bell 412SP *Twin Huey*; 3 Mi-17V-5 *Hip* H; 2 SA319 *Alouette* III; 4 Z-9EH
 TPT 6: **Medium** 4 Mi-171Sh; **Light** 2 AW109A

DEPLOYMENT

CENTRAL AFRICAN REPUBLIC: UN • MINUSCA 16
CYPRUS: UN • UNFICYP 1
DEMOCRATIC REPUBLIC OF THE CONGO: UN • MONUSCO 482; 1 inf bn
GAMBIA: ECOWAS • ECOMIG 50
LEBANON: UN • UNIFIL 870; 1 mech inf bn
MALI: UN • MINUSMA 156; 1 engr coy
SOMALIA: UN • UNSOS 1
SOUTH SUDAN: UN • UNMISS 876; 1 inf bn
SUDAN: UN • UNAMID 4; **UN** • UNISFA 9
SYRIA/ISRAEL: UN • UNDOF 12
WESTERN SAHARA: UN • MINURSO 14

Guinea GUI

Guinean Franc fr		2018	2019	2020
GDP	fr	109.0tr	125.6tr	
	US$	12.1bn	13.4bn	
per capita	US$	910	981	
Growth	%	5.8	5.9	
Inflation	%	9.8	8.9	
Def bdgt	fr	1.77tr	1.79tr	
	US$	197m	191m	
US$1=fr		9010.89	9394.72	

Real-terms defence budget trend (US$m, constant 2015)

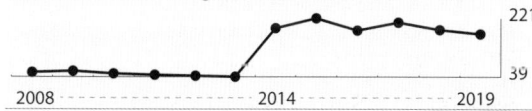

Population 12,186,420

Age	0–14	15–19	20–24	25–29	30–64	65 plus
Male	20.8%	5.3%	4.4%	3.7%	14.0%	1.7%
Female	20.5%	5.2%	4.4%	3.7%	14.1%	2.1%

Capabilities

Guinea's armed forces remain limited in size and capacity, although reforms since 2010 have brought them back under political control and begun a process of professionalisation. SSR, supported by the EU, is ongoing, with improvements seen in units dispatched to Mali. Internal-security challenges reportedly led to the composition of mixed army–gendarmerie units. Piracy in the Gulf of Guinea is a key concern, as is illegal trafficking and fishing. A military-programme law for the period 2015–20 has not been fully implemented due to funding issues. Defence cooperation with France and the US has led to financial and training assistance, including US and French support for the deployment to Mali and training, by France, for a newly created special-forces unit. Guinea participates in multilateral exercises, such as the US-led *Obangame Express*. Much of the country's military equipment is ageing and of Soviet-era vintage; serviceability will be questionable for some types. There is limited organic airlift and France is supporting the development of a light aviation observation capability. Guinea is also attempting to improve its logistics and military-health capacities. There are no significant defence-industrial capabilities.

ACTIVE 9,700 (Army 8,500 Navy 400 Air 800)
Paramilitary 2,600
Conscript liability 9–12 months (students, before graduation)

ORGANISATIONS BY SERVICE

Army 8,500
FORCES BY ROLE
MANOEUVRE
 Armoured
  1 armd bn
 Light
  1 SF bn
  5 inf bn
  1 ranger bn
  1 cdo bn
 Air Manoeuvre
  1 air mob bn
 Other
  1 (Presidential Guard) gd bn
COMBAT SUPPORT
 1 arty bn
 1 AD bn
 1 engr bn
EQUIPMENT BY TYPE
ARMOURED FIGHTING VEHICLES
 MBT 38: 30 T-34; 8 T-54
 LT TK 15 PT-76
 RECCE 27: 2 AML-90; 25 BRDM-1/BRDM-2
 IFV 2 BMP-1
 APC 59
  APC (T) 10 BTR-50
  APC (W) 30: 16 BTR-40; 8 BTR-60; 6 BTR-152
  PPV 19: 10 *Mamba*†; some *Puma* M26; 9 *Puma* M36
ENGINEERING & MAINTENANCE VEHICLES
 ARV T-54/T-55 reported
ANTI-TANK/ANTI-INFRASTRUCTURE
 MSL • MANPATS 9K11 *Malyutka* (AT-3 *Sagger*); 9K111-1 *Konkurs* (AT-5 *Spandrel*)
 RCL 82mm B-10
 GUNS 6+: 57mm ZIS-2 (M-1943); 85mm 6 D-44
ARTILLERY 47+
 TOWED 24: 122mm 12 M-1931/37; 130mm 12 M-46
 MRL 220mm 3 9P140 *Uragan*
 MOR 20+: 82mm M-43; 120mm 20 M-1938/M-1943

AIR DEFENCE
SAM • Point-defence 9K32 *Strela*-2 (SA-7 *Grail*)‡
GUNS • TOWED 24+: 30mm M-53 (twin); 37mm 8 M-1939; 57mm 12 Type-59 (S-60); 100mm 4 KS-19

Navy ε400
EQUIPMENT BY TYPE
PATROL AND COASTAL COMBATANTS • PB 4: 1 Swiftships†; 3 RPB 20

Air Force 800
EQUIPMENT BY TYPE†
AIRCRAFT
FGA (3 MiG-21 *Fishbed* non-op)
TPT • Light 4: 2 An-2 *Colt*; 2 *Tetras*
HELICOPTERS
ATK 4 Mi-24 *Hind*
MRH 5: 2 MD-500MD; 2 Mi-17-1V *Hip* H; 1 SA342K *Gazelle*
TPT 2: Medium 1 SA330 *Puma*; Light 1 AS350B *Ecureuil*
AIR-LAUNCHED MISSILES
AAM • IR R-3 (AA-2 *Atoll*)‡

Paramilitary 2,600 active

Gendarmerie 1,000

Republican Guard 1,600

People's Militia 7,000 reservists

DEPLOYMENT

MALI: UN • MINUSMA 863; 1 inf bn
SOUTH SUDAN: UN • UNMISS 3
SUDAN: UN • UNISFA 2
WESTERN SAHARA: UN • MINURSO 5

Guinea-Bissau GNB

CFA Franc BCEAO fr		2018	2019	2020
GDP	fr	793bn	812bn	
	US$	1.43bn	1.40bn	
per capita	US$	822	786	
Growth	%	3.8	4.6	
Inflation	%	1.4	-2.6	
Def bdgt	fr	n.k	n.k	
	US$	n.k	n.k	
US$1=fr		555.02	581.17	

Real-terms defence budget trend (US$m, constant 2015)

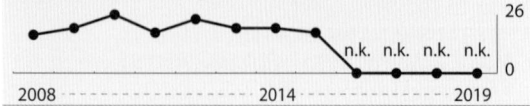

Population 1,879,407

Age	0–14	15–19	20–24	25–29	30–64	65 plus
Male	21.8%	5.4%	4.5%	3.7%	12.0%	1.3%
Female	21.6%	5.6%	4.8%	4.1%	13.4%	1.7%

Capabilities

Guinea-Bissau's armed forces have limited capabilities and are in the midst of both DDR and SSR programmes. There are embryonic schemes to recruit professionals. Defence policy is focused mainly on tackling internal-security challenges, in particular drug trafficking. International defence cooperation has reduced since the 2012 *coup d'état*. The ECOWAS mission in Guinea-Bissau was extended to March 2020. The authorities have looked elsewhere for defence cooperation; in 2017 a letter of intent was signed with Indonesia. Training remains limited and there are problems with recruitment and retention, as well as in developing adequate non-commissioned-officer structures. The number of generals and admirals more than doubled between 2009 and 2017. A pension system was established and funded only in 2015, with international financing. The armed forces participate in multinational exercises, such as the US-led *Obangame Express*. China has donated some non-lethal military and civilian equipment, but much of the country's military equipment is ageing. There is no defence manufacturing sector, and maintenance likely limits military effectiveness.

ACTIVE 4,450 (Army 4,000 Navy 350 Air 100)
Conscript liability Selective conscription
Manpower and eqpt totals should be treated with caution. A number of draft laws to restructure the armed services and police have been produced

ORGANISATIONS BY SERVICE

Army ε4,000
FORCES BY ROLE
MANOEUVRE
Reconnaissance
1 recce coy
Armoured
1 armd bn (sqn)
Light
5 inf bn
COMBAT SUPPORT
1 arty bn
1 engr coy
EQUIPMENT BY TYPE
ARMOURED FIGHTING VEHICLES
MBT 10 T-34
LT TK 15 PT-76
RECCE 10 BRDM-2
APC • APC (W) 55: 35 BTR-40/BTR-60; 20 Type-56 (BTR-152)
ANTI-TANK/ANTI-INFRASTRUCTURE
RCL 75mm Type-52 (M20); 82mm B-10
GUNS 85mm 8 D-44
ARTILLERY 26+
TOWED 122mm 18 D-30/M-30 (M-1938)
MOR 8+: 82mm M-43; 120mm 8 M-1943
AIR DEFENCE
SAM • Point-defence 9K32 *Strela*-2 (SA-7 *Grail*)‡
GUNS • TOWED 34: 23mm 18 ZU-23; 37mm 6 M-1939; 57mm 10 S-60

Navy ε350
EQUIPMENT BY TYPE
PATROL AND COASTAL COMBATANTS 4
PB 4: 2 *Alfeite*†; 2 Rodman 55m

Air Force 100
EQUIPMENT BY TYPE
AIRCRAFT • TPT • Light 1 Cessna 208B

FOREIGN FORCES
Nigeria ECOMIB 100

Kenya KEN

Kenyan Shilling sh		2018	2019	2020
GDP	sh	8.91tr	10.1tr	
	US$	87.9bn	98.6bn	
per capita	US$	1,831	1,998	
Growth	%	6.3	5.6	
Inflation	%	4.7	5.6	
Def bdgt [a]	sh	130bn	126bn	
	US$	1.29bn	1.23bn	
US$1=sh		101.28	102.11	

[a] Includes national-intelligence funding

Real-terms defence budget trend (US$m, constant 2015)

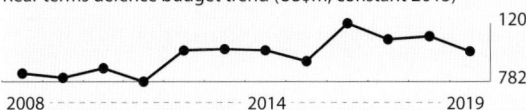

Population 49,142,516
Ethnic groups: Kikuyu ε22–32%

Age	0–14	15–19	20–24	25–29	30–64	65 plus
Male	19.0%	5.7%	4.4%	4.1%	15.3%	1.4%
Female	18.9%	5.7%	4.4%	4.1%	15.2%	1.8%

Capabilities

The armed forces are concerned with threats to regional stability and tackling security challenges, particularly from neighbouring Somalia. A separate coastguard service, established in late 2018 with one vessel, is intended to boost maritime security. A long-standing defence and security agreement with the UK includes a permanent UK training unit, which is to increase support for maritime security and open a counter-IED training centre. There are also significant defence ties with the US and evidence of developing relationships with the Chinese and Jordanian armed forces. Involvement in a number of regional security missions and multinational exercises may also foster improved levels of cooperation and interoperability. Training has received attention, given the need to prepare for AU deployments. Regular operational deployments have increased military experience and confidence. Kenya's armed forces regularly participate in multinational exercises. Kenya remains a key contributor to AMISOM in Somalia, demonstrating limited capacity to project power immediately beyond its own territory. The armed forces also provide smaller contributions to other UN missions and are a leading element of the East African Standby Force. Recent equipment investments have focused on improving counter-insurgency capabilities, including the procurement of helicopters, armoured vehicles and ISR systems. The air force is renewing its fixed-wing transport fleet in order to support regional deployments. There is a limited defence industry focused on equipment maintenance and the manufacture of small-arms ammunition.

ACTIVE 24,100 (Army 20,000 Navy 1,600 Air 2,500)
Paramilitary 5,000

ORGANISATIONS BY SERVICE

Army 20,000
FORCES BY ROLE
MANOEUVRE
  Armoured
  1 armd bde (1 armd recce bn, 2 armd bn)
  Light
  1 spec ops bn
  1 ranger bn 1 inf bde (3 inf bn)
  1 inf bde (2 inf bn)
  1 indep inf bn
  Air Manoeuvre
  1 air cav bn
  1 AB bn
COMBAT SUPPORT
  1 arty bde (2 arty bn, 1 mor bty)
  1 ADA bn
  1 engr bde (2 engr bn)
EQUIPMENT BY TYPE
ARMOURED FIGHTING VEHICLES
  MBT 78 Vickers Mk 3
  RECCE 92: 72 AML-60/AML-90; 12 Ferret; 8 S52 Shorland
  APC 200
    APC (W) 95: 52 UR-416; 31 Type-92; 12 Bastion APC; (10 M3 Panhard in store)
    PPV 105 Puma M26-15
ENGINEERING & MAINTENANCE VEHICLES
  ARV 7 Vickers ARV
  MW Bozena
ARTILLERY 111
  SP 155mm 2+ Nora B-52
  TOWED 105mm 47: 40 L118 Light Gun; 7 Model 56 pack howitzer
  MOR 62: 81mm 50; 120mm 12 Brandt
ANTI-TANK/ANTI-INFRASTRUCTURE
  MSL • MANPATS Milan
  RCL 81mm Carl Gustav
HELICOPTERS
  MRH 37: 2 Hughes 500D†; 12 Hughes 500M†; 10 Hughes 500MD Scout Defender† (with TOW); 10 Hughes 500ME†; 3 Z-9W
AIR DEFENCE • GUNS • TOWED 94: 20mm 81: 11 Oerlikon; ε70 TCM-20; 40mm 13 L/70
AIR-LAUNCHED MISSILES • ASM TOW

Navy 1,600 (incl 120 marines)
EQUIPMENT BY TYPE
PATROL AND COASTAL COMBATANTS 7
  PCO 1 Jasiri with 1 AK630 CIWS, 1 76mm gun
  PCF 2 Nyayo
  PCC 3: 1 Harambee II (ex-FRA P400); 1 Shujaa with 1 76mm gun; 1 Shujaa
  PBF 1 Archangel
AMPHIBIOUS • LCM 2 Galana
LOGISTICS AND SUPPORT • AP 2

Air Force 2,500

FORCES BY ROLE
FIGHTER/GROUND ATTACK
  2 sqn with F-5E/F *Tiger* II
TRANSPORT
  Some sqn with DHC-5D *Buffalo*†; DHC-8†; F-70† (VIP); Y-12(II)†
TRAINING
  Some sqn with *Bulldog* 103/*Bulldog* 127†; EMB-312 *Tucano*†*; *Hawk* Mk52†*; Hughes 500D†
TRANSPORT HELICOPTER
  1 sqn with SA330 *Puma*†

EQUIPMENT BY TYPE†
AIRCRAFT 37 combat capable
  FTR 21: 17 F-5E *Tiger* II; 4 F-5F *Tiger* II
  TPT 17 **Light** 16: 4 DHC-5D *Buffalo*†; 3 DHC-8†; 9 Y-12(II)†; (6 Do-28D-2 in store); **PAX** 1 F-70 (VIP)
  TRG 29: 8 *Bulldog* 103/127†; 11 EMB-312 *Tucano*†*; 5 Grob 120A; 5 *Hawk* Mk52†*
HELICOPTERS
  ATK 3 AH-1F *Cobra*
  MRH 9 H125M (AS550) *Fennec*
  TPT 20: **Medium** 12: 2 Mi-171; 10 SA330 *Puma*†; **Light** 8 Bell 205 (UH-1H *Huey* II)
AIR-LAUNCHED MISSILES
  AAM • **IR** AIM-9 *Sidewinder*
  ASM AGM-65 *Maverick*

Paramilitary 5,000

Police General Service Unit 5,000
EQUIPMENT BY TYPE
ARMOURED FIGHTING VEHICLES
  APC • **PPV** 25 CS/VP3
  AUV some Streit *Cyclone*
PATROL AND COASTAL COMBATANTS • **PB** 5 (2 on Lake Victoria)

Air Wing
EQUIPMENT BY TYPE
AIRCRAFT • **TPT** • **Light** 6: 2 Cessna 208B *Grand Caravan*; 3 Cessna 310; 1 Cessna 402
HELICOPTERS
  MRH 3 Mi-17 *Hip* H
  TPT 5: **Medium** 1 Mi-17V-5; **Light** 4: 2 AW139; 1 Bell 206L *Long Ranger*; 1 Bo-105
  TRG 1 Bell 47G

Coast Guard
Ministry of Interior
EQUIPMENT BY TYPE
PATROL AND COASTAL COMBATANTS 1
  PCC 1 *Doria* with 1 hel landing platform

DEPLOYMENT

CENTRAL AFRICAN REPUBLIC: UN • MINUSCA 15
DEMOCRATIC REPUBLIC OF THE CONGO: UN • MONUSCO 10
LEBANON: UN • UNIFIL 2
MALI: UN • MINUSMA 12
SOMALIA: AU • AMISOM 4,046: 3 inf bn; **UN** • UNSOS 1
SOUTH SUDAN: UN • UNMISS 11
SUDAN: UN • UNAMID 86; 1 MP coy

FOREIGN FORCES
United Kingdom BATUK 350; 1 trg unit

Lesotho LSO

Lesotho Loti M		2018	2019	2020
GDP	M	37.5bn	40.8bn	
	US$	2.71bn	2.74bn	
per capita	US$	1,333	1,339	
Growth	%	2.8	2.8	
Inflation	%	4.7	5.9	
Def bdgt	M	661m	643m	
	US$	47.8m	43.2m	
US$1=M		13.83	14.88	

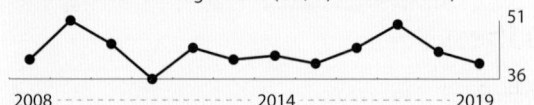
Real-terms defence budget trend (US$m, constant 2015)

Population	1,966,253					
Age	0–14	15–19	20–24	25–29	30–64	65 plus
Male	15.9%	4.9%	4.4%	4.3%	17.2%	2.9%
Female	15.7%	5.1%	4.9%	5.0%	17.1%	2.7%

Capabilities

Lesotho has a small ground force and an air wing for light transport and liaison. A SADC force deployed in country at the end of 2017 to support the government following the assassination of the army chief. The mission concluded at the end of November 2018. Lesotho's armed forces are charged with protecting territorial integrity and sovereignty and ensuring internal security. Lesotho is a SADC member state. The armed forces are a voluntary service. Morale may have been undermined by instability in the country and by the requirement for a SADC force to provide stability. There is no independent capacity to deploy and support an operation beyond national borders. Lesotho's limited inventory is obsolescent by modern standards, and there is little possibility of any significant procurement to replace ageing equipment. The acquisition of light helicopters has been identified as a goal. Barring very limited maintenance, there is no defence-industrial capacity.

ACTIVE 2,000 (Army 2,000)

ORGANISATIONS BY SERVICE

Army ε2,000
FORCES BY ROLE
MANOEUVRE
  Reconnaissance
  1 recce coy

Light
7 inf coy
Aviation
1 sqn
COMBAT SUPPORT
1 arty bty(-)
1 spt coy (with mor)

EQUIPMENT BY TYPE
ARMOURED FIGHTING VEHICLES
MBT 1 T-55
RECCE 30: 4 AML-90; 2 BRDM-2†; 6 RAM Mk3; 10 RBY-1; 8 S52 *Shorland*
ANTI-TANK/ANTI-INFRASTRUCTURE
RCL 106mm 6 M40
ARTILLERY 12
TOWED 105mm 2
MOR 81mm 10

Air Wing 110
AIRCRAFT
TPT • Light 3: 2 C-212-300 *Aviocar*; 1 GA-8 *Airvan*
HELICOPTERS
MRH 3: 1 Bell 412 *Twin Huey*; 2 Bell 412EP *Twin Huey*
TPT • Light 1 Bell 206 *Jet Ranger*

Liberia LBR

Liberian Dollar L$		2018	2019	2020
GDP	L$	3.25bn	3.22bn	
	US$	3.25bn	3.22bn	
per capita	US$	728	704	
Growth	%	1.2	0.4	
Inflation	%	23.5	22.2	
Def bdgt	L$	13.2m	13.9m	12.2m
	US$	13.2m	13.9m	
US$1=L$		1.00	1.00	

Real-terms defence budget trend (US$m, constant 2015)

Population 4,937,804
Ethnic groups: Americo-Liberians 5%

Age	0–14	15–19	20–24	25–29	30–64	65 plus
Male	22.0%	5.4%	4.7%	3.3%	13.2%	1.4%
Female	21.5%	5.4%	4.7%	3.4%	13.5%	1.4%

Capabilities

A revised National Security Strategy was produced in 2017, reportedly clarifying the roles of Liberia's security institutions. The government is emphasising national security as part of its development agenda, in order to fill the gap left by the end of the UNMIL mission in 2018. However, UN-level support continues for the security and justice sectors. The army chief of staff has said that priorities include improving training, operational readiness and personnel welfare. There are plans to establish an air wing to boost the country's search-and-rescue, movement and logistics, medevac and maritime-patrol capacities. Related to this, two pilots graduated from basic flight training in Nigeria in 2018. However, plans to increase establishment strength to 5,000 remain aspirational. US military assistance has in recent years focused on areas such as force health, including schemes to improve recruitment and retention, as well as maritime security and military medicine. A military-cooperation agreement with Nigeria was signed in 2007 and has led to training for soldiers and personnel. The armed forces are able to deploy and sustain small units, such as to the MINUSMA mission in Mali. Equipment recapitalisation will be dependent on finances, as well as the development of a supporting force structure. Liberia has no domestic defence industry, bar limited maintenance-support capacities.

ACTIVE 2,010 (Army 1,950, Coast Guard 60)

ORGANISATIONS BY SERVICE

Army 1,950
FORCES BY ROLE
MANOEUVRE
Light
1 (23rd) inf bde with (2 inf bn, 1 engr coy, 1 MP coy)
COMBAT SERVICE SUPPORT
1 trg unit (forming)

Coast Guard 60
All operational patrol vessels under 10t FLD

DEPLOYMENT

MALI: UN • MINUSMA 116; 1 inf coy
SOUTH SUDAN: UN • UNMISS 2
SUDAN: UN • UNISFA 1

Madagascar MDG

Malagsy Ariary fr		2018	2019	2020
GDP	fr	40.3tr	45.2tr	
	US$	12.1bn	12.6bn	
per capita	US$	459	464	
Growth	%	5.2	5.2	
Inflation	%	7.3	6.7	
Def bdgt	fr	244bn	278bn	
	US$	73.3m	77.2m	
US$1=fr		3334.86	3605.34	

Real-terms defence budget trend (US$m, constant 2015)

Population 26,317,853

Age	0–14	15–19	20–24	25–29	30–64	65 plus
Male	19.8%	5.3%	4.8%	4.2%	14.4%	1.5%
Female	19.4%	5.2%	4.8%	4.2%	14.5%	1.9%

Capabilities

The army dominates the country's modest armed forces, and there remains the risk of military intervention in domestic politics. Ensuring sovereignty and territorial integrity are principal defence aspirations, while maritime security is also an area of focus. Madagascar is a member of SADC and its regional Standby Force. In 2018, the country signed an 'umbrella defence agreement' with India to explore closer defence ties and an intergovernmental agreement with Russia on military cooperation. There is no independent capacity to deploy and support an operation beyond national borders. The equipment inventory is obsolescent and with economic development a key government target, equipment recapitalisation is unlikely to be a key priority. A small number of second-hand transport aircraft and helicopters were acquired in 2019, modestly boosting military mobility.

ACTIVE 13,500 (Army 12,500 Navy 500 Air 500)
Paramilitary 8,100
Conscript liability 18 months (incl for civil purposes)

ORGANISATIONS BY SERVICE

Army 12,500+
FORCES BY ROLE
MANOEUVRE
  Light
  2 (intervention) inf regt
  10 (regional) inf regt
COMBAT SUPPORT
  1 arty regt
  3 engr regt
  1 sigs regt
COMBAT SERVICE SUPPORT
  1 log regt
AIR DEFENCE
  1 ADA regt
EQUIPMENT BY TYPE
ARMOURED FIGHTING VEHICLES
  LT TK 12 PT-76
  RECCE 73: ε35 BRDM-2; 10 FV701 *Ferret*; ε20 M3A1; 8 M8
  APC • APC (T) ε30 M3A1 half-track
ANTI-TANK/ANTI-INFRASTRUCTURE
  RCL 106mm M40A1
ARTILLERY 25+
  TOWED 17: 105mm 5 M101; 122mm 12 D-30
  MOR 8+: 82mm M-37; 120mm 8 M-43
AIR DEFENCE • GUNS • TOWED 70: 14.5mm 50 ZPU-4; 37mm 20 PG-55 (M-1939)

Navy 500 (incl some 100 Marines)
EQUIPMENT BY TYPE
PATROL AND COASTAL COMBATANTS 8
  PCC 1 *Trozona*
  PB 7 (ex-US CG MLB)
AMPHIBIOUS • LCT 1 (ex-FRA EDIC)

Air Force 500
FORCES BY ROLE
TRANSPORT
  1 sqn with An-26 *Curl*; Yak-40 *Codling* (VIP)
  1 (liaison) sqn with Cessna 310; Cessna 337 *Skymaster*; PA-23 *Aztec*
TRAINING
  1 sqn with Cessna 172; J.300 *Joker*; Tetras
TRANSPORT HELICOPTER
  1 sqn with SA318C *Alouette* II
EQUIPMENT BY TYPE
AIRCRAFT • TPT 17: **Light** 15: 1 An-26 *Curl*; 4 Cessna 172; 1 Cessna 310; 2 Cessna 337 *Skymaster*; 1 CN235M; 2 J.300 *Joker*; 1 PA-23 *Aztec*; 1 *Tetras*; 2 Yak-40 *Codling* (VIP); **PAX** 2 B-737
HELICOPTERS
  MRH 3 SA318C *Alouette* II
  TPT • Light 4: 3 AS350 *Ecureuil*; 1 BK117

Paramilitary 8,100

Gendarmerie 8,100

Malawi MWI

Malawian Kwacha K		2018	2019	2020
GDP	K	5.05tr	5.67tr	
	US$	6.90bn	7.52bn	
per capita	US$	350	371	
Growth	%	3.2	4.5	
Inflation	%	9.2	8.8	
Def bdgt	K	37.3bn	50.8bn	51.1bn
	US$	50.9m	67.5m	
US$1=K		732.22	753.36	

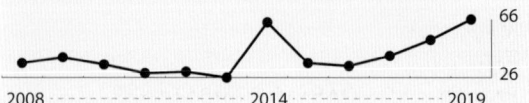
Real-terms defence budget trend (US$m, constant 2015)

Population	20,509,317					
Age	0–14	15–19	20–24	25–29	30–64	65 plus
Male	22.9%	5.5%	4.7%	3.8%	11.5%	1.2%
Female	23.1%	5.6%	4.8%	3.8%	11.8%	1.5%

Capabilities

The army is the largest element of the Malawi Defence Force (MDF). The armed forces are constitutionally tasked with ensuring sovereignty and territorial integrity. Providing military assistance to civil authorities in times of emergencies and support to the police are additional tasks and in recent years the army has been used to help with infrastructure development and attempts to control illegal deforestation. Counter-trafficking is a role for the MDF's small air wing and naval unit. Development plans include enhancing combat readiness and improving military medicine and engineering. Malawi is a member of the SADC and its Standby Force. In 2018, the country signed an 'umbrella defence agreement' with India to explore closer defence ties. The armed forces have contributed to AU and UN peacekeeping operations, including in Côte d'Ivoire and the DRC. There is no independent capacity to deploy and support an operation beyond national borders. The UK provided training and support for the armed forces' deployment to the DRC, where troops contribute to the Force Intervention Brigade. Although the military inventory is obsolescent, there are no public requirements for modernisation. Apart from limited maintenance facilities, the country has no defence industry.

ACTIVE 10,700 (Army 10,700) Paramilitary 4,200

ORGANISATIONS BY SERVICE

Army 10,700
FORCES BY ROLE
MANOEUVRE
  Mechanised
  1 mech bn
  Light
  1 inf bde (4 inf bn)
  1 inf bde (1 inf bn)
  Air Manoeuvre
  1 para bn
COMBAT SUPPORT
  3 lt arty bty
  1 engr bn
COMBAT SERVICE SUPPORT
  12 log coy
EQUIPMENT BY TYPE
ARMOURED FIGHTING VEHICLES
  RECCE 66: 30 *Eland-90*; 8 FV701 *Ferret*; 20 FV721 *Fox*; 8 RAM Mk3
  APC • PPV 31: 14 *Casspir*; 9 *Marauder*; 8 *Puma* M26-15
ARTILLERY 107
  TOWED 105mm 9 L118 Light Gun
  MOR 81mm 98: 82 L16A1; 16 M3
AIR DEFENCE • GUNS • TOWED 72: **12.7mm** 32; **14.5mm** 40 ZPU-4

Navy 220
EQUIPMENT BY TYPE
PATROL AND COASTAL COMBATANTS 3
  PB 3: 1 *Kasungu* (ex-FRA *Antares*); 2 *Mutharika* (PRC)

Air Wing 200
EQUIPMENT BY TYPE
AIRCRAFT • TPT • Light 1 Do-228
HELICOPTERS • TPT 8: **Medium** 3: 1 AS532UL *Cougar*; 1 SA330H *Puma*; 1 H215 *Super Puma* **Light** 5: 1 AS350L *Ecureuil*; 4 SA341B *Gazelle*

Paramilitary 4,200

Police Mobile Service 4,200
EQUIPMENT BY TYPE
ARMOURED FIGHTING VEHICLES
  RECCE 8 S52 *Shorland*
AIRCRAFT
  TPT • Light 4: 3 BN-2T *Defender* (border patrol); 1 SC.7 3M *Skyvan*
HELICOPTERS • MRH 2 AS365 *Dauphin* 2

DEPLOYMENT

DEMOCRATIC REPUBLIC OF THE CONGO: UN • MONUSCO 864; 1 inf bn

SOUTH SUDAN: UN • UNMISS 1
SUDAN: UN • UNISFA 2
WESTERN SAHARA: UN • MINURSO 3

Mali MLI

CFA Franc BCEAO fr		2018	2019	2020
GDP	fr	9.54tr	10.3tr	
	US$	17.2bn	17.6bn	
per capita	US$	927	924	
Growth	%	4.7	5.04	
Inflation	%	1.7	0.2	
Def bdgt [a]	fr	403bn	423bn	452bn
	US$	726m	727m	
US$1=fr		555.19	581.37	

[a] Defence and interior-security budget

Real-terms defence budget trend (US$m, constant 2015)

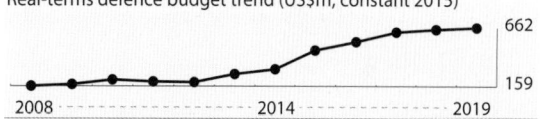

Population 18,985,881
Ethnic groups: Tuareg 6–10%

Age	0–14	15–19	20–24	25–29	30–64	65 plus
Male	24.1%	5.2%	3.9%	3.0%	11.0%	1.5%
Female	23.8%	5.5%	4.5%	3.7%	12.4%	1.5%

Capabilities

The armed forces are focused on countering rebel and Islamist groups. A defence-reform process is ongoing, with assistance from external partners. A 2015–19 military-programming law aims to improve recruitment and training. Mali is supported by neighbouring states in the G5 Sahel partnership, and benefits from training assistance from the EU, France and the US. France maintains bases, personnel and equipment in Mali as part of *Operation Barkhane*, while some other states supporting *Barkhane* also deploy personnel and equipment in-country. The EU Training Mission, whose mandate has been extended to May 2020, continues to train Malian troops including at the Koulikoro training centre, and has also delivered training to the air force. The armed forces also participate in multinational exercises, particularly those focused on counter-terrorism capabilities. There are no deployments of formed units abroad. The air force has no combat aircraft and only a small number of attack helicopters. Strengthening air capability is a priority and contracts have been signed with Brazil for light attack aircraft, France for transport helicopters and Russia for attack helicopters. Equipment and maintenance capabilities are limited and the serviceability of some vehicles is in doubt. There is no defence manufacturing sector.

ACTIVE 13,000 (Army 13,000) Paramilitary 7,800

ORGANISATIONS BY SERVICE

Army ε13,000
FORCES BY ROLE
The remnants of the pre-conflict Malian army are being reformed into new combined-arms battlegroups, each of

which comprise one lt mech coy, three mot inf coy, one arty bty and additional recce, cdo and cbt spt elms

MANOEUVRE
  Light
    9 mot inf bn
    1 inf coy (Special Joint Unit)
  Air Manoeuvre
    1 para bn
COMBAT SUPPORT
  1 engr bn
COMBAT SERVICE SUPPORT
  1 med unit
EQUIPMENT BY TYPE
ARMOURED FIGHTING VEHICLES
  LT TK 2+ PT-76
  RECCE BRDM-2†
  APC 85:
    APC (W) 23+: 4+ *Bastion* APC; 10+ BTR-60PB; 9 BTR-70
    PPV 62: 29 *Casspir*; 24 Stark Motors *Storm Light*; 4 Streit *Gladiator*; 5+ Streit *Python*
ARTILLERY 30+
  TOWED 122mm D-30
  MRL 122mm 30+ BM-21 *Grad*

Air Force

FORCES BY ROLE
TRANSPORT
  1 sqn with BT-67; C295W; Y-12E
TRAINING
  1 sqn with *Tetras*
TRANSPORT/ATTACK HELICOPTER
  1 sqn with H215; Mi-24D *Hind*; Mi-35M *Hind*
EQUIPMENT BY TYPE
AIRCRAFT 4 combat capable
  ISR 1 Cessna 208 *Caravan*
  TPT • Light 11: 1 BT-67; 1 C295W; 7 *Tetras*; 2 Y-12E (1 An-24 *Coke*; 2 An-26 *Curl*; 2 BN-2 *Islander* all in store)
  TRG 4 A-29 *Super Tucano** (6 L-29 *Delfin*; 2 SF-260WL *Warrior** all in store)
HELICOPTERS
  ATK 4: 2 Mi-24D *Hind*; 2 Mi-35M *Hind*
  TPT • Medium 2 H215 (AS332L1) *Super Puma*; (1 Mi-8 *Hip* in store); Light (1 AS350 *Ecureuil* in store)

Paramilitary 7,800 active

Gendarmerie 1,800
FORCES BY ROLE
MANOEUVRE
  Other
    8 paramilitary coy
    1 air tpt gp (2 sy coy; 1 tpt coy)
EQUIPMENT BY TYPE
ARMOURED FIGHTING VEHICLES
  APC • PPV 1+ RG-31 *Nyala*

National Guard 2,000
FORCES BY ROLE
MANOEUVRE
  Reconnaissance
    6 (camel) cav coy

EQUIPMENT BY TYPE
ARMOURED FIGHTING VEHICLES
  APC • PPV 1+ RG-31 *Nyala*

National Police 1,000

Militia 3,000

DEPLOYMENT

DEMOCRATIC REPUBLIC OF THE CONGO: UN • MONUSCO 4

FOREIGN FORCES

All under MINUSMA comd unless otherwise specified
Albania EUTM Mali 4
Austria 2 • EUTM Mali 47
Bangladesh 1,295; 1 inf bn; 1 engr coy; 2 sigs coy; 1 tpt coy
Belgium 38 • EUTM Mali 15
Benin 260; 1 mech inf coy
Bhutan 5
Bosnia-Herzegovina 2
Bulgaria EUTM Mali 5
Burkina Faso 1,704; 2 inf bn
Burundi 2
Cambodia 292; 2 eng coy; 1 EOD coy
Cameroon 2
Canada 5
Chad 1,423; 1 SF coy; 2 inf bn
China 421; 1 sy coy; 1 engr coy; 1 fd hospital
Côte d'Ivoire 161; 1 sy coy
Czech Republic 7 • EUTM Mali 120
Denmark 2
Egypt 1,103; 1 sy bn; 1 MP coy
El Salvador 211; 1 hel sqn with 3 MD-500E
Estonia 3 • *Operation Barkhane* 50 • EUTM Mali 10
Ethiopia 1
Finland 4 • EUTM Mali 3
France 25 • *Operation Barkhane* 1,750; 1 mech inf BG; 1 log bn; 1 tpt unit with 1 CN235M; 1 hel unit with 4 *Tiger*; 7 NH90 TTH; 4 SA342 *Gazelle* • EUTM Mali 13
Gambia 3
Georgia EUTM Mali 1
Germany 370; 1 obs; 1 sy coy; 1 int coy; 1 UAV sqn • EUTM Mali 174
Ghana 156; 1 engr coy
Greece EUTM Mali 2
Guatemala 2
Guinea 863; 1 inf bn
Hungary EUTM Mali 7
Indonesia 9
Ireland EUTM Mali 20
Italy 2 • EUTM Mali 7
Jordan 66
Kenya 12
Latvia 9 • EUTM Mali 3
Liberia 116; 1 obs; 1 inf coy(-)

Lithuania 37 • EUTM Mali 2
Luxembourg EUTM Mali 2
Mauritania 6
Mexico 3
Moldova EUTM Mali 2
Montenegro EUTM Mali 1
Nepal 154; 1 EOD coy
Netherlands 4 • EUTM Mali 1
Niger 1,237; 1 inf bn
Nigeria 83; 1 fd hospital
Norway 91; 1 tpt flt with 1 C-130J
Pakistan 14
Portugal 2 • EUTM Mali 11
Romania 18 • EUTM Mali 1
Senegal 1,276; 2 inf bn; 1 engr coy
Serbia EUTM Mali 3
Sierra Leone 21
Slovenia EUTM Mali 8
Spain EUTM Mali 200
Sri Lanka 203; 1 sy coy
Sweden 240; 1 int coy • EUTM Mali 6
Switzerland 4
Togo 937; 1 inf bn; 1 fd hospital
Tunisia 82; 1 tpt flt with 1 C-130J-30
Ukraine 2
United Kingdom 2 • *Operation Barkhane* 90; 1 hel flt with 3 CH-47SD *Chinook* HC5; • EUTM Mali 8
United States 9
Yemen 2

Mauritius MUS

Mauritian Rupee R		2018	2019	2020
GDP	R	482bn	507bn	
	US$	14.2bn	14.4bn	
per capita	US$	11,228	11,361	
Growth	%	3.8	3.7	
Inflation	%	3.2	0.9	
Def bdgt [a]	R	7.54bn	7.76bn	8.86bn
	US$	222m	220m	
US$1=R		33.94	35.23	

[a] Police service budget

Real-terms defence budget trend (US$m, constant 2015)

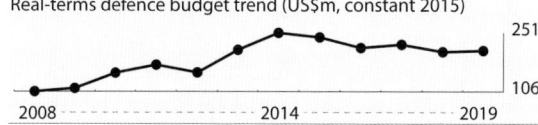

Population 1,371,946

Age	0–14	15–19	20–24	25–29	30–64	65 plus
Male	10.0%	3.6%	3.6%	4.0%	23.5%	4.4%
Female	9.6%	3.5%	3.6%	3.9%	24.1%	6.2%

Capabilities

The country has no standing armed forces; instead, security tasks are met by the police force's Special Mobile Force (SMF), formed as a motorised infantry battalion. The SMF is tasked with ensuring internal and external territorial and maritime security. India provides support to the Mauritian National Coast Guard, which is a branch of the police force. The SMF trains along traditional military lines but has no ability to deploy beyond national territory. There is no defence industry, beyond very limited maintenance facilities.

ACTIVE NIL Paramilitary 2,550

ORGANISATIONS BY SERVICE

Paramilitary 2,550

Special Mobile Force ε1,750
FORCES BY ROLE
MANOEUVRE
  Reconnaissance
  2 recce coy
  Light
  5 (rifle) mot inf coy
COMBAT SUPPORT
  1 engr sqn
COMBAT SERVICE SUPPORT
  1 spt pl
EQUIPMENT BY TYPE
ARMOURED FIGHTING VEHICLES
  IFV 2 VAB with 20mm gun
  APC • APC (W) 12: 3 *Tactica*; 9 VAB
ARTILLERY • MOR 81mm 2

Coast Guard ε800
EQUIPMENT BY TYPE
PATROL AND COASTAL COMBATANTS 17
  PCC 2 *Victory* (IND *Sarojini Naidu*)
  PCO 1 *Barracuda* with 1 hel landing platform
  PB 14: 10 (IND Fast Interceptor Boat); 1 P-2000; 1 SDB-Mk3; 2 *Rescuer* (FSU *Zhuk*)
AIRCRAFT • TPT • Light 4: 1 BN-2T *Defender*; 3 Do-228-101

Police Air Wing
EQUIPMENT BY TYPE
HELICOPTERS
  MRH 9: 1 H125 (AS555) *Fennec*; 2 *Dhruv*; 1 SA315B *Lama* (*Cheetah*); 5 SA316 *Alouette* III (*Chetak*)

Mozambique MOZ

Mozambique New Metical M		2018	2019	2020
GDP	M	876bn	946bn	
	US$	14.4bn	15.1bn	
per capita	US$	475	484	
Growth	%	3.3	1.8	
Inflation	%	3.9	5.6	
Def bdgt	M	7.86bn	7.94bn	
	US$	129m	127m	
US$1=M			60.88	62.70

Real-terms defence budget trend (US$m, constant 2015)

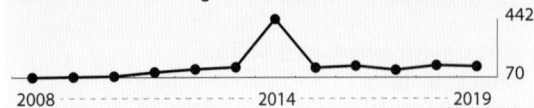

Population 27,910,300

Age	0–14	15–19	20–24	25–29	30–64	65 plus
Male	22.3%	5.8%	4.9%	3.9%	10.8%	1.3%
Female	22.0%	5.8%	5.1%	4.3%	12.2%	1.6%

Capabilities

The country faces a growing internal threat from Islamist groups, with attacks being carried out in the north of the country. The armed forces are tasked with ensuring territorial integrity and internal security, as well as tackling piracy and human trafficking. The integration of RENAMO personnel into the military is a long-standing objective. Talks between the government and Renamo continued in July 2019 to further this goal, though some armed attacks have been blamed on RENAMO dissidents. Mozambique has defence relationships with China, Portugal and Russia. In 2017, the UN raised concerns that Mozambique was receiving defence support from North Korea, a claim the government denied. The defence ministry is reportedly to implement a military HIV policy, including more screening, to try to reduce HIV incidence. The armed forces have no capacity to deploy beyond Mozambique's borders without assistance. Soviet-era equipment makes up the majority of the inventory and maintaining this will be problematic, not least in the absence of any local defence industry. Moreover, Mozambique's recent economic performance will likely limit the government's ability to recapitalise.

ACTIVE 11,200 (Army 10,000 Navy 200 Air 1,000)
Conscript liability 2 years

ORGANISATIONS BY SERVICE

Army ε9,000–10,000
FORCES BY ROLE
SPECIAL FORCES
  3 SF bn
MANOEUVRE
  Light
    7 inf bn
COMBAT SUPPORT
  2–3 arty bn
  2 engr bn

COMBAT SERVICE SUPPORT
  1 log bn
EQUIPMENT BY TYPE†
Equipment estimated at 10% or less serviceability
ARMOURED FIGHTING VEHICLES
  MBT 60+ T-54
  RECCE 30 BRDM-1/BRDM-2
  IFV 40 BMP-1
  APC 326
    APC (T) 30 FV430
    APC (W) 285: 160 BTR-60; 100 BTR-152; 25 AT-105 Saxon
    PPV 11+: 11 Casspir; some Tata Motors MRAP
ANTI-TANK/ANTI-INFRASTRUCTURE
  MSL • MANPATS 9K11 Malyutka (AT-3 Sagger); 9K111 Fagot (AT-4 Spigot)
  RCL 75mm; 82mm B-10; 107mm 24 B-12
  GUNS 85mm 18: 6 D-48; 12 PT-56 (D-44)
ARTILLERY 126
  TOWED 62: 100mm 20 M-1944; 105mm 12 M101; 122mm 12 D-30; 130mm 6 M-46; 152mm 12 D-1
  MRL 122mm 12 BM-21 Grad
  MOR 52: 82mm 40 M-43; 120mm 12 M-43
AIR DEFENCE • GUNS 290+
  SP 57mm 20 ZSU-57-2
  TOWED 270+: 20mm M-55; 23mm 120 ZU-23-2; 37mm 90 M-1939; (10 M-1939 in store); 57mm 60 S-60; (30 S-60 in store)

Navy ε200
EQUIPMENT BY TYPE
PATROL AND COASTAL COMBATANTS 12
  PBF 8: 2 DV 15; 6 HSI 32
  PB 4: 3 Ocean Eagle 43 (capacity 1 Camcopter S-100 UAV); 1 Pebane (ex-ESP Conejera)
UNMANNED AERIAL VEHICLES
  ISR • Light 1 S-100 Camcopter

Air Force 1,000
FORCES BY ROLE
FIGHTER/GROUND ATTACK
  1 sqn with MiG-21bis Fishbed; MiG-21UM Mongol B
TRANSPORT
  1 sqn with An-26 Curl; FTB-337G Milirole; Cessna 150B; Cessna 172; PA-34 Seneca
ATTACK/TRANSPORT HELICOPTER
  1 sqn with Mi-24 Hind†
EQUIPMENT BY TYPE
AIRCRAFT 8 combat capable
  FGA 8: 6 MiG-21bis Fishbed; 2 MiG-21UM Mongol B
  ISR 2 FTB-337G Milirole
  TPT 6: Light 5: 1 An-26 Curl; 2 Cessna 150B; 1 Cessna 172; 1 PA-34 Seneca; (4 PA-32 Cherokee non-op); PAX 1 Hawker 850XP
HELICOPTERS
  ATK 2 Mi-24 Hind†
  TPT • Medium 2 Mi-8 Hip
AD • SAM • TOWED: (S-75 Dvina (SA-2 Guideline) non-op‡; S-125 Pechora SA-3 Goa non-op‡)

Namibia NAM

Namibian Dollar N$		2018	2019	2020
GDP	N$	192bn	200bn	
	US$	14.5bn	14.4bn	
per capita	US$	6,013	5,842	
Growth	%	-0.1	-0.2	
Inflation	%	4.3	4.8	
Def bdgt	N$	5.96bn	5.88bn	
	US$	450m	422m	
US$1=N$		13.24	13.94	

Real-terms defence budget trend (US$m, constant 2015)

Population 2,581,689

Age	0–14	15–19	20–24	25–29	30–64	65 plus
Male	18.2%	5.4%	4.8%	4.3%	14.6%	1.7%
Female	17.9%	5.3%	4.8%	4.4%	16.3%	2.2%

Capabilities

The defence authorities aim to develop a small, mobile professional force. According to the constitution, the Namibian Defence Force's (NDF's) primary mission is territorial defence. Secondary roles include assisting the civil power in domestic support operations, assisting the AU and the SADC and supporting UN missions. The NDF Development Strategy 2012–22 states that the NDF design should be based on a conventional force with a force-projection capability. Namibia is a member of the AU and the SADC, with which the navy exercises as part of its Standing Maritime Committee. There is a permanent commission on defence and security with Zambia that meets annually. An MoU on training and cooperation was signed with Botswana in late 2018. While the NDF receives a comparatively large proportion of the state budget, the government has acknowledged that funding problems led training to almost cease, especially for recruits, though the services continued training at low levels. Namibia has deployed on AU and UN missions, but there is only limited capacity for independent power projection. The NDF is equipped for the most part with ageing or obsolescent systems, which it has ambitions to replace. However, economic difficulties make this unlikely in the near term. The country has a limited defence manufacturing sector covering armoured vehicles, tactical communications and ammunition, as well as some broader industrial business interests.

ACTIVE 9,900 (Army 9,000 Navy 900) Paramilitary 6,000

ORGANISATIONS BY SERVICE

Army 9,000
FORCES BY ROLE
MANOEUVRE
  Reconnaissance
    1 recce regt
  Light
    3 inf bde (total: 6 inf bn)
  Other
    1 (Presidential Guard) gd bn
COMBAT SUPPORT
  1 arty bde with (1 arty regt)
  1 AT regt
  1 engr regt
  1 sigs regt
COMBAT SERVICE SUPPORT
  1 log bn
AIR DEFENCE
  1 AD regt
EQUIPMENT BY TYPE
ARMOURED FIGHTING VEHICLES
  MBT T-54/T-55†; T-34†
  RECCE 12 BRDM-2
  IFV 7: 5 Type-05P mod (with BMP-1 turret); 2 *Wolf Turbo 2* mod (with BMP-1 turret)
  APC 61
    APC (W) 13: 10 BTR-60; 3 Type-05P
    PPV 48: 20 *Casspir*; 28 *Wolf Turbo 2*
ENGINEERING & MAINTENANCE VEHICLES
  ARV T-54/T-55 reported
ANTI-TANK/ANTI-INFRASTRUCTURE
  RCL 82mm B-10
  GUNS 12+: 57mm ZIS-2; 76mm 12 ZIS-3
ARTILLERY 72
  TOWED 140mm 24 G-2
  MRL 122mm 8: 5 BM-21 *Grad*; 3 PHL-81
  MOR 40: 81mm; 82mm
AIR DEFENCE
  SAM • **Point-defence** FN-6 (CH-SA-10)
  GUNS 65
    SP 23mm 15 *Zumlac*
    TOWED 50+: 14.5mm 50 ZPU-4; 57mm S-60

Navy ε900
EQUIPMENT BY TYPE
PATROL AND COASTAL COMBATANTS 7
  PSO 1 *Elephant* with 1 hel landing platform
  PCC 3: 2 *Daures* (ex-PRC *Haiqing* (Type-037-IS)) with 2 FQF-2300 A/S mor; 1 *Oryx*
  PB 3: 1 *Brendan Simbwaye* (BRZ *Grajaú*); 2 *Terrace Bay* (BRZ *Marlim*)
AIRCRAFT • TPT • Light 1 F406 *Caravan II*
HELICOPTERS • TPT • Medium 1 S-61L

Marines ε700

Air Force
FORCES BY ROLE
FIGHTER/GROUND ATTACK
  1 sqn with F-7 (F-7NM); FT-7 (FT-7NG)
ISR
  1 sqn with O-2A *Skymaster*
TRANSPORT
  Some sqn with An-26 *Curl*; *Falcon* 900; Learjet 36; Y-12
TRAINING
  1 sqn with K-8 *Karakorum**
ATTACK/TRANSPORT HELICOPTER
  1 sqn with H425; Mi-8 *Hip*; Mi-25 *Hind D*; SA315 *Lama* (*Cheetah*); SA316B *Alouette* III (*Chetak*)

EQUIPMENT BY TYPE
AIRCRAFT 12+ combat capable
　FTR 8: 6 F-7NM; 2 FT-7 (FT-7NG)
　ISR 5 Cessna O-2A *Skymaster*
　TPT 6: **Light** 5: 2 An-26 *Curl*; 1 Learjet 36; 2 Y-12; **PAX** 1 *Falcon* 900
　TRG 4+ K-8 *Karakorum**
HELICOPTERS
　ATK 2 Mi-25 *Hind* D
　MRH 5: 1 H425; 1 SA315 *Lama* (*Cheetah*); 3 SA316B *Alouette* III (*Chetak*)
　TPT • Medium 1 Mi-8 *Hip*

Paramilitary 6,000

Police Force • Special Field Force 6,000 (incl Border Guard and Special Reserve Force)

DEPLOYMENT
SOUTH SUDAN: UN • UNMISS 2
SUDAN: UN • UNISFA 5

Niger NER

CFA Franc BCEAO fr		2018	2019	2020
GDP	fr	5.16tr	5.42tr	
	US$	9.30bn	9.44bn	
per capita	US$	414	405	
Growth	%	6.5	6.3	
Inflation	%	2.7	-1.3	
Def bdgt	fr	128bn	101bn	
	US$	230m	176m	
US$1=fr		555.20	573.62	

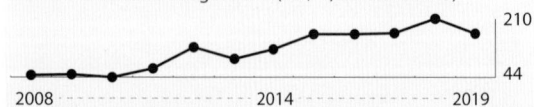
Real-terms defence budget trend (US$m, constant 2015)

Population 20,501,509
Ethnic groups: Gourma 55.3%; Djerma Sonrai 21%; Touareg 9.3%; Peuhl 8.5%; Kanouri Manga 4.6%; other or unspecified 1.3%

Age	0–14	15–19	20–24	25–29	30–64	65 plus
Male	24.4%	5.5%	4.2%	3.3%	11.5%	1.4%
Female	23.9%	5.6%	4.4%	3.4%	11.2%	1.3%

Capabilities
Maintaining internal and border security are key roles for the armed forces, in light of the regional threat from Islamist groups. Defence-policy developments in recent years have helped professionalisation. The country is a member of the G5 Sahel group and part of the Multi-National Joint Task Force fighting Boko Haram in the Lake Chad Basin. France has conducted joint counter-terrorism operations with Niger's armed forces. Niamey hosts air contingents from France, Germany (an air-transport base to supply its troops in neighbouring Mali) and the US, which maintains a detachment of UAVs. Niger's armed forces are combat experienced and relatively well trained, and there is training support from France, Italy and the US. Deployment capabilities are limited to neighbouring countries without external support. Operations in austere environments have demonstrated adequate sustainment and manoeuvre capacity. However, the armed forces are generally under-equipped and under-resourced for the tasks they face. Apart from limited maintenance facilities, the country has no domestic defence-industrial capability.

ACTIVE 5,300 (Army 5,200 Air 100) **Paramilitary 5,400**
Conscript liability Selective conscription, 2 years

ORGANISATIONS BY SERVICE

Army 5,200
3 Mil Districts
FORCES BY ROLE
MANOEUVRE
　Reconnaissance
　　4 armd recce sqn
　Light
　　7 inf coy
　Air Manoeuvre
　　2 AB coy
COMBAT SUPPORT
　1 engr coy
COMBAT SERVICE SUPPORT
　1 log gp
AIR DEFENCE
　1 AD coy
EQUIPMENT BY TYPE
ARMOURED FIGHTING VEHICLES
　RECCE 134: 35 AML-20/AML-60; 90 AML-90; 2+ *Bastion Patsas*; 7 VBL
　APC 45
　　APC (W) 24: 22 Panhard M3; 2 WZ-523
　　PPV 21 *Puma* M26-15; some *Puma* M36
ANTI-TANK/ANTI-INFRASTRUCTURE
　RCL 14: **75mm** 6 M20; **106mm** 8 M40
ARTILLERY • MOR 40: **81mm** 19 Brandt; **82mm** 17; **120mm** 4 Brandt
AIR DEFENCE • GUNS 39
　SP 20mm 10 Panhard M3 VDAA
　TOWED 20mm 29

Air Force 100
EQUIPMENT BY TYPE
AIRCRAFT 2 combat capable
　ATK 2 Su-25 *Frogfoot*
　ISR 6: 4 Cessna 208 *Caravan*; 2 DA42 MPP *Twin Star*
　TPT 7: **Medium** 1 C-130H *Hercules*; **Light** 5: 1 An-26 *Curl*; 2 Cessna 208 *Caravan*; 1 Do-28 *Skyservant*; 1 Do-228-201; **PAX** 1 B-737-700 (VIP)
HELICOPTERS
　ATK 2 Mi-35P *Hind*
　MRH 5: 2 Mi-17 *Hip*; 3 SA342 *Gazelle*

Paramilitary 5,400

Gendarmerie 1,400

Republican Guard 2,500

National Police 1,500

DEPLOYMENT

CENTRAL AFRICAN REPUBLIC: UN • MINUSCA 10

DEMOCRATIC REPUBLIC OF THE CONGO: UN • MONUSCO 3

MALI: UN • MINUSMA 1,237; 1 inf bn

FOREIGN FORCES

France *Operation Barkhane* 500; 1 FGA det with 4 *Mirage 2000D*; 1 tkr/tpt det with 1 C-135FR; 1 C-160R; 1 UAV det with 2 MQ-9A *Reaper*

Germany *Operation Barkhane* 2 C-160

Italy MISIN 96

United States 800; 1 ISR UAV sqn with MQ-9A *Reaper*

Nigeria NGA

Nigerian Naira N		2018	2019	2020
GDP	N	129tr	145tr	
	US$	398bn	447bn	
per capita	US$	2,033	2,222	
Growth	%	1.9	2.3	
Inflation	%	12.1	11.3	
Def bdgt	N	567bn	594bn	878bn
	US$	1.75bn	1.83bn	
US$1=N		324.19	325.00	

Defence budget: ten-year perspective (US$bn, constant)

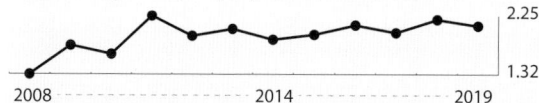

Population 208,679,114

Ethnic groups: North (Hausa and Fulani) Southwest (Yoruba) Southeast (Ibo); these tribes make up ғ65% of population

Age	0–14	15–19	20–24	25–29	30–64	65 plus
Male	21.5%	5.6%	4.6%	3.6%	13.6%	1.5%
Female	20.6%	5.4%	4.4%	3.6%	13.7%	1.7%

Capabilities

Nigeria is the region's principal military power and faces numerous security challenges, including from Boko Haram and militants in the Delta. The challenge from Boko Haram, and the relative weaknesses exposed in the armed forces, have led to reform initiatives. There have been operational changes, including attempts to implement counter-insurgency tactics and generate forward-operating bases and quick-reaction groups. Nigeria is central to several regional security initiatives and is part of the Multi-National Joint Task Force. It is a key member of the ECOWAS Standby Force. Military and security assistance is either discussed or under way with Germany, the UK and the US. The UK bases its British Defence Staff West Africa in Nigeria. Efforts have been made to improve training, notably in the air force, with the establishment of Air Training Command and Ground Training Command. Contractors have also been used to improve training levels. Nigeria is able to mount regional operations, though its deployment capacities remain limited. Deliveries of attack helicopters continue and there is a plan to acquire JF-17 combat aircraft, while an effort has been made to refurbish stored aircraft. A number of small coastal-patrol boats have been acquired in recent years in light of security requirements in the Delta region. Nigeria is developing its defence-industrial capacity, including local production facilities for small arms and protected patrol vehicles.

ACTIVE 143,000 (Army 100,000 Navy 25,000 Air 18,000) **Paramilitary 80,000**

Reserves planned, none org

ORGANISATIONS BY SERVICE

Army 100,000

FORCES BY ROLE

SPECIAL FORCES
1 spec ops bn
3 (mobile strike team) spec ops units
1 ranger bn

MANOEUVRE

Armoured
1 (3rd) armd div (1 armd bde, 1 arty bde)

Mechanised
1 (1st) mech div (1 recce bn, 1 mech bde, 1 mot inf bde, 1 arty bde, 1 engr regt)
1 (2nd) mech div (1 recce bn, 1 armd bde, 1 arty bde, 1 engr regt)
1 (81st) composite div (1 recce bn, 1 mech bde, 1 arty bde, 1 engr regt)

Light
1 (6th) inf div (1 amph bde, 2 inf bde)
1 (7th) inf div (1 spec ops bn, 1 recce bn(-), 1 armd bde, 7 (task force) inf bde, 1 arty bde, 1 engr regt)
1 (8th Task Force) inf div (2 inf bde)
1 (82nd) composite div (1 recce bn, 3 mot inf bde, 1 arty bde, 1 engr regt)
1 (Multi-National Joint Task Force) bde (2 inf bn(-))

Other
1 (Presidential Guard) gd bde (4 gd bn)

AIR DEFENCE
1 AD regt

EQUIPMENT BY TYPE

ARMOURED FIGHTING VEHICLES
MBT 315: 174 Vickers Mk 3; 100 T-55†; 10 T-72AV; 31 T-72M1
LT TK 154 FV101 *Scorpion*
RECCE 341: 89 AML-60; 40 AML-90; 70 EE-9 *Cascavel*; 50 FV721 *Fox*; 20 FV601 *Saladin* Mk2; 72 VBL
IFV 32: 10 BTR-4EN; 22 BVP-1
APC 593+
  APC (T) 315: 250 4K-7FA *Steyr*; 65 MT-LB
  APC (W) 172+: 10 FV603 *Saracen*; 110 AVGP *Grizzly* mod/*Piranha* I 6x6; 47 BTR-3UN; 5 BTR-80; some EE-11 *Urutu* (reported)
  PPV 106+: 14 *Caiman*; some CS/VP3; some *Marauder*; 7+ *Maxxpro*; 8 Proforce *Ara-1*; 13 Proforce *Ara-2*; 23

REVA III 4×4; 10 Streit *Spartan*; 9 Streit *Cougar* (*Igirigi*); 25 Streit *Typhoon*
AUV 108 *Cobra*
ENGINEERING & MAINTENANCE VEHICLES
ARV 17+: AVGP *Husky*; 2 *Greif*; 15 Vickers ARV
VLB MTU-20; VAB
ANTI-TANK/ANTI-INFRASTRUCTURE
MSL • MANPATS *Shershen*
RCL 84mm *Carl Gustav*; 106mm M40A1
ARTILLERY 514+
SP 155mm 39 *Palmaria*
TOWED 104: 105mm 49 M-56; 122mm 48 D-30/D-74; 130mm 7 M-46; (155mm 24 FH-77B in store)
MRL 122mm 41: 9 BM-21 *Grad*; 25 APR-21; 7 RM-70
MOR 330+: 81mm 200; 82mm 100; 120mm 30+
AIR DEFENCE
SAM • Point-defence 16+: 16 *Roland*; *Blowpipe*; 9K32 *Strela-2* (SA-7 *Grail*)‡
GUNS 89+
SP 23mm 29 ZSU-23-4 *Shilka*
TOWED 60+: 20mm 60+; 23mm ZU-23; 40mm L/70

Navy 25,000 (incl Coast Guard)
Western Comd HQ located at Apapa; Eastern Comd HQ located at Calabar; Central Comd HQ located at Brass
EQUIPMENT BY TYPE
PRINCIPAL SURFACE COMBATANTS 1
FRIGATES • FFGHM 1 *Aradu*† (GER MEKO 360) with 8 single lnchr with Otomat Mk1 AShM, 1 octuple *Albatros* lnchr with *Aspide* SAM, 2 triple 324mm ASTT with A244/S LWT, 1 127mm gun (capacity 1 med hel)
PATROL AND COASTAL COMBATANTS 125
CORVETTES • FSM 1 *Erinomi*† (UK Vosper Mk 9) with 1 triple lnchr with *Seacat*† SAM, 1 twin 375mm Bofors ASW Rocket Launcher System A/S mor, 1 76mm gun
PSOH 4: 2 *Centenary* with 1 76mm gun; 2 *Thunder* (ex-US *Hamilton*) with 1 76mm gun
PCFG 1 *Sirit* (FRA *Combattante* IIIB) with 2 twin lnchr with MM38 *Exocet* AShM, 1 76mm gun
PCF 2 *Siri* (FRA *Combattante* IIIB) with 1 76mm gun
PCO 1 *Kyanwa* (ex-US CG *Balsam*)
PCC 2 *Ekpe*† (GER Lurssen 57m) with 1 76mm gun
PBF 33: 21 *Manta* (Suncraft 17m); 4 *Manta* MkII; 3 *Shaldag* II; 2 *Torie* (Nautic Sentinel 17m); 3 *Wave Rider*
PB 78: 1 *Andoni*; 1 *Dorina* (FPB 98); 2 FPB 110 MkII; 7 *Okpoku* (FPB 72); 1 *Karaduwa*; 1 *Sagbama*; 2 *Sea Eagle* (Suncraft 38m); 15 *Stingray* (Suncraft 16m); 40 Suncraft 12m; 4 Swiftships; 2 *Town* (of which one laid up); 2 *Yola*†
MINE WARFARE • MINE COUNTERMEASURES 2:
MCC 2 *Ohue* (ITA *Lerici* mod)
AMPHIBIOUS 4
LC • LCVP 4 *Stingray* 20
LOGISTICS AND SUPPORT 1
AX 1 *Prosperity*

Naval Aviation
EQUIPMENT BY TYPE
HELICOPTERS
MRH 2 AW139 (AB-139)
TPT • Light 3 AW109E *Power*†

Special Boat Service 200
EQUIPMENT BY TYPE
FORCES BY ROLE
SPECIAL FORCES
1 SF unit

Air Force 18,000
FORCES BY ROLE
Very limited op capability
FIGHTER/GROUND ATTACK
1 sqn with F-7 (F-7NI); FT-7 (FT-7NI)
MARITIME PATROL
1 sqn with ATR-42-500 MP; Do-128D-6 *Turbo SkyServant*; Do-228-100/200
TRANSPORT
2 sqn with C-130H *Hercules*; C-130H-30 *Hercules*; G-222
1 (Presidential) gp with B-727; B-737BBJ; BAe-125-800; Beech 350 *King Air*; Do-228-200; *Falcon* 7X; *Falcon* 900; Gulfstream IV/V
TRAINING
1 unit with *Air Beetle*†
1 unit with *Alpha Jet**
1 unit with L-39 *Albatros*†*; MB-339A*
1 unit with *Super Mushshak*; DA40NG
1 hel unit with Mi-34 *Hermit* (trg)
ATTACK HELICOPTER
1 sqn with Mi-24/Mi-35 *Hind*†
TRANSPORT HELICOPTER
1 sqn with H215 (AS332) *Super Puma*; (AS365N) *Dauphin*; AW109LUH; H135
EQUIPMENT BY TYPE†
AIRCRAFT 60 combat capable
FTR 12: 10 F-7 (F-7NI); 2 FT-7 (FT-7NI)
ELINT 2 ATR-42-500 MP
ISR 1 Beech 350 *King Air*
TPT 34: Medium 5: 1 C-130H *Hercules* (4 more in store†); 1 C-130H-30 *Hercules* (2 more in store); 3 G.222† (2 more in store†); Light 20: 3 Beech 350 *King Air*; 1 Cessna 550 *Citation*; 8 Do-128D-6 *Turbo SkyServant*; 1 Do-228-100; 2 Do-228-101; 5 Do-228-200 (incl 2 VIP); PAX 9: 1 B-727; 1 B-737BBJ; 1 BAe 125-800; 2 *Falcon* 7X; 2 *Falcon* 900; 1 Gulfstream IV; 1 Gulfstream V
TRG 118: 58 *Air Beetle*† (up to 20 awaiting repair); 3 *Alpha Jet* A*; 10 *Alpha Jet* E*; 2 DA40NG; 23 L-39ZA *Albatros*†*; 12 MB-339AN* (all being upgraded); 10 *Super Mushshak*
HELICOPTERS
ATK 16: 2 Mi-24P *Hind*; 4 Mi-24V *Hind*; 3 Mi-35 *Hind*; 2 Mi-35P *Hind*; 5 Mi-35M *Hind*
MRH 11+: 6 AW109LUH; 2 Bell 412EP; 3+ SA341 *Gazelle*
TPT 22: Medium 11: 2 AW101; 5 H215 (AS332) *Super Puma* (4 more in store); 3 AS365N *Dauphin*; 1 Mi-171Sh; Light 11: 4 H125 (AS350B) *Ecureuil*; 1 AW109; 2 AW109M; 1 Bell 205; 3 H135
UNMANNED AERIAL VEHICLES 2+
CISR • Heavy 1+ CH-3
ISR 1: Medium (9 *Aerostar* non-operational); Light 1+ *Tsaigami*
AIR-LAUNCHED MISSILES
AAM • IR R-3 (AA-2 *Atoll*)‡; PL-9C
ASM AR-1
BOMBS • INS/GPS guided FT-9

Paramilitary ε80,000

Security and Civil Defence Corps 80,000
EQUIPMENT BY TYPE
ARMOURED FIGHTING VEHICLES
APC 80+
  APC (W) 74+: 70+ AT105 *Saxon*†; 4 BTR-3U; UR-416
  PPV 6 *Springbuck* 4x4
AIRCRAFT • TPT • Light 4: 1 Cessna 500 *Citation* I; 2 PA-31 *Navajo*; 1 PA-31-350 *Navajo Chieftain*
HELICOPTERS • TPT • Light 5: 2 Bell 212 (AB-212); 2 Bell 222 (AB-222); 1 Bell 429

DEPLOYMENT

CENTRAL AFRICAN REPUBLIC: UN • MINUSCA 2
DEMOCRATIC REPUBLIC OF THE CONGO: UN • MONUSCO 9
GAMBIA: ECOWAS • ECOMIG 197
GUINEA-BISSAU: ECOWAS • ECOMIB 100
LEBANON: UN • UNIFIL 1
MALI: UN • MINUSMA 83; 1 fd hospital
SOUTH SUDAN: UN • UNMISS 12
SUDAN: UN • UNISFA 4
WESTERN SAHARA: UN • MINURSO 6

FOREIGN FORCES
United Kingdom 80 (trg teams)

Rwanda RWA

Rwandan Franc fr		2018	2019	2020
GDP	fr	8.19tr	9.20tr	
	US$	9.51bn	10.2bn	
per capita	US$	787	825	
Growth	%	8.6	7.8	
Inflation	%	1.4	3.5	
Def bdgt	fr	92.3bn	101bn	121bn
	US$	107m	112m	
US$1=fr			861.09	901.11

Real-terms defence budget trend (US$m, constant 2015)

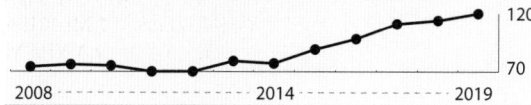

Population 12,461,248
Ethnic groups: Hutu 80%; Tutsi 19%

Age	0–14	15–19	20–24	25–29	30–64	65 plus
Male	20.5%	5.3%	4.6%	4.0%	13.6%	1.0%
Female	20.1%	5.3%	4.6%	4.1%	15.6%	1.5%

Capabilities

Rwanda is one of the principal security actors in East Africa, with disciplined and well-trained armed forces. Their principal missions are to defend territorial integrity and national sovereignty. The country fields a relatively large army, but units are lightly equipped, with little mechanisation. Rwanda signed a Mutual Defence Treaty with Kenya and Uganda in 2014 and participates in the East African Standby Force. A law on downsizing and demobilising elements of the armed forces was published in October 2015 and there have in recent years been official retirement ceremonies for those reaching rank-related retirement ages. The lack of fixed-wing aircraft limits the armed forces' ability to independently deploy much overseas beyond personnel. There have been some acquisitions of modern artillery and armoured vehicles. There is limited maintenance capacity but no defence manufacturing sector.

ACTIVE 33,000 (Army 32,000 Air 1,000) Paramilitary 2,000

ORGANISATIONS BY SERVICE

Army 32,000
FORCES BY ROLE
MANOEUVRE
  Light
    2 cdo bn
    4 inf div (3 inf bde)
COMBAT SUPPORT
  1 arty bde
EQUIPMENT BY TYPE
ARMOURED FIGHTING VEHICLES
  MBT 34: 24 T-54/T-55; 10 *Tiran*-5
  RECCE 106: ε90 AML-60/AML-90; 16 VBL
  IFV 35+: BMP; 15 *Ratel*-90; 20 *Ratel*-60
  APC 60+
    APC (W) 20+: BTR; *Buffalo* (Panhard M3); 20 WZ-551 (reported)
    PPV 40 RG-31 *Nyala*
  AUV 30 *Cobra*
ENGINEERING & MAINTENANCE VEHICLES
  ARV T-54/T-55 reported
ANTI-TANK/ANTI-INFRASTRUCTURE
  MSL • SP HJ-9A (on *Cobra*)
ARTILLERY 177+
  SP 17: **122mm** 12: 6 CS/SH-1; 6 SH-3; **155mm** 5 ATMOS 2000
  TOWED 35+: **105mm** some; **122mm** 6 D-30; **152mm** 29 Type-54 (D-1)†
  MRL 10: **122mm** 5 RM-70; **160mm** 5 LAR-160
  MOR 115: **81mm**; **82mm**; **120mm**
  AIR DEFENCE SAM • Point-defence 9K32 *Strela*-2 (SA-7 *Grail*)‡
  GUNS ε150: **14.5mm**; **23mm**; **37mm**

Air Force ε1,000
FORCES BY ROLE
ATTACK/TRANSPORT HELICOPTER
  1 sqn with Mi-17/Mi-17MD/Mi-17V-5/Mi-17-1V *Hip* H; Mi-24P/V *Hind*

EQUIPMENT BY TYPE
HELICOPTERS
ATK 5: 2 Mi-24V *Hind* E; 3 Mi-24P *Hind*
MRH 12: 1 AW139; 4 Mi-17 *Hip* H; 1 Mi-17MD *Hip* H; 1 Mi-17V-5 *Hip* H; 5 Mi-17-1V *Hip* H
TPT • Light 1 AW109S

Paramilitary

District Administration Security Support Organ ε2,000

DEPLOYMENT

CENTRAL AFRICAN REPUBLIC: UN • MINUSCA 1,388; 2 inf bn; 1 fd hospital
SOUTH SUDAN: UN • UNMISS 2,786; 3 inf bn; 2 hel sqn
SUDAN: UN • UNAMID 1,136; 2 inf bn; UN • UNISFA 5

Senegal SEN

CFA Franc BCEAO fr		2018	2019	2020
GDP	fr	13.0tr	14.0tr	
	US$	23.5bn	23.9bn	
per capita	US$	1,441	1,428	
Growth	%	6.7	6.0	
Inflation	%	0.5	1.0	
Def bdgt	fr	193bn	201bn	
	US$	347m	343m	
US$1=fr		555.20	584.07	

Real-terms defence budget trend (US$m, constant 2015)

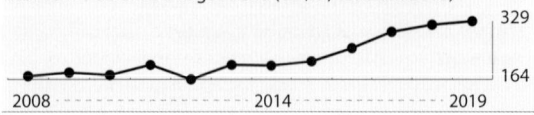

Population 15,377,009

Ethnic groups: Wolof 36%; Fulani 17%; Serer 17%; Toucouleur 9%; Man-dingo 9%; Diola 9% (of which 30–60% in Casamance)

Age	0–14	15–19	20–24	25–29	30–64	65 plus
Male	20.5%	5.5%	4.7%	4.0%	12.4%	1.3%
Female	20.3%	5.4%	4.8%	4.2%	15.2%	1.7%

Capabilities

Senegal's armed forces have strong international relationships and are experienced in foreign deployments. Their focus is internal and border security, including counter-insurgency in the country's south and Islamist activity in neighbouring states, as well as combating narcotics trafficking. The government in 2019 was looking to develop a strategy to combat urban organised crime. Under the 'Horizon 2025' programme, the defence authorities intend to reorganise and re-equip key defence organisations and renew infrastructure. Areas for improvement include mobility and firepower. Despite limited resources, there are plans to improve operational capabilities and training. France remains Senegal's principal defence partner and retains a military presence in the country. French military forces deliver training assistance, including in search and rescue, and in 2019 transferred France's air-logistics hub to upgraded facilities at Blaise Diagne airport. The US also provides security assistance, including to the national police and gendarmerie. A US-funded counter-terrorism training centre was opened in September 2018. The UK trains personnel in tasks relating to international peacekeeping operations. The armed forces are able to deploy personnel using organic airlift, but short-notice movements of heavy equipment would be problematic without external assistance. Modernisation of the air force is a priority, and Senegal is on track to revive a modest jet capability with the order of four L-39NG light attack aircraft, having also ordered a small number of turboprop trainers. Bar limited maintenance facilities, the country has no domestic defence-industrial capability.

ACTIVE 13,600 (Army 11,900 Navy 950 Air 750)
Paramilitary 5,000
Conscript liability Selective conscription, 24 months

ORGANISATIONS BY SERVICE

Army 11,900 (incl conscripts)
7 Mil Zone HQ
FORCES BY ROLE
MANOEUVRE
 Reconnaissance
  5 armd recce bn
 Light
  1 cdo bn
  6 inf bn
 Air Manoeuvre
  1 AB bn
 Other
  1 (Presidential Guard) horse cav bn
COMBAT SUPPORT
 1 arty bn
 1 engr bn
 3 construction coy
 1 sigs bn
COMBAT SERVICE SUPPORT
 1 log bn
 1 med bn
 1 trg bn
EQUIPMENT BY TYPE
ARMOURED FIGHTING VEHICLES
 ASLT 27 PTL-02 *Assaulter*
 RECCE 145: 30 AML-60; 74 AML-90; 10 M8; 4 M20; 27 RAM Mk3
 IFV 26 *Ratel*-20
 APC 91
  APC (T) 12 M3 half-track
  APC (W) 22: 2 *Oncilla*; 16 Panhard M3; 4 WZ-551 (CP)
  PPV 57: 8 *Casspir*; 39 *Puma* M26-15; 10 *Puma* M36
ENGINEERING & MAINTENANCE VEHICLES
 ARV 2 *Puma* M36 ARV
ANTI-TANK/ANTI-INFRASTRUCTURE
 MSL • MANPATS *Milan*
ARTILLERY 82
 TOWED 20: **105mm** 6 HM-2/M101; **155mm** 14: ε6 Model-50; 8 TR-F1
 MRL **122mm** 6 BM-21 *Grad* (UKR *Bastion*-1 mod)
 MOR 56: **81mm** 24; **120mm** 32
AIR DEFENCE • GUNS • TOWED 39: **14.5mm** 6 ZPU-4 (tch); **20mm** 21 M693; **40mm** 12 L/60

Navy (incl Coast Guard) 950

FORCES BY ROLE

SPECIAL FORCES
1 cdo coy

EQUIPMENT BY TYPE

PATROL AND COASTAL COMBATANTS 5
PCO 1 *Fouladou* (OPV 190 Mk II)
PCC 1 *Njambour* (FRA SFCN 59m) with 2 76mm gun
PBF 1 *Ferlo* (RPB 33)
PB 2: 1 *Conejera*; 1 *Kedougou*

AMPHIBIOUS • LANDING CRAFT 2
LCT 2 *Edic 700*

LOGISTICS AND SUPPORT 1
AG 1

Air Force 750

FORCES BY ROLE

MARITIME PATROL/SEARCH & RESCUE
1 sqn with C-212 *Aviocar*; CN235; Bell 205 (UH-1H *Iroquois*)

ISR
1 unit with BN-2T *Islander* (anti-smuggling patrols)

TRANSPORT
1 sqn with B-727-200 (VIP); F-27-400M *Troopship*

TRAINING
1 sqn with R-235 *Guerrier**; TB-30 *Epsilon*

ATTACK/TRANSPORT HELICOPTER
1 sqn with AS355F *Ecureuil* II; Bell 206; Mi-35P *Hind*; Mi-171Sh

EQUIPMENT BY TYPE

AIRCRAFT 1 combat capable
TPT 10: **Light** 8: 1 BN-2T *Islander* (govt owned, mil op); 1 C-212-100 *Aviocar*; 2 CN235; 2 Beech B200 *King Air*; 2 F-27-400M *Troopship* (3 more in store); **PAX** 2: 1 A319; 1 B-727-200 (VIP)
TRG 7: 1 R-235 *Guerrier**; 6 TB-30 *Epsilon*

HELICOPTERS
ATK 4: 2 Mi-24V *Hind* D; 2 Mi-35P *Hind*
MRH 1 AW139
TPT 8: **Medium** 2 Mi-171Sh; **Light** 6: 1 AS355F *Ecureuil* II; 1 Bell 205 (UH-1H *Iroquois*); 2 Bell 206; 2 PZL Mi-2 *Hoplite*

Paramilitary 5,000

Gendarmerie 5,000

EQUIPMENT BY TYPE

ARMOURED FIGHTING VEHICLES
RECCE 13: 2 *Bastion Patsas*; 11 RAM Mk3
APC 56
  APC (W) 24: 7 *Bastion* APC; 5 EE-11 *Urutu*; 12 VXB-170
  PPV 32: 24 *Ejder Yalcin*; 8 *Gila*

DEPLOYMENT

CENTRAL AFRICAN REPUBLIC: UN • MINUSCA 113; 1 atk hel sqn

DEMOCRATIC REPUBLIC OF THE CONGO: UN • MONUSCO 7

GAMBIA: ECOWAS • ECOMIG 250

MALI: UN • MINUSMA 1,276; 2 inf bn; 1 engr coy

SOUTH SUDAN: UN • UNMISS 2

FOREIGN FORCES

France 350; 1 *Falcon* 50MI
Spain Operation Barkhane 60; 1 C-130H *Hercules*

Seychelles SYC

Seychelles Rupee SR		2018	2019	2020
GDP	SR	22.0bn	23.2bn	
	US$	1.58bn	1.64bn	
per capita	US$	16,575	17,052	
Growth	%	4.1	3.5	
Inflation	%	3.7	2.0	
Def exp	SR	n.k	n.k	
	US$	n.k	n.k	
US$1=SR		13.91	14.11	
Population	95,321			

Age	0–14	15–19	20–24	25–29	30–64	65 plus
Male	9.8%	3.3%	3.4%	4.0%	27.8%	3.3%
Female	9.3%	3.0%	3.0%	3.5%	24.9%	4.7%

Capabilities

The Seychelles maintains one of the smallest standing armed forces in the world. Its proximity to key international shipping lanes is of strategic significance. The Seychelles People's Defence Force (PDF) primarily focuses on maritime security and counter-piracy operations. The country hosts US military forces conducting maritime-patrol activities on a rotational basis, including the operation of unarmed UAVs. India maintains strong defence ties with the Seychelles, donating equipment, providing maintenance and supporting efforts to enhance its maritime-patrol and surveillance capability. There are ongoing plans to improve defence cooperation with China, which has already led to some equipment deliveries. The Seychelles continues to participate in and host a number of multinational maritime-security exercises. The PDF does not deploy overseas and has a limited capacity to deploy and support troops operating in the archipelago. Modern platforms in the air force and coastguard comprise donations from China, India and the UAE. There are limited maintenance facilities but no domestic defence manufacturing sector.

ACTIVE 420 (Land Forces 200; Coast Guard 200; Air Force 20)

ORGANISATIONS BY SERVICE

People's Defence Force

Land Forces 200

FORCES BY ROLE
SPECIAL FORCES
  1 SF unit
MANOEUVRE
  Light
  1 inf coy
  Other
  1 sy unit
COMBAT SUPPORT
  1 MP unit
EQUIPMENT BY TYPE
ARMOURED FIGHTING VEHICLES
  RECCE 6 BRDM-2†
ARTILLERY • MOR 82mm 6 M-43†
AIR DEFENCE • GUNS • TOWED 14.5mm ZPU-2†; ZPU-4†; 37mm M-1939†

Coast Guard 200 (incl 80 Marines)
EQUIPMENT BY TYPE
PATROL AND COASTAL COMBATANTS 10
  PCO 3: 1 *Andromache* (ITA *Pichiotti* 42m); 2 *Topaz* (ex-IND *Trinkat*)
  PBF 3: 1 *Hermes* (ex-IND *Coastal Interceptor Craft*); 2 *Wave Rider*
  PB 4: 2 *Le Vigilant* (ex-UAE Rodman 101); 1 *Etoile* (*Shanghai* II mod); 1 *Fortune* (UK *Tyne*)

Air Force 20
EQUIPMENT BY TYPE
AIRCRAFT
  TPT • Light 5: 1 DHC-6-320 *Twin Otter*; 2 Do-228; 2 Y-12

Sierra Leone SLE

Sierra Leonean Leone L		2018	2019	2020
GDP	L	32.4tr	37.9tr	
	US$	4.08bn	4.23bn	
per capita	US$	539	547	
Growth	%	3.5	5.0	
Inflation	%	16.9	15.7	
Def bdgt	L	107bn	96.0bn	137bn
	US$	13.4m	10.7m	
US$1=L		7937.68	8968.37	

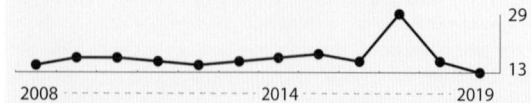
Real-terms defence budget trend (US$m, constant 2015)

Population	6,466,064				
Age	0–14	15–19	20–24	25–29	30–64	65 plus
Male	20.8%	5.0%	4.1%	3.7%	13.5%	1.5%
Female	20.8%	5.2%	4.4%	4.0%	14.8%	2.2%

Capabilities

The armed forces' primary task is to ensure internal and border security and provide forces for continental peacekeeping missions. With international support, there remains a focus on building defence institutions, generating formal defence documentation and improving planning functions. The UK is heavily involved in supporting the development of Sierra Leone's security institutions and improving training. UK training is also intended to boost the capacity of the police force, so that military support is only needed in major emergencies. Freetown's Horton Academy trains local and regional personnel in SSR issues, as well as general military training tasks for local staff. Defence ties with China include personnel exchanges and capacity-building for peacekeeping operations. The armed forces' ability to deploy anything other than small units is constrained by force size and logistics-support capacity. With the budget mainly directed to personnel costs, capability in areas including air and maritime surveillance remains limited. There is no domestic defence-industrial capability.

ACTIVE 8,500 (Joint 8,500)

ORGANISATIONS BY SERVICE

Armed Forces 8,500
FORCES BY ROLE
MANOEUVRE
  Reconnaissance
  1 recce unit
  Light
  3 inf bde (total: 12 inf bn)
COMBAT SUPPORT
  1 engr regt
  1 int unit
  1 MP unit
  1 sigs unit
COMBAT SUPPORT
  1 log unit
  1 fd hospital
EQUIPMENT BY TYPE
ARMOURED FIGHTING VEHICLES
  APC • PPV 4: 3 *Casspir*; 1 *Mamba* Mk5
ANTI-TANK/ANTI-INFRASTRUCTURE
  RCL 84mm *Carl Gustav*
ARTILLERY 37
  TOWED 122mm 6 Type-96 (D30)
  MOR 31: 81mm ε27; 82mm 2; 120mm 2
HELICOPTERS • MRH 2 Mi-17 *Hip* H/Mi-8 *Hip*†
AIR DEFENCE • GUNS 14.5mm 3

Maritime Wing ε200
EQUIPMENT BY TYPE
PATROL AND COASTAL COMBATANTS • PB 2: 1 *Shanghai* III†; 1 *Isle of Man*

DEPLOYMENT

CENTRAL AFRICAN REPUBLIC: UN • MINUSCA 3
LEBANON: UN • UNIFIL 3
MALI: UN • MINUSMA 21
SOMALIA: UN • UNSOM 2; UN • UNSOS 1
SOUTH SUDAN: UN • UNMISS 1
SUDAN: UN • UNAMID 4; UN • UNISFA 4

Somalia SOM

Somali Shilling sh		2018	2019	2020
GDP	sh	4.72bn	4.96bn	
	US$	4.72bn	4.96bn	
per capita	US$	n.k.	n.k.	
Growth	%	2.8	2.9	
Inflation	%	n.k.	n.k.	
Def bdgt	US$	n.k.	n.k.	
US$1=sh		1.00	1.00	
Population	11,500,692			

Age	0–14	15–19	20–24	25–29	30–64	65 plus
Male	21.3%	5.4%	4.5%	3.8%	14.5%	0.9%
Female	21.3%	5.4%	4.3%	3.6%	13.6%	1.4%

Capabilities

Internal stability remains fragile following decades of conflict and insurgency, with al-Shabaab and other extremist groups active in the country. Deployed international forces look to provide security, stabilisation and capacity-building assistance, with a transition plan in place for the country to assume full security responsibility. The Somali National Army (SNA) remains weak in terms of both organisation and military capability. US forces are deployed independently to Somalia and target militant groups. Plans to professionalise, legitimise and unite the loose collections of clan-based militia groups that form the SNA have yet to be fully realised. Although training programmes have been delivered by a number of countries, organisations and private-security companies, there are no common training standards throughout the army. There is no capacity to deploy beyond national borders, while there is minimal national infrastructure available to support domestic operations. The equipment inventory is limited, and government plans to re-establish and equip Somalia's air and maritime forces remain unfulfilled. There is no domestic defence-industrial capability.

ACTIVE 19,800 (Army 19,800)

ORGANISATIONS BY SERVICE

Army 19,800 (plus further militias (to be integrated))

FORCES BY ROLE
COMMAND
 4 div HQ
MANOEUVRE
 Light
 Some cdo bn(+)
 12 inf bde (3 inf bn)
 2 indep inf bn
 Other
 1 gd bn
EQUIPMENT BY TYPE
ARMOURED FIGHTING VEHICLES
 APC 47+
  APC (W) 38+: 25+ AT-105 *Saxon*; 13 *Bastion* APC; Fiat 6614
  PPV 9+: *Casspir*; MAV-5; 9+ *Mamba* Mk5; RG-31 *Nyala*
 AUV 12 *Tiger* 4×4

Paramilitary

Coast Guard
All operational patrol vessels under 10t FLD

FOREIGN FORCES

Under UNSOM command unless stated
Burundi AMISOM 5,073; 6 inf bn
Djibouti AMISOM 1,872; 2 inf bn
Ethiopia AMISOM 4,323; 6 inf bn
Finland EUTM Somalia 10
Ghana UNSOS 1
Italy EUTM Somalia 128
Kenya AMISOM 4,046; 3 inf bn • UNSOS 1
Mauritania UNSOS 1
Pakistan UNSOS 1
Portugal EUTM Somalia 4
Romania EUTM Somalia 1
Serbia EUTM Somalia 6
Sierra Leone 2 • UNSOS 1
Spain EUTM Somalia 20
Sweden EUTM Somalia 9
Turkey 1 • 200 (trg base)
Uganda 627; 1 sy bn • AMISOM 6,022; 7 inf bn • UNSOS 1
United Kingdom 3 • UNSOS 13 • EUTM Somalia 3
United States Africa Command 500

TERRITORY WHERE THE GOVERNMENT DOES NOT EXERCISE EFFECTIVE CONTROL

Data presented here represents the de facto situation. This does not imply international recognition as a sovereign state. Much of this equipment is in poor repair or inoperable

Somaliland

Army ε12,500
FORCES BY ROLE
MANOEUVRE
 Armoured
 2 armd bde
 Mechanised
 1 mech inf bde
 Light
 14 inf bde
COMBAT SUPPORT
 2 arty bde
COMBAT SERVICE SUPPORT
 1 spt bn
EQUIPMENT BY TYPE†
ARMOURED FIGHTING VEHICLES
 MBT T-54/55
 RECCE Fiat 6616
 APC • APC(W) Fiat 6614

ARTILLERY • MRL various incl BM-21 *Grad*
AIR DEFENCE • GUNS • 23mm ZU-23-2

Ministry of the Interior

Coast Guard 600
All operational patrol vessels under 10t FLD

Puntland

Army ε3,000 (to be integrated into Somali National Army)

Maritime Police Force ε1,000
EQUIPMENT BY TYPE
AIRCRAFT • TPT 4: **Light** 3 Ayres S2R; **PAX** 1 DC-3
HELICOPTERS • MRH SA316 *Alouette* III
PATROL AND COASTAL COMBATANTS
All operational patrol vessels under 10t FLD

South Africa RSA

South African Rand R		2018	2019	2020
GDP	R	4.87tr	5.12tr	
	US$	368bn	359bn	
per capita	US$	6,354	6,100	
Growth	%	0.8	0.7	
Inflation	%	4.6	4.4	
Def bdgt	R	47.9bn	50.5bn	53.8bn
	US$	3.62bn	3.54bn	
US$1=R		13.24	14.27	

Defence budget: ten-year perspective (US$bn, constant)

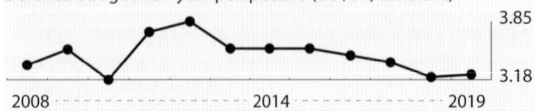

3.85 / 3.18
2008 — 2014 — 2019

Population	55,918,443					
Age	0–14	15–19	20–24	25–29	30–64	65 plus
Male	14.1%	4.2%	4.2%	4.7%	19.8%	2.5%
Female	14.0%	4.2%	4.4%	4.7%	19.7%	3.4%

Capabilities

While on paper the region's most capable armed forces, economic problems have undermined effectiveness. According to the 2017/2018 Defence Annual Report, funding constraints meant that the level of ambition set for the armed forces was not 'sustainable' and should the funding trajectory continue downward, a lower capability than that outlined in the 2015 Defence Review was the likely outcome. This caution was reiterated in the 2019 Annual Performance Plan. Roles include protecting the state and maintaining territorial integrity, as well as supporting the police service in specific circumstances. The Department of Defence Strategic Plan 2015–2020 is the force's primary policy instrument. This maps out five strategic-planning milestones, the first of which is to arrest the decline of critical military capabilities. South Africa contributes to UN operations and has been a key component of the Force Intervention Brigade in the DRC since its inception. It is a member of the SADC Standby Force. Historically, South African forces have also played a significant role in training and supporting other regional forces. The SANDF can independently deploy its forces across the continent, deploys regularly on peacekeeping missions, and participates in national and multinational exercises. Equipment availability on some deployments, such as helicopter units in the DRC, has been a cause for concern. While the SANDF has a well-established modernisation plan, the ability to deliver on this is hindered by funding problems and a number of programmes are behind schedule. Budget cuts are likely to have an adverse effect on training. There is concern in the army over the obsolescence of principal equipment. South Africa has the continent's most capable defence industry, including the state-owned Armaments Corporation of South Africa and weapons manufacturer Denel. However, budget cuts and reduced domestic procurement have increasingly required South Africa to look to export markets. A National Defence Industry Council was launched in 2016 to support arms exports. The possibility of defence-industrial cooperation with Russia was mooted in 2019.

ACTIVE 74,850 (Army 37,600 Navy 7,000 Air 9,650 South African Military Health Service 7,600 Other 13,000)

RESERVE 15,050 (Army 12,250 Navy 850 Air 850 South African Military Health Service Reserve 1,100)

ORGANISATIONS BY SERVICE

Space
EQUIPMENT BY TYPE
SATELLITES • ISR 1 *Kondor-E*

Army 37,600
FORCES BY ROLE
Regt are bn sized. A new army structure is planned with 3 mixed regular/reserve divisions (1 mechanised, 1 motorised and 1 contingency) comprising 12 brigades (1 armoured, 1 mechanised, 7 motorised, 1 airborne, 1 airlanded and 1 sea landed)
COMMAND
 2 bde HQ
SPECIAL FORCES
 2 SF regt(-)
MANOEUVRE
 Reconnaissance
 1 armd recce regt
 Armoured
 1 tk regt(-)
 Mechanised
 2 mech inf bn
 Light
 8 mot inf bn
 1 lt inf bn
 Air Manoeuvre
 1 AB bn
 1 air mob bn
 Amphibious
 1 amph bn
COMBAT SUPPORT
 1 arty regt
 1 engr regt
 1 construction regt
 3 sigs regt

COMBAT SERVICE SUPPORT
  1 engr spt regt
AIR DEFENCE
  1 ADA regt

Reserve 12,250 reservists (under-strength)
FORCES BY ROLE
MANOEUVRE
  Reconnaissance
  3 armd recce regt
  Armoured
  4 tk regt
  Mechanised
  6 mech inf bn
  Light
  14 mot inf bn
  3 lt inf bn (converting to mot inf)
  Air Manoeuvre
  1 AB bn
  2 air mob bn
  Amphibious
  1 amph bn
COMBAT SUPPORT
  7 arty regt
  2 engr regt
AIR DEFENCE
  5 AD regt
EQUIPMENT BY TYPE
ARMOURED FIGHTING VEHICLES
  MBT 24 *Olifant* 2 (133 *Olifant* 1B in store)
  ASLT 50 *Rooikat*-76 (126 in store)
  IFV 534 *Ratel*-20/*Ratel*-60/*Ratel*-90
  APC • PPV 810: 370 *Casspir*; 440 *Mamba*
ENGINEERING & MAINTENANCE VEHICLES
  ARV *Gemsbok*
  VLB *Leguan*
  MW *Husky*
ANTI-TANK/ANTI-INFRASTRUCTURE
  MSL
    SP ZT-3 *Swift*
    MANPATS *Milan* ADT/ER
  RCL 106mm M40A1 (some SP)
ARTILLERY 1,240
  SP 155mm 2 G-6 (41 in store)
  TOWED 155mm 6 G 5 (66 in store)
  MRL 127mm 6 *Valkiri* Mk II MARS *Bataleur*; (26 *Valkiri* Mk I and 19 *Valkiri* Mk II in store)
  MOR 1,226: **81mm** 1,190 (incl some SP on *Casspir* & *Ratel*); **120mm** 36
UNMANNED AERIAL VEHICLES
  ISR • Light up to 4 *Vulture*
AIR DEFENCE
  SAM • Point-defence *Starstreak*
  GUNS 40
    SP 23mm (36 *Zumlac* in store)
    TOWED 35mm 40: 22 GDF-002; 18 GDF-005A/007

Navy 7,000
Fleet HQ and Naval base located at Simon's Town; Naval stations located at Durban and Port Elizabeth
EQUIPMENT BY TYPE
SUBMARINES • TACTICAL • SSK 2 *Heroine* (Type-209/1400 mod) with 8 533mm TT with SUT 264 HWT (1 additional boat in refit since 2014, awaiting funds to complete)
PRINCIPAL SURFACE COMBATANTS • FRIGATES 4:
  FFGHM 4 *Valour* (MEKO A200) with 2 quad lnchr with MM40 *Exocet* Block 2 AShM (upgrade to Block 3 planned); 2 16-cell VLS with *Umkhonto*-IR SAM, 1 76mm gun (capacity 1 *Super Lynx* 300 hel)
PATROL AND COASTAL COMBATANTS 4
  PCC 3: 2 *Warrior* (ISR *Reshef*) with 1 76mm gun; 1 *Warrior* (ISR *Reshef*)
  PB 1 *Tobie* (2 additional in reserve)
MINE WARFARE • MINE COUNTERMEASURES 2
  MHC 3 *River* (GER *Navors*) (Limited operational roles; training and dive support)
LOGISTICS AND SUPPORT 2
  AORH 1 *Drakensberg* (capacity 2 *Oryx* hels; 100 troops)
  AGHS 1 *Protea* (UK *Hecla*) with 1 hel landing platform

Maritime Reaction Squadron
FORCES BY ROLE
MANOEUVRE
  Amphibious
  1 mne patrol gp
  1 diving gp
  1 mne boarding gp
COMBAT SERVICE SUPPORT
  1 spt gp

Air Force 9,650
Air Force HQ, Pretoria, and 4 op gps
Command & Control: 2 Airspace Control Sectors, 1 Mobile Deployment Wg, 1 Air Force Command Post
FORCES BY ROLE
FIGHTER/GROUND ATTACK
  1 sqn with *Gripen* C/D (JAS-39C/D)
GROUND ATTACK/TRAINING
  1 sqn with *Hawk* Mk120*
TRANSPORT
  1 (VIP) sqn with B-737 BBJ; Cessna 550 *Citation* II; *Falcon* 50; *Falcon* 900
  1 sqn with C-47TP
  2 sqn with Beech 200/300 *King Air*; C-130B/BZ; C-212
ATTACK HELICOPTER
  1 (cbt spt) sqn with AH-2 *Rooivalk*
TRANSPORT HELICOPTER
  4 (mixed) sqn with AW109; BK-117; *Oryx*
EQUIPMENT BY TYPE
AIRCRAFT 50 combat capable
  FGA 26: 17 *Gripen* C (JAS-39C); 9 *Gripen* D (JAS-39D)
  TPT 24: **Medium** 7: 2 C-130B *Hercules*; 5 C-130BZ *Hercules*; **Light** 13: 3 Beech 200C *King Air*; 1 Beech 300 *King Air*; 3 C-47TP (maritime); 2 C-212-200 *Aviocar†*; 1 C-212-300 *Aviocar†*; 2 Cessna 550 *Citation* II; 1 PC-12; (9 Cessna 208 *Caravan* in store) **PAX** 4: 1 B-737BBJ; 2 *Falcon* 50; 1 *Falcon* 900

TRG 59: 24 *Hawk* Mk120*; 35 PC-7 Mk II *Astra*
HELICOPTERS
ATK 11 AH-2 *Rooivalk*
MRH 4 *Super Lynx* 300
TPT 69: **Medium** 36 *Oryx*; **Light** 33: 25 AW109; 8 BK-117
AIR-LAUNCHED MISSILES • AAM • IIR IRIS-T
BOMBS • Laser-guided GBU-12 *Paveway* II

Ground Defence
FORCES BY ROLE
MANOEUVRE
  Other
  12 sy sqn (SAAF regt)

South African Military Health Service 7,600; ε1,100 reservists (total 8,700)

DEPLOYMENT

DEMOCRATIC REPUBLIC OF THE CONGO: UN • MONUSCO • *Operation Mistral* 1,131; 1 inf bn; 1 atk hel sqn; 1 hel sqn
MOZAMBIQUE CHANNEL: Navy • 1 FFGHM
SUDAN: UN • UNAMID (*Operation Cordite*) 3
ZIMBABWE: Army • 118; 1 engr coy

South Sudan SSD

South Sudanese Pound SSP		2018	2019	2020
GDP	ssp	649bn	812bn	
	US$	4.58bn	3.68bn	
per capita	US$	353	275	
Growth	%	-1.1	7.9	
Inflation	%	83.5	24.5	
Def bdgt [a]	ssp	13.0bn	15.5bn	21.9bn
	US$	91.5m	70.1m	
US$1=ssp		141.71	220.52	

[a] Security and law-enforcement spending

Real-terms defence budget trend (US$m, constant 2015)

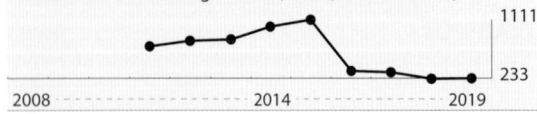

Population	10,280,287					
Age	0–14	15–19	20–24	25–29	30–64	65 plus
Male	21.3%	6.0%	5.0%	4.1%	13.8%	1.4%
Female	20.5%	5.9%	4.3%	3.5%	13.2%	1.0%

Capabilities

South Sudan has been in a state of civil war with armed opposition groups since 2013, with significant challenges remaining to the 2018 peace agreement. This included an aspiration for a Revitalized Transitional Government of National Unity. A 2017 ceasefire improved the overall security situation, though several groups continue to operate. Progress on professionalising and restructuring the rebranded South Sudan People's Defence Force (SSPDF) remains unclear, though allegations continue of child-soldier recruitment. In 2018, South Sudan reportedly signed a defence agreement with South Africa, including scope to cooperate on procurement and training. There is no capacity to deploy and sustain military units beyond national borders. Equipment is primarily of Soviet origin with some light arms of Chinese origin, and there have been efforts to expand the small air force in recent years. Sanctions remain in place, with both the EU and UN arms embargoes widened in 2018 to include all types of military equipment. South Sudan has no established domestic defence industry but has reportedly sought to develop an ammunition-manufacturing capacity in recent years.

ACTIVE 185,000 (Army 185,000)

ORGANISATIONS BY SERVICE

Army ε185,000
FORCES BY ROLE
3 military comd
MANOEUVRE
  Light
  8 inf div
COMBAT SUPPORT
  1 engr corps
EQUIPMENT BY TYPE
ARMOURED FIGHTING VEHICLES
  MBT 80+: some T-55†; 80 T-72AV†
  APC • PPV Streit *Typhoon*; Streit *Cougar*; *Mamba*
ANTI-TANK/ANTI-INFRASTRUCTURE
  MSL • MANPATS HJ-73; 9K115 *Metis* (AT-7 *Saxhorn*)
  RCL 73mm SPG-9 (with SSLA)
ARTILLERY
  SP 122mm 2S1 *Gvozdika*; **152mm** 2S3 *Akatsiya*
  TOWED 130mm Some M-46
  MRL 122mm BM-21 *Grad*; **107mm** PH-63
  MOR 82mm; **120mm** Type-55 look-alike
AIR DEFENCE
  SAM
    Short-range 16 S-125 *Pechora* (SA-3 *Goa*) (reported)
    Point-defence 9K32 *Strela*-2 (SA-7 *Grail*)‡; QW-2
  GUNS 14.5mm ZPU-4; **23mm** ZU-23-2; **37mm** Type-65/74

Air Force
EQUIPMENT BY TYPE
AIRCRAFT 2 combat capable
  TPT • Light 1 Beech 1900
  TRG ε2 L-39 *Albatros**
HELICOPTERS
  ATK 5: 2 Mi-24V *Hind*; 3 Mi-24V-SMB *Hind*
  MRH 9 Mi-17 *Hip* H
  TPT 3: **Medium** 1 Mi-172 (VIP); **Light** 2 AW109 (civ livery)

FOREIGN FORCES

All UNMISS, unless otherwise indicated
Albania 2
Australia 19
Bangladesh 1,619; 1 inf coy; 2 rvn coy; 2 engr coy
Benin 4
Bhutan 4

Bolivia 1
Brazil 13
Cambodia 83; 1 MP unit
Canada 11
China, People's Republic of 1,057; 1 inf bn; 1 engr coy; 1 fd hospital
Denmark 10
Ecuador 2
Egypt 4
El Salvador 3
Ethiopia 2,138; 3 inf bn
Fiji 5
Germany 14
Ghana 876; 1 inf bn
Guatemala 6
Guinea 3
India 2,396; 2 inf bn; 1 engr coy; 1 fd hospital
Indonesia 4
Japan 4
Jordan 5
Kenya 11
Korea, Republic of 275; 1 engr coy
Kyrgyzstan 2
Liberia 2
Malawi 2
Moldova 4
Mongolia 872; 1 inf bn
Namibia 2
Nepal 1,744; 2 inf bn
New Zealand 4
Nigeria 12
Norway 17
Pakistan 11
Paraguay 3
Peru 2
Philippines 2
Poland 1
Romania 6
Russia 6
Rwanda 2,786; 3 inf bn; 2 hel sqn
Senegal 2
Sierra Leone 1
Sri Lanka 173; 1 fd hospital; 1 hel sqn
Sweden 2
Switzerland 1
Tanzania 10
Togo 3
Tunisia 3
Uganda 1
Ukraine 4
United Kingdom 299; 1 engr coy
United States 7
Vietnam 68
Zambia 13
Zimbabwe 6

Sudan SDN

Sudanese Pound sdg		2018	2019	2020
GDP	sdg	1.36tr	2.01tr	
	US$	34.3bn	30.9bn	
per capita	US$	817	714	
Growth	%	-2.2	-2.6	
Inflation	%	63.3	50.4	
Def exp	sdg	n.k	n.k	
	US$	n.k	n.k	
US$1=sdg		39.73	65.21	

Population 44,350,744

Ethnic and religious groups: Muslim 70% mainly in North; Christian 10% mainly in South; Arab 39% mainly in North

Age	0–14	15–19	20–24	25–29	30–64	65 plus
Male	21.6%	5.9%	4.6%	3.7%	12.9%	1.6%
Female	20.9%	5.8%	4.3%	3.6%	13.7%	1.4%

Capabilities

In April 2019, President Omar Al-Bashir was overthrown after 30 years in power and months of protests. By August, opposition forces and the armed forces comprised a Sovereign Council that is due to lead a transition to civilian rule. The armed forces remain focused on internal security as well as border issues in the south, although in August there was agreement with South Sudan to reopen borders. There are also ongoing concerns regarding opposition groups operating in the south, including in Darfur, with the government relying on paramilitary forces to provide internal security. The UN maintains two significant peacekeeping missions in Sudan. Sudan is part of the Saudi-led coalition intervention in Yemen. A defence agreement with Iran in 2008 reportedly included assistance in developing the domestic arms industry. The armed forces are conscript-based and will have gained operational experience from internal-security deployments and the Saudi-led coalition. By regional standards, Sudan's armed forces are relatively well equipped, with significant holdings of both ageing and modern systems. While there is a UN arms embargo in place, it is limited to equipment used within the Darfur region. Recent acquisitions have been Russian and Ukrainian government surplus, apart from new Chinese jet trainers. The state-run Military Industry Corporation manufactures a range of ammunition, small arms and armoured vehicles for the domestic and export market. The majority of the corporation's products are based on older Chinese and Russian systems.

ACTIVE 104,300 (Army 100,000 Navy 1,300 Air 3,000) **Paramilitary 20,000**
Conscript liability 2 years for males aged 18–30

RESERVE NIL Paramilitary 85,000

ORGANISATIONS BY SERVICE

Space
EQUIPMENT BY TYPE
SATELLITES • ISR 1 SRSS-1

Army 100,000+
FORCES BY ROLE
SPECIAL FORCES
  5 SF coy
MANOEUVRE
  Reconnaissance
  1 indep recce bde
  Armoured
  1 armd div
  Mechanised
  1 mech inf div
  1 indep mech inf bde
  Light
  15+ inf div
  6 indep inf bde
  Air Manoeuvre
  1 air aslt bde
  Amphbious
  1 mne div
  Other
  1 (Border Guard) sy bde
COMBAT SUPPORT
  3 indep arty bde
  1 engr div (9 engr bn)
EQUIPMENT BY TYPE
ARMOURED FIGHTING VEHICLES
  MBT 465: 20 M60A3; 60 Type-59/Type-59D; 305 T-54/T-55; 70 T-72AV; 10 *Al-Bashier* (Type-85-IIM)
  LT TK 115: 70 Type-62; 45 Type-63
  RECCE 206: 6 AML-90; 70 BRDM-1/2; 50–80 FV701 *Ferret*; 30–50 FV601 *Saladin*
  IFV 152+: 135 BMP-1/2; 10 BTR-3; 7 BTR-80A; WZ-523 IFV
  APC 415+
    APC (T) 66: 20-30 BTR-50; 36 M113
    APC (W) 349+: 10 BTR-70M *Kobra* 2; 50–80 BTR-152; 20 OT-62; 50 OT-64; 3+ *Rakhsh*; 10 WZ-551; WZ-523; 55-80 V-150 *Commando*; 96 Walid
ANTI-TANK/ANTI-INFRASTRUCTURE
  MSL • MANPATS 9K11 *Malyutka* (AT-3 *Sagger*); HJ-8; 9K135 *Kornet* (AT-14 *Spriggan*)
  RCL 106mm 40 M40A1
  GUNS 76mm ZIS-3; **100mm** M-1944; **85mm** D-44
ARTILLERY 860+
  SP 66: **122mm** 56 2S1 *Gvozdika*; **155mm** 10 Mk F3
  TOWED 128+: **105mm** 20 M101; **122mm** 21+: 21 D-30; D-74; M-30; **130mm** 75 M-46/Type-59-I; **155mm** 12 M114A1
  MRL 666+: **107mm** 477 Type-63; **122mm** 188: 120 BM-21 *Grad*; 50 *Saqr*; 18 Type-81; **302mm** 1+ WS-1
  MOR 81mm; **82mm**; **120mm** AM-49; M-43; W86
AIR DEFENCE
  SAM • Point-defence 4+: 9K32 *Strela*-2 (SA-7 *Grail*)‡; FN-6; 4+ 9K33 *Osa* (SA-8 *Gecko*)
  GUNS 966+:
    SP 20: **20mm** 8 M163 *Vulcan*; 12 M3 VDAA
    TOWED 946+: 740+ **14.5mm** ZPU-2/**14.5mm** ZPU-4/**37mm** Type-63/**57mm** S-60/**85mm** M-1944; **20mm** 16 M167 *Vulcan*; **23mm** 50 ZU-23-2; **37mm** 80 M-1939; (30 M-1939 unserviceable); **40mm** 60

Navy 1,300
EQUIPMENT BY TYPE
PATROL AND COASTAL COMBATANTS 11
  PBR 4 *Kurmuk*
  PB 7: 1 13.5m; 1 14m; 2 19m; 3 41m (PRC)
AMPHIBIOUS • LANDING CRAFT 5
  LCVP 5
LOGISTICS AND SUPPORT 3
  AG 3

Air Force 3,000
FORCES BY ROLE
FIGHTER
  2 sqn with MiG-29SE/UB *Fulcrum*
FIGHTER/GROUND ATTACK
  1 sqn with FTC-2000*
GROUND ATTACK
  1 sqn with Su-24M/MR *Fencer*
  1 sqn with Su-25K/Su-25UB *Frogfoot*
TRANSPORT
  Some sqn with An-30 *Clank*; An-32 *Cline*; An-72 *Coaler*; An-74TK-200/300; C-130H *Hercules*; Il-76 *Candid*; Y-8
  1 VIP unit with *Falcon* 20F; *Falcon* 50; *Falcon* 900; F-27; Il-62M *Classic*
TRAINING
  1 sqn with K-8 *Karakorum**
ATTACK HELICOPTER
  2 sqn with Mi-24/Mi-24P/Mi-24V/Mi-35P *Hind*
TRANSPORT HELICOPTER
  2 sqn with Mi-8 *Hip*; Mi-17 *Hip* H; Mi-171
AIR DEFENCE
  5 bty with S-75 *Dvina* (SA-2 *Guideline*)‡
EQUIPMENT BY TYPE
AIRCRAFT 56 combat capable
  FTR 22: 20 MiG-29SE *Fulcrum* C; 2 MiG-29UB *Fulcrum* B
  ATK 17: 6 Su-24M/MR *Fencer*; 9 Su-25K *Frogfoot*; 2 Su-25UB *Frogfoot* B; (15 A-5 *Fantan* in store)
  ISR 2 An-30 *Clank*
  TPT 24: **Heavy** 1 Il-76 *Candid*; **Medium** 6: 4 C-130H *Hercules*; 2 Y-8; **Light** 13: ε3 An-26 *Curl*; 2 An-32 *Cline*; 2 An-72 *Coaler*; 4 An-74TK-200; 2 An-74TK-300; **PAX** 4: 1 *Falcon* 20F (VIP); 1 *Falcon* 50 (VIP); 1 *Falcon* 900; 1 Il-62M *Classic*
  TRG 21+: 6 FTC-2000*; 11 K-8 *Karakorum**; some SAFAT-03; 3 UTVA-75
HELICOPTERS
  ATK 40: 25 Mi-24 *Hind*; 2 Mi-24P *Hind*; 7 Mi-24V *Hind* E; 6 Mi-35P *Hind*
  MRH ε3 Mi-17 *Hip* H
  TPT 27: **Medium** 23: 21 Mi-8 *Hip*; 2 Mi-171; **Light** 4: 1 Bell 205; 3 Bo-105
UNMANNED AERIAL VEHICLES
  CISR • Heavy CH-3; CH-4
AIR DEFENCE • SAM • Medium-range: 90 S-75 *Dvina* (SA-2 *Guideline*)‡
AIR-LAUNCHED MISSILES • AAM • IR R-3 (AA-2 *Atoll*)‡; R-60 (AA-8 *Aphid*); R-73 (AA-11A *Archer*); **ARH** R-77 (AA-12A *Adder*)

Paramilitary 20,000

Popular Defence Force 20,000 (org in bn 1,000); 85,000 reservists (total 105,000)
mil wing of National Islamic Front

DEPLOYMENT

SAUDI ARABIA: *Operation Restoring Hope* 3 Su-24M/MR *Fencer*

YEMEN: *Operation Restoring Hope* 950; 1 mech BG; T-72AV, BTR-70M *Kobra* 2

FOREIGN FORCES

All UNAMID, unless otherwise indicated
Bangladesh UNISFA 2
Benin UNISFA 2
Bhutan UNISFA 2
Bolivia UNISFA 4
Brazil UNISFA 3
Burkina Faso UNISFA 1
Burundi UNISFA 4
China, People's Republic of 6
Ecuador UNISFA 3
Egypt 11
El Salvador UNISFA 1
Ethiopia 826; 1 inf bn • UNISFA 4,131; 3 inf bn; 2 arty coy; 1 engr coy; 1 sigs coy; 8 fd hospital; 1 hel sqn
Gambia 132; 1 inf coy
Ghana 4 • UNISFA 9
Guatemala UNISFA 3
Guinea UNISFA 2
India UNISFA 5
Indonesia UNISFA 4
Iran 1
Kenya 86; 1 MP coy
Kyrgyzstan UNISFA 1
Liberia UNISFA 1
Malawi UNISFA 2
Malaysia 2 • UNISFA 2
Mongolia UNISFA 3
Namibia UNISFA 5
Nepal UNISFA 8
Nigeria UNISFA 4
Pakistan 906; 1 inf bn • UNISFA 1
Peru UNISFA 4
Russia UNISFA 2
Rwanda 1,136; 2 inf bn • UNISFA 5
Sierra Leone 4 • UNISFA 4
South Africa 3
Sri Lanka UNISFA 7
Tanzania 667; 1 inf bn • UNISFA 4
Togo 2
Uganda UNISFA 1
Ukraine UNISFA 6
Zambia UNISFA 4
Zimbabwe 3 • UNISFA 6

Tanzania TZA

Tanzanian Shilling sh		2018	2019	2020
GDP	sh	129tr	144tr	
	US$	56.9bn	62.2bn	
per capita	US$	1,040	1,105	
Growth	%	7.0	5.2	
Inflation	%	3.5	3.6	
Def bdgt	sh	1.73tr	1.91tr	
	US$	758m	827m	
US$1=sh		2275.46	2309.14	

Real-terms defence budget trend (US$m, constant 2015)

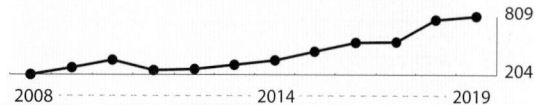

Population	56,985,045					
Age	0–14	15–19	20–24	25–29	30–64	65 plus
Male	21.8%	5.6%	4.5%	3.8%	13.0%	1.3%
Female	21.3%	5.5%	4.5%	3.8%	13.1%	1.8%

Capabilities

Non-state actors pose the principal threat to Tanzania's security, with terrorism, poaching and piracy of concern. A developing relationship with China has led to a series of procurements and training contacts. There are also defence-related ties with Israel, Pakistan and Russia. The armed forces take part in multinational exercises in Africa and have provided some training assistance to other African forces. Training relationships also exist with extra-regional armed forces, including the US. Tanzania's contribution to the UN's Force Intervention Brigade in the eastern DRC, notably its special forces, will have provided many lessons for force development as well as direct combat experience. However, there is only a limited capacity to project power independently beyond the country's borders. Budget constraints have limited recapitalisation ambitions and, although heavy equipment is ageing, airlift capacity has improved with the delivery of new helicopters. There are local ammunition facilities, but otherwise Tanzania relies on imports for its military equipment.

ACTIVE 27,000 (Army 23,000 Navy 1,000 Air 3,000)
Paramilitary 1,400
Conscript liability Three months basic military training combined with social service, ages 18–23

RESERVE 80,000 (Joint 80,000)

ORGANISATIONS BY SERVICE

Army ε23,000
FORCES BY ROLE
SPECIAL FORCES
 1 SF unit
MANOEUVRE
 Armoured
 1 tk bde
 Light
 5 inf bde

COMBAT SUPPORT
  4 arty bn
  1 mor bn
  2 AT bn
  1 engr regt (bn)
COMBAT SERVICE SUPPORT
  1 log gp
AIR DEFENCE
  2 ADA bn
EQUIPMENT BY TYPE†
ARMOURED FIGHTING VEHICLES
  MBT 45: 30 T-54/T-55; 15 Type-59G
  LT TK 57+: 30 FV101 *Scorpion*; 25 Type-62; 2+ Type-63A
  RECCE 10 BRDM-2
  APC • APC (W) 14: ε10 BTR-40/BTR-152; 4 Type-92
ANTI-TANK/ANTI-INFRASTRUCTURE
  RCL 75mm Type-52 (M20)
  GUNS 85mm 75 Type-56 (D-44)
ARTILLERY 344+
  TOWED 130: **122mm** 100: 20 D-30; 80 Type-54-1 (M-30); **130mm** 30 Type-59-I
  GUN/MOR 120mm 3+ Type-07PA
  MRL 61+: **122mm** 58 BM-21 *Grad*; **300mm** 3+ A100
  MOR 150: **82mm** 100 M-43; **120mm** 50 M-43

Navy ε1,000
EQUIPMENT BY TYPE
PATROL AND COASTAL COMBATANTS 14
  PCC 2 *Mwitongo* (ex-PRC *Haiqing*)
  PHT 2 *Huchuan* each with 2 single 533mm ASTT
  PB 10: 2 *Nguguri*; 2 *Shanghai* II (PRC); 2 VT 23m; 4 *Mambwe* (Damen Fast Crew Supplier 3307)
AMPHIBIOUS 3
  LCM 2 *Mbono* (ex-PRC *Yunnan*)
  LCT 1 *Kasa*

Air Defence Command ε3,000
FORCES BY ROLE
FIGHTER
  3 sqn with F-7/FT-7; FT-5; K-8 *Karakorum**
TRANSPORT
  1 sqn with Cessna 404 *Titan*; DHC-5D *Buffalo*; F-28 *Fellowship*; F-50; Gulfstream G550; Y-12 (II)
TRANSPORT HELICOPTER
  1 sqn with Bell 205 (AB-205); Bell 412EP *Twin Huey*
EQUIPMENT BY TYPE†
AIRCRAFT 17 combat capable
  FTR 11: 9 F-7TN; 2 FT-7TN
  ISR 1 SB7L-360 *Seeker*
  TPT 12: **Medium** 2 Y-8; **Light** 7: 2 Cessna 404 *Titan*; 3 DHC-5D *Buffalo*; 2 Y-12(II); **PAX** 3: 1 F-28 *Fellowship*; 1 F-50; 1 Gulfstream G550
  TRG 9: 3 FT-5 (JJ-5); 6 K-8 *Karakorum**
HELICOPTERS
  MRH 1 Bell 412EP *Twin Huey*
  TPT 2: **Medium** 1+ H225M; **Light** 1 Bell 205 (AB-205)
AIR DEFENCE
  SAM
    Short-range 2K12 *Kub* (SA-6 *Gainful*)†; S-125 *Pechora* (SA-3 *Goa*)†

Point-defence 9K32 *Strela*-2 (SA-7 *Grail*)‡
GUNS 200
  TOWED 14.5mm 40 ZPU-2/ZPU-4†; **23mm** 40 ZU-23-2; **37mm** 120 M-1939

Paramilitary 1,400 active
Police Field Force 1,400
18 sub-units incl Police Marine Unit

Air Wing
EQUIPMENT BY TYPE
AIRCRAFT • TPT • Light 1 Cessna U206 *Stationair*
HELICOPTERS
  TPT • Light 4: 2 Bell 206A *Jet Ranger* (AB-206A); 2 Bell 206L *Long Ranger*
  TRG 2 Bell 47G (AB-47G)/Bell 47G2

Marine Unit 100
EQUIPMENT BY TYPE
PATROL AND COASTAL COMBATANTS
All operational patrol vessels under 10t FLD

DEPLOYMENT
CENTRAL AFRICAN REPUBLIC: UN • MINUSCA 445; 1 inf bn(-)

DEMOCRATIC REPUBLIC OF THE CONGO: UN • MONUSCO 961 1 SF coy; 1 inf bn

LEBANON: UN • UNIFIL 159; 1 MP coy

SOUTH SUDAN: UN • UNMISS 10

SUDAN: UN • UNAMID 667; 1 inf bn; UN • UNISFA 4

Togo TGO

CFA Franc BCEAO	fr	2018	2019	2020
GDP	fr	2.98tr	3.20tr	
	US$	5.36bn	5.50bn	
per capita	US$	670	671	
Growth	%	4.9	5.1	
Inflation	%	0.9	1.4	
Def bdgt	fr	58.0bn	61.9bn	
	US$	104m	107m	
US$1=fr		555.24	581.36	

Real-terms defence budget trend (US$m, constant 2015)

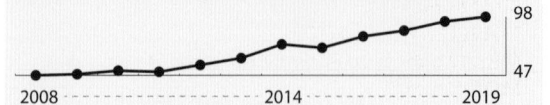

Population	8,390,953				
Age	0–14	15–19	20–24	25–29	30–64	65 plus
Male	20.0%	5.1%	4.4%	4.1%	14.4%	1.5%
Female	20.0%	5.1%	4.4%	4.1%	14.8%	2.0%

Capabilities

Defence authorities are increasingly concerned by the challenge from piracy and other illicit maritime activities in the Gulf of Guinea. Regional cooperation is being strengthened as a result. France contiues to deliver military training, including peacekeeping training for Togolese personnel participating in MINUSMA. There is also a peacekeeping training centre in Lomé. The US Africa Contingency Operations Training and Assistance programme has also provided training assistance. Togo's deployment capabilities are limited to its region without external support. Financial challenges limit military capabilities, including air-transport and maritime capacities. There are limited maintenance facilities, but no defence manufacturing sector.

ACTIVE 8,550 (Army 8,100 Navy 200 Air 250)
Paramilitary 750
Conscript liability Selective conscription, 2 years

ORGANISATIONS BY SERVICE

Army 8,100+
FORCES BY ROLE
MANOEUVRE
  Reconnaissance
  1 armd recce regt
  Light
  2 cbd arms regt
  2 inf regt
  1 rapid reaction force
  Air Manoeuvre
  1 cdo/para regt (3 cdo/para coy)
  Other
  1 (Presidential Guard) gd regt (1 gd bn, 1 cdo bn, 2 indep gd coy)
COMBAT SUPPORT
  1 cbt spt regt (1 fd arty bty, 2 ADA bty, 1 engr/log/tpt bn)
EQUIPMENT BY TYPE
ARMOURED FIGHTING VEHICLES
  MBT 2 T-54/T-55
  LT TK 9 FV101 *Scorpion*
  RECCE 86: 3 AML-60; 7 AML-90; 29 *Bastion Patsas*; 36 EE 9 *Cascavel*; 6 M8; 3 M20; 2 VBL
  IFV 20 BMP-2
  APC 34
    APC (T) 4 M3A1 half-track
    APC (W) 30 UR-416
ANTI-TANK/ANTI-INFRASTRUCTURE
  RCL 75mm Type-52 (M20)/Type-56; **82mm** Type-65 (B-10)
  GUNS 57mm 5 ZIS-2
ARTILLERY 30+
  SP 122mm 6
  TOWED 105mm 4 HM-2
  MRL 122mm Type-81 mod (SC6 chassis)
  MOR 82mm 20 M-43
AIR DEFENCE • GUNS • TOWED 43 **14.5mm** 38 ZPU-4; **37mm** 5 M-1939

Navy ε200 (incl Marine Infantry unit)
EQUIPMENT BY TYPE
PATROL AND COASTAL COMBATANTS 3
  PBF 1 *Agou* (RPB 33)
  PB 2 *Kara* (FRA Esterel)

Air Force 250
FORCES BY ROLE
FIGHTER/GROUND ATTACK
  1 sqn with *Alpha Jet**; EMB-326G*
TRANSPORT
  1 sqn with Beech 200 *King Air*
  1 VIP unit with DC-8; F-28-1000
TRAINING
  1 sqn with TB-30 *Epsilon**
TRANSPORT HELICOPTER
  1 sqn with SA315 *Lama*; SA316 *Alouette* III; SA319 *Alouette* III
EQUIPMENT BY TYPE†
AIRCRAFT 10 combat capable
  TPT 5: **Light** 2 Beech 200 *King Air*; **PAX** 3: 1 DC-8; 2 F-28-1000 (VIP)
  TRG 10: 3 *Alpha Jet**; 4 EMB-326G *; 3 TB-30 *Epsilon**
HELICOPTERS
  MRH 4: 2 SA315 *Lama*; 1 SA316 *Alouette* III; 1 SA319 *Alouette* III
  TPT • Medium (1 SA330 *Puma* in store)

Paramilitary 750

Gendarmerie 750
Ministry of Interior
FORCES BY ROLE
2 reg sections
MANOEUVRE
  Other
  1 (mobile) paramilitary sqn

DEPLOYMENT

LIBERIA: UN • UNMIL 1
MALI: UN • MINUSMA 937; 1 inf bn; 1 fd hospital
SOUTH SUDAN: UN • UNMISS 3
SUDAN: UN • UNAMID 2
WESTERN SAHARA: UN • MINURSO 2

Uganda UGA

Ugandan Shilling Ush		2018	2019	2020
GDP	Ush	105.3tr	116.0tr	
	US$	28.1bn	30.7bn	
per capita	US$	724	770	
Growth	%	6.1	6.2	
Inflation	%	2.6	3.2	
Def bdgt	Ush	1.47tr	2.07tr	3.62tr
	US$	393m	547m	
US$1=Ush		3743.98	3781.15	

Real-terms defence budget trend (US$m, constant 2015)

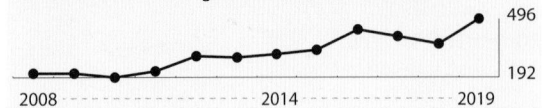

Population 42,169,690

Age	0–14	15–19	20–24	25–29	30–64	65 plus
Male	23.8%	5.6%	4.8%	4.0%	10.7%	0.9%
Female	23.9%	5.8%	4.9%	4.0%	10.7%	1.1%

Capabilities

Uganda's armed forces are well equipped and are important contributors to East African security. Operational experience and training have led to improvements in administration and planning, as well as in military skills including counter-IED and urban patrolling. A number of years spent targeting the Lord's Resistance Army has also ensured experience in counter-insurgency tactics. There are plans to establish a National Defence College. Uganda is one of the largest contributors to the East Africa Standby Force and in 2014 signed a Mutual Defence Treaty with Kenya and Rwanda. Training levels are adequate, particularly for the special forces, and are improving after recent experiences. There is regular training with international partners, including at Uganda's own facilities, and Ugandan forces have gained experience at the US Joint Readiness Training Centre. Airlift is limited, though the country was able to deploy an armoured element to southern Sudan in 2013. Rotary-wing aviation has improved in recent years, partly due to US assistance. While logistical support remains superior to that of many other regional states, the motorised infantry still lacks sufficient transport and logistics capacity. Uganda's mechanised forces are relatively well equipped in these areas, though heavy equipment is disparate and ageing. Improvements include the arrival of MRAP and other protected vehicles. There is limited defence-industrial capacity, though there is some manufacturing of light armoured vehicles. Uganda's 2015–19 Security Sector Development plan included the establishment of an engineering centre at Magamaga, as well as a defence-research centre at Lugazi.

ACTIVE 45,000 (Ugandan People's Defence Force 45,000) **Paramilitary 1,400**

RESERVE 10,000

ORGANISATIONS BY SERVICE

Ugandan People's Defence Force ε40,000–45,000

FORCES BY ROLE
MANOEUVRE
Armoured
1 armd bde
Light
1 cdo bn
5 inf div (total: 16 inf bde)
Other
1 (Special Forces Command) mot bde
COMBAT SUPPORT
1 arty bde
AIR DEFENCE
2 AD bn
EQUIPMENT BY TYPE†
ARMOURED FIGHTING VEHICLES
MBT 239+: 185 T-54/T-55; 10 T-72B1; 44 T-90S; ZTZ-85-IIM
LT TK ε20 PT-76
RECCE 46: 40 Eland-20; 6 FV701 Ferret
IFV 31 BMP-2
APC 150
 APC (W) 58: 15 BTR-60; 20 Buffel; 4 OT-64; 19 Bastion APC
 PPV 92: 42 Casspir; 40 Mamba; 10 RG-33L
AUV 15 Cougar
ENGINEERING & MAINTENANCE VEHICLES
ARV T-54/T-55 reported
VLB MTU reported
MW Husky
ARTILLERY 333+
SP 155mm 6 ATMOS 2000
TOWED 243+: 122mm M-30; 130mm 221; 155mm 22: 4 G-5; 18 M-839
MRL 6+: 107mm (12-tube); 122mm 6+: BM-21 Grad; 6 RM-70
MOR 78+: 81mm L16; 82mm M-43; 120mm 78 Soltam
AIR DEFENCE
SAM
 Short-range 4 S-125 Pechora (SA-3 Goa)
 Point-defence 9K32 Strela-2 (SA-7 Grail)‡; 9K310 Igla-1 (SA-16 Gimlet)
GUNS • TOWED 20+: 14.5mm ZPU-1/ZPU-2/ZPU-4; 37mm 20 M-1939

Marines ε400

All operational patrol vessels under 10t FLD
FORCES BY ROLE
MANOEUVRE
Amphibious
1 mne bn

Air Wing

FORCES BY ROLE
FIGHTER/GROUND ATTACK
1 sqn with MiG-21bis Fishbed; MiG-21U/UM Mongol A/B; Su-30MK2 Flanker
TRANSPORT
1 unit with Y-12
1 VIP unit with Gulfstream 550; L-100-30

TRAINING
  1 unit with L-39 *Albatros*†*
ATTACK/TRANSPORT HELICOPTER
  1 sqn with Bell 206 *Jet Ranger*; Bell 412 *Twin Huey*; Mi-17 *Hip* H; Mi-24 *Hind*; Mi-172 (VIP)
EQUIPMENT BY TYPE
AIRCRAFT 16 combat capable
  FGA 13: 5 MiG-21bis *Fishbed*; 1 MiG-21U *Mongol* A; 1 MiG-21UM *Mongol* B; 6 Su-30MK2 *Flanker*
  TPT 6: **Medium** 1 L-100-30; **Light** 4: 2 Cessna 208B; 2 Y-12; PAX 1 Gulfstream 550
  TRG 3 L-39 *Albatros*†*
HELICOPTERS
  ATK 1 Mi-24 *Hind* (2 more non-op)
  MRH 5: 2 Bell 412 *Twin Huey*; 3 Mi-17 *Hip* H (1 more non-op)
  TPT 4: **Medium** 2: 1 Mi-172 (VIP), 1 Mi-171 (VIP); **Light** 2 Bell 206A *Jet Ranger*
AIR-LAUNCHED MISSILES
  AAM • IR R-73 (AA-11A *Archer*); SARH R-27 (AA-10 *Alamo*); ARH R-77 (AA-12 *Adder*) (reported)
  ARM Kh-31P (AS-17A *Krypton*) (reported)

Paramilitary ε600 active

Border Defence Unit ε600
Equipped with small arms only

DEPLOYMENT

SOMALIA: AU • AMISOM 6,022; 7 inf bn; **UN** • UNSOM 627; 1 sy bn; **UN** • UNSOS 1
SOUTH SUDAN: UN • UNMISS 1
SUDAN: UN • UNISFA 1

Zambia ZMB

Zambian Kwacha K		2018	2019	2020
GDP	K	279bn	313bn	
	US$	26.7bn	23.9bn	
per capita	US$	1,503	1,307	
Growth	%	3.7	2.0	
Inflation	%	7.0	10.0	
Def bdgt	K	3.50bn	5.07bn	6.57bn
	US$	334m	387m	
US$1=K		10.46	13.09	

Real-terms defence budget trend (US$m, constant 2015)

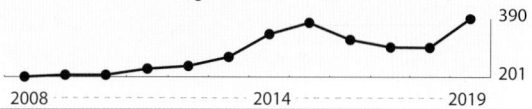

Population	16,929,953					
Age	0–14	15–19	20–24	25–29	30–64	65 plus
Male	23.0%	5.4%	4.6%	3.8%	12.1%	1.0%
Female	22.8%	5.4%	4.6%	3.8%	12.1%	1.3%

Capabilities

Zambia faces no immediate external threat, though its border with the Democratic Republic of the Congo presents a security challenge. China has become an important investor in the country over the past decade, including military training and weapons sales. Ensuring territorial integrity and border security, and a commitment to international peacekeeping operations, are the armed forces' key tasks. Given equipment obsolescence and a comparatively small establishment strength, there could be challenges in adequately fulfilling this role. Zambia is a member of the AU and SADC and the services have participated in exercises with international and regional partners including for the SADC Standby Force. Zambia's largest peacekeeping contribution is to the MINUSCA operation in the Central African Republic. As well as growing defence ties with China, in April 2017 Zambia signed a defence deal with Russia for equipment spare-parts support. The armed forces are all-volunteer. The US has provided funding and material support for army and air-force pre-deployment training for the CAR peacekeeping mission. The armed forces have limited capacity to self-deploy and sustain forces beyond national borders. While there is a need to modernise the equipment inventory, funds remain limited. The country has no defence-industrial base, apart from limited ammunition production.

ACTIVE 15,100 (Army 13,500 Air 1,600) Paramilitary 1,400

RESERVE 3,000 (Army 3,000)

ORGANISATIONS BY SERVICE

Army 13,500
FORCES BY ROLE
COMMAND
  3 bde HQ
SPECIAL FORCES
  1 cdo bn

MANOEUVRE
  Armoured
  1 armd regt (1 tk bn, 1 armd recce regt)
  Light
  6 inf bn
COMBAT SUPPORT
  1 arty regt (2 fd arty bn, 1 MRL bn)
  1 engr regt
EQUIPMENT BY TYPE
Some equipment†
ARMOURED FIGHTING VEHICLES
  MBT 30: 20 Type-59; 10 T-55
  LT TK 30 PT-76
  RECCE 70 BRDM-1/BRDM-2 (ε30 serviceable)
  IFV 23 Ratel-20
  APC • APC (W) 33: 13 BTR-60; 20 BTR-70
ENGINEERING & MAINTENANCE VEHICLES
  ARV T-54/T-55 reported
ANTI-TANK/ANTI-INFRASTRUCTURE
  MSL • MANPATS 9K11 Malyutka (AT-3 Sagger)
  RCL 12+: **57mm** 12 M18; **75mm** M20; **84mm** Carl Gustav
ARTILLERY 182
  TOWED 61: **105mm** 18 Model 56 pack howitzer; **122mm** 25 D-30; **130mm** 18 M-46
  MRL 122mm 30 BM-21 Grad (ε12 serviceable)
  MOR 91: **81mm** 55; **82mm** 24; **120mm** 12
AIR DEFENCE
  SAM • MANPAD 9K32 Strela-2 (SA-7 Grail)‡
  GUNS • TOWED 136: **20mm** 50 M-55 (triple); **37mm** 40 M-1939; **57mm** ε30 S-60; **85mm** 16 M-1939 KS-12

Reserve 3,000
FORCES BY ROLE
MANOEUVRE
  Light
  3 inf bn

Air Force 1,600
FORCES BY ROLE
FIGHTER/GROUND ATTACK
  1 sqn with K-8 Karakorum*
  1 sqn with L-15*
TRANSPORT
  1 sqn with MA60; Y-12(II); Y-12(IV); Y-12E
  1 (VIP) unit with AW139; CL-604; HS-748
  1 (liaison) sqn with Do-28
TRAINING
  2 sqn with MB-326GB; MFI-15 Safari
TRANSPORT HELICOPTER
  1 sqn with Mi-17 Hip H
  1 (liaison) sqn with Bell 47G; Bell 205 (UH-1H Iroquois/AB-205)
AIR DEFENCE
  3 bty with S-125 Pechora (SA-3 Goa)
EQUIPMENT BY TYPE†
Very low serviceability
  AIRCRAFT 21 combat capable
    TPT 25: **Medium** 2 C-27J Spartan; **Light** 21: 5 Do-28; 2 MA60; 4 Y-12(II); 5 Y-12(IV); 5 Y-12E; **PAX** 2: 1 Gulfstream G650ER; 1 HS-748
    TRG 51: 15 K-8 Karakorum*; 6 L-15*; 10 MB-326GB; 8 MFI-15 Safari; 12 SF-260TW
  HELICOPTERS
    MRH 5: 1 AW139; 4 Mi-17 Hip H
    TPT • Light 12: 9 Bell 205 (UH-1H Iroquois/AB-205); 3 Bell 212
    TRG 5 Bell 47G
  UNMANNED AERIAL VEHICLES 3+
    ISR • Medium 3+ Hermes 450
  AIR DEFENCE
    SAM • Short-range S-125 Pechora (SA-3 Goa)
  AIR-LAUNCHED MISSILES
    AAM • IR PL-5E-II
    ASM 9K11 Malyutka (AT-3 Sagger)

Paramilitary 1,400

Police Mobile Unit 700
FORCES BY ROLE
MANOEUVRE
  Other
  1 police bn (4 police coy)

Police Paramilitary Unit 700
FORCES BY ROLE
MANOEUVRE
  Other
  1 paramilitary bn (3 paramilitary coy)

DEPLOYMENT

CENTRAL AFRICAN REPUBLIC: UN • MINUSCA 932; 1 inf bn

DEMOCRATIC REPUBLIC OF THE CONGO: UN • MONUSCO 8

SOUTH SUDAN: UN • UNMISS 13

SUDAN: UN • UNISFA 4

Zimbabwe ZWE

Zimbabwe Dollar Z$		2018	2019	2020
GDP	US$	42.8bn	97.5bn	
	Z$	21.0bn	12.8bn	
per capita	US$	1,434	860	
Growth	%	3.5	-7.1	
Inflation	%	10.6	161.8	
Def bdgt	US$	420m	547m	
	Z$	206m	71.9m	
US$1=Z$		2.04	7.60	

Real-terms defence budget trend (US$m, constant 2015)

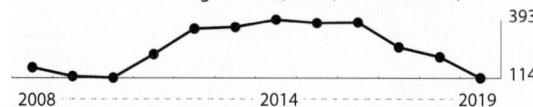

Population 14,277,281

Age	0–14	15–19	20–24	25–29	30–64	65 plus
Male	19.0%	5.4%	4.5%	4.4%	13.8%	1.8%
Female	19.4%	5.5%	4.8%	4.4%	14.1%	2.7%

Capabilities

Political instability and a weak economy are the key challenges for the state. The August 2018 presidential election resulted in victory for Emmerson Mnangagwa, though it saw troops deployed on the streets amid unrest, which continued into 2019. Ensuring sovereignty, territorial integrity and border security, and providing internal-security support to the police, are tasks for the armed forces. They also take an active political role. Zimbabwe is a member of the AU and the SADC, and takes part in SADC Standby Force exercises. There are defence ties with China, and an emergent defence relationship with Belarus, while Russia in mid-2019 reportedly said it would consider alternative payment means for military cooperation. In 2018, a 'special allowance' was paid to military personnel to boost overall pay. Military leaders have identified training as a development priority. Small numbers of personnel have deployed on peacekeeping operations, but there is no capacity to sustain a force far beyond national borders. Recapitalising an obsolescent equipment inventory is also a priority. This, however, will depend on economic recovery, and perhaps the extent to which China and Russia will provide support. State-owned small-arms and munitions manufacturer Zimbabwe Defence Industries has struggled after nearly two decades of Western sanctions, but there are plans to revive the plant.

ACTIVE 29,000 (Army 25,000 Air 4,000) **Paramilitary 21,800**

ORGANISATIONS BY SERVICE

Army ε25,000
FORCES BY ROLE
COMMAND
 1 SF bde HQ
 1 mech bde HQ
 5 inf bde HQ
SPECIAL FORCES
 1 SF regt
MANOEUVRE
 Armoured
 1 armd sqn
 Mechanised
 1 mech inf bn
 Light
 15 inf bn
 1 cdo bn
 Air Manoeuvre
 1 para bn
 Other
 3 gd bn
 1 (Presidential Guard) gd gp
COMBAT SUPPORT
 1 arty bde
 1 fd arty regt
 2 engr regt
AIR DEFENCE
 1 AD regt
EQUIPMENT BY TYPE
ARMOURED FIGHTING VEHICLES
 MBT 40: 30 Type-59†; 10 Type-69†
 RECCE 115: 20 Eland-60/90; 15 FV701 Ferret†; 80 EE-9 Cascavel (90mm)
 IFV 2+ YW307
 APC • APC (T) 30: 8 ZSD-85 (incl CP); 22 VTT-323
ENGINEERING & MAINTENANCE VEHICLES
 ARV T-54/T-55 reported; ZJX-93 ARV
 VLB MTU reported
ARTILLERY 254
 SP 122mm 12 2S1 Gvozdika
 TOWED 122mm 20: 4 D-30; 16 Type-60 (D-74)
 MRL 76: 107mm 16 Type-63; 122mm 60 RM-70
 MOR 146: 81mm/82mm ε140; 120mm 6 M-43
AIR DEFENCE
 SAM • Point-defence 9K32 Strela-2 (SA-7 Grail)‡
 GUNS • TOWED 116: 14.5mm 36 ZPU-1/ZPU-2/ZPU-4; 23mm 45 ZU-23-2; 37mm 35 M-1939

Air Force 4,000
FORCES BY ROLE
FIGHTER
 1 sqn with F-7 II†; FT-7†
FIGHTER/GROUND ATTACK
 1 sqn with K-8 Karakorum*
 (1 sqn Hawker Hunter in store)
GROUND ATTACK/ISR
 1 sqn with Cessna 337/O-2A Skymaster*
ISR/TRAINING
 1 sqn with SF-260F/M; SF-260TP*; SF-260W Warrior*
TRANSPORT
 1 sqn with BN-2 Islander; CASA 212-200 Aviocar (VIP)
ATTACK/TRANSPORT HELICOPTER
 1 sqn with Mi-35 Hind; Mi-35P Hind (liaison); SA316 Alouette III; AS532UL Cougar (VIP)
 1 trg sqn with Bell 412 Twin Huey, SA316 Alouette III
AIR DEFENCE
 1 sqn

EQUIPMENT BY TYPE
AIRCRAFT 45 combat capable
  FTR 9: 7 F-7 II‡; 2 FT-7‡
  ISR 2 O-2A *Skymaster*
  TPT • Light 25: 5 BN-2 *Islander*; 7 C-212-200 *Aviocar*; 13 Cessna 337 *Skymaster**; (10 C-47 *Skytrain* in store)
  TRG 33: 10 K-8 *Karakorum**; 5 SF-260M; 8 SF-260TP*; 5 SF-260W *Warrior**; 5 SF-260F
HELICOPTERS
  ATK 6: 4 Mi-35 *Hind*; 2 Mi-35P *Hind*
  MRH 9: 8 Bell 412 *Twin Huey*; 1 SA316 *Alouette* III
  TPT • Medium 2 AS532UL *Cougar* (VIP)
AIR-LAUNCHED MISSILES • AAM • IR PL-2; PL-5 (reported)
AD • GUNS 100mm (not deployed); **37mm** (not deployed); **57mm** (not deployed)

Paramilitary 21,800

Zimbabwe Republic Police Force 19,500
incl air wg

Police Support Unit 2,300
PATROL AND COASTAL COMBATANTS
All operational patrol vessels under 10t FLD

DEPLOYMENT
SOUTH SUDAN: UN • UNMISS 6
SUDAN: UN • UNAMID 3; **UN •** UNISFA 6

FOREIGN FORCES
South Africa 118; 1 engr coy

Arms procurements and deliveries – Sub-Saharan Africa

Significant events in 2019

MARCH
A400M SUPPLY CHAIN

South African company Denel stated that it will wind down its contribution to Airbus's A400M supply chain in order to save money. The company made a ZAR1.7 billion (US$128.4 million) loss in 2017–18 and has struggled to deliver parts on time. Denel's involvement with the A400M began in 2005 when South Africa signed a contract for eight aircraft, which it cancelled in 2009 due to cost increases.

MAY
SU-25 REPLACEMENT

Sudan's air-force commander said that he had requested funding for a multi-role fighter to replace the Su-25K *Frogfoot* ground-attack aircraft. Sudan is reportedly interested in Russia's Su-30MK and Su-35 as potential replacements. He also said that Sudan plans to acquire a Russian-manufactured S-300 air-defence system. Sudan's last significant aerospace import was six FTC-2000 jet training aircraft from China's Guizhou Aircraft Industry Corporation in 2018. Sanctions currently prevent Sudan importing fighter aircraft and air-defence systems from Western states.

JUNE
***ARA* 2 EXPORT**

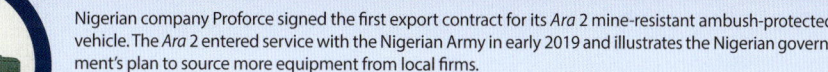

Nigerian company Proforce signed the first export contract for its *Ara* 2 mine-resistant ambush-protected vehicle. The *Ara* 2 entered service with the Nigerian Army in early 2019 and illustrates the Nigerian government's plan to source more equipment from local firms.

JULY
PARAMOUNT / SAMI

Paramount Group, headquartered in South Africa, signed a collaboration agreement with Saudi Arabian Military Industries (SAMI). The firms will jointly develop defence technologies, as well as SAMI's industrial capability. Paramount Group has already established a joint venture with Kazakhstan Engineering to manufacture armoured-vehicles.

SEPTEMBER
DENEL TURNAROUND PLAN

State-owned company Denel received a ZAR1.8bn (US$129.1m) cash injection from the South African government as part of a 'turnaround plan'. This has included changes to the firm's structure and governance. Denel is responsible for a number of significant South African defence projects, including the long-delayed *Project Hoefyster* armoured-vehicle programme.

Figure 32 France: naval exports to sub-Saharan African states

France's naval-shipbuilding industry, particularly state-owned shipbuilding giant Naval Group (formerly DCNS), has in the past decade had significant export success in Asia, Europe and the Middle East. However, smaller French shipyards have also made inroads in the patrol-craft market, notably in sub-Saharan Africa. This has not been confined to francophone nations. Many regional states have large coastlines and exclusive economic zones. But budgets are often tight, and navies and coastguards have to compete for funding with ground and air forces conducting operations against insurgents. Because of this, smaller patrol craft capable of operating in the maritime littoral may be seen as satisfying a number of capability requirements, and seem to be the preferred platform for many navies. France has several shipyards producing ocean-going offshore-patrol vessels, though there is emerging competition from Chinese firms who have sold patrol craft to countries such as Cameroon, Nigeria and Tanzania.

Table 24 France: naval exports to sub-Saharan African states, 2011–Nov 2019

Order date	Customer	Class	Type	Quantity	Shipyard	Deliveries
2011	Nigeria	*Okpoku* (FPB 72 MkII)	Patrol boat	3	OCEA	2012
2011	Benin	*Alibori* (FPB 98)	Patrol boat	3	OCEA	2012
2012	Senegal	*Kedougou* (Raidco OPV 45)	Patrol boat	1	Raidco Marine	2015
2012	Senegal	*Ferlo* (Raidco RPB 33)	Fast patrol boat	1	Raidco Marine	2013
c. 2012	Nigeria	*Dorina* (FPB 98 MkI)	Patrol boat	1	OCEA	2013
2013	Togo	*Agou* (Raidco RPB 33)	Fast patrol boat	2	Raidco Marine	2014
Sep 2013	Mozambique	Ocean Eagle 43	Patrol boat	3	CMN	2016
		HSI 32	Fast patrol boat	3		
Jan 2014	Côte d'Ivoire	*L'Emergence* (Raidco 33m)	Fast patrol boat	3	Raidco Marine	2014–16
2015	Senegal	*Fouladou* (OPV 190 Mk II)	Offshore-patrol craft	1	OCEA	2016
2015	Mozambique	HSI 32	Fast patrol boat	3	CMN	2017
Dec 2016	Nigeria	*Okpoku* (FPB 72 MkII)	Patrol boat	2	OCEA	2017
Dec 2016	Nigeria	*Nguru* (FPB 110 MkII)	Patrol boat	2	OCEA	2018
2017	Nigeria	*Okpoku* (FPB 72 MkII)	Patrol boat	2	OCEA	2018
Nov 2019	Senegal	OPV 58	Guided-missile patrol craft with surface-to-air missiles	3	Kership	n.k.
Total				**33**		

Chapter Ten
Military cyber capabilities

The Military Balance has in recent editions carried, for some states, short statements of factors (such as national plans and organisations) deemed relevant to determining national capabilities for military cyber operations. We have this year dispensed with this method. Instead, and in line with work emerging from the Institute's research into measuring the national cyber capabilities of states, we are in this edition outlining more systematically the factors that we judge useful in understanding a nation's military cyber capability and that we will in future integrate in our Military Balance+ database.

Definitions

Cyberspace is the realm of computer networks in which information is stored, shared and communicated online. A cyber capability entails the use of cyberspace to deliver an effect, which can be defensive in nature (such as protection and resilience) or offensive (such as influence, coercion, disruption and destruction). These effects can be intended to achieve numerous national objectives, including in the economic, national-security and diplomatic realms. The starting point for the Military Balance+ is to consider cyber capabilities designed for a military purpose.

Some states – for example China, France, Singapore and the United States – have created higher-level military commands and substantial dedicated force structures. Even in these cases, there can be the added complication of overlaps, in terms of doctrine and force structure, between cyber operations and information warfare/operations. Other states, such as Israel and the United Kingdom, rely more heavily on structures that integrate their military and civilian capabilities.

This complicates analysis for the *Military Balance*, since much cyber capability that might be used for a military purpose is civilian-owned, while some military-owned capability might be used for non-military purposes. Even in cases of cyber attacks across borders, such as Iran's attack on Saudi Aramco in 2012 or Russia's attack on Ukraine's power grid in 2016, it is unclear in each case just how much the armed forces of these countries were involved. In many countries with a cyber-offensive capability, these assets sit largely in covert agencies or military-related intelligence agencies, rather than in the armed forces per se.

Nonetheless, there is a military-owned subset of national cyber capabilities, specifically designed for military outcomes, that we can look to measure – even if the relative size of this subset varies from state to state (it is quite substantial in China and the US). It is this that we will include in the Military Balance+: military-owned cyber capability.

Measuring military-owned cyber capability

As part of its broader research on cyber power, the IISS is looking to measure cyber capabilities and capacity in order to identify cyber-capable states, as well as examining the constraining or enabling factors that permit an understanding of how such a capability might be used. In order to analyse important state capability in cyberspace, we have developed a taxonomy that focuses on enablers, including indicators of capability from the civilian sector and the armed forces. These have been tested by a process of conducting research reports on select states. The categories are: strategy and doctrine; command and control (including intelligence, surveillance and reconnaissance); cyber empowerment and dependence; cyber security and resilience; global leadership in cyberspace; and military capability for cyber coercion.

It is also important to consider the degree to which cyber capabilities are integrated into the fabric of national strategy and military operations, as well as their integration in terms of command and control and between civilian and military authorities, and also within alliances. Important too is research and development, and human capacity.

Developing indicators

With this in mind, it is possible at this stage to set out some indicators that could be examined in order to assess capability. The nature of cyberspace and cyber-enabled capabilities and the organisations that employ them mean that some information may be hard to obtain, but more is objectively measurable than may be expected, particularly when it comes to cyber protection.

Table 25 presents a number of indicators of organisational arrangements (proxy indicators for capability) of the sort that the Military Balance+ could use. In generating this table, we have refined further the categories used in the assessment of select states' capabilities, so that we can more accurately measure the military-owned subset of their national cyber capacity. Of course, there are a range of supporting capabilities residing in the civilian sector that enable military cyber operations, but these are deliberately excluded from the Military Balance+ taxonomy. We test these indicators using the United States as an example.

Table 25 Military cyber capabilities: a potential collection plan

Overall information category	Possible assets	Demonstration case: United States
▪ Military strategy/doctrine ▪ Command and control and integration	▪ National-security and cyber-strategy documents detailing the military role in cyberspace; cyber-doctrine document(s) ▪ National- and command-level formations ▪ Integrating bodies, such as national-security councils ▪ Military cyber-intelligence capacity	▪ National Security Strategy 2018 ▪ Cyber Command ▪ JP 3-13 Information Operations ▪ JP 3-12 Cyberspace Operations ▪ 133 Cyber Mission Teams (establishment strength of 6,000 people, 8–10 specialist designations for cyber-operations personnel) ▪ Indo-PACOM J6
▪ Extent of a military force's digital dependence/enabling	▪ Space-based intelligence, surveillance, target-acquisition and reconnaissance (ISTAR) capability ▪ Global operations and therefore reliance on global communications capabilities ▪ Significant investments in digitally enabled technology ▪ Ability to independently access and manoeuvre in space	▪ Space Command; satellite constellations for global positioning system (GPS); global space situational-awareness architecture ▪ Sovereign space-launch capacity (with limits) ▪ Reported anti-satellite (ASAT) capability ▪ Global operations at reach supported with reach-back capabilities; blue-force-tracker systems

Overall information category	Possible assets	Demonstration case: United States
■ Protection and resilience of military networks	■ Automated joint-force cyber situational-awareness system; military computer emergency-response teams (MIL CERTs) ■ Military cyber-security exercises	■ Department of Defense cyber exchange ■ CERT teams across all services ■ *Cyber Flag* exercise ■ NATO and Allied cyber exercises ■ Defensive military deployments
■ Military capacity for cyber coercion	■ Decision-making framework ■ Recent reported uses of cyber military force	■ Reported Presidential Policy Directive 2.0 revisions ■ Reported 2019 attack on Iran's missile command-and-control system
■ Military research and development and human capacity	■ Research institutes (government and military affiliated) ■ Military exercises in cyber defence or offensive actions ■ Active recruitment	■ Defense Advanced Research Projects Agency (DARPA); Intelligence Advanced Research Projects Activity (IARPA); Homeland Security Advanced Research Projects Agency (HSARPA); Idaho National Laboratory, Argonne National Laboratory; Federally-funded research and development centres ■ National Defense University's College of Information and Cyberspace ■ Professional courses ■ *Cyber Flag* exercise

PART TWO
Explanatory notes

The Military Balance provides an assessment of the armed forces and defence expenditures of 171 countries and territories. Each edition contributes to the provision of a unique compilation of data and information, enabling the reader to discern trends by studying editions as far back as 1959. The data in the current edition is accurate according to IISS assessments as of November 2019, unless specified. Inclusion of a territory, country or state in *The Military Balance* does not imply legal recognition or indicate support for any government.

General arrangement and contents

The introduction is an assessment of global defence developments and key themes in the 2020 edition. There are three analytical essays, followed by a graphical section analysing comparative defence statistics by domain, as well as key trends in defence economics.

Regional chapters begin with analysis of the military and security issues that drive national-defence policy developments, and key trends in regional defence economics. These are followed by focused analysis, for certain countries, of defence policy and capability issues, and defence economics. Next, detailed data on regional states' military forces and equipment, and defence economics, is presented in alphabetical order. Graphics assessing important regional arms procurements and deliveries complete each region.

The book closes with comparative and reference sections containing comparisons of expenditure and personnel statistics.

The Military Balance wall chart

The Military Balance 2020 wall chart is an assessment of land-attack cruise-missile development and proliferation, highlighting by country the platforms they are integrated onto, manufacturer, in-service date, payload type and range. It also provides information on Missile Technology Control Regime membership by year. The graphical display is complemented by a timeline showing major arms-control, missile-development, entry into service, first operational use and withdrawal from service events.

Using The Military Balance

The country entries assess personnel strengths, organisation and equipment holdings of the world's armed forces. Force-strength and equipment-inventory data is based on the most accurate data available, or on the best estimate that can be made. In estimating a country's total capabilities, old equipment may be counted where it is considered that it may still be deployable.

The data presented reflects judgements based on information available to the IISS at the time the book is compiled. Where information differs from previous editions, this is mainly because of changes in national forces, but it is sometimes because the IISS has reassessed the evidence supporting past entries. Given this, care must be taken in constructing time-series comparisons from information given in successive editions.

Abbreviations and definitions

Qualifier	
'At least'	Total is no less than the number given
'Up to'	Total is at most the number given, but could be lower
'About'	Total could be higher than given
'Some'	Precise inventory is unavailable at time of press
'In store'	Equipment held away from front-line units; readiness and maintenance varies
Billion (bn)	1,000 million (m)
Trillion (tr)	1,000 billion
$	US dollars unless otherwise stated
ε	Estimated
*	Aircraft counted by the IISS as combat capable
-	Part of a unit is detached/less than
+	Unit reinforced/more than
†	IISS assesses that the serviceability of equipment is in doubt[a]
‡	Equipment judged obsolete (weapons whose basic design is more than four decades old and which have not been significantly upgraded within the past decade)[a]

[a] Not to be taken to imply that such equipment cannot be used

Country entries

Information on each country is shown in a standard format, although the differing availability of information and differences in nomenclature result in some variations. Country entries include economic, demographic and military data. Population figures are based on demographic statistics taken from the US Census Bureau. Data on ethnic and religious minorities is also provided in some country entries. Military data includes personnel numbers, conscript liability where relevant, outline organisation, number of formations and units, and an inventory of the major equipment of each service. Details of national forces stationed abroad and of foreign forces stationed within the given country are also provided.

Arms procurements and deliveries

A series of thematic tables, graphics and text follow the regional data. These are designed to illustrate key trends, principal programmes and significant events in regional defence procurements. More detailed information on defence procurements, organised by country, equipment type and manufacturing company, can be found on the IISS Military Balance+ database (*https://www.iiss.org/militarybalanceplus*). The information in this section meets the threshold for a *Military Balance* country entry and as such does not feature information on sales of small arms and light weapons.

Defence economics

Country entries include defence expenditures, selected economic-performance indicators and demographic aggregates. All country entries are subject to revision each year as new information, particularly regarding actual defence expenditure, becomes available. On pp. 529–34, there are also international comparisons of defence expenditure and military personnel, giving expenditure figures for the past three years in per capita terms and as a % of gross domestic product (GDP). The aim is to provide a measure of military expenditure and the allocation of economic resources to defence.

Individual country entries show economic performance over the past two years and current demographic data. Where this data is unavailable, information from the last available year is provided. All financial data in the country entries is shown in both national currency and US dollars at current – not constant – prices. US-dollar conversions are calculated from the exchange rates listed in the entry.

Definitions of terms

Despite efforts by NATO and the UN to develop a standardised definition of military expenditure, many countries prefer to use their own definitions (which are often not made public). In order to present a comprehensive picture, *The Military Balance* lists three different measures of military-related spending data.
- For most countries, an official defence-budget figure is provided.
- For those countries where other military-related outlays, over and above the defence budget, are known or can be reasonably estimated, an additional measurement referred to as defence expenditure is also provided. Defence-expenditure figures will naturally be higher than official budget figures, depending on the range of additional factors included.
- For NATO countries, a defence-budget figure, as well as defence expenditure reported by NATO in local currency terms and converted using IMF exchange rates, is quoted.

NATO's military-expenditure definition (the most comprehensive) is cash outlays of central or federal governments to meet the costs of national armed forces. The term 'armed forces' includes strategic, land, naval, air, command, administration and support forces. It also includes other forces if they are trained, structured and equipped to support defence forces and are realistically deployable. Defence expenditures are reported in four categories: Operating Costs, Procurement and Construction, Research and Development (R&D) and Other Expenditure. Operating Costs include salaries and pensions for military and civilian personnel; the cost of maintaining and training units, service organisations, headquarters and support elements; and the cost of servicing and repairing military equipment and infrastructure. Procurement and Construction expenditure covers national equipment and infrastructure spending, as well as common infrastructure programmes. R&D is defence expenditure up to the point at which new equipment can be put in service, regardless of whether new equipment is actually procured. Foreign Military Aid (FMA) contributions are also noted.

For many non-NATO countries the issue of transparency in reporting military budgets is fundamental. Not every UN member state reports defence-budget data (even fewer report real defence expenditures) to their electorates, the UN, the IMF or other multinational organisations. In the case of governments with a proven record of transparency, official figures generally conform to the standardised definition of defence budgeting, as adopted by the UN, and consistency problems are not usually a major issue. The IISS cites official defence budgets as reported by either national governments, the UN, the OSCE or the IMF.

For those countries where the official defence-budget figure is considered to be an incomplete measure of total military-related spending, and appropriate additional data is available, the IISS will use data from a variety of sources to arrive at a more accurate estimate of true defence expenditure. The most frequent instances of budgetary manipulation or falsification typically involve equipment procurement, R&D, defence-industrial investment, covert weapons programmes, pensions for retired military and civilian personnel, paramilitary forces and non-budgetary sources of revenue for the military arising from ownership of industrial, property and land assets. There will be several countries listed in *The Military Balance* for which only an official defence-budget figure is provided but where, in reality, true defence-related expenditure is almost certainly higher.

Percentage changes in defence spending are referred to in either nominal or real terms. Nominal terms relate to the percentage change in numerical spending figures, and do not account for the impact of price changes (i.e. inflation) on defence spending. By contrast, real terms account for inflationary effects, and may therefore be considered a more accurate representation of change over time.

The principal sources for national economic statistics cited in the country entries are the IMF, the OECD, the World Bank and three regional banks (the Inter-American, Asian and African Development banks). For some countries, basic economic data is difficult to obtain. GDP figures are nominal (current) values at market prices. GDP growth is real, not nominal growth, and inflation is the year-on-year change in consumer prices. When real-terms defence-spending figures are mentioned, these are measured in constant 2015 US dollars.

General defence data
Personnel
The 'Active' total comprises all servicemen and women on full-time duty (including conscripts and long-term assignments from the Reserves). When a gendarmerie or equivalent is under control of the defence ministry, they may be included in the active total. Only the length of conscript liability is shown; where service is voluntary there is no entry. 'Reserve' describes formations and units not fully manned or operational in peacetime, but which can be mobilised by recalling reservists in an emergency. Some countries have more than one category of reserves, often kept at varying degrees of readiness. Where possible, these differences are denoted using the national descriptive title, but always under the heading of 'Reserves' to distinguish them from full-time active forces. All personnel figures are rounded to the nearest 50, except for organisations with under 500 personnel, where figures are rounded to the nearest ten.

Other forces
Many countries maintain forces whose training, organisation, equipment and control suggest that they may be used to support or replace regular military forces, or be used more broadly by states to deliver militarily relevant effect; these are called 'paramilitary'. They include some forces that may have a constabulary role. These are detailed after the military forces of each country, but their personnel numbers are not normally included in the totals at the start of each entry.

Units and formation strength

Company	100–200
Battalion	500–1,000
Brigade	3,000–5,000
Division	15,000–20,000
Corps or Army	50,000–100,000

Forces by role and equipment by type
Quantities are shown by function (according to each nation's employment) and type, and represent what are believed to be total holdings, including active and reserve operational and training units. Inventory totals for missile systems relate to launchers and not to missiles. Equipment held 'in store' is not counted in the main inventory totals.

Deployments
The Military Balance mainly lists permanent bases and operational deployments, including peacekeeping operations, which are often discussed in the regional text. Information in the country-data sections details, first, deployments of troops and, second, military observers and, where available, the role and equipment of deployed units. Personnel figures are not generally included for embassy staff, standing multinational headquarters, or deployments of purely maritime and aerospace assets, such as Iceland Air Policing or anti-piracy operations.

Land forces
To make international comparison easier and more consistent, *The Military Balance* categorises forces by role and translates national military terminology for unit and formation sizes. Typical personnel strength, equipment holdings and organisation of formations such as brigades and divisions vary from country to country. In addition, some unit terms, such as 'regiment', 'squadron', 'battery' and 'troop', can refer to significantly different unit sizes in different countries. Unless otherwise stated, these terms should be assumed to reflect standard British usage where they occur.

Naval forces
Classifying naval vessels according to role is complex. A post-war consensus on primary surface combatants revolved around a distinction between independently operating cruisers, air-defence escorts (destroyers) and anti-submarine-warfare escorts (frigates). However, ships are increasingly performing a range of roles. For this reason, *The Military Balance* classifies vessels according to full-load displacement (FLD) rather than a role-classifica-

tion system. These definitions will not necessarily conform to national designations.

Air forces

Aircraft listed as combat capable are assessed as being equipped to deliver air-to-air or air-to-surface ordnance. The definition includes aircraft designated by type as bomber, fighter, fighter/ground attack, ground attack and anti-submarine warfare. Other aircraft considered to be combat capable are marked with an asterisk (*). Operational groupings of air forces are shown where known. Typical squadron aircraft strengths can vary both between aircraft types and from country to country. When assessing missile ranges, *The Military Balance* uses the following range indicators:
- Short-range ballistic missile (SRBM): less than 1,000 km;
- Medium-range ballistic missile (MRBM): 1,000–3,000 km;
- Intermediate-range ballistic missile (IRBM): 3,000–5,000 km;
- Intercontinental ballistic missile (ICBM): over 5,000 km.

Attribution and acknowledgements

The International Institute for Strategic Studies owes no allegiance to any government, group of governments, or any political or other organisation. Its assessments are its own, based on the material available to it from a wide variety of sources. The cooperation of governments of all listed countries has been sought and, in many cases, received. However, some data in *The Military Balance* is estimated. Care is taken to ensure that this data is as accurate and free from bias as possible. The Institute owes a considerable debt to a number of its own members, consultants and all those who help compile and check material. The Director-General and Chief Executive and staff of the Institute assume full responsibility for the data and judgements in this book. Comments and suggestions on the data and textual material contained within the book, as well as on the style and presentation of data, are welcomed and should be communicated to the Editor of *The Military Balance* at: IISS, Arundel House, 6 Temple Place, London, WC2R 2PG, UK, email: *milbal@iiss.org*. Copyright on all information in *The Military Balance* belongs strictly to the IISS. Application to reproduce limited amounts of data may be made to the publisher: Taylor & Francis, 4 Park Square, Milton Park, Abingdon, Oxon, OX14 4RN. Email: *society.permissions@tandf.co.uk*. Unauthorised use of data from *The Military Balance* will be subject to legal action.

Principal land definitions

FORCES BY ROLE

Command:	free-standing, deployable formation headquarters (HQs).
Special Forces (SF):	elite units specially trained and equipped for unconventional warfare and operations in enemy-controlled territory. Many are employed in counter-terrorist roles.
Manoeuvre:	combat units and formations capable of manoeuvring. These are subdivided as follows:
Reconnaissance:	combat units and formations whose primary purpose is to gain information.
Armoured:	units and formations principally equipped with main battle tanks (MBTs) and infantry fighting vehicles (IFVs) to provide heavy mounted close-combat capability. Units and formations intended to provide mounted close-combat capability with lighter armoured vehicles, such as light tanks or wheeled assault guns, are classified as light armoured.
Mechanised:	units and formations primarily equipped with lighter armoured vehicles such as armoured personnel carriers (APCs). They have less mounted firepower and protection than their armoured equivalents, but can usually deploy more infantry.
Light:	units and formations whose principal combat capability is dismounted infantry, with few, if any, organic armoured vehicles. Some may be motorised and equipped with soft-skinned vehicles.
Air Manoeuvre:	units and formations trained and equipped for delivery by transport aircraft and/or helicopters.
Amphibious:	amphibious forces are trained and equipped to project force from the sea.
Other Forces:	includes security units such as Presidential Guards, paramilitary units such as border guards and combat formations permanently employed in training or demonstration tasks.
Combat Support:	combat support units and formations not integral to manoeuvre formations. Includes artillery, engineers, military intelligence, nuclear, biological and chemical defence, signals and information operations.
Combat Service Support (CSS):	includes logistics, maintenance, medical, supply and transport units and formations.

EQUIPMENT BY TYPE

Light Weapons:	small arms, machine guns, grenades and grenade launchers and unguided man-portable anti-armour and support weapons have proliferated so much and are sufficiently easy to manufacture or copy that listing them would be impractical.
Crew Served Weapons:	crew served recoilless rifles, man portable ATGW, MANPADs and mortars of greater than 80mm calibre are listed, but the high degree of proliferation and local manufacture of many of these weapons means that estimates of numbers held may not be reliable.
Armoured Fighting Vehicles (AFVs):	armoured combat vehicles with a combat weight of at least six metric tonnes, further subdivided as below:
Main Battle Tank (MBT):	armoured, tracked combat vehicles, armed with a turret-mounted gun of at least 75mm calibre and with a combat weight of at least 25 metric tonnes.
Light Tank (LT TK):	armoured, tracked combat vehicles, armed with a turret-mounted gun of at least 75mm calibre and with a combat weight of less than 25 metric tonnes.
Wheeled Assault Gun (ASLT):	armoured, wheeled combat vehicles, armed with a turret-mounted gun of at least 75mm calibre and with a combat weight of at least 15 metric tonnes.
Armoured Reconnaissance (RECCE):	armoured vehicles primarily designed for reconnaissance tasks with no significant transport capability and either a main gun of less than 75mm calibre or a combat weight of less than 15 metric tonnes, or both.
Infantry Fighting Vehicle (IFV):	armoured combat vehicles designed and equipped to transport an infantry squad and armed with a cannon of at least 20mm calibre.

Armoured Personnel Carrier (APC):	lightly armoured combat vehicles designed and equipped to transport an infantry squad but either unarmed or armed with a cannon of less than 20mm calibre.
Airborne Combat Vehicle (ABCV):	armoured vehicles designed to be deployable by parachute alongside airborne forces.
Amphibious Assault Vehicle (AAV):	armoured vehicles designed to have an amphibious ship-to-shore capability.
Armoured Utility Vehicle (AUV):	armoured vehicles not designed to transport an infantry squad, but capable of undertaking a variety of other utility battlefield tasks, including light reconnaissance and light transport.
Specialist Variants:	variants of armoured vehicles listed above that are designed to fill a specialised role, such as command posts (CP), artillery observation posts (OP), signals (sigs) and ambulances (amb), are categorised with their parent vehicles.
Engineering and Maintenance Vehicles:	includes armoured engineer vehicles (AEV), armoured repair and recovery vehicles (ARV), assault bridging (VLB) and mine warfare vehicles (MW).
Nuclear, Biological and Chemical Defence Vehicles (NBC):	armoured vehicles principally designed to operate in potentially contaminated terrain.
Anti-Tank/Anti-Infrastructure (AT):	guns, guided weapons and recoilless rifles designed to engage armoured vehicles and battlefield hardened targets.
Surface-to-Surface Missile Launchers (SSM):	launch vehicles for transporting and firing surface-to-surface ballistic and cruise missiles.
Artillery:	weapons (including guns, howitzers, gun/howitzers, multiple-rocket launchers, mortars and gun/mortars) with a calibre greater than 100mm for artillery pieces and 80mm and above for mortars, capable of engaging ground targets with indirect fire.
Coastal Defence:	land-based coastal artillery pieces and anti-ship-missile launchers.
Air Defence (AD):	guns, directed-energy (DE) weapons and surface-to-air missile (SAM) launchers designed to engage fixed-wing, rotary-wing and uninhabited aircraft. Missiles are further classified by maximum notional engagement range: point-defence (up to 10 km); short-range (10–30 km); medium-range (30–75 km); and long-range (75 km+). Systems primarily intended to intercept missiles rather than aircraft are categorised separately as Missile Defence.

Principal naval definitions

To aid comparison between fleets, the following definitions, which do not always conform to national definitions, are used:

Submarines:	all vessels designed to operate primarily under water. Submarines with a dived displacement below 250 tonnes are classified as midget submarines (SSW); those below 500 tonnes are coastal submarines (SSC).
Principal surface combatants:	all surface ships designed for combat operations on the high seas, with an FLD above 1,500 tonnes. Aircraft carriers (CV), including helicopter carriers (CVH), are vessels with a flat deck primarily designed to carry fixed- and/or rotary-wing aircraft, without amphibious capability. Other principal surface combatants include cruisers (C) (with an FLD above 9,750 tonnes), destroyers (DD) (with an FLD above 4,500 tonnes) and frigates (FF) (with an FLD above 1,500 tonnes).

Patrol and coastal combatants:	surface vessels designed for coastal or inshore operations. These include corvettes (FS), which usually have an FLD between 500 and 1,500 tonnes and are distinguished from other patrol vessels by their heavier armaments. Also included in this category are offshore-patrol ships (PSO), with an FLD greater than 1,500 tonnes; patrol craft (PC), which have an FLD between 250 and 1,500 tonnes; and patrol boats (PB) with an FLD between ten and 250 tonnes. Vessels with a top speed greater than 35 knots are designated as 'fast'.
Mine warfare vessels:	all surface vessels configured primarily for mine laying (ML) or countermeasures. Countermeasures vessels are either: sweepers (MS), which are designed to locate and destroy mines in an area; hunters (MH), which are designed to locate and destroy individual mines; or countermeasures vessels (MC), which combine both roles.
Amphibious vessels:	vessels designed to transport personnel and/or equipment onto shore. These include landing helicopter assault vessels (LHA), which can embark fixed- and/or rotary-wing air assets as well as landing craft; landing helicopter docks (LHD), which can embark rotary-wing or V/STOL assets and have a well dock; landing platform helicopters (LPH), which have a primary role of launch and recovery platform for rotary-wing or V/STOL assets with a dock to store equipment/personnel for amphibious operations; and landing platform docks (LPD), which do not have a through deck but do have a well dock. Landing ships (LS) are amphibious vessels capable of ocean passage and landing craft (LC) are smaller vessels designed to transport personnel and equipment from a larger vessel to land or across small stretches of water. Landing ships have a hold; landing craft are open vessels. Landing craft air cushioned (LCAC) are differentiated from Utility craft air cushioned (UCAC) in that the former have a bow ramp for the disembarkation of vehicles and personnel.
Auxiliary vessels:	ocean-going surface vessels performing an auxiliary military role, supporting combat ships or operations. These generally fulfil five roles: replenishment (such as oilers (AO) and solid stores (AKS)); logistics (such as cargo ships (AK) and logistics ships (AFS)); maintenance (such as cable-repair ships (ARC) or buoy tenders (ABU)); research (such as survey ships (AFS)); and special purpose (such as intelligence-collection ships (AGI) and ocean-going tugs (ATF)).
Weapons systems:	weapons are listed in the following order: land-attack cruise missiles (LACM), anti-ship missiles (AShM), surface-to-air missiles (SAM), heavy (HWT) and lightweight (LWT) torpedoes, anti-submarine weapons (A/S), CIWS, guns and aircraft. Missiles with a range less than 5 km and guns with a calibre less than 57mm are generally not included.
Organisations:	naval groupings such as fleets and squadrons frequently change and are shown only where doing so would aid qualitative judgements.

Principal aviation definitions

Bomber (Bbr):	comparatively large platforms intended for the delivery of air-to-surface ordnance. Bbr units are units equipped with bomber aircraft for the air-to-surface role.
Fighter (Ftr):	aircraft designed primarily for air-to-air combat, which may also have a limited air-to-surface capability. Ftr units are equipped with aircraft intended to provide air superiority, which may have a secondary and limited air-to-surface capability.
Fighter/Ground Attack (FGA):	multi-role fighter-size platforms with significant air-to-surface capability, potentially including maritime attack, and at least some air-to-air capacity. FGA units are multi-role units equipped with aircraft capable of air-to-air and air-to-surface attack.
Ground Attack (Atk):	aircraft designed solely for the air-to-surface task, with limited or no air-to-air capability. Atk units are equipped with fixed-wing aircraft.
Attack Helicopter (Atk hel):	rotary-wing platforms designed for delivery of air-to-surface weapons, and fitted with an integrated fire-control system.

Anti-Submarine Warfare (ASW):	fixed- and rotary-wing platforms designed to locate and engage submarines, many with a secondary anti-surface-warfare capability. ASW units are equipped with fixed- or rotary-wing aircraft.
Anti-Surface Warfare (ASuW):	ASuW units are equipped with fixed- or rotary-wing aircraft intended for anti-surface-warfare missions.
Maritime Patrol (MP):	fixed-wing aircraft and unmanned aerial vehicles (UAVs) intended for maritime surface surveillance, which may possess an anti-surface-warfare capability. MP units are equipped with fixed-wing aircraft or UAVs.
Electronic Warfare (EW):	fixed- and rotary-wing aircraft and UAVs intended for electronic warfare. EW units are equipped with fixed- or rotary-wing aircraft or UAVs.
Intelligence/ Surveillance/ Reconnaissance (ISR):	fixed- and rotary-wing aircraft and UAVs intended to provide radar, visible-light or infrared imagery, or a mix thereof. ISR units are equipped with fixed- or rotary-wing aircraft or UAVs.
Combat/Intelligence/ Surveillance/ Reconnaissance (CISR):	aircraft and UAVs that have the capability to deliver air-to-surface weapons, as well as undertake ISR tasks. CISR units are equipped with armed aircraft and/or UAVs for ISR and air-to-surface missions.
COMINT/ELINT/ SIGINT:	fixed- and rotary-wing platforms and UAVs capable of gathering electronic (ELINT), communications (COMINT) or signals intelligence (SIGINT). COMINT units are equipped with fixed- or rotary-wing aircraft or UAVs intended for the communications-intelligence task. ELINT units are equipped with fixed- or rotary-wing aircraft or UAVs used for gathering electronic intelligence. SIGINT units are equipped with fixed- or rotary-wing aircraft or UAVs used to collect signals intelligence.
Airborne Early Warning (& Control) (AEW (&C)):	fixed- and rotary-wing platforms capable of providing airborne early warning, with a varying degree of onboard command and control depending on the platform. AEW(&C) units are equipped with fixed- or rotary-wing aircraft.
Search and Rescue (SAR):	units are equipped with fixed- or rotary-wing aircraft used to recover military personnel or civilians.
Combat Search and Rescue (CSAR):	units are equipped with armed fixed- or rotary-wing aircraft for recovery of personnel from hostile territory.
Tanker (Tkr):	fixed- and rotary-wing aircraft designed for air-to-air refuelling. Tkr units are equipped with fixed- or rotary-wing aircraft used for air-to-air refuelling.
Tanker Transport (Tkr/Tpt):	platforms capable of both air-to-air refuelling and military airlift.
Transport (Tpt):	fixed- and rotary-wing aircraft intended for military airlift. Light transport aircraft are categorised as having a maximum payload of up to 11,340 kg; medium up to 27,215 kg; and heavy above 27,215 kg. Light transport helicopters have an internal payload of up to 2,000 kg; medium transport helicopters up to 4,535 kg; heavy transport helicopters greater than 4,535 kg. PAX aircraft are platforms generally unsuited for transporting cargo on the main deck. Tpt units are equipped with fixed- or rotary-wing platforms to transport personnel or cargo.
Trainer (Trg):	fixed- and rotary-wing aircraft designed primarily for the training role; some also have the capacity to carry light to medium ordnance. Trg units are equipped with fixed- or rotary-wing training aircraft intended for pilot or other aircrew training.
Multi-role helicopter (MRH):	rotary-wing platforms designed to carry out a variety of military tasks including light transport, armed reconnaissance and battlefield support.
Uninhabited Aerial Vehicles (UAVs):	remotely piloted or controlled unmanned fixed- or rotary-wing systems. Light UAVs are those weighing 20–150 kg; medium: 150–600 kg; and large: more than 600 kg.

Reference

Table 26 List of abbreviations for data sections

AAA	anti-aircraft artillery
AAM	air-to-air missile
AAR	search-and-rescue vessel
AAV	amphibious assault vehicle
AB	airborne
ABM	anti-ballistic missile
ABU/H	sea-going buoy tender/with hangar
ABCV	airborne combat vehicle
ac	aircraft
ACV	armoured combat vehicle
ACS	crane ship
AD	air defence
ADA	air-defence artillery
ADEX	air-defence exercise
adj	adjusted
AE	auxiliary, ammunition carrier
AEM	missile support ship
AEV	armoured engineer vehicle
AEW	airborne early warning
AFD/L	auxiliary floating dry dock/small
AFS/H	logistics ship/with hangar
AFSB	afloat forward staging base
AFV	armoured fighting vehicle
AG	misc auxiliary
AGB/H	icebreaker/with hangar
AGE/H	experimental auxiliary ship/with hangar
AGF/H	command ship/with hangar
AGHS	hydrographic survey vessel
AGI	intelligence collection vessel
AGM	space tracking vessel
AGOR	oceanographic research vessel
AGOS	oceanographic surveillance vessel
AGS/H	survey ship/with hangar
AH	hospital ship
AIP	air-independent propulsion
AK/L	cargo ship/light
aka	also known as
AKEH	dry cargo/ammunition ship
AKR/H	roll-on/roll-off cargo ship/with hangar
AKS/L	stores ship/light
ALCM	air-launched cruise missile
amb	ambulance
amph	amphibious/amphibian
AO/S	oiler/small
AOE	fast combat support ship
AOR/L/H	fleet replenishment oiler with RAS capability/light/with hangar
AOT/L	oiler transport/light
AP	armour-piercing/anti-personnel/transport ship
APB	barracks ship
APC	armoured personnel carrier
AR/C/D/L	repair ship/cable/dry dock/light
ARG	amphibious ready group
ARH	active radar homing
ARL	airborne reconnaissance low
ARM	anti-radiation missile
armd	armoured
ARS/H	rescue and salvage ship/with hangar
arty	artillery
ARV	armoured recovery vehicle
AS	anti-submarine/submarine tender
ASBM	anti-ship ballistic missile
ASCM	anti-ship cruise missile
AShM	anti-ship missile
aslt	assault
ASM	air-to-surface missile
ASR	submarine rescue craft
ASTT	anti-submarine torpedo tube
ASW	anti-submarine warfare
ASuW	anti-surface warfare
AT	tug/anti-tank
ATBM	anti-tactical ballistic missile
ATF	tug, ocean going
ATGW	anti-tank guided weapon
Atk	attack/ground attack
ATS	tug, salvage and rescue ship
AUV	armoured utility vehicle
AVB	aviation logistic support ship
avn	aviation
AWT	water tanker
AX/L/S	training craft/light/sail
BA	Budget Authority (US)
Bbr	bomber
BCT	brigade combat team
bde	brigade
bdgt	budget
BG	battlegroup
BMD	ballistic-missile defence
BMEWS	ballistic missile early warning system
bn	battalion/billion
bty	battery
C2	command and control
casevac	casualty evacuation
cav	cavalry
cbt	combat
CBRN	chemical, biological, radiological, nuclear, explosive
cdo	commando
C/G/H/M/N	cruiser/with AShM/with hangar/with SAM/nuclear-powered
CISR	combat ISR
CIMIC	civil military cooperation
CIWS	close-in weapons system
COIN	counter-insurgency
comd	command
COMINT	communications intelligence
comms	communications
coy	company
CP	command post
CPX	command post exercise
CS	combat support
CSAR	combat search and rescue
CSS	combat service support
CT	counter-terrorism
CV/H/L/N/S	aircraft carrier/helicopter/light/nuclear powered/VSTOL
CW	chemical warfare/weapons
DD/G/H/M	destroyer/with AShM/with hangar/with SAM
DDR	disarmament, demobilisation and reintegration
DE	directed energy
def	defence
det	detachment
div	division
ECM	electronic countermeasures
ELINT	electronic intelligence
elm	element/s
engr	engineer
EOD	explosive ordnance disposal
EPF	expeditionary fast transport vessel
eqpt	equipment
ESB	expeditionary mobile base
ESD	expeditionary transport dock
EW	electronic warfare
excl	excludes/excluding
exp	expenditure
FAC	forward air control
fd	field
FF/G/H/M	frigate/with AShM/with hangar/with SAM
FGA	fighter ground attack
FLD	full-load displacement
flt	flight
FMA	Foreign Military Assistance
FS/G/H/M	corvette/with AShM/with hangar/with SAM
Ftr	fighter
FTX	field training exercise
FY	fiscal year
GBU	guided bomb unit
gd	guard
GDP	gross domestic product
GLCM	ground-launched cruise missile
GMLS	Guided Missile Launching System
gp	group
HA/DR	humanitarian assistance/disaster relief
hel	helicopter
how	howitzer
HQ	headquarters
HUMINT	human intelligence
HWT	heavyweight torpedo
hy	heavy
IBU	inshore boat unit
ICBM	intercontinental ballistic missile
IFV	infantry fighting vehicle
IIR	imaging infrared
IMINT	imagery intelligence
imp	improved
indep	independent
inf	infantry
info ops	information operations

INS	inertial navigation system	MRBM	medium-range ballistic missile	sat	satellite
int	intelligence	MRH	multi-role helicopter	SDV	swimmer delivery vehicles
IOC	Initial operating capability	MRL	multiple rocket launcher	SEAD	suppression of enemy air defence
IR	infrared	MS/C/D/I/O/R	mine sweeper/coastal/drone/inshore/ocean/river	SF	special forces
IRBM	intermediate-range ballistic missile			SHORAD	short-range air defence
ISD	in-service date	msl	missile	SIGINT	signals intelligence
ISR	intelligence, surveillance and reconnaissance	mtn	mountain	sigs	signals
		MW	mine warfare	SLBM	submarine-launched ballistic missile
ISTAR	intelligence, surveillance, target acquisition and reconnaissance	n.a.	not applicable	SLCM	submarine-launched cruise missile
		n.k.	not known	SLEP	service-life-extension programme
JOINTEX	joint exercise	NBC	nuclear, biological, chemical	SP	self-propelled
LACM	land-attack cruise missile	NCO	non-commissioned officer	Spec Ops	special operations
LC/A/AC/H/M/PA/P/L/T/U/VP	landing craft/assault/air cushion/heavy/medium/personnel air cushion/personnel/large/tank/utility/vehicles and personnel	nm	nautical mile	SPAAGM	self-propelled anti-aircraft gun and missile system
		nuc	nuclear		
		O & M	operations and maintenance	spt	support
		obs	observation/observer	sqn	squadron
LCC	amphibious command ship	OCU	operational conversion unit	SRBM	short-range ballistic missile
LGB	laser-guided bomb	OP	observation post	SS	submarine
LHA	landing ship assault	op/ops	operational/operations	SSA	submersible auxiliary support vessel
LHD	amphibious assault ship	OPFOR	opposition training force		
LIFT	lead-in ftr trainer	org	organised/organisation	SSAN	submersible auxiliary support vessel (nuclear)
LKA	amphibious cargo ship	OPV	offshore patrol vessel		
LLI	long-lead items	para	paratroop/parachute	SSBN	nuclear-powered ballistic-missile submarine
lnchr	launcher	PAX	passenger/passenger transport aircraft		
LoA	letter of acceptance			SSC	coastal submarine
log	logistic	PB/F/G/I/M/R/T	patrol boat/fast/with AShM/inshore/with SAM/riverine/with torpedo	SSG	guided-missile submarine
LoI	letter of intent			SSI	inshore submarine
LP/D/H	landing platform/dock/helicopter			SSGN	nuclear-powered guided-missile submarine
LRIP	low-rate initial production				
LS/D/L/LH/M/T	landing ship/dock/logistic/logistic helicopter/medium/tank	PC/C/F/G/H/I/M/O/R/T	patrol craft/coastal/fast/guided missile/with hangar/inshore/with CIWS missile or SAM/offshore/riverine/with torpedo	SSK	attack submarine (hunter-killer)
				SSM	surface-to-surface missile
				SSN	nuclear-powered attack submarine
lt	light	pdr	pounder	SSR	security-sector reform
LWT	lightweight torpedo	pers	personnel	SSW	midget submarine
maint	maintenance	PG/G/GF/H	patrol gunboat/guided missile/fast attack craft/hydrofoil	str	strength
MANPAD	man-portable air-defence system			surv	surveillance
MANPATS	man-portable anti-tank system			sy	security
MAREX	maritime exercise	PGM	precision-guided munitions	t	tonnes
MBT	main battle tank	PH/G/M/T	patrol hydrofoil/with AShM/SAM/with torpedo	tac	tactical
MC/C/CS/D/I/O	mine countermeasure coastal/command and support/diving support/inshore/ocean			tch	technical
		pl	platoon	temp	temporary
		PKO	peacekeeping operations	tk	tank
MCM	mine countermeasures	PoR	programme of record	tkr	tanker
MCMV	mine countermeasures vessel	PPP	purchasing-power parity	TMD	theatre missile defence
MD	military district	PPV	protected patrol vehicle	torp	torpedo
MDT	mine diving tender	PRH	passive radar-homing	tpt	transport
mech	mechanised	prepo	pre-positioned	tr	trillion
med	medium/medical	PSO/H	peace support operations or offshore patrol ship/with hangar	trg	training
medevac	medical evacuation			TRV	torpedo recovery vehicle
MH/C/D/I/O	mine hunter/coastal/drone/inshore/ocean	ptn	pontoon bridging	TT	torpedo tube
		quad	quadruple	UAV	unmanned/uninhabited aerial vehicle
mil	military	R&D	research and development		
MIRV	multiple independently targetable re-entry vehicle	RCL	recoilless launcher	UCAC	utility craft air cushioned
		recce	reconnaissance	UCAV	unmanned combat air vehicle
mk	mark (model number)	regt	regiment	utl	utility
ML	minelayer	RFI	request for information	UUV	unmanned/uninhabited underwater vehicle
MLU	mid-life update	RFP	request for proposals		
mne	marine	RIB	rigid inflatable boat	veh	vehicle
mod	modified/modification	RL	rocket launcher	VLB	vehicle launched bridge
mor	mortar	ro-ro	roll-on, roll-off	VLS	vertical launch system
mot	motorised/motor	RRC/F/U	rapid-reaction corps/force/unit	VSHORAD	very short-range air defence
MoU	memorandum of understanding	RV	re-entry vehicle	V/STOL	vertical/short take-off and landing
MP	maritime patrol/military police	rvn	riverine	WFU	withdrawn from use
MR	maritime reconnaissance/motor rifle	SAM	surface-to-air missile	wg	wing
		SAR	search and rescue		
		SARH	semi-active radar homing		

Table 27 International comparisons of defence expenditure and military personnel

	Defence spending (current US$m)			Defence spending per capita (current US$)			Defence spending % of GDP			Active armed forces (000)	Estimated reservists (000)	Active paramilitary (000)
	2017	2018	2019	2017	2018	2019	2017	2018	2019	2020	2020	2020
North America												
Canada	18,627	19,125	18,723	523	533	518	1.13	1.12	1.08	67	36	5
United States	598,722	631,161	684,568	1,833	1,917	2,063	3.07	3.07	3.19	1,380	849	0
Total	**617,349**	**650,286**	**703,291**	**1,704**	**1,781**	**1,911**	**2.92**	**2.92**	**3.04**	**1,447**	**885**	**5**
Europe												
Albania	110	133	142	36	43	46	0.86	0.88	0.92	8	0	1
Austria	3,159	3,391	3,248	361	386	368	0.76	0.74	0.73	23	144	0
Belgium	4,513	4,845	4,832	393	419	415	0.91	0.91	0.93	26	0	5
Bosnia-Herzegovina	156	171	167	41	45	43	0.89	0.85	0.83	11	0	0
Bulgaria	677	959	2,074	95	136	296	1.17	1.47	3.13	37	3	0
Croatia	687	966	1,051	160	226	247	1.25	1.59	1.73	15	18	3
Cyprus	397	431	403	325	348	322	1.79	1.76	1.66	15	50	1
Czech Republic	2,247	2,710	2,940	211	254	275	1.04	1.11	1.19	23	0	0
Denmark	3,780	4,559	4,592	674	785	786	1.15	1.29	1.32	15	44	0
Estonia	544	645	691	434	518	558	2.06	2.12	2.22	7	28	0
Finland	3,565	3,757	3,999	646	678	720	1.41	1.37	1.48	22	216	3
France	48,704	53,160	52,268	726	789	773	1.88	1.91	1.93	204	39	101
Germany	41,789	45,510	48,548	519	566	604	1.14	1.15	1.26	181	29	0
Greece	4,731	4,857	4,835	439	451	450	2.32	2.23	2.26	143	222	4
Hungary	1,469	1,724	1,993	149	175	203	1.05	1.07	1.17	28	20	12
Iceland	55	39	55	162	115	159	0.22	0.15	0.23	0	0	0
Ireland	1,040	1,118	1,116	208	221	218	0.31	0.29	0.29	9	4	0
Italy	26,666	28,701	27,133	429	461	435	1.37	1.38	1.36	166	18	176
Latvia	531	724	712	273	377	374	1.77	2.10	2.03	7	11	0
Lithuania	817	1,057	1,065	289	378	385	1.74	2.00	1.98	21	7	16
Luxembourg	280	403	344	471	665	557	0.45	0.58	0.49	1	0	1
Macedonia, North	114	125	152	54	59	71	1.04	0.98	1.20	8	5	8
Malta	64	70	84	155	156	185	0.50	0.48	0.56	2	0	0
Montenegro	75	79	74	117	129	121	1.57	1.45	1.37	2	0	10
Netherlands	10,114	11,254	12,097	592	656	703	1.21	1.23	1.34	35	5	6
Norway	6,196	6,756	6,723	1,165	1,258	1,240	1.56	1.56	1.61	23	40	0
Poland	9,381	11,893	11,378	259	310	297	1.90	2.03	2.01	124	0	73

Table 27 International comparisons of defence expenditure and military personnel

	Defence spending (current US$m) 2017	Defence spending (current US$m) 2018	Defence spending (current US$m) 2019	Defence spending per capita (current US$) 2017	Defence spending per capita (current US$) 2018	Defence spending per capita (current US$) 2019	Defence spending % of GDP 2017	Defence spending % of GDP 2018	Defence spending % of GDP 2019	Active armed forces (000) 2020	Estimated reservists (000) 2020	Active paramilitary (000) 2020
Portugal	2,527	2,573	2,682	233	248	260	1.14	1.07	1.13	27	212	25
Romania	3,643	4,359	4,964	169	203	232	1.73	1.82	2.04	70	53	57
Serbia	546	704	906	77	99	129	1.24	1.39	1.76	28	50	4
Slovakia	1,118	1,300	1,867	205	239	343	1.17	1.22	1.75	16	0	0
Slovenia	474	594	630	241	283	300	0.98	1.10	1.16	7	2	0
Spain	13,354	15,059	12,921	273	305	260	1.01	1.05	0.92	120	15	76
Sweden	5,935	6,193	6,384	596	617	631	1.10	1.11	1.21	15	10	0
Switzerland	4,786	4,811	5,369	581	580	643	0.70	0.68	0.75	21	135	0
Turkey	7,885	8,380	8,103	98	103	99	0.92	1.09	1.09	355	379	157
United Kingdom*	52,352	56,003	54,769	808	860	837	1.98	1.98	2.00	148	80	0
Total	**265,084**	**290,014**	**291,312**	**422**	**461**	**462**	**1.37**	**1.40**	**1.44**	**1,962**	**1,836**	**736**
Russia and Eurasia												
Armenia	435	513	644	143	169	213	3.78	4.13	4.79	45	210	4
Azerbaijan	1,542	1,709	1,787	155	170	176	3.73	3.64	3.79	67	300	15
Belarus	531	599	650	56	63	68	0.97	1.00	1.04	45	290	110
Georgia	307	321	311	62	65	63	2.28	2.20	1.96	21	0	5
Kazakhstan	1,265	1,500	1,588	68	80	84	0.78	0.87	0.93	39	0	32
Kyrgyzstan	n.k.	n.k.	n.k.	n.k.	n.k.	n.k.	n.k.	n.k.	n.k.	11	0	10
Moldova	31	38	42	9	11	12	0.45	0.45	0.36	5	58	1
Russia [a]	45,715	45,151	48,206	321	318	340	2.89	2.72	2.94	900	2,000	554
Tajikistan	174	180	187	21	21	21	2.43	2.40	2.30	9	0	8
Turkmenistan*	n.k.	n.k.	n.k.	n.k.	n.k.	n.k.	n.k.	n.k.	n.k.	37	0	5
Ukraine	2,798	3,257	3,831	64	74	87	2.58	2.56	2.56	209	900	88
Uzbekistan	n.k.	n.k.	n.k.	n.k.	n.k.	n.k.	n.k.	n.k.	n.k.	48	0	20
Total**	**52,797**	**53,270**	**57,247**	**186**	**187**	**200**	**2.52**	**2.41**	**2.56**	**1,435**	**3,758**	**851**
Asia												
Afghanistan	2,169	2,031	1,906	64	58	53	10.72	10.35	10.17	181	0	92
Australia	24,446	26,311	25,466	1,052	1,121	1,074	1.76	1.85	1.85	57	21	0
Bangladesh	2,930	2,531	3,551	19	16	22	1.12	0.88	1.12	163	0	64
Brunei	327	365	435	738	811	950	2.70	2.69	3.49	7	1	1
Cambodia*	791	964	1,045	49	59	63	3.57	3.95	3.91	124	0	67
China	154,353	170,504	181,135	111	122	130	1.28	1.28	1.28	2,035	510	660
Fiji	51	51	56	55	55	61	0.95	0.93	0.99	4	6	0

Table 27 **International comparisons of defence expenditure and military personnel**

	Defence spending (current US$m)			Defence spending per capita (current US$)			Defence spending % of GDP			Active armed forces (000)	Estimated reservists (000)	Active paramilitary (000)
	2017	2018	2019	2017	2018	2019	2017	2018	2019	2020	2020	2020
India	58,026	57,830	60,543	45	45	46	2.19	2.13	2.06	1,456	1,155	1,586
Indonesia	8,781	7,368	7,429	34	28	28	0.87	0.72	0.67	396	400	280
Japan	45,892	47,011	48,590	361	373	386	0.94	0.95	0.94	247	56	14
Korea, DPR of	n.k.	n.k.	n.k.	n.k.	n.k.	n.k.	n.k.	n.k.	n.k.	1,280	600	189
Korea, Republic of	35,876	39,215	39,764	701	763	770	2.21	2.28	2.44	599	3,100	9
Laos	n.k.	n.k.	n.k.	n.k.	n.k.	n.k.	n.k.	n.k.	n.k.	29	0	100
Malaysia	3,501	3,890	3,330	112	122	103	1.10	1.08	0.91	113	52	23
Mongolia	85	104	96	28	34	31	0.76	0.82	0.70	10	137	8
Myanmar	2,168	1,928	2,060	39	35	37	3.53	2.81	3.12	406	0	107
Nepal	336	431	387	11	14	13	1.34	1.49	1.30	97	0	15
New Zealand	2,353	2,353	2,722	522	518	594	1.17	1.16	1.33	9	2	0
Pakistan	9,746	11,411	10,314	48	55	49	3.28	3.63	3.66	654	0	291
Papua New Guinea	72	64	79	10	9	11	0.32	0.27	0.33	4	0	0
Philippines	2,727	2,592	3,493	26	24	32	0.88	0.80	0.99	142	131	11
Singapore	10,288	10,944	11,268	1,747	1,825	1,846	3.04	3.01	3.11	51	253	8
Sri Lanka	1,863	1,795	1,668	83	80	73	2.12	2.02	1.93	255	6	62
Taiwan	10,489	10,864	10,940	446	461	464	1.82	1.84	1.87	163	1,657	11
Thailand	6,292	6,724	7,103	92	98	103	1.38	1.33	1.34	361	200	94
Timor-Leste	25	21	31	20	16	23	1.02	0.75	1.07	2	0	0
Vietnam*	4,372	4,800	5,214	45	49	53	1.99	1.99	2.00	482	5,000	40
Total **	**387,760**	**412,102**	**428,624**	**96**	**101**	**105**	**1.44**	**1.43**	**1.43**	**9,326**	**13,286**	**3,731**
Middle East and North Africa												
Algeria	10,077	9,591	10,394	246	230	246	6.02	5.52	6.02	130	150	187
Bahrain	1,480	1,480	1,501	1,049	1,026	1,018	4.19	3.92	3.93	8	0	11
Egypt	3,212	2,900	3,351	33	29	33	1.88	1.68	1.54	439	479	397
Iran	20,928	21,900	17,428	255	264	207	4.86	4.91	3.80	610	350	40
Iraq	19,271	17,259	20,471	492	429	497	9.99	7.81	9.12	193	0	145
Israel	18,892	19,612	19,273	2,276	2,328	2,254	6.25	6.13	5.82	170	465	8
Jordan	1,635	1,635	1,691	160	156	159	5.16	4.87	4.62	101	65	15
Kuwait	5,763	6,179	6,398	2,004	2,119	2,165	4.82	4.36	4.65	18	24	7
Lebanon	1,366	2,122	1,928	300	348	330	3.65	3.95	3.38	60	0	20
Libya	n.k.	n.k.	n.k.	n.k.	n.k.	n.k.	n.k.	n.k.	n.k.	n.k.	n.k.	n.k.

Table 27 **International comparisons of defence expenditure and military personnel**

	Defence spending (current US$m)			Defence spending per capita (current US$)			Defence spending % of GDP			Active armed forces (000)	Estimated reservists (000)	Active paramilitary (000)
	2017	2018	2019	2017	2018	2019	2017	2018	2019	2020	2020	2020
Mauritania	145	159	160	39	41	41	2.94	3.04	2.82	16	0	5
Morocco	3,492	3,651	3,633	103	106	105	3.19	3.09	3.05	196	150	50
Oman	8,687	8,947	8,973	2,537	2,561	2,517	12.30	11.29	11.71	43	0	4
Palestinian Territories	n.k.	n.k.	n.k.	n.k.	n.k.	n.k.	n.k.	n.k.	n.k.	0	0	n.k.
Qatar	n.k.	n.k.	n.k.	n.k.	n.k.	n.k.	n.k.	n.k.	n.k.	17	0	5
Saudi Arabia	89,067	86,400	78,400	3,117	2,611	2,331	12.93	10.99	10.06	227	0	25
Syria	n.k.	n.k.	n.k.	n.k.	n.k.	n.k.	n.k.	n.k.	n.k.	169	0	100
Tunisia	833	881	993	73	76	85	2.33	2.37	2.67	36	0	12
United Arab Emirates	n.k.	n.k.	n.k.	n.k.	n.k.	n.k.	n.k.	n.k.	n.k.	63	0	0
Yemen	n.k.	n.k.	n.k.	n.k.	n.k.	n.k.	n.k.	n.k.	n.k.	40	0	0
Total**	**185,348**	**182,716**	**174,592**	**443**	**421**	**390**	**6.06**	**5.46**	**5.13**	**2,533**	**1,683**	**1,031**
Latin America and the Caribbean												
Antigua and Barbuda	6	7	7	66	74	74	0.43	0.44	0.43	0	0	0
Argentina	6,172	4,317	3,265	139	97	72	0.96	0.83	0.73	74	0	31
Bahamas	99	85	92	299	255	275	0.81	0.68	0.73	1	0	0
Barbados	39	40	38	134	138	131	0.78	0.79	0.74	1	0	0
Belize	23	23	23	64	60	59	1.29	1.26	1.17	2	1	0
Bolivia	543	503	479	49	44	42	1.44	1.24	1.13	34	0	37
Brazil	29,245	27,551	27,467	141	132	131	1.42	1.48	1.49	367	1,340	395
Chile	4,426	4,701	4,566	249	262	253	1.59	1.58	1.55	77	40	45
Colombia	10,150	10,570	10,451	213	219	215	3.27	3.21	3.19	293	35	188
Costa Rica	390	451	433	79	90	86	0.67	0.75	0.71	0	0	10
Cuba	n.k.	n.k.	n.k.	n.k.	n.k.	n.k.	n.k.	n.k.	n.k.	49	39	27
Dominican Republic	496	603	621	46	59	60	0.62	0.70	0.69	56	0	15
Ecuador	1,565	1,698	1,590	96	103	95	1.50	1.57	1.47	40	118	1
El Salvador	146	141	145	24	23	23	0.59	0.55	0.54	25	10	17
Guatemala	260	255	337	17	15	20	0.35	0.33	0.41	18	64	25
Guyana	58	61	68	79	82	91	1.61	1.56	1.64	3	1	0
Haiti	7	8	13	1	1	1	0.09	0.13	0.15	1	0	0
Honduras	267	331	341	30	36	37	1.18	1.41	1.40	15	60	8
Jamaica	146	230	262	49	82	93	0.99	1.49	1.67	6	3	0
Mexico	4,568	5,314	5,085	37	42	40	0.40	0.44	0.40	236	82	132
Nicaragua	84	82	78	14	13	13	0.60	0.62	0.63	12	0	0

Table 27 International comparisons of defence expenditure and military personnel

	Defence spending (current US$m)			Defence spending per capita (current US$)			Defence spending % of GDP			Active armed forces (000)	Estimated reservists (000)	Active paramilitary (000)
	2017	2018	2019	2017	2018	2019	2017	2018	2019	2020	2020	2020
Panama	746	738	305	199	194	209	1.20	1.14	1.17	0	0	26
Paraguay	273	311	288	39	44	40	0.70	0.74	0.71	14	165	15
Peru	2,166	2,286	2,206	70	73	70	1.01	1.03	0.96	81	188	77
Suriname	n.k.	n.k.	n.k.	n.k.	n.k.	n.k.	n.k.	n.k.	n.k.	2	0	0
Trinidad and Tobago	1,125	921	904	923	758	746	5.05	4.09	4.00	4	0	0
Uruguay	515	481	442	153	143	131	0.86	0.81	0.74	21	0	1
Venezuela	741	n.k.	n.k.	24	n.k.	n.k.	0.51	n.k.	n.k.	123	8	220
Total	**64,257**	**61,707**	**60,008**	**103**	**98**	**94**	**1.18**	**1.18**	**1.16**	**1,555**	**2,152**	**1,269**
Sub-Saharan Africa												
Angola	3,233	2,158	1,705	110	71	54	2.65	2.04	1.86	107	0	10
Benin	117	90	68	11	8	6	0.92	0.63	0.48	7	0	5
Botswana	490	518	537	221	230	235	2.82	2.78	2.87	9	0	0
Burkina Faso	192	313	361	10	16	18	1.56	2.21	2.47	11	0	0
Burundi	64	65	62	6	5	5	1.87	1.89	1.73	30	0	21
Cameroon	411	430	424	16	17	16	1.17	1.11	1.10	25	0	9
Cape Verde	10	11	11	17	20	19	0.55	0.56	0.53	1	0	0
Central African Rep	31	31	33	5	5	6	1.47	1.36	1.40	9	0	1
Chad	176	182	206	15	12	13	1.75	1.65	1.87	33	0	5
Congo	490	293	301	99	58	58	5.48	2.51	2.60	10	0	2
Côte d'Ivoire	829	931	898	34	35	33	2.17	2.16	2.02	27	0	n.k.
Dem Republic of the Congo	285	297	329	3	3	4	0.76	0.63	0.67	134	0	0
Djibouti	n.k.	n.k.	n.k.	n.k.	n.k.	n.k.	n.k.	n.k.	n.k.	10	0	3
Equatorial Guinea	n.k.	n.k.	n.k.	n.k.	n.k.	n.k.	n.k.	n.k.	n.k.	1	0	0
Eritrea	n.k.	n.k.	n.k.	n.k.	n.k.	n.k.	n.k.	n.k.	n.k.	202	120	0
Ethiopia	461	437	518	4	4	5	0.61	0.54	0.57	138	0	0
Gabon	267	261	269	151	123	124	1.79	1.55	1.59	5	0	2
Gambia	n.k.	n.k.	n.k.	n.k.	n.k.	n.k.	n.k.	n.k.	n.k.	4	0	0
Ghana	189	216	233	7	8	8	0.32	0.33	0.35	16	0	0
Guinea	200	197	191	16	17	16	1.94	1.63	1.43	10	0	3
Guinea-Bissau	n.k.	n.k.	n.k.	n.k.	n.k.	n.k.	n.k.	n.k.	n.k.	4	0	0
Kenya	1,198	1,286	1,231	25	27	25	1.52	1.46	1.25	24	0	5
Lesotho	56	48	43	28	24	22	2.08	1.76	1.58	2	0	0

Table 27 International comparisons of defence expenditure and military personnel

	Defence spending (current US$m)			Defence spending per capita (current US$)			Defence spending % of GDP			Active armed forces (000)	Estimated reservists (000)	Active paramilitary (000)
	2017	2018	2019	2017	2018	2019	2017	2018	2019	2020	2020	2020
Liberia	14	13	14	3	3	3	0.52	0.41	0.43	2	0	0
Madagascar	67	73	77	3	3	3	0.58	0.61	0.62	14	0	8
Malawi	38	51	67	2	3	3	0.61	0.74	0.90	11	0	4
Mali	655	726	727	37	39	38	4.26	4.22	4.12	13	0	8
Mauritius	234	222	220	172	163	161	1.76	1.56	1.53	0	0	3
Mozambique	93	129	127	4	5	5	0.74	0.90	0.84	11	0	0
Namibia	452	450	422	182	178	163	3.33	3.10	2.94	10	0	6
Niger	172	230	176	9	12	9	2.12	2.47	1.86	5	0	5
Nigeria	1,525	1,750	1,827	8	9	9	0.41	0.44	0.41	143	0	80
Rwanda	109	107	112	9	9	9	1.19	1.13	1.10	33	0	2
Senegal	309	347	343	21	23	22	1.48	1.48	1.43	14	0	5
Seychelles	n.k.	n.k.	n.k.	n.k.	n.k.	n.k.	n.k.	n.k.	n.k.	0	0	0
Sierra Leone	23	13	11	4	2	2	0.62	0.33	0.25	9	0	0
Somalia	n.k.	n.k.	n.k.	n.k.	n.k.	n.k.	n.k.	n.k.	n.k.	20	0	0
South Africa	3,651	3,622	3,540	67	65	63	1.04	0.98	0.99	75	0	15
South Sudan	97	91	70	7	9	7	2.83	2.00	1.90	185	0	0
Sudan	n.k.	n.k.	n.k.	n.k.	n.k.	n.k.	n.k.	n.k.	n.k.	104	0	20
Tanzania	532	758	827	10	14	15	1.00	1.33	1.33	27	80	1
Togo	89	104	107	11	13	13	1.86	1.95	1.94	9	0	1
Uganda	434	393	547	11	10	13	1.64	1.40	1.78	45	10	1
Zambia	337	334	387	21	20	23	1.30	1.25	1.62	15	3	1
Zimbabwe	272	206	72	20	15	5	1.24	0.98	0.56	29	0	22
Total**	**17,800**	**17,387**	**17,092**	**17**	**16**	**16**	**1.12**	**1.04**	**0.99**	**1,594**	**213**	**248**
Summary												
North America	617,349	650,286	703,291	1,704	1,781	1,911	2.92	2.92	3.04	1,447	885	5
Europe	265,084	290,014	291,312	422	461	462	1.37	1.40	1.44	1,962	1,836	736
Russia and Eurasia	52,797	53,270	57,247	186	187	200	2.52	2.41	2.56	1,435	3,758	851
Asia	387,760	412,102	428,624	96	101	105	1.44	1.43	1.43	9,326	13,286	3,731
Middle East and North Africa	185,348	182,716	174,592	443	421	390	6.06	5.46	5.13	2,533	1,683	1,031
Latin America and the Caribbean	64,257	61,707	60,008	103	98	94	1.18	1.18	1.16	1,555	2,152	1,269
Sub-Saharan Africa	17,800	17,387	17,092	17	16	16	1.12	1.04	0.99	1,594	213	248
Global totals	**1,590,396**	**1,667,483**	**1,732,166**	**216**	**223**	**230**	**2.00**	**1.98**	**2.02**	**19,852**	**23,812**	**7,871**

* Estimates. **Totals exclude defence-spending estimates for states where insufficient official information is available in order to enable approximate comparisons of regional defence-spending between years [a] 'National Defence' budget chapter. Excludes other defence-related expenditures included under other budget lines (e.g. pensions).
Defence Spending as % of GDP includes US foreign military financing programmes

Table 28 Index of country/territory abbreviations

AFG ... Afghanistan	GEO ... Georgia	NPL ... Nepal
ALB ... Albania	GER ... Germany	NZL ... New Zealand
ALG ... Algeria	GF ... French Guiana	OMN ... Oman
ANG ... Angola	GHA ... Ghana	PT ... Palestinian Territories
ARG ... Argentina	GIB ... Gibraltar	PAN ... Panama
ARM ... Armenia	GNB ... Guinea-Bissau	PAK ... Pakistan
ATG ... Antigua and Barbuda	GRC ... Greece	PER ... Peru
AUS ... Australia	GRL ... Greenland	PHL ... Philippines
AUT ... Austria	GUA ... Guatemala	POL ... Poland
AZE ... Azerbaijan	GUI ... Guinea	PNG ... Papua New Guinea
BDI ... Burundi	GUY ... Guyana	PRC ... China, People's Republic of
BEL ... Belgium	HND ... Honduras	PRT ... Portugal
BEN ... Benin	HTI ... Haiti	PRY ... Paraguay
BFA ... Burkina Faso	HUN ... Hungary	PYF ... French Polynesia
BGD ... Bangladesh	IDN ... Indonesia	QTR ... Qatar
BHR ... Bahrain	IND ... India	ROC ... Taiwan (Republic of China)
BHS ... Bahamas	IRL ... Ireland	ROK ... Korea, Republic of
BIH ... Bosnia-Herzegovina	IRN ... Iran	ROM ... Romania
BIOT ... British Indian Ocean Territory	IRQ ... Iraq	RSA ... South Africa
BLG ... Bulgaria	ISL ... Iceland	RUS ... Russia
BLR ... Belarus	ISR ... Israel	RWA ... Rwanda
BLZ ... Belize	ITA ... Italy	SAU ... Saudi Arabia
BOL ... Bolivia	JAM ... Jamaica	SDN ... Sudan
BRB ... Barbados	JOR ... Jordan	SEN ... Senegal
BRN ... Brunei	JPN ... Japan	SER ... Serbia
BRZ ... Brazil	KAZ ... Kazakhstan	SGP ... Singapore
BWA ... Botswana	KEN ... Kenya	SLB ... Solomon Islands
CAM ... Cambodia	KGZ ... Kyrgyzstan	SLE ... Sierra Leone
CAN ... Canada	KWT ... Kuwait	SLV ... El Salvador
CAR ... Central African Republic	LAO ... Laos	SOM ... Somalia
CHA ... Chad	LBN ... Lebanon	SSD ... South Sudan
CHE ... Switzerland	LBR ... Liberia	STP ... São Tomé and Príncipe
CHL ... Chile	LBY ... Libya	SUR ... Suriname
CIV ... Côte d'Ivoire	LKA ... Sri Lanka	SVK ... Slovakia
CMR ... Cameroon	LSO ... Lesotho	SVN ... Slovenia
COG ... Republic of Congo	LTU ... Lithuania	SWE ... Sweden
COL ... Colombia	LUX ... Luxembourg	SYC ... Seychelles
CPV ... Cape Verde	LVA ... Latvia	SYR ... Syria
CRI ... Costa Rica	MDA ... Moldova	TGO ... Togo
CRO ... Croatia	MDG ... Madagascar	THA ... Thailand
CUB ... Cuba	MEX ... Mexico	TJK ... Tajikistan
CYP ... Cyprus	MHL ... Marshall Islands	TKM ... Turkmenistan
CZE ... Czech Republic	MKD ... Macedonia, North	TLS ... Timor-Leste
DJB ... Djibouti	MLI ... Mali	TTO ... Trinidad and Tobago
DNK ... Denmark	MLT ... Malta	TUN ... Tunisia
DOM ... Dominican Republic	MMR ... Myanmar	TUR ... Turkey
DPRK ... Korea, Democratic People's Republic of	MNE ... Montenegro	TZA ... Tanzania
DRC ... Democratic Republic of the Congo	MNG ... Mongolia	UAE ... United Arab Emirates
ECU ... Ecuador	MOR ... Morocco	UGA ... Uganda
EGY ... Egypt	MOZ ... Mozambique	UK ... United Kingdom
EQG ... Equitorial Guinea	MRT ... Mauritania	UKR ... Ukraine
ERI ... Eritrea	MUS ... Mauritius	URY ... Uruguay
ESP ... Spain	MWI ... Malawi	US ... United States
EST ... Estonia	MYS ... Malaysia	UZB ... Uzbekistan
ETH ... Ethiopia	NAM ... Namibia	VEN ... Venezuela
FIN ... Finland	NCL ... New Caledonia	VNM ... Vietnam
FJI ... Fiji	NER ... Niger	YEM ... Yemen, Republic of
FLK ... Falkland Islands	NGA ... Nigeria	ZMB ... Zambia
FRA ... France	NIC ... Nicaragua	ZWE ... Zimbabwe
GAB ... Gabon	NLD ... Netherlands	
GAM ... Gambia	NOR ... Norway	

Table 29 Index of countries and territories

Country	Page
Afghanistan AFG	250
Albania ALB	86
Algeria ALG	340
Angola ANG	460
Antigua and Barbuda ATG	398
Argentina ARG	398
Armenia ARM	183
Australia AUS	251
Austria AUT	87
Azerbaijan AZE	184
Bahamas BHS	401
Bahrain BHR	342
Bangladesh BGD	254
Barbados BRB	402
Belarus BLR	187
Belgium BEL	88
Belize BLZ	402
Benin BEN	461
Bolivia BOL	403
Bosnia-Herzegovina BIH	90
Botswana BWA	462
Brazil BRZ	405
Brunei BRN	256
Bulgaria BLG	91
Burkina Faso BFA	463
Burundi BDI	464
Cambodia CAM	257
Cameroon CMR	465
Canada CAN	43
Cape Verde CPV	467
Central African Republic CAR	467
Chad CHA	469
Chile CHL	409
China, People's Republic of PRC	259
Colombia COL	412
Congo, Republic of COG	470
Costa Rica CRI	415
Côte d'Ivoire CIV	471
Croatia CRO	93
Cuba CUB	415
Cyprus CYP	94
Czech Republic CZE	96
Democratic Republic of the Congo DRC	472
Denmark DNK	98
Djibouti DJB	473
Dominican Republic DOM	417
Ecuador ECU	418
Egypt EGY	344
El Salvador SLV	420
Equatorial Guinea EQG	475
Eritrea ERI	475
Estonia EST	100
Ethiopia ETH	477
Fiji FJI	268
Finland FIN	101
France FRA	103
Gabon GAB	478
Gambia GAM	479
Georgia GEO	188
Germany GER	108
Ghana GHA	480
Greece GRC	111
Guatemala GUA	422
Guinea-Bissau GNB	482
Guinea GUI	481
Guyana GUY	423
Haiti HTI	424
Honduras HND	424
Hungary HUN	114
Iceland ISL	116
India IND	269
Indonesia IDN	275
Iran IRN	348
Iraq IRQ	352
Ireland IRL	116
Israel ISR	354
Italy ITA	118
Jamaica JAM	426
Japan JPN	279
Jordan JOR	357
Kazakhstan KAZ	190
Kenya KEN	483
Korea, Democratic People's Republic of DPRK	284
Korea, Republic of ROK	286
Kuwait KWT	359
Kyrgyzstan KGZ	192
Laos LAO	290
Latvia LVA	122
Lebanon LBN	361
Lesotho LSO	484
Liberia LBR	485
Libya LBY	363
Lithuania LTU	123
Luxembourg LUX	125
Macedonia, North MKD	125
Madagascar MDG	485
Malawi MWI	486
Malaysia MYS	291
Mali MLI	487
Malta MLT	127
Mauritania MRT	365
Mauritius MUS	489
Mexico MEX	427
Moldova MDA	193
Mongolia MNG	294
Montenegro MNE	127
Morocco MOR	366
Mozambique MOZ	490
Multinational Organisations	128
Myanmar MMR	295
Namibia NAM	491
Nepal NPL	297
Netherlands NLD	129
New Zealand NZL	298
Nicaragua NIC	429
Nigeria NGA	493
Niger NER	492
Norway NOR	131
Oman OMN	368
Pakistan PAK	299
Palestinian Territories PT	370
Panama PAN	431
Papua New Guinea PNG	303
Paraguay PRY	431
Peru PER	433
Philippines PHL	304
Poland POL	133
Portugal PRT	136
Qatar QTR	371
Romania ROM	138
Russia RUS	194
Rwanda RWA	495
Saudi Arabia SAU	373
Senegal SEN	496
Serbia SER	140
Seychelles SYC	497
Sierra Leone SLE	498
Singapore SGP	306
Slovakia SVK	143
Slovenia SVN	144
Somalia SOM	499
South Africa RSA	500
South Sudan SSD	502
Spain ESP	145
Sri Lanka LKA	309
Sudan SDN	503
Suriname SUR	436
Sweden SWE	149
Switzerland CHE	151
Syria SYR	376
Taiwan (Republic of China) ROC	311
Tajikistan TJK	209
Tanzania TZA	505
Thailand THA	314
Timor-Leste TLS	317
Togo TGO	506
Trinidad and Tobago TTO	436
Tunisia TUN	379
Turkey TUR	153
Turkmenistan TKM	210
Uganda UGA	508
Ukraine UKR	211
United Arab Emirates UAE	381
United Kingdom UK	157
United States US	45
Uruguay URY	437
Uzbekistan UZB	215
Venezuela VEN	439
Vietnam VNM	318
Yemen, Republic of YEM	383
Zambia ZMB	509
Zimbabwe ZWE	511